VOLUME V

THE COLLECTED SCIENTIFIC PAPERS OF PAUL A. SAMUELSON

Edited by Kate Crowley

THE MIT PRESS
Cambridge, Massachusetts, and London, England

Printed and bound in the United States of America.

Library of Congress Cataloging-in-Publication Data
(Revised for vol. 5)

Samuelson, Paul Anthony, 1915–
The collected scientific papers of Paul A. Samuelson.

Vol. 3 edited by R. C. Merton; v. 4 edited by H. Nagatani and K. Crowley; v. 5 edited by Kate Crowley.
Includes bibliographies.
1. Economics—Collected works. I. Title.
HB33.S2 330 65-28408
ISBN 0-262-19251-9 (v. 5)

THE COLLECTED SCIENTIFIC PAPERS OF PAUL A. SAMUELSON

CONTENTS

Volume V

Part IV. Stochastic Theory

Part VII. Biographical and Autobiographical Writings

Part VIII. Current Economics and Policy

AUTHOR'S PREFACE

A scholar's work is never done—until he himself is finished. Here is a fifth volume of my scientific papers, and still there are more to come. In a rash moment I acceded to the Sloan Foundation's kind invitation to write a scientific autobiography dealing with the growth of economic science in my lifetime.

Again and again I have had to alibi for my putting off that job, with the plaintive query: "How can I write *about* science while busily engaged in *doing* science?"

Kate Crowley, who shared with Hiroaki Nagatani the editing of Volume 4 of my scientific papers, this time has performed editorial labors alone. She has saved from my rejection various popularizations, arguing persuasively that historians of our times will need to know how scholars reacted from year to year to the important problems of the age.

As with earlier volumes, offset reproduction provides the reader with the articles as they actually appeared. A few misprints have been corrected. Crowley has classified papers under a few convenient headings and has provided all needed bibliographic information.

The same gratitude I and readers felt in the past to Joseph E. Stiglitz, Robert C. Merton, and Hiroaki Nagatani and Kate Crowley is now owed to Kate Crowley. Her editorial task was all the harder for having to be done from across the Atlantic Ocean. I am truly grateful.

Paul A. Samuelson
Cambridge, Massachusetts
January 1986

EDITOR'S PREFACE

Paul Samuelson has been true to his academic code. Although it was only three years ago that he wrote that "it is a sin not to publish," it is obvious that he had held that conviction for a long time. When that precept appeared in print, four volumes of his *Collected Scientific Papers*, containing 293 of his papers, had already been published. In 1966, after the publication of Volumes 1 and 2, Seymour Harris wrote to Professor Samuelson predicting that "in 1985 there will be two more massive volumes." Harris probably thought he was being generous in his prediction. Yet he was off by an entire volume. Volume 3 appeared in 1972, Volume 4 in 1977, and now, in late 1985, Volume 5 is ready to go to press.

This massive volume contains 96 articles, all of Paul Samuelson's scientific contributions from 1977 in 1985, as well as papers of a biographical nature and papers on current topics. The papers are grouped into eight parts. Obvious typographical and mechanical errors have been corrected.

My transatlantic commute to put this volume together was possible only because of the help of my parents, who made Francesca so happy. I am truly grateful to them.

Kate Crowley
Delft, The Netherlands
December 1985

PART I

Economic Theory

9 Bergsonian welfare economics

Paul A. Samuelson

As I write, the new welfare economics is just over four decades old. This subject, in its essentials as we know it today, was born when the 24-year-old Abram Bergson – then still a Harvard graduate student – wrote his classic 1938 *Quarterly Journal of Economics* article. To one like myself, who before 1938 knew *all* the relevant literature on welfare economics and just could not make coherent sense of it, Bergson's work came like a flash of lightning, describable only in the words of the pontifical poet:

> Nature and Nature's laws lay hid in night:
> God said, Let Newton be! and all was light.

King Alphonse claimed that if he had been in on the Creation, he could have done a better job. By sheer good luck, as a fellow graduate student and comrade at arms, I *was* in on Bergson's creation: but time has shown that I have not been able to do a better job of it; nor, I believe, has anyone else[1] – and this despite the quite confused rumors that Kenneth Arrow's Impossibility Theorem rendered Bergson's "social welfare function" somehow nonexistent or self-contradictory.

Here I hope to set the record straight as only a living witness and participant can. After a few introductory sections that sketch the historical setting of modern welfare economics, I provide under the heading "Existence and Property of a Bergsonian Social Welfare Function" an analytical exposition of some of the fundamentals of the Bergsonian welfare economics.

Conception and gestation

Mine was the best spectator's seat for Bergson's creative travail. I was the coarse stone against which he honed his sharp axe – the semiabsorbing, semireflecting surface against which he bounced off his ideas.

I owe thanks to the National Science Foundation for financial aid, and to Aase Huggins and Kate Crowley for editorial assistance.

"What can Pareto mean by this 1898 use of the French singular when he speaks of 'the social optimum'?" Bergson would ask himself and me. In the end the innovator demonstrated the wisdom of what Gertrude Stein was to declare on her deathbed: "What is the question?" points the way to what is the answer.

From 1930 to 1938 a host of writers were rediscovering in an unsystematic way the finding of John Stuart Mill, Edgeworth, Pareto, and other earlier writers – that those who lose from various deviations from ideal free-trade situations can bribe or buy off those who gain, so that there does exist a movement from the status quo which by unanimity *could* make *everyone* better off. Prominent among such rediscoverers of "compensationism" were Abba Lerner, Harold Hotelling, Jacob Viner, Nicholas Kaldor, R. F. Harrod, John Hicks, myself, and many others. The *necessary condition(s)* for an optimum, that such a *universal* improvement *not* be possible, Ian Little came in 1950 to call "Pareto optimality," a felicitous and useful coinage. But just what accomplishment this necessary condition was necessary for, that question was not clarified until 1938 when Bergson defined and clarified the concept of an *individualistic social welfare function* – which ethically orders the various states of the world and which lets "individual tastes 'count,' in the sense of agreeing with individuals' orderings *when those orderings are unanimous* and *resolving them ethically* when they are not unanimous."

The skeleton key to understanding provided by Bergson in 1938 was logically what mathematicians call a "weakly separable function." Thus, for (bread^1, wine^1) and (bread^2, wine^2) the "private goods" consumed respectively by two nonenvying and nonsympathizing people, Person^1 and Person^2, the Bergson (individualistic and ordinal) Social Welfare Function (BISWF), could be described by the separable indicator function

$$W = w[U^1(\text{bread}^1, \text{wine}^1), U^2(\text{bread}^2, \text{wine}^2)]$$
$$w[A^1, A^2] \geq w[B^1, B^2] \qquad \text{if } A_1 \geq B_1, A_2 \geq B_2$$
$$U^i(a_1^i, a_2^i) \geq U^i(b_1^i, b_2^i) \qquad \text{if } a_1^i \geq b_1^i, a_2^i \geq b_2^i \qquad (i = 1, 2) \tag{1}$$

As I shall explicate, any one cardinal indicator of ethical preferences such as that above can be replaced by an infinity of different renumberings or stretchings of the $w[\cdot]$ and $U^i(\cdot)$ functions. (Indeed, to underline the completely *ordinal* nature of the BISWF, my analytical account shows that it can be given solely in *indifference-contour and marginal-rate-of-substitution* form; and it is also expressed in terms of a "complete ordering" symbolism à la Debreu.)

This concept of the social welfare function enabled one to understand for the first time the germ of truth in Adam Smith's paradigm of the Invisible Hand: namely, that when conditions of returns and tastes, nonexternalities, and nonmonopolies are right, the algorithm of Walrasian competition can be combined with the device of ideal lump-sum transfers to achieve the maximum of a prescribed well-behaved individualistic social welfare function.

It took more than a decade after 1938 for the Bergsonian message to be understood within the profession. For a long time scholars confused two versions of the New Welfare Economics:

1. The narrow version that emphasized and stopped short at "compensation payments" made by gainers to losers (or determined to be *capable* of being made, *even if not actually made*) – an approach that when stripped of its pretensions was revealed to merely catch up to the concept of Pareto optimality.

2. Bergson's synthesis of the Old Welfare Economics of the additive-hedonistic type with the more general notion of a Social Welfare Function that introduces, from outside positivistic economic science, ethical norming of alternative states of the world. Within this broad genus, interest attaches to those species that involve ethics of *individualistic* type rather than of *paternalistic* type. Benthamite hedonism is only one of many varieties within the individualistic species. Bergson not only clarified the relationship of this general New Welfare Economics to the previous Old Welfare Economics; but, as well, his 1938 analysis enabled scholars to understand how the narrow "New Welfare Economics" of Hicks, Kaldor, Scitovsky, and a dozen others reached only the state of necessary conditions rather than that of necessary-and-sufficient conditions. By means of Bergson's analysis, the practioners of the narrow welfare economics could not only apprehend the crucial distinction between necessary condition(s) and sufficient condition(s) – but he also provided them with an understanding of for what the sufficient conditions may suffice.

Prior history

The Old Welfare Economics flourished in the nineteenth century. Bentham, Sidgwick, and the general run of neoclassical economists – Edgeworth, Marshall, Wicksell, Böhm-Bawerk, Walras, Carver, and Pigou – believed that cardinal utility was a scientifically definable magnitude for each person. With appropriate interpersonal constants these intrapersonal utilities could be added to form Total Social Utility, a magnitude that manifestly ought to be maximized.

Most neoclassical economists remained confused on what this all implied for laissez-faire. Many vulgarly believed that this mandated laissez-faire. Bastiat, L. von Mises, and lesser lights are examples. Some – Wicksell is a good example – realized that only *after* the initial distribution of endowments of dollar-voting power were *ethically proper* would that which perfect competition accomplished be a desirable accomplishment.[2] Still others were confused.[3]

I have recorded somewhere in print how in the year 1935 as a puzzled student I could not get satisfactory answers anywhere in the Harvard Yard or the University of Chicago quadrangle to the simple question: "Exactly why is it *right* for price to equal marginal cost?" Jacob Viner, Frank Knight, Joseph Schumpeter, Wassily Leontief, Paul Sweezy, and other leading economists of the time had written material with a bearing upon this question. But none could give me a clear understanding. Lest it be thought that my own experience was singular, recall that several years later Ragnar Frisch could engage in a public controversy with Harold Hotelling concerning the cogency of what Hotelling had alleged in this regard. When Thomas Kuhn comes to amplify his taxonomy of *The Structure of Scientific Revolutions,* he will find that in addition to the division between scholars who believe in conflicting paradigms, there is always a normal state of science in which confusion and ambiguity play a role.

This unsatisfactory state of the Old Welfare Economics reached a climax with the 1932 publication of Lionel Robbins's *An Essay on the Nature and Significance of Economic Science.* This well-written and brief work fit in with the postivistic strain of modern times. Darwin and Biblical criticism contributed to the decay of Victorian religious orthodoxy. By the end of the century, positivism is well represented in the passionate writings of Vilfredo Pareto. The time was overripe within the Anglo-Saxon tradition for nihilistic questioning of the inherited Bentham–Edgeworth hedonistic utilitarianism. When Robbins sang out that the emperor had no clothes – that you could not prove or test by any empirical observations of objective science the normative validity of comparisons between different persons' utilities – suddenly all his generation of economists felt themselves to be naked in a cold world. Most of them had come into economics seeking the good. To learn in midlife that theirs was only the craft of a plumber, dentist, or cost accountant was a sad shock.

It was to salvage something from the ruins that the narrow new welfare economists worked toward the concept of production efficiency and consumption efficiency. Actually, as we now know, these various concepts of Pareto optimality were not only already in Pareto's post-1894 writings, but in fact with care we can detect in the works of J. S. Mill, Ricardo, and other early writers explicit glimpses of the notion that interferences with competition bring gains to those who benefit which are less in an objective sense than the losses brought to those who suffer. That this may be so is the germ of truth not quite isolated by Adam Smith when enunciating his doctrine of the Invisible Hand.

The Invisible Hand doctrine cannot cogently be used to deduce the optimality of laissez-faire, although many have fallen into this confusion. What is saying the same thing, the Pareto-optimality property of competitive equilibrium is no theoretical argument for laissez-faire, and is in many situations no cogent practical argument for favoring the use of competition. After Bergson laid the foundations for modern welfare economics in 1938, all these issues could be properly sorted out.

I do not think it is interesting at this point to review the pretentious claims made for the narrow version of compensationist economics and the retreats that subsequently had to be made. Nor is it useful to go into the various tests proposed by Hicks and Kaldor, Scitovsky, and myself to determine whether a particular policy change is or is not a good thing.

Although the matter is not clearly thought out, what gives some lasting relevance to this muddled literature was its tacit dependence upon a vague asymptotic theorem of the following sort.

> *Heuristic theorem.* Most technical changes or policy choices directly help some people and hurt others. For some changes, it is possible for the winners to buy off the losers so that everyone could conceivably end up better off than in the prior status quo. Suppose that no such compensatory bribes or side payments are made, but assume that we are dealing with numerous inventions and policy decisions that are quasi-independent. Even if for each single change it is hard to know in advance who will be helped and who will be hurt, in the absence of known "bias" in the whole sequence of changes, there is some vague presumption that a hazy version of the law of large numbers will obtain: so as the number of quasi-independent events becomes larger and larger, the chances improve that any random person will be on balance benefited by a social compact that lets events take place that push out society's utility possibility frontier, even though any one of the events may push some people along the new frontier in a direction less favorable than the status quo.

My language and logic have purposely been left fuzzy to model the actual thought processes economists muddled through some four decades back.

Dissemination of Bergsonian welfare economics

One of the first to follow Bergson's road was Oskar Lange in his 1942 *Econometrica* article, "Foundations of Welfare Economics." This unnecessarily stressed *additive* hedonism of the BSWF, what the mathematician calls "strong separability" rather than "weak separability." Evidently, Lange had not yet freed himself from his mid-1930s misconception that cardinal measurement of utility was intrinsically necessary for welfare economics.

My *Foundations of Economic Analysis* treatment of welfare economics in Chapter 8 still reads as a convenient summary of the Bergsonian *Weltanschauung*. Jan van de Graaf's *Theoretical Welfare Economics* (1957) provides an elegant and useful treatment of the same subject. Bergson's own 1966 *Essays in Normative Economics* not only reproduces his 1938 classic but also contains valuable extensions and further developments.

In my writing on the subject, here and elsewhere, the reader will notice that I have not shown much interest in the process by which particular social welfare functions arise and are deemed to be of interest or relevance. I have been satisfied to consider it not to be the task of economics as such to pass judgments on whether this social welfare function is in some sense more important than that social welfare function. Abram Bergson's writings show that he has been interested in exploring the topics that I have been content to turn over to disciplines other than my own.

In completing this general introduction to the analytical discussion that follows, I should not ignore an important misunderstanding of welfare economics and of Bergsonian welfare economics. In 1951, Kenneth Arrow published his classic, *Social Choice and Individual Values*. This founded an important branch of mathematical politics and has spawned some hundreds of papers on social choice. In particular, Arrow proved the impossibility of existence of a well-behaved "Constitutional Function," one that was supposed to provide an answer in the way of decision to any ballots given as inputs by K individuals who are permitted to vote according to *any and all possibilities of the rankings of various states of the world*. This Impossibility Theorem is a landmark in the history of ideas. It ends for all time our hope that there exists some ideal form of democracy, one that has eluded us up to this time but can be found in the future if only we continue an intelligent search for it. Arrow has earned a Nobel Prize at least twice over – once for his important breakthroughs in the economics of risk bearing, and once for this Impossibility Theorem in the theory of social choice.

Unfortunately, what I and Bergson and Ian Little have called a "Constitutional Function" – other and perhaps better names could be given to it – Arrow happened to call a "social welfare function." He used the same name for his unicorn that Bergson and other writers had used for their existent animals. So it is not particularly surprising that Arrow's readers, learning that he had proved the impossibility of a "social welfare function," should have formed the mistaken inference that there cannot exist a reasonable and well-behaved Bergsonian social welfare function.

By now this has all been sorted out in the advanced literature. But plenty of signs still abound that the misunderstanding lives on. All I can do is call attention once again to this spurious matter of confusion.[4] The rest of this chapter analyzes the content of Bergsonian welfare economics.

Existence and property of a Bergson social welfare function

1. To be brief, I start with the case of $j = 1, 2, \ldots, J$ "private" goods, each to be split up among $k = 1, 2, \ldots, K$ men. Man k has the consumption vector $(x_1^k, \ldots, x_J^k) = \mathbf{x}^k$. A *state of the world* is given by $\mathbf{x} = (\mathbf{x}^1; \mathbf{x}^2; \ldots; \mathbf{x}^K) = (x_1^1, \ldots, x_J^1; x_1^2, \ldots, x_J^2; \ldots; x_1^K, \ldots, x_J^K) = (x_j^k)$

A *Bergsonian social welfare function* (BSWF) is a *complete order* that ethically orders all the states of the world. Thus, if there are many states of $\mathbf{x}$, given by $\mathbf{a}, \mathbf{b}, \mathbf{c}, \ldots$, between every pair of states, we have a relationship "at least as good ethically as," written as $\gtrsim$, which is transitive. With standard technicalities understood, we have a *complete binary ordering* that obeys *transitivity*.

α For *any* pair, say $\mathbf{a}$ and $\mathbf{b}$, just one of the three cases holds:
- $\mathbf{a} \gtrsim \mathbf{b}$ and $\mathbf{b} \gtrsim \mathbf{a}$: "indifference" ($\mathbf{a} \sim \mathbf{b}$, $\mathbf{b} \sim \mathbf{a}$)
- $\mathbf{a} \gtrsim \mathbf{b}$ and not $\mathbf{b} \gtrsim \mathbf{a}$: "strong preference" ($a > b$)
- $\mathbf{b} > \mathbf{a}$ and not $\mathbf{a} \gtrsim \mathbf{b}$: "strong preference" ($b > a$)
- (Thus, $\mathbf{a} \sim \mathbf{a}$; etc.)

β For any three states,
- $\mathbf{a} \gtrsim \mathbf{b}$ and $\mathbf{b} \gtrsim \mathbf{c}$ implies that $\mathbf{a} \gtrsim \mathbf{c}$
- ($\mathbf{a} \gtrsim \mathbf{b}$ and $\mathbf{b} > \mathbf{c}$ implies that $\mathbf{a} > \mathbf{c}$; $\mathbf{a} > \mathbf{b}$ and $\mathbf{b} \gtrsim \mathbf{c}$ implies that $\mathbf{a} > \mathbf{c}$; etc.)

There need not exist a scalar function $z(\mathbf{x})$ with the property that $\mathbf{a} \sim \mathbf{b}$ if and only if $z(\mathbf{a}) = z(\mathbf{b})$. However, if the sets that satisfy $\mathbf{x} \gtrsim \mathbf{a}$ and $\mathbf{a} \gtrsim \mathbf{x}$ have specified simple topological properties, there will always exist an infinity of such $z(\mathbf{x})$ functions, each such "cardinal welfare indicator" being a monotone stretching of any other – as with $Z(\mathbf{x}) = f[z(\mathbf{x})]$, $f'[z] > 0$.

For us it will do if *each* state $\mathbf{x}$ can be found to be ethically indifferent to a state in which *every person gets the same scalar number of units, z, of every good.* Thus, we posit a root for z of the relation

$$(x_1^1, \ldots, x_J^1; \ldots; x_1^K, \ldots, x_J^K) \sim (z, \ldots, z; \ldots; z, \ldots, z) \tag{1.1}$$

This then defines a ("nonsubjective") "scalar indicator" of ethical welfare, $z(x_1^1, \ldots, x_J^1; \ldots; x_1^K, \ldots, x_J^K)$. For brevity, assume that $z(\cdot)$ is a smooth twice-differentiable function of its KJ arguments, with partial derivatives $\partial z/\partial x_j^k$:

$$\text{grad } z = \nabla z(\mathbf{x}) = [z_j(\mathbf{x})] \tag{1.2}$$

$$\text{Hessian } z = \nabla^2 z(\mathbf{x}) = [z_{ij}(\mathbf{x})] \tag{1.3}$$

Remark. Since units of goods are arbitrary, so is this z metric. But any choice of units – tons rather than loaves of bread, drops rather than quarts of wine, . . . – will serve indifferently. (If some subsets of goods had been irreplaceable for life, a z root would not always have had to exist. I also ignore lexigraphic orderings and other well-known complications.) Until later sections I have no need for the $z(\cdot)$ function.

2. Now we focus down from the general BSWF to the narrow *individualistic* BISWF. Let the men first be *atoms – sans* envy or altruism. Man k has "tastes" that depend only on his $\mathbf{x}^k$ and not on others' $\mathbf{x}^s$ when $s \neq k$. He has "his" complete ordering of states of the world, written as $\overset{k}{\gtrsim}$. This has the properties α and β above (but of course generally does not give the *same* decisions about points as the ethical ordering $\gtrsim$ did). Being atomistic, he has

$$(\mathbf{b}^1; \mathbf{b}^2; \ldots; \mathbf{b}^k; \ldots; \mathbf{b}^K) \overset{k}{\gtrsim} (\mathbf{a}^1; \mathbf{a}^2; \ldots; \mathbf{a}^k; \ldots; \mathbf{a}^K)$$

if

$$(\mathbf{c}^1; \ldots; \mathbf{c}^{k-1}; \mathbf{b}^k; \mathbf{c}^{k+1}; \ldots; \mathbf{c}^K) \overset{k}{\gtrsim} (\mathbf{c}^1; \ldots; \mathbf{c}^{k-1}; \mathbf{a}^k; \mathbf{c}^{k+1}; \mathbf{c}^K)$$

for *any* $(\mathbf{c}^1; \mathbf{c}^2; \ldots; \mathbf{c}^{k-1}; \mathbf{c}^{k+1}; \ldots; \mathbf{c}^K)$. So to speak, for man k, there is essential relevance only for "his own" J-dimensional subspace, $(x_1^k, \ldots, x_J^k)$, out of the KJ-dimensional full space, $(x_1^1, \ldots, x_J^1; \ldots; x_1^k . \ldots; \ldots x_J^k)$. This means that we can record *all* intraperson information about the K atoms by knowledge of their separate respective complete orders over (their own) J private-goods spaces: $\mathbf{a}^k \overset{k}{\gtrsim} \mathbf{b}^k$, $\mathbf{c}^k \overset{k}{\gtrsim} \mathbf{b}^k$, and so on $(k = 1, \ldots, K)$.

Remark. Later we can make use for each man of a scalar function that is a "cardinal utility indicator" of *his* well-being: we assume that one can *always* solve for the *scalar* root, $z^k, \ldots$, each person's indifference relation:

$$(z^k, \ldots, z^k) \overset{k}{\sim} (x_1^k, \ldots, x_J^k) = \mathbf{x}^k$$

$$z^k = z^k(\mathbf{x}^k) \qquad (k = 1, \ldots, K) \tag{2.1}$$

$$\nabla z^k(\mathbf{x}^k) = [z_j^k(\mathbf{x}^k)] = [\partial z^k(x_1^k, \ldots, x_J^k)/\partial x_j^k] \tag{2.2}$$

$$\nabla^2 z^k(\mathbf{x}^k) = [z_{ij}^k(\mathbf{x}^k)] = [\partial z^k(x_1^k, \ldots, x_J^K)/\partial x_i^k\, \partial x_j^k] \tag{2.3}$$

3. Now we must explicate the implications of the individualistic dogma that the "individuals' tastes are to count when they are unanimous and to be ethically resolved when they are not." This means that the ethical $\gtrsim$ is constrained to agree with the separate $\overset{k}{\gtrsim}$'s when they *all* happen to agree about two states of the world.

γ If for *all k*, $\mathbf{a}^k \overset{k}{\sim} \mathbf{b}^k$ $(k = 1, \ldots, K)$, then necessarily

$$\mathbf{a} = (\mathbf{a}^1; \ldots; \mathbf{a}^k; \ldots; \mathbf{a}^K) \sim \mathbf{b} = (\mathbf{b}^1; \ldots; \mathbf{b}^k; \ldots; \mathbf{b}^K)$$

This forces the BISWF to be "weakly separable" in the men's tastes. When I come to use the $z(\mathbf{x})$ and $z^k(\mathbf{x}^k)$ functions, it will be seen that weak-separability implies that $z(\mathbf{x})$ can be written in the form

$$z(x_1^1, \ldots, x_J^1; \ldots; x_1^K, \ldots, x_J^K) \equiv z[z^1(x_1^1, \ldots, x_J^1), \ldots, z^K(x_1^K, \ldots, x_J^K)] \quad (3.1)$$

where $z[z^1, \ldots, z^K]$ is a function of K scalar variables that records *all* the ethical information needed for interpersonal comparisons and judgments.

Specifically, we can infer by repeated substitutions of indifference that the only *independent* interpersonal ethical judgments that we need record about the BISWF are those involving states in which, for each man k, the goods he consumes are in the same scalar quantity, z^k. I use the symbol $(\gtrsim)$ for $\gtrsim$ as applied to such special states.

This means that we need only define $(\gtrsim)$ over the K-dimensional space of $\hat{z} = (z^1, z^2, \ldots, z^K)$, where a vector of these scalars adequately stands for

$$\begin{aligned}\hat{\mathbf{a}} &= (a^1, a^1, \ldots, a^1; a^2, \ldots, a^2; \ldots; a^K, \ldots, a^K)\\ &= (a^1, a^2, \ldots, a^K)\\ \hat{\mathbf{b}} &= (b^1, b^1, \ldots, b^1; b^2, \ldots, b^2; \ldots; b^K, \ldots, b^K)\\ &= (b^1, b^2, \ldots, b^K) \qquad \text{etc.}\end{aligned}$$

Since $K \ll KJ$, the economy in mustering ethical judgments is significant. It is this same weak-separability economy that permits *decentralized* market algorithms to function optimally and that lets optimal interpersonal redistributions be made solely in terms of a single good or in terms solely of abstract purchasing power.

Let me sketch how any two arbitrary states of the world can be decided upon once we know the $K \overset{k}{\gtrsim}$ orderings and the ethical $(\gtrsim)$ ordering in the $(z^1, \ldots, z^K)$ reduced space of K dimensions. For general $\mathbf{a}$ and $\mathbf{b}$, solve for respective K scalars

$$\hat{a} = (a^1, a^2, \ldots, a^K) \quad \text{and} \quad \hat{b} = (b^1, b^2, \ldots, b^K)$$

$$(a^k, a^k, \ldots, a^k) \overset{k}{\sim} (a_1^k, \ldots, a_J^k) = \mathbf{a}^k \qquad (k = 1, \ldots, J)$$

$$(b^k, b^k, \ldots, b^k) \overset{k}{\sim} (b_1^k, \ldots, b_J^k) = \mathbf{b}^k$$

Then find out how $(a^1, \ldots, a^K) = \hat{\mathbf{a}}$ and $(b^1, \ldots, b^K) = \hat{\mathbf{b}}$ are ethically ordered by $(\gtrsim)$. The answer found for $(\gtrsim)$ judgments then provides the needed answer for $\gtrsim$ as applied to the original $\mathbf{a}$ and $\mathbf{b}$!

Although Bergson did not in 1937 use the Debreu–Arrow notation and symbolism about complete orders, the foregoing discussion fairly describes his 1938 thought in that language. Before relaxing the *atomistic* simplifications, I sketch his 1938 thought in terms of observable marginal-rates-of-(ethical)-substitution functions.

4. It will be useful sometimes to renumber the KJ variables in $(x_1^1, \ldots; \ldots; \ldots; \ldots, x_J^K) = \mathbf{x}$ and write this vector as $\mathbf{x} = (y_1, \ldots, y_Q) = \mathbf{y}$, where $Q = KJ$. Then, under standard regularity conditions, such as (2.1)–(2.3) and (1.1)–(1.3), we can replace $\gtrsim$ by an equivalent symbolism that uses only marginal-rates-of-substitution functions denoting slope elements of ethical indifference. Any good may be taken as reference *numéraire* – say $x_1^1 = y_1$. Then we write, for a general BSWF, its marginal rates of substitution as

$$\begin{aligned} -\partial x_1^1/\partial x_j^k &= R^{jk}(x_1^1, \ldots; \ldots; \ldots, x_J^K) \\ &= R^{jk}(\mathbf{x}) = R^{jk}(\mathbf{x}^1; \ldots; \mathbf{x}^K) \end{aligned} \tag{4.1}$$

What is just the same in easier notation is

$$-\partial y_1/\partial y_i = R^i(y_1, \ldots, y_Q) = R^i(\mathbf{y}) \qquad (i = 2, \ldots, Q = KJ) \tag{4.2}$$

In order that the BSWF have "integrable" contours of indifference in KJ space, the foregoing MRS functions must satisfy well-known standard Antonelli–Allen integrability conditions, $\frac{1}{2}(Q-1)(Q-2)$, in independent number:

$$R_j^i(\mathbf{y}) - R^j(\mathbf{y})R_1^i(\mathbf{y}) = R_i^j(\mathbf{y}) - R^i(\mathbf{y})R_1^j(\mathbf{y}) \qquad (i, j = 2, \ldots, Q;\ i \neq j) \tag{4.3}$$

Recall that

$$R_j^i(\mathbf{y}) = \partial R^i(y_1, \ldots, y_Q)/\partial y_j; \quad \text{etc.}$$

We know from the standard theory of Pfaffian differentials that with (4.3) assured, the following expression admits of an "integrating factor," $\gamma(\mathbf{y})$, that defines an "exact differential" of an existent "cardinal BSWF indicator":

$$dy_1 + \sum_{j=2}^{Q} R^j(\mathbf{y})\, dy_j = \gamma(y_1, \ldots, y_Q)^{-1}\, dZ(y_1, \ldots, y_Q) \tag{4.4}$$

Indeed, we can pin down from the infinity of existent $\gamma(\mathbf{y})$ factors and $Z(\mathbf{y})$ indicator functions a unique $z(\mathbf{y})$ function if we require that (4.2) be equivalent to the ratio of $z(\mathbf{y})$'s "marginal social utilities" and satisfy the arbitrary *boundary conditions* of (4.5b), along loci where each person consumes the same number of units of one good as of any other, namely:

$$-\partial y_1/\partial y_i = R^i(\mathbf{y}) = [\partial z(\mathbf{y})/\partial y_i]/[\partial z(\mathbf{y})/\partial y_i] \qquad (i = 2, \ldots, Q) \tag{4.5a}$$

$$z(y, y, \ldots, y; y, \ldots, y; \ldots; y, \ldots, y) \equiv y \tag{4.5b}$$

5. How does this simplify when Bergson narrows the BSWF to being a BISWF? Now we have the atomistic (individualistic) property of the men, respected by the ethical judge:

$$R^{ik}(\mathbf{x})/R^{1k}(\mathbf{x}) = {}^kR^i(\mathbf{x}^k) \quad \text{independently of } \mathbf{x}^s, \quad s \neq k \tag{5.1}$$

where $R^{11}(\mathbf{x}) \equiv 1$.

All this involves $(K-1)J$ weak-separability conditions

$$\partial[R^{ik}(\mathbf{x})/R^{1k}(\mathbf{x})]/\partial x_j^s \equiv 0 \qquad \text{if } s \neq k \tag{5.2}$$

In the presence of these weak-separability conditions holding, it can be shown that many less than the $\frac{1}{2}(KJ-1)(KJ-2)$ integrability conditions of (4.3) are now *independently* needed. We can parallel for each man what was done for the whole KJ social space in (4.3), (4.4), and (4.5). Briefly, for each man we have $\frac{1}{2}(J-1)(J-2)$ integrability conditions

$${}^kR_j^i(\mathbf{x}^k) - {}^kR^j(\mathbf{x}^k){}^kR_1^i(\mathbf{x}^k) = {}^kR_i^j(\mathbf{x}^k) - {}^kR^i(\mathbf{x}^k){}^kR_1^j(\mathbf{x}^k)$$
$$(i, j = 2, \ldots, J;\ k = 1, \ldots, K) \tag{5.3}$$

These being satisfied, we have defined existing exact differentials of existent $z^k(\mathbf{x}^k)$ functions

$$[dz^k(\mathbf{x}^k)]/\gamma^k(\mathbf{x}^k)] = dx_1^k + \sum_2^J {}^kR^j(\mathbf{x}^k)\,dx_j^k \qquad (k = 1, \ldots, k) \tag{5.4}$$

$$z^k(z, \ldots, z) \equiv z \tag{5.5}$$

6. Now, as in Section 4, we need only observe interpersonal ethical judgments in the K-dimensional space of $(\hat{a}, \hat{b}, \hat{c}, \ldots)$, which adequately denote the $(\mathbf{a}, \mathbf{b}, \mathbf{c}, \ldots)$ points of the full space. Thus, in terms of the scalars $(z^1, \ldots, z^K)$, which stand for $(\hat{z}_1, \ldots, \hat{z}_K)$ but omit for brevity the circumflexes, we have interpersonal-ethical integrable MRS functions:

$$-\partial z^1/\partial z^k = E^k(z^1, \ldots, z^K) = E^k(\mathbf{z}) \qquad (k = 2, \ldots, K) \tag{6.1}$$

These need satisfy only $\frac{1}{2}(K-1)(K-2)$ integrability conditions:

$$E_s^k(\mathbf{z}) - E^s(\mathbf{z})E_1^k(\mathbf{z}) = E_k^s(\mathbf{z}) - E^k(\mathbf{z})E_1^s(\mathbf{z})$$
$$(k, s = 2, \ldots, K;\ k \neq s) \tag{6.2}$$

These guarantee the existence of an exact differential

$$dz^1 + \sum_{k=2}^{K} E^k(\mathbf{z})\,dz^k = dz[z^1, \ldots, z^K]/\hat{\gamma}(z^1, \ldots, z^K) \tag{6.3}$$

Subject to the boundary condition

$$z[z, \ldots, z] \equiv z \tag{6.4}$$

the $z[z^1, \ldots, z^K]$ function is uniquely defined.

Thus, we have finally arrived at *a nonsubjective cardinal indicator of ethical social welfare that is individualistically weakly separable,* as in (3.1):

$$z = z[z^1(x_1^1, \ldots, x_J^K), z^2(x_1^2, \ldots, x_J^2), \ldots, z^K(x_1^K, \ldots, x_J^K)]$$
$$= z[z^1, \ldots, z^K] = z(\mathbf{x}) \tag{6.5}$$

Remark. A general BSWF in $Q = KJ$ variables must have its $Q-1$ marginal-rate-of-substitution functions, $R^{1+i}(\mathbf{y})$, satisfy $\frac{1}{2}(KJ-1)\cdot(KJ-2)$ integrability conditions. If it is also an atomistic BISWF, it satisfies $K(J-1)(K-1)J$ weak-separability conditions. The sum of these, $\frac{1}{2}(KJ-1)(KJ-2) + K(J-1)(K-1)J$, represents many more conditions than are truly an *independent* set. Actually, as has been indicated above and as I hope to write up for publication, only $\frac{1}{2}(K-1)(K-2)+\frac{1}{2}(J-1)(J-2)$ integrability conditions can be *independently* specified in addition to the $K(J-1)(K-1)J$ weak-separability conditions. For K and J large, this saves us virtually 100 percent of the drudgery of verifying the integrability conditions. Furthermore, the (6.2) conditions need hold only for a limited set of points and then with (5.3) they guarantee that (4.3) holds *everywhere* in the space of Q dimensions!

7. Geometry may help a reader understand the power of the individualistic weak-separability axiom. To stay in three-dimensional space that one can visualize, I assume two persons only, $K = 2$: he and she. Person 1, he, consumes (bread^1, wine^1) $= (x_1^1, x_2^1)$ and lacks envy or altruism. Person 2, she, is a teetotaler consuming only (bread^1) $= x_1^2$; she is an atom sans envy and altruism. Individuals' tastes are to "count" ethically.

Use the lower corner on the floor of a cubical room as your origin. Use the two sides of the floor emerging from that origin-corner as your axes to measure *his* consumptions (x_1^1, x_2^1). Use the vertical line above the origin-corner as your third axis for her bread consumption x_1^2. Then Bergson's *general* BSWF provides indifference contours (i.e., surfaces) that fill the space like nested soup bowls with their bottoms faced toward the origin.

But now assume that each person's tastes are ethically to "count." A tremendous economy of ethical specification immediately applies. Now draw on the floor, for the space of (bread^1, wine^1) or (x_1^1, x_2^1), *his* personal indifference curves dictated by his atomistic tastes. Each such Person 1 indifference curve can be given a number equal to its ordinary distance from the origin-corner as measured along the diagonal drawn on the floor between the origin-corner and its opposite corner. For *her,* the loci of personal indifference are given by all points that are the same bread^2 height above the floor. These loci of hers can be numbered by that x_1^2 coordinate.

The Ethical Observer's power to arbitrarily specify shapes of ethical-indifference contours is seriously reduced by the individualistic axiom. Thus, erect a thin glass wall that rises vertically above the floor's diagonal (splitting the cubical room into two geometrically equal prismatic volumes). The interpersonal judgments required for the BISWF from the ethical preceptor consist of no more and no less than the ethical-interpersonal indifference curves chalked in on the thin glass partition. Each such curve specifies how much must be her increased bread^2 to compensate ethically for balanced reductions in his (bread^1 = wine^1). There is no avoiding such interpersonal judgments if we are to be provided with a complete ethical ordering of all the states of the world. But once they are made in this small (glass-partition) part of the vast three-dimensional space, *all the rest* of the interpersonal judgments are already implied!

Mathematically, the weak-separability conditions on the slope elements of ethical indifference – slope elements that fill the interior of the room like myriad thumbtacks oriented at each interior point – are partial differential equations that have solution functions uniquely determined once the values of those functions are specified along the boundary conditions (the agreement on the floor with *his* autonomous indifference curves; the agreement on the glass partition with the interpersonal ethical-indifference curves). Twist a set of wires into the shape of each one of the floor's indifference curves. Raise any such wire vertically evenly above its profile on the floor: any such lifting will provide a locus of points ethically indifferent. So the whole space is filled with such twisted wires. Can these one-dimensional wires be "integrated" to form two-dimensional indifference *surfaces of ethical indifference?* The answer is necessarily, Yes.

Note. For $Q = 3$, *generally* one integrability condition would have to be imposed. But when the BSWF is a BISWF, we had no need to specify *any* integrability condition – since neither the floor's two-dimensional indifference curves nor the glass wall's two-dimensional indifference curves need any such reciprocity conditions. Weak separability has done the work for us!

8. Now a Bergson Individualistic Social Welfare Function has been carefully devised (1) in terms of *ordinal* ethical ordering, (2) honoring people's autonomous tastes when those lead to unanimity, and (3) providing the irreducibly required *inter*personal ethical orderings. We have arrived at a position to dispose of a misunderstanding concerning whether a certain odd Axiom of Neutrality makes any sense as a requirement; and concerning whether, whatever its foolishness, it was actually implied in the earlier writings of such Bergsonians as Samuelson (1947) or Bergson (1938). [See Samuelson (1977) for a rebuttal of Kemp and Ng (1976, 1977).] If it were not that a number of writers in the social choice vineyard (Kemp and Ng, Parks, Hammond, Pollak, . . .) attach disproportionate importance to this issue, I would be even briefer in disposing of it here.

Note that my BISWF is *not* formulated in terms of "an ethical *ranking*" determined as an output of a function whose input variables are individual *rankings*. It is not the case, and not intended to be the case, that sign $\{z(\mathrm{x}) - z(\mathrm{y})\}$ for the BISWF is always determinable from knowledge alone of

$$[\mathrm{sign}\{z^1(\mathrm{x}) - z^1(\mathrm{y})\},\ \mathrm{sign}\ \{z^2(\mathrm{x}) - z^2(\mathrm{y})\},\ \ldots,\ [\mathrm{sign}\{z^K(\mathrm{x}) - z^k(\mathrm{y})\}]$$

Why should it be? To call such a requirement an Axiom of Neutrality is to dignify it beyond its merits in the present context.

In axiomatics more than almost anywhere else must the watchword be: By their fruits shall you know assumptions. *Caveat emptor.* The poisoned apple borne by the axiom above (when combined with some harmless regularity conditions) is that some *one* single person's tastes must rule *dictatorially*. It tells us something about the state of present-day "social choice" writing that such an axiom would be considered even momentarily as applying to Bergsonian welfare economics or to the Old Welfare Economics.

Consider the simplest case of two persons, between whom a fixed total of a single private good is to be allocated.

$$x_1^1 + x_1^2 = x \qquad x_1^k \geq 0$$

Suppose that they are deemed ethically "alike" and that Jesus, long before Abram Bergson was born, considers the *bonum bonorum* to be at the maximum of a symmetric, strictly quasi-concave (ordinal!) function of their respective consumptions. Then Jesus's BISWF will judge it better to go from $y = (x, 0)$ to $y = (\frac{1}{2}x, \frac{1}{2}x)$. We know that there is no self-contradiction in this *final* decision; and many would say, no absurdity in this ethos. Also, Jesus has let the individuals' tastes "count," in the sense of not judging more of x_1^k bad for a person. No paternalism or merit wants here. (And, actually, coming together in a Rawlsian convention under a veil of ignorance, risk-averse individuals might all by *unanimous* vote always opt for such completely egalitarian taxes.)

Now how do the lobbyists for the Axiom of Neutrality view all this? They say,

Since $[\text{sign}(\frac{1}{2}x - x), \text{sign}(\frac{1}{2}x - 0)] = [-, +]$, and
since $[\text{sign}(0 - x), \text{sign}(x - 0)] = [-, +]$,
Jesus has committed himself to giving *everything* to Man![1]

Jesus's amused answer, and mine, is this: Neither Bergson, nor Lange, nor Samuelson, nor Little, nor de Graaf – nor Buddha, nor Father Divine, nor the Wizard of Oz, Pareto, Bentham, Edgeworth – expected an *ordinal* social welfare function of individualistic type (that respects people's tastes when they are unanimous) to obey such an odd axiom-on-signs.

Moral: I blow on my soup to cool it off and, *without contradiction,* I blow on my hands to warm them up.

9. It is inhuman to be an atom, sans envy and altruism. It is also unrealistic. What happens to the *individualistic* social welfare function when people are more human?

We can still define a BISWF, as a species of the genus BSWF. Now each person's $\succeq^k$ ordering involves *all* the goods, x_j^s items as well as x_j^k items. Now we write the cardinal indicator of man k's preferences in a general form lacking any separability properties:

$$z^k = z^k(\mathbf{x}^1, \ldots, \mathbf{x}^k, \ldots \mathbf{x}^K) = z^k(\mathbf{x}) \tag{9.1}$$

$$y \equiv z^k(y, \ldots, y; y, \ldots, y; \ldots; y, \ldots, y) \tag{9.2}$$

Each of these is *formally* indistinguishable from a general BSWF. As long as we stay with a BSWF, and not a BISWF, there is *no* necessary relation between any of (9.1) and the BSWF of (1.1):

$$z = z(\mathbf{x}^1, \ldots, \mathbf{x}^K) \quad (9.3)$$

$$y = z(y, \ldots, y; \ldots; y, \ldots, y) \quad (9.4)$$

What if the ethical observer still wishes to be individualistic in the sense that persons' tastes are to "count" when they are unanimous and to be ethically resolved when they are not? Then (9.3) takes the form like that in (3.1), but with each $z^k(\mathbf{x})$ function there now involving $\mathbf{x}^s$ as well as $\mathbf{x}^k$ items:

$$z = z[z^1(\mathbf{x}); \ldots; z^K(\mathbf{x})] \quad (9.5)$$

$$y = z[y; \ldots; y] \quad (9.6)$$

In *general,* the BISWF of (9.5) written for nonatomistic people is mathematically indistinguishable from the BSWF of (1.1)–(1.3). This is a fairly devastating observation from the standpoint of economists enamored of the market. In general, when there are *no* weak separability properties, there is no useful role for *decentralized* pricing mechanisms[5] – either à la von Mises and Schumpeter or à la Lerner and Lange.

An all-powerful ethical mind could use its perfect computer to select the best state of the world. Pareto-optimal states can still be identified. But most states of the world might well be trivially Pareto optimal. And, in any case, the perfect computer will not only screen out all non-Pareto-optimal points but as well must do the job itself of picking out of those that remain the one that is ethically best. There are, in general, no lump-sum algebraic transfers of goods or of dollars that can be given to people in the justified confidence that men can be counted on to harness their self-interest to achieve the Ethical Observer's orchestrated maximum.

Alas, for much of conventional political economy.

10. Fortunately for the vanity of economists, the presence of *some* externalities in preferences and values does not render useless the atomic private-good model that can utilize decentralized market pricing. Thus, if there are only trace elements of "paternalism" – or, to use a less pejorative language, of "merit wants" – one might still hope to get a tolerable approximation to the optimum by a system of markets-cum-lump-sum transfers plus a few adjustments to take account of the externality complications.

One man's trace element is another man's mountain. So there may well be problems in deciding when the remarks of this section are of relevance.

11. Economists have studied some special patterns of *external* interdependences. My 1954 "Pure Theory of Public Expenditure" represents a logical culmination of the "voluntary theory of public exchange" doctrines associated historically with Erik Lindahl (1919), Knut Wicksell (1896), and other writers in the Austrian and Italian utility literature.[6]

I sketch a few of its properties as they relate to Bergsonian welfare economics and Pareto optimality. Now, in addition to the J private goods of Sections 2 and 3 and relation (3.1), namely $(x_1^k, \ldots, x_J^k)$, I introduce a category of M "public goods":

$$(x_{J+1}, \ldots, x_{J+M}) \equiv (x_{J+1}^k, \ldots, x_{J+M}^k) \qquad (k = 1, \ldots, K) \qquad (11.1)$$

The essence of any such public good, x_{J+m}, is that it enters into the indifference curves of more than one person.

Each person's tastes are summarizable by

$$z^k = z^k(x_1^k, \ldots, x_J^k; x_{J+1}, \ldots, x_{J+M}) = z^k(\mathbf{x}^k; \bar{\mathbf{x}}) \qquad (11.2)$$

$$y = z^k(y, \ldots, y; y, \ldots, y) \qquad (11.3)$$

If the BSWF is to be "individualistic" and respect tastes, so that it is to be a BISWF, then it becomes

$$z = z(z^1[\mathbf{x}^k; \bar{\mathbf{x}}], \ldots, z^K[\mathbf{x}^K; \bar{\mathbf{x}}]) \qquad (11.4)$$

$$y = z(y, \ldots, y) \qquad (11.5)$$

Although it is hard to find a decentralized price–tax mechanism that will motivate people to reveal their preferences[7] and help achieve the ethical optimum, it is easy to write down in the 1954 fashion the conditions of the optimum. For brevity, I make some overly strong assumptions.

Assume that $z[z^1(\ \ ), \ldots] \equiv z(\mathbf{x})$ and that all $z^k(\mathbf{x}^k, \bar{\mathbf{x}})$ functions are strictly monotone-increasing, smooth, strictly quasi-concave functions of their positive arguments, and that every good is *essential* to every person. Also, assume there is a smooth *concave* production-possibility frontier technologically connecting the *totals* of the $J + M$ goods

$$\sum_1^K x_1^k = T\left(\sum_1^K x_2^k, \ldots, \sum_1^K x_J^k, x_{J+1}, \ldots, x_{J+M}\right) \qquad (11.6)$$

$$T_q(a_2, \ldots, a_{J+M}) = \partial T(a_2, \ldots, a_{J+M})/\partial a_q < 0 \qquad (q = 2, \ldots, J+M)$$

Then it is a necessary and sufficient condition for the ethical maximization of $z(x; \bar{x})$ in (11.4) that the following 1954 relations be satisfied:

$$\frac{z_j^k(x^k; \bar{x})}{z_1^k(x^k; \bar{x})} = -T_j\left(\sum_1^K x_2^k, \ldots, \sum_1^K x_J^k, x_{J+1}, \ldots, x_{J+m}\right) \qquad (j = 2, \ldots, J; k = 1, \ldots, K) \qquad (11.7)$$

$$\sum_1^K \frac{z_{J+m}^k(\mathbf{x}^k; \bar{\mathbf{x}})}{z_1^k(\mathbf{x}^k; \bar{\mathbf{x}})} = -T_{J+m}\left(\sum_1^K x_2^k, \ldots; \ldots, x_{J+m}\right) \qquad (m = 1, \ldots, M) \qquad (11.8)$$

$$\frac{z_k[z^1(\mathbf{x}^1;\bar{\mathbf{x}});\ \ldots\ ;z^K(\mathbf{x}^K;\bar{\mathbf{x}})]z_1^k(\mathbf{x}^k;\bar{\mathbf{x}})}{z_1[z^1(\mathbf{x}^1;\bar{\mathbf{x}});\ \ldots\ ;z^K(\mathbf{x}^K;\bar{\mathbf{x}})]z_1^1(\mathbf{x}^1;\bar{\mathbf{x}})} = 1$$

$$(k = 2, \ldots, K) \qquad (11.9)$$

The relations (11.6)–(11.8) alone do not define a unique state of the world. They define only the Pareto-optimality utility-possibility frontier involving a $(K - 1)$-fold infinity of Pareto-optimal possibilities. The final interpersonal relations (11.9) render the interpersonal ethical judgments to select out of this infinity the single best state of the world (best according to this specified BISWF, of course).

12. Where there are no public goods and only private goods, with $M = 0$, (11.8) would be vacuous and market pricing can be used to achieve the ethical optimum when we assume (a) the atomistic case of an individualistic social welfare function, a BISWF free of envy and altruism; and (b) that the laws of technical returns are those most favorable to viable competition – constant returns to scale, convex technology, and so forth – and each person's indifference contours are strictly convex and involve every good as an essential item; and where we introduce an optimal set of lump-sum transfers to ensure that dollar votes are ethically commensurable.

I make some (overstrong) assumptions about the various slopes and curvatures. The people's tastes are given by strictly quasi-concave functions

$$z^k = z^k(x_1^k, \ldots, x_J^k; x_{J+1}, \ldots, x_{J+M}) = z^k(\mathbf{x}^k;\bar{\mathbf{x}}) \qquad (12.1)$$

$$z_q^k(\mathbf{x}^k;\bar{\mathbf{x}}) > 0 \qquad (q = 1, \ldots, J, J+1, \ldots, J+M)$$

$$\lim_{x_q^k \to 0} \frac{z_q^k(\mathbf{x}^k;\bar{\mathbf{x}})}{z_{q'}^k(\mathbf{x}^k;\bar{\mathbf{x}})} = \infty, \qquad \lim_{x_q^k \to \infty} \frac{z_q^k(\mathbf{x}^k;\bar{\mathbf{x}})}{z_{q'}^k(\mathbf{x}^k;\bar{\mathbf{x}})} = 0$$

$$(q \neq q'; q, q' = 1, \ldots, J, \ldots, J+M)$$

The weakly separable BISWF also satisfies similar properties: $z[z^1, \ldots, z^K]$ is strictly quasi-concave, with positive partials and obeys limit relations like the last set.

Finally, $T(x_2, \ldots,)$ is a strictly concave function with negative partial derivatives; and so on.

Set $p_1 \equiv 1$ as *numéraire* and let $(p_2, \ldots, p_J)$ be market prices for the remaining $J - 1$ private goods. Each person k, given his lump-sum payment L^k, expressed in terms of the first, *numéraire* good, acts to maximize $z^k(\mathbf{x}^k)$:

$$\text{subject to } x_1^k + \sum_2^J p_j^k x_j^k = L^k \qquad (k = 1, \ldots, K) \qquad (12.2)$$

$$\max_{x_j^k} z^k(\mathbf{x}^k) = z^k(X^k[L^k; 1, p_2, \ldots, p_J]) \qquad (12.3)$$

where the kth person's single-valued demand functions each depend on the parameters

$$[L^k; 1, p_2, \ldots, p_j] \equiv [L^k; p]:$$
$$x_j^k = X_j^k[L^k; 1, p_2, \ldots, p_J] = x^k[L^k; \mathbf{p}]$$
$$(j = 1, \ldots, J; \quad k = 1, \ldots, K) \quad (12.4)$$

Whatever the values that $[L^k]$ take in (12.1) and (12.2), the consumers' demand maximizations will assure that the following hold:

$$\frac{z_j^k(\mathbf{x}^k)}{z_1^k(\mathbf{x}^k)} = p_j \qquad (j = 2, \ldots, J; \quad k = 1, \ldots, K) \qquad (12.5)$$

If the technological return conditions in (11.6) are suitable for perfect competition, then the market mechanism can be used to assure equality of p_j to marginal (social) cost. Or this may result from Pareto–Barone or Lerner–Lange bureaucratic planning. In any case, we have

$$p_j = -T_j\left(\sum_1^K x_2^k, \ldots\right) \qquad (j = 2, \ldots, J) \qquad (12.6)$$

To ensure that all goods produced are consumed, the ethical planners must make the $(L^1, \ldots, L^K)$ vector satisfy

$$\sum_1^K X_1^k[L^k; \mathbf{p}] = T\left(\sum_1^K X_2^k[L^k; \mathbf{p}], \ldots, \sum_1^K X_J^k[L^k; \mathbf{p}]\right) \qquad (12.7)$$

Under my strong assumptions on convexity (which are stronger than those spelled out by early writers such as Pareto), we are guaranteed that the pricing model's relations (12.1)–(12.7) will define an equilibrium for this system of atomistic individuals as a result of a proper (unique) choice of $(L^1, \ldots, L^K)$; and one of these competitive equilibria does achieve the desired ethical maximum of $z(\mathbf{x})$.

As will be discussed later, Pareto sensed correctly that each such competitive solution is Pareto optimal[8] (and, what is exactly the same thing, *could* represent the *optimum optimorum* of *some* existent BISWF). Also – as Pareto at least vaguely realized, Lerner clearly realized, and Arrow proved in our time – the *optimum optimorum* called for by *any* given specified BISWF is capable (under my *strong* assumptions!) of being effectuated by a competitive equilibrium achievable through an appropriate choice of (L^K).

Of course, a BSWF that is *not* a BISWF need not be achievable by pricing in decentralized competitive markets.

13. Now restore the condition that M be positive and there be at least one public good. This "externality" kills off any simple use of the pricing system.

Lindahl (1919) naively believed something like the following:

a In (12.3) we are to replace $(\mathbf{x}^k)$ by $(\mathbf{x}^k; \bar{\mathbf{x}})$ and write $z^k(\mathbf{x}^k; \bar{\mathbf{x}})$. (There can be no objection to that.)

b For the M public goods and for each kth person, let us define respective "pseudo-tax-prices," $(p^K_{J+1}, \ldots, p^k_{J+M})$. (The name is mine and is meant to sound a warning.)

c Adjoin to (12.2) and (12.3) relations that *pretend* each person can buy as much or little of any public good at its pseudo-tax-price to him:

$$x^k_1 + \sum_2^J p_j x^k_j + \sum_1^M p^k_{J+M} x_{J+M} = L^k \qquad (k = 1, \ldots, K) \qquad (13.1)$$

$$\frac{z^k_{J+M^k}(\mathbf{x}^k; \bar{\mathbf{x}})}{z^k_1(\mathbf{x}^k; \bar{\mathbf{x}})} = p^k_{J+m} \qquad (m = 1, \ldots, M; \quad k = 1, \ldots, K) \qquad (13.2)$$

$$\frac{z^k_j(\mathbf{x}^k; \bar{\mathbf{x}})}{z^k_1(\mathbf{x}^k; \bar{\mathbf{x}})} = p_j \qquad (j = 1, \ldots, J) \qquad (13.3)$$

Equations (13.1), (13.2), and (13.3) generate $J + M$ pseudo-demand functions for each man k:

$$x^k_q = X^k_q[L^k; 1, p_2, \ldots, p_J; p^k_{J+1}, \ldots, p^k_{J+M}]$$
$$= X^k_q[L^k; \mathbf{p}; \bar{\mathbf{p}}^k] \qquad (k = 1, \ldots, K; \quad q = 1, \ldots, J, \ldots, J + M) \qquad (13.4)$$

d Equate to each public good's marginal cost the *sum* of its pseudo-tax-price taken over all the people: that is, adjoin to (12.6):

$$P^1_{J+m} + \cdots + p^K_{J+m}$$
$$= -T_{J+m}\left(\sum_1^K x^k_2, \ldots, \sum_1^K x^k_J, x_{J+1}, \ldots, x_{J+M}\right) \qquad (m = 1, \ldots, M) \qquad (13.5)$$

$$p_j = -T_j\left(\sum_1^K x^k_2, \ldots, \sum_1^K x^k_J, x_{J+1}, \ldots, x_{J+M}\right) \qquad (13.6)$$

e The total pseudodemand of each public good given in (13.4) must equal that public good's common value:

$$X^k_{J+m}[L^k; 1, \mathbf{p}; \bar{\mathbf{p}}^k] = x_{J+m} \qquad (k = 1, \ldots, K; \quad m = 1, \ldots, M) \qquad (13.7)$$

f Finally, there must be a *feasible* choice of $(L^1, \ldots, L^K)$, a vector picked to assure that all which is produced and supplied must be demanded and consumed.

$$\sum_1^K X^k_1[L^k; \mathbf{p}, \mathbf{p}^{-k}]$$
$$= T\left(\sum_1^K X^k_2[L^k; \mathbf{p}, \mathbf{p}^{-k}], \ldots, x_{J+1}, \ldots, x_{J+M}\right) \qquad (13.8)$$

These Lindahl pseudo-tax-price functions, (13.1)–(13.8), do define a solution for each feasible choice of L^k's under my strong assumptions.

Every one of these $(K - 1)$-infinity-fold of Lindahl solutions can be shown to define a point of Pareto optimality – and, under my strong assumptions, *all* Pareto-optimal points can be generated by the Lindahl equations for proper choice of (L^k). And, of course, the ethical maximum of the specified BISWF will be achievable formally by the one best selection of the (L^k) lump-sum transfers.

However, what Lindahl never sufficiently realized, people will not be motivated to act in accordance with the "Lindahl" relations (13.2) if they are smart enough to realize that (13.5) is to hold! It pays you to *hide* your true tastes for a public good, not to reveal them as you are selfishly motivated to do with regard to a private good.

14. There is another pattern of altruism or envy that economists have found interesting to analyze. In it, I am not an atom. The private bread and wine I eat affect me. The private bread and wine you eat also affect me.

But my altruism and envy are themselves "individualistic." If *you* (privately) feel as well off with (4 of your bread, 2 of your wine) and (3 of your bread, 3 of your wine), then *I* feel equally well off (on your account) in these alternative situations.

To avoid infinite regress, economists sometimes postulate in this situation a "first-order level of atomic tastes": prior to my envy or altruism concerning your $\mathbf{x}^s$, I as man k have a *first-order* utility indicator function ${}^{(1)}z^k(\mathbf{x}^k)$, like that in (2.1):

$$\begin{aligned} {}^{(1)}z^k &= {}^{(1)}z^k(\mathbf{x}^k) \qquad (k = 1, \ldots, K) \\ y &\equiv {}^{(1)}z^k(y, \ldots, y) \end{aligned} \tag{14.1}$$

To introduce empathy and make your $\mathbf{x}^s$ matter to me, I define for me (or any person k) a *second-order* utility indicator function, ${}^{(2)}z^k(\mathbf{x})$, *that is weakly separable* in my own first-order tastes and every other person's first-order tastes:

$$\begin{aligned} {}^{(2)}z^k &= {}^{(2)}z^k[{}^{(1)}z^1(\mathbf{x}^1); {}^{(1)}z(\mathbf{x}^2), \ldots, {}^{(1)}z(\mathbf{x}^K)] \qquad (k = 1, \ldots, K) \\ y &\equiv {}^{(2)}z^k[y; \ldots ; y] \end{aligned} \tag{14.2}$$

One could even envisage a countable infinity of higher-order values or tastes, each dependent on the next lower-order taste function:

$$\begin{aligned} {}^{(h+1)}z^k &= {}^{(h+1)}z^k\{{}^{(h)}z^1[\cdot], \ldots, {}^{(h)}z^K[\cdot]\} \\ &= {}^{(h+1)}z[{}^{(1)}z^1(\mathbf{x}^1), \ldots, {}^{(1)}z^K(\mathbf{x}^k)] \\ &\qquad (h = 1, 2, \ldots ; k = 1, \ldots, K) \end{aligned} \tag{14.3}$$

Note that, by induction, we can verify that each of these higher-order functions is weakly separable in terms of the *same* first-order functions of people's atomic tastes. So each is weakly separable in a meaningful sense.

There might even be a limit set of functions:

$$\begin{aligned} &\lim_{h \to \infty} {}^{(h)}\bar{z}[{}^{(1)}z^1(\mathbf{x}^1), \ldots, {}^{(1)}z^k(\mathbf{x}^k)] \\ &\quad = \bar{z}^k[{}^{(1)}z^1(\mathbf{x}^1), \ldots, {}^{(1)}z^K(\mathbf{x}^K)] \qquad (k = 1, \ldots, K) \end{aligned} \tag{14.4}$$

A good reference for this hierarchy of utility functions is that of Tintner (1946). Just as nothing very interesting seemed to come from speaking of "the probability of a (person's subjective) probability," so cascading higher-order utilities has not seemed to lead to anything very novel or interesting. So I shall couch my exposition here in terms of h equal to 2, or equal to *any* integer, or equal to infinity as in (14.4). Notationally, I shall omit the superscript in ${}^{(1)}z(\mathbf{x}^k)$ and the h superscript in ${}^{(h)}\bar{z}[\quad]$ (whatever be the relevant final h).

As far as individuals' tastes and values are concerned, we have arrived at a special kind of nonatomic people, those who are "quasi-atomic" in the sense of having for *their* personal indifference contours the *same* weakly separable structure – the same "atoms" in their "molecules":

$$\begin{aligned} \bar{z}^k &= \bar{z}^k[z^1(\mathbf{x}^1), \ldots, z^k(\mathbf{x}^k)] \qquad (k = 1, \ldots, K) \\ y &= \bar{z}^k[y, \ldots, y] \end{aligned} \tag{14.5}$$

What individualistic BISWF does this imply for the ethical observer? Clearly, the BISWF must *also* have the common weakly separable structure, the same atoms as building blocks but of course with its own molecular composition:

$$\begin{aligned} z &= z[z^1(\mathbf{x}^1), \ldots, z^K(\mathbf{x}^K)] \\ y &= z[y, \ldots, y] \end{aligned}$$

Remember that no superscript, $(k = 1, \ldots, K)$, means that the utility function is a *social* welfare function of some ethical norming system.

What makes this common-atomic case interesting is that, despite its "externalities," it may still lend itself to use of decentralized pricing mechanisms.

15. The quasi-atomistic structures of the preceding section can involve either benevolent sympathy [in which my $\bar{z}^k$ rises when your $z^s(\mathbf{x}^s)$ rises], or envy [in which my $\bar{z}^k$ falls when your $z^s(\mathbf{x}^s)$ rises], or elements of both. The case most clearly seen to be favorable to the use of competitive pricing in decentralized markets is that of positive sympathy or altruism.

For, in this case, the final BISWF has *all* the properties of the atomic BISWF case. Indistinguishable from (3.1) will be the present

$$\begin{aligned} &z = z[z^1(\mathbf{x}^1), \ldots, z^K(\mathbf{x}^K)] \\ &\partial z[\cdot]/\partial z^k > 0, \qquad \partial z^k(x_1^k, \ldots, x_J^h)/\partial x_j^k > 0 \end{aligned} \tag{15.1}$$

The market demand functions generated by giving each man k the money to spend at given market prices, $(1, p_2, \ldots, p_J)$, are *strictly atomic* even though the person's "values" are quasi-atomic. Let me explain. Because $\bar{z}^k[\ldots, z^k(\mathbf{x}^k), \ldots, z^s(\mathbf{x}^s), \ldots]$ has the indicated weak-separability property, maximizing it, for given income of k, given prices, and *given quantities* for others, means that his maximizing his *private* (first-order) tastes will do the trick (of course with some implied harmless "simultaneity"). Man k solves

$$\max_{x^k} z^k(\mathbf{x}^k) \text{ subject to} \sum_1^J p_j x_j^k = L^k = z^k(\mathbf{X}^k[L^k; 1, p_2, \ldots, p_J]) \quad (15.2)$$

where his demand functions are roots of the atomic equations

$$\sum_1^J p_j x_j^k = L^k; \quad \frac{z_j^k(\mathbf{x}^k)}{z_1^k(\mathbf{x}^k)} = p_j \qquad (j = 2, \ldots, J) \qquad (15.3)$$

Reminder: Weak separability makes $z^k(\mathbf{x}^k)$ independent of x_j^s, $s \neq k$!

There will always exist one choice of $(L^1, L^2, \ldots, L^K)$ that will achieve the maximum of (15.1)'s $z[\bar{z}^1(\mathbf{x}^1), \ldots, \bar{z}^K(\mathbf{x})]$ by assuring that the interpersonal equity relations hold:

$$\frac{z_k[z^1, \ldots]z_1^k(\mathbf{x}^k)}{z_1[z^1, \ldots]z_1^1(x^1)} = 1 \qquad (k = 2, \ldots, K) \qquad (15.4)$$

Remark. The set of points that are Pareto optimal vis-à-vis the quasi-atomic vector of functions $\{\bar{z}^k[z^1(\mathbf{x}^1), \ldots, z^K(\mathbf{x}^K)]\}$ will have *shrunk* relative to the set of points that are Pareto optimal vis-à-vis the atomic vector of functions $\{z^1(\mathbf{x}^1), \ldots, z^K(\mathbf{x}^K)\}$. Why? Because altruistic people may well *voluntarily* give up some of their own (L^k) to others – for that's what makes them "selfishly" happy.[9]

16. An extreme case is that of Perfect Consensus. Everyone then has the *exact same* $\bar{z}^k[\mathbf{x}]$ function. So the BISWF must exactly agree with this common values function. So the set of Pareto-optimal points shrinks to the *single* "best state of the world," to the maximum of the agreed-on BISWF.

Theological zealots argue that this is the way the world should be. In Samuelson (1956), I gave a fanciful example of family consensus that generates a peaceful collective utility function with weakly separable demands for pappa, mamma, brother, and sister. What I regarded as a fanciful polar case, I understand Gary Becker has proposed as a serious sociological archetype.

17. Suppose that we reverse altruism, replacing it by envy? Then $\partial\bar{z}^k/\partial x_j^s < 0$ for $s \neq k$. Just as positive empathy shrinks the set of Pareto-optimal states of the world, sadism and envy widen the set. A limiting case is that of a zero-sum game: pure *power* rather than welfare prevails. It does not matter how few or many chapeaux I have – as long as I have many more than you!

In the zero-sum case, *every* state of the world is Pareto optimal. Despite any formal difference between a BSWF and a BISWF, they are in substance exactly the same thing.

Use of decentralized pricing would be hopeless in seeking the best state of the world if the BISWF shared these malevolence properties and delighted in inequalities and resentments. Direct computation or selection would be needed to arrive at such an odd best state of the world.

18. Despite the widening of the Pareto-optimal set brought by envy, the pricing system could still be used in the quasi-atomic model provided that the degree of intraperson envy is not too large and that $\partial z[\ldots, z^k, \ldots]/\partial z^k > 0$. The Ethical Observer need work only in the K-dimensional space of $\{z^1, \ldots, z^K\}$, where $z^k = z^k(\mathbf{x}^k)$. By choice of the (L^k) set, He or She can swing the system into any and every such point. The best state of the world will be found along the *atomic* Pareto-optimality set.

What only seemingly complicates matters are cases where too much for one man is so resented by the rest that the individualistic Ethical Observer is virtually forced into resenting it: this means that some $\partial z/\partial x^k$ become negative; and then $\partial z/\partial \bar{z}^k$ must be negative in such regions.

If you plot the ethical (interpersonal) indifference curves in the (z^1, z^2) space, where $K = 2$, those curves bend back and have positive slopes in some regions. However, just as atoms avoid consuming too many chocolates if that makes them sick, the Ethical Observer faced with choice along a negatively inclined (z^1, z^2) trade-off locus of feasibility will then most assuredly avoid oversatiated branches of the indifference curve with positive slope.

19. This section explains what has been mentioned in note 1, the resurrection for ethics of *additive* hedonism by John Harsanyi (1955) through a consideration of rational *stochastic* choice axioms. Harsanyi advances persuasive reasons why the weakly separable BISWF of (3.1) or (15.1), call it $z[z^1(\mathbf{x})], \ldots, z^K(\mathbf{x})]$, should have a monotone stretching that makes it *linear:*

$$\begin{aligned} V(x) &= Z\{z[z^1(\mathbf{x}), \ldots, z^K(\mathbf{x})]\}, \qquad Z'\{z\} > 0 \gtreqless Z''\{z\} \\ &\equiv \sum_1^K \lambda^k V^k(\mathbf{x}), \qquad \lambda^k > 0 \end{aligned} \tag{19.1}$$

In case the individuals are atoms, without envy or altruism and consuming only private goods, then of course $z^k(\mathbf{x})$ and $V^k(\mathbf{x})$ can be replaced by $z^k(\mathbf{x}^k)$ and $V^k(\mathbf{x}^k) \equiv Z^k\{z^k(\mathbf{x}^k)\}$, where $Z^k\{\cdot\}$ is a strictly monotone-increasing stretching that is allowed to be of any curvature.

Recall some fundamentals about individual stochastic decision making. You face alternative states of the world ($\mathbf{a}, \mathbf{b}, \ldots$), and you believe that each obtains with respective (subjective, personal) probabilities of $p(\mathbf{a})$, $p(\mathbf{b}), \ldots$, where $p(\mathbf{a}) + p(\mathbf{b}) + \cdots = 1$ because some one of the mutually exclusive, exhaustive set of possible states of the world must "occur." You are able to order consistently, according to which you "like better" all such "prospects". Your "stochastic ordering," designated by $\succsim$, obeys certain natural rules: It is transitive, not self-contradictory; you prefer 2 chocolates with certainty to 1 chocolate with certainty . . . ; you prefer a 50–50 chance of either 2 or 3 chocolates to a certainty of 1 chocolate . . . ; and so on. Finally, in accordance with Frank Ramsey (1931), Jacob Marschak (1950), L. J. Savage (1954), and other writers in the tradition that goes from 1738 (Daniel Bernoulli) to 1944 (von Neumann and Morgenstern), you choose to obey a natural "independence axiom": If you prefer prospect A to prospect B, then you will prefer a 50–50 chance of A or C to a 50–50 chance of B or C (it being understood that C never occurs except when neither A nor B occurs).

It follows that you *must* react in your stochastic decision making so as to maximize the "Expected (or "mean") value" of your (existent) utility function defined for each state of the world. You act to maximize

$$\text{Exp } V^k = p(a)V^k(\mathbf{a}) + p(b)V^k(\mathbf{b}) + \cdots \tag{19.2}$$

where $V^k(\cdot)$ is a well-defined metric (up to an arbitrary scaling and origin constant, $\alpha V^k + \beta$, $\alpha > 0$).

So far, "you" have been one of our individuals. But let us suppose that the Ethical Observer is no less "rational" or "consistent" than is any one fallible human being. The Ethical Observer then also has a utility metric, $[V(\mathbf{a}), V(\mathbf{b}), \ldots]$, written without a superscript. The BSWF then must, in stochastic situations, be expressible in the form

$$\text{Exp } V = p(\mathbf{a})V(\mathbf{a}) + p(\mathbf{b})V(\mathbf{b}) + \cdots \tag{19.3}$$

where

$$V(\mathbf{x}) = Z\{z(\mathbf{x})\}, \qquad Z'\{\cdot\} > 0 \gtreqless Z''\{\cdot\} \tag{19.4}$$

So far I have been talking about any general BSWF. Now let me concentrate on an individualistic BISWF, in which individuals' tastes are to rule when individuals are unanimous (and where, we have seen, weak separability is implied). Harsanyi in effect argues:

> If your individualistic ethic respects people's tastes in non-stochastic situations, the same logic suggests you will want to respect people's tastes in stochastic situations. Thus, just as you don't second guess individuals when they say they prefer beans to caviar, when consenting adults want not to gamble you respect their (ex ante, probabilistic) preferences.

This persuasive reasoning leads to the following axiom system:

- α Individuals behave consistently in stochastic situations so as to become maximizers of their *Expected* utilities.
- β The Ethical Observer similarly behaves consistently and maximizes Expected social utility.
- γ In the individualistic case, weak separability is imposed so that individual's tastes rule when they are unanimous on

nonstochastic situations (and, when they are not, are ethically resolved).

δ In the individualistic case, where stochastic elements can occur, weak separability in individuals' Expected utilities is imposed on the BISWF Expected utility function, so that whenever all say "We prefer the stochastic prospect A to B," the ethical judgment must be rendered, "A is ethically preferred to B."

Harsanyi's new element is to adjoin γ to the earlier axioms. This requires the following functional equation, weakly separable in the expected values:

$$\text{Exp } V = \phi[\text{Exp } V^1, \ldots, \text{Exp } V^K] \tag{19.5}$$

where ϕ is a strictly monotone-increasing function of its arguments. This is a strong – not unreasonable! – requirement.

To understand how $\phi[\cdot]$ relates to $z[\cdot]$ and to derive the implications of (19.5), consider the case where, with 50–50 odds, the K persons get their personal utilities respectively of

$$[\alpha^1, \alpha^2, \ldots, \alpha^K] \quad \text{or} \quad [\beta^1, \beta^2, \ldots, \beta^K]$$

where

$$\alpha^k = V^k(\mathbf{a}) = Z^k\{z^k(\mathbf{a})\}$$
$$\beta^k = V^k(\mathbf{b}) = Z^k\{z^k(\mathbf{b})\}$$
$$p(\mathbf{a}) = \tfrac{1}{2} = p(\mathbf{b}) \qquad (k = 1, \ldots, K)$$

Then (19.5) becomes

$$\tfrac{1}{2}V[\alpha^1, \ldots, \alpha^K] + \tfrac{1}{2}V[\beta^1, \ldots, \beta^K] \equiv \phi[\tfrac{1}{2}\alpha^1 + \tfrac{1}{2}\beta^1, \ldots, \tfrac{1}{2}\alpha^K + \tfrac{1}{2}\beta^K] \tag{19.6}$$

The functional equation (19.6), after we impose the overstrong condition that it be twice differentiable, implies that $V[y^1, \ldots, y^K]$ and $\phi[y^1, \ldots, y^K]$ be *linear* and be the *same* function:

$$V[y^1, \ldots, y^K] \equiv \lambda^0 + \lambda^1 y^1 + \cdots + \lambda^K y^K \equiv \phi[y^1, \ldots, y^K] \tag{19.7}$$

To prove that (19.6) implies (19.7), differentiate (19.6) with respect to α^s and β^k; equating both sides then requires that $\phi[\cdot]$ have all vanishing second derivatives and be linear. Q.E.D.

Thus, we have proved the Harsanyi contention that the (stochastic) BISWF must be of the form

$$z[z^1(\mathbf{x}), \ldots, z^K(\mathbf{x})] = \text{a monotone-increasing function of } \lambda^1 V^1(\mathbf{x}) + \cdots + \lambda^K V^K(\mathbf{x}) = V(\mathbf{x}) \tag{19.8}$$

where $V(\mathbf{x})$ is the utility whose Expected value is to be ethically maximized, and where $V^k(\mathbf{x})$ is a monotone-increasing stretching of $z^k(\mathbf{x})$.

20. John Chipman (1976) has given a magisterial review of Pareto's attempts to relate competitive equilibrium to welfare optimality. What was later to be called Pareto optimality was definitely glimpsed by Pareto in the years after 1894 [as it had been in Edgeworth (1881) in connection with the "contract" curve there]. Pareto's attempts at mathematical proof are, to put it kindly, obscure. Why does this matter? For one thing, if you do not manage to get your proof of a theorem right, you are not able to understand the theorem's precise limitation of application.

I have reread for the present essay the English translations of Pareto. This confirms my view of 45 years ago – that a fresh treatment of welfare economics was still needed. After, and only after, you have worked out a clear understanding of this subject are you able to recognize the bits of the puzzle that Pareto had already discerned. Nor will this surprise historians of science such as Robert Merton (1973) or Thomas Kuhn (1962): they have learned to expect multiple discoverers and rediscoverers of important scientific phenomena and theories. Thus, no less than 12 scientists can be said to be discoverers of the law of the conservation of energy. The fact that some of their writings were known to others in the group does not preclude legitimate claims to independent discovery if, as is often the case with early pioneers, the expositions are unclear and even defective in spots.

Let it be agreed at the beginning that Pareto was remarkably ahead of his time.

21. Pareto (1894) deals with optimal production conditions. Although I shall skip that topic here, it is worth mentioning that Pareto in this article discovers much of marginal productivity theory that is important in Wicksteed's famous *Essay on the Coordination of the Laws of Distribution*. Pareto's work seems to antedate that of Barone, his disciple; so Walras' 1896 third edition treatment, which Walras seemed to owe in large measure to Barone, essentially traces back to Pareto. Thus, my ordered list of discoverers of the general equilibrium theory of marginal productivity would include J. B. Clark, V. Pareto and P. H. Wicksteed, Barone and Walras, Wicksell, ...

Pareto (1903) represents his matured thought, with a fair sample of its obscurity. My notation will resemble that of Chipman (1976) in an understandable way. It is enough to consider Pareto's simplest case of competitive exchange with fixed production endowments of private goods by the persons: (a^k_j), a K by J nonnegative matrix, with row sums and column sums that are positive.

I begin by making the strong assumptions on slopes and curvatures made in (12.1): smoothness, nonsatiation, and strict quasi-concavity for every atomic person and for the BISWF; every good a private good and an essential item in the sense of (12.1)'s limit relations. We moderns know that these assumptions suffice to guarantee the existence of a competitive solution (with positive prices). There may well be multiple solutions.

Pareto is correct to assert at the turn of the century:

Any observed competitive solution is Pareto optimal.

I am also correct to assert after mid-century:

Every *Pareto*-optimal point, under our strong curvature and nonexternality assumptions, can be achieved by a competitive equilibrium provided the laissez-faire "endowments" of income are altered by suitable algebraic lump-sum transfers, $(\lambda^1, \lambda^2, \ldots, \lambda^K = -\lambda^1 - \lambda^2 - \cdots - \lambda^{K-1})$, where

$$\sum_1^J p_j x_j^k - \sum_1^J p_j a_j^k = \lambda^k \qquad (k = 1, \ldots, K) \tag{21.1}$$

To prove this, all Pareto had to do was note that competitive equilibrium must fall on Edgeworth's contract locus, the locus of points of mutual tangency so that from each such point no mutually beneficial move is possible. And note that any finite movement from a contract-curve point must harm *at least one* person (and *possibly* all persons).

For a mathematical proof that the first-order conditions for Pareto optimality are implied by the first-order conditions effectuated under perfect competition, Pareto had need only to describe the following procedure. The equations necessary for competitive equilibrium are now

$$x_1^k + \cdots + p_J K_J^k - a_1^k - \cdots - p_J a_J^k = \lambda^k \qquad (k = 1, \ldots, K) \tag{21.2}$$

$$\frac{z_j^k(\mathbf{x}^k)}{z_1^k(\mathbf{x}^k)} = p_j \qquad (j = 2, \ldots, J; \quad k = 1, \ldots, K) \tag{21.3}$$

$$\sum_1^K x_j^k = \sum_1^K a_j^k \qquad (j = 1, 2, \ldots, J) \tag{21.4}$$

$$\Lambda = \lambda^1 + \lambda^2 + \cdots + \lambda^K = 0 \tag{21.5}$$

Remark. The first equation in (21.4) follows redundantly from all the other equations and could be omitted in any listing of *independent* relations. For arbitrary choices of $(\lambda^2, \ldots, \lambda^K)$ not too large in absolute value, one (or more) solution(s) are determined: $(\bar{x}_j^k; \bar{p}_j)$.

For a feasible $(\bar{x}_j^k)$ to be Pareto optimal, it is necessary (and, under my strong assumptions, sufficient) that the tangencies be realized

$$\frac{z_j^k(\mathbf{x}^k)}{z_1^k(\mathbf{x}^k)} = \frac{z_j^1(\mathbf{x}^1)}{z_1^1(\mathbf{x}^1)} \qquad (j = 2, \ldots, J; \quad k = 2, \ldots, K) \tag{21.6}$$

All Pareto had to say, in the *Cours, Manual,* or 1903 polemic, is that the competitive relations (21.3) do imply the needed (21.6) welfare optimality conditions.

Mind you, a proper proof requires discussion of *second*-derivative conditions as well as *first*-derivative conditions. (In other words, *my* repeated assertions that quasi-concavity turns necessary conditions into sufficiency conditions needs explicit proof, something not hard to give in our times but quite beyond Pareto's knowledge of *un*bordered determinants.) Pareto never adequately dealt with secondary curvature conditions, for which I do not fault him in this review. It is his obscurities on *basics* that I here concentrate on. And I do that because these confusions clouded his pre-1913 expositions of what a SWF is all about.

22. Instead of simply identifying the (21.6) relations contained in (21.3), Pareto stubbornly worked with a hybrid sum (or its differential)

$$\Pi(\mathbf{x}) = \frac{z^1(\mathbf{x}^1)}{z_1^1(\bar{\mathbf{x}}^1)} + \frac{z^2(\mathbf{x}^2)}{z_1^2(\bar{\mathbf{x}}^2)} + \cdots + \frac{z^K(\mathbf{x}^K)}{z_1^K(\bar{\mathbf{x}}^K)} \tag{22.1}$$

Here, $\Pi(\mathbf{x})$ is my shorthand for $\Pi(\mathbf{x}, \bar{\mathbf{x}})$ and $z_1^k(\mathbf{x}) \equiv \partial z^k(\mathbf{x})/\partial x_1^k$.

For a positivist $\Pi(\mathbf{x})$ smacks of being a Benthamistic Social Welfare Function. It adds together what Pareto might be expected to regard as cheese and chalk – the weighted utility of man k to the weighted utility of man s. And Pareto squeamishly avoids ever writing down the sum $\Pi(\mathbf{x})$ or the sum of differentials that total up to $d\Pi(\mathbf{x})$. Such forebearance cannot, however, succeed in exorcising the devil.

But actually that does not seem to be what Pareto is aiming at. His total differential

$$\begin{aligned} d\Pi(\mathbf{x}) &= \sum_1^K \frac{dz^k(\mathbf{x}^k)}{z_1^k(\bar{\mathbf{x}}^k)} \\ &= \sum_1^K \frac{\Sigma_1^J z_j^k(x_1^k, \ldots, x_J^k)\, dx_j^k}{z_1^k(\bar{x}_1^k, \ldots, \bar{x}_J^k)} \end{aligned} \tag{22.2}$$

is intended solely to help him prove the Pareto-optimality property. It is an artifice that I would compare with a Lagrangean multiplier expression so beloved by advanced calculus texts in their dealings with constrained maxima problems. (Strangely, Pareto seems not to employ the Lagrangean multiplier technique, albeit one would suppose that he was familiar with this standard procedure that seems made to order for his kind of problem.)

At the equilibrium point itself, where Pareto equates $\mathbf{x}$ to $\bar{\mathbf{x}}$ and *there* evaluates (22.1)'s expression, he finds that $d\Pi(\mathbf{x})$ (which has the dimensionality of the *numéraire* good itself, of dx_1) *vanishes;*

$$\begin{aligned} d\Pi(\mathbf{x})|_{x=\bar{x}} &\equiv d\Pi(\mathbf{x}, \bar{\mathbf{x}})|_{x=\bar{x}} \\ &= \sum_1^J \sum_1^K \frac{z_j^k(\bar{\mathbf{x}}^k)}{z_1^k(\bar{\mathbf{x}}^k)}\, dx_j^k && (22.3) \\ &= \sum_1^J \bar{p}_j \sum_1^K dx_j^k \qquad \text{by (21.3)} && (22.4) \end{aligned}$$

$$d\Pi(\mathbf{x})|_{x=\bar{x}} = \sum_{1}^{J} \bar{p}_j \, d\left(\sum_{1}^{K} x_j^k\right) = \sum_{1}^{J} \bar{p}_j \cdot (0) \qquad \text{by (21.4)} \tag{22.5}$$

$$= 0 \tag{22.6}$$

Note that the z_j^k/z_1^k ratios have common values of $\bar{p}_j$ in competitive equilibrium. And if the total endowment of a good is given, the feasible variation in its *total* consumption must vanish by virtue of

$$\sum_{1}^{K} x_j^k = \sum_{1}^{K} a_j^k, \qquad d\left(\sum_{1}^{K} x_j^k\right) = d\left(\sum_{1}^{K} a_j^k\right)$$

$$\equiv 0 \qquad (j = 1, \ldots, J) \tag{22.7}$$

Why is it important to prove that $d\Pi(x, \bar{x}) = 0$ at $x = \bar{x}$? And why important to prove – if only Pareto had been able to do so! – that $d^2\Pi(x) = d^2\Pi(x, \bar{x}) <$ at $x = \bar{x}$? Remember that $\Pi(x)$ is a positively weighted sum of the people's individual (allegedly cardinal) utilities. If such a sum genuinely reaches its maximum at the competitive equilibrium, then manifestly there exists *no* movement away from the equilibrium along which *every* z^k $(\mathbf{x}^k)$ grows! So $(\bar{x}_j^k)$ is then indeed a Pareto-optimal point.

23. Let me motivate a defense for Pareto's trucking with the devil of *adding inter*personal utilities. It involves only mathematical artifice and no philosophical capitulation. It is, however, defective in its unnecessary dependence on *concavity* of *cardinal* utility instead of properly relying only on *quasi-concavity* of any *ordinal* indicator of people's utility.

Actually, if $z^k(\mathbf{x}^k)$ is strictly quasi-concave, in a finite neighborhood of $\bar{\mathbf{x}}^k$ there exists an (infinity of) stretchings of $z^k(\mathbf{x}^k)$ which will yield a *strictly concave* $Z^k(\mathbf{x}^k)$ in that neighborhood. If we and Pareto agree to use such strictly concave individual utilities, one way of tracing out the utility-possibility frontier of points near $\bar{\mathbf{x}}$ is to vary the positive weights, $(\omega^1, \omega^2, \ldots, \omega^K)$, and maximize for each choice of the ω's the positive sum

$$\max_{\mathbf{x}} \Phi(\mathbf{x}) = \max_{\mathbf{x}_j^k} \sum_{1}^{k} \omega^k Z^k(\mathbf{x}^k) \tag{23.1}$$

subject to

$$\sum_{1}^{K} x_j^k = \sum_{1}^{K} a_j^k \qquad (j = 1, \ldots, J)$$

One choice of ω weights is $[\omega^k] = [1/Z_1^k(\bar{\mathbf{x}}^K)]$ and for it, we and Pareto can verify that $(\mathbf{x}^k) = (\bar{\mathbf{x}}^k)$ is indeed a solution of the implied first-order extremal conditions:

$$\frac{Z_j^k(\mathbf{x}^k)}{Z_1^k(\mathbf{x}^k)} = \frac{Z_j^1(\mathbf{x}^1)}{Z_1^1(\mathbf{x}^1)} \qquad (j = 2, \ldots, J; \quad k = 2, \ldots, K) \tag{23.2}$$

$$\sum_{1}^{K} x_j^k = \sum_{1}^{K} a_j^k \qquad (j = 1, \ldots, J; \quad k = 1, \ldots, K) \tag{23.3}$$

By using Pareto's $[1/Z_1^k(\mathbf{x}^k)]$ coefficients as our ω's, we've selected for $\Phi(\mathbf{x})$ precisely $\Pi(\mathbf{x}) = \Pi(\mathbf{x}, \bar{\mathbf{x}})$ as defined in (22.1).

What is good about this version of Pareto's proof of the Pareto-optimality property of competitive exchange is that it enables us not only to derive Pareto's first-order conditions properly; it also can provide a rigorous proof that the critical point represents a *local* true maximum. The critical point, one realizes, is actually a *global* maximum, but it would be a delicate task to ensure that quasi-concave $z^k(\mathbf{x}^k)$ can be globally stretched into a single concave $Z^k(\mathbf{x}^k)$ (or into an appropriate sequence of such).

I have lingered on Pareto's $\Sigma_1^K dz^k(\mathbf{x}^k)/z^k(\bar{\mathbf{x}}^k)$ discussions not because they are very appealing in their own right but to help clarify the mysteries of discussions by Pareto and by Barone (1908).

24. There is a still better approach to a proof of competitive equilibrium's being Pareto optimal that stays in the spirit of Pareto's several skirmishes with the problem. Instead of $\Pi(\mathbf{x}, \bar{\mathbf{x}})$, it works with a related $\Lambda(\mathbf{x}, \bar{\mathbf{x}})$ function. I offer it not for its own sake, since my Section 21 has already provided straightforward proof, but rather to help in the interpretation of Pareto's historic writings.

Let me begin with a fresh start. Consider Pareto's observed competitive-equilibrium point, $(\bar{x}_j^k)$. It was achieved within the initial endowments $(\Sigma_1^K a_j^k) = (a_j)$. If it was a laissez-faire point, as most of the writings of Pareto and neoclassical economists concentrate on, it is a solution to the following equations when $(\lambda^1, \lambda^2, \ldots, \lambda^K) = (0, 0, \ldots, 0)$.

$$0 = x_1^k + \sum_2^J p_j x_j^k - \left(a_1^k + \sum_2^J p_j a_j^k\right) - \lambda^k \qquad (k = 1, \ldots, k) \quad (24.1)$$

$$\frac{z_j^k(\mathbf{x}^k)}{z_1^k(\mathbf{x}^k)} = p_j \qquad (j = 2, \ldots, J) \quad (24.2)$$

$$0 = \sum_1^K x_j^k - \sum_1^K a_j^k \qquad (j = 1, 2, \ldots, J) \quad (24.3)$$

$$-\Lambda = \lambda^1 + \lambda^2 + \cdots + \lambda^K = 0 \quad (24.4)$$

A laissez-faire solution may be called $(\bar{x}_j^k)$ to distinguish it from the infinity of *interventionist* competitive solutions, $(\bar{x}_j^k)$, which are achieved with choices of $(\lambda^2, \ldots, \lambda^K)$ not all equal to zero. For Pareto or Smith to prove that the laissez-faire solution is Pareto optimal is not to prove much about it. *That* does not warrant the Bastiat–Mises–Friedman inference that $(\bar{x}_j^k)$ is "a good thing." There are infinities of non-Pareto-optimal points that are "ethically better" than the laissez-faire point in the view of "almost all" ethical systems – even those of "individualistic type."

Mathematically, this is a precise statement:

Given *any* $z[z^1(\mathbf{x}^1), \ldots, z^K(\mathbf{x}^K)]$ with well-behaved properties, for *almost all* (a^k_j) endowment points, no laissez-faire solution can provide the feasible maximum to $z[\cdot]$.

So let us in 1980 widen Pareto's focus. We consider not only $(\bar{x}^k)$ laissez-faire points but also $(\bar{x}^k)$ points that are the competitive solution for some choice of $(L^2, \ldots, L^K)$ in (24.1) and (24.4). Scorza and Cassel are dead wrong to doubt that each such point is Pareto optimal. Here help will be given to explicate Pareto's purported proof of this by use of his Λ function. [*Reminder:* To prove that a $(\bar{x}^k_j)$ is a Pareto-optimal point does not mean "it is a good thing." Unless the (L^k) intervention that generated it was at the singular level(s) needed to maximize the BISWF in question, there will exist infinities of $\mathbf{x}$ points for which $z[\cdot]$ is greater than at this $\bar{\mathbf{x}}$!]

Pareto (1894) in effect makes this observation pertinent to our present problem. "Unless $(\bar{x}^k_j)$ is Pareto Optimal, society will be able to provide it with *less* of total endowment of the *numéraire* good and the same total endowments for all the other goods." So write the saving achieved on the total endowment of the first good as Λ:

$$\Lambda = a_1 - \sum_1^K x^k_1$$

$$= \sum_1^K (a^k_1 - x^k_1) \tag{24.5}$$

Let us now maximize this saving achievable while we achieve the levels of well-being $[z^k(\bar{x}^k)]$ for every person and stay within the endowment totals of the non-*numèraire* goods.

We solve the new maximum problem,

$$\max_{x^k_j} \Lambda(x) = \max_{x^k_j} \sum_1^K (a^k_1 - x^k_1) \tag{24.6}$$

subject to

$$z^k(\mathbf{x}^k) \geq z^k(x^k) \qquad (k = 1, \ldots, K) \tag{24.6$'$}$$

$$\sum_1^K x^k_j \leq \sum_1^K a^k_j = a_j \qquad (j = 2, \ldots, J) \tag{24.6$''$}$$

If the competitive equilibrium is Pareto optimal, and only then, will max Λ equal zero and be achieved at $(x^k_j) = (\bar{x}^k_j)$. For if there were any positive saving possible, competitive equilibrium could be improved upon for every individual by giving each some of the achievable saving.

Under my overstrong curvature and satiation conditions on the contours of $z^k(\mathbf{x}^k)$, this last maximum problem is solved for $\mathbf{x}^*$, the root of the following equations for the critical point of the Lagrangean expression.

$$L(\mathbf{x};\boldsymbol{\alpha},\boldsymbol{\beta}) = \sum_1^K (a_1^k - x_1^k) + \sum_1^K \alpha^k[z^k(\mathbf{x}^k) - z^k(\bar{\mathbf{x}}^k)] + \sum_2^J \beta_j \sum_1^K (a_j^k - x_j^k) \tag{24.7}$$

At $L(\cdot)$'s critical point,

$$\begin{aligned} \partial L/\partial x_1^k &= 0 = -1 + \alpha^k z_1^k(\mathbf{x}^k) && (k = 1, \ldots, K) \\ \partial L/\partial x_j^k &= 0 = \alpha^k z_j^k(\mathbf{x}^k) - \beta_j && (k = 1, \ldots, K;\ j = 2, \ldots, J) \\ \partial L/\partial \alpha^k &= 0 = z_K^k(\mathbf{x}^k) - z^k(\bar{\mathbf{x}}^k) && (k = 1, \ldots, K) \\ \partial L/\partial \beta_j &= 0 = \sum_1^K a_j^k - \sum_1^k x_j^k && (j = 2, \ldots, J) \end{aligned} \tag{24.8}$$

Eliminating (α^k, β_j) from the first two sets of (24.8) leaves us with the last two sets and with

$$\frac{z_j^k(\mathbf{x}^k)}{z_1^k(\mathbf{x}^k)} = \frac{z_j^1(\mathbf{x}^1)}{z_1^1(\mathbf{x}^1)} \qquad (j = 2, \ldots, J;\quad k = 2, \ldots, K) \tag{24.9}$$

Any $\mathbf{x}^*$ root is, under my strong conditions, unique. So these necessary conditions are also sufficient (since the maximum patently exists and is an interior one). From the nature of $(\bar{x}_j^k)$ as a competitive solution, we recognize at sight that $\mathbf{x}^* = \bar{\mathbf{x}}$ is indeed a solution of (24.8)–(24.9). And for it Λ is indeed zero.

There remains only to show that the Λ saving magnitude is the sum (with sign reversed to keep our problem a maximum rather than minimum formulation) of the lump-sum transfers $(\lambda^1, \lambda^2, \ldots, \lambda^K)$ in (24.1).

$$-\Lambda = \lambda^1 + \lambda^2 + \cdots + \lambda^K \tag{24.10}$$

To verify this, multiply each endowment relation of (24.3) respectively by p_j; then from their sum subtract the sum of the k relations in (24.1) and observe that you will be left with (24.4)'s right-hand side.

Just as $\partial\Pi(x)/\partial x_1^k$ equals unity at $\mathbf{x} = \bar{\mathbf{x}}$, so does $-\partial\Lambda(\mathbf{x})/\partial x_1^k$ equal unity at $\mathbf{x} = \bar{\mathbf{x}}$ (it being understood that all other x_1's are held constant in this variation). Thus, even though the degrees of freedom of x in $\Pi(\mathbf{x})$ and in $-\Lambda(x)$ are not the same, these two Paretian functions are closely related up to the first order.

25. In his forties Pareto began to emancipate himself from *cardinal* (as opposed to *ordinal*) utility: to concentrate on the indifference contours' curvatures and to ignore the noninvariant utility metric. He never quite integrated his new thinking, never quite purged from his mind his old thinking. In part this was because he lacked mathematical knowledge of bordered quadratic forms relevant for constrained extrema – a lack he shared with most mathematicians of his day.

Rather than belabor these invariant-curvature niceties, let me show why they matter. Suppose that a million people have (well-behaved) rectangular hyperbola for atomic indifference curves in their private goods (x_1^k, x_2^k). Suppose that a single person has for his indifference curves quarter circles, an *admissible* case of *nonconvex* indifference contours in his (x_1^K, x_2^K) space ($K = 1{,}000{,}001$).

Now competitive equilibrium fails utterly. For given endowments (a_j^k), there is no market-clearing intersection of supply and demand to determine an equilibrium p_2. But Pareto optimality is still well defined no matter what K is!

Thus, with $K = 2$ and $(a_1, a_2) = (4, 4)$, the point $(x_1^1, x_2^1; x_1^2, x_2^2) = (1, 1; 3, 3)$ is Pareto optimal. It is also Bergson optimal for a BISWF of the form

$$V = [x_1^1 x_2^1]^{1/4} + \sqrt{3}[\tfrac{1}{2}(x_1^2)^2)^2 + \tfrac{1}{2}(x_2^2)^2]^{1/4}$$

What went wrong? Pareto never correctly stated the curvature conditions necessary and sufficient for Pareto optimality, distinguishing them from the curvature conditions necessary and sufficient for competitive equilibrium. And modern textbook writers, aware that Arrow and Debreu have provided conditions under which Pareto-optimal and competitive points can be interrelated, usually neglect to reproduce the fine print in which certain assumptions of the argument are specified.

Ironically, in Pareto's somewhat confused extensions of the theory of production to handle increasing returns to scale, he had already sensed some similar formal difficulties that mar the use of (Lerner–Lange) *competitive role playing* by the socialist bureaucrats.

26. To complete this brief survey of Pareto's pre-Bergson contribution to welfare economics, I call attention to the notice in Chipman (1976) of Pareto (1913). Here Pareto finally does consider the genuine sum of utilities across persons, at least as part of "sociology" (which is Pareto's catchall for that which is not rational economics). It is not clear that Pareto is returning to a Benthamite or Old Welfare Economics social welfare function. Rather he is doing at least two things.

1. As in my Sections 14–18 discussion of quasi-atomic higher-order individual tastes, Pareto considers how "do-gooders and humanitarians" want to act in accordance with (what is in my notation)

$$\alpha^{1k}V^1(\mathbf{x}^1) + \alpha^{2k}V^2(\mathbf{x}^2) + \cdots + \alpha^{Kk}(\mathbf{x}^K) \qquad (k = 1, \ldots, K) \qquad (26.1)$$

2. But, since some people k are do-gooders and some people s are (like Pareto) less altruistic, these different α weights are discordant between people. Pareto envisages a "government" that second-guesses and compromises between them, applying *its* superweights $[\alpha^{1G}, \alpha^{2G}, \ldots, \alpha^{kG}, \ldots, \alpha^{KG}]$ to form

$$\alpha^{1G} \sum_{1}^{K} \alpha^{k1} V^k(\mathbf{x}^k) + \cdots + \alpha^{KG} \sum_{1}^{K} \alpha^{kK} V^k(\mathbf{x}^k)$$
$$= \left(\sum_{s} \alpha^{SG}\alpha^{ST}\right) V^1(\mathbf{x}^1) + \cdots + \left(\sum_{s} \alpha^{SG}\alpha^{SK}\right) V^K(\mathbf{x}^K)$$
$$= \sum_{1}^{K} \beta^k V(\mathbf{x}^k)$$

Rather than this resultant Social Function being a social *welfare* function (of ethical-norming nature), for Pareto this may simply have been a positivistic function to account for the behavior of quasi-democratic government – in Chipman's felicitous phrase merely "an expression of the revealed preferences of a centrally organized society, as exhibited by its observed behavior."[10]

To sum up what Pareto had accomplished in 1913, 25 years before Bergson's 1938 formulation, let me say:

1. Pareto may or may not have given in 1913 an Old Welfare Economics social welfare function of Bentham's additive-hedonistic form.
2. Or Pareto may have tried to account for the behavior resulting from group and governmental interactions by collective utility and indifference fields.

In all likelihood, Pareto never had to make up his mind on just what he was hoping to accomplish.

27. I mention a new topic. Abba Lerner (1944), and other writers, have tried to argue in this vein:

Our knowledge of people's actual and proper λ's in Benthamite expressions $\Sigma_1^K \lambda^k V^k(\mathbf{x}^k)$ is (necessarily) imperfect. But in the absence of any knowledge or presumption that people's initial endowments are correlated with their λ^k deservingnesses, it is valid to infer, "An *egalitarian* division of a given (conserved) total output, $x = x^1 + \cdots + x^k$, is in a defendable probability sense best."

In my 1964 salutation to Lerner's sixtieth birthday, I used pre-Rawlsian arguments to buttress this insight. [Later, Kenneth Arrow reminded me that the pre-Rawlsian argument of Samuelson (1964) had already appeared in Vickery (1945)!] Here is how the argument goes.

I am any person k. What tax charter will each of us want for society if, under the Rawlsian veil of ignorance, we suppose that the probability distribution determining *my* initial endowment a^k and others' endowments a^s is *symmetric* in ($k, s = 1, \ldots, K$)? If each of us is risk averse with concave $V^k(\mathbf{x}^k)$, I and everyone will then opt for egalitarian progressive taxation.[11] Q.E.D. [This holds even if our $V^k(x^k)$ functions are all different, and known only to be concave.]

Rawls, Sen, Varian, and others have extended such arguments to include questions such as this:

What if I don't know whether I'll be a man, woman, cockroach, or teetotaler. Gathered together under the veil of ignorance to form a social contract, we each selfishly may be able to arrive at unanimous agreement on what is "fair" and an ethically best state of the world or generator of best future states.

28. The argument I presented to Lerner was not quite the one he had originally desired. Perhaps it can be given a valid formulation in its own right, along the following lines. [For brevity, I shall assume that all $V^k(\cdot)$ functions are the *same* unknown concave function, $V(\cdot)$; and shall assume that $J = 1$, so there is a single scalar good to divide up. The simplifications are inessential.]

Without redistributive taxes, the BISWF would take on the value

$$\lambda^1 V(a^1) + \cdots + \lambda^K V(a^K) \tag{28.1}$$

Suppose that you as Legislator do not know what the values of (λ^k, a^k) are but know only that the λ's and a's obey *independent* probability distributions.

$$\text{Prob}\{a^1 < \alpha^1, \ldots, a^K < \alpha^K, \lambda^1 < \beta^1, \ldots, \lambda^K < \beta^K\} = P(a^1, a^2, \ldots, a^K)Q(\lambda^1, \ldots, \lambda^K) \tag{28.2}$$

and where $P(\cdot)$ is *symmetric* in its arguments.

You as Legislator want to vote on the degree of tax progression, t, which moves every person with initial a^k toward the mean, $\Sigma_1^K a^k/K = \mu$, by the fraction t of that distance.

If $t = 0$, we have laissez faire. If $t = 1$, we have complete egalitarian taxation. For every t, we assume no deadweight loss, with $\Sigma_1^K a^k = \Sigma_1^K x^k$.

The Expected value of social utility becomes a function of the parameter t alone once the probability distributions $P(\cdot)$ and $Q(\cdot)$ are given. We have for this Expected social utility:

$$v(t) = \text{Exp} \sum_1^K \lambda^k V(x^k)$$

$$= \int \cdots \int \sum_1^K \lambda^k V([1 - t]a^k + t\mu)\, d[P(a^1, \ldots)Q(\lambda^1, \ldots)] \tag{28.3}$$

It is easy to show that $v(t)$ is concave and that $v(t)$ achieves its minimum at $t = 1$, where

$$v'(1) = V'(\mu) \sum_1^K \left[\int \cdots \int \lambda^k\, dQ(\lambda^1, \ldots)\right]\left[\int \cdots \int (a^k - \mu)\, dP(a^1, \ldots)\right]$$

$$= V'(\mu) \sum_1^K [\text{Exp}(\lambda^k)] \cdot 0 = 0 > v''(1) \tag{28.4}$$

What confidence we should have in the axiom of $P(a^1, \ldots)Q(\lambda^1, \ldots)$ *probabilistic independence* is not a question of deductive logic.

29. My final topic reiterates the warning against confusing (a) Arrow's proof that a Constitutional Function with certain desirable properties does not exist, with (b) a belief that well-behaved Bergson Social Welfare Functions do not exist. In the spirit of Samuelson (1967), I make one more try.

Consider two people: He and She. Consider three states of the world: *A, B,* and *C*. Preference orderings on these states will, for simplicity, permit no ties of indifference. Always $A > B$ or $B > A$, with $A \sim B$ never encountered.

First, contemplate the BISWF problem. He has his preference ordering $>^k$, for $k = 1$. She has hers, for $k = 2$. Either can have any *one* of the six possible orderings of (A, B, C). I write these six possibilities as *ABC, ACB, BAC, BCA, CAB, CBA*. If He has any one of six, and She has any one of six, between them there are 36 different pairs of orderings that could be the actual one that confronts the Ethical Observer. Whichever *one* of the 36 the Ethical Observer is confronted with – and it will be one precise one – the Observer must come up with a BISWF ordering that (a) agrees with theirs whenever they are unanimous and (b) resolves the choice ethically when they disagree.

Does such a BISWF exist? Yes. I can write down, for any pair of specified individuals' orderings, a well-behaved BISWF. Indeed, more than one admissible BISWF exists for most pairs of individuals' preferences, and it is not for me to appraise the relative merits of alternative admissible BISWFs.

I shall now display the *existent* BISWFs and shall do so in the context where Arrow's Impossibility Theorem does apply (apply to show there is no Arrow Constitutional Function, even though there do exist BISWFs in abundance).

Rather than go through 36 different specifications, I can deal with six only. Since labels are arbitrary, I can by relabeling make His ordering always be (*ABC*). So the one case confronting the Ethical Observer must be one of the six cases corresponding to Her six alternative possible orderings: *ABC, ACB, BAC, BCA, CAB, and CBA*. I examine each in turn and write out the existent BISWFs for each:

ABC: Here they are unanimous on $(ABC)^k, k = 1, 2$. So the social ordering or BISWF, written without a superscript, must be the sole choice of (*ABC*). *Conclusion:* In this first of six cases, yes, a BISWF does exist.

ACB: I propose for the reader's testing that the following two BISWFs do exist: (*ABC*) and (*ACB*). *Note:* Since the individuals are unanimous that *A* is better than *B,* and that *A* is better than *C,* the BISWF is required to agree to that. But since the individuals disagree on the merits of *B* versus *C,* the Ethical Observer can resolve their difference in either of two ways: decreeing *B* better ethically than *C*, or vice versa. *Conclusion:* Again the existence of a BISWF has been affirmed; actually the above two exist.

BAC: This is like the previous case. He and She are unanimous that *B* is better than *C* and that *A* is better than *C*. They have one disagreement on whether *A* is better than *B*, or vice versa. *Conclusion:* A BISWF does exist in this case; actually two of them, (*ABC*) and (*BCA*).

BCA: Now there are two disagreements between Him and Her. They only agree unanimously that *B* is better than *C*. The Ethical Observer can go in favor of either person in each of the two disagreements. So you might think there are four existent BISWFs. Actually, though, we must not forget transitivity, which will rule out one of the four contingencies as self-contradictory,[12] leaving us with the three existent BISWFs: (*ABC*), (*BCA*), and (*BAC*).

CAB: As with the previous case there are here two disagreements between Him and Her. They only agree unanimously that *A* is better than *B*. They disagree on whether *C* is better than *A* or better than *B*, and the ethical resolution of the discordance can go in favor of either one of each of these pair comparisons. Again, insisting on transitivity of the resulting BISWF, we find that there do indeed exist three alternative BISWFs: (*ABC*), (*CAB*), and (*ACB*).

CBA: This is the case where She and He perversely differ in every respect. So every state of the world must be Pareto optimal. The Ethical Observer is free to pick any of the six possible transitive orderings in order to resolve the ethical normings. Hence, in this last case, as in all of our previous cases, there do exist well-behaved BISWFs: (*ABC*), (*ACB*), (*BAC*), (*BCA*), (*CAB*), and (*CBA*).

Summary. I have now shown constructively that well-behaved Bergson social welfare functions do exist, exactly as Bergson and Samuelson have always defined them.

30. I have now proved that a BISWF always exists in a two-person three-state universe. Does an Arrow Constitutional Function, an ACF, with well-behaved properties exist for that universe? After I describe how such an ACF is defined, we will see why none can exist with Arrow's postulated good properties.

A BISWF is defined for *only one* of the six alternative taste patterns prevailing. An ACF is defined so that *no matter which of the six* orderings

She fills out for Her voting ballot, the Constitutional Function or Vote-Scoring Machine must come out with its answer – its social ordering, which, remember, must then be a selection of one of the six possible orderings *ABC, ACB, BAC, BCA, CAB,* or *CBA*.

Arrow posits the following axioms as a well-behaved ACF.

1. For every possible pattern of votes or orderings on the part of the K (=2 in our example) that people put into the ACF as inputs, it must be wired to come out with a definite social ordering as output – a social ordering that is *transitive*.
2. When the people are *unanimous* on any choice among a pair of states of the world, the ACF must agree with them. When some differ, it must resolve their difference in *its* chosen way.
3. In making its above choice among a pair of states, say among A or B, the preferences involving other states – B or C, A or C, and the actual feasible occurrence of such other states – cannot have any relevance.
4. The ACF must not be "dictatorial" in the sense of *always* giving one of the k persons the deciding choice.

Still other axioms could be added, or different combinations and permutations of these and other axioms could be posited. But it will suffice to show that there exists no ACF satisfying these four axioms of (1) unlimited domain, (2) Pareto unanimity principle, (3) independence of irrelevant alternatives, and (4) nondictatorship.

An ACF must be a selection of one each from the following six input orderings and their possible output orderings as given in the previous section on BISWF:

Her input	*ABC*	*ACB*	*BAC*	*BCA*	*CAB*	*CBA*
Possible BISWFs	*ABC*	*ABC*	*ABC*	*ABC*	*ABC*	*ABC*
		ACB	*BAC*	*BCA*	*CAB*	*CBA*
				BAC	*ACB*	*ACB*
						BAC
						BCA
						CAB

There are plenty of Constitutional Functions we can select from the table, but none will be "well behaved" in the Arrow sense.

How many possible CFs are there? There are $1 \times 2 \times 2 \times 3 \times 3 \times 6$ or 216 in all, representing all possible independent choices of one each from the elements in the six columns of the table. But each one of the 216 is found to violate one or more of the reasonable axioms.

Let us sample to verify this. Suppose that we pick the *ABC* element from the top of every column and define our CF by that set of choices.

Clearly, this CF gives Him his way every time. He is a dictator. So that CF is no ACF.

Let us try again. To avoid dictatorship, each person must be given the decisive choice in at least one case where the two differ in ordering a pair of states. Since our example involves only three pairs of states – *A* versus *B*, *A* versus *C*, *B* versus *C* – our ACF must resolve differences in favor of one of the people twice and in favor of the other person once. Since the gender label is arbitrary, in mock chivalry let us give Her the decisive role in two pairs and Him that role in one.

Thus, let Him prevail only when there is discordance over *A* and *B*. This defines our CF, and we must examine it to see whether it is an ACF. Here is its decision in the cases of the six possible ballots for Her (and, it is understood, for His constant ABC ballot):

Her input	*ABC*	*ACB*	*BAC*	*BCA*	*CAB*	*CBA*
CF output	*ABC*	*ACB*	*ABC*	Null	*CAB*	*CAB*

Corresponding to *BCA* there is no possible social ordering that is transitive and agrees with our stipulated rules; He to prevail on the *A* versus *B* choice; She to prevail on the rest. For, applying these rules to the *BCA* ballot gives us: *A* socially better than *B* (to please Him); *B* socially better than *C* (to please Her); *C* better than *A* (to please Her) – but this is a contradiction to social transitivity (how can *C* be better than *A* when *A* is better than *B*, which is better than *C!*).

Symbolically, the fifth item is null because our rules produce the following contradiction to transitivity:

$$A > \mathrm{B} > C > A \quad \text{or} \quad ABCA, \qquad \text{a contradiction} \qquad (30.1)$$

Lest the reader thinks the above contradiction comes from giving Him dominance only on his choice between his very best and next best, let us derive a similar contradiction from the cases where He prevails on his choice between *B* or *C*. Now the table is similarly uncompletable:

Her input	*ABC*	*ACB*	*BAC*	*BCA*	*CAB*	*CBA*
CF output	*ABC*	*ABC*	*BAC*	*BCA*	null	null

Finally, and this exhausts the possible essentially different cases, consider the case where He gets his way only on the choice between *A* or *C* (between his actual most preferred and least preferred states). This uncompletable table obtains:

Her input	*ABC*	*ACB*	*BAC*	*BCA*	*CAB*	*CBA*
CF output	*ABC*	*ACB*	*BAC*	*BAC*	*ACB*	null

Thus, without bothering to enumerate all 216 cases, we have shown that in *no* possible case will there exist a definable Arrow Constitutional Function satisfying the four plausible axioms.[13] And, despite this, a BISWF does exist to ethically norm the states of the world while respecting the actual (one out of the six possible) individuals' orderings that do obtain.

31. My task is done. Space did not permit me to address topics of only secondary importance. Thus, I have not dealt with "consume*r's* surplus," which is only a subspecies in the "revealed preference" zoo. I have not dealt with "consume*rs'* surplus" either and must refer the reader to a more general treatment of how to make inferences from aggregate data on $\Sigma_1^K x_j^k$ in Samuelson (1950). Samuelson and Swamy (1973) sum up the easier problem of interpreting index numbers based on one person's ($\mathbf{p}$, x_j^k) observations. Frank Ramsey's theory of the "second best" (or, better, of the feasible "first best" when a person can be subjected only to excise taxes on goods and services), as in Ramsey (1927), takes simplest form in a one-person society, or in "a good society," where initial endowments have been rectified in the background. These and many other topics, such as the existence of "cheat-proof" algorithms in game situations, would take me too far afield.

Enough has been said to honor the magnificent edifice of Bergsonian welfare economics.

Notes

1 A possible qualification to this comes from what I have called the quantum jump of progress in modern welfare economics due to John Harsanyi (1955). He showed there that *individualistic* ethics applied to *stochastic* (i.e., probabilistic) states can lead back naturally to the *additive* hedonism of Bentham, Edgeworth, and the "old" welfare economists (Pigou, Marshall, Wicksell, etc.). In terms of the notation in my later equation (1), the BISWF there can then be written in terms of *strongly* separable functions, namely as $\lambda_1 U^1(\text{bread}^1, \text{wine}^1) + \lambda_2 U^2(\text{bread}^2, \text{wine}^2)$, where the *only* remaining judgment required of the ethical judge is the ratio of the λ's once the metrics of the U's have been specified.

2 Marshall's 1890 *Principles of Economics* noted, but did not emphasize, that the existence of *multiple* solutions to a microsystem would cast doubt that all such (quite different) solutions could *simultaneously* each be ethically optimal. So why should a system with a unique competitive equilibrium have accorded to that equilibrium social optimality?

3 Thus, Walras, and Frank Knight in my time, sometimes believed that perfect competition "maximized each person's utility subject to the constraints on everybody of being a price-taking competitor." That this is a confusion and irrelevancy is simplest seen in the case where competitive equilibrium is unique: Its outcome then is the *only* possible outcome, as much the *worst* feasible state of the world as the *best*. What Knight had in the back of his mind was that, somehow, a one-price competitive regime involves some im-

portant personal freedom. Walras seems to have had a related fuzzy notion about "commutative justice" independently of "distributive justice." As a rich man I ought ethically to give to poor men, but it is ethically right for me not to do so and to use *my* private property as I wish.

4 Relevant to this are Bergson (1954, chap. 2), Little (1952), and Samuelson (1967).

5 A competitive equilibrium may exist under lighter conditions than my assumptions. Externalities aside, it can be proved to be Pareto optimal. However, a socialist's desired Bergson optimum, which will of course be a Pareto-optimal point, need not be realizable as a competitive solution when (a) laws of returns are not appropriate, and (b) when some people's indifference contours violate quasi-concavity. I return to this later.

6 Richard Musgrave (1959) and Leif Johansen (1965) are standard references on the public goods model.

7 Vickery (1961), Groves and Ledyard (1975), Tideman and Tulloch (1976), and others in our time have tried to work out alternatives to the Lindahl solution that will motivate people not to try to be "free riders" in their use of and rates for public goods. My exposition here parallels Samuelson (1954, 1956, 1964) and overlaps with Johansen (1965).

8 Perhaps Pareto's *literary* exposition is, for once, better than his mathematical. Thus his *Manual* (chap. 6, §33–8) adequately recaptures tangencies of indifference contours along the "contract curves [of Pareto optimality]" in Edgeworth's 1881 *Mathematical Psychics*.

9 Some ideologically conservative people seriously propose that redistribution of income and wealth should be limited to what people *want* to give in *private* charity.

10 We should not expect too much from a paper as short as this 1913 fragment of Pareto. But, on reflection, we realize that no integrable social preference field is likely to emerge from the game-theoretic interactions of group politics. Samuelson (1956) shows by the concept of "a good society" how strict are the requirements (in the way of optimizing lump-sum transfers) if family or group demand behavior of weakly separable members is to satisfy the Slutsky–Antonelli reciprocity conditions of transitive preferences. In particular, as Pareto the cynic knew, observations from political compromises are unlikely to be Pareto optimal and hence could not have been generated by any quasi-individualistic social function of the type Pareto here attributes to "government."

11 Redistribution of $\Sigma_1^K a^k$ may involve deadweight transfer loss as $\Sigma_1^K x^k$ is lowered. This realistic fact will cause each of us to opt for less than complete egalitarianism, unless each and every one of us is a Maxaminer in the Rawls (1971) manner. See my contribution to the Vickery *Festschrift* (1976), where I analyze what Arthur Okun was to call the "leaky bucket experiment"; and where it is shown that following Rawls's Maxaminer dogma would force all parties to the social compact into more egalitarianism than any of them would want.

12 Thus, suppose that He is given his way on the A and B disagreement and She is given her way on the A and C disagreement. This would lead to "C better than A, A better than B, and B better than C," a contradiction to transitivity of the BISWF.

13 Some had hoped to get around the Impossibility Theorem by invoking a *cardinal* intensity for each individual's private ordering. Samuelson (1967) has

argued that a new Impossibility Theorem will be found to obtain in the realm of intensity orderings. So there is no escape from the Arrow nullity in that direction.

References

Arrow, Kenneth. 1951. *Social Choice and Individual Values,* 2d ed. New York: Wiley, 1963.

Barone, Enrico. 1908. ''Il ministerio della produzione nello stato colletivista,'' *Giornale degli Economisti,* pp. 267–93, 391–414. Translated in F. A. Hayek (ed.), *Collectivist Economic Planning.* London: Routledge and Kegan Paul, 1935.

Bastiat, F. 1850. *Economic Harmonies.*

Bentham, J. 1789. *An Introduction to the Principles of Morals and Legislation.* Payne; also Clarendon Press, Oxford, 1907.

Bergson, Abram. 1938. ''A Reformulation of Certain Aspects of Welfare Economics,'' *Quarterly Journal of Economics* 52, 310–34.

Bergson, Abram. 1954. ''On the Concept of Social Welfare,'' *Quarterly Journal of Economics* 68, 233–52.

Bergson, Abram. 1966. *Essays in Normative Economics.* Cambridge, Mass.: Harvard University Press.

Bernoulli, Daniel. 1738. ''Specimen theoriae novae de mensura sortis.'' English translation: ''Exposition of a New Theory on the Measurement of Risk,'' *Econometrica* 22, 23–6 (1954).

Chipman, John. 1976. ''The Paretian Heritage,'' *Revue Europeene des Sciences Sociales et Cahiers Vilfredo Pareto* 14, 65–171.

Debreu, Gerard. 1959. *Theory of Value.* New York: Wiley.

Edgeworth, F. Y. 1881. *Mathematical Psychics.* London: C. Keagan Paul.

Graaf, Jan van de. 1957. *Theoretical Welfare Economics.* Cambridge: Cambridge University Press.

Groves, T., and J. Ledyard. 1975. ''Optimal Allocation of Public Goods: A Solution to the 'Free Rider'.'' Discussion paper 144, Center for Mathematical Studies, Economics and Management Science, Northwestern University, Evanston, Ill.

Harrod, R. F. 1938. ''Scope and Methods of Economics,'' *Economic Journal* 48, 383–412.

Harsanyi, John. 1955. ''Cardinal Welfare, Individualistic Ethics, and Interpersonal Comparisons of Utility,'' *Journal of Political Economy* 63, 309–21.

Hicks, J. R. 1939. ''The Foundations of Welfare Economics,'' *Economic Journal* 49, 696–712.

Hotelling, H. 1938. ''The General Welfare in Relation to Problems of Taxation and of Railway and Utility Rates,'' *Econometrica* 6, 242–69.

Johansen, L. 1965. *Public Economics.* Chicago: Rand McNally.

Kaldor, Nicholas. 1939. ''Welfare Propositions of Economics and Interpersonal Comparisons of Utility,'' *Economic Journal* 49, 549–52.

Kemp, M. C., and Y.-K. Ng. 1976. ''On the Existence of Social Welfare Functions, Social Orderings and Social Decision Functions,'' *Economica* 43, 59–66.

Kemp, M. C., and Y. K. Ng. 1977. ''More on Social Welfare Functions: The Incompatibility of Individualism and Ordinalism,'' *Economica* 44, 89–90.

Kuhn, Thomas. 1962. *The Structure of Scientific Revolutions*. Chicago: University of Chicago Press.
Lange, O. 1942. "The Foundations of Welfare Economics," *Econometrica* 10, 215–28.
Lerner, A. P. 1934a. "Concept of Monopoly and the Measurement of Monopoly Power," *Review of Economic Studies* 1, 157–75.
Lerner, A. P. 1934b. "Economic Theory and Socialist Economy," *Review of Economic Studies* 2, 51–61.
Lerner, A. P. 1944. *Economics of Control*. New York: Macmillan.
Lindahl, Erik. 1919. *Die Gerechtigkeit der Besteuerung, eine Analyse der Steuer Prinzipen auf Grundlage der Grenznutzentheorie*. Lund.
Little, Ian. 1950. *A Critique of Welfare Economics*. Oxford: Clarendon Press.
Little, Ian. 1952. "Social Choice and Individual Values," *Journal of Political Economy* 60, 422–32.
Marschak, Jacob. 1950. "Rational Behavior, Uncertain Prospects and Measurable Utility," *Econometrica* 18, 111–41.
Marshall, A. 1890. *Principles of Economics*. London: Macmillan.
Merton, Robert K. 1973. *The Sociology of Science*. Chicago: University of Chicago Press.
Mises, Ludwig von. 1920. "Die Wirtschaftsrechnung im sozialistischen Gemeinwesen," *Archiv fur Sozialwissenschaften*, pp. 86–121. Translated in F. A. Hayek (ed.), *Collectivist Economic Planning*. London: Routledge & Kegan Paul, 1935.
Musgrave, Richard. 1959. *The Theory of Public Finance*. New York: McGraw-Hill.
Neumann, J. von, and O. Morgenstern. 1944. *Theory of Games and Economic Behavior*. Princeton, N.J.: Princeton University Press.
Pareto, Vilfredo. 1894. "Il massimo di utilita data dalla libera concorrenza," *Giornale degli Economisti* 2, 9, 48–66.
Pareto, Vilfredo. 1896, 1897. *Cours d'économie politique*, vols. 1 and 2. Lausanne: F. Rouge.
Pareto, Vilfredo. 1903. "A proposito del massimo di ofelimita," *Giornale degli Economisti* 2, 26, 177–8.
Pareto, Vilfredo. 1909. *Manuel d'économie politique*. Paris: M. Giard et E. Brière. English translation: *Manual of Political Economy*. New York: Augustus Kelly, 1971.
Pareto, Vilfredo. 1913. "Il massimo di utilita per una colletivita in sociologia," *Giornale degli Economisti* 3, 46, 337–41.
Pigou, A. C. 1932. *Economics of Welfare*. London: Macmillan.
Pollak, Robert A. 1979. "Bergson–Samuelson Social Welfare Functions and the Theory of Social Choice," *Quarterly Journal of Economics* 93, 73–92.
Ramsey, Frank. 1927. "A Contribution to the Theory of Taxation," *Economic Journal* 37, 47–61.
Rawls, John. 1971. *A Theory of Justice*. Cambridge, Mass.: Harvard University Press.
Robbins, Lionel. 1932. *An Essay on the Nature and Significance of Economic Science*. London: George Allen & Unwin.
Samuelson, Paul A. 1938. "Welfare Economics and International Trade," *American Economic Review* 38, 261–66; reprinted in Joseph E. Stiglitz (ed.), *The Collected Scientific Papers of Paul A. Samuelson*, vol. 2. Cambridge, Mass.: MIT Press, 1966, chap. 60.

Samuelson, Paul A. 1947. *Foundations of Economic Analysis.* Cambridge, Mass.: Harvard University Press.
Samuelson, Paul A. 1950. "The Evaluation of Real National Income," *Oxford Economic Papers* (N.S.) 2, 1, 1–29; reprinted in *CSP,* vol. 2, chap. 77.
Samuelson, Paul A. 1954. "The Pure Theory of Public Expenditure," *Review of Economics and Statistics* 36, 4, 387–9; reprinted in *CSP,* vol. 2, chap. 92.
Samuelson, Paul A. 1956. "Social Indifference Curves," *Quarterly Journal of Economics* 70, 1–22; reprinted in *CSP,* vol. 2, chap. 78.
Samuelson, Paul A. 1964. "A. P. Lerner at Sixty," *Review of Economics and Statistics* 31, 169–78; reprinted in Robert C. Merton (ed.), *The Collected Scientific Papers of Paul A. Samuelson,* vol. 3. Cambridge, Mass.: MIT Press, 1972, chap. 183.
Samuelson, Paul A. 1967. "Arrow's Mathematical Politics," in S. Hook (ed.), *Human Values and Economic Policy.* New York: New York University Press. Reprinted in *CSP,* vol. 3, chap. 167.
Samuelson, Paul A. 1973. "Invariant Economic Index Numbers and Canonical Duality: Survey and Synthesis" (with S. Swamy), *American Economic Review* 64, 566–93. Reprinted in Hiroaki Nagatani and Kate Crowley (eds.), *The Collected Scientific Papers of Paul A. Samuelson,* vol. 4. Cambridge, Mass.: MIT Press, 1977, Chap. 209.
Samuelson, Paul A. 1976. "Optimal Compacts for Redistribution," in R. E. Grieson (ed.), *Public and Urban Economics.* Lexington, Mass.: Lexington Books (D. C. Heath). Reprinted in *CSP,* vol. 4, chap. 257.
Samuelson, Paul A. 1977. "Reaffirming the Existence of 'Reasonable' Bergson-Samuelson Social Welfare Function," *Economica* 44, 81–8.
Savage, L. J. 1954. *Foundations of Statistics.* New York: Wiley.
Scitovsky, Tibor. 1941. "A Note on Welfare Propositions in Economics," *Review of Economic Studies* 9, 77–88.
Scorza, Gaetano. 1903. "A proposito del massimo di ofelimita data dalla libera concorrenza," *Giornale degli Economisti* 2, 41–62.
Sen, Amartya. 1971. *Collective Choice and Social Welfare.* San Francisco: Holden-Day.
Tideman, T. N., and G. Tullock, 1976. "A New and Superior Process for Making Social Choices," *Journal of Political Economy* 84, 1145–59.
Tintner, G. 1946. "A Note on Welfare Economics," *Econometrica* 14, 69–78.
Vickery, W. 1945. "Measuring Marginal Utility by Reactions to Risk," *Econometrica* 13, 319–33.
Vickery, W. 1961. "Counterspeculation, Auctions, and Competitive Sealed Tenders," *Journal of Finance* 16, 8–37.
Viner, Jacob. 1937. *Studies in the Theory of International Trade.* New York: Harper & Bros.
Wicksell, Knut. 1896. *Finanztheorestische Unterschungen.*
Wicksell, Knut. 1934. *Lectures on Political Economy.* Translated by E. Classen from the 3rd edition published in Swedish; edited by Lionel Robbins. London: Routledge & Kegan Paul.
Wicksteed, P. H. 1894. *An Essay on the Coordination of the Laws of Distribution.* London: Macmillan.

Reaffirming The Existence of "Reasonable" Bergson–Samuelson Social Welfare Functions

By P. A. SAMUELSON
Massachusets Institute of Technology

It is a pity that David Ricardo is not alive to tell us whether he would agree with Pierro Sraffa's 1960 proposed 'standard commodity" as a good approach to Ricardo's desired "standard measure of value". Fortunately, Abram Bergson and I are alive and kicking and available to record our reactions to the recent axioms proposed by Kemp and Ng (1976) (who refer to a similar unpublished 1973 Washington University paper by R. R. Parks) as "reasonable" for an ethical system of the individualistic Bergson–Samuelson type to satisfy.

Let me record at the beginning, after careful reflection and consultation with various authorities, the following reactions.

(a) I must regard Axiom 3 of Kemp–Ng as anything but "reasonable" to impose on a Bergson–Samuelson Individualistic Social Welfare Function (B–S ISWF). As Oscar Wilde might put it, "For any ethical observer to understand Axiom 3 is to reject it".

I believe that Plato, Aristotle and Hobbes would be interested in Arrow's "Impossibility Theorem" on ideal democracy. I doubt that such ethical philosophers as Bentham, Kant, Sidgwick or Rawls would be jarred by the Kemp–Ng "impossibility theorem", once they perceive how it transparently follows from the gratuitous Axiom 3.

(b) Granted that I or any writer in the Bergson tradition would not wish to adopt the proferred Axiom 3 and that the jury would approve of this considered decision, what about the semantic question of whether post-1938 writers in that tradition have seemed to use the words, "individual tastes are to count or to be respected" and the words "the B–S ISWF is to be purely 'ordinal' and not at all 'cardinal' ", in such a way as to imply that the Kemp–Ng Axiom 3 does validly obtain?

If this semantic indictment could be sustained—and some research in the relevant writings leads me to believe that it cannot be—the charge would not be a serious one: in almost forty years, it seems to have occurred to only three sophisticated people to be led astray! As Pareto used to say, who would ever let substantive matters be determined by philology?

In any case, since the question of word usage has been raised, the Kemp and Ng article provides an appropriate occasion to clarify the record on the sense in which the B–S ISWF is to be understood to "ordinally" "depend on" the "ordinal" preferences of individuals. My later discussion deals with this matter.

(c) Granted that ethical systems will not wish to be restricted by Axiom 3 and that their wording is clear (or made clear) on that, there is no reason why those economists engrossed in social choice theory may not wish to explore other "social choice" functions than those of proposed ethical systems. In the absence of a proposed ethical ordering capable of adjudicating whether any movements should be made that both hurt and help some individuals, who is to stop anyone from exploring in the manner of Kemp–Ng and Pollak (1976) what are the consequences of *any* sets of axioms that might be put on a social choice function defined for given individuals' tastes and values? It is a free universe. Why should I want to repudiate Pollak's new suggestion that the name "mathematical politics" be applied to such questions raised in the context of *given* individuals' tastes and values, and not confine the name as I did in the 1967 Hook Symposium (Samuelson, 1967) only to the quite different Arrow problem in which any and all different tastes and values of individuals are to be put into Arrow's Constitutional Voting-Machine Function for it to arrive at final social decisions? There I was concerned to demonstrate the logical difference between a B–S ISWF and an Arrow Constitutional Voting-Machine Function (A CV–MF), a distinction blurred in K. J. Arrow (1951). Kemp and Ng, Pollak and I are all agreed that here we are in the domain of given individuals' tastes and values and not in the wider and different Arrow domain of all that their tastes and values might be—even though certain logical similarities of axioms and theorems may be discerned in the two domains. I am happy to leave moot the question of how widely mathematical politics should be usefully defined.

An initial warning is, however, in order. Sometimes when we are considering one domain of applicability—say, gasoline blending—we may by lucky chance find that the axioms appropriate to some other domain of applicability—say, von Neumann axioms on probability blendings in stochastic decision-making—happen also to apply. We then turn the crank of deductive logic and, so to speak, get a nice free ride with respect to valid theorems and corollaries that are analogous to those in the other domain of applicability. Several fruitful examples of this could be referred to. And Pollak's analysis, stimulated by the Kemp and Ng discussion, is one further example in which many of the May and Sen results for the wide-domain Arrow problem have a counterpart in the narrower domain shared with the Bergson SWF.

But there is this pitfall that one must beware of in making use of such analogies. An axiom that seems perfectly "reasonable" in one context may really lack "reasonableness" in another context, and yet this fact may be obscured by the fact that a spurious appearance of reasonableness may arise because of an uncritical taking over of the analogies. Thus, the Axiom 3 that is so abhorrent from an ethical viewpoint has been called by Pollak an axiom of "neutrality and independence". These are what Gilbert Ryle called "persuasive" appellations. At first blush, who could be against "neutrality" or consider it unreasonable? Against the historical background of colonial oppression and exploitation, other things equal, what person would be opposed to "independence"? To put matters so crudely here is to warn the reader against the treachery of words and analogies. But often the pitfalls and fallacies are more insidious. We shall see that Axiom 3 is anything but a harmless and reasonable axiom in the context of ethical judgments.

But, not to prejudge that issue which is under debate, consider a logically similar case: an "independence axiom" is what does the trick in justifying ordinal decision-making in stochastic situations by means of maximizing the mathematical expected value of a cardinal utility function of all possible outcomes. On reflection, because we realize that the state of the world that obtains when heads rather than tails occurs is a mutually exclusive alternative to the state that obtains when tails occurs, we realize that in this probability context the crucial independence axiom does appeal to good sense (as virtually a "sure-thing" axiom). But let us try to apply the same logic of independence to a different, and only partially analogous, situation. Suppose you prefer "getting an extra tyre while losing an olive" to "the *status quo*" when you already have three tyres in the "*status quo*". Does that reasonably mean that you *have* to prefer "getting an extra tyre while losing one olive" to the "*status quo*" when that *status quo* involves your having two or less tyres for your auto? "Of course not", you will reply; which is only to say that the assumption of independence of ordinal preference concerning a subset of goods often makes much less sense than independence makes in connection with probabilistic alternative outcomes.[1] This warning is very much in order because I have found that I could trap people into provisionally accepting the Kemp–Ng Axiom 3 by interrogating them about it before they had become familiar with the context of the problem: later they recanted and accused me of having taken advantage of their innocence by deceptive exposition. I had to plead guilty of Machiavellianism in the good cause of illuminating this trap.

I. Reductio ad Absurdum?

Before giving an example of an existent reasonable ordinal B–S ISWF in a context that has enough texture to make the distinction between an Individualistic Social Welfare Function and a general Paternalistic Social Welfare Function meaningful and interesting, let us consider a much simpler context in which the distinction is vacuous. Suppose society has a fixed total number of chocolates that could be partitioned between two specified selfish hedonists: say, 80 and 20, 50 and 50, 20 and 80, or more generally as any of two non-negative real variables (X chocolates to Person 1 or x chocolates to Person 2), where $X+x=100$ and neither is negative.

Every admissible state of the world is now Pareto-optimal. So long as any ethical system is reduced to pronouncing on which point on the line-segment of admissible points is socially or ethically optimal, there is no restriction whatsoever now imposed on a SWF by the requirement that it be ISWF (i.e., be "of individualistic type, other things equal", respecting individuals' tastes).

What is the meaning of the new Axiom 3 in this context? It says, "If it is ethically better to take something (say 1 chocolate or, alternatively, say 50 chocolates) from Person 1 who had *all* the chocolates in order to give to Person 2 who had none, then it *must* be ethically preferable to give *all* the chocolates to Person 2".

One need not be a doctrinaire egalitarian to be speechless at this requirement. Is it "reasonable" to put on an ethical system such a straightjacket? Few will agree that it is.

Is there some semantic or philological reason for failure to agree to satisfy Axiom 3 to be judged by the jury to be a lapse from *ordinalism* in ethical judging? "No" is I believe the proper answer to such a question—even though one senses why someone might be tempted to yield to confusion in the matter. It is the proper answer because we must not confuse *cardinality* in the measurement of X and of x (which are measured in grammes of chocolates or centimetres on a graph) with cardinality of "ethical utility". An egalitarian like Rawls (or like Bentham confronted with "like" persons) can express his ethical-indifference contours in the (X, x) quadrant completely ordinally: his asserted symmetry around the 45° line of those observable, non-introspective contours must lead, when he asserts that those contours are convex (an ordinal, observable curvature property), to the theorems of egalitarian allocation. [Suppose the persons are known to be risk-averse, an ordinal fact about their stochastic odds taking; it can be described in terms of a cardinal-metric von Neumann function for each of them (although it *need not* be so described). J. C. Harsanyi (1955) has given reasons why the ethical observer of individualistic type might wish to "respect" individuals' risk reactions by making the B–S SWF an "additively independent" ethically-weighted sum of the individuals' respective von Neumann functions. Again, there is *nothing* non-ordinal about all this; but, unlike the proposed Axiom 3, the new axioms proposed by Harsanyi do possess appeal and do impose straightjackets on the B–S ISWF that are deemed "reasonable". Cf. Samuelson (1965).]

In pronouncing that redistribution is good up to the point of equal-chocolate income but not beyond, the ethical observer must not be understood necessarily to be arguing, "The cardinal intensity of 1's sacrifice of 51 chocolates is so much greater than that of his sacrifice of 50, and the cardinal intensity of 2's gain in utility from 51 rather than 50 chocolates is so great, that by our taking into account these cardinalities (and only by doing so), the ethical system judges one redistribution to be worthwhile and not the other". Rather, the ethical observer explains: "The ordinally defined, observable ethical marginal rate of substitution between 1's chocolates and 2's chocolates achieves under symmetry the value of one only on the (X, x) axis of symmetry. For some positive values of h up to the critical $h^* = 50$, $(100-h,\ 0+h)$ is ethically ordinally preferred to $(100, 0)$; for $h > h^*$, $(100-h,\ 0+h)$ is ethically worse than (50, 50). And this is true even though the sign pattern of individual's algebraic gains from (100, 0) is $(-, +)$ both for $h < 50$ and $h > 50$!" It is monstrously "unreasonable" to require, as Axiom 3 does, that wherever $(-, +)$ occurs it must be treated ethically the same regardless of what (X, x) intensities (intensities that are in *commodity* space, not ethical or subjective spaces!) are involved in the background. Moreover, it is a strained semantic interpretation of words like "dependence only on individual's ordinal preferences" to think that this implies a prior agreement to require the sign pattern $(-, +)$ to be always treated in the same way.

What is not in dispute is the logical correctness of the Kemp and Ng allegation that stipulating the strong Axiom 3 leads to *always* favouring some one person if that person is ever favoured (subject of course to lexicographic ties). Their impossibility theorem holds if they are granted the axiom that many will deem preposterous. Agreed to is the fact that, under an additional "symmetry" or "anonymity" axiom, which rules out any one person's tastes becoming ethically dominant, Axiom 3 leads to a null existence of any SWF. It is the very correctness of their logic that alerts those with well-defined ethical orderings to the inappropriateness of Axiom 3. "By their fruits must ye know them" applies above all to axiom systems. Once Machiavelli explains to people the implications of Axiom 3, they come to understand their desire to reject it.

The reader can now see why the question mark should be removed from the title of this section so that it comes to read "A Reductio Ad Absurdum".

II. Example of an Existent ISWF

A one private-good world of selfish persons is ill-adapted to convey the content that SWFs may have for welfare policies. This is so for the reason that with one such good virtually all states of the world are already Pareto-optimal; hence little new is to be gained from the optimality analysis of modern welfare economics.

Here is a richer example to show the inadmissibility of Axiom 3, while at the same time displaying the meaningful content of the individualistic ethical requirement that "... individuals' tastes are to 'count' in the sense of being 'respected' when all persons are in agreement on a move and are only to be supplemented for moves involving tradeoffs between different individuals, tradeoffs that can be resolved only by specified ethical norms or judgments".

We contemplate two persons, 1 and 2; two goods, food and clothing. For expositional simplicity each person displays unitary income elasticities of demand (i.e., *homothetic* indifference contours). Each is free of altruism or envy, self-mindedly indifferent to the food and clothing consumptions of other people.

Figure 1(a) shows Person 1's indifference contours in terms of his food and clothing, written in large letters as (F, C). Knowing one contour in 1(a), the reader can supply all the rest as radial blowups of the homothetic field.

Figure 1(b) shows Person 2's homothetic indifference contours in his (f, c) space. These are selected as parallel straight lines to show that strong convexity of contours is not necessarily presupposed.

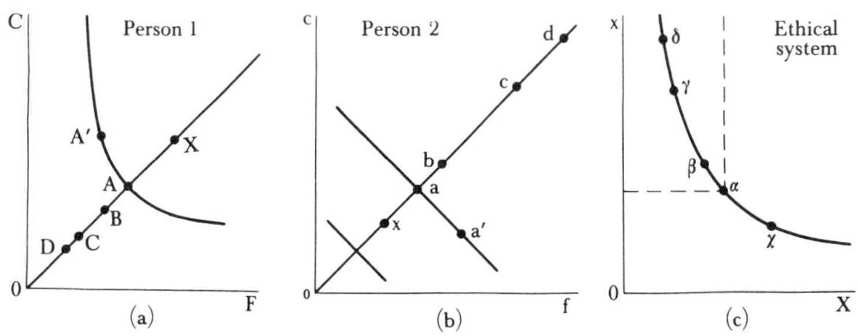

FIGURE 1

Although Figures 1(a) and 1(b) are shown in the respective two-spaces (F, C) and (f, c), each gives *full* information on the relevant person's transitive, non-lexicographic, purely ordinal preferences in the four-dimensional space (F, C, f, c)—once we remember my no-envy no-altruism specification.

Now introduce an ethical ordering of all states of the world, dramatized by an ethical observer's ordinal contours in (F, C, f, c) space. This B–S ISWF is to be complete, transitive, and in this example non-lexicographic. It is also to be restricted to being of individualistic type: such a B–S ISWF, by definition, has the Pareto property that whenever both persons deem a point in four-space to be better than another point, so will the ethical observer (who, other things being truly equal in this special instance, does "respect" their tastes). There is no other requirement, other than this "tree" or "separability" property *à la* Pareto, imposed on a B–S ISWF.

Figure 1(c) records the *complete* information on the ethical deservingnesses of the two persons implied by the existence of this example's well-defined instance of a B–S ISWF. To understand 1(c), concentrate on the related points $(A, a; \alpha)$ in 1(a), 1(b) and 1(c) respectively. Compare them with the related points $(B, b; \beta)$, These two states of the world are stipulated by this ISWF to be "ethically indifferent". Indeed, the points $(C, c; \gamma)$ and $(D, d; \delta)$ are also stipulated to be ethically indifferent to each other and to $(A, a; \alpha)$ or $(B, b; \beta)$. For any running variables, X and x, depicting distances from the origin on the specified respective rays OA and oa, we can always for any given X find that x such that $(X, x; \chi)$ is just ethically indifferent to $(A, a; \alpha)$. The axes of 1(c) depict these observed commodity scalars, X and x, which are observable without regard to any person's cardinal intensity of utility or to any ethical observer's cardinal intensity of ethical feeling. Indeed, through every point in the (X, x) space, there is an ethical indifference contour; in our example we assume homotheticity in that (X, x) space, so that one contour defines everything.

We now have, from knowledge of the three contours of 1(a), 1(b) and 1(c), codified all there is to know (and it is everything) about this existent ISWF.

Remark: (A', a') is ethically indifferent to (A, a). But, unlike the previous ethical information that was at the *arbitrary* determination of the ethical observer, this last bit of information comes to us as a derivable theorem, deducible from our Pareto axiom that the ethical system is indeed one of "individualistic type". This tree-property or separability axiom tells us that since A is indifferent to A' for Person 1, and a is indifferent to a' for Person 2, it follows that (A', a') must be ethically indifferent to (A, a) in the four-space (F, C, f, c). This requirement is quite another thing from Axiom 3 of Kemp and Ng, as all discussants realize.

III. Discussion of the Example's ISWF

First, *it* does exist. Second, it is purely *ordinal* in its definition. *No* cardinal intensities are ever involved. Third, it is non-lexicographic and could be represented by an *infinity* of cardinal ethical numberings in four-space of the Individual Ethical Observer's ethical-indifference contours.[2] Fourth, this SWF has a rich texture, with important implied policy conditions for welfare optimality.[3]

Fifth, the example most definitely violates Axiom 3. Only if 1(c)'s contour were a vertical line, making Person 1 an ethical dictator, or a horizontal line, in effect giving ethical primacy to Person 2, could Axiom 3 be respected. A glance at Figure 1(c) will show why the contour there must violate Axiom 3. The latter says that *all* the points south-east of α there must represent a gain if any point does: but the drawn contour denies this, claiming that only the points south-east of α that are above the contour represent a gain, those below representing a loss. If, and only if, we replaced the drawn contour through α by a vertical line or alternatively by a horizontal line, could we honour the bizarre Axiom 3.

Points on any vertical line east of another vertical line would be ethically superior; but ties along any one vertical line could be broken by the lexicographic ordering which says that, since Person 1 is indifferent concerning points on that vertical line, we are to use Person 2's preferences for more northward points to break ties. A similar caveat holds for the case of horizontal lines in Figure 1(c). Since no contours can simultaneously be both vertical and horizontal, a further axiom of symmetry or "anonymity" would with Axiom 3 lead only to a null solution, as Kemp and Ng properly assert.

IV. Conclusion

My verdict is that the existence, reasonableness and appropriate naming of Bergson–Samuelson Social Welfare Functions have stood up well under the new investigation by Kemp and Ng.

Still, as we know from Thomas Kuhn's paradigm on the historical development of science, often progress is made only funeral by funeral. So it is appropriate that established ideas be subject to unsparing probing and testing like that provided by Kemp and Ng.

ACKNOWLEDGMENTS

I owe thanks to the National Science Foundation for financial aid. Friendly correspondence with Murray Kemp is gratefully acknowledged, as are helpful discussions with Robert Pollak of the University of Pennsylvania and Hiroaki Nagatani of the MIT Graduate School. Abram Bergson read a first draft of this paper and empowers me to record his general agreement with my rejection of the proposed Kemp–Ng axiom system, particularly their odd Axiom 3. I have to insist that the adjective "Bergson–Samuelson" must be understood in the sense of "Darwin–Huxley", not "Darwin–Wallace".

NOTES

[1]Readers familiar with axiomatizing personal probabilities and subjective stochastic decision-making will understand the role of an "independence" axiom in the writings of Ramsey, J. Marschak, L. J. Savage, Milnor and Herstein and others; topological implications of "independence" in more general contexts have been explored by Georgescu-Roegen, Debreu, Samuelson, Komolgorov and many others going back to the early nineteenth-century functional equation of Abel.

[2]Actually, in parody of Irving Fisher's "ideal index number" formula, I constructed this B–S ISWF to agree with "a geometric (ethical) mean of Person 1's harmonic mean of his (F, C) and

Person 2's arithmetic mean of his (f, c)". I hardly dare write down the formula $\omega = (0.5F^{-1}+0.5C^{-1})^{-0.5}(0.5f+0.5c)^{0.5}$ for fear some hasty reader will think I am introducing cardinal intensities into the ethical ordering. But I run the risk. Further, the example may assume that each person, confronted with any food and clothing prices, will always require, as a recompense for wagering half his income on the appearance of heads from the toss of a fair coin, a promised gain that will end him at tails with a doubling of his income. This is of course a special assumption, but a possible one; and one that is purely ordinal in its nature. With cunning, the ISWF has been selected so that those who agree with the Harsanyi argument of the last footnote will not find this ISWF abhorrent: indeed, the unitary elasticity contour of Figure 1(c) can be replaced by any isoelastic contour and still meet Harsanyi's requirement (which, in this context, requires the ethical observer to be *ex ante* indifferent between $(F, C, f, c) = (2, 2, 2, 2)$ with certainty and heads and tails outcomes of $(1, 1, 1, 1)$ and $(4, 4, 4, 4)$ respectively!). I must emphasize for the benefit of any reader of Kemp and Ng that none of this involves a surreptitious departure from ordinality: ordinality in a stochastic context is still ordinality, and it leaves non-stochastic ordinality non-cardinal.

[3]Thus, wartime food and clothing rationing, with non-transferable ration tickets, will leave society inside the Pareto utility possibility frontier by violating interpersonal equality of marginal rate of substitution between food and clothing. The example's "ideal index" is, however, singular in that it happens to elude Bergson's subtle 1938 perception that, when persons' tastes differ, the equality of money income that may be ethically optimal for an egalitarian ISWF at one set of relative prices will be thereby recognized to be non-optimal at another set of prices. To remove this singularity of Bernoulli logarithmic functions, as applied to $\log \omega$, merely suppose that Persons 1 and 2 have constant and unequal relative risk aversions so that, to risk half his money income on occurrence of tails, man 2 must be promised as a gain on heads a multiple of his income that is larger or smaller than 1. Then we do verify that, for a food–clothing price ratio other than unity, equal money incomes is no longer optimal—now that figure 1(c)'s Cobb–Douglas contour has been replaced by a more general contour.

The differences in tastes alerts us to a basic ambiguity in the Rawls notion of Maxmin—i.e., of choosing *ex ante* that social compact which betters the wellbeing of the person who ends worse off. As "I" initially contemplate the possibility that "I" may turn out to be Person 1 rather than Person 2, how do "I" determine for each and every point in $(\bar{F}, \bar{C}, \bar{f}, \bar{c})$ space which person would be "worst off"? Who is the "I" that can make this decision? And "whose" tastes are to be used? We are at sea until these questions can be resolved. With diffidence, one may propose recourse to a Bergson–Harsanyi interpersonal function of the form $a\,\Phi\{(0.5\bar{F}^{-1}+0.5\bar{C}^{-1})^{-1}\}+(1-a)\phi(0.5\bar{f}+0.5\bar{c})$, where the Rawlsian must somehow supply the proper positive fractional value for a, and where Φ and ϕ are risk-definable von Neumann utilities. Until the right a is knowable, we are still at sea. (Note: suggesting that $a=\frac{1}{2}$ or $1 \div$ the number of persons is an evasion of the conundrum, not a solution! Perhaps there is some appeal in the following definition: 1 is "worse off" than 2 if 1 envies (f, c) while 2 does not envy (F, C); i.e. when $F^{-1}+C^{-1} > f^{-1}+c^{-1}$ and $f+c > F+C$.)

REFERENCES

Arrow, K. J. (1951, 1963). *Social Choice and Individual Values.* New Haven, Conn.: Yale University Press.

Harsanyi, J. C. (1955). Cardinal welfare, individualistic ethics and interpersonal comparisons of utility. *Journal of Political Economy*, **63,** 309–321.

Kemp, M. C. and Ng, Y-K (1976). On the existence of social welfare functions, social orderings and social decision functions. *Economica,* **43,** 59–66.

Pollak, R. A. (1976). Bergson–Samuelson social welfare functions and the theory of social choice. Unpublished Working Paper, University of Pennsylvania.

Samuelson, P. A. (1965). 1965 postscript. In *Collected Scientific Papers of Paul A. Samuelson* (J. E. Stiglitz, ed.), I, pp. 124–126. Cambridge, Mass.: MIT Press.

—— (1967). Arrow's mathematical politics. In *Human Values and Economic Policy* (S. Hook, ed.) New York: University Press.

When it is ethically optimal to allocate money income in stipulated fractional shares

PAUL A. SAMUELSON

MASSACHUSETTS INSTITUTE OF TECHNOLOGY

1. INTRODUCTION AND SUMMARY

It is tempting for an egalitarian to recommend equal *money* incomes for all; or, for one who perceives differing degrees of need and deservingness, to stipulate some optimal fractions of total money income to be allocated among Persons 1, 2, . . . , *j*, . . . , *J*. Such a rule of invariant fractional money-income shares is known to be, in general, a *shibboleth* incompatible with true continual maximization of a Bergson Social Welfare Function which is defined in terms of the many real goods and services that the various people consume.[1]

I owe thanks to the National Science Foundation for financial aid; also to Kate Crowley and Vicki Elms for editorial assistance. My ancient debts to Abram Bergson and Robert Bishop will be obvious.

[1] See Bergson (1938, n. 15; 1966; Chapter 3 Addendum) and Samuelson (1947, p. 225) for explication of this now obvious general implication of asymmetry among individuals' preferences. Relevant lines from the latter include these:

> . . . the rule of equality of income (measured in dollars, numeraire, abstract purchasing power) applied to individuals of different tastes, but made to hold in all circumstances, is actually inconsistent with any determinate, definite *W* function. Equality becomes a fetish or shibboleth, albeit a useful one, in that the means becomes the end, and the letter of the law takes precedence over the spirit.

The present paper shows that what is in general a shibboleth will be formally optimal in a definable category of cases. In particular, if people have *different* nonstochastic tastes, but all display the same *constant vectoral relative risk aversions* of exact logarithmic or Bernoullian degree, then a Bentham–Bergson–Harsanyi Social Welfare Function will be maximized by the rule of invariant money-income fractional shares. Less singularly, if people have identical nonstochastic tastes and the *same* constant degree of *vectoral relative risk aversion* (not necessarily that of Bernoulli), then invariant money fractions will also be optimal. Also, in Santa Claus cases of Kantian symmetry, equal shares almost trivially obtain at the optimum, a case open to some generalizings.

2 SOCIAL WELFARE FUNCTIONS

DEFINITION *of an individualistic social welfare function* Suppose there are J persons $(1, 2, \ldots, J)$, who, for simplicity, are free of envy, altruism, and all consumption externalities. The jth person consumes the vector of n goods and services $(x_1{}^j, \ldots, x_n{}^j) = \mathbf{x}^j$, the tastes and demands for which are derivable from maximizing a cardinal indicator of utility, $U^j(\mathbf{x}^j) = U^j(x_1{}^j, \ldots, x_n{}^j)$.

The most general Bergson Social Welfare Function would involve an ethical norming or ordering of all states of the world, $\mathbf{X} = (x_1{}^1, \ldots, x_n{}^1, \ldots, x_1{}^J, \ldots, x_n{}^J) = (\mathbf{x}^1, \ldots, \mathbf{x}^J)$, summarizable by a cardinal indicator

$$\begin{aligned} W &= \omega(\mathbf{x}^1, \mathbf{x}^2, \ldots, \mathbf{x}^J) = \omega(\mathbf{X}) \\ &= \omega(x_1{}^1, \ldots, x_n{}^1, x_1{}^2, \ldots, x_n{}^2, \ldots, x_1{}^J, \ldots, x_n{}^J). \end{aligned} \tag{1}$$

For the decision of equal incomes as optimal in one situation implies a certain relative well-being as between vegetarians and non-vegetarians; at different relative prices between vegetables and non-vegetables an equal distribution of income can no longer be optimal.

... equality of money income where there is diversity of tastes involves the equality of nothing important. It is in lesser degree like the Anatole France aphorism concerning the equality of the law in its treatment of rich and poor. Before Bergson's treatment one could have sensed, but not analyzed definitively, this subtlety.

What is said about equality of income can as well be said about any non-50–50 invariant fractional shares, $(\alpha_1, \alpha_2, \ldots)$, $\sum \alpha_j = 1$. Actually, this *Foundations* passage involves both an understatement and an overstatement: an overstatement because in the singular Bernoulli case discussed here, despite asymmetry of nonstochastic tastes, invariant fractional shares constitute no shibboleth—and similarly for some other generalizations developed here; an understatement because, even when relative prices do not change or are irrelevant, equality at one set of society's endowments need not imply equality at another set (as when wartime scarcity mandates ethical fair-sharing, compatibly with ethical toleration of some inequality in an affluent peacetime).

Note that a lower-case boldface symbol, such as $\mathbf{x}^j$, is an $n \times 1$ column vector; a capital-letter boldface symbol, such as $\mathbf{X}$, is an $n \times J$ rectangular matrix.

When individuals' tastes are to be "respected," Bergson defines an *Individualistic* Social Welfare Function as one with the *weak-separability* or "tree" property[2]

$$W = w[U^1(\mathbf{x}^1), U^2(\mathbf{x}^2), \ldots, U^J(\mathbf{x}^J)], \qquad \partial w/\partial U^j > 0 \qquad (j = 1, \ldots, J). \quad (2)$$

Bergson (1938), Lange (1942), Samuelson (1947), and others have recognized that Bentham's hedonistic additive function represented that special case of (1), and of (2), which takes the form

$$W = \lambda_1 V^1(x_1{}^1, \ldots, x_n{}^1) + \cdots + \lambda_J V^J(x_1{}^J, \ldots, x_n{}^J) = \sum_1^J \lambda_j V^j(\mathbf{x}^j), \qquad \lambda_j > 0. \quad (3)$$

Here $(\lambda_1, \ldots, \lambda_n)$ are, so to speak, ethical weight factors whose respective numerical magnitudes depend on the particular version of the $U^j(\mathbf{x}^j)$ cardinal indicator of the respective persons' utilities suitable to serve as $V^j(\mathbf{x}^j)$'s in (3).

DEFINITION *of a Bentham–Bergson–Harsanyi additive SWF* Harsanyi (1955) has presented persuasive arguments for (3)'s being more than one highly special case of (2), being instead a rather natural extension to the stochastic domain of (2)'s basic philosophy that "individuals' tastes are to be respected."[3] Indeed,

[2] See Bergson (1938), Lange (1942), Samuelson (1947), and Graaf (1959) for explicit treatments of *individualistic* social welfare functions. The general idea was much exploited by Pareto around the turn of the century; however, the notion that one should not give far-sighted glasses to myopic people goes back a long way. In the 1930s, Lerner (1934a,b, 1944), Kaldor (1939), Hicks (1939), and other writers, anxious to save something from the rubble of conventional welfare economics left after the positivist attack by Robbins (1932), made implicit (and sometimes confused) use of the *individualistic function* concept. Chipman (1976) has professed to find explicitly in Pareto (1896–1897, 1909, 1913, and earlier writings) the concept of a social welfare function $\omega(\mathbf{X})$ or $w[U^1(\ ), \ldots, U^J(\ )]$. This, I believe, involves an act of sympathetic charity since Pareto's many writings are often obscure on what we now call Pareto optimality, and since expressions such as $\theta_1(\delta U^1) + \theta_2(\delta U^2) + \ldots$ are sometimes used by Pareto as positivistic-politics constructs and sometimes as vague Lagrange multiplier expressions relevant to the first-order conditions for being on the ("Pareto-optimal" points of the) utility-possibility frontier. Alas, during Pareto's most productive quarter century, he was able to conduct no dialogue with competent peers and consequently his expositions suffer from impatience, repetition, and obscurity—so that only his genius shines through.

[3] Harsanyi (1955) at first escaped the notice it deserves as a classic. Strotz (1958) was led to somewhat similar results by axiomatizing welfare economics along the lines of the axiomatization of probabilistic inference by Chernoff. See Samuelson (1965, pp. 124–126) for my own belated recognition of the 1955 Harsanyi advance. Diamond (1967) gives a dissenting view (as J. Rothenberg and F. Fisher implicitly had done on other grounds in their 1961–1962 controversy with Strotz).

(a) if individuals' *nonstochastic* tastes are to count, as in (2);

(b) if individuals' *stochastic* tastes are to count, in the sense that when they *all* ex ante prefer one stochastic option to another, so will the Social Welfare Function;

(c) if each individual wants to make stochastic decisions which satisfy the aesthetic *consistency* or independence axioms of Ramsey (1931), Marschak (1950), and Savage (1954) that lead to *maximizing the expected value* of his existent Neumann cardinal utility function defined for all $\mathbf{x}^j$ outcomes

$$\max E\{N^j(\mathbf{x}^j)\}, \quad U^j(x^j) \equiv f_j[N^j(x^j)]; \qquad f_j'[\ ] > 0, \quad f_j''[\ ] \gtreqless 0; \tag{4}$$

(d) if the ethical observer wishes to make his stochastic decisions so as also to obey the Ramsey–Marschak–Savage consistency (or "sure-thing") axioms, thus acting to achieve

$$\max E\{N(\mathbf{x}^1, \ldots, \mathbf{x}^J)\} = \max E\{N(\mathbf{X})\}, \tag{5}$$

where $N(\mathbf{X})$ is a definable cardinal function unique up to scale and origin constants and representing some stretching of $\omega(\mathbf{X})$ in (1); then it follows from (a)–(d) that the form of (3) must obtain for $N(\mathbf{X})$, namely

$$N(\mathbf{X}) \equiv \sum_1^J \lambda_j N^j(x_1{}^j, \ldots, x_n{}^j) = \sum_1^J \lambda_j N^j(\mathbf{x}^j), \tag{6}$$

where the $N^j(\mathbf{x}^j)$ are observable from revealed personal risk choices and will be strictly concave if people are strictly risk averse.

Combining (a)–(d), we can infer that Harsanyi in effect stipulates the following functional identity on an existent $N[N^1, \ldots, N^J]$ function

$$E\{N[N^1(\mathbf{x}^1), \ldots, N^J(\mathbf{x}^J)]\} \equiv N[E\{N^1(\mathbf{x}^1)\}, \ldots, E\{N^J(\mathbf{x}^J)\}]. \tag{7}$$

When $N^j(\mathbf{x}^j)$ takes only the values a^j and b^j with 50–50 probabilities, (7) becomes

$$\tfrac{1}{2}N[a^1, \ldots, a^J] + \tfrac{1}{2}N[b^1, \ldots, b^J] \equiv N[\tfrac{1}{2}a^1 + \tfrac{1}{2}b^1, \ldots, \tfrac{1}{2}a^J + \tfrac{1}{2}b^J]. \tag{8}$$

Subtract the first term on the left from both sides to find that both sides of the new expression must be independent of $[a^1, \ldots, a^J]$; setting the requisite partial derivatives equal to zero gives

$$\begin{aligned} \tfrac{1}{2}N_j[\tfrac{1}{2}a^1 + \tfrac{1}{2}b^1, \ldots, \tfrac{1}{2}a^J + \tfrac{1}{2}b^J] &\equiv \tfrac{1}{2}N_j[a^1, \ldots, a^J] \\ &\equiv \tfrac{1}{2}c_j, \quad \text{a constant} \qquad (j = 1, \ldots, J), \end{aligned} \tag{9}$$

where by notational definition

$$N_j[z_1, \ldots, z_J] \equiv \partial N[z_1, \ldots, z_J]/\partial z_j.$$

Therefore,

$$N[z_1, \ldots, z_J] \equiv c_0 + c_1 z_1 + \cdots + c_J z_J \tag{10}$$

just as (6) asserts when we choose to set arbitrary c_0 inessentially at zero and identify the c's as λ's.

3. CONSTANCY OF RELATIVE RISK AVERSION

Constant (Scalar) Relative Risk Aversion

From various investigations, such as those of Pfanzangl (1959), R. Schlaifer (unpublished), Pratt (1964), Arrow (1964), Samuelson (1969a,b), Merton (1969), and many others, the ordinary concept of constant relative risk aversion is well understood in its application to a single measure of income or wealth. A standard theorem can state the equivalence of any of the following definitions of the term.

THEOREM *on constant (scalar) relative risk aversion* Any one of the following properties implies all the others:

(i) The person acts to maximize

$$E\{(x^\gamma - 1)/\gamma\}, \qquad 1 \geq \gamma,$$

where x is a positive scalar;

(ii) he acts to maximize

$$E\{U(x)\},$$

where $xU''(x)/U'(x) = d \log U(x)/d \log x = \gamma - 1 \leq 0$;

(iii) $\frac{1}{2}U(\beta_H x) + \frac{1}{2}U(\beta_T x) - U(x) \equiv 0$ defines

$$\psi(\beta_H, \beta_T) \equiv \psi(\beta_T, \beta_H) = 1,$$

where $\psi(\beta_H, \beta_T)$ is independent of x and must be expressible in the form

$$\tfrac{1}{2}\exp[\gamma \log_e \beta_H] + \tfrac{1}{2}\exp[\gamma \log_e \beta_T] = 1 \geq \gamma.$$

When $\gamma = 1$, the person is *risk neutral*, with linear utility, $U = a + bx$ and with $\beta_H = 2 - \beta_T$. For $\gamma < 1$, the person is risk averse and $\beta_H > 2 - \beta_T$. As $\beta_H \beta_T \rightarrow \infty$, $\gamma \rightarrow -\infty$, and the person becomes infinitely risk averse and approximates indefinitely closely to a *minimaxer* (or, more accurately, a maximiner). For $\beta_H = \beta_T^{-1}$, we are in the Bernoulli case of logarithmic utility, $U = a + b \log X$: here, $\gamma = 0$ and $(x^\gamma - 1)/\gamma$ becomes a 0/0 indeterminate form, evaluable by l'Hôpital's rule as $\gamma \rightarrow 0$; l'Hôpital's rule applied to (iii)'s final relation also yields $\beta_H = \beta_T^{-1}$ as $\gamma \rightarrow 0$. For $\gamma = \frac{1}{2}$, we have Cramer's square-root utility function, which is unbounded above (as with all cases of positive γ). Cross-sectional observations on market trade-offs between securities' mean returns and their risks suggested a negative γ as most realistic, with β_T in $\psi(\beta_H, \beta_T) = 1$ being bounded below by a positive fraction and $(x^\gamma - 1)/\gamma$ being bounded above.

Proof of the theorem is direct The mutual equivalence of (i) and (ii) is immediate. That (i) implies (iii) is immediate. That (iii) implies (ii), and hence its equivalent (i), follows from the fact that it implies

$$\frac{\partial}{\partial x}\left\{-\frac{\partial\beta_H}{\partial\beta_T}\right\} \equiv 0 \equiv \frac{\partial}{\partial x}\left\{\frac{\partial\psi(\beta_H, \beta_T)/\partial\beta_T}{\partial\psi(\beta_H, \beta_T)/\partial\beta_H}\right\}, \tag{11}$$

$$0 \equiv \frac{\partial}{\partial x}\left\{-\frac{\partial\beta_H}{\partial\beta_T} - \log\beta_T + \log\beta_H\right\} \equiv \frac{\partial}{\partial x}\{\log U'(\beta_T x) - \log U'(\beta_H x)\}$$

$$\equiv x^{-1}\left\{\frac{\beta_T x U''(\beta_T x)}{U'(\beta_T x)} - \frac{\beta_H x U''(\beta_H x)}{U'(\beta_H x)}\right\} \equiv x^{-1}\{A(\beta_T x) - A(\lambda\beta_T x)\}, \quad \lambda = \beta_H/\beta_T,$$

where $A(z) = zU''(z)/U'(z)$. For the last brace to vanish for all choices of $(\beta_T x)$ and λ requires that each term in the brace be a constant, or that $zU''(z)/U'(z)$ be a constant as (ii) requires.[4]

Remark It appears that (iii) need not be specified as holding for *all* possible arbitrary choices of β_T. It seems to be enough to require (iii) to hold for a limited number of specified fractional β_T's, perhaps even for only a single value. Thus, set $\beta_T = \frac{1}{2}$, and suppose that β_H is observed always to be $(\frac{1}{2})^{-1}$ independently of x. The identity

$$\tfrac{1}{2}U(\tfrac{1}{2}x) + \tfrac{1}{2}U(2x) - U(x) \equiv 0 \tag{12}$$

has only one monotone-increasing solution for $U(x)$, up to a linear transformation, namely $U(x) = z + b\log x$. A formal solution of (12) would appear to permit our replacing b by an arbitrary function of $\log_{1/2} x$, $\Pi(\log_{1/2} x)$, so long as $\Pi(z)$ is periodic in z with a unit period, $\Pi(z) \equiv \Pi(z \pm 1)$. However, unless $\Pi(z)$ were a strict constant, the derivative of $U(x) = a + \Pi(\log_{1/2} x)$ $\log x$ could not help becoming negative for some sufficiently small value of x: hence $U(x) = a + b\log x$ is the only admissible monotone-increasing solution of (12). The reader may also verify that there is only a linear well-behaved concave solution, $U(x) = a + bx$ of

$$\tfrac{1}{2}U(x - \tfrac{1}{2}) + \tfrac{1}{2}(x + \tfrac{1}{2}) - U(x) \equiv 0. \tag{13}$$

Likewise any specific values for $\overline{\beta}_T$ and $\overline{\beta}_H$ in

$$\tfrac{1}{2}U(\overline{\beta}_T x) + \tfrac{1}{2}U(\overline{\beta}_H x) - U(x) \equiv 0 \tag{14}$$

lead to $a + b[(x^\gamma - 1)/\gamma]$ as admissible solutions for $U(x)$.

[4] An alternative proof that (iii) implies (ii) comes from realizing that, when β_H is, from $\frac{1}{2}U(\beta x) + \frac{1}{2}U(f[\beta;\, x]x) \equiv U(x)$, the most general function of β_T and x, namely $f[\beta_T;\, x]$, then $-\frac{1}{2}\partial^2 f(1;\, x)/\partial\beta_T{}^2$ equals $-xU''(x)/U'(x)$. This last expression must be a constant independent of x as in (ii) if $f[\beta_T;\, x]$ is to be free of x. Q.E.D.

Constant (Vectoral) Relative Risk Aversion

People do not consume scalar money income. They consume a vector of goods and services, $\mathbf{x}^j = (x_1{}^j, \ldots, x_n{}^j)$, for the jth person.

How do we generalize the notion of constant relative risk aversion from a scalar to a vector? Years ago Robert Bishop of MIT pointed out the way. We examine how a person reacts to risk of money incomes spendable at different absolute (and relative) prices. What can be shown to be the same thing, we require that gains and losses expressed as scaled-up or scaled-down intensities of any initial vector of goods and services induce the same decision of preference or indifference when both the initial vector endowment and the intensities of gains and losses are increased in the same proportion.

All this is made definite by the following theorem of Stiglitz (1969) and Samuelson (1969a,b) generalizing the equivalencies already encountered in the case of constant (scalar) relative risk aversion.

THEOREM *on constant (vectoral) relative risk aversion* Anyone of the following properties implies all the others:

(i) The person acts to achieve

$$\max E\{[H(x_1, \ldots, x_n)^\gamma - 1]/\gamma\},$$

where $H(\lambda x_1, \ldots, \lambda x_n) \equiv \lambda H(x_1, \ldots, x_n)$ is a first-degree-homogeneous concave function;

(ii) the person acts to achieve

$$\max E\{U(x_1, \ldots, x_n)\},$$

where $\partial U(x_1, \ldots, x_n)/\partial x_i \equiv U_i(x_1, \ldots, x_n)$ are all homogeneous functions of the same nonpositive degree, namely with

$$\sum_{k=1}^{n} \frac{\partial \log[U_i(x_1, \ldots, x_n)]}{\partial x_k} = \gamma - 1 \leq 0 \qquad (i = 1, \ldots, n);$$

(iii) the person acts to maximize $E\{U(\mathbf{x})\}$, where

$$\tfrac{1}{2}U(\beta_T \mathbf{x}) + \tfrac{1}{2}U(\beta_H \mathbf{x}) - U(\mathbf{x}) \equiv 0$$

defines $\psi(\beta_H, \beta_T) \equiv \psi(\beta_T, \beta_H) = 1$ independently of $\mathbf{x}$ and where $\psi(\beta_H, \beta_T)$ is expressible in the form

$$\tfrac{1}{2}\exp[\gamma \log_e \beta_H] + \tfrac{1}{2}\exp[\gamma \log_e \beta_T] = 1 \geq \gamma;$$

(iv) the person acts to maximize the expected value of the Roy *indirect utility* function

$$\max E\{[I^\gamma H^*(p_1, \ldots, p_n)^\gamma - 1]/\gamma,$$

where

$$H^*(p_1/I, \ldots, p_n/I) \equiv \max_{x_i} H(x_1, \ldots, x_n) \qquad \text{s.t.} \ \sum_1^n (p_k/I)x_k = I$$

$$= \max_{x_i} \frac{H(x_1, \ldots, x_n)}{\sum_1^n (p_k/I)x_k} \equiv IH^*(p_1, \ldots, p_n)^{-1},$$

and where $H^*(\mathbf{p})$ is a concave homogeneous function of degree one;

(v) the person acts to maximize the expected value of the *indirect utility* function, $U^*(p_1/I, \ldots, p_n/I)$, where the partial derivatives of U^*, $\partial U^*(y_1, \ldots, y_n)/\partial y_i = U_i^*(y_1, \ldots, y_n)$, should all be homogeneous functions of the same nonpositive degree,

$$\sum_{k=1}^n \frac{\partial \log U_i^*(y_1, \ldots, y_n)}{\partial \log y_i} = \gamma - 1 \leq 0, \qquad (i = 1, \ldots, n);$$

(vi) the person acts to maximize the expected value of the Roy *indirect utility* function $U^*(p_1/I, \ldots, p_n I) = U^*(\mathbf{p}/I)$, where

$$\tfrac{1}{2}U^*(\mathbf{p}/\beta_H) + \tfrac{1}{2}U^*(\mathbf{p}/\beta_T) - U^*(\mathbf{p}) \equiv 0$$

defines

$$\psi(\beta_H, \beta_T) \equiv \psi(\beta_T, \beta_H) = 1 \qquad \text{independently of } \mathbf{p},$$

where $\psi(\ \ )$ can be expressed as

$$\tfrac{1}{2}\exp[\gamma \log_e \beta_H] + \tfrac{1}{2}\exp[\gamma \log_e \beta_T] = 1.$$

Proof of the theorem is straightforward As part of the oral tradition at MIT in the early 1960s, Bishop had posed the problem of (v) in its risk-neutral form (where $\beta_H = 2 - \beta_T$), and had inferred that (v) implied homothetic preference and (i) with $\gamma = 1$. Stiglitz (1969) demonstrated that (vi) implied (i) globally.[5] That (i) implies all the rest is immediate; that (iv) implies (i) and all the rest is immediate once we utilize duality theory. That (ii) and (i) are essentially equivalent follows from integrating the linear partial-differential equations of (ii); likewise to prove the equivalence of (iv) and (v).

[5] The present theorem, due to Stiglitz (1969) and also to Samuelson (1969a,b), has global validity throughout the whole of the nonnegative $(x_1, \ldots, x_n)$ or $(p_1, \ldots, p_n)$ orthant. Stiglitz (1969) also gives more general results of local validity: in the manner of Gorman (1953) or Theil (1954), he considers the risk-neutral case where all the Engel curves are straight lines in certain subregions of the nonnegative orthant for $(x_1, \ldots, x_n)$; however, as argued in Samuelson (1965, n. 2), if the Engel's loci are *always* to be straight lines, they must be straight lines through the origin—which is the homothetic case. Likewise, if constant vectoral risk aversion is to obtain globally, the only solution to the function equations of (iii) or (vi) are those corresponding to homothetic tastes. Since completing this paper, I have chanced on the valuable work of Rothblum (1975), which gives references to numerous writers who have worked independently of the Bishop, Stiglitz, and Samuelson investigations.

The part of a rigorous proof that is at all difficult is the demonstration that either (iii) or (vi) imply all the rest. Actually, from the scalar theorem, we know that (iii) implies there exists a $N(x_1, \ldots, x_n)$ whose expected value is maximized and that takes the form

$$a + bN(x_1, \ldots, x_n) = \theta(x_2/x_1, \ldots, x_n/x_1) + \gamma^{-1}[x_1{}^{\gamma}\tau(x_2/x_1, \ldots, x_n/x_1) - 1]. \tag{15}$$

Then, for $\gamma < 1$ and for x_1 either large or small, nonconstancy of θ would contradict *every* $\partial N/\partial x_i$ being *always* positive. With θ an ignorable constant, (15) is seen to be essentially of the form given in (i). A similar argument applies dually to show that (vi) implies (v).

4. OPTIMALITY CONDITIONS

The General Case

Suppose we have prescribed totals of each good to allocate among the J persons so as to maximize a Bentham–Bergson–Harsanyi social welfare function:

$$\max_{x_i{}^j} \sum_1^J \lambda_j U^j(\mathbf{x}^j) \qquad \text{s.t.} \quad \left(\sum_{j=1}^J x_i{}^j\right) = \sum_1^J \mathbf{x}^j = (\bar{x}_i) = \bar{\mathbf{x}} > 0$$

$$= V(\bar{x}_1, \ldots, \bar{x}_n; \lambda_1, \ldots, \lambda_J) = \sum_1^J \lambda_j U^j(\mathbf{x}^{j*}), \tag{16}$$

where $(\bar{\mathbf{x}}^{j*}) = (x_i^{j*})$ satisfy

$$\frac{\partial U^j(\mathbf{x}^{j*})/\partial x_i{}^j}{\partial U^j(\mathbf{x}^{j*})/\partial x_1{}^j} = \pi_i \qquad (i = 2, \ldots, n; \quad j = 1, \ldots, J), \tag{17a}$$

$$\frac{\lambda_j\, \partial U^j(\mathbf{x}^{j*})/\partial x_1{}^j}{\lambda_1\, \partial U^1(\mathbf{x}^{1*})/\partial x_1{}^1} = 1 \qquad (j = 2, \ldots, J). \tag{17b}$$

The conditions in (17) are both necessary and sufficient provided some regularity conditions are imposed on the $U^j(\mathbf{x}^j)$ functions—as for example that they all be *strictly* quasi concave, and satisfy strong Inada conditions such that as any $x_i{}^j \to 0$, $\partial U^j(\mathbf{x}^j)/\partial x_i{}^j \to \infty$ and as any $x_i{}^j \to \infty$, $\partial U^j(\mathbf{x}^j)/\partial x_i{}^j \to 0$.

From standard welfare economics and duality theory, we know that the following market-clearing algorithm can provide the solution to (16):

$$\max_{I^j} \sum_1^J \lambda_j U^{j*}(I^j; \bar{p}_1, \ldots, \bar{p}_n) \qquad \text{s.t.} \quad \sum_{j=1}^J I^j = \sum_{i=1}^n \bar{p}_i \bar{x}_i$$

$$= \sum_1^J \lambda_j U^{j*}(I^{j*}; \bar{p}_1, \ldots, \bar{p}_n), \tag{18}$$

where the optimal (I^{j*}) are each functions of the given parameters

$$I^{j*} = \Phi^j(p_1, \ldots, p_n; \bar{x}_1, \ldots, \bar{x}_n; \lambda_1, \ldots, \lambda_J) \equiv p_1\Phi^j(1, \mathbf{p}/p_1; \bar{\mathbf{x}}; \lambda) \quad (19)$$

and where, by definition of the quasi-concave *indirect dual* utility function,

$$U^{j*}(I^j, p_1, \ldots, p_n) \equiv U^{j*}(1, \mathbf{p}/I^j)$$

$$= \max_{x_i{}^j} U^j(x_1{}^j, \ldots, x_n{}^j) \qquad \text{s.t.} \quad \sum_1^n p_i x_i = I^j$$

$$x_i^{j*} = -\frac{\partial U^{j*}(1, \mathbf{p}/I^j)/\partial p_i}{\partial U^{j*}(1, \mathbf{p}/I^j)/\partial I^j} = \Phi_i{}^j(\mathbf{p}/I^j)$$

and where the $\bar{\mathbf{p}} = (\bar{p}_1, \ldots, \bar{p}_n)$ are market-clearing prices satisfying

$$\sum_{j=1}^J \Phi_i{}^j([\mathbf{p}/p_1]/[I^j/p_1]) = \bar{x}_i \qquad (i = 2, \ldots, n). \quad (20)$$

Relations (19) and (20) are assured to have at least one solution for $(\mathbf{X}^*; \bar{\mathbf{p}}/\bar{p}_1; I^{1*}/\bar{p}_1, \ldots, I^{J*}/\bar{p}_1)$ under our regularity conditions. However, in the general case where the $U^j(\mathbf{x}^j)$ functions do not correspond to homothetic demand and are different for each j, the optimal (I^{j*}/I^{1*}) may give rise to multiple solutions of the general equilibrium problem; only one of these solutions can be the optimal one for $\mathbf{X}^*$. Even if demands are all homothetic, if they differ enough among persons, multiplicity of solution may hamper the practicability of using market pricing to attain the welfare optimum. Indeed, as shown in the Musgrave *Festschrift* piece of Samuelson (1974), the optimal $\mathbf{X}^*$ could correspond to a general equilibrium solution of (19) and (20) that is locally and globally unstable.

As will be discussed in a later section, in the Santa Claus case of perfect symmetry, where $U^j(\mathbf{x}) \equiv U^1(\mathbf{x})$ and $\lambda_j \equiv \lambda_1$, the welfare optimum must be at the Kantian point of perfect symmetry

$$x_i^{j*}/\bar{x}_i \equiv 1/J, \qquad I^{j*}\Big/\sum_{k=1}^J I^{k*} \equiv 1/J,$$
$$\frac{\bar{p}_i}{\bar{p}_1} \equiv \frac{\partial U^j(\bar{\mathbf{x}}/J)/\partial x_i{}^j}{\partial U^j(\bar{\mathbf{x}}/J)/\partial x_1{}^j} \qquad (j = 1, \ldots, J; \quad i = 2, \ldots, n). \quad (21)$$

In this case of "balanced income effects," the relevant general equilibrium solution will be unique.

Singular Case of Bernoulli's Logarithmic Risk Aversion

Now assume all people have constant (vectoral) risk aversion of exactly Bernoulli's degree. (The is testable by their being just willing to risk half their chocolates and gloves on the fair toss of a coin provided they are promised twice the amount of their chocolates and gloves when they win: i.e., $\beta_H = \beta_T^{-1}$ in our earlier theorems.)

The relevant optimality problem of (16) now specializes to

$$\max_{x_i{}^j} \sum_1^J \lambda_j \log H^j(\mathbf{x}^j) \qquad \text{s.t.} \quad \sum_1^J \mathbf{x}^j = \bar{\mathbf{x}}$$

$$\equiv \max_{\alpha^j} \sum_1^J \lambda_j \log[(\alpha_j I)H^{j*}(\bar{\mathbf{p}})^{-1}] \qquad \text{s.t.} \quad \sum_1^J \alpha_j = 1$$

$$\equiv \sum_1^J \lambda_j \log[IH^*(\bar{\mathbf{p}})^{-1}] + \max_{\alpha_j} \sum_1^J \lambda_j \log \alpha_j \tag{22.1}$$

$$\equiv \sum_1^J \lambda_j \log[IH^*(\bar{\mathbf{p}})^{-1}] + \sum_1^J \lambda_j \log\left(\lambda_j \Big/ \sum_1^J \lambda_k\right), \tag{22.2}$$

where

$$H^j(\mathbf{x}^j) \quad \text{is first-degree-homogeneous and concave,} \tag{23.1}$$

$$H^{j*}(\mathbf{p}) \quad \text{is likewise, being } H^j(\ )\text{'s "dual" defined by} \tag{23.2}$$

$$H^{j*}(\mathbf{p}) = \min_{x_i} \frac{\sum_1^n p_i x_i}{H^j(x_1, \ldots, x_n)}, \tag{23.3}$$

$$I = \sum_1^n \bar{p}_i \bar{x}_i, \qquad \alpha_j = I^j/I, \tag{23.4}$$

$\bar{\mathbf{p}}$ represents market-clearing prices satisfying (19) and (20). (23.5)

The equivalence of (22.2) and (21.1) gives the implied optimality of invariant fractional money-income shares:

$$\alpha_j{}^* \equiv \lambda_j \Big/ \sum_1^J \lambda_k \qquad \text{for all} \quad (\bar{x}_i). \tag{24}$$

This follows from the singular property of the logarithmic function that

$$\sum \log[f_j(\lambda_j, \alpha_j) g_j(\lambda_j, \beta)] \equiv \sum \log g(\lambda_j, \beta) + \sum \log f_j(\lambda_j, \alpha_j) \tag{25}$$

with the implication that the second term's extremum is independent of the variable β. The last term in (22.2) looks much like "entropy" in discussions of information theory and statistical mechanics.

We may summarize this singular Bernoulli case (which is a variant of the Cobb–Douglas case found in Chipman (1974) to be capable of aggregation):

THEOREM[6] *on singular logarithmic risk aversion* When all persons have constant (vectoral) risk aversion of Bernoulli degree, so each maximizes $E\{\log H^j(x^j)\} \equiv E\{\log \beta^{-1} H^j(\beta x^j)]\}$, the optimal allocation of fixed totals of society's goods is achievable by specifying invariant fractional shares of *money* income, $(\alpha_1^*, \ldots, \alpha_J^* = 1 - \alpha_1^* - \alpha_2^* - \cdots)$.

None of this requires similarity of individuals' nonstochastic tastes! Note that x_i^{J*}/x_i^{1*} varies among the goods. However, $\sum_1^n \bar{p}_i x_i^{j*} / \sum_1^n \bar{p}_i x_i^{1*}$ is always the same no matter how the relative components of $(\bar{x}_1, \ldots, \bar{x}_n)$ vary.

Proof of this theorem has already been provided by the demonstrated equivalence of (22.1) and (22.2), by virtue of (25)'s decomposition of the logarithmic expressions.

It follows from this exact theorem that, if all people have relative (vectoral) risk aversions that are never very far from that of constant Bernoullian degree, the optimal income fractions (α_j^*) will alter very little as social endowments change a great deal.

Constant (Vectoral) Relative Risk Aversion and Uniform Tastes

Less singularly, we find another class of cases in which invariant income shares are optimal. Suppose all people have the same nonstochastic tastes; and all have the same constant relative (vectoral) risk aversion, not necessarily of Bernoullian degree, $\beta_H \gtrless \beta_T^{-1}$.

Now (16) takes the equivalent of the form

$$\max_{x_i^j} \sum_1^J \lambda_j H(\mathbf{x}^j)^\gamma/\gamma \qquad \text{s.t.} \quad \sum_1^J \mathbf{x}^j = \bar{\mathbf{x}}$$

$$= \max_{\alpha_j} \sum_1^J \lambda_j \alpha_j^\gamma I^\gamma H^*(\bar{\mathbf{p}})^{-\gamma}/\gamma \qquad \text{s.t.} \quad \sum_1^J \alpha_j = 1$$

$$= [I^\gamma H^*(\bar{\mathbf{p}})^{-\gamma}/\gamma] \max_{\alpha_j} \sum_1^J \lambda_j \alpha_j^\gamma \qquad \text{s.t.} \quad \sum_1^J \alpha_j = 1 \tag{26.1}$$

[6] I came upon this singular result by chance when giving as an example of a Bergson Social Welfare Function the following parody of Fisher's "ideal index": $w = [\frac{1}{2}x_1{}^1 + \frac{1}{2}x_2{}^1]^{1/2}[\frac{1}{2}(x_1{}^2)^{-1} + \frac{1}{2}(x_2{}^2)^{-1}]^{-1/2}$. Invariant fractional shares, $\alpha_1^* = \alpha_2^* = \frac{1}{2}$, turned out singularly to be optimal for this "ideal index," whose logarithm is of the Bentham–Bergson–Harsanyi additive form. Curiously, relative prices remain at unity for $\bar{x}_2/\bar{x}_1$ in a wide range around unity; this is because $\exp U^1 = \frac{1}{2}x_1{}^1 + \frac{1}{2}x_2{}^1$ happens to be weakly quasi concave, with linear indifference contours. However, for $\bar{x}_2/\bar{x}_1$ large enough, it will be ethically optimal to have Person 1 consume none of the now-scarce first good; even so, the ratio $x_2{}^2/x_1{}^2$ becomes so excessive that $\bar{p}_2/\bar{p}_1$ must fall to get all of the redundant second good demanded. Nonetheless, equal α_1^* and α_2^* stays optimal despite the change in relative prices! At the proofreading stage, I therefore had to alter the final footnote of Samuelson (1977), suggesting that, for $\gamma \neq 0$, $[\frac{1}{2}x_1{}^2 + \frac{1}{2}x_2{}^1]^\gamma \gamma^{-1} + [\frac{1}{2}(x_1{}^2)^{-1} + \frac{1}{2}(x_2{}^2)^{-1}]^{-\gamma}\gamma^{-1}$, the *non*optimality of invariant α_j^* would obtain. Around equation (29) I return to the subtleties raised by this footnote.

$$= [I^{\gamma}H^*(\bar{\mathbf{p}})^{-\gamma}/\gamma]\left[\sum_1^J \lambda_j^{1/(1-\gamma)}\right]\Big/\left[\sum_1^J \lambda_k^{\gamma/(1-\gamma)}\right], \tag{26.2}$$

where

$H(\mathbf{x})$ is homogeneous-first-degree and concave, (27.1)

$H^*(\mathbf{p})$ is likewise, being H's dual, (27.2)

$$H^*(\mathbf{p}) = \min_{x_i} \frac{\sum_1^n p_i x_i}{H(x_1, \ldots, x_n)}, \tag{27.3}$$

$$I = \sum_1^n \bar{p}_i \bar{x}_i, \qquad \alpha_j = I^j/I, \tag{27.4}$$

$\bar{\mathbf{p}}$ represents market-clearing prices satisfying (19) and (20). (27.5)

The equivalence of (26.2) and (26.1) gives the implied optimality of fractional money-income shares.

$$\alpha_j^* = \lambda_j^{\gamma/(1-\gamma)}\Big/\left[\sum_1^J \lambda_k^{\gamma/(1-\gamma)}\right]. \tag{28}$$

For $\gamma \to 0$, l'Hôpital's rule applied to $\log \alpha_j^*$ yields (24) from (28).

We may summarize this case of identical tastes and constant (vectoral) risk aversion.

THEOREM *on uniform tastes and constant (vectoral) risk aversion* When all people have identical tastes and the same constant relative (vectoral) risk aversion, each acting to maximize $E\{H(\mathbf{x}^j)^{\gamma}/\gamma\} \equiv E\{H(\theta\mathbf{x}^j)^{\gamma}\theta^{-\gamma}/\gamma\}$, the social optimum of a Bentham–Bergson–Harsanyi welfare function is achievable by specifying invariant fractional shares of money income, $(\alpha_1^*, \alpha_2^*, \ldots, \alpha_J^* = 1 - \alpha_1^* - \alpha_2^* - \cdots)$. Now, with tastes uniform and necessarily homothetic, $x_i^{j*}/x_i^{1*} \equiv (\alpha_j^*\bar{x}_i)/(\alpha_1^*\bar{x}_i) \equiv \alpha_j^*/\alpha_1^*$, for all i

$$\alpha_j^* = \lambda_j^{\gamma/(1-\gamma)}\Big/\left[\sum_1^J \lambda_k^{\gamma/(1-\gamma)}\right] > 0, \qquad \sum_j^J \alpha_j^* = 1.$$

Any change in the (λ_j/λ_1) coefficients, and hence in the optimal income fractions, will have no effect on relative prices or people's relative consumptions in this case of uniform homothetic tastes.

No further proof of this theorem is needed beyond the recognition that (26.1) is factorable and is thus equivalent to (26.2).

Unlike the singular Bernoulli case with its differences in tastes, the case dealt with in this last theorem is more intuitively understandable. With tastes homothetic and uniform among people, the complexities of a vector as against a scalar essentially evaporate: whatever the composition of endowments totals ($\bar{x}_i$), mere Pareto optimality will force the relevant equilibrium to involve every person consuming x_i^j/x_1^j in the same proportions as $\bar{x}_i/\bar{x}_1$.

We are in effect back in the scalar realm, with only α_j variable in $\alpha_j\bar{x}_i = x_i^j$. Relative prices are never affected by changes of α_j in $p_i/p_1 = [\partial H(\bar{\mathbf{x}}/\bar{x}_1)/\partial x_i]/[\partial H(\bar{\mathbf{x}}/\bar{x}_1)\partial x_1]$; and when changes in $\bar{\mathbf{x}}/\bar{x}_1$ do alter relative prices, they are altered for everybody in the same way.

Nonoptimality of Invariant Fractional Shares Even When Changes in Relative Prices Do Not Occur or Are Irrelevant

The cited items, Bergson (1966) and Samuelson (1947) both stress the crucial role played by shifting relative prices in making it mandatory that income shares (α_j^*/α_1^*) alter as social endowments alter. The results of the previous section seem to confirm this emphasis.

Nevertheless, as hinted at in footnotes 1 and 6, nonoptimality of invariant fractions may well occur even in the absence of relative price changes. Indeed, the case mentioned in footnote 6 would involve different optimal values for (α_1^*, α_2^*) when $\bar{x}_2/\bar{x}_1$ is raised a bit above unity—this despite the fact that $\bar{p}_2/\bar{p}_1$ stays at 1 for sizeable shifts of $\bar{x}_2/\bar{x}_1$ away from 1.

To clinch the point that changes in relative prices do not constitute the whole story, consider the case where

(1) only scalars of real incomes are involved, chocolates, (x^1, x^2); or

(2) what is much the same case, where $\bar{\mathbf{x}}/\bar{x}_1$ never changes and each person has the same homothetic tastes

$$U^j = f_j[H(x_1^j, x_2^j)] \qquad (j = 1, 2). \tag{29}$$

In this last case we know that relative prices never change, even when $f_2''[H] \not\equiv f_1''[H]$; and we know that it suffices to solve, for

$$U^j = f_j[x^j H(\bar{x}_1, \bar{x}_2)] \equiv U_j(x^j),$$

the optimality problem

$$\max_{x^j} \sum_1^2 \lambda_j U_j(x^j) \qquad \text{s.t.} \quad x^1 + x^2 = \bar{x}. \tag{30}$$

For fixed (λ_1, λ_2), fixed β, and varying $(\bar{x}_1, \bar{x}_2) = (\bar{x}, \beta\bar{x})$, the optimal solution need not have the property

$$x^{2*}/x^{1*} = \text{constant invariant to changes in } \bar{x}. \tag{31}$$

Thus, let the persons have different degrees of relative risk aversion so that (30) becomes equivalent to

$$\max_{x^j} [\lambda_1(x^1)^{1/2} + \lambda_2(x^2)^{1/3}] \qquad \text{s.t.} \quad x^1 + x^2 = \bar{x}. \tag{32}$$

Then, the larger is $\bar{x}$ the greater for fixed (λ_2/λ_1) will be $x_1{}^*/x_2{}^*$. This violates the optimality of invariant fractional shares.

Actually, if invariant shares are to be optimal for arbitrary choices of λ_2/λ_1 in $\lambda_1 U_1(x^1) + \lambda_2 U_2(x^2)$, it is necessary that the latter belong to the Bergson (1936) CES family, namely

$$\begin{aligned} U^j(\mathbf{x}^j) &= c_j[H(\mathbf{x}^j)^\gamma - 1]/\gamma, \qquad 1 > \gamma \\ \sum \lambda_j U^j(\mathbf{x}^j) &= a_\gamma + b_\gamma \sum [b_j H(\mathbf{x}^j)]^\gamma. \end{aligned} \tag{33}$$

In a sense, therefore, the theorems of the last two sections involve necessity as well as sufficiency.

However, as the remaining sections will show, if the vector (λ_j/λ_1) is to be frozen, it is possible to define cases of symmetry, and of symmetry's generalization, where invariant fractional shares do remain optimal.

5. SYMMETRY SITUATIONS AND GENERALIZATIONS

Perfect Symmetry

To remain a philosopher one must let cowardice keep breaking in. From Kant to Rawls, philosophers have manufactured ethics out of the thin air of disguised symmetry assumptions. Without symmetry, they are at sea without a compass—or, better, at sea where there is no definable magnetic-compass direction. With symmetry (*and* with quasi concavity!) the principle of Sufficient Reason yields a definite optimum at the point of symmetry. Natch.

This may be expressed by the following theorem.

THEOREM *on symmetry* Let the most general Bergson SWF of (1) have

(a) symmetry as between persons and

(b) be quasi concave (i.e., have iso-ω contours in the $n \times J\ x_i{}^j$ space that are convex).

Then

$$\begin{aligned} \max_{x_i{}^j} \omega(\mathbf{x}^1, \mathbf{x}^2, \ldots, \mathbf{x}^J) \qquad \text{s.t.} \quad \sum_1^J \mathbf{x}^j = \bar{\mathbf{x}} \\ = \omega(\bar{\mathbf{x}}/J, \bar{\mathbf{x}}/J, \ldots, \bar{\mathbf{x}}^J/J) \end{aligned}$$

COROLLARY For $\lambda_1 = \lambda_2 = \cdots = \lambda_J$ and $U^j(\mathbf{x}) \equiv U(\mathbf{x})$, a quasi-concave function,

$$\max_{x_i{}^j} \sum_1^J U(\mathbf{x}^j) \qquad \text{s.t.} \quad \sum_1^J \mathbf{x}^j = \bar{\mathbf{x}}$$

$$= \sum_1^J U(\bar{\mathbf{x}}/J).$$

Remark $U(y_1, \ldots, y_n)$ is quasi concave iff

$$U(y_1, \ldots, y_n) \geq A \qquad \text{forms a convex set in} \quad (y_1, \ldots, y_n). \tag{34}$$

When $U(y)$ is strictly quasi concave, the contour defined by $U(y_1, \ldots, y_n) = A$ is a strictly convex frontier of the convex set. The optimum point with $\alpha_j{}^* = x_i^{j*}/\bar{x}_i = J^{-1}$ is *unique* when $\omega(\ )$ or $U(\ )$ are *strictly* concave monotonic *strongly* increasing functions.

By (personal) symmetry of a function, we mean

$$\omega(\mathbf{x}^1, \mathbf{x}^2, \ldots, \mathbf{x}^J) \equiv \omega(\mathbf{x}^2, \mathbf{x}^1, \ldots, \mathbf{x}^J) \equiv \omega(\mathbf{x}^J, \mathbf{x}^1, \ldots, \mathbf{x}^2) \tag{35}$$

and likewise for every permutation of the vectors $(\mathbf{x}^1, \mathbf{x}^2, \ldots, \mathbf{x}^J)$.

Remark Suppose $\omega(\mathbf{X})$ were convex, as when $\sum U(\mathbf{x}^j)$ and $U(\ )$ possess "increasing marginal utility" and each person displays "risk preference." The point of symmetry is then the *worst* rather than *best* state of the world. The social optimum of maximum Bentham–Bergson–Harsanyi $\omega(\mathbf{X})$ occurs when *all* $\bar{\mathbf{x}}$ is given to one person—*any* person. Invariant fractional income shares are optimal, with $(\alpha_j{}^*) = (1, 0, \ldots, 0), (0, 1, 0, \ldots, 0)$, etc. [Actually, whatever $x_i{}^j$ were initially meted out, such people would spontaneously gamble until, with probability one, laissez faire would entail one victor with all the spoils. To argue that such an outcome is what most would "regret," is in effect to deny that the ethical observer wishes to adhere to the individualistic social welfare concept, preferring to them "paternalism" or what Musgrave calls "merit wants."]

Local First-Order Symmetry

Symmetry is too strong a requirement on $\omega(\mathbf{X})$ for $\alpha^j = J^{-1}$ to be optimal. Writing $\partial\omega(\mathbf{X})/\partial x_i{}^j$ as ${}_j\omega_i(\mathbf{X})$, it suffices that

$$\frac{{}_j\omega_i(\bar{\mathbf{x}}/J, \ldots, \bar{\mathbf{x}}/J)}{{}_1\omega_i(\bar{\mathbf{x}}/J, \ldots, \bar{\mathbf{x}}/J)} \equiv 1 \qquad (j = 2, \ldots, n; \quad i = 1, \ldots, n). \tag{36}$$

Symmetry of $\omega(\mathbf{x}^1, \ldots, \mathbf{x}^J)$ implies (36). But (36) does not actually imply global symmetry; rather (36) merely implies what might be called local first-order symmetry. (*Example*: imagine a 2-good indifference-curve field with slopes of -1 on the 45° line; it need not possess global symmetry around the 45° line. Q.E.D.)

However, once we limit $\omega(\mathbf{X})$ to be of (3)'s Bentham–Bergson–Harsanyi form, symmetry of $\sum \lambda_j U^j(\mathbf{x}^j)$ is necessary as well as sufficient if $\alpha_j \equiv J^{-1}$ is to be ethically optimal for all choices of $(\bar{x}_1, \ldots, \bar{x}_n)$.

It will suffice to consider first the 1-good case, $n = 1$. Now (36) becomes

$$\frac{\lambda_j d[U^j(x)]/dx}{\lambda_1 d[U^1(x)]/dx} \equiv 1, \qquad U^j(x) \equiv a_j + \lambda_j^{-1} U(x),$$
$$\sum_1^J \lambda_j U^j(x^j) \equiv \sum_1^J \lambda_j a_j + \sum_1^J U(x^j). \qquad \text{Q.E.D.} \tag{37}$$

For the n-good case, we similarly require for every arbitrary vector $\mathbf{x}$

$$\frac{\lambda_j d[U^j(x)]/dx}{\lambda_1 d[U^1(x)]/dx} \equiv 1 \qquad (j = 2, \ldots, J; \quad i = 1, \ldots, n). \tag{38}$$

Therefore

$$U^j(\mathbf{x}) \equiv a_j + \lambda_j^{-1} U(\mathbf{x}),$$
$$\sum_1^J \lambda_j U^j(\mathbf{x}^j) \equiv \sum_1^J \lambda_j a_j + \sum_1^J U(\mathbf{x}^j). \qquad \text{Q.E.D.}$$

Nonequal Sharings

One nose, one person. So reckons the naive quantum mechanics of philosophical individualism. However, if nutritional requirements for a 6-foot Norwegian differ from those for a 5-foot Malayan, does fair rationing involve equal calories per person or equal "fractions of nutritional need?" Clearly, there arise cases where symmetry analysis must be amplified or generalized.

Thus, let person 1 represent a larger family than any of the rest, being in effect the embodiment of two normal consuming people. If the subutilities of the two inner-people add to form person 1's utility, and if each of them happened to be just like each outer-person $(2, 3, \ldots, j, \ldots, J)$, it must be intuitively obvious that person 1 should receive twice the vector they receive—namely

$$\mathbf{x}^{j*} = \bar{\mathbf{x}}/(J+1), \qquad (j = 2, \ldots, J), \qquad \mathbf{x}^{1*} = 2\bar{\mathbf{x}}/(J+1). \tag{39}$$

Again, the principle of invariant fractional income shares obtains (indeed, obtains in the strong form of all people consuming goods in the same proportions as total endowments).

This far-fetched example alerts us to the following way of generalizing for additive Bentham–Bergson–Harsanyi functions the local first-order symmetry concepts of (38).

THEOREM *on constant (vectoral) fractional shares under generalized symmetry* Suppose

$$U^j(\mathbf{x}^j) \equiv a_j + \lambda_j^{-1} C_j U(\mathbf{x}^j/C_j), \qquad C_j > 0,$$
$$c_j = C_j \Big/ \sum_1^J C_k \qquad (j = 1, \ldots, J),$$

and $U(\mathbf{x})$ is concave and monotone strongly increasing; then

$$\begin{aligned}
\max_{x^j} \sum_1^J \lambda_j U^j(\mathbf{x}^j) \qquad \text{s.t.} \quad \sum_1^J \mathbf{x}^j = \bar{\mathbf{x}} \\
= \sum_1^J \lambda_j a_j + \max_{x^j} \sum_1^J C_j U(\mathbf{x}^j/C_j) \\
= \sum_1^J \lambda_j a_j + \sum_1^J C_j U(c_j \bar{\mathbf{x}}/C_j) \\
= \sum_1^J \lambda_j a_j + \left(\sum_1^J C_j\right) U(\bar{\mathbf{x}}/\textstyle\sum_1^J C_k),
\end{aligned} \tag{40}$$

where

$$x_i^{j*} \equiv c_j \bar{x}_i, \qquad (i = 1, \ldots, n; \quad j = 1, \ldots, J),$$
$$\alpha_j^* = c_j \qquad \text{independently of} \quad (\bar{x}_1, \ldots, \bar{x}_n).$$

To prove this theorem, we solve for the unique roots of the necessary first-order maximizing conditions, involving $\partial U^j(\mathbf{x}^j)/\partial x_i^j = U_i^j(\mathbf{x}^j)$ and $\partial U(\mathbf{z})/\partial z_i = U_i(\mathbf{z})$:

$$\begin{aligned}
1 &= \lambda_j U_i^j(\mathbf{x}^j)/\lambda_1 U_i^1(\mathbf{x}^1), \qquad (j = 2, \ldots, J; \quad i = 1, \ldots, n) \\
&= \frac{C_j^{-1} \lambda_j \lambda_j^{-1} C_j U_i(c_j\{\bar{\mathbf{x}}/\sum_1^J C_k\}/c_j)}{C_1^{-1} \lambda_1 \lambda_1^{-1} C_1 U_i(c_1\{\bar{\mathbf{x}}/\sum_1^J C_k\}/C_1} = \frac{U_i(\bar{\mathbf{x}}/\sum_1^k C_k)}{U_i(\bar{\mathbf{x}}/\sum_1^k C_k)}.
\end{aligned} \tag{41}$$

Remark: If we drop the B–B–H additivity requirement and shift attention from (38) to the more general (36), the conditions of this last theorem become sufficient but overly strong to be necessary. Thus, the following example has invariant optimal fractional vectoral shares, $\mathbf{x}^{j*} = \alpha_j^* \bar{\mathbf{x}}$:

$$\begin{aligned}
W &= \log H(\mathbf{x}^1) + \log[H(\mathbf{x}^2)^{1/4} H(\mathbf{x}^3)^{1/4} + H(\mathbf{x}^4)^{1/2}]^2 \\
H(\theta\mathbf{x}) &\equiv \theta H(\mathbf{x}), \qquad H(\mathbf{x}) \quad \text{strictly quasi concave,} \\
\alpha_1^* &= \tfrac{1}{2}, \qquad \alpha_1^* = \tfrac{1}{8} = \alpha_3^*, \qquad \alpha_4^* = \tfrac{1}{4}.
\end{aligned} \tag{42}$$

However, (42) is not a Bentham–Bergson–Harsanyi additive function. If we insist on B–B–H functions and that, for *any* choice of $(\lambda_1, \ldots, \lambda_J)$, parameters invariant fractional vectors are to be optimal, then (36) implies

$$U^j(\mathbf{x}^j) \equiv a_j + b_j[H(\mathbf{x}^j)^\gamma - 1]\gamma^{-1}, \qquad \gamma \leq 1, \tag{43.1}$$

$$1 \equiv \frac{\lambda_j \partial U^j(\alpha_j \bar{\mathbf{x}})/\partial x_i^j}{\lambda_1 \partial U^1(\alpha_1 \bar{\mathbf{x}}) \partial x_i^1} = \frac{\lambda_j b_j \alpha_j^{\gamma-1}[\partial H(\bar{\mathbf{x}})/\partial x_i]}{\lambda_1 b_1 \alpha_1^{\gamma-1}[\partial H(\bar{\mathbf{x}})/\partial x_i]} = \frac{\lambda_j b_j \gamma_j^{\gamma-1}}{\lambda_1 b_1 \gamma_1^{\gamma-1}}, \tag{43.2}$$

$$\alpha_j^* = (\lambda_j b_j)^{1/(1-\gamma)}\left[\sum_1^J (\lambda_k b_k)^{1/(1-\gamma)}\right]. \tag{43.3}$$

6. QUALIFICATIONS

For brevity I have assumed away all consumption externalities: envy, altruism, public goods, etc. A complete analysis would have to take account of realistic externalities.

The present analysis has concentrated exclusively on the problem of allocating a given available total vector of society's consumption goods $(\bar{x}_1, \ldots, \bar{x}_n)$ among a set of specified persons. When one must take account of production of outputs out of inputs, some of which must be provided by the persons themselves—as for example, irksome skilled labor—proper analysis must become more complicated. Indeed, the original perceptions in Bergson (1938) of that nonoptimality of equal money incomes, in the sense of equal $\sum x_i^j p_i - \sum$ factor returns, come in the context of the variable input case.

The cautious reader will take warning of the special features required for simple income-sharing to be even approximately optimal.

REFERENCES

Arrow, K. J. (1964). *Aspects of the Theory of Risk-Bearing.* Helsinki: Yrjö Jahnssonin säätio. Reproduced as Chapters 2 and 3 in *Essays in the Theory of Risk-Bearing.* Chicago: Markham, 1971.

Bergson, A. (1936). Real Income, Expenditure Proportionality, and Frisch's 'New Methods of Measuring Marginal Utility,' *Review of Economic Studies* **4**, 33–52.

Bergson, A. (1938). A Reformulation of Certain Aspects of Welfare Economics, *Quarterly Journal of Economics* **52**, 310–334.

Bergson, A. (1966). *Essays in Normative Economics.* Cambridge, Massachusetts: Belknap Press of Harvard Univ. Press.

Bergson, A. (1976). Taste Differences and Optimal Income Distribution: A Paradox Illustrated. Discussion Paper 82, Harvard Inst. of Econ. Res. Harvard Univ.

Chipman, J. S. (1974). Homothetic Preferences and Aggregation, *Journal of Economic Theory* **8**, 1, 26–38.

Chipman, J. S. (1976). The Paretian Heritage, *Revue European de Sciences Sociales et Journal Cahiers Vilfredo Pareto* **14**, No. 37, 65–171.
Diamond, P. A. (1967). Cardinal Welfare, Individualistic Ethics and Interpersonal Comparison of Utility: Comment, *Journal of Political Economy* **75**, 765–766.
Fisher, F. M. and J. Rothenberg.(1961 and 1962). How Income Ought to be Distributed: Paradox Lost [and] Paradox Enow, *Journal of Political Economy* **69** and **70**, 162–180 and 88–93.
Gorman, W. M. (1953). Community Preference Fields. *Econometrica* **21**, 63–80.
de V. Graaf, J. (1967). *Theoretical Welfare Economics*. London and New York: Cambridge Univ. Press.
Harsanyi, J. C. (1955). Cardinal Welfare, Individualistic Ethics, and Interpersonal Comparisons of Utility, *Journal of Political Economy* **63**, 309–321.
Hicks, J. R. (1939). The Foundations of Welfare Economics, *Economic Journal* **49**, 696–712.
Kaldor, N. (1939). Welfare Propositions of Economics and Interpersonal Comparisons of Utility, *Economic Journal* **49**, 549–552.
Kemp, M., and Ng Y-K (1976). On the Existence of Social Welfare Functions, Social Orderings and Social Decision Functions, *Econometrica* **43**, 59–66.
Lange, O. (1942). The Foundations of Welfare Economics, *Econometrica* **10**, 215–228.
Lerner, A. P. (1934a). The Concept of Monopoly and the Measurement of Monopoly Power, *Review of Economic Studies* **1**, 157–175.
Lerner, A. P. (1934b). Economic Theory and Socialist Economy, *Review of Economic Studies* **3**, 51–61.
Lerner, A. P. (1944). *Economics of Control*. New York: Macmillan.
Marschak, J. (1950). Rational Behavior, Uncertain Prospects, and Measurable Utility, *Econometrica* **18**, 111–141; Errata, *Econometrica* **18**, 312.
Merton, R. C. (1969). "Lifetime Portfolio Selection under Uncertainty: The Continuous-Time Case, *Review of Economics and Statistics* **51**, 247–257.
Pareto, V. (1896, 1897). *Cours d' Economie Politique*, Vol. I. Lausanne: F. Rouge, editeur, 1896; Vol. II. Lausanne: F. Rouge, librarie-editeur, 1897.
Pareto, V. (1909). *Manuel d'Economie Politique*. Paris: V. Giard et E. Briere.
Pareto, V. (1913). Il massimo di utilità per una collettività in Sociologia, *Giornale degli Economisti* **3**, 337–341.
Pfanzangl, J. (1959). A General Theory of Measurement—Applications to Utility, *Naval Research Logistics Quarterly* (Office Naval Res.) **6**, 283–294.
Pratt, J. W. (1964). Risk Aversion in the Small and in the Large, *Econometrica* **32**, 122–136.
Ramsey, F. (1931). *Foundations of Mathematics*. London: Kegan Paul.
Robbins, L. (1932). *An Essay on the Nature and Significance of Economic Science*. New York: Macmillan.
Rothblum, V. G. (1975). Multivariate Constant Risk Posture, *Journal of Economic Theory* **10**, 309–312.
Samuelson, P. A. (1947). *Foundations of Economic Analysis*. Cambridge, Massachusetts: Harvard Univ. Press.
Samuelson, P. A. (1956). Social Indifference Curves, *Quarterly Journal of Economics* **70**, 1, 1–22. Reproduced in *The Collected Scientific Papers of Paul A. Samuelson*, Vol. II, Chapter 78, pp. 1073–1094. Cambridge, Massachusetts: MIT Press, 1966.
Samuelson, P. A. (1969a). Risk-Taking with Respect to Commodities. Mimeo. Referred to by Stiglitz (1969).
Samuelson, P. A. (1969b). Lifetime Portfolio Selection by Dynamic Stochastic Programming, *Review of Economics and Statistics* **51**, 4, 239–246. Reproduced in *The Collected Scientific Papers of Paul A. Samuelson*, Vol. III, Chapter 204, pp. 883–890. Cambridge, Massachusetts: MIT Press, 1966.

Samuelson, P. A. (1974). A Curious Case Where Reallocation Cannot Achieve Optimum Welfare, in Warren L. Smith and John M. Culbertson, eds., *Public Finance and Stabilization, Essays in Honor of Richard A. Musgrave*. (New York: North Holland/American Elsevier), 145–150.

Samuelson, P. A. (1977). Reaffirming the Existence of 'Reasonable' Bergson–Samuelson Social Welfare Functions, *Economica* **44**, 81–88.

Savage, L. J. (1954). *Foundations of Statistics*. New York: Wiley.

Stiglitz, J. E. (1969). Behavior towards Risk with Many Commodities, *Econometrica* **37**, 660–667.

Strotz, R. H. (1958). "How Income Ought to Be Distributed: A Paradox in Distributive Ethics, *Journal of Political Economy* **66**, 189–205.

Thiel, H. (1954). *Linear Aggregation of Economic Relations*. Amsterdam: North-Holland Publ.

A Chapter in The History of Ramsey's Optimal Feasible Taxation and Optimal Public Utility Prices

Paul A. Samuelson

Robert K. Merton has taught us that simultaneity of scientific discovery is the rule not the exception. A slow publisher like Darwin was bound to have his Wallace. Even a genius like Newton must expect to encounter a genius like Leibniz. No less than a dozen different scholars, Tom Kuhn has shown, can be said to have discovered the law of conservation of energy. And so it is in economics. Jevons, Menger, and Walras separately glimpsed marginal utility theory and general equilibrium. J. B. Clark, Wicksteed, Walras, Pareto, Barone, and Wicksell each perceived marginal productivity and before their time von Thünen had already approached it (just as Gossen, before Jevons and unknown to him, had stumbled toward utility theory). Hicks-Allen had their Slutsky; and Slutsky had his Antonelli. Torrens had his Ricardo; and Ricardo had his West and Malthus.

Here I sample some memories concerning rediscoveries of Frank Ramsey's 1927 taxation theorem, an analysis that still remains about the only substantive contribution to the theory of the second best (a subject better titled the "theory of the *feasible* first best.") The exercise has some interest for its own sake. It has further interest from the standpoint of the sociology and history of science.

1. Questions

I lectured at the University of Copenhagen in September 1948. My friend Jørgen Gelting, not yet a professor at Aarhus, put to me at least two interesting questions. He asked my opinion about Lindahl's 1919 model of public goods. I knew only Musgrave's diagram from it: this plots on the horizontal axis the scale of expenditure for the public good, on the vertical axis the fractions of its cost that each of two citizens are willing to pay, and finds the Lindahl equilibrium level of the public good where the sum of the fractions just equals unity. My dissatisfaction with the fundamental meaning of the Lindahl construction led, half a dozen years after Gelting's question, to my 1954 paper on optimal public expenditure, a paper that launched an industry (and proved its point that mathematics could be useful in economics!).

Jørgen Gelting's second question is the concern of the present memoir. "What do you think of Ramsey's tax rule that we should tax to reduce every good in the same proportion?" My reply was a cool one. I had always found Ramsey's underlying model to be too ambiguous, too ill defined. What gave me pause, however, was Gelting's information that on his trip to the States after World War II he had heard Harold Hotelling lecture on what seemed to be much the same as the Ramsey tax analysis, in the course of which Hotelling reported that it was John Hicks who had also independently arrived at Ramsey's rule.

2. Doubts

My interest was aroused. But first I ought to report the standard doubts I uttered.

1. The equal-percentage-reduction rule sounds arbitrary on the face of it. Where is the intuitive basis? Why not reduce luxuries more than necessities?

2. Isn't Ramsey's rule negated by what we know to be the optimality of an income tax (on *inelastic* effort), a lumpsum tax of the well-known Lerner type?

3. Doesn't the rule fail in the well-known Ricardo and Henry George case when a tax on inelastic land can produce zero deadweight loss?

4. How I measure the percentage reduction in any good and service must depend upon the arbitrary *origin* I use in defining its quantity: a cut in daily work from 8 to 6 hours is a 25 percent reduction looked at one way; looked at another way, it is a $12\frac{1}{2}$ percent *increase* in leisure. When I go from producing 10 oranges and consuming 11 to producing 12 oranges and consuming 10, my algebraic import of oranges passes through an *infinite* percentage reduction and a change in sign. Can a sound rule be based on the sand of arbitrary origins?

5. Finally, Ramsey's definition of his model is cryptic to the point of making it unjudgeable. He speaks of keeping the marginal utility of money constant – a red flag to me since my 1934-5 days in studying Marshall's *Principles*. If there existed in the background ideal lumpsum taxes that would rectify different people's different marginal utilities, Ramsey's main problem of "optimal *feasible* taxation" would hardly have arisen in the first place.

But Gelting had planted the seed of doubt in my mind. Frank Ramsey was a genius. (His work on optimal saving I knew well and, with reservations, admired. Ramsey's cryptic axiomatization of personal probability and expected cardinal utility was not yet rediscovered by Marschak, Little, and McKenzie.) Hotelling and Hicks I admired. Could three such able men be making a fuss about nothing? And *independently* doing so? Hardly likely.

3. Conversion

I was hooked. As my Guggenheim fellowship took me from Denmark to Holland I brooded over the matter. Having no books or journals, I could only chew on my own cud. How would I formulate the problem and give its solution?

I first disposed of my own objections, working backwards.

5. To provide a firm economic background, contemplate a single person: Robinson Crusoe. He produces food and clothing, (q_1, q_2), at constant returns to scale from labor, L. Along with these private goods and services that he buys, government provides him with a public good q_0, in a $\bar{q}_0$ magnitude exogenously specified. His tastes are summarized by indifference contours in the $(q_1, q_2, -L)$ space once $\bar{q}_0$ is specified. The government must put taxes on q_1, q_2, and L to finance the $\bar{q}_0$ in real resource terms.

Ambiguity is banished.

4. No arbitrary origin need bother one in this scenario. If (food, clothing, labor) are to be taxed, that is a *different constitutional restriction* than if (food, clothing, leisure), $(q_1, q_2, 24-L)$ are to be taxed. We ought to get a different result for the optimum if $24-L$ rather than L is the admissible object of taxation. Likewise if q_j minus (exempt amount of q_j) is to be the object of taxation, this changed origin ought to give a different (and worse!) best feasible solution.

Objection 4 is no objection, but rather a virtue.

3. In the Henry George and Ricardo case where labor always is inelastic in supply, working up to say 8 hours indifferently and never more, obviously there should be a single tax on Crusoe's labor. There is no deadweight loss. The common percentage reduction in everything is (perhaps) zero?

Verdict: Ramsey's equal-percentage-cut rule is not absurd (but it still needs careful formulating since the need to get labor to produce $\bar{q}_0$ must lower q_1 and q_2 and with L frozen must do so according to their Engel's laws and not in the same percentage amounts).

2. Since there is no land in my Ramsey scenario, all that was said in 3. above applies to the present point involving a feasible lumpsum tax that can finance the government expenditure.

1. No truth is intuitive until you've recognized what is truth. By repetition, one develops intuition. Besides, Ramsey's rule of equal-percent-reduction is an asymptotic one. It is meant to apply when $\bar{q}_0$ is incipiently small, which is a limiting case we have little intuition about.

Only the neglect of Engel's laws, of income effects, remains a worry.

4. Resolution

By now I had an open mind. I was still tormented by the cogent demonstration in M. W. F. Joseph (1939) – call it Objection 6 – that *deadweight* tax loss depends on *substitution* effects (on *curvature* of the indifference contours) and not on tax incidence with its necessary contaminating *income effects*. And I was still tormented by what can be called Objection 7, the fact that, if *all* private outputs and inputs fell in the same proportions, this would *not* seem to provide the extra resources needed to produce the new public good $\bar{q}_0$. Ramsey, I came to believe, didn't have it quite right (or had it right only in special Marshallian contexts where income effects were zero because some good like q_1 had "constancy of its marginal utility").

In the days between Copenhagen and the 1948 September Econometric Society meeting at the Hague I blessed Jørgen Gelting for having set me an interesting and important problem. Once posed, the problem straightforwardly solved itself.

Ramsey's rule did need correction. The correct optimality conditions involved Slutsky-Hicks *compensated substitution* coefficients not Marshallian *ceteris paribus* coefficients. Objections 6 and 7 do cogently rebut Ramsey's simple rule, and turned out to vindicate my improved version of his analysis.

The next sections sketch my few-goods analysis. Then after a section devoted to some independent rediscoverers of Ramsey, I sketch the n-good general case. The final section draws some lessons for substantive tax policy and for the history of science.

5. A Firmly Based Ramsey Model

First I write down the special scenario I intially worked out that made Ramsey's 1927 result most nearly correct. To eliminate considerations of interpersonal equity, I consider Robinson Crusoe to be the only person in society.

Special Marshallian assumptions

i) One of the two private goods has literally *constant marginal utility.* (Alternatively, it could have been labor that is assumed to have constant marginal disutility.)

ii) Utilities of all the goods and the disutility of labor are *additively* independent.

Crusoe's utility can therefore be written in the following special form (after a convenient choice of q_1 units):

$$U = q_1 + U_2(q_2) - V(L) + U_0(\bar{q}_0) \tag{5.1}$$

$$U_2' > 0, \quad U_2'' < 0; \qquad V' > 0, \quad V'' > 0$$

Society's production relations can be written (after a convenient choice of L, q_0, and q_2 units) as

$$L = \bar{q}_0 + q_1 + q_2, \quad q_j \geqq 0 \tag{5.2}$$

The pre-tax prices at which production takes place and the government buys can be written in lower-case letters as

$$(p_0; p_1, p_2; w) = (1; 1, 1; 1) \tag{5.3}$$

The post-tax prices that Crusoe the consumer actually faces can be written in capital letters as $(P_1, P_2; W)$. Pertaining to a public good whose $\bar{q}_0$ quantity is determined by political decision and not by consumer choice in the market, q_0's post-tax price P_0 might as well be its pre-tax p_0.

The consumer's demand for $(q_1, q_2; L)$ satisfies the following budget equation and tangency relations of marginal utility:

$$P_1 q_1 + P_2 q_2 - WL = 0 \tag{5.4a}$$

$$U_2'(q_2) = P_2/P_1$$

$$V'(L) = W/P_1 \tag{5.4b}$$

To finance its $\bar{q}_0$ program in real and money terms, the government must collect its excises on goods and services, $(P_1 - 1,\ P_2 - 1;\ -1 - W) = (t_1, t_2; t_w)$: these tax rates multipled by the quantities the consumer demands must equal government's expenditure on $\bar{q}_0$:

$$(P_1 - 1)q_1 + (P_2 - 1)q_2 + (1 - W)L = 1\bar{q}_0 \tag{5.5}$$

$$p_0 = P_0 = 1$$

For each choice of taxes, of $(P_1 - 1,\ P_2 - 1,\ 1 - W)$, there results an equilibrium of equations (5.2), (5.4), and (5.5). Ramsey's problem of *optimal feasibility* is to select $(P_1 - 1,\ P_2 - 1,\ 1 - W)$ so as to maximize U in (5.1).

We deal here with a problem of the "second best" because the trivial first best solution of a *lumpsum* tax is specified not to be constitutionally or practically feasible. (That first best solution, which keeps the cost of q_0 to society down to its irreducible sacrifice in private individual utility, involves setting $(P_1 - 1, P_2 - 1, 1 - W)$ at zero, instead putting on the left side of (5.4a)'s budget relation a lumpsum tax equal to $p_0\bar{q}_0$. Note that the resulting reductions in (q_1, q_2, L) are *not* in the same percentage degree even when $\bar{q}_0$ is incipiently small, showing that Ramsey's rule does arouse intuitive suspicions as contradicting Engel's laws of income effects.

Before writing down the analytical and graphical solutions, I should call attention to an odd feature of the problem. *The number of taxes is redundant*. Doubling all P's and W for Crusoe in (5.4a) alters the stated levels of the tax rates and the discrepancies from pre-tax prices; but substantively that is a spurious change since it leaves Crusoe in real terms exactly where he was previously. Therefore, whatever can be achieved by the constitutionally admissible pattern of $(2+1)$ tax rates, $(P_1-1, P_2-1, 1-W)$, can also be achieved by leaving one good or service free of any tax! To give Ramsey rope, I confine myself to $(0, P_2-1, 1-W)$, setting $P_1=p_1=1$ and achieving maximum utility by finding the optimum values for these real tax rates. (Remark: Understanding this feature of tax redundancy suffices to dispose of the deadhorse contention that somehow direct taxes on services can be presumed to be better than indirect taxes on goods consumed.)

This scenario of Ramsey's problem I could now pose in briefer form. Relations (1)-(5) can be boiled down to

$$u[\bar{q}_0] = \underset{q_2, L}{\mathrm{Max}}\,[U_0(\bar{q}_0)+(L-\bar{q}_0-q_2)+U_2(q_2)-V(L)] \text{ s.t.} \tag{5.6a}$$

$$[U_2'(q_2)-1]q_2+[1-V'(L)]L = \bar{q}_0 \tag{5.6b}$$

By Lagrangean multiplier technique or otherwise, we immediately deduce the *equal-"net"-elasticities*[1] optimality conditions:

$$\frac{U_2'(q_2)-1}{-q_2U_2''(q_2)} = \frac{1-V'(L)}{LV''(L)} \tag{5.6c}$$

For $\bar{q}_0$ small, (5.6b) and (5.6c) will together determine a *unique* Ramsey configuration for (L^*, q_2^*) near to the zero-$\bar{q}_0$ laissez faire configuration (L^{**}, q^{**}). (There will generally also be a second solution far away from the laissez faire solution: in 1982 we could call it the "Arthur Laffer solution;" it does not provide even a local maximum for utility and we can ignore it. If $\bar{q}_0$ is set too high, there will be no feasible solution for the program, a case that in the 1950s could have been called the "Colin Clark case.") After (q_2^*, L^*) are determined, use of (5.2) enables us to solve for q_1^*.

Goods $q_3, q_4, \ldots$ could be added to the problem by adding terms like $U_3(q_3)+U_4(q_4)+\ldots$ to (5.6a), adding terms like $[U_3'(q_3)-1]q_3+[U_4'(q_4-1)]q_4+\ldots$ to (5.6b), and finally adding new $[U_j'(q_j)-1]/[-q_jU_j''(q_j)]$ equalities to (5.6c). (We'll see that (5.6c) is also a theory of optimal public utility pricing, a Ramsey result constantly being rediscovered.)

1. Warning: Two kinds of net-elasticity equalities will be encountered: one set like (5.6c) here, which can apply to the net vertical difference between dd and ss schedules; a quite different set appropriate to ideal utility pricing subject to a partial cost recovery constraint. As will be shown, when ss curves are horizontal the first looks like the second.

6. Diagrammatic Solution

Figure 1 shows the graphical solution. For drafting simplicity I've made the schedules straight lines (corresponding to quadratic U). My other purpose for using straight lines is to make Ramsey's equal-percentage rule *globally exact* rather than merely an asymptotic approximation for $\bar{q}_0$ "small."

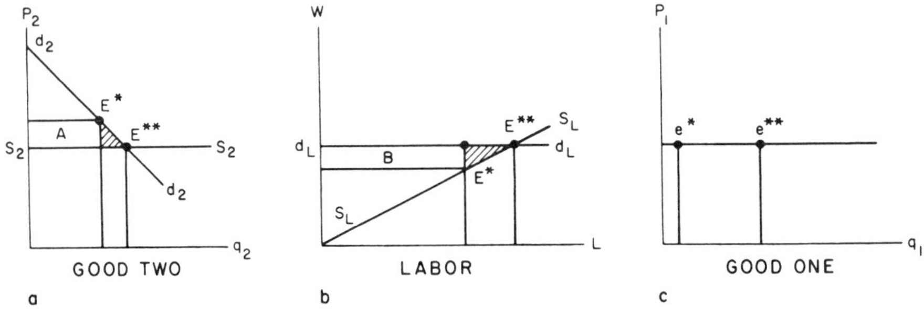

Figure 1. *Crusoe's utility is maximized when deadweight loss (sum of shaded triangles) is minimized subject to fixed* $A+B$ *areas needed to finance specified public good(s). For straight lines this means equal-percentage cuts in all private goods and services, save for* q_1 *(the private good with constant marginal utility).*

In 1(a) and 1(b), the E^{**} points represent the original laissez faire equilibrium with $\bar{q}_0=0$. The E^* points represents Crusoe's Ramsey equilibrium with specified positive $\bar{q}_0$. Note that *the* E^* *points are shifted westward by the same percentage amounts.* The sum of the areas A and B represent the size of the $\bar{q}_0$ program. (The shaded triangles represent deadweight loss; the sum of such triangular areas has been minimized by following Ramsey's rule. My special Marshallian assumptions make these consumer-surplus areas *exact* measures.)

But now look at 1(c). It's e^{**} and e^* points represent the before-tax-program and after-tax-program level for the background private good q_1. The percentage cut in q_1 definitely violates Ramsey's equal-percentage rule: where the common drop in (q_2, L) is 25 percent, for q_1 the drop is over 80 percent. (Ramsey's lawyer can validly assert for the record: "The sum $\bar{q}_0+\bar{q}_1$ does drop by the common 25 percent." But how was Ramsey's reader to know that? And what is its significance?[2] Let the record also

2. In Figure 1a I realized that the *ss* curve(s) did not have to be horizontal. Thus, I was able to vary the scenario to let L have constant marginal disutility and supposed that each q_j was produced by labor on its own specialized land that was in fixed supply. (I didn't like the resulting model because taxing those lands' rents would be equivalent to ideal lumpsum taxing, and would really make a mockery of Ramsey's feasibility restrictions. But no matter.) Then the *ss* supply curves sloped upward: but, so long as the vertical differences between the *dd*

show that Ramsey only claimed his rule would hold when government merely spends on transfers.

In sum, my first Copenhagen pass at the problem pinpointed how Ramsey's analysis had suppressed the *income effects* which post-1934 economists knew were an integral part of the Hicks-Slutsky *substitution effects* that lay at the heart of taxation's distortions. For the (q_1, q_2, L) case I could swiftly provide the needed correct analysis; and later during my Guggenheim travels, primarily at the newly started up Rand Corporation, I was able to pretty up the general n-good analysis of Section 8 to come.

7. Coincidences

I interrupt the derivation of substantive science to report on the sociology and history of science. Already Ramsey, Hicks and Hotelling, had quasi-independently arrived at some similar results on an important topic that Jørgen Gelting planted in my consciousness. A week later I attended the September Econometrica meetings at the Hague. Imagine my surprise to hear, through the imperfect filter of my graduate student knowledge of French, Marcel Boiteux giving a paper on what seemed close to the Ramsey problem. Moreover, he was clearly arriving at correct results that did involve Slutsky-Hicks substitution coefficients.

Boiteux, a graduate of the *École normal superieure*, was then on the threshold of a brilliant career as a scientist and public utility executive. Although he had the title of a professor, in fact he had not yet been called to a chair; and, as I recall, he did not in the crowded Paris of the time enjoy office and research facilities that one normally takes for granted. However, he was part of a Paris renaissance in economic theory associated with people like Pierre Massé, Maurice Allais,[3] Gerard Debreu, Edmund Malinvaud and others outside the Faculty of Law.

---

and *ss* curves are a linear function of the respective q_j, the deadweight triangles of consumer-and-producer surpluses would be minimized by Ramsey's rule applied to all the private goods but labor.

The rest of this paper deals primarily with a single public good, q_0. My own analysis, and that of Ramsey's Appendix, considered any number of such goods and let some of them be producible just like certain private goods. This last possibility would require some schedules in Figure 1 to be shifted by the amount of the respective public goods, a complication that is left to the reader.

3. Maurice Allais is a fountain of original and independent discoveries. In any catalogue of Mertonian coincidences of discovery, the case of the golden rule deserves mention. Before World War II, J. A. Schumpeter, F. P. Ramsey, J. E. Meade, G. C. Evans, O. Lange and others, had recognized that maximum steady-state consumption producible by a fixed supply of primary factor(s) can be achieved only when produced inputs have reached a configuration compatible with a zero interest rate. Allais, T. Swan, E. S. Phelps, and others provided rigorous

I mentioned to Boiteux in private conversation the possible overlap between his problem and the work of Frank Ramsey, a name he was not familiar with. I daresay it would not have been easy in the Paris of 1948 to get access to the 1927 *Economic Journal.* In any case, neither of the two papers that grew out of his Hague presentation, Boiteux (1951, 1956), make reference to Ramsey.[4] Besides my inadequacy in French, I received less benefit from the Hague lecture because of my uneasiness with the use of differentials. Although I had to admit that a completely rigorous mode of handling them did exist, they had once led me into confusion in connection with a paper on observable group demand, Samuelson (1938, 1965); and in connection with Schumpeter's lectures on Divisia index numbers they had impressed me as treacherous constructs. So I still continued to regard the Ramsey issue as an open problem even after the Paris conversation with Allais (and, I think, Debreu).

After visits to the LSE and Cambridge, I saw John Hicks and Ian Little at Oxford. But by then Ramsey had receded to the background of my consciousness. Only years later, when perusing Ursula Hicks, *Public Finance* (1947, Ch. X, 167-80), was I able to glimpse the nature of her husband's rediscovery of Ramsey as a result of his knowledge of Hotelling (1932).

My purpose here is to describe the background to my own unpublished 1951 memorandum to the United States Treasury on optimal (Ramseyan) taxation. It would require a much longer discussion to trace the later rediscoverers of Ramsey's rules (or of aspects of those rules). Such an account would at a minimum include such names as Peter Diamond and James Mirrlees, Alan Walters, Jacques Drèze, Jacques Lesourne, Serge Kolm, Arnold Harberger, William Baumol and David Bradford, and many other writers in the field of public utility regulation and antitrust prosecution.[5]

extensions to systems whose primary factors grow at a (Harrod natural) exponential rate, so that maximum consumption per capita requires a golden-rule configuration in which the interest rate and growth rates are equalized along with the shares of profit and of capital formation being equalized. Had Allais's earliest writings been in English, a generation of economic theory would have taken a different course. I ought to mention also that Allais's generalizations of consumer surplus concepts have direct relevance to the Ramsey problem.

4. Boiteux, like Debreu at the same time, was among other things concerned to define a measure of (deadweight) loss for a system. This quest did not much interest me. For Crusoe, two situations can be said to have truly the same loss coefficient if and only if they lie on his same indifference contour. So we are back in the standard problem of revealed preference. For a more-than-one-person society, how "far it is inside" its (non-metric) utility-possibility frontier seems intrinsically ambiguous for reasons adumbrated in Samuelson (1950).

5. The June 1970 *American Economic Review* carried three articles of relevance here: Baumol and Bradford (1970), A. P. Lerner (1970), and A. Dixit (1970). The first gives some historical background, but with some inevitable gaps. Drèze (1964) is valuable, both as a report on French work and for its own synthesis and innovations.

There is value for the historian of science, and for all interested in the psychology of scientific discovering, to have personal accounts of the stages by which a breakthrough in analysis took place. My own resistance to Ramsey is just as valuable from this point of view as acceptance and extensions. The next section gives my substantive analysis for the general case performed during the 1948-9 Guggenheim Fellowship period following my autumn return to the States.

8. Ramsey Optimum With Income Effects

Assumptions. My general model wrote Crusoe's utility as

$$U = U(\bar{q}_0, q_1, \ldots, q_n) \tag{8.1}$$

$$\partial U/\partial q_j = U_j(\ ) > 0, \quad (j=1,\ldots,n)$$

where $U(\ )$ is quasi concave in the $(q_1,\ldots,q_n)$ private variables. These private variables represent goods when they are positive; irksome services with their algebraic signs reversed are also covered by my notation.[6] (For brevity, I henceforth write $\bar{q}_0$ as q_0: the reader is to understand that q_0 is given to Crusoe exogenously.)

Technology is summarized by

$$p_0q_0 + \sum_1^n p_jq_j = 0, \ (p_0,\ldots,p_n) > 0 \tag{8.2}$$

where the real cost ratios (p_j/p_i) are technical constants whose magnitudes depend on the units chosen for the q's. We can select units to make all $(p_0,\ldots,p_n)$ equal to unity. (After 1948-9 I generalized (8.2) to constant returns without invariant unit costs.)

Crusoe faces after-tax prices for the private goods

$$(P_1,\ldots,P_n) = (p_1+t_1,\ldots,p_n+t_n)$$

$$t_j = P_j - p_j \gtreqless 0, \quad (j=1,\ldots,n)$$

Subject to his budget equation

$$Y = \sum_1^n P_jq_j = 0 \tag{8.3a}$$

6. To give Ramsey's rule its best chance, back in 1948-9 I actually wrote utility with the public good(s) utility as additively separable: $f(q_1,\ldots,q_n)+u_0(q_0)$. I tamper with the historical record because I learned something interesting in the course of this 1982 review: the optimal pattern of *incipient* taxes is independent of any contamination of private tastes from finite q_0, as will be seen in (8.8) to come. Later I shall comment on what difference it makes not to assume separability in the form of $U=g[q_0, f(q_1,\ldots,q_n)]$. Also, in 1948-9, I made q_0 a vector rather than a scalar, an inexpensive generalization.

Crusoe's demand functions are derived by

$$u[q_0] = \underset{q_1,\ldots,q_n}{\text{Max}}\ U(q_0, q_1,\ldots,q_n)\ s.t.\ \sum_1^n P_j q_j = Y,\ Y = 0 \tag{8.3b}$$

$$= U^*(q_0; P_1,\ldots,P_n, Y) \tag{8.3c}$$

$$= U(q_0, q^1[q_0; P_1,\ldots,P_n, Y],\ldots,q^n[q_0; P_1,\ldots,P_n, Y])$$

where $U^*(\ )$ is the indirect utility function (whose use was becoming popular in the late 1940s) and where the demand functions were known to have the following properties

$$\frac{-\partial U^*/\partial P_i}{\partial U^*/\partial Y} = -\frac{U_i^*(q_0; P, Y)}{U_{n+1}(q_0; P, Y)} \equiv q^i[q_0; P, Y] \tag{8.4a}$$

$$\equiv q^i[q_0; mP, mY],\ m > 0,\ (i=1,\ldots,n) \tag{8.4b}$$

$$\sum_1^n P_j q^j[q_0; P, Y] \equiv Y \tag{8.4c}$$

$$S[q_0; P, Y] = (S_{ij}) = (q_j^i + q^j q_{n+1}^i)$$

$$\equiv (S_{ji}) \tag{8.4d}$$

$$P'S[q_0; P, Y] = 0 \tag{8.4e}$$

$$X'S[q_0; P, Y]X < 0 \quad \text{for } X \neq aP \tag{8.4f}$$

Of course, Y is to be set equal to zero wherever it appears—in order to meet Ramsey's implicit feasibility restriction that lumpsum taxes are not admissible to finance the public good expenditure. The condition that the government must finance its public-good expenditure(s) by its excise tax collections requires that

$$\sum_1^n t_j q^j[q_0; p_1+t_1,\ldots,p_n+t_n, 0] = p_0 q_0 \tag{8.5}$$

Indirect utility formulation. Ramsey's problem now boils down to

$$u[q_0] = \underset{t_1,\ldots,t_n}{\text{Max}}\ U^*(q_0; p_1+t_1,\ldots,p_n+t_n, 0) \tag{8.6a}$$

$$\text{s.t.} \sum_1^n t_j q^j[q_0; p+t, 0] = p_0 q_0$$

$$= U^*(q_0; p_1+t_1[q_0],\ldots,p_n+t_n[q_0]) \tag{8.6b}$$

where $(t_j[q_0])$ are the optimal feasible taxes at each q_0 level. They depend of course on the technical coefficients $(p_0,\ldots,p_n)$, each of which can be written as unity. The optimal $t_j[\ ]$ must be roots of the first-order variational conditions derivable by the Lagrangean multiplier technique

$$U_i^* = \lambda\left(q^i + \sum_1^n t_j q_i^j\right), \qquad (i=1,\ldots,n) \tag{8.6c}$$

Using (8.4)'s properties for the $q^i[\ ]$ functions, we can rewrite this as

$$\sum_1^n q_i^j t_j = \alpha q^i \tag{8.6d}$$

With use of (8.5) we can eliminate the Lagrangean multiplier α from (8.6d) and write down the n relations determining the n unknowns, $(t_1,\ldots,t_n)$, as

$$\sum_1^n q_i^j[q_0;\, p+t, 0]t_j = q^i[q_0;\, p+t, 0]\left(\sum_1^n \sum_1^n t_r q_r^s[q_0;\, p+t, 0]/q_0\right),$$
$$(i=1,\ldots,n) \tag{8.7}$$

Incipient tax limits. Ramsey's problem is formally solved by (8.7). However, the result is not very intuitive. To prepare the way for analysis of "small" tax and expenditure programs, I divide all t's by q_0 and rewrite (8.7) as

$$\sum_{j=1}^n q_i^j(t_j/q_0) = \left[\sum_1^n \sum_1^n (t_r/q_0)q_r^s(t_s/q_0)\right]q^i, \qquad (i=1,\ldots,n) \tag{8.8}$$

Letting $q_0 \to 0$, we have

$$\lim_{q_0 \to 0} (t_j) = 0 \tag{8.9a}$$

$$\lim_{q_0 \to 0} (t_j/q_0) = t_j'[0] = \dot{t}_j \text{ for short} \tag{8.9b}$$

After the limits are taken in (8.7) these become just enough relations to determine the $(\dot{t}_1,\ldots,\dot{t}_n)$, namely

$$\sum_{j+1}^n q_i^j[0; p, 0]\dot{t}_j = q^i[0; p, 0]\sum_1^n \sum_1^n \dot{t}_r q_r^s[0; p, 0]\dot{t}_s, \qquad (i=1,\ldots,n) \tag{8.10}$$

Although (8.10) appears to involve quadratic equations, they can be written as linear equations by restoring an auxiliary Lagrangean variable, β, to arrive at $n+1$ linear relations in the $n+1\,(\dot{t}_j, \beta)$ unknowns.

$$\sum_{1}^{n} q_i^j t_j - \beta q_i = 0, \quad (i=1,\ldots,n) \tag{8.11}$$

$$\sum q^j t_j = 1$$

A unique solution for optimal incipient taxes is thus defined by (8.11) near the laissez faire solution.

Substitution coefficients. The result now reached is formally complete and provides a logical solution to the problem posed by A. C. Pigou, Ramsey's mentor. But it still lacks intuitive content. And it fails to connect up with Frank Ramsey's provocative equal-percentage rule. A quantum jump in my own feeling of accomplishment came when I found how to tie up this analysis in terms of Marshall–Cournot *ceteris paribus* coefficients, $\partial q_i/\partial P_j$, with Slutsky–Hicks *substitution* coefficients

$$(\partial q_i/\partial P_j)_{U=\bar{U}} = \frac{\partial q_i}{\partial P_j} + q_j \frac{\partial q_i}{\partial Y} = S_{ij} = S_{ji} \tag{8.12}$$

At last my intuitions about Engel's laws of income effects were vindicated once I generalized Ramsey's analysis and corrected it for income effects. The reader interested in the psychology of scientific discovering should be alerted to the fact that my biggest thrill of analytical *surprise* (and hence feeling of achievement) came at the step between (8.13a) and (8.13b). By adding and subtracting the same magnitude to $\sum t_j q_i^j$, I was able to convert the problem to the realm of *substitution* coefficients. Explicitly,

$$\sum_{j=1}^{n} t_j q_i^j = \sum_{j=1}^{n} t_j (q_i^j + q^i q_{n+1}^j) - q^i \left(\sum_{k=1}^{n} t_k q_{n+1}^k \right) \tag{8.13a}$$

$$= \sum_{j=1}^{n} (S_{ji}) t_j - a q^i, \quad (i=1,\ldots,n)$$

$$= \sum_{j=1}^{n} S_{ij}[q_0;\, p+t, 0] t_j - a q^i [q_0;\, p+t, 0] \tag{8.13b}$$

Combining (8.7) and (8.8) with (8.13a), I reach the goal of Ramseyan optimality tax conditions with income effects explicitly displayed:

$$\sum_{j=1}^{n} S_{ij}[q_0;\, p+t, 0](t_j[q_0]/q_0)$$

$$= q^i [q_0;\, p+t, 0] \sum_{1}^{n} \sum_{1}^{n} S_{rs}(t_r[q_0]/q_0)(t_s[q_0]/q_0), \quad (i=1,\ldots,n) \tag{8.14}$$

Because of redundancy, (8.14) could validly hold for $(i=2,\ldots,n)$ and $t_1[q_0] \equiv 0$. Also, if $(t_{r+1},\ldots,t_n)$ were arbitrarily given to us at $(\bar{t}_{r+1},\ldots,\bar{t}_n)$, the first r relations of (9.14) with the summations running over $(1,\ldots,r)$, would be the necessary and sufficient condition for constrained optimality of $(t_1,\ldots,t_r)$.

Taking the limit, $q_0 \to 0$, I then devise the essentially linear relations for the tax derivates (or "incipient taxes"), $(\dot{t}_j)=(t'_j[0])$:

$$\sum_{j=1}^{n} \bar{S}_{ij}\dot{t}_j = q_i \sum_1^n \sum_1^n \bar{S}_{rs}\dot{t}_r\dot{t}_s, \qquad (i=1,\ldots,n) \tag{8.15}$$

$$(\bar{S}_{ij}) = (S_{ij}[0;\, p+0,0]),\ (\bar{q}^j) = (q^j[0;\, p+0,0])$$

Note that the presence of q_0 in the $q^i[q_0, p+t, 0]$ demand function does not affect the optimal $(\dot{t}_j)$ pattern, a fact I should have noticed in 1948.

Equivalent local maximum problem. The solutions to (8.15) are recognized to be maximizing solutions to

$$\operatorname*{Max}_{t_j} \sum_1^n \sum_1^n \bar{S}_{ij}\dot{t}_i\dot{t}_j \quad \text{s.t.} \quad \sum_1^n \bar{q}_j\dot{t}_j = 1$$

$$= \sum_1^n \sum_1^n \bar{S}_{ij}t'_i[0]t'_j[0] \tag{8.16}$$

However, the intuitive meaning of (8.14) and the (8.16) maximum problem I perceived to come from the Taylor–Maclaurin expansion of (8.3b)'s $u[q_0]$:

$$u[q_0] = u[0]+u'[0]q_0+\tfrac{1}{2}u''[0]q_0^2+\text{remainder} \tag{8.17}$$

For q_0 small, unless $u'[0]$ is maximized by the choice of $(\dot{t}_j)$, we can't be dealing with a truly optimizing set of arcs, $(t_j[q_0])$. However, calculation shows that $u'[0]$ is indifferently the same for all feasible choices of initial taxings.

A similar argument shows that the arcs can't be optimal near $q_0=0$ unless the $(\dot{t}_j)$ do maximize $u''[0]$.

Writing out

$$u[q_0] = U^*(q_0;\, p+t[q_0], 0) \tag{8.18}$$

and respecting the $\sum^n q^j[\,]t_j[q_0]$ constraint, shows that $u''[q_0]$ is proportional to (8.16)'s quadratic form, $\dot{t}'\bar{S}\dot{t}$. (When U is given an admissible arbitrary stretching, u will also undergo that stretching. However, that merely changes the proportionality factor linking $u''[q_0]$ and $\dot{t}'\bar{S}\dot{t}$, a reassuring finding that only ordinal utility is needed for Crusoe.)

Dominating interpersonal equity. Not only did (8.14)–(8.18) free me from any need to deal with differentials, it also reaffirmed my intuition that Ramsey's optimizing small taxes were solving a problem in farthings while the pounds were going askew. Ramsey dealt with the second-degree term in Taylor's expansions, not the first-degree term. He worried about small triangular areas, squares of small fractions. As soon as Crusoe lives in a society with at least one other person, the normative problem of taxing to optimize a Bergsonian social welfare function involves *interpersonal equity* considerations that enter critically into the first-degree term of the Taylor expansion. When all taxes have in them a common epsilon factor, then as that epsilon goes to zero, $u'[0]$ is found to depend on differences in the marginal social significances of various persons' dollars. Around 1950, Marcus Fleming and James Meade had already perceived this basic fact of the predominance of "equity effects" over "substitution-distortion effects." My own remarks on the topic, as in Samuelson (1958, p. 333), were a direct outgrowth of Gelting's siccing me onto the Ramsey problem.

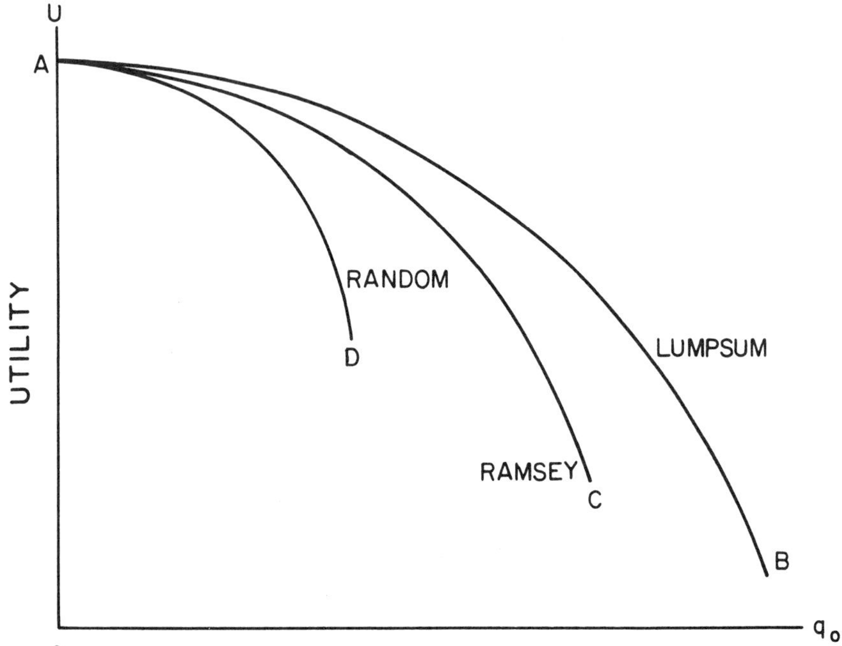

Figure 2.

Diagram of local effects. Figure 2 returns to the one man world of Robinson Crusoe. It deals with the case mentioned in footnote where his utility from private goods is strongly separable from his utility from public goods. For different levels of q_0, the resulting level of private utility is indicated. At the laissez faire point A, it is at its maximum. Outer curve AB shows how private utility falls off under ideal lumpsum taxation. The curve AC shows how it falls off under optimal Ramsey (feasible) taxation when only goods and services can be taxed. Finally AD shows the results of some arbitrary nonoptimal pattern of excises. The tangency of all three curves dramatizes the point that, up to first powers of q_0, the pattern of taxing is indifferent. Only at the curvature level does the pattern of taxing matter.

Correct rule at last. We can now examine how all (q_i) change with q_0. By definition

$$q_i[q_0] = q^i[q_0; p_1 + t_t[q_0], \ldots, p_n + t_n[q_0], 0] \tag{8.19a}$$

$$\begin{aligned}\dot{q}_i &= q_i'[0] = \sum_{j=1}^{n} q_j^i \dot{t}_j + q_0^i \\ &= \sum_j (q_j^i + q^j q_{n+1}^i)\dot{t}_j - \left(\sum_j q^j \dot{t}_j\right) q_{n+1}^i + q_0^i \\ &= \sum_j S_{ij}\dot{t}_j + (q_0^i - q_{n+1}^i) \qquad (8.19b) \\ &= \beta q^i + (q_0^i - q_{n+1}^i), \text{ from (8.15)} \qquad (8.19c)\end{aligned}$$

My final result is attained:

$$\frac{q_i'[0]}{q_i[0]} = \beta - \frac{\partial q^i[0; p, 0]/\partial Y}{q^i[0; p, 0]} + \frac{\partial q^i[0; p, 0]/\partial q_0}{q^i[0; p, 0]}, \quad (i = 1, \ldots, n) \tag{8.20}$$

The last two terms correct Ramsey's equal-percentage rule. The middle term is the income effect that we expect to enter the problem when resources must be shifted to public goods. After all, intuition is preserved! In wartime we do cut down more on "luxuries" than on "necessities" in order to finance military output. The final term, added in 1982 to my 1948-9 researches to take account of the fact that in 1982 I do let public goods alter private-good demand, agrees with expectations by me, Pigou, Ramsey, or anyone else.

Jørgen Gelting's question is answered at long last.

Pure transfers and the rule. My need to work with models that have a firm foundation has often served me well. And this has been such a case. Scientists, however, must sometimes fly as well as walk. My pedantry in dismissing as silly a case where Crusoe puts excises on himself only to transfer their revenue back to himself in a lumpsum way made me replace with a realistic case Ramsey's bizarre case of taxing only in order to make *transfers* (to "rentiers and pensioners"). Now in 1982 I see that it is a legitimate problem to find out just how silly such a distortion is, and to see what is the case when that silliness is kept to a feasible minimum.

So let me no longer treat $\bar{q}_0$ as my parameter that departs from zero. Let the size of the tax program, T, be that parameter. And, for simplicity, suppose that $\bar{q}_0$ is a fraction k of T, while the fraction $1-k$ of T is the amount transferred back to Crusoe as a lumpsum Y transfer. Now $\dot{q}_i$ denotes $q_i'[T]$ at $T=0$; and likewise for $\dot{t}_i$ as $t_i'[T]$ when $T=0$.

The government's budget equation and Crusoe's demand functions then become

$$\sum_1^n q_j t_j = T = q_0 + Y$$

$$= kT + (1-k)T \tag{8.21}$$

$$q_i = q^i[kT;\ p + t[T], (1-k)T], \quad (i=1,\ldots,n) \tag{8.22}$$

Differentiating (8.22) with respect to T and utilizing (8.20)'s earlier findings, I get

$$\dot{q}_i = \sum_{j=1}^n q_i^i \dot{t}_j + kq_0^i + (1-k)q_{n+1}^i$$

$$= \beta q^i - q_{n+1}^i + kq_0^i + (1-k)q_{n+1}^i \tag{8.23}$$

Our final general result becomes

$$\frac{q_i'[0]}{q_i[0]} = \beta - k\frac{\partial q^i[0;\ p,0]/\partial Y}{q^i[0, p, 0]} + k\frac{\partial q^i[0;\ p,0]/\partial q_0}{q^i[0;\ p,0]}, \quad (i=1,\ldots n) \tag{8.24}$$

But now comes what I am ashamed to report as a surprise. For his *pure transfer* case, $k=0$, Ramsay's formula of equal-percentage cut would be completely correct even when income effects are properly handled.

Complete model of optimal price regulation. In 1948 I was content to treat the level of tax and expenditure as an exogenous parameter. The pure theory of public expenditure, Samuelson (1954; 1969, Appendix on the Optimal Markup Theorem), helped complete the theory. Also, I had soon realized that the net-elasticity-equalization theorem, which held for any exogeneous level of subsidy to the public utility or government agency, could be sharpened by a model that *deduced* endogenously the optimal amount of subsidy. My result is so general, and so obvious, that it must be somewhere in the literature if only in bits and pieces. Here is a brief sketch of how it goes in the simplest scenario.

Alfred Marshall (1920, Book III, Ch. 4), in a rare lapse into confusion, argued: Increasing cost industries should be taxed to subsidize decreasing cost industries. He arrived at this result by adding areas of consumer's surplus, but unaccountably failed also to add in producers' surplus. By Marshall's fallacious mode of reasoning, he could as legitimately have deduced: in a world of constant returns to scale, where some industries have constant-cost supply curves and some have rising supply curves, Crusoe could improve his world by taxing the latter to subsidize the former — a false assertion whose validity would negate the Pareto-optimality of competitive pricing in an externality-free model. Marshall is plain wrong. Besides confusing a generation, Marshall confused his pupil A. C. Pigou, as in Pigou (1912, 1920). It took the Herculean labors of Allyn Young (1913) (and, later, Frank Knight (1924) and Dennis Robertson (1924)) to clean the soiled stables.

Marshall obscured two valid but distinguishable points. Externalities do raise a rebuttable presumption in favor of interfering with laissez faire. And the introduction of increasing-return-to-scale activities into a competitive constant-returns world also creates such a presumption in favor of optimal regulated price.

We are back with a Ramsey problem of the second best, but now in slightly generalized form. To give Marshall most rope and abbreviate the exposition, I give my optimum-regulation model for the Crusoe case where all goods have additive (concave) utilities and where his labor has constant disutility at the level that can be taken to be unity. There are two categories of goods: $(q_1,\ldots,q_n)$ that do obey constant returns to scale (and "convexity" of technology); and $(q_{n+1},\ldots,q_m)$ public-utility goods that display some increasing-returns-to-scale features.

For Robinson Crusoe's utility I specify

$$U = \sum_1^n U_j(q_j) + \sum_{n+1}^m U_j(q_j) - L \tag{8.25}$$

For technology I parameterize the degree of divergence from constant returns to scale characterizing the public utility sectors by the parameter x, writing

$$L = \sum_1^n L_j + \sum_{n+1}^m L_j = \sum_1^m C_j(q_j) \tag{8.26}$$

where

$$C_j(q_j) = q_j, \qquad (j=1,\ldots,n) \tag{8.26a}$$

$$C_{n+i}(q_{n+i}) = q_{n+i} + xf_{n+i}(q_{n+i}), \qquad (i=1,\ldots,m-n) \tag{8.26b}$$

$$f_{n+i}(0) = 0 \tag{8.26c}$$

$$f_{n+i}(q_{n+i}) = a_1 + b_i g_{n+i}(q_{n+i}), q_{n+i} > 0 \tag{8.26d}$$

$$g''_{n+i}(q_{n+i}) < 0, \ (a_{n+i}, b_{n+i}, x) \geqq 0$$

When $a_{n+i}>0$, that public utility industry has "initial fixed costs" that have to be incurred in the steady state if it produces any positive amount however small. If $b_{n+i} > 0$, the utility has falling marginal costs. In either case, charging marginal costs will not cover full costs in the steady state. Competition not being viable in some sectors, we can seek the pattern of best price to marginal cost discrepancies for the society as a whole.

Problem: What pattern of optimal excises, $(t_1,\ldots,t_n,\ldots,t_m)$ should be put as wedges between the prices consumers pay and the marginal costs producers incur in order to meet all steady-state costs and maximize Robinson Crusoe's total utility?

When some a_{n+i} is positive and x is very large, it will pay to shut down q_{n+i} completely. However, if all $U'_{n+i}(0)$ begin above unity and x is sufficiently small, we can be sure that our optimizing solution will be an interior one with all goods to be produced in positive amounts. This is the case I shall focus on, one for which the maximum will be unique.

Now we have a variant of Ramsey's second best. The problem can be posed as follows:

$$u[x] = \sum_1^m U_j(q_j[x]) - \sum_1^m C_j(q_j[x])$$

$$= \operatorname*{Max}_{q_1,\ldots,q_n} \left[\sum_1^m U_j(q_j) - \sum_1^m C_j(q_j) \right] \qquad (8.27)$$

subject to the side constraint that the total of excise tax collections just cover the shortfall of marginal-cost receipts in comparison with full unit cost outlays; or, what is the same thing, that marginal-utility pricing to the consumers just cover total cost outlays for the system.

$$\sum_1^m U'_j(q_j)q_j = \sum_1^m C_j(q_j) \qquad (8.27a)$$

By Lagrange multiplier technique, we derive the necessary and sufficient variational conditions

$$U'_i - C'_i = \lambda[U'_i - C'_i] + \lambda q_i U''_i, \quad (i=1,\ldots,m) \qquad (8.27b)$$

This gives the now-familiar[7] Ramsey condition of percentage markdown of marginal

7. Baumol and Bradford (1970) purport to read apprehension of this rule in Dupuit of 1854, writers on railroads of almost a century ago, and in Joan Robinson (1933) and W. A. Lewis (1949). To do this they give quotations showing apprehension of related propositions — namely that it may be better to keep a decreasing cost activity in existence by a pattern of price discrimination than to insist upon uniform prices, and that there is a presumption of less

cost below price varying inversely with demand elasticity as in Samuelson (1969, p. 121)

$$P_i\left(1-\frac{1}{\alpha|E_i|}\right) = MC_i, \quad (i=1,\ldots,m) \tag{8.27c}$$

$$\alpha > 1,\ |E_i| = q_iU_i''/U_i';\ P_i = U_i',\ MC_i = C_i'$$

Warning: these elasticities are *industry* elasticities; for competitive industry q_1, a small firm might have infinite demand elasticity but industry $|E_1|$ will not be infinite.

The present model does not leave the factor α as an exogenously specifiable parameter, but instead deduces its optimizing value in accordance with (8.27a)'s overall constraint. The full set of optimizing conditions can be summarized as follows:

$$\frac{U_1'(q_1)-C_1'(q_1)}{q_1U_1''(q_1)} = \ldots = \frac{U'(q_m)-C_m'(q_m)}{q_mU_m''(q_m)}$$

$$= \frac{\sum_1^m C_j(q_j)-\sum_1^m q_jC_j'(q_j)}{\sum_1^m (q_j)^2U_j''(q_j)} = \frac{x[\sum_1^m f_j(q_j)-\sum_1^m q_jf_j'(q_j)]}{\sum_1^m (q_j)^2U_j''(q_j)} \tag{8.28}$$

The implications of this analysis are definite and important. It means that competitive industries as well as public utilities must end up marking up price over marginal cost, a point that Hotelling, Bonbright, Lerner, Wicksell, Cassel, and other historic exponents of marginal cost pricing for public utilities have perhaps understressed.

In the case where all b_i in (8.26d) are zero, so that only initial "fixed costs" occasion the departures from constant return to scale, the present model of social pricing becomes precisely that of my Ramsey exhaustive expenditure formulation. Thus, as $x \to 0$, the incipient ($t_i'[0]$) pattern obeys the Ramsey-Samuelson modified percentage-cut rule:

$$\frac{q_i'[0]}{q_i[0]} = \beta - \frac{\partial q_i[0,p,0]/\partial Y}{q_i[0,p,0]} \quad (i=1,\ldots,n,\ldots,m) \tag{8.29}$$

To keep my model at Marshall's 2-dimensional level, I made L have constant marginal disutility, thus annihilating the final income effects in (8.29). However, they really do belong there. (When some b_i are positive, the incipient change in quantities, ($q_i'[0]$), depend in a more complicated way on the $f_j(q_i)$ functions' derivatives.)

---

distortion when things inelastic in demand are raised in price. (Albert Gallatin's *Free Trade Memorial* of 1832 contains the last vague perception.) However, Baumol and Bradford seem to have had to provide much charity to read into the words they quote the Ramsey markup rule.

Remark: No $C_j''(q_j)$ terms appear in (8.28)'s denominators. If this had been the original Ramsey problem, and if some competitive industries had rising marginal costs—as when each good is produced by labor working on a land specific to itself so that $L_j = C_j(q_j)$—then (5.6c) would generalize into a "net elasticity equalization" different from (8.28), namely into

$$\frac{U_1'(q_1) - C_1'(q_1)}{q_1[U_1''(q_1) - C_1''(q_1)]} = \cdots = \frac{U_m'(q_1) - C_m'(q_1)}{q_m[U_m''(q_m) - C_m''(q_n)]} \tag{8.30}$$

No wonder the literature has involved rediscoveries and "misplacement" of theorems in view of the subtle differences in assumptions of various models and the paucity of unifying analyses.

9. Concluding Reflections

Substance. Here are som things learned from this chapter in the history of thought.

1. To think a *voluntary* tax is a virtue is to have things just backwards. When a tax makes you stop buying, that distorts your pattern while collecting no revenue. Somehow the needed revenue has to be raised: other things equal (equity and so forth) the more *inelastic* a good's substitution coefficient the more it should be taxed; to the extent that the height of a tax drives people toward black market substitutes, that is precisely the kind of elasticity that the theory tells us should augur toward lower tax rates. (By contrast, taxing tobacco and alcohol in the hope of curbing their use is defensible as good policy when we paternalistically *don't* trust our actual demand tastes as indicators of the true utility that ought to be maximized for society.)

2. The harm done by taxing any one thing grows quadratically. So it is better to tax two things lightly than one heavily. Better still to tax three, four, . . ., all things—*ceteris paribus*. There is a rebuttable presumption against exempting any positive amount of a good from taxation, since that implies higher marginal tax rates and greater distortion.

3. For small fiscal programs, the tax distortion is very small indeed. So any tax pattern is tolerable. With public goods in minimal need, considerations of equitable redistribution should initially outweigh efficiency considerations: social equity gains that begin linearly outweigh cost distortions that begin quadratically. The margin at which redistribution ceases to be beneficial is reached when the final loss of efficiency matches the final gain deemed for equity. (Cf. Samuelson (1976, p. 187).)

4. Activities subject to increasing returns to scale cannot cover their full long-run costs through marginal cost pricing. A "public good" problem necessarily arises and a presumption in favor of public utility regulation and even subsidy. Finding the

optimal pattern of discrepancies between prices and marginal costs is a variant of our Ramseyan problem.

Adding a new small element of initial fixed costs somewhere in Crusoe's system should motivate him to raise taxes on constant-returns-to-scale activities to subsidize the new activity. If constitutionally only goods and services can be taxed, the optimal pattern of incipient-tax-and subsidy will cut all goods — whether competitive or public utility goods — in the Ramsey-Samuelson percentage way of (8.20) that respects income effects. The Ramsey and Boiteux analysis tells how a utility should price its many products to achieve the highest Crusoe maximum compatible with any specified degree of recovery of total costs:

> A utility should set prices as if it were a discriminating monopolist of the T. O. Yntema (1928) or J. Robinson (1933) type. But it should do so under the pretence that its goods' demand elasticities are all blown up from their actual magnitudes by a common proportionality factor, the size of that constant to grow toward infinity as amount of subsidy occasioned by increasing returns becomes vanishingly small.

Psychology of Science. Frank Ramsey was a genius by all tests for genius. He was precocious; deep; versatile. No need for me to evaluate his contributuons to logic, philosophy, and mathematics. All three of his contributions to economics, mentioned in my introduction, I and other economists have found to be seminal: they point beyond themselves. Paradoxically, we find them so stimulating because they are imperfect. You might almost say that Ramsey was too clever by half. Like Willard Gibbs in thermodynamics, what Ramsey saw clearly he felt no need to explain so that the reader can perceive all its implications.[8]

It is cant to say that Ramsey is all the better for his imperfections. Even genius can be improved upon. And the body of economic science would be the richer if Ramsey

8. I should put in the record a story about Ramsey told me years ago at Harvard's Society of Fellows by the late I. A. Richards, founder of basic English with G. K. Ogden. More than sixty years ago, as I write, Richards visited Ogden's rooms at Cambridge University. Their conversation was interrupted by a big hulk of a schoolboy from Winchester mumbling some thoughts about essence and being. (Frank Ramsey was the son of a Cambridge mathematical physicist; Frank's younger brother later became Archbishop of Canterbury.) Richards reported this dialogue.

Ogden: That sounds like Kant.
Ramsey: Who is Kant, sir?
Ogden: Author of this book [Critique of Pure Reason?].
Ramsey: But I don't know German, sir.
Ogden: Then borrow this dictionary as well.

Richards was curious enough to ask Ogden later how it all turned out. Ogden reported: "He was back a week later, saying 'Kant almost got it right, sir, but. . .'."

had worked out the details and underpinnings of his contributions. It is a pity that Hotelling, the two Hicks's, and Boiteux seem not to have been aware of Ramsey's 1927 analysis. No fault of theirs. But I do reproach myself that for over three decades I did not publish my lectures and memoranda. It is a sin not to publish.

Science's imperfection is the young scholar's opportunity. Who gives one an important puzzle bestows the greatest gift of all. My debt to Jørgen Gelting has been accumulating at compound interest for more than a third of a century and I return this token payment with gratitude.[9]

References

Baumol, W. J. and D. F. Bradford, "Optimal Departures from Marginal Cost Pricing," *American Economic Review*, June 1970, 60, pp. 265-83.

Boiteux, M., "Le 'Revenu distribuable' et les pertes économiques," *Econometrica*, April 1951, 19, pp. 112-33.

Boiteux, M., "Sur la gestion des monopoles publics astreints à équilibre budgétaire," *Econometrica*, January 1956, 24, p. 22.

Diamond, P. A. and J. A. Mirrlees, "Optimal Taxation and Public Production; I-Production Efficiency," *American Economic Review*, March 1971, 61, pp. 8-27 and II-Tax Rules, *American Economic Review*, June 1971, 61, pp. 261-78.

9. My references only sample a copious literature. Ramsey (1927) is of course a prime source. Since Pigou was Ramsey's mentor, who posed to him the problem, Pigou (1928, 1929, 1947) deserves notices as being for a long time practically the only place where Ramsey's results received notice in the literature. I have already referred to Boiteux (1951, 1956). Drèze (1964) provides a useful summary of his work and of related work by French-language writers. Baumol and Bradford (1970) fill in some of the history, particularly where utilities goods pricing is concerned. Quoting from Samuelson (1964), they jogged John Hicks' memory of his 1946 Chapel Hill conversation with Harold Hotelling, in which he developed an equal-percentage rule from

$$\text{Min}\,\tfrac{1}{2}\textstyle\sum\sum q_{ij}dp_i dp_j \text{ subject to } G=\sum q_i dp_i$$

leading to

$$dq_i = \textstyle\sum q_{ij}dp_j = \lambda q_i$$

Apparently Samuelson (1969), my 1966 IEA Biarritz paper, had not come to their attention. In the same *AER* symposium with Baumol and Bradford, A. P. Lerner (1970) and A. Dixit (1970) bring to a close what may be called the pre Diamond-Mirrlees phase of the subject. P. A. Diamond and J. A. Mirrlees (1971) is the spring from which all modern discussions flow. But for space limitations here I would include a three-dimensional diagram, involving (q_1, q_2, L) in the general case with no special Marshallian separability assumptions, that I gave before the Harvard Graduate Economics Club at Harkness Commons in 1952: it elucidates sans calculus the crucial feature of best feasible taxing.

Dixit, A. K., "On the Optimum Structure of Commodity Taxes," *American Economic Review*, June 1970, 22, pp. 229-34.

Drèze, J. H., "Some Postwar Contributions of French Economists to Theory and Public Policy, with Special Emphasis on Problems of Resource Allocation," *American Economic Review*, June 1964, 54, pp. 1-64.

Hicks, U., *Public Finance*, (Cambridge Handbook Series) Pittman, London 1947.

Hotelling, H., "Edgeworth's Taxation Paradox and the Nature of Demand and Supply Functions," *Journal of Political Economy*, October 1932, 40, pp. 577-616.

Hotelling, H., "The General Welfare in Relation to Problems of Taxation and of Railway and Utility Rates," *Econometrica*, July 1938, 6, pp. 242-69.

Joseph, M. F. W., "The Excess Burden of Indirect Taxation," *Review of Economic Studies*, June 1939, 6, pp. 226-31.

Knight, F. H., "Some Fallacies in the Interpretation of Social Cost," *Quarterly Journal of Economics*, 1924, 38, pp. 582-606.

Kuhn, T. S., *The Structure of Scientific Revolutions*, The University of Chicago Press 1962 and 1970.

Lerner, A. P., "Distributional Equality and Aggregate Utility: Reply," *American Economic Review*, June 1970, 60, pp. 442-43.

Lewis, W. A., *Overhead Costs*, Rinehart & Co., New York 1949.

Marshall, A., *Principles of Economics*, Book 5, chapter XIII, 8th ed., Macmillan, London 1920.

Merton, R. K., *The Sociology of Science, Theoretical and Empirical Investigations*, ed. Norman W. Storer, The University of Chicago Press 1973.

Pigou, A. C., *Wealth and Welfare*, Macmillan 1912.

Pigou, A. C., *Economics of Welfare*, Macmillan 1920.

Pigou, A. C., *A Study in Public Finance*, Macmillan 1928, 1929 and 1947.

Ramsey, F. P., "A Contribution to the Theory of Taxation," *Economic Journal*, March 1927, 37, pp. 47-61.

Robertson, D. H., "Those Empty Boxes," *Economic Journal*, March 1924, 34, pp. 16-31.

Robinson, J., *The Economics of Imperfect Competition*, Macmillan, London 1933.

Samuelson, P. A., "The Empirical Implications of Utility Analysis," *Econometrica*, October 1938, 6, pp. 344-356 and 1965 Postscript in *The Collected Scientific Papers of Paul A. Samuelson* (henceforth referred to as *CSP*) chapter 3, volume 1, p. 34, ed. Joseph E. Stiglitz, The MIT Press, 1966.

Samuelson, P. A., "Evaluation of Real National Income," *Oxford Economic Papers*, January 1950, 2, pp. 1-29; reprinted in *CSP* chapter 77, volume 2, ed. Joseph E. Stiglitz, The MIT Press 1966.

Samuelson, P. A., "The Pure Theory of Public Expenditure," *The Review of Economics and Statistics*, November 1954, 36, pp. 387-89; reprinted in *CSP* chapter 92, volume 2.

Samuelson, P. A., "Aspects of Public Expenditure Theories," *The Review of Economics and Statistics*, November 1958, 40, pp. 332-38; reprinted in *CSP* chapter 94, volume 2.

Samuelson, P. A., "Principles of Efficiency — Discussion," *American Economic Review* (Papers and Proceedings of the 76th Annual Meeting of the American Economic Association) May 1964, 54, pp. 93-96;

reprinted in *CSP* chapter 164, volume 3, ed. Robert C. Merton, The MIT Press 1972.

Samuelson, P. A., "Pure Theory of Public Expenditure and Taxation," in J. Margolis and H. Guitton, eds., *Public Economics: An Analysis of Public Production and Consumption and their Relations to the Private Sectors: Proceedings of a* 1966 *Conference Held by the International Economics Association*, Macmillan, London 1969, pp. 98-123; reprinted in *CSP* chapter 172, volume 3.

Samuelson, P. A., "Optimal Compacts for Redistribution," in R. E. Grieson, ed., *Public and Urban Economics*, Lexington Books, D. C. Heath and Co. 1976, pp. 179-90; reprinted in *CSP* chapter 257, volume 4, eds. Hiroaki Nagatani and Kate Crowley, The MIT Press 1977.

Yntema, T. O., "The Influence of Dumping on Monopoly Price," *Journal of Political Economy*, December 1938, 36, pp. 686-98.

Young, A. A., "Pigou's Wealth and Welfare," *Quarterly Journal of Economics*, 1912–13, 27, pp. 672-86.

6

Pseudo-Maximization to the Rescue of Derived Factor Demand of a Competitive Industry

Paul A. Samuelson

Exactly forty-two years ago, when I was an undergraduate taking Jacob Viner's first course in graduate economic theory, his celebrated 301 at the University of Chicago, a brilliant comet visited the seminar. Later I learned this was Fritz Machlup. I term him a comet because his was a strange and new face in the heavens; but actually Machlup twinkled like a star of the first magnitude. After Viner made some remarks, not completely complimentary, about Böhm-Bawerk's tedious discrete-horse markets, Machlup intervened with great courtesy and élan, pointing out that in the *Excursi* of later editions, Böhm had worked out the continuous-variable supply and demand intersections so beloved of Marshall's Anglo-Saxon readers.

That was the first of many benefits I received from Fritz's scholarship: like the dividends on consols, Machlup's contributions to modern economics continue to accrue, not with the long gaps of Haley's comet but fortunately with its predictable regularity.

Although I did not know it then, Machlup must already have written by the time of that Viner seminar his 1935 paper "The Common Sense of the Elasticity of Substitution." This article could serve as a model for any would-be scholar. It makes clear much that was murky. It is a *tour de force* of skillful exposition—unpretentious, modest, punctilious in its scholarly attributions. At the same time it had depth, pointing to problems still to be solved (some of which I found still waiting resolution a third of a century later when, for the Hicks *Festschrift,* I tackled Machlup's vital concept of *intercommodity* substitutions).

Now I hope to provide some simplification, clarification, and generalization (all Machlupian earmarks!) to one of the problems involved in the original discussions of the elasticity of substitution by Hicks (1932), Joan Robinson (1933), Kahn (1933, 1935), Meade (1934), Paul Douglas (1934), Pigou (1934), Tarshis (1933), Abba Lerner (1933, 1934, 1936), Paul Sweezy (1933), Machlup (1935, 1936), Champernowne (1935), Milton Friedman (1936), Mosak (1938), Roy Allen (1938), and others. (I invite the reader to savor the above names.) Aside

I owe thanks to the NSF for financial aid, and to Vicki Elms for editorial assistance.

from tackling the problems of (a) relative shares of factors in a one-product aggregative economy, and (b) their shares in a general equilibrium mode involving Machlup-Hicks intercommodity substitutions, these early writers hoped to employ the elasticity of substitution concepts (c) *to analyze a single competitive industry's demand for two or more factors of production.* This last venture had, by the late 1930s, bogged down in a swamp of hard-to-handle and inconclusive matrices. More recently, advances in duality theory by Shephard (1953, 1970), Samuelson (1947, 1953, 1960, 1962, 1965, 1968, 1972, 1974), Uzawa (1962), McFadden (1963), Diewert (1971a,b), Hicks (1936, 1963, 1970), Sato and Koizumi (1970, 1973a, b), Akerlof and Burmeister (1970), Silberberg (1971), Vázquez and Puu (1973), Sakai (1975), and others have provided some much needed simplification to the analysis.

However, the last word has by no means yet been said. It is a pleasure to use a concept near to Fritz Machlup's heart—that of *maximizing*—to yield some enormous simplifications and also some fresh, verifiable testings of the model.

A Frankenstein-Samuelson Monster

Machlup is of course famous for his 1940's defense of marginalism. He insists that firms *really do* try to maximize their profits and that we economists will have to recognize the validity of this instance of the "economic principle" even if it complicates our analysis (rather than enormously simplifying it, as is actually the case). Carl Menger, the Abraham of the Austrian School and Machlup's spiritual grandsire, had insisted a century ago in his polemics against the Historical School on the methodological dogma of rational individualism, upon which all sound economic analysis *must* be based. Machlup as Joseph has found no need to alter the faith of his forefathers. Far from it.

If I were to allege to Fritz that hydrogen molecules maximize utility or that salt economizes on love, he would regard these as pathetic examples of the "Pathetic Fallacy" (according to which rocks have broken hearts and willow trees weep) and he might urge me to go on the wagon. Or he might indulge my excursion into poetry as perhaps a sign of evolving senility. None the less, my serious proposal in the present effort is to fabricate (or "forge") a function to be maximized for an industry that is a collection of a multitude of independent and competitive firms. The magnitude that is thought of as being maximized will be found to be measurable in dollars[1] and is closest in concept to "net utility" or "consumers' surplus." One must warn, however, that there are no normative or welfare connotations implied by this mechanical construction.

Why do I construct such a monstrosity? Because scientists must be opportunists and exploit every advantage the data offer. As I explained in my Nobel Lecture, Samuelson (1971), enormous unification and simplification can be procured whenever an economic problem can, by serendipity, be formulated as a maximum or minimum problem. Voltaire said that if God had not existed, we would have had to invent Him. I say, "Since this competitive industry's comparative-statics can be shown to behave as if the industry had a soul and an integrable mind, expediency urges us to pretend it has. Pretend? Operationally speaking, in effect it does maximize—else we could not successfully pretend it does. Abraham, Isaac, and Jacob be hanged if they don't approve."

The Industry Problem

Returning to sobriety, consider with Hicks (1932) and Robinson (1933, ch. 22) the following one-industry situation.[2]

output = neoclassical production function of 2 or more inputs

$$q = Q(x_1, x_2, \ldots) = Q(\mathbf{x}): \quad \text{a monotone increasing function} \quad (6.1.1)$$

$$\equiv m^{-1}Q(mx_1, mx_2, \ldots): \quad \text{1st-degree homogeneity} \quad (6.1.2)$$

$$Q(\mathbf{a}+2\mathbf{b}) - Q(\mathbf{a}+\mathbf{b}) \leqslant Q(\mathbf{a}+\mathbf{b}) - Q(\mathbf{a}): \quad \text{"diminishing returns" or concavity} \quad (6.1.3)$$

$$\partial Q/\partial x_i = Q_i, \ \partial^2 Q/\partial x_i \partial x_j = Q_{ij} \quad \text{is well-defined;} \quad \text{smoothness} \quad (6.1.4)$$

$$p = P[q], \quad P'[q] > 0: \quad \text{Cournot-Marshall industry demand}$$

$$q = Q[p], \quad Q'[\ ]P'[\ ] \equiv 1 \quad \text{for equilibrium pairs} \quad (6.2)$$

where the warning in note 2 about the distinction between $Q(\ )$ and $Q[\ ]$ should be noted.

$$y_1, y_2, \ldots: \quad \text{factor prices of } x_1, x_2, \ldots, \text{given to each firm}$$

$$0 = s_i(x_i, y_i; \ldots), (i = 1, 2, \ldots): \quad \text{supply schedules of factors} \quad (6.3)$$

Except for the assumption in (6.1.4) of smooth differentiability, the above assumptions are sufficient (and, actually, necessary) for viable competition in this Hicks-Robinson industry. Darwinian competition will then impose the marginal productivity conditions:

$$y_i = P[Q(x_1, x_2, \ldots)]\,[\partial Q(x_1, x_2, \ldots)/\partial x_i] \qquad (i = 1, 2, \ldots) \quad (6.4.1)$$

$$P[Q(\mathrm{x})]\,Q(\mathrm{x}) \equiv y_1x_1 + y_2x_2 + \ldots \tag{6.4.2}$$

So long as $P'[q] < 0$, it can be shown that (6.4) implies reduced form factor demand functions

$$x_i = X^i(y_1, y_2, \ldots) \qquad (i = 1, 2, \ldots) \tag{6.5}$$

These will be single valued functions for all positive (y_j) provided the conditions of (6.1.2)-(6.1.4) are strengthened so that the smooth iso-Q contours approach the axes asymptotically in Inada fashion.

So far, the properties of (6.5), such as the sign of $\partial X^i(\ )/\partial y_i$, have not been explored. And, thus far, no connection of (6.4) or (6.5) with a maximum problem has been exposed.

Consider now what would have replaced (6.4) if this Marshallian industry had been run by a "monopolist" (e.g., by a sole seller given exclusive rights to provide the product q to customers). The monopolist's maximum problem would have replaced (6.4) by

$$\begin{aligned} &\mathrm{Max}_{x_i}\left\{Q(\mathrm{x})P[Q(\mathrm{x})] - y_1x_1 - y_2x_2 - \ldots\right\} \\ &\equiv \mathrm{Max}_{x_i}\left\{R[Q(\mathrm{x})] - y_1x_1 - y_2x_2 - \ldots\right\} \\ &\equiv R[Q(\mathrm{x}^*)] - y_1x_1^* - y_2x_2^* - \ldots \\ &\equiv -\Pi^*(y_1, y_2, \ldots) \end{aligned} \tag{6.6.1}$$

where $(x_1^*, x_2^*, \ldots, q^*)$ are functions of $(y_1, y_2, \ldots)$ given by roots of the extremal conditions

$$R'[Q(x_1, x_2, \ldots)]\,[\partial Q(x_1, x_2, \ldots)/\partial x_i] - y_i = 0 \qquad (i = 1, 2, \ldots) \tag{6.6.2}$$

$$R[q] \equiv qP[q] \qquad R'[q] \equiv P[q] + qP'[q] \qquad R''[q] < 0 \tag{6.6.3}$$

$$P[Q(\mathrm{x})]\,Q(\mathrm{x}) - y_1x_1 - y_2x_2 - \ldots = -Q(\mathrm{x})^2P'[Q(\mathrm{x})] > 0 \tag{6.6.4}$$

In (6.6) I assumed that the monopoly is viable with positive output, upon which it is seen to necessarily earn a surplus profit.[3]

The problem in (6.6) is certainly a maximum problem: Menger and Machlup would not find it a camel hard to swallow. Its properties are by now old hat, as in Samuelson (1947, ch. 4) Thus, the relations (6.6.2) can be solved for the following reduced-form demands

$$x_i = \partial \Pi^*(y_1, y_2, \ldots)/\partial y_i \qquad (i = 1, 2, \ldots) \tag{6.7.1}$$

$$\partial^2 \Pi^*(\ )/\partial y_i^2 < 0 \tag{6.7.2}$$

$[-\partial^2 \Pi^*(\ )/\partial y_i \partial y_j]$ is positive definite with principal minors all positive.

Constructing The Industry's Maximand

We can reduce our (6.4.1) relations to the amenable maximization case of (6.6.2) once we realize that $P[q]$ in (6.4.1) can be the derivative of an existent function and can therefore play exactly the role that $R'[q]$ did in (6.6.2). Define

$$Y[q] \equiv \int_{q_0}^{q} P[v]\,dv : \qquad \text{the area under the demand curve} \tag{6.8.1}$$

$$Y'[q] \equiv P[q] \tag{6.8.2}$$

$$\partial Y[Q(x_1, x_2, \ldots)]/\partial x_i \equiv P[Q(x_1, \ldots)]\,[\partial Q(x_1, \ldots)/\partial x_i] \qquad (i = 1, 2, \ldots) \tag{6.8.3}$$

For

$$\begin{aligned} Y[Q(x_1, x_2, \ldots)] &\equiv Y(x_1, x_2, \ldots) \\ \partial Y[Q(x_1, x_2, \ldots)]/\partial x_i &\equiv Y_i(x_1, x_2, \ldots) \end{aligned} \tag{6.8.4}$$

for short,

$$\begin{aligned} Y_i(x_1, x_2, \ldots) &\equiv P[Q(x_1, x_2, \ldots)]\,[\partial Q(x_1, x_2, \ldots)/\partial x_i] \\ [Y_{ij}(x_1, x_2, \ldots)] &= [(P)(\partial^2 Q/\partial x_i \partial x_j) + (P')(\partial Q/\partial x_i)(\partial Q/\partial x_j)] \end{aligned} \tag{6.8.5}$$

is negative definite.

Now the basic Hicks-Robinson industry equilibrium of (6.4) can be cast in the following maximizing form

$$\text{Max}_{x_i}\left\{Y(x_1, x_2, \ldots) - y_1 x_1 - y_2 x_2 - \ldots\right\}$$
$$= Y(x_1^*, x_2^*, \ldots) - y_1 x_1^* - y_2 x_2^* > 0 \qquad (6.9.1)$$
$$= -X(y_1, y_2, \ldots) \qquad (6.9.2)$$

the industry's *dual* function; and where $(x_1^*, x_2^*, \ldots)$ are optimal values of (x_j^*) for given (y_j),

$$x_i^* = \partial X(y_1, y_2, \ldots)/\partial y_i \qquad (i = 1, 2, \ldots)$$
$$= X_i(y_1, y_2, \ldots) \qquad (6.9.3)$$

for short; and where (x_j^*) are the roots of the extremal first-order maximum conditions equivalent to (6.4.2):

$$y_i = Y_i(x_1, x_2, \ldots) \equiv P[Q(x_1, x_2, \ldots)] \frac{\partial Q(x_1, x_2, \ldots)}{\partial x_i}$$
$$[Y_{ij}(\mathbf{x})] \text{ and } [X_{ij}(\mathbf{y})] \equiv [Y_{ij}(\mathbf{x})]^{-1} \qquad \text{negative definite} \qquad (6.9.4)$$

Under our strong regularity conditions on $Q(\mathbf{x})$, such that its contours are smooth and asymptotic to the axes, demands are unique and smooth.

There is an interesting moral from this rigorous model. It shows that maximization can be *simultaneously* postulated both for small firms *and* for the industry aggregate they belong to! This raises a question much debated in modern biology.

Is evolution a drama played out, as some writers insist, by the *selfish gene?* Or, does reciprocal altruism—among families, clans, parents, and the like—play a vital role so to be itself subject to selection and fitness survival? Our exact analysis shows that it need not always be a case of one or the other—the selfish gene *or* the selfish family. Both, or neither, might be involved. (Indeed, with a countable infinity of units one might, as in Samuelson (1968, Equations 17-20), construct an *endless* hierarchy of higher and lower stages, *each* of which involves maximization at its level.) In principle, revealed preference methods can be used to test and refute hypothesized models of maximization. Thus, econometricians or biometricians can measure whether observations on (6.5) do satisfy approximately the Maxwell reciprocity relations, $\partial X^1(\ )/\partial y_2 \equiv \partial X^2(\ )/\partial y_1$, that enable (6.5) to be written as (6.9.3).

Much of biology, like much of Parsonian sociology, impresses the experienced economist as empty talk about untestable tautologies of *extrema* language. The young science of economics has perhaps some good examples to set for some of the older sciences (and still has some stables of its own that need cleaning!).

Easy Fruits of Maximization

From the maximizing formulation, we at once infer some basic facts:

1. A rise in an input price will, when other input prices are constant (*or* where some other inputs' quantities rather than prices are held constant), lower the amount of it demanded by the industry:[4]

$$(\Delta x_1)(\Delta y_1) \leqslant 0 \qquad X_{11}(y) < 0 \tag{6.10}$$

2. A rise in one input's price may raise or lower the amount the industry demands of another input. Unlike the case where q is held constant, there is no presumption toward "substitutability" rather than complementarity. Robinson (1933) found this out the hard way, deriving the criterion for $n = 2$ that $\partial x_2/\partial y_1 \lesseqgtr 0$ depending on whether industry-product demand elasticity is absolutely greater than the Hicks-Robinson elasticity of substitution, $\eta \gtrless \sigma$ in Hicks notation. Since the sign of $\partial x_2/\partial x_1$ is opposite in the polar cases where q and where p are frozen, one infers without breaking $\partial x_2/\partial y_1$ down into scale-and-substitution effects that all sign patterns are possible. Whatever the sign pattern of $\partial x_2/\partial y_1$, one can assert from the maximizing formulation above the following:

> The algebraic value of $\partial x_i/\partial y_j$ and $\partial x_j/\partial y_i$ must be equal. And likewise for the dimensionless elasticity expressions $k_i[\partial \log x_i/\partial \log y_j]$ or $[\partial \log x_i/\partial \log y_j]/k_j$:

$$X_{ij}(y) \equiv X_{ji}(y) \qquad k_i\frac{Ex_i}{Ey_j} \equiv k_j\frac{Ex_j}{Ex_i} \tag{6.11}$$

and so on, where $k_i = x_i y_i/\Sigma_1^n x_j y_j$ and Ez denotes $dz/z = d \log z$, as in $Eq/Ep = p[q]/p'[q]q = -\eta$, or in $Ex_i/Ey_j = \partial \log X_i(y)/\partial \log y_j$.[5]

This analysis dispells the "paradox" of Richard Nelson (1957), who thought it strange that a rise in the price of wheat farm labor could ***raise*** the wheat land rents of farmers. Nelson's case can be shown to be a simple variant of the problem solved in Robinson (1933), so that her criterion $\eta \gtrless \sigma$ is identical with Nelson's criterion $\eta \gtrless$ ratio of Average Variable Cost Curve's Elasticity to Marginal Cost Curve's Elasticity.[6] The methods of Samuelson (1960) can show the two problems' complete equivalence. Since *any* pattern of complementarity between two factors is possible, nothing should surprise us.

3. From the maximizing formulation alone, we know from Samuelson (1947) that the more comprehensive weak-axiom inequality holds:

$$(\Delta y_1)(\Delta x_1) + (\Delta y_2)(\Delta x_2) + \ldots \leqslant 0 \tag{6.12}$$

And all this holds even if we dispense with definable partial derivatives and marginal products. Thus, in the case of fixed proportions,

$$q = \text{Min}\,[x_1/a_1, x_2/a_2, \ldots]$$

$$p^* = a_1 y_1 + a_2 y_2 + \ldots$$

$$x_1^* = a_i q^* = a_i p^{-1}\left[\sum_1^n a_j y_j\right] = a_i X'\left[\sum_1^n a_j y_j\right]$$

$$\partial x_i^*/\partial y_i = a_i^2 X''\left[\sum_1^n a_j y_j\right] < 0$$

as in (6.10) above. Similarly, $\partial x_i^*/\partial y_j = a_i a_j X''[\ \ ] < 0$.

In terms of smooth derivatives, $[-X_{ij}(\mathbf{y})]$ and $[-Y_{ij}(\mathbf{x})]$ are positive definite with all their principal minors positive:

$$\partial x_i/\partial y_i < 0 \qquad (\partial x_i/\partial y_i)(\partial x_j/\partial y_j) - (\partial x_i/\partial y_j)^2 > 0\,, \ldots, \text{and so on.} \tag{6.13}$$

4. A maximum problem like (6.9) or (6.6) is known to be subject to the Le Chatelier-Samuelson inequalities. Therefore, we get as a bonus the Marshall-Hicks principle of derived demand: "The demand for labor will be more elastic if the supply of land responds elastically to any change in its price induced by a rise in wage." That is:

$$0 > \left(\frac{\partial x_1}{\partial y_1}\right)_{x_2 = \bar{x}_2} \geqslant \left(\frac{\partial x_1}{\partial y_1}\right)_{y_2 = \bar{y}_2} \qquad n \geqslant 2 \tag{6.14}$$

If space permitted, the analysis of Samuelson (1960) could be used to derive various generalizations of these shorter run and "rationing" phenomena, only a sampling of which is provided in sections 6A-4 and 6A-5 of the mathematical appendix to this chapter.

Throughout the rest of this chapter, I shall derive various duality and equilibrium relations. The nonmathematical reader may wish to skim some of this material. Let me call the attention of any parting guests to the fact that this one-industry model could be easily generalized to the case of a cluster of industries that use the same inputs. Thus, replace $p = P[q(\mathbf{x})]$ by

$$\begin{aligned} p_s &= Y_s[q_1, \ldots, q_m] \qquad (s = 1, \ldots, m) \\ &= \partial Y[\mathbf{q}]/\partial q_s \end{aligned} \tag{6.15.1}$$

where $Y[\mathbf{q}]$ is a definable "payoff" function measured in utils.

$$q_s = Q^s(x_{1s}, x_{2s}, \ldots) \equiv m^{-1} Q^s(mx_{1s}, mx_{2s}, \ldots) \tag{6.15.2}$$

and so on. Then (6.4.1) and (6.9) can be replaced by

$$\mathrm{Max}_{x_{is}} \left\{ Y[Q^1(x_{11}, \ldots), Q^2(x_{12}, \ldots), \ldots] - y_1 \sum_{s=1}^{m} x_{1s} - y_2 \sum_{s=1}^{m} x_{2s} - \ldots \right\}$$

$$= -X(y_1, y_2, \ldots) \tag{6.16.1}$$

$$x_i = x_{i1} + x_{i2} + \ldots = \partial X(y_1, y_2, \ldots)/\partial_{y_i} \qquad (i = 1, 2, \ldots) \tag{6.16.2}$$

$$[X_{ij}(\mathbf{y})] \text{ negative definite} \tag{6.16.3}$$

The function dual to $X(y)$ of (6.16.1) can be defined as $Y(\Sigma_1^m x_{1s}, \Sigma_1^m x_{2s}, \ldots)$, which is an aggregate function for the complex of industries.

Pursuing this line we shall reach the model of general equilibrium of Samuelson (1968), which tries to embrace the intercommodity substitutions of Machlup (1935) and achieves its greatest simplicity when all consumers have uniform homothetic tastes. (Those who skip the mathematical appendix to this chapter may perhaps still want to look at its concluding section.)

Methodological Caveats

To say, "Total revenue for a firm or industry rises when it raises price if and only if it has elasticity of demand less than unity in absolute value," is not to assert a true or false empirical proposition. Repeating the tautological *definition* of "Marshallian demand elasticity" in the above manner is useful, at best, in its *implicit* suggestion that Gregory King was correct in his noting that, "In the real world, demand may be *either in*elastic or *e*lastic (and, in seventeenth-century England, tended for grain to be inelastic)."

In what sense is the following Robinson-Allen proposition useful or interesting?

"Cross-elasticity has algebraic sign of 'Elasticity of Substitution minus Industry Demand Elasticity.'"

$$Ex_2/Ey_1 = k_2(\sigma_{12} - \eta) \tag{6.17}$$

where k_2 is the proportion of *total* factor incomes going to the second factor. Or, for q held constant, we have

$$(Ex_2/Ey_1)_{\bar{q}} = k_2\sigma_{12} \tag{6.18}$$

It is illusory to say, "The sign of σ_{12} 'explains' the sign of $(Ex_2/Ey_1)_{\bar{q}}$." They are essentially the same thing, and it is no "explanation" to give a thing as a cause for itself. The proposition in (6.17) has at least this use (although the interpretation I am about to give is late in being recognized). Since it can be shown that σ_{12} must be positive for $n = 2$ (and, for $n > 2$, must "average out" positive), one is at least alerted to the fact that (6.17) is of mixed sign and *could* be anything. We are warned against false dogmatism!

A second use comes from the fact that we *might* have *separate* knowledge about industry technology and industry market structure. When we know that demand for q is *very inelastic*, we can be sure that at least one factor has positive cross-elasticity with any factor whose price has changed; and, by Marshall-Hicks reasoning, we can bet that a factor's own-elasticity is low.

But, as Pigou (1934, p. 240) noted[7] in realistic despair, taxonomy only sets out for the asking the questions whose answers we'd like to know.

Far more useful than deductive propositions (which merely nominate for questioning questions that could be asked of the data) are testable and refutable hypotheses that can be proposed as descriptions of the regularities of the economic observables. Examples are the hypotheses of (6.13) that $\partial X_i(\mathrm{y})/\partial y_i < 0$ and $[\partial X_i(\mathrm{y})/\partial y_j]$ is a symmetric negative-definite matrix and that the testable relation (6.12) holds.

I doubt that Fritz Machlup agrees with my viewpoint. But let me illustrate it on what Hicks in *Value and Capital* (1939, p. 311) calls the Fundamental Equation of Value Theory (his capital letters). If a person with income M, facing prices $(p_1, \ldots, p_n)$, buys goods $(x_1, \ldots, x_n)$ satisfying the demand relations, $x_i = D^i(M; p_1, \ldots, p_n)$, with $\partial D^i(\ )/\partial p_j = D^i_j(\ )$ and $\partial D^i/\partial M = D^i_0(\ )$, then Hicks's "fundamental" relations take the form:

$$[D^i_j(M; \mathbf{p}) + D^j(M; \mathbf{p})D^i_0] = [x_{ij}(\ )] \tag{6.19}$$

where $[x_{ij}(\ )]$ is a symmetric matrix of "substitution terms" defined by the final n rows and columns of the inverse of the bordered matrix

$$\begin{bmatrix} 0 & p_j \\ p_i & u_{ij} \end{bmatrix}$$

where, at equilibrium,

$$\lambda p_i = u_i(\mathbf{x}) \qquad \sum_1^n p_j x_j = M$$

The equalities of (6.19) merely *name* the substitution terms defined on their right. At most, one might be led from (6.19) to realize that $(\partial U/\partial p_j) + x_j(\partial U/\partial M)$ vanishes, so that a change in p_j alone accompanied by a change in income, $dM/dp_j = x_j$, is truly "compensatory." But that is not a fact of fundamental interest for its own sake. What is fundamental is not the relation (6.19), but rather the symmetry relations and the inequalities that the matrix in (6.19) satisfies: we should speak of the "fundamental inequalities and symmetries of the theory of ordinal maximizing by a consumer," namely[8] that

$$\sum_1^n \sum_1^n z_i x_{ij}(M; \mathbf{p}) z_j < 0 \tag{6.20}$$

for *all* $\mathbf{z}$ *not* proportional to $\mathbf{p}/M$. Hence, $x_{11} < 0$, and so on.

If one must speak of a "fundamental equality," the best single one might be the equality of marginal utility per dollar spent in every use, which Stigler (1965, p. 85) attributes to Gossen and which implies (6.19). In my notation, and with various modern adaptations (such as omitting Gossen's additive-independence), it would become

$$\frac{u_1(\mathbf{x})}{p_1} = \ldots = \frac{u_n(\mathbf{x})}{p_n} = \frac{\sum_1^n x_j u_j(\mathbf{x})}{M} \tag{6.21}$$

But (and this is the view that I would urge on Machlup), (6.21) is fundamental precisely to the degree that it does give us the revealed-preference hypotheses of the matrix of (6.19), implied inequalities of (6.20).

My same point can be made less technically in connection with the supply response of a competitive firm facing unchanged factor prices. If its total cost curve is $C(q)$ and is convex, then almost everywhere the MC equality holds, $p = C'(q)$; this equality is useful to the degree that it provides us with the testable knowledge on supply response, $dq/dp > 0$ or $\Delta q \Delta p \geqslant 0$–a conclusion implied by the fact that $C''(q) > 0$ holds almost everywhere where the above equality holds.

6A-1. Duality and Homotheticity

To save space I shall from now on use mathematics more freely: equations will be numbered by sections. Returning to the one-good industry of Cournot and Marshall, I call attention to one special feature of (6.4) or (6.8) and (6.9) that results from the first-degree homogeneity of $Q(\mathbf{x})$: the function $Y(x_1, x_2, \ldots)$ has *homothetic* contours, whose slopes are constant when the ratios of the xs, as denoted for example by $\mathbf{x}/x_1$, are constant. That is,

$$y_i/y_1 = Y_i(\mathbf{x})/Y_1(\mathbf{x}) \equiv M^i(\mathbf{x}/x_1) \qquad (i = 2, \ldots) \qquad (6A.1.1)$$

It can then be shown that the dual function defined in (6.9.2) must also have homothetic contours, namely

$$x_i/x_1 = X_i(\mathbf{y}) \equiv M^{*i}(\mathbf{y}/y_1) \qquad (i = 2, \ldots) \qquad (6A.1.2)$$

We see this by solving (6A.1.1) uniquely for $\mathbf{x}/x_1$ in terms of $\mathbf{y}/y_1$.

It follows that we are entitled to rewrite $X(\mathbf{y})$ in a canonical form dual to $Y(\mathbf{x}) \equiv Y[Q(\mathbf{x})]$, namely as

$$X(y_1, y_2, \ldots) \equiv X[P(y_1, y_2, \ldots)] \qquad (6A.1.3.1)$$

where again the distinction between brackets and parentheses in $X(\ )$ and $X[\ ]$ is to be noted.

$$X_i(y_1, y_2, \ldots) \equiv X'[P(y_1, y_2, \ldots)]P_i(y_1, y_2, \ldots) \qquad (6A.1.3.2)$$

$$\equiv Q[P(y_1, y_2, \ldots)]P_i(y_1, y_2, \ldots) \qquad (6A.1.3.3)$$

where

$$p = P[q] \equiv X'[q]$$

$$q = P^{-1}[p] \equiv Q[p] \equiv X'[p] \qquad (6A.1.3.4)$$

$$P'[\ ]Q'[\ ] \equiv X''[\ ]Y''[\ ] \equiv 1$$

and where $P(y_1, y_2, \ldots)$ is the *production dual* to $Q(x_1, x_2, \ldots)$, namely the homogeneous-first-degree, concave *minimum-unit-cost-of-production* function, defined by Shephard (1953) and others as

$$P(y_1, y_2, \ldots) \equiv \text{Min}_{x_i} \frac{y_1 x_1 + y_2 x_2 + \ldots}{Q(x_1, x_2, \ldots)} \tag{6A.1.4.1}$$

$$Q(x_1, x_2, \ldots) \equiv \text{Min}_{y_i} \frac{x_1 y_1 + x_2 y_2 + \ldots}{P(y_1, y_2, \ldots)} \tag{6A.1.4.2}$$

$$Q_i(\mathrm{x}) = y_i/p \qquad P_i(\mathrm{y}) = x_i/q \tag{6A.1.4.3}$$

To exploit this production duality within the framework of overall industry duality, we note that (6.9) can be rewritten in a form more symmetric between quantities and prices, (x_j, q) and (y_j, p), namely

$$\text{Max}_{x_i} \left\{ Y[Q(x_1, x_2, \ldots)] - y_1 x_1 - y_2 x_2 - \ldots \right\}$$
$$= -X[P(y_1, y_2, \ldots)] \equiv -\int_{P[q^0]}^{P(\mathrm{y})} Q[p]\, dp \tag{6A.1.5.1}$$

$$\text{Max}_{y_i} \left\{ X[P(y_1, y_2, \ldots)] - x_1 y_1 - x_2 y_2 - \ldots \right\}$$
$$= -Y[Q(x_1, x_2, \ldots)] \tag{6A.1.5.2}$$

where $P[q]$ and $Q[p]$ are the inverse and dual functions already noted in (6A.1.3.4).

Remark: For $n = 1$, and with $Q(x_1) \equiv x_1$, we trivially have in $Y[Q(x_1)] \equiv Y[x_1]$ and $X[P(y_1)] \equiv X[y_1]$, respectively, the area vertically under the demand curve and the negative of the consumer-surplus area measured to the left of the demand curve.

The extremal first-order maximum conditions provide Legendre transformation relations of duality

$$Y[Q(\mathrm{x})] + X[P(\mathrm{y})] \equiv \sum_1^n y_j x_j \tag{6A.1.5.3}$$

for

$$y_i = Y_i(\mathrm{x}) = Y'[Q(\mathrm{x})]\, Q_i(\mathrm{x}) \qquad x_i = X_i(\mathrm{y}) = X'[P(\mathrm{y})]\, P_i(\mathrm{y}) \tag{6A.1.5.4}$$

Also

$$\partial Y[\ ]/\partial\alpha + \partial X[\ ]/\partial\alpha \equiv 0 \tag{6A.1.5.5}$$

if α is a parameter in $Y[Q(\mathbf{x};\alpha);\alpha]$ and $X[P(\mathbf{x};\alpha);\alpha]$.

Since $X_i(\mathbf{y})$ and $Y_i(\mathbf{x})$ are inverse functions, their Jacobians must be inverse matrices. For I, the identity matrix,

$$\begin{aligned} I &= [\partial x_i/\partial y_j]\,[\partial y_i/\partial x_j] \\ &\equiv [X_{ij}(\mathbf{y})]\,[Y_{ij}(\mathbf{x})] \\ &\equiv [X'[P]P_{ij} + X''[P]P_iP_j]\,[Y'[Q]Q_{ij} + Y''[Q]Q_iQ_j] \end{aligned} \tag{6A.1.5.6}$$

where, as indicated in (6A.1.3.4),

$$X''[\ ]\,Y''[\ ] = 1 \tag{6A.1.5.7}$$

for (p, q) equilibrium pairings. Also,

$$[\partial x_i/\partial y_j] \equiv [X_{ij}(\mathbf{y})] \equiv [X_{ij}(\mathbf{y})]^T \tag{6A.1.5.8}$$

and so on; where A^T is the transpose of the matrix A. Of course, in (6A.1.5.7), a similar symmetry holds for $[\partial y_i/\partial x_j]$. In (6A.1.5.6), $[\partial \log x_i/\partial \log y_j]$ and $[\partial \log y_i/\partial \log x_j]$ must also be inverses; but these last dual elasticity matrices, which it is often convenient to write as $[Ex_i/Ey_j]$ and $[Ey_i/Ex_j]$, will obviously not be symmetric.

6A-2. Duality and Elasticities-of-Substitution-or-Complementarity

For $n \geqslant 2$, the Allen (1938, pp. 503-9) *partial elasticities*, $[\sigma_{ij}]$, are useful. Exploiting duality theory, Sato and Koizumi (1973a) give appropriate modification to the related $[s_{ij}]$ definitions suggested in Hicks (1970). In my notation, which uses σ^*_{ij} for the 1973 c_{ij} coefficients, we have the dual families of coefficients:

$$\sigma_{ij}(\mathbf{y}/y_1) = \frac{P(\mathbf{y})P_{ij}(\mathbf{y})}{P_i(\mathbf{y})P_j(\mathbf{y})} = \sigma_{ji}(\mathbf{y}/y_1) \tag{6A.2.1}$$

$$\sigma^*_{ij}(\mathbf{x}/x_1) = \frac{Q(\mathbf{x})Q_{ij}(\mathbf{x})}{Q_i(\mathbf{x})Q_{ij}(\mathbf{x})} = \sigma^*_{ji}(\mathbf{x}/x_1) \tag{6A.2.2}$$

For $n = 2$, it can be shown that $\sigma_{12}(y/y_1)\overset{*}{\sigma}_{12}(x/x_1) = 1$ for equilibrium pairings of $(y/y_1, x/x_1)$. For $n = 3$, Hicks (1970) shows how $[\sigma_{ij}]$ and $[\overset{*}{\sigma}_{ij}]$ can be related.

Earlier, Allen (1938) related his $\sigma_{ij}(y/y_1)$ to the bordered matrices of $Q(x)$ for any n. Sato and Koizumi (1973a, equations 13) relate these coefficients by means of dual bordered determinants.

Here I shall present an alternative procedure, one that avoids bordered determinants and is capable of dealing directly with either the industry problem or with the $[\sigma_{ij}]$ and $[\overset{*}{\sigma}_{ij}]$ relationships for their own sake. My exposition goes as follows:

$$\sigma_{ij}(y/y_1) = [y_j P_{ij}/P_i]\,[y_j P_j/P]^{-1}$$

$$= \left[\frac{\partial \log P_i}{\partial \log y_j}\right] k_j^{-1}$$

$$= \frac{\partial[\log x_i + \log q]}{k_j\,\partial \log y_j} \tag{6A.2.3}$$

by the duality of (6A.1.4.3)

$$= [k_j^{-1} Ex_i/Ey_j] + [(Eq/Ep)(k_j/k_j)]$$

$$= k_j^{-1}(Ex_i Ey_j) + (Eq/Ep) \tag{6A.2.4}$$

$$[Ex_i/Ey_j] = [\sigma_{ij} + (Eq/Ep)]\,k_j$$

Note that (6A.2.4) is precisely the Allen-Robinson relation of (6.17), derived here without explicit inversion of any matrix relations.

In duality's usual two-for-the-price-of-one way, we immediately write down the counterpart of (6A.2.3) and (6A.2.4) as applied to $\overset{*}{\sigma}_{ij}$, namely

$$[Ey_i/Ex_j] = [\overset{*}{\sigma}_{ij} + (Ep/Eq)]\,k_j \tag{6A.2.5}$$

Note that use has been made of the fact that (Ep/Eq) is dual to (Eq/Ep).

Since (6A.2.4) and (6A.2.5) are inverse matrices, our avoiding bordered determinants gives us the following infinity of relations between $[\sigma_{ij}]$ and $[\overset{*}{\sigma}_{ij}]$,

$$[\sigma_{ij}k_j + \lambda k_j]\,[\overset{*}{\sigma}_{ij}k_j + \lambda^{-1}k_j] \underset{\lambda}{\equiv} I \tag{6A.2.6}$$

Since (6A.2.6) holds for any negative λ, it must hold for the simplest case where industry has *unitary* elasticity of demand: $P[q] = a/q$, $Eq/Ep = -1$, Ep/Eq

$= 1/(-1) = -1$. This gives us $n \times n$ unbordered matrices convenient for relating the dual families of elasticities:

$$[(\sigma_{ij} - 1)k_j]\,[(\sigma^*_{ij} - 1)k_j] = I \tag{6A.2.7}$$

We can check by considering the Cobb-Douglas case where $Q(\mathbf{x})$ and $P(\mathbf{y})$ are self-dual. For this case, (6A.2.6) becomes $(-I\lambda)(-I\lambda^{-1}) = I$.

6A-3. Polar Cases of Zero or Infinite Elasticity of Industry Demand

For completeness, one may analyze these limiting cases to relate the above analysis to the bordered matrices of Allen (1938) and Sato and Koizumi (1973a). First, note that we can write down by duality (6.18) and its dual counterpart, each respectively corresponding to $Eq/Ep = 0$ and $Ep/Eq = 0$.

$$(Ex_i/Ey_j)_{\bar{q}} = \sigma_{ij}(\mathrm{y}/y_1)k_j \tag{6A.3.1}$$

$$(Ey_i/Ex_j)_{\bar{p}} = \sigma^*_{ij}(\mathrm{x}/x_1)k_j \tag{6A.3.2}$$

Consider inverse systems relating $(p, x_1, \ldots, x_n)$ and $(q, p_1, \ldots, p_n)$, where I replace **y** by **p** to emphasize that this section deals only with polar cases. If we adopt the convenient convention of writing $x_0 = p$ and $p_0 = q$, we have:

$$\begin{aligned} Q(x_1, \ldots, x_n) &= p_0 \\ x_0 Q_i(x_1, \ldots, x_n) &= p_i \qquad (i = 1, \ldots, n) \end{aligned} \tag{6A.3.3}$$

By duality, the inverse to (6A.3.3) takes the form

$$\begin{aligned} P(p_1, \ldots, p_n) &= x_0 \\ p_0 P_i(p_1, \ldots, p_n) &= x_i \qquad (i = 1, \ldots, n) \end{aligned} \tag{6A.3.4}$$

These pairs of relations make no use of the industry's demand curve, $P[q]$ or $Q[p] = P^{-1}[p]$.

It is easy to verify that the following are line integrals (of *exact* differentials) that are independent of path.

$$\int \sum_0^n p_j dx_j = \int d\left\{x_0 Q(x_1, \ldots, x_n)\right\} \tag{6A.3.5}$$

$$(\partial p_0/\partial x_{0+j}) \equiv Q_{0+j}(\mathbf{x}) \equiv (\partial P_{0+j}/\partial x_0) \qquad (j = 1, \ldots, n)$$
$$(\partial p_{0+i}/\partial x_{0+j}) \equiv Q_{ij}(\mathbf{x}) \equiv (\partial p_{0+j}/\partial x_{0+i}) \qquad (i, j = 1, \ldots, n) \tag{6A.3.6}$$

$$\int \sum_0^n x_j\, dp_j = \int d\left\{p_0 P(p_1, \ldots, p_n)\right\} \tag{6A.3.7}$$

And so on, as in (6A.3.6).
So (6A.3.3) and (6A.3.4) are related dually by a Legendre transformation:

$$\mathrm{Min}_{x_0} \mathrm{Max}_{x_i} \left\{x_0 Q(x_1, \ldots, x_n) - p_0 x_0 - \sum_1^n p_j x_j\right\}$$
$$= p_0 P(p_1, \ldots, p_n) = qP(\mathbf{p}) \tag{6A.3.8}$$

$$\mathrm{Min}_{p_0} \mathrm{Max}_{p_i} \left\{p_0 P(p_1, \ldots, p_n) - x_0 p_0 - \sum_1^n x_j p_j\right\}$$
$$= q_0 Q(x_1, \ldots, x_n) = pQ(\mathbf{x}) \tag{6A.3.9}$$

$$[x_i] = [\partial\left\{p_0 P(p_1, \ldots, p_n)\right\}/\partial p_i] \qquad (i = 0, 1, \ldots, n)$$
$$= \mathrm{grad}\left\{p_0 P(\mathbf{p})\right\}$$
$$[p_i] = [\partial\left\{x_0 Q(x_1, \ldots, x_n)\right\}/\partial x_i] \qquad (i = 0, 1, \ldots, n) \tag{6A.3.10}$$
$$= \mathrm{grad}\left\{x_0 Q(\mathbf{x})\right\}$$

$$\begin{bmatrix} 0 & Q_j \\ Q_i & Q_{ij} \end{bmatrix} \begin{bmatrix} 0 & P_j \\ P_i & P_{ij} \end{bmatrix} \equiv I \tag{6A.3.11}$$

From (6A.3.11) and the definitions of σ_{ij} and σ^*_{ij}, we can derive

$$\begin{bmatrix} 0 & 1 & \ldots & 1 \\ 1 & & & \\ \cdot & & & \\ \cdot & & & \\ \cdot & & \sigma^*_{ij}(\mathbf{x}/x_1) & \\ 1 & & & \end{bmatrix} \begin{bmatrix} 1 & 0 & \ldots & 0 \\ 0 & & & \\ \cdot & & & \\ \cdot & & & \\ \cdot & & k_j \delta_{ij} & \\ 0 & & & \end{bmatrix} \begin{bmatrix} 0 & 1 & \ldots & 1 \\ 1 & & & \\ \cdot & & & \\ \cdot & & & \\ \cdot & & \sigma_{ij}(\mathbf{p}/p_1) & \\ 1 & & & \end{bmatrix} \begin{bmatrix} 1 & 0 & \ldots & 0 \\ 0 & & & \\ \cdot & & & \\ \cdot & & & \\ \cdot & & k_j \delta_{ij} & \\ 0 & & & \end{bmatrix} = I \tag{6A.3.12}$$

These are essentially the bordered-matrix relations of Sato and Koizumi (1973a, equations 13).

Remark: Either of the polar cases, zero clasticity of industry demand or infinite elasticity, results in a degeneracy of determinateness. When $Eq/Ep = 0$, factor inputs $\mathbf{x}$ cannot all be independently inelastic in supply to the industry; even when $(x_1, \ldots, x_n, q)$ are compatibly given to the industry, p is not determinate and neither is the absolute level of $(y_1, \ldots, y_n)$; only price ratios, (y_j/y_1) or (y_j/p) are then determinate. Dually, when industry demand is infinitely elastic (as in a one-product Solow-Douglas economy), all factor prices cannot be in real terms *independently* prescribed to the industry: when $(y_1, \ldots, y_n)$ are prescribed consistent with the factor-price frontier relation, $1 = P(\mathbf{y}/p)$, the scale of q and of $(x_1, \ldots, x_n)$ is indeterminate; only the ratios, (x_j/x_1) and (x_j/q) are then determinate. It is interesting to analyze "mixed" cases where some factor prices are given to the industry, $(y_1, \ldots, y_r)$, $1 \leqslant r < n$; and where the remaining set of factor quantities are given to the industry, $(x_{r+1}, \ldots, x_n)$, $1 \leqslant n - r < n$. Then the remaining variables $(x_1, \ldots, x_r; y_{r+1}, \ldots, y_n : p, q)$ are determinate in all cases, even in the polar cases of zero or infinite industry elasticity. The next section analyzes the case of mixed variables.

6A–4. Factor-supply Responses and Le Chatelier Principle

It is customary to consider more and more inputs as fixed in the short run. As the run is made longer and longer, less and less such inputs are fixed, their prices instead being given as constants to a small industry.

Consider

$$x_i = X_i(y_1, \ldots, y_n) \qquad (i = 1, \ldots, n)$$

with partitioned Jacobian matrix

$$J_n = \begin{bmatrix} \alpha & \beta \\ \beta' & \gamma \end{bmatrix} \tag{6A.4.1}$$

where α is a symmetric negative definite matrix, γ is a $(n - r) \times (n - r)$ negative definite matrix; and where J_n is itself a symmetric negative definite matrix.

Consider the alternative *mixed* set of relations

$$\begin{aligned} x_i &= X^i(y_1, \ldots, y_r; x_{r+1}, \ldots, x_n) \qquad (i = 1, \ldots, r \geqslant 1) \\ &\equiv X_i(y_1, \ldots, y_r; x_{r+1}, \ldots, x_n) \end{aligned} \tag{6A.4.2}$$

$$y_i = X^i(y_1, \ldots, y_r; x_{r+1}, \ldots, x_n) \qquad (i = r+1, \ldots, n > r)$$

$$\equiv -X_i(y_1, \ldots, y_r; x_{r+1}, \ldots, x_n)$$

where $X(y_1, \ldots, y_r; x_{r+1}, \ldots, x_n)$ is an existent "potential" function, whose semicolon serves to distinguish it from $X(y_1, \ldots, y_n)$ of (6.9.2). The Jacobian matrix of the relation of (6A.4.2) can be shown to be expressible in terms of the submatrices of J_n, as in Samuelson (1960), namely as

$$J_r = \begin{bmatrix} \alpha - \beta'\gamma^{-1}\beta & -\gamma^{-1}\beta \\ \beta'\gamma^{-1} & \gamma^{-1} \end{bmatrix}$$

$$= \left[\begin{array}{c|c} I & 0 \\ \hline 0 & -I \end{array}\right] [\partial^2 X(\mathbf{z})/\partial z_i \partial z_j] \qquad (6A.4.3)$$

where $\mathbf{z} = (y_1, \ldots, y_r; x_{r+1}, \ldots, x_n)$.

Since γ is negative definite, so must be γ^{-1}. Therefore, the diagonal coefficients of J_r can be shown to be negative (this even though J_r is not itself a negative definite matrix!). We infer that $\alpha - \beta'\gamma^{-1}\beta$ is negative definite since it is dual to γ^{-1}, which is negative definite. We also infer the symmetry of the terms $+\partial x_i/\partial x_{r+j}$ and $-\partial y_{r+j}/\partial y_i$.

One way of expressing the generalized Le Chatelier principle is to note that a quadratic form made up of α is "more negative (if anything)" than one made up of $\alpha - \beta'\gamma^{-1}\beta$. Hence, as r drops from n to ever lower values in the shorter run, we have

$$(\partial x_i/\partial y_i)_n \leqslant (\partial x_i/\partial y_i)_{n-1} \leqslant \ldots \leqslant (\partial x_i/\partial y_i)_r \qquad (i < r < n)$$

$$(6A.4.4)$$

For $n = 2$, γ is a scalar and $\beta'\gamma^{-1} \equiv (\partial y_2/\partial x_1)_{\bar{x}_2}$ must agree in sign with $(\partial x_2/\partial y_1)_{\bar{y}_2} = \beta' \equiv \beta$, just as was already indicated in connection with the mention in note 6 of the Nelson (1957) unconscious rediscovery of the Robinson (1933) cross-elasticity sign criterion.

6A-5. Effects of Supply Elasticity of Factors

Marshall (1920, pp. 385-7, 853, Note XV) gave the classic analysis of the four conditions that make for elastic demand, Ex_i/Ey_i in our notation. Hicks (1932, 241-6) gave the definitive discussion of these four conditions, correcting

Marshall's erroneous belief that low k_i will always reduce $|Ex_i/Ey_i|$ (even when the elasticity of substitution exceeds $|Eq/Ep|$, which is false).

Our present discussion throws light on the third condition, which points out that $|Ex_i/Ep_i|$ will be greater when the elasticity of supply for x_j is positive and great. $X_1(p_1;x_2)$ in (6A.4.2) corresponds to zero-elastic supply of x_2, while $X_1(p_1, p_2)$ corresponds to infinite-elastic supply of x_2; the Le Chatelier principle thus guarantees the correctness of Marshall's third condition as applied to extreme polar cases. I can now indicate briefly how intermediate degrees of positive supply elasticity in (6.3) will accord with the Marshall-Hicks third rule. (Space does not permit full treatment of the general case where the supply relation for x_2 may have a negative slope, as with "backward-bending" and "forward-falling" supply; nor does the question of *proper* "stability conditions" receive in note 1 of the appendix the full treatment it needs.)

Equation (6.3) made the supply of x_2 to an industry depend only on y_2, and not on other y_j, which does seem rather special. However, this is usually done in the literature and that lends interest to such an assumption.

Let (6.3) be written as a *rising* supply relation

$$y_i = \pi_i + s_i'(x_i) \qquad s_i' > 0 \tag{6A.5.1}$$

Here $(\pi_1, \ldots, \pi_n)$ are parameters of upward-vertical shifts of the respective supply schedules. The integrals of $s_i'(x_i)$ are defined by

$$s_i(x_i) = \int_{x_i^0}^{x_i} s_i'(t)\, dt \tag{6A.5.2}$$

We again have a maximum formulation

$$\begin{aligned} \text{Max}_{x_i} &\left\{Y(x_1, \ldots, x_n) - \sum_1^n \pi_j x_j - \sum_1^n s_j(x_j)\right\} \\ &= Y(x^*) - \sum_1^n \pi_j x_j^* - \sum_1^n s_j(x_j^*) \\ &= -X(\pi_1, \ldots, \pi_n) \end{aligned} \tag{6A.5.3}$$

where the optimal amounts demanded satisfy the gradient relations

$$Y_i(x_1, \ldots, x_n) - s_i'(x_i) = \pi_i \qquad (i = 1, \ldots, n) \tag{6A.5.4}$$

$$x_i = X_i(\pi_1, \ldots, \pi_n) \tag{6A.5.5}$$

For brevity, write $(\partial x_i/\partial \pi_j) = (\dot{x}_{ij})$, a symmetric matrix by virtue of (6A.5.3) through (6A.5.5). Then the linear equations satisfied by $\dot{x}_{ij}$ are seen to be

$$[Y_{ij} - s_j''\delta_{ij}]\,[\dot{x}_{ij}] = I \tag{6A.5.6}$$

where $[\delta_{ij}] = I$.

It is now easy to verify the Marshall-Hicks rule that, "Increased supply elasticity of x_2, which means *lower* positive s_j'', will increase own-demand elasticity for factor 1, $|\partial x_1/\partial \pi_1|$ (or $|\partial x_1/\partial y_1|$ if $s_1'' \equiv 0$)."

Straightforward differentiation of $\dot{x}_{11}$ with respect to s_2'' in (6A.5.6) leads, as in Dorfman, Samuelson, and Solow (1958, p. 254) to

$$\partial(-\dot{x}_{11})/\partial s_2'' = -\dot{x}_{12}\dot{x}_{21} = -\dot{x}_{12}^2 \leqslant 0 \tag{6A.5.7}$$

Here, a change in s_2'' is thought of as a change in the supply slope of the curve going through the same (unchanged) equilibrium point.

Thus, we verify for $n \geqslant 2$ the Marshall-Hicks third rule, in agreement with Sato and Koizumi (1970). Hicks (1932, p. 245) did not mention the fact brought out in (6A.5.7) that the effect can be *zero* in the case where $\dot{x}_{12} = 0$ (as in Mrs. Robinson's case where $\sigma = \eta$). Likewise in Sato and Koizumi (1970, pp. 111-12), $\partial\lambda/\partial e_j > 0$ would seem to be better if written as $\partial\lambda/\partial e_j \geqslant 0$. We may also note that, even when the supply curve is forward-falling[1] with $s_2''(x_2) < 0$, the third rule may still apply. Indeed, even when we have a steeply backward-bending supply curve, with s_2'' near negative infinity and the maximizing formulation vitiated, we may still opportunistically predict that $\dot{x}_{11}$ will be near to that given by $(\partial x_1/\partial y_1)_{\bar{x}_2}$ and that Marshall's third rule is still operative.

6A-6. Machlup's 1935 Discussion

The present notation can clear up any questions left open in Machlup (1935). I follow his Roman numeral sectioning.

I. Here he considers exclusively a single output that, in effect, constitutes the whole (macro- *and* micro-) economy: $q = Q(x_1, x_2) \equiv m^{-1}Q(mx_1, mx_2)$, where x_1 and x_2 are labor and ("homogeneous") "capital," each *inelastic in supply*. Labor's share in total product is $k_1 = x_1Q_1(x_1, x_2)/Q(x_1, x_2)$, with capital's share, $k_2 = 1 - k_1$.

To study how a change in x_1 alone, or in x_1/x_2, alters k_1, his diagram at the bottom of page 204 unfortunately implicitly defines an elasticity of substitution that is a variant of that of Hicks (1932) and of the equivalent definition of Robinson (1933): their coefficient measures the change in $k_1/(1-k_1)$ whereas Machlup's measures the change in k_1 alone. Obviously, when k_1 is unchanged, all three coefficients are unity. Machlup's measure, call it σ_M to contrast it from $\sigma_H = \sigma_R$, has the virtue that sign $[\sigma_M - 1]$ = sign $[\sigma_H - 1]$. Thus, for the Cobb-Douglas case of $x_1^{3/4}x_2^{1/4}$, all three σs are unity; but for the CES family, $[a_1x_1^\gamma + a_2x_2^\gamma]^{1/\gamma}$, $1 > \gamma \neq 0$, σ_H and σ_R are constants equal to $(1-\gamma)^{-1}$, but $\sigma_M - 1$ varies with k_1 and x_2/x_1 although agreeing in sign with $(1-\gamma)^{-1} - 1$. It can be verified that $\sigma_H - 1 = (\sigma_M - 1)[1 + (k_1/k_2)(\sigma_M - 1)]k_1$. Since Machlup never actually proposes using his diagram's σ_M except as a test of when $\sigma_H = 0$, 1, or ∞, I shall ignore its difference with σ_H and the complications thereby encountered in M. Friedman (1936).

II. Under Machlup's one-good economy, we can provide for him his desired relation between labor-demand-elasticity and the elasticity of substitution: when $x_2 = \bar{x}_2$ and $Eq/Ep = -\infty$,

$$(-Ex_1/Ep_1) = \sigma_{12}/(1-k_1) > \sigma_{12} = \sigma_H = \sigma_R \tag{6A.6.1}$$

This agrees with the general formula in Hicks (1932, p. 244), being a special case of it.

Machlup's concern lest σ_H and σ_R be different coefficients can be put completely to rest when $n = 2$ and Q is homogeneous-first-degree.

Robinson (1933, p. 260) was merely meaning to enunciate a correct conclusion:

$$\begin{aligned} \text{sign of } [(-Ex_1/Ey_1) - \sigma_{12}] &= \text{sign of } [\sigma_{12} - (-Eq/Ep)] \\ &= \text{sign of } [Ex_2/Ey_1] \end{aligned} \tag{6A.6.2}$$

Equation (6A.6.2) is clearly implied by Hicks (1963, p. 374, equation 4). It agrees with (6A.6.1) when $(-Eq/Ep) = \infty$. If elasticity of supply of x_2 is allowed to be positive, the equality in (6A.6.1) should be replaced by ">". Again, all this agrees with Hicks (1932, p. 244).

Machlup (1935, p. 205) rightly chides Douglas (1934, p. 133) for liking elasticity of labor demand while disliking elasticity of substitution: after all, (6A.6.1) does relate them.

III. Machlup (1935, p. 206) rightly points out that agreement in sign of $\partial[k_1Q]/\partial(x_1/x_2)$ and $[(Ex_1/Ey_1) - 1]$ provides no "explanation," but is merely a reiteration. He nods, however, in thinking that a large value of σ_{12} in $\sigma_{12}/(1-k_1)$ provides a *deeper* "explanation." Actually, one can invert (6A.6.1) and write $\sigma_{12} = (1-k_1)(-Ex_1/Ey_1)$. It is no better—but, notice, *no worse!*—to "explain" large σ_{12} by large $(-Ex_1/Ey_1)$ than vice versa. Actually, in the relation $y_1/p = Q_1(x_1/x_2, 1) = f(x_1/x_2)$, there is but one *empirical* function involved:

its properties we can point to, but they are their own "explanation" or "description."

IV, V, VI. Here, Machlup relaxes his one-product assumption. He considers in a vague way many products and the *intercommodity* substitutions that an increase in total x_1 will generate when $\bar{x}_2$ is constant.

To illustrate Machlup's insistence on intercommodity substitution, consider the following special case of Samuelson (1968, Part II). Three goods, corn, cotton, and ballet, are produced by labor and land. (Avoid "capital" to avoid its extraneous complications.) Cobb-Douglas functions characterize each industry: one-third corn cost *always* goes to wages; two-thirds cotton cost goes to wages; one hundred per cent of ballet costs goes to wages. Now suppose everyone spends equal thirds of income on each of the three goods.

What will a Kuznets observe of this "macro" economy? *Always* two-thirds of national income goes to wages and one-third to land rent.[2] It is *precisely as if* a Solow-Douglas production function holds for the macroeconomy—$\bar{q} = (\Sigma x_1)^{2/3}(\Sigma x_2)^{1/3}$.

Robinson (1936), Lerner (1936), and Hicks are correct to point out to Machlup that their *formal* σ measures—but now applied to some *aggregate* production function—still serve to show how aggregate wage share changes. But Machlup is right to insist, as Hicks (1963, p. 298) agreed, that the relevant coefficient of the aggregate function is a *complicated* function of both *intra*- and *inter*commodity substitutions.

We see this best when we leave Cobb-Douglas production functions behind. Suppose labor and land in *fixed proportions* produce the goods: 1 labor and 2 land for each 1 corn; 2 labor and 1 land for 1 cotton; 1 labor and 0 land for 1 ballet. Again, everyone spends one-third on each good. Then, for fixed totals of labor and land, $\Sigma x_1 = L$ and $\Sigma x_2 = T$, *everything* is determinate (relative shares, relative prices, quantities, etc.).

Thus, begin with 300 labor and 150 land. It can be shown that 50 labor and 100 land produce 50 corn; 100 labor and 50 land produce 50 cotton; 150 labor produce 150 ballets. Each corn and each cotton is three times as dear as each ballet. Again, what Kuznets *initially* observes is two-thirds to wages and one-third to rents.

But now increase the labor supply—say from 300 to 301 or to 400 or to 3 million. To get it all "absorbed," Machlup correctly insists that *only* intercommodity substitutions can do the trick when technical substitutability is zero. And here it can do the trick!

Higher L/T means lower Wage/Rent, W/R. It means cheapening of ballet most; but, also, some cheapening of cotton relative to corn. All the relatively labor-using goods have their physical demands expanded: when W/R falls enough, the new equilibrium is achieved. Note that Kuznets records a *drop* in the aggregate share of labor $\bar{\alpha}$. Evidently the *overall* $\bar{\sigma}$ is less than one.[3] (Why does $\bar{\alpha}$

drop? Why is $\bar{\sigma} < 1$? Because lowered W/R lowers α_j for corn, cotton, and all industries using both factors: hence $(\alpha_1 + \alpha_2 + \alpha_3)/3$ falls.)

The reader can verify that increasing T/L, from 150/300 to 0.51 or to 1 or to 3 will lower R/W and land-rent's share. Indeed, when land is more than twice labor (which is the maximum ratio used in *any* industry), land becomes redundant in supply and a free good with zero share in income. Again, $\bar{\sigma} < 1$.

My assumption of uniform-homothetic tastes is needed if I am to reduce Machlup's general equilibrium to the case of an aggregate production function for all of society. But, in general, my assumption is too strong a one for realistic economic theory. Machlup would be quite right to insist that general equilibrium is more complicated than in this model.

VII. This leads to, and justifies, Machlup's questioning the necessary symmetry, in qualitative sign or algebraic quantity, of the effect on factor shares of an increase in labor or an increase in land (the *other* factor in my exposition).

Lerner (1936) never met Machlup's valid point. Instead Lerner concentrated on a banality: any arc elasticity between A and B, call it $(\log a - \log b)/(\log \alpha - \log \beta)$ is of course the same as between B and A; we need only reverse signs consistently, or work with instantaneous derivatives $d \log t/d \log \theta$ and not care about the direction in which the slope is traversed. What Lerner never faced up to was the fact that, (1) once we leave the two-input first-degree-homogeneous case, or (2) increase the number of goods and number of people with different tastes, (3) we no longer end up with a *single* relation between factor-price and factor-quantity ratios and (4) we certainly can not any longer calculate the change in $\bar{\alpha}_1$ from a coefficient definable only along an (one!) isoquant.

Thus, suppose we find W/R is a function of total labor and total land and *not* of their ratio. The *single* curve relating W/R and L/T along which Lerner purports to measure Marshallian elasticity simply does not exist. So, Lerner ought to have agreed with Machlup's point that $\partial\bar{\alpha}/\partial L$ and $\partial(1 - \bar{\alpha})/\partial T$ need not even be of the same sign.

VIII. Let me add that when one comes to generalize σ to $(\sigma_1, \sigma_2, \ldots, \sigma_n)$ in the n-factor case, as in Samuelson (1968, Part I), one confirms Machlup's denial that $\sigma_1 = \sigma_2 = \ldots = \sigma_n$ necessarily.[4]

What Schumpeter would call the general "vision" of Machlup's 1935 article has been seen to be fully vindicated by the present investigation.

Notes

1. Strictly speaking, if the industry's demand price, $p = P[q]$, is measured in $\$/q$, then the $Y[q]$ of (6.8) will be measured in \$. The "real" meaning of such \$ will depend upon what Cournot-Marshall presuppose in their partial equilibrium

analysis. My own taste is for not defending partial equilibrium, but for reaching past it toward a more general equilibrium.

2. There is no single standard notation. Hicks (1932, 1963, 1970) uses $(a, b, \ldots; p_a, p_b, \ldots; x, p_x, \ldots)$ or $(a_1, a_2, \ldots; p_1, p_2, \ldots; x, p_x, \ldots)$ where I here use $(x_1, x_2, \ldots; y_1, y_2, \ldots; q, p)$. Using capital letters to denote a function, as in $q = Q(x_1, x_2, \ldots)$, I use subscripts in $Q_i(\ )$ and $Q_{ij}(\ )$ to represent $\partial Q(x_1, x_2, \ldots)/\partial x_i$ and $\partial^2 Q(x_1, x_2, \ldots)/\partial x_i \partial x_j$; for brevity, I sometimes write $Q(x_1, x_2, \ldots)$ as $Q(\mathbf{x})$, boldface representing vectors or matrices. The careful use of brackets, as against parentheses, rules out ambiguity in expressions such as $Y(x_1, x_2, \ldots) \equiv Y[Q(x_1, x_2, \ldots)]$ and $q = Q[p] \equiv Q[P(\mathbf{y})]$, or $Y_i(\mathbf{x}) \equiv Y'[Q(\mathbf{x})]\, Q_i(\mathbf{x})$. With good notation, one is able to write $y_i = Y_i(x_1, x_2, \ldots)$ and their inverse functions $x_i = X_i(y_1, y_2, \ldots)$ and, at equilibrium, $[X_{ij}(\mathbf{y})]^{-1} = [Y_{ij}(\mathbf{x})] \equiv [Y_{ji}(\mathbf{x})]$. Elasticities can be denoted by $Ep/Eq = d \log P / d \log q$, or $Ex_i/Ey_j = y_j X_{ij}(\mathbf{y})/X_i(\mathbf{y})$. Thus Ez is short for $dz/z = d \log z$ or for $\partial z/z$.

Warning: my (x_j) variables are *industry* input totals, not a firm's; my (y_j) variables are input prices, presumably in \$, and not real prices relative to the industry's p as numeraire. My demand relations do not hold industry q constant; nor do they assume infinite elasticity of industry demand such as would keep its price unchanged; these limiting poles can be approximated as I make the industry's elasticity of demand become almost 0 or almost infinite.

3. The attentive reader will realize that, if any firm were free to imitate the constant-returns $Q(\mathbf{x})$, entry would occur to deprive any one firm of its monopoly possession of the industry's demand curve: the only final industry equilibrium would be the competitive industry solution given by (6.4) rather than (6.5); the indeterminateness of interindustry allocation among zero-profit firms is of no importance, contrary to the apprehensions of Sraffa (1926), Kaldor (1934), and other post-Marshallian worriers. To make the present formal point, suppose entry is legally closed.

4. For $n = 2$, Hicks (1932, p. 244) had derived this result: in his notation, it would read, $-\lambda = \kappa(-\eta) + (1 - \kappa)(-\sigma) < 0$. To prove this for $n = 3$, Hicks (1963, 1970) uses the trick that inputs (2, 3) can be made into a composite single (Hicksian) input if their relative prices are frozen: and so $n = 2$ arguments suffice. Allen (1938, p. 508) gives formulas for this result for any n, utilizing symmetric bordered determinants and quasi-concavity conditions implied on them; and for cross-elasticities, Allen generalizes to $n \geqslant 2$ the Robinson-Nelson criteria about to come, namely replacing $\eta \gtrless \sigma$ by $\eta \gtrless \sigma_{ij}$.

5. Curiously, Hicks (1932, 1963, 1970) and later writers put no stress on these reciprocity conditions (which are *not* for any conscious firm decision maker). Perhaps the use of overesteemed Ex_1/Ey_j elasticities deflected attention from symmetry conditions. Allen (1938) gives formal results that point in the desired direction. And actually, if anyone had commented on the symmetry, $\partial\{P[\ ]Q(\ )\}/\partial x_i \equiv \partial\{P[\ ]Q(\ )\}/\partial x_j$, so that $\int \Sigma y_j dx_j$ is an exact line integral independent of the path that equilibrium moves along between endpoints,

the point would have been obvious without the industry maximand or any bordered matrices.

6. Here, in present notation, is a demonstration that Nelson's ratio of elasticities is precisely Hicks's elasticity of substitution,

$$AVC = \bar{y}_1 x_1 / Q(x_1, \bar{x}_2) \qquad MC = \bar{y}_1 \frac{\partial x_1}{\partial q} = \bar{y}_1 / Q_1(x_1, \bar{x}_2)$$

$$\frac{\text{Elas. } AVC}{\text{Elas. } MC} = \frac{[\partial \{\ln \bar{y}_1 + \ln x_1 - \ln Q(x_1, \bar{x}_2)\} / \partial \log x_1]}{[\partial \{\ln \bar{y}_1 - \ln Q_1(x_1, \bar{x}_2)\} / \partial \log x_1]} \frac{[\partial \log x_1 / \partial \log q]}{[\partial \log x_1 / \partial \log q]}$$

$$= \frac{1 - x_1 Q_1 Q^{-1}}{-x_1 Q_{11} Q^{-1}} = \frac{x_2 Q_2 Q^{-1}}{x_2 Q_{12} Q_1^{-1}}$$

using Euler's theorems

$$= \frac{Q_1 Q_2}{Q\, Q_{12}} = \sigma \text{ of } 1932\text{-}3 \qquad\qquad Q.E.D.$$

It is easy to show that $(\partial x_2 / \partial y_1)$ with y_2 constant, Robinson's object of study, must for $n = 2$ have exactly the same algebraic sign as $(\partial y_2 / \partial y_1)$ with x_2 constant: one has only to apply the algebra of Samuelson (1960), or of (6A.4.3) in the appendix to this chapter.

7. The explanatory emptiness of taxonomic descriptions in terms of elasticity and elasticity-of-substitution coefficients was already forcefully argued in Marion E. Crawford's 1937 Radcliffe undergraduate honors thesis on the elasticity of substitution. A terse reprise of this truth reappears in Samuelson (1974).

8. Note that my quarrel with Hicks's language in no way demeans his accomplishment, but rather spotlights its true magnificence. For $n = 2$, the standard textbook case, the sole content of preference theory can be summed up by the two-variable demand function, $x_1 = D^1(P_1/M, P_2/M)$, which must be (a) nonnegative, (b) as also must be $1 - (p_1/M)D^1(p_1/M, p_2/M)$; then the *only* other requirement, stemming from $x_{11}(\;) < 0$, is (c) that $[\partial \log x_1 / \partial \log p_1](1 - k_1) < k_1(\partial \log x_1 / \partial \log p_2)$. How many students know this? How many professors?

Notes

1. Some element of *monopoly* is probably present *outside* this industry if x_2 is supplied to it along a forward-falling supply curve. The case of a back-

ward-bending negatively sloped supply curve for x_2 could arise when owners of x_2 are choosing between it and leisure in a budget-constraint maximization problem offstage. If $0 > \partial x_2/\partial y_2 \gg -1$ along a steeply backward-bending supply curve, $s_2''(x_2)$ will be so greatly negative as to make $\partial^2 \{Y(x_1, x_2) - y_1 x_1 - x_2 - s_2(x_2)\}/\partial x_2^2 > 0$, in violation of the industry's macimum achievement. Hence, $\dot{x}_{22} = \partial x_2/\partial \pi_2$ would be "perversely" positive, "in violation" of some presumed (dynamic?) stability conditions. Yet Marshall's third rule would apply! When x_2's supply curve is negatively sloped, somewhere between the case of a gently forward-falling curve and the case of a steeply backward-bending one, we reach the critical point where $|Y_{ij} - s_j'' \delta_{ij}|$ changes sign, making $[\partial x_i/\partial \pi_j]$ all go through infinity and change sign. (Remark: When a change in s_2'' is regarded as changing $\partial x_1/\partial y_1$, the exact meaning is murky; one useful interpretation is to imagine the supply curve of x_2 pivoting ever more steeply through the same previous equilibrium point (x_2, y_2), and then asking what this does to the slope of the demand curve for x_1 at the same old equilibrium point (x_1, y_1). The literature leaves all this in a hazy state.)

2. Explanation: $[(1/3) + (2/3) + (1)]/3 = 2/3$. The problem is only a bit more complicated if wages get spent in three fixed fractions different from rent's three fixed fractions. Thus, if wages are spent only on corn and land rents only on ballet, Kuznets will observe that three-fifths of national income always goes to wages (but now with no cotton produced). Let the wage shares in the industries be $(\alpha_1, \alpha_2, \alpha_3)$; the expenditure fractions of wage earners and retainers be $(\omega_1, \omega_2, \omega_3)$ and (ρ_1, ρ_2, ρ_3). Then the aggregate wage share, $\bar{\alpha}$, is given by $\Sigma_1^3 \rho_j \alpha_j / [1 - \Sigma_1^3 \omega_j \alpha_j + \Sigma_1^3 \rho_j \alpha_j] = [0 + 0 + 1]/[1 - 1/3 + 1] = 3/5$.

3. See Samuelson (1968, Equation 20) for the definitions of the *aggregate* production function, $\bar{q} = \bar{Q}(L, T)$ that Kuznets will find himself observing and for which Hicks could compute his $\bar{\sigma}$. Warning: Only if everyone has uniform homothetic tastes (albeit not necessarily of fixed-fractional-expenditure type) are we assured that such a nicely defined function exists. To prove it does, suppose as in Samuelson (1968, Part II), there are M industries, each with first-degree homogeneous, concave production functions: $q^m = Q^m(x_1^m, \ldots, x_n^m)$. Then subject to $\Sigma_1^M x_j^m \leqslant x_j$, maximize $u[q^1, \ldots, q^M] \equiv u[Q^1(\ ), \ldots, Q^M(\ )]$ and call the result $u(x_1, \ldots, x_n)$. If $u[\ ]$ is first-degree homogeneous and concave, this aggregate $u(x_1, \ldots, x_n)$ has *all* the properties of a one-good neoclassical production function, being first-degree homogeneous and concave. (Moreover, it may be everywhere differentiable even when the constituent $Q^m(\ )$ functions are not.) See Akerlof and Burmeister (1970) for a needed correction of my slip in Samuelson (1968, p. 475) where I wrongly argued that differences in industry factor intensities will augment $u(x_1, x_2)$'s overall $\bar{\sigma}$: when $Q^m(x^m)$s have greater σs than does $u[q^1, q^2]$, factor-intensity differences lower $\bar{\sigma}$, as is shown in R. Jones (1965) and Dixit (1976, p. 129). My pen also slipped in claiming that $\bar{\sigma} \geqslant \text{Min}\,[\sigma^1, \sigma^2]$ and σ of $u[\ ]$, as in note 2 of the chapter proper.

4. Robinson (1933, pp. 149–50) scolds Machlup for saying that, hoarding of money aside, "the elasticity of demand for all commodities together . . . is unity." One understands her dislike for such a Quantity-Theory hypothesis, and her defense of Hicks's infinite-elasticity of real demand for a one-good macro-economy. Still, as Marshall (1923, Appendix C) suggested, Machlup's case is a possible case. Thus, apply it and ask how, with land fixed and *money* wage rate prescribed, the demand for labor behaves. Then, as in my (6A.2.7) but with $n = 2$ and $x_2 = \bar{x}_2$, the Hicks-Robinson algebra could be validly applied by Machlup. (Example: with pq a constant and WL a constant fraction of it, the demand for labor has unitary elasticity; this is just what Robinson's own relation (6A.6.2) asserts when $\sigma = \eta = 1$, so that $(-Ex_1/y_1)$ also equals 1.) Robinson does not provide argument to deny this, and there is none; what she can argue is that the case is not of much actual interest in a depression decade.

In VIII, Machlup rightly indicates, as did Shove's 1933 *Economic Journal* review of Hicks (1932), reproduced in Hicks (1963, pp. 249-67), that "capital" is not just a second factor parallel to "labor."

References

Akerlof, G.A., and E. Burmeister. 1970. "Substitution in a General Equilibrium Framework," *Journal of Economic Theory* 2, pp. 411–422.

Allen, R.G.D. 1938. *Mathematical Analysis for Economists.* (London: Macmillan).

Champernowne, D.G. 1935. "A Mathematical Note on Substitution," *Economic Journal* 45, pp. 246-258.

Crawford, M.S. 1937. *A Mathematical Reconsideration of the Elasticity of Substitution.* Undergraduate Honors Thesis, Radcliffe College.

Diewert, E.W. 1971a. "An Application of the Shephard Duality Theorem: A Generalized Leontief Production Function," *Journal of Political Economy* 63, pp. 481-507.

——. 1971b. "A Note on the Elasticity of Derived Demand in the N-Factor Case," *Economica* 38, pp. 192-198.

Dixit, A.K. 1976. *The Theory of Equilibrium Growth.* (London: Oxford University Press).

Dorfman, R., P.A. Samuelson, and R.M. Solow. 1958. *Linear Programming and Economic Analysis.* (New York: McGraw-Hill).

Douglas, P.H. 1934. *Theory of Wages.* (New York: Macmillan; and Kelley & Millman).

Friedman, M. 1936. "Further Notes on Elasticity of Substitution. I. Note on Dr. Machlup's Article," *Review of Economic Studies* 3, pp. 147-148.

Hicks, J.R. 1932. *Theory of Wages* (1st edition). (London: Macmillan), 2nd edition, 1963.

——. 1933. "A Note on Mr. Kahn's Paper [Elasticity of Substitution]," *Review of Economic Studies* 1, pp. 78-80.
——. 1934. "A Note on the Elasticity of Supply," *Review of Economic Studies* 2, pp. 31-37.
——. 1936. "Distribution and Economic Progress, A Revised Version," *Review of Economic Studies* 4, pp. 1-12.
——. 1939. *Value and Capital.* (London: Oxford University Press).
——. 1963. *Theory of Wages* (2nd edition). (London: Macmillan), 1st edition, 1932.
——. 1970. "Elasticity of Substitution Again: Substitutes and Complements," *Oxford Economic Papers* 22, No. 3, pp. 289-296.
Jones, R. 1965. "The Structure of Simple General Equilibrium Models," *The Journal of Political Economy* LXXIII, December, pp. 557-572.
Kahn, R.F. 1933. "The Elasticity of Substitution and the Relative Share of a Factor," *Review of Economic Studies* 1, pp. 72-77.
——. 1935. "Two Applications of the Concept of Elasticity of Substitution," *Economic Journal* 45, pp. 242-245.
Kaldor, N. 1934. "Equilibrium of the Firm," *Economic Journal* 44, pp. 60-76.
Lerner, A.P. 1933. "Notes on Elasticity of Substitution. II. The Diagrammatical Representation," *Review of Economic Studies* 1, pp. 68-70.
——. 1934. "Notes on the Elasticity of Substitution. II [Reply to L. Tarshis]," *Review of Economic Studies* 1, pp. 147-148.
——. 1936. "Further Notes on Elasticity of Substitution," *Review of Economic Studies* 3, pp. 150-151.
McFadden, D. 1963. "Constant Elasticity of Substitution Production Functions," *Review of Economic Studies* 30, pp. 73-83.
Machlup, F. 1935. "The Commonsense of the Elasticity of Substitution," *Review of Economic Studies* 2, pp. 202-213. (Reproduced as chapter 6 in *Selected Economic Writings of Fritz Machlup,* 1976. (New York: New York University Press), pp. 119-130.)
——. 1936. "Further Notes on Elasticity of Substitution. IV. Reply," *Review of Economic Studies* 3, pp. 151-152.
——. 1976. *Selected Economic Writings of Fritz Machlup,* edited by George Bitros. (New York: New York University Press).
Marshall, A. 1920. *Principles of Economics* (8th edition). (London: Macmillan).
——. 1923. *Money Credit and Commerce.* (London: Macmillan).
Meade, J.E. 1934. "Elasticity of Substitution and the Elasticity of Demand for One Factor of Production," *Review of Economic Studies* 1, pp. 152-153.
Mosak, J.L. 1938. "Interrelations of Production, Price, and Derived Demand," *Journal of Political Economy* 46, pp. 761-787.
Mundlak, Y. 1968. "Elasticities of Substitution and the Theory of Derived Demand," *Review of Economic Studies* 35, pp. 225-236.
Muth, R. 1964. "The Derived Demand Curve for a Productive Factor and the Industry Supply Curve," *Oxford Economic Papers* 16, No. 2, pp. 221-234.

Nelson, R.R. 1957. "Increased Rents from Increased Costs: A Paradox of Value Theory," *Journal of Political Economy* 65, pp. 387-393.

Pigou, A.C. 1934. "The Elasticity of Substitution," *Economic Journal* 44, pp. 232-241.

Robinson, J. 1933. *Economics of Imperfect Competition.* (London: Macmillan), chapter 22.

——. 1936. "Dr. Machlup's Commonsense of the Elasticity of Substitution," *Review of Economic Studies* 3, pp. 148-150.

Sakai, Y. 1975. "Substitution and Expansion Effects in the Theory of the Firm: New Results in an Old Framework," *Seikei Ronso* 25, pp. 95-118.

Samuelson, P.A. 1947. *Foundations of Economic Analysis.* Cambridge, Mass.: Harvard University Press).

——. 1953. "Prices of Factors and Goods in General Equilibrium," *Review of Economic Studies* 21, pp. 1-20. (Reproduced as chapter 70 in *Collected Scientific Papers,* Vol. II., 1966.)

——. 1960. "Structure of a Minimum Equilibrium System," in Ralph W. Pfouts, ed., *Essays in Economics and Econometrics: A Volume in Honor of Harold Hotelling.* (Chapel Hill: University of North Carolina Press), pp. 1-33. (Reproduced as chapter 41 in *Collected Scientific Papers,* Vol. I, 1966.)

——. 1962. "Parable and Realism in Capital Theory: The Surrogate Production Function," *Review of Economic Studies* 29, pp. 193-206. (Reproduced as chapter 28 in *Collected Scientific Papers,* Vol. I, 1966.)

——. 1965. "Using Full Duality to Show That Simultaneously Additive Price and Indirect Utilities Implies Unitary Price Elasticity of Demand," *Econometrica* 33, pp. 781-796. (Reproduced as chapter 134 in *Collected Scientific Papers,* Vol. III, 1972.)

——. *Collected Scientific Papers of Paul A. Samuelson.* Vol. I and II, edited by Joseph E. Stiglitz, 1966; Vol. III, edited by Robert C. Merton, 1972; Vol. IV, edited by Hiroaki Nagatani and Kate Crowley, 1977. (Cambridge, Mass.: MIT Press).

——. 1968. "Two Generalizations of the Elasticity of Substitution," in J.N. Wolfe, ed., *Value, Capital and Growth: Papers in Honor of Sir John Hicks.* (Edinburgh: Edinburgh University Press), pp. 467-480. (Reproduced as chapter 133 in *Collected Scientific Papers,* Vol. III, 1972.)

——. 1971. "Maximum Principles in Analytical Economics," (Nobel Memorial Lecture, Stockholm, 1970) in *Les Prix Nobel en 1970.* (Stockholm: Nobel Foundation), pp. 273-288. (Reproduced in *American Economic Review* 62, 1972, pp. 249-262; also reproduced as chapter 130 in *Collected Scientific Papers,* Vol. III, 1972.)

——. 1972. "Unification Theorem for the Two Basic Dualities of Homothetic Theory," *Proceedings of the National Academy of Science* 69, pp. 2673-2674. (Reproduced as chapter 4 in *Collected Scientific Papers,* Vol. IV, 1977.)

——. 1973. "Relative Shares and Elasticities Simplified: Comment," *American*

Economic Review 63, pp. 770-771. (Reproduced as chapter 5 in *Collected Scientific Papers,* Vol. IV, 1977.)

——. 1974. "Complementarity, An Essay on the 40th Anniversary of the Hicks-Allen Revolution in Demand Theory," *Journal of Economic Literature* 12, pp. 1255-1289. (Reproduced as chapter 1 in *Collected Scientific Papers,* Vol. IV, 1977.)

Samuelson, P.A., and S. Swamy. 1974. "Invariant Economic Index Numbers and Canonical Duality: Survey and Synthesis," *American Economic Review* 64, pp. 566-593. (Reproduced as chapter 2 in *Collected Scientific Papers,* Vol. IV, 1977.)

Sato, R. and T. Koizumi. 1970. "Substitutability, Complementarity and the Theory of Derived Demand," *Review of Economic Studies* 37, pp. 107-118.

——. 1973a. "On the Elasticity of Substitution and Complementarity," *Oxford Economic Papers* No. 25.

——. 1973b. "Relative Shares and Elasticities Simplified: Reply," *American Economic Review* 63, p. 772.

Shephard, R.W. 1953, 1970. *Theory of Cost and Production Functions.* (Princeton, N.J.: Princeton University Press).

Shove, G.F. 1933. Book review of J.R. Hicks, *The Theory of Wages* in *Economic Journal* 43, pp. 460–472. (Reproduced in Hicks (1932), pp. 249-267.)

Silberberg, E. 1971. "The Le Chatelier Principle as a Corollary to a Generalized Envelope Theorem," *Journal of Economic Theory* 3, pp. 146-155.

Sraffa, P. 1926. "The Laws of Returns under Competitive Conditions," *Economic Journal* 37, pp. 535-550. (Reproduced as chapter 9 in G.J. Stigler and K.E. Boulding, eds., *Readings in Price Theory.* Chicago: Richard D. Irwin, 1952.)

Stigler, G.J. 1965. *Essays in the History of Economics.* (Chicago: University of Chicago Press).

Sweezy, P.M. 1933. "Notes on Elasticity of Substitution. I. A Note on Relative Shares," *Review of Economic Studies* 1, pp. 67-70.

Tarshis, L. 1933. "Notes on the Elasticity of Substitution. I," *Review of Economic Studies* 1, pp. 144-147.

Uzawa, H. 1962. "Production Functions with Constant Elasticities of Substitution," *Review of Economic Studies* 29, pp. 291-299.

Vázquez, A., and T. Puu. 1973. "Factor Demand Functions in Long-Run Equilibrium," *Revista Internazionale di Scienze Economiche e Commerciale* 20, pp. 1209-1228.

St. Petersburg Paradoxes: Defanged, Dissected, and Historically Described

By PAUL A. SAMUELSON

Massachusetts Institute of Technology

I owe thanks to the National Science Foundation for financial aid and to Kate Crowley for valuable editorial assistance.

THE St. Petersburg paradox constitutes a fascinating chapter in the history of ideas. What other subject can link together Edward Gibbon and the father-in-law of Thomas Mann? Or can, in the conceit of Maynard Keynes, link together the Bernoullis and Darwin?[1]

Substantively, the Petersburg paradox served as a dramatic paradigm, alerting people to the fact that their utility of gain exceeded their utility of equivalent money lost. As a byproduct, the discussion generated an interest of its own: the idiocies it evoked from various writers are scarcely less fascinating than the lasting insights. Yet when I came recently to review the matter, I found to my surprise that no one seems to have provided anything like a complete survey of the subject. The standard sources provide us with tantalizing glimpses: the useful 1954 English translation of the classic Latin work of Daniel Bernoulli [4, 1738]; the references and discussion in histories of probability, such as those of Isaac Todhunter [39, 1865] and Leonid Maistrov [17, 1966]; the selective but perspicacious accounts in the work of Keynes [15, 1921] and George Stigler [37, 1950]; the new lease on life given to the subject by Karl Menger [19, 1934] with the discussion there of Super-Petersburg paradoxes creatable when the utility function is unbounded; the recent observation by Kenneth Arrow [2, 1971] that not all stochastic processes can be ordered by the expected value of their utility outcomes when such Mengerian super-paradoxes are allowed to exist. The number of post-Mengerian writers is large, including L. S. Shapley [36, 1972], D. L. Brito [6, 1975], Samuelson [28, 1960], Robert J. Aumann [3, 1975], and many others.

Given my own limited linguistic abilities and leisure time, I have not been able to provide anything like a definitive survey, one that checks back on and quotes copiously from the original sources. After all, the list of writers connected with the St. Petersburg paradox reads like a veritable who's who in probability and the social sciences. Here is but a sample: Nicholas Bernoulli (1687–1759), Montmort (1678–1719), Gabriel Cramer (1704–

[1] "The continuity and oneness of modern European thought may be illustrated, if such things amuse the reader, by the reflection that Condorcet derived from Bernoulli, that Godwin was inspired by Condorcet, that Malthus was stimulated by Godwin's folly into stating his famous doctrine, and that from the reading of Malthus on *Population* Darwin received his earliest impulse" [15, Keynes, 1921, p. 83, n. 1].

1752), Daniel Bernoulli (1700–1782), Buffon (1707–1788), Condorcet (1743–1794), d'Alembert (1717–1783), Euler (1707–1783), Poisson (1781–1840), A. A. Cournot (1801–1877), Bertrand (1822–1900), J. M. Keynes (1883–1946), and Karl Menger (1902–).

As a compromise, I have provided first a general critical account of the Petersburg problem. This reflects my original debunking attitude, before I was seduced by the antiquarian charms of the problem. Subject to the irreducible difficulties of the topic's mathematical technicalities, this bird's-eye view can provide a self-contained description of the essentials. Then, in the numbered sections of the *Historical Notes,* I provide a self-contained chronology of the subject, not hesitating to offer my own critical remarks and to mention interesting digressions.

Serious scholars will not be satisfied to rely on the secondary rather than primary sources, particularly since experience confirms that what seem to be foolish views in brief and selective quotations from an author often appear less bizarre in their full context.

I. *The Ordinary*[2] *St. Petersburg Paradox*

"The dollar I win is not as worthwhile to me as the dollar I lose, and that is why I will shun a bet at 'fair' odds (and, of course, at 'unfair' odds)." This is how the Peters and Pauls of the world explain to themselves why they behave as they do, make risk-averse decisions as if to maximize in stochastic situations the expected value of *a strictly concave* ["utility"] *function of money wealth* rather than to maximize the expected value of *money wealth* itself.

Although a Watsonian behaviorist or a revealed-preference zealot might consider the gloss redundant, the "explanation" provided is harmlessly valid. From the now-perceived axiom that Paul will avoid finite fair bets, he can *deduce* that his utility function is not linear, and that he will not pay as high a price to play the *compound* risky games of gain that their straightforward mathematical-expectation-of-money-gains would require.

The St. Petersburg paradox refers to only one such compound game, a dramatic and even over-dramatic case. Here are its essentials:

> Peter offers to let Paul toss a fair coin an indefinite number of times, paying him 2 ducats if heads first come up at the first toss, 4 ducats if it first comes up at the second toss, . . . , 2^i ducats for heads first coming up at the ith toss, . . . , and so forth *ad infinitum.* Hence, if Paul has linear utility, he could be made to pay for the "fair price of playing the game" the value of the mathematical expectation of the gains
>
> $$E\{2^i\} = \frac{1}{2}2 + \frac{1}{4}4 + \ldots + \frac{2^k}{2^k} + \ldots \qquad (1)$$
> $$= (1 + 1 + 1 + \ldots) = \infty$$

According to the mythological history of ideas, Paul, only *after* recoiling in horror at the thought that he would be willing to pay such an infinity, learns about himself that he has strictly-concave utility and will not accept small fair bets. This reverses the first argument given here: from behavior when faced with the compound Petersburg game, people learn about how they will react to simple games (or wagers or investments).

[2] By contrast to the "ordinary" paradox of 1713–38, there is the Super-Petersburg paradox of Menger [19, 1934], in which the gains at the ith toss grow enough faster than 2^i to make expected utility infinite when utility is unbounded—even though it is strictly concave. This important Menger addition to the literature receives parallel treatment in later sections.

An English translation of Menger's classic 1934 article appears in the 1967 Morgenstern *Festschrift,* along with a few new thoughts by Karl Menger. My specific page citations will be to the English Menger [20, 1967] rather than to the German Menger [19, 1934].

The example, one hesitates to call it a paradox, is over-dramatic in that most Pauls might have been spared the notion of a game with an *infinite* number of plays (whatever that is supposed to mean in a real life situation). To those who regard infinity as just a way of talking about limit relations in which something finite gets big and bigger, the paradigm could be reformulated.

> Peter offers to let Paul toss a fair coin n times, n an integer specified in advance. If heads never comes up in the n tosses, Paul gets nothing. If it comes up for the first time at toss i, $1 \leq i \leq n$, Peter pays Paul 2^i. Paul, asking himself whether he would pay 10^{23} ducats when $n = 10^{23}$, finds on reflection that he never would pay so gigantic a sum. So, he clarifies in his mind that, even for $n = 1$, he would not pay the expected-money-gain of n to play with Peter (and, incidentally, that he would not change places with Peter and himself offer the house odds on the game!).

Thus the ordinary person infers that his marginal utility is essentially a decreasing function of his wealth.

The argument is roundabout, but can be made into an acceptable syllogism, and I have no quarrel with it.

A different line of reasoning, which is less to my liking, runs as follows:

> Because of the need to avoid the St. Petersburg paradox, it is necessary (or plausible? or desirable?) in axiomatizing stochastic choice theory to assume the axiom that people do not (cannot? must not? ought not?) have linear utility.

The civil liberties of gamblers seem to have been cut by Occam's Razor of the *a priori* economist. Models should adapt to people, not people to models. Economists were not born to have an easy, tidy, or aesthetic life. I know one Paul who, on reflection, does not enjoy linear utility. But why couldn't he have done so? The consequences of assuming linear utilities are worth pausing over as preparation for discussing Karl Menger's Super-Petersburg paradoxes, by which (a) people are to learn that they in fact have *bounded* utility:

$$U(W) < M < \infty \qquad (2)$$
$$\lim_{W \to \infty} U(W) = M$$

And, as preparation to discuss the warrant—which is more questionable in my view—by which (b) economists are empowered to assume the axiom that people have bounded utility, "lest a Super-Petersburg paradox be 'encountered'."

Digression on Linear Utility

A few words to analyze the behavior of Peters and Pauls with linear utilities may be of interest. Suppose we face such a citizen of St. Petersburg, Paul, with wealth of so many rubles or ducats, W_1. Suppose Peter has many more rubles, W_0, perhaps because Peter is a conglomerate of stock owners in a vast casino: $W_0 >> W_1$. Both W's are finite, since I don't quite know what an infinite wealth means in a real-life situation. This does not preclude us from letting W_1 grow large, or W_0/W_1 grow large. Since, in the beginning, we don't know what a negative W means, we assume initial (W_0, W_1) to be finite positive numbers. For simplicity, we can assume wealths are measured in terms of the stakes at each toss in the Petersburg games, ducats or rubles or dollars as the case may be.

Now suppose that Peter has $W_0 \geq 1$ and offers Paul the option to play a finite Petersburg game for $n = 1$. Unless $W_1 \geq 1$, Paul cannot effectively agree to play, being unable to guarantee to pay 1 ducat, the fair price to receive 2 ducats if heads comes up at the first and only toss. However, if $W_1 \geq 1$, $W_0 \geq 1$, an effective equilibrium is possible for the game's being played at a positive intensity level.

Similarly, for $W_1 \geq 2$ and $W_0 \geq 2$, the 2-toss game can be played at a positive intensity level. If Paul does not have a W_1 of at least 2, he can't assure a referee (or court) that he can pay the needed fair price; and if Peter does not have a W_0 of at least 2 (or $2^n - n$, when $n = 2$), he cannot assure Paul and the referee that he can pay what he has contracted to pay in the worst possible contingency.

Similarly, for $W_1 \geq 3$ and $W_0 \geq 5$, a game for $n = 3$ can be feasibly played. Generally, for $W_1 \geq n$ and $W_0 \geq 2^n - n$, a game of n can be played.

I have to agree with the legion of early writers on the infinite–St. Petersburg game that, with finite (W_1, W_0) the *infinite* game cannot *feasibly* be played by both parties (or either party) whatever their utilities and desires. So the paradox aborts even before it dies. (This does not deny that, by a hypothetical thought experiment, a Paul or Peter may imagine how much he would pay for a game of n tosses if his W were large enough.)

Nor does the above argument deny that, by halving the stakes at each toss as many times as is needed, the game can then be played by Paul and Peter with given finite (W_1, W_0) for n arbitrarily large, provided only that the stake per toss, h, is made small enough so that $(W_1/h, W_0/h) \geq (n, 2^n - n)$. It is worth mentioning that it is the Peters and not the Pauls who are likely to become bottlenecks in keeping n limited, since $2^n - n >> n$ as n grows. Although the commentators on the paradox have mostly concentrated on Paul's dilemmas, I have always felt it is Peter's dilemma that is the even more interesting one. By reducing h to $W_0/(2^n - n)$, n can be set as high as one wishes. Moreover, now that we are subdividing the stakes, the deadweight loss in playing the Petersburg game between two risk averters can be made small.[3]

From our glimpse of those with linear utility and without risk aversion, we understand why the ordinary Petersburg paradox can never be a relevant threat to ordinary folk with risk aversion.

Theorem. No matter what their finite positive (W_1, W_0) is, for no positive stake h and number of plays n will Peters and Pauls with strictly concave utilities be able to agree to play a [Petersburg, or any] *fair* game at any positive intensity level. *A fortiori* the infinite-game Petersburg activity can never spontaneously occur or be competitively viable at positive intensity levels.

Even though some such fair games may be *feasible,* they will never be willingly entered into, since they fabricate unnecessary variability for both risk-averse parties.

Still, we could imagine some intermediary, say, the Ford Foundation—which is prepared to provide an outright subsidy to enable the game to take place. Call $f_1(W_1; n, h)$ the maximum amount that risk-averse Paul will pay to play the finite game

[3] See Samuelson [28, 1960] for a demonstration that, as the stake at each toss is made small and smaller, even with bounded and strictly concave $U_1(W_1)$, the multiple of the stake that Paul will pay to play the game goes to n and, as $n \to \infty$, goes to infinity. This holds even if $h(2^n - n)$ or hn are kept bounded. A similar result can be shown for Peter, as will be shown in equations (3) to (6) to come. Menger [20, 1967, p. 211; 21, 1973, pp. 57–58, n. 25] seems to suggest that this 1960 result is the same as his 1934 result about the necessity that $U_1(W_1)$ be bounded if his Super-Petersburg game is not to be equivalent to giving Paul an infinite amount of wealth. The two results seem to me to be quite distinct, Menger's being the more interesting one. The 1960 result is a "local" property of smooth $U_1(\,)$ around initial W_1, and holds whether $U_1(\,)$ is bounded or unbounded as W_1 becomes large.

of n tosses; and $f_0(W_0; n, h)$ the minimum amount that risk-averse Peter will take to play the game.

It can be shown with a little effort that $U_1''(W)/[dU_1/d \log W] < \epsilon < 0$ implies

$$f_0(W_0; n, h) > nh > f_1(W_1; n, h) > 0, \quad (n = 1, 2, \ldots) \tag{3}$$

$$\lim_{n \to \infty} f_0(W_0; n, h) \geq \lim_{n \to \infty} nh > \lim_{n \to \infty} f_1(W_1; n, h) \tag{4}$$

However, as is hinted in Bertrand [5, 1889] and shown in Samuelson [28, 1960],

$$\lim_{h \to 0} \left\{\frac{1}{h} f_0(W_1; n, h)\right\} = n = \lim_{h \to 0} \left\{\frac{1}{h} f_1(W_1; n, h)\right\} \tag{5}$$

General Games

Now consider a more general case in which a fair coin is to be tossed n times. If heads first comes up at toss $(1, 2, \ldots, i, \ldots, n)$, Peter agrees to pay Paul positive prizes of $(X_{1n}, X_{2n}, \ldots, X_{in}, \ldots, X_{nn})$ respectively, or zero if heads never comes up. To compute how much each will respectively require as payment in order to be induced to play the game, namely f_1 and f_0 respectively, we solve an equation for each person that gives him the same expected utility when he plays and when he doesn't. Each f_1[4] and f_0 are the respective roots of

$$U_1(W_1) = \sum_{i=1}^{n} 2^{-i} U_1(W_1 - f_1 + X_{in}) + 2^{-n} U_1(W_1 - f_1) \tag{6}$$

$$U_0(W_0) = \sum_{i=1}^{n} 2^{-i} U_0(W_0 + f_0 - X_{in}) + 2^{-n} U_0(W_0 + f_0) \tag{7}$$

$$f_1 = f_1(W_1, n; X_{1n}, \ldots, X_{nn}) = f_1(W_1, n) \text{ for short} \tag{6'}$$

$$f_0 = f_0(W_0, n; X_{1n}, \ldots, X_{nn}) = f_0(W_0, n) \tag{7'}$$

For $U_1''(\,) < 0$ and $U_0''(\,) < 0$,

$$f_0(W_0, n) > \sum_1^n 2^{-i} X_{in} > f_1(W_1, n) \tag{8}$$

The standard St. Petersburg game has $X_{in} \equiv 2^i h$ and

$$\sum_1^n 2^{-i} X_{in} = \sum_1^n 2^{-i} 2^i h = nh \qquad \lim_{n \to \infty} \sum_1^n 2^{-i} 2^i h = \infty \tag{9}$$

Thus, *Figure* 1 gives a self-contained picture of the situation for $n = 1$, a one-toss Petersburg game: in *Figure* 1a is shown how much of f_1^* we must add to Paul's initial W_1 to compensate him for foregoing the option of receiving with even-odds $h2^1$ or 0; in *Figure* 1b is shown how much of f_1 Paul would pay to play the game and still be as well off as at initial f_1. Writers use both concepts, f_1 and f_1^*.

An interesting special case is that of con-

[4] In D. Bernoulli [4, 1738] and Menger [19, 1934 or 20, 1967, p. 217] a concept different from f_1 is used. Instead of asking what Paul will pay rather than not play the game (which is f_1), they for the most part ask, "How much will Paul have to be given to make him as well off as if he received the game's positive gains." I write the latter as f_1^*, the root of

$$U(W_1 + f_1^*) = \sum_1^n 2^{-i} U_1(W_1 + 2^i h) + 2^{-n} U_1(W_1)$$
$$f_1^* = g(W_1; X_{1n}, \ldots, X_{nn}) = g(W_1, 2h, \ldots, 2^n h) = g(W_1; n, h)$$

Menger [20, 1967, p. 222] recognizes that f_1 and f_1^* are not equal, asserting that ". . . in fact, the first is usually smaller than the second." Actually one verifies that $f_1 = g(W_1 - f_1; n, h)$. This would be less than $g(W_1; n, h)$ if it were necessarily the case that always $\partial g(W_2; n, h)/\partial W_1 > 0$. For absolute risk aversion that grows with W_1, a possible case even though many writers presumably think it empirically unlikely or bizarre, $\partial g(\,)/\partial W_1 < 0$ and $f_1 > f_1^*$. As will be seen in my later discussion of the Super-Petersburg paradox, I believe that there is much advantage in concentrating on f_1 as well as on f_1^*.

[Important warning: For f_1^* to be finite, it is *necessary* that $U_1''(W)$ be negative for "most" large W. It is *not*, however, sufficient to make f_1^* finite that $U_1''(W)$ be everywhere negative and that $U_1'(W)$ fall monotonically toward zero. Thus, for large W, let $U_1(W)$ be exactly $(W-1)/\log(W-1)$. Then it can be verified that, for large W, $U_1'(W)$ falls steadily to zero. But the evaluation of $U(W + f_1^*)$ now gives us, for sufficiently large initial W_1, the divergent harmonic series $A[1 + 2^{-1} + 3^{-1} + \ldots + n^{-1} + \ldots]$. Q.E.D.]

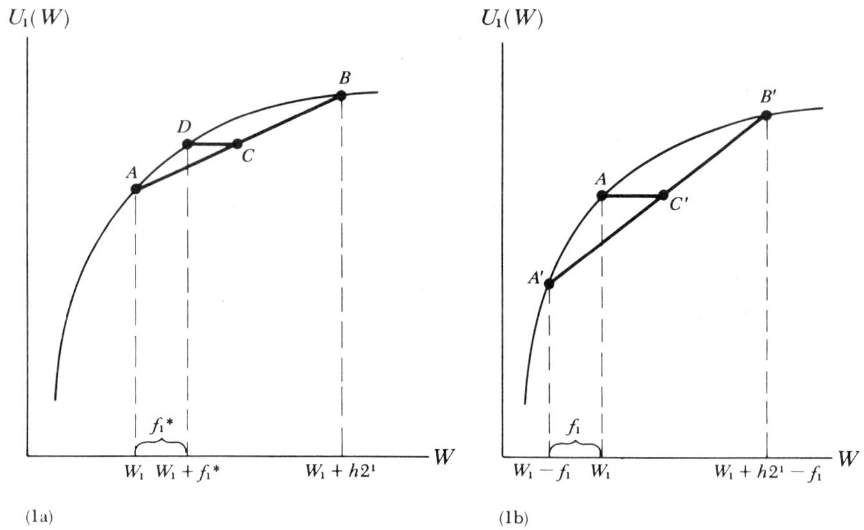

Figure 1. In (1a), Paul begins with W_1 at A. With $n = 1$, Petersburg game gives him 2^{-1} chance of being at B with $W_1 + h2^1$ dollars, and ½ chance of staying at A: this 50–50 option has utility at C (halfway between A and B). Beginning with certainty at D, due west of C, is just as good as C. So f_1^* equals exact distance that D is east of A—the amount of money needed to compensate Paul for foregoing Petersburg game with $n = 1$.

In (1b), we find just how much A and B must *each* be moved west, to A' and B' with halfway point C' at A's level. That unique westward dollar shift gives f_1, the \$ amount Paul will pay for the privilege of playing the game. If AB were on straight line $U_1(W)$ locus, f_1 and f_1^* would each equal "expected dollar gain, \$½ $h2^1$," as C and D coincide and C' and A coincide.

stant-relative-risk-aversion. $U(W) = \log W$ or $U(W) = W^\gamma/\gamma$, $1 > \gamma \neq 0$. For all these, $f_1(W_1, n)$ takes the special form

$$f_1(W_1, n) = W_1\ \phi_1(h/W_1, n; \gamma_1) \equiv W_1\ \phi_1(h_1, n; \gamma_1) \tag{10}$$

where h_1 is defined in (10) as the stake in ratio to wealth and where $\phi_1(\ )$ is the positive unique root of

$$1 = \sum_1^n 2^{-i}(1 - \phi_1 + 2^i h_1)^{\gamma_1} + 2^{-n}(1 - \phi_1)^{\gamma_1},\ 0 \neq \gamma_1 < 1 \tag{11}$$

For $\gamma_1 = 0$, we of course use $U_1(W_1) = \log W_1$.

It can be shown that

$$\lim_{n\to\infty} \phi_1(h_1, n; \gamma_1) = \phi_1(h_1; \gamma_1) < 1, \quad \gamma_1 \leq 0 \tag{12}$$

$$\partial\phi_1(h_1; n, \gamma_1)/\partial\gamma_1 > 0, \quad -\infty < \gamma_1 < 1 \tag{13}$$

For $\gamma_1 \to 0$, we approach the ϕ_1 ( ) solution for the log W_1 case. For $\gamma_1 \to -\infty$, we approach the minimax case (in which Paul will pay only zero to play the game). (For $0 < \gamma_1 < 1$, equation (11) may have no root for ϕ_1 on the admissible interval [0,1]. Thus, for $\gamma_1 = 1/2$, Cramer's case, and $n = 1$, if we make h_1 big enough, Paul will give up all his W_1 as f_1 and still be ahead to take the Petersburg gamble—which leads us to the topic of bankruptcy.)

Bankruptcy

So long as γ_1 is restricted to be non-positive, Paul will never pay more than a fraction of his W_1 to play the game, $\phi_1(h_1, n; \gamma_1) < 1$. Therefore, the referee need never concern himself about the feasibility of collecting the fee that Paul is willing to contract to play the game. However, the fee that Peter will want to require can be made to exceed what Paul could pay out of his finite W_1: we need only freeze the stake per toss, and let n be set very large.

However, for n and h small enough and W_1 and W_0 large enough, the game can be feasible. Still, with γ_1 and γ_0 both less than unity, there is no "danger" that the game will ever be played (even for n finite or unity). The referee need never worry about the possible enforcability of a contract that will never come into existence.

Suppose for the sake of the argument we banish all problems having to do with the ability (and desire!) of Peter to engage in the contract at Paul's needed price, $f_1()$. [Perhaps a convenient grant from the Ford Foundation will permit the thought experiment to take place for finite n.] Then, as just seen, there still can arise serious problems of Paul's bankruptcy if Paul has γ_1 a positive proper fraction. Paul is still risk averse, but he is now more risk tolerant than a person with Bernoullian logarithmic utility. Thus, now, Paul might have $U(W) \equiv 2W^{1/2}$, the Cramer [11, 1728] case.

The point is the one already made—that equation (11) may have no meaningful solution for ϕ_1 and $f_1(\,)$ if h is too large and $0 < \gamma_1 < 1$. To find a meaningful solution, Paul must ask himself: "What if I pay an f_1 greater than my wealth and, as must sometimes happen, I end up 'owing' more than I can pay? What is *my* evaluation of negative-wealth outcomes?" Aside from this being a feasibility problem for the referee and the creditor Peter, this is a problem for Paul that we must analyze.

To come to grips with the bankruptcy problem, it is helpful to leave the case of constant-relative-risk aversion with its concentration exclusively on non-negative wealth outcomes. A more useful case is one like that of constant-absolute-risk aversion. For it

$$U_1(W_1) = -e^{-aW_1}, \qquad a > 0; \quad -\infty < W_1 < +\infty \tag{14}$$

For it, Paul's willing price is independent of his initial wealth, being the root f_1 of

$$\begin{aligned} \exp[-aW_1] &= \sum_1^n 2^{-i}\exp[-aW_1 - f_1 + 2^i h] \\ &\quad + 2^{-n}\exp[-aW_1 - f_1] \\ 1 &= \sum_1^n 2^{-i}\exp[-a(-f_1 + 2^i h)] \\ &\quad + 2^{-n}\exp[af_1] \end{aligned} \tag{15}$$

$$f_1 = f_1(h, n), \; \partial f_1(h, n)/\partial W_1 \equiv 0 \tag{16}$$

$$\lim_{n\to\infty} f_1(h, n) = f_1(h) < \infty \tag{16'}$$

$$\lim_{h\to 0} \frac{1}{h} f_1(h, n) = n$$

For $W_1 < f_1$ and n finite, there is a positive probability that Paul will not be able to pay the f_1 he has promised to pay. Technically, he will be bankrupt; he knows of this possibility in advance, and so do Peter and the referee. Even for n infinite, with $W_1 + 2h < f_1$, there is at least a .5 probability that Paul will become bankrupt.

Once bankruptcy can happen, we lose the zero-sum-of-money-gains property for the game: terminal W_0 for Peter cannot equal his initial W_0 plus Paul's computed contractual loss; as an asset to Peter, bankrupt Paul's I.O.U. is worthless.

However, by the device of a subsidizing Ford Foundation we can still investigate what Paul would be willing to promise to pay for a Petersburg game of n tosses or an infinite number of tosses. We must ask what it means for Paul to have a negative terminal wealth $(W_1 - f_1 + 2^i h)$: what does U_1(negative number) really mean?

There are at least two possibilities. First, when we say that Paul evaluates −\$5,000 at $-\exp[a\$5{,}000]$ we can mean exactly that the "shame" of going bankrupt for \$5,000 is greater than the shame of going bankrupt for \$4,000; and the extra shame of doing so is greater than the extra shame of going bankrupt for \$4,000 rather than \$3,000. The concave function $U_1(W_1) = -e^{-aW_1}$ really describes Paul's decision behavior even with respect to making unfulfillable promises!

A second interpretation will often be more realistic and is implicit in folk statements like the following: "You might as well be hanged for a sheep as a lamb." "You can only die once." "One stain utterly besmirches honor." These considerations destroy the assumption of uniformly strict concavity of utility. Now

$$\begin{aligned} U_1(W_1) &= -e^{-aW_1}, \quad W_1 > 0 \qquad (17)\\ &\equiv -e^{-a0} = -1, \quad W_1 \le 0 \\ U_1(W_1) &= -\exp[-a\,\mathrm{Max}(W_1, 0)] \end{aligned}$$

Actually, if "dishonor" has a lexicographic penalty connected with it, $U_1(-|x|)$ might be defined to be identically less than $U_1(0)$ by a finite or infinite amount.

The equation to determine $f_1(W_1; n, h)$ now involves a non-concave $U_1(W_1)$ function, taking the form

$$\begin{aligned} &U_1(W_1) \qquad (18)\\ &= \sum_1^n 2^{-i} U_1(\mathrm{Max}[W_1 - f_1 + 2^i h, 0]) \\ &+ 2^{-n} U_1(\mathrm{Max}[W_1 - f_1, 0]) \end{aligned}$$

Such an f_1 will exceed the old f_1 whenever Paul can know that promising to pay more need not involve his actually having to pay more.

Peter knows all this, and his new f_0 will be gauged accordingly. Hence, it is a theorem that recognition of the possibility of bankruptcy makes it, if anything, more impossible for any two "risk averters" to agree to play a Petersburg game at positive intensity. Even if Peter and Paul have linear utility (or even have $U(\ )$ so convex as to make them risk takers), neither will agree to play for a stake h that is so large relative to (W_1, W_0) as to yield a positive probability that someone will fail to live up to contract. (A proper side payment to compensate for this understood contingency will, in effect, create a new game—fair to each person, but no longer zero-sum—that is no longer of standard Petersburg type, in that "true" prizes are no longer proportional to 2^i.)

I conclude these desultory remarks on bankruptcy with the observation that ancient writers who grapple with the St. Petersburg paradox by bringing in bankruptcy considerations do not deserve to be dismissed with contempt. Such considerations are part of any full treatment of the problem.

Summing Up for Ordinary Petersburg Game

1. If people did have constant marginal utility, their decisions about playing simple and compound games would be very different from what they'd be with declining marginal utilities. With constant marginal utility a Paul with a thousand dollars, facing a Peter with a million dollars, would be willing to pay a paltry \$19 for the privilege of doubling up dollar bets on a fair coin at least 19 times. And Peter, if only he had constant marginal utility, would be willing (and able!) to offer the privilege at that price. (Of course neither party would knowingly enter into a contract with someone who patently cannot fulfill his promises; but that will not be relevant

when Paul and Peter are assumed to be this affluent.)

2. Most Peters in real life would not risk so much for so little (a possible loss of $528,288 for a maximum gain of $19!). *A fortiori*, with such evident risk aversion and concavity of utility, they will not agree to make Petersburg-like wagers with each other for still higher stakes and a permitted number of plays greater than $n = 19$: what real Peters will ask, real Pauls won't pay.

3. Thus, it is not "the fear lest a Petersburg infinity should arise" that permits us to rule out linear utility: it is merely the fact that marginal utility diminishes (if it does!) that rules out constancy of marginal utility. Aversion to simple "fair" bets alerts us less dramatically but adequately to the concavity of utility, which the Petersburg paradox over-dramatically alerts us to.[5]

II. *Menger's Super-Petersburg Paradox*

After 1738, nothing earthshaking was added to the findings of Daniel Bernoulli and his contemporaries until the quantum jump in analysis provided by Karl Menger [19, 1934]. He points out that it is not enough merely to make marginal utility decline steadily to zero as wealth grows. That may suffice to keep finite the amount that Pauls will require to compensate them for giving up the privilege of playing an infinite version of the ordinary Petersburg case. But, unless utility is actually bounded by a finite level M, Menger shows one can always fabricate a Super-Petersburg game, in which the payoffs at the nth toss grow enough faster than $2^n h$ to make the compensation Paul needs again be infinite.

One salutes Karl Menger for this important new insight. One thanks him for providing a new dramatic way of seeing that you have bounded utility—if indeed you do have it. But just as I question whether the ordinary Petersburg game is (a) perhaps over-dramatic to provide the insight it provides, and whether it is (b) really a relevant threat that is conclusive in compelling every person to have declining marginal utility—so I shall now proceed to analyze the super-paradox in a parallel fashion. One must ask:

(1) Would Menger's construction of a super-game, with its revealed fact of infinity for the money compensation that Paul needs to forego playing that game, $f_1^* \to \infty$ as $n \to \infty$, shock a Bernoulli who believed his U_1 obeyed log W_1 into abandoning that belief in unbounded utility?

(2) If not, *should* it *necessarily* have shocked him into such abandonment?

(3) Could not simple, one-game options accomplish *all* that the more dramatic infinite-game options can legitimately accomplish?

(4) Finally, what about the contention that we analysts "have to" assume bounded utilities *lest we lay our system open to the threat* of a Mengerian Super-Petersburg paradox?

My answers to the above questions will in the end be as follows:

A. Yes, any of us may on careful reflection be free to possess unbounded utility functions, $U(W_1) \to \infty$ as $W_1 \to \infty$. The implied Mengerian infinity for f_1^* will then seem a "natural" outcome and not a *reductio ad absurdum*.

B. Whether we have Max $U(W_1) < \infty$ or $= \infty$ can be cogently revealed by simple

[5] Thus, as is mentioned in Stigler [37, 1950, n. 127], Cournot [10, 1843] essentially makes the acute observation that is tantamount to strictly concave utility: if ticket i pays you $2^i h$ with probability 2^{-i} and zero otherwise, the bigger is i the less people will pay for the ticket. The full paradox can add nothing essential to the insight that $f_1(i)$ drops steadily to zero as $i \to \infty$. See my later discussion of Shapley [36, 1972] in the *Historical Notes* for the arithmetic of this example, with its startling display of how quickly Peter's liability rises to astronomical heights.

non-Petersburg thought experiments, each involving but *one* toss of a specifiable coin.

C. If in fact all or some people have unbounded utilities, nonetheless the risk-averse Peters and Pauls of the world will never (repeat, never) choose to engage in any Super-Petersburg game at any positive intensity levels. Peters will always ask more than Pauls will ever offer to pay, with the result: In competitive equilibrium, the number of Menger games played—even with *finite* n—will be exactly zero.

I begin with discussion of B as an adequate answer to question (3) of the previous paragraphs.

Single-Toss Experiments

How Paul evaluates the utility of great wealth, the properties of $U_1(W_1)$ for large W_1, can be deduced from a number of different behavior patterns or thought experiments. One simple test is to pick the increment between two arbitrary utility levels, $W_1 = A$ and $W_1 = B > A$, as a unit for utility, namely $U_1(B) - U_1(A) = 1$. We can now determine from Paul's behavior what the critical probability must be such that he would pay $B - A$ for the privilege of gaining $W - A$, for all W above A. We solve for the root p in

$$U_1(B) = pU_1(W) + (1 - p)\ U_1(A) \qquad (19)$$

$$p = \frac{U_1(B) - U_1(A)}{U_1(W) - U_1(A)} \qquad (20)$$
$$= p(W; B, A), \quad \partial p/\partial W < 0$$

If we adopt the harmless convention of setting $U_1(A) = 0$, $U_1(B) = 1$, our utility is computable from Paul's revealed preferences concerning different W's, namely by the observable reciprocal probability

$$U_1(W) = p(W; B, A)^{-1} \qquad (21)$$

If, on reflection, Paul agrees that, no matter how high W is offered to be, he will not accept a p lower than a critical positive p^*, then his utility is bounded by $1/p^*$:

$$0 < \lim_{W\to\infty} p(W; B, A)^{-1} = 1/p^* \qquad (22)$$
$$> p(W; B, A)^{-1} \text{ for any } W > A$$

Most Pauls I know about confess that they do, by this test, have bounded utility. The fear of kidnapping goes up with W (at least up to a point). Their desire to gloat over poorer neighbors becomes satiated. The difficulty of finding time to "enjoy" one's wealth may itself be limiting.

On the other hand, large wealth is "power" rather than potential for consumption of ordinary goods and services. A manic and insatiable desire for power may be the essence of the demand for power; and the game of acquiring and holding power may be the essence of the regularities of behavior that need to be described and analyzed.

I see no reason to be dogmatic in the matter and to follow older writers who denounce this or that mode of behavior as "insane," or even eccentric and implausible. A person, it seems to me, has the right to say after considered reflection that there is no p^* above zero that will bound his needed roots to equation (19) once he has become adjusted to having very large W. When people have low W, they exaggerate the desirability of slightly higher W and denigrate the desirability of much higher W; but that is only to acknowledge transient hysteresis which, like standing (Coulomb) friction, distorts in non-permanent ways the appearances of our long-run reversible $U_1(W)$ relations. Also, if all of us in a society gain higher W's, with about the same distributions, we may not satiate as quickly as one person will.

Hence, the theoretical economist must leave moot the question whether $U_1(W_1)$ is necessarily bounded above. It is up to the guinea pigs to decide, not up to the zoo keeper or observer. This provides justification for my conclusion A above and my answer to the posed question (2) above.

Analyzing the Super-Petersburg Option

With utility bounded above, the $f_1{}^*$ needed to compensate Paul for losing the option of playing the Menger super-game can for no finite n exceed an upper bound. Therefore, as $n \to \infty$, $f_1{}^* \to$ a finite positive number. So, if there were something horrendous or mind-boggling about the outcome $f_1{}^* \to \infty$ as $n \to \infty$, that calamity is indeed averted, as Menger has so rigorously shown, only by assuming $U_1(W_1) \leq M < \infty$.

However, to any Paul with unbounded $U_1(W_1)$ and with p^* in equation (22) equal to zero, there is nothing paradoxical or even odd about his $f_1{}^* \to \infty$. He enjoys high W_1 so much that this is the compensation he needs. (As economist observers we must remind ourselves that there is no danger that any Peter would want to offer such a game or even be able to do so. Even the Ford Foundation or the Federal Reserve can command only a limited *real* W!) To pretend that the Paul in question would be shocked at the outcome of the thought experiment is to deny that he really meant that his p^* is zero. It is like the Cretan joke: "I'm glad I don't like olives. Because if I liked them I'd eat them—and I hate them." It is true that people who abhor oysters and olives sometimes wonder to the point of doubt that others really do like them.

It may be argued that, in the notation of my footnote 4, it is the f_1 concept rather than the $f_1{}^*$ concept that we should be talking about to give the paradoxes their full melodramatic value. "Would one really *pay* an infinite number of dollars or all one's W_1 to play *any* game? That is the interesting question and not how much Santa Claus would have to pay Paul to persuade him not to take the free gift of some defined super-game."

I concede merit to such a suggestion. And that is why my early exposition departed from the practice of D. Bernoulli [4, 1738] and K. Menger [19, 1934] and concentrated on f_1 rather than on $f_1{}^*$. Let us see how bounded and unbounded utilities affect f_1 and its limit values.

First, even with unbounded utility, as with log W_1, it is *not* the case that f_1 can be made to approach ∞ as $n \to \infty$ by a Menger super-game. Instead, it is "pathology" enough that f_1 can be made to approach indefinitely close to W_1 itself as $n \to \infty$. Are we to recoil at such a revealed implication of unbounded utility? Even if we are, it is worth remembering that one did *not* need a super-game, nor even an infinite n, to demonstrate this: by increasing the stake h in the ordinary Petersburg game, with fixed n we find for the unbounded Bernoulli case, log W_1:

$$\lim_{h \to \infty} f_1(W_1;\ n,\ h) = W_1 \tag{23}$$

What keeps f_1 bounded above by W_1 itself is the fact that log W_1 is unbounded *below* for positive W_1. Much of our instinctive surprise or disgust at the results of linear utility maximization does not come so much from our feeling that our $U_1(W_1)$ fails to grow linearly at *high* W_1; it comes rather from our abhorrence for starvation and dishonor, phenomena that reflect grave departures from linearity of $U_1(W_1)$ at *low* W_1.

Again, a Paul who does on reflection have a log W_1 function will not share the spectator's surprise or abhorrence that he can be made to pay *almost* all his W_1 on some attractive Menger option. And another Paul, who feels that there is a minimum of W_1 needed for subsistence, W_s, and whose $U_1(W_1)$ equals log $(W_1 - W_s)$, can be made to pony up f_1 arbitrarily near to $W_1 - W_s$. Witnesses to the experimental fact that f_1 never exceeds some number less than W_1 cannot validly infer that it was an upper finite bound on utility that caused this; rather, as just seen, it may be the *absence* of a lower bound that is the important cause. As I have had occasion to remark in print before, the behavior of $U_1(W_1)$ at low W_1 has often failed to receive the emphasis it deserves because of preoccupation with its behavior at high W_1.

In connection with Petersburg paradoxes about the possible large size of f_1, bounding $U_1(W_1)$ below makes the paradox (if it is one) more likely. Thus, replace $\log W_1$ by $\text{Max}[0, \log(1 + W_1)]$, a well-defined $U_1(W_1)$ function on $-\infty < W_1 < \infty$. Since there is no penalty to making f_1 greater than W_1—it is now only an empty promise to pay!—one can easily construct a finite ordinary Petersburg game, with a finite n, that will make f_1 equal to all one's W_1 or exceed it by as much as we desire. Thus, as $h \to \infty$, $f_1 \to \infty$ even for $n = 1$, a single-toss game! Only the letter of an infinite paradox is achieved; the spirit of a paradox is quite lacking.

Finally, I must analyze the threat of our being able to construct a Super-Petersburg game if all Pauls and all Peters in fact had utility unbounded above. Suppose, with D. Bernoulli, that everyone has $U = \log W$. Is the threat of a super-game's arising other than an idle threat? Is it a relevant threat? I believe not.

To study the equilibrium intensity level of super-games in a competitive market, assume many Peters, each with fortunes large relative to many Pauls: $W_0 >> W_1 = 1$. Define a Mengerian game of n tosses, with payments from Peter to Paul of $(e^{2h} - 1, e^{4h} - 1, \ldots, e^{2^n h} - 1, 0)$ with respective probabilities $(2^{-1}, 2^{-2}, \ldots, 2^{-n}, 2^{-n})$. Since the example is structured to give Paul utilities of outcomes that grow in exact proportion to 2^i, clearly the $f_1{}^*$ that must be paid Paul as compensation for foregoing such a bonanza is given by

$$\log(1 + f_1{}^*) = \sum_1^n (ih) = nh \tag{24}$$

$$\lim_{n \to \infty} f_1{}^* = \infty$$

So what? Who will give him such compensation? Certainly not Peter. No Peter will ever play this Mengerian game with him for any value of n, much less for $n = \infty$. Who compensates people for what there is no chance of their getting? No one.

Utility Boundedness for Completeness of Orderings?

Menger's analysis has alerted writers like Arrow [2, 1971, pp. 63–69] to the fact that, in order to be able to have a complete ordering of all probabilistic outcomes of options in terms of their expected utilities,

> . . . [it] turns out, somewhat surprisingly, to imply that the utility function must be bounded; we cannot have utilities which are indefinitely large in either the positive or negative direction.
>
> The argument depends interestingly on the very problem that originally gave rise to Daniel Bernoulli's original paper [4, 1738] . . . the 'St. Petersburg paradox'. . . . Bernoulli suggested that maximizing expected utility . . . [where], for example, the utility of a quantity of money was equal to its logarithm . . . [would give a f_1 that was] finite and in fact reasonably small.
>
> But this solution is in fact incomplete. If the utility function is unbounded, one can always construct an action with an infinite utility as was first observed by the mathematician Karl Menger [19, 1934]. . . .
>
> . . . [Thus, we have proved] the following theorem: UTILITY BOUNDEDNESS THEOREM. Any utility function which satisfies the conditions of the Expected Utility Theorem[6] must be bounded from above and below.

[6] Arrow [2, 1971, p. 53] states:
EXPECTED UTILITY THEOREM: It is possible to define a real-valued utility function over actions [or decisions with their implied respective possible outcomes, each with specifiable probabilities], with the following properties: (1) $a^1 \succ a^2$ [*i.e.*, action 1 definitely preferred to action 2] if and only if $U(a^1) > U(a^2)$; (2) $U(a) = E\{U[a(s)]\}$ [*i.e.*, equals the expected value of utilities of outcomes implied by action a].

Arrow's argument has been worth quoting in some detail. That unbounded utility can lead, for certain probability distributions, to infinite or undefined expected utility, is indisputable; and, of course, it has been known quite independently of Menger's super-paradox. (An example is a log-normal probability for wealth and $U(W) = -W^{-1}$, with $E\{U\} = -\infty$ no matter how high is the geometric mean of outcomes.) This raises the point that a complete transitive ordering over *all* probability distributions is never possible if $U(W)$ is unbounded—since two options might both have $E\{U(\ )\} = \infty$ while being non-indifferent; and, also, the Continuity Axiom of ordinal stochastic preferences will be violated (as my discussion of Arrow in the later footnote 14 explains).

Those who are tempted to insist upon both an upper and lower bound for utility must sacrifice the property of utility concavity and general risk aversion everywhere. They gain the property that, for any defined probability distribution of W_1 outcomes, a transitive ordering is well defined. Thus, even for Lévy distributions with no finite integral moments, $E\{U_1(W_1)\}$ is finite, being bounded by the bounds of $U_1(W_1)$. However, we have now lost all *general diversification* theorems (like those in Samuelson [30, 1967; 31, 1976]).

Repeatedly I have still had to raise the questions: Do people *ever get faced* with probability distributions that leave them with undefined expected utilities? How often do such options arise? If ever they should, might not new lexicographic orderings be found to break ties between infinitely-good or infinitely-bad alternatives?

There is no need to bore readers with repetitions of the same point, particularly since my purpose is to raise questions, not to sell one particular set of answers to them. What needs emphasis here is this: the *last* place that could ever generate real-world probability distributions with the infinite ranges and moments that keep $E\{U(W)\}$ from being finite would be in the St. Petersburg marketplace of zero-sum gambling games! Mother Nature might present Paul with a Cauchy distribution for extreme positive gains in the right-hand tail: Peter, the casino owner, would never be willing to do so or even ever be able to do so.

Only by inadvertence is the St. Petersburg paradox, ordinary or super, germane to the genuine problems of the current section. Which is only to notice once again that, often in intellectual history, the accidental plays a crucial role in the progression of thought and ideas.

Conclusion

When you have defanged a paradox with the texture of the St. Petersburg puzzle, the problem does not disappear or fade away into banality. As my *Historical Notes* illustrate, so many points were raised by commentators on the problem that the St. Petersburg paradox enjoys an honored corner in the memory bank of the cultured analytic mind.

Historical Notes

1. *Christenings.* The problem gets its name, the "St. Petersburg" paradox, from the fact that Daniel Bernoulli's basic article of the early 1730's appeared in that city in 1738. (However, the only explicit appearance in Bernoulli [4, 1738] of a Petersburg merchant, Caius, seems to be in connection with an insurance problem

there rather than in connection with the game involving 2^{-i} probabilities and 2^{i} gains.) An excellent 1954 English translation of Bernoulli [4, 1738] appears in *Econometrica*, with some editorial footnotes by Karl Menger; any page references I give refer to this translation, Bernoulli [4, 1738, p. 23] meaning page 23 of the 1954 translation.

I have relied primarily on Todhunter [39, 1865] as a useful reference for the history of the problem. Menger also provides some historical remarks [19, 1934], in addition to representing the first substantive quantum jump over D. Bernoulli in two centuries. Other secondary sources appear in my bibliography.

2. *Bouquet of Bernoullis.* A preliminary word on the many Bernoullis may be useful. James (or Jacob or Jacques) Bernoulli (1654–1705), the oldest brother of the first generation, has immortal fame from his posthumous *Ars Conjectandi* (1713), which among other excellences asserts the Law of Large Numbers. After James comes Nicholas (Sr.), of interest here only as father of Nicholas (Jr.). Third comes John (or Johann or Jean) Bernoulli (1667–1748), teacher of Euler and codifier of much of the post-Newtonian calculus—for example, the so-called l'Hôpital's rule for evaluating 0/0 seems to be due to John and to have been "sold" to that nobleman. John's genius was matched by his vanity: he may even have predated manuscripts to rob his son Daniel of priority in one or another matter, a phenomenon presumably rare in the annals of parental relationships. Daniel (1700–1782), the major figure in the Petersburg problem, has innumerable other discoveries to his credit—such as kinetic theory, aerodynamics, actuarial science, analysis of inoculation, ... His cousin Nicholas (1687–1759) was an important scientist in his own right: as we have seen, his correspondence around 1713 with Montmort, and his later correspondence with Cramer and Daniel Bernoulli, had an important role in the pre-1738 history of the Petersburg problem. Later Bernoullis named John or James need not concern us here.

The Bernoulli and Euler school stems originally from the Leibniz rather than Newton branch of mathematics. But it was in fact they, and not Newton's countrymen, who fulfilled and developed his tradition, paving the way for Lagrange, Laplace, Gauss, Cauchy, Poincaré, and nineteenth century giants.

3. *Mathematical puzzles.* Prior to the 1738 publication, the Petersburg problem had first arisen purely as a problem in probability in a letter from Nicholas Bernoulli to Montmort, some time around 1713, commenting on the first edition of 1708 of Montmort's treatise and suggesting a number of combinatorial or expectational problems. The "Petersburg" doubling-of-stakes infinite game was one such problem, and the solution in terms of a divergent series was considered by Montmort to be rather easy.

Already for a century such combinatorial algebra was familiar, and it is worth describing the pre-1713 state of the art—what we might call the "Pascal mathematical expectation of money" stage, prior to the Bernoulli-Cramer stage of "moral expectation" or "mathematical expectation of the utility of money."

4. *Potted history.* According to convenient legend, probability theory began around 1654 when the nobleman gambler, Chevalier de Méré, presented to Pascal (1623–1662), and through him to Fermat (1601–1665), certain gambling problems. This version plays down the role of earlier probability works by Cardano (1501–1576), Kepler (1571–1630), and Galileo (1564–1642). It perhaps does not do justice to the intellectual interests of de Méré, and somewhat exaggerates

the novelties of Pascal (as for example, neglecting earlier appearances of the Pascal binomial-coefficients triangle constructed according to certain simple partial-difference equations). It also underplays the importance of Huygens, Newton, and other early writers on probability.

Pascal can be taken as a convenient name for those mathematicians who seemed to base behavior decisions on the "expected value of money (wealth or income)," $E\{W\}$. Only after elapse of almost a century did the Petersburg commentators argue that it is more realistic (and perhaps more "rational") to base decisions on expected value of a strictly-concave (from-below) utility function of money wealth, $E\{U_1(W_1)\}$.

The de Méré "Problem of Points," for which see Todhunter [37, 1865, index], was solved by Pascal and Fermat in terms that we can interpret as a finite Petersburg game where Paul or Peter have linear utility. Thus, suppose Paul and Peter have each anted up 2 ducats, with winner Paul to take all if 2 heads come up before 2 tails come up, and Peter to win if 2 tails come up first. Heads come up once and the game is interrupted. How should a referee divide the 4 ducats "fairly" between Paul and Peter?

The answer can be shown to be that Paul is to take 3 ducats and Peter 1 ducat. This is equivalent to solving for f_1 and f_1^*, as defined in my text's equations, the following general Petersburg game, for $n = 2$:

$$W_1 = 2^{-1}(W_1 - f_1 + 4) + 2^{-2}(W_1 - f_1 + 4) + 2^{-2}(W_1 - f_1) \tag{4.1}$$

$$W_1 + f_1^* = 2^{-1}(W_1 + 4) + 2^{-2}(W_1 + 4) + 2^{-2}(W_1) \tag{4.2}$$

$$f_1 = f_1^* = 3 \tag{4.3}$$

Note that $U_1(W_1)$ does not explicitly appear here, because when $U_1 = a_1 + b_1 W_1$, a_1 and b_1 can be cancelled out.

5. *Cramer resolution.* Despite my earlier contentions that we today do not need the over-dramatic Petersburg games to recognize our actual diminishing marginal utility, $U_1''(\,) < 0$, I know of no written remark to this literal effect prior to the Petersburg resolution in Cramer [11, 1728], as quoted in Bernoulli [4, 1738]. Gabriel Cramer of Geneva, in effect, first replaces linear utility, $U_1 = W_1$ by $U_1 = \text{Min}\,[W_1, 2^{24}]$ on the arbitrary supposition that above 2^{24} ducats further wealth adds zero incremental utility; or, second, he replaces $U_1 = W_1$ by what he regards as more realistic, by $U_1 = W_1^{1/2}$. He solves in effect, alternatively, for

$$\text{Min}\,[W_1 + f_1^*, 2^{24}] = \sum_1^\infty 2^{-i}\,\text{Min}\,[W_1 + 2^{i-1}, 2^{24}], \quad f_1^* = 13 \text{ ducats} \tag{5.1}$$

$$(W_1 + f_1^*)^{1/2} = \sum_1^\infty 2^{-i}(W_1 + 2^{i-1}), \quad f_1^* = 2.9 \text{ ducats} \tag{5.2}$$

These answers depend of course on the initial W_1 chosen. Cramer, presumably on the basis of introspection and knowledge of his fellow-men, believes that 2.9 ducats is nearer to the truth for real-world Pauls than is 13 ducats, and *a fortiori* nearer than is infinity ducats.

6. *Classic logarithmic utility.* Now for Daniel Bernoulli's own solution by means of logarithmic utility. Starting out from the assumption that "a poor man generally obtains more utility than a rich man from an equal [money] gain," [4, 1738, p. 24], he rather airily postulates that a small *"increase in wealth . . . will always result in an increase in utility which is inversely proportionate to the quantity of goods already possessed"* [4, 1738, p. 25, italics in original]. This result he holds to be "highly probable," holding "in the absence of the unusual," namely that marginal utility halves when wealth doubles:

$$dU/dW = KW^{-1}, \qquad (6.1)$$

$$U = K \log_e W + constant. \qquad (6.2)$$

Few economists will today swallow this gratuitous postulate, but to novitiates such argumentation apparently carries some plausibility (as with the Weber-Fechner law in experimental psychology).

Daniel acknowledges his cousin Nicholas's contention that Paul will not pay infinity ducats to play the Petersburg game, indeed agreeing that ". . . any fairly reasonable man would sell his chance, with great pleasure, for twenty ducats" [4, 1738, p. 31]. Bernoulli shows how his logarithmic utility leads to a finite payment; and, since log W represents constant-relative-rich aversion at a greater rate than does Gabriel Cramer's $W^{1/2}$, Daniel would arrive at even fewer ducats[7] for $f_1{}^*$ than would Gabriel, whose theory is "so similar to mine that it seems miraculous that we independently reached such close agreement on this sort of subject" [4, 1738, p. 33]. Robert K. Merton, who studies multiple independent discoveries in science, would find this a nice but not surprising example of coincidence. A 1954 or 1977 reader of Bernoulli's 1738 paper will be struck by its modernity of tone.

7. *Buffon's practical objections.* It is natural to lump together the early critics of the Cramer-Bernoulli resolution of the Petersburg paradox by a proposed maximizing of the expected value of utility of wealth rather than of money wealth itself. They include d'Alembert, Buffon, Fontaine, and perhaps Condorcet.

Buffon (1707–1788), the prolific naturalist and philosopher, famous for his geometrical needle problem in probability and much else, combines a number of heterodox views on the Petersburg phenomenon. (*Cf.* Todhunter [39, 1865, pp. 345–46].) From his 1730 discussions with Cramer until his 1770 publication, Buffon reflects views of others as well as his own views. Here are samples.

First, as with Fontaine's contemporaneous views and Poisson's later view, Buffon limits i in the infinite sequence 2^i to no more than 29 on the ground that Peter's W_0 out of which he pays Paul is neces-

[7] Modern writers on portfolio theory who try to fit utility functions of the class W^γ/γ to market observations on risk-return trade-offs infer even greater risk aversion among investors at large than Bernoulli's log W_1, and an implied even smaller $f_1{}^*$. Thus, $\gamma = -1$ or -2, implying U_1 as $-W_1{}^{-1}$ or $-W_1{}^{-2}$, may be more realistic than Cramer's $W_1{}^{1/2}$ or Bernoulli's log W_1. Some modern writers believe the data display decreasing *absolute* risk aversion as W_1 grows but increasing relative risk aversion. *I.e.*,

$$d\{d \log U'(W)/dW\}/dW > 0 > d\{d \log U'(W)/d \log W\}/dW.$$

If utility is bounded on the W interval $(-\infty,\infty)$, neither such law could hold uniformly: (1) at low enough W, people would, so to speak, be heedless of bankruptcy and be more absolutely risk tolerant than at higher W; but, of course, if $U(W)$ is bounded above, absolute-risk-aversion must *ultimately* fall. Relative-risk-aversion is not well-defined for nonpositive W: Arrow [2, 1971, chap. 3, *c.* p. 98] observed, $WU''(W)/U'(W)$ can oscillate on the $(0,\infty)$ interval for W. (If it is required to move in one direction only, and $U(W)$ is to be concave and bounded on $[0,\infty]$, relative-risk-aversion would *have to* be rising rather than falling as with the splicing together of $W^{.5}$ for $0 \leq W < 1$ with $1.5 - .5W^{-1}$ for $1 \leq W < \infty$, to achieve $U(W)$ differentiable everywhere.) However, there is no analytic reason why, for *all sufficiently high* W, relative-risk-aversion could not be falling or constant (even though $U(W)$ is bounded). It becomes an empirical matter. As Arrow points out, if safe money and risky securities were held solely for portfolio reasons, and if the historical tendency were for the ratio of cash to total W to increase as W itself increases, this would be conclusive evidence for increasing relative-risk-aversion. If, however, the writers Arrow cites *are* correct in their frequent contentions that people hold relatively more cash when they are wealthy because of the *transaction* convenience of cash, the evidence for increasing relative-risk-aversion becomes cloudy. It must in any case reckon with the (also cloudy!) counterevidence of cross-sectional portfolio observations, which seem to show that the very rich hold minute fractions of wealth in zero-interest cash.

The life-cycle fact that people's W may increase with age can confuse the issue: there is some evidence that as people approach retirement, their relative risk-aversion grows, which may lead to a spurious observed crude correlation between relative-risk-aversion and W that is positive. Correcting for age, we may perhaps be left with a true partial correlation that is 0 or even negative.

sarily finite,[8] and a prize of 2^{29} is "more money . . . than the whole of the kingdom of France could furnish" [38, Todhunter, 1865, p. 346]. Now we have a variant of my finite games, with $n=29$ and finite $f_1^*(W_1;29,1)$ or $f_1(W_1;29,1)$ accordingly. Still, should not Buffon have worried whether actual Paul will *need* to be paid even this much f_1^*? Or whether, for *any* stake h, Paul will need an f_1^* up to Peter's W_0, however large that might be?

Second, Buffon agrees with d'Alembert that any probability below some small positive fraction can be set equal to zero. He adds only the specification of that critical magnitude: $p<1/10{,}000$ is zero, because no man of 56 in good health expects to die in one day and that actuarial probability around 1750 was agreed to be of such an order of magnitude. Condorcet, taking Buffon seriously, proposed still another critical threshold value for p: he argues that no one takes seriously the difference in the probability of dying in a week at age 47 from that at age 37; so $52^{-1}\,[480^{-1}-580^{-1}]=144{,}768^{-1}$ is the critical threshold reported in Todhunter [39, 1865, pp. 386–87]. Why a week and not a minute or year? Stigler [37, 1950, n. 126] reports the force of male mortality at 56 two centuries later, as $p=1/2$ of $1/10{,}000$; in view of limited improvements in old-age life expectancies by 1950, a halving would seem dubious, raising doubts about the accuracy of the older estimate.

Various of the absurdities involved in the concepts of "surprise" introduced in Shackle [35, 1949] seem to adhere to the Buffon and d'Alembert concepts of negligible small probabilities. Gibbon tellingly rebutted Buffon by asking whether you'd be indifferent to having to draw with 9,999 others, one to be put to death.[9] Do 56-year-old men cancel their term insurance each morning? Do insurance companies charge them nothing if they don't? Should immortal 21-year olds cancel their term insurance each month? Recognizing that 2^{-13} and 10^{-4} are of comparable magnitude, do real world Paul's require $\Sigma_1^{13}\ 2^{-i}U_1(W_1+2^ih)$ for $U_1(W_1+f_1^*)$ to play the infinite game? Or do they agree in advance (!) to quit at $n=14$, where they will "never" get to?

Third, Buffon rules out $n=\infty$ on the grounds that in finite time only a finite number of tosses can be made ". . . allowing only two minutes for each game [or toss]. . . ." So goes the argument reported in Todhunter [39, 1865, p. 346]. However, if we accept Buffon's argument of the previous paragraph, this paragraph's argument loses its terror: "never" [*almost* never!] will the game take more than 26 minutes. The *expected* duration of play of the Petersburg game is of course finite and surprisingly small

$$E\{n\}=\sum_1^{\infty}2^{-i}i=2 \tag{7.1}$$

If Peter and Paul agree to quit when either runs out of time, they can solve the de Méré Problem of Points on how to divide the antes. If they have linear utilities, they will require that Paul and Peter each put up (presumably in the form of interest bearing bonds, now that "time is scarce") nh ducats for a game to last at least n tosses, but subject to termination at any toss with "fair division" of any outstanding antes. The problem then degenerates into their decision to make one more toss at ever higher stakes, something they will

[8] Poisson [23, 1837] later emphasizes Peter's W_0 limitation and Paul's taking this into account. Shapley [36, 1972] emphasizes the "con game" feature of any assumed infinite Petersburg game.

[9] Keynes [15, 1921, p. 322] quotes Gibbon's sardonic words: "If a public lottery were drawn for the choice of an immediate victim, and if our name were inscribed on one of the ten thousand tickets, should we be perfectly easy?" In connection with the name of Gibbon, I should mention that Thomas Mann married the daughter of Alfred Pringsheim, professor of mathematics at Munich and 1896 translator of Bernoulli [4, 1738] into German.

not want to do if their utilities are more concave than linear utility. If agreement breaks down before the first toss, we infer non-linearity of utility. If it does not break down until some later point, Friedman-Savage [13, 1948] arguments might suggest existence of $U_1(W_1)$ functions with inflexion points in a W_1 interval where $U_1''(W_1)$ is positive: or, more plausibly, one might infer a "positive love of gambling," a persistent deviation from $E\{U_1(W_1)\}$ maximization, or an incoherent attitude concerning subjective probabilities.

A modern computer can speed up the time needed to play any game whose length is n tosses. But, on reflection, I confess that I am troubled by the relevant question of whether one could in finite time recognize a given irrational number on the unit interval. One cannot after all, throw an ideal dart with a point of *zero* width at random onto the unit interval and then "read off" the irrational point's numeral in the dyadic number system. The theory of elastic materials tells us that the point of every cone breaks off; in any case the words "read off" have reason to be put in quotation marks. We are left with the the feasibility requirement that Peter, Paul, and the referee understood in advance that n will not be able to exceed some large integer; this rules out those perfect systems for avoiding losses, in which one doubles up on bets "until" one "must" win.

Fourth, Buffon relies on an odd argument concerning the "relative value" of an equal money gain and money loss, which seems to lead inadvertently to Bernoulli's log W_1 rather than to linear $U_1(W_1)$. Buffon claims that, with $W_1 = 100$, a gain of 50 brings me only $1/3 = 50/150$; but an equal loss of 50 involves $1/2 = 50/100$. (Todhunter [39, 1865, p. 346] asks why not 50/50?) Since $1/2 > 1/3$, I am supposed to shun fair money bets; and so, of course, I'll not agree to $\Sigma_1^\infty 2^{-i}$ as my f_1 or f_1^*.

Buffon's implicit argument obviously is tempting to amateurs. Bentham somewhere says in effect: "Since £100 on £1,000 is more than it is on £10,000, we ought to favor redistribution of £100 from the latter rich men to the former poor men." The Weber-Fechner and Bernoulli laws of constant relative or "proportional effect" are constantly being rediscovered by such semantic syndromes. Mathematically, one need only agree with the functional equation

$$U_1(W_1 + hW_1) - U_1(W_1) \equiv U_1(A + hA) - U_1(A) \tag{7.2}$$

Then multiplying and dividing both sides by the initial wealths W_1 and A and taking limits as h goes to zero, one is trapped into the implied Bernoulli relation

$$U_1'(W_1) \equiv [AU_1'(A)]/W_1 = c/W_1 \tag{7.3}$$

$$U_1(W_1) = c \log W_1 + d, \quad c > 0,\ d \gtrless 0 \tag{7.4}$$

8. *D'Alembert's aberrations.* D'Alembert (1717–1783), a great physicist and prolific Encyclopedist, made a spectacle of himself in his many odd contentions about probabilities. So notorious were his positions that the sedate Todhunter loses patience and is reduced to saying at one point that an argument of d'Alembert's ". . . contains errors which seem extraordinary even for him."

D'Alembert's best remembered aberration is his insistence that on two independent tosses of a fair coin, the probabilities of two heads are 1/3 and of two tails 1/3. Orthodox writers would deduce these as 1/4 from writing down the 4 "equally likely" cases: HH, TH, HT, TT. D'Alembert, apparently applying some Pauli exclusion principle before its time, would consolidate the two intermediate cases into one, applying to it so to speak the Carnap label "coins that disagree in face." If the coin is biased away from probability of heads of $p=1/2$, one would indeed rather bet that two tosses will be alike than be different. But then one would not expect two heads to occur with the same probability as two tails. Richard Stone has somewhere shown that d'Alembert's (1/3, 1/3, 1/3) answer can be derived if one assumes that "p is equally likely to be anywhere on the interval [0, 1]." Did d'Alembert ever think of Stone's defense?[10]

D'Alembert seems also to have thought that, after observing a run like HHH, we should expect on the fourth toss a probability for tails of more than 1/2. Was this an anticipation of Marbe's errors on "maturing of odds," that nonsensical version of "the law of averages," according to which "tails are 'due' after heads have appeared too often"? And was d'Alembert speaking about a "fair" coin "fairly" tossed? Since he believed that two tosses of the same coin is not the same as one toss of two coins, one is in doubt. Actually, if I witnessed 10 heads in a row, I'd think I had learned something and would probably bet that the eleventh event is more likely to be heads than tails—perhaps because the single coin is built to have $p>1/2$, or because all 11 coins come from a mint that biases each to have $p>1/2$. But it is unclear that d'Alembert thinks in these terms.

Naturally, so opinionated a mind can be expected to have novel views on the Petersburg problem. And d'Alembert does not disappoint. He begins by calling it a "scandal" [39, Todhunter, 1865, p. 259] that the Cramer-Bernoulli problem and other solutions stand and that they have not been cleared up. D'Alembert proceeds to convert this notion of scandal into a self-fulfilling prophecy.

One specious argument is that the infinity of f_1 or f_1^* comes from the infinity of n. D'Alembert seems to think this follows from the valid fact that a game with $n+1$ deserves a higher f_1^* than one with n. Illogically, he has assumed that every infinite series of positive terms must be divergent. How did he overlook the fact that Cramer's and Bernoulli's solutions involve *finite* sums for convergent infinite series?

Moreover, true to his style, d'Alembert years later considers a variant game, which instead of paying 2^i at the ith toss pays only i. He notes that the series $\Sigma_1^\infty 2^{-i}i$ is convergent, just as was shown in (7.1) dealing with the expected number of tosses in the Petersburg game. But it never occurs to him to retract or revise his previous formulations.

D'Alembert considers, but rejects, the view of Fontaine [and Buffon and of Poisson later] that f_1^* cannot be infinite because Peter's finite W_0 will not enable him to fulfill his contractual payments under the infinite game. For, says d'Alembert in effect, suppose we replace ∞ by $n=100$: Paul will not agree on $f_1=f_1^*=100\ h$. So something else must be afoot other than the infinity of n. This is fair enough, and one might have thought this would push d'Alembert in the direction of the Cramer-Bernoulli formulation. But d'Alembert has his own different resolution in mind. (Parenthetically, Todhunter's pp. 261–62 rebuttal to the above argument seems more relevant for the game's referee than for Peter or Paul: Todhunter quotes Condorcet's later contention that $f_1=f_1^*=f_0=nh$ is the only price of the game that *will not in a long series of such games systematically transfer W from one player to the other*—a true implication of the Law of Large Numbers, but not relevant to whether either should agree to play the game at all.)

D'Alembert deserves the dubious credit for propagating rather than originating the view that *all probabilities below some critical positive fraction are to be treated as if they were zero.* It is reasonable for me

[10] I now learn from private conversation with Professor Stone that he did indeed invent this defense for d'Alembert.

to ignore the small probability that I shall find a dollar on my way to work. But why a rational man would want to ignore the small probability of a great disaster d'Alembert never seems to have thought about. Terms like $2^{-13}2^{13}$ d'Alembert finds convenient to set equal to $(2^{13}) \times 0$ in order that $\Sigma_1^\infty 2^{-i}2^i$ not be divergent and instead be 13!

For some people all things are possible. For d'Alembert many things are virtually impossible—"metaphysically possible," he agrees, but "physically impossible," he claims. Thus, d'Alembert says that Peter should not agree to give John (Jean) 1 crown for the privilege of receiving 2^{100} crowns from John if heads occurs for the first time on the hundredth toss of a (fair?) coin. Indeed Peter should not if he enjoys negative $U''(W)$. But, if his utility is linear, he would be ill advised to say that 2^{-100} is zero and its product with 2^{100} is also zero. D'Alembert actually thinks that the event, although not "necessarily" zero, is in fact "certainly" zero. "It is *metaphysically* possible [*i.e.*, possible] to throw two sixes with two dice a hundred times running; but it is *physically* impossible because it has never [?] happened and never will [??] happen."

I have already discussed in connection with Buffon what the effect of disregarding small probabilities is on the Petersburg calculations. It remains here only to mention that d'Alembert has further odd suggestions to make $\Sigma 2^{-i}2^i$ convergent: arbitrarily, he proposes to replace 2^{-i} by $2^{-i}(1+\beta i^2)^{-1}$, or by $2^{-i}2^{-i}$ or $2^{-i}2^{-i+1}$, or by $2^{-i}[1+\beta(K-i)^{-j+½}]$. One wonders why.

As mentioned already, d'Alembert later replaces 2^i by i, yielding the convergent sum of $2^{-i}i$ already given in (7.1). Perhaps dimly realizing that he is here contradicting his earlier remarks about any infinite series having to be infinite, d'Alembert is said by Todhunter [39, 1865, p. 281] to question that the expected value of a random variable is to be the sum of all its possible values each weighted by its probability. One wonders that d'Alembert does not sacrifice the scandal that $2+2=4$.[11]

Finally, and enough is enough, d'Alembert read Laplace's calculations for $E\{W_1\}$ in which the coin has an unknown bias between heads and tails, so that instead of being known to be at 1/2, p is anywhere on the unit interval. This somehow leads d'Alembert to suggest replacing 2^{-i} in $2^{-i}2^i$ by a sequence of fractions whose value at each i depends on what occurred on earlier tosses, leading to an expression dominated by a convergent geometric series and therefore finite. I know of no commentator who has hitherto been able to make sense of this.

If forced to find a defense for d'Alembert, I would suggest the following. Since d'Alembert sometimes professes to believe that successive tosses are not independent in their probabilities, let us postulate the following simple Markov process:

$$\begin{aligned}&\text{Prob}\{\text{H at toss } t+1 \mid \text{H at toss } t\} \quad (8.1)\\ &\quad = \text{Prob}\{\text{T at toss } t+1 \mid \text{T at toss } t\}\\ &\quad = \frac{1}{2}\lambda < \frac{1}{2}, \quad 1 > \lambda\end{aligned}$$

To start off the Petersburg game fairly, let H and T be equally likely at the first toss.

Now the game will tend to end sooner, albeit it could by rare chance go on for an indefinitely large time. One easily verifies

$$\begin{aligned}&\text{Prob}\{(t\text{ T's in a row}\} \quad (8.2)\\ &\quad = \frac{1}{2}\lambda\ \text{Prob}\{(t-1)\text{T's in a row}\}\\ &\quad = \text{Prob}\{t-1)\text{T's in a row}\}\\ &\qquad - \text{Prob}\{(t-1)\text{T's followed by H}\}\\ &\quad = \lambda^{t-1}2^{-t} \text{ if Prob}\{\text{first T}\} = \frac{1}{2}\end{aligned}$$

[11] It is meaningless to question the *definition*: $E\{g(x)\} = \int g(x)d[\text{Prob}\{X \le x\}]$. D'Alembert would make more sense if he were merely questioning whether people *act* to maximize the expected value (or "first moment") of *any* function of outcomes. Prior to 1950, I took such a view until converted by L. J. Savage to the Ramsey-Marschak "independence axioms." *Cf.* Samuelson [26, 1950; 27, 1952], Jacob Marschak [18, 1950], Savage [32, 1954].

$$\text{Prob}\{(t-1)\text{T's followed by H}\} \quad (8.3)$$
$$= \text{Prob}\{\text{game ends at } t \text{ tosses}\}$$
$$= \lambda^{t-2}2^{-t+1} - \lambda^{t-1}2^{-t}$$
$$= (2-\lambda)\lambda^{t-2}2^{-t}$$

It follows that

$$E\{W_1\} = 2^{-1}2 + (2-\lambda)2^{-2}2^2 \quad (8.4)$$
$$+ (2-\lambda)\lambda 2^{-3}2^3$$
$$+ \ldots + (2-\lambda)\lambda^{i-2}2^{-i}2^i + \ldots$$
$$= 1 + (2-\lambda)\sum_0^\infty \lambda^i$$
$$= 1 + (2-\lambda)(1-\lambda)^{-1}, \; 0 \le \lambda < 1$$

If $\lambda = 0$, the game is sure to end in 2 tosses, and $E\{W_1\} = 2^{-1}2 + 2^{-1}4 = 3$. Were λ above 1, there would be positive serial correlation; $E\{W_1\}$, which is already on the border of divergence when $\lambda = 1$, will be even more rapidly divergent so that $E\{W_1\}n^{-1} \to \infty$ as $n \to \infty$.

In casting this pearl before d'Alembert, I may be defending him against his conscious will. This does give d'Alembert his finite $E\{W_1\}$. But will Paul be willing to pay so much for f_1? or require so much for f_1^*? Definitely not, if $U_1''(W_1) < 0$.

To explain d'Alembert's perversities, recall that he lived in an age of amateurs. Outside of the Bernoulli circle, there were few well-trained pros. Beyond this, even within physics d'Alembert was a brilliant, but erratic, theorist. It was part of his psychological profile not to be prosaically clear-headed, and to strive to be different.

9. *Condorcet.* Condorcet (1743–1794), prolific *philosophe,* believed in the indefinite perfectibility of mankind, but fell victim to the French Revolution. Malthus's father was a convert to his views, and it was to refute them that Malthus developed his population theory. Analytically, Condorcet is best remembered for his pre-Arrow demonstration of the possibility of intransitivity of simple majority voting; thus, let A rank 3 events in the order (α, β, γ); B rank them in the order (β, γ, α); C rank them in the order (γ, α, β). Then in a vote between α and β, α wins 2 to 1. Likewise β wins over γ 2 to 1. But γ wins over α 2 to 1—a seeming contradiction.

Condorcet wrote widely on probability, if obscurely. He particularly analyzed the probability of correct verdicts of tribunals and juries, what J. S. Mill considered the underworld of probability analysis. Todhunter regards his addiction to Bayes' Theorem as excessive. We have already noted Condorcet's acceptance of the notions of Buffon and d'Alembert concerning the ignorability of small positive probabilities. He also concurred with earlier writers that Peter's finite W_0 limits f_1^* to a finite bound.

With respect to Petersburg problems, Condorcet asserts that, for $n = 1$, stake of h, and a fair coin, the only tenable *long run* value for f_1 and f_0 must be $h = .5(2h) + .5(0)$. This number, independently of the tastes of Paul or Peter, is the only number that keeps wealth from systematically being transferred between Peter and Paul in a *large number of Petersburg games.* James Bernoulli's Law of Large Numbers makes Condorcet's rediscovery or reassertion of this truth strictly unnecessary, but not useless. Still, at best the recognition of this truth is relevant only for the referee, since neither Peter nor Paul will play the game if they have $U_k(W_k)$ more concave than W_k. Alternatively, the Condorcet remark about the outcome of a large number of games might be relevant to the problem of the Ford Foundation in allocating its subsidy between Peter and Paul to cover the difference between h and f_1 and between f_0 and h.

Condorcet applies the same reasoning when $n >> 1$, finding that $\Sigma_1^n 2^{-i}2^i = n$ is the critical price that will result in no systematic transfer of W between Peter and Paul when a great number of games of n tosses are played.

Condorcet does recognize that Peter stands to lose a great deal with small probability; that Paul stands to win a little with great probability.

Condorcet seems almost to state an interesting theorem: "At fair odds, it is 'better' (in the sense of 'less bad') to have a relatively large gain with small probability than to have a small gain with large probability."

Is this correct? For quadratic utility, the theorem is *not* true as stated. The two options are equally bad in utility terms. However, for positive U''', as with constant-relative-risk aversion or constant-absolute-risk aversion, a version of the theorem is indeed correct.

Here is a proof. Consider fixed positive increments of wealth, $0 < L << G$. What is asserted is that, necessarily

$$\frac{L}{L+G}U(W+G)+\frac{G}{L+G}U(W-L) \quad (9.1)$$
$$> \frac{L}{L+G}U(W-G)+\frac{G}{L+G}U(W+L)$$

For $U(W)=W^{\gamma}/\gamma$, $U(W)=\log W$, $G<W$ and L/G small, the result is verified to be valid. For $U(W)=-e^{aW}$, it is also true.

For $U'''(\ )>0$, it is locally true in the following sense:

$$V(\epsilon)=\frac{L}{L+G}[U(W+\epsilon G) \quad (9.2)$$
$$-U(W-\epsilon G)]$$
$$+\frac{G}{L+G}[U(W-\epsilon L)-U(W+\epsilon L)]$$
$$V(0)=0$$
$$V'(0)=2\frac{LG-GL}{L+G}U'(W)=0$$
$$V''(0)=0\frac{LG[G-L]}{L+G}U''(W)=0$$
$$V'''(0)=2\frac{LG[G^2-L^2]}{L+G}U'''(W)$$

Therefore $V(\epsilon)$ has sign of $U'''(W)$ for $0<\epsilon<\delta$. (9.3)

So, if $U'''(W)>0$, the Condorcet theorem is valid locally around W_1. Again, we are reminded that Peter's problem is even greater than Paul's, not only with respect to his needed liquidity but also with respect to his unwillingness to play the game.

10. *Stigler on Cournot et al.* The nineteenth century added comparatively little to the St. Petersburg discussion.[12] I content myself here with commenting on Stigler's discussion of some of these writers.

Stigler [38, 1965, pp. 108–115] reviews the Cramer and Bernoulli $E\{U_1(W_1)\}$ resolutions of the paradox, relating the latter's $\log W_1$ to the Weber-Fechner and Marshall discussions of psychology and economics. Stigler [38, 1965, p. 113] seems critical of the Poisson or Buffon concern to replace $\Sigma_1^{\infty}2^{-i}2^i$ by some finite series, asserting that "Bernoulli was right in seeking the explanation in utility (or, alternatively, as Cournot did in market appraisals), and he was wrong only in making a special assumption with respect to the [$\log W_1$] shape of the utility curve for which there was no evidence and which he submitted to no tests." Like Keynes, Stigler [37, 1950, n. 128] seems to think Bertrand's belief that by subdivision of stakes "fear of insolvency may be reduced without limit" is somehow a valid point scored against Poisson and others concerned for Peter's solvency.

On Cournot, Stigler is most interesting, saying [38, 1965, p. 112], "Cournot, here as in demand theory, refused to look at utility and resorted to the market evaluation of the game. . . . He reformulated the problem: the state . . . issues tickets: No. 1 pays $1.00 if the first throw is heads; No. 2 pays $2.00 if the first head comes on the second throw; etc. He argued that no one would buy the high-numbered tickets."

One welcomes Cournot to the ranks of those interested in revealed preference.

[12] Laplace [16, 1812], Poisson [23, 1837], Cournot [10, 1843], and Bertrand [5, 1889] receive merited notice from Keynes, Stigler, and other writers. Schumpeter [34, 1954] cites as relevant 1832 work of Hermann and 1865 work of F. A. Lange; Menger [19, 1934] cites 1806 work of Lichtenberg, 1842 work of Fries, and 1882 work of Czuber.

Whatever the shortcomings of his postulated partial-equilibrium demand functions relating price and quantity of a single good, Cournot's hypothesis is a good one, that the sequence of roots, $(x_1^*, x_2^*, x_3^*, \ldots)$ is diminishing in

$$U_1(W_1 + x_i^*) = 2^{-i}U_1(W_1 + h2^{i-1}) + (1 - 2^{-i})U_1(W_1) \quad (10.1)$$

This follows from the strong concavity of $U_1(W_1)$, as can be seen from the implied positive sign of $(\partial/\partial p)\{pU_1(W_1 + hp^{-1}) + (1 - p)U_1(W_1)\}$. As a converse, if $(x_1^*, x_2^*, \ldots)$ is a decreasing sequence at *all* W_1, we can infer that $U_1'(W_1)$ diminishes with W_1. Q.E.D. (Note: if $x_2^* < x_1^*$ for all W_1, the same qualitative truth is assured!)

11. *Keynes's commentary and novel "risk" concept.* The commentary of Keynes on other Petersburg writers has already been commended [15, 1921, chap. 26]. He adds a few new wrinkles of his own, and we may say of him what he said [15, 1921, p. 284, n. 1] of Cournot: Keynes "never touched a subject without contributing something to it, but . . . ."[13]

[13] Keynes of Tilton, like Homer, has been known to nod. The former is only half right to write [15, 1921, p. 320] that ". . . poor men should not gamble and that millionaires should do nothing else." True, tycoons bankrupt clerks more often than vice versa: but that is only because there is so little to win from clerks. With negative $U_i''(W_i)$, *no one* should gamble, rich or poor. The Keynes [15, 1921, p. 320, n. 1] argument that the social welfare view negates the millionaires' view that gambling should take place is thus unnecessary. Moreover, the social welfare view against gambling is defectively stated: gambling is bad not primarily because gambling-to-ruin *most often* transfers dollars from high-marginal utility domiciles among clerks to low-marginal-utility domiciles among tycoons: a gamble is socially bad even on a stake level that will ruin neither party, and hence where the dollars are *equally likely* to go from rich to poor or poor to rich; what's bad about gambling is that, even at *balanced* probabilities, the dollars that go upward represent less incremental utilities than the dollars that go downward. (Even if you believe the rich are born more exquisite utility receptacles than the poor, gambling to ruin is socially bad despite the greater *probability* that a clerk will contribute to a tycoon.)

Keynes writes: ". . . the theoretic dispersal of what element of paradox remains must be brought about, I think, by a development of the theory of risk. It is primarily the great *risk* of the wager which deters us [Pauls] . . ." [15, 1921, p. 319]. Keynes is here proposing a new (and dubious) concept of "risk."

Keynes words on "risk" are so brief they can essentially be reproduced in full [15, 1921, pp. 314–15]:

> . . . the theory of 'mathematical expectation' has been very seldom disputed . . . d'Alembert has been almost alone in casting serious doubts upon it (although he only brought himself into disrepute by doing so). . . . Is it certain that a larger good, which is extremely improbable, is precisely equivalent ethically to a smaller good which is proportionately more probable?
>
> There seems, at any rate, a good deal to be said for the conclusion that, other things being equal, that course of action is preferable which involves least risk. . . . [T]he absence of risk increase[s] *pro tanto* the desirability of the action to which [it] refer[s]. . . .
>
> The 'risk' may be defined in some such way as follows. If A is the amount of good which may result, p its probability $(p + q = 1)$, and E the value of the 'mathematical expectation,' so that $E = pA$, then the 'risk' is R, where $R = p(A - E) = p(1 - p)A = pqA = qE$. This may be put another way: E measures the net immediate sacrifice which should be made in the hope of obtaining A; q is the probability that this sacrifice will be made in vain; so that qE is the 'risk.' The ordinary theory supposes that the ethical value of an expectation is a function of E only and is entirely independent of R.

Since Keynes has not spelled out exactly how he would define his "risk" in the general situation of several algebraic gains and losses with their respective defined probabilities $(A_1, \ldots, A_n; p_1, \ldots, p_n = 1 - \Sigma_1^{n-1} p_j)$, it will be best to stay with his case of a single monetary gain A, that will obtain with probability p. Thus, we consider $(A_1, A_2; p_1, p_2) \equiv (A, 0; p, 1 - p)$. This case has the virtue of being equivalent to the simplest Petersburg game, with one specifiable money gain payable if a general coin turns up one way, or with zero gain if the coin does not turn up that way.

What would Paul, possessed of initial money wealth, W_1, require as a payment, $f_1{}^*$, to make him indifferent between facing the $(A, 0; p, 1-p)$ option or not facing it?

Three different answers have been given: the maximum-expected-money-gain approach of Pascal and pre-Petersburg-paradox writers; the maximum-expected-utility-of-money approach of post-Petersburg writers such as D. Bernoulli, Cramer, Bentham, Marshall, Ramsey, von Neumann–Morgenstern, Savage, and mainstream modern economists; the view inferable from Keynes's notion that people normally wish for maximum dollar return *ceteris paribus* and for minimum Keynes's "risk" *ceteris paribus*.

Here then are three different measures of $f_1{}^*$, call them F_1, F_2, F_3. Being in principle observable for each specified $(A; p)$ pair of numbers—or, more generally, for each specified triplet of numbers $(A; p; W)$—one can hope to test what the differences are between the three alternative models and perhaps even hope to let the empirical facts decide between the different models.

The Pascal solution is easily computed as follows:

$$\begin{aligned} 1(W+F_1) &= p(W+A) \\ &\quad + (1-p)(W+0) \\ F_1 &= \phi_1[p, A; W] \equiv \phi_1[p, A] \equiv pA \end{aligned} \tag{11.1}$$

The Cramer-Bernoulli solution is less easily computed, as we have seen, but is definable in principle as follows:

$$E\{U(W+F_2)\} = E\{U(W+A_i)\} \tag{11.2}$$

with F_2 the root of

$$\begin{aligned} 1U(W+F_2) &= pU(W+A) \\ &\quad + (1-p)U(W+0) \end{aligned}$$

$$F_2 = \phi_2[p, A; W] < pA, \quad \text{for } 0 < p < 1 \text{ and } U''(W) < 0 \tag{11.3}$$

Here, the exact shape of the strictly-concave $U(W)$ function, or of its falling marginal utility, $U'(W)$, determines the exact short-fall of $\phi_2[p, A; W]$ below $\phi_1[p, A]$. Obviously for $U(W)$ linear and $U''(W) \equiv 0$, the two solutions, $\phi_1[\ ]$ and $\phi_2[\ ]$, agree. However, if people are averse to chance dispersion as such and are partial to steady and secure returns, the curvature of $U(W)$ will be the reflection of that fact.

Now we come to Keynes's novel third model. Taking him literally, we must write F_3 as the following general function:

$$\begin{aligned} F_3 &= \phi_3(p, A; W) \equiv \phi_3(p, A) \\ &= K(\text{expected money gain, "risk"}) \\ &= K(pA),[1-p]pA; \ \partial K(\ )/\partial(pA) > 0; \\ &\quad \partial K(\ )/\partial([1-p]pA) < 0 \end{aligned} \tag{11.4}$$

Keynes's proposed decision procedure is independent of initial wealth, W. In general, therefore, the resulting $\phi_3(p, A)$ differs from $\phi_2(p, A)$. The latter will be free from W only in the special case of constant-absolute-risk-aversion, when $U(W) \equiv -e^{-\alpha W}$. Although $\phi_1(p, A)$ is similarly independent of W, F_3 is less than F_1 in the same way that (11.3) showed F_2 to be less than F_1. Abhorrence of chancy variation is thus captured by the novel Keynes 1921 model alternative to the standard $E\{U(\ )\}$ model. (Indeed, if he had used *RA* rather than *A*, Keynes would be suggesting one version of the mean-variance model.) However, Keynes's new risk model fails to satisfy the "sure-thing" and "independence" axioms of stochastic choice theory whenever it differs from that theory as applied to $U(W) - - e^{-\alpha W}$. For more than half a century, nothing useful seems to have come from Keynes's 1921 innovation of his new "risk" concept.

12. *Karl Menger's contribution.* My text has already outlined the great debt in the discussion of the St. Petersburg paradox

that we owe to Menger [19, 1934] with its demonstration that, unless $U_1(W_1)$ is bounded, Paul's needed compensation, f_1^*, can be made to be infinity by a proper stepping up of the gains at each throw (*i.e.*, of $X_{in} = X_i$ in my general notation). Here I wish only to add some unsystematic comments on the Menger article.

In the 1967 translation of Menger [19, 1934], the author mentions in the new initial footnote Morgenstern's report that "this paper played a primary role in persuading J. von Neumann to undertake a formal treatment of utility, which was incorporated in the second and third editions of von Neumann and Morgenstern's, *Theory of Games and Economic Behavior*" [22, 1944, 1947, 1953]. Menger also mentions that his paper was conceived in 1923 before he could have known of Frank Ramsey's 1926 sketch of axiomatized personal-probability-cum-personal-utility in Ramsey [25, 1931], a formulation independently arrived at by Bruno de Finetti [12, 1937], Savage [32, 1954], Marschak [18, 1950], and no doubt others. Actually, however, Menger does not much discuss Ramseyan problems like: "How do I, Paul, decide that this coin will on the next throw or sequence of throws have a property like 'probability of heads equals probability of tails, regardless of what face appeared in previous tosses'? Why should I, Paul, act to maximize the *first moment* of an existent function of wealth outcomes rather than the *median* of such a function?" And so forth. Savage and Marschak, better than von Neumann–Morgenstern or Menger, address themselves to these questions along lines implicit in Ramsey [25, 1931] and involving what are called various "independence axioms" in Samuelson [27, 1952].

Menger [19, 1934, pp. 214–15] does touch upon the question of whether single games can have meaningful "probabilities" attached to them, in connection with his footnote 5 discussion of Fries. Also, if I understand Menger [19, 1934, pp. 222–26], it is a matter of empirical verification that people do tend toward "undervaluation of choices with high probabilities," perhaps because of some love for gambling, suspense, and even danger. At the other extreme from treating true p's near one as if they were not so near to one, Menger takes it as an empirical propensity that people tend to "undervalue very small probabilities," treating true p's near zero as if they were nearer to zero. Perhaps so—although I think they *exaggerate* small p's of vastly pleasant events. And, I would add, perhaps when a p is near to one-half, people tend to treat it as if it were nearer one-half than it is ("equiprobability of the unknown," *etc.*). It is difficult to be definite here. Thus, it is not easy for me to learn from sampling experience that a probability is really about 10^{-4}; therefore a jury of observers may infer that probabilities I truly regard as 10^{-4} I apparently treat as if they were 10^{-5}, whereas in fact it may be the case that I am not able to judge that the probability is really about 10^{-4}.

Mention may be made of the fact that, if I am careless, I may choose between two acts so that the probability that my decision will put me ahead is large. But, when I think about this philosophy, I realize that it *distorts* my decisions away from what I really want to accomplish, namely the maximization of expected value of my utility. An empiricist who describes "slips of the tongue" need not glorify them into "intended" modes of speech, even though they do occur with some regularity and pattern. And a Freudian will want to study closely "mere slips."

Menger's general non-dogmatic approach, in which any commonly observed behavior is treated as admissible, is congenial to my notions. However, I myself would be a bit more sparing in use of such phrases as ". . . he will not, if he is sane . . ." [19, 1934, p. 212]; ". . . behavior of normal individuals . . ." [19, p. 213]; ". . . no normal person would risk his total fortune . . ." [19, p. 217]; ". . . behavior of normal people . . ." [19, p. 222]; ". . . it is clear that a normal man will risk only a limited part of his total wealth to buy chances in games . . ." [19, p. 224]. Presumably these are intended only to describe what the reader will agree are *correct empirical propositions about most people,* and to this sense I have no objection.

An excellent sampling of Menger is provided in Arrow [2, 1971, p. 23]. Menger [19, 1934] is a modern classic that, despite my quibbles, stands above all criticism.

13. *Post-Menger writers.* These can be treated very briefly. I have already mentioned the developments associated with the names of Ramsey, de Finetti, Savage, and Marschak in defining both the personal p's and the personal $U(W)$ in expressions like $\Sigma p_j U(W_j)$. By the accidental fact that von Neumann and Morgenstern happened to need "utility payoffs" and mixed-strategy probabilities in their Zero-Sum-Transferable-Payoffs solutions of game theory, a repopularization of expected-utility maximization took place. However, in any case, Abraham Wald's extensions of the traditional R. A. Fisher and Neyman-Pearson versions of statistics were bound to bring into renewed prominence Bayesian probabilities in the decision calculus. Relevant references include von Neumann and Morgenstern [22, 1944, 1947, 1953], Wald [40, 1950], Schlaifer [33, 1959], Raiffa and Schlaifer [24, 1961], and Arrow [2, 1971].

On the Petersburg problem, relatively little of recent work needs to be noticed here other than Samuelson [28, 1960], Arrow [2, 1971], Coolidge [9, 1949], Shapley [36, 1972], Brito [6, 1975], and Aumann [3, 1975].

Samuelson [28, 1960] demonstrates the point of Bertrand [5, 1889] and Keynes [15, 1921], that subdividing the stakes preserves the infinity implied by the St. Petersburg paradox even when the Cramer-Bernoulli or Menger $U_1(W_1)$ functions depict strongly concave utility and bounded utility. The readers of Bertrand and Keynes may wish to remind those authors that the total numbers of grains of sand or of molecules are themselves *finite* numbers, so that (W_1, W_0) still remain limited when expressed in such numeraire units. And those readers may wonder whether Bertrand and Keynes believe that there is any paradox *left to be resolved* in their regained infinity for the limit to f_1/h as $n \to \infty$.

My own position is simple. If for each finite n we make the stake per toss small enough, we can prove that Paul's $f_1(W_1, n, h)$ and $f_1{}^*(W_1, n, h)$ approximate as closely as we may wish to n times h. Therefore, by the double limit process, in which $h \to 0$ and $n \to \infty$, we prove that

$$\lim_{n\to\infty} [\lim_{h\to 0} \{f_1(W_1, n, h)/h\}] \tag{13.1}$$

$$= \lim_{n\to\infty}[n] = \infty \tag{13.2}$$

$$\lim_{n\to\infty} [\lim_{h\to 0} \{f_1{}^*(W_1, n, h)/h\}] = \lim_{n\to\infty}[n] = \infty \tag{13.3}$$

where $f_1(\ )$ and $f_1{}^*(\ )$ are roots of the equations in my footnote 4 above.

I see nothing paradoxical about this infinity result. Those who ask a silly question must expect to get a silly answer. And those who contrive an infinity process must expect to generate infinity limits. No Paul or Peter will reproach himself if he behaves in such a way that, when $h \to 0$ and $n = h^{-1}c \to \infty$, carrying h to zero, his needed $f_1(\ )$ and $f_1{}^*(\ )$ will approach the *constant* ducats magnitude of $c < W_1$. Why should Bertrand, Keynes, or any of us deem there to be *any* paradox in this necessary prosaic fact?

This 1960 demonstration, once understood, boils down merely to the truism that, *for small enough stakes, concave utility leads to nearly the same behavior as linear utility,* a useful observation already made by D. Bernoulli in 1738!

Arrow [2, 1971] makes mention of the St. Petersburg paradox in several places: *i.e.*, pages 6, 23, 28–29, 63–69. In his earliest references, from a classic 1951 essay, he approves of the Menger line of argument that, with $U_1(W_1)$ unbounded above, Paul's f_1^* can be made indefinitely large, writing [2, p. 23]: "This is rejected as contrary to intuition"; and [2, pp. 28–29]: "If, as seems natural, we demand that all utilities [including those of lottery options, for which my f_1^* is an equivalent needed payment] be finite, then Menger's argument leads to the conclusion that no utility should exceed some fixed upper bound."

In his later 1965 Finnish lectures, Arrow seems to take a stronger line. Thus, Arrow [2, 1971, p. 64] argues that unbounded $U_1(W_1)$ in the Super-Petersburg game context ". . . leads to a contradiction" [within Arrow's axiom system].[14] What I take this to mean is that, if $U_1(W_1)$ is not bounded both above and below, certain well-defined probability options will have no finite $E\{U_1(W_1)\}$ and cannot therefore be part of a *complete* ordering dependent upon expected utility. As I have indicated elsewhere, a person who came to us with $U_1(W_1) = \log W_1$ might have to be deemed admissible even if he had to resort to something other than $E\{U_1(W_1)\}$ for ordering some of his options. The fact that a thought experiment can be contrived in which his $f_1^* \to \infty$ does not seem to me to be of great moment: in real life, no Peter or Karl will contrive such an actual experiment to *actually confront him with.* I agree that the theoretical axiom formulation has a less neat model to handle this postulated Paul: but that is tough doughnuts for the theorist, not for Paul, whose only personal problem is deciding how to choose among options that have no finite expected utilities.

Despite, my contention that the Petersburg super-paradox need never have played a role in alerting theorists to the problems for ordering when utility is unbounded, this should not lessen my admiration for Menger's work for its own sake and for the historic fact that it *did* serve that alerting purpose.

Coolidge [9, 1949, pp. 172–74] mentions two rather delightful oddities in Buffon. Thus Coolidge [9, p. 172] writes: "Buffon assumes that after each day when the sun has risen the probability that it will rise the next day is doubled [by which is undoubtedly meant, the probability that it will *not* rise the next day is halved: PAS]. Assuming that it has already risen 2,190,000 times [since Genesis?], the probability that it will rise the next day is $1 - 2^{-2,190,000}$."

Coolidge (like Laplace earlier) properly scorns this odd mode of inductive inference, which is such as to make Bayes look like a genuis. What Coolidge (and, apparently, Buffon) did not notice was the effect on the Petersburg game if its objective probabilities of a head at each toss were not independent but rather behaved in such a way as to make Buffon's mode of

[14] One of the considerations that Arrow considers as telling against unbounded utility is that it will lead to a violation of the Continuity Axiom in stochastic choice: For any 3 descending options, A, B, and C, there must always be an intermediate probability, p, such that a p-choice-at-A-and-a-$(1-p)$-choice-at-C, written as A_pC, is *indifferent* to B. Now let $U_1(W)$ be unbounded above. Let A be the opportunity to play Menger's Super-Petersburg game; let B be \$2 with certainty, and C \$1 with certainty. Then there is no such intermediate p: actually, any positive p will make A_pC better than B; but for $p=0$, B of \$2 is definitely better than A of \$1—a clear contradiction to the Continuity Axiom, and one that Arrow believes should perturb most reflective people. It would not, however, perturb a Pascal-Wagerer with unbounded utility: such a person would satisfy the Continuity Axiom with respect to *all finite* probability situations; but he would *want* to violate the Continuity Axiom precisely where he does violate it (I mean, even on careful reflection he would *want* to do so). Incidentally, if $U(W)$ is bounded on $(-\infty,\infty)$, it must have at least one Friedman-Savage inflexion point. In that case, stochastic-reaction "demand" functions may well involve ties, jumps, and discontinuities to parameter shifts.

inductive inference a correct one. The new Petersburg game is still of indefinitely many possible tosses; its mathematical expectation to Paul is still a divergent sum, but at a slower rate than in the standard game; oddly, although the probability of Paul's winning a small (early-toss) prize is reduced, Paul is now *worse off*, since it turns out that there is a positive probability that the game will *never* end and never pay Paul anything!

Now, instead of considering the divergent limit of $\Sigma_1^n 2^i 2^{-i} = n$, we consider[15] the divergent limit of

$$B_n = 2^1 p_1 + 2^2 p_2 + \ldots + 2^n p_n \qquad (13.4)$$

$$= 2^1 2^{-1} + 2^1 2^{-1}$$

$$+ \sum_{i=3}^{n} (2^i 2^{-i})[\prod_{j=1}^{i-2} (1 - 2^{-j})]$$

$$< \sum_{i=1}^{n} (2^i 2^{-i}) = n$$

The last inequality holds because the bracketed terms are clearly less than unity (but with a non-zero limiting value). The divergence of the B_n sequence follows from the ascertainable truth of the last parenthetical fact. Hence

$$\lim_{n \to \infty} (2^n 2^{-n}) \prod_1^{n-2} (1 - 2^{-j}) = a > 0 \qquad (13.5)$$

$$\lim_{n \to \infty} (B_n / n) = b > 0 \qquad (13.6)$$

Also, since

$$p_i < 2^{-i}, \quad i \geq 3 \qquad (13.7)$$

therefore

$$\sum_1^n p_i < \sum_1^n 2^{-i}, \quad n \geq 3 \qquad (13.8)$$

$$\lim \sum_1^n p_i < 1 = \sum_1^n 2^{-i} \qquad (13.9)$$

This demonstrates that, under the postulated Buffon tendency of a long run of tails to make more tails so likely, there is a substantial probability that the infinite Petersburg game will never end—to the pleasure of Peter and the discomfort of Paul.

In Coolidge's second novel comment on Buffon, he writes [9, 1949, p. 173]: "Buffon had the bright idea of having a child throw a coin 2,048 times. [Todhunter [39, 1865, p. 346] says 2,084 times, of which 1,061 and 494 times Paul wins on the first and second toss.] The total payment [from my Peter to my Paul on as many Petersburg games as were completed] was [twice] 10,057 crowns, so that the average was about [twice] 5 [or about twice 10,057 ÷ 2,048]. Peter should offer about [twice] 5 crowns to come into the game, not an infinite sum." Coolidge makes no sense of this odd conclusion, and later rightly questions Buffon's replacing $\Sigma 2^{-i} 2^i$ by the *ad hoc* result $\Sigma 2^{-i}(9/5)^i$, merely because replacing 2 by (9/5) makes the last infinite series sum to [twice] 5.

Of course Buffon's calculated ratio is nonsensical as a proposed estimate of the mathematical expectation of Paul per infinite Petersburg game. In 2,048 tosses, Paul may win anything from 0 to $2^{2{,}048}$. Why take the result of 1 arbitrary sample? And how did Buffon score uncompleted games? If Buffon correctly applies the "method of fair division" between Paul and Peter for games interrupted before their finish, he will find that half the time on the 2,048th toss the sequence shows a T and an incomplete game: with probabilities $(2^{-1}, 2^{-2}, \ldots, 2^{-2{,}048})$ the *last* run of T's will be of lengths (0, 1, 2, . . . , 2,048), each leaving Peter owing Paul the "fair" liability of $(0, 2^{1 \times \infty}, 2^{2 \times \infty}, \ldots, 2^{2{,}048 \times \infty})$; adding these terminal liabilities to what Peter has paid Paul for completed games, Buffon would have to pay infinity half the time: therefore, Paul's expected money gain will indeed be infinite (either per game or per opportunity to play as many games as can be played and with

[15] To derive (13.4), define Prob{T|all previous i occurrences were T's only} $= \pi_i$. Then Prob{i T's occur in i tosses} $= \gamma_i = \pi_{i-1} \gamma_{i-1} = \pi_{i-1} \pi_{i-2} \ldots \pi_1 \gamma_1$. Therefore, Prob{game ends with H first at i^{th} toss} $= P_i = (1 - \pi_{i-1})\gamma_{i-1}$. Since Buffon assumes that $\pi_i = 1 - 2^{-i}$, $\gamma_1 = 2^{-1}$, we have (13.4)'s $p_i = 2^{-(i-1)}[1 - 2^{-(i-2)}] \ldots [1 - 2^{-1}]2^{-1}$.

fair terminal adjustment). More generally, Buffon might have computed for general N and n, $E\{$Paul's gains from as many completed n-toss-games of Petersburg type as can be completed in N tosses, with or without "fair" terminal payments$\} = G_{n,N}$ or $G'_{n,N}$. Although $G'_{n,N}$ and $G'_{n,N}/N$ for fixed N approach finite limits as $n \to \infty$, still as $n \to \infty$ and as N also $\to \infty$, the limit is infinite. Furthermore, $G_{n,N}$ and G_n/N each go to ∞ as $n \to \infty$. Consequently, Buffon's Monte Carlo experiments are childish ways to avoid the true infinity in the Petersburg expectations: adultishly understood, they confirm the need to replace Paul's linear $U_1(W)$ by sufficiently concave $U_1(W)$ if Paul's needed compensation for foregoing ordinary-Petersburg options, $f_1{}^*(n, n)$, is to stay bounded, no matter how great n and N jointly become.

Shapley [36, 1972], as the words "con game" in his title suggest, reasserts with great force the point already made by Fontaine, Buffon, Poisson, and in fact the great majority of writers who deal with the Petersburg problem at any length —namely, that Peter must be understood by a thoughtful Paul to have but a finite W_0. So, even if Paul had linear utility, the $f_1{}^*$ root to the following relevant Poisson [23, 1837] equation would be finite and surprisingly small:

$$\begin{aligned} U_1(W_1 + f_1{}^*) &= \sum_1^k 2^{-i} U_1(W_1 + 2^{i-1}) \qquad (13.2)\\ &\quad + U_1(W_1 + W_0)\, 2^{-k} W_0,\\ &\quad 2^{k-1} \le W_0 < 2^k\\ &\approx \sum_1^k 2^{-i} U_1(W_1 + 2^{i-1})\\ &\quad + U_1(W_1 + W_0)\, W_0{}^{-1},\\ &\quad k \approx \log_2 W_0 \end{aligned}$$

For $U_1(W_1) \equiv bW_1 + a$, this becomes

$$\begin{aligned} f_1{}^* &= \frac{1}{2}k + W_0 2^{-k} \qquad (13.3)\\ &\approx \frac{1}{2}k + 1,\ k >> 1\\ &\approx \frac{1}{2}\log_2 W_0 + 1 \end{aligned}$$

For W_0 equal to the U.S. 1972 GNP of about $\$(1.4)10^{11}$ Shapley reckons that Paul will pay less than 25¢, since $\log_2[(1.4)10^{12}] \approx 47$¢. Since we are talking about wealth and not calendar-year income, Shapley might have safely raised $(1.4)10^{11}$ to $5(10^{11})$ with resulting $f_1{}^*$ remarkably modest, perhaps 27 cents.

If Peter of Las Vegas can be expected to pay off only $W_0 = \$10{,}000$, linear $U_1(W_1)$ calls for $f_1{}^*$ of only about 11¢. For such a Paul to rationally require $f_1{}^*$ of \$1,000, Shapley finds Paul must believe Peter can pay $\$10^{60204}$ or 10^{120408}¢.

Shapley is correct that bankruptcy conditions do contaminate people's notions about the described game, and may thus interfere with our identifying that it is curvature of utility which could *alone* make $f_1{}^*$ finite. Shapley's being right in what he contends does not make D. Bernoulli and Menger wrong in what they contend.

Aumann [3, 1975], essentially agreeing with Menger that people will empirically verify that they do have bounded utility, points out as earlier commentators on Fontaine and Buffon had done, that *thought experiments* concerning a Peter conceived to have as large a W_0 as one wishes to pretend, will convince most of us that our $f_1{}^*$ is bounded far below W_0. As W_0 grows, $f_1{}^*$ does not, for finite n or for indefinitely growing n, in fact grow as it would with linear utility. So, *allowing* for the bankruptcy considerations, one can still use the Petersburg paradigm to convince oneself of the *empirical* fact that $U_1''(W_1)$ is strongly negative. Presumably Shapley would not disagree with this, or with Aumann's point that other probability densities can provide actual or thought experiments that will convince Paul he does not *empirically* require the $f_1{}^*$ of full $E\{$money gain$\}$.

Finally, mention should be made of Brito [6, 1975] who, appealing to Becker's model on the allocation of scarce time, argues that $U_1(W_1)$ is likely to be [or is necessarily to be?] bounded because it takes extra time to achieve extra pleasure and time is bounded. Aumann makes the valid point that power and not time-requiring consumptions may be the "reason" one wants extra W_1. Moreover, it seems to me the Becker argument can boomerang: precisely because time is so precious, Paul requires ever more W_1 and command over the time of indefinitely more *other* people so that Paul can squeeze out ever more pleasure from his 24 hour day; adding one "net" minute to Paul's life may be worth everything in the universe and more to him. Who can logically rule that out?

14. *Finale.* Let me conclude with this banality: If you make something (infinitely) large in a problem, why be surprised by the non-paradoxical fact that this may imply that something else must be (infinitely) large? Even with bounded Mengerian utility, the amount of bread becomes indefinitely large that you must give me so as to compensate for my passing up the privilege of playing a large-n Petersburg game for stakes that consist of **h** as a *vector* of bread *and* butter, when my concave utility function is as follows:

$$U(\text{butter, bread}) = U(x_1, x_2) = -\exp[-x_1^{.5} + e^{-x_2}] \quad (14.1)$$

For this function, f_1^* *measured in units of bread* $\to \infty$ as $n \to \infty$ when $\mathbf{h} = (h \text{ butter}, h \text{ bread})$ and h is large enough. Indeed, for n large but finite enough to forestall Brito objections, and Peter so well-stocked with bread-and-butter sandwiches as to forestall Shapley objections, f_1^* of infinity need not be enough compensation for a Mengerian Paul with (14.1) utility to forego playing the feasible Petersburg game! This infinity does not frighten Paul, nor, I believe, should it surprise anybody who thinks the analysis through.

At bottom, the "paradox" is no paradox. Nor is my previous sentence. Nor. . . .

References

1. D'ALEMBERT, JEAN LEROND. "Doutes et questions sur le calcul des probabilités," in *Mélanges de Littérature d'Histoire et de Philosophe.* Volume V. Amsterdam: Chatelain, 1773.
2. ARROW, KENNETH J. *Essays in the theory of risk-bearing.* Chicago: Markham, 1971. This contains his classic 1951 essay as Chapter 1, and his classic 1952 essay on Securities in Optimal Risk-Taking as Chapter 4, and his 1963 Helsinki lectures as Chapters 2 and 3.
3. AUMANN, ROBERT J. *The St. Petersburg Paradox: A discussion of some recent comments.* The Economics Series, Institute for Mathematical Studies in the Social Sciences. Stanford University Working Paper No. 60, September, 1975.
4. BERNOULLI, DANIEL. "Specimen Theoriae Novae de Mensura Sortis," in *Commentarii Academiae Scientiarum Imperialis Petropolitanae.* Volume V. (1738). Translated by L. SOMMER as "Exposition of a New Theory on the Measurement of Risk," *Econometrica,* Jan. 1954, *22*(1), pp. 23–36.
5. BERTRAND, JOSEPH. *Calcul des probabilités.* Paris, 1889.
6. BRITO, D. L. "Becker's Theory of the Allocation of Time and the St. Petersburg Paradox," *J. Econ. Theory,* Feb. 1975, *10*(1), pp. 123–26.
7. BUFFON, G. L. L. "Essai d'Arithmétique Morale," in *Supplément à l'Historie Naturelle.* Vol. IV. 1777.
8. CONDORCET, M. [LE MARQUIS DE.] *Essai sur l'application de l'analyse à la probabilité des décisions rendues à la pluralité des voix.* Paris: *De l'Imprimerie royale,* 1785.
9. COOLIDGE, J. W. *The mathematics of great amateurs.* New York: Dover Publications, [1949] 1963.
10. COURNOT, ANTOINE AUGUSTIN. *Ex-*

position de la théorie des chances et des probabilités. Paris: L. Hachette, 1843.

11. CRAMER, GABRIEL. Letter to N. Bernoulli (1728), published fully by D. BERNOULLI [4, 1738, pp. 33–35].
12. DE FINETTI, BRUNO. "La prévision: ses lois logiques, ses sources subjectives," *Annales de l'Institut Henri Poincaré,* 1937, *7,* pp. 1–68. Translated by H. E. KYBURG in *Studies in subjective probability.* By HENRY E. KYBURG AND HOWARD E. SMOKLER. New York: Wiley, 1964, pp. 95–158.
13. FRIEDMAN, MILTON AND SAVAGE, LEONARD J. "The Utility Analysis of Choices Involving Risks," *J. Polit. Econ.,* August 1948, *56,* pp. 279–304.
14. HICKS, JOHN R. AND WEBER, WILHELM. *Carl Menger and the Austrian School of Economics.* Oxford: Clarendon Press, 1973.
15. KEYNES, JOHN MAYNARD. *A treatise on probability.* London: Macmillan, 1921.
16. LAPLACE, PIERRE SIMON. "Théorie Analytique des Probabilités" (1812), in *Oeuvres de Laplace.* Volume VII. Paris, 1886.
17. MAISTROV, LEONID E. *Probability theory: A historical sketch.* Translated and Edited by SAMUEL KOTZ. New York: Academic Press, [1966] 1974.
18. MARSCHAK, JACOB. "Rational Behavior, Uncertain Prospects and Measurable Utility," *Econometrica,* April 1950, *18,* pp. 111–41.
19. MENGER, KARL. "Das Unsicherheitsmoment in der Wertlehre," *Z. Nationalökon,* 1934, *51,* pp. 459–85.
20. ———. "The Role of Uncertainty in Economics," Chapter 16 in *Essays in mathematical economics in honor of Oskar Morgenstern.* Edited by MARTIN SHUBIK. Princeton: Princeton University Press, 1967. Translated from *Z. Nationalökon.,* [19, 1934].
21. ———. "Austrian Marginalism and Mathematical Economics," Chapter 3 in *Carl Menger and the Austrian School of Economics.* Edited by J. R. HICKS AND W. WEBER. Oxford: Clarendon Press, 1973, pp. 38–60.
22. VON NEUMANN, JOHN AND MORGENSTERN, OSKAR. *Theory of games and economic behavior.* Third edition. Princeton: Princeton University Press, [1944, 1947] 1953.
23. POISSON, SIMÉON D. "Recherches sur la Probabilité des Jugements en matière Criminelle et en matière Civile, in *Précédées des Règles Generales du Calcul des Probabilités,* Paris: Bachelier, 1837.
24. RAIFFA, HOWARD AND SCHLAIFER, ROBERT. *Applied statistical decision theory.* Boston: Harvard University, Graduate School of Business, Division of Research, 1961.
25. RAMSEY, FRANK. "Truth and Probability" in *The foundations of mathematics and other logical essays.* Edited by R. B. BRAITHWAITE. London: Paul, Trench, Trubner, 1931.
26. SAMUELSON, PAUL A. "Probability and the Attempts to Measure Utility," *The Economic Review (Keizai Kenkyu),* July 1950, *1,* pp. 167–73 (English and Japanese). Republished as Chapter 12 in *Collected scientific papers.* Vol. I [29, 1966, pp. 117–26].
27. ———. "Probability, Utility, and the Independence Axiom," *Econometrica,* Oct. 1952, *20*(4), pp. 670–78. Republished as Chapter 14 in *Collected scientific papers.* Vol. I [29, 1966, pp. 137–45].
28. ———. "The St. Petersburg Paradox as a Divergent Double Limit," *Int. Econ. Rev.,* Jan. 1960, *1*(1), pp. 31–37. Republished as Chapter 15 in *Collected scientific papers.* Vol. I [29, 1966, pp. 146–52].
29. ———. *The collected scientific papers of Paul A. Samuelson.* Volume I.

Edited by JOSEPH E. STIGLITZ. Cambridge, Mass.: MIT Press, 1966.

30. ———. "General Proof That Diversification Pays," *J. Financial Quant. Anal.*, March 1967, *2*(1), pp. 1–13. Republished as Chapter 201 of *The collected scientific papers of Paul A. Samuelson.* Vol. III. Edited by ROBERT C. MERTON. Cambridge, Mass.: MIT Press, 1972, pp. 848–60.
31. ———. "Limited Liability, Short Selling, Bounded Utility, and Infinite-Variance Stable Distributions," *J. Financial Quant. Anal.*, Sept. 1976, *11* (3), pp. 485–503.
32. SAVAGE, LEONARD J. *The foundations of statistics.* New York: Wiley, 1954.
33. SCHLAIFER, ROBERT. *Introduction to statistics for business decisions.* New York: McGraw-Hill, 1959.
34. SCHUMPETER, JOSEPH A. *History of economic analysis.* New York: Oxford University Press, 1954.
35. SHACKLE, G. L. S. *Expectation in economics.* London: Cambridge University Press, 1949.
36. SHAPLEY, L. S. *The Petersburg Paradox—A con game?* RAND Report, P-4940. Santa Monica, Calif.: Rand Corporation, 1972.
37. STIGLER, GEORGE J. "The Development of Utility Theory," Parts I and II. *J. Polit. Econ.*, August and Sept. 1950, *58*, pp. 307–27; 373–96. Republished as Chapter 5 in *Essays in the history of economics* [38, 1965], pp. 66–155.
38. ———. *Essays in the history of economics.* Chicago: University of Chicago Press, 1965.
39. TODHUNTER, ISAAC. *A history of the mathematical theory of probability.* New York: Cambridge University Press, 1865. Reprint. New York: Chelsea, [1949] 1961.
40. WALD, ABRAHAM. *Statistical decision functions.* New York: Wiley, 1950.

SECOND THOUGHTS ON ANALYTICAL INCOME COMPARISONS

Paul A. Samuelson

Swamy (1984) and Keren–Weinblatt (1984)[1] earn thanks for identifying a logical error in my analysis[2] of international real-income measures, and for constructive discussions of sufficiency and necessity conditions. The global result stated by me, erroneous as an alleged *logical* necessity, is suggested by the Keren and Weinblatt geometry to be at best a plausible presumption as the countries in comparison are far enough apart in levels of well-being, as their income elasticities diverge sufficiently from unity, and provided their price differences are not too great.[3]

Fig. 1 below presents a summary of the possibilities that takes into account the valid criticisms and breaks some new ground. But first a recasting of emphasis is in order.

I. NEW KNOWLEDGE AND PROBLEMS

My 1974 discussion had its origin in a desire to adjudicate between certain contending experts in the field of international income comparisons. To help decide, for example, whether a Laspeyres quantity index ought to stand alone or be spliced with a Paasche index I felt a need to determine the relations between computations and theoretical concepts in a simple 2-good world.

In the last decade, thanks primarily to the magisterial researches of the University of Pennsylvania team of Kravis–Heston–Summers,[4] we have new light on the various magnitudes and we have new questions to ask. Let me highlight a few that seem important. At the same time, I shall catalogue some explanations and mention a few researchable theoretical questions.

(1) *Bias in exchange-rate-based estimates.* Suppose representative person A in America has \$15,000 of income. Suppose B in India has 3,000 rupees of income. Suppose the exchange rate is 10 Indian rupees to the dollar, $e_{BA} = 10\,R/\$$. Then

[1] I owe thanks to Professors Keren and Weinblatt for helping me to avoid new errors.

[2] In a 1976 submission to this JOURNAL, Dr Subramaniam Swamy, MP, had already made the same correction, which can be summarised as follows. There are two measures of real income of a poor B relative to a rich A: A_q, the fraction of A's income that B would need at A's prices to be as well off as B actually is; and B_q, the ratio of B's actual income to what A would need to be as well off at B's prices as A actually is. For A_q to exceed B_q, it is *not* a sufficient condition that the luxury good be cheaper relative to the necessity good in the rich country (the Engel–Gerschenkron effect). Even when B_q does exceed A_q, my new Fig. 1 shows that the Engel–Gerschenkron effect is a sufficient condition for both of them to fall in the [Paasche index, Laspeyres index] interval, a theorem that I should have enunciated in 1974 and that the Keren–Weinblatt geometry makes intuitive....

[3] I.e. points in the non-empty Keren–Weinblatt triangle that reverse the $A_q > B_q$ inequality are B' points that cannot be 'too far away' from homotheticity. If the luxury good is very much a luxury good along both A's and B's Engel's paths, A_q is seen to be likely to exceed B_q by the Keren–Weinblatt triangle–trapezoid geometry.

[4] Kravis *et al.* (1978, 1982, 1983).

the crude way the World Bank Atlas or other statisticians calculate relative Indian–American real incomes is by the exchange-rate-based estimator

$$\frac{\Sigma_1^n p_j^B q_j^B / e_{BA}}{\Sigma_1^n p_j^A q_j^A} = \frac{3{,}000/10\,R/\$}{\$15{,}000} = \frac{\$300}{\$15{,}000} = 0{\cdot}02. \tag{1}$$

What seems to stand up as well in 1984 as in 1974, is that such a calculation grossly underestimates a poor country's well-being compared to the rich. My brother Robert Summers, to whom I an indebted for much that I have learned on these subjects, tells me that the systematic bias in exchange-rate-based estimators is quite uniform (the only exceptions being observed after 1973 for certain countries not too far from the U.S. level of affluence). For a very poor country, the bias has been estimated to be a twofold or threefold underestimate.

Why? How to explain the one-way persistent bias? The conventional explanation is worth re-examining.

(2) *Perfect Cassel-like purchasing-power parity.* Suppose every good trades perfectly freely in competitive markets. Tariffs, quotas, all transport costs are zero. Then of course the crude formula (1) would not be crude: it would give an exact estimator of both of my 1974 concepts A_q and B_q, which would be equal when the price vectors $\mathbf{P}^A$ and $\mathbf{P}^B$ are proportional to each other. The Laspeyres quantity index and the Paasche index, L_q and P_q, would be equal to each other and to A_q and B_q.

Item by item, the price ratios between countries would be equal to a common factor: normalised by the exchange rate these would become

$$\frac{p_1^B/e_{BA}}{p_1^A} = \frac{p_2^B/e_{BA}}{p_2^A} = \dots = \frac{p_n^B/e_{BA}}{p_n^A} = 1. \tag{2}$$

Now let's be a mite more realistic. All tariffs and quotas are still kept at zero. But small transport costs must be met: let them all be about 1 % or less. Now trade still balances between A's region and B's. Loosely half the goods are exported by A to B and the other half exported by B to A. Let B's export goods be $(1, \dots, r)$ and A's export goods be $(r+1, \dots, n \approx 2r)$. Then, to a good approximation, we will have so long as these goods flow between A and B

$$\frac{p_1^B/e_{BA}}{p_1^A} \approx \dots \approx \frac{p_r^B/e_{BA}}{p_r^A} \approx 0{\cdot}99,$$

$$\frac{p_{r+1}^B/e_{BA}}{p_{r+1}^A} \approx \dots \approx \frac{p_n^B/e_{BA}}{p_n^A} \approx 1{\cdot}01.$$

$$\text{Average } \frac{p_j^B/e_{BA}}{p_j^A} \approx 1{\cdot}00. \tag{3}$$

All this holds even when A is a rich country with high wage rates and B a very poor country – so long as labour cannot migrate from B to A and trade is almost frictionless.

The basic fact of life is that (3) is systematically violated in real life and in one direction. If B is poor and A is rich,

$$\text{Average } \frac{p_j^B/e_{BA}}{p_j^A} < 1. \tag{4}$$

Robert Summers informs me that when his group divides all goods into those tradeable and those not tradeable – an admittedly crude dichotomy based on putative transport costs and frictions – they typically find

$$\text{Average}\,\frac{p_i^B/e_{BA}}{p_i^A}\,\text{for tradeables} \approx 0{\cdot}6 < 1 \tag{5}$$

$$\text{Average}\,\frac{p_i^B/e_{BA}}{p_i^A}\,\text{for non-tradeables} \approx 0{\cdot}25 \ll 1.$$

No doubt if I did this for Norway and nearby Sweden, these averages would be nearer to unity and on either side of unity.

(3) *Goods' immobility and productivity intercorrelations.* We face the apparent fact that *rich countries have improved their productivities most and lowered their costs most in goods that trade most easily.*[1]

To get a fit to the stylised facts takes a little ingenuity. Here is a sketch of such an explanatory model.

(*a*) There is a category of immobile goods, Group 0, produced primarily by labour in the same way everywhere. (It is dangerous to call these 'services', but one often tends to do so. Often they are said to be of high income elasticity; but Summers warns me that the factual warrant for this last is equivocal.)

(*b*) For all other goods the rich countries have generated a substantial gain in absolute productivity. But these split up into two categories: Group 1, those of relatively less productivity gain in *A* as compared to *B*; and those in Group 2 with relatively more of productivity gain in *A* as compared to *B*.

Some of each of these categories can overcome the transport cost barrier and move in trade. Those in Group 1 that trade form *B*'s comparative-advantage exports (and these may in part have an important dependence on natural resources localised in the poorer region). Those in Group 2 that trade form *A*'s comparative advantage exports (and these may tend to be peculiarly capital intensive in nature as in the Heckscher–Ohlin theory and in Bhagwati (1984, Fig. 2)).

The model I have sketched qualitatively fits the facts about bias in exchange-rate-based computations. *It does so without committing itself to any systematic interdependence between* (1) *income elasticities of goods and* (2) *their tradeability group affiliations.* Therefore, most of my 1974 analysis concerning the presumed dearness or cheapness of luxuries in rich as compared to poor countries was perhaps dispensable.

In any case, the Kravis–Heston–Summers calculations done for the linear expenditure system of the A_q and B_q measures – which of course are related to the standard Hicks' *compensating* and *equalising* measures of consumers' surplus – show them to be in rather close agreement, certainly in closer agreement than that between exchange-rate-based estimators and Kravis-team estimators based on

[1] Bhagwati (1984) makes the point in connection with his Fig. 1 that the relevant productivities need not merely be those of the Ricardian labour-only models: thus, they could be Bhagwati's Hicks-neutral parameters of 'total-factor productivity' applied to labour-and-capital Ohlin production functions. Later, I refer to Bhagwati's second, and even more interesting, paradigm to explain the cheapness of services in poor countries.

observations of actual local prices and on interpolations for like countries, and closer than Paasche and Laspeyres indexes are to each other.

Therefore, much of my concentration on the $[B_q, A_q]$ ordering was perhaps an overemphasis. Indeed my curiosity about the relative ordering of A_q and B_q blinded me in 1974 to my more definitive finding – namely that the observable Laspeyres and Paasche indexes, L_q, P_q, do provide bounds for *both* the A_q and B_q measures of relative well-being in what I called the Gerschenkron–Engel case (defined as when the richer country has a higher price ratio for the goods that are 'necessaries' in the sense of having income elasticities below unity). The main Kravis–Heston–Summers finding of bias in exchange-rate-based measures, stands whether the Gerschenkron–Engel pattern obtains or not.

II. METHODOLOGY OF EXPLANATION

A researchable project can throw light on how the standard Ricardian and Haberlerian trade theory has to be augmented to account for the downward bias in exchange-rate-based estimations. To understand the exchange-rate-based estimators' downward bias, Kravis *et al.* (1978, p. 87) name and discuss a 'productivity differential' model that Ricardo and later writers at least glimpsed. It is that which I underline in footnote 1 p.269. They cite Ricardo's *Principles* (Everyman's edition, p. 87) for this remark that '. . . prices of home commodities, and those of great bulk, though of comparatively small value, are, independently of other causes, higher in those countries where manufacturers flourish'. As will be seen, Ricardo would be too sweeping if he identified improvement in manufacturing in A with an inevitable rise in A's real income relative to B's; and, even if A's manufacturing innovations did lower B_q and A_q during an epoch, Ricardo would have no temptation to insist that his theory required that A's non-tradeables show less productivity improvements than its tradeables. As the authors make clear, their 'productivity differential' doctrine[1] is an empirical (testable) hypothesis about paces of technical improvements in two different sectors.

If, as the next section suggests, the Ricardian trade theory is itself neutral on the likelihood of productivity improvement being greater or less in the sector of tradeable goods rather than untradeables, what other than reiteration of that empirical fact can be offered? Here are a few diffident suggestions, not pretending to be particularly novel or worked out.

Darwinian–Toynbeean challenge process. Suppose we hypothesise (1) that productivity improvement correlates with intensity of competition from whatever source. And (2) that countries that are rich are rich because somehow they have been endowed with greater ability to respond to competitive challenges. In this case, from the fact that tradeable goods involve a country in more challenges, in challenges from all countries, we can deduce that tradeables generally should display greater productivity improvements in any fixed time epoch than non-

[1] Kravis *et al.* (1978, p. 87) cite, in addition to Ricardo, such names as Viner, Harrod and Balassa. The last two do assert the empirical likelihood of greater productivity differences in the tradeable than in the non-tradeable sectors. Samuelson (1964) makes similar points and works out rigorously the relation between countries' wage levels, exchange rates, and Ricardian cost ratios.

tradeables do and that the countries that have become rich should display their greatest productivity differentials in the tradeables sector.

Crude and obvious as this model is, it does provide a 'productivity differential' paradigm that is methodologically satisfying in a way that the general Ricardo–Viner theory does not pretend to be.

'A man's a man' paradigm. A different hypothesis, but still one that meets the methodological aesthetics of the problem, is that which links non-tradeables empirically with goods of high direct-labour intensity. By contrast to such 'direct-human services', goods involving fabrication of raw materials and durable produced inputs may be goods that can peculiarly benefit from science and innovation in their productivity aspects. So long as 'past labour' in them has already been embodied 'in' them, such goods may travel easily and tend to be tradeables. This provides an empirical, but natural, link between greater-than-average productivity improvements and greater-than-average tradeability.[1]

Bhagwati (1984, Fig. 2) postulates that rich countries differ from poor countries only in having much more K/L in the same Ohlin production functions of the form $F^j(L_j, K_j) = K_j f_j(L_j/K_j)$. If the regions' factor endowments are disparate enough, the poor region must specialise on tradeables that are relatively labour intensive while the rich region specialises on tradeables that are relatively capital intensive. With the wage/K-rent ratio lower in the poor country, all non-tradeables (such as services) that are more labour intensive than the tradeables will be especially cheap in the poor countries. Q.E.D.

Note that Bhagwati's result about services being relatively cheap in the poorer countries envisages a definition of 'services' that makes them virtually synonymous with items of high labour intensity – as when a masseur kneads my muscles by hand. Bhagwati's exposition is clearcut and above criticism. However, in actual operation, the term 'services' has multiple meanings and ambiguities. Often all of services are classified as non-tradeables; and all of commodities, except construction, are treated as tradeables. On the Kravis–Heston–Summers (1983) definition, services are found by them *not* to be of income elasticity well in excess of unity, bringing into question the old A. G. B. Fisher and Collin Clark taxonomy of the historical succession of employment from agriculture to manufacturing to services.

To get the principal Kravis–Heston–Summers finding of relatively low price levels for poorer countries by Bhagwati's route, we have to add a second axiom to his first axiom that labour in rich countries works with a generous endowment of non-labour factors: this second axiom is that non-tradeables average out to be of higher labour intensity than tradeables, a hypothesis that is borne out in the Kravis–Heston–Summers (1983) analysis.

Johnsonian economics. Tibor Barna reviewed Kravis–Heston–Summers (1982) in this JOURNAL, vol. 93 (June, 1983), pp. 430–1. There he takes note that '... price levels are lower in poor countries as the result of lower prices for non-tradeable goods, and especially services.' Neither the physiocrats nor Dr Samuel Johnson would have been surprised by the positive correlation of prices with real

[1] Nicholas Kaldor's belief that manufactures, by contrast to services and agriculture, are peculiarly prone to productivity growth and increasing returns, is a variant of this general paradigm.

incomes, Barna observes: Dr Johnson on his visit to the Hebrides in 1773, had sagely stated that a comparison of real product in terms of money 'measures an unknown quantity by an uncertain standard', a remark noticed by Colin Clark and quoted by Kravis–Heston–Summers (1982, p. v). Also, Barna suggests, Johnson 'believed that the low price of necessities was due to poverty rather than abundance'.

The morning our schoolform studied Johnson we read less and more into him. Measuring an unknown quantity by an uncertain standard, we took to be pleasant rhetoric warning against oversimplification of complicated reality. When Johnson reacted to the information that an egg on Skye cost but a pence with the observation that this signified not that eggs were cheap but pence hard to come by, our class took this to be a recognition not of an esoteric property of tradeables versus non-tradeables, but of the prosaic fact that demand functions are homogeneous of degree zero – as in current jokes that, by 1999 your monthly income will be a million dollars but the busfare to pick it up will be a thousand dollars. Scotland was Johnson's Araby, his first venture to strange territory, as he later testified. From the beginning he was struck with the poverty of the place, and had to reconcile this with the lowness of (some) prices by the paucity of income.

If Dr Johnson and the physiocrats recognised that 'the low price of necessities was due to poverty rather than abundance', they were in the good company of Samuelson (1974) and Barna (1983). But were they correct that goods of low income elasticity do tend to be relatively cheap in poorer regions? Kravis–Heston–Summers (1978) put my 1974 'Gerschenkron–Engel' effect (which alleged this) to the test and found it not supported by the data; indeed they found that the reverse of this effect would also be dubious.[1] As an example of how unsturdy common sense can be, I have had to be disabused of the notion that, in a rich country like the United States, food, with its low income elasticity is relatively dear: actually, it turns out to be cheap.

Commonly we travellers from a rich country are struck by how little we could live on if only we would go native in our tastes and scale of expenditures. This has a bearing, but not a strong bearing, on the essential Kravis–Heston–Summers finding; and it is not inconsistent with the experience of travellers from the outposts to the metropolitan centre, that insisting upon living in Rome as one had done in Gaul would be very expensive indeed.[2]

Asymmetry in transport costs? If the goods poor countries ship to rich involve

[1] Their conclusion that there is no systematic relation brings into question the reverse contention made in Theil and Suhm (1981), a work which mines the same 1978 Kravis–Heston–Summers data by a different process. The Kravis–Heston–Summers 1982 data reconfirms earlier doubts on both my 1974 thesis and the 1981 Theil–Suhm counter-thesis.

[2] When I first read Barna's thought-arousing words, I worked out a model to explain cheap prices in poor countries along quite different lines. Transport costs between Skye and London are so steep, relative to differences in *comparative* (not *absolute*) advantage, as to make Skye practically autarkic. Under the gold standard poor Skye inhabitants have such high time preference as to use up most of their gold to pay for one-time imports. By the Quantity Theory their meagre gold gives them a relatively low price level. Q.E.D.

This is a neat theory to explain the Kravis–Heston–Summers fact, involving no asymmetry between tradeables and non-tradeables. It also helps explain the notorious complaints in colonies that they are 'short of money'. But, on reflection, I judge the theory's net algebraic merits to be low.

heavier transport-costs than do the goods that the rich ship to the poor, that should explain relatively low price levels in poor countries. Thus, if an LDC has bulky exports and compact imports, which are carried in the same ships, competition will allocate most of the joint shipping costs to the LDC goods. It is as if, in equation (3) above, we had to average not 0·99 and 1·01 to get 1·00, but rather to average 0·2 and 1·00 to get 0·60.

This alternative explanation, which differs from the Harrod–Balassa–Samuelson and the Bhagwati explanations, has as far as I know little factual warrant. Years ago Major Wright tried to make consistent the complaints of LDCs and of rich countries that each of them had (simultaneously!) deteriorating terms of trade by suggesting that ocean transport was becoming relatively more expensive over time. However, the Kravis–Heston–Summers measured effects seem much too large to be explicable by transport-cost asymmetries.

Consider the alternative scenario where poor countries produce staples for export to rich urban countries. The latter, in the fashion of A. Smith, Allyn Young and Ohlin, produce manufactures under conditions of increasing returns and ship them expensively to the poor countries. In such a model, it would be the rich countries that tend to have the lower price levels, which would be 180° off from the Kravis–Heston–Summers finding.

III. THE NICE COBB–DOUGLAS TEST CASE

Here is a beautifully simple model to test contentions on. It involves Ricardian labour costs for all goods in both countries. It involves Millian demands: uniform positive fractions of income (k_j), spent on the respective goods whether in A or B; $\Sigma_1^n k_j = 1$. Goods $(1, \ldots, m)$ move perfectly *freely* in trade; goods $(m+1, \ldots, n)$ are perfectly *untradeable*. Labour supplies in A and B are fixed at (L^A, L^B).

The tradeable goods can be numbered in order of their comparative advantages for A as against B:

$$\frac{C_1^B}{C_1^A} > \frac{C_2^B}{C_2^A} > \ldots > \frac{C_m^B}{C_m^A}. \tag{6}$$

Where do the non-tradeables' C_{m+i}^B/C_{m+i}^A ratios fall in terms of the above chain? *A priori*, I don't see that we have any right to say. With non-sharp Bayesian priors, we might regard each and all of them to be distributed 'at random' along the chain – until some sufficient reason or presumption is presented to do otherwise. Thus, if C_{m+i}^B/C_{m+i}^A 'tends' to be below C_m^B/C_m^A, we have almost a case of overkill for those who want to verify downward bias in the exchange-rate-based estimation of A_q and B_q. Contrariwise, if C_{m+i}^B/C_{m+i}^A tends to exceed C_1^B/C_1^A, the opposite bias is found. The exact conditions for 'neutrality' are complicated. The basic Ricardo–Mill theory itself is neutral on all this.

With the labour supply totals for the two regions given, the system has a determinate equilibrium. For it, with some effort, we can compute the relative *per capita* real incomes as

$$A_q = B_q = \left[\frac{(\Sigma_1^m p_j^B q_j^B)/e_{BA}}{\Sigma_i^m p_j^A q_j^A}\right]^{\Sigma_1^m k_j} \left[\prod_{i=m+1}^{n} \left(\frac{C_i^A}{C_i^B}\right)^{k_i}\right]$$

$$= \left[\frac{W^B/e_{BA}}{W^A}\right]^{1-k} \left[\prod_{m+1}^{n} \left(\frac{C_i^A}{C_i^B}\right)^{k_i/k}\right]^k, \qquad (7)$$

$$0 < k = \sum_{m+1}^{n} k_i < 1.$$

W^B and W^A are nominal wage rates expressed in respective local currencies: $(W^B/e_{BA})/W^A$ is their real ratio in any common currency.

The true measure is an exact weighted geometric mean between the exchange-rate-based measure in the left-hand bracket and the Cobb–Douglas geometric mean of relative costs for non-tradeables as contained in the right-hand bracket.

It will be helpful to add the well-known inequalities that relate a region's real wage to its average level of labour productivity:[1]

$$\min_j (C_j^A/C_j^B) = (C_1^A/C_1^B) \leqslant (W^B/e_{BA})(W^A) \leqslant (C_m^A/C_m^B) = \max_j (C_j^A/C_j^B). \qquad (8)$$

Again, why should (7)'s mean of (C_{m+i}^A/C_{m+i}^B) chance always to be greater than (8)'s differently calculated mean of tradeables' (C_j^A/C_j^B)? And yet that is what does appear to obtain in the real world.

The case of three goods – two tradeables and one untradeable – is simple enough to calculate out mentally while driving to work. So long as

$$(L^B/C_2^B k_2)/(L^A/C_1^A k_1)$$

is within the range of maximum and minimum of tradeables' (C_j^A/C_j^B) ratios, any invention that raises world real tradeables' income leaves its sharing between A and B unchanged. So, in the Cobb–Douglas case it is paradoxical that an invention in A's tradeable realm results in no downward bias by the exchange-rate-based estimator.

Ordinarily, changes in the realm of tradeables will have interactions on non-tradeables. What enables us to have no such complicating interactions is to assume merely that the Cobb–Douglas property holds for the whole complexes of tradeables and non-tradeables. It suffices to have for each person's utility function

$$u = T(q_1, \ldots, q_m)^{1-k} N(q_{m+1}, \ldots, q_n)^k, \quad 0 < k < 1, \qquad (9)$$

where $T(\ )$ and $N(\ )$ are first-degree-homogeneous and concave utility functions in their respective tradeables and non-tradeables arguments.

Suppose that innovation in A causes C_1^A to drop. Elasticity optimists would expect that to raise A's real income, lowering A_q and B_q. And, since (9)'s group Cobb–Douglas property keeps the true non-tradeables' component of relative well-being from being at all changed, here is a case where the exchange-rate-based estimator would have the conventional downward bias.

[1] We can interpret (8) as asserting that $(W^B/e_{BA})/W^A$ will be a *generalised internal mean* of the perfectly tradeables' cost ratios. Paradoxically, letting C_1^B/C_1^A fall while others stay unchanged need not lower the $(W^B/e_{BA})/W^A$ mean.

Elasticity pessimists are aware that innovation in A can be immiserating to it. For this case the exchange-rate-based estimator is biased upward compared to the true rise in A_q and B_q, a reversal of the conventional bias reported by Kravis–Heston–Summers.

Suppose A has innovational reductions in untradeables' C^A_{m+i}. The exchange-rate-based estimators will give A no credit for these in the Cobb–Douglas cases. So, again, such estimators could theoretically be upward biased in comparing poor and rich countries, another reversal of the conventional bias.

In the end we see that the 'productivity differential' interpretation of the commonly observed downward bias in exchange-rate-based estimators must boil down in this Ricardo-Mill case to the testable hypothesis that, for whatever reason, as a country gets rich its productivities improve less in the untradeable sector than in the tradeable. This is a fact to wonder at, and to provide interpretations for.

Kravis–Heston–Summers do not have to juggle with two true measures – my A_q and B_q (as defined in footnote 2 on p. 267). They are able to work with one measure because they utilise the Geary–Khamis adjustment procedure that they describe in (1978, pp. 73–84). My pure Cobb–Douglas case, with two tradeables and one untradeable, should be a good test example to investigate just how tolerable is the Geary–Khamis system's degree of approximation.[1]

IV. LOCAL AND GLOBAL RELATIONSHIPS

In concluding, I must acknowledge that Swamy and Keren–Weinblatt are right to reject the 1974 contention concerning the necessity of B_q's being globally less than A_q. However, it is a researchable programme to investigate whether there is a valid local version of the asserted relation.

Fig. 1 suggests the corrections and amplifications that at a minimum are needed for my 1974 Fig. 2. The poor person (in India, for example) is at B on the base indifference curve shown: BE is the income-consumption path of Engel, along which the price ratio of the luxury and necessity goods is the same as in B. The affluent person (in America, for example), according to the 1974-posited Gerschenkron–Engel effect, must have her/his A point fall below BE and above the indifference curve's arc BZ. However, the present version can be agnostic on the Gerschenkron–Engel effect and therefore presents the region above BE as well as below it.

Now there is shown six regions (I – VI) into which the point A could fall vis-à-vis the specified point B. In each region there is shown the ordering relations among the Laspeyres and Paasche quantity indexes and the true A_q and B_q money-metric-utility indexes that involve A's and B's price ratios respectively.

Thus, along BE all four measures are equal: $A_q = B_q = L_q = P_q$. Again, along the BZ indifference contour, A_q and B_q are equal at unity and lie in the interval $[P_q, L_q]$. Everywhere in the Gerschenkron–Engel domain below BE – i.e. both in Region II and Region I – the $[P_q, L_q]$ interval brackets both A_q and B_q; however, only in Region II, drawn just below BE, is B_q necessarily below A_q as asserted in

[1] Kravis–Heston–Summers (1982, Table 9–8) provides evidence that the Geary–Khamis estimates agree well with those from a Linear Expenditure System fitted to the data.

my 1974 discussion. My 1974 diagram should have allowed for the possibility of the *BN* boundary shown as separating Region I's points (for which $A_q < B_q$) from Region II's point (for which B_q is indeed below A_q). As Professors Keren and Weinblatt have pointed out to me in correspondence, the region below *BN* might in more complicated cases have alternating sub-regions in which the (A_q, B_q) orderings reverse themselves several times.

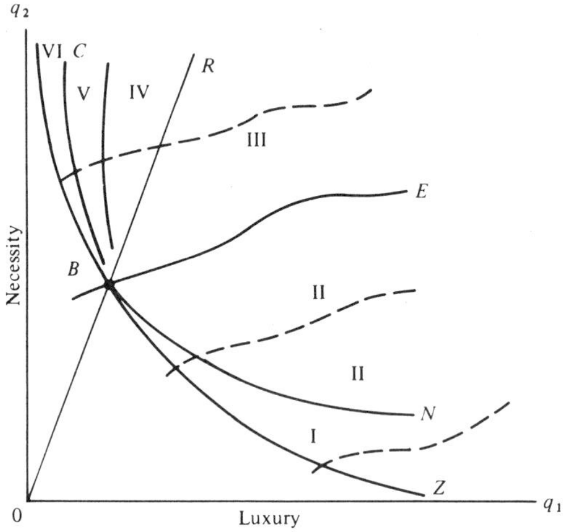

Fig. 1. If the affluent person is in Region II, we have the 1974 orderings: $P_q < B_q < A_q < L_q$. In I, we have $P_q < A_q < B_q < L_q$; in III, $A_q < L_q < P_q < B_q$; in IV, $A_q < P_q < L_q < B_q$. In VI we have $P_q < B_q \gtreqless A_q < L_q$, while V could be one of a number of transition regions with orderings intermediate between those of IV and VI. Research is needed to determine whether *BN* must be tangential to the *BZ* indifference contour.

For each set of indifference curves, specified and frozen in their shapes, a definite set of regions like those shown in Fig. 1 can be defined. What needs to be subjected to rigorous analysis is whether directly below *BE* there has to be (tends to be?) a Region II as shown. Is its boundary *BN* tangential to the indifference curve at *B*, as shown in Fig. 1? The Keren–Weinblatt geometry can be applied to specimen examples, to suggest possible counter-examples, and to infer possible necessities.

As a supplement to geometry, here is a sketch of how the Newtonian calculus might be applied. Consider a second indifference curve that is arc distance x above the point *B* along *BE*. And let *A* be a variable point that is arc distance y below the second indifference curve's intersection with *BE*. Then, all our magnitudes are defined as definite functions of x and y once the preference structure is specified and frozen.

$$\left.\begin{aligned} A_q &= a(x,y), \\ B_q &= b(x,y), \\ L_q &= \lambda(x,y), \\ P_q &= \pi(x,y), \\ (L_q P_q)^{\frac{1}{2}} &= I(x,y). \end{aligned}\right\} \tag{10}$$

One should then be able to prove

$$\pi(x,y) \leqslant \min[b(x,y), a(x,y)] \leqslant \max[b(x,y), a(x,y)] \leqslant \lambda(x,y), (x,y) > 0,$$
$$\pi(x,0) = b(x,0) = a(x,0) = \lambda(x,0),$$
$$\pi(0,y) < b(0,y) = a(0,y) = 1 < L(0,y), \quad y \gtrless 0. \tag{11}$$

One can also investigate whether the following relationships obtain

$$b_x(x,\epsilon) \leqslant a_x(x,\epsilon) \quad \text{for} \quad x > 0 \quad \text{and} \quad 0 < \epsilon \ll 1,$$
$$b_x(\epsilon,y) \geqslant a_x(\epsilon,y) \quad \text{for} \quad y > 0 \quad \text{and} \quad 0 < \epsilon \ll 1,$$

where $b_x(x,y) = \partial b(x,y)/\partial x$, etc.

The calculation will be straightforward but intricate.

Swamy (1983) is right to refer to the findings in Samuelson–Swamy (1974, p. 482 ff.) and Samuelson (1953, p. 8, n. 1) that Fisher's Ideal Quantity Index number, or any symmetric mean of the Laspeyres and Paasche indexes, may provide a locally high-order contact or approximation to 'true' economic index numbers. In the present context, this raises the researchable question whether $a(\epsilon,\epsilon) - I(\epsilon,\epsilon)$ and $b(\epsilon,\epsilon) - I(\epsilon,\epsilon)$ have one more vanishing derivative at $\epsilon = 0$ than do $a(\epsilon,\epsilon) - \lambda(\epsilon,\epsilon)$, $a(\epsilon,\epsilon) - \pi(\epsilon,\epsilon)$, $b(\epsilon,\epsilon) - \lambda(\epsilon,\epsilon)$, $b(\epsilon,\epsilon) - \pi(\epsilon,\epsilon)$.

Swamy has made the valid point that knowledge of Engel's paths through A and B enable us to improve approximations to A_q and B_q. Readers of Wald and Frisch, and of Afriat, Varian, Houthakker, and Samuelson, will appreciate the usefulness of such knowledge. However, in my 1974 text, I assumed no such knowledge although I approved of the Kravis–Heston–Summers *simultaneous* analysis of their many countries.

In this connection I must mention the genuine breakthroughs of W. E. Diewert (1983) with his concepts of 'superlative' index numbers and 'flexible functional forms'.[1] Thus, to handle non-homothetic preferences, better than the Ideal index will be a *translog quantity* index, calculable from the $(\mathbf{P}^A, \mathbf{Q}^A; \mathbf{P}^B, \mathbf{Q}^B)$ data alone, and with the nice property that this index function's indifference contours agree with the true indifference contours when $|\mathbf{Q}^A - \mathbf{Q}^B|$ is small up to a higher number of partial derivatives. Kravis–Heston–Summers, I suspect, could with advantage chain together their diverse countries' data by such graduation formulas and get a standard against which to evaluate the goodness of their somewhat *ad hoc* Geary–Khamis graduations.

Massachusetts Institute of Technology

Date of receipt of final typescript: September 1983

References

Bhagwati, J. (1984). 'Why services are cheaper in in poorer countries.' Economic Journal, vol. 94, this issue.

Diewert, W. E. (1983). 'The theory of the cost of living index and the measurement of welfare change.' Discussion Paper no. 83–05. Department of Economics, University of British Columbia, February.

Keren, M. and Weinblatt, J. (1984). 'A note on Samuelson's analytical notes on international real income measures.' Economic Journal vol. 94, this issue.

[1] Diewert (1983) gives a superb summary of modern index number theory with full references to earlier works. Theorem 13 is of special interest.

Kravis, I., Heston, A. and Summers, R. (1978). *International Comparisons of Real Product and Purchasing Power*. Baltimore: Johns Hopkins University Press.

——, —— and —— (1982). *World Product and Income: International Comparisons of Real Gross Product, Phase III*. Baltimore: Johns Hopkins University Press.

——, —— and —— (1983). 'The share of services in economic growth,' in F. G. Adams and B. G. Hickman (eds.) *Global Econometrics: Essays in Honor of Lawrence R. Klein*. Cambridge, Mass: MIT Press, pp. 188–218.

——, Kenessy, A., Heston, A. and Summers, R. (1975). *A System of International Comparisons of Gross Product and Purchasing Power*. Baltimore: Johns Hopkins University Press.

Samuelson, P. (1953). 'Consumption theorems in terms of overcompensation rather than indifference comparisons.' *Economica*, New Series, vol. 20, (February), pp. 1–9.

—— (1964). 'Theoretical notes on trade problems.' *The Review of Economics and Statistics*, vol. 46, (May), pp. 145–54.

—— (1974). 'Analytical notes on international real-income measures.' ECONOMIC JOURNAL, vol. 84, (September), pp. 595–608.

—— and Swamy, S. (1973). 'Invariant economic index numbers and canonical duality: Survey and synthesis.' *American Economic Review*, (August), pp. 566–593.

Swamy, S. (1984). 'Samuelson's analytical notes on international real income measures – a comment.' ECONOMIC JOURNAL, vol. 94, this issue.

Theil, H. and Suhm, F. E. (1981). *International Consumption Comparisons: A System-wide Approach*. New York: North Holland.

Unattainability of Integrability and Definiteness Conditions in the General Case of Demand for Money and Goods

By PAUL A. SAMUELSON AND RYUZO SATO*

Two fallacies have long permeated classical monetary theories: one, that demand for money is not subject to the analysis of marginal utility; two, that money is like coffee, music boxes, or any other good in its marginal utility analysis. One way to avoid these fallacies, not the only way and in the end not the best way, is to use the model of Samuelson (1947), which puts steady-state money and prices directly in the utility function along with steady-state goods like coffee and music boxes. This model does capture the difference between money and goods —the fact that money is not wanted for its own sake but only for the advantage of being able to make transactions—by insisting that increasing money and all prices in the same proportions will *ceteris paribus* leave the utility function unchanged. Thus the model does encapsulate the germ of truth in the Quantity Theory.[1]

Demand theory for ordinary goods has observable empirical implications. Pareto and Marshall began the investigation of these; Slutsky advanced the search by a quantum jump; and, finally in our modern times, *complete* observable implications of the corpus of demand theory have been derived, in that sense closing the theory for all times. No such closure has been achieved for demand theory inclusive of money (despite some imperfect attempts in the literature). The present paper suggests why such attempts are destined to fail in the *general* case. Mathematics has the useful function in science of helping establish what is true, what can be established. Mathematics can also perform the needed function of helping identify what cannot be established.

Does this analysis mean that a monetarist might be right in believing that the amount of M held could be independent of the interest rate r that provides the opportunity-cost hurdle that the desirability of holding a cash balance must overcome? No, our nihilistic presumption applies only to the demands for goods and leaves the usual Slutsky-Hicks presumptions concerning money intact. (More precisely, we establish that the demand for coffee might in a model involving money have positive income elasticity and still show Giffen-like positive price elasticity! Money, however, cannot show such perversity.)

This paper also considers a number of cases of "separable" demands in which *complete* integrability and definiteness conditions can be derived for observational testing, for refutation or nonrefutation. Also we generalize the model involving money and an interest rate, (M, r), to a model involving a vector of assets of differing degrees of liquidity, each element of which has a characteristic respective yield that defines the opportunity cost relevant to holding it: $(M_1, \ldots, M_N; r_1, \ldots, r_N)$.

Study of this money model yields, serendipitously as a byproduct, insight into the consequences of Veblen and Scitovsky phenomena in which tastes are themselves affected by relative prices.

*Departments of Economics, Massachusetts Institute of Technology, E-52, 383, Cambridge, MA 02139; and Brown University, Providence, RI 02912 and J. F. Kennedy School of Government, Harvard University, Cambridge, MA 02138, respectively. This work was in part supported by the National Science Foundation. We acknowledge useful comments on an earlier version by Robert Clower, John G. Riley, Jerome L. Stein, Fumitake Mimura, Don Patinkin, Peter W. Howitt, and Shunichi Tsutsui.

[1]In Section IX, we comment selectively on related work by C. E. V. Leser (1943), Don Patinkin (1956, 1965), Cliff Lloyd (1964), Per Meinich (1964), Richard Dusansky and P. J. Kalman (1972, 1974), Robert Clower and John Riley (1976), Clower and Peter Howitt (1978), Robert Pollak (1977), Howitt and Patinkin (1980), Dusansky (1980), and others. Also, in Section VII, we comment on the paper by R. L. Basmann, D. J. Molina and D. J. Slottje (1983).

I. The Money-Goods Model

Quantities of ordinary goods, coffee and such, we write as $(x_1,\ldots,x_n)=\mathbf{X}$; their respective prices are $(p_1,\ldots,p_n)=\mathbf{P}$. The steady-state stock of money is the zero-th good, M. To hold a unit of it in the steady state you must forego the positive yield on earning assets you might otherwise have held, r: thus, subtracted from your disposable steady-state income, Y, is not only p_1x_1 for your coffee expenditure but also rM for your expenditure incurred to hold the ("average") cash balance M.

You face the following maximum problem

$$(1)\quad \underset{M,\mathbf{X}}{\text{Max}}\, U[M,x_1,\ldots,x_n;p_1,\ldots,p_n]$$

$$=\underset{M,\mathbf{X}}{\text{Max}}\, U[M,\mathbf{X};\mathbf{P}]=\underset{M,\mathbf{X}}{\text{Max}}\, U[1,\mathbf{X};\mathbf{P}/M]$$

(2) subject to

$$rM+\sum_1^n p_jx_j=Y=rM+\mathbf{P}\cdot\mathbf{X}$$

$$(3)\quad =U[Yh^0(r;\mathbf{P},Y),h^1(r;\mathbf{P},Y),\ldots,$$
$$h^n(r;\mathbf{P},Y);\mathbf{P}]=U[\mathbf{h}(r;\mathbf{P},Y);\mathbf{P}/Y]$$

$$(4)\quad =U^*[r;\mathbf{P},Y]=U^*[r;\mathbf{P}/Y,1],\qquad r>0,$$

where the demand functions $\mathbf{h}(r;\mathbf{P},Y)$ have the following contrasting homogeneities for goods and for money

$$(5a)\quad x_i=h^i(r;\mathbf{P},Y)\equiv h^i(r;\mathbf{P}/Y,1),\qquad (i=1,\ldots,n);$$

$$(5b)\quad M/Y=h^0(r;\mathbf{P},Y)\equiv h^0(r;\mathbf{P}/Y,1)$$
$$=r^{-1}\left[1-\sum_1^n (P_j/Y)h^j(r;\mathbf{P}/Y,1)\right].$$

Note that coffee or any x_i continues in this money model to have the property of being homogeneous of degree zero in prices and income, as in conventional moneyless theory. By contrast, the demand for M is deduced to be homogeneous of degree *one* in prices and income (as is relevant to the ancient Quantity Theory of Copernicus, Locke, Hume, Thornton, Marshall, Ricardo, and Irving Fisher).[2]

To establish the validity of the many assertions in (3)–(5), we shall be making here some stronger simplifying assumptions than are needed in a truly general analysis. We can stay in the realm of calculus *interior equalities*, and out of the Kuhn-Tucker world of *boundary* extrema, by stipulating the following:

(6a) $U[M,\mathbf{X};\mathbf{P}]$ is strictly quasi concave in $[M,\mathbf{X}]$, having strictly convex indifference contours that are smoothly differentiable;

(6b) the various partial derivatives exist as continuous functions, and throughout we use numerical subscripts to a function to denote such derivatives

$$\partial U/\partial M=U_0[M,\mathbf{X};\mathbf{P}]$$
$$\equiv U_0[1,\mathbf{X};\mathbf{P}/M]M^{-1}>0$$

$$\partial U/\partial x_i=U_i[M,\mathbf{X};\mathbf{P}]$$
$$\equiv U_i[1,\mathbf{X};\mathbf{P}/M]>0,\qquad (i=1,\ldots,n);$$

$$\partial U/\partial p_i=U_{n+i}[M,\mathbf{X};\mathbf{P}]$$
$$=U_{n+i}[1,\mathbf{X};\mathbf{P}/M]M^{-1},\qquad (n+i=n+1,\ldots,2n);$$

$$\partial^2U/\partial M^2=U_{00},\qquad \partial^2U/\partial x_i\,\partial x_j=U_{ij},$$
$$\partial^2U/\partial M\,\partial x_i=U_{0i},$$
$$\partial^2U/\partial p_i\,\partial x_j=U_{n+i,j},\ldots;$$

$$(6c)\qquad \mathbf{A}>0,\ U[\mathbf{A};\mathbf{P}]=U[\mathbf{B};\mathbf{P}]\quad \mathbf{B}>0.$$

[2] Many moneys used in history—gold is only one example—have a direct utility for their own sake as well as serving a transaction and store-of-wealth need. Marshall and early writers wouldn't expect such moneys to be "strictly neutral" in any run; when we speak of the simple Quantity Theory, we therefore refer to the polar case of fiat money or of a purely conventional material object that is of indifference for its own sake.

Relations (6) assure a *unique* interior solution to (1)'s maximum problem: strong convexity rules out ties and smoothness makes the h functions differentiable; (6c)'s "Inada" conditions rule out boundary maxima; etc.

Under our overstrong curvature conditions, the first-order *necessary* variational conditions are also *sufficient*. Avoiding mention of any nonobservable Lagrangean multiplier variables, we can write the maximizing conditions in a form that shows their invariance when $U[M,\mathbf{X},\mathbf{P}]$ is subjected to any monotone-increasing stretching, $u[M,\mathbf{X};\mathbf{P}] = f(U[M,\mathbf{X};\mathbf{P}])$ with $f'(U)>0 \lesseqgtr f''(U)$:

$$(7a) \qquad \frac{U_i[M,\mathbf{X};\mathbf{P}]}{U_0[M,\mathbf{X};\mathbf{P}]} = \frac{p_i}{r}, \qquad (i=1,\ldots,n);$$

$$(7b) \qquad rM + \sum_1^n p_j x_j = Y.$$

Using the homogeneity property of U in (1), and the implied (6) homogeneity properties of U's partials, we can rewrite (7) in a form that displays (5)'s assertions about the homogeneities of the $\mathbf{h}(r,\mathbf{P},Y)$ functions:

$$(8a) \qquad \frac{U_i[M/Y,\mathbf{X};\mathbf{P}/Y]}{U_0[M/Y,\mathbf{X};\mathbf{P}/Y]} = \frac{p_i/Y}{r}, \quad (i=1,\ldots,n);$$

$$(8b) \qquad r(M/Y) + \sum_1^n (p_j/Y)x_j = 1.$$

Under our assumptions, the $(n+1)$ equations of (8) can be solved for a unique solution for the $(n+1)$ real unknowns, $[M/Y, x_1,\ldots,x_n]$ in terms of the $n+1$ prescribed real parameters $[r, p_1/Y,\ldots,p_n/Y] = [r,\pi_1,\ldots,\pi_n] = [r,\Pi]$.

II. Review of Conventional Moneyless Model

In the standard demand model, $U[M/Y, x_1,\ldots,x_n; p_1/Y,\ldots,p_n/Y]$ involves no p_j/Y parameters beyond the semicolon and $M/Y = x_0$ is an ordinary good with price $p_0/Y = r$; thus the partial derivatives $U_{n+i}[\ ]$ and $U_{j,n+i}[\ ]$ vanish in the moneyless model. It is well known for the moneyless model, under our strong simplifying assumptions, that its full empirical implications are summarized in the following $(n+1)$-by-$(n+1)$ negative semidefinite matrix:

Symmetry, for $i, j = 0,1,\ldots,n$,

$$(9) \qquad \mathbf{S} = \left[H_j^i(rY;\mathbf{P};Y) + H^j(rY;\mathbf{P};Y)H_{n+1}^i(rY;\mathbf{P};Y)\right] = \mathbf{S}^T$$

where $H_0^i = \partial H^i(p_0,\mathbf{P},Y)/\partial p_0$,

$H_{n+1}^i = \partial H^i/\partial Y$, etc.

Homogeneity

$$(10) \qquad [p_0\mathbf{P}]\mathbf{S} = 0;$$

Negative semidefiniteness

$$(11) \qquad \mathbf{Q}^T\mathbf{S}\mathbf{Q} < 0 \quad \text{for} \quad \mathbf{Q}^T \neq a[p_0\mathbf{P}]$$

almost everywhere in $(r,\mathbf{P}/Y)$.

Duality theory can be used to deduce $\mathbf{S}$'s symmetry from the symmetry of U^*'s Hessian matrix. With no money in the model, Roy (1942) and others have shown

$$(12) \qquad x_i = -\frac{U_i^*[p_0,p_1,\ldots,p_n,Y]}{U_{n+1}^*[p_0,p_1,\ldots,p_n,Y]} = H^i[p_0,\ldots,p_n,Y], \quad (i=0,1,\ldots,n);$$

$$(13) \qquad \mathbf{S} = \left[H_j^i + H^jH_{n+1}^i\right] = \left(U_{n+1}^*\right)^{-3}\Big[-U_{ij}^*\left(U_{n+1}^*\right)^2 + \left(U_i^*U_{n+1,j}^* + U_j^*U_{i,n+1}^*\right)\left(U_{n+1}^*\right) - U_i^*U_j^*U_{n+1,n+1}^*\Big] = \left[H_i^j + H^iH_{n+1}^j\right] = \mathbf{S}^T.$$

That $\mathbf{S}$ is singular follows from U^*'s homogeneity. That any principal minor of $\mathbf{S}$ is almost everywhere negative definite follows from U's strong quasi concavvity, with its implied similar property for $-U^*[p_0/Y,\ldots, p_n/Y,1]$.[3]

Unfortunately, once prices and money enter our model's utility function, it is conceptually impossible to unscramble contaminating effects of price on U_{n+i}/U_k. The simplicities of demand theory are lost.

IIII. Money's Contaminations

Duality theory rests on the basic envelope theorem of maximization theory, as in Samuelson (1947). To handle our many relations, we find it convenient to use the following Lagrangean expressions:

$$(14) \quad L = U[M,\mathbf{X};\mathbf{P}] + \lambda\left(Y - rM - \sum_1^n p_j x_j\right),$$

$$(15) \quad \partial L/\partial Y = \lambda = U^*_{n+1}[r;\mathbf{P},Y],$$

$$(16a) \quad \partial L/\partial r = -\lambda M = U_0^*[r;\mathbf{P},Y],$$

$$(16b) \quad M = -\frac{U_0^*[r;\mathbf{P},Y]}{U^*_{n+1}[r;\mathbf{P},Y]} = Yh^0(r;\mathbf{P}/Y,1),$$

$$(17a) \quad \partial L/\partial p_i = U_{n+i}[M,\mathbf{X};\mathbf{P}] - \lambda x_i = U_i^*[r;\mathbf{P},Y],$$

$$(17b) \quad x_i = -\frac{U_i^*[r;\mathbf{P},Y]}{U^*_{n+1}[r;\mathbf{P},Y]} + \frac{U_{n+i}[M,\mathbf{X};\mathbf{P}]}{\lambda}$$

$$= -\frac{U_i^*[r;\mathbf{P},Y]}{U^*_{n+1}[r;\mathbf{P},Y]} + Y\frac{U_{n+1}[M,\mathbf{X};\mathbf{P}]}{MU_0[M,\mathbf{X};\mathbf{P}] + \sum_1^n x_j U_j[M,\mathbf{X};\mathbf{P}]}$$

$$= h^i(r;\mathbf{P},Y) = h^i(r;\mathbf{P}/Y,1), \quad (i=1,\ldots,n).$$

Note that the breakdown between the two terms on (17b)'s right-hand side can generally not be made from observational data contained in the empirical $[h^i(r;\mathbf{P}/Y,1)]$ functions.

It follows that the following discrepancies generally will not vanish

$$(18) \quad [s_{ij} - s_{ji}] = \left[\left(h^i_j + h^j h^i_{n+1}\right) - \left(h^j_i + h^i h^j_{n+1}\right)\right].$$

Here $\partial h^i/\partial r = h^i_0(r;\mathbf{P},Y)$, etc. Moreover, these discrepancies involve the higher derivatives of the unidentifiable contamination terms, $U_{n+1}[M,\mathbf{X};\mathbf{P}]/U_k[M,\mathbf{X};\mathbf{P}]$.

In short, once money enters into the model in an essential way, demand theory not only loses its crown jewels (of testable well-behaved curvature and perhaps reciprocity relations), but worse than that, in a sense it loses its *raison d'etre* as a theory. The facts could be said to be left to tell their own story, except that our analysis has essentially demonstrated that the facts are left with no story to tell. All they can do is glare at us; all we can do is glare back and try to remember their multivariousnesses.

IV. Money and a Single Good

Here all is well behaved. We contemplate

$$(19) \quad \max_{M,x_1} U[M,x_1;p_1] = \max_{M/p_1,x_1} U[M/p_1,x_1;1] = \max_{x_0,x_1} U[x_0,x_1;1]$$

$$\text{subject to} \quad rM + p_1x_1 = Y = \sum_0^1 p_j x_j$$

$$= U\left[H^0(p_0,p_1,Y), H^1(p_0,p_1,Y)\right]$$

$$= U\left[H^0(rp_1,p_1,Y), H^1(rp_1,p_1,Y)\right]$$

$$= U^*[r;p_1,Y] = U^*[r;p_1/Y,1].$$

Warning: Here $H^0 = M/p_1$ and not M/Y as in (5b). It is apparent that, if we work

[3]See Sato (1981) for a more abstract version of the integrability conditions in terms of Lie groups.

with $(x_0, p_0) = (M/p_1, rp_1)$, (19) becomes exactly the form of a standard moneyless system.

Hence, we can deduce the full empirical implications of such a standard system, which can be summarized by

$$\text{(20a)} \quad H^1(r; p_1, Y) = (Y/p_1) - rH^0(r; p_1, Y),$$

and almost everywhere,

$$\text{(20b)} \quad \frac{1}{p_1}\frac{\partial H^0(r; p_1, Y)}{\partial r} + H^0(r; p_1, Y)\frac{\partial H^0(r; p_1, Y)}{\partial Y} < 0.$$

Since money's "price," the interest rate r, does not enter explicitly into the utility function, M will always respond in the conventional function to a compensated *increase* in its price: that is, if we raise r, and at the same time raise Y by M times the change in r, utility will remain constant and there will always be a negative "substitution effect" in the Slutsky-Hicks fashion (no matter how $\mathbf{P}$ contaminates U!).

Equivalent to (20b) is

$$\text{(21)} \quad (\partial M/\partial r)_{\text{comp.}} = (\partial M/\partial r) + M(\partial M/\partial Y) < 0.$$

We shall see in Section VI that (21) is valid in the general case, no matter how large is n and without regard to special separability features.

The demand behavior for the good x_1 will, when $n=1$, be just as well behaved as is the demand for money itself (for M or for x_0, as in (20b)). For $n=1$, we can also write: almost everywhere

$$\text{(22a)} \quad 0 > \frac{\partial x_1}{\partial p_1} + x_1\frac{\partial x_1}{\partial Y} = h_1^1(r; p_1, Y) + h^1(r; p_1, Y)h_3^1(r; p_1, Y),$$

$$\text{(22b)} \quad 0 = (\partial U/\partial p_1)_{\text{comp.}}$$

The contaminating term(s) to the right of the semicolon in $U[M,\mathbf{X};\mathbf{P}]$ can be got rid of for $n=1$, when we use (19)'s trick of writing $U[M, x_1; p_1]$ as $U[M/p_1, x_1; 1] = U[x_0, x_1; 1]$.

We shall see that, although (20b) will hold for $n \geq 1$, alas, (22b) will not be assured for $n > 1$ when there are no Santa Claus separability properties.

V. Weak Separability

Complete integrability and Slutsky-curvature conditions can be derived in two cases; when the goods in the utility function are weakly separable, or when the prices in U are weakly separable. These respective cases are

$$\text{(23)} \quad U[M,\mathbf{X};\mathbf{P}] \equiv U[M, g(\mathbf{X});\mathbf{P}] = U[1, g(\mathbf{X}); \mathbf{P}/M]$$

$$\text{(24)} \quad U[M,\mathbf{X};\mathbf{P}] \equiv U[M,\mathbf{X}; p(\mathbf{P})] = U[M/p(\mathbf{P}),\mathbf{X};1]$$

$$p(a\mathbf{P}) \equiv ap(\mathbf{P}), \text{ first-degree homogeneous.}$$

This second case, much discussed by Don Patinkin, Per Meinich, and others, easily reduces to the conventional moneyless model of our Section II. Assume we know the form of the $p(\mathbf{P})$ function and define a new set of left-hand variables:

$$\text{(25a)} \quad x_0 = M/p(\mathbf{P}),\ \mathbf{X} = (x_1, \dots, x_n), \quad p_0 = rp(\mathbf{P}),\ \mathbf{P} = (p_1, \dots, p_n).$$

Then

$$\text{(25b)} \quad p_0x_0 + \sum_1^n p_jx_j \equiv rM + \sum_1^n p_jx_j = Y,$$

$$\text{(25c)} \quad U[x_0, x_1, \dots, x_n; 1] \equiv U[M,\mathbf{X}; p(\mathbf{P})] \equiv U[M/p(\mathbf{P}),\mathbf{X};1].$$

Looking at the left-hand sides of (25b) and (25c), we see only the components of a conventional moneyless demand model—in $n+1$ goods, consisting of n regular commodities and one real-money magnitude. As in (12) and (13),

$$(26a)\quad x_i = H^i[p_0; \mathbf{P}, Y],\ (i = 0,1,\dots,n),$$

$$(26b)\quad \mathbf{S} = \left[H^i_j + H^j H^i_{n+1}\right] = \mathbf{S}^T,$$

$$(26c)\quad [p_0\mathbf{P}]\mathbf{S} = 0,$$

$$(26d)\quad Q^T\mathbf{S}Q < 0 \text{ almost everywhere, for } Q^T \neq a[p_0\mathbf{P}].$$

These tests of (26) can be applied to the observed $\mathbf{h}[r;\mathbf{P},Y]$ demand vector by utilizing the identities.

$$(27)\quad x_i = h^i[r;\mathbf{P},Y] \equiv H^i[rp(\mathbf{P});\mathbf{P},Y],\quad (i=1,\dots,n),$$

$$M = Yh^0[r;\mathbf{P},Y] \equiv p(\mathbf{P})H^0[rp(\mathbf{P});\mathbf{P},Y],$$

$$\left[H^i_0, H^i_j, H^i_{n+1}\right] = \left[h^i_0/p(\mathbf{P}), h^i_j - rh^i_0/p(\mathbf{P}) \times\{\partial p(\mathbf{P})/\partial p_j\}, h^i_{n+1}\right].$$

Warning: if $p(\mathbf{P})$ is not known to us in advance—and why would it be?—and why even be known to exist?—the (27) observations do not seem to be sufficient to "identify" the form or even existence of the $p(\mathbf{P})$ function and the (26) tests cannot be performed!

More satisfactory is the complete resolution of testable consequences of (23)'s weakly separable-quantities case. Here we see how to perform a two-stage maximization procedure.

1) Recognize first that the full optimum is not achieved unless the amount spent on real goods along, $\hat{Y} = Y - rM$, buys the consumer the highest level of $g(\mathbf{X})$. So, first solve the moneyless conventional problem (in n, not $n+1$, variables):

$$(28)\quad \operatorname*{Max}_{\mathbf{X}} g(\mathbf{X}) \quad \text{subject to } \mathbf{P}\cdot\mathbf{X} = \hat{Y} = g(\mathbf{H}\{\mathbf{P},\hat{Y}\}).$$

To remind ourselves that the $\mathbf{H}\{\mathbf{P},\hat{Y}\}$ vector involves n and not $n+1$ elements, we use curly rather than square brackets. From Section II's moneyless theory we know that

$$(29)\quad \mathbf{S} = \left[H^i_j + H^j H^i_{n+1}\right] = \mathbf{S}^T,$$

$$\mathbf{PS} = 0,\ \mathbf{Q}^T\mathbf{SQ} < 0 \text{ for } \mathbf{Q}^T \neq a\mathbf{P} \text{ almost everywhere.}$$

2) In the second stage of the maximization procedure, with $(r,\mathbf{P},Y)$ regarded as fixed, we optimize how Y should be divided between M and $\hat{Y}$, recognizing how any $\hat{Y}$ will itself be optimally allocated among real commodities, and recognizing finally that the realization of both stages of the maximization must succeed in solving our full-optimality problem, so that

$$\operatorname*{Max}_{M,\mathbf{X}} U[1, g(\mathbf{X}); \mathbf{P}/M] \quad \text{subject to } rM + \mathbf{P}\cdot\mathbf{X} = Y$$

$$(30a)\quad = U[1, g(\mathbf{h}\{r;\mathbf{P},Y\}); \mathbf{P}/M(r;\mathbf{P},Y)] = \operatorname*{Max}_{M,\hat{Y}} U[1, g(\mathbf{H}\{P,\hat{Y}\}); \mathbf{P}/M] \quad \text{subject to } rM + \hat{Y} = Y,$$

$$(30b)\quad = U[1, g(\mathbf{H}\{\mathbf{P}, Y - rM(r,\mathbf{P},Y)\}); \mathbf{P}/M(r;\mathbf{P},Y)].$$

The reader who carefully studies the identity of (30a) to (30b) will be able to verify the two-stage-maximization identities

$$(31a)\quad x_i = h^i\{r;\mathbf{P},Y\} \equiv H^i\{\mathbf{P}, Y - rM(r;\mathbf{P},Y)\}.$$

If he or she differentiates both sides of these identities partially with respect to p_j, and then with respect to compensated changes in r, the reader will be able to solve explicitly for the following:[4]

(31b) $$H^i_{n+1} = -r^{-1}\left(h^i_0 + Mh^i_{n+1}\right)/(M_r + MM_Y), \quad (i=1,\dots,n),$$

where $M_r + MM_Y < 0$, $r > 0$,

(32a) $$H^i_j = h^i_j - M_j\left(h^i_0 + Mh^i_{n+1}\right)/(M_r + MM_Y), \quad (i, j=1,\dots,n),$$

(32b) $$\mathbf{S} = \left[H^i_j + H^j H^i_{n+1}\right] = \left[h^i_j + h^j h^i_{n+1} - \left(M_j + h^j M_Y\right)\left(h^i_0 + Mh^i_{n+1}\right)/(M_r + MM_Y)\right] = \mathbf{S}^T,$$

negative semidefinite almost everywhere.

With some reflection the reader would note that (32b) is a modification of the simple Slutsky expression. This expression now includes the following: a compensated price change on money $(M_j + h^j M_Y)$, a compensated interest rate change on money $(M_r + MM_Y)$, and a compensated interest rate change on the ith good $(h^i_0 + Mh^i_{n+1})$.

These, at last, are $(n-1)(n-2)/2$ independent reciprocity conditions that the observable $\mathbf{h}(r;\mathbf{P},Y)$ goods' demand functions must satisfy when $g(\mathbf{X})$ exists. Moreover, unlike $p(\mathbf{P})$, if the $g(\mathbf{X})$ function exists, that fact can be ascertained from the demand data; and those data provide us with the integrable differential forms that do "identify" the exact form of $g(\mathbf{X})$—of course, up to an arbitrary stretching of g, and with unambiguous marginal rate of substitution functions $g_j(\mathbf{X})/g_1(\mathbf{X})$ identifiable from p_j/p_1 data.

Worth mentioning is the following beautifully simple case that is weakly separable in both prices and quantities, and with $[p(\mathbf{P}), g(\mathbf{X})]$ functions that are first-degree homogeneous and are Shephard (1953) duals to each other. This case has the pleasing feature that it makes sense in the homothetic case for the person to possess a single price-index function which validly measures *at all income levels* the economists' notion of a true cost-of-living index. On the other hand, a painful price has to be paid for this logical consistency in that all experience tells us that real people do not have homothetic preferences.

Now we have

(33) $$U[M,\mathbf{X};P] = U[M, g(\mathbf{X}); p(\mathbf{P})] = U[M/p(\mathbf{P}), g(\mathbf{X}); 1],$$

where

(34a) $$\min_{\mathbf{X}} \mathbf{P}\cdot\mathbf{X}/g(\mathbf{X}) = p(\mathbf{P}): \text{concave}$$
$$= a^{-1}p(a\mathbf{P}): \text{first-degree homogeneous}$$

(34b) $$\min_{\mathbf{P}} \mathbf{P}\cdot\mathbf{X}/p(\mathbf{P}) = g(\mathbf{X}): \text{concave}$$
$$= a^{-1}g(a\mathbf{X}): \text{first-degree homogeneous.}$$

From duality theory

(35a) $$x_i/g(\mathbf{X}) = [\partial \ln p(\mathbf{P})]/\partial p_i,$$

(35b) $$p_i/p(\mathbf{P}) = [\partial \ln g(\mathbf{X})]/\partial x_i.$$

Clearly, we can treat (33) as a two-good moneyless system

$$\max_{x_0, x_1} U[x_0, x_1; 1] \quad \text{subject to } \sum_0^1 p_j x_j = Y$$
$$= U^*[p_0, p_1, Y] = U^*[p_0/Y, p_1/Y, 1]$$

(36a) $$= U\left[H^0(p_0, p_1, Y), H^1(p_0, p_1, Y); 1\right]$$

(36b) $$\equiv \max_{M,g} U[M/p(\mathbf{P}), g; 1]$$

subject to $rM + p(\mathbf{P})g = Y$

(36c) $$= U[M\{r; p(\mathbf{P}), Y\}/p(\mathbf{P}), g\{r; p(\mathbf{P}), Y\}; 1].$$

[4]Symbolically, each side of (31a) is subjected to $\partial/\partial p_j$ and to the compensated operation $(\partial/\partial r + M\partial/\partial Y)$. *Remark*: A compensated interest rate change on money $(M_r + MM_Y)$ is strictly negative for the general case as proved in Section VI (see 39e)).

In (36) $M\{r;\, p(\mathbf{P}), Y\}$ satisfies the single Slutsky-Hicks curvature condition

$$(37a) \qquad M_r + MM_Y < 0.$$

Also, from (35a), for $(i = 1, \ldots, n)$,

$$(37b) \quad x_i/g = h^i\{r; \mathbf{P}, Y\}$$

$$/[Y - rM\{r;\, p(\mathbf{P}), Y\}]\, p(\mathbf{P})^{-1}$$

$$= \partial[\ln p(\mathbf{P})]/\partial p_i, \quad (i = 1, \ldots, n),$$

with $[\partial^2\{\ln p(\mathbf{P})\}/\partial p_i\, \partial p_j]$ having to be symmetric and thereby implying $n(n-1)/2$ reciprocity condition on the $[\mathbf{X}/g, \mathbf{P}/Y]$ observable demand interrelations. Also, under our original strong quasi-concavity assumption, there will be (almost everywhere) the $n-1$ negative-semidefiniteness curvature conditions on the testable Hessian matrix of $\ln p(\mathbf{P})$.

VI. Well-Behaved Substitution Effect for Money

Invoking no separability properties for $U[M, \mathbf{X}; \mathbf{P}]$ and letting there be any number of goods along with money, we can now show why a rise in the interest rate that is compensated by a rise in income just big enough to leave your utility intact must cause you to hold less money—a direct violation of extreme monetarism. The easiest approach is via the program of minimizing the expenditure needed to achieve a fixed level of utility:

$$(38a) \qquad \min_{M, \mathbf{X}} [rM + \mathbf{P} \cdot \mathbf{X}]$$

$$\text{subject to} \qquad U[M, \mathbf{X}; \mathbf{P}] = \overline{U}$$

$$(38b) \qquad = E^*[r; \mathbf{P}|\overline{U}]$$

$$(38c) \qquad = rg^0(r; \mathbf{P}|\overline{U}) + \sum_1^n p_j g^j(r; \mathbf{P}|\overline{U}).$$

We wish to show that the $g^0(r; \mathbf{P}|U)$ demand function for money falls as the interest rate rises,

$$g_0^0 = \partial g^0(r; \mathbf{P}|\overline{U})/\partial r < 0 \text{ almost everywhere}$$

$$= Y\left[h_0^0(r; \mathbf{P}, Y) + h^0(r; \mathbf{P}, Y) \times \left\{h_{n+1}^0(r; \mathbf{P}, Y) + h^0(r; \mathbf{P}, Y)\right\}\right]$$

$$= M_r + MM_Y < 0.$$

First, we prove this property for general finite changes in r alone, with $(p_1, \ldots, p_n)$ and U held constant at $(\overline{\mathbf{P}}; \overline{U})$. Then for all $(M, \mathbf{X})$ that satisfy

$$(39a) \qquad U(M, \mathbf{X}; \overline{\mathbf{P}}) = \overline{U}$$

to optimal g responses to $r = r^1$ and $r = r^2$, (M^1, X^1) and (M^2, X^2), satisfy

$$(39b) \quad r^1 M^1 + \overline{\mathbf{P}} \cdot \mathbf{X}^1 \leq r^1 M^2 + \overline{\mathbf{P}} \cdot \mathbf{X}^2,$$

$$(39c) \quad r^2 M^2 + \overline{\mathbf{P}} \cdot \mathbf{X}^2 \leq r^2 M^1 + \overline{\mathbf{P}} \cdot \mathbf{X}^1.$$

These inequalities, which will be strong inequalities if $r^1 \neq r^2$ and our earlier sections' regularity conditions are stipulated for U, follow from (38)'s defined minimum program.

Now if one subtracts respective sides of (39b) from those of (39c) and cancels, one derives

$$(39d) \quad 0 \geq (r^2 - r^1)(M^2 - M^1)$$

$$= \Delta r \Delta M = (\Delta r)^2 [\Delta M/\Delta r].$$

Again, the inequality will be a strong one for $r^2 \neq r^1$.

With M a smooth function of r, by letting $(\Delta r) \to 0$, we denote

$$(39e) \quad \lim_{\Delta r \to 0} [\Delta M/\Delta r] = g_0^0(r; \mathbf{P}|\overline{U})$$

$$\equiv M_r + MM_Y < 0 \text{ almost everywhere.}$$

In conventional moneyless models, one can deduce for *any good* that compensated $\Delta p_j \Delta x_j$ is nonpositive. But only, so to speak, for $\Delta p_0 \Delta x_0$ can one validly arrive at this conclusion once money enters the utility function along with its contaminating U_{n+i}/U_j effects. Thus, (39b) and (39c) would not be valid if disparate values of **P** were put into (39b) and (39c).

In summary, for a money model $g_j^j(r; \overline{P}|\overline{U})$ can be assured to be negative only for $j=0$.

VII. Theoretical Chaos when People Judge Quality by Price

Thorstein Veblen (1899) pointed out that people often want goods not so much because they are directly useful as because they are expensive. Tibor Scitovsky (1945) called attention to the fact that often we consumers judge the quality of goods by the prices charged for them: if Fords are cheap relative to Cadillacs and pork chops, we may regard that as a signal for the low worth of a Ford car.

Analytically, our indifference contours for (bread, Ford cars, pork chops) now depend on some relative prices, as on $p_{\text{Ford}}/p_{\text{pork}}$. Any indicator of utility, U, now becomes a function of price(s) as well as quantities:

$$(40)\quad U(\text{bread, Ford, pork};\ p_{\text{Ford}}/p_{\text{pork}}) = U(x_0, x_1, x_2;\ p_1/p_2).$$

Although the context for this price contamination is different from that of our money models, the analytics look similar. Thus, recall a model involving two goods and money:

$$(41a)\quad U(M, x_1, x_2; p_1, p_2) \equiv U(M/p_2, x_1, x_2; p_1/p_2, 1),$$

$$(41b)\quad \equiv U(x_0, x_1, x_2; p_1/p_2, 1).$$

Comparison of (40) and (41b) shows them to be formally identical. When our previous analysis showed that theory can tell us virtually nothing useful about (41b)'s demand functions, $\mathbf{h}(p_0, p_1, \mathbf{Y})$, that demonstration warns us that theory is powerless to say interesting things about the Veblen-Scitovsky demand functions. As the elementary textbooks warn us, chic shops "may do better in moving a slow-selling item if they *raise* its price" (Samuelson, 1948, p. 474). We may now have $\partial x_1/\partial p_1 > 0$ even though $\partial x_1/\partial Y > 0$; and we aren't surprised if reciprocity conditions fail.

It will be instructive to consider two real goods, (x_1, x_2), whose marginal rates of substitution depend on the p_2/p_1 price ratio, $R[x_1, x_2; p_2/p_1]$:

$$(42a)\quad R[x_1, x_2; p_2/p_1] > 0 \quad \text{for } [x_1, x_2; p_2/p_1] > 0.$$

Almost everywhere in the positive (x_1, x_2) quadrant, no matter what fixed value p_2/p_1 takes, we posit

$$(42b)\quad 0 > R_2[x_1, x_2; p_2/p_1] - R[x_1, x_2; p_2/p_1]R_1[x_1, x_2; p_2/p_1] = \Delta[x_1, x_2; p_2/p_1].$$

Also

$$(42c)\quad \lim_{x_1 \to 0} R[x_1, x_2; p_2/p_1] = \infty, \qquad \lim_{x_2 \to 0} R[x_1, x_2; p_2/p_1] = 0.$$

Then, for each positive $(p_2/p_1, Y/p_1)$, there is a unique (x_1^*, x_2^*) demanded

$$(43)\quad x_1^* = h^1(1, p_2/p_1, Y/p_1) = h^1(p_1, p_2, Y),$$

$$x_2^* = h^2(1, p_2/p_1, Y/p_1) = h^2(p_1, p_2, Y).$$

These *direct* demand functions of (43) can be regarded as solutions of the *implicit* equations

$$(44a)\quad p_2/p_1 = R[x_1, x_2; p_2/p_1],$$

$$(44b)\quad Y/p_1 = x_1 + x_2 R[x_1, x_2; p_2/p_1].$$

But, of course, mere knowledge of the observable demand functions, of (43)'s

$h^i(p_1, p_2, Y)$ functions, does *not* give us knowledge of the $R[x_1, x_2; p_2/p_1]$.

(How could we get knowledge of $R[x_1, x_2; p_2/p_1]$ and of the indifference contours generated by any p_2/p_1 point? *Direct interrogation* of the consumer could give it in principle. For each p_2/p_1, he would compare for us any pair of (x_1, x_2) points. For p_2/p_1 given, he'd report

$$(a_1, a_2) \text{ better than } (b_1, b_2), \mathbf{A} \succ \mathbf{B}$$

$$\text{or} \quad (b_1, b_2) \text{ better than } (a_1, a_2), \mathbf{B} \succ \mathbf{A}$$

$$\text{or} \quad (a_1, a_2) \text{ and } (b_1, b_2) \text{ indifferent}, \mathbf{A} \sim \mathbf{B}.$$

Also, his $\mathbf{A} \succ \mathbf{B}$ and $\mathbf{A} \sim \mathbf{B}$ orderings would obey transitivity, etc.)

If the p_2/p_1 contamination of $R[\ ]$ were "weak," so that $R_3[\ ]$ is close enough to zero, (44a) could assuredly be solved for

$$(45) \qquad p_2/p_1 = f(x_1, x_2)$$

where $f(x_1, x_2)$ is a single-valued function. Also,

$$(46) \qquad f_2(x_1, x_2) - f(x_1, x_2) f_1(x_1, x_2) = \Delta(x_1, x_2)$$

will be assuredly negative wherever $R_3(x_1, x_2; p_2/p_1)$ is sufficiently near zero, since by the Implicit Function theorem

$$(47a) \quad f(x_1, x_2) \equiv R[x_1, x_2; f(x_1, x_2)],$$

$$(47b) \quad \Delta(x_1, x_2) \equiv \Delta[x_1, x_2; f(x_1, x_2)] / \{1 - R_3[x_1, x_2; f(x_1, x_2)]\}.$$

If (47b)'s numerator is required by (42b) to be negative, then where $R_3[x_1, x_2; f(x_1, x_2)]$ is sufficiently small, $\Delta(x_1, x_2)$ will be assuredly negative. For such *weak Veblen effects*, observed demand will still be well behaved.

However, let $R_3[x_1, x_2; p_2/p_1]$ become a sizable positive number. Then raising good 2's relative price will so much enhance good 2's relative marginal utility as to *reverse the curvature* of the reduced-form (pseudo!) indifference contours inferred by the naive observer of the (45) relation. Now $\Delta(x_1, x_2)$ has the opposite sign to $\Delta[x_1, x_2; f(x_1, x_2)]$ because (47b)'s denominator has become negative. No wonder that $\partial x_2/\partial p_2$ can be positive when $\partial x_2/\partial Y$ is positive: actually, the naive observer of (45) and (43) price-quantity interrelations will infer that he is observing a masochistic *minimizer* rather than a *homo economicus* who maximizes; each observed tangency of a budget line to a (pseudo) indifference contour will be a point of global minimum rather than maximum.

Qualification. There is no reason why R_3 shouldn't take on values that equal one at some places and that both exceed and fall short of one at other places. That means that no single-valued $f(x_1, x_2)$ function may exist. But, regardless of that, the *direct* demand functions of (43) are guaranteed to exist as single-valued smooth functions by our strong sufficiency conditions of (42) and of (6). The point is that they need not have conventional slope and curvature conditions.

With but two goods, there were no integrability conditions to be upset by Veblenesque effects. With three or more goods, the slightest Veblenesque effects will destroy the razor's-edge condition in which observable reciprocity effects necessarily obtain.

The case $n = 3$ will suffice. Consider the (not-directly-observable) *MRS* functions:

$$(48) \quad p_2/p_1 = R^2[x_1, x_2; p_2/p_1],$$

$$p_3/p_1 = R^3[x_1, x_2, x_3; p_2/p_1],$$

$$Y/p_1 = x_1 + \sum_2^3 R^j[x_1, x_2, x_3; p_2/p_1] x_j.$$

Under our regularity conditions, (48) is compatible with

$$(49) \quad x_j = h^j(p_1, p_2, p_3, Y) = h^j(1, p_2/p_1, p_3/p_1, Y/p_1), \qquad (j = 1, 2, 3).$$

For every positive p_2/p_1, the following two-by-two matrix is everywhere symmetric and almost everywhere negative-definite:

$$\text{(50a)} \quad (a_{ij}) = (R^i_j - R^j R^i_i) = (a_{ji}).$$

Almost everywhere

$$\text{(50b)} \quad (q_1 \quad q_2)(a_{ij})\begin{pmatrix} q_1 \\ q_2 \end{pmatrix} < 0$$

$$\text{for } (q_1 \quad q_2) > 0.$$

If Veblenesque effects are "weak," so that $1 - R^2_4$ is positive, the Implicit Function theorem assures us that (48) can be replaced by

$$\text{(51)} \quad p_j/p_1 = f^j(x_1, x_2, x_3) \quad (j = 2,3)$$

$$Y/p_1 = x_1 + \sum_2^3 f^j(x_1, x_2, x_3)x_j.$$

However, it will *not* (generally) be the case that the reciprocity relation of (50a), $a_{12} = a_{21}$, will have the following valid counterpart

$$\text{(52)} \quad f^2_3(x_1, x_2, x_3) - f^3(x_1, x_2, x_3)f^2_1(x_1, x_2, x_3) = \Delta_{23}(x_1, x_2, x_3)$$

$$\text{(53)} \qquad = \Delta_{32}(x_1, x_2, x_3).$$

Of course, $\Delta_{23} - \Delta_{32}$ will "almost vanish" if $R^2_4[x_1, x_2, x_3; f^2(x_1, x_2, x_3)]$ "almost vanishes." Also

$$\text{(54)} \quad \Delta_{22}(x_1, x_2, x_3) = f^2_2 - f^2 f^2_1$$

can be counted on to stay negative when R_4 remains sufficiently small. But as R_4 deviates more and more from zero, all bets are off concerning the signs of observed demand changes. Wherever $R^2_4[x_1, x_2, x_3; p_2/p_1]$ deviates from unity

$$\text{(55)} \quad (f^i_j - f^j f^i_1) = (R^i_j - R^j R^i_1) + (R^i_4[f^2_j - f^j f^i_1]).$$

Although the first matrix on the right (if it were observable) would have to be that of a symmetric matrix almost everywhere negative definite, the second (also unobservable) matrix generally spoils the conventional story. See, however, R. L. Basmann et al. for a special Fechner-Thurstone family of preferences, where the $f^j(\mathbf{X})$ functions are indistinguishable from the standard noncontamination case.

VIII. Multiple Money

Now replace a single money asset, M, with its opportunity cost of holding, r, by a whole vector of assets of different degrees of liquidity and usefulness for transaction purposes and steady-state holding: $(M_1, \ldots, M_k, \ldots, M_N) = \mathbf{M}$ with relevant interest-yield costs respectively of $(r_1, \ldots, r_k, \ldots, r_N) = \mathbf{R}$. Thus, in the steady state, I may hold some cash, M_1, with zero yield-return; its r_1 that measures what it costs me per dollar per annum in foregone income is a large positive amount. But, also, I hold a money market fund asset, M_2, that in the steady state adds to my utility; since, however, it yields me a high nominal return per annum—in 1981 a safe rate of as much as 18 percent—the f_2 that measures its foregone-income opportunity cost to me is lower than r_1 (possibly even being negative, depending on what convention we use for measuring opportunity costs). My demand problem is this: confronted by income Y, by prices of goods $\mathbf{P}$, and by vector of $\mathbf{R}$ costs for holding different moneys, I pick $(\mathbf{M}, \mathbf{X})$ so as to maximize my steady-state utility.

We generalize our old one-money utility function of Samuelson (1947) in the following natural way:

$$\text{(56)} \quad U[M_1, \ldots, M_N, x_1, \ldots, x_n; P_1, \ldots, P_n] = U[\mathbf{M}, \mathbf{X}; P] \equiv U[a\mathbf{M}, \mathbf{X}; aP]$$

$$\partial U/\partial x_i = U_i[\mathbf{M}, \mathbf{X}; \mathbf{P}] > 0, \qquad (i = 1, \ldots, n)$$
$$= U_i[a\mathbf{M}, \mathbf{X}; a\mathbf{P}]$$

$$\partial U/\partial p_i = U_{n+i}[\mathbf{M}, \mathbf{X}; \mathbf{P}], \qquad (i = 1, \ldots, n)$$
$$= U_{n+i}[a\mathbf{M}, \mathbf{X}; a\mathbf{P}]a$$

$$\partial U/\partial M_k = U_{-k}[\mathbf{M}, \mathbf{X}; \mathbf{P}] > 0, \; (k = 1, \ldots, N)$$
$$= U_{-k}[a\mathbf{M}, \mathbf{X}; a\mathbf{P}]a.$$

As before, U is to be strongly concave in $[\mathbf{M},\mathbf{X}]$; etc.

We write our $n+N$ demand functions for goods and for moneys as

$$(57)\quad x_i = h^i(r_1,\ldots,r_N;\, p_1,\ldots,p_n,Y), \qquad (i=1,\ldots,n)$$
$$= h^i(\mathbf{R};\mathbf{P},Y) = h^i(\mathbf{R};\mathbf{P}/Y,1)$$
$$M_k = Yh^{-k}(r_1,\ldots,r_N;\, p_1,\ldots,p_n,Y), \qquad (k=1,\ldots,N)$$
$$= Yh^{-k}(\mathbf{R};\mathbf{P},Y) = Yh^{-k}(\mathbf{R};\mathbf{P}/Y,1).$$

When there is only one money, $N=1$, our old $h^0(r;\mathbf{P}/Y,:1)$ becomes the same thing as our present notation's $h^{-1}(\mathbf{R},\mathbf{P}/Y,1)$.

These optimal amounts demanded, $(\mathbf{M}^*,\mathbf{X}^*)$, are the roots of the following variational equations:

$$(58a)\quad U_i[\mathbf{M}/Y,\mathbf{X};\mathbf{P}/Y]b^{-1} = p_i/Y, \qquad (i=1,\ldots,n)$$

$$(58b)\quad U_{-k}[\mathbf{M}/Y,\mathbf{X};\mathbf{P}/Y]b^{-1} = r_k, \qquad (k=1,\ldots,N)$$

$$b = \sum_{k=1}^{N} M_k U_{-k}[\mathbf{M},\mathbf{X};\mathbf{P}] + \sum_{j=1}^{n} x_j U_j[\mathbf{M},\mathbf{X};\mathbf{P}]$$
$$= \sum_{k=1}^{N} (M_k/Y) U_{-k}[\mathbf{M}/Y,\mathbf{X};\mathbf{P}/Y] + \sum_{j=1}^{n} x_j U_j[\mathbf{M}/Y,\mathbf{X};\mathbf{P}/Y].$$

The $(n+N)$ right-hand functions of (58) can be solved for our unique demand functions (57): these variational conditions are sufficient as well as necessary for solution to the following natural maximum problem.

$$(59a)\quad \max_{\mathbf{M}\cdot\mathbf{X}} U[\mathbf{M},\mathbf{X};\mathbf{P}] \text{ subject to } \mathbf{R}\cdot\mathbf{M}+\mathbf{P}\cdot\mathbf{X}=Y,$$
$$(59b)\quad = U^*[\mathbf{R};\mathbf{P},Y] = U^*[\mathbf{R};\mathbf{P}/Y,1],$$
$$(59c)\quad = U[\mathbf{h}(\mathbf{R};\mathbf{P}/Y,1);\mathbf{P}],$$

where $\mathbf{h}(\mathbf{R};\mathbf{P},Y) = [Yh^{-1}(\mathbf{R};\mathbf{P},Y),\ldots, Yh^{-N}(\mathbf{R};\mathbf{P},Y), h^1(\mathbf{R};\mathbf{P},Y),\ldots, h^n(\mathbf{R};\mathbf{P},Y)]$.

Students of rational macroeconomic policy will find confirmed in this neoclassical analysis their doubts concerning the validity of monetarists' prescriptions of simple rules. Should the Federal Reserve stabilize the trend-growth of M_1 or M_2 inclusive of money market fund assets? In the early 1980's, the crude empirical correlation between nominal *GNP* and M_2 exceeded the correlation between *GNP* and M_1. However, the relative sizes of these $\bar{R}^2$s would seem a poor guide to the kind of causality relevant for policy. The present model would explain a great 1979–81 increase in money market fund assets as a rational reaction to an increase in their nominal and real yields from one-digit to two-digit per annum rates; if that rise contributed toward a high $\bar{R}^2$ between *GNP* an M_2, this model would not expect that fact to increase confidence in M_2 as an important Granger-Sims causal factor of future *GNP* movements. In short, the present model is a model for understanding *variations* in various M_k *velocities* of circulation, not a model leading one to expect quasi constancy of such diverse velocities.

An important fruit of a theory is its suggestiveness concerning the likely pattern of comparative statics that will occur. Since the signs of $[\partial x_i/\partial p_i, \partial x_i/\partial Y]$ were seen to be nonidentifiable when the vector M consisted of a single element, we must, of course, expect that a multimoney model (with $N>1$) will suffer from the same deficiency.

Fortunately, the Slutsky-like matrix of M_k responses to changes in $[r_1,\ldots,r_N]$ parameters is as well behaved in the multimoney model as in the one-money model.[5] The following N-by-N matrix is symmetric and negative definite:

$$(60a)\quad \boldsymbol{\sigma}=\left[\frac{\partial h^{-k}(\mathbf{R};\mathbf{P},Y)}{\partial r_q}+h^{-q}(\mathbf{R};\mathbf{P},Y)\frac{\partial h^{-k}(\mathbf{R};\mathbf{P},Y)}{\partial Y}\right]=\boldsymbol{\sigma}^T,$$

$$(60b)\quad (z_1,\dots,z_N)\boldsymbol{\sigma}(z_1,\dots,z_N)^T<0 \quad \text{for } (z_1,\dots,z_N)\neq 0.$$

No separate proof of this is needed. Since **P** is being held constant when elements of **R** change, and since no elements of **R** contaminate the U function, we may rely on classical moneyless demand analysis for results like (60) and for similar results on inverse demand functions in which $(M_1,\dots,M_N;\, p_1,\dots,p_n)$ are the independent variables. For such mixed-variables dualities, see Samuelson (1960).

The reader can explore special cases involving *weak separability*: as in the case of $N=1$, these special cases permit identifying testable reciprocity and curvature conditions.

What remains of the Quantity Theory when a vector of moneys replaces a single M? Its germ of truth still obtains. Every nominal price and wage, instead of being ultimately proportional to the quantity of externally prescribed M, now becomes a homogeneous (first-degree) function of the prescribed vector, $\mathbf{M}=(M_k)$. Only if one has an endogenous theory involving endogenous long-run invariances for the (M_k/M_1) ratios can a single scalar set the absolute scale for the system. Note that in a proper general equilibrium formulation there is no need for a Quantity Equation of Exchange with hypothetically constant velocity of circulation. Instead, the present neoclassical principles give an endogenous theory of how the velocity or velocities will vary in function of interest rates and other variables of the equilibrium.

[5] Robert Clower reminds us that what is called an increase in interest rates—some kind of a simultaneous increase in different kinds of interest rates—cannot be expected to have unambiguous sign responses on the part of each and every one of our many Ms. Agreed. What we can expect, and what the mathematical analysis confirms, is that a balanced (compensated) increase in any subset of the $[r_1,\dots,r_N]$ vector will, in the Hicksian fashion, have a definite negative effect on the Hicksian composite-commodity $\Sigma r_k M_k$, made up of the respective rs and Ms in question. No more can be expected to obtain. (All or some of the x_i goods flows might be in some degree inventoriable. So our vector of Ms might desirably be augmented by such inventory stocks. The present paper does not tackle the resulting problems in comparative statics.)

IX. False Starts

Here we shall merely mention some earlier studies that might be misinterpreted by hasty readers as having solved the problem shown here to be generally unsolvable.

One early model, that of C. E. V. Leser, seems to give a "generalized set of Slutsky equations" (1943, p. 130). However, the z_{rs} terms in them are precisely of the "contaminations" form we have noted in this paper, involving unobservable expressions that in our notation would be written as U_{n+i}/U_j. Moreover, we do not really understand this 1943 model. In our notation, it seems to be expressible as

$$(61)\quad \underset{x_1,\dots,x_n,L}{\text{Max}}\; U[x_1,\dots,x_n;\, L/p_1,\dots,L/p_n]$$

$$\text{subject to}\quad \sum_1^n p_j x_j+L=M.$$

In the steady state, if L does not equal M, we seem to deny the steadiness of the state; if L does equal M, $(x_1,\dots,x_n)$ can be a positive vector only if some other source of steady-state income is specified—wage income, interest income, or something. Modern dynamic analysis, of the kind that weds Miguel Sidrauski (1967) to Frank Ramsey (1928) would suggest a calculus-of-variations approach to a changing cash balance, $M(t)$. A typical program would involve

$$(62)\quad \underset{M(t),\mathbf{X}(t)}{\text{Max}}\; \sum_0^\infty U[M(t),\mathbf{X}(t);\mathbf{P}],$$

$$\text{subject to}\quad \sum_{j=1}^n p_j x_j(t)+rM(t)=Y(t)+M(t)-M(t-1).$$

Samuelson (1947, equations (117)) circumspectly refrained from trying to obtain *compensated demand* coefficients. He was content to point out the well-behaved negative sign of the Slutsky term $(\partial M/\partial r)+M(\partial M/\partial Y)$.

Richard Dusansky and Peter Kalman (1972, 1974), citing writings of Samuelson, Lloyd, Meinich, Hadar, and Patinkin, derive Slutsky reciprocity relations. Despite certain words of exposition that seem to refer to a general $U[M,\mathbf{X};\mathbf{P}]$ function, it is clear that valid observationally testable results would crucially depend on the weak-separability cases—as for example their case of $U[M/p(\mathbf{P}),\mathbf{X};1]$ that was considered in our Section V. They also point out that when $U[M,\mathbf{X};\mathbf{P}]$ departs from homogeneity of degree zero in the variables $[M,\mathbf{P}]$ in such a way as to make the marginal rates of substitutions, U_{n-k}/U_n, also depart, then various "money illusions" are involved and the Quantity Theory's neutral money properties have to be qualified—a valid point too obvious to be itself controversial.

X. Final Reflections

The model that puts money and prices into the utility function in a homogeneous way has the merit of capturing some of the basic features of money. That doesn't mean it is an optimal model. It is not. Despite its helpfulness, we should be under no illusions on this point.

Money is useful to you in real life because it enables you to have a steadier and better adjusted time stream of consumptions: music boxes when and where you want to hear music; time profiles of coffee consumption with less variance because you don't run out of liquid cash to buy; better bargains available for ready cash; less uncertainty as to where your next meal is to come from, and fewer past disappointments concerning hoped for consumption goods. A really deep analysis, therefore, will put in its utility functions time profiles of real consumption goods: $[\mathbf{X}(t),\mathbf{X}(t+1),\ldots,\mathbf{X}(t+T),\ldots]$.

A larger average steady-state money balance,

$$(63)\quad \overline{M}=T^{-1}\sum_{t=0}^{T}M(t),\qquad T\to\infty$$

will give a higher expected value to

$$(64)\quad U[\ldots,X(t),X(t+1),\ldots].$$

But, as an ultimate *desideratum*, money is no more in the utility function than is penicillin or any other intermediate good. We must, therefore, regard our $U[M,\mathbf{X};\mathbf{P}]$ function as already the result of some behind-the-scenes optimizing and time-averaging. With this understanding and caveat, we can regard the present model as a useful scaffolding of analysis even if it is not itself at the deepest level.

Some other qualifications should be made explicit. This paper has analyzed effects of a change in the interest rate on $\mathbf{X}$ real-good consumptions or on M money holding while "income" is being held constant. Actually, a permanent rise in the interest rate might itself induce a rise in the *rentier's* steady-state income. (Or, for one whose sole asset is an acre of land with a fixed perpetual real annual payment, a rise in r will cause *no* change in steady-state Y, the induced drop in land's capitalized value just matching the rise in r and leaving annual spendable Y intact.) We make no pronouncement on these incidence questions. If you know the form of the $\mathbf{h}(r;\mathbf{P},Y)$ functions, then you are in a position to analyze any combination of $(r;\mathbf{P},Y)$ changes that are presented to you.

Ever since 1947, a number of writers have been bothered by the present steady-state analysis. "Why," they may ask, "does rM enter on the left-hand side of (2)'s budget equation, with M entering nowhere else?" And actually a number of writers have tried to follow the example of J. R. Hicks (1939) and of Don Patinkin (1956) and envisage a model involving successive weekly periods. At the beginning of the week, you have begun with $M(t)$ of money holding. Your "income" that you can spend in the week (paid, say, at the beginning of the week) is $Y(t)$. You must decide how much of goods, $\mathbf{X}(t)$, you'll buy to consume during the week; and you must decide how much $M(t+1)$ to end the week with. Provided prices are constant over time, $P(t)\equiv\mathbf{P}$, all you need is a utility function that orders the $[M(t+1),\mathbf{X}(t)]$ vector. Under stationary conditions your maximum problem becomes, for any given t,

$$\text{(65a)} \quad \underset{M(t+1),\mathbf{X}(t)}{\text{Max}} U[M(t+1),\mathbf{X}(t);\mathbf{P}]$$

$$= \underset{M(t+1),\mathbf{X}(t)}{\text{Max}} U[1,\mathbf{X}(t);\mathbf{P}/M(t+1)],$$

subject to

$$\text{(66)} \quad M(t+1)+\mathbf{P}\cdot\mathbf{X}(t)=M(t)+Y(t),$$

$$\text{(65b)} \quad =U^*[1;\mathbf{P},M(t)+Y(t)]$$

$$=U^*[1;\mathbf{P}/\{M(t)+Y(t)\},1],$$

$$\text{(65c)} \quad =U[\{M(t)+Y(t)\} \times h^0(1;\mathbf{P}/\{M(t)+Y(t)\}, \mathbf{h}(1;\mathbf{P}/\{M(t)+Y(t)\}].$$

Our point is that the U in (65a) is *exactly* of the form analyzed in this paper; the *indirect utility* function in (65b) is *exactly* of the form analyzed here, except, of course, that the budget equation in (66) puts $M(t)+Y(t)$ where we had put Y and it puts our r equal to unity; and, finally, the optimizing demand functions in (65c) are *exactly* of the form we have already derived, once $[r;\mathbf{P},Y]$ are replaced as arguments by $[1;\mathbf{P}, M(t)+Y(t)]$.[6]

Therefore, our present analysis handles both the Samuelson (1947) steady-state model and the Patinkin-Hicks week-by-week model. All of our negative results on identifiability apply to *both models*.

A further negative word needs to be said about the week-by-week model. In the form given it has defects that can be removed. And it also has intrinsic defects. First, writers like Cliff Lloyd (1964) and Dusansky and Kalman (1972; 1974) ought preferably to put an interest rate, r, somewhere into their analysis. Instead of taking $Y(t)$ income as given for the week, one would take the week as beginning with a stock of *total* assets $A(t)$. This can be "spent" on the week's real goods, $\mathbf{P}\cdot\mathbf{X}(t)$; or it can be held, all or in part, as an earning asset, $K(t)$, earning $rK(t)$ extra by the end of the week; or part of it can be held during the week as zero-yielding useful cash, $M(t)$, desired for its "convenience" in making $\mathbf{P}\cdot\mathbf{X}(t)$ transactions; or what's left over can be carried into next week's initial assets $A(t+1)$.

Now we can build up our "budget equation" from the identity:

$$\text{(67)} \quad A(t+1)=A(t)+[A(t)-\tilde{M}(t)]r + \tilde{Y}(t)-\mathbf{P}\cdot\mathbf{X}(t),$$

where $\tilde{Y}(t)$ is the period's noncapitalizable extraneous income, and $r[A(t)-\tilde{M}(t)]$ is the yield of earning assets. The budget relation becomes at the equilibrium $A(t)=A(t+1)$

$$\text{(68)} \quad r\tilde{M}(t)+\mathbf{P}\cdot\mathbf{X}(t)=\tilde{Y}(t)+A(t)r.$$

Then, subject to this,

$$\text{(69)} \quad \underset{\tilde{M}(t),\mathbf{X}(t)}{\text{Max}} U[1,\mathbf{X}(t);\mathbf{P}/\tilde{M}(t)]$$

will yield the observable demand functions:

$$\text{(70a)} \quad \tilde{M}=\{\tilde{Y}(t)+rA(t)\} \times h^0(r;\mathbf{P}/\{\tilde{Y}(t)+rA(t)\},1),$$

$$\text{(70b)} \quad x_i=h^i(r;\mathbf{P}/\{\tilde{Y}(t)+rA(t)\},1) \quad (i=1,\ldots,n).$$

Remark: $K(t)$ could itself be put in the utility function along with M; your earning assets could also be one kind of "liquidity."

Note that the present dynamic formulation avoids the flaw involved in the conventional week-by-week model of (65a); in that model, determining terminal $M(t+1)$ essentially involves determining how much to *save* and yet it gives the reader the impression that its decisions have to do with prudent cash-balance management. In (65a), the dependence of U on $M(t+1)$ is not so much a matter that hinges on how near you are to a bank, how liquid your portfolio of stocks

[6] If a steady state is to exist uniquely for $Y(t)=Y$, one would have to equate the given $M(t)$ to the optimized $M(t+1)$ at M^*, the root of

$$M=(Y+M)h^0(1;\mathbf{P}/[Y+M],1).$$

and bonds is, or how unsynchronized and unpredictable are your outpayments and inpayments; the dependence of U on $M(t+1)$ there could merely reflect how much you weigh subsequent weeks' needs against that of the current week (will you be retired then? Do you have a Fisher-Böhm subjective time preference rate that is high or low?...).

Warning: Avoid the temptation to think of the week's money holding, $\tilde{M}(t)$, as being quantitatively the *same* thing as the $\Sigma p_j x_j(t)$ spent during the week. Twins might be equally well off when Twin A spends \$100 on $\mathbf{P}\cdot\mathbf{X}(t)$ and holds on the average \$10 in barren cash, while Twin B spends \$95 on $\mathbf{P}\cdot\mathbf{X}(t)$ and holds \$20 in barren cash. To let them be indifferent, Twin B's time profile of $\mathbf{X}(t)$ must be supposed to be a more "convenient" one than Twin A's profile of $\mathbf{X}(t)$. If the reader does not understand this distinction, he misses the point of the $U(1,\mathbf{X};\mathbf{P}/M)$ model.

Here we have analyzed the consumer as *price taker*. For a neoclassical closed model of monetary general equilibrium, see Samuelson (1968). For weak money "contaminations" presumably the usual existence theorems on existence of a competitive equilibrium will serve for a money economy with some appropriate modifications.[7]

[7]The following example serves as a warning that a system may have no positive-price equilibrium. Suppose all people are alike in maximizing an infinite lifetime Ramsey utility integral, with integrand

$$Ue^{-\bar{r}t} = [(p_1/p_2)\ln x_1 + \ln x_2 + M/p_2]e^{-\bar{r}t}.$$

They each have the same positive money and goods endowments initially, $(\bar{x}_1, \bar{x}_2, \bar{M})$. Then

$$p_1/p_2 = (\partial U/\partial x_1)/(\partial U/\partial x_2) = (p_1/p_2)(x_2/x_1)$$

$$r/p_2 = (\partial U/\partial M)/(\partial U/\partial x_2) = x_2/p_2.$$

If $\bar{x}_1 \neq \bar{x}_2$, there cannot be a positive-price equilibrium. This case does not violate the general existence theorem of Lionel McKenzie (1955), for the reason that he permits an equilibrium to involve a zero price—as in the following when $\bar{x}_1 > \bar{x}_2$:

$$0 = (p_1/p_2)^* = (p_1/p_2)^*(x_2^*/x_1^*), \quad p_1^* = 0,$$

$$r^*/p_2^* = \bar{r}/\bar{p}_2 = x_2^*/M^*$$

$$x_2^* = \bar{x}_2, \quad M^* = \bar{M}, \quad x_1^* \leq \bar{x}_1, \quad p_2^* = \bar{r}\bar{M}/\bar{x}_2.$$

In concluding, we call attention to the open question whether, in the general nonseparable case, there are any testable consequences on the (5) observable demand functions of the (1)–(2) money-and-prices-in-the-utility-function model. Since there are such consequences for the case of money and a single good, and for the case of money and a weakly separable composite of goods, one will not give up hope that there exist such testable consequences until a definite *impossibility theorem* is proved or is shown to be false.

REFERENCES

Basmann, R. L., Molina, D. J. and Slottje, D. J., "Budget Constraint Prices as Preference Changing Parameters of Generalized Fechner-Thurston Direct Utility Functions," *American Economic Review*, June 1983, *73*, 411–13.

Clower, Robert W. and Howitt, Peter W., "The Transactions Theory of the Demand for Money: A Reconsideration," *Journal of Political Economy*, June 1978, *86*, 449–66.

______ **and Riley, John G.,** "The Foundations of Money Illusion in a Neoclassical Micro-Monetary Model: Comment," *American Economic Review*, March 1976, *66*, 184–85.

Dusansky, Richard, "Utility Function Transformations and Money Illusion: Reply and Further Results," *American Economic Review*, September 1980, *70*, 823–25.

______ **and Kalman, Peter J.,** "The Real Balance Effect and the Traditional Theory of Consumer Behavior: A Reconciliation," *Journal of Economic Theory*, December 1972, *5*, 336–47.

______ **and** ______, "The Foundations of Money Illusion in a Neoclassical Micro-Monetary Model," *American Economic Review*, March 1974, *64*, 115–22.

Hicks, J. R., *Value and Capital*, Oxford: Clarendon Press, 1939.

Howitt, Peter W. and Patinkin, Don, "Utility Function Transformations and Money Illusion: Comment," *American Economic Review*, September 1980, *70*, 819–22.

Leser, C. E. V., "The Consumer's Demand for Money," *Econometrica*, April 1943, *11*,

123–40.

Lloyd, Cliff, "The Real-Balance Effect and the Slutsky Equation," *Journal of Political Economy*, June 1964, *72*, 295–99.

McKenzie, Lionel, "Competitive Equilibrium with Dependent Consumer Preference," in *The Second Symposium on Linear Programming*, National Bureau of Standards and Department of the Air Force, Washington, 1955.

Meinich, Per, "Money Illusion and the Real Balance Effect," *Statsøknomisk Tideskrift*, 1964, *28*, 9–16, 20–21.

Patinkin, Don, *Money, Interest, and Prices*, 1st; 2nd eds., Evanston: Row, Peterson and Company, 1956; 1965.

Pollak, Robert A., "Price Dependent Preferences," *American Economic Review*, March 1977, *67*, 64–75.

Ramsey, Frank P., "A Mathematical Theory of Saving," *Economic Journal*, December 1928, *38*, 543–59.

Roy, R., *De l'utilité*, Paris: Herman, 1942.

Samuelson, Paul A., *Foundations of Economic Analysis*, Cambridge: Harvard University Press, 1947 (Enlarged edition, 1983).

______, *Economics*, 1st edition, New York: McGraw-Hill, 1948.

______, "Structure of a Minimum System," in Ralph W. Pfourts, ed., *Essays in Economics and Econometrics: A Volume in Honor of Harold Hotelling*, Chapel Hill: University of North Carolina Press, 1960, reproduced in J. E. Stiglitz, ed., Vol. 2, *The Collected Scientific Papers of Paul A. Samuelson*, Cambridge: MIT Press, 1972, ch. 44.

______, "What Classical and Neoclassical Monetary Theory Really Was," *Canadian Journal of Economics*, February 1968, *1*, 1–15, reproduced in J. E. Stiglitz, ed., Vol. 3, *The Collected Scientific Papers of Paul A. Samuelson*, Cambridge: MIT Press, 1972, ch. 176.

______ **and Swamy, S.,** "Invariant Economic Index Numbers and Canonical Duality: Survey and Synthesis," *American Economic Review*, September 1974, *64*, 566–93.

Sato, Ryuzo, *Theory of Technical Change and Economic Invariance: Application of Lie Groups*, New York: Academic Press, 1981.

Scitovsky, Tibor, "Some Consequences of the Habit of Judging Quality by Price," *Review of Economic Studies*, No. 2, 1945, *12*, 100–05.

Shephard, R. W., *Cost and Production Functions*, Princeton: Princeton University Press, 1953.

Sidrauski, Miguel, "Rational Choice and Pattern of Growth in a Monetary Economy," *American Economic Review Proceedings*, May 1967, *57*, 534–44.

Slutsky, E., "Sulla Teoria del Bilancio del Consumatore," *Giornale degli Economisti*, 1915, *51*, 1–26, translated as "On the Theory of the Budget of the Consumer," in G. L. Stigler and K. Boulding, eds., *Readings in Price Theory*, Homewood: Richard Irwin, 1952.

Veblen, Thorstein, *The Theory of the Leisure Class: A Study in the Evolution of Institution*, London; New York: Macmillan, 1899.

Balanced-Growth Equilibrium in the General Multi-Class Saving Model

(macroeconomic distribution theory/neoclassical imputation/neoKeynesian identities)*

Paul A. Samuelson

Abstract. N permanent classes of rentiers each save a characteristic fraction of their profit incomes; M classes of workers save a characteristic fraction of their wage and profit incomes; labor (in efficiency units) grows at a positive exponential rate, and total investment is always equal to full-employment saving generated by the model. With short-run output and profit determined by a simple neoclassical one-sector model — or by a von Neumann-Sraffa finite activities model involving only one scalar capital good and no other joint production — the system has determinate transient trajectories, which from a wide set of initial capitals of all the classes do approach asymptotically nearby long-run equilibrium states. The implied balanced-growth equilibrium is either of *primal* (Pasinetti) type or of *dual* (non-Pasinetti) type, depending upon whether a definable non-linear mean of the workers' saving fractions is below the highest rentier saving fraction multiplied by the fraction of income going to profits when the interest rate is at its primal level, a generalization in the manner of Vaughan and Pasinetti of the standard 2-class criterion to any number of classes. Certain symmetric dualities hold in either of the two alternative regimes; each regime has its characteristic comparative statics.

Background

The dynamic system of Samuelson and Modigliani ([1966] patterned on the saving assumptions pioneered by Pasinetti [1962]), can be written as

$$\dot{k}_c^i = [s_c^i r - n]\, k_c^i, \qquad (i=1, \ldots, N) \tag{1.1}$$

$$\dot{k}_w^j = [s_w^j r - n]\, k_w^j + s_w^j \lambda_j y[1-\alpha], \qquad (j=1, \ldots, M) \tag{1.2}$$

$$\lambda_j > 0, \quad \sum_1^M \lambda_j = 1, \quad L'[t]/L[t] \equiv n > 0$$

* I owe thanks to the National Science Foundation for financial aid and to Kate Crowley for editorial assistance.

(1.3) $$k=\sum_1^N k_c^i+\sum_1^M k_w^j;\qquad \alpha=r/(y/k)\ \text{profits' relative share}$$

(1.4) $$y=f(k)\geqq 0,\qquad r=f'(k),\qquad f''(k)<0\ \text{a.e.}$$

(1.4′) $$f'(k)\ \text{goes from}\ \infty\ \text{to 0 as}\ k\ \text{goes from 0 to}\ \infty.$$

Here n is the exponential growth rate of total labor (inclusive of Harrod neutral technical change); λ_j is the fraction of labor always with saving propensity s_w^j; $k_c^i[t]$ and $k_w^j[t]$ are the amounts of capital owned by the respective classes, normalized by division by $L[t]$. Notationally, $\dot{x}$ stands for dx/dt or for $dx[t]/dt=x'[t]$.

By convention, we can require

(2) $$s_c^1>s_c^2>\cdots>s_c^N\geqq 0,\qquad s_w^1>s_w^2>\cdots>s_w^M>0.$$

Independently of knowledge of $f(k)$, we shall find it convenient to define the following weighted non-linear *mean* fraction of workers' income saved, $\bar{s}_w$:

(3.1) $$\bar{s}_w/s_c^1=M[s_w^1/s_c^1,\ldots,s_w^M/s_c^1],\qquad \text{defined for}\ 0<s_w^1/s_c^1<1$$

(3.2) $$\operatorname{Min}(x_1,\ldots,x_m)\leqq M[x_1,\ldots,x_m]\leqq \operatorname{Max}(x_1,\ldots,x_m)<1$$

$$(M[x_1,\ldots,x_m]^{-1}-1)\stackrel{\text{def}}{=}\left(\sum_1^M\frac{\lambda_j}{x_j^{-1}-1}\right)^{-1},$$

a weighted harmonic mean of $x_j^{-1}-1$, with λ_j weights,

(3.3) $$\partial M[s_w^1/s_c^1,\ldots,s_w^M/s_c^1]/\partial s_w^j>0,\qquad \text{for}\ 0<s_w^1/s_c^1<1.$$

Here $M[\ ]$ is a generalized, monotone-increasing mean in its domain of definition. For $s_w^1/s_c^1\geqq 1$, $\bar{s}_w$ is undefined (but could be defined simply as s_c^1).

Long-Run Equilibria and Short-Run Dynamics

By themselves (1.1), (1.2) and (1.3) yield an undetermined system, not defining for given initial $(k_c^i[0],k_w^j[0])$ a determinate subsequent motion, transient or long-run, for $(k_c^i[t],k_w^j[t];k[t],r[t],y[t]/k[t])$. However, when we adjoin (1.4) — or some other additional (non-neoclassical) relations — the system's subsequent motions become determinate.

Its trajectories have a variety of fixed points of long-run equilibrium. These fixed points must satisfy (1.1)—(1.3) and (1.4), with all $(\dot{k}_c^i,\dot{k}_w^j)$ set equal to zero on the left-hand side of (1.1) and (1.2). Whatever the relations provided for (1.4) or in place of (1.4), it is necessary that a fixed point satisfy

(4.1) $$0=[r-(n/s_c^i)](\bar{k}_c^i/\bar{k}),\qquad (i=1,\ldots,N)$$

(4.2) $$0=[r-(n/s_w^j)](\bar{k}_w^j/\bar{k})+\lambda_j[(y/k)-r], \qquad (j=1,\ldots,M)$$

(4.3) $$1=\sum_1^N(\bar{k}_c^i/\bar{k})+\sum_1^M(\bar{k}_w^j/\bar{k}).$$

Here (y/k) and r are understood to be constants in long-run equilibria.

Any such solution can have at most one of $(\bar{k}_c^1/\bar{k},\ldots,\bar{k}_c^N/\bar{k})$ non-zero. Any solution with a non-zero $\bar{k}_c^{1+i}/\bar{k}$ is locally unstable, to be dominated for any positive perturbation of $k_c^1[0]$. Therefore, we can ignore all such locally unstable fixed points.

Remarks. An example of an existent, but locally unstable fixed point of a different kind, is one with $s_c^1 \gg s_w^1 > 0$ and $\bar{k}_c^1=0<\bar{k}$. For ever so small positive $k_c^1[0]$, the system departs from the fixed point forever. An example of a motion that never settles down to any fixed point would be provided by a system that approaches a limit cycle surrounding some equilibrium point, $(\bar{k}_c^1, \bar{k})>0$.

Denote any "non-dominated" equilibrium point by $\bar{x}=(\bar{k}_c^i, \bar{k}_w^j; \bar{k}, \bar{r}, \bar{y})$. Then the following theorem can be verified for the system obeying (1.1)—(1.4′):

Theorem. (i) For each choice of parameters $(s_c^i, s_w^j, \lambda_j)$, there is exactly one non-dominated equilibrium, which must be of the form

(i.1) $$\bar{x}=(a_1,0,\ldots,0;b_1,\ldots,b_M;\bar{k},\bar{r},\bar{y}),$$

$a_1 \geqq 0$ and all other non-zero elements being positive. Also, in accordance with duality,

(i.2) $$\bar{r}\leqq n/s_c^1, \qquad \bar{r}<n/s_w^1;$$

(i.3) $$(\partial\bar{r}/\partial s_c^1)(\partial\bar{r}/\partial s_w^j)=0, \qquad (j=1,\ldots,M)$$

(ii) Equilibrium is inside the *primal* (Pasinetti) regime, at x^* with

(ii.1) $$a_1=k_c^{1*}>0, \qquad r^*=n/s_c^1=f'(k^*)<n/s_w^1;$$

(ii.2) $$k_w^{j*}/k^*=\lambda_j\frac{[y/k]^*-r^*}{[n/s_w^j]-r^*}=\lambda_j\frac{[f(k^*)/k^*]-f'(k^*)}{[n/s_w^j]-f'(k^*)}$$
$$=\lambda_j\frac{[1-\alpha(k^*)]/\alpha(k^*)}{[s_c^1/s_w^j]-1}$$

if and only if

(ii.3) $\bar{s}_w < \alpha(k^*) s_c^1$, where $\bar{s}_w$ is defined as in (3)

and $\alpha(k^*) = k^* f'(k^*)/k^*$.

(iii) Equilibrium is inside the *dual* (non-Pasinetti) regime if and only if either

(iii.1) $s_w^1 \geqq s_c^1$ or $\bar{s}_w > s_c^1\,\alpha(k^*)$

where $\bar{s}_w$ is as defined in (3).

The dual equilibrium x^{**}, has the properties

(iii.2) $k_c^{1**} = 0, \quad r^{**} = f'(k^{**}) < n/s_c^1$;

k^{**} is the unique admissible positive root of

(iii.3) $$1 = \sum_1^n \lambda_j \frac{[f(k)/k] - f'(k)}{[n/s_w^j] - f'(k)},$$

or of the equivalent relation

(iii.3′) $$\alpha(k) = M\,[f'(k)\,s_w^1/n, \ldots, f'(k)\,s_w^M/n]$$

where $M[\ ]$ is as defined in (3);

(iii.4) $$k_w^{j**}/k^{**} = \lambda_j \frac{[y/k]^{**} - r^{**}}{[n/s_w^j] - r^{**}}, \quad (j = 1, \ldots, M)$$

$$= \lambda_j \frac{[f(k^{**})/k^{**}] - f'[k^{**}]}{[n/s_w^j] - f'[k^{**}]}.$$

From (iii.3) we realize that

$$\frac{f(k^{**})}{k^{**}} = \text{linear weighted average of } \left[\frac{n}{s_w^j}\right]$$

$$= \left\{\sum_1^M \frac{\lambda_j}{[n/s_w^j] - r^{**}} \frac{n}{s_w^j}\right\} \div \sum_1^M \frac{\lambda_j}{[n/s_w^j] - r^{**}}.$$

Any of the above relations that do not involve terms with $f(k)$, $f'(k)$, or $\alpha(k)$ are *necessary* truths, holding *outside* the simple neoclassical specifications of (1.4); but, of course, the system is incomplete even in its long-run steady-state behavior until something definite is supplied in place of (1.4). Also, if (1.4′)'s strict "regularity" conditions are not hypothesized, there can be "boundary" equilibria, with $\bar{k}$ either zero or infinite. Under the not-implausible assumption that $\alpha(k)\to 0$ as $k\to\infty$ even when (1.4′) holds, for small enough n the system's r^{**} will fall below n itself, betokening "permanent inefficiency" of the Phelps-Koopmans type (PHELPS [1966]).

Where $\bar{s}_w$ exactly equals $s_c^1\,\alpha(k^*)$, the system is in both regimes simultaneously, primal and dual, with $r^*=r^{**}$, $k^*=k^{**}$, etc.

Needed Correction

This formulation is in complete agreement with the correction of Samuelson-Modigliani by VAUGHAN [1971]. (Professor Modigliani wishes to be understood as concurring in this agreement.) Instead of writing the criterion for separating the regimes as (ii.3), namely

$$\bar{s}_w \lesseqgtr s_c^1\,\alpha(k^*), \tag{ii.3}$$

Vaughan writes the equivalent relation as

$$\pi=\sum_1^M \frac{s_w^j\,\lambda_j}{s_c^1-s_w^j}\lesseqgtr\frac{\alpha(k^*)}{1-\alpha(k^*)}. \tag{4}$$

This is indeed a needed correction to the erroneous Samuelson-Modigliani criterion, which in terms of present notation took the mistaken form

$$s_w^1 \lesseqgtr s_c^1\,\alpha(k^*). \tag{5}$$

My harmonic mean of (3.2) was patterned after Vaughan's π.

The present discussion is also fully in the spirit of Pasinetti's [1974] use of a linear weighted average of the s_w^j, with weights *proportional* to each working class's share in equilibrium (Pasinetti [1974]). Writing this as s_{w*}, we see its difference in definition from $\bar{s}_w$ of (3). The latter, like Vaughan's π, can be computed once and for all prior to any knowledge of technology and of what $[y/k]$ would end up being in any regime's equilibrium.

No particular formulation of several equivalent formulations is better than any other. *All* the valid criteria consist essentially of tests to see whether, for any nominated primal solution, $(r^*=n/s_c^1,\ [y/k]^*)$,

$$\sum_1^M \lambda_j\,\frac{[y/k]^*-[n/s_c^1]}{[n/s_w^j]-[n/s_c^1]}\ \begin{matrix}<\\ \text{or}\\ >\end{matrix}\ 1. \tag{6}$$

If " > " holds, we have an unpermissible contradiction to the requirement that k_c^1/k be non-negative.

Under (1.4′)'s strong monotonicity assumption on $f'(k)$ and $f(k)/k$, once we rule out (or in) a nominated primal equilibrium, we rule in (or out) an existent unique, locally-stable, dual equilibrium; and vice versa, symmetrically. When there are many heterogeneous capital goods, both under neoclassical smoothness and under Neumann-Sraffa activities models, the criterion ruling out a nominated primal equilibrium $(k^*, [y/k]^*)$ does not tell us whether some other primal equilibrium state holds, or some dual state, or which of many alternative dual states holds. The system's configuration is undetermined until its technology and pricing behavior equations are hypothesized.

Non-Neoclassical Generalizations

Examining the system (1.1)—(1.4), one sees that essentially the same results can sometimes hold for a non-neoclassical activities model of type discussed by VON NEUMANN [1945—1946], SRAFFA [1960], LEONTIEF [1953], or ROBINSON [1956]. Although smooth differentiability of marginal productivity theory can be dispensed with, the scenario avoids formidable "foresight" and "aggregation" problems only if there is still but one scalar capital good (no longer "malleable").

As an example, postulate two activities. Activity 1 produces 1 of consumer goods or machines from 1 of labor *and* $b_1 = .5\ (\rho+\delta)^{-1}$ of machines, each machine depreciating exponentially at rate δ. Activity 2 produces 1 of consumer goods or 1 of new machines out of a_2 labor alone. For Activity 1 ever to be viable at a positive profit rate its saving of direct labor, in comparison with Activity 2's a_2, must be great enough to justify machines used up in production. This requires that $a_2 > 1$.

Thus for $a_2 = 2$, Activities 1 and 2 will be indifferently profitable when $r = \rho$. For $r > \rho$, Activity 2 will predominate. For $r < \rho$, competition requires use of Activity 1 alone. Let us set $a_2 = 2$.

Now we must replace the differentiable neoclassical relations of (1.4), $y = f(k)$ and $r = f'(k)$, by the following set-correspondence. Define

(7.1) $\hat{f}(k) = .5 + \rho k, \quad 0 < k < b_1$

(7.2) $\quad = 1 - \delta k, \quad b_1 < k < \infty$

(7.3) $\hat{f}'(k) = \rho, \quad 0 < k < b_1$

(7.4) $\hat{f}'(k) = -\delta, \quad b_1 < k < \infty$

(7.5) $\hat{f}'(b_1) =$ any number at least as great as $-\delta$ and no greater than ρ

(7.6) $\hat{f}'(0) =$ any number at least as great as ρ.

Now replace (1.4) by the non-neoclassical relations of (7)

$$(1.4^{\#}) \qquad y=\hat{f}(k), \qquad r=\hat{f}'(k)$$

Relations (1.1), (1.2), (1.3), and (1.4 #) now generate a determinate dynamic motion through almost all $(k_c^i[t], k_w^j[t])$ points.

For n small compared to s_c^1 but not compared to s_w^1, the system will approach a primal equilibrium

$$(8) \qquad r^*=n/s_c^1, \qquad k^*=b_1, \qquad n<s_c^1\,\rho, \qquad n>s_w^1\,\hat{f}(k^*)/k^*.$$

Such a determinate income distribution would be congenial to microeconomics albeit not "neoclassical" in J. B. Clark's sense.

However, if we now shrink n enough, the system will approach a dual equilibrium beyond the golden-rule state, with Phelps-Koopmans inefficiency:

$$r^{**}=-\delta, \qquad k^*>b_1$$

Not only for very small n, but also for very large n, the system approaches a dual equilibrium:

$$r^{**}=\rho, \qquad 0<k^{**}<b_1, \qquad n \gg \mathrm{Max}\,(s_c^1, s_w^1).$$

The commonsense explanation is simple. If the system must strain to be able to widen capital in balance with rapidly expanding population, it will have to use much of the Activity 2 with a minimal capital/output ratio and only a little of Activity 1. With both activities coexisting, the profit rate must be ρ, which is the rate just large enough to pay the labor at the real wage set in Activity 2 and have just enough left over to pay for replacing the machines that permit economy of direct labor needed. Such a dual equilibrium seems no less "Keynesian" than a primal equilibrium.

Complete details of other equilibria possible for all choices of (s_c^i, s_c^j) can be left to the interested analyst. Full proofs and demonstrations can also be left to other occasions. Most of the steps are economically intuitive. (Example: Since $s_c^1>s_c^2$, $(k_c^2/k_c^1)^{-1}[d(k_c^2/k_c^1)/dt]=-|s_c^1-s_c^2|\; r(t)<0$ and $k_c^2/k_c^1 \to 0$ as $t\to\infty$.) However, it can be more complicated to prove even local stability of a system that can involve any number of variables, and recourse must be had to more sophisticated methods.

Conclusion

There are further alternatives to the present analysis worthy of exploration. Particularly is this needed in the case of short-run analysis. Thus, there is a zeroth axiom underlying the present system, that of equality of saving and investment *at full employment in every* run of time however short. Suppose employment is no longer given as the exogenous function $L[t]$: instead $L[t]$ becomes an unknown function, restricted only to be no greater than some prescribed trend of labor supply. Suppose, as in a Keynesian fashion (KALDOR [1955—1956]), $\dot{k}[t]$ is given in the short run as an exogenous function, perhaps fluctuating so as to average out in the longer run to about that warranted by longer-run trends. Provided nominal wage rates, prices, and interest rates are stipulated to have certain short-run rigidities, the resulting solution for $L[t]$ may involve underemployment equilibrium in the short run.

Specifically, postulate the truth of (1.1), (1.2), (1.3), and either (1.4) or (1.4 $^{\#}$). But drop the notion of L as an exogenously given function, instead requiring it to be part of the solution of the system. By way of compensation, stipulate that $\dot{k}$ be an exogenously given function $I[t]$. Then the resulting system differs from the Kaldorian model cited, denying that model's full employment; instead, it becomes like that of KALECKI ([1938, 1942], Samuelson [1964, 1976]), involving unemployment and with short-run dynamic stability that would be unaffected even by the extreme case in which s_w^M exceeded s_c^1.

More realistic than any of these simple alternatives, I think would be a model that replaces the oversimplified saving assumptions of (1.1) and (1.2) by more realistic models taking account of net assets and life cycles, and that elaborates (1.4) and (1.4 $^{\#}$) to allow for a more realistic degree of oligopoly and imperfection of competition.

References

KALDOR, N. [1955/1956], Alternative Theories of Distribution. *Rev. of Econ. Studies*, 23, 83 – 100. Reproduced as the final chapter in N. Kaldor, Vol. I.

KALECKI, M. [1938], The Determinants of Distribution of the National Income. *Econometrica*, 6, 97 – 112.

– [1942], A Theory of Profits. *Economic Journal*, 52, 256 – 267.

LEONTIEF, W. W. [1953], *Studies in the Structure of the American Economy*, New York.

VON NEUMANN, J. [1945/1946], A Model of General Equilibrium. *Rev. of Econ. Studies*, 13, 1 – 9, a translation of a pre-1936 German paper.

PASINETTI, L. [1962], Rate of Profit and Income Distribution in Relation to the Rate of Economic Growth. *Rev. of Econ. Studies* 29, 267 – 279. Reproduced as Ch. V in Pasinetti, L., *Growth and Income Distribution: Essays In Economic Theory*, London 1974.

– [*op. cit.* 1974], *Growth and Income Distribution*, Ch. VI, 141 – 142.

PHELPS, E. S. [1966], *Golden Rules of Economic Growth: Studies of Efficient and Optimal Investment*, pp. 55 – 68. New York.

ROBINSON, J. [1956], *Accumulation of Capital*, London.

SAMUELSON, P. A. [1964], A Brief Survey of Post-Keynesian Developments, especially p. 344, in R. Leckachman (ed.), *Keynes' General Theory: Report of Three Decades*, London.

– [1976], Interest Rate Determinations and Oversimplifying Parables: A Summing Up, especially Section 1.2: in M. Brown, K. Zarembka (eds.), *Essays in Modern Capital Theory*, Rotterdam.

– and MODIGLIANI, F. [1966], The Pasinetti Paradox in Neoclassical and More General Models, *Rev. of Econ. Studies* 33, 269–301. Reproduced in Vol. III, *Collected Scientific Papers of Paul A. Samuelson*, R.C. Merton (ed.), MIT Press, Cambridge, Mass., 1972, Ch. 146.

SRAFFA, P. [1960], *Production of Commodities by Means of Commodities*, London.

VAUGHAN, R.W. [1971], The Pasinetti Paradox in Neoclassical and More General Models: A Correction. *Rev. of Econ. Studies*, 38, 271.

Paul Douglas's Measurement of Production Functions and Marginal Productivities

Paul A. Samuelson

Massachusetts Institute of Technology

"... he was the greatest labor economist in the first 50 years of this century." [GLEN CAIN]

If Nobel Prizes had been awarded in economics after 1901, as they were in physics, chemistry, medicine, peace, and literature, Paul H. Douglas would probably have received one before World War II for his pioneering econometric attempts to measure marginal productivities and quantify the demands for factor inputs. The Cobb-Douglas function, $P = bL^kC^{1-k}$ or $Q = bV_1^{k_1} \ldots V_n^{k_n}$ with $\Sigma_1^n k_j = 1$, receives thousands of citations in present-day economics. Controversies still rage over the admissibility of aggregation in the theory of capital and in connection with the production function. And, it was Douglas, I seem to recall, who first introduced into our vocabulary the adjective "cross-sectional" for studies that use observations at one point in time as a scatter for estimating functional relationships.

From 1927 to 1976, when he died in his eighty-fifth year still with his boots on and with his posthumous article (Douglas 1976) in press, Paul Douglas persevered in his studies whenever public service gave him the leisure to do so. Not long before he died, and after his health was already in a precarious state, I was astonished to pick up my M.I.T. phone and hear the voice of my old teacher, still looking for able assistants to replace those who had died, retired, and grown disabled on the quest for the Holy Grail.

I owe thanks to the National Science Foundation for financial aid and to Aase Huggins and Kate Crowley for editorial assistance.

Douglas felt at the beginning that his work met with unfriendly opposition, a feeling of martyrdom that abated over the years but never quite disappeared. Indeed, I doubt that he ever appreciated the degree to which his scientific contribution had become part of every economist's toolbox; nor, perhaps, was he sufficiently aware of the new impetus to measurement that Robert Solow brought to his problem 30 years after 1927, when the empirical studies of productivity trends by Colin Clark, Abramovitz, John Kendrick, Fabricant, Denison, Maddison, and others were made interpretable in terms of a time-shifting Wicksell-Douglas-Cobb function or more general form. Today we all speak of the "residual"—the part of product growth attributable to technical change and not to inputs—testimony to the power of an analytical idea.

Henry Schultz aside, Douglas's colleagues—Knight, Simons, Viner—probably displayed inadequate interest in empirically measuring and describing real-world phenomena. Nonetheless, as I resurvey the early criticisms that Douglas's work received at the hands of Slichter, M. Copeland, J. M. Clark, Schumpeter, Frisch, Mendershausen, Durand, and other eminent contemporaries,[1] I have to conclude that like Ricardo's early critics (Torrens, Malthus, Ricardo himself, . . .) they made good points that needed to be made: for example, aggregating physical capital does raise deep questions, as Joan Robinson has more recently insisted; assuming no technical progress in U.S. manufacturing for 1899–1922 did shock Schumpeter and should have done so; the data of inputs in Douglas's 3-dimensional scatter were almost collinear, making "identification" of separate factors' marginal products treacherous and raising legitimate doubts concerning the robustness of specifying the Cobb-Douglas (C-D) formula; and so forth.

Along with Jacob Mosak, Gregg Lewis, Martin Bronfenbrenner, and others now eminent as economists, I attended Douglas's classes in those years when his classic 1934 *Theory of Wages* was being completed for publication. It is remarkable how many of the words that I have been rereading in his 1927–76 writings we heard from his own lips during those fascinating classroom hours: the same poetry, anecdotes, rebuttals and defenses!

I shall use my limited space here to review Douglas's achievement, indicate what his successors added to his procedures, and comment on the recurring puzzle concerning Wicksell's independent early discovery of the L^kC^{1-k} function and Douglas's confusion concerning Wicksteed's role. Finally, I shall ventilate some uneasinesses concern-

[1] See the index to Douglas (1934) for many of these critiques or refer to Douglas (1965, 1972, 1976; Gunn and Douglas 1941) for his defenses and rebuttals.

ing the meaning of the cross-sectional investigations. Space does not permit an adequate treatment of the aggregation issue, concerning which the last word has not yet been said.

The 1927 Beginning

However documented was Gilbert's meeting with Sullivan, we know how fame brushed against Cobb when Douglas spent a sabbatical at Amherst in 1927. Out of Douglas's many similar accounts I quote this sample from his 1972 autobiography:

> . . . in 1927, . . . at Amherst, I charted on a logarithmic scale three variables . . . for American manufacturing for the years 1889 to 1922: an index of total fixed capital . . . (C), an index of the total number of wage earners employed in manufacturing (L), and an index of physical production in manufacturing (P). I noticed that the index of production lay between those for capital and labor and that it was from one-third to one-quarter of the relative distance between the lower index of labor and the higher index of capital. After consulting with my friend Charles W. Cobb, the mathematician, we . . . chose the Euler formula of a simple homogeneous function of the first degree, which that remarkable Englishman Philip Wicksteed had developed some years before ($P = bL^{k}C^{1-k}$). We found the values of k and $1-k$ by the method of least squares to be 0.75 and 0.25, and that b was merely 1.01.
>
> The production values computed by this formula came close to the actual values with a very low average error. Furthermore, such deviations from the actual values as did occur were largely accounted for by known inaccuracies in the data themselves and by the business cycle. . . . A final test was that the actual shares of the total product received by labor and capital according to the National Bureau of Economic Research were almost the same as their exponents, namely 74.1 per cent for labor. [Pp. 46–47]

I select this account because it is the one that most clearly misidentifies the roles of Wicksteed and Wicksell, illegitimately attributing to the former what belonged only to the latter, namely, pre-1927 use of the $L^{k}C^{1-k}$ form of a first-degree-homogeneous function. Only in his posthumous paper did Douglas (1976, p. 904) explicitly credit Wicksell with the C-D formula, clouding, however, the acknowledgment by the remark ". . . a form that had also been used by Wicksteed [*sic*] and Wicksell."

Actually, despite Douglas's many accounts, Wicksteed never used the *special species*, bL^kC^{1-k}, of the *general genus* of first-degree-homogeneous functions

$$\begin{aligned} f(L,C) &\equiv Lf(1,C/L) \equiv L\phi(C/L) \\ &\equiv Cf(L/C,1) \equiv C\psi(L/C) \qquad (1) \\ x^{-1}\phi(x)/\psi(x^{-1}) &\equiv 1. \end{aligned}$$

Douglas was a most generous scholar. He quixotically put Cobb's name before his own and foolish posterity accepted that convention. Gunn, Bronfenbrenner, Schoenberg, and myriad other collaborators similarly received pride of place out of alphabetical order or seniority. Also, Douglas knew and cited the very pages in Wicksell's lectures—the 1913 German translation since the 1934 English translation was not yet available—where the production function is written in "C-D" form as $P = a^{\alpha}b^{\beta}$ with $\alpha + \beta = 1$. Why then did Douglas not accord, from 1934 on, unique priority to Wicksell for the C-D function?[2]

[2] Not to burden the text, I put in a footnote the gist of Douglas's other writings that bear on this Wicksteed-Wicksell issue. Cobb-Douglas (1928, pp. 151–52) said that the ". . . [neoclassical, marginal-productivity] theory . . . [is] due to J. B. Clark [1899], Wicksteed, et al. . . . ;" and that, among the wide class of first-degree-homogeneous functions $f(L,C)$ that vanish whenever one or both factors vanish, ". . . let us make a definite choice . . . of the function $P' = bL^kC^{1-k}$ . . . [a species in which] the marginal productivity of labor is proportional to the production per unit of labor . . . [and likewise for capital]." Though Douglas (1934) gave no specific citation to pre-1927 writers for the bL^kC^{1-k} formula, Douglas (1948, p. 6) said, "We, Cobb and I, were both familiar with the Wicksteed analysis and Cobb was, of course, well versed in the history of Euler's theorem. At his suggestion, therefore, the sum of the exponents was tentatively made equal to unity in the formula $P = bL^kC^{1-k}$." Again, one reads in Douglas (1967, p. 16): "I am no mathematician, so I then went to my friend, Charles W. Cobb. . . . Almost immediately he remembered the Euler theorem of a simple homogeneous function of the first degree and suggested it [*sic*] as a first approximation $P = bL^1C^{1-k}$. . . . We remembered that this simple function [*sic*] had been suggested and indeed laid down over thirty years before by that extraordinary genius Philip Wicksteed in his *Coordination of the Laws of Distribution* [1894] and, later in his *Common Sense of Political Economy* [1933]. . . . The same theorem had also been treated very elegantly by Leon Walras." In contradiction to this assertion by Douglas, Walras was actually confusedly critical of Wicksteed for espousing the general homogeneous function. Finally, Douglas (1976, p. 904) said that, at Cobb's suggestion, ". . . the formula $P = bL^kC^{1-k}$ was adopted, a form that had also been used by Wicksteed [*sic*] and Wicksell. This, following Euler [*sic*], was a simple homogeneous function of the first degree." Here at long last is a proper recognition of Wicksell, confounded, however, by confusion with Wicksteed and Euler. Actually, as had to be obvious after the 1934 English translation of Wicksell's *Lectures,* Wicksell had employed the $a^{\alpha}b^{1-\alpha}$ formula more than a quarter of a century before 1927. In the recent Scandinavian journals, Olsson (1971) called attention to the appearance of it in Wicksell (1916); Velupillai (1973) then traced it back to Wicksell (1900) and even earlier to Wicksell (1896). If θ is Wicksell's period of investment and T is primary land invested with L at the beginning of the production period, then output at θ periods later of $bL^kT^{1-k}\,\theta^{\gamma}$, $\gamma > 0$, $0 \leq k \leq 1$, is a proper example of an economic C-D function; by contrast, $L^{1/3}\,T^{1/3}\,\theta^{1/3}$ is not. Nor are $bL^{2/3}\,\theta^{1/3}$, $bL^{2/3}\theta^{1/2}$, $bL^{2/3}\theta^{1/6}$, unless we may consider there to be a factor before the $L^{2/3}$ factor of the form $b = \beta T^{1/3}$, with T either unity or constant at some agreed-upon level, $\bar{T}$. The point is that θ is *not* an input logically parallel to L and T.

After much pondering, I can offer only one hypothesis to cover the facts best, a hypothesis for which there is also other evidence: Often in the 1927–76 period Douglas momentarily became confused between the broad *genus* of homogeneous functions and the narrow *species* of the C-D form. (At other times he shows recognition of their differences; actually, in 1926, before the Cobb meeting, Douglas's assistant, Sidney Wilcox, had given him the form $[L^2 + C^2]^{1/2\epsilon} L^k C^h$, $\epsilon + k + h = 1$, a form that includes the C-D formula as a special case when $\epsilon = 0$ [but which, alas, does not preserve everywhere convex isoquants when ϵ is not zero!]; see Douglas 1934, pp. 224–25.) Confusing homogeneity—Euler's theorem and all that—with the singular C-D case of constant relative shares and unity of what Hicks (1932) would later call the "elasticity of substitution," Douglas sometimes credited Wicksteed, J. B. Clark, Walras, and all the neoclassicals with already knowing the C-D form. Wicksell was honored in Douglas (1934, pp. 54–55) for something else—for his heuristic proof of Euler's theorem that homogeneity implies proper "adding up" and that uniform departures from constant returns to scale would result (1) in monopoly and destruction of competition if increasing returns to scale were universal and (2) in pulverization of the industry into an infinity of infinitesimal firms if decreasing returns to scale prevailed for firms that can be replicated ad infinitum.[3] Douglas's words on Wicksell reveal confusion concerning the generality of the $L^k C^{1-k}$ form, enough confusion to explain why he saw nothing special in Wicksell's use of this form.

Leaving to Robert K. Merton the further study of the history and sociology of simultaneity and independence in scientific discovery (à la Darwin-Wallace or Newton-Leibnitz), we might turn to ask: "How did Cobb chance on the sum-of-exponents formula?" Wicksell (1896, 1900, 1901, 1916) had backed into it, beginning with simplest square-root examples such as $bL^{1/2}$. If I were Cobb and Douglas asked me for a first-degree homogeneous function, my simplest first reply would be $P = aL + bK$. Since this linear form would deny the law of diminishing returns, I would next turn to $b\sqrt{LK}$, the unweighted geometric mean and from there to the weighted geometric mean that is the C-D formula.

On resurveying the history, I now realize that the data Douglas

[3] Reserved for another occasion must be my resolution of the puzzle that exercised Barone, Walras, Pareto, Wicksell, Wicksteed, Hicks, and others. Can we relax the assumption of first-degree homogeneity for the production function of the observed *competitive industry*? Is it not enough to assume "merely" that all viable *competitive firms* enjoy only "*local*" (not *global*) first-degree homogeneity at the equilibrium bottom of their U-shaped cost curves? What these writers fail to bring out properly is that such an assumption about numerous such firms implies syllogistically that the *industry* function is essentially (i.e., *asymptotically*) first-degree homogeneous (see Samuelson 1967, pp. 129–35; 1973, pp. 329–35; 1976, p. 481, problem 10).

presented Cobb practically commanded the C-D formula. Let me explain.

If the arcs $[L(t), C(t), P(t)]$ stream out of a common base point forming distinct trends on semilog paper over the interval (1899–1922), and $P(t)$ is always *exactly* one-fourth the way up from $L(t)$ to $C(t)$, then the unique solution to the functional equation

$$\frac{\log [P(t)] - \log [L(t)]}{\log [C(t)] - \log [L(t)]} \equiv \frac{1}{4}, \; 1899 \leq t \leq 1922 \qquad (2a)$$

is

$$P(t) \equiv bL(t)^{3/4}K(t)^{1/4} \qquad (2b)$$
$$b = 1.0 \text{ if } L(1899) = C(1899) = P(1899) = 1.$$

The empirical value for b of 1.01 merely reflected the inexactness of the regression for the initial base year.

None of the authors began with the axiom of constant relative shares

$$0 < \frac{L[\partial f(L,C)/\partial L]}{f(L,C)} \equiv k < 1, \qquad (3a)$$

from which one could deduce the formula

$$f(L,C) \equiv bL^kC^{1-k}, \; 0 < k < 1. \qquad (3b)$$

Nor did they begin with unitary Hicks-Robinson elasticity of substitution:

$$1 = \sigma = \frac{f_Lf_C}{ff_{LC}} = -\frac{d \log [L/C]}{d \log [f_L/f_C]} \qquad (3c)$$

where $[f_L, f_C]$ represent the factors' respective partial derivatives calculated from (1). Cobb (and Wicksell before him) noticed that L^kC^{1-k} led to constant competitive wage share in national income of k. Also, like Dalton [1920] before them, Cobb and Douglas recognized that labor's demand elasticity, for capital fixed, was $1/(1 - k)$ when its share was a constant of k.

Douglas was glad to find that Pigou (1933) confirmed his own estimate that the general demand for labor was highly elastic; it salved Douglas's conscience as a liberal to be able to believe that a slight cut in real wage rates would benefit rather than hurt labor's total real income. Douglas never squared his notions about an elastic *real demand curve for labor as a whole* (a concept he shared with reactionaries such as T. N. Carver and E. Cannan) with the post-1936 Keynesian notion of a demand for labor that shifts with investment multiplicands and which depends crucially on how much of a drop in general prices is itself induced by a contrived cut in *money* wage rates.

The Magnum Opus

One lingers on the 1927 breakthrough because so much was accomplished at the very beginning. However, the 1934 *Theory of Wages* is a rewarding classic in its own right. Not only does it present Douglas's econometric measurements on the *supply* of factors of production,[4] but in addition it offers a rich menu dealing with the history of the subject.[5]

Supplementing the 1899–1922 time series, Douglas (1934) presents similar 1890–1926 evidence for Massachusetts analyzed by Cobb and also time series on New South Wales by Aaron Director, who for a time labored in the Douglas workshop (alongside a future Socialist party candidate for the vice-presidency, Maynard Krueger). Time-series investigations by others for New Zealand and South Africa are later reported on by Douglas. Although the significance for marginal products of production functions with time trends removed is unclear, Douglas and Cobb reported such results for any light they might give for understanding production movements.

Paul Douglas was adept at explaining away most errors of fit. We students used to jest admiringly that his multiple correlation coefficients of .97 probably overflowed above 1.00 once he turned his serious attention to explaining observed squared errors; thus, the recorded depression C_t *in place* was probably in excess of the true capital stock *used*, . . . , etc. (I ought to report, though, that as a stunt I fitted the inadmissible form $P = aL + bK$ to his 1899–1922 data and got the same multiple correlation coefficient of $R = .97$ that he got from the C-D form, a lesson to me about collinearity that I have never ceased to profit from. As a by-product I mastered the Doolittle ritual in that Haskell Hall toil, an investment in human capital that I have not yet succeeded in amortizing.)

Cross-Section Investigations

A new love began to occupy Douglas after his 1934 book was finished. The last years before his country and the Marines called him away from research he devoted to cross-section studies. These studies across industries—performed with Grace Gunn, Marjorie Hansaker,

[4] See the companion piece on this topic by Albert Rees (this volume); also the generous address on Douglas at the University of Wisconsin of Glen Cain (1977), from which my opening quotation is taken.

[5] My own first paper, Samuelson (1937), dealing esoterically with use of life-cycle saving data to infer cardinal additive utility à la Fisher and Ramsey, I now realize was triggered by Douglas's book and classroom discussion of Landry's theory of interest. History of doctrine to split hairs over what Ricardo (should have) meant is one thing; it is another to benefit from the many conflicting ideas nominated by past writers.

Patricia Daly Ogburn, Martin Bronfenbrenner, Ernest Olson, and many others—are summarized by Douglas's last will and testament to the economics profession in his 1947 Presidential Address, delivered just when he received the nod to campaign in 1948 as a Democrat for the U.S. Senate seat from Illinois.

Do these cross-section studies make sense? What sense? I am not sure.

First, let us take a case where they could make sense. Suppose corn is produced along a Hotelling line out of immobile labor and land. If we can observe the same mode of production everywhere but with the ratio of labor to land and corn to land falling steadily as we move uptown and encounter higher wage/rent ratios, then the observed spatial arcs $[L(s), C(s), P(s)]$, like (2)'s temporal arcs, could provide us the scatter to which we can fit a *unique* first-degree-homogeneous production function. Such a cross-sectional study I could understand.

But Douglas does nothing like that. Rather, imagine that there are three industries in society producing, respectively, the goods corn, cloth, and caviar. Each is produced by *its own* first-degree-homogeneous neoclassical function, $f_i(L_i, C_i)$. Suppose society's total L and C are divided into observable (L_i, C_i) breakdowns, $\Sigma_1^3 L_i = L$ and $\Sigma_1^3 C_i = C$. Even if we could observe physical quantities (q_1, q_2, q_3), what scatter across *disparate* industries would give us an *aggregate* production function? Will even the knowledge of the price data of that one period, $(P_1, P_2, P_3; W$, the wage; R, the rental or price of the nonlabor factor), help?

Let me take the case most favorable to Douglas, unrealistic as it is. (1) Assume everyone has the same homothetic tastes so every dollar is spent alike whatever the income distribution. (2) Assume each industry has its own neoclassical production function. (3) Assume that no problems of measuring aggregated "capital" arise, because a homogeneous physical magnitude is malleable for every use ("leets," steel spelled backward, in Mrs. Robinson's caustic terminology). (4) Assume perfect competition, with observable goods and factor prices $(P_1, \ldots, P_n; W, R)$.

Then there does exist a neoclassical first-degree-homogeneous *aggregate* function, which out of total labor and capital produces total real product:

$$\begin{aligned} \mathbf{Q} &= \mathbf{f(L,C)} \\ &= \max_{L_i, C_t} u[f_1(L_1, C_1), \ldots, f_n(L_n, C_n)] \\ &\quad \text{subject to } \sum_1^n C_j = C, \ \sum_1^n L_j = L \end{aligned} \tag{4}$$

where

$$u[q_1, \ldots, q_n] \equiv \lambda^{-1} u[\lambda q_1, \ldots, \lambda q_n]$$

is a first-degree-homogeneous function precisely measuring "output as a whole." On this, see my articles for the Hicks and Machlup *Festschrifts* (Samuelson 1968, pp. 473–77; 1978, p. 114, n. 3).

I have given the cross-section caper all the rope it can use. What can one do with it on the basis of the following observations: $(P_1q_1, L_1, RC_1; \ldots, P_nq_n, L_n, RC_n; R, W, P_1, \ldots, P_n)$. Certainly, a properly weighted average of all industries' relative wage shares should give the aggregate wage share:

$$\mathbf{k} = \frac{WL}{\Sigma_1^n P_i q_i} = \sum_1^n \omega_j \frac{WL_j}{P_j q_j} \text{ where } \omega_j = \frac{P_j q_j}{\Sigma_1^n P_i q_i}. \qquad (5)$$

But this is a triviality. What warrant is there for putting such a $\mathbf{k}$ into bL^kC^{1-k} and pretending that $\mathbf{f(L,C)}$ of (4) is "approximated" by such a pretension? I can think of no justification. A follower of Douglas might wish to derive comfort from the fact that, in many different times, a Bowley will report pretty much the same relative wage share for a particular country like the United States or the United Kingdom. But why cannot such a fact, or alleged fact, stand on its own bottom, gaining and losing nothing from being coupled with an aggregate neoclassical production function?

My point is this: the dispersion of industries is *not* the scatter needed for the aggregate $\mathbf{f(L,C)} = \mathbf{Q}$ function; on the latter, Douglas has at best, in any chosen year, only one observed point; and from one point no one can infer elasticities of demand, of substitution, or anything else. The reader may convince himself of this by the following consideration: suppose every $f_i(L_i, C_i)$ in (3) is different from Cobb-Douglas, instead being of CES form with σ_i's that all *differ* from unity by the same amount. Still the *same* scatter as in the universal C-D case would be observed by Douglas and Gunn or Bronfenbrenner or Olson! No hint of the true $\partial^2\mathbf{f(L,C)}/\partial\mathbf{L}\partial\mathbf{C}$ is inferrable.[6]

[6] Fig. 2 of Bronfenbrenner-Douglas (1939, p. 781) might, after modification and interpretation, be of some help in connection with the problem of my n. 3 above, which deals with relations of firms in the *same* industry; I am unable to see how it can give *across-industry* scatters a relevance to society's aggregate production function (even when that aggregate function happens to exist). My severe criticism may, therefore, not tell against the kind of cross-sectional studies of Griliches-Ringstad (1971) that deal with *different firms* producing the *same industry's* good. Professor Griliches has been kind enough to suggest the following additional references: Marschak and Andrews (1944, 1945); Mundlak and Hoch (1965); M. Nerlove (1965); Drèze, Zellner, and Kmenta (1966). The CES function referred to in my text seems first to have been discovered by Bergson (1936), but in connection with consumer indifference contours: writing it as $[aL^\gamma + bC^\gamma]^{1/\gamma}$, $\gamma < 1$, Bergson showed it to be the only case with both homothetic contours and capability of being numbered by additive-independent sums, $U_1(L) + U_2(C) = [aL^\gamma + bC^\gamma]\gamma^{-1}$ or $[a(L-1)^\gamma + b(C-1)^\gamma]\gamma^{-1}$; also, it has the same income elasticity of marginal utility whatever the prices or income. For $\gamma = 1$, we have infinite substitutability or *E*-of-*S*, $\sigma = (1-\gamma)^{-1} = \infty$; for $\gamma \to -\infty$, we have fixed proportions and zero *E*-of-*S*, $\sigma = (1-\gamma)^{-1} \to 0$; for $\gamma \to 0$, evaluating the indeterminate form gives the C-D case, $\sigma = (1-\gamma)^{-1} \to 1$. I have heard it said that H. D. Dickinson and Champernowne, as well as Solow (1956) and Arrow et al. (1961), represent post-

A Strategic Counterexample

Is this too skeptical an appraisal? Should I not concede that, at the least, these cross-sectional investigations have tested—and verified triumphantly—the hypothesis that the C-D exponents do sum to unity to a good approximation as the neoclassical marginal-productivity wants them to do? On examination I find that, when one specifies $Q = bL^kC^h$ and lets the cross-sectional data decide whether $k + h = 1$, that result tends to follow purely as a cross-sectional *tautology* based on the *residual* computation of the nonwage share. Even if the data had been generated by an existent aggregate C-D function, the post-1934 methodology does not give an unbiased estimate of the proper **k** and $1 - \mathbf{k}$; finally one sees the answer to the puzzle that cross-sectional estimates yield k's that look low, being nearer to ½ than are the aggregate shares and the time-series estimate.

An example will bring this out. Let there be four industries, not necessarily competitive or with constant returns to scale. Out of GNP or national income of 100, let the dollar values (and value addeds) of the industries be, respectively, $(10, 20, 30, 40) = (P_jq_j)$, with respective wage bills of $(6, 12, 24, 32) = (WL_j)$, and residually computed profit returns to "property" or to the nonlabor factor of (4, 8, 6, 8). No one can stop us from labeling this last vector as (RC_j), as J. B. Clark's model would permit—even though we have no warrant for believing that noncompetitive industries have a common profit rate R and use leets capital (C_j) in proportion to the $(P_jq_j - WL_j)$ elements!

Now subject the data to the least-square logarithmic regression estimation procedures of cross-sectional Douglasism, which follow the suggestion of David Durand (1937) of treating k and h as unconstrained parameters in

$$P_jq_j = \log\beta + k\log(WL_j) + h\log(P_jq_j - WL_j) + \text{error}_j\ (j = 1, 2, 3, 4). \tag{6}$$

Since industries 1 and 2 have identical wage shares of 0.6 and industries 3 and 4 have identical shares of 0.8, the regression will afford a *perfect fit* to the scatter if one put a straight line on double-log paper through the two *pooled* pairs of observations. Then

$$\hat{\mathbf{k}} = \frac{\log(10 + 20)/(4 + 8) - \log(30 + 40)/(6 + 8)}{\log(6 + 12)/(4 + 8) - \log(24 + 32)/(6 + 8)} = \frac{\log(1/2)}{\log(3/8)} = 0.707 \tag{7}$$

Bergson independent rediscoveries of the CES family. The CES family can be shown to be the general solution to the following partial differential equation: The elasticity of demand when we vary any factor alone is to be inversely proportional to the share of the remaining factors; the special C-D case is where the proportionality factor is $\sigma = 1$.

$$\hat{\mathbf{h}} = 1 - \hat{\mathbf{k}} = 0.293. \tag{8}$$

Why has the freedom to make h differ from $1 - k$ been rejected by the scatter? Because nature really favors constant returns to scale? Nonsense: she has not shown us her petticoat. Profit and wages add up to total $P_j q_j$ along any fixed ray not because Euler's theorem is revealed to apply on that ray but rather because of the accounting identity involved in the residual definition of profit: with Pq_j a trivial first-degree-homogeneous sum of WL_j and RC_j along any L_j/C_j ray, how can its form of $(WL_j)^k\ (RC_j)^h$ give other than $k + h = 1$?

This example of perfect fit is contrived to be overstrong, to bring out dramatically what is less obviously present in more realistic samples. Several suspicions have been uncovered, which will have to be cleared up if future credence is given to such cross-section-of-industries exercises:

1. The smallness of $1 - k - h$ is an artifact of the tautologies, not a robust test of the conditions for competition and the relevance of marginal productivity.

2. If a true $\mathbf{k}$ and $1 - \mathbf{k}$ exist—a big if—the proposed regressions do not provide unbiased estimates of them. (The example's true $\mathbf{k}$ is $0.74 = [0.1 + 0.2]\ [0.6] + [0.3 + 0.4]\ [0.8]$, not 0.707. The least-squares procedure to get 0.707 takes no account of the greater value weight of industries 3 and 4; if they were expanded a trillionfold, Douglas's computers would still produce 0.707 instead of 0.800! Since realism probably calls for a bell-shaped distribution of k_j's around some central value, failing to give due weight to industries' value weights ought to bias both $\mathbf{k}$ and $1 - \mathbf{k}$ toward ½.)

3. The across-industry scatter at a point of time provides *at best* only one observation on the true aggregate $\mathbf{f(L,C)}$ even when the latter exists. The elasticity of aggregate wage demand could be anything far from $1/(1 - \mathbf{k})$ and still the *same* point-of-time industry scatter could be observed.

It is a late hour to raise these doubts about the Emperor's clothes, but not until undertaking the present assignment did this child give the matter of across-industry fitting the careful attention it deserves and does not seem to have received.[7] We honor a great scholar by

[7] Bronfenbrenner (1939, 1944) and Reder (1943) have registered understandable qualms; concerning them I have to be overly brief. Bronfenbrenner (1939) makes the valid deductive point: if C-D obtains with $Q = bL^k C^{1-k}$ and $0 < k < 1$, inelastic Marshallian demand cannot obtain for $(L, W/P_Q)$ or for $(L/C, \partial Q/\partial L)$. To this Douglas could reply: "Were the observed $(L, W/P_Q)$ truly inelastic, my attempted fit to it to the scatter of $[L/C, b(C/L)^{1-k}]$ would fail for all k. So my method could be self-checking." As referee, I could agree but with a qualification: "Douglas might get what 'looks like' a good fit to the $[L/C, Q/C]$ scatter, while not sufficiently noting how poor might still be the more relevant fit to *higher* derivatives like $[L/C, \partial Q/\partial L]$." To isolate the main point of Reder (1943), consider firms producing the same product under pure competition in

taking his efforts seriously, not by fobbing them off with fulsome, inattentive praise. I hope that someone skilled in econometrics and labor economics will audit and evaluate my critical findings.

Successors to Douglas

Economic statisticians were confronted with rises in output that fully matched the rises in one of the inputs alone. In sharp contrast to Douglas's 1899–1922 manufacturing sample, which showed the rise in the capital/output ratio called for by the statical Clark theory, Kuznets, Abramovitz, and others often found no such change in the capital/output ratio as capital "deepened" relative to labor.

Reality commanded that technical change, or t itself, be put into the production function, so that it takes the Solow (1957) form

$$Q = F(L, K; t), \quad \partial f(\qquad)/\partial t \geqslant 0. \tag{9}$$

---

the product market and with a common good's price, P_Q. To simplify, let them all have the same (leets) capital stock, $\bar{C}_1 = \bar{C}_2 = \ldots = \bar{C}_n = \bar{C}$ and the same *intra*-firm production function of Clarkian type: $Q_j = C_j f(L_j/C_j) = f(L_j/C) = f(L_j)$, if we adopt the convention of $\bar{C} = 1$. Reder posits that the firms have different degrees of *monopsony* power in local labor markets. Hence, L_j's differ and so must the Q_j's or $f(L_j)$s. Reder correctly asserts that the observed (labor, real-wage) scatter, $(L_j, W_j/P_Q)$, will then *not* be generated by the marginal-productivity partial derivatives of Douglas's estimated across-firms production function, the latter being fitted to Douglas's scatter of (L_j,Q_j) or $(L_j/P_Q Q_k)$. Suppose the latter fall *exactly* on a straight line with slope α when double-log paper is used to chart ($\log Q_j$, $\log L_j$); then Douglas gets $\hat{f}(L)$ exactly bL^α, $0 < \alpha < 1$. Reder can say that observed labor share, $k = \Sigma_1^n W_j L_j / P_Q \Sigma_1^n q_j$, need not equal α and indeed must fall below α under posited universal monopsony. Douglas, however, has this defense: "My regression procedure will reveal Reder's shortfall of k from α *if* it is there; but in fact it has not turned up in any of several studies (both cross-sectional and time-series). And, since I use data on L_j and $W_j L_j$ and $P_Q q_j$, my data could reveal the exact departures of the $(W_j/P_Q,L_j)$ scatter from the $[\partial f(L_j)/\partial L, L_j]$ scatter. Moreover, I have correctly identified the true production function and am able to estimate precisely Reder's degree-of-monopsony values from calculable $(W_j/P_Q)f'(L_j/C)$ ratios!" Bronfenbrenner (1944) abandons Douglas's across-firms regressions of the double-log form, $\log (P_j Q_j) = \beta' + k \log (L_j) + (k \log (P_j Q_j - W_j L_j) + \text{error}_j$. Instead he proposes a new across-firm regression of "net-product type." In Reder's case of $Q = \Sigma_1^n q_j, P_j = P_Q, C_1 = \ldots = C_n = 1$, where intrafirm technology is of the same $q_j/C = f(L_j/C) = b(L_j/C)$ form, but where zero monopsony obtained and where free entry with zero monopsony of capital equalized the profit rate and made profit's share RC_j, Bronfenbrenner would be regressing $P_Q q_j - RC_j$ against L_j; or, what is then the same thing, regressing observed WL_j against L_j. Naturally he must get a ray through the origin of slope W for a perfect fit in the (L_j, WL_j) quadrant. *This* he calls *his* new "interfirm 'production' function." Why use the words "production function" for such an accounting-tautology or competition-arbitrage relation (or, where the C_j's differ, why call the observed multiple-regression relation, $P_Q q_j = WL_j + RC_j + \text{zero-error}_j$ an *inter*-firm "production function")? The question asks itself. As applied to data on $[L_j, P_j Q_j - WL_j$ or $P_j Q_j - W_j L_j]$ generated by industries and firms of different technologies and facing different degrees of goods'-market and factors'-market monopolistic and monopsonistic imperfections, what does high or low R^2 for Douglas's double-log or for Bronfenbrenner's linear fit tell us about "empirical verification of marginal-productivity distribution theory"?

However, with $C(t)/L(t)$ showing strong collinear growth with the variate t itself, there would be no hope of "identifying" reasonable parameters for (k, a) in $be^{at}L^kC^{1-k}$, at least from $[Q(t), L(t), C(t)]$ data alone.

Abramovitz (1956), eschewing refined theory, had combined $L(t)$ and $C(t)$ into a linear weighted sum, $\alpha L(t) + \beta C(t)$, called "total resources." Comparing this fabrication with $Q(t)$, he showed how we must invoke a positive role of technical change (i.e., of t itself) as a proxy for productivity improvements in (9)'s version of (1)'s production function.

Solow, having won theoretical fame in 1956, in 1957 sought empirical fortune by supplementing the $[Q(t), L(t), C(t)]$ data by independent relative-share data on $[W(t)L(t)/P(t)Q(t)] = [\rho(t)]$. Stipulating that this represented observations on marginal products

$$\frac{W(t)L(t)}{P(t)Q(t)} = \frac{\partial f[L(t), C(t); t]}{\partial L(t)} \frac{L(t)}{f[L(t), C(t); t]}, \text{ marginal product} \quad (10)$$

$$f[L, C; t] \equiv \lambda^{-1} f[\lambda L, \lambda C; t], \text{ first-degree homogeneity,}$$

Solow (1957) showed that U.S. GNP data for 1909–49 were consistent with Hicks-neutral technical change, with

$$f[L(t), C(t); t] \equiv A(t) f[L(t), C(t)] \equiv A(t) f\left[1, \frac{C(t)}{L(t)}\right] L(t). \quad (11)$$

Since $[\rho(t)]$ was virtually constant at the level around 2/3, Solow could determine the exogenous "residual" productivity function, $A(t)$, approximately by

$$A(t) = \frac{Q(t)}{L(t)^{2/3} C(t)^{1/3}} \quad (12a)$$

or, pretty much equivalently, from cumulating over time,

$$\frac{A(t+1) - A(t)}{A(t)} = \frac{Q(t+1) - Q(t)}{Q(t)} - \rho(t) \frac{L(t+1) - L(t)}{L(t)} - [1 - \rho(t)] \frac{C(t+1) - C(t)}{C(t)}. \quad (12b)$$

Solow not only validated Abramovitz's pragmatic picture, he provided it with a shiny new theoretical frame, and thereby launched a hundred studies of the "residual," the factor $A(t)$ or e^{at} in front of neoclassical production functions. Not the least amusing of the subsequent findings is that of Weitzman (1970) for the USSR: the land of the labor theory of value turned out to have an especially high $1 - k$ for capital! And its residual for technological creativity and imitativeness turned out to be especially low in comparison with the anarchic capitalistic system! (This would all be more ironical if it were not the case that countries as alike as Norway and Sweden differ considerably in the importance of the measured residual; and countries different in almost every way are often measured to have similar residuals! Moreover, scholars who have continued Weitzman's kind of analysis have differed with his pessimistic estimate for the residual even though they have confirmed his suspicion of σ as being less than C-D's unity.)

Let me conclude by examining whether Kaldor and neo-Keynesians are right in suggesting that the Cobb-Douglas results are a cooked-up foregone conclusion from the nature of the statistical methodology! Obviously, so long as Bowley's law of (almost) constancy of labor's share holds, no Clarkian can get a good fit with a function far away from Cobb-Douglas so long as shifts in the $C(t)/L(t)$ ratio are not serendipitously just offset by labor-saving rather than capital-saving biases in technical change!

A follower of Douglas would want to say, "If the data were generated by Clarkian functions, those functions would have to be near Cobb-Douglas if the only change in them was of a 'purely labor-augmenting' kind and if $C(t)/L(t)$ in *efficiency* units varied during the period of observation." Actually this last "if" is *not* strongly realized in the historical data, and hence we cannot rule out the possibility that some other model could generate the same observations, perhaps one of a dozen from Kaldor's own stable. Nor does it rule out the induced labor-saving syndrome of Marx, Hicks (1932), and Fellner (1967), which was finally given logical coherence in the analysis of Samuelson (1965, 1966) and Phelps-Drandakis (1966) of the Charles Kennedy and the von Weizsäcker versions of choices between investing in labor-economizing or capital-economizing efforts.[8]

Vale!

Enough has been said to validate the encomium for Paul Douglas quoted earlier from Glen Cain. The last word should be about Paul Douglas, the person and scholar.

I can see him now, all 250 pounds of his pre-Marines self stretched out in Roman fashion on the Cobb Hall classroom desk, puffing furiously on his cigarette, his seersucker suit wrinkled and his shirt collars pointing up convexly toward the heavens. High noon it was for Hutchins's University of Chicago, and for Douglas as a creative

[8] To make sense of the notion that deepening of capital relative to labor induces labor-saving innovations to offset rising W/R costs, see Samuelson (1965, 1966) and Phelps-Drandakis (1966) with their references to von Weizsäcker and Kennedy.

scholar. For me and my lucky classmates it was dawn of a more exciting day.

Since then I have encountered some of the best teachers in the world and some of the worst. But only after youth had stolen away did I learn to measure its ineffable joys.

References

Abramovitz, Moses. "Resource and Output Trends in the United States since 1870." *A.E.R.* 46 (suppl.; May 1956): 5–23.

Arrow, K. J.; Chenery, H. B.; Minhas, B. S.; and Solow, R. M. "Capital-Labor Substitution and Economic Efficiency." *Rev. Econ. and Statis.* 43 (August 1961): 225–50.

Bergson, Abram. "Real Income, Expenditure Proportionality, and Frisch's 'New Methods of Measuring Marginal Utility.'" *Rev. Econ. Studies* 4 (October 1936): 33–52.

Bronfenbrenner, Martin. "The Cobb-Douglas Function and Trade-Union Policy." *A.E.R.* 29 (December 1939): 793–96.

———. "Production Functions: Cobb-Douglas, Interfirm, Intrafirm." *Econometrica* 12 (January 1944): 35–44.

Bronfenbrenner, Martin, and Douglas, P. H. "Cross-Section Studies in the Cobb-Douglas Function." *J.P.E.* 47, no. 6 (December 1939): 761–85.

Cain, Glen G. "A Tribute to Paul H. Douglas, 1892–1976, Labor Economist and Senator." Paper presented at the Labor Economics Workshop, University of Wisconsin, October 11, 1977.

Clark, John Bates. *The Distribution of Wealth; A Theory of Wages, Interest and Profits*. New York: Macmillan, 1899.

Cobb, Charles W., and Douglas, P. H. "A Theory of Production." *A.E.R.* 18 (suppl.; March 1928): 139–65.

Dalton, Hugh. *Some Aspects of the Inequality of Incomes in Modern Communities.* London: Routledge, 1920.

Douglas, Paul H. *The Theory of Wages.* New York: Macmillan, 1934.

———. "Are There Laws of Production?" *A.E.R.* 38 (March 1948): 1–41.

———. "Comments on the Cobb-Douglas Production Function." In *The Theory and Empirical Analysis of Production: Studies in Income and Wealth,* edited by Murray Brown. Vol. 31. New York: Nat. Bur. Econ. Res., 1967.

———. *In the Fullness of Time: The Memoirs of Paul H. Douglas.* New York: Harcourt, Brace, Jovanovich, 1972.

———. "The Cobb-Douglas Production Function Once Again: Its History, Its Testing, and Some Empirical Values." *J.P.E.* 84, no. 5 (October 1976): 903–15.

Drèze, Jacques; Zellner, Arnold; and Kmenta, J. "Specification and Estimation of Cobb-Douglas Production Function Models." *Econometrica* 34 (October 1966): 784–95.

Durand, David. "Some Thoughts on Marginal Productivity, with Special Reference to Professor Douglas' Analysis." *J.P.E.* 45, no. 6 (December 1937): 740–58.

Fellner, William J. "Comment on the Induced Bias." *Econ. J.* 77 (September 1967): 662–64.

Griliches, Zvi, and Ringstad, Vidar. *Economies of Scale and the Form of the Production Function: An Econometric Study of Norwegian Manufacturing Establishment Data.* Amsterdam: North-Holland, 1971.

Gunn, G., and Douglas, P. H. "The Production Function for American Manufacturing." *A.E.R.* 31 (1941): 67–80.

Hicks, J. R. *The Theory of Wages.* London: Macmillan, 1932.

Marschak, Jacob, and Andrews, W. H., Jr. "Random Simultaneous Equations and the Theory of Production." *Econometrica* 12 (July–October 1944): 143–205.

———. "Errata." *Econometrica* 13 (January 1945): 91.

Mundlak, Y., and Hoch, I. "Consequences of Alternative Specifications in Estimation of Cobb-Douglas Production Functions." *Econometrica* 33 (October 1965): 814–28.

Nerlove, Marc. *Estimation and Identification of Cobb-Douglas Production Functions.* Amsterdam: North-Holland, 1965.

Olsson, Carl-Axel. "The Cobb-Douglas or the Wicksell Function?" *Econ. and Hist.* 14 (1971): 64–69.

Phelps, Edmund S., and Drandakis, E. M. "A Model of Induced Invention, Growth, and Distribution." *Econ. J.* 76 (December 1966): 823–40.

Pigou, A. C. *The Theory of Unemployment.* London: Macmillan, 1933.

Reder, Melvin W. "An Alternative Interpretation of the Cobb-Douglas Function," *Econometrica* 11 (July–October 1943): 259–64.

Rees, Albert. "Douglas on Wages and the Supply of Labor." *J.P.E.*, this volume.

Samuelson, Paul A. "A Note on Measurement of Utility." *Rev. Econ. Studies* 4 (February 1937): 155–61. Reproduced in *The Collected Scientific Papers of Paul A. Samuelson.* Vol. 1, edited by J. E. Stiglitz. Cambridge, Mass.: M.I.T. Press, 1966.

———. "A Theory of Induced Innovation along Kennedy-Weizsäcker Lines." *Rev. Econ. and Statis.* 47 (November 1965): 343–56. Reproduced in *The Collected Scientific Papers of Paul A. Samuelson.* Vol. 3, edited by R. C. Merton. Cambridge, Mass.: M.I.T. Press, 1972.

———. "Rejoinder: Agreements, Disagreements, Doubts, and the Case of Induced Harrod-Neutral Technical Change." *Rev. Econ. and Statis.* 48, no. 4 (November 1966): 444–48.

———. "The Monopolistic Competition Revolution." In *Monopolistic Competition Theory: Studies in Impact, Essays in Honor of Edward H. Chamberlin*, edited by Robert E. Kuenne. New York: Wiley, 1967. Reproduced in *The Collected Scientific Papers of Paul A. Samuelson.* Vol. 3.

———. "Two Generalizations of the Elasticity of Substitution." In *Value, Capital, and Growth. Papers in Honour of Sir John Hicks*, edited by J. N. Wolfe. Edinburgh: Edinburgh University Press and Chicago: Aldine, 1968. Reproduced in *The Collected Scientific Papers of Paul A. Samuelson.* Vol. 3.

———. "A Quantum Theory Model of Economics: Is the Coordinating Entrepreneur Just Worth His Profit?" In *Development and Planning, Essays in Honor of Paul Rosenstein-Rodan*, edited by J. Bhagwati and R. S. Eckaus. London: Allen & Unwin, 1973. Reproduced in *The Collected Scientific Papers of Paul A. Samuelson.* Vol. 4, edited by H. Nagatani and K. Crowley. Cambridge, Mass.: M.I.T. Press, 1978.

———. *Economics.* 10th ed. New York: McGraw-Hill, 1976.

———. "Pseudo-Maximization to the Rescue of Derived Factor Demand of a Competitive Industry." In *Breadth and Depth in Economics, Fritz Machlup—the*

Man and His Ideas, edited by Jacob S. Dreyer. Lexington, Mass.: Lexington, 1978.

Solow, Robert M. "The Production Function and the Theory of Capital." *Rev. Econ. Studies* 23, no. 2 (1956): 101–8.

———. "Technical Change and the Aggregate Production Function." *Rev. Econ. and Statis.* 39 (August 1957): 312–20.

Velupillai, Kumaraswamy. "The Cobb-Douglas or the Wicksell Function." *Econ. and Hist.* 16 (1973): 11–113.

Weitzman, Martin L. "Soviet Postwar Economic Growth and Capital-Labor Substitution." *A.E.R.* 60 (September 1970): 672–92.

Wicksell, Knut. "Ein neues Prinzip der gerechen Besteurung." *Finanztheoretische Untersuchungen*, Jena (1896). Translated as "A New Principle of Just Taxation." In *Classics in the Theory of Public Finance*, edited by R. A. Musgrave and A. T. Peacock. London: Macmillan, 1958.

———. "Marginal Productivity as the Basis of Distribution in Economics." *Ekon. Tidskrift* (1900): 305–37. Reproduced in *Selected Papers on Economic Theory*. London: Allen & Unwin, 1958.

———. *Lectures on Political Economy*. Vol. 1. London: Macmillan, 1934. Swedish, 1901; German, 1913; English, 1934.

———. "The 'Critical Point' in the Law of Decreasing Agricultural Productivity." *Ekon. Tidskrift* (1916), pp. 285–92. Reproduced in *Selected Papers on Economic Theory*.

Wicksteed, P. H. *An Essay on the Coordination of the Laws of Distribution*. London: Macmillan, 1894.

———. *Common Sense of Political Economy*. 2 vols. London: Routledge, 1933.

1 Rigorous Observational Positivism: Klein's Envelope Aggregation; Thermodynamics and Economic Isomorphisms

Paul A. Samuelson

Twenty or more years ago, Edwin G. Nourse, the first chairman of the Council of Economic Advisers and a respected agricultural economist at the Brookings Institution, wrote to Alvin Hansen to ask "Who originated the word 'macroeconomics'?" Hansen wrote back "I don't know. Probably Samuelson."

I know there is much that I will have to answer for at Saint Peter's Gate. But when I read carbons of this correspondence, I was pretty sure that I was not guilty as charged. Familiar as the distinction between *microeconomics* and *macroeconomics* is today, the expressions are not old ones. I confirmed that *macroeconomics* is not in the index of the first (1948) edition of my textbook *Economics.* I suspected that the word was a coinage of Ragnar Frisch, who was so ingenious in originating and naming concepts. I did a little research in the 1952 *Guide to Econometrica.* Sure enough, there was a classification there involving *macroeconomics.* And, as I vaguely recall, listed under that category were articles from the early 1930s by Frisch, Jan Tinbergen, and others. However, when I perused the bound volumes of those early issues, I discovered that Frisch and Tinbergen seemed not to have actually used the word in question. The compilers of the *Guide* had (properly) used hindsight in making their classification of earlier articles.[1]

So I was stumped. And I was challenged to do some further cursory research on the appearance of *macroeconomics.* Moreover, I realized that *macroeconomics* as used today has two primary meanings. The first deals, for example, with Keynesian notions of effective demand, of fluctuations in output as a whole. At the pre-Keynesian neoclassical level, this first concept involves the notion of the "price level," as distinct from individual prices and price ratios and as determinable by a Fisherian equation of exchange, $MV = PQ$. The second important meaning we now give to *macroeconomics* is at the real level of pure theory. With J. B. Clark, we speak of a society with a production function that produces (aggregate) output out of its total labor, land, and capital. In this second sense, a micro system of general equilibrium that is very simple becomes a macromodel. Trade theory is full of two-good, two-factor models, involving Marshallian bales and indifference contours for a country.

To return to the hunt for origins of the term *macroeconomics*: Its earliest appearance turned up by my desultory explorations was in the second sense of the term—in connection with simple, aggregated micro models. The lead article in the April 1946 *Econometrica*, written by the 25-year-old Lawrence R. Klein, had the word in its title: Macroeconomics and the Theory of Rational Behavior. I am sure more assiduous researchers will turn up references prior to 1946; until they do, Laurie Klein can be regarded as Columbus.

Envelope Aggregation

Over 35 years later, we can sum up on the 1946 Klein program for aggregation.[2] There are many different kinds of aggregation—some rigorous, some approximate, some erroneous or incomplete. Klein put his emphasis on what I here characterize as *envelope aggregation.*

Let me briefly mention some other kinds of aggregation. Ricardo and other classical writers are sometimes assumed to work with a "dose of labor and capital." This reduces two inputs, L and K, to a new single input, $\mathrm{Min}(L/a,\ K/b) \equiv V$. This so-called Leontief (1936) aggregation is not in Klein's focus.

Hicks (1939) holds the ratio P_3/P_2 constant at $\bar{\Pi}$ in demand functions for three goods: $D^i(M;\ P_1,\ P_2,\ P_3)$. Hicks shows that the first good, and the composite spent on the remaining goods, obey well-behaved two-good demand:

$$D^1(M;\ P_1\ \ P_2,\ \ \bar{\Pi}P_2) \equiv D^1(M;\ P_1,\ P_2),$$

where the latter obeys all of the Slutsky conditions. Again, Klein's focus is not on this.

One last example of aggregation that does not concern Klein can be given. Suppose each of $j = 1, \ldots, J$ persons has a simple propensity-to-consume function: $C_j = a_j + b_j Y_j$. Then, even if the bs differ capriciously, suppose that whatever business-cycle forces affect total income, $Y = \sum_j Y_j$, always do so consistently with definite distributional laws: $Y_j = f_j(Y)$. It will follow that total consumption, $C = \sum_j C_j$, obeys an invariant function of total income:

$$C = F(Y) = \sum_j [a_j + b_j f_j(Y)], \tag{1}$$

$$F'(Y) = \sum_j b_j f_j'(Y). \tag{2}$$

The collective marginal propensity to consume depicts no property of a collective mind with thrift propensities; it is merely a definable average of disparate minds. Legitimate as this could be, it is not what Klein has in mind.

What is Klein's concern? He does want to replace multivarious relations between $(x_1, \ldots, x_n)$ and $(y_1, \ldots, y_m)$ by fewer relations between some scalar X and some scalar Y—as, for example, $Y = F(X)$. This goal he shares with the other theorists I have mentioned and with the Bureau of Labor Statistics and other government agencies that provide us with statistical measures of aggregates (index numbers of price levels, output or input measures, and the like).

But Klein insists on an additional criterion for his aggregate functions: If economic theory says that the individual firms and families at the microscopic level are maximizers or minimizers who equate market prices of goods or factors to partial derivatives of their respective micro functions, then the surrogate macro function constructed from these micro functions should have its partial derivatives equaling *its* macro prices. An example is the marginal productivity wage. If each product has

$$q_j = f_j(L_j, \ldots), \tag{3}$$

$$\frac{W}{P_j} = \frac{\partial f_j(L_j, \ldots)}{\partial L_j}, \tag{4}$$

then Klein seeks for $\sum q_j = Q, \sum L_j = L, \ldots$

$$Q = F(L, \ldots), \tag{5}$$

$$\frac{W}{P_Q} = \frac{\partial F(L, \ldots)}{\partial L}. \tag{6}$$

The correspondence between equations 4 and 6 is what is characteristic of envelope aggregation. (I supply this term for it because, as will be seen, an envelope property is what is involved.)

Motivations

Remember, Klein was a Berkeley undergraduate. Like Francis Dresch, George Danzig, Kenneth May, Ronald Shephard, and many other students of that generation, Klein benefited from the influence of two noneconomists: the mathematician Griffith C. Evans and the statistician Jerszy Neyman. Around 1925, Evans went beyond his specialty of functional analysis to explore mathematical economics (Evans 1930, 1934). His ideas were important for diverse topics: integrability conditions, aggregation and Divisia indexes, and time-phased input-output models (which W. W. Leontief and P. Sraffa were to cultivate in depth). In particular, Klein puzzled over the approach to aggregation along the lines of Divisia indexes by Francis W. Dresch.

Klein was a student of mine at the Massachusetts Institute of Technology. He was MIT's first Ph.D. in economics—and still our fastest, provided you penalize Robert Mundell for graduate study elsewhere than at MIT. Between wartime tasks at the Radiation Laboratory, I was revising for publication my Well's Prize Harvard thesis. *Foundations of Economic Analysis* (Samuelson 1947) contained a chapter on special topics such as aggregation. Already in 1936, on a trip back to Chicago, I had unsuccessfully tried to interest Henry Schultz in Jacobian conditions for rigorous aggregation (functional dependences of separability). Also, I spent countless hours pursuing testable regularities that aggregate demand data ($\Sigma_j q_1^j$, $\Sigma_j q_2^j, \ldots$, $p_1, p_2, \ldots$) must theoretically obey. Only in relatively recent times did Hugo Sonnenschein (1972) demonstrate how empty of such laws aggregate functions will be if we are not given data on $(I^1, I^2, \ldots)$ and if endowment breakdowns of q_i totals by individuals $(\bar{q}_i^j)$ cannot be known.

Finally, Klein had gone to the Chicago Cowles Commission from MIT. I suspect that Jacob Marschak and Leo Hurwicz had urged him to try to give his aggregate models greater trustworthiness by trying to anchor them in the individuals' maximizing behavior of economic theory.[3]

Already, A. A. Könus, G. Haberler, H. Staehle, R. G. D. Allen, A. P. Lerner, Leontief, and Frisch had shown the value of basing index numbers on the theory of indifference curves rather than on the mechanical tests of Irving Fisher, F. Y. Edgeworth, W. Persons, the earlier Frisch, and the official compilers of indexes. It was natural for Klein to attempt to bring production theory in line.

I add that, implicitly at least, there had always been envelope aggregation involved in such classical concepts as the total of corn produced for each total of labor applied (under the invisible hand of competition) to diverse acres of land, and in such neoclassical concepts as the supply curve for an industry.

Crusoe's Exact Case

Provide R. Crusoe with totals of primary factors: $(V_1, V_2, \ldots, V_I)$. They can be allocated among $j = 1, \ldots, J$ different single-good industries:

$$q_j = F^j(V_{1j}, V_{2j}, \ldots), \quad \sum_j V_{ij} \leq V_i > 0 \leq V_{ij}. \tag{7}$$

Suppose Crusoe has a quasi-concave indicator of the utility of the goods he consumes: $u = u[q_1, \ldots, q_J]$. Then it is an easy envelope theory that we can define for Crusoe a derived utility function that depends only on his factor totals, $(V_1, V_2, \ldots)$.
Thus,

$$\begin{aligned} U(V_1, V_2, \ldots) &= \operatorname*{Max}_{V_{ij}} u[q_1, q_2, \ldots, q_j, \ldots] \\ &= \operatorname*{Max}_{V_{ij}} u[F^1(V_{11}, V_{21}, \ldots), F^2(V_{12}, V_{22}, \ldots), \ldots] \\ \text{s.t.} \sum_j V_{ij} &\leq V_i \quad (i = 1, 2, \ldots, I). \end{aligned} \tag{8}$$

What is important for Klein's requirement is that the slopes of the indifference contours of the constructed aggregate utility yield the factor-price ratios needed to define functional distribution among the factors; that is,

$$\frac{W_2}{W_1} = \frac{\partial U(V_1, V_2, \ldots)/\partial V_2}{\partial U(V_1, V_2, \ldots)/\partial V_1}, \text{ etc.} \tag{9}$$

Trivial Generalizations of Symmetry

If Crusoe is joined by Friday, with equal ownership of each V_j total, and with $u[q_1, q_2, \ldots]$ tastes of exactly Crusoe's form, then the aggregate $U(V_1, V_2, \ldots)$ that works for the whole can also stand for the representative person.

Classroom expositions often use Santa Claus cases like this one to make the portrayal of complicated general equilibrium look simple. A century ago, Friedrich von Wieser's *Natural Value* improved on the Crusoe metaphor by using the metaphor of the perfect communist state. This led, via V. Pareto, E. Barone, L. von Mises, F. Taylor, A. P. Lerner, O. Lange, F. von Hayek, A. Bergson, and L. Kantorovitch, to fruitful debate on the role of market pricing in socialist planning.

To appreciate when a theorem is not true, realize that indifference curves and factor endowments that differ among people will vitiate the existence of a social surrogate with the sought Klein properties.

Uniform Homotheticity

Does Klein set out to hunt a unicorn or chimera? Does his quarry exist? In general, no aggregate that is an exact surrogate will exist. Only if we can tolerate some approximations can we, in general, succeed in the hunt. Perhaps an antelope or a cow can approximate to a unicorn. But there are sufficient conditions that ensure exact surrogates. Here is the rock-bottom example.

A Crusoe world with fixed supplies of two goods, x and y, could have its sole price ratio predicted by the slope of Crusoe's indifference contour at that point:

$$\frac{P_x}{P_y} = r(x, y) = \frac{\partial u(x, y)/\partial x}{\partial u(x, y)/\partial y}. \tag{10}$$

Now add Friday. Knowing x^1, y^1, x^2, y^2, $X = x^1 + x^2$, and $Y = y^1 + y^2$, we cannot in general validly write

$$p_x/p_y = R(X, Y) = R(x^1 + x^2, y^1 + y^2). \tag{11}$$

Reallocating x^1 and x^2 within the same total of $x^1 + x^2$ will alter real-world p_x/p_y, falsifying equation 11, unless the persons' $[r^1(x^1, y^1), r^2(x^2, y^2)]$ marginal-rate-of-substitution functions are of special form.

We require

$$p_x/p_y = r^1(x^1, y^1) = r^2(x^2, y^2) \equiv r(x^1 + x^2, y^1 + y^2). \tag{12}$$

If this identity is to hold throughout the (x, y) non-negative orthant, it is necessary and sufficient that

$$r^1(a, b) \equiv r(a/b) \equiv r^2(a, b). \tag{13}$$

This is the singular case of *uniform homothetic* demand. (Both adjectives are required.) William Gorman (1953) and Henri Theil (1957) have presented a weaker condition for aggregative invariance under limited local reallocations of the $(x^1 + x^2, y^1 + y^2)$ totals, namely that the persons have straight-line Engel's paths with the same positive slopes at common price ratios. But, globally throughout the non-negative orthant, the only straight lines that will not be bent by the axes are straight lines through the origin—the uniform homothetic case of Samuelson (1956).

When Klein (1946a, p. 103) suggested Cobb-Douglas-type functions, his instinct was a good one. But, as just seen, it is homotheticity and general homogeneous functions that are in order and not merely the special species of Cobb-Douglas type.

Dresch's use of Divisia indexes can also be shown to have a certain rationale through their connection with homogeneous functions. If Divisia index integrals are to enjoy the indispensable independence-of-path property, they must be applied to homothetic structures.

In particular, let $[p_1, \ldots, p_n]$ be proportional to the gradient of $f(x_1, \ldots, x_J)$,

$$[\partial f(x_1, \ldots, x_J)/\partial x_j] \equiv [f_1(x), \ldots, f_J(x)],$$

where these partials are well defined on $x \geq 0 \neq x$.

The integral

$$\int \sum_j \left(p_j \Big/ \sum_k p_k x_k \right) dx_j = \int \sum_j \left(f_j(x) \Big/ \sum_k f_k(x) x_k \right) dx_j \tag{14}$$

will be the same for every path beginning at $(x_1^0, \ldots, x_J^0)$ and ending at $(x_1^1, \ldots, x_J^1)$ if and only if $f(x)$ can be written in the form

$$f(x_1, \ldots, x_n) \underset{\lambda}{\equiv} \phi[x_1 \psi(x_2/x_1, \ldots, x_J/x_1)], \quad \Phi''[\ ] \gtreqless 0. \tag{15}$$

The next section shows the purest case of uniform homotheticity.

The Santa Claus Case

In connection with the Hicks Festschrift and my memorial notice for Paul Douglas (Samuelson 1968, 1979), I show how simple general equilibrium can become if every dollar is spent in the same way by people who have uniform homothetic tastes.[4]

Suppose individuals, $k = 1, \ldots, K$, have inelastic factor supplies, V_i^k, whose $i = 1, \ldots, I$ totals can be allocated among goods $j = 1, \ldots, J$, in amounts V_{ij}. These goods have production functions

$$q_j = Q^j(V_{1j}, \ldots, V_{ij}, \ldots, V_{Ij}) \quad (j = 1, \ldots, J), \quad V_{ij} \geq 0, \tag{16}$$

$$\sum_{k=1}^{K} V_i^k = \sum_{j=1}^{J} V_{ij} \quad (i = 1, \ldots, I), \quad V_i^k \geq 0. \tag{17}$$

With uniform homothetic tastes, any person k acts to maximize the first-degree-homogeneous utility function

$$u^k = u[q_1^k, \ldots, q_J^k] \quad (k = 1, \ldots, K). \tag{18}$$

All consumptions end up subject to individual budget restrictions and

$$\sum_{k=1}^{K} q_j^k = q_j = Q^j(V_{1j}, \ldots, V_{Ij}) \quad (j = 1, \ldots, J), \quad q_j^k \geq 0. \tag{19}$$

The multivarious general equilibrium relations, $JI + JK + TJ$ in number,

$$p_j \frac{\partial Q^j(V_{1j}, \ldots)}{\partial V_{ij}} = W_i \quad (i = 1, \ldots, I; j = 1, \ldots, J), \tag{20}$$

$$\frac{\partial u^k[q_1^k, \ldots]/\partial q_j^k}{\partial u^k[q_1^k, \ldots]/\partial q_1^k} = \frac{p_j}{p_1} \quad (k = 1, \ldots, K; j = 2, \ldots, J), \tag{21}$$

$$\sum_{j=1}^{J} p_j q_j^k = \sum_{i=1}^{I} W_i V_i^k \qquad (k = 1, \ldots, K), \tag{22}$$

$$\sum_{k=1}^{K} q_j^k = Q^j(V_{1j}, \ldots, K_{Ij}) \quad (j = 1, \ldots, J), \tag{23}$$

can be summarized by the I relations from equation 8's $U(V_1, \ldots)$ function:

$$\frac{\partial U\left(\sum_k V_1^k, \ldots, \sum_k V_I^k\right)}{\partial V_i} = \frac{W_i}{P_U} \quad (i = 1, \ldots, I) \tag{24}$$

where W_i/P_U is the real wage of V_i in terms of the $u[\ ]$ measure of output.

The economy becomes a simple Clark sausage machine for producing real-dollar pleasure out of the given factor supplies. The imputation of real income among factors is given by the marginal product the sausage machine defines for the factors. Successful aggregation can go no further.

The reader may be amused to contemplate the simplest possible case of general equilibrium. It is the double Cobb-Douglas case, where all calculations can be done in one's head. Assume constant imputed marginal product shares for factors i in industry j:

$$1 = s_{1j} + \cdots + s_{ij} + \cdots + s_{Ij} \quad (j = 1, \ldots, J). \tag{25}$$

Assume constant fractional shares of expenditure on each of the J goods:

$$e_1 + e_2 + \cdots + e_j + \cdots + e_J = 1. \tag{26}$$

Then

$$U = bV_1^{\Sigma_j s_{1j} e_j} \cdots V_I^{\Sigma_j s_{Ij} e_j}, \tag{27}$$

$$\frac{W_i}{W_1} = \frac{V_1}{V_i} \frac{\sum_j s_{ij}}{\sum_j s_{1j}} \quad (i = 2, \ldots, I), \tag{28}$$

$$\frac{P_j}{P_1} = \frac{q_1}{q_j} \frac{e_j}{e_1} \quad (j = 2, \ldots, J). \tag{29}$$

The Prose Long Spoken

I go from the strongest case for aggregation to the more general sphere, where a version of envelope aggregation has long been utilized at the implicit level. Every time we add marginal curves laterally to define a resultant marginal curve, we are employing envelope aggregation. I describe two familiar instances.

Marshall analyzes the supply of tea. Suppose tea relies solely on lands good only for it. Each amount of homogeneous labor made available to the tea industry gets optimally allocated (by rent charging . . .) on the land. The lateral sum of the separate acres' marginal-cost or supply curves provides Marshall's long-and-intermediate-run SS curve for the industry.

Change tea to corn and you have Ricardo's case. The corn industry has what we would call a production function. Aggregation is involved, implicitly by Ricardo and explicitly by post-Wicksell economists. The marginal productivity of the aggregate (L, Q) relation gives the real wage; Ricardian rent can be measured as a triangular-area residual.

Labor Theory of Value as Attempted Aggregation

When labor alone timelessly hunts deer and beaver, Smith's labor theory of value applies. If boy labor differs from man labor, and both differ from girl and woman labor, Marx tries to rescue Smith's theory by defining each person's labor hour as containing so many units of lowest-common-denominator labor. Thus, if boys have the lowest productivity, Marx would *try* to use their labor as the lowest common denominator: for example, one unit in boy labor, two such input units in man labor, three units in girl labor, and five lowest-common-denominator units in an hour of woman's labor. This way, Mozart has 10^9 of my units in him.

But such envelope aggregation usually is not valid. I beat Mozart at quaternions. I have 10^3 Mozart units in me. Which is right: Does Samuelson/Mozart equal 1/1 billion, or 1,000? As soon as the ratio of labor efficiencies becomes an endogenous variable for general equilibrium to resolve, the trick of reducing heterogeneous labor inputs to a lowest common denominator will not work. The labor theory of value is *kaput*. (James Mill, admitting that old trees sell for more than their labor of planting, tried to save the labor theory of value by making "time and capital" honorary congealed labor. That way lies comedy.)

Methodology of Operational Positivism

Clerk Maxwell wrote down the equations that light and electromagnetism must follow. When physicists complained about the mathematical complexity of Maxwell's exposition, Heinrich Hertz properly chastized them by observing that the content of Maxwell's theory was that of his equations, no more and no less. Similarly, the economic theory of consumption is no more and no less than the Slutsky or revealed-preference restrictions it obeys. Envelope aggregation stands or falls with, and is, the maximizing equilibrium relations that obtain in a competitive market. If Soviet economic planning were capricious, with no resemblance to decentralized pricing or to realization of planning maxima, Klein could never expect the partial derivatives of Soviet aggregates to have any systematic relation to wage shares or goods prices. (There is a moral here for Klein's 1946 hope to handle imperfect competition in the aggregation process: Unless the deviations from perfect competition are very balanced, what envelope aggregation adds to crude aggregation will be very hard to obtain.)

Werner Heisenberg was led to his 1925 matrix mechanics by taking a hard-boiled Machian approach to what it is that we can observe. He thought he was following in Einstein's footsteps, in that Einstein's 1905 Special Theory of Relativity can be formulated antiseptically in terms of axioms on what can be observed: the impossibility of measuring "ether drift"; the constancy of speed of light observed to emanate from a body independently of its own velocity. However, in the last half of his life Einstein increasingly used language that people could be forgiven for interpreting as showing some indifference toward what has been and will be observed. Some Einstein admirers have admired him for these anti-Machian sentiments.

In my youth I did not agree with this. After 45 years of observing what does and does not turn out to be fruitful in economic science, I still dissent. Einstein was right to suspect that simple systems will be found to explain much of physics. He was right to reserve judgment about fragmentary experiments that seemed to contradict details of his beautiful synthesis. He was right to eschew piecemeal patchwork. But he would have been wrong to shrug off important empirical discrepancies that were observed repeatedly. And Bohr and other great contemporaries of Einstein were right to carry on with their probabilistic models in defiance of Einstein's hunch that someone might later come up with a better theory.

Although not every branch of science benefits from an axiomatic approach based on observational relations—successful immunology, for example, seems to have had to proceed largely on an *ad hoc* basis—there are some branches that do. Classical thermodynamics is an archetype. Essentially, it is isomorphic with envelope aggregation. For this reason I put in a self-contained appendix to this chapter an economist's way of formulating the relations of that important subject. Inasmuch as Lawerence Klein has been one of the economists who have provided generalizations of the thermodynamic Le Chatelier principle, this is a fitting place to show how the economist's practice of framing theoretical axioms in terms of strict observables can be carried out for classical thermodynamics, the most chastely elegant branch of physics and chemistry.

Appendix: Some Axiomatic Foundations For Thermodynamics

1. Mechanics

Classical mechanics, from Galileo through Newton, Euler, Lagrange, and Hamilton, deals with motions of apples, planets, pendulums, bicycles, and general systems of particles. Implicit in Galileo's analysis of freely falling bodies, and made explicit by Leibniz, is the law of conservation of (mechanical) energy for a (frictionless) system. A frictionless pendulum has the greatest kinetic energy (squared velocity) at the bottom of its swing, when its potential energy is minimal. The sum of a conservative system's kinetic and potential energies is a constant along any motion, conserving the initial value of that sum.

No observed system is completely without friction. As actual systems lose mechanical energy, a rise in "temperature" occurs. Thus, as a weight moves from rest at a higher altitude to rest at a lower altitude, turning thereby a paddle wheel in a fluid, it increases that fluid's temperature. It loses total mechanical energy, and that loss is offset by a rise in the fluid's temperature.

2. Thermodynamics

Classical thermodynamics is the subject that deals with such interactions of mechanics and "temperatures." That part of the subject's development dealt with here is associated with Rumford, Sadi Carnot, Kelvin (William Thomson), Mayer, Joule, Helmholtz, Clausius, Maxwell, Gibbs, Carathéodory, Born, Tisza, and many others. Although there is extensive overlap between my formulation and those of these authors, mine is idiosyncratic in that the formal relations that are important in analytical economics have motivated my choice of physical axioms and the order of their introduction. In the end, of course, the system derived here is isomorphic with that of conventional phenomenological thermodynamics.

3. Program

I have eschewed all reference to statistical mechanics, kinetic theory, quantum mechanics, Brownian motion, and other microscopic observations. This abstention is solely for the purpose of characterizing the logical structure of macroscopic (phenomenological) thermodynamics.

I avoid the word *heat*, not because there is any objection in principle to giving a name to certain differences between *work* and *energy* magnitudes, but to forestall implicit theorizing.

I avoid differentials, exact or inexact, such as $-pdv$, or $-pdv + tds$, ds, dQ, or $-\int pdv$. I do work with derivatives—partial derivatives like $\partial p/\partial v$, with temperature held constant, and ordinary derivatives like $p'[x]$, where $p[x]$ is a well-defined arc along which the behavior of pressure is specified.

For the most part, I do not employ the language of engineering. When I utilize the area of a closed curve in the (pressure, volume) plane, I do not relate it to the "cycle" some engine might be performing. This does not mean that I share Max Born's repugnance against basing thermodynamics on axioms couched in terms of the impossibility of perpetual-motion machines of various kinds. What's wrong with that, aesthetically or methodologically? The mathematical axioms that I do hypothesize undoubtedly can be put into equivalent engineering language.

Finally, much of thermodynamics might as appropriately be called thermo-*statics*. My approach tries (necessarily without complete success, as it itself makes clear) to deal with equilibrium relations, obviating the need to execute *reversible* motions. The irreducible notion of *irreversible* movements is introduced at the beginning to define certain "insulated" or "adiabatic" contours. Then the results of one short Joule experiment, it is shown, do have to be assumed known at some later stage. Beyond that, no irreversibility phenomena are required, nor for that matter any reversibility phenomena as such.[5] (In section 16, I do digress to show how internal energy functions can be defined solely by observing spontaneous irreversible equalizations of empirical temperature.)

4. Walls

Assume that any substance, for example a specified mass of water vapor, can be enclosed in walls that define a measurable volume. The surrounding wall may be of two kinds. The pressures of two substances on each side of a rigid wall need not be equal. When we wish to, we can work with a *nonrigid* wall that lets volume expand or contract to cause internal pressure to come into equality with some measurable external pressure. Similarly, our wall may be insulating or *noninsulating* (thermal conducting). By use of Dewar "thermos" flasks, a fluid that looks to the eye red-hot can persist next to external substances that are blue-hot or cold to the touch. By contrast to such an insulating wall, we have noninsulating walls such that one observes that substances they separate show observable changes in properties until finally they approach compatible states. From such reproducible observations one builds up the notion of "equality of temperature" of two substances and of "inequality of (empirical) temperatures."

In considering nonsimple substances that involve the masses of more than one chemical substance—of $M_1, M_2, \ldots$ rather than M alone—we assume that there are impermeable and semipermeable walls that either do or do not let some of the M_i in an internal system interchange with that external system outside the walls. Again, one learns from observation that two substances inside and outside a wall permeable to M_i will in general not stay unchanged in observable properties; rather, their properties will gradually change until they each come to states of compatible rest—equilibrium states. So just as the primitive notion of "temperature differences" can be built up out of crude observational experience, the primitive notion of Gibb's "differences in chemical potential of each mass" can be built up.

Until later, I ignore multivarious masses and concentrate on simple substances with a single M, encloseable in a volume of measurable V—for example, H_2O in liquid, gaseous, or solid form.

5. Overview

Here is a brief preview of my axiomatic procedure. Axiom 1 posits the existence of what familiar expositions call "isotherms." Axiom 2 posits the existence of a second set of observable contours, the "adiabatics." Axiom 3 posits a proportionality property of pressure-volume areas of the curvilinear parallelograms formed by intersections of the two families of contours. Axiom 2 has something of the conventional second law of thermodynamics in it; axiom 3 adds to the others much of the content of the first and second laws. Although the three axioms do together cover most of what holds for thermostatics (that is, for equilibrium states of compatible rest), they fail to determine a privileged zero-origin for Absolute temperature. Carnot's maximal efficiency between two Kelvin temperatures cannot be deduced from this triad of axioms. Yet the triad does define unique Absolute-temperature differences (called "canonical temperature"), canonical entropy, and canonical internal energy, whose differences *along adiabatics* will agree with

Joule's conventional internal energy (and which, by a unique choice of zero-origin for canonical temperature, we can make agree completely with Joule energy). So, if as axiom 4 I posit knowledge of one irreversible experiment—for example, knowledge of how much altitude an external weight loses in making a paddle wheel turn to stir a fluid enough to raise its pressure a small specified amount, while its volume is held constant—then my four-axiom system comes full circle and has all the properties of conventional macroscopic thermodynamics.[6]

6. "Zeroth" Law of Thermodynamics

Maxwell and Fowler emphasized that, if substance A is in temperature equilibrium with both B and C independently, then one can predict before observing the fact that B and C will stay in compatible equilibrium with each other after insulating walls between them are replaced by noninsulating walls. The same logical relationship (of things "equal" to a common thing being "equal" to each other) holds for pressure (and, for that matter, for the chemical potential of mass M_i, namely μ_i). Something more is involved here methodologically than the truth that holds for arithmetic scalars: $1 + 5 = 2 + 4$ and $3 + 3 = 2 + 4$ implies that $1 + 5 = 3 + 3$. It is a refutable hypothesis whether every observable state of a substance can be arrayed in a one-dimensional temperature ordering that can be put in unique correspondence to the one-dimensional temperature ordering of any other substance. And likewise with respect to the ways masses $(M_1, M_2, \ldots)$ interact across permeable walls. I leave moot whether the pressure a fluid exerts on its external environment can, by definition, be related from the beginning to the scale of arithmetic numbers so that there is no need for Maxwell's zeroth axiom to be separately assumed to hold for pressures.

7. Isotherms

A simple substance of unit mass cannot always have its equilibrium states uniquely defined by points in its (pressure, specific volume) space: $(p, V/M) \equiv (p, v)$. But if we make an inessential simplification of avoiding certain reversal phenomena (such as the reversal of water's contraction of volume at lower temperatures that occurs near its freezing temperature under ordinary room atmospheres), we can use the (p, v) space to frame our needed axioms.

AXIOM 1: There is an observable "equation of state." For any substance whose state is characterized by (p, v) coordinates, there exist one-dimensional contours of states that are compatibly in equilibrium when in contact with each other through rigid noninsulating walls. These loci, called *isotherms*, exist and can be written in the form

$$f(p, v) = \vartheta \quad \text{or} \quad F[f(p, v)] = F[\vartheta], \tag{7.1}$$

$$F'[\vartheta] > 0 \gtreqless F''[\vartheta]. \tag{7.2}$$

Similarly, between two or more substances, each of whose states are respectively characterized by (p_1, v_1), (p_2, v_2), ... coordinates, the equations of state for each imply when all are in contact through noninsulating walls that

$$f_1(p_1, v_1) = f_2(p_2, v_2) = \cdots = \vartheta \tag{7.3}$$

or

$$F[f_1(p_1, v_1)] = F[f_2(p_2, v_2)] = \cdots = F[\vartheta] \tag{7.4}$$

where the arbitrary stretching of one "empirical temperature" into another is given by $F[\vartheta]$, which has the property given in the relation 7.2.

Remarks: I could avoid working with even one arbitrary empirical temperature metric—ϑ, $F[\vartheta]$, $f_i(p_i, v_i)$, ...—by working with the observable invariant isotherm slopes:

$$\left(\frac{\partial p_i}{\partial v_i}\right)_{\text{temp}} = R_i(p_i, v_i). \tag{7.5}$$

Also, instead of choosing from $[p, v, \vartheta]$ the pair $[p, v]$ to specify the system's state, we could even more conveniently use $[\vartheta, v]$ as independent variables to specify its state. Then equation 7.3 would be written

$$p_1 = \Pi_1(\vartheta, v_1), \quad p_2 = \Pi_2(\vartheta, v_2), \ldots. \tag{7.6}$$

More complicated systems involving different chemical masses, with variables $(V, M_1, M_2, \ldots, p, \mu_1, \mu_2, \ldots)$, have further equations of state that are in principle identifiable by observation of what is required for states to be compatible in equilibrium when connected by permeable walls.

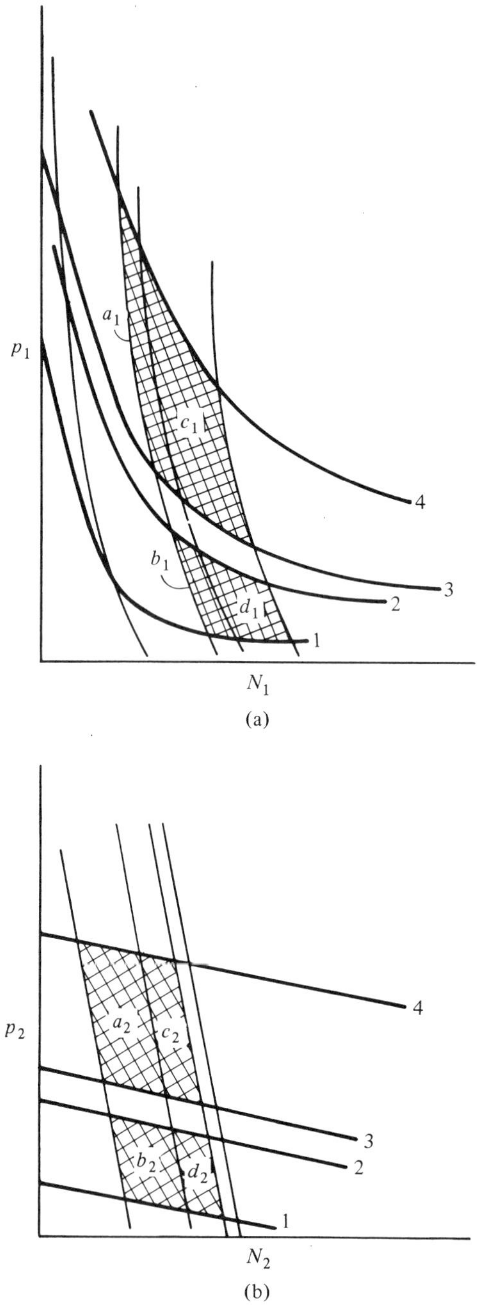

Figure 1
The four isotherms marked 1, 2, 3, and 4 for the substance in part a will respectively be in equilibrium with points on the four isotherms for the substance in part b. Each substance's four steeper adiabatics mark off with respective isotherms shaded areas that must have the proportionality property: $a_1/b_1 = c_1/d_1$ and $a_2/b_2 = c_2/d_2$. Also, between substances, areas formed by compatible isotherms must have the proportionality property: $a_1/b_1 = a_2/b_2$.

8. Adiabatic Contours

Figures 1a and 1b show dashed contours also. These are definable by specified operational procedures, and may be called adiabatics if none of the connotations familiar with that name are prematurely read into them.

Another name for any one of these contours would be this: Starting from an arbitrary point (p^0, v^0), the other points on its adiabatic contour are those frontier points that bound the region of (p, v) points that can never be reached from (p^0, v^0) when the substance is surrounded by perfectly insulating walls, no matter what mechanical work we do on the system—that is, no matter how we stir its fluids by paddle-wheel motions, or push its piston walls back and forth rapidly or indefinitely slowly.

It is a fact of nature—a fact about "irreversibility," if you wish—that adiabatics exist and can be taken as given by observation. Nature might have been constructed otherwise. So our second axiom asserts the existence of "adiabatic contours."

AXIOM 2: For each simple substance, there exist well-defined adiabatic contours in its (p_i, v_i) space. Thus, for any (p_i^0, v_i^0) initial point, there exist a set of points that could never be reached from it by any mechanical movement of its insulating walls or by any mechanical stirrings of its contents or other processes that can be performed on it by the use of external mechanical work. The remaining points in the (p_i, v_i) space can be reached from (p_i^0, v_i^0) by performing such external mechanical work on it. The limit points of this second "available set" form the one-dimensional adiabatic contour going through (p_i^0, v_i^0).

Mathematically, an empirical numbering of the adiabatics can be defined for each substance by the empirical functions

$$a_1(p_1, v_1) = \text{constants}, \quad a_2(p_2, v_2) = \text{constants}, \ldots \tag{8.1}$$

or by arbitrary monotone stretchings of any such empirical measures:

$$A_1[a_1(p_1, v_1)], A_2[a_2(p_2, v_2)], \ldots \tag{8.2}$$

$$A_i'[\ ] > 0 \gtreqless A_i''[\ ] \quad (i = 1, 2, \ldots). \tag{8.3}$$

Remarks: To avoid use of an arbitrary empirical numbering of the adiabatic contours, I could have worked with observable invariant adiabatic slopes in the (p_i, v_i) planes, namely with

$$0 \geq \left(\frac{\partial p_i}{\partial v_i}\right)_{ad} = \alpha_i(p_i, v_i) \quad (i = 1, 2, \ldots). \tag{8.4}$$

By use of limitingly slow movements of the surrounding insulating walls—that is, by what are called quasi-static, reversible movements—the exact shapes of the adiabatic contours could be determined experimentally. As an alternative to my exposition, if you had available to you Joule's first law of thermodynamics, ensuring the existence of an internal energy function, $u_i(p_i, v_1)$, then you could deduce the adiabatic slopes of equation 8.4 from the fact that the difference between u_i at two points on the same adiabatic must equal the integral $-\int p_i[x]v_i'[x]dx$, evaluated on the arc of the adiabatic between those points. This implies

$$\alpha_i(p_i, v_i) = \frac{-p_i - \partial u_i(p_i, v_i)/\partial v_i}{\partial u_i(p_i, v_i)/\partial p_i}. \tag{8.5}$$

The existence of the equation of state and its exact functional form, unlike those of the adiabatic, cannot be deduced from mere knowledge of $u_i(p_i, v_i)$—that is to say, it cannot be deduced from the first law of thermodynamics alone.

9. The Proportional-Area Property

Axioms 1 and 2, which assert the existence of knowable isotherms and adiabatics, do not exhaust the verifiable regularities of nature. Brute experience shows that isotherms and adiabatics are always related in a singular way involving a proportional-area property.

From the way things are, any four areas on the (p_i, v_i) diagram formed by intersections of any four isotherms with any four adiabatics must be in proportion. Thus, for the marked areas in figures 1a and 1b,

$$\frac{a_1}{b_1} = \frac{c_1}{d_1}, \quad \frac{a_2}{p_2} = \frac{c_2}{d_2}. \tag{9.1}$$

Moreover, if the four temperatures used are compatible ones between the two substances—so that points in each diagram on an isotherm marked with, say, 3 are in compatible thermal equilibrium with each other, and likewise for those on the respective isotherms marked 4—then between substances we must have

$$\frac{a_1}{b_1} = \frac{a_2}{b_2}. \tag{9.2}$$

This is a basic regularity of nature, which among other things could have been deduced from the conventional axioms concerning the first and second laws of thermodynamics. I begin with this observational fact as my axiom 3, which goes as follows.

AXIOM 3: The ("Carnot-circuit") areas defined between specified isotherms and adiabatics, as measured by $\int p[x]v'[x]dx$ integrals taken along the defined $(p[x], v[x])$ arcs, must have the equiproportionality property, both within a simple substance and between any two substances in compatible equilibria.

Axiom 3 is singularly restrictive on the facts. If nature had not displayed it, we should never have expected it to prevail. (To be sure, it would not be easy to imagine how the world would behave if it did admit of perpetual-motion machines of different kinds. A whimsical Einstein might assert that God could hardly have invented a different world, thereby answering Bohr's objection: "Who are we to tell Him his business?")

My overview noted that axioms 1–3 can generate the full set of thermostatic equilibrium relations that obtain in nature. But the point of my present selected order of imposition of axioms is to identify what observable facts of thermodynamics *cannot* be deduced from thermostatic equilibrium relations. In particular, a preferred origin of zero Absolute temperature cannot be deduced from axioms 1–3. We must add to them some subset of the (Carathéodory-Joule) first law of thermodynamics to be able to deduce a privileged Absolute Zero for canonical temperature and to be able to deduce a measurable "heat" and Carnot's coefficient of universal efficiency attainable at best between two specified empirical temperatures.

10. Diagrammatic Recapitulation

Figure 1a shows the isotherms and adiabatics for some specified mass of a gas. These contours look like those of a "perfect gas," but that coincidence plays no part in the development. (The facts that adiabatics must be steeper than the isotherms and that neither can be positively sloped constitute one version of the so-called Le Chatelier principle.) Figure 1a verifies the equiproportionality-of-areas property: $a_1/b_1 =$

a_2/b_2, and so on. Figure 1b shows isotherms and adiabatics for another simple substance. They are drawn as straight lines for expositional convenience only; but, locally, linearity is an admissible physical case. Again, figure 1b shows the $a_2/b_2 = c_2/d_2$ property of axiom 3.

When the two substances are in contact through noninsulating (rigid) walls, any isotherm of figure 1a is compatible with but one particular isotherm of figure 1b. Points on respective contours marked 1, 2, 3, and 4 in figure 1a are found by observation to be compatible in equilibrium with contours marked 1, 2, 3, and 4 in figure 1b.[7] It will be seen that, between the substances, axiom 3's area property is satisfied: a_1/b_1 is indeed equal to a_2/b_2 or to c_2/d_2.

Remark: When the isotherms alone are drawn on the diagram, there is no way to say when "one of them is halfway between two others." I could have used $1^2 = 1$, $2^2 = 4$, $3^2 = 9$, and $4^2 = 16$ to label the isotherms—then 9 would certainly not be "halfway" between 16 and and 4; and, actually, the isotherm marked 3 in figure 1a or 1b is not in any useful sense halfway between those marked 2 and 4.

The same lack of a natural metric holds for the adiabatics drawn by themselves. Only when axiom 3 interrelates them in its special way will our *p*-*v* areas provide a natural canonical metric for the isotherms (canonical temperature differences) and for the adiabatics (canonical "entropy" differences). (Although each numbered isotherm in figure 1a does relate exactly to the labeled isotherm in 1b, there is complete independence between 1a's and 1b's respective adiabatics.)

Figure 2a shows how the nonmetric empirical ordering, ϑ, can be converted into a privileged metric of canonical temperature, $T_c - T_c^0$:

$$T_c - T_c^0 = \Theta[\vartheta], \quad \Theta'[\;] > 0 \gtreqless 0 \tag{10.1}$$

where the $\Theta[\;]$ function is made definite by use of the horizontally shaded areas. We may choose our scale unit of canonical temperature arbitrarily—say, by calling the freezing point of water at standard atmospheric pressure 0 and its boiling point 1. (This convention is to hold as applied to other substances than water. Their canonical temperature is 0 when they are in equilibrium with icewater, even if their own melting point is much lower or higher.) Neither substance in figure 1a or 1b is water. Figure 2a's substance is the same as 1b's, as can be seen from its axes being labeled with (p_2, v_2).

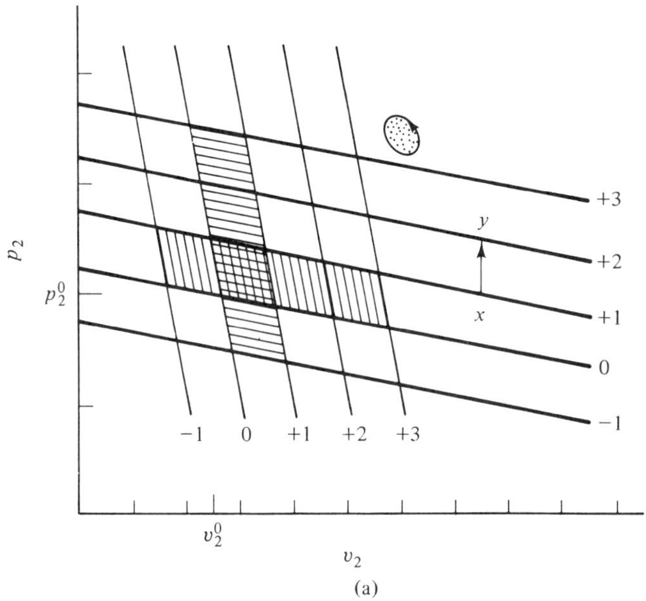

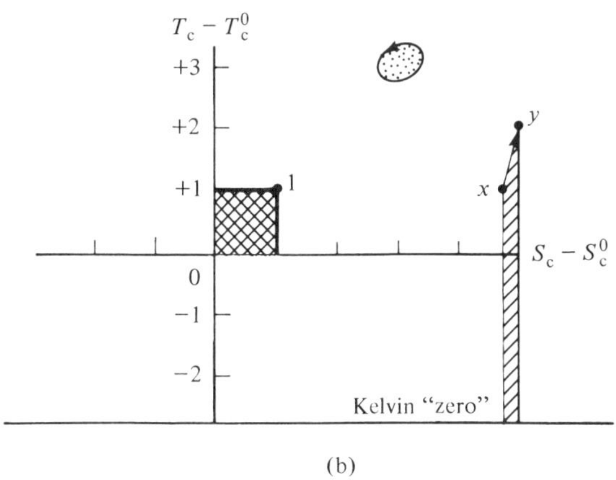

Figure 2
Part a of this figure is figure 1b, but now with the proportionality-of-area property used to define the metric of equally spaced isotherms and adiabatics. This gives the metrics for canonical temperature (shown in part b on the $T_c - T_c^0$ vertical axis) and canonical entropy (shown in part b on the horizontal axis). The area between the arbitrary "zero" point and the "unity" point must be the same in both diagrams, by construction. Every closed area in part a maps into a closed area in part b with the same area, by construction. Note the dot-shaded circular areas. To find a natural Kelvin "zero" that converts any canonical temperature to unique Absolute temperature, consider external Joule work observed to be required to move from x to y in part a (by frictional stirring or otherwise.) The xy arrow in part b must have the area under it equated to the Joule work measured, which provides the equation for $\bar{\theta}^*$ that makes $T_c - T_c^0 + \bar{\theta}^*$ equal to T.

Pick the (p_2^0, v_2^0) point marked "0" as our arbitrary origin for canonical temperature. Pick the (p_2^1, v_2^1) point marked "1" as our unit-scaling point. The doubly shaded area thus selected gives us our unit for canonical temperature (and, as we will see, for our canonical entropy and canonical "internal energy").

Using the two arbitrarily selected adiabatics, as we measure off the isotherms that divide their areas in equal amounts, as shown by the blocks, we deduce the canonical numberings +3, +2, +1, 0, and −1 for the isotherms. These are the defined canonical temperatures, $T - T^0$, for those isotherms; thus, the $\Theta[\vartheta]$ function in equation 10.1 can be defined as accurately as we wish.

Similarly, using the arbitrarily selected base isotherms, we can divide the areas between them into equal blocks of subareas with adiabatic boundaries, as shown by the vertically shaded blocks. Thus, we deduce the canonical numberings for the adiabatics: +3, +2, +1, +0, −1. Call this $s - s^0$, or, for substance 2, $s_2 - s_2^0$. (If the two substances are plotted with equal areas for their (0, 1) points, entropies will be dimensionally addable across substances.)

11. Canonical Internal Energy

Figure 2b plots the canonical (T_2^c, s_2) space. Every point in (p_2, v_2) maps into a unique (T_2^c, s_2), and vice versa. Moreover, by axiom 3's area property, the (T_2^c, s_2) space relates to the (p_2, v_2) space in the exact way to make the area inside any closed curve in 2a exactly equal to the area inside the implied closed curve in figure 2b. More precisely, by construction, the signed area formed by traversing the closed contour in figure 2a in the counterclockwise direction must exactly equal the signed area traversed by going in the counterclockwise direction around the implied closed contour in figure 2b.[8]

Mathematically, around closed arcs that map into each other on $0 \le x \le 1$, $(p[x], v[x])$, and $(T_c[x], s[x])$,

$$\int_0^1 p[x]v'[x]dx = \int_0^1 (T_c[x] - T_c^0)s'[x]dx. \tag{11.1}$$

(Here I have omitted the subscript 2 on p, v, T_c, and s, since axiom 3 makes this property hold for any substance.)

Around any closed arc of equilibrium-compatible points, the following line integral vanishes independent of path:

$$-\int \{p[x]v'[x]dx + (T_c[x] - T_c^0)s'[x]dx\} = 0. \tag{11.2}$$

Therefore, between any two points, such as $(p^0, v^0) = (p[x^0], v[x^0])$ and $(p, v) = (p[x], v[x])$, the following line integral is independent of the path connecting (p^0, v^0, T_c^0, s^0) and (p, v, T_c, s):

$$u_c^*(p, v) - u_c^*(p^0, v^0)$$
$$= \int_{x^0}^{x} \{-p[y]v'[y] + (T_c[y] - T_c^0)s'[y]\}dy. \tag{11.3}$$

Thus, axiom 3 enables us to define canonical (internal) energy differences as the sum of $\int -pdv$ and $\int (T_c - T_c^0)ds$ line integrals. As equation 11.3 shows, we can express all this as simple definite integrals of a single x variable.

Remark: Instead of specifying (p^0, v^0) and (p, v), we could have picked from (p, v, T_c, s) the specified pair (v, s) and written u_c^* as a function of them; or we could have specified the pair (T_c, v), and written u_c^* as a function of them; or we could have picked the pair (T_c, p) and written the internal energy (of the unit mass) as a function of them. Finally, just as we have been able to use (p, v) as our independent variables in regions where volume-temperature relations do not change direction, we could have picked (T_c, s) as the independent variables to define u^* in that region. Most generally, for a given mass, any one choice from the conjugate pairs $(-p, v)$ and (T_c, s) can be selected as independent variables; the $4 = 2^2$ pairs of independent variables that are always admissible then become (v, s), (v, T_c), $(-p, s)$, and $(-p, T_c)$.

12. Nonuniqueness of Canonical Energy Differences

There has been defined no natural, privileged zero for canonical temperature. Instead of T_c, we could use $T_c + \overline{\Theta}$, $-\infty < \overline{\Theta} < \infty$. Indeed, we can add to equation 11.3's integral an arbitrary linear term $\overline{\Theta}s'[x]$ and still get an (energy) integral that is independent of path. So it is natural to free ourselves from the tyranny of the particular (p^0, v^0) arbitrary origin that we happened to use. Instead of the unique, arbitrary $u^*(p, v)$ of equation 11.3, we can generalize to a one-parameter family of canonical internal energies:

$$u_c(p,v) - u_c(p^0,v^0) = u_c^*(p,v) - u_c^*(p^0,v^0) + \overline{\Theta}(s - s^0)$$
$$= \int \{-p[x]v'[x] + (T_c[x] - T_c^0 + \overline{\Theta})s'[x]\}dx. \tag{12.1}$$

A numerical example is illuminating. Consider figure 1a, whose isotherms and adiabatics resemble those of a "perfect gas." These isotherms and adiabatics can be given empirical numbers that respectively satisfy the following formulas:

$$pv = \text{constants} = \vartheta, \tag{12.2}$$

$$pv^3 = \text{constants} = \sigma. \tag{12.3}$$

Axiom 3's area proportionalities can be verified by elementary integrations. This assures us that, after we select a (p^0, v^0) as our local arbitrary origin and a (p^1, v^1) as our arbitrary unity point, we can define canonical temperature and canonical entropy by the following formulas:

$$T_c - T_c^0 = \frac{pv - p^0v^0}{p^1v^1 - p^0v^0}, \tag{12.4}$$

$$s - s^0 = \frac{\ln(pv^3) - \ln([p^0][v^0]^3)}{\ln([p^1][v^1]^3) - \ln([p^0][v^0]^3)}. \tag{12.5}$$

Then our $u^*(p,v)$ and our family of canonical internal energy functions can be defined by line integrals that are independent of path and yield

$$u^*(p,v) - u^*(p^0,v^0) = \frac{3}{2}\frac{pv - p^0v^0}{p^1v^1 - p^0v^0}, \tag{12.6}$$

$$u_c(p,v) - u_c(p^0,v^0) = u_c^*(p,v) - u^*(p^0,v^0)$$
$$= \frac{3}{2}\frac{pv - p^0v^0}{p^1v^1 - p^0v^0} + \overline{\Theta}\frac{\ln(pv^3/p^0[v^0]^3)}{\ln(p^1[v^1]^3/p^0[v^0]^3)}. \tag{12.7}$$

An engineer confronted with these formulas would simplify them by choosing to set

$$\overline{\Theta} = p^0v^0/(p^1v^1 - p^0v^0). \tag{12.8}$$

Then his canonical energy simplifies to be proportional to the product of p and v. But it is purely an accident that he can find for a "perfect gas" such a simplifying choice. How any actual substance (even a rarefied gas) will behave when very cold cannot be predicted from how much its volume shrinks between the boiling and freezing points of water.

Figure 2b shows how arbitrary are the $\int T_c ds$ areas in their dependence on where one bases the horizontal axis by arbitrarily choosing an origin for canonical temperature. The shaded area "under" the curve would have been much larger if a large $\overline{\Theta}$ had been arbitrarily added to $T_c - T_c^0$.

13. Joule Internal Energy

Joule's experimental vindication of the first law of thermodynamics can give us a privileged origin for canonical temperature. Joule established that, in moving any enclosed insulated system from one state (p_1^0, v_1^0) to another (p, v), always exactly the same external work (or sacrifice of external mechanical energy) is implied—no matter whether the movement is accomplished quickly or slowly, reversibly or irreversibly, quasi-statically or otherwise, and no matter whether the task is done by stirring fluids against friction, by moving walls against internal pressure, by generating electric currents that pass through resistances and warm up the internal fluids and solids, or by other means. Thus, Joule can in principle supply us with still another internal energy function. Call it $u_J(p,v) - u_J(p^0,v^0)$. It must not be confused with $u_c^*(p,v) - u_c^*(p^0,v^0)$. As yet, we have no warrant for identifying it with any one of the infinity of canonical energy functions defined in equation 12.1.

When I add a fourth axiom to axioms 1–3, I will be able to show that Joule internal energy is in fact one of our family of canonical energies. So, if we have even one small Joule (irreversible) experiment on any one substance or system of substances, we shall be able to identify a privileged $\overline{\Theta}^*$ to provide us with Kelvin's Absolute Zero for temperature. At long last, axioms 1–4 will cover essentially the same ground as conventional thermodynamics. I have shown we can get along with no use of the concept of "heat." Note that I never wrote down "Q", or "dQ", or "$đQ$", or "dQ/T". Though we do not need the "heat" concept for axioms 1–3, axiom 4 restores the right to use it wherever we find it useful.

But first we must add the axiom that, together with axioms 1–3, assures us that there will be a unique choice of $\overline{\Theta}^*$ that converts

$$\begin{aligned} u_J(p,v) - u_J(p^0,v^0) &\equiv u_c^*(p,v) - u_c^*(p^0,v^0) + \overline{\Theta}^*[s - s^0] \\ &\equiv u_c^*(p,v) - u_c^*(p^0,v^0) + \overline{\Theta}^*[s(p,v) - s(p^0,v^0)] \end{aligned} \tag{13.1}$$

into a valid entity.

14. The Final Axiom

Now, for the first time, consider the measurable amount of external work needed to move the system from one adiabatic to another (possibly to a close-by contour). Let $(p^{\dagger}, v^{\dagger})$ and $(p^{\dagger\dagger}, v^{\dagger\dagger})$ be on different adiabatics, and label the two points so that by external mechanical work operating through the insulated walls of the the system we can move from $(p^{\dagger}, v^{\dagger})$ to $(p^{\dagger\dagger}, v^{\dagger\dagger})$. Select units of work that agree with the units of $\int p\, dv$ integrals. Join the points by arcs

$$(p[x], v[x], (T_c[x] - T^0), s[x]), \quad 0 \leq x \leq 1$$

and let the work, $W_J[x]$, be an observable measurement.

Warning: How quickly or slowly Joule makes his measurements has nothing to do with the "speed" with which we traverse the arcs or with their geometric "lengths." $W_J[x]$ is taken to be observed. Its derivative, $W_J'[x]$, is taken to be an observable positive number, as for example $W_J'[0]$ at $x = 0$.

AXIOM 4: Select out of the one-parameter infinity of canonical energies the one that has its parameter $\overline{\Theta}^*$ in equation 12.1 such that it will agree with the measured Joule energy, $u_J(p, v) - u_J(p^0, v^0)$, or (what is the same thing) with $W_J[x]$, on the arc connecting $(p^{\dagger}, v^{\dagger})$ and $(p^{\dagger\dagger}, v^{\dagger\dagger})$. In particular, if we write $u_c^*(p[x], v[x]) - u_c^*(p^{\dagger}, v^{\dagger})$ as $W_c^*[x]$ and $u_c(p[x], v[x]) - u_c(p^{\dagger}, v^{\dagger})$ as $W_c[x] = W_c[x; \overline{\Theta}] = W_c^*[x] + \overline{\Theta}(s[x] - s^0)$, this imposes the single (point) condition to determine $\overline{\Theta}^*$ as the root of

$$W_c'[0] = W_c^{*\prime}[0] + \overline{\Theta}^* s'[0] = W_J'[0], \tag{14.1}$$

$$\overline{\Theta}^* = (W_J'[0] - W_c^{*\prime}[0])/s'[0]. \tag{14.2}$$

This uniquely identifies the $\overline{\Theta}^*$ that converts canonical temperature with its arbitrary origin into Kelvin Absolute temperature, T, with its natural origin. Specifically,

$$T = T_c - T_c^0 + \overline{\Theta}^*. \tag{14.3}$$

Axioms 1–4 imply that the chosen canonical energy agrees everywhere with the observable Joule energy:

$$u_c[p,v] - u_c^0[p^0,v^0]$$
$$= u_c^*[p,v] - u_c^*[p^0,v^0] + \overline{\Theta}^*[s(p,v) - s(p^0,v^0)]$$
$$\equiv u_J[p,v] - u_J[p^0,v^0]. \quad (14.4)$$

To see why, recall that the adiabatics that Joule's $u_J(p,v)$ would define must be the same ones that our $u_c(p,v)$'s will all define. The isotherms Joule's function will define, by the relation

$$\left(\frac{\partial U_J}{\partial s}\right)_v = T, \quad (14.5)$$

must yield the same observable equations of state defined by

$$\left(\frac{\partial u_c^*}{\partial s}\right)_v = T_c - T_c^0 \quad \text{or} \quad \left(\frac{\partial[u_c^* + \Theta^* s]}{\partial s}\right)_v = T_c - T_c^0 + \overline{\Theta}^*. \quad (14.6)$$

To see that my axioms 1–4 imply testable, refutable restrictions on the observations, note that they could be falsified if any exception to Joule's first law could be observed: If you could go from $(p^\dagger, v^\dagger)$ to $(p^{\dagger\dagger}, v^{\dagger\dagger})$ with two different expenditures of external mechanical work performed on the system surrounded by insulating walls, that would invalidate the system defined by axioms 1–4.

Figure 2b shows how the crucial $\overline{\Theta}^*$ can be determined from a single irreversible measurement. In the beginning we have no Absolute Zero axis at the bottom of figure 2b. We know from any elementary physics text that, on the Celsius scale, it should come at a distance below the melting point of water (marked "0" in figure 2a) that is about 2.7316 times the distance by which the melting point is below the boiling point of water (marked "1" in figure 2a).[9]

Now consider a Joule experiment that takes the system from x to y in figure 2a. Since the volumes are the same in this northward movement, and since by hypothesis the system is surrounded by an insulating wall, suppose that the transition occurs by a paddle wheel's stirring the fluid until it is warmed enough to raise its pressure from x to y. We measure how much external work in the form of a falling external weight is needed to turn the paddle wheel the requisite amount. We record the numerical external work, which Joule treats as the increment to his internal energy u_J.

By Axiom 4, that numerical work must equal an observable area in figure 2b. The arc *xy* in figure 2a maps into the arc *xy* in figure 2b. Under axiom 4, we must put our Absolute Zero axis for T_c (that is, for $T = T_c - T_c^0 + \overline{\Theta}^*$) just far enough below *ab* so that the area *zyxa* just equals our Joule experiment's numerical work. (Thereafter, axioms 1–4 enable us to predict the numerical results of all-new Joule experiments. The system is far from a tautology; it is a set of falsifiable hypotheses about reality.)

15. Additivity

Some axiomatic treatments of thermodynamics stipulate a separate axiom that entropy and energy be additive magnitudes. No fifth axiom to this effect need be stipulated in addition to the present axiom 1–4. Areas are addable. It comes as a theorem of the axiom system that entropies and internal energies are addable. Thus, twice the mass, M, at unchanged pressure (p) and unchanged temperature (ϑ or T), will imply twice the canonical entropies and energies. First-degree homogeneity applies to all the extensive functions:

$$S = Ms, \quad U_c = Mu_c, \quad V = Mv. \tag{15.1}$$

More specific,

$$s - s^0 = s(p, T) = (S - S^0)/M, \tag{15.2}$$

$$u_c - u_c^0 - u_c(p, T) - (U_c - U_c^0)/M, \tag{15.3}$$

$$v = v(p, T) = V/M. \tag{15.4}$$

Also, consider different masses of the same substance, $\overline{M}'$ and $\overline{M}''$, each contained with fixed volumes by rigid impermeable walls. If, first, the walls are insulating, the observed pressures and specific volumes, $(p', v'; p'', v'')$, are independent. What can we predict for equilibrium if, now, the rigid wall separating the two masses of the same substance is made to be noninsulating? Although the two subsystems' pressures can still differ, their temperatures must, in equilibrium, be equal. From the empirical equations of state, for $V'/M' = \overline{v}'$ and $V''/M'' = \overline{v}''$ given, we have

$$\vartheta = f(\overline{v}', p') = f(\overline{v}'', p''). \tag{15.5}$$

Here we have three unknowns (ϑ, p', p''), two known parameters $(\bar{v}', \bar{v}'')$, and only two equations. From the data given we are unable to determine a unique (p', p'') equilibrium. A one-dimensional continuum of admissible equilibria is determined by equation 15.5. Those same (p', p'') equilibria can be generated by an alternative formulation involving the canonical entropies and canonical energies of the two subsystems.

Every total of canonical entropies, $S' + S''$, must divide itself between the two subsystems so as to minimize the summed internal energies, $U' + U''$. The equilibria configurations of equation 15.5 all belong to the minimizing solution of the following problem:

$$\min_{p', p''} [\overline{M}' u_c^*(p', \bar{v}') + \overline{M}'' u_c^*(p'', \bar{v}'')]$$
$$\text{subject to } \overline{M}' s(p', \bar{v}') + \overline{M}'' s(p'', \bar{v}'')$$
$$= S \, (= S' + S''). \tag{15.6}$$

Call the minimized value $\mathscr{W}_c^*(\overline{V}'/\overline{M}', \overline{V}''/\overline{M}'', S, \overline{M}', \overline{M}'')$. Then, for every assigned total S, we have equilibrium solutions for $(p', p'', T_c - T_c^0)$ given by the envelope relations

$$p' = -\frac{\partial \mathscr{W}_c^*(\bar{v}', \bar{v}'', S, \overline{M}', \overline{M}'')}{\partial \bar{v}'},$$
$$p'' = -\frac{\partial \mathscr{W}_c^*(\bar{v}', \bar{v}'', S, \overline{M}', \overline{M}'')}{\partial \bar{v}''}, \tag{15.7}$$
$$T_c - T_c^0 = \frac{\partial \mathscr{W}_c^*(\bar{v}', \bar{v}'', S, \overline{M}', \overline{M}'')}{\partial S}.$$

If we like, we can replace $u_c^*[\ ]$ by $u_c[\ ] = u^* + \overline{\Theta}(s - s^0)$. This adds to $\mathscr{W}^*(\ )$ the term $\overline{\Theta}(S - S^0)$, and to $T_c - T_c^0$ the term $\overline{\Theta}$. If $\overline{\Theta} = \overline{\Theta}^*$, so that $u_c(\ )$ becomes Joule's $u_J(\ )$, the same formalism holds.

16. Time Rise in Entropy

Instead of minimizing $U' + U''$ for fixed $S' + S''$, so long as $\overline{\Theta}$ is enough positive to keep $T - T^0 + \overline{\Theta}$ positive we can as well maximize entropy, $S' + S''$, for fixed total energy, $U' + U''$, and generate the same equilibria. Which is a better formulation? At the level of thermostatics it makes no difference, since the same infinity of $(p', p'', T_c - T_c^0)$ points represent the possible equilibria respecting the equation of state and the assigned specific volumes. But it does make a difference if dynamically we are to be able to predict the actual unique terminal state that a prescribed initial state will spontaneously lead to.

For temporal movements, from a prior equilibrium to a new equilibrium achieved dynamically spontaneously and under assurance that no external work has been done on the combined system, the combined total Joule internal energy of the system may be dynamically assumed to remain constant in time. If that can be stipulated—and to do so takes us outside of the thermostatics here axiomatized—then it will be seen to be more convenient to maximize summed entropy for the assigned initial summed Joule internal energy. (Warning: Now we must use $u_J(\ )$'s, not any old one of the $u_c(\ )$'s.)

Return to the system just discussed, which has masses $\overline{M}'$ and $\overline{M}''$ of the same substance. First, it has them in rigid, impermeable insulating walls that define fixed specific volumes $(\overline{v}', \overline{v}'')$ and permit unequal temperatures. Our four unknowns begin at $(p_a', \vartheta_a'; p_a'', \vartheta_a'')$.

Now let the connecting wall be made noninsulating. Eventually, in brute fact, the system will change dynamically, from initial a, until it comes to rest at a rendezvous terminal equilibrium, b $(p_b', \vartheta_b' = \vartheta_b'', p_b'')$. Axioms 1–4 do not have enough dynamic content to answer this specific question about behavior over real time. But if we are told dynamically that summed Joule internal energy cannot change in the absence of external work done on the system, that will provide the minimal new knowledge about dynamic behavior over time to enable us to reduce equation 15.5's or 15.7's one-dimensional continuum of admissible equilibrium rendezvous to the single true physical rendezvous.

How? If the minimized $U_J' + U_J''$ in equation 15.5 must have the same total as the given initial $U_J' + U_J''$, namely $\overline{M}'u_J(\overline{v}', p_a') + \overline{M}''u_J(\overline{v}'', p_a'')$—for the reason that external mechanical energy has not been changed—then we can solve for the unique S in equations 15.6 and 15.7 that satisfies this requirement. That is, we can solve for S_b the implicit equation

$$\mathscr{W}_J(\overline{v}', \overline{v}'', S, \overline{M}', \overline{M}'') = \overline{M}'u_J(\overline{v}', p_a') + \overline{M}''u_J(\overline{v}', p_a''). \tag{16.1}$$

Then, putting this S_b into equation 15.7 gives us our unique terminal equilibrium state $(p_b', p_b'', \vartheta_b)$.

Rather than solve an implicit equation, we can more elegantly utilize the maximum-entropy formulation:

$$\mathscr{S}(\bar{v}',\bar{v}'',\bar{U}_J,\overline{M}',\overline{M}'') = \operatorname*{Max}_{p',p''}[\overline{M}'s(p',\bar{v}') + \overline{M}''s(p'',\bar{v}'')] \tag{16.2}$$

subject to

$$\overline{M}'u_J(p',\bar{v}') + \overline{M}''u_J(p'',\bar{v}'') = \overline{M}'u_J(p'_a,\bar{v}') + \overline{M}''u_J(p''_a,v''_a) = \bar{U}_J.$$

Then the following envelope relations give our proper unique terminal equilibrium:

$$p'_b = \frac{\partial\mathscr{S}(\bar{v}',\bar{v}'',\bar{U}_J,\overline{M}',\overline{M}'')/\partial\bar{v}'}{\partial\mathscr{S}(\bar{v}',\bar{v}'',\bar{U}_J,\overline{M}',\overline{M}'')/\partial\bar{U}_J}, \tag{16.3}$$

$$p''_b = \frac{\partial\mathscr{S}(\bar{v}',\bar{v}'',\bar{U}_J,\overline{M}',\overline{M}'')/\partial v''}{\partial\mathscr{S}(\bar{v}',\bar{v}'',\bar{U}_J,\overline{M}',\overline{M}'')/\partial\bar{U}_J}, \tag{16.4}$$

$$T^{-1} = \partial\mathscr{S}(\bar{v},\bar{v},\bar{U}_J,\overline{M}',\overline{M}'')/\partial\bar{U}_J. \tag{16.5}$$

The same formalism would enable us to predict where the system will reach a third equilibrium if, after it is at rest at b, we unlock its rigid separating wall and let its subvolumes adjust until pressure equality obtains as well as temperature equality. The variables v' and v'' then adjust to maximize $S' + S''$ for unchanged $U'_J + U''_J$ and $V' + V''$.

17. Nonsimple Systems

So far I have been considering simple substances. Each is simple because its state depends only on the variables V, S, M, with intensive properties that depend only on specific variables $(V/M, S/M) = (v, m)$. Readers of Born and Carathéodory will suspect that my two-variable systems enabled me to avoid the complexity of Pfaffian differential expressions and the problem of whether they satisfy "integrability conditions" and can be made to be proportional to exact differentials. That suspicion is only partially justified. Thus, as soon as I consider equilibria between two or more simple substances, each contained within its impermeable walls or even between subsystems that involve a single simple substance, my functions are already in a space of variables with dimensionality much greater than 2. If I wrote down the usual Pfaffian for such systems, they would indeed be testable for integrability conditions of the type that interested Carathéodory explicitly and conventional physicists implicitly. The point I must make is this: Axioms 1–3 do imply, as theorems, the requisite independence-of-path integrals in the higher-than-two-dimensional spaces.

Still, a word is needed for systems that are neither themselves simple substances nor equilibrium combinations of enclosed simple substances. Thus, consider chemical problems where two or more different chemical masses (M_1 for hydrogen and M_2 for oxygen, for example) interact. They (and their implied chemical compounds) share a volume and provide the observer with a fluid whose pressure and (empirical) temperature depend on more than two specific variables. Thus, 7.3's equation of state might now have to be written as

$$\vartheta = F(p; V, M_1, M_2) \equiv F(p; 1, M_1/V, M_2/V). \tag{17.1}$$

Now that we have added a new intrinsic variable, a second independent equation of state will be observable. In conventional terms, what Gibbs called "chemical potentials"—(μ_1, μ_2), corresponding respectively to (M_1, M_2)—are new variables an observer could measure. (Remark: Conventionally, the measurable Joule energy function would be used, but here axioms 1–4 could be used after natural generalizations.)

The second independent equation of state might be observed as

$$\lambda_1 = \phi(p; V, M_1, M_2) = \phi(p; 1, M_1/V, M_2/V). \tag{17.2}$$

Finally, brute experimentation could be taken as establishing adiabatic contours in the $(p, M_1/V, M_2/V)$ space. For any point (p^0, m_1^0, m_2^0) in that space, two mutually exclusive sets of (p, m_1, m_2) are determinable. The first set is the points that cannot be reached from (p^0, m_1^0, m_2^0) by any expenditure of external mechanical work; the second set is those points that can be so reached. (The process of reaching them involves what is conventionally called an irreversible process, but that need not detain us.) The frontier separating these sets (whose points technically belong to the first set) defines the adiabatic contours.

The existence of these adiabatics is a question of physics, not of Pfaffian mathematics. We might just as well axiomatize their existence, as I did in the two-dimensional case, where there never arises the mathematical "integrability conditions" (to ensure the existence of an "integrating factor" that converts a Pfaffian differential form into an "exact differential").

The adiabatic contours, assumed given to the logician by empirical observations, are of the form

$$A(p; M_1/V, M_2/V, \ldots) = \text{constants} = \bar{A}. \tag{17.3}$$

With even empirical numberings of the contours eschewed, adiabatic contours can be defined by their observable slope functions:

$$\left(\frac{\partial p}{\partial m_1}\right)_{\text{ad}} = A^1(p, m_1, m_2),$$

$$\left(\frac{\partial p}{\partial m_2}\right)_{\text{ad}} = A^2(p, m_1, m_2), \tag{17.3'}$$

. . . .

From axiom 2's postulated existence of equation 17.3, we have implied the following integrability conditions:

$$\alpha_{ji} = \alpha_{ij} = \frac{\partial A^i(p; m_1, m_2, \ldots)}{\partial m_i} - A^j(p; m_1, m_2, \ldots)\frac{\partial A^i(p; m_1, m_2, \ldots)}{\partial p} \tag{17.4}$$

where $[\alpha_{ij}]$ is assumed to be an observably symmetric matrix.

Here is a sketch of how the new axiom system must go for nonsimple as well as simple systems.

AXIOM 1: Independent equations of state are observable, and are as numerous as different chemical masses.

AXIOM 2: A set of adiabatic contours is observable, as in equation 17.3.

AXIOM 3: The different contours of axioms 1 and 2 cannot be independent of each other, but instead must be interrelated so that generalized areas and volumes respect observable proportionality conditions. These imply that conjugate canonical entropy and canonical temperature variables $[S_c - S_c^0, T_c - T_c^0]$ are definable by path-independent integrals

$$\int (T_c[x] - T_c^0) S_c'[x]dx - \int \left(p[x]dV + \sum_{j=1}^{J} \lambda_j[x] M_j'[x] \right) dx \tag{17.5}$$

independent of the arc path that joins $(p^0, V^0, M_1^0, M_2^0, \ldots, M_J^0)$ to $(p, V, M_1, M_2, \ldots, M_J)$. The important point is that the (T_c, S) variables so defined must be invariant monotone stretchings of the observable (arbitrarily defined) empirical numberings of the respective isotherms and adiabatics of equations 17.1 and 17.3[10]

Space prevents me from considering other nonsimple systems. Besides chemical systems, magnetic and electric systems and still more general systems can also be made subject to thermodynamic axioms. We augment the extensive variables $(V, S, M_1, M_2, \ldots)$ to any set $(Y_1, Y_2, Y_3, Y_4, Y_5, \ldots)$; at the same time the former's conjugate intensive variables

$(-p, T, \mu_1, \mu_2, \ldots)$ are augmented to the general set of variables conjugate to $(Y_1, Y_2, \ldots)$, namely $(y_1, y_2, \ldots)$. Legendre transformations, and various formalisms involving mixed functions

$$\phi(Y_1, \ldots, Y_r; y_{r+1}, \ldots, y_J) - \sum_1^r y_j Y_j + \sum_{r+1}^{j} Y_j y_j,$$

can be shown to apply. The letter and spirit of my three or four Axioms require only various natural adaptations.

18. Conclusion

Space limits force heuristic brevity. In the end, one's admiration for conventional pre-Carathéodory thermodynamics is enhanced. And it is gratifying to see that this most elegant paradigm of nature, thermostatics and thermodynamics, can be antiseptically formulated solely in terms of the observable measurements. It is now clear that, by an independent path, economic theory has arrived at an isomorphic logical structure.

Acknowledgments

I owe thanks to the National Science Foundation for financial aid and to Aase Huggins for editorial assistance.

Notcs

1. Frisch and Tinbergen had used the closely related word *macrodynamics*. In physics, particularly in relating thermodynamics and statistical mechanics, *microscopic* and *macroscopic* had been familiar since the mid-nineteenth century at least. Thus, Maxwell, Boltzmann, Poincaré, Lohnschmidt, Zermelo, Ehrenfest, and others wrestled with the paradox that objects that are subject to time-reversible laws at the microscopic level somehow seem at the macroscopic level to be characterized by time-asymmetric properties (such as necessary increase in entropy with the passage of time). I can remember arguing in Gottfried Haberler's 1936 Harvard seminar how Carl Menger's methodological dictum, that economic theory must build on individual's behavior, might be valid at the microsoopic level without contradicting the possible usefulness of macroscopic regularities. Professor Hendrik Houthakker has verified my surmise of a reference to macroeconomics antedating 1946, namely Pieter de Wolff (1941).

2. Klein (1946a) evoked useful replies from Kenneth May (1946) and Shou Shan Pu (1946), to which he replied in Klein 1946b. At about the same time, independently, Leontief (1946, 1947) was exploring requirements for weak and strong separability. Subsequently a vast literature on aggregation emerged, associated with R. M. Solow, H. A. J. Green, H. Theil, W. M. Gorman, P. A. Samuelson, F. M. Fisher, J. V. Robinson, John Chipman, and many others.

3. I am not able to judge whether the empirical reliability has or has not been greater for macro models that try to follow economic theory in specifying their relations. Some *ad hoc* models without theoretical underpinnings have worked tolerably well. Some models based on theory have performed badly. What the preponderance of experience has been I do not know.

4. If stochastic elements are involved, tastes for risk would have also to be uniformly homothetic; since each person has only 24 hours a day, it would seem to be hard to make tastes for leisure (as against work) fit into a homothetic framework.

5. In theoretical economics there is no "irreversibility" concept, which is one reason Georgescu-Roegen (1971) is critical of conventional economics. I have benefited over the years from discussions with MIT colleagues, particularly Laszlo Tisza and the late Joseph Keenan. Edwin Bidwell Wilson, Willard Gibb's last assistant, was my teacher at Harvard, and to him I owe my interest in the formal relations between economics and thermodynamics. Although I learned of the Carathéodory formulation years after my own ideas were formed, his approach is the one I find most congenial, even though I think there is some merit in considering at least once the present alternative to it. My present exposition overlaps, but goes beyond, my axiomatic appendix on thermodynamics in the Harold Hotelling *Festschrift* (Samuelson 1960). For the Carathéodory approach, see Carathéodory 1909, 1925; Born 1921, 1949; and Wilson 1957. The last takes notice of Norman Ramsey's "negative temperature" (negative T^{-1}) for spin systems, a possibility here ignored.

6. Of course, Nernst's so-called third law of thermodynamics requires separate stipulation concerning how the contours behave as the system becomes ever colder.

7. It could even be the case that, in figure 1b, the numbers 1, 2, 3, and 4 could be *reversed* in order: the colder 1b's substance, the greater could be its volumes at fixed pressures—as with water near its freezing point.

8. Must the closed arc be traversed limitingly slowly, so that the movement is a quasi-static reversible one? Such a question comes naturally to those familiar with the conventional axiomatic treatments. But once one understands the alternative present approach, one sees that all we are doing is measuring magnitudes defined by paired equilibrium states. Our computer can run the arcs as quickly as it pleases; there is no necessary correspondence between the $-\int pdv$ calculations and any real-time "cycle" of any physical "engine." The reversibility-irreversibility issue has no further relevance once we are given adiabatic contours. (This does not mean that axiom 4 will not reintroduce at least one physical measurement along what is an irreversible movement in real time. When a paddle wheel does work against friction and changes a fluid's temperature, you cannot physically reverse that action. But what does a well-defined integral $\int f(x)dx$ care about that?)

9. Warning: Figures 1b and 2a do not refer to water. For example, water would have horizontal isotherms around its "O" melting temperature where ice and water coexist as phases, rather than having the negatively sloped parallel isotherms shown in figure 2a. Nonetheless, for the actual substance shown in 2a, the zero and unity reference states have been selected to be those that would be in temperature and pressure equilibrium with water at freezing and evaporating points under standard atmospheric pressure.

10. I have here taken the Gibbs $(\lambda_1, \ldots, \lambda_5)$ as observable magnitudes. More fundamentally, we might treat them the way we do empirical temperature, ϑ. When any equation of state 17.2 is not satisfied, we observe a dynamic flow of mass through semipermeable or permeable walls; static equilibrium is observed only when equation 17.2 is satisfied. So we can infer an empirical scale of each λ_j, namely

$$\vartheta_j = \Theta_j[\lambda_j], \quad \Theta_j'[\ ] > 0 \gtreqless \Theta_j''[\ ], \quad (j = 0, 1, \ldots, J).$$

Expanding the $\vartheta_0 = \vartheta$, empirical temperature specification of axiom 3, we would have to specify logical conditions that guarantee independence of path for integrals of the form

$$\int\left(-p[x]V'[x]+\sum_{1}^{j}\Theta_j^{-1}[\vartheta_j]M_j'[x]+\Theta_0^{-1}[\vartheta]G'[\bar{A}]\right)dx.$$

These are generalized proportionality-of-area properties. Such properties are "in-the-large integrability condition." So in the end the present approach does seem to reduce to much the same logic as the admirable Carathéodory system. Multiplying axioms is not a sign of decadence or inelegance; the point is to unbundle the separable contents of the final axiom system—to show the independence of the separate axioms and recognize the wider models that would satisfy various subsets of the axioms.

Bibliography

Born, M. 1921. Critical reflections on the traditional exposition of thermodynamics. *Phys. Z.* 22 : 218, 249, 282.

Born, M. 1949. *Natural Philosophy of Cause and Chance.* Oxford: Clarendon. Chapter 5, appendixes 6–10.

Carathéodory, C. 1909. Investigations on the foundation of thermodynamics. *Math. Ann.* 67 : 355.

Carathéodory, C. 1925. The determination of the internal energy and the absolute temperature by means of reversible processes. *S. B. Preuss. Akad. Wiss.* 39.

de Wolff, P. 1941. Income elasticity of demand, a micro-economic and a macro-economic interpretation. *Economic Journal* 51 : 140–145.

Evans, G. C. 1930. *Introduction to Mathematical Economics.* New York: McGraw-Hill.

Evans, G. C. 1934. Maximum production studied in a simplified economic system. *Econometrica* 2: 37–50.

Georgescu-Roegen, N. 1971. *The Entropy Law and the Economic Process.* Cambridge, Mass.: Harvard University Press.

Gorman, W. M. 1953. Community preference fields. *Econometrica* 21: 63–80.

Hatsopoulos, G. N., and J. H. Keenan. 1965. *Principles of General Thermodynamics.* New York: Wiley.

Hicks, J. R. 1939. *Value and Capital.* Oxford: Clarendon.

Klein, L. R. 1946a. Macroeconomics and the theory of rational behavior. *Econometrica* 14: 93–108.

Klein, L. R. 1946b. Remarks on the theory of aggregation *Econometrica* 14: 303–312.

Leontief, W. W. 1936. Composite commodities and the problem of index numbers. *Econometrica* 4: 39–59.

Leontief, W. W. 1946. A note on the interrelation of subsets of independent variables of a continuous function with continuous first derivatives. *Bull. Am. Math. Soc.* 53: 343–350.

Leontief, W. W. 1947. Introduction to a theory of the internal structure of functional relationships. *Econometrica* 15: 361–373.

May. K. O. 1946. The aggregation problem for a one-industry model. *Econometrica* 14: 285–298.

Pu, Shou Shan. 1946. A note on macroeconomics. *Econometrica* 14: 229–302.

Samuelson, P. A. 1947. *Foundations of Economic Analysis.* Cambridge, Mass.: Harvard University Press.

Samuelson, P. A. 1956. Social indifference curves. *Q. J. Econ.* 70: 1–22.

Samuelson, P. A. 1960. Structure of a minimum system. In Hotelling *Festschrift*, ed. R. W. Pfouts. Charlotte: University of North Carolina Press. Reproduced as chapter 44 in *Collected Scientific Papers of Paul A. Samuelson* (Cambridge, Mass.: MIT Press, 1966).

Samuelson, P. A. 1966. *Collected Scientific Papers*. Cambridge, Mass.: MIT Press. Volume 1, chapters 42, 43, 44, appendix to chapter 44.

Samuelson, P. A. 1968. Two generalizations of the elasticity of substitution. In *Value, Capital and Growth* (Hicks *Festschrift*), ed. J. N. Wolfe. Edinburgh University Press.

Samuelson, P. A. 1979. Paul Douglas's measurement of production functions and marginal productivities. *J. Pol. Econ.* 87: 923–939.

Sonnenschein, H. 1972. Market excess demand functions. *Econometrica* 40: 549–563.

Theil, H. 1957. Linear aggregation in input-output analysis. *Econometrica* 25: 346–349.

Tisza, L. 1966. *Generalized Thermodynamics*. Cambridge, Mass.: MIT Press.

Wilson, A. H. 1957. *Thermodynamics and Statistical Mechanics*. Cambridge University Press. Chapter 4.

PART II

Marx, Keynes, and Schumpeter

1983: MARX, KEYNES AND SCHUMPETER*

Paul A. Samuelson

The cloth of history is woven with an endless seam. I myself knew a man who knew a man who had known Napoleon. Newton was born the year that Galileo died. Both John Maynard Keynes and Joseph A. Schumpeter were born in 1883, the year that Karl Marx died.

Thünen's Bicentennial

Actually 1983 gives us four anniversaries to commemorate. Along with those of Keynes, Schumpeter and Marx, we have this June the bicentennial of Johann Heinrich von Thünen. Thünen's life exactly parallels that of Schumpeter but for a century: 1783 rather than 1883 for birth; 1850 rather than 1950 for death. Thünen is the least known of the four scholars even though as a microeconomist he is the greatest of them all. I have in mind not merely that Thünen clearly anticipated the spirit and the letter of John Bates Clark's marginal productivity theory of distribution -- which Thünen certainly did do half a century before Clark. What is insufficiently recognized is the grandeur of Thünen's general equilibrium model.

In 1803, before Thünen was legally old enough to drink or vote, already he had the vision of a central town surrounded by a homogeneous endless plain. Using data from his own Junker estate, Thünen deduced the rings of specialization that competition would establish around the town. Nearest to town, on the high-rent limited acres there, rural goods most expensive to transport will be grown. Farther out will come goods cheaper to transport. Land rent will fall steadily with radial distance from town, until rent reaches zero at the external margin of farthest cultivation. This complicated problem in nonlinear programming, involving an uncountable infinity of variables, Thünen understood would get solved by the algorithm of competition. Elsewhere, Samuelson 1983, I have provided the modern reformulation of Thünen that has been long overdue. And therefore I desist tonight from further mention of Thünen -- except to serve warning that no present-day economist should be put off by his weird doctrine of the natural wage as the geometric mean of labor's subsistence wage and its average product.

The Genius of Keynes

It is hard to ride three horses at once. Should I give 15 minutes to Marx, and then 15 minutes to each of Keynes and Schumpeter, leaving 5 minutes at the end for graceful wrapup? Or, rather, should I run down a list of points and compare the three of them?

Which scholar was the tallest? Which the shortest? History does not record Karl Marx's height and a close reading of the vast biographical literature can only permit the guess that Karl was the shortest and Maynard the tallest.

*Distinguished Lecture presented at the Tenth Annual Meeting of the Eastern Economic Association, March 10, 1983, Boston, Mass. Samuelson is Professor of Economics, Massachussetts Institute of Technology Cambridge, Mass. 02139. The editorial assistance of Aase Huggins and the Sloan Foundation for partial support is acknowledged.

It is a matter of record that Schumpeter and Keynes left no legitimate offspring. Although to Eleanor Marx, Karl's and Jenny's youngest daughter, it was dreadfully important that Karl and not Friedrich Engels fathered the illegitimate son of the Marx family's housekeeper, the only interest we have in this matter today is in calibrating commentators on Marx by how they handle this incident.

Even better to judge a new biographer Marx is to examine how he deals with Marx's antisemitism. Keynes, Schumpeter and Marx all displayed some of the racial bigotries of their respective times and circles. Since we have a more complete sample of Marx's correspondence, our modern sensibilities are most offended by his tasteless remarks about Ferdinand Lasalle's hair color and texture. But evidence of selfhate among assimilating members of minority groups is by now an old story. More interesting is how each biographer explains or explains away the young Marx's identification of predatory capitalistic behavior as peculiarly associated with Judaism.

My primary interest is in our heroes' scholarship not their pulchritude or social manners. From this viewpoint it does not matter that Keynes could be rude, that he wore loud brown shoes, and was to himself ugly. Or that Schumpeter was courtly, and Marx sometimes difficult. All three were billiant, recognized early to be precocious. That Schumpeter by the age of 30 should have written three great books and received a Columbia honorary degree is truly remarkable. Bertrand Russell, as brilliant a mind as philosophy and mathematics can offer, testified that Maynard Keynes was the most brilliant conversationalist he ever heard. Higher praise than that is not possible. Long before Karl Marx had found his vocation, Moses Hess described him as the coming man of the new generation.

All three men were prodigious workers. Russell believed Keynes worked himself to an early death. Despite his pretence of never working hard, I can testify that Joseph Schumpeter drove himself hard, working every weekend, summer, and at night after keeping tedious office hours for mediocre students. Karl Marx strained his own health with incessant sedentary study; and his inability in the final 15 years of his life to get Das Capital finished must be attributed not to lack of effort but rather to sheer inability to make good his intention of explaining the rate of competitive profit by means of his idiosyncratic paradigm concerining the rate of surplus value.

Which of the three was the greatest economist? That is a naive question. But if you insist on asking it, my considered reply would have to be that John Maynard Keynes was scientifically the greatest economist of this century. Only Adam Smith and Léon Walras can be mentioned in the same breath with him. Karl Marx can be mentioned in the same breath with Mohammed and Jesus, but it is of scientific scholarship that I speak and not of political movements and ideology.

Without Joseph Schumpeter, valuable insights into the laws of motion of political change and economic development would be lost to us, along with one strand of business-cycle theorizing. Without Schumpeter we would know less about our subject's history. Still the 1983 corpus of economic science would not be qualitatively different from what it is now. Whereas, without the shift in analytical paradigm that Keynes exploded in the 1930s, one could not even phrase the modern defenses of Say's Law or the critiques of Keynesianism that are so important a part of today's economics.

Thus, when at long last Milton Friedman came to write down in the 1970 Journal of Political Economy what his monetarism was analytically, it turned out to be one specialization of the general Keynesian identities and behavior functions and not a very plausible one at that. The goatskins that contained the old wine were of post-1933 fabrication. When Benjamin Friedman analyzed in 1976 what the monetarists Karl Brunner and Allen Meltzer said their preferred theory was, again the paradigmatic equations were of a formal structure never seen in the pre-1933 literature -- and revealed themselves to be qualitatively indistinguishable from the models of the Keynesian James Tobin.

Post Keynes, ergo different from neoclassical macroeconomics. I know. I was there. I heard the University of Chicago tradition -- heard it from the lips of Frank Knight, Jacob Viner, Henry Simons, Lloyd Mints, Aaron Director, Milton Friedman, George Stigler, and Albert Hart. My hearing was good and I was a devout Yeshiva student, a dedicated Jesuit. Believe me, Don Patinkin is right. There was less there than met the ear. Dennis Robertson's Cambridge handbook on Money, and Alfred Marshall's unitary-elasticity demand for money were the alpha and omega of that allegedly subtle oral tradition. At the LSE and Harvard, the same macro economics prevailed.

A.C. Pigou put the matter well. In order to understand the macroeconomic world and to refute Keynes' extreme hypothesis of permanent unemployment equilibrium, Pigou had to replace his own Theory of Unemployment modes of analysis in favor of new modes never dreamed of in the pages of Léon Walras (or of the Gerard Debreu memoirs to come.)

Albert Einstein admitted the explanatory power of quantum mechanics as developed by Planck, Einstein himself, Bohr, Schrodinger, Heisenberg, and Born. But Einstein remained convinced that the probability notions of quantum theory did not say the last word on the subject. I suspect that 1999 post-Keynesian eclecticism will be as different from the 1983 variety as that variety is different from the 1939 version. If Einstein turns out to be right, Planck and Heisenberg will not be stripped of their greatness.

Keynes' role in the history of our subject is equally secure. That is why, when Time magazine asked me if Keynes is dead, I replied: Yes, Keynes is dead. And so are Newton and Darwin.

Marx's Serendipitous Beef with Smith

Enough of praise for Keynes. It is Karl Marx who needs refurbishing with mainstream economists. Marx gets too good a press with noneconomists. In consequence we economists miss noticing his one considerable theoretical achievement.

If you retain one thing from this lecture, let it be the following solemn admonition. NEVER MAKE A JOKE. This is as fatal in science as it is in politics.

My pen once referred to Karl Marx as "..a minor post-Ricardian .. a not uninteresting precursor of Leontief's input-output ..." That was worse than a crime. It was a blunder. So sincere a scholar as Maurice Dobb went to his grave, knowing that he could have nothing to learn from so frivolous a pen. That I consider a pity, since I regard Marx as a scholar deserving of analysis on his objective merits and without regard to the deification or denigration meted out to him in various regions and ideologies.

In the Festschrift for Lloyd Metzler, Samuelson 1974 , I appraised Marx as a mathematical economist, eschewing Michio Morishima's hyperbole but hailing Marx's most original contribution in Capital's Volume II Tableaus of Simple and Expanded Reproduction. Marx's critics have missed this achievement, while at the same time his partisans have been praising his sterile paradigm that seeks to understand the general level of macroeconomic profit by means of the detour through the irrelevant swamp of equal-percentage-markup of wages in every industry.

Only after years of reflection did I come to realize that Marx was led to his tableau breakthrough by error. In all four volumes of Capital, Marx struggled against what he considered to be a fatal flaw in Adam Smith's theory.[1] Smith said often:

> Price of any product breaks into its wage component, interest component, and rent component. A nation's total income is the sum of all such components -- the wages its labor earns, the rent its land earns, the interest earned on its stock of capital. (Uncertainty and stochastic complications are here being ignored, so that competition is perfect and the interest rate and the profit rate are the same thing.)

Nonsense, replied Marx. The price of corn, along with wages-rent-interest, includes the cost of the farmer's seed, his horses, and other used-up instruments of husbandry. Four components, not three, make up Marx's price.

Smith, however, had already anticipated Marx's objection even though Marx never could understand the argument. Smith explained, in The Wealth of Nations, Book 1, Chapter 6 and elsewhere, that any instruments of husbandry, such as a horse that gets used up in producing corn, is itself made up of the same three parts: the rent of land upon which the horse is reared, the wages of labor there, and the profits of the farmer rearing the horse. Smith even uses the mot juste of "value added." Smith is right, as Simon Kuznets, Wassily Leontief, and Pierro Sraffa have shown in our day.

Each stage's fourth component of used-up capital goods is decomposable ultimately into Smith's three basic components. Marx could never quite grasp this. He could just perceive the value-added resolution in the singular case where capital goods do not themselves need capital goods as inputs. But Marx feared a vicious circle of infinite regress in the more general case already glimpsed in his 1858 Grundrisse, where all goods as outputs need, along with their need for labor and land, some produced goods as inputs.

Let us throw no stone at Marx for being worried about Smith's procedure. Smith does provide only a wave of the hand by way of proof. And not until 1898, after both Marx and Engels were dead, did the obscure Russian economist V.K. Dimitriev 1904 provide the rigorous modern solution by way of solving steady-state simultaneous equations.

Let us rather be grateful that Marx began in confusion. For that did lead him to his steady-state tableaus of reproduction. And these, without Marx's realizing it, did provide Adam Smith with the rigorous vindication that Marx so badly wanted and the tableaus do offer us basic insight into input-output equilibrium.

Marx's Tableau

If you are an economic theorist about to go to jail, and you can take with you only two chapters out of the scores of chapters in Capital's three volumes, my advice is to hold on to the final two chapters in Volume II. From Chapters XX and XXI there, I shall sketch the nature of Marx's theoretical breakthrough.

There will be three goods in the present scenario: coal, a raw material or capital good that is never used for final consumption; corn, a consumption good that provides workers with their needed wage subsistence; finally, caviar, a luxury good that capitalists spend their profit incomes on.

Take your ball pens out and write on your thumbnails the few technical and taste numbers that rule this scenario.

To produce 1 unit of coal output, assume that we need 1/3 unit of coal input along with 1 unit of direct labor. To produce 1 unit of corn output, assume that we also need 1/3 of coal input and 1 of labor input. Caviar is assumed to be produced by direct labor alone: with appropriate choice of units, 1 of caviar output requires 1 of labor.

I postulate that the real subsistence wage to keep each of 300 workers alive and reproducing their labor power is 1/3 unit of corn per period. We can then calculate for Marx that the profit rate must in the steady state be 50% per period. If there are 300 workers, the system must produce 100 of corn, 66 2/3 of coal, and 150 of caviar. Coal and corn sell for 3 wage units each, caviar sells for 1.5.

Here is how Marx's tableau ought to go.

Tableau I: Simple Reproduction
(rate of profit of 50%)

	C_j		V_j		$S_j = .5(C_j+V_j)$			
Coal	50	+	50	+	50	=	150	
Corn	100	+	100	+	100	=	300	
								525
Caviar	0	+	150	+	75	=	225	
	150		300		225			
				525				

Remark 1: For stationary equilibrium, the first row sum must equal the first column sum; and likewise for the other respective row and column sums.

Remark 2: I have used as numeraire wage units. No harm in that; you may use your own scale convention. So each of the 300 laborers gets a nominal wage of 1. In those units the corn they buy costs them 3 units, and therefore they do end up with exactly their needed 1/3 of subsistence corn.

Now we can use Marx's own brain child to refute his suspicion that there is something rotten in Adam Smith's tripartite decomposition of price. The coding by underlining shows that Marx's fourth component of price -- used-up coal in this example -- is itself resolvable by the value-added computation into wages-interest-rent and nothing else.

Here are the taxonomic relations for (Kuznets) Net National Product or Income, NNP, written in the three equivalent modern ways:

(1) NNP = 300 wages + 225 profit

(2) = 525 final product of corn and caviar

(3) = Coal value-added of (150-50)
plus
Corn value-added of (300-100)
plus
Caviar value-added of (225-0)

$$= S_jC_j + \underline{(V_j + S_j)} - C_j = S_j\underline{(V_j + S_j)}$$

Marx's Detour

We have praised Marx. Let us be fair. Is there anything in his contribution that a well-informed Thomas Kuhn would have to declare to be a revoluntionary paradigm different from the neoclassical or mainstream-economics paradigm? Are the models of Smith, Ricardo, Marx and the classicals different from those of Marshall, Wicksell, Solow and Arrow? My answer is a decided No.

I won't stop to argue the point but will merely refer you to my canonical version of the classical system, Samuelson 1978 .

There it was shown that Smith, Malthus, Ricardo, Mill, and Marx had essentially one system in common. That common system, when you decribe it fully, is seen to be after all a system of supply and demand qualitatively no different from those of present-day textbooks.

Actually, I have given Marx the benefit of modern knowledge and he would not thank me for it. In 1867 Marx thought he could improve on the coal-corn-caviar tableau that I showed you. He thought that bourgeois is economists like Smith and me lacked understanding of that 50% rate of profit which each industry earned. Marx proposed a new theory purporting to provide deeper understanding of the rate of profit. Neither he, nor anyone else since 1867, has succeeded in showing that better understanding can indeed come from the new paradigm based on a common rate of surplus value for every industry. But let's look at what his novel paradigm was supposed to be.

Live direct labor is supposedly what produces surplus: that is Marx's starting point. So, in the three industries, he has capitalists markup the direct wage outlays by the same percentage amounts -- by the common rate of surplus value. Here is the correct way for me to write Marx's idiosyncratic 1867 version of his tableau, for the coal-corn-caviar technologies, the corn-subsistence wage, the capitalists' penchant for caviar, and with my numeraire defined in terms of wage units.

Tableau II: Reproduction 1867 Style

(Rate of surplus value of 100%)

	c_j		v_j		$s_j = 1.00v_j$			
coal	50	+	50	+	50	=	150	
corn	100	+	100	+	100	=	300	
								600
caviar	0	+	150	+	150	=	300	
	150		300		300			
				600				

Unlike me, Marx would start out with this Tableau II rather than with my Tableau I. Only in his 1894 Volume III did he describe a "transformation" algorithm purporting to go from it to my bourgeois tableau. However, as he himself sensed, his 1894 algorithm was not quite right and would not lead back to my correct Tableau I. Thus the 1894 transformation (by relating column 3's total to the total of columns 1 and 2) would arrive at a false profit rate of (50+100+150)/(50+50+100+100+0+150), which is 66 2/3% rather than the correct 50%.

Forget Marx's minor error, which was corrected by Bortkiewicz in 1907, by Winternitz and Dobb around 1950, and subsequently by Seton, Morishima, me and many others. Concentrate on this: Arithmetic slips aside, we learn nothing new and worthwhile from the novel paradigm even when it is done right!

What was in Marx's mind? Ronald Meek, William Baumol, Ernest Mandel and others have tried to defend or explain Marx along the following lines:

1. From the 1867 version of Tableau II, we reckon up all the third-column surpluses and put them in a pot. Their total, in ratio to the total of the first two columns, gives us the macroeconomic average rate of profit.

2. Then, in actual microeconomic life, competition insures that industries get out of the total profit pot their respective profit shares in proportion not to their respective wage outlays, but rather in proportion to their respective wages-and-capital-goods outlays.

Of course there is no such macro pot into which the 1867 micro items are all put. And there is no such pot out of which 1894 (or 1776, or 1983) micro items are withdrawn. It is all a figment. An unnecessary figment. A misleading figment. The laws of motion of capitalism are blurred by the detour and so is the still picture of the competitive outcome.

To explicate the sterility of the 1867 paradigm, I'll flesh out my example to make it include the realistic fact that every economic system has a variety of technical blueprints to choose from. I now stipulate that 1 unit of coal output can be produced not only by 1/3 unit of coal and 1 of labor but also by any one of the following respective (coal, labor) input pairs:

(*) $$(1/4,3);\ (1/3,1);\ (1/2,2/3);\ \ldots\ ;\ (1-[1/2]^N,\ [1/2]^N[N^{-1}+1/3]$$

Here the integer N can go as high as some specified number. Like Joan Robinson or John von Neumann, I am stipulating a finite number of optional alternative techniques or activities for competition to choose from rather than insisting on the J.B. Clark neoclassical game.

Now we can learn what it really takes to give workers a wage higher than the two tableaus' subsistence level. If workers will hold in their numbers, or capitalists will desist from caviar consumption enough to amass a plentitude of capital goods, then and only then will the laws of competitive capitalism mete out a maximal real wage and exorcize the profit rate of 50%.

Thus, if the integer N in (*) above is at all large, the workers' wage can rise from 1/3 of corn per period almost to 3 of corn per period -- a ninefold improvement. Marx's insistence that direct labor is alone productive does credit to his warm heart but dulls his reasoning brain.

Foul, you will cry? Samuelson has forgotten about reswitching? No: fair, I say. Although this simple example does not admit of reswitching, its point does not hinge on that fact. A universal truth needs to be comprehended once we stop prattling about metaphysical pots and face up to competitive arbitrage.

> Any economy that starts out in a non-golden-rule technology can move into that golden-rule maximal-wage state only by intertemporal substitution along the way, in which someone sacrifices something of present-time consumption in favor of greater future consumption.

The above is a theorem, not a brief for capitalism. It is an valid in Peking as in Manchester. In Xanadu as on Robinson Crusoe's island. As valid for Garegnani as for Burmeister.

Expanding Reproduction

Keep the same technology as in Tableau I's stationary case, and the same subsistence-corn real wage. But replace the zero saving propensity of the stationary case by the assumption that capitalists always save a constant positive fraction of their profit incomes. This can define a balanced exponential growth tableau. (Just as there were two alternative tableaus in the stationary case, the 1867 Marx version and the alternative bourgeois version with the profit rates equalized, so there will be two versions here. However, in the case that I shall work out where all profits are saved and the resulting two industries left happen to have the same organic compositions of capital, Tableau IV can be omitted as merely duplicating Tableau III.)

When at work out Marx's tableous property, will they still be found to vindicate Adam Smith's three-part accounting decomposition in the growth case as in the stationary case? Yes. The value-added approach goes through just as before; the flow of product approach also checks through nicely provided we are careful to include in final products net capital formations of coal and of corn.

Here are two adjacent periods of the expanded-reproduction tableau. The initial period has been normalized so as to have the same 300 of labor supply as in Tableaus I and II. As before, I use for my numeraire wage units. To make the most dramatic test case, I assume capitalists save everything, eschewing all luxury caviar consumption and causing the system to grow exponentially at the same rate as the unchanged interest rate of 50% per period.

Tableau III: Reproduction With Balance Growth
(Profit rate and growth rate 50%; 100% saving rate)

Initial Period									
	C_j		V_j		S_j=.5(C_j+V_j)				
coal	150	+	150	+	150	=	450	= 300 + (450-300)
corn	150	+	150	+	150	=	450	= 300 + (450-300)
caviar	0	+	0	+	0	=	0	
	300		300		300			
				600				
Next Period								
coal	225	+	225	+	225	=	675	= 450 + (675-450)
corn	225	+	225	+	225	=	675	= 450 + (675-450)
caviar	0	+	0	+	0	=	0	
	450		450		450			
				900				

I have underlined the wage-interest income items on the left. On the right I have underlined the final product flows. Thus for the initial period there is the increment of total coal stock, <u>450-300</u>; and the increment of corn advances, <u>450-300</u>; and the 300 corn consumed by workers out of their wage advances received at the beginning of the period.

In summary, here are Smith's vindicated accounting relations:

(4) $NNP_t = Wages_t + Profits_t + 0 \text{ Land Rent}$

$= 300 + .5(600) + 0 = \underline{300} + \underline{300} = \underline{600}$

(5) $= \text{Summed Values-Added} = S_j \; (C_j + V_j + S_j) - C_j$

$= \underline{(450-150)} + \underline{(450-150)} + \underline{(0-0)} = \underline{600}$

(6) $= Consumptions_t + \text{Net Capital } Formations_t$

$= \underline{300} + \underline{(450-300)} + \underline{(450-300)} = \underline{600}$

It is a pity that Marx did not perceive and articulate this vindication of Smith and abandon the 1867 alternative paradigm as being not really necessary or helpful.

Insights From Conventional Sources

An anniversary is an occasion for celebration not for the pouring of cold water. As Dr. Johnson said, one is not under oath on these occasions. Let me stipulate in lawyer's language that Marx does sometimes proposed seminal insights into the evolution of the market economy.

Here is an example. Marx thought that innovation and accumulation were moving England toward fixed capital such as machines and structures, and relatively away from variable capital in the sense of wage-fund advances. He felt that this would reduce the demand for labor and either slow down wage increases or even lower wages.

Cheers for Karl. The only thing we can fault him for is not realizing sufficiently that such a process would negate his own law of the falling rate of profit.

What needs to be asked is this: Does this insight about a downward shifting of the demand for labor somehow flow from the 1867 rate-of-surplus-value paradigm? Is bourgeois economics incapable of generating and explaining this same hypothesis?

Answer 1. No, the 1867 novelty did not originate the hypothesis. Karl never uses <u>mehrwert</u> to arrive at it.

Answer 2. On reflection you will realize that non-Marxians arrive at the specified result when they posit that (a) labor and capital goods have an elasticity of substitution less than unity, and (b) labor-sparing inventions are occurring (either exogenously or as induced by rising wage rates).

The same point has to be made when someone extolls the classical writers for insights denied to later day neoclassicists. When Ricardo shocked his readers by pointing out in his third edition that invention of machinery could reduce the demand for labor, that ought not to shock readers of Frank Ramsey or Knut Wicksell -- even though it did shock McCullough and Ricardo's laissez-faire disciples. The effect is simply another ho-hum possibility under the heading of (b) just above.

In leaving this logical audit of Marx's hypothesis, I ought to warn that Marx may have been 180°, off in his suspicion that nineteenth century innovation was tending to lower labor's relative share of total income.

Schumpeter's Vision

Enough on Marx as an economic theorist's theorist. And I have already praised Keynes enough. For all his world fame, Schumpeter's stock on the bourse of scholarly reputations was too long selling below its intrinsic worth.

Like other students of Schumpeter and like his academic colleagues and friends, I tended to regard as a bit comical his early celebrity as the chap who believed that the rate of interest would be zero in the stationary state. The same went for his 1939 fascination with the fol de rol of Kondratieff long waves, superimposed on the decade-length sinusoidal undulations of the major Juglar business cycle and on the Kitchin-Crum workaday 40-month National Bureau cycles. Among us professionals the recent revival of Kondratieff moonshine -- in its disparate Rostow, Forrester, Shonihara, and Christopher Freedman reincarnations -- does not make us look back more kindly on Schumpeter's Ptolemaic epicycles.

Schumpeter was right to insist that his basic vision of dynamic economic development would be little changed if the stationary state had a rendezvous not with a zero interest rate but with a positive Irving Fisher or Modigliani interest rate. And he was right in insisting that nothing in his own theory called for superimposed sine waves. Where we can disagree is with his contention that the facts cried out for him to adopt a three-wave schema. At the age of 20 I thought it odd that a great mind would be satisfied to explain the virulence of the Great Depression by the happenstance that all three cycles just happened to be in their downward phase.

For his cycle-cum-development theory of the business cycle connected with the entrepreneurial process of innovation, Joseph Schumpeter belongs on Mt. Olympus along with such business-cycle greats as Bagehot, Mitchell, Aftalion, Hawtrey, Spiethoff, Wicksell, Cassel, Robertson, Slutsky, J.M. Clark, Frisch, Hansen, Tinbergen, Kalecki, Haberler, Metzler, Warburton, Friedman, Klein, and honored others.

Schumpeter's second great claim to fame is as historian of economic analysis and as biographer. His 1954 posthumous book is a classic, even though it is a prodigiously uneven work and a sadly incomplete one. Too little time was accorded Schumpeter and posterity is the loser. One learns to tolerate his patronizing omniscience and to appreciate his provocative interpretations and undoubted erudition.

Paradoxically, however, the very greatest contribution that the economist Schumpeter made to the history of ideas was not strictly in the field of economics but had to do with the evolutionary trends in the post-capitalistic order. Capitalism, Socialism and Democracy reads better 40 years after its publication than it did in 1942 or 1950.

It is a great book. And this despite the fact that its main thesis does not quite convince. The demise of capitalism is not really speeded up the more successfully it fills its economic mission. That is not plausible in terms of logic; and the facts of 1900-1942, or for that matter 1942-1983, do not make it plausible.

But Schumpeter's sense that self-interest will lead voters and elites to use the power relations of government and other non-market collusions to alter the laissez-faire equilibrium does commend itself both to logic and to the facts of history old and new. Although Mancur Olson came to Harvard years after Schumpeter died, Olson's recent The Rise and Decline of Nations is very much in the Schumpeter vein with its stress on the Pareto-non-optimal harm occasioned by groups seeking their own interest.

Schumpeter's centennial has already coaxed out of me several reinterpretations of his work, as in Samuelson 1980, 1981 . Therefore I shall desist with the remark that Schumpeter's over-narrow definition of what capitalism is, coupled with an over-broad definition of socialism, made him too cavalier in his expectations that capitalism would die and be succeeded by socialism.

Schumpeter was uncharacteristically naive in awarding Lange and Lerner victory over Ludwig von Mises on the issue of whether rational economic calculation would be possible under socialism. Of course Mises was wrong in his sweeping rejection. But Schumpeter of all people should have understood the importance of uncertainty, stochastic error, and dynamic innovation in all social life. And this might have been expected to lead him to award the victory to Hayek for his insistence on the difficulty of pooling information when command and bureaucracy limit the workings of the market. Had Schumpeter lived another third of a century he would also have realized what Oskar Lange had to learn the hard way, that few socialist societies will play the Barone-Lerner-Lange game of simulated decentralized market pricing.

Final Fun and Games

My time is almost up. We know how we feel about our three giants. How did they feel about each other?

Keynes is easiest to classify. He went whole hours not thinking about Joseph Alois Schumpeter. For Karl Marx Keynes had confident contempt, referring to Das Kapital as the bible of communism

> ...above and beyond criticism, an obsolete textbook which I know to be not only scientifically erroneous but without interest or application for the modern world... Even if we need a religion how can we find it in the turbid rubbish of the Red bookstores?

Joan Robinson thinks that Keynes might have developed his 1936 General Theory earlier and better if only, like Michael Kalecki, Keynes had known the works of Marx. She does not make her case. Others who knew not Marx -- Richard Kahn, J.M. Clark, Bertil Ohlin, Ragnar Frisch, ... -- came as close as Kalecki did to Keynes's notion that the equilibrium level of output and unemployment is determined by the adequacy of investment desires relative to the saving scheduled at each level of income. Marx's reproduction tableaus are seen on examination to be anticipations of Kuznetsian national-income accounting, no more Keynesian than they are Hayekian, as much like Leontief, Keynes' critic, as like Sraffa, Keynes' protégé.

The Schumpeter-on-Marx Puzzle

In his indifferent contempt for Marx, Keynes was not atypical of the generation that taught me. New Left students of the 1960s were ill-informed to think that Marxism was a spectre that haunted the dreams of mainstream economists in the first half of the twentieth century. My teachers slept well.

Schumpeter, an exception, praised Marx as a great scholar. That is clear. What is not clear is why Schumpeter thought Marx to be great. You will search Schumpeter's writing in vain for a cogent argument. Moreover, I was Schumpeter's pupil. I attended his formal Harvard lectures and seminars. Many an hour I whiled away in his company -- as at the old Merle cafe across the street from Harvard's Widener Library, where economists used to drop in for coffee and gossip. But I never heard Schumpeter give reasons for placing Marx high as an economist.

It is as if what Schumpeter thought great in Marx was Marx's chutspah. Karl aimed so high. Claimed so much. But by this criterion every asylum is full of genius.

Marx purported to have a grand dynamics of development. So did Schumpeter. But Schumpeter's paradigm and Weltanschauung was quite other than Marx's, economically beneficent not malignant. If one man's economic vision was right, the other's had to be grossly wrong. Thus Marx feared technological unemployment. Schumpeter, Marx's alleged admirer, is all too cavalier in pooh-poohing its possibility.

Each Marxian insight Schumpeter despises. As a putdown of his Anglo-Saxon contemporaries, Schumpeter engaged in overpraised of Marx's totality. I have to report that overpraise was a characteristic Schumpeter ploy -- as when I heard him give a flowery introduction at Harvard for Ludwig von Mises, a scholar whose merits could not have been as low as Schumpeter privately placed them.

Schumpeter's rivalry with Keynes is easy to characterize. Few hours went by in which he did not measure himself against Keynes. In the late 1920s he regarded himself as in a race with Keynes to produce a treatise on money. That Schumpeter should have shelved the manuscript after the Keynes' Treatise on Money appeared is interesting. The Treatise, we now realize, was not a great book; it was at best a stepping stone to a great book; and in places it was an idiosyncratic deadend. Some feeling of dissatisfaction with Schumpeter's own manuscript, I believe, must have been involved. It is a question whether the posthumous publication of this German manuscript would have pleased its author. (On the macroeconomic theory of money, Schumpeter did have some ideas linking up spending flows with the flow of income; but no deep linkage with the stock of money seems to have been achieved by him.)

It was the reception of the General Theory that put Schumpeter's nose out of joint. Arthur Smithies reported that Schumpeter never discerned any scientific merit in Keynes' paradigm. Yet economists all over the world, including some of Schumpeter's own best pupils, praised Keynes and followed him. How to account for this if no scientific merit was involved? Schumpeter's rationalization was that it was Keynes's political message that won for him his false fame. In this Schumpeter was quite wrong; surprisingly wrong in that, long before Thomas Kuhn had hit upon his theory of scientific revolutions, Schumpeter had already stated that it takes a new theory to kill an old theory, not a new fact. What Schumpeter could not accept was the notion implicit in Keynes, that equilibrium could prevail without all markets clearing. Young people like me took this for granted: this was the usefulness of the Keynesian model that it let us understand the world as if, because of not-very-fully-described rigidities, its equilibria involved changing degrees of unemployment and supply-demand discrepancies. The modern preoccupation with giving macroeconomics more articulated microeconomic foundations is in accord with Schumpeter's reservations about Keynes. But it is a shame that Schumpeter had to forego using the new useful paradigm just because he could not reconcile it with older paradigms and with an understood firm foundation.

Finally, what would Marx's attitude be toward Schumpeter and Keynes? We can make pretty good guesses about the answer to this hypothetical question. Marx has few good words to say for any contemporary or successor. Beyond that, Marx would have been repelled by Schumpeter's conservative ideology and attitudes. Schumpeter's playfulness would have annoyed him.

Keynes, Marx would have taken more seriously. But that means he would have been even weighter in his denouncing of Keynes. Marxians of the 1930s hated the General Theory. They denounced it as a covert way of getting the real wage down. Wht they could not stand was the notion that capitalism could be saved merely by some fiscal and monetary palliatives. If the system was condemned to die by its own self-induced cancers, a shaman who came forth with a laetrile that could reverse the cosmic time table of history had to be reviled as a charlatan. If the medicine man were correct in his claims for his magic, that would be an even worse offense.

Images of Fame

My time is up. I conclude with pictures of the gods and with the totems that made them gods.[2] To be a great scientist, you don't have to produce shelves of books. You just have to produce at least one great idea.

First, here is a picture and signature of Thunen. Under Thunen's picture is the natural wage, formula w = ap, that made Thunen infamous not famous.

Second comes the picture and signature of Karl Marx. I follow it not with the tableau that makes him great, which is Tableau I that you have already seen. I follow Marx's portrait with Tableau II, which is what he and his followers wrongly think makes him great.

Third comes the picture of Keynes. It does not have the element of caricature that we so often see, but I think it is a good likeness of the hero just after the Treatise and just before the General Theory. Under the picture are the relations that make Keynes great: they are the equivalent of the Hicks-Hansen IS-LM diagrams, and Alex Leijonhufvud has it all quite wrong when he argues that Keynes is greater than Keynesianism. The cash value of a scientific theory is in its application.

Finally comes the picture of my old teacher. This portrait better than the photographs of earlier dates, catches Schumpeter as I remember him. I have put below the picture equations that encapsulate his vision of a process of periodic development, driven by oscillatory impulses from the side of innovation.

People speak of 1984 as an important date. For us economists the vintage year is 1983.

Footnotes

1. Adam Smith is currently being reevaluated upwards. Not only were the doubts of him by Marx wrong, as my current discussion shows. In addition the corrections of Smith that Ricardo thought needed turn out to be largely misapprehensions and errors on Ricardo's part. When Professor Samuel Hollander comes to prepare revised editions of his two books on Smith and Marx, he will have to reverse the balance and recognize that the canonical classical model that is common to all the writers and to Marx is already definitely in the Wealth of Nations. Schumpeter, Keynes and Marx would all have changes to make in their written evaluation of Smith and Ricardo.

2. Not included here are the portraits that were flashed on the screen along with characteristic tags of wisdom associated with each author.

References

Dimitriev, V.K., Economic Essays on Value, Competition, and Utility, (English translation of 1904 Russian book), (London: Cambridge University Press, 1974).

Friedman, B., "The Theoretical Nondebate About Monetarism," Kredit Kapital, 9(3) 1976, pp. 347-67.

Friedman, M., "A Theoretical Framework for Monetary Analysis," Journal of Political Economy, 78 (March-April, #2), 1970, pp. 193-238.

Marx, K., Grundrisse, (1858).

_____ Capital, I (1867), II (1885), III (1894).

_____ Theories of Surplus Value (so-called Volume IV of Capital, written largely in the 1860s), 1905.

Olson, M., The Rise and Decline of Nations (New Haven: Yale University Press, 1982).

Pigou, A.C., Theory of Unemployment, (London: Macmillan, 1933).

Samuelson, P.A., "Marx as Mathematical Economist: Steady-State and Exponential Growth Equilibrium," in G. Horwich and P. Samuelson, eds., Trade, Stability, and Macroeconomics, Essays in Honor of Lloyd A. Metzler, (New York: Academic Press, 1974), pp. 269-307. Reprinted in Collected Scientific Papers of Paul A. Samuelson, vol. 4, ch. 225, pp. 231-69, (Cambridge, Ma.: MIT Press, 1977).

_____ "The Canonical Classical Model of Political Economy," Journal of Economic Literature, XVI (December) 1978, pp. 1415-34.

_____ "Schumpeter's Capitalism, Socialism and Democracy," in Schumpeter's Vision: Capitalism, Socialism and Democracy after 40 years, A. Heertje, ed. (UK: Praeger Publishers, 1981).

_____ "Schumpeter as Economic Theorist," in Schumpeterian Economics, H. Frisch, ed. (UK: Praeger Publishers, 1982).

_____ "Thunen at 200," Journal of Economic Literature, December 1983.

Schumpeter, J.A., Capitalism, Socialism and Democracy, (N.Y.: Harper and Row, 1942, 1949).

305

THE KEYNES CENTENARY

Sympathy from the other Cambridge

Maynard Keynes was a great Englishman of the first half of the twentieth century, and one of the world's three greatest economists of all time. Only Adam Smith and Leon Walras can be mentioned in the same breath with him.

When I came into economics 50 years ago I would never have guessed that Keynes would earn this place in history. Yes, he was then the single most famous economist in the world. He had written a vast Treatise on Money, and a fine Tract on Monetary Reform. He even understood the Indian rupee. What makes you a celebrity, however, is not what earns you a permanent place at the top of the scholarly pole. The Economic Consequences of the Peace was more than half right in its warnings against the dire consequences of the punitive Versailles peace treaty. Perhaps it was its exaggerations—and the fine writing—that made the book a runaway best seller and gave Keynes the nest-egg ante to sit in on the highstakes game of international speculation. It is only economists who know that, on the technical analysis of the capacity of Germany to pay war reparations, the young Scandinavian Bertil Ohlin was more nearly right than the brilliant Keynes. What led to Keynes's exaggerations was an undue reliance on the classical economics he was later to caricature: J. S. Mill and Alfred Marshall had not really mastered their basic foreign-trade theory.

As the lawyers say, I am laying the basis for an objective appraisal of Keynes as scientist. By freely recognising the imperfections that are there in the Keynesian record, I come into court with cleaner hands and can with greater credibility make the tall claims on his behalf that simple justice requires.

The unreliable seer?

Since Keynes had the notorious reputation for always changing his mind, how could he always have been right? The charges, like the jokes about economists, are a little tiresome. "When a Royal commission solicits opinions from five economists", the story runs, "they get six answers—two from Mr Keynes". President Harry Truman is supposed to have summed it up well: "What I want is a one-armed economist". For him none of this pussyfooting around—on the one hand this and on the other hand that. Some sage, I expect it was I, gave the proper rebuttal. The prince will find that one-armed economists generally come in two disjoint sets: those with a left arm only, and those with only a right; and then the prince must call in an eclectic two-armed economist like myself to adjudicate between their divergent claims.

Knowing the guild of economists all too well, I must depose that the trouble with us is not that charged by Shaw of disagreeing too much among ourselves. In truth our forecasts are too boringly similar. And what we agree on is this, that our last consensus was wrong and is to be replaced by the new one. Roy Blough's dictum has stood the test of time: "Economists are like six eskimos in a bed. You can be sure only that they'll all turn over together". Keynes provided his own impeccable defence of being protean. "When my information changes, I alter my conclusions. What do you do, sir?"

Out of idle curiosity I once made a desultory study of Keynes's lifetime variability, using for controls such contemporaries as Joseph Schumpeter, Gustav Cassel, Frank Knight, Lord Robbins, and

Sumner Slichter. I found nothing left to rationalise or apologise for. Anecdotes do not a science make!

Judging right

Consistency as such is of course no virtue. Although I know hundreds of economists, only a few of them manage to be wrong all the time. Even a stopped clock is periodically right, but at times that only those with a good watch can identify. Scientists must be judged by their long-run means of forecasts and not just by their standard deviations.

On this score Keynes had a remarkably good batting average. With only a little vacillation, he correctly warned Winston Churchill against the disastrous 1925 restoration of the pound's parity at the pre-1914 level. (From the researches of Churchill's biographers, we know now that he was fearful of disregarding Keynes's advice but was talked down by the City establishment.) At the time of the Macmillan committee, Keynes was on the side of the angels, but he had nobody else on his side.

Almost 40 years ago I pointed out the paradox that Keynes the cosmopolitan was at the same time the most provincial of British patriots. He never really cared for Americans. (Did Bernie Baruch snub him at the Crillon? Were FDR's hands that coarse?) In Second-World-War Washington this ill-concealed distaste sometimes threatened to upset hardwon concessions and benevolences. It was not nice, I understand, to witness Keynes's meetings with Senator Vincent, who was both an American and a lawyer. In my reveries I used to conjure up encounters between M. Keynes of Eton and A. Lincoln of the log schoolhut.

Keynes and the New Deal

The paradox is not that Keynes should disrelish Americans. I feel the same way about Californians—an arrogant mixture of envy and contempt. The paradox is that the ideas and paradigms that Keynes generated out of his insular background were really better suited to America than to Britain. Ours was a great continental economy, virtually closed to international trade and balance-of-payments constraints. Franklin Roosevelt—who was a Keynesian as Dr Johnson's dog was an infidel (he had not thought on the matter)—at first by instinct and then under the prodding of the Keynesian Hansens, Eccleses, Curries, Colms, and Gilberts, applied the fiscal-policy therapies called for by Keynes in the General Theory.

The American academic orthodoxy—my beloved teachers: Schumpeter, Viner, Knight, Leontief, Chamberlin—disapproved of the New Deal. Keynes clapped both hands. As John the Baptist to the later coming of Milton Friedman's flexible exchange rates, Keynes hailed Roosevelt's sabotaging of the 1933 international economic conference and his suspension of the dollar's fixed parity. History has approved.

It is a myth which will not die that deficit financing was tried in the 1930s and was found to fail, that it took the Second World War to bring back prosperity. America's real GNP accounts show that the 1933-37 recovery was the strongest, on a sustained basis, in all history. It was able to be so because it started from so low a base. And for this same reason, its sharp reducing of unemployment still left the unemployment rate high in 1937 or 1940 compared to pre-1929 or 1950s levels. The definitive researches of Professor E. C. Brown show that fiscal multiplicands worked in the 1930s just about the way theory says they ought to have, no less and no more.

Keynes, where art thou now?

I think the Keynes record in predictions is not quite as good as his friends and enemies think it to be. His creation, Bretton Woods, was after all flawed at its core: the set of exchange rates right for the pre-OPEC era could not stay right; and the process by which such basic under- and overvaluations could be recognised to be wrong and be made right had to involve, under Bretton Woods, a long field day for speculators and the kind of chronic currency overvaluations that we Kennedy-Johnson economists had to suffer under for periods measured in decades and not months.

However, a birthday party is not the place to enlarge on pimples and scars. So good was Keynes's judgment that a whole industry has grown up around the preoccupation: "What would Keynes do now if he were alive?" In his home university, the effect was clearly baleful. Maynard never cared for mathematical economics or statistics: ergo, don't alter the good old tripos.

Isaac Newton put British mathematics and science on the map. Alas, it took a generation for British scholarship to recover from the stultifying brilliance of Newton. It was on the continent, in the hands of the Bernoullis and Euler, that Newtonian dynamics flourished. And, say it I must, it was on the North American continent that advances in the Keynesian art largely took place in the postwar decades. The Radcliffe committee testimony testifies to the moribund state of the subject in the home counties.

Worse than any errors or influence bequeathed by Keynes was the licence given people to defend their own prejudices under the banner of what Keynes would really be for. A protean authority can be appealed to by contradictory causes. Besides, the same syndrome operates in the case of Keynes that we used to hear in the 1930s: "Adolf Hitler is all right. But it is the wicked Goering, or Goebbels, or . . . who is to blame for the excesses." Similarly, one wearies of hearing "Keynes is a genius. A little eccentric but at bottom wise. It is the Keynesian disciples (the Hungarians, mathematicians, Marxists, cranks, American enthusiasts . . .) who disseminate in his name the dangerous nonsense".

Also, just as there is the doctrine of the two Karl Marxs—the young Hegelian and the old economist—there is the comfortable notion that late in life Keynes came to his senses, and if only he had been spared more years he would have led his band back into the promised land of classical Egypt. Some of his last letters do point that way. But some point in the opposite direction. And several of the letters that conservative friends like David McCord Wright interpreted as blessing their own viewpoints, I read as polite brushoffs.

All too many scholars are Bourbons: after the age of 29 they learn nothing and forget nothing. The Keynesians I admire—like Franco Modigliani, James Tobin, Robert Solow—are not the same in this decade as they were in the last, and next decade they will be something else again. Why should we refuse the same privilege to Keynes?

Keynes versus his system

Preoccupation with the man's views is encouraged by another syndrome that used to be in vogue. Not only is Keynes supposed to be better than his *epigone,* according to the thesis I am about to deflate, Keynes is better than the Keynesian system. So to speak, Sir Isaac is a genius but watch out for the Newtonian system. Professor Axel Leijonhufvud's bestseller of 1968 tells it all in the title: On Keynesian Economics [Ugh] and the Economics of Keynes [Hosannahs]. What James Meade, Roy Harrod, John Hicks, Brian Reddaway, A. P. Lerner, Oskar Lange, Paul Samuelson, A. C. Pigou, and Joan Robinson all agreed on as the analytical core of the General Theory, Mr Leijonhufvud decides is only a mathematical perversion of Keynes's thought. The real McCoy of Keynes is rather to be found in the subtle nuances of Keynes's perceptions: the notions of "bearishness" and "liquidity" that try to form themselves in the Treatise, the ineffable importance of expectations. It is these, Leijonhufvud avers, that constitute the genius of Keynes and not the embalmed simplicities of the Hicks-Hansen LM and IS schedules of the textbooks.

It won't wash. Yes, Keynes was a genius. Yes, some of his ideas were inchoate and would not have lent themselves usefully to diagramming and symbolic manipulation. Yes, by the time of the Radcliffe committee many of his British admirers were still frozen in the Model T version of his system. And yes, Keynes resented excessive simplifying of his paradigms.

Nevertheless, in science it is not the incoherent, inchoate and ineffable that has a cash value. If that were so, Goethe would be a greater scientist than either Einstein or Newton. What matters is the Kuhnian paradigm that people who are not geniuses can use. That which so many scholars independently agreed upon cannot be independent of the text that Keynes wrote down for them to read.

What is remarkable is not the cogency of the case that Leijonhufvud manages to muster, which is rather flimsy, but rather how strong was the latent demand in the 1970s for a work to debunk Keynesianism.

Harry Johnson put the same point in a different way. The appeal of monetarism was not in its superior ability to predict. For only a brief period did reality reel into the gunsights of the regression equations of the monetarists. And certainly it was not the analytical subtlety of monetarism or its theoretical correctness that explained its vogue; for, as Johnson stressed, monetarism is bad neoclassical economics in its denial that the velocity of circulation of money is systematically speeded up by rises in interest rates. You cannot beat something with nothing, and much of monetarism's appeal was an offset to populist Keynesianism. I cannot but agree.

Comparing the emperor and his garments is measuring cheese against chalk. But if it comes to that, the Leijonhufvuds have things 180° wrong. Keynes in the late 1930s was often worse than his system. The heat of debate made him embrace in letters to Irving Fisher and John Hicks positions based on misunderstandings of his own model. (When stating that a test of whether you were not Keynesian was whether, like classicists, you believed that an increase in investment demand would raise the interest rate, Homer nodded: in the Keynes paradigm, the fact that the interest rate is related to liquidity preference does not deny that improved yields on investment projects will expand nominal incomes and force up interest rates when the central bank keeps the stock of money constant.)

The scientific legacy

Scholarship is a Darwinian jungle. In the short run we are all dead as scientists. Macroeconomics was the creation of John Maynard Keynes, even the macroeconomics that his opponents use today to refute the views of his adherents. It is not just that the name "macroeconomics" itself dates only to the last five years of Keynes's lifetime. But the replacement of models in which all markets clear by relationships that involve job-seekers who cannot find jobs is the hallmark of writings for the past half century. What had been implicit in business cycle descriptions was made explicit and scientifically respectable. When the venerable A. C. Pigou came to demonstrate that permanent Keynesian unemployment was avertable, the 1940 arguments he found to use were couched in the Keynesian constructions that had not been available to Pigou before publication of the General Theory. When Professor Milton Friedman opened up the black box of his monetarism for the 1970 readers of the Journal of Political Economy, what he exhibited from it was one version of the Keynesian paradigm. In 1976 when Professor Benjamin Friedman of Harvard wrote down for the monetarists Karl Brunner and Allen Meltzer what their model of monetarism was, it turned out not to be qualitatively distinguishable from a James Tobin Keynesian model.

Now that is scientific immortality, the kind of immortality that Newton, Maxwell, Planck, Einstein and Heisenberg possess, the only kind of immortality that a scientist can win in the non-zero-sum battle against ignorance. Any good scientist rates a *Festschrift* on reaching the age of 60. But only a great innovator like John Maynard Keynes merits commemorative articles and symposia a long hundred years after his birth.

The House That Keynes Built

On his 100th birthday, Keynesian economics still lives.

By PAUL A. SAMUELSON

WHEN I was asked some years ago whether Keynes was dead, I had to reply: "Yes, Keynes is dead. And so are Newton and Darwin." My point was that John Maynard Keynes had become part of history. Of course, most people born 100 years ago are already part of history, especially those who have been dead for almost four decades.

But by coupling the name of Keynes with two great men who altered the course of human thought, I was emphasizing the fact that Keynes was one of history's political economists — in the top class along with Adam Smith. Economics remains permanently different because of Keynes's innovations in the big-picture analysis of government fiscal and monetary policy now known as macroeconomics.

My colorful teacher, Joseph A. Schumpeter, who taught me postgraduate economics at Harvard, also has a birthday centennial this year. By every test he was a great scholar. He forumlated a theory of the business cycle and of economic development based on the crucial role of the innovating entrepreneur. Beyond narrow economics, Schumpeter earned a niche in the history of political economy by his insightful prediction that capitalism's very successes would undermine its appeal to the electorates. But it is in no sense demeaning to Schumpeter's high achievements to place him outside the class that contains Newton, Darwin and Keynes.

KEYNES is associated in the popular mind with free and easy government spending. And, during the Great Depression of the 1930's, he did in fact advocate unbalanced budgets as a device to create jobs and get the capitalist machine running again. Young economists by the hundreds rallied to his banner. I know, I was one of them.

But Lord Keynes was not the first, nor the last, to advocate public works in times of slump. Adolf Hitler knew as little of economics as he knew of morality. Still, his sprint to rearm Germany and mount a campaign of revenge and conquest did succeed in bringing Germany to a state of full employment from the situation in 1932, when one in four Germans, like one in four Americans, was without hope of finding a job.

The history of science shows that being an important influence in politics is not a way of holding lasting fame in the annals of scholarship. Adam Smith is remembered in our modern universities because he laid the foundations for the mainstream microeconomics which we still teach — the economics of prices, profits and the corporation — and not because he preached the gospel of laissez faire, for which today's politicians love to remember him.

John Maynard Keynes likewise enjoys within the academic profession of economics a scientific reputation that is quite distinct from his celebrity as an adviser to British and American heads of state on the use of stimulative fiscal policy.

Inventing Macroeconomics

A simple prescription for the Government to lower tax rates and increase spending actually did make good sense in the early 1930's when grass grew on main street and one bank failure led to another. By wartime 1942 and peacetime 1952, however, such simple Keynesianism was dead, as dead as the view that the mountains are 5,000 years old and that all matter is water, air, fire and stone.

What remains alive, however, is the apparatus of thought born with Keynes which recognizes that the supply of jobs and the supply of workers who want jobs are not automatically brought into balance in the short run by economic forces — and that governments need not stand idly by and let workers suffer long bouts of high unemployment.

Before Keynes, when I was learning my microeconomics as an undergraduate at the University of Chicago in the early 1930's, we had no handle on this problem. We had to attribute the persistent unemployment to uppity workers who insisted on wages that were just too high. But that was not a satisfactory explanation.

What perplexed us, and should have perplexed us more than it did, was how to explain why the crestfallen workers seen in the Chicago breadlines had been less uppity in the palmy days of 1928. We mistakenly tried to blame the high American tariffs for the huge unemployment of the Great Depression or blame Federal Reserve policy for feeding the great stock market boom that preceded the Depression.

What made Keynes different from the village print-some-money cranks whom we have always with us, was the fact that his 1936 volume, "The General Theory of Employment, Interest and Money," did not take a narrow look at one or two isolated parts of the economy. He tackled the whole thing in one brilliant analytic formulation and provided economists with new ways of looking at how the entire gross national product is determined and how wages and prices and the rate of unemployment are determined along with it.

This was the advent of "macroeconomics," a study that is now so commonplace in the profession. The origins of the word are murky. Twenty years ago Edwin Nourse, who had been the first chairman of the Council of Economic Advisers, wrote to Alvin Hansen, a Harvard economics professor, asking, "Who invented the word macroeconomics?" Hansen replied (and sent me a carbon copy): "I don't know. Probably Samuelson."

I knew that was not so. The Keynesian revolution did indeed create a new branch of economics and one that needed a name, but the first edition of my textbook, "Economics," in 1948 — which was one of the first economics texts books to draw heavily on Keynesian analysis — did not even contain the word. And it took hours of library research to verify that the expression dates from the last years of Keynes's life, surfacing in the technical literature of economics after 1940.

SCIENCE is a Darwinian jungle — the survival of the fittest. New theories kill off old. Measurements test expectations, refuting most pet notions and corroborating a few survivors.

By 1939, Keynes himself was shedding his depression skins, shifting away from viewing unemployment as the primary problem, to focusing attention on the rising problems of inflation. His pamphlet on how Britain should pay for World War II to avoid inflation developed a new theory of "demand inflation" — whereby prices rise endlessly as labor and capital between them try to enjoy more than 100 percent of the output producible at full employment.

And as Keynes's own thinking underwent changes, so American scholars who call themselves Keynesians — or, more accurately, post-Keynesians — have gone far beyond 1936 Keynesianism. Franco Modigliani of M.I.T., while still a young man in the early 1940's, showed that people's spending depended not only on their current incomes, as Keynes had said, but also on their accumulated holdings of liquid wealth — money, bank accounts and other very liquid assets — plus other assets such as equities, long-term bonds and homes. James Tobin of Yale, in the 1950's, improved on Keynes's theory of the demand for money and showed how interest rates affect money velocity — the rate at which money changes hands in the economy.

Moreover, the shadow of Keynes stands behind the most successful of econometric models of today. The Wharton Model at the University of Pennsylvania and the D.R.I. model in Harvard are a far cry from the 1936 "Model T" version of Keynes, but in basic methodology they are much closer to Keynes's models formulated in his "General Theory" than to the neoclassical texts that I was brought up on.

KEYNESIAN thinking was obviously not always well received, especially in the early days. A scientific theory, fortunately, benefits not only from its friends but also from its enemies. And the adversary process of scholarship that has produced the monetarist theories of Milton Friedman and others has helped to sharpen the modern application of Keynes's thoughts rather than to destroy them.

Monetarism emphasizes the critical importance of the money supply in determining the level of total output of goods and services in a nation's economy. This sharply contradicts the Great Depression version of Keynesian economics, which had downplayed the role of money and put its major emphasis on fiscal policy and the flows of income. Monetarism demonstrated the importance of the money supply both on the basis of historical evidence and plausible economic analysis.

I applaud this emphasis. Like Tobin, Modigliani and other American eclectic post-Keynesians, I was sharply critical of the Neanderthal Keynesianism that still dominated British economics as recently as 20 years ago.

I am not a monetarist, however. My reason and my reading of experience will not permit me to believe in a one-factor theory of causation. Actually, when monetarists like Milton Friedman of Chicago and his disciple, Karl Brunner of the University of Rochester, spelled out the mechanisms underlying their theory, these mechanisms were seen as a variant of Keynesian analysis.

I seriously doubt that freezing the growth rate of the money supply for all time is the best way to run an economy. And it was with forebodings that I heard in the fall of 1979 the Federal Reserve announce that henceforth it would bind itself to an inflexible growth rate of the money supply.

The stock of monetarism on the bourse of practical forecasting and of academic opinion took a severe buffeting from 1979 until last August when Paul A. Volcker's Federal Reserve temporarily removed the corset of monetarism. I applauded this move in advance and indeed regarded it as overdue.

But in all candor I feared that the nation might be in a Catch-22 situation where the attempt to lower interest rates — both real and nominal — by the Federal Reserve might lead Wall Street denizens, brain-washed by various simple versions of monetarism, to fear a new outbreak of inflation, thus pushing long-term rates higher. I was similarly concerned that, as a consequence, the attempt to ease credit by the Fed might instead cause bonds to be dumped and end up tightening the available credit for housing and other durable-goods investments.

Fortunately, Wall Street reacted in the more old-fashioned Keynesian way. Bond prices soared, carrying equities upward with them in last August's Henry Kaufman market. Again in last October's Volcker market, equities and bonds zoomed upward.

The Legacy of Keynes

One must not forget the birthday child at the centennial party, concentrating only on his partisans and enemies. Enough has been said to show that, in its evolved form, Keynesian economics is still very much alive and constitutes one of the three main theories of 1980's macroeconomics — along with monetarism and the new school of rational expectations (which denies that any government policies can have a real effect on the economy once people catch on to them).

Keynes himself was, in a word, brilliant. Son of a learned Cambridge don and an activist mother (the Mayor of the town of Cambridge), he ran away with all the honors at Eton College (a prestigious boys school near Windsor Castle) and Cambridge University. With Virginia Woolf, Vanessa Bell and Lytton Strachey, he founded the precious Bloomsbury Set. As a youngster he virtually ran the British Treasury in World War I.

Wider fame came to him when he resigned from the Versailles peace delegation and warned that the punitive Versailles Treaty would only end in another rising within Germany. Hitler proved him right 15 years later.

In 1925, Keynes also warned Winston Churchill, then Chancellor of the Exchequer, against the folly of England's going back onto the gold standard at the punitive prewar exchange rate of $4.87 for the pound. Churchill, with misgivings that did him credit, was forced by the banking establishment to disregard Keynes's advice. The rest, alas, is history — a subsequent decade of mass unemployment and the eventual eclipse of Britain as a leading economic power.

Keynes was a canny speculator. He ran a successful insurance company, endowed the ballet and enriched King's College, his alma mater. Despite himself, he became respectable, masterminded World War II British finances, and set up the 1944 Bretton Woods system of fixed exchange rates, which lasted until 1971 — and which some now would like to resurrect. He died a peer, Lord Keynes of Tilton.

For 20 years, American conservative opinion considered Keynes a radical. Herbert Hoover, who often attacked Roosevelt's deficit spending — invented the pejorative term "Marxist-Keynesian."

Actually, Keynes was an elitist exponent of the middle classes. Like Bertrand Russell, he recognized even before Stalin's hegemony the totalitarian inefficiencies of a system run in the name of the working class.

An optimist who lived at a time when the world economy was running so badly that clever gimmicks could still work wonders, Keynes's object was to save capitalism from itself. In the end, his prescription in its most simple form self-destructed, as the obligation to run a full-employment humanitarian state caused modern economies to succumb to the new disease of stagflation — high inflation along with joblessness and excess capacity.

Economists of the most diverse views are constantly asking themselves: What would Keynes advise if he were now alive. And usually — whether the economist is a free-marketeer like Friederich von Hayek or one with strong interventionist leanings like John Kenneth Galbraith — they pay Keynes the supreme compliment of believing that if brought back to earth, Maynard would be favoring just what each of them happens to favor.

One also might wonder what Lord Keynes would prescribe for the huge structural deficit of Ronald Reagan, with the crowding out of investment that it implies once the American economy reattains high levels of employment.

But for all his persuasiveness, could he really sell increased tax rates to the President? Keynes fancied he could teach heads of state, even those who were not very good at understanding economics.

For whatever good or ill Keynes may have wrought in economic ideology, when asked late in life what he would do differently if given a chance to live his life over again, his only reply was, "I'd have drunk more champagne."

On his hundredth birthday which takes place on June 5, (it also happens to be Adam Smith's 260th birthday) we can all join in a symbolic toast for a life well fulfilled.

PAUL A. SAMUELSON

Succumbing to Keynesianism

In the Chicago economics classrooms of the 1930s, markets always cleared. Yet some students and teachers knew they had to reconcile theoretical dogma with the depression misery around them.

In 1968 I wrote an article entitled "What Classical and Neoclassical Monetary Theory Really Was." It was an exercise in remembering. I cast my mind back some thirty-five years to recall what it was that we used to think about macroeconomics in those olden times.

Memory is notoriously unreliable. Hindsight can contaminate what you think happened earlier. So a really professional student of the history of science—I have in mind a virtuoso of the subject like Don Patinkin—takes all claims from memory with a grain of salt. "Show me your documents, reprints, contemporaneous lecture notes," he correctly insists before he awards credits for scientific novelty and innovation. For better or worse, however, the 1968 reconstruction seems to have served a useful purpose and has been reproduced in various anthologies of the subject.

I want to engage here in a related exercise. This time I seek to dredge my memory not in order to capture past scientific understandings, but rather to try to recall past puzzlements and vague dissatisfactions with received theories and paradigms. This is a study that ought to delight Thomas Kuhn, because it tries to deal with the dynamics of transitions in paradigms. I seek to explain to myself, and to my posterity in an overlapping-generations model of scientific development, why I was vulnerable to the heretical analyses of Keynes' *General Theory*. My resistances to the new

Nobel laureate PAUL A. SAMUELSON is Institute Professor of Economics at MIT. This article was presented as the Horowitz Lecture in Jerusalem in March 1984.

virus, if I can remember them, will perhaps be of as much interest as any capitulations.

Even a scholarly purist like Patinkin may find the present endeavor of interest. It is less pretentious than the 1968 effort, in that this is a tale of recognized inadequacies. Moreover, in narrating most of my findings I believe I am serving as a partial sample of all the economists of my generation rather than testifying only to what was peculiar to my own *Weltanschauung* and research effort.

As things really happen

History, I have come to believe, never gets things quite right. History is not generally written by survivors. It is written by those who follow the survivors, and it has to be as biased as the samples of retained records are biased. All this was brought home to me one summer when I was still a lad. In those days it was safe to play in Chicago's Jackson Park. One Saturday a pal asked me if I wanted to make half of fifty dollars. During the Great Depression that was real money, so I was game. Thurston, the Great Magician, was playing the Tivoli Theatre that week and had a standing offer to pay that amount to anyone who could explain how he sawed a woman in half and put her back together in full sight of the audience. My friend Bill Partridge had attended every performance that week and had gone up on the stage in accordance with Thurston's invitation. There he had learned, by quick observation, that the legs of the sawed woman were not those of the *ex ante* and *ex post* unsawed woman. I came into the act because Bill feared Thurston had spotted him as a repeater and would withdraw the offer at the final performance. I verified with my own eyes the anatomical substitutions. My own value-added was to decide to come armed with a postage stamp. At the final run I spoke up to claim the reward, pasting the stamp on the original legs as I did so. Thurston, perspiring only a little, had me help him with the sawing. Then, in full sight of the audience and me, he palmed the stamp and commanded the ushers to remove me quietly from the stage.

My rational expectation had been frustrated by fraud. So I hung around the stage door and theater exit. Person after person, leaving the theater, remarked to me how magically Thurston had defied my explanations. Ever since, I have known that historians never get things right—even when they see things happening before their eyes. All the more reason to have a Rip van Winkle like me tell a chronicler like Axel Leijonhufvud how it really was in history.

There will never be a better time. I am not getting any younger. And there are precious few in the relevant cohort. A James Tobin, who began his studies in the academic year when the *General Theory* was launched, is too young. A Howard Ellis, or even a Gottfried Haberler, is too old. People like Alvin Hansen, who worked in the *ancien régime* and also the brave new world, are (alas) mostly dead. Scarcity imparts value.

Schizophrenic times, desperate reconciliations

I began the study of economics on January 2, 1932. America, indeed the world, was in deep depression, though this had not quite yet contaminated any of the books assigned to me at the University of Chicago. Nor were the lectures I heard from Aaron Director, Lloyd Mints, Henry Simons, or Frank Knight as yet affected analytically by the bankruptcy of banks and the foreclosures of mortgages that were going on around us. Paul Douglas, always a populist do-gooder, did worry about unemployment but he had been doing that even in the palmy 1920s.

Professor Conrad Blythe of Auckland once told me that it was hard learning Keynesian economics at a time when the total unemployment in New Zealand was seventy-five people! Oddly, even though the outside world of the 1930s was being wracked by increasing joblessness and excess capacity, in Chicago it was easy learning pre-Keynesian economics in which all markets always cleared. We handled the situation by being schizophrenic. For no twenty-four hours were we unaware of the Great Depression. In witness of this, Frank Knight gave a famous speech in which he declared that there was at hand a simple choice between communism and fascism—and, as for himself, he would have to opt for communism. None of this affected his ongoing polemics in capital theory, in which he insisted that the period of production was either zero or infinity.

At the same time that Jacob Viner, Knight, and Simons maintained a theoretical belief in Say's Law, they were motivated to sign manifestos in 1931 calling for anti-depression fiscal deficits. (Arthur F. Burns, no radical at any stage in his career known to me, once boasted that he had written for the New York *Herald Tribune* a demand for deficit spending. Only my later Harvard mentors—Schumpeter, Chamberlin, and

Leontief, to say nothing of their elders, Bullock, Carver, Gay, and Burbank—resisted deviating into good sense during the depression gale.)

A convert takes his religion seriously. From age 16 to 19 I was puzzled. I knew there were no jobs. Throughout my college career I earned exactly $3.00; it was for a Saturday's stint delivering luxury fruits, but I was not called back and the University Placement Service had no leads for me to pursue. People who still held their jobs were lucky and knew it. How could all this be in a market-clearing model? Walras-Debreu paradigms, like Marshall-Cassel paradigms, have no room in them for lucky and unlucky transactors. Under rent controls you know that reality is not on the demand curve because those who can't get a flat would gladly make payments to a lucky tenant to induce him to give up his. Similarly, if one in ten job applicants garnered a job at the depressed 1932 rates, all the others would have been glad to bribe him to turn it over to them.

Clearly I was ripe to accept, a few years later, Keynes' proposal that money wage rates be accepted as if they were "sticky." This was not a perfect bicycle, but it was the best wheel in town. But at the time I worked desperately to fit all this into my classical system. In despair I fabricated the hypothesis that people already on the job must have developed special skills that made them more valuable to their employers than the unemployed alternatives were. Since the unemployed would work at wage rates deeply below those that prevailed, I realized that this human-capital reed would not bear the weight to explain what needed to be explained.

Not always did I agree with my parents. But one remark my mother made stuck in mind: "Don't you know, son, that times are really good only during a war?" Certainly the booming 1914–1918 Gary steel mills had propelled my family into the comfortable middle classes. And, even before the nationwide slowdown following 1929, real estate investments in Florida and elsewhere had been eroding the family net worth. Full employment only in wartimes was not at all consistent with Richard Ely's *Outline of Economics* or with Dennis Robertson's Cambridge handbook on *Money*, our beginners' textbooks.

Two different tensions: ethical and scientific

Kuhn's *Structure of Scientific Revolutions* does well to call attention to times when new empirical findings contradict or challenge the comfortable complacencies of an established school or camp. But more needs to be studied on the competitive process whereby paradigms do get modified and abandoned under the bombardment of anomalous and aberrant observations. There are no crucial experiments that instantly annihilate a theory. But theories do get nickled and dimed away until their adherents are ripe for seduction by different theories.

It would not be of great scientific interest if I were to belabor the fact that, during the Great Depression, the widespread suffering I saw aroused my humanitarian sympathies. What is of scientific interest is how the observed, omnipresent hardships constituted a challenge to my belief in the economic theories I was engaged in mastering. Freud has rationalized what the history of scholarship has recorded, that the brain can consciously or unconsciously shrug off the disagreements registered by the facts with the nice theories we have come to cherish. During the Great Depression, the naggings of the heart were an irritant that kept calling the bluffs of the complacent subconscious.

So a few words on the depression miseries will serve a scientific purpose. When economists are shown distresses dealt out in the market, they accept them remarkably cheerfully. Lots of the unemployed don't want to work. Many of them are unemployable. When we lie in the stochastic beds that we have made for ourselves, it must be expected that some of them will be hard ones. So go our usual rationalizations.

After 1929 it was the sturdy middle classes, and not just the lumpen proletariat, who were down and out. It was not all that unfashionable or disreputable to be bankrupt. By the last Hoover years, the states and localities had run out of money for relief. In middle-class neighborhoods like mine, you constantly had children at the door, asking by mouth or with a note for a dime, a quarter, or a potato: saying, in a believable fashion, we are starving. Virtually all the banks I knew shut down. In my part of the world you had to buy change! We used to rib my older brother about his $200 pen, the one he had been given as an inducement to put what he had saved for his college education into a particular bank. If he eventually received three cents on the dollar, he was lucky.

Read Homer Hoyt's *One Hundred Years of Chicago Land Values* and you will realize that in the early 1930s no real estate changed hands in that city. Do I exaggerate? Very well, I exaggerate—but only a little. Ernest Henderson and Robert Moore started the great Sheraton hotel chain with virtually no cash. All they had to do was assume some mortgage obligations that had long been in default and carried negligible personal liability.

Apparent poverty midst plenty

It certainly looked as if the economic system no longer occupied its full-employment equilibrium state, its neoclassical equilibrium. It seemed to be stuck in a deadweight-loss rotten equilibrium, one which threatened to get still more rotten in a self-fulfilling cumulative downturn. (Of course all this is here expressed in terminology that would not have been standard in 1932 or before 1936.) Economists, students like me and scholars like my teachers, couldn't face their mirrors in the morning without some story to rationalize what was happening and provide conformity with our regnant academic models. The high tariff was a crutch I at one time leaned on to explain how the depression could have occurred. Longer lasting was an attempt to tie up the depression with some kind of overshoot and undershoot in the money supply and the price level.

At some time in my freshman or sophomore year, I got the impression from my teachers that it was the Hawley-Smoot tariff that had caused the Great Depression. Being gullible and yet desperately aware of the need for reconciliation of reality with market-clearing dogma, I grabbed for this lifeline. Imagine, then, my dismay to hear Aaron Director speculate one day in class that the deadweight loss traceable to all tariffs and quotas could hardly equal 10 percent of national income *in toto*. At that time of poverty in the midst of plenty, real GNP was already down from its 1929 peak by several times that estimate. So I had lost my first crutch of rationalization.

Like all beginners in economics, I found the process of multiple-bank-expansion of money more fascinating than it really is. Since old-fashioned macroeconomics had nothing on its stage other than the supply of money and the price level, one of the ways to rationalize the Great Depression was to blame it on the authorities who let the total of M decline. By now it has been amply debunked that there was at Chicago around the time of 1940–1950, or in the 1932–5 time of Milton Friedman and me, a subtle, fruitful oral tradition concerning the demand for money. There was no such oral tradition at Chicago in the classrooms of Viner, Mints, Knight, or Simons; nor in the students' corridors of Albert Hart, George Stigler, Allen Wallis, Milton Friedman, Russ Nicholls, Homer Jones, Jacob Mosak, Lee Bach, Martin Bronfenbrenner, Paul Samuelson, Gregg Lewis, or anyone else.

But there was an important oral tradition in America of that time, shared with central and private bankers not absent from the Chicago corridors. It was pre-Keynesian and is in danger of getting lost. It had two important elements.

To understand the first, recall that M and M′ were the symbols then used to denote currency and bank-deposit money in Fisher-like quantity equations:

$$MV + M'V' = PQ$$

With the banks failing around us and with banks reluctant to lend and creditworthy borrowers reluctant to borrow, we tended to regard the M'/M ratio as a countercyclical quasi-endogenous variable. And of course it was standard pre-1930 wisdom to expect V and V′ to be similar countercyclical variables.

It was simply not on the agenda for serious discussion and debate that the Federal Reserve would suspend all concern for its legal reserve requirements and take whatever actions were necessary to force (M,M') up enough to make nominal and real GNP rise sufficiently to end the depression. I do not defend this tacit presupposition of all policy discussions. But I do describe it as a fact. I suspect that any brave soul who came into court with the advice that the Fed should simply ignore such feasibility constraints in the interest of ending the depression would have been laughed out of court, dismissed as an unsound fellow not worth listening to.

Too few readers of the history of the period realize that, whatever crimes the Fed was guilty of then, it certainly did not *decrease* the total of "high-powered reserves money" in the early 1930s. If it is a crime for the Fed not to have increased high-powered money by enough, however much that would have had to be—to offset and compensate for the reduction in the multiplier relating $M+M'$ to reserve money that was entailed by the severity of the depression and by the cascade of bank failures and fear of further runs on banks—then the Federal Reserve is subject to indictment. But it is not justice to apply the standards of conduct dictated only by hindsight and which were beyond even the contemplation of the brightest and best of the earlier time.

When you read whig history of the Great Depression, remember that whig history is the perversion of actual history that comes from the pens of those seeking to dictate how the might-have-beens could have been arranged to better achieve their vision of progress.

Eroding faith in the potency of money policy

Why didn't we all become monetary cranks in 1932–35 and simply advocate that the Fed flood the system with new Ms? However potent such policy would have been if pushed hard in 1931–32, we began to be seduced by an oral tradition that in deep depression, new effective M would be hard or impossible to engineer.

While Rome burned, we at Chicago fiddled with so-called 100 percent money. One alleged advantage of that doctrinaire crotchet of my Chicago teachers—Viner being a good-sense dissenter—was that any fractional-reserve system would be subject to a *varying* effective fraction. Only 1.00 was a fraction that (almost by definition) could and would never change.

From practical bankers at first, and from academics only later toward the middle of the 1930s, I began to hear a different dissenting argument that became part of an important oral tradition: "You can lead a horse to water but you can't make him drink. Banks aren't able to get loaned up with zero excess reserves if there are insufficient would-be borrowers from the banks of the requisite creditworthiness." When bread was scarce, Marie Antoinette said, Let them eat cake. My orthodox teachers said, in effect, "If banks can't find loans to make in depression times, let them get rid of their excess reserves and get 'loaned up' by acquiring government bonds."

As a student I bought this line of argument. But not without the uneasy recognition that this could involve bidding down the interest rate on gilt-edged Treasury securities so much as to lower equivalently the velocity of M+M′. I wish I could remember in what year I heard Henry Simons say, "Just what is accomplished by open-market operations that add M to the system and at the same time subtract from it an equivalent amount of near-money substitutes?" (Into the ears of Chicago babes were being directed in the early 1930s, not 1956 Friedman or 1940 Clark Warburton questions, but rather Keynesian *General Theory* questions—and of the polar liquidity-trap type to boot.)

Indeed, during this period I heard Frank Knight give one of his rare analyses of current macroeconomics. Its date is unclear in my mind, but I seem to recall that it took place in Haskell Hall, where the business school was located. Its contents may have been similar to that of his 1941 *Review of Economics & Statistics* paper entitled "The Business Cycle, Interest and Money: A Methodological Approach." In any case, through the filter of imperfect memory, I later attributed to him something like the following view:

Normally, equilibrium economics prevails (Say's Law and all). But occasionally, when a depression disturbance has somehow been able to become big enough, vicious circles of expectation can temporarily become perverse enough so that the usual remedies and comparative statics (of the "elasticity optimists") cannot be counted on. Either no therapy will be effective or, at the least, unconventional therapies may be needed.

Presumably, such abnormal periods are rare.

Rationalizations, rationalizations; doubts, doubts

Freud tells us that memories, like dreams, often serve a purpose that is independent of their ostensible truth and meaning. This version attributed to Knight would give a neoclassical student license to look for an alternative paradigm—at least for the duration of the depression emergency.

My point is that what was atrophying in the face of depression behavior of the economic system was the confidence in Say's Law—that a competitive system, left to itself, would generate whatever reductions in interest rates were necessary to keep total MV+M′V′ spending at the level needed this year to banish joblessness. Atrophying was the belief that real-world competition would, without a helping hand, lower real wage rates to the level needed to generate ordinary jobs for all. Why, one asked oneself fruitlessly, should the real wage needed to clear the market in 1933 be *lower* than in 1929? Population and capital stock were virtually unchanged. Technology was not lost; if anything, some new options had been added.

Naturally, as a recent convert to general equilibrium, I toyed with the notion that the one in four who could not find work in the United States and Germany were *voluntarily* unemployed. Why such a sudden shift toward leisure *after* 1929? Why had workers suddenly turned uppity all over the world? If the general demand for labor was given by the marginal-product relation in the aggregate production function (à la Paul Douglas or A. C. Pigou), why had $\partial Q(L,K)/\partial LK$ shifted so much downward when K and the laws of knowledge had changed so little since 1929? *Voluntary* unemployment satisfied Hayek in the 1930s as an explanation, but my reason had to reject it as unuseful and for that matter downright misleading.

Let me repeat the point already made: how inadequate conventional economics seemed to be in squaring with the obvious facts. Often what I was learning in the classroom seemed to go against what warm-hearted noneconomists were urging ought to be done. Neoclassical economics seemed to be requiring me to warn them that their therapies would add to sufferings rather than subtract from them. Within the university itself, and in dialogue with people on the street, I felt a tension between the paradigm of mainstream economics and the commonsense views of amateurs. What really troubled me was how unconvincing my own arguments sounded in my ears.

Actually, few of us American pre-Keynesians went to such ridiculous extremes as did Lionel Robbins and Friedrich Von Hayek during the Great Depression. Von Hayek's 1931 *Prices and Production* did pique analysts' curiosity. But its author never could tie up his metaphors concerning artificial lengthenings of the period of production through overissue of M, followed by a resultant shortening of the period, with the actual depression process taking place in the real world; and few believed Hayek when he warned that providing people with funds to enable them to spend on consumption would only make the depression worse. Only the most conservative of American economists advocated letting the system sweat out the problems. The trouble was, we weren't sure what policies to advocate to help the depression come to an end.

Outside of academia, there were plenty of monetary cranks who were advocating printing of money by the government. Telling them the result would be inflation was not very effective in those days when it was a manifest goal of policy in many quarters to get the price index back to its 1925 level of 100. (In this connection I can still recall the overrated Bernard Baruch's testimony for price controls during World War II; he and everybody else present seemed stumped when one of the Congressmen innocently asked, "Why do you want to keep prices down when we haven't yet got back to 1925's 100?")

If Frederic Bastiat had stood on a park soapbox and given one of his sermons on social harmonies, warning against the notion that a hurricane can make the community better off by encouraging spending on rebuilding, he would have been hooted at. Instead, I can remember little fables that went the rounds, to some puzzlement and considerable applause. A baker counterfeits bills in order to buy clothes. That gives the tailor money to spend, which after several rounds results in his buying bread. This permits the baker to extinguish the money he has illegitimately printed. Everyone is better off; the tailors and bakers get work; all of us fill our stomachs with bread and cover our backs with clothes. And who is hurt?

Of course this is fable and not science. It is a Bagehot multiplier process but with no systematic leakage through saving, and hence no damping that creates a finite rather than infinite Kahn multiplier. (I never knew of Richard Kahn's 1931 article on the multiplier until I was assigned it at Harvard in 1936!)

From the mouths of oracles

When I had observed that there were people ready to replace those lucky enough to have a regular job, and with almost as much effectiveness and at a much lower wage if that were necessary, it naturally made me wonder why all the unemployed bakers and tailors could not get together and take in each others' laundry for a comfortable living. During the Great Depression, Frank Graham of Princeton even seriously proposed a supplementary division of labor manned by the unemployed and utilizing surplus factories, financed if not by ordinary money then by some kind of scrip. The manifest difficulties in getting such enterprises started and keeping them viable brought home to me how far from realism was the usual Walrasian assumption of constant returns to scale, with every seller free to throw more of his goods on the market without sensibly altering the ruling market prices. Obviously, any good theory of effective demand, once we got it, would have to presuppose Chamberlinian imperfect competition rather than auction-market purity of competition.

Speaking of issuers of scrip, I must recall how the heretics of the underworld of economics were then obsessed with the problem of *hoarding*. It was feared that even if currency was dropped down from biplanes, anxious people couldn't be counted on to spend it. So more than one reformer advocated dated money that would lose its value with time: if its real-interest yield were made negative enough, then it would surely get spent.

The parable of the counterfeiting baker made it not

implausible to regard public works as essentially costless. I think it was the battleship Missouri that was built during the Great Depression, and which proved useful in World War II. The reactionary head of the Harvard economics department would not admit in 1936 that the Missouri had cost nothing—had perhaps cost less than nothing, considering the extra Kuznets national income it brought into being, but he could not explain the logic of his contention. (By the way, when he would solemnly proclaim that a dollar of expenditure was a dollar of taxation, we would slap our thighs with glee; I can remember Robert Bishop's whispering: "There are only two billion exceptions to that theorem." When Milton Friedman proclaims in the 1980s that a dollar of expenditure is a dollar of taxation, he obviously takes for granted what we would not let Burbank take for granted in the 1930s—that the natural rate of unemployment is what a system is going to experience on the average, and that it is not a level that can be affected by macro policy. Just as the precession of the perihelion of Mercury provided an aberrant exception to Newton's simple theory of gravitation, the ongoing pattern of economic history of the 1930s provided an aberrant exception to the Walras model that would make Friedman's contention unquestionable.)

Non-Euclidian economics: Social Security

A few years later, when Keynes' *General Theory* came along, one had a handle to deal with these problems. I think particularly of the mechanics of Social Security finance. When Marion Crawford Samuelson worked as research assistant to Seymour Harris on this topic, she found that different paradigms gave diametrically opposed results. If the system always stayed spontaneously at full employment, with whatever people wanted to save at that level being effectively converted into net capital formation, then fully funding Social Security would bring into existence a larger stock of capital, and out of its fruits retirement consumption would be the more easily provided. (For simplicity, this assumes that the government program provides the thrift which people would not themselves have been providing.)

Suppose, however, that the tax revenues collected to fund Social Security fully produced a budget surplus that was not automatically accompanied by a lowering of the real rate of interest sufficient to induce a matching increment of private capital formation. If the effect of that were to increase unemployment and lower income, then the effective level of investment-saving achieved would not be that of her first paradigm. Indeed, if the accelerator-induced reduction in net capital formation outweighed the increment of capital formation induced by lower interest rates, the attempt to fund Social Security fully might leave the system with less capital formation when people come to retire.

If you read many modern treatments of Social Security—as, for example, in the writings of Martin Feldstein or in Samuelson—the paradigm used presupposes that markets do always clear at full employment. Whether that is a useful paradigm to invoke for the 1980s is not my primary business to discuss on the present occasion. But I am required to state that the feel of the 1930s was very much against such a paradigm.

Learning to love a new theory

Pressure of other research interests keeps me from keeping up on the fine points of methodology and the philosophy of science. Sometimes I am not sure of the exact difference between Karl Popper and Imre Lakatos. Therefore, when by chance I recently read Douglas W. Hands' *Second Thoughts on Lakatos*, I was somewhat taken aback to see the allegation that a theory is progressively useful only if it predicts some new facts that are in some degree empirically borne out by the data. Taken literally, this strange doctrine seems to say that, if the facts of the Great Depression (mass unemployment, worsening of the situation due to Hoover's attempts to increase tax rates, etc.) were known before Keynes wrote his book, then there is no worth in his theory even if his theory describes and explains those known facts better than the preceding paradigm did.

Surely, this cannot put the matter right. I have no reason to deny that there is something more impressive about Einstein's predicting deflection of a star's rays by the sun *before* the 1919 eclipse expedition takes place than his theory's predicting the already known facts; we rightly regard that as an important advance in science and a tribute to that novel theory.

This leads me to another point. I would rather have a theory with good foundations than one with incomplete or hazy foundations. But it is better to have a theory with imperfect foundations that gives some fit to the facts than to have an impeccable theory that doesn't at all fit the facts.

When Keynes' *General Theory* came along, there were parts of it I didn't understand at first. There were parts that, perhaps, I never could understand. There were parts that I was willing to ignore or to replace by alternative relations. But in science you must be opportunistic, not be a perfectionist. In 1983, on the centennial of Schumpeter's birth, I criticized him for getting no benefit from the *General Theory* because he was not able to square it with a Walras-Debreu formulation of the world. *That was his own loss.*

I am not saying that a theory is the better for its imperfections. By its descriptive fruits we measure the value of a theory. And it is not a small thing, either in economics or in physics, to have a theory that can usefully describe the known facts *after* we know them. Better an ill-founded theory that fits the relevant facts than a well-founded one that doesn't.

Being converted to a new scientific theory is not like falling in love. Falling in love, poets tell us, is a one-time thing. Before you are in love, you are not. After, you are. And forever.

I have told why one might have been attracted to Keynes' *General Theory*, softened up to give it an experimental whirl. But a few drinks don't make you a hopeless addict.

What I want to point out is that American events of the period from 1936 to 1941 were even more conducive to respect for the Keynesian model than were the pre-trough years. By 1938, short-term interest rates had been forced so low that the liquidity-preference functions of Keynes seemed required by the facts of the day. Lowering the short-term interest by the central bank, à la Hawtrey, could not seem a promising tool when that merely implied a Treasury bill rate down from 3/8 to 3/8 of 1 percent to 3/8 of 3/8 of 3/38 of 1 percent. (I often tell the story of asking a government official why so many millions of dollars of overdue Treasury bills remained outstanding. "Do you know a better way of holding a million dollars?" he asked. I really didn't.)

So, affection blossomed into love.

But in science that way lies danger. In science one asks of every theory, "What have you done for me lately?"

The Keynesianism I like is not that of 1936 or 1948. It is the evolved and evolving apparatus that rediscovers money when money is mattering more and forgets liquidity traps when they are far away.

COMMENT

Paul A. Samuelson

It is unrewarding to debate about what the man Keynes would think in 1983 about the doctrines of Lucas, Sargent, and other rational expectationists. Keynes died when he died, and the curve recording the state of his macrodynamic methodologies was not one of those smooth trajectories that lend themselves to confident reliance on Taylor–Maclaurin or other long-distance extrapolations.

It is more rewarding to regard Keynes as an example of a scholar of brilliant good sense. One can then ask, 'How should an informed scholar appraise the new classical school in its rational expectationist version?' This of course is a tall order. Since rational expectations is one of the four important macro paradigms with a sizeable present-day following, the task as described in this paragraph is one that a vast number of articles are constantly being written about. There must be some special reason why, at the centennial celebrations of the birth of John Maynard Keynes, this ongoing research endeavor is especially in season – more in season for example than at a similar festival to honor Joseph Schumpeter's hundredth birthday.

That special reason is not hard to find. Keynes's 1936 *General Theory* had a revolutionary impact precisely because the novel paradigm that it proposed led to analysis and therapies so different from those of pre-1929 classical and neoclassical economics. The new classical economics of rational expectationists is a return with a vengeance to the pre-Keynesian verities.

Utilizing Keynesian methods and insights, I find the modern world poorly described by the depression Keynesian mode. I do not find that the market-clearing neutral-money new classical theory models of the short and intermediate run work well. But if I had to choose between these two extreme archetypes, a ridiculous Hobson's choice, I fear that the one to jettison would have to be the Ur-Keynesian model, which indeed was not one that commanded the main allegiance of Keynes himself.

In short, what Keynes would have thought of the modern classical school is what I think of it: markets do not clear perfectly in the short run and policy interventions can have appreciable real effect for quite a while. But people learn faster these days and the easy Keynesian victories are long behind us.

REVOLUTION AND COUNTERREVOLUTION

Anyone who mastered the *General Theory* in, say, the years 1936–39 was led to believe in quite a different paradigm to explain and understand the world from the models that pre-Keynesians had believed in. When I say pre-Keynesians I mean neoclassical economists in the broad sense of the word neoclassical. I agree with Kaldor that Marshall did not have quite the same view of general equilibrium that Walras did; but their differences fade into insignificance in comparison with the difference between a three-equation macro system of the *General Theory* type and any of the versions of economics that I was taught before 1935.

The 'new classical economics' of Robert Lucas, Tom Sargent, Robert Barro and others is truly a counterrevolution and the same cannot be said of 'monetarism'. If I can believe in Lucas market clearing, then I can no longer believe in the behavior equations and relations of the *General Theory* and this holds both for positivistic description or prediction and for policy diagnosis and therapeutic recommendation. Even Milton Friedman found the new rational expectationism at first unwelcome, since it denied the real evils of systematic mismanagement of money.

I was somewhat saddened to read many of the papers prepared for this conference and to hear much of our discussion. Like the Bourbons so many of us have learned nothing and forgotten nothing. In my observation the way of the world has changed much since the 1930s. Because I regard myself as a serious Keynesian, a post-Keynesian, I have had continually to modify my paradigms and insights. That is not pleasant to do, or easy to do. But it has to be done in the interest of science and I experience no serious qualms of conscience in constantly adapting my Keynesianism to the new cut of the world. To cease to be an old-fashioned Keynesian is not to become a monetarist: I have lost my faith, not my reason.

Having lived through the various stages of unreconstructed Keynesianism, let me describe my view of them.

DEPRESSION KEYNESIANISM

Back in 1938 when the short-term rate of interest in the U.S. was $\frac{3}{8}$ of $\frac{3}{8}$ of 1 per cent, it was sensible to believe in an almost infinitely elastic liquidity preference schedule and to be skeptical about the potency of conventional monetary policy. In the early 1930s when banks were failing, firms were going bankrupt, and mortgages were in delinquency on a macro scale, it was sensible to worry about liquidity traps, vicious cycles of wage cuts and debt deflation, inelastic marginal efficiency schedules. The textbook paradigm of deep-depression Keynesianism (which Maynard himself only occasionally believed in) deserved serious scrutiny then.

The comparative statics of the depression paradigm is about as different from that of Walras's system as one could imagine. Take for example the vital issue of Roosevelt's social security system, which was adopted in 1935. The reasoning of Jevons in the Victorian age, that Britain's coal mines would become exhausted and that she therefore should pay off her public debt, was ludicrous reasoning in the depression version of Keynesian economics. To finance the system in the way it was then decided to do, by essentially pay-as-you-go non-actuarial funding, made more sense: pay-as-you-go would add rather than subtract from the capital stock available to help support workers when they became old; to follow Jevons's orthodox advice might in the Walras–Say paradigm increase the capital stock of future generations, but in the depression whilst the paradox of thrift was valid, following that same advice would most certainly backfire.

NEOCLASSICAL SYNTHESIS

By 1940 simple-minded Keynesianism of the depression paradigm variety had become outmoded hat. It was right that it should be followed by a general model of the *General Theory* in which government policy could hope to use the levers of fiscal and monetary policy to cause the *IS* and *LM* curves of the Keynesian system to shift so as to achieve an equilibrium intersection nearer to full employment and with a mix between capital formation and real consumption that could be shifted toward investment by greater emphasis upon expansionary credit policy and on austere fiscal policy. This post-Depression Keynesian paradigm worked in the Roosevelt–Truman years, and it even continued to work in Europe and Japan into the 1950s and 1960s. If a Lucas had said then that the 1949 devaluation of the principal currencies *vis-à-vis* the dollar would soon be found out and would spend itself completely in price-level changes with few favorable real effects of any duration, he would rightly have been laughed out of court by informed observers of how the world then worked.

Let me stick with my practical example of how to devise a good social security system, bringing the analysis forward in time. It is saying the same thing to say that Milton Friedman was at this time working out the monetarists' paradigm as an alternative to Keynesianism or to say that Friedman was belatedly discovering for himself the elements of Keynesian liquidity theory and demand for money, and was converging toward the post-Keynesian models of Tobin, Solow, Samuelson, and Modigliani. In the systems of all of these scholars, it would have been deemed feasible to accomplish the Jevonian task of adding to public thrift by means of an austere overbalanced fiscal budget, but with the proviso that the fiscal surplus would not be permitted to abort its own thriftiness by causing an insufficiency of effective demand; instead room would be made for 'crowding in', by the Federal Reserve central bank following an easy money policy that could ensure that the ample fraction of resources left over from full-employment consumption demands would be channelled into effective capital formation.

In social security terms, the system could now afford full actuarial funding without fear of the paradox of thrift. And, social security aside, in the miracle economies of the Common Market and Japan, high investment equilibria were maintained throughout much of the 1950s and 1960s. I recognize that neo-Keynesians of the Kaldor–Robinson–Pasinetti–Garegnani school could not countenance this possibility in terms of their preferred fixed-capital. But what killed off the golden epoch of the 1950s and 1960s was not some confirmatory scientific findings pointing in the direction of the doubts of the neo-Keynesian school. Most of the economic world simply stopped paying much attention to their models.

STAGFLATION

What ended the honeymoon of functional finance and, in Leijonhufvud's accurate words, lost to the camp of Keynesianism many of the able economists of younger ages was the dilemma of stagflation. By the end of the 1960s, and with a vengeance after 1973, inflation rates showed a damnable tendency to accelerate at higher and higher (so-called) natural rates of unemployment. The mixed economy was sick; and it was that sickness that opened the way for the virus of the Lucas rational-expectationist new classical economics.

The sickness of the mixed economy, which must be kept distinct from the imperfections of us economists and the decline in our self-esteems and reputations, I must repeat, is in its fundamentals the problem of stagflation. For more than a decade I have been arguing that this stagflation is a basic feature of the humane welfare state that has replaced ruthless capitalism. It changes drastically the behavior equations of the modern macro world, and it itself has to be understood as much in terms of microeconomic incentives and behaviors as in terms of conventional macroeconomics.

As a description of what happens in the real world and as a tool for intermediate-run macro prediction, the Lucas–Sargent–Barro model is a poor tool. Those members of their school who venture an occasional prediction have terrible cricket batting averages. (Barro I recall at a 1974

Federal Reserve academic consultants' meeting had the grossest squared-error of unemployment estimate that I had heard that year; with apologies for picking on him as one daring occasionally to venture a view, I mention a recent Goldman-Sachs report trying to test the Barro view that when Reaganomics promises large structural deficits in the mid-1980s, that will lead us rational bequeathers to step up our private savings now: there have of course been no such stepups discernible in private savings. I have had fun with the Barro–Rush regressions purporting to predict nominal GNP changes from surprises in M: until these regressions were tamed by autocorrelation corrections barely consonant with their spirit, they led to fantastic extrapolations. Sargent's resurrections of 1923 currency stabilizations, I must report, although they have not been useful in leading us to expect Reagan victories over inflation at little real cost, have in my view slightly prepared us for somewhat better anti-inflation success than earlier Tobin and R. J. Gordon regressions had suggested to me. However, thus far the dicta by the rational expectationists on the miracle that can be expected to follow the establishment of credibility have themselves lacked credibility (and, often, have lacked operational meaning).)

SUMMING UP

Having written on Keynes so many times in this centenary year, I fear to repeat myself. Let me say again that the Keynesian system is better than Keynes the man. Even when we are forced into empirical and policy inferences that are quite the reverse of those appropriate for 1936, we modern economists are using the tools that were not part of economics before Keynes wrote. When Friedman writes down a monetarist model or Meltzer writes down one of his versions, readers note that there is a complete isomorphism with models written down by Keynesians like Tobin or Modigliani – and all of them are different, distinctly different at the methodological level, from the Walras–Debreu or Knight–Viner models of my pre-Keynesian schooling.

Yes, the Keynes model needed, and needs, better exact foundations. But as a student I learned by 1937 that it is better to have a model with inexact foundations that gives you a good grip to handle reality than to wait for better foundations or to continue to use a model with good foundations that is not usefully relevant to explain the phenomena that we have to explain.

The fiction that Keynes assumed rigid wages was found to be a useful fiction. That was so even if one could be persuaded by his purported demonstration that wage cutting might induce such perverse dynamic effects as to be incapable of helping the unemployment problem.

Yes, American Keynesians like me believed that imperfections of competition and deviations from strict constant returns to scale are an important part of the Keynesian under-employment equilibrium story. We knew that the Fortune 500 corporations were there to stay and we also knew that Chamberlin–Robinson diagrams didn't explain why the system was so Pareto-nonoptimal in 1933 and so much more nearly Pareto-optimal in 1929 or 1952. Keynes-cum-Chamberlin-and-Means would have been better than Keynes alone, but we pragmatists were grateful for what we had.

In closing I warn us Keynesians against the vice of complacency. Let us not be *un*reconstructed Keynesians. Let us be *reconstructed* Keynesians – reconstructed by the reconstruction of the world itself.

DISCUSSION

The discussion opened on a point of fact, the claims on p. 184 of Professor Leijonhufvud's paper concerning Keynes's assumptions about expectations in the *General Theory*. First, it was argued that Keynes modelled long-term expectations in real terms. It was pointed out that (expected) quasi rents are measured in monetary terms. Secondly, while it is true that *for convenience* Keynes assumed in Chapter 3 that short-run expectations were realized (in Chapter 5 he discussed what would happen if they were not), it is incorrect to imply that he used a perfect foresight model throughout the *General Theory*. It was added that the expectations of firms were missing from modern macroeconomics displaced, first, by labour's expectations of prices and now by expectations about the monetary regime (an inclusion which must be welcomed in its own right). In the framework of Chapter 21 of the *General Theory all* those elements are present. It is too general a framework to cope with at any particular time as it is important to focus attention on the area where expectations are most volatile at any particular time. Nevertheless, in a general framework, all three types of expectations must be included.

Next it was pointed out that there are two forms of rational expectations, the weak form which is true but tautological and the strong form which Lucas used. The latter implied a very particular relationship between the past, the present and the future, the sort of exact relationship that would not even be necessarily true in physics. Keynes argued that there were certain relevant phenomena for which no probability distributions existed. This ruled out the strong form of rational expectations and ensured that money matters in our sorts of economies in both the short run and the long run. He also argued that economies could be analysed by models which assumed stationary expectations and by those that assumed shifting expectations, stressing that it was the models which changed as the purposes for which they were created changed, not the underlying economy itself.

Keynes dealt with uncertainty and expectations in Chapter 12 where he was discussing the stock market. This approach was fundamentally different from that of the rational expectations school but not that different from the qualifications to rational expectations that Lucas, for example, had to make in order to explain business cycles. There are a limited number of people who are well informed, there is a range of people with differing degrees of information, and the first group make money from the second. They do so because uncertainties about the future are so great that it is better use of their scarce time to be thinking how to make money out of mugs than it is to think about whether it is better to sink an oil well. In retrospect the chapter does not read that well because Keynes greatly exaggerated the impact of stock market volatility on the real economy. (If he were writing today he would have applied the same principles to exchange rates.)

It was next argued that rational expectations is an assertion about how people learn to form expectations about events that can be specified in the form of probability distributions, the sort of uncertainty that is related to earthquakes, rainfall, that is to say, uncertain events that are exogenous to the economic system. This excludes endogenous uncertainty, expectations about other people's decisions, especially in oligopolistic settings (for example, Keynes's example of a beauty contest). The point is not that you cannot fool everybody all the time, as Friedman pointed out, but that people may fool themselves. Keynes wished to design policies which would prevent this happening.

As a point in the history of thought, while the Phillips curve may have been a crucial feature of post war Keynesianism in the United States, that was never true of the United Kingdom. Phillips' article was not well received by British Keynesians when it was first published because the basic model was thought to be far too mechanical, that the market determining wages was too complicated to be modelled in this way. It never became an article of faith.

The discussion moved to the proposition that the theory of rational expectations emphasizes the extent to which the effectiveness of public policy may be determined by the reaction to it of public opinion. Keynes, of course, was well aware of this. Thus he referred to the possibility that an expansionary fiscal policy might weaken industrial confidence if its purpose was not properly understood. Later, rational expectations – to use the modern term – came to be regarded as *favourable* to Keynesian policies. For example, the confidence felt in automatic stabilizers would help to ward off fears of cumulative recession. By contrast, monetarists hold that rational expectations will render public action impotent if this action is foreseen. Why is there this difference? The explanation must lie largely in the fact that a rise in monetary expenditure is assumed by monetarists to vent itself wholly – after perhaps a short lag – in raising prices. Expansion will be inflationary and the aim will be to cheat – or impose an 'inflation tax'. If, however, people are aware beforehand of the intentions of the public authorities, they will take protective action, as far as contracts permit, and will thus frustrate the policy. By contrast the usual Keynesian assumption was that output would rise with rising expenditure. It would not then be a case of the authorities fooling the people. Co-operation rather than confrontation was envisaged.

The difference between the two predictions must obviously reflect differences in what is assumed about the degree of slack in the economy when expenditure is increased.

Professor Leijonhufvud had referred to the debacle of Keynesianism. There had also been a debacle of monetarism. For the rise in OECD unemployment to the huge figure of over 30 million was clearly not anticipated by monetarist advisers. Nor is there any convincing monetarist solution. This does not mean that the right course is simply to revert to the earlier policy and increase expenditure until full employment, in some sense, has been reached. As has long been recognized by some economists, expansion on that scale would need to be accompanied by changes of regime, notably in the labour market.

While one of the discussants did not wish to sound too much like an unreconstructed Bourbon and while it had to be conceded that American Keynesians were too slow to introduce price and inflationary expectations in their models and too quick to embrace the Phillips curve as Friedman's missing equation in macro models, there were two points about this history which should be made. First, no United States administration deliberately took a ride up the Phillips curve in order to obtain lower unemployment at the expense of higher inflation. None of them wanted higher inflation and various of them adopted wage-price policies during expansions in order to limit the possible inflationary results of expansionary policies. The mistakes made in 1968 were done against the advice of Keynesian advisers and other economists and for not entirely discreditable political reasons by President Johnson. In the 1970s the Federal Reserve Board were faced with the agonizing dilemma of how much to accommodate external shocks of unprecedented magnitude associated, for example, with OPEC and the Iranian revolution.

Secondly, on a matter of history of thought, mainstream Keynesians did not believe that demand could be expanded indefinitely with a finite inflationary cost. The Phillips curve was meant to describe a less abrupt transition from the realm of non explosive inflation to excess demand inflation than was implied by the abrupt change in the simpliste model in the *General Theory*. Samuelson and Solow were quite explicit in 1960 about the possibilities of choosing a point on the short-run Phillips curve that would shift the curve itself in the longer run in various directions, including the accelerationist's one. Moreover, it has been a long standing Keynesian view that it is very difficult at all times to maintain price stability and full employment simultaneously without also having an incomes policy.

It was pointed out that as far as forecasting was concerned Keynesian models have done very well, much better than rational expectations models. The proof was that the people who build the first type of models were making millions! The basic difference between the Keynesians, on the one hand, and the rational expectations school and the monetarists, on the other, related to the efficiency of discretionary policies. In the long run it may turn out that they have a role to play but it will be necessary to be far less ambitious as to what may reasonably be expected from them.

Disappointment was expressed at the failure to separate two entirely different issues: rational expectations and 'market clearing' or full wage-price flexibility. The former is increasingly, in some form or other, accepted in decent macroeconomic theory. It is only necessary to mention the work by John Taylor on staggered wage contracting as an example. Anyone must make *some* assumption about expectations. Recent refinements of the original rational expectations models prove to be extremely rich and appropriate for such questions as regime changes, short-term and long-term interest rates and their relation to budget deficits or the exchange rate implications of potential changes in monetary and fiscal policy.

Where the real difference of opinion resides is in the assumptions about wage/price flexibility. It is in this area that the New Classical Economics fails to offer a convincing macroeconomic account of what is occurring and where Keynesian economics insists on the right facts but still owes a persuasive explanation.

Professor Leijonhufvud replied to the discussion as follows:

He said he found it difficult to respond. One of the problems with Keynesian economics is that there are more kinds of Keynesians than you could shake a stick at; he knew because he had tried. Professor Pasinetti said that he (Professor Leijonhufvud) had not answered the question, what would Keynes have thought of rational expectations? He tended to think that Keynes would have had no big objection to making short-run nominal expectations endogenous but he would have objected to the very attempt to make long-run real expectations about real profits endogenous. He would have thought it science fiction to have done so (not that Keynes disliked s.f. – he once favourably reviewed a book of H. G. Wells and ended by saying 'it [was] a large and meaty egg laid by a glorious hen').

Professor Leijonhufvud referred to his 1968 book and his critique of the interpretation of Keynes which said that unemployment was due to the downward inflexibility of nominal wages, an argument that *any* pre-Keynesian economist would have used to explain unemployment. He felt that in the 1960s Keynesian economics was getting into trouble because it refused to straighten out some conceptual problems in its structure. The models which he learned in school did show a clear lineage back to Keynes but there was no inevitability that the arguments needed to develop as they did and land us in the mess that we are in today – there were several different futures, as it were, with the *General Theory* as starting point. His 1968 book was an attempt to go back and see what other alternative futures could have been read into Keynes.

In the paper there is a little diagram, which Professor Leijonhufvud calls the Swedish flag diagram, see p. 187, in which stocks and adjustment failures are classified as nominal, mixed and real. Many Keynesians hold on to some nominal wage rigidity, whether from implicit contract theory or elsewhere, because they think it is what makes them characteristically Keynesians. Professor Leijonhufvud thinks that the move over to this mish-mash and away from Keynes's intertemporal equilibrium story makes Keynesian economics an easy prey to monetarism. Many reacted to his paper by saying that he is a monetarist or a rational expectationist, but he is not, he is one of the other kind of Keynesians you can shake a stick at (and an ageing one at that).

Chapter One

Schumpeter as an Economic Theorist

PAUL A. SAMUELSON

SCHUMPETER was a universalist in economics. Mention a field in the subject of political economy, and you will find his name already established there: economic theory, macroeconomic business cycles, methodology, econometrics, Marxian economics, economic history, *Dogmengeschichte*—the list is only countably finite.

In a discipline that is undergoing dynamic development and being swept by gales of creative destruction, it is lucky if a scholar of age 67 is even remembered or curtsied to. Yet, at the time of his death, a citation index shows that Joseph Schumpeter was the scholar most often cited in the whole field of economics. As he himself might put it, 'This is a remarkable performance.' It is one that ought to have brought him satisfaction and fulfilment. But his was an enterpreneurial nature whose appetite for scientific achievement grew by what it fed upon.

The Wagnerian hero does not strive to be a Jack-of-all-trades and Schumpeter, I venture to suspect, would have traded his Popeship for a Keynesian revolution. Moreover, often we want what it is that we are not. A beautiful woman wishes to be clever, a sage to be an Olympic athlete. Norbert Wiener would trade ten mathematical theorems and three lemmas for one biological discovery. I have retold Schumpeter's story about his three wishes in life—to be the greatest lover in Austria, the best horseman in Europe, and the greatest economist in the world—and his regret of having failed to fulfil the second wish. It is not a joke that Joseph Schumpeter aspired to scholarly greatness, however lighthearted his tone and amusing his stories. As with Sigmund Freud and Abraham Lincoln, from the time of puberty there was a little clock in Schumpeter's breast ticking with the impulse for scholarly fame. Before I knew of Robert J. Merton's sociology of scientists, before I had myself articulated that the coin we scholars work for is our own applause, the example of my old Harvard teacher taught me this not-really-dirty little secret about the motives that run scientists.

Yes, Schumpeter may have envied a Keynes. Or a Ricardo, who changed the course of one of intellectual history's rivers. But we know that Schumpeter also had a certain condescension and contempt towards the economist who comprised his scientific birthright for a mess of populist pottage. And it is sad that Schumpeter's great 1942 *Capitalism, Socialism and Democracy* did not have greater worth in its author's own eyes.

I suspect that, in Schumpeter's heart of hearts, the scholar he admired most was the economic theorist, Ragnar Frisch. To have innovated in the many corridors of pure theory as Frisch had done—and then himself to surpass such magnificent performance by creating his own Newtonian *Principia*—that might have brought fulfilment to Joseph Schumpeter's insatiable soul.

Nihil Nisi?

As the centenary of Joseph Schumpeter's birth looms close, we are in a orgy of discussions of him and his works. To prepare for this symposium, to contribute a chapter to Professor Heertje's symposium volume, *Schumpeter's Vision Capitalism, Socialism and Democracy after 40 Years*, and to clarify my own thinking on the economic future at century's end for the Mexico City World Economic Congress, I have found myself preoccupied with Schumpeter's thought and person. It is a pleasant orgy, and a rewarding one. But it is boring to say the same thing twice and to have to engage in elegant variation merely to avoid exact repetition.

Already I have written much on Schumpeter. For his sixtieth *Festschrift* in the 1943 *Review of Economics and Statistics*, I wrote to clarify the logic and taxonomy of statics and dynamics. At the same time I both defended the *logic* of the *possibility* of zero interest rate in the stationary state and, as much as was meet in a scholar's own *Festschrift*, queried the importance of Schumpeter's dogma on that point. Shortly after Schumpeter's death in January 1950, I contributed a chapter to Seymour Harris's 1951 memorial volume, *Joseph Schumpeter: Social Scientist*, and returned there to the subject of his own interest theory.

I was honoured to have my memoir on 'Schumpeter as a teacher and economic theorist' appear along with the excellent essays by Arthur Smithies, Gottfried Haberler, Wolfgang Stolper, Paul Sweezy, Herbert von Beckerath, Arthur Marget, Erich Schneider, and others. As I re-read my words, I feel they catch much of what that remarkable man was. Still a problem of decorum does arise, a delicate question of whether and how to apply the doctrine of *de morituri nihil nisi bonum*. Should one's pen write of a beloved teacher that he was a 'showman' (or, a bit of a poseur)? What warts—beloved warts—should be airbrushed out of the photograph?

Within the family one speaks freely of Mama's engaging foibles, Brother's accident-proneness, Aunt Sophie's tone-deafness. But that does not mean that you should sell your Grandfather for a wisecrack. For a reserved and dignified scholar like Frank Taussig, the eulogist encounters few problems. With an engaging extrovert like Schumpeter, who loved to *épater* the bourgeoisie, aristocracy, priesthood, proletariat and the universal set, how acute the problem has to be for biographers. As Paul Sweezy used to say, 'You hate to hear outsiders criticize Schumpie; but within the inner circle, you find much to criticize.'

Moses Outside the Promised Land

There is an element of anticlimax in my assignment for today—to talk about Schumpeter as an economic theorist. Since Schumpeter's most theoretical work was his first German book of 1908—*Das Wesen und Hauptinhault der theoretischen Nationalökonomie*—my inadequate mastery of German disqualifies me for the assigned task. Also, though much of the world regarded Schumpeter as the very essence of an economic theorist, he regarded himself as in a sense a theorist *manqué*. When singing the praises of more exact methods in our beloved science of economics, Schumpeter claimed he was entitled to do so with a better right since his own work was primarily not in the airy heights of mathematical theory. He would have loved to team up, later in life with someone like Nicholas Georgescu-Roegen, to write a profound treatise on modern economic theory. After that he could toss off his mathematical logic, complete his sociology, and in well-earned old age write his novel.

If it was not given to Moses to enter into the Promised Land, it is understandable that he should have tended to exhalt the promise of that fair country. So with Schumpeter. His schemata of three interacting cycles—the intermediate Juglar wave, superimposed on the shorter Kitchen cycle and the longer Kondratieff cycle—seemed less commanded by the facts of economic history than by Schumpeter's fascination with the mysteries of harmonic analysis. If a Ragnar Frisch came up with a new inflection-point technique for identifying cyclical phases, Schumpeter's admiration for Newtonian dynamics made him a favourable consumer to buy his theories. Chamberlin and Robinson, through their geometrical novelties, gained Schumpeter's support for their new theories of imperfect competition. Leon

Walras's comprehensive equations of general equilibrium represented the pinnacle of economics for Schumpeter. Böhm-Bawerk's tortured numerical examples tended to be put to a discount, perhaps because they were the sort of thing Schumpeter himself could so easily do. My own early work in *revealed preference*, Schumpeter, if anything, overvalued, because it brought into economics some of the elegance and economy of the most exact sciences and of mathematical logic itself.

Eclectic Methodologist

Young Schumpeter was a stormy petrel. He did not mind giving offence. He was not a good Austrian, in that he whored after mathematical economics, praised American and English economics, and questioned some of the established verities of Böhm-Bawerk. All this is in character.

One might then expect Schumpeter to take an extreme position in the debate between the German Historical School and the theorists of Austria and England. Perhaps to thumb his nose at his teachers, Schumpeter might have been expected to embrace Marxism; or to speak up for empiricism; or to denounce all grubbing in the facts. But it was not so. From the beginning his methodology took the eclectic road of good sense. In his view, inductive facts need to interact with simplifying theories whose logical implications are rigorously deduced with the help of advanced mathematics; probability techniques must be applied to interpret that which is ephemeral and singular in the empirical data from that which is persistent. Ricardo and Menger have merit. But so do Schmoller and List. Even Karl Marx, especially for his *chutzpah* in attempting to devise a dynamic theory for all aspects of the social universe, deserves praise.

Before there was a Vienna Circle, Schumpeter and Pareto embraced a separation of positivist science from normative aspiration. Before Tom Kuhn entered kindergarten, Schumpeter emphasized: It takes a theory to kill a theory; no dirty single fact can do so and, given our need to have a systematic way of thinking about complicated reality, our present theories will hold their place even in the face of cascades of *ad hoc* discordant observations.

At the same time that Schumpeter hailed the new, he warned against the Whig historians' propensity to criticize the historic great because they did not wear present-day beards and cravats and did not know all we have since learned. Each generation is entitled to its own mistakes, which if made by a Newton or Ricardo can be of interest in their own right. (I would add that this does not absolve us from the responsibility of naming as mistakes that which is mistaken.)

This core of good sense—unlike Schumpeter, I can never identify good sense with *common sense*—sometimes got concealed under Schumpeter's patronizing affectation of omniscience. It is not quite the case that Schumpeter's posthumous *History of Economic Doctrines* (1954) contains the lines, 'I shall not weary the reader with discussions of the 83 economists whose views dominated Rome from 100 B.C. to 53 A.D., for the reason that she or he will know much more about them than I do.' But somewhat similar passages do occur, and experience shows that readers will make an error if they think that Schumpeter is dropping names of authorities he has not tackled. The erudition he parades was erudition—*his* erudition.

PREVIEW

Since I was Schumpeter's student and friend for the last fifth of his life, I shall begin by recording some of my memories from his lectures and oral discourses. My account accords him less than full credit since what is memorable in a scholar is what is unexpected. The countless doctrines that he early appreciated at their correct worth are lost to memory, and one hardly remembers his judgements on people that merely agree with the conventional wisdom.

Then, in the last part of this paper, I stop chattering about theorists and Schumpeter's theoretical views. I actually do some economic theorizing, applying standard modern tools to Schumpeter's own paradigm of the interest rate. Although what I do here seems never to have been done in its entirety, it does not really have to be done. I show in the end that my extended analysis, using the standard neoclassical model of Solow, leads precisely to the conclusions and emphases arrived at briefly by Gottfried Haberler, Schumpeter's affable younger colleague. My elaborate Ramsey dynamics only corroborate what Haberler's (1951) simple Fisherine diagram showed. Nonetheless, as we approach the Schumpeter centennial year, a little excess of attention to his analysis can be forgiven.

Personal Likes

I can recall some of the theorists Schumpeter especially admired. He adored his brilliant young colleague Wassily Leontief. He had great respect for Leontief's teacher at Berlin, L. von Bortkiewicz, honouring his Herculean labours in trying to keep clean the Augean stables of economics, but regretting that more of von Bortkiewicz's energies did not go into creative innovations all his own. On the other hand, the corrosive common-sensical criticisms of an Edwin Cannan, Schumpeter rather underrated, being turned off by Cannan's antipathy to anything fancy and by his overconclusive simplifications. Knut Wicksell, Schumpeter beatified. But Wicksell's more highly publicized rival, Gustav Cassel, Schumpeter despised as a plagiarist, saying: 'Cassel is 10 per cent Walras and 90 per cent water.' He did faint-praise Cassel's textbook, as exactly what was needed on the Continent at the time. (I think Cassel, for all his personal faults, pretensions, and over-simplifications is now underrated as an original analyst.)

Before the world took much notice of American economists, Schumpeter singled out J. B. Clark for attention and respect. He found Irving Fisher amusing for his solemn do-goodism and health faddisms, but that never diminished his reverence for Fisher's theoretical innovations in value theory and interest determination. Schumpeter studied carefully the works of Carver, Fetter (who took him to his first and probably only football game), Walker, H. L. Moore, Allyn Young, Davenport, and Wesley Mitchell. Frank Taussig was an uncle figure with whom Joseph Schumpeter did not joke. As widowers, each twice bereft, they shared Taussig's massive Scott Road house in the 1932–37 years before Schumpeter married the economic historian Elizabeth (Boody) Firuski.

Frank Knight, Jacob Viner, Henry Schultz, J. M. Clark—leaders of American economics when I began my studies—Schumpeter went for whole lecture hours without much discussing. (In the autumn of 1935 I apparently became something of a joke because I so often talked about Frank Knight, whose intellect dominated the Chicago barnyard where I began my studies.) Harold Hotelling, Frisch, Tinbergen,[1] R. G. D. Allen, Hicks, Bowley, Divisia, Amoroso, Barone, Georgescu-Roegen, A. P. Lerner, Chamberlin, R. F. Kahn, Joan Robinson, von Stackelberg, Zeuthen, Lange, and Wald were mathematical economists whom Schumpeter applauded. The new and exciting *Review of Economic Studies* he recommended to his Ec 11 classes. He spoke of the brilliant Pierro Sraffa, whom he had met when the latter was young, leading me to draw the false inference that Sraffa was a bit of a lazy dilettante because of his inherited wealth.

Although Schumpeter recognized that the 1924–33 'cost controversy' was mostly a catching-up of the Marshallians to 1838 Cournot, Schumpeter

---

[1] I have commented elsewhere on Schumpeter's rapturous amazement that business cycles—his Kondratieffs and Juglars—might be produced by Frisch and Tinbergen using imaginary numbers involving $\sqrt{(-1)} = \mathrm{i}$. He could understand sin t as a cycle; and that $\mathrm{d}^2y/\mathrm{d}t^2 = -y$ had the oscillatory solution $y(t) = y(0)\cos t + y'(0)\sin t$. But that its solution could be generated by the oscillations of $ae^{it} + be^{-it}$ smacked to him of delicious black magic. Had he understood why $(\mathrm{e}^{it} - \mathrm{e}^{-it})/2\mathrm{i}$ can be short for sin t, the mysticism would have vanished, as it would if he had realized that the complex number $5 + 3\mathrm{i}$ can be regarded as a way to depict the coordinates (5, 3) of a vector that obeys certain natural laws of addition and multiplication: then only real numbers would be needed to handle the real numbers of pig-iron and price data.

overvalued the lasting importance of that controversy. It is I think indicative of a certain uneasiness in his own handling of the tools of mathematical economics that, to his final hour, Schumpeter believed he could justify against the criticism of Viner's draftsman, Y. K. Wong, Viner's contention that the long-run cost curve should go through the *bottoms* of the U-shaped short-run curves. Schumpeter conceded that Wong (and, later, Harrod) were correct in the *two-dimensional* picture of the envelope. But in three dimensions—output, unit cost, planned scale of plant(?)—Schumpeter professed he could find normative significance in bottom-of-the-U points. I cannot reproduce his argument because I have always found it hard to formulate and remember false arguments.[2]

Aside from this erroneous identification of the minimum-unit-cost point with efficiency optimization, I can recall another Napoleonic claim of Schumpeter that I should have written down in my lecture notes because I could never reconstruct the steps of his alleged syllogism. After correctly informing his Harvard Ec 11 students that truly joint costs can never be allocated meaningfully between joint products, Schumpeter went on to say: 'Nevertheless, when recently I sat down with [some forgotten expert] over drinks, I showed how it could be done by means of an infinite series . . . [? in which the costs that wool does not bear are initially attributed to mutton, after which . . ., and so on until all costs are in the end fully and uniquely allocated]. . . .' I hope St Peter confronted Joseph with the case, TC = min[mutton, wool/2], and asked for its meaningful series-expansion imputation into f(mutton) + g(wool).

Alfred Marshall's *Principle of Economics* was the admitted classic of the 1890–1930 period. It was typical of Schumpeter's love for theory that he rejected Marshall's view that the reader could skip the footnotes and appendixes. If time were short, Schumpeter advised, read them and skip the *text*!

Schumpeter's older Harvard colleague, Edwin Bidwell Wilson, mathematical physicist and last student of J. Willard Gibbs, devoted part of his 1936–37 seminar to Marshall's Mathematical Appendix. I was then struck by how patchy these notes are and how hard it was for us economists to answer Wilson's proper questions about them. I came to realize that

[2] Schumpeter's own Bonn student, Erich Schneider, had provided, in the same 1931 volume of the *Zeitschrift für Nationalökonomie* that carried Viner's famous cost article, a graph involving *total* cost curves demonstrating the envelope tangencies that Wong properly insisted on. I may retell the story that, as late as 1935, Viner insisted to his Chicago class: 'Although Wong is mathematically right, I can draw the envelope curve through the bottoms of the U's.' My cheeky rebuke as a nineteen year old was, 'Yes Professor Viner, you can, with a *thick* pencil!' As a twenty-five year old, I realized that I might better have added: 'Or, of course, if your U-shaped short-run curves are V-shaped, with *cornered* minima, and provided the economies of plant enlargement aren't too rapid.'

Marshall, despite his reputation as a synthesizer, was in fact primarily a *miniaturist* who lacked the energy and will to shape a coherent masterwork in analytical economics. It went against the grain to admit that Schumpeter was right in elevating Leon Walras above Marshall and the rest as the Newton of economics who discovered the system of the world in his paradigm of general equilibrium. All the more credit is due the youthful Schumpeter, since after 1900 the moon of Pareto was serving to eclipse the sun of Walras. All hats off to Pareto, but as Lagrange lamented in eulogizing Newton, there is alas only one system of the economic world to discover and Walras had already done that when Pareto was still a schoolboy.

Marshall, having managed to bury Jevons, kept Francis Edgeworth in the shade for four decades. Schumpeter accorded Edgeworth his due. 'If you don't write books, and merely squander your genius in articles, you won't command your true value in the markets of scholarship,' Schumpeter used to say. He therefore rejoiced when the Royal Economic Society brought out Edgeworth's collected papers in three large books. The cases of Einstein and Frank Ramsey (the latter's three immortal contributions to economics appeared in separate articles) suggest that Schumpeter's emphasis on books can be refuted—at least by a genius. Still, Edgeworth's own important innovations in statistics—which, despite their obscurity of exposition, anticipated much of R. A. Fisher's maximum likelihood and went beyond Karl Pearson's large-sample asymptotics—were never part of one unified book and have failed to receive the credit they deserve. In any case Schumpeter practised what he preached. He was usually engaged on an ambitious book. And, although he published articles every year, he resisted temptation to make small contributions to economic science.

Maturity and Youth

Schumpeter stayed alive as a theorist. That means he improved in his understanding, sloughing off old skins or covering them up with new. That also means that he is sometimes a bit inconsistent in his expositions of any one date. I was struck in reading his last years' work on welfare economics: in some places he betrays clear understanding of Pareto optimality; in other places he accepts L. Robbins' view that economists have virtually nought to say in this domain; in no one place does he provide a unified grasp of the subject's final status. All this is merely to say that Schumpeter was human. Even Pareto, who innovated in replacing one cardinal measure of utility by any numberings of the indifference contours that preserve ordinal rankings, often forgot about his own innovations and reverted back in his definitions of complementarity to operations on the cardinal utility he had already thrown out into the trash.

Progression in Schumpeter's thought offers special problems. Schumpeter had respect for the past. To tamper with Smith's 1776 text in the light of 1913 scientific findings he would have considered foolish. Schumpeter's own youthful classics are part of the past. What right does J. A. S. have in 1934 to second-guess the thought of J. A. S. of 1912? For better or worse, a classic should be left to stand. Besides, Mertonian study of the sociology of science suggests that you will retain a higher ranking in the history of a scholarly discipline if you stand your ground. Never complain and never explain. Newton's warts are part of his picture and to use an airbrush to shade them out is to distort the portrait and rob it of interest.

For the rest of this survey of Schumpeter as a theorist, I am going to stop talking about him as a connoisseur of theory and patron of theorists. I am going to discuss in a theoretical way one of Schumpeter's own most famous—you might say most notorious—theories. I refer to Schumpeter's paradigm of a zero rate of interest in equilibrium when innovational development is ruled out. If this view is correct, it is only as a result of innovation that society accords any income to people who do not work for wages or receive rents for the land resources they own. A bourgeois class that receives permanent net income from its ownership of machines, factories and inventories continues to exist only to the extent that innovations do not flag.

Many of my comments will have to be critical. All of them might have been written in, say, 1934 when Schumpeter was 51 and his theory was at least a quarter of a century old. Since Schumpeter rarely discussed his own theories, and nowhere repudiated them, one's pen tends to write almost angrily: 'Do you mean to say in 1934 that . . .?' Yet the argument is really with a 1912 text. I find no useful way to evade this problem. So I must ask the reader to realize that what seems like strong criticism is not really that of a student directed against his beloved friend and benefactor, but rather is a pungent verdict by a later generation on the preliminary scientific findings of an earlier generation.

T. S. Eliot was told, 'We know more than the classics.' Much as this message pained him, if it is scientists we are talking about, Eliot must accept this fact. But even scientists must recognize the epsilon of truth in Eliot's rejoinder: 'Yes, and it is the classics that we know.' The greatest of scientists was honest in saying that he took off from the shoulders of giants. I can be as objective in weighing the merits and demerits of Schumpeter's 1912 paradigm because it was Joseph Schumpeter who taught me how to administer justice.

EVALUATING SCHUMPETER'S ZERO-INTEREST-RATE DOCTRINE

The Ramsey (1928) and Solow (1956) one-sector paradigm can illustrate Schumpeter's contentions. It was this I had in mind in earlier expositions (Samuelson, 1943, 1951). In view of Schumpeter's youthful admiration for J. B. Clark, my modelling is a fair one.

Technology

Output, $Q(t)$, is the sum of consumption, $C(t)$, and net investment: $C(t) + K'(t)$. It is produced by a first-degree-homogeneous, concave, smooth neoclassical production function whose variables are land, labour, and a homogeneous stock of capital ('leets' in Joan Robinson's sardonic lingo), $[T, L, K(t)]$:

$$\begin{aligned} Q(t) = C(t) + K'(t) &= \mathrm{F}[T, L, K(t)] \\ &= T\mathrm{f}[L/T, K(t)/T] \end{aligned} \tag{1}$$

where $\mathrm{f}[L, K]$ is a smooth, strictly concave function.

It suffices to consider land and labour as 'primary' factors not producible within the system, instead being given in constant amounts, $[T, L]$, which by appropriate definition of units could each be taken to be unity. With the understanding that labour supply is fixed, $\mathrm{f}[L, K]$ can be written as $\mathrm{f}[K]$, with $\mathrm{f}''[K] < 0$.

Competitive Imputation

In the absence of uncertainty and technical change, [real wage rate, interest or profit rate, rent] are given respectively by the competitive marginal-productivity relations:

$$w(t) = \partial \mathrm{f}[L, K(t)]/\partial L, \qquad L \equiv 1 \equiv T \tag{2a}$$

$$\begin{aligned} r(t) = [\partial K'/\partial K] &= \partial \mathrm{f}[L, K(t)]/\partial K, \qquad L \equiv 1 \\ &= \mathrm{f}'[K] \end{aligned} \tag{2b}$$

$$\begin{aligned} R(t) &= Q(t) - w(t)L - r(t)K(t) \\ &= \partial \mathrm{F}[T, L, K(t)]/\partial T, \qquad [T, L] \equiv [1, 1] \end{aligned} \tag{2c}$$

Golden-Rule State

Schumpeter's theory of a zero rate of interest in the circular-flow equilibrium posits that, for given primary factors of $[T, L]$, there is a *finite* golden-rule K^s, a Schumpeter point such that

$$0 = r^s = f'[K^s] \tag{3}$$

Before Ramsey, Meade, Allais, Phelps, von Weizsäcker, and other analysts of the 'golden-rule state of maximal per capita consumption', Schumpeter recognized that his zero-interest-rate equilibrium would maximize the aggregate steady-state real consumption of fixed-supply primary factors of production. The competitive breakdown of this aggregate between wages and rent would depend on technology and endowment of land relative to labour, w and Q/L being the greater the greater is the T/L ratio.

Falling Rate of Interest

In the absence of innovation, if $K(0)$ begins below K^s, Schumpeter may be presumed to be supposing that positive accumulation of $K'(t)$ will always be forthcoming and will soon bring the interest rate down to zero:

$$\lim_{t \to \infty} [K(t), r(t), Q(t)] = [K^s, 0, \text{maximal } Q] \tag{4}$$

And then equilibrium will persist happily ever afterwards forever.

If $K(0)$ begins above K^s, a possibility I do not remember Schumpeter having recognized, $r(0)$ begins negative and decumulation brings it up to zero.

Innovational Development

But now let us introduce the possibility of gales of creative self-destruction. A parameter of technological improvement, $\theta(t)$, is put in the production function:

$$f[L, K(t); \theta] \qquad \text{with} \qquad \partial f[L, K(t); \theta(t)]/\partial[\theta(t)] > 0 \tag{5}$$

$\theta(t)$ increases as t increases. The increases in θ may be jerky; or they may be quasi-periodic; or they could be near to random. In any case, so long as such innovations are going on, the competitive interest will be perturbed above[3] zero by development.

[3] Only in preparing this paper did I notice what Schumpeter did not emphasize: namely, technical change can *lower* the interest rate rather than raise it; e.g. when $\partial^2 f[L, K; \theta]/\partial\theta\partial K < 0$ and the prior zero interest rate turns negative as innovation makes the stock of leets become redundant.

For land and labour fixed, output will grow for two reasons: first, improved technology will raise product directly; secondly, the induced rise of the interest rate above zero will in Schumpeter's scenario cause capital to grow.

A Schumpeter Cycle

I can even construct a regular cycle of Schumpeterian developmental evolution. Thus, assume that $\theta'(t)$ is a positive periodic function of time:

$$\theta'(t) \equiv \theta'(t + \tau)$$

Or let technical advance be almost periodic. Or let it be bunchy in time like an autocorrelated error function. Or, even if technical change is purely random (as white as the driven snow of 'white noise'), the economic system will then show quasi-realistic autocorrelated fluctuations in the fashion of the Wicksell–Frisch rocking horse subject to random impulsive shocks.

The reader can verify this in the case of a quadratic production function, and where we postulate that $K'(t)$ accumulates at a rate proportional to the deviation of r from 0. This gives, after appropriate choice of units,

$$f[K; \theta] = \theta(t)K(t) - \tfrac{1}{2}K(t)^2 \tag{6}$$
$$r = \theta - K \tag{7}$$
$$K'(t) = \alpha r(t), \qquad \alpha > 0 \tag{8}$$

Then, if $\theta'(t)$ is sinusoidal with period τ, it can be shown that investment becomes ultimately sinusoidal with the same period (but with a lag). Profits, growth of output, and other variables will display behaviour a bit like that observed by the National Bureau of Economic Research.

Summary

Seventy years after Schumpeter glimpsed his basic model, I have produced this instance to show that it involves no *logical* contradictions. We observe a system that evolves cyclically, displaying a rising trend of real wage and output and cyclical fluctuations in the profit rate around a flat long-run trend.

Note, however, that Schumpeter had no real need to put into his system that which economists have found to be most novel and shocking in Schumpeter. I refer to the *zero* rate of interest. How Böhm-Bawerk must have smarted at that saucy conception of Schumpeter. And we all know how vehemently Frank Knight rejected in the 1930s the very notion of a zero rate of interest.

My point is a simple one. Suppose Schumpeter had believed in a *positive* rate of subjective time preference *à la* Böhm, Irving Fisher, Pigou, Cassel, and other orthodox neoclassical writers. Call it ρ, and let it be positive (as when Pigou's representative Englishman is born with a psychological rate of subjective time preference of 4 per cent: $\rho = 0.04$).

> Schumpeter's model of cyclical development would have been little different with a positive rather than a zero floor for the interest rate! Output would still grow cyclically, while real wage and interest rates would still vary in the same quasi-cycles.

To see this, replace the proportionality of accumulation to the interest rate by its proportionality to the deviation of the interest rate above the time preference rate:

$$K'(t) = \alpha[r(t) - \rho] \qquad (9)$$

Then $\rho > 0$ merely gives a positive asymptote to which the interest rate may descend in the absence of innovation, rather than a zero asymptote. It is still fits and starts of innovation that create dynamic development and cycles. The scenario for the economy is still essentially a cheerful one, even if golden-rule perfection is not being attained or even aimed at.

Simplifications

Though my model is in the sense just described even more general than Schumpeter's 1912 schemata, it quite fails to catch some qualitative properties of the Schumpeterian scenarios. My transient positive profit is merely the competitive interest rate generated as innovation makes every item of capital more productive. My profit is temporary, but it is a phenomenon of perfect competition equilibrium.

Schumpeter's innovators, by contrast, are *temporary monopolists*. Their transient profits come because rivals are not yet able to do what they can do. To understand them you need to read pages in Chamberlin on imperfect competition, or in Cournot and Marshall on monopoly.[4] As knowledge and

[4] Schumpeter early admired Cournot's 1838 analysis of monopoly, duopoly, and oligopoly. It was Schumpeter who edited the last symposium in which Wicksell participated, which dealt critically with A. L. Bowley's duopoly analysis. Illustrative of Schumpeter's felt need to believe in the stability of capitalism and, by extension, to rule out instability of bilateral monopoly, was the ambivalent doctrine on duopoly that Schumpeter maintained from 1925 to his death in 1950. He believed that the Cournot determinate solution is the correct one, except when it is not!—and then the collusive joint-profit-maximization solution of Wicksell is the correct and determinate solution. I am still amazed that such feckless eclecticism could satisfy him. Was it a case of the heart superseding the head?

methods are gradually imitated by rivals, oligopoly will atrophy and degenerate into competitive imputation. So to speak, I have aped with changes in *quantity* of K and its productivity what Schumpeter contrives by changes in *quality* of market structure and entrepreneurial power. Keeping this qualification in mind, we are pleased to see how much of the Schumpeterian epic this dynamic Clark–Solow model can capture.

Imperfect Competition Theory

This qualification also explains why Schumpeter should have always had so keen an interest in the analysis of imperfect competition. His laudatory views on Joan Robinson and Edward Chamberlin reflect this.

John Kenneth Galbraith's giant corporations fit well into the modified version of Schumpeter's model that he arrived at in his final years. But unlike Galbraith, Schumpeter insisted that these giants were constitutional monarchs, who reigned only so long as they desisted from trying to rule. 'What have you done for us lately?' is the question ever put to the Fortune-500 companies. Those with disappointing replies are evicted from the choice rooms of capitalism's hotel: those suites are always full, but with a changing roster of guests, each of whom must earn his place in every epoch.

The *countervailing power* that runs Schumpeter's jungle is the competition of giant seller against giant seller. And even a pygmy can challenge a giant, and hope to become a giant.

When I look at the great fortunes amassed since World War II, I understand them through Schumpeter's spectacles. David Packard or Edwin Land or Sheikh Yamani have each become as rich as Rockefeller. The Marxian paradigm of the falling rate of profit or rising organic competition of capital throws no light on the Pareto distribution of incomes and their genie coefficient of concentration. The strictly competitive model of Hicks, Solow, and J. B. Clark, as well as the Kaldorian and Kaleckian widow's cruses, equally withhold insight on the trends and causes of income inequality.

Progression in Schumpeter's View?

I am not sure that I can document what I have described as a change in Schumpeter's view on innovators and on the welfare economics of oligopoly that took place between the autumn of 1935 when I first attended his Harvard lectures and his mature thought in his final years. In 1935 he believed Du Pont could not long hold its innovational lead. General Electric,

General Motors, IBM, and AT&T all had limited life expectancy as producers of enterpreneurial profit—which is essentially the only source of profit he then gave diplomatic recognition to.

By 1950 Schumpeter was prepared to concede that a bureaucratic corporation might be able to continue to innovate. Moreover, the *statical* deadweight loss transiently arising from the Fortune-500 innovational oligopoly power, Schumpeter came to believe, was more than compensated for by the consumers' surplus they created from their dynamic innovations. Their monopolists' Danegeld was a bargain in Schumpeter's recalculation.

Schumpeter's final logic ought to have predisposed him to accord to Hayek the final victory over Lerner and Lange in the debate over whether a socialist state could play the game of parametric pricing. To find new *cost* technologies and husband scarce knowledge as it is forever newly arriving, the letter of Walrasian equations achievable by Lerner–Lange auctioneers and bureaucrats serves as nothing compared to what Hayek's real-life speculators and profit receivers are led by the invisible hand of market competition to contribute. I do not remember Schumpeter as pronouncing on this point, but on my reading it should be congenial to his *Weltanschauung*.

How Vital is Money Creation?

The present model is unrelievedly microeconomic in its ignoring of money supply and nominal spending behaviour. It thus fails to do justice to what was considered important in Schumpeter's model, namely his insistence that innovational development be financed by money *creation*, which in turn leads to unanticipated inflation that cuts the real consumption people can purchase with their previous nominal incomes, thereby procuring the 'forced saving' that offsets the incremental innovational investment. Dennis Robertson and other writers of the 1920s on forced saving were thus anticipated by Schumpeter. Even though many orthodox economists were shocked by Schumpeter's notion that inflation could advance progress, Viner and Hayek have shown that forced-saving notions occur as early as 1803 in Henry Thornton. Keynes's *General Theory*, preoccupied with the *ex post* identity of saving with investment, needlessly denied the importance of forced saving; similarly the recent school of rational expectationists do well to insist that inflation foreseen is less effective than unexpected inflation in releasing resources from consumption for investment.

We can add money to the Solow–Ramsey model. Whether we do or do not, it confirms doubt that there *has* to be money creation for capitalism to work in its characteristic way. When the banking system keeps aggregate money inelastic in supply, innovational investment can still pull resources out of the old circular flow by competing with older kinds of investment and reinvestment for the limited quota of funds (and, in essence, resources). A disciple of Schumpeter has no need to insist upon the same degree of business-cycle overshoot relative to innovation under different policy regimes.

QUALIFICATION AND EXTENSION

Approach Towards Zero Interest Rate

My equations (1)–(4) demonstrate that Schumpeter's paradigm of an interest rate that is zero in innovationless equilibrium is not a logically impossible one. That does not mean that Schumpeter himself ever provided an adequate demonstration of this fact, and does not answer the question of whether he understood how to reply to the legitimate queries on the matter. Also, for a thing to be logically possible does not mean that it is necessarily *likely* or probably *relevant*.

There are also models, as simple as the Clark–Solow model that I have just analysed, in which the interest rate only *asymptotically* goes to zero but never quite reaches there. Frank Knight exaggerated the necessity or likelihood of such models in the 1930s, but that is no reason to refuse them careful analysis.

Thus, instead of having output attain a maximum at a *finite* stock of capital, at $K^s < \infty$, suppose $f[\bar{L}, K] \equiv f[K]$ only approaches its upper bound at $K = \infty$. Then

$$\begin{aligned} &\lim_{K\to\infty} f[K] = B < \infty \\ &f'[K] > 0, \qquad 0 < K < \infty \\ &\lim_{K\to\infty} f'[K] = 0, \qquad \lim_{K\to\infty}\int_{\epsilon}^{K} f'[x]\,dx < \infty \end{aligned} \tag{10}$$

Any constant-elasticity-of-substitution (CES) function, with Hicksian σ less than unity, will have this property. An easy CES example is the 'harmonic mean':

$$F[T, K, L] = (aT^{-1} + bK^{-1} + cL^{-1})^{-1} \tag{11}$$

This really alters Schumpeter's vision of cyclical evolution very little. True, net investment never quite ceases after innovation ceases. But it does trickle away to an ignorable infinitesimal. And quasi-periodic or even white-noise perturbations in innovation (i.e. in $\theta'(t)$ above) will still produce a quasi-regular pattern of cyclical evolution.

Therefore, even if we take the view of Schumpeter's fair-minded critic, Gottfried Haberler—namely, that it is hard to conceive of *zero* net productivity of capital being quite reached—Schumpeter's theoretical system remains intact in its important logical properties.

Unbounded Output

Knight went farther than Haberler. For him, $f'[K]$ falls very slowly indeed. That is Knight's empirical allegation, and for which he gives a bag of uneven arguments. (It is as if Knight believes σ is virtually infinite; or that $T(t)$ and $L(t)$ are not exogenously given as 'primary factors' but are, in the von Neumann fashion, themselves producible and produced at constant returns to scale *within* the economic system. Then, as Kaldor cogently noted in his critique of Knight, the innovationless system could approach positive exponential growth and an asymptote of positive interest rate would be possible.)

Whatever the slowness at which the interest rate would drop, Knight seems to assert the further view that $f'[K]$ cannot fall so fast with K as to make $f[K]$ bounded. As with the Cobb–Douglas function, where $\sigma \equiv 1$ and relative factor shares are constant,

$$\lim_{K\to\infty} f[K] = \infty, \qquad \lim_{K\to\infty} f'[K] = 0 \tag{12}$$

Again, a lawyer for Schumpeter can make good a defence for the view that this need not change his vision. Thus, if utility in a Ramsey integral attains an upper bound at finite consumption levels, investment will peter out in the absence of innovation.[5]

Now, however, there is no guarantee that pure profit falls towards zero in the absence of development. Nor is there even guarantee that the *fractional share* of profit falls towards zero. Schumpeter's startling doctrine of euthanasia of the rentier, which differs from Keynes's *General Theory* version in that Schumpeter's leads to no lasting unemployment problem and happily splashes workers and landowners with real income, now could be invalidated. My lament over this would be limited, since in any case there is

[5] However, now that $U(C) \leq U(f[K^s])$, with $f'[K^s] = r^* > 0$, as $t \to \infty$, we find $r(t) \to r^* > 0$. Also, as $\theta(t) \to \infty$, utility satiation will be achieved and the behaviour equations of the truly affluent society would have to be altered beyond recognition by traditional economists. If $U(\infty) = B < \infty$, and $f[K]$ is Cobb–Douglas, Ramsey's optimized integral could still be convergent, and Schumpeterian evolution would still involve an interest rate that falls towards zero except when innovation transiently elevates it.

no likelihood that innovation will cease (and perhaps no great reason to expect it to fall substantially). Why agitate oneself about a quarrel over contrafactual asymptotes?

Logical Confusions?

Even if technology could permit the interest rate to become zero, Schumpeter never spelled out correctly why and exactly how this would come about. This may have been only inadvertence. But my reading of his 1912 classic (and later discussions) raises doubt that Schumpeter perceived the problem correctly. Schumpeter seems to have had a vague notion that, in the absence of development, the interest rate *logically* could have no equilibrium other than zero.

If he held such a view, he was in error. I have used the Clark–Solow model to show that $r(t)$ going to zero is a *logically possible* case. That same model can serve to show that a zero interest rate is not *logically necessary*. It is a puzzle that Schumpeter did not perceive this and concede it.

My example of a subjective rate of time preference of $\rho > 0$ has already made the point. True, Schumpeter might have the empirical hunch that $\rho = 0$. But if that were the basis for his notion of a zero interest rate, in his polemics with Böhm-Bawerk he might have been expected to marshal the factual evidence for so unconventional a view. Instead his arguments, inconclusive as they may seem to a careful reader, appear to be theoretical in character. (Later I review some of the 1912 points.)

Suppose Böhm were to put this question to Schumpeter: 'If the physical net productivity of capital never falls below a positive constant, do you still insist that the equilibrium real rate of interest would be zero?'

It is unflattering to say so, but I fear that Schumpeter would still have answered 'yes'. Somehow, he thought, the present K input that produced the postulated future fruits would have imputed to itself so much value as to make its subsequent net yield zero. But, as I see it, no finite value for K could do that. And, unlike the case of land, which I shall deal with presently, there is no reason for an infinity to rear its head in the model's depiction of K. (I return below to Schumpeter's 1912 exposition on this issue.)

Infinite Capitalization of Land

Permanent productive land will have an infinite value when the interest rate is zero:

$$P_T T/r = \infty \qquad \text{if} \qquad r = 0 > P_T T \tag{13}$$

This would shock many critics of Schumpeter. Blunt Edwin Cannan dismissed the problem of proving that the rate of interest must be positive, taking it for granted that there has to exist a (finite) ratio between the stock value of a flow.

Suppose Schumpeter conceived of a Robinson Crusoe who lived forever. Or, better, conceived of a Swiss Family Robinson that as a clan will live forever and that empirically is free of systematic time preference. Then there is nothing absurd about land's having a value higher than any multiple of its annual net rent. Two acres of land will be worth twice one acre; but no acres will ever be permanently sold for finite annual incomes.

We think land's value must be finite because we think of each person as dying. We expect that people do not attach as much importance to their remote heirs as they do to their own old age and to their immediate children and grandchildren. Empirically, we introduce the elements of subjective time preference that seem realistic and which are inconsistent with Schumpeter's idealized scenario.

We then face a model of overlapping generations and the Modigliani life-cycle model for wealth and saving applies. As I showed in my A. P. Lerner *Festschrift* contribution, with permanent land in the picture, a Turgot–Modigliani paradigm will yield a positive interest rate that is just large enough to make the amount of wealth that people will want to hold (out of their savings and inheritances) equal to society's valuation of all earning assets. At r too low, land and leets will be worth more than people want to continue to own; as people try to sell assets and spend proceeds on increments of consumption, asset prices will drop and r will return towards equilibrium r^*. At r above r^*, people of all ages will not be able to hold on the average as much as they need to plan to hold to fulfil their expected retirement consumption needs; they will try to save more, bidding up asset values, enhancing the stock of K leets and lowering the $f'[K]$ yield back down to r^*.

So, realistically, a positive interest rate seems indicated for Schumpeter's circular-flow equilibrium. Nonetheless, since the logical issue has been debated, in the next section I shall use Ramsey's 1927 model of optimal saving to vindicate Schumpeter's *logic* of a zero interest rate.

A RAMSEY MODEL FOR SCHUMPETER

To the Clark–Solow capital technology, I add a concave utility function for Schumpeter's society. The undiscounted integral of this utility integrand, extended over the *infinite* future, is to be maximized. Thus, we have

$$\max \int_0^\infty U(c)\,dt = \max_{K(t)} \int_0^\infty U(f[K] - K')\,dt \tag{14}$$

$$K(0) = K^0 < K^s, \qquad f'[K^s] = 0 > f''[K], \qquad f[K^s] \geq f[K]$$
$$U'(C) > 0 > U''(C), \qquad U(f[K^s]) = U(B) \geq U(f[K])$$

As is well known, $K(t)$ will grow by positive accumulation from initial K^0 gradually towards the golden-rule Schumpeter turnpike K^s. This means that the interest rate falls asymptotically towards zero, doing so at the optimal rate given by the Ramsey–Keynes 'energy integral':

$$U(B) = U(f[K] - K') + K'U'(f[K] - K') \tag{15}$$

This first-order differential equation in K has, from each initial K^0, a solution that asymptotically approaches Schumpeter's zero-interest golden-rule state. By standard mathematical methods that I need not review here, the following asymptotic limits can be shown to hold—in close agreement with the heuristic relations (1)–(4) presented earlier:

$$\lim_{t\to\infty} \left\{K(t), K'(t), r(t), \frac{K'(t)}{r(t)}, \frac{K'(t)}{K^s - K(t)}\right\} = \{K^s, 0, 0, \alpha, \beta\} \tag{16}$$

$$\alpha = \left\{\frac{U'(f[K^s])}{U''(f[K^s])f''[K^s]}\right\}^{1/2}, \qquad \beta = \left\{\frac{f''[K^s]U'(f[K^s])}{U''(f[K^s])}\right\}^{1/2} \tag{17}$$

The integral of present-discounted value of land, calculated along the system's path to equilibrium, will diverge to infinity as the interest rate decays exponentially to zero. But that is only as it should be in a system where decision-making is made on an infinite-lifetime basis.

Corrections

This concrete Schumpeter model permits us to correct any possible misapprehensions. Thus, suppose $r(t)$ or $f'[K(t)]$ can never fall below a positive number $\bar{r}$. Then with utility unsatiable, $U'[C] > 0$, Ramsey's integral will be infinite and no Schumpeter circular-flow equilibrium becomes possible. Böhm would then be right to reject any contention of a zero equilibrium rate of interest.

Also, suppose we realistically attach to Schumpeter's people finite lifetimes. And suppose that their bequeathing motivations are realistically limited: some of their Modigliani life-cycle wealth they want to leave to children and grandchildren, but they definitely fail to give like consideration to consumption by their descendants a million years from now. Then my earlier remarks about a Turgot–Modigliani model apply to negate a zero rate of interest.

Derailings

There would be some interest in dissecting Schumpeter's own 1912 expositions, to trace where his logic nods, what are his idiosyncratic definitions and views of empirical reality, and how he entraps himself in his own rhetoric. I have not the time to do this adequately. With diffidence, I mention a few of the highlights.

First, Schumpeter glimpses the golden-rule maximizing property of the zero-interest configuration. Thus Schumpeter (1912, p. 35) observes that a person who departs from the zero-interest state '. . . would discover in due course that he had obtained a smaller total satisfaction than he might have done.' This is at least a vague perception that $U(\mathrm{f}[K])$ is at its maximum when K is at the K^s where $\mathrm{f}'[K^s] = 0$. And it reflects a glimpse of the truth that $\int_0^\infty U(\mathrm{f}[K] - K')\mathrm{d}t$ is larger if $K(t) \equiv K^s$ than for any other $K(t)$ path emanating from $K(0) = K^s$.

Second, Schumpeter out-Smiths Adam Smith. He thinks that rational circular-flow competition most assuredly *achieves* the optimum glimpsed above. Only irrational 'children and primitive men', who are ignorable, will fail to be led by the invisible hand of competition to the golden-rule state. This is logically quite unwarranted, except if there is gratuitously slipped into the premises of the argument that all decision bodies live foreover and happen to perceive complete time-symmetry in their esteemings of future consumptions in 1912, 2012, and 9999. . . 912! There is no sign that the logical issues have been thought through and sorted out from the empirical plausibilities.

Third, it can be shown that, when we specify a zero interest rate, the resulting competitive-arbitrage conditions of steady-state pricing will permit the total value of society's consumption to be decomposed into the factor-returns of labour and land (the 'primary' non-reproducible inputs). Smith asserted this (and, when the interest rate is not zero, showed how the interest return on non-primary inputs must be included as a third return). Marx, worried about the infinite regress when it takes iron to produce coal and coal to produce iron, grappled with this truth over tens of thousands of words. Schumpeter blithely asserts this truth. Since Dimitriev's 1898 Russian essay, students of Leontief and Sraffa are in a position to demonstrate that it is indeed truth.

Fourth, Schumpeter erroneously thinks that the zero-interest-rate *premise* needed for the theorem's conclusion is itself a *guaranteed* property of innovationless circular-flow competition. He errs. Competitive arbitrage has no intrinsic tendency of its own to compete interest out of existence. All it does is equalize between every effort the market-sustainable interest rate. Schumpeter (1912, p. 29ff.) gratuitously asserts that *all* final values are imputed back to land rent[6] and labour wages *alone*—a truth only true on the stipulation of zero interest rate. To deduce zero interest from a syllogism that is valid only if you have already stipulated a zero interest rate is the height of self-deception. At best Schumpeter's comments only serve to show that there is a *self-consistency* about the golden-rule state (even though, we remind him, that is only *one of an infinity* of self-consistent steady states!).

Fifth, Schumpeter falls into the attractive fallacy of automatic synchronization that entrapped J. B. Clark, Frank Knight, and Henry George. Böhm-Bawerk's turn-of-the-century polemics against Clark had to be replicated in the 1930s by Hayek's polemics against Knight to refute this fallacy. In the steady-state circular flow, the same inputs are followed by the same outputs. An observer sees simultaneously an input and an output: ergo, he is tempted to cry blunderingly that there is no time lag between inputs and outputs and no tempting temporary gain in consumption to be had by departing from the circular flow. In truth the steady state only stays steady because people choose not to fail to do that which keeps it steady.

A Lionel Robbins is wrong to assert that a zero interest rate robs people of the incentive to stay in it: our Ramsey paradigm demonstrates that Robbins is wrong.[7] But a Robbins is right to insist that staying in a steady state does require that it continues to be the more attractive of the multiplicity of choices open to you in every new period of the process.

Sixth, Schumpeter does not reconcile his doctrine that *all* value is decomposable into land rent and labour wages with a *possible* technological case: 100 rice ripen into 110 rice in one year's time without need for any labour or scarce land. (You may say, 'Surely, land is needed, eventually if not now.' Do not say it. Let Schumpeter accept the challenge and observe what he does with the rope Böhm and we give to him.)

Schumpeter's answer might start out in terms of these words (which I put

---

[6] Schumpeter on p. 166 of the 1934 English version of 1912 *The Theory of Economic Development*—my few page references will always be to this source—rejects by logic any view of Böhm that, if the interest rate is zero, the rent yield of land must evaporate: for, on an infinite base a zero yield can form a finite product: $0 \times \infty$ can equal a finite positive number. But this formality fails to meet our *empirical* rejection of infinite value for land. Our senses tell us that people do not live forever; they do buy and sell land *in the circular flow* at predictable ages and at predictable finite 'number of years' purchase'. The young Schumpeter somehow doped himself into identifying innovationless competitive equilibrium with clans that live forever!

[7] Robbins (1930) may however be considered to have more of a point in connection with the issue of *whether a decentralized pricing mechanism can sustain the golden-rule state* with each producer's integrals of present-discounted-value being *finite*. See Samuelson (1943, 1951, 1971), Whitaker (1972), and McCrae (1947).

into his mouth). 'With more rice next year, the price of each grain falls. Thus, 110 then sell for the total of marks 100 now will sell for. So 100 marks today still get you 100 marks tomorrow. The rate of interest is zero *sans* innovations. Q.E.D.' Around p. 170, Schumpeter (1912) repeatedly makes the point that (*when* the interest rate is truly zero) the greater magnitude of the forest is *already* imputed back in value to the saplings: so these foreseen changes in time only conserve the already calculated value of the process. Without labour and land, zero Kuznet product is being produced and it is correctly decomposable into zero real rent and zero real wages.

But this is pure self-deception. Real rice *is* being produced net. Kuznets can measure it. You can eat 10 rice every year and still not impair your circular-flow income. With land redundant and labour not needed, Kuznets measures national income of zero in terms of primary-factors' income. To this he adds permanent real interest income of 10 rice per year. No hocus-pocus of backward imputation—of forest to sapling, or rice grain to rice grain—evades the naive fact of productive interest.

Empirically, Schumpeter may deny to Böhm that there always exists positive technical productivity of capital at the margin. But *logically* he must throw in the towel: when 100 rice as input yields 110 rice output at the end of the year, *no* steady-state (real!, 'own'!) rate of interest can obtain other than 10% per year. A zero equilibrium rate becomes a contradiction (and settling down of the system to a steady state may no longer occur).

Seventh, and this will be my final point as patience ebbs, although Schumpeter correctly perceives the need to keep our thinking straight on the difference between (1) our being in a steady state, and (2) the process of getting into a steady state, Schumpeter himself often makes errors of logic in *denying that the differences between a magnitude in two adjacent alternative steady states may themselves be relevant for understanding what are the market pricings in each of these alternative steady states*. For a Leets model, the ratio $(f[K^2] - f[K^1])/(K^2 - K^1)$ involves only (alternative) steady-state magnitudes. But it has good relevance to the r^2 or the r^1 that you would measure in each such steady state! And, in the Leets model, it has considerable relevance to the optimal path of development that a socialist planner would aim for in maximizing the social utility over time of the ongoing society. One can hardly criticize a 1912 genius for occasional failures in understanding these subtleties. But respect for truth compels one to note in dissecting that genius's work wherein the pathologies originated.

Schumpeter à la Sraffa

My earlier 'leets' model of Solow–Ramsey type can help make clear the error in believing that competitive arbitrage makes it a requirement of steady-state circular flow that the profit rate be zero.

I replace continuous time by discrete time: $K(t)$ by K_t, $t = 0, 1, 2, \ldots$; $K'(t) = \mathrm{d}K(t)/\mathrm{d}t$ by $K_{t+1} - K_t$. For convenience I replace the net-product function $f[K_t]$ by the gross-product function $g[K_t] \equiv f[K_t] + K_t$. To avoid Sraffian joint products, I assume leets are used up in one use as input: we have 100 per cent depreciation and a working capital model.

Now (1) and (2b) take the form

$$C_{t+1} + K_{t+1} = g[K_t], \qquad g''[K] < 0 \tag{18}$$

$$1 + r_t = \partial K_{t+1}/\partial K_t = g'[K_t], \qquad g'[K^s] = 0 + 1 \tag{19}$$

In steady-state equilibrium, we have

$$(C_{t+1}, K_{t+1}, r_{t+1}) \equiv (C_t, K_t, r_t) \equiv (C, K, r) \tag{20}$$

Prices of consumption and leets are the same, P. The steady-state wage rate and rent rate are W and V. The interest rate per period is r.

The Leontief–Sraffa conditions of price equal to competitive unit costs—which could also be called the Ricardo–Dimitriev–Smith conditions—are as follows for the consumption-good sector and the leets sector:

$$PC = (WL_C + VT_C + PK_C)(1 + r) \tag{21a}$$

$$P(K_K + K_C) = (WL_K + VT_K + PK_K)(1 + r) \tag{21b}$$

where $L = L_C + L_K$, $T = T_C + T_K$, $K = K_C + K_K$. Remember that the Ramsey–Solow 'one-sector' model involves both industries with the same technique:

$$(L_C, T_C, K_C)/C \equiv (L_K, T_K, K_K)/(K_C + K_K), \qquad L_C + L_K = L \tag{21c}$$

Schumpeter's pivotal error of imputation is to think that competitive arbitrate requires that $(1 + r)$ be $(1 + 0)$ in (21a) and (21b). We know better. We know that $1 + 0$ is only one of an infinity of arbitrage-proof equilibria. One must look to the behaviour equations of saving-investing, and not those of competition or to the definition of circular flow, to find conditions determining the relevant choicc of $1 + r$ from the admissible set.

In Part I of Sraffa's (1960) classic, the six ratios in (21c) are taken as technically given. The unknowns of $(W/P,\ V/P,\ r)$ become determinate only if three further equations are specified from outside (21)–(23). However, here (21c)'s ratios are not exogenously prescribed, but instead are specified to satisfy the neoclassical production function:

$$K_{t+1} = G[T_t, L_t, K_t], \qquad K = G[T, L, K] \tag{22a}$$

$$1 = G[T_K/K, L_K/K, K_K/K] \tag{22b}$$

No competitive steady state could survive if the technique used could be replaced by a known technique that could produce a surplus profit beyond the interest rate $1 + r$. Therefore, we adjoin to (21a)–(21c) the following two marginal-productivity relations:

$$1 + r = G'[K] = \partial G[T, L, K]/\partial K \qquad (21d)$$
$$W/P = (1 + r)^{-1}\, \partial G[T, L, K]/\partial L \qquad (21e)$$

Along with these there is a third such marginal-productivity relation for land. But it is redundant, being implied by the formula for residual rent already implied in (21a)–(21e).

Schumpeter missed the discount factor $(1 + r)^{-1}$ in (21e)'s Wicksell–Taussig discounted-marginal-product relation. And in (21d)'s Jevons–Wicksell relation, Schumpeter failed to mention that $1 + r$ need *not* be $1 + 0$. That need obtain only in the special case where K is always guaranteed to have grown to reach K^s after innovation ceases. This is a possible case, but not an inevitable one, and certainly not so probable a case as Schumpeter's quill proclaimed it to be.

We still lack in relations (18)–(22) one final relation to make steady-state r and all our variables determinate. Schumpeter, implicitly thinking of perpetual-life actors with 'neutral' subjective time preference, supplies the missing equation by having $K(t)$ accumulate to the golden-rule level of K^s. Pigou and Fisher postulated a subjective rate of time preference, ρ, that sets the asymptote for $r(t)$. Classical economists (Smith, Ricardo) similarly closed their long-run system by having $r(t)$ fall to ρ while population grows or shrinks when $W(t)/P(t)$ differs from some postulated subsistence-wage level, $\bar{W}$. Marxians, usually ignoring land as if it were redundant, get their missing equation by similarly specifying a $\bar{W}$ level at which labour supply is reproduced from the reserve army of the unemployed.

FINALE

As I re-read my words, they strike me as overly critical and insufficiently appreciative. Joseph Schumpeter will not stay dead and exalted. His memory is so vivid, his thought so lively, that one finds oneself arguing with unseemly vigour as if he were a mere mortal.

This is not the first time I felt an urge to go back and paint in more favourable brush strokes, not for the purpose of eulogizing but simply to redress the balance properly. Thus, at Mexico City I had to say explicitly that Schumpeter was anti-Hitler and anti-Nazi, because some who read my remarks about his belief that market capitalism would not prevail unless politically imposed mistakenly equated his distrust of Stalin with sympathy for Hitler. When evaluating *Capitalism, Socialism and Democracy* (1942), and finding in the end reasons to doubt Schumpeter's belief that capitalism's *success* would be its undoing, I had to state explicitly, lest I be misunderstood, that it is a great book.

Here, in closing, I must make a similar disclaimer. My failure to agree that a zero interest rate is the inevitable equilibrium when innovation does not occur, and my discussion of some limitations in Schumpeter's mathematical expertise, in no sense lessens his claim to have been one of the few most important economic theorists of the twentieth century. His fame is secure.

ACKNOWLEDGEMENT

I owe thanks to the National Science Foundation for financial aid, and to Kate Crowley and Aase Huggins for editorial assistance.

REFERENCES

Haberler, G. (1951) Schumpeter's theory of interest. In *Schumpeter: Social Scientist* (Ed.) S. Harris, Cambridge, MA: Harvard University Press.
Heertje, A. (Ed.) (1981) *Schumpeter's Vision: Capitalism, Socialism and Democracy after 40 years.* New York: Praeger.
Kaldor, N. (1960) *Essays on Economic Stability and Growth*. London: Duckworth.
Kaldor, N. (1960) *Essays on Value and Distribution*. London: Duckworth.
Kaldor, N. (1964) *Essays on Economic Policy*. 2 volumes, London: Duckworth.
Macrae, C. D. (1974) Equilibrium, efficiency, and the golden rule. *Quarterly Journal of Economics*, **88**, 143–8.
Ramsey, F. (1928) A mathematical theory of savings. *Economic Journal*, **38**, 543–59.
Robbins, L. (1930) On a certain ambiguity in the conception of stationary equilibrium. *Economic Journal*, **40**, 194–214.
Samuelson, P. A. (1943) Dynamics, statics, and the stationary states. *Review of Economics and Statistics*, **25**, Essays in Honor of Joseph Schumpeter. Reprinted (1966) in *The Collected Scientific Papers of Paul A. Samuelson*, Vol. 2. Cambridge, MA: MIT Press.
Samuelson, P. A. (1951) Schumpeter as a teacher and economic theorist. In *Joseph Schumpeter: Social Scientist* (Ed.) Harris, S. Cambridge, MA: Harvard University Press. And (1951) *Review of Economics and Statistics*, **33**, 98–103. Reprinted (1966) in *The Collected Scientific Papers of Paul A. Samuelson*, Vol. 2, Chap. 116. Cambridge, MA: MIT Press.
Samuelson, P. A. (1979) Land and the rate of interest. In *Theory for Economic Efficiency: Essays in Honor of Abba P. Lerner* (Eds.) Greenfield, Levenson, Hamovitch and Rotwein. Cambridge, MA: MIT Press.
Schumpeter, J. A. (1908) *Das Wesen und Hauptinhalt der theoretischen Nationalökonomie (Nature and Main Content of Theoretical Economics)*. Leipzig: Verlag von Duncker und Humblot.
Schumpeter, J. A. (1912) *Theorie der wirtschaftlichen Entwicklung*. Leipzig. English translation (1934) *Theory of Economic Development, An Inquiry into Profits, Capitalism, Credit, Interest and the Business Cycle* (*Harvard Economic Studies*, Vol. XLVI). Cambridge, MA: Harvard University Press.
Schumpeter, J. A. (1942) *Capitalism, Socialism and Democracy*. New York: Harper & Row.
Schumpeter, J. A. (1954) *History of Economic Doctrines*. Oxford: Oxford University Press.

Solow, R. M. (1956) A contribution to the theory of economic growth. *Quarterly Journal of Economics*, **70**, 65–94.
Sraffa, P. (1960) *Production of Commodities by Means of Commodities*. Cambridge: Cambridge University Press.
Whitaker, J. K. (1972) Private wealth as an obstacle to Pareto optimality. *Review of Economics and Statistics*, **39**, 325–29.

Chapter One

Schumpeter's Capitalism, Socialism and Democracy

PAUL A. SAMUELSON

THE MAN

These are impressionistic reflections about my old teacher, Joseph Schumpeter. He deserves a more coherent analysis but alas I lack the free time to attempt that here. Nor shall I confine my attention to his last book alone.

It is a great book. Somewhere I wrote that the books Schumpeter toiled over longest turned out to be less important than those that gushed out in the heat of inspiration. Probably I was wrong. Perhaps I had in mind the contrast between his 1914 little gem on historical doctrines and the stillborn treatise on money to which he devoted the 1920s in self-styled competition with John Maynard Keynes; or the contrast between the pedantic two-volume 1939 *Business Cycles* and the 1942 *Capitalism, Socialism and Democracy*.

But, from the text of *CSD* one learns that part of it goes back to the mid-1930s, even though we graduate students thought that 'Schumpie'—what we called him, at first behind his back, and only later to his face—was solely engaged then on his *Business Cycles*. The great Mozart arias may seem to have soared out of the composer's quill but that is not cogent evidence of their comparative gestation periods.

One of Schumpeter's poses was that he did not work hard. He always had time for a cup of coffee at the disreputable Merle Cafe across from the Harvard Yard, and a spare hour in which to suffer fools gladly. Demand creates a responsive supply in the lonely barnyard of the graduate school, and the anteroom to Schumpeter's office was as crowded as Freud's must have been. Nights and weekends Schumpeter wrote.

He was a driven man. Driven by the ambition for accomplishment, by the itch for lasting scholarly fame, Schumpeter below the surface of theatrical gallantry was daily grading himself—and daily finding himself wanting. Since his standards were high and his aspirations insatiable, no scratching could assuage his itch.

When did Schumpeter have time between the tasks of teaching and writing to do the reading needed to build up the erudition displayed in his works? He must have been a fast reader with a remarkable memory for whatever was once read.

Even so, by choice Schumpeter died early from overwork. When the adrenalin is always running, you burn up 500 days each year and are allotted proportionally fewer years. No doubt this was a Faustian gamble, willingly entered into and happy in its net outcome.

THE MESSAGE

A 400-page book contains many messages. The thesis in *CSD* that principally interests me can be indicated, to use Schumpeter's description, 'in one short and imperfect sentence':

> Capitalism, whilst economically stable, and even gaining in stability, creates, by rationalizing the human mind, a mentality and style of life incompatible with its own fundamental conditions, motives and social institutions, and will be changed, although not by economic necessity and probably even at some sacrifice of economic welfare, into an order of things which it will be merely a matter of taste and terminology to call Socialism or not.

These words have the Schumpeterian flavour, even though a 70-word sentence is not 'short' and occurs more commonly in his German than in his English prose. Granted, many of the ideas we associate with Schumpeter's name had antecedents in the past; this thesis seems peculiarly his own. What are its objective merits?

Firstly, if it is true, it is important. The more successful Peter the Great is in effectuating for Mother Russia an industrial revolution, the nearer comes the death of that new capitalistic order and the nearer in time the onset of the socialist order that is next in turn. Such is the allegation.

Secondly, there are some facts that Schumpeter's paradigm does seem to fit. Observing the behaviour of New Left students at the end of the 1960s in Berkeley, Harvard, Heidelberg and Paris, I was impelled to write in the course of a 1970 *Newsweek* column:

It is just twenty years since Joseph Schumpeter died. Although it is not my practice to tout profitable speculations, today I'd like to suggest that Schumpeter's diagnosis of the probable decay of capitalism deserves a new reading in our own time. The general reader cannot do better than begin with his 1942 *Capitalism, Socialism and Democracy*.

Sour Smell of Success

Nothing that has happened in recent years at Berkeley or Harvard would have come as a surprise to those who have absorbed this work. And if there are good clubs in the great beyond, one can picture Schumpeter—a spry 87-year-old by this time, martini glass in hand—reading the New York Review of Books and chuckling in clinical amusement. Only his Viennese veneer keeps him from saying, 'I told you so.' The successes and rationalism of bourgeois capitalism will breed a swarm of discontented intellectuals—to fan the flames of hostility toward an efficient but unlovable system with no mystique to protect it.

THESIS AND ANTITHESIS

Joseph Schumpeter was long dead when I wrote those words. The prophecies implicit in *CSD* were formulated a quarter of a century *before* their fulfilment occurred. This adds to our admiration for Schumpeter's acumen. For, in science, it is somehow more impressive when an Einstein tells you in 1915 that observations during a *future* 1919 eclipse will reveal a shift of light's path as it passes near the sun's gravitational field, than if he tells you only in 1920 that what you *did* observe does indeed accord with his theory. If I or Schumpeter were to develop in 1970 or 1980 the quoted thesis to explain the 1968 happenings, that would be less impressive than for Schumpeter to have done so in 1942, prior to the fact itself. You will remind me, however:

> Scientific inference is a tandem chicken–egg–chicken . . . sequence. From earlier inductive observations, we formulate our theoretical hypotheses, testing them and modifying them on later observations that we are lucky enough to make or that we contrive to observe because our provisional hypotheses suggested such observations would be of peculiar interest. Einstein already knew of *past* observations on the anomaly of the planet Mercury's aphelion and had framed his relativity theory in accordance . . . And Schumpeter, already in 1942, had observed the post-1929 withering away of capitalist democracy as the Great Depression made it vulnerable to the onslaughts of Hitlerism and Stalinism . . .

Precisely. One can always benefit from a sermon on the hypotheticological methods of 20th-century scientists. But my point concerning how remarkably early Schumpeter arrived at his fundamental insight remains untouched by these caveats. There is still something to wonder at—which means there is an interesting puzzle here that deserves to be studied in depth.

Let me make my case.

Yes indeed, Joseph Schumpeter did by 1942 know about the Great Depression. He could not have been unaware of the popular thesis that Franklin Roosevelt saved capitalism, whose existence in many countries had been threatened by fascist and communist movements that thrived on the mass unemployment and bankruptcies engendered by the Great Depression. Having been threatened by death once—you will go on to argue—capitalism might well be deemed to be subject to similar threats in the period after the Second World War. From which you will infer that a prophecy to that effect by Schumpeter in 1942 is not all that remarkable.

If you argue in that way, you quite miss the point. That capitalism will die because of its economic malperformance is a possible hypothesis to submit to testing at the bar of History. But it is not Schumpeter's hypothesis! Instead it is almost the negation of *his* hypothesis. For Schumpeter, capitalism is to be killed by its *successes*, not its failures; by its *good* performance, not its bad.

That Russia should turn communist in the wake of a disastrous war Schumpeter would take as obvious. That a long period of depression or of stagnation after the Second World War could undermine capitalism and usher in socialism is a proposition Schumpeter would not have sought to make his own. It was the implausibility of this proposition's antecedent—the implausibility that capitalism would *economically breed its own bad performance*—that constituted his contention. And Schumpeter shared this complacent contention with many who professed optimism about the postwar cyclical outlook, either out of conservative wishful thinking or careful analysis of accumulating wartime liquidity and consumption needs.

What distinguishes Schumpeter from others hopeful about postwar economic conditions is his assertion that capitalism's success will not protect it from dying, but *instead will be the very cause of its demise.*

That I am faithfully stating his position is attested by Schumpeter's own summary, at the beginning of *CSD*'s section entitled 'Can Capitalism Survive?' On page 61, he writes: 'The thesis I shall endeavor to establish is that

> [T]he actual and prospective performance of the capitalistic system is such as to negative the idea of its breaking down under the weight of economic failure, but that its very success undermines the social institutions which protect it, and "inevitably" creates conditions in which it will not be able to live and which strongly point to socialism as the heir apparent.'

If you will compare this passage with the 70-word 'short and imperfect sentence' that I earlier quoted to encapsulate Schumpeter's basic vision, you will see that they are essentially the same (albeit this last passage covers less of the ground).

Fatal to the notion that Joseph Schumpeter arrived at his vision of how the capitalist order was to generate its own demise *by empirical induction from the unrest of the 1930s* is the fact, which I have until now artfully concealed, that Schumpeter's 70-word enunciation of his schemata is not taken from his 1942 book but instead dates back to his 1928 *Economic Journal* article, 'The instability of capitalism'.

In the palmy days of the 1920s' new epoch of perpetual prosperity Schumpeter had already announced his prophecy.[1]

The Great Depression is rather a refutation than a confirmation of Schumpeter's thesis. The events from 1928 to 1942 surely mock Schumpeter's 1928 guess that capitalism is 'economically stable, and even gaining in stability.'

We are left in the end with a more remarkable phenomenon. Even *before* the world's most capitalistic society, that of the United States, showed any signs of age or decay, Schumpeter had already, in 1928, arrived at his prediction of its psychosomatic demise as a result of self-induced will not to resist dying.

This is almost too much of a good thing. To predict from a few facts already seen many new facts yet to come is the apex of good science. But to predict something about a domain before you have seen anything of it smacks of superhuman powers or of chance serendipity. (It is like the case of de Tocqueville, who correctly foresaw in the 1830s the weakness of future American presidents. But he did so while lacking recognition that the American presidents before his time—Washington, Jefferson, Madison, Jackson—averaged out as remarkably strong presidents!)

A RED HERRING

It is well, I think, to differentiate the thesis that is characteristically Schumpeter's and which is what I am engaged in appraising here from a somewhat

[1] Since so many of Schumpeter's seminal ideas go back to the 1903 to 1913 period, his third decade of life—the epoch for scholars he glorified as 'that sacred period of fertility'—a pre-1928 formulation cannot be ruled out.

I fell into the trap of believing that Schumpeter generated his thesis out of the observations of the post-1929 collapse. In my World Economic Congress speech in Mexico City, August 1980, I wrote: 'The Great Depression showed Schumpeter how prone the political systems of Europe and North America were to depart from the conventional patterns and practices of constitutional democracy.'

different thesis popular with certain historians. The late Crane Brinton, expert in French history at Harvard, used to make the point that revolutions do not come when a region is at its poorest. When people are down and out, they do not have the energy to burst out of their lethargy. Therefore, Brinton asserted, revolutions are more likely to occur after a regime has begun to make some progress towards raising the standard of life. The French Revolution broke out in the most prosperous region of Europe, not in the poorest. (There is evidence, however, of French agricultural distress in the decades prior to the 1789 Revolution. To this degree, the simple Brinton thesis of progress as conducing towards instability is contradicted or at least is laid open to the need for qualification and dilution.) Forcing the thesis and ignoring the more important factor of the Czar's army being defeated in the First World War, you might try to claim that it was the burst of industrial development in Russia early in this century that led to the 1917 February Revolution.

Whether Schumpeter would have agreed with this, I can't say. He did know Brinton at Harvard's Dunster House (but Brinton's name does not appear in *CSD*, nor does Brinton's explicit thesis). But even if Schumpeter would have concurred with Brinton, it is not the Brinton hypothesis that we associate with the name of Schumpeter. Here I confine my attention to the peculiarly Schumpeterian twist, which alleges that it is capitalism's economic success that leads to its political failure.

AD HOMINEM

How can we explain Schumpeter's early genesis—almost too early genesis—of his basic sociological–political paradigm? The effort to find an explanation is interesting for its own sake. In addition, that effort may help to clarify what the content of Schumpeter's thesis really is, and help suggest procedures by which we can hope to test, corroborate or refute its contention and perhaps improve upon its formulation and content.

I am on treacherous ground in studying a scholar's biography to illuminate his thought. My old friend, the economic historian Alexander Gerschenkron, who was also the Harvard colleague of Schumpeter in Schumpeter's last few years of life, was dead set against all biography of scholars. 'Let their works stand for themselves, and don't look for dirty underwear', was Gerschenkron's dictum. Schumpeter himself thought otherwise. In his 1948 Presidential Address to the American Economic Association, 'Science and Ideology', Schumpeter set out to 'look for ideological elements in three of the most influential structures of economic thought, the works of Adam Smith, of Marx, and of Keynes' (p. 353). To ascertain 'what kind of ideology we are to attribute to him [Adam Smith]', Schumpeter wrote: 'Proceeding on the Marxist principle we shall look to his social location, that is, to his personal and ancestral class applications and in addition to the class connotation of the influences that may have helped to form what we call his vision.'

Even if we bless the effort to apply psychobiography to Schumpeter, adding to the shaky methods of Marx the even more problematic methods of Freud, I am ill-equipped for the job. Children never know their parents. I knew Schumpeter for only the last 15 years of his 67-year life, and never had the intimate knowledge of him that Wolfgang Stolper or Paul Sweezy enjoyed. Gottfried Haberler, Wassily Leontief, Edward Mason and Arthur Smithies have told us much about their colleague, but the still more that they can bear witness to should be recorded while yet there is time.

If biography of class and personality cannot be done well, better not do it at all? That is a defensible rule. I violate it with the explicit warning that all my inferences are dubious. If I have little confidence in them, the reader should have less.

I begin by presenting a popular stereotype about Schumpeter, one that I myself fabricated in 1969. For the second time I quote from an earlier *Newsweek* column, this time in its entirety.

MEMORIES (June, 1969)

When Diaghilev revived his ballet company he had the original Bakst sets redone in even more vivid colors, explaining, 'so that they would be as brilliant as people remember them.' Recent events on college campuses have recalled to my inward eye one of the great happenings in my own lifetime.

It took place at Harvard back in the days when giants walked the earth and Harvard Yard.

Joseph Schumpeter, Harvard's brilliant economist and social prophet, was to debate with Paul Sweezy on 'The Future of Capitalism'. Wassily Leontief was in the chair as moderator, and the Littauer Auditorium could not accommodate the packed house.

Let me set the stage. Schumpeter was a scion of the aristocracy of Franz Josef's Austria. It was Schumpeter who had confessed to three wishes in life: to be the greatest lover in Vienna, the best horseman in Europe, and the greatest economist in the world. 'But, unfortunately,' as he used to say modestly, 'the seat I inherited was never of the topmost caliber.'

Half mountebank, half sage, Schumpeter had been the *enfant terrible* of the Austrian school of economists. Steward to an Egyptian princess, owner of a stable of race horses, onetime Finance Minister of Austria, Schumpeter could look at the prospects for bourgeois society with the objectivity of one whose feudal world had come to an end in 1914. His message and vision can be read in his classical work of a quarter century ago, *Capitalism, Socialism, and Democracy*.

Whom the Gods Envy

Opposed to the foxy Merlin was young Sir Galahad. Son of an executive of J.P.

Morgan's bank, Paul Sweezy was the best that Exeter and Harvard can produce. Tiring of the 'gentlemen's C' and of the good life at Locke-Ober's with Lucius Beebe, Sweezy had early established himself as among the most promising of the economists of his generation. But tiring of the conventional wisdom of his age, and spurred on by the events of the Great Depression, Sweezy became one of America's few Marxists. (As he used to say, you could count the noses of American academic economists who were Marxists on the thumbs of your two hands: the late Paul Baran of Stanford; and, in an occasional summer school of unwonted tolerance, Paul Sweezy.)

Unfairly, the gods had given Paul Sweezy, along with a brilliant mind, a beautiful face and wit. With what William Buckley would desperately wish to see in his mirror, Sweezy faced the world. If lightning had struck him that night, people would truly have said that he had incurred the envy of the gods.

So much for the cast. I would have to be William Hazlitt to recall for you the interchange of wit, the neat parrying and thrust, and all made the more pleasurable by the obvious affection that the two men had for each other despite the polar opposition of their views.

Meeting of Opposites

Great debaters deserve great moderators, and that night Leontief was in fine form. At the end he fairly summarized the viewpoints expressed.

'The patient is capitalism. What is to be his fate? Our speakers are in fact agreed that the patient is inevitably dying. But the bases of their diagnoses could not be more different.

'On the one hand there is Sweezy, who utilizes the analysis of Marx and of Lenin to deduce that the patient is dying of a malignant cancer. Absolutely no operation can help. The end is foreordained.

'On the other hand, there is Schumpeter. He, too, and rather cheerfully, admits that the patient is dying. (His sweetheart already died in 1914 and his bank of tears had long since run dry.) But to Schumpeter, the patient is dying of a psychosomatic ailment. Not cancer but neurosis is the patient's complaint. Filled with self-hate, he has lost the will to live.

'In this view capitalism is an unlovable system, and what is unlovable will not be loved. Paul Sweezy himself is a talisman and omen of that alienation which will seal the system's doom.'

All this I had long forgotten. And a few years ago when I reread Schumpeter's book, I graded him down for his gloomy views on the progress that would be made by the mixed economy—capitalism in an oxygen tent, as Schumpeter put it. His failure to predict the miraculous progress of the postwar years earned Schumpeter a C in my eyes.

However, 1969 university happenings reveal an alienation of privileged youth entitling Schumpeter to a report-card recount.[2]

---

[2] After that column appeared, several readers wrote nice notes to tell how much they had liked it. I was struck with the finding that all my correspondents seemed to be over 50, from which I concluded that such reminiscence had a limited audience. However, half a dozen years later, when I was making an informal luncheon talk in the Lowell House junior common room, a sophomore addressed me belligerently, saying: 'It was on account of you that I came to Harvard. Your column of memories of great debates enticed me, and I've not found it true that there are such bright memories to be had here.' My reply was, 'Wait 30 years for them to brighten up.' I also realized that Schumpeter's thought still held relevance for the present, and future.

SECOND THOUGHTS

The above analysis needs revision. It classifies too confidently Schumpeter as an aristocrat. Psychobiology has to do better than that. Even if I had been correct in type-casting Schumpeter as a fossil from a pre-capitalistic epoch, at best that could only explain his cheerful objectivity in uttering gloomy prophecies about the future of capitalism. It is easy to utter gloomy prophecies. Cranks do so all the time. My account failed to specify exactly how and why Schumpeter could cogently claim that capitalism would endogenously generate its own demise out of its very successes.

I did, however, specify one possible line of causation. You could call it the 'spoiled, rich dissident' syndrome. According to this special mechanism, as the Schumpeterian entrepreneur goes from shirt-sleeves to shirt-sleeves in three generations, the detailed stages of his dynasty run as follows: farmer or labourer; small merchant; tycoon; diplomat and public servant; and finally parlour-pink or terrorist.

How much truth is there in this strain of the argument? On reflection, I would say, only a little. It is not just that Paul Sweezy serves only imperfectly to exemplify this paradigm. For if that were all, we could supplement Sweezy with Samuel Bowles, son of the Chester Bowles who went from the highly successful advertising agency of Bowles and Benton to be Ambassador to India and Assistant Secretary of State. The fact that someone like Samuel Bowles was a leading radical economist at Harvard around 1970 could be used to give some plausibility to the model and still other confirmatory anecdotes could be marshalled in which Patty Hearst plays a bit part.

Affluent elite institutions like Harvard and Yale did display more campus unrest than was to be seen in landgrant universities of the Middle West. During the 1960s, when a more radical course competed with the mainstream introductory economics course, a census revealed that those who opted for the radical course came from families with incomes that on average were higher than those in the university at large. Other bits of like evidence can be supplied.

The reasons, though, why I think the thesis will not wash include the following: the most radical American college students come on the average from parents who already have themselves possessed ideologies somewhat critical of market capitalism. Sometimes these parents are successful capitalists. More often, such parents are professional people rather than businessmen or corporate executives. If you look at the children of Paul Sweezy's Harvard class of 1931, a class which predated the meritocracy democratization of Harvard and did contain many who were to be capitalists, I doubt that children of this affluent set showed much pinkness of ideology.

In any case, I doubt that Joseph Schumpeter himself put considerable weight on this particular straw.[3] Schumpeter took it for granted that intellectuals were a source of disaffection in any capitalist society. He recognized that the affluence characteristic of modern industrial economies made possible the existence of an intellectual class of some size. But would he have thought it more likely that the son of a successful entrepreneur would become a dissident than the son of an immigrant tailor would? No, according to my recollection.

When European capitalism seemed to be succeeding less well than American capitalism, as in the 1920s, did Schumpeter believe that dissident intellectuals were being recruited at a greater relative rate in America than in Europe? I doubt that he had any such unrealistic expectations. Furthermore, Schumpeter as cynic discounted heavily the political importance of the intelligentsia, both as scribblers and as chatterers. Had Schumpeter been alive these last 30 years, to observe in Japan the continued omnipresence of Marxist terminology among journalists and teachers, I doubt that he would have been astonished that alongside this there should be recurrent victories at the polls of the ruling conservative party. What I do think might cause in him some squirming and some need to recast his paradigm would be the following phenomenon that is virtually independent of the content of Japanese intellectuals' ideological leanings:

> The fantastic material success of Japan's mixed economy—its characteristic amalgam of capitalism and bureaucracy—far from undermining that mixed economy to the point of harakiri, instead did succeed in keeping the ruling powers in power despite a number of scandals and external shocks.

As I write these words, Ronald Reagan has been elected President on a conservative platform. Was it the successes of the mixed economy that led to this repudiation of New Dealism? Or was it the mixed economy's failure? Surely, it was a rational and not an irrational reaction to America's inflation and stagnation during the 1970s that led voters to repudiate Jimmy Carter, the heir to the Roosevelt–Truman–Kennedy tradition. Reagan may not be able to do better, but pragmatic voters are ready to try out new methods in the best tradition of scientific logic; and those of us who disagree with them do not do so primarily on logical grounds.

Am I denying any empirical triumphs for Schumpeter's thesis? That

[3] Opposite to the notion that intellectual dissidents are themselves rich is Ludwig von Mises's notion that those who can't hack it in the competitive commercial struggle for existence become the whiners and complainers who seek to subvert the capitalistic order.

would be unjust. At Mexico City in August 1980, I was able to say on his behalf:

> As *Capitalism, Socialism and Democracy* approaches its fortieth birthday, what stands up best in its analysis is this striking thesis of Schumpeter that capitalism's very success will be its undoing. Joseph Schumpeter, looking down from Valhalla on the Iranian revolution against the Shah, must be crowing, 'I told you so!' In his view the same fate would have been meted out to Peter the Great were it not that the feudal elements of superstition and religion conspired to protect Peter from the Shah's destiny.
>
> Schumpeter, like Thorstein Veblen, does not really document conclusively the interesting dogmas that he promulgates. Like Oliver Twist, we readers ask for, 'More'.

Against Schumpeter's favourable case of the Shah in Iran, we might have to balance Ataturk, who successfully modernized the Ottoman society, even altering its alphabet and secularizing its cultural life. Empirical science is a more tedious business than speculative brainstorming is.

After pondering over how Schumpeter arrived at his thesis, I am inclined to the view that it was not primarily a clever inference from empirical observations. So, to echo Max Planck's work, as an act of desperation we are led to dig deeper into Schumpeter's own biography.

UNDER THE MICROSCOPE

Firstly, Schumpeter was more than an aristocrat—*and less!* He was not born in Vienna, but rather in the province of Moravia (now Czechoslovakia), son of a textile manufacturer; his mother was the daughter of a physician. What evidence there is I do not know for von Beckerath's[4] assertion: 'Born to a fairly affluent family of Moravia, with aristocratic connections . . .' His mother, widowed when Joseph was four, did marry a Viennese general, when Schumpeter was ten. As a stepson, his years until 23 were spent on the fringe of higher Viennese society. Von Beckerath's appellation of Schumpeter as of the class 'gentleman-bourgeois' seems merited, but one would not say that the adult Schumpeter had the vacant good looks associated with

---

[4] When this paper was at the revision stage, I received a reprint of Frank Meissner's *The Schumpeters of Trieve*. It documents that he came from a Catholic family of textile entrepreneurs. (In my recollection Schumpeter considered himself a Lutheran in his later years; when he formally ceased being Catholic I do not know. The Meissner account refutes what was always a dubious rumour—that Joseph Schumpeter may have had some original Jewish connections. It also reveals no aristocratic 'connection'.)

court circles. There was always something of the outsider[5] about him. Except that Schumpeter was not Jewish, he shared some of the insecurities and strengths of those other Moravians, Freud and Mahler.

Many of Schumpeter's best friends—maybe most of them—were intellectuals. When I give him the label aristocrat–bourgeois–intellectual, the ordering is monotone increasing in weightiness.

To understand Schumpeter's Wagnerian vision of capitalistic self-death, I don't think we should look to the facts of economic history. Consider that Vienna was a dying culture even before 1914. Its brilliance was that of the feverish tubercular genius of the arts. That Ludwig Wittgenstein should have had five siblings who committed suicide was more than par for the course, but it is indicative.

I am not yet done. Ludwig von Mises, who was as different from the urbane and cynical Schumpeter as you could imagine, was already convinced before the First World War that capitalism was being killed from within by its enemies. He enunciated no Schumpeterian thesis, nor indeed any interesting thesis at all to explain that fact believed in with paranoid passion.

Moreover, we learn from von Mises why Carl Menger, the Abraham of the Austrian School, was so sterile as a scholar the last 25 years of his life. Already, when Schumpeter was still in knee pants, Menger was convinced that the liberal economic order was doomed to be succeeded by the interfering state. So in a sense the less interesting part of Schumpeter's thesis—the assertion that capitalism is dying—involves little mystery as to its genesis: it only reflects the conventional wisdom of Schumpeter's own teachers and colleagues.

What is impishly Schumpeter's personal twist is the part of his thesis that asserts that *success of capitalism is what constitutes its own undermining*. How did Schumpeter arrive at that notion? Did the facts in the Austrian–Hungarian Empire of 1870 to 1925 suggest that hypothesis? Did the facts in the England that Schumpeter admired call for it, or the facts in America of the first part of the 20th century?

---

[5] At the November 1980 Viennese symposium on Schumpeter, Professor Erich Streissler in his paper 'Schumpeter's Vienna and the Role of Credit in Innovation' confirmed my *a priori* surmise that the young Joseph Schumpeter was considered something of an unreliable upstart. Dr Streissler quotes 'the first society' in Vienna as considering him 'impossible'. So much the better for Schumpeter, we now say looking back on those old times: but my earlier thesis of Schumpeter as a secure feudal aristocrat, with no regrets over capitalism's possible demise, is contradicted.

SCHUMPETER'S INADEQUATE ARGUMENTATION

As I said in my Mexico City address one wants more in the way of argumentation from Schumpeter than he gives us. I shall review briefly some of his reasoning in *CSD* and then address the problem of whether we can cogently supply for Schumpeter the buttressing argument that he has not supplied for himself.

Schumpeter at different times reads different meanings into the expression 'capitalism'. It is a tricky word and most of us will be surprised to learn that the word itself goes back barely more than a hundred years.

At times Schumpeter gives *capitalism* a very narrow meaning, if anything too narrow. Capitalism is thus associated closely with the innovation process elaborated in Schumpeter's own scientific writings. Or, it is supposed to be intrinsically connected with the ability of a banking system to create new money for the purpose of financing innovational activity. Personally, I find it very easy to imagine a capitalistic order in which the total money supply is rigidly controlled à la Chicago and in which the Walrasian equilibrium is stably maintained over time, either without important innovation, or with innovation being provided by large corporations that are subject to the checks and balances of other large corporations. If Joseph Schumpeter cannot concede this to be capitalism, then that only shows his human weakness in succumbing to infatuation for his own special theories.

At other times Schumpeter uses capitalism in too broad a sense. Everything that you and I associate with post-Renaissance modernism—for example, the development of Newtonian science—Schumpeter's rhetorical pen tends to regard as part and parcel of capitalism. There is nothing startling in the statement that modernism of the last few centuries tends to disintegrate the cake of custom, tends to undermine reverence for established hierarchies of order and social stratification. Who would care to deny that? Part, therefore, of what seems paradoxical, perverse, startling and interesting in Schumpeter's thesis comes from verbal vagueness. If a translator explains to us that modernism undermines custom and historic order, we yawn. And we feel some element of anticlimax and disillusionment if the translator goes on to explain to us that such a banality is all that is substantively implied in Schumpeter's dictum that the very success of capitalism will undermine its political stability and continued existence.

Such a vague thesis is of little interest. So I move on to consider the more interesting thesis of whether the private-property market system, as it is understood by economists who do not accept Schumpeter's theory of zero-interest-rate equilibrium, is likely to be politically damaged by its own successful operation.

PERSONAL DOUBTS

My own studies of political economy began in 1932 when the American economy was in collapse. Under Herbert Hoover, hundreds of banks were closing down. Bankruptcies were rampant. One out of four workers was jobless, and this was a great depression that did not spare the middle class. In no sense could the years 1929 to 1932 be considered an epoch of capitalism's success. Whether or not Schumpeter would consider this era of capitalistic failure to be the result of *political* instability as against *economic* instability, the citizenry at large regarded the period as one of failure. If Schumpeter is right that capitalistic success jeopardizes continuation of capitalism, reversing the direction of movement along his regression we are entitled to attribute to him the paradoxical hypothesis: failure of capitalism ought to enhance the longevity of capitalism.

The subsequent facts, of course, quite contradict any such hypothesis. By the end of Hoover's term, more than half of the rural editors in the United States favoured nationalization of the banking system. The road was paved for the victory of Franklin Roosevelt's New Deal.

I would interpret the transition from the pre-1929 virtual laissez-faire order to the mixed economy of the welfare state less as a movement from 'capitalism towards socialism' than Schumpeter would. But let us grant Schumpeter the rope he needs for his argument. Certainly the facts of the 1930s, both in America and abroad, seem contradictory to Schumpeter's paradoxical thesis.

I realize that my example is slightly strained. A lawyer for Schumpeter might offer the following defence: when Schumpeter says 'an increase in A causes B to increase', he doesn't have to be regarding the relation as a *completely reversible* one. I bring up the example of the 1930s not in order to foreclose such a defence or settle the issue. Rather, the case is mentioned as relevant to my own autobiographical reason for querying the plausibility of the Schumpeter paradox.

REFORMULATING THE QUESTION

Let me go on to survey different times and different places. Successful functioning of a market system is neither a necessary nor a sufficient condition for promoting its longevity. Malfunctioning of a market system from whatever causes is neither a necessary nor a sufficient condition for its demise. Agreed. The question we should therefore want to address along with Schumpeter is the following. Given that capitalism may ultimately become extinct whatever be its failures or successes in operation, does experience and plausible analysis lend credence to the view that *the forces of mortality operating against capitalism*, and which will determine its expected longevity, will be intensified by successful performance of the system?

If Schumpeter still insists upon giving an affirmative answer to the question put in this way and if in the end we find ourselves having to agree with him, that would indeed be an important finding, all the more important in view of its element of paradox.

However, on reflection, I suspect that *the totality of the facts point away from Schumpeter's answer*. Since facts are rarely conclusive in economics, we must supplement them by examining which modes of logical analysis seem most plausibly relevant. Here too I find the prosaic paradigm more plausible than Schumpeter's paradoxical one. *It seems reasonable that governments which are in power during times of economic progress, other things being equal, have a greater probability of being re-elected to stay in power.* The fruits of this prosaic syllogism seem on the whole to be *corroborated* by cross-sectional and time-series surveys on how politics and economics interact.

Schumpeter's own Austria had an economy that worked out badly after the First World War. Its economy seems to have been working out much better after the Second World War. That should incline you to bet that the post-Second World War regime would have a longer life expectancy than that following the First World War. For once, economic history has been content to fulfil our expectations.

ACCOUNTING FOR SCHUMPETER'S VIEW

This leaves the reader with a question: how did Schumpeter come to form the thesis that I have been trying to test? If induction and deduction command such a thesis, we are confronted with no mystery. But if, as I have been arguing, neither facts nor theorizing suggest his thesis, we are left with a puzzle.

So let us look again into Schumpeter's biography. Just prior to 1928 when Schumpeter wrote the *Economic Journal* article containing the 70-word formulation of his thesis, many economists all over the world fell for the notion that we were then in a 'new era' of lasting prosperity. We should not censure Schumpeter if he succumbed at that time to the view that capitalism was becoming increasingly stable economically. Thus, even Alvin Hansen the stagnationist concluded his 1927 *Business Cycle Theory* with the surmise that '. . . the cycle phenomenon itself, at least in its extreme manifestations, will be seen to have been a disease which came and passed in the few swift centuries during which the world was made over from a rural, local economy to a highly industrialized world economy' (p. 206).

Although we can exculpate Schumpeter for having fallen into the complacency of the 1920s, what are we to think of his failure in 1942 to follow Hansen's example in changing his mind as a result of subsequent economic history? Here are my tentative explanations, based upon Schumpeter's biography, for his continued complacency concerning the *economic stability* of capitalism and indeed for his compulsion to insist upon a distinction between capitalism's *economic stability* in the face of its *political instability*.

From Schumpeter's early twenties, as we see in his very first 1908 book and again in the famous first chapter of his 1912 *Theory of Economic Development*, Schumpeter developed an inordinate admiration for circular-flow equilibrium. I believe he was right to consider Leon Walras the greatest of all economists; and in my view he awarded Walras the laurel wreath for the right reason, namely Walras's Newtonian accomplishment of formulating the system of general equilibrium.

But I think one should admire without being carried away. Schumpeter always showed resistance to any doubts that economic equilibrium, if only the system could be left alone to work out its destiny, would be stable. As an instance in point, I remember how bothered Schumpeter was when I showed him the complete set of Keynesian equations in Lawrence Klein's MIT thesis, *The Keynesian Revolution*. What bothered Schumpeter was that here was a complete equation system that somehow violated voluntary full employment. His instinct—not incorrect but not usefully relevant to policy dilemmas in, say, 1938—was to look for some price rigidity in the scenario and, having located it, to shrug off the phenomenon with the remark: 'Of course, if you introduce rigidities in your system, you can fabricate involuntary deviations from full employment for it.'

Schumpeter in *CSD* rejects the notion of Keynes and Hansen that laissez-faire capitalism might generate a tendency towards excessive unemployment. In a sense, 1945 to 1980 events have vindicated Schumpeter's hunch. But his discussion in *CSD* and elsewhere does not adequately provide reasons why we should agree with his rejection. According to my personal recollection, Schumpeter for many years after the 1936 appearance of Keynes's *General Theory* did not really understand its analysis and allegations. Alvin Hansen corroborated this impression when he told me that Schumpeter's questions at oral PhD examinations at Harvard revealed a lack of comprehension on Schumpeter's part of what 'hoarding' assumptions are involved in the *General Theory*. Hansen went on to say that by the 1940s Schumpeter's questions at such examinations betrayed some deepening of his understanding.[6] Signs of such deepening are not easy to find in *CSD*.

To sum up, an important source of Schumpeter's need to insist upon the economic stability of capitalism as distinct from its political instability I attribute to Schumpeter's excessive confidence in capitalism's purely-economic stability.

SCHUMPETER'S AMBIGUOUS VIEW OF MARX

There has always been a puzzle connected with Joseph Schumpeter's repeated praises of Karl Marx. In 1970 I wrote 'A foreword: Schumpeter and Marx' for Alexander Balinsky's book *Marx's Economics: Origin and Development*, an item that inadvertently seems to have been left out of the third volume of *The Collected Scientific Papers of Paul A. Samuelson*. I commented there on the mystery of Schumpeter's favourable opinion. Although Schumpeter admired Marx for the *pretension*(!) of his effort, how can a person who if anything exaggerates capitalism's stability honestly applaud Marx's efforts to deny that stability?

Part of the puzzle will disappear once we recognize that some of Schumpeter's praise of Marx is only patronizing and superficial, designed more to *épater la bourgeoisie* than intended as serious approbation. When you turn your attention from Schumpeter's broad florid praise of Marx to Schumpeter's actual detailed specific evaluations—as, for example, his rather contemptuous dismissal in *The History of Economic Analysis* of Marx's fear of technological unemployment—there is no admiration there to puzzle us.

Schumpeter regards Karl Marx as being learned, bold to speculate, and broad in his dynamic vision. Schumpeter himself was learned, bold to speculate, and broad in his dynamic vision. So perhaps we should leave it there and consider Schumpeter to be primarily awarding Marx the highest form of narcissistic praise—as a veritable chip off the new block. It still remains true that Schumpeter was of all my teachers the one whose *economics* was essentially farthest from Marx's: the labour theory of value he considered a joke; Marxian surplus value degenerated to zero in Schumpeter's stationary state; the poor grew richer along with the rich as a result of Schumpeterian

[6] After Schumpeter's *Business Cycles* appeared in 1939, Lloyd Metzler proposed at Harvard that graduate students hold a serious seminar to discuss it. Schumpeter agreed to attend. Although Metzler was the gentlest of critics, Schumpeter for once lost his temper under the barrage of critical questionings. To the persistent Keynesian question, 'Do you assume *full* employment?', Schumpeter never gave a serious answer, fobbing off his audience with the facetious remark: 'I'd never dream of wearing a waistcoat that is out of fashion, so of course I don't assume full employment.' But, frictions aside, didn't he?

development; business cycles had no Marxian tendency to worsen as Schumpeter's entrepreneurs checked each other by competition.

GAME-THEORETIC POLITICAL VULNERABILITY OF LAISSEZ FAIRE

I believe Schumpeter's intuition was correct that the relatively laissez-faire economy embodied in Walrasian general equilibrium (even when we allow it some Chamberlin–Galbraith deviations from perfect competition) is prone to be interfered with by the political process. What I am sceptical about is Schumpeter's claim that this proneness to interference is actually intensified by successful economic advance.[7]

I can agree with Schumpeter that we are each of us going to die; and, at the same time without inconsistency, disagree with him if he were to argue that exercise and weight-control paradoxically add to longevity. My Schumpeter critique will gain in plausibility if I can supply him with an alternative explanation for the vulnerability of pure capitalism to change—an alternative explanation, that is, to his view of capitalism's own success as the alleged cause of change.

People in the advanced economies of Western Europe, North America, Japan and Australia enjoy a high standard of living. They have a lot to lose, particularly those in the upper two-thirds of the income and wealth distribution. I see little reason to doubt that this does serve politically to limit the rate at which the state infringes on the market economy.

Firstly, there is the obvious point that capitalism has often been changed, democratically and by force, often because of its failures. Depressions and hyperinflations, whatever be our diagnoses of their peacetime or wartime

[7] Successful advance does, to be sure, involve disturbance by innovators of various established interests. One could imagine that Main Street shop-keepers who are displaced by innovating chainstores and mail-order houses might possibly form a political faction that leads to a displacement of conventional capitalism by some kind of a fascistic socialism. But Schumpeter is least in a position to advance this syndrome to rationalize his thesis of capitalist success as the predisposer of its demise. According to *his* characteristic *economic* theory, the fruits of innovation *soon* go to wage earners and landowners, the only groups in society who possess the *primary* factors of production who are the ultimate benefiters from innovation. Remember also that Schumpeter disbelieves in mass unemployment—at least prior to the point where government has already got into the act to interfere with capitalism. If he switches his argument—and instead alleges that government interferences will convert what would otherwise be *successful* capitalistic innovation into *unsuccessful* deadweight loss of unemployment and overcapacity—his interesting paradoxes disappear and with them our necessary scepticism. See my Mexico City paper, in which I argue that Schumpeter's exaggerated fears of the inefficiencies of 'capitalism in an oxygen tent' caused him to underestimate the miracle-growth performance in the *1950s and 1960s* of the *mixed economy*!

causes, have often unseated regimes.

Then too, if we broaden our definition of failure to go beyond the behaviour of broad real aggregates of output and income, if we include failure of a market system to provide what electors deem a fair and equitable *degree of equality* of income and opportunity—if we do this, we can assert with propriety and confidence that *often failure of capitalism is what can be expected to result in its demise.*

No one should know better than Joseph Schumpeter that the behaviour equations of Walrasian equilibrium never promised us a rose garden of egalitarianism. Bastiat, von Mises, Hayek and Friedman can emit purple prose to play down, or deny, laissez faire's *actual* degree of inequality; and they may urge readers to tolerate that outcome in preference to feasible alternatives. But their words are persuasive primarily to those who draw the prizes in the Darwinian competitive jungle, and are ignored by those who draw the blanks (or think they do).

My final point is offered to Schumpeter as a better explanation of why pure capitalism is indeed politically unstable. It is an explanation congenial to Schumpeter's self-interest theory of politics.

That same self interest which provides the gasoline to run the competitive machine of Adam Smith and Leon Walras, according to the theory of games, will inevitably in the broadened context of political democracy lead to group coalitions that use the state to alter the economic imputations of the laissez-faire regime.

John Adams, Alexander Hamilton and Thomas Babington Macaulay feared that, under universal suffrage, the poorer 51 per cent of the populace would use the state to gang up on the richest 49 per cent. John von Neumann shows that this is a correct theorem in the non-zero-sum theory of games. It is only (1) the ensuing deadweight loss, (2) the existence of non-economic sentiments and traditions, and (3) the power of money to defend politically the possessors of money that limit the degree to which capitalism is interfered with by the political state.

FINAL FOREBODING

In concluding, this needs to be said: what capitalism is succeeded by is not necessarily 'socialism' in any of the conventional senses of that word. There Schumpeter trod on uncertain ground.

Speaking for myself, what I find to wonder at is not that the considerable efficiencies of the market mode of organizing society have been interfered with in this century. What is to be wondered at is how restrained and orderly that process has been for the advanced nations in the mid 20th century. To say this is not to express optimism. On the contrary, as I look around the world at the recent developments in the mixed economies, I confess to some anxiety as to whether the combining of equity and progress may not be in jeopardy at the century's end.

That I have extended to my old teacher and friend bountiful criticisms is the highest form of praise. A century after Schumpeter's birth, we take his writings seriously and treat them as living contributions to contemporary debate.

ACKNOWLEDGEMENT

I owe thanks to the National Science Foundation for financial aid, and to Aase Huggins and Kate Crowley for editorial assistance.

REFERENCES

Hansen, A. (1927) *Business Cycle Theory*. Boston: The Ginn Co.
Harris, S.H. (Ed.) (1951) *Schumpeter, Social Scientist*. Cambridge: Harvard University Press.
Keynes, J.M. (1936) *The General Theory of Employment, Interest and Money*. London: Macmillan.
Klein, L. (1947) *The Keynesian Revolution*. New York: Macmillan.
Meissner, F. (1978) The Schumpeters and industrialization of Trieve. *Zeitschrift für die gesamte Staatswissenschaft*, **135,** 2.
Merton, R.C. (Ed.) (1972) *The Collected Scientific Papers of Paul A. Samuelson*. Cambridge, MA: MIT Press.
Samuelson, P.A. (1969) Memories. *Newsweek*, June. Reprinted in Samuelson, P.A. (1973) *The Samuelson Sampler*.
Samuelson, P.A. (1970) A foreword: Schumpeter and Marx. In *Marx's Economics: Origins and Development* (Ed.) Balinsky, A. Lexington, MA: D.C. Heath.
Samuelson, P.A. (1970) Joseph Schumpeter. *Newsweek*, April. Reprinted in Samuelson, P.A. (1973) *The Samuelson Sampler*.
Samuelson, P.A. (1973) *The Samuelson Sampler*. Esp. pp. 259–261 and 265–267. Glen Ridge, NJ: Thomas Horton.
Samuelson, P.A. (1980) *The World Economy at Century's End*. Mexico City, World Economics Congress (August).
Schumpeter, J.A. (1908) *Das Wesen und der Hauptinhalt der theoretischen Nationalökonomie (Nature and Main Content of Theoretical Economics)*. Leipzig: Verlag von Duncker und Humblot.
Schumpeter, J.A. (1912) *Theorie der wirtschaftlichen Entwicklung*. English translation (1934) *Theory of Economic Development*. Cambridge, MA: Harvard University Press.
Schumpeter, J.A. (1914) *Economic Doctrine and Method*. English translation (1967) Oxford: Oxford University Press.
Schumpeter, J.A. (1928) The instability of capitalism. *Economic Journal*, **38,** 361–386.
Schumpeter, J.A. (1939) *Business Cycles: A Theoretical, Historical and Statistical Analysis of the Capitalist Process* (2 volumes). New York: McGraw-Hill.
Schumpeter, J.A. (1942) *Capitalism, Socialism and Democracy*. (2nd edition, 1949.) New York: Harper and Row. 5th edition, 1976, London: Allen and Unwin.
Schumpeter, J.A. (1949) Science and ideology. Presidential Address to the American Economic Association. *American Economic Review* (March).

Schumpeter, J.A. (1954) *History of Economic Analysis* (Ed.) Schumpeter, E.B. 1260 pp. New York: Oxford University Press.
von Beckerath, H. (1951) Joseph A. Schumpeter as a sociologist. In *Schumpeter, Social Scientist* (Ed.) Harris, S.H. p. 110. Cambridge, MA: Harvard University Press.
von Neumann, J. & Morgenstern, O. (1944) *Theory of Games and Economic Behavior*. Princeton, NJ: Princeton University Press.

311

A Foreword

SCHUMPETER AND MARX

History is not so much a well-made play in set acts as a continuous performance of successive *ad lib* players. The year that Galileo died, Newton was born. In the year that Karl Marx died, 1883, Joseph Schumpeter was born. Precocious, he grew up in a Viennese environment where Marxians barked outside the academic gates.

And so we meet in Schumpeter that rarest of birds: a neoclassical economist who both *knew* the works of Marx and *admired* him. (By knowing Marx I do not mean that he had cut most of the pages of *Das Kapital*'s volume 1 and could quote the purple passages from the *Communist Manifesto*. And by admiration, I mean no less than that Schumpeter regarded Marx as one of the greatest social scientists who ever lived.)

To illustrate how rare it is for an economist to admire Marx in spite of *dis*liking his political goals, consider another scholar also born in 1883—Maynard Keynes. There is precious little evidence that Keynes interrupted many games of bridge to master the "turbid rubbish" of the German autodidact. Yet Keynes also disdained the bourgeois world of Queen Victoria. And only down the block, so to speak, from his Bloomsbury arrondissement lived the Fabian socialists. But perhaps the dullness of Sidney and Beatrice Webb, and the soufflé texture of Bernard Shaw's economics, turned his stomach and mind against the paradigms of socialism.

But *why* did Schumpeter have so high an opinion of Marx? This puzzle takes on a renewed interest now that there is a thirst for Marxism among the new generation; and, also, now that Schumpeter's stock is experiencing a flurry of revival on the bourse of intellectual history.

Let me state that, although I often heard Schumpeter praise Marx, I was never able to perceive from his remarks either an explication of the merits which made Marx deserving of the accolades, or—what is not quite the same thing—even the reasons why Schumpeter came to admire him. To use a characteristic Schumpeter evasion, his case for Marx was stronger than the sum of its parts.

We do not need an economist to praise Marx's sociology, history, and philosophy. (Nor, to digress, a non-economist to praise Marx's economics!)

But Schumpeter *qua* economist actually rejected Marx's theory of surplus value as providing either (1) a valid (or logical) theory of "exploitation," or (2) insightful clues into the "laws of motion and transformation of capitalism." What is left then of Marx the economist? Fragmentary, and somewhat contradictory, reflections on overproduction, underconsumption, and periodic business cycles. Suggestive insights concerning technological innovation and the displacement of workers by machines. Certain pre-Leontief models of reproduction and balanced growth. To use another Schumpeter phrase, this is "respectable" work. But just that.

What I finally decided to be Marx's excellence in Schumpeter's eyes was not his "schema" but his grand "vision" of social change. Where a Macaulay conceived of whig society as the culmination of all evolution, and a Hayek looks back upon the epoch of Calvin Coolidge as a reattainable golden age, Marx peered at the social order from out the window of the British Museum to chant: This too will pass away. And it did. And it will.

Paul A. Samuelson
M. I. T.

The Normative and Positivistic Inferiority of Marx's *Values* Paradigm*

PAUL A. SAMUELSON
Massachusetts Institute of Technology
Cambridge, Massachusetts

I. Introduction

Professor Nguyen [5] honors my 1971 postmortem on Marx's "transformation problem," Samuelson [10], by auditing its logic and results. It is gratifying that Nguyen's procedures (1) "will in general confirm Samuelson's result;" (2) give, for *values*, the result "found to be exactly that given in Samuelson's paper;" (3) give, for *prices*, "precisely that given in Samuelson's Table 3B;" and (4) show that "The conclusion reached by Professor Samuelson is . . . demonstrated in a fairly straight-forward fashion . . ." by a matrix characteristic-value formulation.

But, Professor Nguyen points out, Baumol [1] and Morishima [3;4] do not agree that my exposition was optimal. And Nguyen states that his result is not in complete agreement with my "erase-and-replace" description of how one goes from Marx's 1867 *values* to pre-1867 and post-1867 competitive *prices* "to the extent that the two 'alternative and discordant systems' that Professor Samuelson contemplated are shown [by Nguyen's analysis] to be not entirely arbitrary as was indicated by him [Samuelson] . . ." in his 1970 and 1971 papers.

I can add many names to the list of writers who found my "erase-and-replace" characterization as somehow overdramatic. One of the latest is a distinguished Soviet economist of Novosibirsk, K. Valtukh [20, 179] who dubs my 1971 analysis a "polemic outburst."

What I can most usefully do here is to relate the Nguyen analysis to previous discussions of the transformation program, and show that it precisely fits in with my intended contrast between alternative and inconsistent paradigms. Then, constructively, I can use the occasion to show why the *values* paradigm fails as a normative guide to policy and as a positivistic description of how a competitive system will display its statical and historical laws of motion and development.

The reader will be able to verify that no cogent derivation in Morishima [3;4], Baumol [1], Valtukh [20], or Nguyen [5] in any sense negates the truth of propositions proved by me or hypothesized by my pen.

*I owe thanks to the National Science Foundation for financial aid, and to Aase Huggins for editorial assistance.

II. Analysis

To produce 1 of good j a period from now, you must have as inputs now a_{0j} of direct labor and $(a_{1j},a_{2j},...,a_{nj})$ of goods 1,2,...,n. (Note that I have restored Nguyen's transposition of a_{ij} notation to its customary form.) Each unit of labor needs, if it is to be available in the steady state, the stipulated vector of subsistence wage-goods $(m_1,...,m_n)$.

In 1971, I derived the implied rate of profit, R^*, and the implied vector of *real* prices, $(P_j/W)^*$, as roots of the relations

$$[P_j/W] = \mathbf{a_0}(1+R)[\mathbf{I}-\mathbf{a}(1+R)]^{-1} \tag{1a}$$

$$W/(\sum_1^n P_j m_j) = 1. \tag{1b}$$

But I could indifferently have used the eigenvector formulation of the basic 1957 Seton [18] paper that I cited. It introduces as "feeding coefficients," which summarize the amounts of the goods needed as subsistence inputs to maintain the needed labor, the matrix which Nguyen calls **B** in his treatment of my 3-good example. In traditional notation **B** is $[m_i a_{0j}]$.

In place of (1) above, I could have written the Seton-Nguyen equivalent form

$$[P_j/W][(a_{ij}+m_i a_{0j})(1+R)] = [P_j/W] \tag{2a}$$

$$[P_j/W][m_i] = 1, \text{ normalization.} \tag{2b}$$

Substitution confirms that (1) and (2) are completely equivalent, and it is no coincidence that Nguyen verifies the correctness of my 1971 numbers for real prices and profit rate. Neither formulation is better than the other, substantively or for throwing light on what Marx did or should have done.

Now for the paradigm of marked-up Marxian values. Denoting the common rate of surplus value, used to mark up wage payments in all industries by r^*, I derived the resulting real marked-up values, (p_j/w) and r^*, as roots of

$$[p_i/w] = \mathbf{a_0}(1+r)[\mathbf{I} - \mathbf{a}]^{-1} \tag{3a}$$

$$w/(\sum_1^n p_j m_j) = 1. \tag{3b}$$

Nguyen, using the Seton matrix with **a** augmented by the feeding coefficient component of the matrix **B**, writes this paradigm as the roots of the eigenvector relations

$$[p_j/w][a_{ij}+m_{ij}a_{0j}(1+r)] = [p_j/w] \tag{4a}$$

$$[p_j/w][m_i] = 1, \text{ normalization.} \tag{4b}$$

Just as (1) and (2) are easily shown to be identical, (3) and (4) are easily shown to be identical. Just as (1a) and (2a) are alternative incompatible equilibrium regimens, so (3a) and (4a) are alternative incompatible equilibrium regimens.

Using an eigenvector formulation rather than a solved-out formulation does not one whit whitewash the arbitrariness of the (2) and (4) paradigms. Whether Baumol [1] is right or half-right in his allegation that Marx thought that one could understand the essence of the (1) or (3) solution *only after* one contemplates Marx's novel (2) or (4) paradigm, any such belief on Marx's part is an illusory belief. (Whether Baumol would be right in alleging that the chap who wrote me a letter last week thought he was trisecting the angle, we must be clear that a general angle can't be trisected by means of a compass and straight edge alone.)

To clinch the point that an eigenvector description has no power to alter the merits and demerits of economic alternatives, consider the bizarre third paradigm that appeared in Samuelson [12, 65] in response to Leontief's oral suggestion of a *reductio ad absurdum.* Instead of having a regime that marks up all outlays by the same percentage factor, let me here give an eigenvector formulation of a third Napoleonic regime, different from the regimen of *prices* and of *values*, a regimen that marks up only outlays on raw-material inputs and not on labor inputs. If 100ρ is the percent rate of markup on raw materials, (2a) and (4a) are shoved aside in favor of the following relations for ρ^* and real prices $(\pi_j/\omega)^*$:

$$[\pi_j/\omega][a_{ij}(1+\rho) + m_i a_{0j}] = [\pi_j/\omega],\ a \geq \text{ and indecomposable} \tag{5a}$$

$$\sum_{1}^{n} (\pi_j/\omega)m_j = 1. \tag{5b}$$

I do not know anyone who would not consider the system (5) a bizarre system. Whether (5) in its relation to (1) or (2) is, in Nguyen's words, "entirely arbitrary," I am content to leave moot: (5) is arbitrary enough to lack normative and descriptive interest, even though it meets Nguyen's test of using the same (a_{0j}, a_{ij}, m_i) coefficients as (1) and (2) do.

How should a new Napoleon characterize the "transformation" between bizarre (5) and bourgeois (2)? Although they both involve $[a_{ij}]$ and $[m_i a_{0j}]$ coefficients, their behavior equations are contradictory. To go from (5) to (2) or from (2) to (5) is to reject one and accept the other — much as we do when we reject phlogiston and accept Kelvin-Clausius-Gibbs thermodynamics. The form that Bortkiewicz's noble effort took, in Bortkiewicz [2], most unfortunately concealed the erase-and-replace nature of the choice between paradigms.

But, protests a follower of the new Napoleon who (to use a Baumol attribution) claims that understanding of competitive (2) can come only from *prior* contemplation of (5):

A Morishima will rise to prove the fundamental Napoleonic theorem:

"If and only if ρ exceeds zero in (5) will the profit rate R in (2) be able to be positive."

What are we the jury of scientists to say in response to these Napoleonic objections? I believe we are justified in saying that there are a multitude of *equivalent* technical tests that assure that a system satisfies the Hawkins-Simon conditions that it be "net productive" and capable of supporting a positive profit rate; and there are a multitude of such tests, which are not remotely "Marxian", and which assure that the stipulated subsistence wage vector is compatible with one of those feasible positive profit rates. Morishima's "Fundamental Marxian Theorem" is just as uninteresting as the Fundamental Napoleonic Theorem.

III. Inferiority of the *Values* Paradigm: Invention

It is well to give two basic examples to show that only *after* one has solved the bourgeois (real prices, profit rate) paradigm can one know how to calculate the irrelevant *values* and Napoleonic paradigms.

First, consider the laws of motion of competitive capitalism in reacting to a technical change. Corn in my 1971 Bortkiewicz example can now be produced in two ways: by 4/15 of coal and 120 of labor as of old; but also now alternatively by 8/15 of coal and 25 of labor. All the other a_{0j} and a_{ij} coefficients remain unaltered, as do all the (m_i) wage-subsistence coefficients.

What will be the new actual equilibrium? The new profit rate, R^*? The new real prices $[P_1/W, P_2/W, P_3/W]^*$?

In case someone thinks that of relevance or of importance for its own sake, what will the new rate of surplus value r^* be? What will the new marked-up real values $[p_1/w, p_2/w, p_3/w]^*$ be that tell workers what things would cost them in a state run along the lines of the Marxian paradigm? (I won't belabor the point by asking the equally redundant questions: What will ρ^* and $(\pi_j/\omega)^*$ now be in the Napoleonic regime? "Who wants to know?" would be the appropriate response to such inquiries.)

If Baumol believed there was merit in Marx's alleged need to "explain" *profit* by rate of surplus value calculations, he'd have to be able to show that only by solving anew the (3) or (4) relations could one properly arrive at the correct new solutions to (1) or (2) relations. Of course, as Morishima's text knows, the truth is the reverse of this. The competitive regime will eschew the new invention even though it could raise the capitalists' rate of surplus value from 66 2/3% up to over 100%. Competition will make the old technology outcompete the new by offering a higher rate of profit at the equilibrium real subsistence wage, 25% versus the barely 23% of the new technology.

> Conclusion: the values paradigm is indeed an irrelevancy to describe positivistically the statics and dynamics of competitive capitalism.

But should society pass up this new technology that can yield a higher real wage in the zero-profit steady state? I must explain at some length the sense in which it may be rational for society to do so.

Actually, the old technology is one that is intertemporally Pareto-efficient. Any planned state, that maximizes a Ramsey social welfare function of the new type $\Sigma_0^\infty U[c_1(t), c_2(t), c_3(t)]/(1.25)^t$ will end up using the old technology rather than the new.

Actually, if the Soviet Union had this choice of technologies, and its labor supply grew by 25% per period, the only way it could pay labor the stipulated needed subsistence of corn per labor unit would be by using the old technology despite its inferior productivity in terms of (undated!) socially necessary labor.[1] See Weizsäcker and Samuelson [21].

John Roemer [6] provides an instructive example of the harm to clear understanding that can come from a preoccupation with Marxian values and with steady state analysis. Roemer classifies inventions into those which are "socially desirable" and those which are not. The invention mentioned here is of the category Roemer labels "socially desirable." He then points out, correctly, that a competitive regime may fail to adopt an invention that meets his test of being socially desirable and it may insist on adopting an invention that he

1. The equilibrium profit rate, $R^* = .25$, whatever its role as a factor of "exploitation" or discounting, does have a technocratic characterization. Consider a vector of existent gross [coal, corn, velvets], $= [Q_1(t), Q_2(t), Q_3(t)]$. Consistent with the technological and subsistence coefficients, $(a_{0j}, a_{ij}, m_i]$, there is a balanced rate of growth $[Q_j(t)]$ is capable of, so that it becomes $[Q_j(t+1)] = \lambda[Q_j(t)]$, where λ is a scalar that is a function of the two ratios $[Q_j(t)/\Sigma_1^3 Q_i(t)]$. There is a maximum value that λ can attain, $1 + G^*$. By von Neumann-like reasoning, we easily show that $R^* = G^*$

dubs socially undesirable. His readers may be forgiven for being tempted to believe that a defect in the price-profit regimen has been uncovered by Marxian insights.

Alas, Virgil nodded. An ideal planned utopia, using the most powerful techniques of optimal-control dynamic programming, often will also want to spurn new technical options that raise the equilibrium rate of surplus value, r^*, at the previous real wage rate. Thus, face China today with a new invention dubbed socially desirable by Roemer. It may well be the case that it will take another half century before rational Chinese planners could afford to adopt the invention that can raise its golden-rule zero-population-growth consumption level — and this even if its population is strictly constant and its planners are optimally optimizing present versus future consumption benefits and sacrifices. The dual variables of pre-Marx prices-and-profits may correctly tell it now to adopt the so-called socially undesirable invention, and at the proper time later tell it to adopt an invention that Roemer's pejorative terminology favors. See Samuelson [13] for demonstration that Marxian variables such as rate of surplus value cannot provide the normative efficiency that profit-including prices can give.

One example can deflate the pejorative terminology of its pretensions. Begin with situation A and then introduce new technical options B and C.

A. First 1 of corn output needs 1 input of labor and 1/2 of corn. Labor receives its stipulated subsistence wage of 1/4 corn per labor unit. Perforce the profit rate is 33 1/3% per period. The rate of surplus value, for those interested, is 100%: (1/2 corn - 1/4 corn)/(1/4 corn). Now disturb the equilibrium with two new inventions.

B. Now 1 of corn can be produced by 2.1 of labor alone. Roemer would dub this a "socially undesirable" invention. Adopting it would raise the rate of profit to 90% from 33 1/3%. But it would lower the rate of surplus value, r^*, from 100% to 90%. And, what interests us for its own sake, adopting B would lower the per-laborer corn output, producible by the system in a "golden-rule" state with a constant population, from A's 1/2 corn per laborer to B's 1/(2.1) corn.

C. The second invention, which Roemer would dub "socially desirable", enables 1 of corn to be produced by .1 of labor and .8 of corn. But, when capitalists must pay workers the real wage of 1/4 corn, C can only earn them a profit rate of 21 7/33%. Since A earns them 33 1/3%, Roemer is correct to point out that the C invention will not win its way under the laissez faire rules of the game. This even though C could yield a rate of surplus value of 700%! And, in the golden-rule state of a stationary population, C can outyield A and B in corn per capita (providing 2 corn per laborer versus 1/2 and 1/2.1 respectively).

To show that there is nothing necessarily wrong about adopting the B that Roemer labels as socially undesirable, consider a socialist utopia run by Ramsey's omniscient Philosopher-Planners who know how to solve the optimal control problems of weighing present corn pleasures against future.

Let a revolution break out, displacing laissez faire. At the same time, let B and C inventions become known. Let the labor supply be frozen to give Roemer his postulated rules of the game. What will happen?

Immediately, the optimal control solution will mandate that the "socially undesirable" invention B be adopted. In this numerical example, it must be blended with the C invention and A must be dropped. (In other examples, B and some other known technology will be mandatory until, periods later, the system has accumulated enough corn capital to be able to "afford" the C technique. When that time comes, the profit-including dual variables of dynamic programming will give the signal to introduce C in a way that the 1867 magnitudes cannot.) Immediately the real wage imputable to labor's worth to society will rise, holding down the rise in society's own-corn-rate of interest produced by the two inventions. Then, as society optimally accumulates toward its golden-rule rendezvous the interest rate will fall so low as to make B no longer optimal to use. In this example A never comes back into use, it being "dominated" by C and B. Increasingly C comes into relative use — as it should when the corn/labor ratio becomes larger and larger. Q.E.D.

I ought to conclude this too-brief discussion with a warning. Under realistic laissez-faire, the short run impact of adopting invention B will raise the demand for labor, bidding up its real wage and holding down the rise in profit rate until the requisite increase in labor/capital ratio can be coaxed out. Neither Marx, nor Okishio, nor Samuelson, nor Roemer can predict from steady-state analysis what an invention's *transient* incidence on profit and wage rates will be.

The stables of Marxian economics are clogged with the misleading doctrine of "unequal exchange". It should not be left to non-Marxians to clean up this matter. One aspect of the misunderstanding parallels what is involved here in the Roemer taxonomic classification. Clarification is provided by a theorem which is provable only by going *outside* steady-state analysis:

> When a laissez faire system cannot go spontaneously from a status quo non-golden-rule-configuration to a golden-rule configuration, such a transition necessarily involves some tradeoff of consumption sacrificed at an earlier date in return for an increment of (possibly permanent) consumption at a later date. This technological fact, which is independent of "reswitching," is as true under socialism as capitalism. Therefore, it is no valid social reproach that an invention will not be adopted now even though its adoption would permit permanent improvement later. Nor in trade theory is it a valid reproach that a positive profit rate leads to a steady-state production pattern that is "dominated in the steady state" by another golden-rule pattern.

Again the *prices* regime of Ricardo, Walras, von Neumann and Sraffa comes through with flying colors while the *values* regime waits lamely to take its cue from that of *prices*.

IV. Subsistence-vector Changes

As a second example of the inferiority and irrelevance of the *values* paradigm, suppose labor supply can be maintained either by the old (m_j) vector of corn only, or alternatively by a new (m_j) vector involving only the third good.

The third good in the 1907-1971 example, the luxury good velvets, involves a lower component of non-labor to labor cost than does corn. (Coal, by contrast, has a higher component of non-labor to labor cost than corn does.) Therefore, if the competitive system is given the new option of paying the subsistence wage not in corn but in terms of velvets, "it" will prefer to do so if the new subsistence velvet wage is less than the real velvet wage that previously prevailed in the 25%-profit equilibrium. By this shift the system can wrest a higher ("exploitative") rate of profit, higher than the previous 25% profit rate. So this will be done, just as in British history the white potato replaced bread from grain as the effective staple.

But what happens to the Marx rate of surplus value r^* (which is Morishima's defined coefficient of exploitation)? As the velvet real subsistence wage is lowered a little, but enough to raise the system's R^*, we calculate that r^* falls! Have the avaricious capitalists lost their marbles? Have the ferocious tigers changed their spots in favor of sweet altruism? Of course not. It is merely that the Marx-Morishima coefficient of surplus-value exploitation is a poorly devised measure to describe the laws of motion of Darwinian capitalism and what is ordinarily meant by "exploitation." What was proposed in 1867 as an innovative improvement was actually a detour and cul-de-sac. Folderol about eigenvalues does not conceal this fact but to the objective economist only reveals it.

V. Conclusion

Each argument brought forward to justify working with an 1867 model involving a uniform rate of markup on direct labor alone, on examination, discredits itself. Using an eigenvalue formulation, the present paper confirms this basic fact.[2]

In the interest of brevity, I refer the reader to other articles in *Collected Scientific Papers of Paul A. Samuelson* [17] in which I have patiently and good temperedly reviewed the analytical issues. The reader may also be referred to Ian Steedman [19], who writes sympathetically from within the *non*-neoclassical tradition and has also come to similar findings.

Being fully appreciative of Professor Nguyen's valuable audit, I am required in the end to insist that to point out that Marx's values regime uses the same (a_{0j}, a_{ij}, m_i) coefficients as are used in the conventional prices regime does not absolve Marx of the charge that he has introduced an arbitrary detour. The crazy Napoleonic regime also uses exactly those same data and still earns my charge of gratuitous arbitrariness. It is by misuse of data that a paradigm earns rejection.

2. I owe the reader a brief explanation of the contribution by Dr. K. Valtukh [20]. His notations can be related to those used here most simply in the admissible case where all his turnover periods happen to be unity,

$$\alpha_{ij} \equiv 1 \equiv \alpha_j^1:$$

$$[P_j, Q_i, C_i, W, L;\ a_{0j}, a_{ij}, m_i; R]$$

$$\equiv [\bar{P}_j, Q_i, Y_i, \bar{p}^1, L;\ 1_j, a_{ij}, a_i^1;\ r].$$

His relations, as numbered by him, then translate into my matrix notations as follows:

$$Q = aQ + C;\ Q, C \geq 0,\ a \geq 0 \tag{1}$$

$$a_0 Q = L \leq L^{max};\ a_0 \geq 0 \tag{2}$$

$$W = Pm \tag{3}$$

$$P = [Wa_0 + Pa](1+R) > 0. \tag{4}$$

Logically, from (1)-(4) follow Valtukh's further relations, as translated into my notations:

$$PQ = PaQ + Pma_0 L + R[PaQ + Pma_0 L] \tag{10}$$

$$PQ = PaQ + Pma_0 L + P[C - ma_0 L] \tag{11}$$

$$R[PaQ + Pma_0 L] = P[C - ma_0 L]. \tag{12}$$

On the supposition that the R^* root of (1)-(4) is positive, $C - ma_0 L$ will be a non-negative non-zero vector of profit receivers' consumption.

Note that all of the above is derived without mentioning any of Marx's 1867 novel concepts — such as a "rate of surplus value" common to all industries. Therefore, the reader is under no temptation to find optimal Dr. Valtukh's encapsulating sentence (20,184, lines 7-8): "This means that profit is nothing else but the form of surplus value." The reader can thus skip without peril the following pages in which the non-proportionability of $a_0[I-a]^{-1}$ to $a_0(1+R^*)\,[I - a(1+R^*)]^{-1}$ is adumbrated and some deficiencies in my ideology are bruited.

References

1. Baumol, W. J., "The Transformation of Values: What Marx 'Really' Meant." *Journal of Economic Literature*, March 1974, 51-62.

2. Bortkiewicz, L. von., "On the Correction of Marx's Fundamental Theoretical Construction in the Third Volume of *Capital*," *Jahr. Nationalökonomie Statistik*, 1907, 370-85; reprinted in English in Sweezy, P., ed. *Karl Marx and the Close of his System by Eugen von Böhm-Bawerk and Böhm-Bawerk's Criticism of Marx by Rudolf Hilferding with an Appendix by L. von Bortkiewicz.* New York: Augustus M. Kelley, 1949.

3. Morishima, M. *Marx's Economics: A Dual Theory of Growth.* London & New York: Cambridge University Press, 1973.

4. ———, "The Fundamental Marxian Theorem: A Reply to Samuelson." *Journal of Economic Literature*, March 1974, 71-74.

5. Nguyen, D., "Notes on Professor Samuelson's Analysis of the Marxian Transformation Problems." *Southern Economic Journal*, July 1982.

6. Roemer, J., "Technical Change and the Tendency of the Rate of Profit to Fall." *Journal of Economic Theory*, December 1977, 403-424.

7. Samuelson, P. A., "Prices of Factors and Goods in General Equilibrium." *The Review of Economic Studies*, 1953-1954, 1-20; reprinted as Chapter 70 in *The Collected Scientific Papers of Paul A. Samuelson*, Vol. II, The MIT Press, Cambridge, 1966.

8. ———, "Wages and Interest: A Modern Dissection of Marxian Economic Models." *The American Economic Review*, December 1957, 884-912; reprinted as Chapter 29 in *The Collected Scientific Papers of Paul A. Samuelson*, Vol. I, The MIT Press, Cambridge, 1966.

9. ———, "The 'Transformation' from Marxian 'Values' to Competitive 'Prices': A Process of Rejection and Replacement." *Proceedings of the National Academy of Sciences, U.S.A.*, September 1970, 423-425; reprinted as Chapter 154 in *The Collected Scientific Papers of Paul A. Samuelson*, Vol. III, The MIT Press, Cambridge, 1972.

10. ———, "Understanding the Marxian Notion of Exploitation: A Summary of the So-Called Transformation Problem Between Marxian Values and Competitive Prices." *Journal of Economic Literature*, June 1971, 399-431; reprinted as Chapter 153 in *The Collected Scientific Papers of Paul A. Samuelson*, Vol. III, The MIT Press, Cambridge, 1972.

11. ———, "The Economics of Marx: An Ecumenical Reply." *Journal of Economic Literature*, March 1972, 51-57; reprinted as Chapter 227 in *The Collected Scientific Papers of Paul A. Samuelson*, Vol. IV, The MIT Press, Cambridge, 1977.

12. ———, "Samuelson's 'Reply on Marxian Matters.'" *Journal of Economic Literature*, March 1973, 64-68; reprinted as Chapter 228 in *The Collected Scientific Papers of Paul A. Samuelson*, Vol. IV, The MIT Press, Cambridge, 1977.

13. ———, "Optimality of Profit-Including Prices Under Ideal Planning: Marx's Model." *Proceedings of the National Academy of Sciences*, July 1973, 2109-111; reprinted as Chapter 226 in *The Collected Scientific Papers of Paul A. Samuelson*, Vol. IV, The MIT Press, Cambridge, 1977.

14. ———, "Insight and Detour in the Theory of Exploitation: A Reply to Baumol." *Journal of Economic Literature*, March 1974, 62-70; reprinted as Chapter 229 in *The Collected Scientific Papers of Paul A. Samuelson*, Vol. IV, the MIT Press, Cambridge, 1977.

15. ———, "Rejoinder: 'Merlin Unclothed, A Final Word'." *Journal of Economic Literature*, March 1974, 75-77; reprinted as Chapter 230 in *The Collected Scientific Papers of Paul A. Samuelson*, Vol. IV, The MIT Press, Cambridge, 1977.

16. ———. "Marx as Mathematical Economist: Steady-State and Exponential Growth Equilibrium," in *Trade, Stability, and Macroeconomics, Essays in Honor of Lloyd A. Metzler*, edited by G. Horwich and P. Samuelson. New York: Academic Press, 1974, 269-307; reprinted as Chapter 225 in *The Collected Scientific Papers of Paul A. Samuelson*, Vol. IV, The MIT Press, Cambridge, 1977.

17. ———. *The Collected Scientific Papers of Paul A. Samuelson.* Vol. I, Cambridge: The MIT Press, 1966, Vol. II, Cambridge: The MIT Press, 1966, Vol. III, Cambridge: The MIT Press, 1972 and Vol. IV, Cambridge: The MIT Press, 1977.

18. Seton, F., "The Transformation Problem." *Review of Economic Studies*, June 1957, 149-160.

19. Steedman, I. *Marx after Sraffa.* London: NLB, 1977.

20. Valtukh, K., "The Marxian Price of Production Theory in a Formalised Exposition." *Social Sciences, USSR Academy of Sciences*, 1980, 179-198.

21. Weizsäcker, C. C. von and P. A. Samuelson, "A New Labor Theory of Value for Rational Planning Through Use of the Bourgeois Profit Rate." *Proceedings of the National Academy of Sciences, U.S.A.*, June 1971, 1192-94; reprinted as Chapter 155 in *The Collected Scientific Papers of Paul A. Samuelson*, Vol. III, The MIT Press, Cambridge, 1972.

313

Marx without Matrices: Understanding the Rate of Profit

Paul A. Samuelson

Karl Marx proposed in *Capital* (1867, Vol. I) a new paradigm: *the rate of surplus value*, reckoned as a percentage markup on direct-wage payments alone; its purpose to provide deep understanding and explanation of the competitive *rate of profit*, reckoned as a percentage return or markup on all capitalists' outlays, whether on wages or on raw materials and durable equipment.

The new paradigm shocked mainstream economists, who realized that the competitive arbitrage that equalized the rates of profit in two industries would make unequal Marx's rates of surplus value (save in the singular case where the two industries happened to display the same fractional importance of wage costs to total outlays). This gave rise to criticism and rejection, to confusion and debate, to the attempt by Marx (published by his editor Friedrich Engels) of a defense and reconciliation in *Capital* (1894, Vol. III) under the heading of what has been called "the transformation problem" (between Marxian *values* and bourgeois *prices*). Since the 1907 emendation of Marx by Ladislaus von Bortkiewicz, there has been a thriving intellectual industry dealing with the vectors, matrices, and eigenvalues of input-output systems.

Here I propose to sidestep all the purely *logical* complexities of the transformation problem. I want to clear the decks so we can bear down on the *substantive* problem: What does Marx's innovative paradigm of the rate of surplus value tell us about the laws of motion of competitive capitalism? What new understanding does it give us of labor exploitation, of the distribution of income between wages and property, of the inequality of wealth and incomes? The final verdict turns out to be, No new understanding.

1.1 The One-Department Simplification

Logical simplification can be bought at the price of neglecting inessential microeconomic detail. If corn were the only industry, no mainstream economist would have to be offended by the monstrosity of differing rates of profit between industries. By definition there could arise no transformation-problem difficulty or complication and no need for matrix algebra. We are provided with a crystal-clear test case.

If Marx's new paradigm triumphantly handles this test case, *if* concentrating on his *rate of surplus value* (his *coefficient of labor exploitation*) imparts in the one-department case understanding of why capitalism's wage rates are so low and have a tendency to fall lower still and why the law of the declining rate of profit does apply—*if* this vindication of Marx is the consequence of the simple arithmetic of the one-department case—then fair-minded economists of any ideology will be prepared to pay the price of some distortion in microeconomic detail from use of Marx's paradigm in return for the strong light it throws on the macroeconomic big picture. If, if, and if. . . . Here I put the matter to the test.

1.2 Case of Direct Labor Only

First, to produce 1 unit of corn at the end of the period, C_{t+1}, you need $\mathbf{a_0}$ of direct labor at the beginning of this period. Your primitive production function is

$$\mathbf{a_0}C_{t+1} = L_t. \tag{1}$$

Second, suppose labor power has a subsistence real wage rate needed to keep it available and being reproduced. Measured in corn, let the specified subsistence real wage be $\mathbf{m}$. Then steady-state equilibrium requires equality of the real wage to the subsistence level

$$\text{wage}/P_{\text{corn}} = \mathbf{m}. \tag{2}$$

For the system to be viable in the steady state, what labor needs to consume, $\mathbf{m}L$, must not exceed what labor can produce, $a_0{}^{-1}L$.

So the condition for viability, for the existence of a positive profit rate and exploitation, is that we must have a *surplus economy* as guaranteed by $\mathbf{I} - \mathbf{a_0 m} > 0$, where $\mathbf{I}$ stands for one, as in $\mathbf{I} + 2 = 3$.

A good way to see this is to realize that, in effect, corn now is produced out of last period's corn: to produce 1 unit of corn now you need $\mathbf{a_0 m}$ of corn 1 period back (just enough to pay your needed labor its needed subsistence):

$$\text{corn}_{t+1} = (a_0 m)^{-1}\text{corn}_t. \tag{3}$$

Unless $(a_0 m)^{-1}$ exceeds unity, the system is not a *surplus* economy that can produce consumption and pay a positive rate of profit, written as $R > 0$.

Under competition, where entry is free and knowledge universal, arbitrage ensures that all capitalists earn the same steady-state equilibrium rate of profit, R^*:

$$P_{\text{corn}} = \text{wage } \mathbf{a_0}(1 + \mathrm{R}^*). \tag{4}$$

Combining (2) and (4), we have for the equilibrium profit rate in a subsistence-wage economy

$$1 + R^* = (a_0 m)^{-1}. \tag{5}$$

This profit rate is seen from (3) also to be the *own-corn marginal productivity*:

$$\frac{\partial \text{corn}_{t+1}}{\partial \text{corn}_t} = 1 + R^*. \tag{6}$$

So much for the pre-1867 bourgeois treatment of this simplest model. What is Marx's new 1867 paradigm?

Marx calls this department's outlays for wages, *variable capital*, v. If there had been outlays on raw materials—on corn for seed—Marx would call that *constant capital*, c. The residual markup garnered by the capitalists, Marx calls surplus, s. In all he has for this case

$$c + v + s = c + v + rv = 0 + \mathbf{a_0 w} + r(\mathbf{a_0 w}), \tag{7}$$

where r is the markup solely on wages, Marx's new rate-of-surplus-value concept.

Since there is no nonlabor outlay or constant capital to be marked up in this first case, Marx's rate of surplus value, r^*, is here exactly the same as the R^* profit rate of Adam Smith and David Ricardo. The lower-case accounting regime of Marx in this first case of direct-labor-only exactly parallels the pre-Marx paradigm, adding nothing and subtracting nothing.

Thus, if 1 corn requires 4 hours of labor and each labor requires 1 of corn for a 12-hour day's subsistence, the equilibrium rates of profit and surplus value are the same, both being 200 percent. Here are the two parallel regimes, in capital letters for mainstream economists and in small letters for Marx:

$$\begin{aligned} C + V + S &= C + V + R^*(C + V) \\ &= 0 + \mathbf{a_0}W + R^*(0 + \mathbf{a_0}W) \\ &= 0 + (\tfrac{1}{3}\text{day})W + 2.00(0 + \tfrac{1}{3}\text{day})W \\ &= W; \end{aligned}$$

$$
\begin{aligned}
c + v + s = c + v + r^*v \\
&= 0 + \mathbf{a_0}w + r^*(\mathbf{a_0}w) \\
&= 0 + (\tfrac{1}{3}\text{day})w + 2.00(\tfrac{1}{3}\text{day})w \qquad (8) \\
&= w.
\end{aligned}
$$

The verdict is that Marx's paradigm equals Smith's, being no better and no worse in this simplest case where there is direct labor only.

1.3 Capital-Good Input and Labor

Now suppose it takes both direct *labor* and *corn* raw material to make corn. For example, to get 1 unit of corn it takes **1/3** day of direct labor and **2/3** of corn as seed. Again the subsistence requirement to reproduce labor power is **1** corn per (12-hour) day.

Ricardo would perceive that this system could no longer *permanently* pay a positive profit rate. We can see this in two equivalent ways. First is the technocrat's approach of von Neumann (1931). How much corn at time t is needed to produce 1 unit of corn at $t + 1$? It takes **2/3** corn for seed and also enough subsistence corn to reproduce **1/3** of a day's labor, which is **1/3** of corn more. In all it takes 1 unit of corn_t to produce 1 unit of corn_{t+1}. The system cannot grow, and also the system cannot pay a surplus to a capitalist class.

The competitive market approach arrives at the same result:

$$W/P_{\text{corn}} = \mathbf{m} = 1, \qquad (9)$$

$$P_{\text{corn}} = (W\mathbf{a_0} + P_{\text{corn}}\mathbf{a})(1 + R), \qquad (10)$$

$$
\begin{aligned}
P_{\text{corn}} &= \mathbf{a_0}(1 + R)[\mathbf{I} - \mathbf{a}(1 + R)]^{-1} \\
&= \frac{1}{3}(1 + R)\left[\mathbf{I} - \frac{\mathbf{2}}{\mathbf{3}}\left(1 + R\right)\right]^{-1}, \qquad (10')
\end{aligned}
$$

where **a** is the input of corn needed to produce 1 unit of itself as output.

Combining (9) and (10′) gives for the equilibrium rate of profit

$$1 + R^* = [a + ma_0]^{-1} = \left[\frac{2}{3} + 1\left(\frac{1}{3}\right)\right]^{-1} = 1 + 0. \qquad (11)$$

Only if some input requirement were reduced, as when an invention lowers $\mathbf{a_0}$ or **a**, or both, can there be room for capitalists' exploitative return. Thus lower **a** to **1/2**, leaving $\mathbf{a_0}$ at **1/3** and **m** at 1. Then Smith and Ricardo deduce from equations (9) through (11) an equilibrium profit rate of 20 percent:

$$1 + R^* = [a + ma_0]^{-1} = \left[\frac{1}{2} + \frac{1}{3}\right]^{-1} = \frac{6}{5} = 1 + 0.20. \tag{12}$$

This conventional paradigm, which is equivalent to

$$\begin{aligned} C + V + S &= C + V + R^*(C + V) \\ &= \left(\frac{1}{2} + \frac{1}{3}\right) + 0.2\left(\frac{1}{2} + \frac{1}{3}\right) = \frac{6}{5}\left(\frac{5}{6}\right) = 1, \end{aligned} \tag{13}$$

Marx proposes to replace by his rate-of-surplus-value paradigm

$$\begin{aligned} c + v + s &= c + v + r^*v \\ &= \frac{1}{2} + \frac{1}{3} + 0.5\left(\frac{1}{3}\right) = 1. \end{aligned} \tag{14}$$

The Marxian paradigm proposes an alternative accounting regime to (9) and (10). I use lower-case symbols to write out his proposed paradigm's accounting regime: in terms of Marx's *rate of surplus value*, r, his marked-up value for corn, $p/w = p$, expressed in wage units or days of labor, is as follows:

$$\begin{aligned} P_{\text{corn}} &= P_{\text{corn}}\mathbf{a} + \mathbf{a_0} + r\mathbf{a_0} \\ &= P_{\text{corn}}\tfrac{1}{2} + \tfrac{1}{3} + r\tfrac{1}{3}, \end{aligned} \tag{15}$$

or

$$\frac{P_{\text{corn}}}{w} = \mathbf{a_0}[\mathbf{I} - \mathbf{a}]^{-1}(1 + r), \tag{15'}$$

$$\frac{w}{P_{\text{corn}}} = \mathbf{m} = 1. \tag{16}$$

Combining (15′) and (16) enables us to solve for the rate of surplus value of 50 percent:

$$1 + r^* = \frac{1}{\mathbf{a_0}[\mathbf{I} - \mathbf{a}]^{-1}\mathbf{m}} = \frac{1 - \mathbf{(1/2)}}{\mathbf{1/3}(1)} = 1 + 0.50. \tag{17}$$

Note that R and r always have the same sign, R being between r and *0* for every surplus economy. (The explanation is that, if the total markup is to be the same, the markup rate on wages-only must exceed that on both wages and raw materials. See Morishima (1973) for elaboration that deals with the n-good model.)

1.4 Trial Balance with Negative Results

$$\frac{P_{\text{corn}}}{W} = \frac{p_{\text{corn}}}{w} = 1 \text{ corn per day.} \tag{18}$$

First, has Marx reached the same substantive equilibrium as his predecessors? Yes. In the two paradigms workers get the same real wage rates; capitalists get the same income:

$$\begin{aligned} &\text{Total capitalists' income in corn} \\ &= r^*\text{wages} = r^*v = r^*mL = 0.5L \\ &= R^*(C + V) = 0.20(C + V) \\ &= R^*[\mathrm{m} + aa_0^{-1}]L = R^*[1 + (0.5)(3)]L \\ &= 0.20[2.5]L = 0.5L. \end{aligned} \tag{19}$$

Second, has some new insight into exploitation—of prediction, explanation, understanding, positivist causation, or normative policy—been imparted by the new 1867 paradigm? Review the analysis, and you will see that the answer is negative on any new insight into the facts or likelihoods.

The ethical proposition that laborers should receive all of the steady-state product neither gains nor loses from the insistence that direct labor is indispensable to production. If direct labor can produce its product only when it has raw materials to work with, that is a solid fact basic to the understanding of how laborers are able to be exploited under competition. (Thus, as in the case where direct labor was the sole input needed for production, no worker who is able and willing to wait to be paid until the end of the production period can be deprived of his full steady-state productivity regardless of how avaricious the capitalists are.)

Since R^* and r^* lead to the same wage/nonwage result, the 1867 insistence on the latter adds nothing macroeconomically, microeconomically, or ethically to our understanding of the present one-technique case. Alas, as soon as other techniques are invented, the new 1867 paradigm *subtracts* from our understanding. The next section shows why.

1.5 Viable Inventions

Along with the option of producing 1 unit of corn with 1/3 of direct labor and 1/2 of corn seed, let a new option be discovered by which 1 unit of corn can be produced with 1/2 of direct labor and 3/10 of corn. If the subsistence real

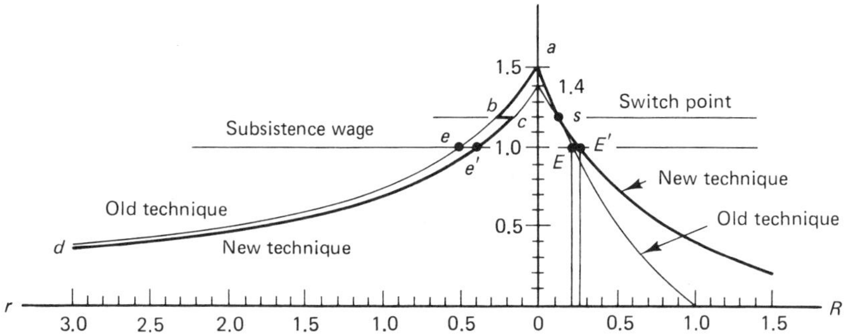

Figure 1.1
On the right, the mainstream economics trade-off between rates of real wage and profit; on the left, the new Marx paradigm involving a rate-of-surplus value. The old paradigm correctly predicts the adoption of new invention even though it lowers the rate-of-surplus value. A Marxian finds the right answer only by returning to the concept of maximized profit rate and disregarding zigzag *bc* at the switchpoint profit rate.

wage is still specified at $\mathbf{m} = 1$ corn per labor-day, which technique will now be used?

If the new technique were used, the rate-of-surplus value would fall—from the old $r^* = 0.50$ to the new $r^* = 0.40$. But the new profit rate would *rise*—from the old $R^* = 0.20$ to the new $R^* = 0.25$! (Recalculating equations (9) through (19) will confirm this.)

The two paradigms seem to tell different stories. Which is the relevant story, the correct one for the case of competitive capitalism? There can be no doubt as to the answer. The bourgeois paradigm of Smith, Ricardo, Pierro Sraffa, and Léon Walras correctly predicts that the new invention will displace the old technique under ruthless competition. Figure 1.1 tells the story. On the left is Marx's *rate-of-surplus value*; on the right is the *rate of profit*. The old equilibrium point E gives way to the higher profit-rate equilibrium point E'. The ASE envelope is well behaved (although it does have a corner at the switchpoint S where the old and new techniques are indifferent).

By contrast, the left-hand diagram has a zigzag *bc* at the switch profit rate of 11.1 percent. Users of the new paradigm, to resolve ambiguity and avoid error, have to peek at the old paradigm and learn that the rate of surplus value *drops* from old e to new e'.

The participants in the competitive market and the adherents to the competitive-profit-prices paradigm are indifferent to the new Marxian paradigm and are rewarded for their indifference.

1.6 Must the Profit Rate Fall?

One claim for the 1867 Marxian paradigm of the rate of surplus value is that, by means of it and only with it, could Marx prove conclusively his law of the falling rate of profit. Our present model can audit this claim and show why it is not valid.

But first note that Simon Kuznets, Frederick Macaulay, Ralph Hawtrey, Sidney Homer, and others who have seriously studied the statistical trends of profit and interest rates in the centuries before and after Marx do not find a downward trend in the profit rate. Instead, in real terms the actual path is a meandering one. (So trendless is the actual path that economists like Frank Taussig and Gustav Cassel exaggerated the constancy of the interest rate and each fabricated special esoteric theories to explain the law of *constancy* of the interest rate.) So it is a doubtful feather in a theorist's hat if he claims to demonstrate why the profit rate *must* fall.

Non-Marxians as well as Marxians were impressed in the nineteenth century with the complexity and proliferation of capital goods: locomotives, turbines, canal locks and docks, and so forth. Marx found a syllogism that purported to derive, from this apparent increase in the ratio of cost outlays other than labor to direct wage payments, a strong presumption that the rate of profit would fall. At the same time that workers were immiserized—as the pace and length of the working day deteriorated and as child labor became ever more necessary—capitalism's own laws of motion would allegedly propel the profit rate downward.

The facts on real wage rates and profits read otherwise in the chronicles of Kuznets et al. But let us audit the Marxian deductive logic.

I begin with some tautologies:

$$\frac{\text{total profits}}{\text{total wealth}} = \frac{\text{total profits}}{\text{total wages}} \times \frac{\text{total wages}}{\text{total wealth}}. \qquad (20)$$

The first of these three ratios is what we mean by the rate of profit, R: it is what invested capital (or wealth) earns divided by that amount of invested capital. The second ratio, at least when applied to our corn-the-only-industry model, is precisely what Marx's *rate of surplus value*, r, is defined as. The third ratio, as we will see, is something that goes down when what Marx calls "the organic composition of capital" goes up.

More precisely, stay with the present model of corn-only. And to keep out logical complexities, stay with the assumption that all nonlabor inputs lack durability: in such a circulating-capital model corn seed is used up completely in the one period. So the rate of turnover is unity.

Under these stark simplifications the total invested wealth is Marx's $c + v$, which is identically the same as bourgeois $C + V$. My earlier tautology now becomes

$$R = r \times \frac{v}{c + v} \equiv r\frac{V}{C + V} \\ = r[1 - \gamma], \tag{21}$$

where the organic composition of capital, γ, is by definition the ratio

$$\gamma = \frac{C}{C + V} \tag{22}$$

The growing plenitude and complexity of nineteenth-century capital—recall those locomotives and other such evidences of "increasing roundaboutness" of modes of production—both Marxians and non-Marxians would hope to identify with a trend toward increasing organic composition of capital, a trend of rising γ.[1]

Tautologically, if r can be supposed to be constant, and if the organic composition of capital rises, then the rate of profit, R, must fall. This constitutes the Marxian purported proof of the alleged downward trend in the profit rate:

$$\frac{\partial R}{\partial \gamma} = \frac{\partial[r(1 - \gamma)]}{\partial \gamma} = -r < 0. \tag{23}$$

I find it strange that such a thin syllogism has been taken so seriously for so long a period of time. The Achilles heel of the argument is located in the arbitrariness of the airy presumption that the rate of surplus value is a *constant* through the dramatic changes of the industrial revolution.[2] To name a concept (in this case the rate of surplus value) is to reify it and give it constancy in the presence of ignorance. But, as students of subjective probability had to learn the bitter way, out of ignorance can come only ignorance. If we don't know whether there are either men or women on Mars, it is gratuitous to opine that their numbers are probably equal since there is insufficient reason to expect the one to exceed the other.

Marx's empty tautology distracts attention from the one thing that can be said about the present version of his model.

THEOREM So long as the steady-state real wage does not rise, the equilibrium rate of profit *cannot fall*. A substantive invention that bludgeons its way into competitive use *must* raise the real wage rate or the profit rate or both.

My numerical example of an invention, shown in figure 1.1, illustrates how misleading the tautology in equation (20) can be. Let's see why.

My new invention happened to be a clearcut case where the organic composition of capital was reduced. There is no empirical law against that occurring in the industrial revolution. "No wonder your profit rate rose," a Marxian may say, "our tautology is useful because that is what it predicts when you reverse our hypothesis about the direction of change for the organic composition of capital."

Not so. The tautology does not apply, either directly or in reverse. As γ changed, it was impossible in the example that r stay the same: r is an endogenous variable, not one given by some exogenous power of bargaining by the capitalist class; technologically, r had to fall—from 50 to 40 percent, as we saw in figure 1.1. Deprived of the pre-Marx paradigm, the Marxian has no way of knowing in which direction and by how much the rate of surplus value will change, and so has no assurance that the change in r will not more than wipe out the postulated change in organic composition of capital.

But this impotence is purely of Marx's own making. The actual answer is a definite one and already known to pre-1867 economists such as Ricardo: the real wage rate and profit rate are in a trade-off relation; with the former set by the subsistence wage, the latter can only rise. In the tautology r cannot move perversely so as to wipe out quantitatively the viable change in $1 - \gamma$—a truth lost in the 1867 purported innovation!

1.7 Concluding Remarks

A subsistence-wage model, in fact, is a poor key to nineteenth-century reality. So much the worse for large parts of classical and Marxist economics. But that is no reason to mishandle the logic of such models.

The notion of exploitation is a complicated one. Relating profits to the denominator of wages rather than to the denominator of wealth solves none of the problems presented by exploitation. Nor can insight into exploitation come from calculating the ratio of the actual competitive real wage to what it could be with the same techniques were profits zero—which is what calculating r means to an a-Marxian agnostic.

Emotive language aside, the Ricardo-Marx model of this chapter could well be formulated for an egalitarian society. Each person could live in retirement on the interest and principal of the assets accumulated from scratch during adult working life. Each person's real income could be determined in equilibrium at precisely that critical level at which population numbers are stationary. If no one is exploiting, no one is being exploited. A determinate positive interest rate is then merely the result of finite human lives, with what that implies for Modigliani-Turgot life cycle consuming.

Supply-demand economics permits the scientist to handle and understand special and general patterns of behavior. Alas, to understand the fortunes of Andrew Carnegie, J. P. Morgan, Albert Hearst, Baron Rothschild, J. D. Rockefeller—to say nothing of the economic circumstances of David Copperfield and Becky Sharp, and of their great-nephews and great-nieces—the $c + v + s$ tableaux, even in their modernized von Neumann formulations, are mostly a digression. Theory, too often, is the opiate of the theorists. That does not have to be.

Elsewhere I have fair-mindedly examined how the Marxian and conventional paradigms fare in handling a variety of test cases. As with the present case of technical change, the Samuelson (1982) verdict is a damning one for the 1867 innovation.

With the full matrix complications, or under all admissible simplifications, the Marxian paradigm of surplus value fails to deliver the goods of description, understanding, prediction, and prescription. It is not that the Emperor has no clothes; rather it is the case that the garments are confining and deceptive, disguising structure and displaying nonexistent bulges and hollows.

1.8 Mathematical Appendix

A 1-good model needs no matrices. However, using boldface type to represent the technological and subsistence-requirements data of the problem, I will hint at how the full matrix study would go.

Thus in the one-technique case the equilibrium that was defined by (10′) will still apply when I add to corn any number of other goods. In matrix terms the equilibrium profit rate is given by the single relation

$$\mathbf{a_0}(1 + R)[\mathbf{I} - \mathbf{a}(1 + R)]^{-1}\mathbf{m} = 1, \tag{A.1}$$

where now $\mathbf{a_0}$ is a row vector, $\mathbf{a}$ is a square matrix, and $\mathbf{m}$ is a column vector.

Always, R^*, the competitive rate of profit, can be interpreted as the highest own-marginal-productivity of a vector of all the goods in producing itself. That is, $1 + R^*$ is defined by the Seton (1957) eigenvector property

$$[\mathbf{a} + \mathbf{ma_0}]\mathbf{Q}^*(1 + R^*) = \mathbf{Q}^*. \tag{A.2}$$

where $\mathbf{ma_0} = [m_i a_{0j}]$ represents the subsistence-wage requirements that must be added to the $[a_{ij}]$ technical requirements in the Seton fashion.

Also

$$1 + R^* = \operatorname*{Max}_{\mathbf{Q}} \lambda \tag{A.3}$$

subject to

$$[Q_i] = \mathbf{Q}(t) \geqq \lambda \mathbf{Q}(t + 1) \tag{A.4}$$

and where all the stipulated constraints on production and subsistence are obeyed.

Joint Products: Durable Goods

Smith and Ricardo recognized that cost would not suffice to determine prices of joint products like wool and mutton; intensity of demand would affect their real prices. The complications of joint products can be ignored in the standard case where each department produces solely one product, and does so with raw material inputs that are used up completely in one use (have a turnover rate of unity per period).

Modern students of Leontief-Sraffa single-produce systems realize that one kind of durability of inputs can be admitted without losing the simplicity of Leontief-Sraffa systems and their nonsubstitution theorem linearities. This is the case of *exponential* depreciation, where the force of mortality and depreciation is the same percentage for each period regardless of the input's age. As suggested in Samuelson (1971, p. 425, n. 37; 1982), the formula for nondurable models

$$\begin{aligned}\mathbf{P} &= [W\mathbf{a_0} + \mathbf{Pa}]\ (1 + R)\\ &= W\mathbf{a_0}(1 + R)\ [\mathbf{I} - \mathbf{a}(1 + R)]^{-1}\end{aligned} \tag{A.5}$$

need only be replaced by

$$\begin{aligned}\mathbf{P} &= [W\mathbf{a_0} + \mathbf{Pa}]\ (1 + R) - \mathbf{P}[a_{ij}(1 - d_{ij})]\\ &= W\mathbf{a_0}(1 + R) + \mathbf{P}[a_{ij}(d_{ij} + R)]\\ &= W\mathbf{a_0}(1 + R)\ [I - a_{ij}(d_{ij} + R)]^{-1},\end{aligned} \tag{A.6}$$

where d_{ij} is the fraction of the ijth intermediate input that is used up in one period's use. When $d_{ij} \equiv 1$, (A.6) becomes (A.5).

With exponential depreciation, we see how Marx's $C + V + S$ formulations should have been handled by his editor.

For the jth industry (A.6) suggests we write

$$\sum_{i=1}^{n} P_i a_{ij} d_{ij} Q_j + W a_{0j} Q_j + R\left(\sum_{i=1}^{n} P_i a_{ij} Q_j + W a_{0j} Q_j\right)$$
$$= \sum_{i=1}^{n} C_{ij} + V_j + R\left(V_j + \sum_{i=1}^{n} C_{ij} d_{ij}^{-1}\right) \tag{A.7}$$
$$= C_j + V_j + R(V_j + C_j \bar{d}_j^{-1}), \quad j = 1, \ldots, n$$

it being understood that $\bar{d}_j^{-1}$ is the weighted mean length of life of the industry's various input items

$$\bar{d}_j^{-1} = \frac{\sum_i C_{ij} d_{ij}^{-1}}{\sum_i C_{ij}}. \tag{A.8}$$

Of course changes in R will alter $\bar{d}_j^{-1}$, as it will V_j/C_j ratios.

Presumably, in terms of the rate of surplus value, Marx would write

$$c_j + v_j + s_j = \sum_{i=1}^{n} p_i a_{ij} d_{ij} Q_j + w a_{0j} Q_j (1 + r), \tag{A. 9}$$

where

$$\left[\frac{p_j}{w}\right] = [a_{0j}]\,[I - a_{ij} d_{ij}]^{-1}\,(1 + r). \tag{A.10}$$

Reswitching in a One-Department Model

Reswitching is the phenomenon that occurs when a particular set of techniques is competitively viable in two different ranges of the profit rate, but not inbetween. A corn-only model, involving no durable capital good but only corn as a raw material used up in the single period of production, cannot exhibit reswitching. This impossibility follows from the linearity of the (real wage, profit rate) trade-off, when $n = 1$ and the real wage is paid *post factum* (at the end rather than the beginning of the period). Also with exponential depreciation, as in (A.6), linearity precludes reswitching.

However, if I admit a durable good into my corn-only model, I can easily specify examples of reswitching. Here is an example with two such options:

1. This involves no durability. To produce 1 unit of corn, we need 1/4 of direct labor and 0.52 of corn seed.

2. Now suppose we can also produce 1 unit of corn by 1 unit of direct labor combined with 1 unit of corn input congealed into a durable tool. Then, along with our output of corn, we get as a joint product one used durable tool: we may suppose that this used tool can produce 2 units of corn without requiring any direct labor.

Which option will be competitively viable? That depends on the profit rate. The durable option can be shown to pay at low interest rates and at high interest rates, but at intermediate interest rates the nondurable technique of option 1 will win out competitively.

Here are the steady-state unit cost relations for corn price, P, as in Samuelson (1959, eq. 22):

Option 1

$$P = (W\bar{a}_0 + P\bar{a}) = \frac{W\bar{a}_0(1 + R)}{1 - \bar{a}(1 + R)}; \tag{A.11}$$

$$\frac{W}{P} = f_1(R) = \frac{1 - 0.52(1 + R)}{0.25(1 + R)}. \tag{A.12}$$

Option 2

$$\begin{aligned} P &= (Wa_0 + Pa)(1 + R) - P_{\text{used}}a \\ &= (W + P)(1 + R) - P_{\text{used}}, \end{aligned} \tag{A.13}$$

$$P = P_{\text{used}}\hat{a}(1 + R) = P_{\text{used}}\frac{1}{2}(1 + R). \tag{A.14}$$

This can be solved to give

$$\frac{W}{P} = \frac{1 - a(1 + R) + a\hat{a}^{-1}(1 + R)^{-1}}{a_0(1 + R)} \tag{A.15}$$

$$= \frac{1 - (1 + R) + 2(1 + R)^{-1}}{1 + R} = f_2(R). \tag{A.16}$$

Under ruthless competition, for each R the option that yields the higher real wage will win out:

$$W/P = \max\,[f_1(R), f_2(R)] = f^*(R). \tag{A.17}$$

Equating $f_1(R)$ to $f_2(R)$ and solving the quadratic equation that is thereby implied, we find

$$\begin{aligned} f^*(R) &= f_2(R), \quad 0 \le R \le \frac{1}{9}, \\ &= f_1(R), \quad \frac{1}{9} \le R \le \frac{2}{3}, \\ &= f_2(R), \quad \frac{2}{3} \le R \le 1, \end{aligned} \tag{A.18}$$

where 1/9 and 2/3 are the roots of the quadratic

$$1.08(1 + R)^2 - 3(1 + R) + 2$$
$$= 1.08\left[(1 + R) - \left(1 + \frac{1}{9}\right)\right]\left[(1 + R) - 1 + \frac{2}{3}\right]. \qquad (A.19)$$

This numerical example of reswitching has a point of interest in the present connection. Reswitching reminds us how ambiguous it is to judge that (1) one technique has a higher or lower organic composition of capital, (2) is more roundabout and time intensive, or (3) is more mechanized than the other. When the system is moved by an invention from option 1 to option 2 and to higher profit rates, is that definitely a decrease in the organic composition of capital? If the same change occurs, but to a lower profit rate, what then? If the reverse occurs, from option 2 to option 1, what definite can be said? To ask these questions is to realize that they admit of no definite answers. What is new here is the demonstration that even a one-department model can display all the complications of the n-department case, complications that the 1867 paradigm cannot handle.

Notes

I owe thanks to the National Science Foundation for aid, and thanks to Kate Crowley and Aase Huggins for editorial assistance.

1. Sraffa and Joan Robinson have alerted scholars to the ambiguity involved in the notion of the organic composition of capital, or in kindred notions of increasing degrees of mechanization or of roundaboutness of modes of production. Seeing a locomotive doesn't tell you whether the capital/output ratio rose on the average between 1800 and 1850. In figure 1.1 I could have given the mathematical appendix example of *reswitching*—of a durable-good alternative that would be commercially superior to my original circulating-capital technique at very high and low interest rates! Which is more mechanized—the machine case or the corn seed case?

2. P. M. Sweezy (1942, ch. 4) provides a useful exposition of the $R/r = 1 - \gamma$ tautology. See H. D. Dickinson (1956–7) for a commendable reexamination of this tautology. In particular, see his p. 127, n. 1 and n. 2, for quotations from Marx and Bortkiewicz that recognize that what changes γ may not leave r constant. Dickinson's own researches point out that certain processes associated with accumulation (non-consuming now so that future output may more nearly attain golden-rule levels) can often be expected to cause the profit rate to fall at the same time that such measures of capital intensity as the organic composition of capital are rising. It is a pity that no modern treatment of the whole matter appears in the literature to show how slight is the insight forthcoming from the rate of surplus value for the (real wage, profit rate) relationships. See the useful Roemer (1977) analysis of Marxian reasonings. In Samuelson (1982) I show how misleading is Roemer's taxonomy of "socially desirable" inventions that competition allegedly will not adopt: in fact, normatively,

competition avoids deadweight loss in the sense of intertemporal Pareto non-optimality; a planned society can rationally eschew inventions that Roemer calls socially desirable.

References

Bortkiewicz, L. von, 1907. On the correction of Marx's fundamental theoretical construction in the third volume of *Capital. Jahrbuch Nationalökonomie Statistik* 34: 370–385.

Dickinson H. D., 1957. The falling rate of profit in Marxian economies. *Review of Economic Studies* 24: 120–130.

Marx, Karl. *Capital.* Vol. I, 1867; Vol. II, 1885; Vol. III, 1894.

Morishima, M., 1973. *Marx's Economies: A Dual Theory of Value and Growth.* Cambridge: Cambridge University Press.

Roemer, J., 1977. Technical change and the tendency of the rate of profit to fall. *Journal of Economic Theory* (December): 403–424.

Samuelson, P. A. *Collected Scientific Papers.* Vol. I, 1965; Vol. II, 1965; Vol. III, 1972; Vol. IV, 1977. Cambridge, Mass.: The MIT Press, chs. 29–32, pp. 113, 117, 152–155, 225–231.

Samuelson, P. A., 1982. The normative and positivistic inferiority of Marx's values paradigm. *Southern Economic Journal* (July): 11–18.

Seton, F., 1957. The transformation problem. *Review of Economic Studies* 24: 149–160.

Sweezy, P. M., 1942. *The Theory of Capitalist Development.* New York: Oxford University Press.

von Neumann, J., 1946. A model of general economic equilibrium (transl. by G. Morgenstern). *Review of Economic Studies* 13: 1–9.

314

Durable Capital Inputs: Conditions for Price Ratios to be Invariant to Profit-Rate Changes

By

Paul A. Samuelson, Cambridge, Mass., U. S. A.

(Received October 30, 1981; revised version received December 28, 1982)

When the profit or interest rate changes, price ratios of goods generally change too. But, as is well known, in the singular case where all industries have the same "organic compositions of capital", price ratios are invariant to changes in R, the profit rate. All this holds in the standard Leontief-Sraffa-Marx model of *circulating* capital, in which every produced input is completely used up in each single period.

Here I provide necessary and sufficient conditions for price invariance in the presence of exponentially-depreciating durable capital inputs. The result is a surprisingly simple criterion: price ratios are invariant to interest rate changes if and only if all industries have (not the same wage fraction of unit cost but) the same capital-to-labor ratio.

However, under realistic age-dependent depreciation schedules, the criteria for price-ratio neutrality become very restrictive; and in these general cases, the present analysis shows that the Sraffian Standard Commodity simply does not exist (even in the subset of situations where the Non-Substitution theorem still obtains). The implications for "reswitching" and for Marx's reproduction tableaux are made clear.

1. Review

Let $[a_{0j}]=\mathbf{a}_0$ be the row vector of direct labor requirements needed to produce each of the respective goods in the steady state: L_j/Q_j is thus assumed to be a given technological constant.

Let $[a_{ij}]=\mathbf{a}$ be the square matrix of input output coefficients, Q_{ij}/Q_j. In the *circulating*-capital model all of the Q_{ij} input is used up in producing (one period later) the Q_j output.

Then competitive real prices are known to be given by solving the following simultaneous equations:

$$P_j/W = [a_{0j} + \sum_{i=1}^{n} (P_i/W)\, a_{ij}]\, (1+R), \qquad (j=1, \ldots, n) \qquad (1.1)$$

In matrix terms, for viable steady-state systems,

$$\mathbf{P}/W = \mathbf{a}_0\, (1+R)\, [I - a_{ij}\, (1+R)]^{-1} = [A_{01}\, (R), \ldots, A_{0n}\, (R)] \qquad (1.2)$$
$$= \mathbf{A}_0\, (\mathbf{R}) > 0.$$

The basic theorem, known essentially from the time of Marx on, is this:

Theorem: If, and only if, the direct-wage component is the same fraction of every good's unit cost, then changes in the interest or profit rate will affect all goods' prices in the same proportion.
An equivalent condition, due to Miyao, is that if and only if the row vector $\mathbf{a}_0$ is the positive eigenvector of $\mathbf{a}$, then for all R

$$A_{0j}\, (R)/A_{01}\, (R) \equiv A_{0j}\, (0)/A_{01}\, (0) = a_{0j}/a_{01}, \qquad (j=1, \ldots, n) \qquad (1.3)$$

The reader may refer to Sraffa (1960, pp. 12—13) and to Miyao (1977).

2. Exponential Depreciation

When some inputs are durable, we are in the domain of joint products. Direct labor, working with leather and a new hammer, produces shoes and a used hammer. Most of the nicc simplicities of the Leontief-Sraffa scenario — as for example the 1949 Non-Substitution Theorem of Georgescu-Roegen (1951) and Samuelson (1951) — are invalidated by jointness of products. (Thus, a change in consumer tastes from wool to mutton will alter the steady-state price ratio of those items; their price ratio is not an invariant.)

But it has been realized for some time that the special case of exponential depreciation yields steady-state price relations essentially like those of the circulating-capital model. By definition, exponential depreciation applies when the force of mortality or depreciation of a capital input is the same fraction independent of its age, being d_{ij} for the ith input used to produce the jth good, where

$$0 \leq d_{ij} \leq 1. \qquad (2.1)$$

See Burmeister and Dobell (1970, Chapter 8), particularly for the case where $d_{ij} = d_i$. The exact model being used here can be spelled out. Outputs $(Q_1, \ldots, Q_n)$ are produced by direct-labor inputs $(L_1, \ldots, L_n)$ and by stocks of produced capital items $(K_1, \ldots, K_i, \ldots, K_n)$, which have respectively been allocated to the j various industries:

$$K_i(t) = \sum_{j=1}^{n} K_{ij}(t), \quad (i = 1, \ldots, n), \quad K_{ij} \geq 0. \tag{2.2}$$

Our time-phased productions functions are

$$Q_j(t+1) = F^j[L_j(t), K_{1j}(t), \ldots, K_{nj}(t)], \quad (j = 1, \ldots, n) \tag{2.3}$$

In the case of fixed coefficients, (2.3) becomes

$$Q_j(t+1) = \text{Min}\,[L_j(t)/a_{0j}, K_{1j}(t)/a_{1j}, \ldots, K_{nj}(t)/a_{nj}]; \quad a_{0j}, a_{ij} \geq 0. \tag{2.4}$$

The change in each stock is the difference between its births (gross new productions) and its deaths (depreciation). Therefore,

$$K_{ij}(t+1) - K_{ij}(t) = Q_{ij}(t+1) - d_{ij}K_{ij}(t) \tag{2.5}$$

where the Q_{ij}'s satisfy the allocation equations for outputs between input uses and net consumptions:

$$Q_i(t) = Q_{i1}(t) + \ldots + Q_{in}(t) + C_i(t), \quad (i = 1, \ldots, n); \quad Q_{ij}, C_i \geq 0. \tag{2.6}$$

In the steady state, we have

$$[Q_i(t), Q_{ij}(t), C_i(t), K_{ij}(t), L_j(t)] \equiv [Q_i, Q_{ij}, C_i, K_{ij}, L_j]. \tag{2.7}$$

Therefore, (2.4)—(2.6) reduce to their steady-state version:

$$\begin{aligned} Q_j &= \text{Min}\,[L_j/a_{0j}, Q_{1j}/(a_{1j}d_{1j}), \ldots, Q_{nj}/(a_{nj}d_{nj})] \\ &= \text{Min}\,[L_j/a_{0j}, K_{1j}/a_{1j}, \ldots, K_{nj}/a_{nj}], \quad (j = 1, \ldots, n) \\ &= \sum_{i=1}^{n} Q_{ji} + C_j. \end{aligned} \tag{2.8}$$

The net-cost price relations, under steady-state competitive conditions, require that each good be priced at its unit cost — wage, plus used-up inputs, plus profit on all money outlays that tie up investable capital. What is the same thing, it involves costs corrected for the amounts of the durable items left over at the end of the period. Now (1.1) becomes

$$P_j = (Wa_{0j} + \sum_{i=1}^{n} P_i a_{ij})(1+R) - \sum_{i=1}^{n} P_i a_{ij}(1-d_{ij}) \tag{2.9}$$

$$= Wa_{0j}(1+R) + \sum_{i=1}^{n} P_i a_{ij}(d_{ij}+R), \qquad (j=1,\ldots,n).$$

Solving these simultaneous relations, we derive the durable-goods version of (2.2) recorded in Samuelson (1971, p. 425, n. 37):

$$\mathbf{P}/W = \mathbf{a}_0(1+R)[I - a_{ij}(d_{ij}+R)]^{-1}$$

$$= \mathbf{A}_0(\mathbf{R}) = [A_{01}(R), \ldots, A_{0n}(R)], \qquad A_{0j}'(R) > 0.$$

Generally, as R rises above zero, the price ratios $A_{0j}(R)/A_{01}(R)$ will change (although not necessarily in a monotonic direction).

Query: What are necessary and sufficient conditions on the $2n^2+n$ coefficients, $[a_{ij}, d_{ij}, a_{0j}]$, such that

$$\frac{A_{0j}(R)}{A_{01}(R)} \equiv \frac{A_{0j}(0)}{A_{01}(0)}, \qquad (j=2,\ldots,n) \tag{2.11}$$

The standard answer in terms of equal organic compositions of capital — equal ratios of wage to nonwage costs — applies only to the non-durability case where $d_{ij} \equiv 1$.

Formally,

$$A_{0j}(R) = (1+R)\sum_{k=1}^{n} a_{0k}\Delta_{kj}(R)/\Delta(R) \tag{2.12}$$

where $\Delta(R)$ is the determinant of $[\mathbf{I} - a_{ij}(d_{ij}+R)]$ and $\Delta_{kj}(R)$ is the cofactor of its jkth element. Clearly, price-ratio invariance occurs if and only if every numerator of (2.12) involves dependence on R through a common $f(R)$ factor that can be factored out of them. I. e., price-ratio invariance comes in the singular case where (2.12) can be reduced to

$$A_{0j}(R) = f(R)\sum_{k=1}^{n} a_{0k}\Delta_{kj}(0)/\Delta(R), \qquad (j=1,\ldots,n). \tag{2.13}$$

As will be shown, under general durability, it is neither necessary nor sufficient that direct labor expense be the same fraction of total unit cost for all industries. Neither is it now the case that the $a_{0j}/A_{0j}(0)$ ratios are to be the same constant, or that $\mathbf{a}_0$ be an eigenvector of $\mathbf{a}$ or of $[a_{ij}d_{ij}]$.

3. Complete Solution in the Two-Good Case

For $n=2$, (2.10) immediately implies

$$P_2/P_1=A_{02}(R)/A_{01}(R)=\frac{(a_{02}+a_{01}a_{12}d_{12}-a_{02}a_{11}d_{11})+(a_{01}a_{12}-a_{02}a_{11})R}{(a_{01}+a_{02}a_{21}d_{21}-a_{01}a_{22}d_{22})+(a_{02}a_{21}-a_{01}a_{22})R} \tag{3.1}$$

For $(\alpha_2+\beta_2 R)/(\alpha_1+\beta_1 R)$ to be independent of R, it is clearly necessary and sufficient that the non-zero α's and β's satisfy

$$\frac{\alpha_2}{\alpha_1}=\frac{\beta_2}{\beta_1} \tag{3.2}$$

Therefore, for $n=2$, our query concerning the necessary and sufficient conditions for price-ratio invariance is completely answered by the following sole requirement on the (a_{ij}, d_{ij}, a_{0j}) coefficients.

Theorem: For $n=2$, price-ratio invariance obtains if and only if the technical coefficients satisfy the fundamental relation

$$\frac{a_{02}+a_{01}a_{12}d_{12}-a_{02}a_{11}d_{11}}{a_{01}+a_{02}a_{21}d_{21}-a_{01}a_{22}d_{22}}=\frac{a_{01}a_{12}-a_{02}a_{11}}{a_{02}a_{21}-a_{01}a_{22}} \tag{3.3}$$

This is one relation involving 10 variables; and therefore we may expect a 9-fold infinity of admissible cases.

I shall present two numerical examples of price-ratio invariance to illustrate the general principles involved and the vital difference between the durable-goods and nondurable-goods cases.

4. Examples

First, let's suppose that input 1 is nondurable, with $d_{11}=d_{12}=1$. But let input 2 have a mean life of two periods, with $d_{21}=d_{22}={}^1/_2$.

From (3.3)'s fundamental relation, we can verify that the following technology does lead to price-ratio invariance:

$$\left[\frac{a_0}{a}\right]=\left[\begin{array}{cc}1 & 1\\ \hline 0 & 2/10\\ 2/11 & 0\end{array}\right] \tag{4.1}$$

Relation (3.1) becomes

$$P_2/P_1=\frac{(1+0.2-0)+(0.2-0)R}{(1+{}^1/_{11}-0)+({}^2/_{11}-0)R}=(1.1)\frac{12+2R}{12+2R}\equiv 1.1. \tag{4.2}$$

In the second example, for variety, let it be the first item that is durable and the second item nondurable: $d_{12}=1/2$, $d_{21}=1$. The $(\mathbf{a}_0, \mathbf{a})$ coefficients that served in (4.1) will no longer satisfy (3.3)'s fundamental relation. However, substitution confirms that the following technology will serve:

$$\left[\frac{a_0}{a}\right]=\left[\begin{array}{cc} 1 & 1 \\ \hline 0 & 2/10 \\ 2/9 & 0 \end{array}\right] \qquad (4.3)$$

Relation (3.1) now becomes

$$\frac{P_2}{P_1}=\frac{(1+1-0)+(0.2-0)\,R}{(1+{}^2/_9-0)+({}^2/_9-0)\,R}=\frac{9}{10}\,\frac{11+2R}{11+2R}\equiv 0.9 \qquad (4.4)$$

Is there some simple ratio identity, like that of equal organic composition in the nondurable case, that these examples can be seen to satisfy?

One's hopes are raised by example 1. When we plug its numbers into (2.10), for $R=0$ we derive

$$[P_1/W, P_2/W]=[A_{01}\,(0), A_{02}\,(0)]=[10/9, 11/9]. \qquad (4.5)$$

And we cannot help but notice that, for example 1,

$$\frac{a_{01}}{(P_1/W)\,a_{11}+(P_2/W)\,a_{21}}=\frac{a_{02}}{(P_1/W)\,a_{12}+(P_2/W)\,a_{22}} \qquad (4.6)$$

both sides being equal to 9/2 where $R=0$.

This suggests the bold conjecture that, equivalent to (3.3)'s fundamental relation is (4.6). This leads to the following:

Theorem: If, and only if, the ratio of wages to total capital outlay is the same in every industry will price-ratio invariance obtain:

$$\frac{WL_j}{(WL_j+\Sigma_i P_i K_{ij})}=\frac{WL_1}{WL_1+\Sigma_i P_i K_{i1}}, \quad (j=2,\ldots,n). \qquad (4.6')$$

Equivalently,

$$\frac{a_{0j}}{\Sigma_i A_{0i}\,(0)\,a_{ij}}=\frac{a_{01}}{\Sigma_i A_{0i}\,(0)\,a_{i1}} \leftrightarrow \frac{A_{0j}\,(R)}{A_{01}\,(R)}\equiv\frac{A_{0j}\,(0)}{A_{01}\,(0)} \qquad (4.6'')$$

The rule suggested by our first example can be tested on our second example. It passes the test with flying colors, the two sides of the expression in (4.6″) both turning out to equal 4.

5. Proof of the Key Theorem

The following lemma points up the general logic of price-ratio invariance.

Lemma. Let the matrix relations

$$\mathbf{P} = \mathbf{a}_0 + \mathbf{P}\mathbf{a}_1 + \mathbf{P}\mathbf{a}_2, \tag{5.1}$$

where $\mathbf{a}_0$ is a (1-by-n) vector and $\mathbf{a}_1$, $\mathbf{a}_2$ are (n-by-n) matrices have the unique solution $\mathbf{P} = \mathbf{A}_0\ (0)$.
Then the relations

$$\mathbf{P} = (\mathbf{a}_0 + \mathbf{P}\mathbf{a}_1)\ \alpha + \mathbf{P}\mathbf{a}_2, \qquad \alpha \geq 1 \tag{5.2}$$

will have a solution with elements whose ratios are independent of α,

$$\mathbf{P} = \beta\ (\alpha)\ \mathbf{A}_0\ (0) \tag{5.3}$$

if and only if there exists a λ such that

$$\mathbf{A}_0\ (0)\ \mathbf{a}_1 = \lambda\ \mathbf{a}_0 \tag{5.4}$$

where

$$\beta\ (\alpha) = \frac{\alpha}{1 + \lambda\ (1 - \alpha)} \tag{5.5}$$

The proof of (5.4)'s sufficiency follows directly from substitution of $\alpha\ [1 + \lambda\ (1 - \alpha)]^{-1}\ \mathbf{A}_0(0)$ into (5.2) and making use of (5.4). The proof of its necessity follows from the requirement that the derivatives of P_j/W with respect to α, evaluated at $\alpha = 1$, be proportional to $\mathbf{A}_0$ itself; and, if (5.4) is violated, this will not be the case.

It will be seen from (2.9) that we shall want to identify $\mathbf{a}_1$ with $\mathbf{a}$, $\mathbf{a}_2$ with $[-(1 - d_{ij})\ a_{ij}]$, α with $1 + R$, and interpret the Lemma's $\mathbf{P}$ as the vector of real prices, $[P_j/W]$. This gives us our desired key theorem.

Theorem: The solution to

$$\begin{aligned} \mathbf{P}/W &= [\mathbf{a}_0 + (\mathbf{P}/W)\ \mathbf{a}]\ (1 + R) - (\mathbf{P}/W)\ [a_{ij}\ (1 - d_{ij})] \\ &= \mathbf{a}_0\ (1 + R)\ [\mathbf{I} - a_{ij}\ (d_{ij} + R)]^{-1} \end{aligned} \tag{5.6}$$

will have elements whose ratios are independent of R if and only if

$$\mathbf{A}_0\ (0)\ \mathbf{a} = \lambda\ \mathbf{a}_0, \tag{5.7}$$

$$\mathbf{P}/W = \frac{1 + R}{1 - R\lambda}\ \mathbf{A}_0\ (0), \qquad R_{\max} = \lambda^{-1}. \tag{5.8}$$

The condition (5.6) is the desired generalization of what equal organic composition of capital must mean in the durable-goods case.

The explicit form of our fundamental criterion for price-ratio invariance, as given in (5.7) puts to rest an inevitable question: How can the criterion $\mathbf{A}_0\,\mathbf{a}$ proportional to $\mathbf{a}_0$ be *independent of the depreciation coefficients* $[d_{ij}]$? We see in (5.7) there is no such independence: hidden inside $\mathbf{A}_0$, as (5.6) displays, are the $a_{ij}d_{ij}$ coefficients!

6. Global Price-Ratio Invariance

Everything said so far applies to a fixed-coefficients model, where there is specified a *single* technologically feasible set of $[a_{ij}, d_{ij}, a_{0j}]$ constants. The analysis then stays in the domain of linear matrix relations. In real economic life there will usually be feasible some choices of alternative technological methods of production. This takes us out of the realm of algebra and into the domain of more complicated inequalities.

When there is a finite number of alternative $[a_{ij}, d_{ij}, a_{0j}]$ coefficients for some jth industry, one must be prepared to encounter different competitive choices of techniques over different subintervals of positive R. At the end-points of such subintervals, we are at "switchpoints" where two techniques are competitively indifferent. (Two different choices of technique will not be competitively indifferent to each other at a set of R's that is of positive measure.)

For *global* price-ratio invariance, it is trivially necessary that *each* viable choice of techniques satisfy our basic criterion of (5.6). Also, as we traverse all feasible positive levels of R, it would be sufficient for global price-ratio invariance if every choice of technique that we encounter does satisfy (5.6)'s local criterion.

Theorem: For global price-ratio invariance, it is necessary and sufficient that on every subinterval of admissible R the viable technique satisfy the necessary and sufficient condition for local price ratio invariance, namely equality in every industry of the capital/labor ratios.

Thus, let $\mathbf{A}_0^R\,(0)$ be the row vector of embodied *total* steady-state labor requirements for the $[\mathbf{a}_0^R, \mathbf{a}^R, d_{ij}^R]$ coefficients that are competitively viable for that profit rate, R. For every such choice of techniques it is necessary and sufficient for price-ratio invariance that

$$\mathbf{A}_0^R\,\mathbf{a}^R \text{ is prop to } \mathbf{a}_0^R \tag{6.1}$$

for all R on the subinterval in question.

Remark: Consider two isolated regions, each with a single choice of techniques that exhibits price-ratio invariance. Now let them intercommunicate. The above theorem would fail if, now, the *only* viable choice of techniques involves at every interest rate *both* regions' previous techniques. However, on reflection, we realize that, either at high or low interest rates, choosing from *only one* region's techniques will be commercially viable.

7. Steady-State Black-Box Production Functions

I owe to Professor Edwin Burmeister's lectures at the University of Virginia the following neat alternative approach. For reasons that will become clear, I can call it the Black-Box Production Function approach.

Begin with the following identity, which holds for any productive economy satisfying the *generalized* Hawkins-Simon condition that $(\mathbf{I}-a_{ij}d_{ij})$ has every principal minor positive along with its determinant:

$$\mathbf{P}W^{-1}=\mathbf{a}_0(1+R)+\mathbf{P}W^{-1}[a_{ij}d_{ij}]+PW^{-1}\mathbf{a}R \tag{2.9}$$

$$=\mathbf{a}_0[\mathbf{I}-a_{ij}d_{ij}]^{-1}(1+R)+\mathbf{PW}^{-1}\mathbf{a}[\mathbf{I}-a_{ij}d_{ij}]^{-1}R \tag{7.1}$$

$$=\mathbf{A}_0(0)(1+R)+\mathbf{PW}^{-1}\mathbf{A}(0)R,\ \mathbf{A}_0(0)\geq 0,\ \mathbf{A}(0)\geq 0 \tag{7.2}$$

$$=\mathbf{A}_0(0)(1+R)[\mathbf{I}-\mathbf{A}(0)R]^{-1}.\quad 0\leq R\leq R^*<\infty \tag{7.3}$$

$$=[\mathbf{A}_0(0)+\mathbf{A}(0)\mathbf{A}_0(0)R+\mathbf{A}(0)\mathbf{A}(0)^2R^2+\ldots](1+R). \tag{7.4}$$

The series in (7.4) is convergent for all competitively feasible R. The row vector $\mathbf{A}_0(0)$ and the matrix $\mathbf{A}(0)$ are explicitly defined by (7.1) and (7.2). They have the same non-negative properties that $(\mathbf{a}_0, \mathbf{a})$ have in a nondurable-goods Leontief-Sraffa system except that there is no need for $\mathbf{A}(0)$ to satisfy Hawkins-Simon conditions. It is enough that $[a_{ij}d_{ij}]$ did, assuring $\mathbf{A}(0)$ to be non-negative and finite.

I can therefore combine the (7.1) approach of Burmeister with Miyao's eigenvector approach.

Theorem: If, and only if, for some γ,

$$\mathbf{A}_0(0)\mathbf{A}(0)=\gamma\mathbf{A}_0(0), \tag{7.5}$$

$$\mathbf{P}/W \text{ is proportional to } \mathbf{A}_0(0) \text{ for all } R, \tag{7.6}$$

namely

$$\mathbf{P}/W = \mathbf{A_0}(\mathbf{R}) = \mathbf{A_0}(0)\,(1+R)\,[\sum_0^\infty \mathbf{A}(0)^i R^i]$$
$$= \mathbf{A_0}(0)\,(1+R)\,[1+\gamma R+(\gamma R)^2+\ldots]$$
$$= \mathbf{A_0}(0)\,(1+R)\,[1-\gamma R]^{-1}$$
$$= \mathbf{A_0}(0)\,(1+R)\,[1-R/R^*]^{-1}, \quad \mathbf{A}(0)\neq 0 \qquad (7.7)$$

Also, from (5.7) in the earlier theorem, each of the following implies the other two:

$$\mathbf{A_0}(0)\,\mathbf{A}(0) = \gamma\,\mathbf{A_0}(0) \quad \text{for some positive } \gamma \qquad (7.8)$$
$$\mathbf{A_0}(0)\,\mathbf{a} = \lambda\,\mathbf{a_0} \qquad (7.9)$$
$$\mathbf{a_0}\,\mathbf{B} = \lambda\,\mathbf{a_0}, \quad \mathbf{B} = [\mathbf{I} - a_{ij}d_{ij}]^{-1}\,\mathbf{a}. \qquad (7.10)$$

In the end, (7.10) does provide us with an eigenvector interpretation for the original $\mathbf{a_0}$ vector of direct labor requirements.

The matrices $\mathbf{A_0}(0)$ and $\mathbf{B}$ have obvious economic interpretations. The latter is the vector of total embodied-labor costs (direct and indirect) of the respective goods in the zero-profit steady state. Since $[I-a_{ij}d_{ij}]^{-1}$ is the multiplier matrix that converts in the steady state the gross outputs $[Q_i]$ and the net consumptions,

$$Q = C + [\sum_{j=1}^{n} Q_{ij}] = C + [a_{ij}d_{ij}]\,Q$$
$$= [I - a_{ij}d_{ij}]^{-1}\,C, \qquad (7.11)$$

setting $\mathbf{C}$ equal to $\mathbf{a}$ itself gives $\mathbf{B}$ as the needed square array of steady-state gross Q's needed to provide the K_{ij} capital goods. Burmeister's matrix $\mathbf{A}(0)$ has no similarly obvious technical interpretation.

However, I can provide the following black-box interpretation for Burmeister's (7.3) relations.

First, in the steady state we observe that the system producing plateaux of $[C_j]$ requires plateaux of $[L_j]$. The observed steady-state ratios seen for the black box of inputs and outputs obey

$$L_j/C_j = A_{0j}(0), \quad (j=1,\ldots,n). \qquad (7.12\text{a})$$

Second, there must permanently be provided for the steady-state system, at the beginning of each and every period, stocks of capital goods (that are being permanently maintained, as their depreciations are matched by new productions):

$$[K_{ij}/C_j] = \mathbf{A}(0) = [A_{ij}(0)]. \qquad (7.12\text{b})$$

To the observer of the black box, who eschews looking into the time-phased technical processes actually going on, all the physical relations and — what is more surprising, all the dual-price relations — look exactly *as if* the system was generated by the following permanent-capital-goods technology:

$$C_j(t+1)+\sum_{i=1}^{n} K_{ji}(t+1)-\sum_{i=1}^{n} K_{ji}(t)$$
$$=\text{Min}\,[L_j/A_{0j}(0), K_{1j}(t)/A_{1j}(0),\ldots, K_{nj}(t)/A_{nj}(0)], \quad (7.13)$$
$$(j=1,\ldots,n).$$

Its steady-state relations would have to be

$$C_j=\text{Min}\,[L_j/A_{0j}(0)\ \ldots, K_{nj}/A_{nj}(0)], \quad (j=1,\ldots,n) \quad (7.14\text{a})$$
$$=L_j/A_{0j}(0)=\ldots=K_{nj}/A_{nj}(0) \quad (7.14\text{b})$$
$$\mathbf{P}=\mathbf{WA}_0(0)(1+R)+\mathbf{PRA}(0) \quad (7.14\text{c})$$
$$=\mathbf{WA}_0(0)(1+R)[\mathbf{I}-\mathbf{A}(0)R]^{-1}. \quad (7.14\text{d})$$

The identity between (7.14d) and (7.3) confirms that the phantom Black-Box Production Functions do generate the actual steady-state observed price relations and dual-quantity relations. In § 9 we shall see how singular to exponential depreciation is this serendipitous black-box property.

8. Defining the Standard Commodity

Now we are in a position quickly to generalize the concept of Sraffa's "Standard Commodity" for the case of durable goods subject to exponential depreciation. When $d_{ij}\equiv 1$, the nondurable case, Burmeister (1968) showed that a's dominant positive characteristic (column) vector, $\mathbf{x}^*$, provides the requisite weights for Sraffa's Standard Commodity — which exists even when price ratios are not invariant to R.

For a non-negative and indecomposable, $\mathbf{x}^*$ is uniquely defined by

$$\mathbf{a}\,\mathbf{x}^*=(1+R^*)^{-1}\,\mathbf{x}^*>0, \quad (8.1\text{a})$$
$$\mathbf{a}_0\,[\mathbf{I}-\mathbf{a}]^{-1}\,\mathbf{x}^*=1, \text{ normalization convention} \quad (8.1\text{b})$$

It is well known that (8.1) implies that the real wage (paid postfactum, at the end of the period) in terms of the *standard* market basket is linearly related to the profit rate:

$$(1+R)\,W/\mathbf{P}\,\mathbf{x}^*=1-(R/R^*). \quad (8.2)$$

Now, with exponential durability, in (8.1)—(8.2), we replace $\mathbf{a}_0$ by $\mathbf{A}_0(0)$, **a** by $\mathbf{A}(0)$, and $\mathbf{x}^*$ by $\mathbf{X}^*$. For **a** indecomposable and productive, $\mathbf{A}(0)$ is positive, and $\mathbf{X}^*$ satisfies

$$R^* \mathbf{A}(0) \mathbf{X}^* = \mathbf{X}^* > 0, \tag{8.3}$$

Multiplying both sides of (7.14c) by the column vector $\mathbf{X}^*/(1+R)$, and using (8.3), we get the desired generalization of Sraffa's Standard Commodity

$$\mathbf{A}_0(0) \mathbf{X}^* = 1 \tag{8.4}$$

$$(1+R)\, W/\mathbf{PX}^* = 1/\mathbf{A}_0(\mathbf{R})\, \mathbf{X}^* (1+R)^{-1} = 1-(R/R^*). \tag{8.5}$$

Remark: If *global* price-ratio invariance obtains, then (as at the end of § 6) reswitching is not possible. This for the reason that straight lines intersect but once.

When *some* price ratio(s), P_j/P_i, are invariant to changes in R, even though Sraffa's $\mathbf{X}^*$ in (8.1) is unique, the set of vectors $(\mathbf{X}^1, \mathbf{X}^2, \ldots)$ whose real wage, $(1+R)\, W/\mathbf{PX}$, is linear in R will contain more than $\mathbf{X}^*$. What Miyao (1977) states about the rank of his defined "labor profile" matrix, $\mathbf{K} = [\mathbf{a}_0 \mathbf{a}^i]$, can be said in the durable good case about the rank of $[\mathbf{A}_0(0)\, \mathbf{A}(0)^i]$.

Thus, in the case of $(P_1/W, P_2/W, P_3/W)$, we can state sufficient conditions for invariance of P_1/P_2 — even though P_3/P_1 varies with R. We apply Miyao-like conditions to $[A_{0j}(0), A_{ij}(0)]$ ratios.

9. Non-Exponential Depreciation: Perfect Current Substitutability Model

How robust are the results for exponential depreciation when actual systems realistically involve forces of depreciation that depend on the equipment's age in ways that are not present in the exponential-depreciation case? As will be shown in the present section, only exponential depreciation gives beautiful generalizations. The general logic of price formation still applies, but now the conditions for price-ratio invariance become very strict indeed. And now in general, there exists no Standard Commodity in Sraffa's desired sense.

It will suffice to consider the next simplest case, after the non-durable and the exponential depreciation cases. The next simplest case involves each K_{ij} tool of age $0, 1, \ldots, \theta, \theta+1, \ldots$ giving rise to a surviving fraction of tools 1 period older of respective amounts

$$\alpha_{ij}{}^0 = 1 \geq \alpha_{ij}{}^1 \geq \alpha_{ij}{}^2 \geq \ldots \geq \alpha_{ij}{}^M > 0 \equiv \alpha_{ij}{}^{M+k}. \tag{9.1}$$

Any tool of whatever age is assumed to have exactly the same current productivity as at any other age. The common gross rental rate of one-period use of the tool is U_{ij} at all ages, where U_{ij} is related to P_i so that a new tool's present-discounted-value, of its future gross rentals, just equals its price of production when new:

$$P_i = U_{ij}\,[1+\alpha_{ij}^{1}\,(1+R)^{-1}+\ldots+\alpha_{ij}^{M}\,(1+R)^{-M}] \qquad (9.2)$$

$$U_{ij}\sum_{\theta=0}^{M}\alpha_{ij}^{\theta}\,(1+R)^{-\theta-1} = U_{ij}/[d_{ij}\{R\}+R] \qquad (9.3)$$

where $d_{ij}\{R\}$ is defined as

$$d_{ij}\{R\} = [\sum_{\theta=0}^{M}\alpha_{ij}^{\theta}\,(1+R)^{-\theta-1}]^{-1}-R. \qquad (9.4)$$

Under exponential depreciation $d_{ij}\{R\}$ is a constant, with

$$\alpha_{ij}^{\theta}=(1-d_{ij})^{\theta},\quad \sum_{0}^{\infty}\alpha_{ij}^{\theta}\,(1+R)^{-\theta}=(1+R)\,(d_{ij}+R)^{-1} \qquad (9.5)$$

$$d_{ij}\{R\}\equiv d_{ij}. \qquad (9.5')$$

Now the simpler pricing equations of (1.1) and (5.6) become the more complicated ones of

$$P_j = Wa_{0j}\,(1+R)+\sum_{i=1}^{n}U_{ij}a_{ij}\,(1+R) \qquad (9.6)$$

$$= Wa_{0j}\,(1+R)+\sum_{i=1}^{n}P_i a_{ij}\,(d_{ij}\{R\}+R). \qquad (9.7)$$

Thus,

$$\mathbf{P} = W\mathbf{a}_0\,(1+R)\,[\mathbf{I}-a_{ij}d_{ij}\{R\}-a_{ij}R]^{-1}>0. \qquad (9.8)$$

It is understood that the system is "productive", in the sense that $[\mathbf{I}-a_{ij}d_{ij}\{0\}]$ satisfies Hawkins-Simon conditions and that every good requires some labor as an input (directly or indirectly). Then every element of the real price vector $\mathbf{P}/W$ decreases as R rises; and, if $a_{ij}d_{ij}\{0\}$ is indecomposable, at some critical positive R^* all real wage rates, W/P_j, vanish.

The conditions for invariance with respect to R of $\mathbf{P}/P_1$ now become stricter. None of our previous theorems, old and new, remain validly applicable. It will suffice to illustrate for the 2-good case how restrictive the conditions for price invariance now become.

We have from (9.6)—(9.8)

$$\frac{P_2}{P_1}=\frac{a_{02}-a_{02}a_{11}\,(d_{11}\{R\}+R)+a_{01}a_{12}\,(d_{12}\{R\}+R)}{a_{01}-a_{01}a_{22}\,(d_{22}\{R\}+R)+a_{02}a_{21}\,(d_{21}\{R\}+R)} \tag{9.9}$$

If all 4 survival vectors

$$[\alpha_{ij}{}^{\theta}]=[1,\alpha_{ij}{}^{1}],\quad M=1 \tag{9.10}$$

involve different $\alpha_{ij}{}^1$ coefficients, the right hand side of (9.8) will involve 5 linearly independent functions of R, and (9.9) cannot be an identity in R.

If $d_{11}\{R\}$ and $d_{22}\{R\}$ involve a common set of α's, at the same time that $d_{12}\{R\}$ and $d_{21}\{R\}$ involve a *different* common set of α's, then it is necessary and sufficient for price-ratio invariance that

$$a_{11}=a_{22}\left(\frac{a_{02}}{a_{01}}\right)^2=\frac{a_{12}}{a_{21}} \tag{9.11}$$

Or, if $d_{11}\{R\}$ and $d_{12}\{R\}$ involve common α's, while $d_{21}\{R\}$ and $d_{22}\{R\}$ involve another set of common α's, then (9.11)'s condition is replaced by

$$\frac{a_{02}}{a_{01}}=\frac{a_{12}}{a_{11}}=\frac{a_{22}}{a_{21}} \tag{9.12}$$

Of course, if all $d_{ij}\{R\}$ involve the same common set of α's, we are back to the criterion of (4.6) and (5.7)

$$\sum_{i=1}^{n}(P_i/W)\,a_{ij}/a_{0j}=\lambda. \tag{9.13}$$

Warning: No simple Black-Box production function can adequately generate the observable steady-state quantity and dual-price relationships now that we've gone beyond the singular case of exponential depreciation. At different R levels, the observed real prices are more complicated polynomials of $(1+R)$ than the polynomials of the nondurable models and of Burmeister's exponential-depreciation surrogates.

Using the convenient abbreviating notation,

$$Ex=x\,(t+1),\qquad E^{-\theta}\,x=x\,(t-\theta)$$

we can summarize the time-phased production function of the present system by

$$EQ_j=\text{Min}\,[L_j/a_{0j},\ \sum_{\theta=0}^{M}\alpha_{ij}{}^{\theta}\,E^{-\theta}\,Q_{1j}/a_{1j},\ldots,\ \sum_{\theta=0}^{M}\alpha_{nj}\,E^{-\theta}\,Q_{nj}/a_{nj}] \tag{9.14}$$
$$=EC_j+\sum_{i=1}^{n}EQ_{ij},\qquad (j=1,\ldots,n).$$

When the system is in balanced growth proportional to $(1+g)^t$

$$(Q_j, Q_{ij}, C_j, L) = (1+g)^t (q_j, q_{ij}, c_j, l), \qquad (9.15)$$

(9.15) implies the linear relations

$$\sum_{j=1}^{n} a_{ij} (d_{ij}\{g\}+g) = q_i - c_i, \qquad (i=1, \ldots, n) \qquad (9.16)$$

$$(1+g) \sum_{j=1}^{n} a_{0j} q_j = l$$

$$\mathbf{q} = [I - a_{ij} (d_{ij}\{g\}+g)]^{-1} \, \mathbf{c}, \qquad g < R^* \qquad (9.17)$$

$$l = a_0 (1+g) [I - a_{ij} (d_{ij}\{g\}+g)]^{-1} c = \mathbf{A}_0 \, (\mathbf{g}) \, \mathbf{c}. \qquad (9.18)$$

For a indecomposable, R^* will be finite; and, if the system is "productive" (capable of growth), R^* will be positive and will satisfy

$$[a_{ij} (d_{ij}\{R^*\}+R^*)] \, \mathbf{X}^* = \mathbf{X}^* > 0 \qquad (9.19)$$

$$\mathbf{P}^* \, [a_{ij} (d_{ij}\{R^*\}+R^*)] = \mathbf{P}^* > 0. \qquad (9.20)$$

The price relations that competitive arbitrage will impose on such a technology are given by (9.8)

$$\mathbf{P} = W\mathbf{a}_0 (1+R) [I - a_{ij} (d_{ij}\{R\}+R)]^{-1}, \qquad R \le R^*.$$

The present general case shows how remarkable and singular it was that the Burmeister Black Box production functions could be fabricated for the case of exponential depreciation. In the general case, the input/output ratios observed for the stationary state *cannot* permit one to infer the technological and pecuniary relations that will prevail for different $(1+g)^t$ growth rates or for different $1+R$ interest rates.

Moreover, with depreciation non-exponential, *no Sraffa Standard Commodity exists.* As shown in (9.19)—(9.20) the dual von Neumann quantity and price vectors, $\mathbf{X}^*$ and $\mathbf{P}^*$, exist; but the real wage, $(1+R)\, W/\mathbf{PX}^*$, is no longer linear: i. e., the following is not linear

$$(1+R)\, W/\mathbf{PX}^* = \frac{1+R}{\mathbf{A}_0\, (\mathbf{R})\, \mathbf{X}^*} \qquad (9.21)$$

Only when the elements $a_{ij} (d_{ij}\{R\}+R)$ are all linear in R will the Sraffa trick generally work. The reader can verify this by considering the case where $n=1$, and where the factor-price frontier is necessarily *non*-linear when $\alpha_{11}{}^1 > 0 = \alpha_{11}{}^2$. One minor implication of the non-existence of a Standard Commodity is the possibility of reswitching even when global price-ratio invariance obtains.

Is all this disturbing? Not really. Sraffa's Standard Commodity is seen on reflection to be without economic interest. As soon as more than one technical option becomes competitively viable, it loses existence. As soon as we leave the classroom and meet real world tools that depreciate differently when old than when new, the Standard Commodity ceases to exist. And really no loss. For Sraffa's Standard Commodity never helped with any *real-world* problem*. In order to grapple with one of Ricardo's hopeless attempts to save the face of the labor theory of value as misapplied to a time-phased system, Sraffa elaborated his notion of a Standard Commodity.

My own response would be to cut Ricardo's losses if David Ricardo himself didn't muster the good sense to do so. The fact that Ronald Meek (1967) and some others have tried to use the Standard Commodity to save the face for Marx's model of uniform rates of surplus value by the different industries is not in my view a valid reason to mourn the news that the Standard Commodity doesn't exist even in a one-technique world of realistic durability. If Karl Marx would not cut *his* losses, objective Marxists and non-Marxists have the necessity to do it for him.

Using letters v_j or V_j to stand for direct wage outlays (so-called "variable capital") and c_j or C_j to stand for used-up capital (so-called "constant capital"), we write down the familiar notations

$$c_j + v_j + s_j = c_j + v_j + r v_j, \quad \text{values} \tag{9.22}$$

$$C_j + V_j + S_j = C_j + V_j + R\,[\text{Capital}_j], \quad \text{prices} \tag{9.23}$$

I can write down what (9.1)—(9.8) now imply for these.

For "values", we write

$$c_j + v_j + r v_j = \sum_{i=1}^{n} p_i a_{ij} d_{ij}\{0\}\, Q_j + w a_{0j} Q_j + r w a_{0j} Q_j = p_i Q_j \tag{9.24}$$

$$(j = 1, \ldots, n)$$

$$[p_j/w] = (1+r)\,\mathbf{a}_0\,[I - a_{ij} d_{ij}\{0\}]^{-1}. \tag{9.25}$$

---

* Morishima (1973, p. 142) properly points out that the formula, rate of profit $=$ rate of surplus value $\times \dfrac{\Sigma V_j}{\Sigma (V_j + C_j)}$ is valid in general only if $(V_j) = W\mathbf{a}_0\mathbf{x}^*$ and $(C_j) = \mathbf{Pax}^*$. However, when there exists no linear right-hand side to (9.21), the last factor will be seen not to capture the complications involved in the organic composition of capital.

For "prices", we have the unwieldly expression

$$C_j + V_j + S_j = C_j + V_j + R\ [\text{Capital}_j] = P_j Q_j$$
$$= \sum_{i=1}^{n} P_i a_{ij} d_{ij}\{0\} Q_j + W a_{0j} Q_j \tag{9.26}$$
$$+ R\left([W a_{0j} Q_j + \sum_{i=1}^{n} P_i a_{ij}] + R^{-1} \sum_{i=1}^{n} P_i a_{ij}\,(d_{ij}\{R\} - d_{ij}\{0\})\right)$$

That the final term is a monstrous melange of technical and compound-interest coefficients is not evidence for the inferiority of bourgeois prices in comparison to Marxian values. Its being a monstrosity is testimony to the lack of usefulness, in the general case, of Marx's peculiar splitup between "variable capital" and his defined "constant capital". Expense incurred to produce a commodity to pay labor needed in the past to produce this good's needed current non-labor input will, under competitive arbitrage, *already* involve an interest-profit markup; and, to ignore that element in one defined component of cost inevitably implies that you must take note of it in another component. As Joan Robinson reminds us, the capital scalar that "bears" interest is a complicated one. This of course means that the "transformation" from the irrelevant simplicity of (9.25) back to (9.26) is a detour through a swamp.

10. General Joint-Production Complexities

Primarily by assuming that each old tool is merely a smaller number of new tools, being otherwise technically *exactly* the same, was the previous section able to sidestep the *intrinsic complexities* of jointness of production introduced by durability of equipment. Realistically, *durability can be expected to force us into the domain of inequalities* and out of the simplicities of the Non-Substitution theorem.

The realistic phenomena of joint products and durability of capital goods have effects not easy to summarize in simple terms. As soon as we leave the singular cases of circulating capital and of exponential depreciation, we lose the existence of a Standard Commodity. In general — but not in every case, as seen in Samuelson (1959, Eq. (22); 1981, Eqs. (A-14) and (A-15)) — we also lose the validity of the Non-Substitution theorem. When prices of goods, including prices of new (and old) tools, are not determinable solely from knowledge of the R profit rate, the W money wage, and the laws of technology, *independently* of the pattern of final demand, it is bootless to look for the singular conditions under which P_i/P_j are unaffected by changes in R.

It does, however, make sense to look for a more general kind of price ratio invariance. Thus, for final demands that are independent of the profit rate — as when we always spend the same fractions of income on each of 2 goods — one might inquire when P_2/P_1 will be invariant with respect to R.

An example will illustrate. Consider the time-phased joint-production model

$$[C_1\,(t+1)^2 + C_2\,(t+1)^2]^{1/2} = L\,(t). \tag{10.1}$$

For steady states in which demands react to prices so as to maximize a homothetic $u\,[C_1, C_2]$ that is independent of R, changes in R will have no effect on P_2/P_1. This is in contrast to a more general case, such as

$$[C_1\,(t+1)^2 + C_2\,(t+2)^2]^{1/2} = L\,(t) \tag{10.2}$$

where P_2/P_1 rises as R grows.

As applied to durable capital goods, we must be prepared to find such final demand contaminations, particularly when new and old tools are not perfect technical substitutes. An example shows how special this paper's models have been in virtue of their obeying the Non-Substitution theorem. Suppose 1 unit of consumer good C_1 requires as input a period earlier 1 new tool and 1 unit of labor. The old tool that is produced as a byproduct of this first industry can, with the aid of 2 units of labor, produce 2 units of a new tool or 2 units of a second consumer good C_2.

Then, without knowing the steady-state intensity of final consumer demand for C_1 and C_2, we cannot for given R determine what will be P_2/P_1 or $(P_1/W_1, P_2/W)$. The time-phased technology obeys

$$C_1\,(t+1) = \text{Min}\,[L_1\,(t), K\,(t)] \tag{10.3}$$
$$C_2\,(t+1) + K\,(t+1) = \text{Min}\,[L_2\,(t)/{}^1/_2,\ J\,(t)/{}^1/_2]$$
$$J\,(t+1) = K\,(t)$$

where K is the level of new tools and J the level of used tools.

Given knowledge of the profit rate R, we cannot determine a unique steady-state value for P_2/P_1 independently of the demand intensities for C_1 versus C_2. By making tastes definite, as for example by assuming the positive fractions $(\alpha_1, 1-\alpha_1)$ are spent on C_1 and C_2 respectively, there will result a determinate steady-state price ratio:

$$P_2/P_1 = f\,(R;\,\alpha_1). \tag{10.4}$$

Neither partial derivative of $f()$ vanishes. Therefore, the general moral is this:

The concept of equal organic compositions of capital becomes an ambiguous one in general realistic cases, even though certain symmetric patterns can still singularly occur.

11. Conclusion

It has been shown that the simplicities of the nondurable Leontief-Sraffa model can for the most part be preserved so long as durability obeys the strict laws of exponential depreciation that is independent of a tool's age. But, as soon as the real world fails to obey the strict rules of this fairy tale, Sraffian Standard Commodities fail to exist and the conditions for price-ratio invariance at all profit rates become both complicated and restrictive.

The complexities are in the nature of things, not a fabrication of the equilibrium analyst. Only the modern paradigm of general equilibrium — as begun by Smith and Ricardo and as improved by Walras, Fisher, Pareto, Dimitriev, von Bortkiewicz, von Neumann, Debreu, Arrow, Leontief, and Sraffa — can do justice to the realities of technology and arbitrage.

References

E. Burmeister (1968): On a Theorem of Sraffa, Economica N. S. *35*, pp. 83—87.

E. Burmeister and A. R. Dobell (1970): Mathematical Theories of Economic Growth, London.

L. von Bortkiewicz (1906, 1970): Wertrechnung und Preisrechnung im Marxschen System, Archiv für Sozialwissenschaft und Sozialpolitik *23* (1906), pp. 1—50, *55* (1907) pp. 10—51, 445—488; reprinted in English under the title "Value and Price in the Marxian System", International Economic Papers 2 (1952), pp. 5—60.

V. K. Dimitriev (1974): Economic Essays on Value, Competition, and Utility, London.

N. Georgescu-Roegen (1951): The Aggregate Linear Production Function and Its Applications to von Neumann's Economic Model, *in:* T. C. Koopmans (ed.): Activity Analysis of Production and Allocation, New York, pp. 98—115.

R. Meek (1961): Mr. Sraffa's Rehabilitation of Classical Economics, Scottish Journal of Political Economics *8*, pp. 119—136; reprinted in R. Meek: Economics and Ideology and Other Essays. Studies in the Development of Economic Thought, London 1967, pp. 143—157.

T. Miyao (1977): A Generalization of Sraffa's Standard Commodity and Its Complete Characterization, International Economic Review *18*, pp. 151—162.

M. Morishima (1973): Marx's Economics — A Dual Theory of Value and Growth, London.

J. von Neumann (1937): Über ein ökonomisches Gleichungssystem und eine Verallgemeinerung des Brouwerschen Fixpunktsatzes, Ergebnisse eines Mathematischen Kolloquiums *8*, pp. 73—83; reprinted in English under the title "A Model of General Economic Equilibrium", Review of Economic Studies *13* (1945), pp. 1—9.

P. A. Samuelson (1951): Abstract of a Theorem Concerning Substitutability in Open Leontief Models, *in:* T. C. Koopmans (ed.): Activity Analysis of Production and Allocation, New York, pp. 142—146; reprinted in J. E. Stiglitz (ed.): The Collected Scientific Papers of Paul A. Samuelson, Vol. 1, Cambridge, Mass. 1966, pp. 515—519.

P. A. Samuelson (1959): A Modern Treatment of the Ricardian Economy: II. Capital and Interest Aspects of the Pricing Process, The Quarterly Journal of Economics *73*, pp. 217—231; reprinted in J. E. Stiglitz (ed.): The Collected Scientific Papers of Paul A. Samuelson, Vol. 1, Cambridge, Mass. 1966, pp. 408—422.

P. A. Samuelson (1971): Understanding the Marxian Notion of Exploitation: A Summary of the So-Called Transformation Problem Between Marxian Values and Competitive Prices, Journal of Economic Literature *9*, pp. 399—431; reprinted in R. C. Merton (ed.): The Collected Scientific Papers of Paul A. Samuelson, Vol. 3, Cambridge, Mass. 1972, pp. 276—307.

P. A. Samuelson (1981): Marx Without Matrixes: Understanding the Rate of Profit, forthcoming in P. Desai (ed.): Festschrift for Alexander Ehrlich.

P. Sraffa (1960): The Production of Commodities by Means of Commodities, Cambridge.

Address of author: Prof. Paul A. Samuelson, Massachusetts Institute of Technology, Department of Economics, Cambridge, MA 02139, U. S. A.

Printed in Austria

PART III

International Economics

A CORRECTED VERSION OF HUME'S EQUILIBRATING MECHANISMS FOR INTERNATIONAL TRADE*

PAUL A. SAMUELSON

1. Introduction

David Hume put to rest in 1752 the fear that free international trade will drain a nation of its money. His doctrine of how an outflow of specie is self-correcting and eventually equilibrating still prevails in our textbooks and treatises after more than two centuries and is still appealed to in our definitive policy debates.

But, actually, Hume's account is both wrong and incomplete. If incompleteness were its only fault, that would be a forgivable blemish in an early masterpiece. Hume's classical followers – Ricardo and Mill, if not Adam Smith – could have been expected to fill in the gaps in Hume's brief exposition. But they did not. Nor did such modern giants as Haberler or Viner do so, though both these authors show clearly that they perceived a need to modify Hume's own syllogisms. And Ohlin, who deserves credit for emphasizing that transfer payments from one country to another will shift demand schedules in both places, did not rectify the classical mechanism that he hoped to supplement with his own innovations.

Never underestimate the blinding power of a beautiful mistake. Hume's inadequate analysis, both because of its brilliant simplicity and its obvious nearness to a correct truth, so satisfied the economists who followed him that they felt no need to provide correct alternative explanations. When Jacob Frenkel and Harry Johnson tried to puff up the case for something they called "the monetary approach to the balance of payments," they cited David Hume as one of its many precursors. But a line-by-line reading of Hume's essay "Of the

*I owe thanks to the National Science Foundation for financial aid, and to Aase Huggins for editorial assistance.

Balance of Trade" will demonstrate that—however close Gervaise, Longfield, Mill, Cairnes, and some other writers had come to the direct effects of money supply on demand-at-unchanged-prices in their momentary *deviations* from mainstream foreign-trade theory—David Hume's treatment of specie flows managed to miss completely that key element.[1]

Once we are alerted to Hume's sins of commission and omission, it is an easy exercise to assign to a modern analyst. Provide a correct version of what Hume sought: a self-equilibrating model of the balance of payments that recognizes the unity of price for competitive goods freely transportable in international trade.

This exercise I propose to provide here—with impressionistic brevity.

2. What Hume said

Here are quotations, selective but complete so far as logic is concerned.

> . . . there still prevails . . . in nations . . . a strong jealousy with regard to the balance of trade, and a fear that all their gold and silver may be leaving them. This seems to me, almost in every case, a groundless apprehension; . . .
>
> Suppose four-fifths of all the money in Great Britain to be annihilated in one night . . . Must not the price of all labour and commodities sink in proportion, and everything be sold as cheap [as in earlier days when *M* was one-fifth]? . . . What nation could then dispute with us in any foreign market, or pretend to navigate or to sell manufactures at the same price, which to us would afford sufficient profit? In how little time, therefore, must this bring back the money which we had lost, and raise us to the level of all the neighbouring nations? Where, after we have arrived, we immediately lose the advantage of the cheapness of labour and commodities; and the farther flowing in of money is stopped by our fullness and repletion. [When *M* rises, the opposite happens.]
>
> . . . Now, it is evident, that the same causes, which would correct these exorbitant inequalities, . . . must preserve money nearly proportionable to the art and industry of each nation. All water, wherever it communicates, remains always at a level . . .
>
> [Similarly, Hume asserts,] it is impossible to heap up money, more than any fluid, beyond its proper level . . .
>
> How is the balance kept [internally] in the provinces of every kingdom among themselves, but by the force of this principle, which makes it impossible for money to lose its level, and either to rise or sink beyond the proportion of labour and commodities which are in each province?[2]

[1] See G. Haberler (1936), J. Viner (1937), B. Ohlin (1933); also J. Frenkel and H. G. Johnson (1974). The latter do give a quotation from another Hume essay, "Of the Jealousy of Trade," but the words cited there do not deal with the essential element of the *money stock's* direct effect on ceteris paribus demand, as stressed for example in Prais (1961), J. J. Polak (1957) or R. Dornbusch (1973).

[2] These quotations are from Hume's 1752 essay "Of the Balance of Trade," and are taken from E. Rotwein, ed., *David Hume: Writings on Economics* (London: Nelson, 1955), pp. 61–5. Hume's essay that follows, "Of the Jealousy of Trade," has no words on the equilibrating macroeconomic mechanism, but does make the nice point that diversity among nations will assure that our nation has [what we would call] comparative advantage in some goods. Hume's April, 1749 correspondence with Montesquieu, Rotwein (1955, pp. 188–9), covers no new ground; his exchange of 1750 with

Now to put Hume in crudest equation form. Let P stand for gold price(s) at home, P^* for price(s) abroad; M^* stands for their (gold) money supply, M for our gold supply; Q and Q^* for the total outputs at home and abroad. Finally, ignoring capital movements, let B be the (algebraic) gold value of our balance of trade—the surplus of our exports over our imports if positive, our deficit if negative.

Crudely put, here is a version of Hume's paradigm:

$$B = f[P/P^*], \quad \frac{df[\;]}{d(P/P^*)} < 0; \tag{1}$$

$$P = kM = (\gamma/Q)M, \quad P^* = k^*M^* = (\gamma/Q^*)M^*; \tag{2}$$

$$\frac{dM}{dt} = -\frac{dM^*}{dt} = B = f[P/P^*]; \tag{3}$$

$$M + M^* = \mu, \text{ the world supply of specie.} \tag{4}$$

Equation (2) states the Quantity Theory of Prices in crudest one-nation form. Equation (3) is the definitional form of the balance of payments or trade when specie is alone used to settle deficits: you lose M^* to us, $-dM^*/dt = B$, when we enjoy a trade surplus of B.

Equation (1) states what Hume regarded as obvious without worrying his head about inelasticities of net demand that violate so-called Marshall–Lerner conditions. As will be seen, this first relation is vitiated by the fact that the same good must have the same price everywhere in a competitive world without transport costs.[3]

Oswald (Rotwein, 1955, pp. 190–199), needlessly denies Oswald's valid point that our P's never rise as much as M alone does, precisely because we are an open trading economy.

Hume (Rotwein, 1955, p. 64, n.1), also has an acute footnote recognizing the equilibrating effect for a deficit country of the depreciation of its exchange rate down to the export *gold point* set by cost of "carriage and insurance" of the specie used as money. He also recognizes that transport costs make possible limited deviations between a good's competitive prices in two places a distance apart. Hume's words show he would understand there being a different water level at the two ends of the Panama Canal; since they are so far apart, the slight friction associated with distance accumulates to a sizable deviation in their equilibrium levels. My exposition will first assume zero transport costs for gold M and for *all* goods. Then I introduce nontraded goods, or goods that trade only when their transport costs are matched by their spatial price differentials. Finally, I briefly treat the case of inconvertible moneys—paper acceptable only at home, or M stuffs so nontransportable as never to enter into international exchange.

[3] It won't help to interpret P and P^* as vectors of prices:

$$P = (p_1, \ldots, p_n); \qquad P^* = (p_1^*, \ldots, p_n^*).$$

Then

$$B = f(P_1, \ldots, P_n; P_1^*, \ldots, P_n^*).$$

Were Hume to claim that raising *all* P_j^* fivefold while holding *all* P_j constant would raise B, we'd still have to ask how *any* P_j^* could stay above its respective P_j under free trade.

Let's give David Hume rope. For fixed total world gold, there is a unique equilibrium distribution of (M, M^*) implied by his system (1)–(4). Although Hume does not explicitly specify that trade balances when prices are equal, $P/P^* = 1$, suppose I do adjoin that relationship:

$$B = 0 = f[1], \qquad P/P^* = 1. \tag{1'}$$

Then in longest-term equilibrium

$$M(t) \to \frac{Q}{Q+Q^*}\mu, \qquad M^*(t) \to \frac{Q^*}{Q+Q^*}\mu, \tag{5}$$
$$B(t) \to 0, \quad P(t)/P^*(t) \to 1.$$

Proof. Substituting the Quantity Theory relations of (2) into (3) and writing $M^*(t)$ as $\mu - M(t)$, (3) becomes the self-correcting differential equation:

$$\frac{dM}{dt} = f\left[\frac{MQ^*}{(\mu - M)Q}\right]. \tag{6}$$

From any initial condition different from $M(\infty) = Q(Q+Q^*)^{-1}\mu$,

$$M(t) \to M(\infty).$$

Indeed, *penultimately*, $M(t) - M(\infty)$ decays away to zero exponentially at the same rate that $B(t)$ or any of the other deviations from equilibrium $[M^*(t) - M^*(\infty), P(t) - P(\infty), P^*(t) - P^*(\infty)]$ decay away to zero. This ultimate speed of adjusting depends of course on how rapidly each change in P/P^* corrects B —the quantitative strength of what some call the Marshall–Lerner criterion— and on how near to the same size are the two countries and are their equilibrium shares of world money supply.[4]

3. Where Davie nodded

As Schumpeter used to put it, we can applaud Hume's performance in specifying a self-correcting mechanism that impressed people for two hundred years. But 1980 is not 1752. And neither was 1900. Hume's model is defective.

To see why, recall a stupid point that is attributed to J. L. Laughlin, bowdlerizing editor of J. S. Mill and first chairman of the Chicago economics department. Laughlin objected, saying in effect:

[4] $M(t) - M(\infty)$ grows penultimately like ae^{-bt}, where

$$b = f'[1][(1/M_\infty) + (1/M^*_\infty)].$$

Note: If $B = 0$ at $f[\pi] = 0$, where $\pi = P_\infty / P^*_\infty$ is not unity, and if in (2) the countries' velocities of circulation are not the same so that on the right γ must be replaced by γ^*, then the formulas in (5) will require obvious modifications. Hume would not be surprised once we called his attention to these possible complications.

In these modern times of cable and quick transport, the specie-flow corrective mechanisms no longer work. Prices of the same goods are virtually *instantaneously* equilibrated. So it's quite impossible for Great Britain's prices to go down by Hume's postulated four-fifths to thereby restore Britain's dearth of M.

We speak of Laughlin's Fallacy. Orthodox writers, such as Haberler and Viner, refute Laughlin with words like the following:

Professor [J.] L. Laughlin has objected that between modern markets which are connected by railroads, telegraph, telephone, etc., price differentials cannot exist long enough to produce sufficiently large movements of goods. This criticism of the classical doctrine can be disposed of by pointing out that modern means of communication equalise prices by inducing transactions between the cheap and dear market; far from being an objection, this statement calls attention to circumstances which make for a rapid functioning of the mechanism. (Haberler, 1936, p. 29)

When, therefore, critics of the classical theory [like Laughlin, 1903] have taken it to task on the ground that it explained the adjustment of international balances by the influence on the course of trade of divergent market prices in different markets of identical [freely] transportable commodities, . . . they have misinterpreted the classical doctrine.

. . . It is relative changes in *supply* prices of identical commodities as between different potential sources of supply, and, above all, relative changes in the actual sales prices of *different* commodities which, through their influence on the direction and extent of trade, exercise a significant role in the mechanism of adjustment of international balances. (Viner, 1937, pp. 316–318)

Haberler and Viner are right to attack Laughlin, but that does not mean Laughlin's critique of the Hume mechanism of the last section misses *its* mark. If $P(t)$ and $P^*(t)$ must be identical, then Equations (1)–(4) are indeed falsified. In effect, Haberler and Viner are agreeing with my present contention that the Hume reasoning is fundamentally defective.

Curiously, as the reader thumbs through the Haberler and Viner texts, she does not find a simple and correct replacement for the defective Hume exposition. To get that alternative, you must infer from between the lines how such a complete account would go. Arnold Collery (1974) has persuaded me that there remains a gap in Viner's exposition. To fill it, you would have to go to the advanced treatise by Viner's student, Jacob Mosak (1944). And even there you will not find the dynamic non-neutral-money adjustments that Frenkel and Johnson (1976) now emphasize shrilly.

Moreover, the Laughlin fallacy still lives, propagating with the vigor of a weed. It could as well be called the Laffer fallacy, or the Wall Street Journal fallacy.

Worse than that. Turn to the advanced modern rebuttals of what is essentially the Laughlin fallacy. You will be a lucky reader if you do not find yourself fobbed off with both or one of the following sophisticated fallacies:

Non-traded goods fallacy. It is by differential movements of 2 countries' nontraded goods' price levels, relative to their necessarily equal price levels of freely traded goods, that we save the faulty Hume mechanism and prove the stability and self-correction of the international trade mechanism. This is alleged to be especially applicable to small, open economies.

Terms-of-trade fallacy. It is not the lowering of price(s) in the deficit country relative to the respective prices in the surplus country of the identical tradeable good(s) that restores equilibrium. What accomplishes the essential equilibrium is the lowering of the price(s) and price level of the deficit country's export goods, relative to the price(s) and price level of the surplus country's export goods—at least this effects the equilibration if the Marshall–Lerner criterion is not perverse.

Neither of these rebuttals is correct logically or applicable in certain important empirical cases. Instead, I shall show:

1. Even with no changes in any relative or absolute prices—here or abroad, between tradeable and nontradeable goods, between export and import goods—a properly reformulated Hume model can be shown to be self-correcting and stable. This can be independent of the Marshall–Lerner criterion, whose importance has to do with microeconomic not macroeconomic stability.
2. If there are zero nontradeable goods, if transport costs and trade impediments are made to shrink to zero, the efficacy and speed of the monetary adjustment is preserved and not emasculated, and indeed may even be *accelerated*.

My words will shock some sophisticated readers. But that is only confirmatory to my charge that the fallacious Hume account has been so seductively plausible as to have eclipsed serious correct analysis. It is a scandal that, as late as 1937, Joan Robinson (1937, pp. 183–209) had to demonstrate that the terms of trade may go either way when a country depreciates its currency and thereby successfully restores micro-equilibrium of the Bickerdike (1920) model. And I do not know where, prior to the exposition of Dornbusch, Fischer, and Samuelson (1977, p. 836) there appeared explicitly in print a demonstration where gold flows *heal themselves faster when zero money is spent on nontradeable goods* than when much is spent on nontradeable items.

A digression. I fault Hume only on his fundamentals. I view as but a venial sin Hume's vagueness concerning his analogy between the equilibrium levels of M and M^* and the common level of water in communicating lakes or vessels. Ignoring friction, I can assert that water in two tubes settles at *identical heights*. That is different from saying, "A rope hanging in its equilibrium shape of a catenary has its parts at *different* heights." What is common in these last cases is the physicist's perception that a self-regulating physical process is involved in each case (and, as it happens, both cases can be subsumed under the principle that the statical equilibrium configuration is that which yields *minimum center of gravity* of the system subject to its constraints).

When I made $\gamma = \gamma^*$ in (2), I made the most favorable case for Hume, and for the notion he shared with such earlier writers as Malynes, Locke, Gervaise, and Cantillon—that M and M^* become respectively proportional to the economic sizes (populations, outputs) of the respective countries. Hume himself realized that a country could change its habits concerning the use of *paper* money and thereby alter γ relative to γ^* and thus affect ultimate M/M^* and make gold M/Q and gold M^*/Q^* be at different heights.

Gold's finding its proper geographical distribution by analogy with the way water finds its own level is merely a persuasive metaphor. If Hume had bothered to think the matter through, he'd have recognized that the analogy would have fit better if he likened the common price of wheat in two places to the common level of water in two places—a P rather than a Q or M analogy.

No later writers have been harmed by Hume's level-of-water analogy.

4. What Hume omitted

Along with the above-described errors of commission note an interesting Humean error of omission.

Hume fails to allow a drop in M to have direct contracting effects on our home country's spending. For him, it is only the changes in home prices relative to those abroad that brings about the healing increase in exports and the reduction in the imports of the deficit nation.

We could modify (1) in the manner of Prais (1961) and Dornbusch (1973) to make Hume more like what Frenkel and Johnson would like for him to have been. Now

$$B = f[P/P^*, M - M(\infty), M^* - M^*(\infty)], \tag{1''}$$

$$\frac{\partial B}{\partial(P/P^*)} < 0, \qquad \frac{\partial B}{\partial[M - M(\infty)]} < 0, \qquad \frac{\partial B}{\partial[M^* - M^*(\infty)]} > 0.$$

Now, even if P/P^* were somehow frozen at unity and (2) somehow relaxed in the short run, (1″) and (3) would constitute a stable, self-correcting mechanism that could work without regard to the Marshall–Lerner condition's determination of a perverse positive value for $\partial B/\partial(P/P^*)$. We could now write

$$\begin{aligned} dM/dt &= f[1, M - M(\infty), -M + M(\infty)], \\ 0 &= f[1, 0, 0], \\ M(t) &\to \frac{Q}{Q + Q^*}\,\mu, \\ M(t) - M(\infty) &\simeq e^{-bt}, \qquad \text{etc.} \end{aligned} \tag{6'}$$

However, rather than patch up the faulty Hume model, the time has come to sketch a correct model.

5. Equilibration sans price changes

Begin with the challenge of tradeable goods only. With zero tariffs and transport costs, the upper and lower "gold points" are only an infinitesimal distance apart and exchange rates can't deviate from their parities. The same holds for all goods: wheat, cloth, cars, ... Their competitive prices must always be exactly the same as a result of quick arbitrage alone:

$$P_j = P_j^*, \qquad (j = 1, 2, \ldots, J). \tag{7}$$

Only factor inputs are immobile between nations. The gold wage rates need not be equal: $W \gtreqless W^*$.

To sidestep the special problems involved in "capital" and time-phasing, if there be a second factor of production, let it be "land." The gold rents of immobile land need not be equal: $R \lesseqgtr R^*$.

Suppose we began in a Ricardian world of constant labor costs. If they were *uniformly* the same in both places, with no comparative advantages being involved, wage rates would be equalized and no profitable trade would occur.

There still would operate a self-correcting specie-flow mechanism. Here is how Hume should have formulated it.

Suppose we begin with twice our quota of world gold. Our initial excess of $M(0)$ will cause us in good Quantity Theory fashion to spend on consumption more than our incomes earned on production—as we try to work our excess money holdings towards their desired level. Abroad, their initial deficiency of $M^*(0)$ causes an opposite deficiency of consumption over output as they try to replenish their M^* balances over time. Short-run equilibrium involves an initial trade deficit, $B(0) < 0$ financed by an outflow of gold from us: $dM/dt = B(0) < 0$. So our $M(t) - M(\infty)$ is being corrected, and their deficiency $M^*(\infty) - M^*(t)$ is being corrected. The $-dM/dt$ hemorrhage ceases only when $[M(t), M^*(t)] \to [M(\infty), M^*(\infty)]$, their long-run normal values. If, as in the present case, the micro-model calls for no changes at all in relative (or even absolute) prices, that does not invalidate the self-correcting specie-flow mechanism.

The above would still hold in a world where, instead of all labor productivities being uniformly the same in all places, labor productivities were twice as great here as abroad so that our money and real wage rates were twice theirs. It would also be true in the more realistic case where we had comparative advantage in some goods and they in others. But now we must examine different cases.

(i) Suppose we *both* produce one of the goods, before the $[M(0), M^*(0)]$ initial disturbance, during the transition, and in the final permanent equilibrium. Then, even if we spend our increment of $M(0)$ differently from how they cut down on their spending, no price or wage changes will ever take place. But still the specie-flow correction works exactly as above.

(ii) Alternatively, suppose we produce goods $(1, 2, \ldots, r)$ and they produce goods $(r + 1, \ldots, J)$. If the switch of $M(0)$ to us, and of $M^*(0)$ away from them, results in our incremental spending going toward the same goods they now cut their spending on—a not implausible Ohlin case in a world of zero transport cost and nonlocalization of demand!—no absolute or relative price changes will be induced. So, again, the specie-flow mechanism does the whole job by itself.

(iii) It could be that our incremental spending goes more toward the goods in which they have a comparative advantage, and their cut in spending is more on our goods than theirs. If so, the initial $[M(0), M^*(0)]$ switch will have turned the terms of trade in their favor: initially, they'll have higher W^*/W than before. This may force us to produce some good $r+1$ or $r+k$, that previously they produced. So our products' prices will start a bit lower relative to their products' prices. ($P_1/P_J = P_1^*/P_J^*$ falls, but never does any P_j/P_j^* fall below unity!) This could add a bit to our initial trade deficit if the Marshall–Lerner conditions are "normal." So more specie will flow out initially. But still the self-correction sketched here will apply—even though money is not "neutral" in the transition phase, and *crude* purchasing-power-parity is violated since our weighted price level drops relative to theirs while exchange-rate parity never changes. Ultimately, gold gets relocated and the terms-of-trade revert to their long-run equilibrium level.

(iv) Finally, it could be that all the initial spending increments go more toward our goods $(1, 2, \ldots)$ than toward theirs. Then, W/W^* will be initially raised. Possibly we no longer produce good r previously produced. Our terms of trade have improved: $P_1/P_J = P_1^*/P_J^*$ rises by the gain in W/W^*. Under normal Marshall–Lerner conditions this subtracts from the size of our initial deficit. We have less initial rate of specie outflow and the transition to new equilibrium takes a bit longer. But the specie-flow mechanism is self-correcting.

Do all these reassuring results in the Ricardian world still hold in a neoclassical Ohlin-Haberler world of labor-cum-land? They do.

If labor/land endowments are close enough together and production-function knowledge the same in all regions, factor prices will be equalized. And through an initial $M(0)/\mu$ perturbation and subsequent correction, they will stay equalized. If our new spending generated by $M(t) - M(\infty)$ excess is directed toward the same goods their $M^*(\infty) - M^*(t)$ deficiency is withdrawn from, all absolute prices of goods and factors will be unaffected by the specie-flow corrections.

$$\frac{dM}{dt} \text{ has the opposite sign to } M(t) - M(\infty);$$
$$M(t) \to M(\infty) \text{ from any initial } M(0). \tag{8}$$

If technologies differ geographically, the same applies without necessary factor-price equalization.

If tastes are not the same at the margin in the different regions, then our $M(0)$ excess and its induced excess of consumption over income may alter the relative prices of the goods we export on balance relative to those we import. So the relative income share earned by the factor we are most abundantly endowed with may initially be perturbed and only gradually be restored to long-run equilibrium levels. Under normal Marshall–Lerner conditions,[5] there may be a slightly larger or smaller initial specie outflow, and a somewhat faster or slower period of adjustment of the self-correcting specie flow.

Warning: My corrected Hume model validates long-run purchasing-power-parity only in applications where the sole disturbance is in (M, M^*) stocks. In the short run, changes in these stocks need not be "neutral." Although P_j/P_j^* never deviates from unity set by zero transport costs and assumed gold-standard constancy of exchange rate, $P_{\text{export}}/P_{\text{import}}$ may change in either direction in the short run and so may any $P_i/P_j = P_i^*/P_j^*$ or W/W^* or Rent/Rent*. Furthermore, if the initial shock comes from something other than an $M/(M + M^*)$ perturbation, all bets are off concerning how some weighted $\sum P_j a_j$ behaves relative to some weighted $\sum P_j^* a_j^*$. With Cassel's bad example before them, why should zealots for the "monetary approach to the balance of payments" put his dunce's cap on their own heads?

6. Impediments to trade

Now I can dispose of the case on nontradeable goods, those with such heavy transport costs as to make them never exported or imported. More generally, with every good having some positive cost of transportation, it becomes an *endogenous* problem to deduce which will be traded and which will not be.

As Ricardo knew, one important reason why gold is used as money domestically and internationally is the fact that its transport costs are unimportant in comparison with those of most goods. I begin by assuming gold has virtually zero transport costs; the gold points virtually coincide, and exchange rate parities never deviate from par.

Now prices of the same goods can deviate from unity within the interval set by transport costs per unit:

$$-t_i^* \leqslant p_i - p_i^* \leqslant t_i, \qquad (i = 1, \ldots, J) \tag{9}$$

where t_i is the (gold) cost of moving a unit of good i from there to here, and t_i^* is the cost of moving it from here to there. These transport costs need not be equal; they need not be constants, but it will suffice here to treat them as given positive constants. (For gold, they are provisionally taken to be zero.)

In long-run equilibrium, those goods with very high t_i or t_i^*, relative to their disparities in comparative advantage and domestic costs of production, will be

[5] Dornbusch and Mussa (1975) have specified an optimal control model in which constancy of the consumption velocity of money is rationally derived. Even if we relax its strong assumptions, so long as an (algebraic) excessive M holding generates an excess of consumption spending over income, equilibrium will be stable.

produced and consumed within the same country. They won't be traded before or after a transitional disturbance. Any good that we do export, say good 1, will be at its "export point" where (9) becomes

$$p_1^* - p_1 = t_1^*.$$

Any good we do import, say good J, obeys (9) in the form of

$$P_J - P_J^* = t_j.$$

Some goods will have such disparities in geographical costs that they will continue to be traded in the same direction throughout the initial perturbation of $M(0)$ and the ensuing transition back to equilibrium. Some goods may cease to be traded and become nontradeable. Some that were nontradeable may now be forced into trade. And some goods may change the direction in which they are traded. All this comes about *endogenously* from the postulated disturbance and induced adjustment.

Even if we could assume that ultimate tastes are the same here and abroad and between rich and poor anywhere (so-called "uniform homothetic demand"), we must now expect transport costs to localize demand. An excess of $M(0)$ here in the California-gold discovery region must raise prices here more than abroad in Yorkshire. The price ratios for permanently nontradeable items, say P_k/P_k^*, are perturbed upward and only gradually recede to their normal long-run level. Now we Californians import goods we previously produced for ourselves as nontradeables: eggs are imported at dollars per egg, ice from abroad can be sold here. Hume and even Laughlin can agree than an index of less tradeable goods, $\sum P_k \alpha_k / \sum P_k^* \alpha_k$, will be bid up initially.

At the same time, easily tradeable goods keep their P_i/P_i^* near unity. So an index of them, relative to nontradeables, also rises: $\sum P_i a_i / \sum P_k a_k$ is perturbed upward and only gradually falls toward normalcy. We shift resources toward nontradeables, away from export goods. We substitute imports for home-produced goods where we can, running a trade deficit. But, to the degree that there are nontradeables whose prices can be bid up here, some of our excess consuming is offset by rises in our incomes and our trade deficit with abroad is thereby lessened.

Nontradeable goods, far from making the equilibration mechanism work, will if anything be presumed *to slow down* the correct version of the Hume specie-flow self-correction process (but not to the point of negating it).

Purchasing-power-parity will ultimately be restored if only an $M/(M^* + M)$ disturbance is involved and if that disturbance impinges on a system with but one micro equilibrium: this means that even an index number of nontradeables will return to its same level relative to an identically weighted index number abroad; this says no more than that, in a neutral-money world system, *every* price anywhere ends up in an exact proportion to world gold supply $\mu = M + M^*$!

During the transition, purchasing-power-parity must be false in the only form of it that experts consider to be useful. I.e., under a gold standard, index numbers of all prices inclusive of nontradeables, if compared geographically with *identical* (!) weights, show that the deficit country has an exchange rate higher than its calculated p-p-p rate. For a speculator to gamble that this will force the deficit country off the gold standard is just like betting that Saudi Arabia's prosperity will force *it* into a depreciation. (In real life, I find p-p-p valuable only if I don't apply it mechanically, but always try to allow for "substantive" changes in the *real* equilibrium relations.)

All this can be formalized. Thus, Dornbusch, Fischer and Samuelson (1977) showed that when we put into the differential equation for $M(t)$ a parameter depending on the percentage importance of nontradeable goods—call it δ—then the greater their importance the *slower* the process of self-correction. I.e.

$$-\frac{dM(t)}{M(t)\,dt} \rightarrow \text{constant that } \textit{diminishes} \text{ with } \delta. \tag{10}$$

In summary, the conventional defenses of Hume against himself and against the Laughlin fallacy are ill thought out, and are often 180° off in their references to the role of nontradeables in the adjustment mechanism.[6]

[6] Here is a mathematical example. Each good gets one-third of anyone's total expenditure. Consumption expenditure (in gold/period) is proportional to the respective holdings of our gold or your gold, M or M^*, with a velocity of $\frac{1}{5}$/period. It costs $(\frac{1}{2}, 1, 2)$ units of L here to produce 1 of (food, housing, clothing). It costs $(2, 1, \frac{1}{2})$ units of your L^* to produce those respective goods. Both labor supplies are equal, $L = L^*$.

With zero transportation costs, $M(\infty) = M^*(\infty) = \frac{1}{2}\mu$. $W(\infty) = W^*(\infty)$. $(P_1, P_2, P_3) = (P_1^*, P_2^*, P_3^*) = (\frac{1}{2}W, 1W = 1W^*, \frac{1}{2}W^*)$. Two-thirds of our L produces food, one-third produces housing. Two-thirds of your L^* produces clothing, one-third produces housing. We export half our food production, import half your clothing production, are self-sufficient in housing.

Now let our gold M double and your gold M^* not change. Eventually, we'll each end with half the 50%-larger world μ supply. Hume errs if he makes our P's initially double and your P^*'s stay the same. Actually, *all* world prices now go up by the 50% rise in μ. So do *both* wage rates. But now our total consumption, $\sum_1^3 P_j C_j$, rises by more than the 50% rise in the nominal value of our total production, $\sum_1^2 P_j Q_j = WL$; our consumption doubles in nominal terms, or by 50% in real terms. Thus, we run a trade deficit. Your nominal incomes rise by 50%, your nominal consumption stays the same as before and your real consumptions each fall by 50%. Now you export half your housing production to us and half of the clothing you had previously been producing for yourself; also, you import only half the food you used to. So your surplus (or half your earlier income) matches our deficit (of half our earlier income): gold flows from us to you.

As we lose gold and fall below holding $2/3$ of world μ, all these discrepancies are reduced but still exist qualitatively: so gold continues to be drained, but at a lower rate. The gold drain ends when

7. Gold's transport costs

My analysis can end with a paradox! Suppose gold's transport costs are appreciable. An example would be a model in which it costs s percent of gold's value to ship it from one country to the other. If all other goods moved freely, arbitrage would impose only the following limits on the gold prices of a good here and abroad:

$$(1 - s) \leqslant P_i / P_i^* \leqslant (1 - s)^{-1}. \tag{11}$$

The exchange rate between an ounce of gold here and an ounce of gold there, expressed as the price in ounces here of 1 ounce delivered there, can be called e: its reciprocal is e^*. Then

$$(1 - s) \leqslant e \leqslant (1 - s)^{-1}, \qquad (1 - s) \leqslant e^* \leqslant (1 - s)^{-1}. \tag{12}$$

A sophisticated reader can test her understanding of the correct Hume analysis by proving that *the world allocation of μ between M and M^* is rendered somewhat indeterminate in the long run by the cost of transporting gold.* And so is the long-run equilibrium deviation of e from unity. Viner (1937, p. 379) realized that there is no need for the gold-standard exchange rate to find its equilibrium at *par* (the geometric mean of the two gold points, where $e = 1 = e^*$), rather than at a random determinate point between the gold points. But I have seen no notice taken anywhere hitherto that $M/(M + M^*)$ is *indeterminate* in long-run equilibrium within a percentage interval determined by the discrepancy between $1 - s$ and one.

Thus, begin with countries the same size, with identical money velocities with each having exactly half the world money supply, $M = M^* = \frac{1}{2}\mu$. And let the past equilibrium be at $e = 1 = e^*$.

Now I wave my wand and transfer a bit of M^* to M. I shall now demonstrate that the correct Hume mechanism does *not* restore the old equilibrium. Instead, to within the limits of the gold points, every P_i and W is bid up in a balanced

---

our M has fallen to our long-run half of expanded world μ. Then the self-correcting mechanism turns itself off.

How will making housing a nontradeable alter the story? We begin as before. But now W is initially bid up by more than W^* is. Now we expand our imports and, diverting L from food production to housing production, expand our housing consumption and reduce our exports to you. Our improved initial terms of trade, $P_{\text{food}}/P_{\text{clothing}} = P^*_{\text{food}}/P^*_{\text{clothing}}$, have contributed to our deficit as we lose export sales and expand clothing costs. But even if the Marshall–Lerner condition only barely held, the excess of our consumption over our production would produce the gold drain that eventually rights itself. On a reduced-form basis we deduce

$$dM/dt = f[M/\mu]; \qquad 0 = f[\bar{x}], \qquad f'[\;] < 0; \qquad M(t)/\mu \to \bar{x}.$$

See my brief mathematical appendix for a proof that handles the continuum Ricardian case.

proportion relative to every P_i^* and W^*, which are bid down in balance. By how much will each P_i exceed each P_i^* initially and forevermore? By the postulated small percentage deviation between $M(0)$ and $M^*(0)$, which measures the permanent rise in e.

Note: This divergence must not exceed the permissible limits set by (8).

$$1 < e(0) = P_i(0)/P_i^*(0) < (1-s)^{-1}, \qquad e(0) = e(\infty). \tag{13}$$

Ever after all variables remain at their perturbed values dictated by p-p-p applied to the small percentage changes in the money supply. By how far from $\frac{1}{2}\mu$ can $M(\infty)$ persist in being? I calculate the limits to be

$$(1-s)\frac{1}{2-s}\mu \leqslant M(\infty) \leqslant \frac{1}{2-s}\mu. \tag{14}$$

For $s = .01$, this gives the narrow interval around $\frac{1}{2}$ of

$$\frac{.99}{1.99}\mu = .4975\mu \leqslant M(\infty) \leqslant .5028\mu = \frac{1}{1.99}\mu. \tag{15}$$

Note: Replace $(2-s)^{-1}$ by $Q(Q + Q^* - sQ)^{-1}$ for the general case.[7]

Under inconvertible paper M and M^*, it is as if $s \to 1$ and then either country is free *permanently* to swell or shrink its money supply as it wishes relative to the other country's given supply.

I leave to the reader the task of working out how transport costs in a good and in gold interact to widen the limits within which the gold prices P_i and P_i^* may deviate; and how a cheaply transportable third good might narrow down the interval set by arbitrage.

8. Summary

David Hume correctly glimpsed how free trade might involve a self-correcting gold-flow mechanism. But he made the mistake of supposing that the Quantity Theory of Money linked every price in a region to the money in that region

[7] The above macroeconomic indeterminacy is not to be confused with multiplicity of *micro* equilibrium. It obtains even when the real equilibrium of price ratios and physical quantities is unique. There is a second, less interesting macro indeterminacy when the long-run equilibrium involves *autarky* with all goods except gold having finite transport costs. Thus, suppose positive σ is the minimum of s_i in $1 - s_i \leqslant P_i/P_i^* \leqslant (1-s_i)^{-1}$ and gold's s is zero. Then $[\mu - M(\infty)]/M(\infty)$ can vary over an interval that shrinks to zero as $\sigma \to 0$. If the long-run equilibrium involves some trade, even ever so little, this second kind of macro indeterminacy disappears.

Why is gold different from other goods? Because it has a low transport cost s? In part that does help to make gold serve as a good money stuff. But also in my model and Hume's, gold is the only good *not* wanted for its own sake but only for its convenience in making transaction purchases. If gold has dental, industrial, and jewelry utilities, the Quantity Theory story needs qualifying in its homogeneity.

alone. This overlooked the forces that keep the competitive prices of the same transportable good virtually the same in all regions. Mesmerized by Hume's elegance, subsequent economists failed to recast Hume's analysis in the correct form that makes it immune to criticism. Instead they left the corrected version implicit, and often provided faulty rebuttals to Hume's critics, rebuttals that gratuitously pretended to locate the equilibrating mechanism in differential movements between a country's nontradeable and tradeable goods or in differential term-of-trade movements between a country's export and import goods.

Such rebuttals fail to notice that (i) the *absence* of nontradeable goods can actually speed up the rate at which an excess of money supply corrects itself; and (ii), even in the absence of any terms-of-trade shifts (or indeed of *any* price changes at all), a gold drain will shut itself off when people run out of the excess money supply that is causing them as a nation to consume more than they produce.

My present analysis is too brief to do justice to the problem. I have been able to analyze only one kind of adjustment to disequilibrium—namely, the adjustment to an initial perturbed stock of money in one or more countries (as, e.g., when the conquistadors splashed Spaniards with new ownership of gold). One defect in early writers is their failure to understand and spell out just which exogenous change they are purporting to analyze. My readers are warned that the present exposition has not gone into the transfer problem, a shift in tastes toward the goods of one of the regions, a specified technical change, a reduction in supply of an important good like oil, and so forth.[8] These need their own analysis in the Hume model and I warn against overpreoccupation with a purely monetary approach to current international problems.

Mathematical appendix

Here is a corrected version for the Hume model in the manageable case of a continuum of goods. I utilize the notations of Dornbusch, Fischer, and Samuelson (1977), setting $e = 1 = e^*$.

Our long-run equilibrium conditions will be shown to impose 6 independent relations on the 6 long-run unknowns: $[\bar{z}_\infty, W_\infty, W^*_\infty, M_\infty, M^*_\infty, \dot{M}_\infty]$. These relations depend on the known value of the constants $(\gamma = V, \gamma^* = V^*, 1 - k, \mu = \bar{G}, L, L^*)$, which refer to velocities, share in total expenditure of nontradeable goods, world gold supply, and regional labor supplies. Our Ricardian labor costs for tradeable goods indexed by z, $0 \leqslant z \leqslant 1$, are at home and abroad respectively given by $a(z)$ and $a^*(z)$, with $A(z) = a^*(z)/a(z)$ a monotone-decreasing

[8] I have covered some of the ground in Samuelson (1971a, 1971b); see also Dornbusch, Fischer, and Samuelson (1977).

function. Tastes are Mill–Cobb–Douglas, with the fraction of expenditure going for tradeable goods produced at home, those with z such that $0 \leqslant z < \tilde{z} < 1$, being given by the monotone-increasing function

$$\vartheta[\tilde{z}] = \int_0^{\tilde{z}} b(z)\,dz, \quad b(z) > 0, \tag{A1}$$

$$\vartheta[1] = k.$$

The fraction of expenditure going for tradeables produced abroad is then $k - \vartheta[\tilde{z}]$, with k going for tradeables: $\vartheta[\tilde{z}] + (k - \vartheta[\tilde{z}]) + (1 - k) = 1$.

Our six relations are

$$WL + W^*L^* = VM + V^*M^* \tag{A2}$$

$$WL = \vartheta[\tilde{z}](VM + V^*M^*) + (1 - k)VM \tag{A3}$$

$$W/W^* = A(\tilde{z}) \tag{A4}$$

$$M + M^* = \mu \text{ or } \overline{G} \tag{A5}$$

$$dM/dt \equiv \dot{M} = WL - VM \tag{A6}$$

$$0 = \dot{M} \tag{A7}$$

Given the monotone nature of the $A(\tilde{z})$ and $\vartheta[\tilde{z}]$ functions, these 6 relations have unique roots for our respective 6 unknowns: $[\tilde{z}_\infty, W_\infty, W^*_\infty, M_\infty, M^*_\infty, \dot{M}_\infty = 0]$.

Actually,

$$\begin{aligned} M_\infty &= m_\infty \mu, \quad M^*_\infty = (1 - m_\infty)\mu \\ W_\infty &= m_\infty \mu/L, \quad W^*_\infty = (1 - m_\infty)\mu \end{aligned} \tag{A8}$$

where $(m_\infty, \tilde{z})$ are unique *real* roots of the following 2 long-run real relations deducible from (A2)–(A7):

$$(L/L^*)A(\tilde{z}) = \frac{\theta[\tilde{z}] + (1 - k)m_\infty V}{k - \vartheta[\tilde{z}] + (1 - k)(1 - m_\infty)V^*}\,; \tag{A9a}$$

$$m_\infty = A(\tilde{z}) \frac{L}{A(\tilde{z})L + L^*} V^{-1}. \tag{A9b}$$

Also, note that from relations (A2)–(A5), we can eliminate the 4 variables $(\tilde{z}, W, W^*, M^*)$, expressing them all in terms of M. Substituting the results into (A6) gives us the reduced-form relation

$$\dot{M} = \mu f[M/\mu], \quad f[m_\infty] = 0 > f'[m_\infty]. \tag{A6$'$}$$

So (A2)–(A7) is equivalent to (A6′)–(A7) as far as long-run M_∞ is concerned.

To determine our 5 short-run unknowns, $[\tilde{z}(t), W(t), W^*(t), M^*(t), \dot{M}(t)]$ in terms of each given $M(t)$, we suspend (A7)'s requirement of long-run trade balance sans specie flow. The remaining 5 independent relations suffice to give our differential equation(s) of self-correction. Again, as far as $M(t)$ alone is concerned, we can use (A6′)'s reduced-form relation

$$\dot{M} = \mu f[M/\mu], \tag{A6′}$$

and derive

$$\lim_{t\to\infty} [\dot{M}(t), M(t)] = [0, m_\infty \mu], \tag{A10}$$

$$\lim_{t\to\infty} \frac{M(t) - m_\infty \mu}{\exp(-f'[m_\infty]t)} = \text{constant.} \tag{A11}$$

Dornbusch, Fischer, and Samuelson (1977) have already given the above relations for $V = V^*$, it being understood that the 1977 Equation (16) refers to the limiting approximation of (A11). When there are no nontradeables, $k = 1$, $\tilde{z}(t)$ never departs from $\tilde{z}_\infty$ and $\dot{M}(t)/[M(t) - M(\infty)]$ is strictly constant. The greater the weight of the nontradeables the *slower* will be the correction of any $M(0) - M(\infty)$ discrepancy, as the 1977 Equation (16) suggested and as can be worked out by evaluating $f'[m_\infty]$ as a function of k when V and V^* take on *any* values.

Non-Ricardian cases, such as those of Heckscher–Ohlin or Jones (1971) and Samuelson (1971), create no new problems for the corrected Humean formulation.

References

Bickerdike, C. F., 1920, "The Instability of Foreign Exchange," *Economic Journal* 30, March, 118–122.

Collery, Arnold, 1974, "Relative Prices in Monetary and 'Classical' Theories of Adjustment of the Balance of Payments," privately circulated.

Dornbusch, Rudiger, 1973, "Devaluation, Money and Nontraded Goods," *American Economic Review* 63, December, 871–880.

Dornbusch, Rudiger, Fischer, Stanley, and Samuelson, Paul A., 1977, "Comparative Advantage, Trade, and Payments in a Ricardian Model with a Continuum of Goods," *American Economic Review* 67, December, 823–839.

Dornbusch, Rudiger, and Mussa, Michael, 1975, "Consumption, Real Balances and the Hoarding Function," *International Economic Review* 16, June, 415–421.

Frenkel, Jacob A., and Johnson, Harry G., 1976, "The Monetary Approach to the Balance of Payments: Essential Concepts and Historical Origins." In Jacob A. Frenkel and Harry G. Johnson, eds., *The Monetary Approach to the Balance of Payments* (London: George Allen & Unwin Ltd.), pp. 21–45.

Haberler, Gottfried, 1936, *The Theory of International Trade* (London: Wm. Hodge & Co.)

Hume, David, 1752, "Of the Balance of Trade," in *Political Discourses*, T. H. Green and T. H. Grose, eds., 1875 of Hume's, *Essays, Moral, Political, and Literary*, Part II (London). See Rotwein (1955) for source of Hume quotations used here.

Jones, Ronald W., 1971, "A Three-Factor Model in Theory, Trade and History," In Jagdish Bhagwati et al., eds., *Trade, Balance of Payments and Growth: Papers in International Economics in Honor of Charles P. Kindleberger* (Amsterdam: North-Holland Publishing Co.), pp. 3–21.

Laughlin, J. L., 1903, *The Principles of Money* (New York).

Mosak, Jacob L., 1944, *General Equilibrium Theory in International Trade*, Cowles Commission Monograph No. 7 (Bloomington, Ind.: Principia Press).

Ohlin, Bertil, 1933, *The Theory of Interregional and International Trade* (Cambridge, Mass.: Harvard University Press).

Polak, Jacques J., 1957, "Monetary Analysis of Income Formation and Payments Problems." In *The Monetary Approach to the Balance of Payments* (Washington, D.C.: International Monetary Fund, 1977), pp. 15–64.

Prais, Sigmund J., 1961, "Some Mathematical Notes on the Quantity Theory of Money in an Open Economy." In *The Monetary Approach to the Balance of Payments* (Washington, D.C.: International Monetary Fund, 1977), pp. 147–61.

Robinson, Joan, 1937, *Essays in the Theory of Employment* (New York: The Macmillan Company), pp. 183–209.

Rotwein, Eugene, ed., 1955, *David Hume: Writings on Economics* (Edinburgh: Thomas Nelson & Sons Ltd.). Hume's essay, "Of the Balance of Trade," appears on pages 60–75.

Samuelson, Paul A., 1971a, "An Exact Hume-Ricardo-Marshall Model of International Trade," *Journal of International Economics* 1, February, 1–18. Reproduced in *Collected Scientific Papers of Paul A. Samuelson* (Cambridge, Mass.: MIT Press, 1972), Vol. III, Ch. 162.

Samuelson, Paul A., 1971b, "On the Trail of Conventional Beliefs about the Transfer Problem." In Jagdish Bhagwati et al., eds., *Trade, Balance of Payments and Growth: Papers in International Economics in Honor of Charles P. Kindleberger* (Amsterdam: North-Holland Publishing Co.). Reproduced in *Collected Scientific Papers of Paul A. Samuelson* (Cambridge, Mass.: MIT Press, 1972), Vol. III, Ch. 163.

Samuelson, Paul A., 1971, "Ohlin Was Right," *Swedish Journal of Economics* 73, 365–84. Reproduced in *Collected Scientific Papers of Paul A. Samuelson* (Cambridge, Mass.: MIT Press, 1977), Vol. IV, Ch. 254.

Viner, Jacob, 1937, *Studies in the Theory of International Trade* (New York: Harper & Brothers Publishers).

Comparative Advantage, Trade, and Payments in a Ricardian Model with a Continuum of Goods

By R. Dornbusch, S. Fischer, and P. A. Samuelson*

This paper discusses Ricardian trade and payments theory in the case of a continuum of goods. The analysis thus extends the development of many-commodity, two-country comparative advantage analysis as presented, for example, in Gottfried Haberler (1937), Frank Graham (1923), Paul Samuelson (1964), and Frank W. Taussig (1927). The literature is historically reviewed by John Chipman (1965). Perhaps surprisingly, the continuum assumption simplifies the analysis neatly in comparison with the discrete many-commodity case. The distinguishing feature of the Ricardian approach emphasized in this paper is the determination of the competitive margin in production between imported and exported goods. The analysis advances the existing literature by formally showing precisely how tariffs and transport costs establish a range of commodities that are not traded, and how the price-specie flow mechanism does or does not give rise to movements in relative cost and price levels.

The formal *real* model is introduced in Section I. Its equilibrium determines the *relative* wage and price structure and the efficient international specialization pattern. Section II considers standard comparative static questions of growth, demand shifts, technological change, and transfers. Extensions of the model to nontraded goods, tariffs, and transport costs are then studied in Section III. Monetary considerations are introduced in Section IV, which examines the price-specie mechanism under stable parities, floating exchange rate regimes, and also questions of unemployment under sticky money wages.

*Massachusetts Institute of Technology. Helpful comments from Ronald W. Jones are gratefully acknowledged. Financial support was provided by a Ford Foundation grant to Dornbusch, NSF GS-41428 to Fischer, and NSF 75-04053 to Samuelson.

I. The Real Model

In this section we develop the basic real model and determine the equilibrium relative wage and price structure along with the efficient geographic pattern of specialization. Assumptions about technology are specified in Section IA. Section IB deals with demand. In Section IC the equilibrium is constructed and some of its properties are explored. Throughout this section we assume zero transport costs and no other impediments to trade.

A. *Technology and Efficient Geographic Specialization*

The many-commodity Ricardian model assumes constant unit labor requirements $(a_1, \dots, a_n)$ and $(a_1^*, \dots, a_n^*)$ for the n commodities that can be produced in the home and foreign countries, respectively. The commodities are conveniently indexed so that relative unit labor requirements are ranked in order of diminishing home country comparative advantage,

$$a_1^*/a_1 > \dots > \dots > a_i^*/a_i > \dots > a_n^*/a_n$$

where an asterisk denotes the foreign country.

In working with a continuum of goods, we similarly index commodities on an interval, say [0, 1], in accordance with diminishing home country comparative advantage. A commodity z is associated with each point on the interval, and for each commodity there are unit labor requirements in the two countries, $a(z)$ and $a^*(z)$, with relative unit labor requirement given by

$$(1) \qquad A(z) \equiv \frac{a^*(z)}{a(z)} \qquad A'(z) < 0$$

The relative unit labor requirement function in (1) is by strong assumption continuous, and by construction (ranking or indexing of goods), decreasing in z. The function $A(z)$ is shown in Figure 1 as the downward sloping schedule.

Consider now the range of commodities produced domestically and those produced abroad, as well as the relative price structure associated with given wages. For that purpose we define as w and w^* the domestic and foreign wages measured in *any* (common!) unit. The home country will efficiently produce all those commodities for which domestic unit labor costs are less than or equal to foreign unit labor costs. Accordingly, any commodity z will be produced at home if

$$a(z)w \leq a^*(z)w^* \tag{2}$$

Thus

$$\omega \leq A(z) \tag{2'}$$

where (3) defines the parameter ω, fundamental to Ricardian analysis,

$$\omega \equiv w/w^* \tag{3}$$

This is the ratio of our real wage to theirs (our "double-factoral terms of trade"). It follows that for a given relative wage ω the home country will efficiently produce the range of commodities

$$0 \leq z \leq \tilde{z}(\omega) \tag{4}$$

where taking (2′) with equality defines the borderline commodity z, for which

$$\tilde{z} = A^{-1}(\omega) \tag{5}$$

$A^{-1}(\ )$ being the inverse function of $A(\ )$. By the same argument the foreign country will specialize in the production of commodities in the range

$$\tilde{z}(\omega) \leq z \leq 1 \tag{4'}$$

The minimum cost condition determines the structure of relative prices. The relative price of a commodity z in terms of any other commodity z', when both goods are produced in the home country, is equal to the ratio of home unit labor costs:

$$\begin{aligned} P(z)/P(z') &= wa(z)/wa(z') \\ &= a(z)/a(z'); \\ &\qquad z \leq \tilde{z}, z' \leq \tilde{z} \end{aligned} \tag{6}$$

The relative price of home produced z in terms of a commodity z'' produced abroad is by contrast

$$\begin{aligned} P(z)/P(z'') &= wa(z)/w^*a^*(z'') \\ &= \omega a(z)/a^*(z''); \\ &\qquad z < \tilde{z} < z'' \end{aligned} \tag{7}$$

In summarizing the supply part of the model we note that any specified relative real wage is associated with an efficient geographic specialization pattern characterized by the borderline commodity $\tilde{z}(\omega)$ as well as by a relative price structure. (The pattern is "efficient" in the sense that the world is out on, and not inside, its production-possibility frontier.)

B. *Demand*

On the demand side, the simplest Mill-Ricardo analysis imposes a strong homothetic structure in the form of J. S. Mill or Cobb-Douglas demand functions that associate with each ith commodity a *constant expenditure share*, b_i. It further assumes *identical* tastes for the two countries or *uniform* homothetic demand.

By analogy with the many-commodity case, which involves budget shares

$$b_i = P_iC_i/Y \qquad b_i = b_i^*$$

$$\sum_1^n b_i = 1$$

We therefore prescribe for the continuum case a given $b(z)$ profile:

$$\begin{aligned} b(z) &= P(z)C(z)/Y > 0 \\ b(z) &= b^*(z) \\ \int_0^1 b(z)\,dz &= 1 \end{aligned} \tag{8}$$

where Y denotes total income, C demand for and P the price of commodity z.

Next we define the fraction of income spent (anywhere) on those goods in which the home country has a comparative advantage:

$$\begin{aligned} \vartheta(\tilde{z}) &\equiv \int_0^{\tilde{z}} b(z)\,dz > 0 \\ \vartheta'(\tilde{z}) &= b(\tilde{z}) > 0 \end{aligned} \tag{9}$$

where again $(0, \tilde{z})$ denotes the range of commodities for which the home country enjoys a comparative advantage. With a fraction ϑ of each country's income, and therefore of world income, spent on home produced goods, it follows that the fraction of income spent on foreign produced commodities is

$$(9') \quad 1 - \vartheta(\tilde{z}) \equiv \int_{\tilde{z}}^{1} b(z)\,dz \qquad 0 \leq \vartheta(z) \leq 1$$

C. *Equilibrium Relative Wages and Specialization*

To derive the equilibrium relative wage and price structure and the associated pattern of efficient geographic specialization, we turn next to the condition of market equilibrium. Consider the home country's labor market, or equivalently the market for domestically produced commodities. With $\tilde{z}$ denoting the *hypothetical* dividing line between domestically and foreign produced commodities, equilibrium in the market for home produced goods requires that domestic labor income wL equals world spending on domestically produced goods:

$$(10) \qquad wL = \vartheta(\tilde{z})(wL + w^*L^*)$$

Equation (10) associates with each $\tilde{z}$ a value of the relative wage w/w^* such that market equilibrium obtains. This schedule is drawn in Figure 1 as the upward sloping locus and is obtained from (10) by rewriting the equation in the form:

$$(10') \quad \omega = \frac{\vartheta(\tilde{z})}{1 - \vartheta(\tilde{z})}(L^*/L) = B(\tilde{z}; L^*/L)$$

where it is apparent from (9) that the schedule starts at zero and approaches infinity as $\tilde{z}$ approaches unity.

To interpret the $B(\ )$ schedule we note that it is entirely a representation of the demand side; and in that respect it shows that if the range of domestically produced goods were increased at constant relative wages, demand for domestic labor (goods) would increase as the dividing line is shifted—at the same time that demand for foreign

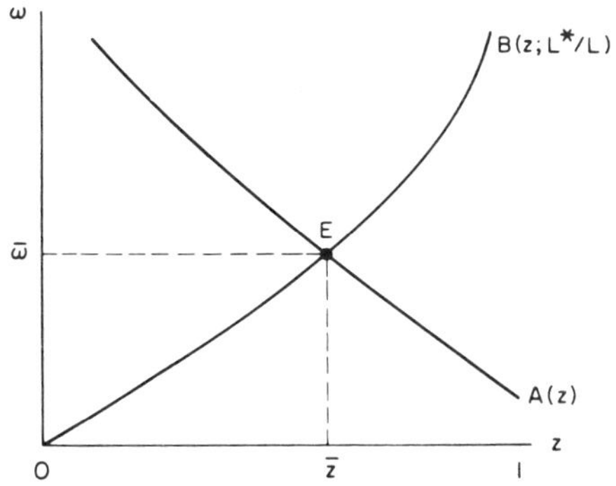

FIGURE 1

labor (goods) would decline.[1] A rise in the domestic relative wage would then be required to equate the demand for domestic labor to the existing supply.

An alternative interpretation of the $B(\ )$ schedule as the locus of trade balance equilibria uses the fact that (10) can be written in the balance-of-trade form:

$$(10'') \quad [1 - \vartheta(\tilde{z})]wL = \vartheta(\tilde{z})w^*L^*$$

This states that equilibrium in the trade balance means imports are equal in value to exports. On this interpretation, the $B(\ )$ schedule is upward sloping because an increase in the range of commodities hypothetically produced at home at constant relative wages lowers our imports and raises our exports. The resulting trade imbalance would have to be corrected by an increase in our relative wage that would raise our import demand for goods and reduce our exports, and thus restore balance.

The next step is to combine the demand side of the economy with the condition of efficient specialization as represented in equation (5), which specifies the competitive margin as a function of the relative wage. Substituting (5) in (10′) yields as a solution the unique relative wage $\bar{\omega}$, at which the world is efficiently specialized, is in bal-

[1]Throughout this paper we refer to "domestic" goods as commodities produced in the home country rather than to commodities that are nontraded. The latter we call "nontraded" goods.

anced trade, and is at full employment with all markets clearing:

$$\bar{\omega} = A(\bar{z}) = B(\bar{z}; L^*/L) \tag{11}$$

The equilibrium relative wage defined in (11) is represented in Figure 1 at the intersection of the $A(\ )$ and $B(\ )$ schedules.[2] Commodity $\bar{z}$ denotes the equilibrium borderline of comparative advantage between commodities produced and exported by the home country ($0 \leq z \leq \bar{z}$), and those commodities produced and exported by the foreign country ($\bar{z} \leq z \leq 1$).

Among the characteristics of the equilibrium we note that the equilibrium relative wages and specialization pattern are determined by technology, tastes, and relative size (as measured by the relative labor force).[3] The relative price structure associated with the equilibrium at point E is defined by equations (6) and (7) once (11) has defined the relative wage $\bar{\omega}$ and the equilibrium specialization pattern $\bar{z}(\bar{\omega})$.

The equilibrium levels of production $Q(z)$ and $Q^*(z)$, and employment in each industry $L(z)$ and $L^*(z)$, can be recovered from the demand structure and unit labor requirements once the comparative advantage pattern has been determined.

We note that with identical homothetic tastes across countries and no distortions, the relative wage $\bar{\omega}$ is a measure of the well-being of the representative person-laborer at home relative to the well-being of the representative foreign laborer.

[2]See the Appendix for the relation of the diagram to previous analyses.

[3]The construction of the $B(\ )$ schedule relies heavily on the Cobb-Douglas demand structure. If, instead, demand functions were identical across countries and homothetic, an analogous schedule could be constructed. In the general homothetic case, however, a set of relative prices is required at each z to calculate the equivalent of the $B(\ )$ schedule; the relative prices are those that apply on the $A(\bar{z})$ schedule for that value of z. In this case the independence of the $A(\ )$ and $B(\ )$ schedules is obviously lost. In the general homothetic case there is still a unique intersection of the $A(\ )$ and $B(\ )$ schedules. For more general nonhomothetic demand structures, it is known that an equilibrium exists; but even in the case of two Ricardian goods there may be *no* unique equilibrium even though there will almost always be a finite number of equilibria. See Gerard Debreu and Stephen Smale. Extensions of our analysis with respect to the demand structure and the number of countries are developed in unpublished work by Charles Wilson.

II. Comparative Statics

The unique real equilibrium in Figure 1 is determined jointly by tastes, technology, and relative size, L^*/L. We can now exploit Figure 1 to examine simple comparative static questions.

A. *Relative Size*

Consider first the effect of an increase in the relative size of the rest of the world. An increase in L^*/L by (10) shifts the $B(\ )$ trade balance equilibrium schedule upward in proportion to the change in relative size and must, therefore, raise the equilibrium relative wage at home and reduce the range of commodities produced domestically. It is apparent from Figure 2 that the domestic relative wage increases *proportionally less* than the decline in domestic relative size.

The rise in equilibrium relative wages due to a change in relative size can be thought of in the following manner. At the initial equilibrium, the increase in the foreign relative labor force would create an excess supply of labor abroad and an excess demand for labor at home—or, correspondingly, a trade surplus for the home country. The resulting increase in domestic relative wages serves to eliminate the trade surplus while

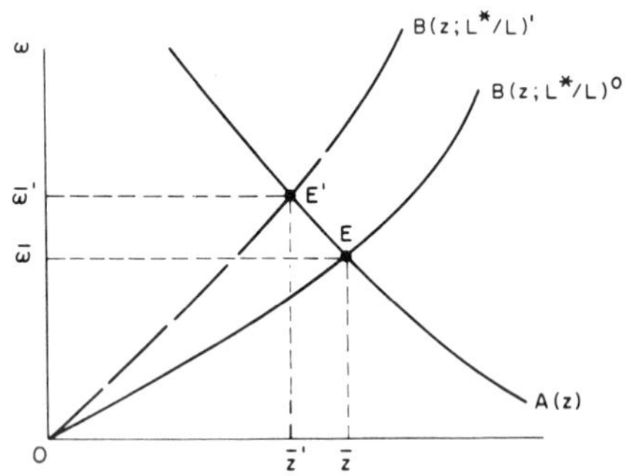

FIGURE 2

at the same time raising relative unit labor costs at home. The increase in domestic relative unit labor costs in turn implies a loss of comparative advantage in marginal industries and thus a needed reduction in the range of commodities produced domestically.

The welfare implications of the change in relative size take the form of an unambiguous improvement in the home country's real income and (under Cobb-Douglas demand) a reduction in real income per head abroad. We observe, too, that from the definition of the home country's share in world income and (10), we have

$$wL/(wL + w^* L^*) = \vartheta(\bar{z}) \tag{12}$$

It is apparent, as noted above, that a reduction in domestic relative size in raising the domestic relative wage (thereby reducing the range of commodities produced domestically) must under our Cobb-Douglas demand assumptions lower the home country's share in total world income and spending—even though our per capita income rises.

B. *Technical Progress*

To begin with, we are concerned with the effects of uniform technical progress. By equation (1), a uniform proportional reduction in foreign unit labor requirements implies a reduction in $a^*(z)$ and therefore a proportional downward shift of the $A(z)$ schedule in Figure 1. At the initial relative wage $\bar{\omega}$, the loss of our comparative advantage due to a reduction in foreign unit labor costs will imply a loss of some industries in the home country and a corresponding trade deficit. The resulting induced decline in the equilibrium relative wage serves to restore trade balance equilibrium, and to offset in part our decline in comparative advantage.

The net effect is therefore a reduction in domestic relative wages, which must fall proportionally short of the decline in relative unit labor requirements abroad. The home country's terms of trade therefore improve as can be noted by using (7) for any two commodities z and z'', respectively, produced at home and abroad:

$$\hat{P}(z) - \hat{P}(z'') = \hat{\bar{\omega}} - \hat{a}^*(z'') > 0 \tag{13}$$

where a "hat" denotes a proportional change. Domestic real income increases, as does foreign real income.[4] The range of goods produced domestically declines since domestic labor, in efficiency units, is now relatively more scarce.

An alternative form of technical progress that can be studied is the international transfer of the least cost technology. Such transfers reduce the discrepancies in relative unit labor requirements—by lowering them for each z in the relatively less efficient country—and therefore flatten the $A(z)$ schedule in Figure 1. It can be shown that such harmonization of technology must benefit the innovating low-wage country, and that it may reduce real income in the high-wage country whose technology comes to be adopted. In fact, the high-wage country must lose if harmonization is complete so that relative unit labor requirements now become identical across countries and all our consumer's surplus from international trade vanishes.[5]

C. *Demand Shifts*

The case with a continuum of commodities requires a careful definition of a demand shift. For our purposes it is sufficient to ask: What is the effect of a shift from high z commodities toward low z commodities? It is apparent from Figure 2 that such a shift will cause the trade balance equilibrium schedule $B(\ )$ to shift up and to the left. It follows that the equilibrium domestic rela-

[4]The purchasing power of foreign labor income in terms of domestically produced goods is $w^* L^*/wa(z) = L^*/a(z)\bar{\omega}$ and in terms of foreign goods $L^*/a^*(z)$. The fact that foreigners' real income per head rises is guaranteed by our Cobb-Douglas demand assumption. In the general homothetic case, a balanced reduction in $a^*(z)$ can be immiserizing abroad if the real wage falls strongly in terms of all previously imported goods; however, the balanced drop in $a^*(z)$ in the general homothetic case *always* increases our real wage.

[5]Complete equilization of unit labor requirements implies that the $A(\ )$ schedule is horizontal at the level $\omega = A(z) = 1$. In this case geographic specialization becomes indeterminate and inessential.

tive wage will rise while the range of commodities produced by the home country declines. Domestic labor is allocated to a narrower range of commodities that are consumed with higher density while foreign labor is spread more thinly across a larger range of goods.

Welfare changes cannot be identified in this instance because tastes themselves have changed. It is true that domestic relative income rises along with the relative wage. Further we note that since $\bar{\omega}$ rises, the relative well-being of home labor to foreign labor (reckoned at the new tastes) is greater than was our laborers' relative well-being (reckoned at the old tastes).

D. *Unilateral Transfers*

Suppose foreigners make a continual unilateral transfer to us. With uniform homothetic tastes and no impediments to trade, neither curve is shifted by the transfer since we spend the transfer *exactly* as foreigners would have spent it but for the transfer. The new equilibrium involves a recurring trade deficit for us, equal to the transfer, but there is no change in the terms of trade. As Bertil Ohlin argued against John Maynard Keynes, here is a case where full equilibration takes place solely as a result of the spending transfers. When we introduce nontraded goods below, Ohlin's presumption will be found to require detailed qualifications, as it also would if tastes differed geographically.

III. Extensions of the Real Model

Extensions of the real model taken up in this section concern nontraded goods, tariffs, and transport costs. The purpose of this section is twofold. First we establish how the exogenous introduction of nontraded goods qualifies the preceding analysis. Next we turn to a particular specification of tariffs and transport costs to establish an equilibrium range of endogenously determined nontraded goods as part of the equilibrium solution of the model. Transfers are then shown to affect the equilibrium relative price structure and the range of goods traded.

A. *Nontraded Goods*

To introduce nontraded goods into the analysis we assume that a fraction k of income is everywhere spent on internationally traded goods, and a fraction $(1 - k)$ is spent in each country on nontraded commodities. With $b(z)$ continuing to denote expenditure densities for traded goods, we have accordingly

$$k \equiv \int_0^1 b(z)\,dz < 1 \tag{14}$$

where z denotes traded goods.[6] As before the fraction of income spent on domestically exportable commodities is $\vartheta(z)$, except that ϑ now reaches a maximum value of $\vartheta(1) = k$.

Equation (1) remains valid for traded goods, but the trade balance equilibrium condition in (10″) must now be modified to:

$$[1 - \vartheta(\tilde{z}) - (1 - k)]wL = \vartheta(\tilde{z})w^*L^* \tag{15}$$

since domestic spending on imports is equal to income less spending on *all* domestically produced goods including nontraded commodities. Equation (15) can be rewritten as

$$\omega = \frac{\vartheta(\tilde{z})}{k - \vartheta(\tilde{z})}(L^*/L) \tag{15'}$$

where k is a constant and therefore independent of the relative wage structure.

We note that (15′) together with (5) determines the equilibrium relative wage and efficient geographic specialization, $(\bar{\omega}, \bar{z})$. Further it is apparent that (15′) has exactly the same properties as (10′) and that accordingly a construction of equilibrium like that in Figure 1 remains appropriate. The equilibrium relative wage again depends on

[6]We can think of the range of nontraded goods as another [0, 1] interval with commodities denoted by x and expenditure fractions on those goods given by $c(x)$. With these definitions we have $\int_0^1 c(x)\,dx \equiv 1 - k$, a positive fraction.

relative size, technology, and demand conditions. In this case demand conditions explicitly include the fraction of income spent on traded goods:

$$(11') \qquad \bar{\omega} = \frac{\vartheta(\bar{z})}{k - \vartheta(\bar{z})} \frac{L^*}{L} = A(\bar{z})$$

This nicely generalizes our previous equilibrium of (11) to handle exogenously given nontraded goods.[7]

Two applications of the extended model highlight the special aspects newly introduced by nontraded goods. First consider a shift in demand (in each country) toward *nontraded* goods. To determine the effects on the equilibrium relative wage we have to establish whether this shift is at the expense of high or low z commodities. In the former case the home country's relative wage increases while in the latter case it declines. If the shift in demand in each country is uniform so that $b(z)$ is reduced in the same proportion for all z in both countries, then the relative wage remains unchanged.

Consider next a transfer received by the home country in the amount T measured in terms of foreign labor. As is well known, and already shown, with identical homothetic tastes and *no* nontraded goods, a transfer leaves the terms of trade unaffected. In the present case, however, the condition for balanced trade, inclusive of transfers, becomes:

$$(16) \qquad T = (k - \vartheta)[\omega L + T] - \vartheta[L^* - T]$$

or, in equilibrium,

$$(16') \qquad \bar{\omega} = \frac{1 - k}{k - \vartheta(\bar{z})}(T/L) + \frac{\vartheta(\bar{z})}{k - \vartheta(\bar{z})}(L^*/L)$$

It is apparent from (16') that a transfer receipt by the home country causes the trade balance equilibrium schedule in Figure 1 to shift upward at each level of z. Accordingly, the equilibrium domestic relative wage increases and the range of commodities produced domestically is reduced. The steps in achieving this result are, first, that at the initial relative wage only a fraction of the transfer is spent on imports in the home country, while foreign demand for domestic goods similarly declines only by a fraction of their reduced income. The resulting surplus for the home country has to be eliminated by, second, an increase in the domestic relative wage and a corresponding improvement in the home country's terms of trade.[8]

The analysis of nontraded goods therefore confirms in a Ricardian model the "orthodox" presumption with respect to the terms of trade effects of transfers.[9]

B. *Transport Costs: Endogenous Equilibrium for Nontraded Goods*

The notion that transport costs give rise to a range of commodities that are nontraded is established in the literature and is particularly well stated by Haberler (1937). In contrast with the previous section we shall now endogenously determine the range of nontraded commodities as part of the equilibrium. We assume, following the "iceberg" model of Samuelson (1954), that transport costs take the form of "shrinkage" in transit so that a fraction $g(z)$ of commodity z shipped actually arrives. We further impose the assumption that $g = g(z)$ is identical for all commodities and the same for shipments in either direction.

The home country will produce commodities for which domestic unit labor cost falls short of foreign unit labor costs adjusted for shrinkage, and we modify (2') accordingly:

$$(17) \qquad wa(z) \leq (1/g)w^*a^*(z)$$

or

$$\omega \leq A(z)/g$$

[7]Diagrams much like Figures 1 and 2 again apply: the descending $A(z)$ schedule is as before; and now the new rising schedule looks much as before. As before, a rise in L^*/L and a balanced drop in $a^*(z)$ will raise $\bar{\omega}$ and lower $\bar{z}$.

[8]At constant relative wages the current account worsens by $[(1 - k - \vartheta) + \vartheta]dT = (1 - k)dT$ which is less than the transfer, since it is equal to the fraction of income spent on nontraded goods.

[9]The pre-Ohlin orthodox view of Keynes, Taussig, Jacob Viner and other writers is discussed in Viner (1937) and Samuelson (1952, 1954). A recent treatment with nontraded goods is Ronald Jones (1975).

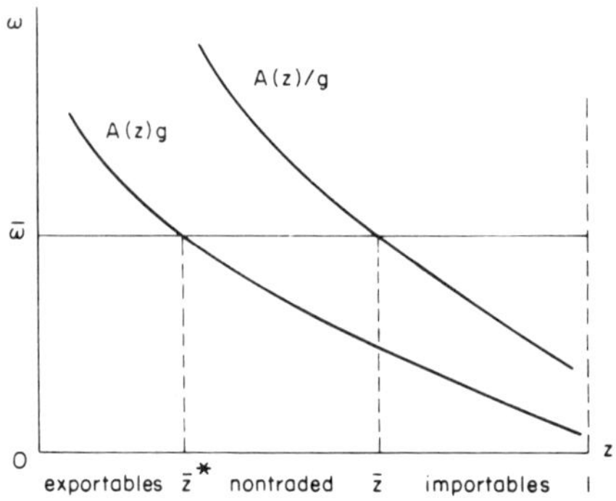

FIGURE 3

Similarly the foreign country produces commodities for which foreign unit labor cost falls short of adjusted unit labor costs of delivered imports:

$$(18) \qquad w^*a^*(z) \leq (1/g)wa(z)$$

$$\text{or} \qquad A(z)g \leq \omega$$

In Figure 3 we show the adjusted relative unit labor requirement schedules $A(z)/g$ and $A(z)g$. It is apparent from (17) and (18) that for any given relative wage the home country produces and exports commodities to the left of the $A(z)g$ schedule, both countries produce as nontraded goods commodities in the intermediate range, and the foreign country produces and exports commodities in the range to the right of $A(z)/g$.

To determine the equilibrium relative wage we turn to the trade balance equilibrium condition in (19)—together with (20) and (21)—which is modified to take account of the endogenous range of nontraded goods:

$$(19) \qquad (1 - \lambda)wL = (1 - \lambda^*)w^*L^*$$

The variable λ is the fraction of home country income spent on our domestically (or home) produced goods—exportables and nontraded—and λ^* is the share of foreigners' income spent on goods they produce. Both λ and λ^* are endogenously determined because the range of goods produced in each country depends on the relative wages.

$$(20) \qquad \lambda(g\omega) \equiv \int_0^{\bar{z}} b(z)dz \qquad \lambda'(g\omega) < 0$$

$$\lambda^*(\omega/g) \equiv \int_{\bar{z}}^1 b(z)dz \quad \lambda^{*\prime}(\omega/g) > 0$$

The dependence of $\lambda(\ )$ and $\lambda^*(\ )$ on the variables specified in (20) and the respective derivatives follow from (21) below.

The limits of integration $\bar{z}$ and $\bar{z}^*$ are derived from the conditions for efficient production in (17) and (18) by imposing equalities and so defining the borderline commodities. Thus, in Figure 3, $\bar{z}$ is the borderline between domestic nontraded goods and imports for the home country, and $\bar{z}^*$ denotes the borderline between foreign nontraded goods and the home country's exports:

$$(21) \qquad \bar{z}^* = A^{-1}(\omega/g) \qquad d\bar{z}^*/d(\omega/g) < 0$$

$$\bar{z} = A^{-1}(g\omega) \qquad d\bar{z}/d(g\omega) < 0$$

Of course, equilibrium $\bar{z}$ and $\bar{z}^*$ are yet to be determined by the interaction of technology and demand conditions.

From (21) an increase in the relative wage reduces the range of commodities domestically produced and therefore raises the fraction of income spent on imports. Abroad the converse holds. An increase in the domestic relative wage increases the range of goods produced abroad and therefore reduces the fraction of income spent on imports. It follows that we can solve:

$$(19') \qquad \bar{\omega} = \frac{1 - \lambda^*(\bar{\omega}/g)}{1 - \lambda(g\bar{\omega})}(L^*/L)$$

$$\equiv \varphi(\bar{\omega}; L^*/L, g) \quad \partial\varphi/\partial\bar{\omega} < 0$$

for the unique equilibrium relative wage as a function of relative size and transport costs:

$$(22) \qquad \bar{\omega} = \bar{\omega}(L^*/L, g)$$

Because (19')'s right-hand side declines as $\bar{\omega}$ rises, a rise in L^*/L must still raise $\bar{\omega}$; a rise in g can shift $\bar{\omega}$ in either direction, depending on the $B(z)$ and $A(z)$ profiles.

The equilibrium relative wage in (22), taken in conjunction with (21), determines the equilibrium geographic production pattern, $\bar{z}$ and $\bar{z}^*$. Since the range of nontraded goods $\bar{z}^* \leq z \leq \bar{z}$ depends in this formulation on the equilibrium relative wage, it is obvious that shifts in given parameters will shift the range of nontraded commodities. Thus, a transfer that raises the equilibrium relative wage at home causes previously exported commodities to become nontraded, and previously nontraded commodities to become importables.

C. *Tariffs*

We consider next the case of zero transport cost but where each country levies a uniform tariff on imports at respective rates t and t^*, with proceeds rebated in lump sum form. This case, too, leads to cost barriers to importing, and to a range of commodities that are not traded, with the boundaries defined by:

$$(23) \qquad \bar{z} = A^{-1}\left(\frac{\omega}{1+t}\right)$$

$$\text{and} \qquad \bar{z}^* = A^{-1}(\omega(1+t^*))$$

From (23) it is apparent that the presence of tariffs in either or both countries must give rise to nontraded goods because in this case $\bar{z} \neq \bar{z}^*$.

The trade balance equilibrium condition at international prices becomes, in place of (19),

$$(24) \qquad (1-\lambda)Y/(1+t) = (1-\lambda^*)Y^*/(1+t^*)$$

where Y and Y^* denote incomes inclusive of lump sum tariff rebates. Using the fact that rebates are equal to the tariff rate times the fraction of income spent on imports, we arrive at the trade balance equilibrium condition in the form:[10]

$$(25) \qquad \omega = \left(\frac{1-\lambda^*}{1-\lambda}\right)\frac{1+t\lambda}{1+t^*\lambda^*}(L^*/L)$$

where λ and λ^* are functions of (ω, t, t^*).

[10]Tariff rebates in the home country are equal to $R = (1-\lambda)Yt/(1+t)$. With $Y \equiv WL + R$ we therefore have $Y = WL(1+t)/(1+\lambda t)$ as an expression for income inclusive of transfers. From equations (20) and (23) we have $\lambda = \lambda[\omega/(1+t)]$ and $\lambda^* = \lambda^*[\omega(1+t^*)]$, having substituted the tariff instead of transport costs as the obstacle to trade.

The implicit relations (25) can be solved for the equilibrium relative wage as a function of relative size and the tariff structure:

$$(26) \qquad \bar{\omega} = \bar{\omega}(L^*/L, t, t^*)$$

From (26) and (23) it is apparent now that the range of nontraded goods will be a function of both tariff rates. It is readily shown that an increase in the tariff improves the imposing country's relative wage and terms of trade. Furthermore, as is well known, when all countries but one are free traders, then one country can always improve its own welfare by imposing a tariff that is not too large.

A further question suggested by (26) concerns the effect of a uniform increase in world tariffs. Starting from zero, a small uniform increase in tariffs raises the relative wage of the country whose commodities command the larger share in world spending. This result occurs for two reasons. First, at the initial relative wage a larger share of spending out of tariff rebates falls on the goods of the country commanding a larger share in world demand. Second, the tariff induces new nontraded goods and therefore increases net demand for the borderline commodity of the country whose residents have the larger income, or equivalently, the larger share in world income.

If countries are of equal size as measured by the share in world income, such a uniform tariff increase has zero effect on relative wages, but of course reduces well-being in both places. Multilateral tariff increases, in this case, unnecessarily create some nontraded goods, and artificially raise the relative price of importables in terms of domestically produced commodities in each country exactly in proportion to the tariff.

IV. Money, Wages, and Exchange Rates

In this section we extend the discussion of the Ricardian model to deal with monetary aspects of trade. Specifically we shall be interested in the determination of exchange rates in a flexible rate system, in the process of adjustment to trade imbalance under fixed rates, and in the role of wage stickiness. The purpose of the extension is to integrate real and monetary aspects of trade.

A. *Flexible Exchange Rates*

The barter analysis of the preceding sections is readily extended to a world of flexible exchange rates and flexible money wages. Assume a given nominal quantity of money in each country, M and M^*, respectively. Further, in accordance with the classical Quantity Theory, assume constant expenditure velocities V and V^*.[11] A flexible exchange rate, and our stipulating the absence of nonmonetary international asset flows, will assure trade balance equilibrium and therefore the equality of income and spending in each country. The nominal money supplies and velocities determine nominal income in each country:

$$(27) \quad WL = MV \quad \text{and} \quad W^*L^* = M^*V^*$$

where W and W^* (now in capital letters) denote domestic and foreign money wages in terms of the respective currencies. Further, defining the exchange rate e as the domestic currency price of foreign exchange, the foreign wage measured in terms of domestic currency is eW^*, and the relative wage therefore is $\omega \equiv W/eW^*$.

From the determination of the equilibrium real wage ratio $\bar{\omega}$ by our earlier "real" relations, we can now find an expression for the equilibrium exchange rates:

$$(28) \quad \bar{e} = (1/\bar{\omega})(\overline{W}/\overline{W}^*) = (1/\bar{\omega})(MV/M^*V^*)(L^*/L)$$

where (27′) defines equilibrium money wages:

$$(27') \qquad \overline{W} = MV/L$$

and

$$\overline{W}^* = M^*V^*/L^*$$

In this simple structure and with wage flexibility, we can keep separate the determinants of all equilibrium real variables from all monetary considerations. Monetary changes or velocity changes in one country will be reflected in equiproportionate changes in prices in that country and in the exchange rate in the fashion of the neutral-money Quantity Theory. However, a real disturbance, as (28) shows, definitely does have repercussions on the nominal exchange rate as well as on the real equilibrium.

Using the results of Section II, we see that an increase in the foreign relative labor force causes, under flexible exchange rates and given $\overline{M}$ and $\overline{M}^*$, a depreciation in the home country's exchange rate as does uniform technical progress abroad. A shift in real demand toward foreign goods likewise leads to a depreciation of the exchange rate as well as to a reduction in real $\bar{\omega}$. A rise in foreign tariffs will also cause our currency to depreciate. Each of these real shifts is assumed to take place while (M, M^*) are unchanged and on the simplifying proviso that real income changes leave V and V^* unchanged.

B. *Fixed Exchange Rates*

In the fixed exchange rates case we assume currencies are fully convertible at a parity pegged by the monetary authorities. In the absence of capital flows and sterilization policy, a trade imbalance is reflected in monetary flows. In the simplest metal money model, the world money supply is redistributed toward the surplus country at precisely the rate of the trade surplus. We assume that the world money supply is given and equal to $\overline{G}$, measured in terms of domestic currency. The rate of increase of the domestic quantity of money is therefore equal to the reduction in foreign money, valued at the fixed exchange rate $\bar{e}$:

$$(29) \qquad \dot{M} = -\bar{e}\dot{M}^*$$

where $\dot{M} \equiv dM/dt$.

For a fixed rate world we have to determine in addition to the real variables $\bar{\omega}$ and $\bar{z}$, the levels of money wages W and W^* as well as the equilibrium balance of payments associated with each short-run equilibrium. In the long run the balance of payments will be zero as money ends up

[11] This is a strong assumption since it makes spending independent of income and nonliquid assets even in the short run.

redistributed internationally to the point where income equals spending in each country. In the short run an initial misallocation of money balances implies a discrepancy between income and spending and an associated trade imbalance. To characterize the preferred rate of adjustment of cash balances in the simplest and most manageable way, we assume that spending by each country is proportional to money holdings.[12] On the further simplifying assumption that velocities are equal in each country, $V = V^*$,[13] world spending is equal to

$$VM + eV^*M^* \equiv V\bar{G} \tag{30}$$

For the tastes and technology specified in Section I, world spending on domestically produced goods is given by

$$V\bar{G}\int_0^{\tilde{z}} b(z)dz \equiv \vartheta(\omega)V\bar{G} \qquad \tilde{z} = A^{-1}(\omega) \tag{31}$$

In equilibrium, world spending on our goods must equal the value of our full-employment income WL:

$$WL = \vartheta(\omega)V\bar{G} \tag{32}$$

Equilibrium requires, too, that world spending on foreign goods equals the value of foreign full-employment income:

$$\bar{e}W^*L^* = [1 - \vartheta(\omega)]V\bar{G} \tag{33}$$

Equations (32) and (33) express what would seem to be the *joint* determination of real and monetary variables. But, in fact, we could have taken the shortcut of recognizing that the real equilibrium is precisely that of the barter analysis developed in Section I. Dividing (32) by (33) and substituting from (11) for the equilibrium relative wage $\bar{\omega}$, we can employ equations (32) and (33) to determine money wage levels.

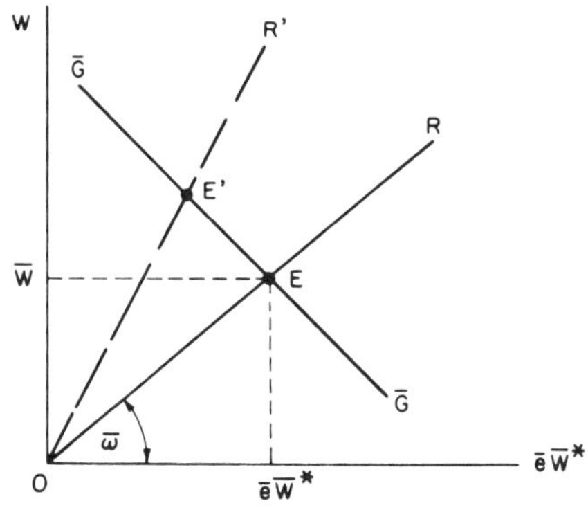

FIGURE 4

The equilibrium determined by equations (32) and (33) can be analyzed in terms of Figure 4. The figure emphasizes the separation of real and monetary aspects of the equilibrium under our assumptions of traded goods only, and no distribution effects. From the ratio of (32) and (33) we obtain the equilibrium relative wage $\bar{\omega}$ as a function of tastes and technology solely from the barter model. This equilibrium relative wage is plotted as the ray OR in Figure 4.

The equality of world income and spending

$$WL + \bar{e}W^*L^* = V\bar{G} \tag{30'}$$

is shown as the downward sloping straight line $\bar{G}\bar{G}$, which is drawn for given velocity, world quantity of money, and labor forces. Point E is the equilibrium where relative prices and the level of wages and prices are such that all markets clear. At a level of wages and prices higher than point E, there would be a world excess supply of goods, and conversely at points below E.

Figure 4 immediately shows some comparative static results. Thus a doubling of both countries' labor forces, from the analysis of the barter model, will leave the relative wage unaffected but will double

[12] The assumption that spending is proportional to cash balances is only one of a number of possible specifications. Conditions for this expenditure function to be optimal are derived in Dornbusch and Michael Mussa. In general, expenditure will depend on both income and cash balances.

[13] In the long-run equilibrium, higher V than V^* leaves us with a smaller share of the world money stock than foreigners, but with nominal and real income *shares* in the two countries the same as when $V = V^*$.

world output. Given unchanged nominal spending $V\overline{G}$, wages and prices will have to halve. This would be shown by a parallel shift of the $\overline{GG}$ schedule halfway toward the origin. A shift in demand toward the home country's output by contrast would rotate the *OR* ray to a position like *OR'* since it raises our relative wage. The ensuing monetary adjustment is then an increase in our money wage and money income and a decline in foreign wages, prices, and incomes (point *E'*).

The real and nominal equilibrium at point *E* in Figure 4 is independent of the short- and long-run distribution of the world quantity of money. The independence of the real equilibrium derives from the uniform homothetic tastes. The independence of the nominal equilibrium is implied by identical velocities. What does, however, depend on the short-run distribution of world money is the transition periods' balance of payments. As in the absorption approach of Sidney Alexander (1952), we know this: when goods markets clear, the trade surplus or balance of payments $\dot{M}$ of the home country is equal to the excess of income over spending, or:

$$(34) \qquad \dot{M} = \overline{W}L - VM$$

With the nominal wage independent of the distribution of world money, equation (34) therefore implies that the trade balance monotonically converges to equilibrium at a rate proportional to the discrepancy from long-run equilibrium:[14]

$$(34') \qquad \dot{M} = V(\overline{M} - M); \ \overline{M} = \vartheta(\overline{\omega})\overline{G}$$

The assumptions of this section were designed to render inoperative most of the traditional mechanisms discussed as part of the adjustment process: changes in the terms of trade, in home and/or foreign price levels, in relative prices of traded and nontraded goods (there being none of the latter), in double factoral terms of trade; and any discrepancies in the price of the same commodity between countries. The features of the adjustment process of this section rely on 1) identical, constant expenditure velocities, 2) uniform-homothetic demand, and 3) the absence of trade impediments. If velocities were constant but differed between countries, the absolute *levels* of money wages and prices, though not *relative* wages or prices, would depend on the world distribution of money. Relaxation of the uniform-homothetic taste assumption would make equilibrium relative prices a function of the distributions of spending. Finally, the presence of nontraded goods would, together with Ricardo's technology, provide valid justification for some of the behavior of relative prices and price levels frequently asserted in the literature; this behavior is studied in more detail in the next section.

C. *The Price-Specie Flow Mechanism under More General Conditions*

We now discuss the adjustment process to monetary disequilibrium and enquire into the price effects associated with a redistribution of the world money supply when there are nontraded goods. Common versions of the Hume price-specie flow mechanism usually involve the argument that in the adjustment process, prices decline along with the money stock in the deficit country, while both rise in the surplus country. There is usually, too, an implication that the deficit country's terms of trade will necessarily worsen in the adjustment process and indeed have to do so if the adjustment is to be successful.

Section IVB demonstrated that the redistribution of money associated with monetary imbalance need have no effects on real variables (production, terms of trade, etc.) and on nominal variables other than the money stock and spending. While this is

[14]Suppose $V > V^*$ and our share of the world money supply is initially larger than our equilibrium share. Then, as we lose M, total world nominal income and nominal *GNP* falls. Always our share of nominal world *GNP* stays the same under the strong demand assumptions. Total world real output never changes during the transition; only regional consumption shares change. Therefore, *both* countries' nominal price and wage levels fall in the transition, but such balanced changes have no real effects on either the transient or the final real equilibrium.

clearly a very special case, it does serve as a benchmark since it establishes that the monetary adjustment process would be effective even in a one-commodity world.

To approach the traditional view of the adjustment process more clearly and provide formal support for that view, we consider an extension to the monetary realm of our previous model involving nontraded goods. We return to the assumption that a fraction $(1 - k)$ of spending in each country falls on nontraded goods, and accordingly equations (32) and (33) become:

$$(32') \qquad WL = \vartheta(\omega)V\overline{G} + (1 - k)\gamma V\overline{G}; \quad \gamma \equiv M/\overline{G}$$

$$(33') \qquad \bar{e}W^*L^* = [k - \vartheta(\omega)]V\overline{G} + (1 - \gamma)(1 - k)V\overline{G}$$

These hold both in final equilibrium, and in transient equilibrium where specie is flowing. Equations (32′) and (33′) imply that the equilibrium relative wage does depend on the distribution of the world money supply. Solving these equations for the equilibrium relative wage we have:

$$(35) \qquad \bar{\omega} = \bar{\omega}(\gamma) \qquad \frac{\partial \bar{\omega}}{\partial \gamma} > 0$$

An increase in the home country's initial share in the world money supply γ raises our relative wage.

Using this extended framework, we can draw on the analysis of the transfer problem in Section II to examine the adjustment that follows an initial distribution of world money between the two countries that differs from the long-run equilibrium distribution.

Suppose our M is initially excessive, say from a gold discovery here. Assume also that the gold discovery occurred when the world was in long-run equilibrium with the previous world money stock. As a result of our excess M, we spend more than our earnings, incurring a balance-of-payments deficit equal to the rate at which our M is flowing out. In effect, the foreign economy is making us a real transfer to offset our deficit. As seen earlier, we, the deficit country, are devoting some of our excess spending to nontraded goods, shifting some of our resources to their production at the expense of our previous exports. We not only export fewer types of goods, but also import more types, and import more of each ($\bar{\omega}$ rises and $\bar{z}$ falls).

During the transition, while the real transfer corresponding to our deficit is taking place, our terms of trade are more favorable than in the long-run state. The new gold raises both their W^* and our W, but in addition, our W is up relative to their W^*. Therefore the price level of goods we continue to produce is up relative to the price level of goods they continue to produce. This is true both for our nontraded goods and for our exportables. The prices of goods we produce rise relative to the prices of goods they produce in proportion to the change in relative wages.

Thus the price levels in the two countries have been changed differentially by the specie flow and implied real transfer. But that does not mean that any traded good ever sells for different prices in two places. In fact the divergence in weighted average (consumer) price levels is due to nontraded goods. The price level will rise in the gold-discovering country relative to the other country the greater is the share of nontraded goods in expenditure, $1 - k$. It is a bit meaningless to say, "What accomplished the adjustment is the relative movements of price levels for nontraded goods in the two countries," since we have seen that the adjustment can and will be made even when there are no such nontraded goods. It is meaningful to say, "The fact that people want to direct some of their expenditure to nontraded goods makes it necessary for resources to shift in and out of them as a result of a real transfer, and such resource shifts take place only because the terms of trade (double-factoral and for traded goods) do shift in the indicated way."

The adjustment process to a monetary disturbance is stable in the sense that the system converges to a long-run equilibrium distribution of money with balanced trade. To appreciate that point, we supplement equations (32′) and (33′) with (34) that continues to describe the monetary adjustment process. We note, however, that now W and W^* are endogenous variables whose levels in the short run do depend on the distribution of the world money supply. A redistribution of money toward the home country would raise our spending and demand for goods, and reduce foreign spending and demand. As before, spending changes for traded goods offset each other precisely so that the net effect is an increase in demand for nontraded goods at home and a decline abroad. As a consequence our wages will rise and foreign wages decline. Therefore, starting from full equilibrium, a redistribution of money toward the home country will create a deficit equal to

$$(36) \quad d\dot{M}/dM = -V(1-\delta) \quad 0 \leq \delta < 1$$

where δ is the elasticity of our nominal wages with respect to the quantity of money and is less than unity.[15] Equation (36) implies that the price-specie flow mechanism is stable.

It is interesting to observe in this context that the presence of nontraded goods in fact *slows down* the adjustment process by comparison with a world of only traded goods (contrary to J. Laurence Laughlin's turn of the century worries). As we saw before, with all goods freely tradeable, wages are independent of the distribution of money, and accordingly $\delta = 0$. Further we observe that the speed of adjustment depends on the relative size of countries. Thus the more equal countries are in terms of size, the slower tends to be the adjustment process.

In concluding this section we note that nontraded goods (and/or localized demand) are essential to the correctness of traditional insistence that the adjustment process necessarily entails absolute and relative price, wage, and income movements. They are, of course, in no way essential to the existence of a stable adjustment process, nor is there at any time a need for a discrepancy of prices of the same commodity across countries in either case.[16]

A final remark concerns the adjustment to real disturbances such as demand shifts or technical progress. It is certainly true that whether the exchange rate is fixed or flexible, real adjustment will have to take place and cannot be avoided by choice of an exchange rate regime. So long as wages and prices are flexible, it is quite false to think that fixed parities "put the whole economy through the wringer of adjustment" while in floating rate regimes "only the export and import industries have to make the real adjustment." It is true, however, that once we depart from flexible wages and prices there may well be a preference for one exchange rate regime over another. The next section is devoted to that question.

D. *Sticky Money Wages*

The last question we address in this section concerns the implications of sticky money wages. For a given world money supply, *downward* stickiness of money wages implies the possibility of unemployment. We assume upward flexibility in wages, once full employment is attained.

We start with a fixed exchange rate $\bar{e}$. The relation between wages and the world quantity of money is brought out in Figure 5. Denote employment levels in each country, as opposed to the labor force, by the new symbols $\bar{L}$ and $\bar{L}^*$, respectively; denote nominal incomes by Y and Y^*. The equality of world income and spending is again shown by the $\overline{GG}$ schedule, the equation of which now is

$$(37) \quad V\bar{G} = Y + \bar{e}Y^* \equiv \overline{W}\bar{L} + \bar{e}\overline{W}^*\bar{L}^*$$

[15]The value of δ can be calculated from equations (32′) and (33′) to be

$$\delta \equiv (1-k)\frac{\gamma(1-\gamma)}{\gamma(1-\gamma)+\vartheta\epsilon}$$

where ϵ is the elasticity of the share of our traded goods in world spending, $\epsilon \equiv -\vartheta'\omega/\vartheta > 0$. The elasticity δ is evaluated at the long-run equilibrium where $\gamma \equiv \vartheta/k$. If $A'(z)$ falls slowly, ϵ will be large.

[16]The continuum Ricardian technology is special in that there can be no range of goods both imported and produced at home. Therefore, the cross elasticity of supply between nontraded goods and exports must be greater than the zero cross elasticity between nontraded goods and imports. Consequently, a transfer must shift the terms of trade (for goods and factors) in the stated orthodox way, favorably for the receiver.

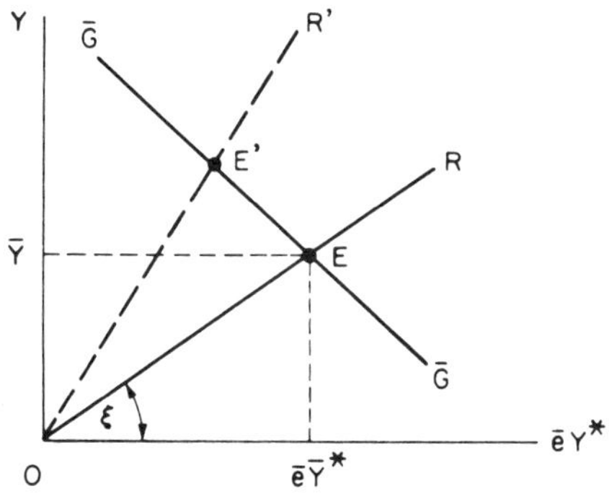

FIGURE 5

where $\overline{W}$ and $\overline{W}^*$ are the fixed money wages set at too high sticky levels. The schedule is drawn for given money wages, a given world quantity of money, and a pegged parity for $\bar{e}$. The ray OR now is predetermined by the given sticky relative wage $\bar{\omega} = \overline{W}/\bar{e}\overline{W}^*$. From equations (32) and (33) the ratio of money incomes $Y/\bar{e}Y^*$ is just a function of the relative wage now given exogenously by rigid money wages and the exchange rate:

$$(38) \quad Y/\bar{e}Y^* = \frac{\vartheta(\omega)}{1 - \vartheta(\omega)} \equiv \xi(\overline{W}/\bar{e}\overline{W}^*) \qquad \xi'(\omega) < 0$$

Point E is the nominal equilibrium where by assumption the world quantity of money is insufficient relative to wage rates to ensure full employment. Although that equilibrium is one with unemployed labor, it is efficient in other respects. Specifically, geographic specialization follows comparative advantage as laid out above, but now labor employed adjusts to sticky wage patterns of specialization.

Employment levels $\overline{L}$ and $\overline{L}^*$ now are determined by (39)

$$(39) \quad \overline{L} = \overline{Y}/\overline{W}, \quad \overline{L}^* = \bar{e}\overline{Y}^*/\overline{W}^*$$

where $\overline{Y}$ and $\overline{Y}^*$ are the equilibrium levels of nominal income determined by equations (37) and (38) or by point E in Figure 5.

Consider now the impact of a foreign increase in money wages. The effect of the implied reduction in our relative wages and the resulting increase in our relative income are shown in Figure 5 by the rotation from OR to OR'.

The new equilibrium is at E' where our money income and employment have risen while income and employment decline abroad. Thus an increase in the foreign wage rate, by moving the terms of trade against us, shifts comparative advantage and employment toward the home country. The extent to which the home country benefits from the adverse terms of trade shift in terms of employment will depend on both the substitutability in demand and the elasticity of the $A(z)$ schedule in Figure 1. We observe, too, that the move from E to E' will bring about a transitory balance-of-payments surplus. Given the initial distribution of money and hence of spending, the foreign decline in income and the increase at home implies that we will spend less than our income and therefore have a trade surplus. This surplus persists until money is redistributed to match the new levels of income at E'.

Next we move to flexible exchange rates. Under flexible rates an increase in the foreign money wage $\overline{W}^*$, given money supplies in each country, will similarly have real repercussion effects on relative prices and employment at home. Now employment in each country is determined by money supplies and prevailing wages:

$$(39') \quad \overline{L} = V\overline{M}/\overline{W}; \quad \overline{L}^* = V\overline{M}^*/\overline{W}^*$$

Given the employment levels thus determined, we know from the analysis of the earlier barter model that there is a unique relative wage at which the trade balance achieves equilibrium. The higher is $\overline{M}^*/\overline{W}^*$, the higher will be employment abroad—and, therefore, the higher will be our relative wage $\bar{\omega}$. It is thus apparent that an increase in the foreign money wage, $\overline{W}^*$, will reduce employment abroad. Employment declines only in proportion to the increase in wages and thus declines by less than it would under fixed exchange rates when specie is lost abroad.

We saw in the barter model that a reduction in effective foreign labor causes a decline in our relative wage, but that the decline in our relative wage falls proportionately short of the foreign reduction in labor. Now, at the initial exchange rate, the increase in foreign wages reduces our relative wage and their employment in the same proportion. The decline in our relative wage is therefore excessive. Domestic goods are underpriced and the exchange rate appreciates to *partly* offset the gain in cost competitiveness. The net effect is therefore a decline in our relative wage and an appreciation of our exchange rate (a decline in e) that falls short of the foreign increase in wages. Since our terms of trade unambiguously deteriorate without any compensating gain in employment, it must be true that welfare declines at home. Abroad, the loss in employment is offset by a gain in the terms of trade, but there too the net effect is a loss in welfare under our strong Mill-Ricardo assumption.

The adjustment to money wage disturbances under fixed and flexible rates differs in several respects. Under fixed rates employment effects are transmitted, while under flexible rates they are bottled up in the country initiating the disturbance. Under fixed rates the terms of trade move one for one with money wage, while under flexible rates exchange rate movements partly offset increases in the foreign money wage rate.

The difference between fixed and flexible rates in relation to the adjustment process is further brought out by an example of a real disturbance. Consider a shift in world demand toward our goods. Under fixed rates the resulting increase in our relative income will, from (38), move us in Figure 5 from E to E'. Employment rises at home and falls abroad. Demand shifts are fully reflected in employment changes. Under flexible rates, by contrast, with given wages and money, a demand shift has no impact on employment—as we observe from (39). At the initial exchange rate the demand shift would give rise to an excess demand for our goods and to an excess supply abroad. Domestic income and employment would tend to rise while falling abroad. The resulting trade surplus causes our exchange rate to appreciate until the initial employment levels and therefore trade balance equilibrium are restored. The demand shift is fully absorbed by a change in the terms of trade and a shift in competitive advantage that restores demand for foreign goods and labor.

Real and nominal equilibria are thus seen to be uniquely definable in our continuum model with constant-velocity spending determinants. The difference between sticky and flexible wage rates under fixed exchange rates is understandable as the difference between (a) having the crucial relative wage $\bar{\omega}$ be imposed in the sticky wage case with employments having then to adjust; or (b) having the full employments be imposed and $\bar{\omega}$ having to adjust. Under floating exchange rates, sticky nominal wages impose employment levels in each country and the crucial relative wage $\bar{\omega}$ then adjusts to those employment levels.

APPENDIX

Historical Remark

Figure 1 seems to be new. G. A. Elliot (1950) gives a somewhat different diagram, one that makes explicit the meaning of Marshall's 1879 "bales" (which, by the way, happen to work only in the two-country constant labor costs case). In terms of the present notations, Elliott plots for the *U.S.* offer curve the following successive points traced out for all ω on the range $[0, \infty]$: on the vertical axis is plotted our total real imports valued in foreign labor units ("our demand for bales of their labor," so to speak), namely,

$$\int_{\bar{z}}^{1} [P^*(z)/w^*]C(z)dz = \int_{\bar{z}}^{1} a^*(z)C(z)dz$$

and on the horizontal axis, our total real exports valued in home labor units ("our supply of bales of labor to them"), namely,

$$\int_{0}^{\bar{z}} [P(z)/w][Q(z) - C(z)]dz = L - \int_{0}^{\bar{z}} a(z)C(z)dz$$

It is to be understood that $\bar{z}$ is a function of ω, namely the inverse function $A^{-1}(\omega)$; also that $C(z)$ are the amounts demanded as a function of our real income L and of the $P(z)/W$ function defined for each, namely $\min[\omega a(z), a^*(z)]$. Because we have a continuum of goods, we avoid Elliott's branches of the offer curve that are segments of various rays through the origin. The reader will discern by symmetry considerations how the foreign offer curve is plotted in the same (L, L^*) quadrant, by varying ω to generate the respective coordinates

$$\left[\int_0^{\bar{z}} a(z)C^*(z)dz,\qquad L^* - \int_{\bar{z}}^1 a^*(z)C^*(z)dz\right]$$

Our model forces the Elliott-Marshall diagram to generate a *unique* solution under uniform-homothetic demand. Unlike our Figure 1, the Elliott diagram can handle the general case of nonhomothetic demands in the two countries; but then, as is well known, multiple solutions are possible, some locally stable and some unstable. The price one pays for this generality is that, as Edgeworth observed, the Marshallian curves are the end products of much implicit theorizing, with much that is interesting having taken place offstage.

REFERENCES

S. Alexander, "The Effects of a Devaluation on the Trade Balance," *Int. Monet. Fund Staff Pap.*, Apr. 1952, *2*, 263–78.

J. S. Chipman, "A Survey of International Trade: Part I: The Classical Theory," *Econometrica*, July 1965, *33*, 477–519.

G. Debreu, "Economies with a Finite Set of Equilibria," *Econometrica*, May 1970, *38*, 387–92.

R. Dornbusch and M. Mussa, "Consumption, Real Balances and the Hoarding Function," *Int. Econ. Rev.*, June 1975, *16*, 415–21.

G. A. Elliott, "The Theory of International Values," *J. Polit. Econ.*, Feb. 1950, *58*, 16–29.

F. Graham, "The Theory of International Balances Re-Examined," *Quart. J. Econ.*, Nov. 1923, *38*, 54–86.

Gottfried Haberler, *The Theory of International Trade*, London 1937.

R. W. Jones, "Presumption and the Transfer Problem," *J. Int. Econ.*, Aug. 1975, *5*, 263–74.

James Laurence Laughlin, *Principles of Money*, New York 1903.

John S. Mill, *Principles of Political Economy*, London 1848.

David Ricardo, *On the Principles of Political Economy and Taxation*, 1817; edited by P. Sraffa, London 1951.

P. A. Samuelson, "The Transfer Problem and Transport Costs: The Terms of Trade When Impediments are Absent," *Econ. J.*, June 1952, *62*, 278–304; reprinted in Joseph Stiglitz, ed., *Collected Scientific Papers of Paul A. Samuelson*, Vol. 2, Cambridge, Mass., ch. 74.

———, "The Transfer Problem and the Transport Costs, II: Analysis of Effects of Trade Impediments," *Econ. J.*, June 1954, *64*, 264–89; reprinted in Joseph Stiglitz, ed., *Collected Scientific Papers of Paul A. Samuelson*, Vol. 2, Cambridge, Mass., ch. 75.

———, "Theoretical Notes on Trade Problems," *Rev. Econ. Statist.*, May 1964, *46*, 145–54; reprinted in Joseph Stiglitz, ed., *Collected Scientific Papers of Paul A. Samuelson*, Vol. 2, Cambridge, Mass., ch. 65.

S. Smale, "Structurally Stable Systems Are Not Dense," *Amer. J. Math.*, 1966, *88*, 491–96.

Frank W. Taussig, *International Trade*, New York 1927.

Jacob Viner, *Studies in the Theory of International Trade*, New York 1937.

C. Wilson, "On the General Structure of Ricardian Models with a Continuum of Goods: Applications to Growth, Tariff Theory and Technical Change," unpublished paper, Univ. Wisconsin-Madison, 1977.

HECKSCHER-OHLIN TRADE THEORY WITH A CONTINUUM OF GOODS

RUDIGER DORNBUSCH
STANLEY FISCHER
PAUL A. SAMUELSON

This paper studies trade theory for the case of a continuum of goods, two factors, two countries, and Cobb-Douglas demand functions. If factor endowments are similar, factor price equalization obtains and geographic patterns of production are indeterminate; nonetheless the effects of changes in factor endowments on prices and welfare in each country are well defined. Factor price equalization does not obtain if factor endowments are far apart, and the geographic pattern of specialization is then determinate. The effects of changes in endowments on the range of goods produced in each country and on prices of goods and factors are analyzed for this case, and the elasticity of substitution in production is shown to play an important role in determining comparative static outcomes.

I. INTRODUCTION

This paper studies Heckscher-Ohlin trade theory in a model with a continuum of goods. In earlier work [Dornbusch, Fischer, and Samuelson, 1977] we formulated a continuum model for the case of Ricardian technology—constant unit labor requirements and labor as the only factor—and showed that the continuum assumption offers great convenience in analyzing standard questions in trade theory. In this paper we report on some applications of the continuum model to the more complicated case of two factors of production.

Section II introduces the model and shows the derivation of the closed-economy equilibrium. Here it is shown that the equilibrium wage-rental ratio fully characterizes the equilibrium of our economy,

* Financial support was provided by grants from the National Science Foundation. We are indebted to an anonymous referee for a speedy and careful report.

even though there is an infinity of goods. In Section III we proceed to an open economy with equalized factor prices. The familiar result that the world economy under factor price equalization is like a single economy is shown, as is the fact that there is no determinate trade pattern. There are nevertheless interesting results relating to growth, world income distribution, and welfare that can be demonstrated for this case.

Section IV develops the analysis of equilibrium in the world economy when factor prices differ internationally, as they will when factor endowments are sufficiently far apart. We show first the determination of equilibrium specialization patterns, and then derive the relationship between relative factor prices and the various regional endowments of factors of production. There is now the possibility—not present in the two-commodity model—of some ambiguity about the effects of growth on relative factor and commodity prices and trade patterns. There is also the fact that specialization will always extend to a range of goods rather than to a single commodity and that accordingly, as we shall show, relative factor prices may move in opposite directions in the two countries.

To pave the way for analysis of the Heckscher-Ohlin continuum model, we recapitulate known results for the case of n goods and m factors. In particular, the case of $n > m$ is of most interest here, since the continuum model involves n as an uncountably infinite number. The exposition simplifies when we assume the following: (1) uniform (strongly quasi-concave) homothetic tastes;[1] and (2) each country has the same concave, first-degree-homogeneous production functions, of the smooth neoclassical type. In the two-factor case ($m = 2$, corresponding to capital and labor), the exposition simplifies when out of any pair of goods, one is always definitely more capital-intensive than the other at *every* factor-price ratio.

One can verify the following results:

For any pattern of factor endowments, a unique pattern of goods and factor pricing is determined. Also, there is a unique equilibrium pattern of world and regional consumptions, with consumption ratios the same in every country when transport costs of goods are literally zero.

If all countries have identical factor-endowment ratios, the pricing and consumption pattern prevailing in every country is what

1. Much of our continuum analysis will be carried out under the further simplifying assumption that uniform homothetic tastes are of the Millian or Cobb-Douglas form: regardless of prices and incomes, every region always spends a fixed function of its income on each respective good. See Samuelson [forthcoming], Wan [1977], and Wilson [forthcoming] for more general models.

would prevail in each and every country under autarky. Real factor returns are, of course, equalized (with or without goods' trade).

However, if there are more goods than factors, it need *not* be the case that each region produces its own autarky-quantum of consumption goods, although that is an admissible pattern of geographical specialization. But, with $n > m$, there will be an $(n - m)$-fold infinity of geographical patterns or production specialization.[2] The indeterminacy is inessential when transport costs are zero.[3]

With $n = m$, the geographical pattern will almost always be unique.

Now let the two countries differ slightly in factor-endowment ratios. Then factor returns will stay equalized, and uniform world pricing and consuming patterns are uniquely determined. Again, with $n > m$, the pattern of production specialization is not geographically determined in a unique way. There will still be an $(n - m)$-fold infinity of indifferent admissible patterns. However, the region with excess labor endowment on average produces goods that are of higher labor intensity than goods produced abroad.

Finally, let the two countries differ more and more in factor-endowment ratios. With n finite, eventually the country with the greater relative capital endowment will find its real rental rate (in terms of every good) falling below that of the other country; as the real rental rate r falls here and the wage-rental ratio w/r rises, the real wage also rises here; and w^*/r^*, w^*, and $1/r^*$ all move in the same direction.[4]

Here is a brief account of Heckscher-Ohlin specialization patterns in the two-factor case. Under our strong assumption, we can rank the goods in order of decreasing relative capital intensity:

$$1, 2, \ldots, j, j + 1, \ldots, n.$$

Good 1 will certainly be produced at home if ours is the capital-rich region with higher w/r. Good n will certainly be produced abroad and be imported by us. As in the analysis of Ricardian comparative advantage, from technology alone, one cannot deduce which other goods

2. See Meade [1950] for discussion of the algebra of the $n = 3 > m = 2$ case. Geometrically, when $n > m$, the production-possibility frontier of any region has straight lines or planes on it; so the tangency between two regions' frontiers, needed to define the world production-possibility frontier, can be along an infinity of points belonging to both regions' flat facets. See also Melvin [1968].

3. When transport costs are positive, the invisible hand of competitive arbitrage will solve the problem that minimizes deadweight loss from cross haulage or non-optimal specialization.

4. An increase in capital in our region, other things equal, lowers both real r and, at least initially, r^*; it raises both real w and initially real w^*; how it ultimately affects r/r^* does not seem to be uniformly predictable.

$2, \ldots, j$ the home region must also produce, and which goods $j, \ldots, n$ we definitely have to import. Where j falls between 1 and n must depend on the full general-equilibrium conditions of reciprocal demand.

In the discrete many-goods case, there are two possible types of equilibria: one in which *no* good is produced by *both* countries; and the other "limbo" case in which the borderline good *is* produced in both countries. The continuum case that we consider in this paper is special in that there is only one type of equilibrium, which we may think of as involving the joint production of the borderline commodity. We proceed now to the closed-economy continuum model.

II. The Closed Economy

There is a continuum of goods, indexed by z (z runs from zero to one), and two factors of production, capital and labor. Supplies of the two factors are fixed exogenously at levels K and N, respectively. Production functions for each of the goods are regularly neoclassical, satisfying the Inada conditions. The goods are indexed in order of decreasing capital intensity of production; there are no factor intensity reversals so that, for instance, good zero is the most capital-intensive in production at all wage-rental ratios.

We assume *uniform* homothetic demand. Our earlier paper's assumption of Millian or Cobb-Douglas demand is again postulated: C-D demand means that the function of income spent on good z, $b(z)$, is the same at all prices and in both countries. The integral over $b(z)$ on the interval $0 \leq z \leq 1$ is thus unity, as all income is spent.

1. The Equilibrium

We now examine the existence and properties of the equilibrium of this economy. For every good, the condition of equality of supply and demand is

$$P(z)Q(z) = b(z)(wN + rK), \tag{1}$$

where $Q(z)$ is the output of good z, $P(z)$ is the price, w is the wage rate, r is the rental rate on capital.

Full employment is assumed, so that total income is equal to the bracketed expression on the right-hand side of (1). By virtue of the assumed constant returns to scale, the value of output of commodity z is equal to $[wN(z) + rK(z)]$, where $N(z)$ and $K(z)$ are the quantities of labor and capital employed in the production of z. Simple manipulation results in (2) as an equivalent statement of the equilibrium condition in market z:

$$x(z) \equiv \frac{N(z)}{N} = \frac{b(z)(\sigma + k)}{\sigma + k(\sigma;z)}, \tag{2}$$

where $\sigma \equiv w/r$ is the wage-rental ratio, k is the aggregate capital-labor ratio, and $k(\sigma;z)$ is the capital-labor ratio in industry z, a function of σ, the wage-rental ratio.[5]

Labor and capital must be fully employed in equilibrium. This fact implies, for labor, that

$$\int_0^1 N(z)dz = N \tag{3}$$

or

$$\int_0^1 x(z)dz = 1 = \int_0^1 \frac{b(z)\,(\sigma + k)}{\sigma + k(z)}\,dz. \tag{4}$$

The full-employment condition for capital is, analogously,

$$\int_0^1 x(z)k(z)dz = k = \int_0^1 \frac{b(z)k(z)(\sigma + k)}{\sigma + k(z)}\,dz. \tag{5}$$

Combining (4) and (5), we obtain the fundamental equilibrium condition for the closed economy:

$$\phi(\sigma;k) \equiv \int_0^1 \frac{b(z)(\sigma + k)}{\sigma + k(z)}\,[k(z) - k]dz = 0. \tag{6}$$

To demonstrate the existence of a unique equilibrium, we consider first the case of Cobb-Douglas production functions. With such production functions distributive shares are constant, and we can substitute in (4) the constant ratios of income shares $\Psi(z) \equiv k(z)/\sigma$ to obtain

$$1 = \int_0^1 b(z)\,\frac{1 + k/\sigma}{1 + \Psi(z)}\,dz \equiv \xi\left(\frac{k}{\sigma}\right). \tag{4$'$}$$

It is immediately apparent that the right-hand side is a uniformly decreasing function of the wage-rental ratio that runs the gamut from $+\infty$ to a number less than one, and that accordingly there exists a unique $\bar{\sigma}$ that solves (4)′ as shown in Figure I.

For the more general case of production functions not restricted to unit elasticities of substitution, it is convenient to look at (6). That at least one equilibrium for this economy exists is established by ob-

5. In what follows, we shall simplify notation and write $k(z)$ instead of $k(\sigma,z)$.

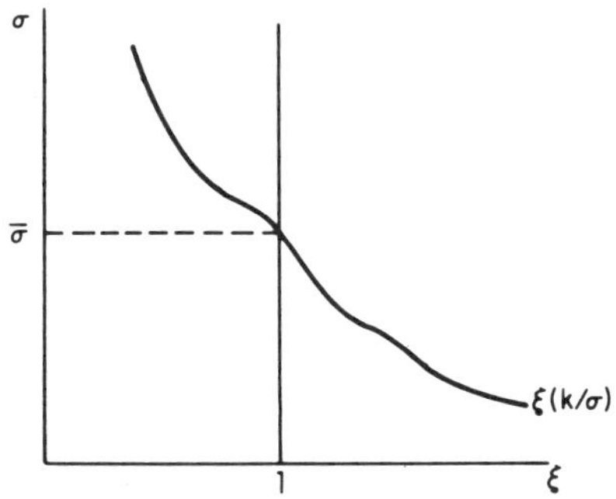

FIGURE I

serving first that, by virtue of the assumption that the production functions are neoclassical, $\phi(\ )$ is continuous in σ; and second, that because each production function satisfies the Inada conditions, there are values of σ such that $k(z)$ is greater than k for all z, and hence that $\phi(\sigma,k)$ is positive at those values of σ, and similarly, that there are values of σ at which $k(z)$ is less than k for all z, so that $\phi(\ )$ is negative at those values of σ. Given that $\phi(\sigma,k)$ is continuous in σ, there is some $\bar{\sigma}$ such that $\phi(\ )$ is equal to zero; $\bar{\sigma}$ is an equilibrium wage-rental ratio.

At such a wage-rental ratio there is full employment of both factors, and the production of each good can be determined from (2) and (3). The equilibrium is in fact unique. To show this, we establish that the derivative of $\phi(\ )$ with respect to σ is positive. Differentiating (6) yields

$$(7)\quad \frac{\partial \phi}{\partial \sigma} = \int_0^1 \frac{b(z)}{[\sigma + k(z)]^2}\left[(k(z) - k)^2 + (\sigma + k)^2 \frac{\partial k(z)}{\partial \sigma}\right] dz > 0.$$

The existence of a unique equilibrium $\bar{\sigma}$ under our strong assumptions is thus established. Given the wage-rental ratio, the rental rate in terms of any good can be determined from the production functions. The relative price structure and the level of income are accordingly determined, as is the demand for each good. We next examine relative price behavior in more detail.

Defining the relative price of commodity z in terms of commodity z', we have

$$\frac{P(z)}{P(z')} = \frac{a(z)w + c(z)r}{a(z')w + c(z')r} = \frac{a(z)[\sigma + k(z)]}{a(z')[\sigma + k(z')]},$$

where $a(z)$ is the unit labor requirement and $c(z)$ the unit capital requirement for commodity z. Taking logs and differentiating, we obtain the familiar result,

$$\frac{d \ln[P(z)/P(z')]}{d\sigma} = \frac{[k(z') - k(z)]}{[\sigma + k(z)][\sigma + k(z')]},$$

so that an increase in the wage-rental ratio lowers the relative price of the capital-intensive good.

Real factor returns are also determined by the wage-rental ratio. An increase in the wage-rental ratio raises the real wage in terms of all commodities and lowers the real rental on capital in terms of all goods.[6]

2. *Comparative Statics*

The equilibrium condition and the relative price structure can now be used to discuss questions of comparative statics. We consider here two applications, changes in the factor endowments, and changes in tastes.

Endowment Changes. We would expect an increase in the capital-labor ratio to reduce the relative return to capital. That result can be demonstrated by differentiating the equilibrium condition in (6), noting that

$$\left.\frac{\partial\phi}{\partial k}\right|_{\phi=0} = -(\sigma + k)\int_0^1 \frac{b(z)}{\sigma + k(z)}\,dz = -1$$

and hence

$$\frac{d\bar{\sigma}}{dk} = 1 \Big/ \frac{\partial\phi}{\partial\sigma} > 0.$$

The increase in the equilibrium wage-rental ratio induced by a higher capital-labor ratio implies changes in relative prices, real factor returns, and resource allocation.[7] The relative price of labor-intensive goods will rise, and the real wage will increase in terms of all com-

6. Defining the real wage and the real rental in terms of commodity z yields

$$\frac{w}{P(z)} = \frac{w}{wa(z) + rc(z)} = \frac{\sigma/a(z)}{\sigma + k(z)}; \quad \frac{r}{P(z)} = \frac{1/a(z)}{\sigma + k(z)}.$$

The elasticities of the real factor prices with respect to the wage-rental ratio are

$$\frac{d \ln(w/P(z))}{d \ln \sigma} = \frac{k(z)}{\sigma + k(z)} \quad \text{and} \quad \frac{d \ln[r/P(z)]}{d \ln \sigma} = -\frac{\sigma}{\sigma + k(z)}.$$

7. For the special case of Cobb-Douglas demand *and* production functions, it can be shown that the elasticity of σ with respect to k is unity. This is directly apparent from (4)′.

modities, while the real return to the more plentiful capital declines in terms of all commodities.

Next we ask how an increase in the capital stock affects the output of each good. The output of good z (per capita) is given by

$$q(z) = \frac{b(z)(w + rk)}{P(z)} = \frac{b(z)(\sigma + k)f(k(z))}{\sigma + k(z)} \tag{8}$$

The effect of an increased k therefore is

$$\frac{dq(z)}{dk} = \frac{b(z)f(k(z))}{\sigma + k(z)}\left[1 + \frac{d\sigma}{dk}\frac{k(z) - k}{\sigma + k(z)}\right] \tag{9}$$

For all low z industries, for which $k(z) > k$, an increase in the aggregate capital stock unambiguously increases physical production. However, it is possible that output in high z industries falls.[8] Note from (9) that if output for any industry falls, it also falls for all those with lower capital intensity. These results simply reflect the income and price effects induced by an expansion in the capital-labor ratio. The income effect raises demand for all goods. The induced increase in the wage-rental ratio lowers the relative price of capital-intensive goods—goods where $k(z) > k$—and thus adds to the demand for those commodities, while reducing demand for relatively labor-intensive goods.

Given that $d\sigma/dk > 0$, capital intensity of production rises in every industry when the overall capital-labor ratio rises. Accordingly, an increase in k must mean that labor is withdrawn in absolute quantity from those high z industries (if any) whose output falls. But it is not necessarily true that labor input is increased for *all* low z industries; that depends on the derivative $\partial k(z)/\partial\sigma$. The more the industry's capital-output ratio responds to a change in the wage-rental ratio (i.e., the higher the elasticity of substitution at that point), the less likely is it that labor is shifted into a particular low z industry. But, on average, labor is shifted into low z industries.

Shifts in Tastes. We ask next about a shift in tastes toward the low z industries. Since we are increasing the demand for capital-intensive goods, we should expect the wage-rental ratio to fall. We conveniently parameterize the change in tastes by adding to each $b(z)$ an amount $\lambda\Delta b(z)$, where λ is a positive scalar, $\int \Delta b(z)dz = 0$, and $\Delta b(z) > 0$ for $0 \le z \le \hat{z}$; and $\Delta b(z) < 0$ for $\hat{z} \le z \le 1$, where $k(\hat{z}) = k$.

8. Of course, it is possible that the output of *all* goods rises. That *must* happen with Cobb-Douglas production functions for every good: in that case a rise in K can be shown to leave real income measured in wage units unchanged. Hence costs, measured in wage units, fall for every good and output increases.

Then

$$\frac{\partial \phi}{\partial \lambda} = \int_0^1 \frac{\Delta b(z)(\sigma + k)(k(z) - k)}{\sigma + k(z)} dz > 0,$$

and accordingly

$$\frac{d\sigma}{d\lambda} < 0.$$

An interesting implication of the shift in demand, and a perhaps surprising one, is that the net effect is not necessarily to raise equilibrium output of all the goods toward which demand shifts. The reason again is the relative price effect, which in this instance implies an increase in the relative price of capital-intensive goods. Since the relative price increases with capital intensity, the substitution effect works against increases in the output of highly capital-intensive commodities and thus for the most capital-intensive goods potentially offsets the shift in demand.

We shall not pursue the properties of the closed-economy equilibrium further because our main interest in it is as a prelude to the open-economy model, to which we now turn.

III. Trading Equilibrium with Equalized Factor Prices

We now put the closed economy of Section II together with another such economy, which differs only in its factor supplies: the foreign capital-labor ratio k^* is smaller than ours. Their labor force is of size N^*.

Initially assume that after the opening of the economies to trade, factor price equalization obtains. The costs of production of all goods will accordingly be identical in both countries after trade opens. Any particular good z can be produced as well (cheaply) in one country as in the other. Given zero transport costs, prices of goods are the same in both countries. Patterns of production are not, however, totally indeterminate, since full employment of both factors requires us, on balance, to produce more capital-intensive goods.

We leave to the Appendix the demonstration that the equilibrium conditions for the world economy are precisely those of the closed economy except that now the capital-labor ratio is $\hat{k} \equiv \pi k + (1 - \pi)k^*$, that is, the respective country's capital-labor ratios weighted by the shares in the world labor force, $\pi \equiv N/(N + N^*)$. The opening of trade with the resulting establishment of a common wage-rental ratio implies, using the result $d\sigma/dk > 0$ of the previous part, that in the capital poor country the wage-rental ratio will rise, while at home it will decline. Prices will be equalized and in the home country the relative price of labor-intensive goods will fall by comparison with autarky, while abroad it will rise.

Production patterns will be indeterminate except in one important respect. Only in a probabilistic sense are we, the capital-rich country, exporters of a *particular* capital-intensive commodity. On *average,* however, we do export capital-intensive commodities, while foreigners export labor-intensive commodities. Equivalently, we are *net* exporters of capital services and *net* importers of labor services. It is this fact that is used now to discuss the effects of endowment changes on income distribution and welfare.

Consider first the benefits from the opening of trade. We noted above that the opening of trade will equalize wage-rental ratios, lowering the relative price of labor in the capital-rich country and increasing the relative price of labor in the capital-poor country. Now we want to show that the opening of trade raises "welfare" for both countries.

We define the welfare function corresponding to our Cobb-Douglas tastes:

$$U = \int_0^1 b(z)[\ln D(z)]dz, \tag{10}$$

where $D(z)$ denotes per capita consumption of commodity z. Substituting for $D(z)$, we have the indirect utility function:

$$U = \int_0^1 b(z)\left[\ln b(z)\frac{\sigma + k}{\sigma + k(z)} f(k(z))\right] dz = U(\sigma,k). \tag{10'}$$

The opening of trade will reduce our wage-rental ratio, since by assumption, we are the capital-rich country. To assess the effect on welfare, we take the derivative of (10′) with respect to σ to obtain

$$\frac{dU}{d\sigma} = \int_0^1 b(z)\left[\frac{1}{\sigma + k} - \frac{1}{\sigma + k(z)}\right] dz. \tag{11}$$

Using (6), with k replaced by $\hat{k}$, and noting that $\int_0^1 b(z)\,dz = 1$, we have

$$\frac{dU}{d\sigma} = \frac{\hat{k} - k}{(\sigma + k)(\sigma + \hat{k})}. \tag{11'}$$

For the home country, $\hat{k} < k$, and σ falls on the opening of trade; thus (11′) shows that the opening of trade makes us better off. For the foreigners, an expression similar to (11′), but with k replaced by k^*, applies. For them, $\hat{k} > k^*$, and σ rises on the opening of trade, which also makes them better off. The magnitude of the gain will depend on the extent of the differences in factor endowments.

We turn next to the income distribution and welfare effects of changes in factor endowments. Consider first the distribution of income. Our share in world income is equal to

$$\frac{wN + rK}{wN + rK + wN^* + rK^*} = \pi \frac{\sigma + k}{\sigma + \hat{k}}. \tag{12}$$

A change in factor endowments would therefore change the international distribution of income. First, a larger labor force would raise the capital-rich country's share in world income. Second, an increase in the foreign capital-labor ratio raises the world capital-labor ratio and thus the wage-rental ratio. Income, therefore, is redistributed away from capital and toward labor. That redistribution must benefit the capital-poor country.

What are the welfare effects of a change in our own capital-labor ratio? Again using the indirect utility function and taking the derivative with respect to k, noting that $\sigma = \sigma(\hat{k})$, we have

$$\frac{\partial U}{\partial k} = \frac{1}{\sigma + k} + \pi \frac{\hat{k} - k}{(\sigma + k)(\sigma + \hat{k})} \frac{d\sigma}{d\hat{k}}. \tag{13}$$

The first term measures the welfare gain of an increase in capital in the closed economy and is of course positive. The second term is negative for the capital-rich country and arises from the international redistribution of income toward the capital-poor country. An increase in the world capital-labor ratio worsens the terms of trade of capital and may do so sufficiently to more than offset the gains from increased productive resources. It can be shown, though, that this possibility cannot arise with elasticities of substitution in production of unity or more.[9]

In summary, the home country, being capital rich and therefore being a net exporter of capital services and importer of labor services, will benefit from a rise in the world wage-rental ratio due to demand shifts or foreign endowment changes. The foreign country, being labor rich, will benefit if the home country accumulates capital or experiences balanced growth or if demand shifts raise the equilibrium wage-rental ratio.

The interesting conclusion of the model with factor price equalization is that, the absence of a determinate production pattern notwithstanding, we can make judgments about welfare effects of

9. Proof of this proposition is omitted for brevity. However, examination of (13) suggests that if $d\sigma/dk$ is low, the second term is less likely to dominate. And $d\sigma/dk$ is inversely related to individual elasticities of substitution in production.

growth or demand changes. The welfare effects are determinate because there is no ambiguity about the fact that the home country is a *net* exporter of capital services and importer of labor services and there is a unique relation between endowments and relative factor and commodity prices.

IV. Trade with Complete Specialization

Now we consider the case where endowments differ sufficiently to give rise to complete specialization. Assuming, as before, that the foreign capital-labor ratio falls short of ours ($k^* < k$), the equilibrium is one where we produce in the capital-intensive range of goods, while foreigners specialize, without overlap, in the range of labor-intensive commodities. The borderline $\bar{z}$ is one of the variables determined as part of the equilibrium along with the two wage-rental ratios. In the equilibrium, we shall produce goods z, $0 \leq z \leq \bar{z}$, and foreigners produce those z in the interval $\bar{z} \leq z \leq 1$.

1. The Equilibrium

The equilibrium is determined by the conditions of trade balance equilibrium and factor market equilibrium in each country. In addition, the cost of production of the borderline commodity $\bar{z}$ is equalized between the two countries. Cost and price equalization at the margin requires that

$$P(\bar{z}) = wa(\bar{z}) + rc(\bar{z}) = P^*(\bar{z}) = w^*a^*(\bar{z}) + r^*c^*(\bar{z}) \tag{14}$$

or

$$\frac{r}{r^*} = \frac{a^*(\bar{z})}{a(\bar{z})} \frac{\sigma^* + k^*(\bar{z})}{\sigma + k(\bar{z})}. \tag{14'}$$

Since the wage-rental ratios differ, with $\sigma > \sigma^*$, the borderline commodity will be produced with a more capital-intensive technique at home compared to that used abroad.

Next we examine the condition of trade balance: the value of our imports is equal to the value of our exports. Our total income is $wN + rK$, and we import all those goods we do not produce, i.e., goods lying in the interval $\bar{z} \leq z \leq 1$. Similarly, foreigners import goods in the range $0 \leq z \leq \bar{z}$. The condition of trade balance is therefore[10]

10. After a little manipulation, (15) can be written in the form

$$\frac{w}{w^*} = \frac{N^*}{N} \frac{(1 + k^*/\sigma^*)}{(1 + k/\sigma)} B(\bar{z}),$$

which is similar to (10′) in our 1977 Ricardian paper.

$$(15)\quad (wN + rK) \int_{\bar{z}}^{1} b(z)dz = (w^*N^* + r^*K^*) \int_{0}^{\bar{z}} b(z)dz.$$

Using (14)′, we can rewrite the trade balance condition as

$$(16)\quad \mathrm{B}(\hat{z}) \equiv \frac{\int_0^{\bar{z}} b(z)dz}{\int_{\bar{z}}^{1} b(z)dz} = \frac{\pi}{1-\pi}\left(\frac{\sigma + k}{\sigma^* + k^*}\right)\left(\frac{a^*(\bar{z})}{a(\bar{z})}\right)\left(\frac{\sigma^* + k^*(\bar{z})}{\sigma + k(\bar{z})}\right).$$

The equilibrium conditions are completed by the requirement of factor market equilibrium in each country:[11]

$$(17)\qquad 0 = \int_0^{\bar{z}} \frac{b(z)}{\sigma + k(z)}[k(z) - k]dz,$$

and

$$(18)\qquad 0 = \int_{\bar{z}}^{1} \frac{b(z)}{\sigma^* + k^*(z)}[k^*(z) - k^*]\, dz.$$

It goes almost without saying that prices of goods are equal in the two countries in the assumed absence of transport costs, and that the costs of production of goods that we do not produce would be higher here than they are abroad.

The equilibrium conditions in (16) to (18) determine the equilibrium wage-rental ratios in each country, $\bar{\sigma}$ and $\bar{\sigma}^*$, and the equilibrium competitive margin $\bar{z}$. The relative price structure, incomes, commodity demands, and factor allocation are associated with the equilibrium relative factor prices. The relative prices and the competitive margin determine trade patterns.

That there is a unique equilibrium of equations (16), (17), and (18), with its implied pricing relationships that we have not written out explicitly, can be established by considering the normative problem that is satisfied by, and only by, the competitive solution. This is shown in Appendix 1.

11. To obtain (17), start from the labor market equilibrium condition,

$$N = \int_0^{\bar{z}} [a(z)b(z)(wN + rK) + (w^*N^* + r^*K^*)]/P(z)\, dz,$$

use (15), and obtain

$$\theta = \int_0^{\bar{z}} \frac{b(z)(\sigma + k)}{\sigma + k(z)} dz,$$

where $\theta \equiv \int_0^{\bar{z}} b(z)dz$. Similar manipulation, starting from the full employment condition for capital shows that

$$\theta k = \int_0^{\bar{z}} \frac{b(z)(\sigma + k)}{\sigma + k(z)} k(z)dz.$$

Equation (17) follows.

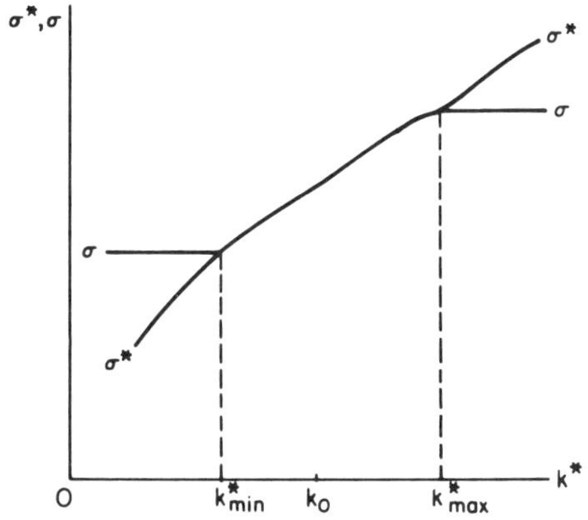

FIGURE II

2. Comparative Statics

We turn now to questions of comparative statics. Specifically we want to establish the effect of endowment changes on relative factor and commodity prices and on trade patterns. In our 1977 paper we showed how growth in one country changes the *equilibrium* dividing line $\bar{z}$ with the growing country increasing the range of goods produced but experiencing a decline in the equilibrium relative wage and terms of trade. In the present model there is a broader range of questions, since in addition to labor growth we can consider balanced growth or growth in the capital-labor ratio. As we shall see presently, there is ambiguity in the effect of growth on factor and commodity prices and in the effect of growth on trade patterns.

Before establishing these results, it is worth asking what the effects of growth are in the standard two-commodity Heckscher-Ohlin model. Figure II summarizes these results in plotting the equilibrium wage-rental ratios as a function of the foreign capital-labor ratio, given our capital stock k_0. The range of factor price equalization is $k^*_{\min}$ to $k^*_{\max}$. For that range of their capital-labor ratio, relative commodity and hence factor prices are such that we are nonspecialized.

A rise in their capital-labor ratio at constant relative prices of goods would, via the Rybczynski effect, create a world excess supply of the capital-intensive good and hence lower its equilibrium relative price and therefore raise the common equilibrium wage-rental ratio. As foreign k^* goes outside the range ($k^*_{\min} \le k^* \le k^*_{\max}$), we become completely specialized in one sector, and consequently our wage-rental ratio is determined by the relative marginal productivities in the producing sector. For the foreign country, though, the wage-rental

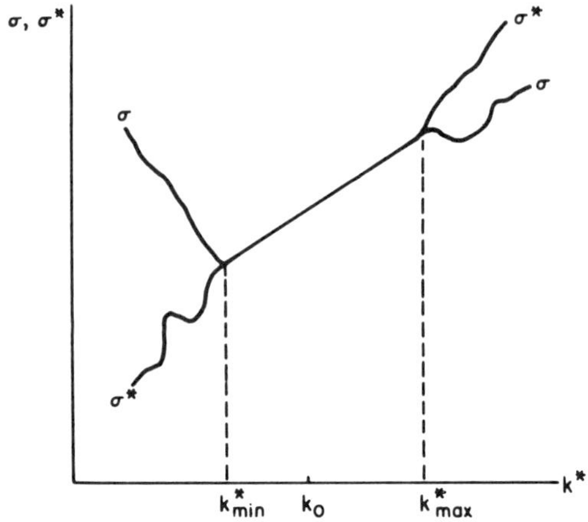

FIGURE III

ratio would continue to be an increasing function of the capital-labor ratio.[12]

One important difference in a multi-commodity model, and in particular in our continuum model, is the fact that we never achieve complete specialization in one single good and that accordingly the relation between relative factor prices and endowments will differ from that in Figure II.[13] The comparative static results of the continuum case are laid out in Table I and are illustrated in Figure III, which is to be compared with Figure II.

Consider first the case where our capital-labor ratio is larger than that abroad, $k^* < k_{\min}$, and where we have complete specialization and unequalized factor returns. A rise in the foreign capital-labor ratio, as Figure III shows, will reduce our wage-rental ratio but will have an ambiguous effect abroad. The interpretation of this result is that at constant relative factor and commodity prices, and hence a given $\bar{z}$, the increased foreign income leads to increased spending on all goods with production concentrated on only the range $\bar{z} \leq z \leq 1$. There will accordingly be excess demand for our goods and an excess supply of foreign goods. In the home country the adjustment takes the form of a decline in the wage-rental ratio and therefore an increase in the relative price of our goods that are capital-intensive. The decline in the wage-rental ratio also leads to the use of more labor-intensive techniques. This adjustment is appropriate since, as Table I shows,

12. For an exposition of these relations see Johnson [1957].
13. On the multi-commodity model see Jones [1974].

TABLE I

COMPARATIVE STATIC RESULTS ($k > k^*$)

		Change in k	Change in k^*	Change in π
Effect on	σ	+	−	+
	σ^*	?	?	+
	$\bar{z}$	?	−	+

we shall concentrate on a narrower range of goods and therefore raise the average capital intensity in the economy. The decline in the wage-rental ratio serves to offset the resulting excess supply of labor and excess demand for capital. Finally, the narrowing of the range of goods produced at home implies that there will be increased output levels so that, in conjunction with the increased relative price, there will be an adjustment to higher foreign real income and spending on our goods.

Consider next the foreign country. Real income has increased, and therefore demand has risen for foreign-produced goods. The increased supply of capital raises potential output, but there is now an excess demand for labor. Suppose for a moment that the elasticity of substitution in production were zero. Then the foreign adjustment could take the form of a shift in the competitive margin, thus increasing capital use, and of a rise in the wage-rental ratio so as to raise the relative price of labor-intensive goods and thus reduce labor demand. It can indeed be shown that for low elasticities of substitution these conclusions hold. If elasticities of substitution are larger than one, though, it becomes possible that an increase in the wage-rental ratio creates an excess demand for capital, as substitution of capital for labor becomes important. This is the source of the ambiguity in the effect of foreign capital growth on their equilibrium wage-rental ratio.

We look now at the case where foreigners are the capital-rich country and experience further growth in their capital-labor ratio. Note that now they produce in the range $0 < z < \bar{z}$, i.e., they produce the relatively capital-intensive goods. Now the foreign wage-rental ratio will rise, but there is uncertainty about our wage-rental ratio and about the change in trade patterns. Abroad, the increase in the wage-rental ratio induces more capital-using techniques, and it lowers the relative price of relatively capital-intensive goods. Both effects operate to absorb the increased capital, but they leave us uncertain about the demand for labor. With no substitutability labor demand would decline, and we would find the foreign country expanding its range of production to encompass more labor-intensive goods. With high substitutability, by contrast, there may be an excess demand for labor requiring a narrowing of the production range. The uncertainty about the effects on trade patterns also leaves us uncertain about the change in the equilibrium wage-rental ratio at home. Again, if substitution elasticities are small, abroad we expect an expansion in the foreign production range, and therefore at home an increase in the wage-rental ratio in order to accommodate ourselves to a more labor-intensive range of products.

Consider finally a balanced increase in our own endowment. This leads to a rise in both countries' wage-rental ratios and to an expansion in the range of goods we produce. The increased range of goods production leaves us with more labor-intensive production that we offset through a rise in the wage-rental ratio. Abroad where the production range shrinks to devote resources more intensively to meet the increased world demand, the more labor-intensive output mix requires a rise in the wage-rental ratio to retain factor market equilibrium.

In the case of balanced growth, analysis of terms-of-trade effects is straight-forward. Here the goods we produce fall in price relative to the borderline commodity, which is the most labor intensive. Abroad all commodities rise in price relative to the borderline commodity, which is the least labor intensive abroad. Accordingly, our terms of trade unambiguously deteriorate.

3. The Borderline Case: Complete Specialization with Factor Price Equalization

We now briefly investigate the borderline case where both countries are completely specialized but factor prices remain equalized. This is the dividing line between the case of overlapping production ranges when endowments are close together and the case of the previous section. The relevant equations are (16) simplified to take account of the common wage-rental ratio and thus the common choice of technique:

$$B(\bar{z}) = \frac{\pi}{1-\pi}\,\frac{\sigma + k}{\sigma^* + k^*}, \tag{16'}$$

as well as the conditions of factor market equilibrium in (17) and (18) with $\sigma^* = \sigma$.

What can be said of the relationship between k and k^* such that we remain on the borderline? The natural conjecture is that an increase in our capital-labor ratio requires an accompanying increase in the foreign relative supply of capital so as to preserve factor price equalization. Perhaps surprisingly that result cannot be demonstrated in general.

It is true that if all production functions are Cobb-Douglas, the borderline has a positive slope. However, an ambiguity arises when elasticities of substitution at home are small and those abroad are large. In such a case an increase in the domestic capital stock may tend to result in a larger increase in σ^* than in σ, requiring a *fall* in k^* to maintain factor price equilibrium (see the discussion of Section IV above).

V. Concluding Remarks

This paper has extended our Ricardian continuum model to the case of two-factor Heckscher-Ohlin trade theory. The extension is rewarding because it introduces, in a still manageable fashion, the scope for relative price changes within a country rather than only changes in relative wages and the terms of trade of the Ricardian composite commodities that emerged in our earlier analysis.

The changes in relative factor and commodity prices induced by such disturbances as demand shifts or endowment changes cannot be determined without ambiguity outside the range of factor price equalization. This ambiguity arises because changes in relative factor supplies can be accommodated either by a shifting of the competitive margin toward more or less capital-intensive goods or by a change in relative factor prices and hence commodity prices. Even under our strong demand assumptions we cannot be certain about the distribution—or even direction—of adjustment between relative factor price changes and changes in trade patterns. Hence the elasticity of substitution in production plays an important role. With elasticities of substitution that are low (equal to or less than unity) the increase in a country's capital-labor ratio will raise the wage-rental ratio, as would be true in the two-commodity model, a closed economy, or under factor price equalization. With high elasticities of substitution, that regularity is no longer assured.

Under factor price equalization the model shows the well-known indeterminacy of geographic specialization. But we can make use of the fact that the capital-rich country is a net exporter of capital services to derive results concerning income distribution and welfare as they are affected by the opening of trade or changes in factor endowments.

The Heckscher-Ohlin variant of our continuum model remains manageable under our demand assumptions because, the multiplicity of goods notwithstanding, the equilibrium can be reduced to three variables—wage-rental ratios in each country and the equilibrium competitive margin. The Stolper-Samuelson theorem ensures that the single wage-rental ratio in each country determines the entire price structure for goods produced in that country, a result only slightly more complex than the Ricardian model.

Appendix 1: The Existence of Equilibrium

The normative problem that is solved by the competitive equilibrium is

(A.1)
$$\Phi(K,N,K^*,N^*) = \max_{\{K(z),N(z),K^*(z),N^*(z)\}} \int_0^1 b(z) \log \{F[K(z),N(z)] + F[K^*(z),N^*(z)]\},$$

subject to

$$\left[\int_0^1 K(z)dz, \int_0^1 N(z)dz, \int_0^1 K^*(z)dz, \int_0^1 N^*(z)dz\right] = [K,N,K^*,N^*] = [y_1, \ldots, y_4] = y.$$

Denoting partial derivatives by numerical subscripts,

$$\frac{\partial\Phi(y_1,y_2,y_3,y_4)}{\partial y_i} = \Phi_i(y), \quad (i = 1, \ldots, 4).$$

we can express our equilibrium unknowns by

(A.2)
$$\omega = w/w^* = \Phi_2(y)/\Phi_4(y)$$
$$\sigma = w/r = \Phi_2(y)/\Phi_1(y)$$
$$\sigma^* = w^*/r^* = \Phi_4(y)/\Phi_3(y).$$

$\bar{z}$ is the root for z in

$$\omega = \left(a^*(z) + \frac{c^*(z)}{\sigma^*}\right) \Big/ \left(a(z) + \frac{c(z)}{\sigma}\right).$$

The Kuhn-Tucker conditions, necessary and sufficient for the maximum and the equilibrium, can be expressed compactly with the help of the following notations:

$$[K(z),N(z),K^*(z),N^*(z)] \equiv [y_1(z), \ldots, y_4(z)] = y(z)$$
$$F(y_1(z),y_2(z)) + F(y_3(z),y_4(z)) \equiv F(y(z))$$
$$\frac{\partial F[y_1(z), \ldots, y_4(z)]}{\partial y_i(z)} \equiv F_i(y(z)), \qquad i = 1, \ldots, 4.$$

Then (A.1) implies that

(A.3)
$$\bar{L}[y(z);\mu] = \frac{b(z)F_i[y(z)]}{F[y(z)]} - \mu_i \geq 0 \qquad (i = 1, \ldots, 4)$$
$$L_{4+i}[y(z);\mu] = y_i - \int_0^1 y_i(z)dz \geq 0; \quad \mu \geq 0, \quad y(z) \geq 0$$
$$\sum_1^4 L_i[y(z);\mu]y_i - \sum_1^4 L_{4+j}\,[y(z);\mu]\mu_j = 0.$$

The μ's are dual variables, proportional to real factor prices of (K,N,K^*,N^*), respectively.

Appendix 2: The Equilibrium with Factor Price Equalization

Let $\alpha(z) \geq 0$ denote the fraction of the world output of good z that we produce; $(1 - \alpha(z))$ is produced by foreigners. Denote our proportion of the world labor force, $N/(N + N^*)$, by π. Equilibrium requires that trade balances. The condition for trade balance is that our income be equal to the value of our production:

$$\text{(A.4)}\quad wN + rK = \int_0^1 \alpha(z)P(z)[Q(z) + Q^*(z)]dz = \int_0^1 \alpha(z)b(z)[(wN + rK) + (wN^* + rK^*)]dz.$$

Rearranging terms, and recalling that $\int_0^1 b(z)dz = 1$, we may write the trade balance as

$$\text{(A.5)}\quad \int_0^1 b(z)(1 - \alpha(z))(\sigma + k)dz = \frac{N^*}{N}\int_0^1 \alpha(z)b(z)(\sigma + k^*)dz = \frac{1-\pi}{\pi}\int_0^1 \alpha(z)b(z)(\sigma + k^*)dz.$$

The remaining equilibrium conditions are those for the factor markets in the two countries:

$$\text{(A.6)}\quad \int_0^1 \frac{k(z)b(z)\alpha(z)[\sigma + \pi k + (1 - \pi)k^*]}{\sigma + k(z)}dz = \pi k$$

and

$$\text{(A.7)}\quad \int_0^1 \frac{k(z)b(z)(1 - \alpha(z))[\sigma + \pi k + (1 - \pi)k^*]}{\sigma + k(z)}dz = (1 - \pi)k^*.$$

The world capital stock per capita is

$$\text{(A.8)}\quad \hat{k} \equiv \frac{K + K^*}{N + N^*} = \pi k + (1 - \pi)k^*.$$

Adding (A.6) and (A.7), we can summarize the two capital market equilibrium conditions by

$$\text{(A.9)}\quad \int_0^1 \frac{k(z)b(z)[\sigma + \hat{k}]}{\sigma + k(z)}dz = \hat{k}.$$

Similarly, the two labor market equilibrium conditions reduce to

$$\text{(A.10)}\quad \int_0^1 \frac{b(z)[\sigma + \hat{k}]}{\sigma + k(z)}dz = 1.$$

Now these are precisely the same equilibrium conditions as equations (5) and (6). A unique equilibrium σ therefore exists. Because

$k > k > k^*$ and we showed earlier that $d\sigma/dk > 0$, we conclude that the wage-rental ratio after the opening of trade is between the two closed economy wage-rental ratios. Furthermore, an increase in the capital stock in either country will increase the equilibrium σ, as long as factor-price equalization continues to obtain.

Appendix 3: Comparative Statics under Complete Specialization

This appendix sketches the derivation of comparative static results for the case of complete specialization without factor price equalization. The equilibrium conditions, repeated here for convenience, are those for balanced trade and equilibrium in factor markets:

$$B(\bar{z}) = \frac{\pi}{1-\pi}\left(\frac{\sigma + k}{\sigma^* + k^*}\right)\left(\frac{a^*(\bar{z})}{a(\bar{z})}\right)\left(\frac{\sigma^* + k^*(\bar{z})}{\sigma + k(\bar{z})}\right) \tag{A.11}$$

$$0 = \int_0^{\bar{z}} \frac{b(z)}{\sigma + k(z)}\,[k(z) - k]dz \tag{A.12}$$

$$0 = \int_{\bar{z}}^1 \frac{b(z)}{\sigma^* + k^*(z)}\,[k^*(z) - k^*]\,dz. \tag{A.13}$$

Differentiating (A.11)–(A.13) yields the following system:

$$[A]\begin{bmatrix} d\bar{z} \\ d\sigma \\ d\sigma^* \end{bmatrix} = [B]\begin{bmatrix} dk \\ dk^* \\ d\pi \end{bmatrix}, \tag{A.14}$$

where $[A]$ and $[B]$ are each 3×3 matrices, with elements a_{ij}, b_{ij}, respectively.

The elements are given by

$$a_{11} = \frac{B'(\bar{z})}{B(\bar{z})} = \frac{b(\bar{z})}{[\int_{\bar{z}}^1 b(z)dz]^2} > 0; \quad a_{12} = \frac{k - k(\bar{z})}{(\sigma + k)(\sigma + k(\bar{z}))} > 0;$$

$$a_{13} = \frac{k^*(\bar{z}) - k^*}{(\sigma^* + k^*)(\sigma^* + k^*(\bar{z}))} > 0;$$

$$a_{21} = \frac{b(\bar{z})}{\sigma + k(\bar{z})}\,[k(\bar{z}) - k] < 0;$$

$$a_{22} = \int_0^{\bar{z}} \frac{b(z)}{[\sigma + k(z)]^2}\left[\frac{\partial k(z)}{\partial \sigma}(\sigma + k) - (k(z) - k)\right]dz > 0;$$

$$a_{23} = 0;$$

$$a_{31} = \frac{-b(\bar{z})}{\sigma^* + k^*(\bar{z})}\,[k^*(\bar{z}) - k^*] < 0; \quad a_{32} = 0;$$

$$a_{33} = \int_{\bar{z}}^{1} \frac{b(z)}{[\sigma^* + k^*(z)]^2}$$

$$= \left[\frac{\partial k^*(z)}{\partial \sigma^*} (\sigma^* + k^*) - (k^*(z) - k^*)\right] dz > 0;$$

$$b_{11} = \frac{1}{\sigma + k} > 0; \quad b_{12} = -\frac{1}{\sigma^* + k^*} < 0; \quad b_{13} = \frac{1}{\pi(1-\pi)} > 0;$$

$$b_{21} = \int_0^{\bar{z}} \frac{b(z)}{\sigma + k(z)} dz > 0; \quad b_{22} = 0 = b_{23};$$

$$b_{31} = 0; \quad b_{32} = \int_{\bar{z}}^{1} \frac{b(z)}{\sigma^* + k^*(z)} dz > 0; \quad b_{33} = 0.$$

Now, substituting the elements a_{ij} and b_{ij} into (A.4) makes it possible to derive the results shown in Table I of the text.

MASSACHUSETTS INSTITUTE OF TECHNOLOGY

REFERENCES

Dornbusch, R., S. Fischer, and P. A. Samuelson, "Comparative Advantage, Trade and Payments in a Ricardian Model with a Continuum of Goods," *American Economic Review,* LXVII (Dec. 1977), 823–29.

Johnson, H. G., "Factor Endowments, International Trade and Factor Prices," *The Manchester School,* XXV, No. 3 (Sept. 1957), 270–83.

Jones, R. W., "The Small Country in a Many-Commodity World," *Australian Economic Papers,* XXXVII (Dec. 1974), 225–36.

Meade, J., "The Equalization of Factor Prices: The Two-Country, Two-Factor, Three-Product Case," *Metroeconomica,* II (Dec. 1950), 129–33.

Melvin, J. R., "Production and Trade with Two Factors and Three Goods," *American Economic Review,* LVIII (Dec. 1968), 1249–68.

Samuelson, P. A., "Two Country Ricardian Analysis for Discrete Goods and for a Continuum of Goods," *Journal of International Economics,* forthcoming.

Wan, H. Y., Jr., "Three Variations on a Theme of Samuelson," mimeo, Cornell University, 1977.

Wilson, C., "On the General Structure of Ricardian Models with a Continuum of Goods: Applications to Growth, Tariff Theory and Technical Change," *Econometrica,* forthcoming.

SUMMING UP ON THE AUSTRALIAN CASE FOR PROTECTION*

PAUL A. SAMUELSON

INTRODUCTION

In 1929 a quasi-official report by several eminent Australian economists—*The Australian Tariff; An Economic Inquiry,* by J. B. Brigden, D. P. Copland, E. C. Dyason, L. F. Giblin, and C. H. Wickens—set off analytical controversy that has helped shape the discovery of what has come to be known as modern international trade theory. I had thought that this whole topic was satisfactorily understood by informed scholars and could be honorably deposited on the shelf of closed history.

G. J. Manger [1976] has, however, uncovered some interesting puzzles. Since Marion Crawford Samuelson, who played a key role forty years ago in the theoretical developments, is not here to consult on doubtful matters of memory, I recently spent an afternoon in the Harvard College libraries reviewing the principal scholarly contributions. Quite aside from Manger's interesting issues, the exercise was a rewarding one. For here is a drama that involved many of the great names of our subject: Ricardo [1815–1823] and Malthus [1815], Torrens [1815] and Stuart Mill [1848]; Sidgwick [1883], Edgeworth [1897], and Bastable [1897] (and, I seem to recall Nicholson and Carver); Simon Patten [1890] and Taussig; Marshall [1879] and Pigou [1906] as well as Allyn Young [1913], Knight [1924] and Robertson [1924]; Brigden [1925, 1927a, 1927b], Benham [1926, 1927, 1935], Copland [1931], and Frank Graham [1923]; Heckscher [1919] and Ohlin [1933], Stolper and Paul Samuelson [1941], Samuelson [1938, 1939], as well as Lerner [1952] and Metzler [1949a, 1949b]; Karl Anderson [1938, 1939] and Marion Crawford Samuelson [1939]; Corden [1957], Reitsma [1958, 1960], Bhagwati and Johnson [1961], Vanek, Kemp and Ronald Jones [1962]; and many others.

The story is worth telling, both in its received and revised versions.

* I owe thanks to the National Science Foundation for financial aid. My debts to the 1976 writings of G. J. Manger of the Department of Economic History of the University of New South Wales will be abundantly evident, as well as to the valuable surveys in Reitsma [1958, 1960].

The Conventional Wisdom

When Prime Minister Bruce asked the authors "... for a Report on the workings of the tariff ...," they disingenuously claimed they "... had to confess that we had no reasoned opinion about it" [Brigden *et al.*, 1929, p. xi]. Working against time and in the face of spatial separation, they came up within twelve months with a 232-page report that heretically concluded:

> The evidence available does not support the contention that Australia could have maintained its present population at a higher standard of living under free trade [p. 1 and also p. 140].

Also, they presented numerical estimates of the cost to Australia of tariffs then prevalent.

Orthodoxy usually closes ranks against heresy. Viner [1929], although somewhat patronizingly admitting that "they have made out a stronger case for their position than I would have supposed possible before reading their report," criticizes its conclusions and modes of reasoning to arrive at them. While admitting the point that protection of manufactures *might* under certain singular conditions increase wage incomes at the expense of land incomes, Viner made the point, in language about compensating losers that Kaldor [1939] was later to rediscover as the basis for his proposed formulation of "new" welfare economics,

> I cannot go far in support of a policy of reducing Jones' income by six shillings in order to increase Smith's income by five, even if Jones is a landowner or capitalist, and Smith a worker [Viner, 1929, p. 308].

Likewise, Gottfried Haberler [1933, pp. 193–95] expressed his disagreements. Admitting that almost anything is possible, he spoke of the unlikelihood that so versatile and so major a factor of production as labor could realistically be hurt by free trade.

It remained for a disciple of Frank Taussig, Karl Anderson [1938], to state the orthodox anti-Australian case most trenchantly. He asserted:

1. Free trade would necessarily maximize Australia's national income as a whole.

2. By virtue of its equalizing marginal value products in every alternative use, free trade would necessarily maximize the *absolute* return of each and every factor.

3. Even if farm goods were subject to strong diminishing returns

because of their dependence on strictly limited land, the Marshall-Pigou argument that their competitive supply should be curtailed in favor of a constant-cost industry like those of manufactured goods, Anderson argued to be false. (If Australia's terms of trade were given from abroad) Anderson believed that competition would lead to the efficient allocation of variable resources between the respective industries.

Marion Crawford Samuelson, in what I believe was originally a term paper for Haberler's Harvard graduate course in international economics, definitively demolished Anderson's first two contentions, granting only his third contention and this (1) on the unrealistic proviso that Australia's wool and other exports would be priced abroad independently of her own export volume and (2) on the further implicit assumption that the case of "increasing returns to scale" could provisionally be ignored. For the first time in the discussions, attention is called to what *must* happen under posited circumstances and not merely to what might or might not do so. Rarely did a criticized scholar more unreservedly and graciously concede to a critic than did Bryn Mawr Professor Karl Anderson to young Radcliffe graduate student Marion Crawford.

Her argument was simplicity itself, crystal clear, illustrating what William Blake had stated (and Frank Ramsey had quoted): "Truth cannot be told so as to be understood without being believed." Her model was this: Australia produces agriculture from labor and land according to classical returns laws, and produces manufactures from labor alone (or with an unimportant reliance on land). Possessed of much land for agriculture, Australia has comparative advantage in the export of such staples and is of finite (albeit limited) importance in the world markets that determine their terms of trade (wool prices versus manufactures' prices, etc.).

It follows that a departure from free trade effected by a protective tariff on manufactures must create a new steady state in which the following occur:

1. There will at first be increased Australian production of protected manufactures, reduced imports of them and of agricultural products, and *higher total real Australian national income* (the terms-of-trade effect of a sufficiently-small tariff).

2. The enhanced demand for labor-intensive manufactures will shift labor out of agriculture, lowering real land rents and total landlord incomes, and *raising real wage incomes both relatively and absolutely*, with the gain to labor being at first greater than the loss

to landowners and only being at more than their expense when the tariff becomes sufficiently too large.[1]

So, it was established for all time that Anderson was wrong in the belief that free trade maximizes each factor's absolute income or total national income as a whole. Even Haberler's more guarded presumption was proved wrong in this plausible model: although labor is here the *only* "versatile" factor transferable to all uses, and although its share could be preponderantly great in the national income with or without protection, its return not only *might* be enhanced by protection but in fact *had to be* so enhanced under the posited conditions.

3. It follows, syllogistically if implicitly, from Marion Samuelson [1939], that only through protection of manufactures could the maximum of population be afforded in Australia if that population was to earn a stipulated real wage in the market place—just as, we shall soon see, Sidgwick, Edgeworth, Patten, Brigden, and Copland had been arguing. This follows, since the free trade that lowers real wage rates at fixed supplies of labor and land, must (since a demand curve's downward shift is a leftward shift) lower the labor population supportable in the market at unchanged land supply and real wage.

The debate was clearly terminated by this magisterial 1939 analysis. And, as numerous commentators have noted, the Stolper-Samuelson breakthrough of 1941 was obviously the beneficiary of this 1939 analysis.[2] So it has become a cliché in the literature that the 1929 *Report* was the progenitor of the post-1940 trade models.[3]

Puzzles and Inconsistencies

Manger [1976] casts doubts on the correctness of the above received version, writing

1. The possibility of a "Metzler paradox," in which a tariff might *worsen* the internal terms of trade of manufactures for agriculture was not mentioned. For the purpose of refuting Anderson's claims and the Haberlerian presumptions of orthodoxy, the phenomenon of Metzler [1949] seems neglectable. In any case, none of the discussants suggested such great inelasticity of foreign reciprocal demand for Australia as to make the paradox likely.

2. To show that appearances can be misleading even when the evidence looks strong, I have to testify that it was Wolfgang Stolper's original insight that the Ohlin [1933] analysis provided some vindication for the view that the U. S. tariff might raise real wages here, and *not* the almost-simultaneous Crawford analysis of the Australian problem, that spawned Stolper-Samuelson [1941]. As Don Patinkin always properly insists, only *after* pioneering work has been completed will the participants understand the nuances and interrelationships of their own innovations.

3. Manger [1976] cites writers for this view that include Metzler [1949], Reitsma [1958, 1960], Corden [1957], Cain [1973], and the Australian version of Samuelson's *Economics* adapted by Hancock and Wallace.

> This paper will attempt to show the 1929 Report cannot be regarded as one of the earliest attempts to formulate a Stolper-Samuelson type redistribution theorem, and the Report did not, in fact, advocate the "Australian-Case for Protection" [of Crawford] as narrowly defined above [1976, p. 2].

He goes on to try to make a distinction between (1) classical or Ricardian theory, which was pre-Heckscher-Ohlin and to which the Report writers subscribed, and (2) neoclassical models of the post-Heckscher-Ohlin type and concerning which Manger [1976] says

> There was no evidence [in the Report] of a neoclassical growth model, a Stolper-Samuelson theorem or a term of trade effect, and on logical grounds there could not have been given their assumptions [p. 3].

> . . . It will be suggested instead the Brigden School based its argument on classical [i.e., *pre*-neoclassical] assumptions, falling back in effect to Ricardian growth and distribution analysis [pp. 2–3].

In brief, we seem to make sense of the writings, so it is argued, only if we assume that Marion Samuelson had not read the 1929 Report and had herself invented the goodies usually attributed to it.[4]

Needed Reformulations

Confronted with Manger's puzzle, I dredged my memory for recollections of forty years ago, reread Marion Samuelson's text closely, and consulted a copy of the 1929 *Report*. I had to conclude that Manger indeed had a point.

1. With great probability, Marion Crawford had never read the 1929 *Report* by Brigden *et al.* She never quotes from it. The last person who charged out the copy in Harvard's Baker Library was from before her time. (The Widener Library copy does not betray records of its users; so the evidence is not conclusive.)

2. I myself never read the *Report,* and already in those days the two of us were thick as thieves—or as thick as the Radcliffe and Harvard rules permitted male and female to be in that bygone time.

3. Most important, there was no need for her to have read it! Her interest, she explicitly tells us, is not primarily in Australia: it is in the sweeping Anderson orthodoxies which, if true, would be vital. The

4. An anecdote is in order. Back in the late 1920s, Thomas Balogh is supposed to have come in on a heated debate between Nicholas Kaldor and a learned scholar, on Pareto's equilibrium system. After Balogh and Kaldor left together, the former is reported to have said to the latter: "I didn't realize you had read Pareto," to which he received the reply: "I haven't. But after he posed the problem, I saw how Pareto's argument had to go."

Australian case suffices to establish her refutations of those overstatements; but it is not even her only illustration, as can be seen from the lines,

> It is perfectly clear that the imposition of a prohibitive tariff on the import of raw silk into the United States would increase the rent of the owners of land suitable for the growth of mulberry trees and the earnings of workers, if there be such, completely specialized in the caring for silk worms. What is true of a narrowly defined factor of production may also be true of the broad categories of land and labor [Marion Samuelson, 1939, p. 149].

Again [1939, p. 148], it would pay organized labor anywhere "to embark on a purposive policy of discrimination designed to render unequal the remunerations in different occupations, just as it always pays a monopolist to discriminate, if he can"—a line of argument demolishing Anderson's claim that equality of marginal products of a factor suffices to maximize its absolute return.[5]

4. Finally, close reading of the *Report* will show that, in various places, it explicitly denies conditions that are posited in the Crawford model. Thus, leaning over backwards and doing so with evident inconsistency, the Report's authors at places assume away any terms-of-trade effects and concede that free trade must raise the national income producible by given suppliers of Australian land and labor. Their hearts, though, seem not to be truly in this concession, and elsewhere I discern signs that theirs is not an unconfused and coherent exposition. As pointed out in Reddaway [1937], they explicitly indulge in various contrafactual or self-contradictory measurements, partly to provide a *reductio.*

Down Under Vindicated

It would be misleading to leave the matter at this stage and quite alien to Marion Samuelson's character to seek credit on her behalf for any undeserved originalities. Those few hours in Baker Library

5. Still another nice touch is her Frisch-like deft demonstration that doing one's best at prices fixed to you does not imply that those are the best feasible prices from your standpoint:

> Under pure competition each individual and each entrepreneur take prices as given parameters, not affected by their own behavior. In terms of these given prices all maximize their respective functions. This does not mean that the resulting situation is an optimal one, any more than it is valid to say that because a Hindu fakir reclines on a bed of spikes in such a way as to minimize his discomfort, he is therefore the happiest of all men. It is not necessarily true that the final prices with which each individual is confronted will be the best set of prices from a welfare point of view [1939, p. 144].

explained away to my satisfaction most of Manger's genuine puzzlements. The explanation is quite simple.

1. Brigden [1925], in the first issue of the *Economic Record,* does have the Crawford model even if the 1929 *Report* does not: the effect of Australia on its own terms of trade is there; the shift from rent to wages is there. True, Marion Crawford Samuelson never read this, any more than she had read the 1929 *Report.* But Sir Douglas Copland had; and Copland [1931], which Anderson cited and Crawford may have read, was much influenced by the 1925 argumentation and even succeeds in connecting it up with earlier notions of Sidgwick [1883] and Patten [1890], and for that matter of Ricardo's friend Torrens. Furthermore, the Crawford model is precisely the Ricardian model that David Ricardo used in his arguments with Malthus on the Corn Laws, and I believe she so regarded it—with the important specified difference that England was supposed to have had little and Australia much land in comparison with labor-land ratios abroad.

2. Benham [1926], in complete contrast to Benham [1935], set back understanding of the Brigden insight. His emphasis on practical-man's estimation of the *quantitative* aspects of the Australian situation helped produce the 1929 Report's concern with inconclusive cost-of-the-tariff measurements and its retreat from the valid qualitative insights rendered earlier by Brigden.[6]

3. Australians like Brigden and Copland resembled Americans like Carey, List (who formed his protectionist notions while living in the United States!), and Patten, in thinking that the standard free trade arguments really applied only to Britain, and that new continents required new theories. They were encouraged in this by their selective quotings of Marshall's muddled notions about taxing decreasing-returns industries to expand industries with constant costs (or with increasing-returns-to-scale). Crawford wisely avoided the decreasing-cost cases, realizing the complications they can raise for viable competition free of externalities. We shall see that, terms-of-trade effects aside, Brigden-Copland-Patten would be in error in believing that protection will do for American and Australian total real incomes what free trade would do for Britain's. They would be right to recognize the true symmetries of the two situations. With total local income maximized at given p's, protecting the *scarcer* factor of

6. See Stolper-Samuelson [1941, p. 65, n. 1] for appropriate acknowledgment to Benham [1935], whose work was located after our paper was completed. Our search of the literature, if conducted today, could also have cited with advantage the valuable insights in Joan Robinson [1941], and Viner [1950].

production can always increase *its* market-imputed real income and relative share: Malthus' Corn Laws would raise land rents of the English gentry; Brigden's and Patten's protection of manufactures would raise the wage income of their intensive-factor, labor.[7]

I must not overglorify my down-under heroes. Undoubtedly, Brigden and Copland had better heuristic insights than their analytical syllogisms could provide proofs for. The refutation of Pigou's boner concerning the overexpansion of decreasing-returns industries, by Allyn Young [1913], Knight [1924], and Robertson [1924], they could have studied with advantage—as Karl Anderson rightfully insisted on. Perhaps this[8] Marshall-Pigou confusion gave them the courage to buck the tide of then current dogmatic orthodoxy, and in that sense served a useful purpose after all.

General Proofs

Here, forty years overdue, are the constructive general proofs of what is sound in the Australian contentions that Marion Samuelson [p. 147] generously attributed to me in 1939. For brevity, I shall largely employ geometric diagrams and now make the simplifying assumption that tastes are everywhere the same (among the poor and rich, the Australians and the foreigners, the workers and the farmers: uniform-homothetic indifference contours).

Figures Ia and Ib show the symmetry between 1815 British Corn Laws and the 1925 Australian or American situations, both on the polar assumption of countries too small to affect their own terms of

7. Manger is right to insist on the nonfixity of the population in the Sidgwick-Patten-Brigden argumentation; but, as is shown by Kemp-Jones [1962] and Samuelson [1953, pp. 10–20], there is nothing alien to neoclassicism in this assumption. Even in those parts of the 1925–1931 Australian discussions that posit fixed coefficients of production rather than smooth substitutability, the Crawford-Stolper-Samuelson-Benham conclusion holds: a rise in P_2/P_1 will raise W_2/W_1 if industry 2 is "more intensive" in factor 2 than is industry 1, a lemma no less "neoclassical" than it is "classical."

8. We must not judge scientists by their worst performances or by the misinterpretations their expositions lead readers into. Marshall [1879] is one of the classics in trade theory, deserving to be included with the major writings of Hume, Torrens [1815], Ricardo, J. S. Mill [1848], Mangoldt, and Edgeworth [1897]. Also, Pigou [1906, p. 58] provides some anticipation of Stolper-Samuelson [1941]: "Protective duties . . . may . . . develop one manufacture, A, at the expense of another, B, and a given factor may play a more important part in the former than in the latter of these . . . and consequently secures a greater proportionate share of the National Dividend." Indeed, my review brought home to me forcibly that class stands out in this as in other matters: when Edgeworth [1897, pp. 401–30] disputes Bastable [1897] on whether protection of a good that a factor is important in producing will raise the amount of it affordable at a pre-assigned real return, it is the first rater Edgeworth who is both right in his conclusion and clear in his reasonings!

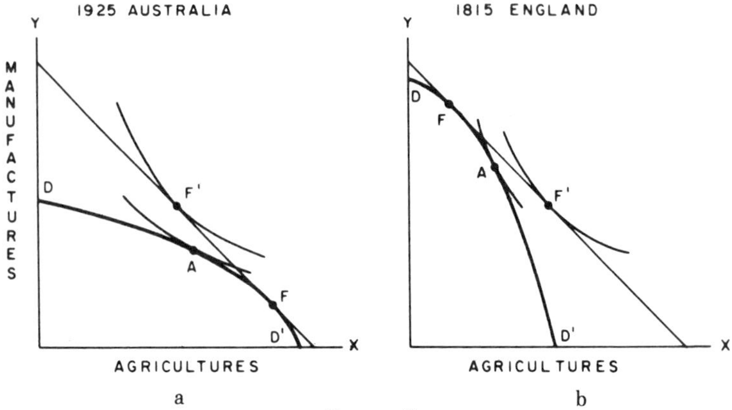

FIGURE I
With goods' prices given, free trade maximizes total Australian or English income, albeit lowering the absolute return of each's most-scarce factor. Marx and institutionalists are wrong to regard free trade as a pro-English ploy.

trade. Free trade maximizes in Ib Britain's national income produced at F and enjoyed at F', with her exporting the manufacturing fruits of her abundant labor factor. In Ia free trade maximizes Australian national income at F and F', but now with her exporting agricultural products of abundant land. Under autarky, each would have lower total incomes and potential living standards: the autarky indifference contour, at A, in each case shows only about nine-tenths the real income level as under free trade at F'. In this contrived example, that is, the "cost" of a completely protective tariff is made to be about one-tenth the free-trade real-GNP level (as measured by the comparative distance along any one specified ray from the autarky to the free trade indifference contour).[9]

Now drop the assumption that the home country cannot affect its terms of trade with the rest of the world. Just as Figures Ia and Ib showed the essential identity of analysis applicable to 1925 Australia and 1815 England once the proper axis interchanges are made to take

9. The mode of calculating the cost of a tariff used in Brigden *et al.* [1929] was not deemed optimal by Reddaway [1937], Corden [1958], and other discussants. The transparent method of calculating a tariff's cost used in my homothetic diagrams can be related by the patient reader to these methods in Corden [1957]; also, that same reader can modify properly the usual Dupuit-Harberger consumers'-surplus calculus to arrive at the present uniform-homothetic case's exact result. Chs. 5, 10, 44, 70, 77–78, 130, 157–58, 164, 183, 208–11, 260–62, in my *Collected Scientific Papers* bear on such measures; also *Foundations*, Chs. 3–8. They indicate why, when we drop homotheticity in favor of realistic general demand analysis (in which different Australian laborers and landowners have varying tastes, as people also do abroad), *no* unique numerical estimate of "cost" can capture the shifts and twists in the *utility-possibility frontier* that varying duty rates can involve.

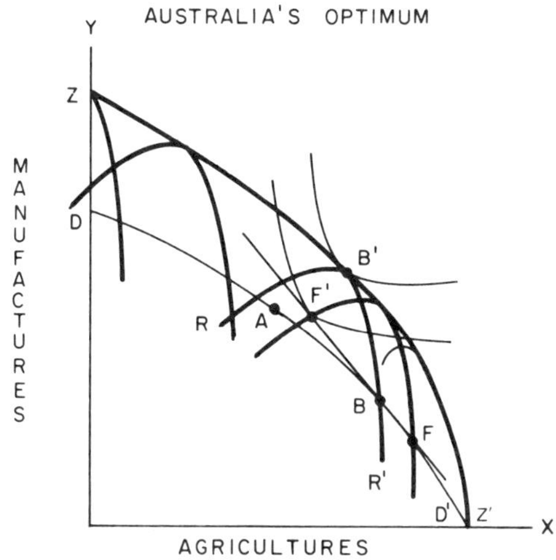

FIGURE II
An optimally small tariff can increase Australia's national income and raise scarce labor's relative share.

account of the different factor that is superabundant, so the careful reader can supplement my Figure II's picture for Australia with the parallel picture for England. (Hint: the more vertical frontier applies in 1815 and export trade is in the southwest rather than northeast direction; etc.)

Now consumption ends up at B', on the *Baldwin Envelope,*[10]

10. For the independent discovery of this Envelope, see Baldwin [1948, 1952]. To generate from the DAD' domestic *p-p frontier* of Figure II its Baldwin Envelope, ZBZ', we use the foreigners' reciprocal-demand locus, ROR', shown here schematically.

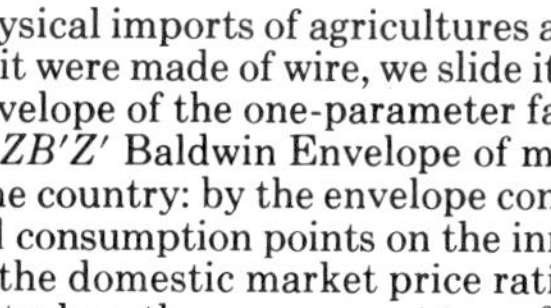

The axes plot algebraic physical imports of agricultures and manufacturing. Keeping ROR' rigidly oriented as if it were made of wire, we slide its 0 origin along the domestic DAD' locus. The outer envelope of the one-parameter family of curves generated by this sliding process is the $ZB'Z'$ Baldwin Envelope of maximal consumptions of the goods available to the home country: by the envelope construction, when we pair corresponding production and consumption points on the inner and outer frontiers, their slopes have to be equal to the domestic market price ratio, P_x/P_y, and hence to each other—as at B and B'. (Note: how the government transfers the proceeds of its tariffs is immaterial under my assumption of uniform-homothetic demand.) For fuller discussion of the envelope construction, see Samuelson [1962, pp. 821–23].

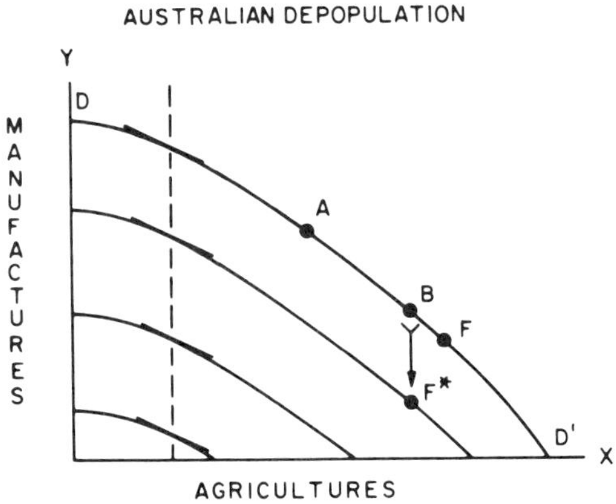

FIGURE III
Slope $-dx/dy$ is proportional to real wage in terms of x. To preserve under free trade high real wage of B's optimal tariff position, Australian population would have to drop enough to move P^* free-trade point due south of B.

$ZB'Z'$. See the figure in footnote 10 for its derivation. Now production takes place at B, inbetween autarky's A and free-trade's F; rather than depress her own terms of trade unduly, Australia uses a tariff or other protective device to hold back on her production of agricultural products, improving her terms of trade, P_x/P_y, along the rest-of-the world's offer curve, $RB'R'$. (When the parallel picture for Britain is drawn, the reader will see that Patten, Brigden, and Copland indeed nodded in viewing free trade as nothing but a self-interested European plot!)

Clearly, the "cost" of the *optimal* tariff to Australia is negative, since compared to the free trade point F', the B' point in II brings about a gain in enjoyable real national income of about one-fifth in this dramatic example. Only when the tariff is much "too high," as Brigden *et al.* evidently suspected the 1929 Australian tariff to be, will there be a positive cost of the tariff.

Our figures can also show exactly what happens to the market-imputed income distribution if we adhere to the Ricardo-Crawford convention that manufactures require negligible scarce land. The reciprocal of the absolute slope of the *p-p frontier*, $-dx/dy$, measures the real wage in agricultural produce; this of course varies with the labor-land intensity attained (in contrast to the unvarying real wage earnable in terms of manufactures).

At free trade's F in Figure III, the scarce factor's real return is *always* less than at autarky's A and less than at the optimal tariff point of B. Q.E.D

(Note: Metzler's paradox cannot negate these truths, since reciprocal demand for Australia must be "elastic" along OB'.)

Finally, Figure III shows the correctness of the Sidgwick-Patten-Brigden contention that, if the Australian population insists upon earning under free trade the same high real wage it earns at Figure II's B under optimal protection, then the population will have to be decimated.

As labor supply shrinks in Australia, its *p-p frontier* shifts in an exact downward direction, forming parallel contours apart by constant vertical distances, and preserving the same slopes along any vertical line. Only at population reduced enough to move the free trade point F down to F^*, *just below* B, will the free-trade wage be at the previous optimally protected height. (Conceivably, this could be a population so small that only agriculture would be viable under free trade.)

Final Caveats

In concluding, I must warn that the analysis by Marion Crawford Samuelson was deliberately designed to avoid the complications that have to arise when, along with labor and land, a "third" factor of scalar or vector capital is needed. Also, her strategic theoretical simplifications were not meant to deny the importance of increasing returns for a new economy like Australia or the nineteenth-century U.S.A.

If Marion Samuelson were alive, she would not have let me resurrect the 1939 analysis, she being the sort who disliked having people make a fuss about such bits of ancient history as an old term paper. Nonetheless, it would be a pity to abide by that judgment. The famous Stokes Theorem in mathematics first appeared in print as a quiz question in the Cambridge Mathematics Tripos; Weierstrasse's breakthroughs in the calculus of variations trace only to his classroom expositions; Lerner's 1933 discovery of factor-price equalization was embalmed in a forgotten LSE seminar paper, until my subsequent work led Lionel Robbins to resurrect and publish it in 1952; and further examples could be multiplied.

Proprieties and personalities aside, following these threads of the Australian-American case for protection, I hope the reader will agree, provides a fascinating case study of the dynamics by which a living science advances, a plum pudding of Mertonian doubletons of quasi-independent analytic discoveries and of Kuhnian retreats and advances in the perception and acceptance of competing paradigms.

Massachusetts Institute of Technology

References

Anderson, Karl, "Protection and the Historical Situation: Australia," this *Journal,* LIII (Nov. 1938), 86–104.

——, "Comment," this *Journal,* LIV (Nov. 1939), 149–51.

Baldwin, R. E., "Equilibrium in International Trade: A Diagrammatical Analysis," this *Journal,* LXII (Nov. 1948), 748–62.

——, "The New Welfare Economics and Gains from International Trade," this *Journal,* LXVI (Feb. 1952), 91–101.

Bastable, C. F., *The Theory of International Trade* (London: Macmillan, 1897 and 1903, 2nd and 4th editions).

Benham, F. C., "The Australian Tariff and the Standard of Living: A Reply," *Economic Record,* II (May 1926), 20–42.

——, "The Australian Tariff and the Standard of Living: A Restatement," *Economic Record,* III (Nov. 1927), 239–48.

——, "Taxation and the Relative Prices of Factors of Production," *Economica N.S.,* II (May 1935), 198–203.

Bhagwati, J., and H. G. Johnson, "A Generalized Theory of the Effects of Tariffs on the Terms of Trade," *Oxford Economic Papers NS,* XIII (Oct. 1961), 225–53.

Brigden, J. B., "The Australian Tariff and the Standard of Living," *Economic Record,* I (Nov. 1925), 29–46.

——, "The Australian Tariff and the Standard of Living: A Rejoinder," *Economic Record,* III (May 1927a), 102–16.

——, "Comment on Mr. Benham's Restatement," *Economic Record,* III (Nov. 1927b), 239–48.

—— *et al., The Australian Tariff: An Economic Inquiry* (Melbourne: 1929).

Cain, N., "Political Economy and the Tariff: Australia in the 1920s," *American Economic Papers* (1973), 1–20.

Copland, D. B., "A Neglected Phase of Tariff Controversy," this *Journal,* XLV (Feb. 1931), 289–308.

Corden, W. M., "The Calculation of the Cost of Protection," *Economic Record,* XXXIII (April 1957), 29–51.

Edgeworth, F. Y., "Review of Bastable," *Economic Journal,* VII (Sept. 1897), 397–403.

Graham, Frank D., "Some Aspects of Protection Further Considered," this *Journal,* XXXVII (Feb. 1923), 199–227.

Haberler, G., *Theory of International Trade* (London: Hodges, 1933).

Heckscher, Eli F., "The Effect of Foreign Trade on the Distribution of Income," *Ekonomisk Tidskrift,* XXI (1919), 497–512; translated as Ch. 13, *Readings in the Theory of International Trade* (Homewood, IL: Richard Irwin, 1949).

Kaldor, N., "Welfare Propositions of Economics and Interpersonal Comparisons of Utility," *Economic Journal,* XLIX (Sept. 1939), 549–52.

Kemp, M. C., and R. W. Jones, "Variable Labor Supply and the Theory of International Trade," *Journal of Political Economy,* LXX (Feb. 1962), 30–36.

Knight, F. H., "Some Fallacies in the Interpretation of Social Cost," this *Journal,* XXXVIII (Aug. 1924), 582–606.

Lerner, A. P., "Factor Prices and International Trade," *Economica NS,* XIX (Feb. 1952), 1–15.

Malthus, T. R., *An Inquiry into the Nature and Progress of Rent* (1815).

Manger, G. J., "The Australian Case for Protection Reconsidered," working paper (Sydney: The University of New South Wales, 19 January 1976).

Marshall, Alfred, *The Pure Theory of Foreign Trade* (1879, for private circulation; facsimile reprint, London: London School of Economics and Political Science, 1930).

Metzler, L. A., "Tariffs, the Terms of Trade and the Distribution of National Income," *Journal of Political Economy,* LVII (Feb. 1949a), 1–29.

——, "The Theory of International Trade," in *A Survey of Contemporary Economics,* H. S. Ellis, ed. (Homewood, IL: Richard D. Irwin for the American Economic Association, 1949b), pp. 210–54.

Mill, J. S., *Principles of Political Economy* (1848).

Ohlin, Bertil, *Interregional and International Trade* (Cambridge: Harvard University Press, 1933).

Patten, S. N., *The Economic Basis of Protection* (1890).

Pigou, A. C., *Protective and Preferential Import Duties* (London: Macmillan, 1906).
Reddaway, W. B., "Some Effects of the Australian Tariff," *Economic Record,* XIII (June 1937), 249–50.
Reitsma, A. J., "Trade and Redistribution of Income: Is There Still an Australian Case?" *Economic Record,* XXXIV (Aug. 1958), 172–138.
——, *Trade Protection in Australia* (Leiden: H. E. Stenfert Kroese, 1960).
Ricardo, David, *The Works and Correspondence of David Ricardo,* P. Sraffa, ed. (Cambridge: Cambridge University Press for the Royal Economic Society, 1815–1823).
Robertson, D. H., "Those Empty Boxes," *Economic Journal,* XXXIV (March 1924), 16–31.
Robinson, J., "Rising Supply Price," *Economica N.S.,* VIII (Feb. 1941), 1–8.
Samuelson, Marion Crawford, "The Australian Case for Protection Re-Examined," this *Journal,* LIV (Nov. 1939), 143–49.
Samuelson, P. A., "Welfare Economics and International Trade," *American Economic Review,* XXVIII (June 1938), 261–66.
——, "The Gains from International Trade," *Canadian Journal,* V (May 1939), 195–205.
——, "Prices of Factors and Gains in General Equilibrium," *Review of Economic Studies,* XXI (1953–54), 1–20.
——, "The Gains from International Trade Once Again," *Economic Journal,* LXXII, (Dec. 1962), 820–29.
Sidgwick, Henry, *Principles of Political Economy* (1883).
Stolper, W. F., and P. A. Samuelson, "Protection and Real Wages," *Review of Economic Studies,* IX (Nov. 1941), 58–73.
Torrens, Robert, *An Essay on the External Corn Trade* (1815).
Viner, J., "The Australian Tariff," *Economic Record,* V (Nov. 1929), 306–15.
——, "Supplementary Note" (to his 1931 "Cost Curves and Supply Curves"), in *Readings in Economic Analysis 2,* R. B. Clemence, ed. (Cambridge, MA: Addison-Wesley, 1950).
Young, Allyn, "Pigou's Wealth and Welfare," this *Journal,* XXVII (Aug. 1913), 672–86.

JUSTICE TO THE AUSTRALIANS

PAUL A. SAMUELSON

My acknowledged debt to Gary J. Manger is so great that I fear to register any dissent lest I seem an ingrate. Therefore, I stay with a few truths that relate to his concerns.[1]

1. By 1920 it was high time to replace the labor-only model of Ricardo-Mill classicism by the formal Ohlin, Haberler, and other multi-factor extensions. Already Ricardo, Torrens, and Malthus recognized that the corn laws could raise landowners' share in English national income—a phenomenon not relevant to the 1-factor-only formal model. The 1925–1931 Australian discussions similarly deviated into good sense *before* international trade theory had, in Manger's happy phrase, "shifted intellectual gears." Tom Kuhn must realize that in real life scientists work with more than one paradigm at a time, including some still getting born and perceived.

2. Ohlin's recognition of oversimplification in purchasing-power-theory will be seen on reflection to be logically and empirically *un*related to the inadequacies of the labor-only models. Similarly, Mill's recognition that "international values" cannot accord with "labor values" is not a point *against* a model involving labor-alone-in-each-country: it is a valid deduction *about* such a classical model. In short, as Kuhn can document, a new and better paradigm may be motivated by criticisms of an old paradigm that are themselves confused and even wrong.

3. Frederic Benham's 1935 paper on how factor prices and goods prices are related is a quantum-advance in the post-Heckscher literature. His jousts with Bridgen on Marion Samuelson's problem do not win for him from me Manger's high marks. But when have teachers been unanimous in making out report-card grades?

4. Manger earns our praise for throwing new light on basic advances in the theory of international trade. My reservations, which are minor, hope to guard against awarding *excessive* credit to post-1938 writers.

MASSACHUSETTS INSTITUTE OF TECHNOLOGY

1. Cf. Manger [1981] and Samuelson [1981]. I list in my brief bibliography only a few relevant references.

REFERENCES

Benham, F. C., "The Australian Tariff and the Standard of Living: A Reply," *Economic Record,* II (May 1926), 20–42, and sequels in *Ibid.,* III (Nov. 1927), 239–48.
Bridgen, J. B., "The Australian Tariff and the Standard of Living," *Economic Record,* I (Nov. 1925), 29–46; and sequels in *Ibid.,* III (May/Nov. 1927), 102–16, 249–51.
Kuhn, T. S., *The Structure of Scientific Revolutions* (Chicago: University of Chicago Press, 1962, 1970).
Manger, G. J., "The Australian Case for Protection Reconsidered: A Reformulation," this *Journal,* XCVI (1981), 161–67.
Ohlin, B., *Interregional and International Trade* (Cambridge, MA: Harvard University Press, 1933).
Samuelson, Marion Crawford, "The Australian Case for Protection Re-examined," this *Journal,* LIV (1939), 143–49.
Samuelson, Paul A., "Summing Up on the Australian Case for Protection," this *Journal,* XCVI (1981), 147–60.

INTEREST RATE EQUALIZATION AND NONEQUALIZATION BY TRADE IN LEONTIEF–SRAFFA MODELS

Paul A. SAMUELSON*

M.I.T., Cambridge, MA 02139, U.S.A.

Received May 1977

A half-dozen theorems and some corollaries concerning equalization of factor prices in a time-phased Leontief–Sraffa system with steady-state profit rates are carefully stated and discussed. An example is the new Mainwaring theorem, that a 1-technique world will either have the normalized price ratio vector independent of the profit rate or uniquely determined by it. Another example is that, when intermediate goods can be imported, unchanged profit rates and changed tastes can negate the nonsubstitution theorem and alter price ratios, since now the world has more than one *primary* (i.e. geographical) labor.

The simplest Leontief–Sraffa case is that in which (i) labor is the only primary factor, nonproducible to order within the system, (ii) all outputs are producible in a time-phased way out of labor and themselves as inputs, (iii) joint production is ruled out. Finally, (iv) we restrict ourselves to steady-state configurations in which the set of all real prices and wages are uniquely determinate once the rate of interest is given at an admissible nonnegative level.

The following two general theorems are well known, and to them we can now add the useful new Mainwaring theorem.[1]

Theorem 1. If two regions are observed producing all n goods in common while connected by free trade, then even if they have common technical knowledge there is no necessity that their steady-state interest rates and real wages should be equalized.

*I owe thanks to the National Science Foundation for partial financial aid, and to Vicki Elms for editorial assistance.

[1]Cf. the preceding article: L. Mainwaring, 'The interest rate equalisation theorem with nontraded goods', with which I am much in agreement. Relevant earlier writings are my 1965 and 1975 papers in the references. The latter gives citations to, and some discussions of, earlier papers by C.J. Bliss, I. Steedman and J.S. Metcalfe, Mainwaring, and others. My notation involves $[a_{0j}]$ for the row vector of direct labor requirements, and $[a_{ij}]$ as the Leontief input/output coefficients, the amount of good i needed for each unit of j output. Some writers use A to denote this last matrix; my $A_{0j}\{r\}$ coefficients are quite different and are self-defined in my text. Real prices are written as $(P_j/w) = (p_j)$, being (p_j') in region $'$ and (p_j'') in region $''$.

Theorem 2. If two regions with the same techniques have the same steady-state interest rate, there can be no observed pattern of mandatory specialization under free trade: they must be capable of producing all goods in common and actually there is then no need for trade at all. So observed patterns of mandatory specialization for even 1 good negates interest rate and real-wage equalization.

To prove the first theorem one need only notice that, at different interest rates, regions with the same technical options may be forced to choose different actual technologies. When two regions use *different* actual technologies, there is of course no reason for them to have equalized factor returns (interest rate or real wages); but at the same time countless examples can be given of quite *different* technologies that happen to imply the same relative prices for all goods (or for any subset). Actually, even if there were only 1 choice of technology – the case Leontief often prefers, and the one discussed in Part I of Sraffa (1960) – we know from the familiar singular case of 'equal organic composition of capital' (when socially necessary *total* embodied labor is proportional for all goods to *direct* labor) that all price ratios can be identical at every interest rate, so that interest rate equalization could never be *universally guaranteed* by free trade alone.

To prove the second theorem, we need only recall the well known non-substitution theorem. With the same interest rate given and only 1 primary factor, the same vector of real prices, $P/w = (P_1/w, \ldots, P_n/w)$ is assured in the same state of technical knowledge, independently of the pattern of positive demand for the goods. Mandatory specialization, however, depends on there being *differences* in relative-cost-ratios, which is ruled out by equalized interest rates.

The truth of these theorems ends forever the hope that one can deduce factor-returns equalization from free trade alone *without making some further specialized assumptions*. That is why Samuelson (1965) specified such a further sufficiency condition.[2] And that is why, if Mainwaring is to be able to deduce global interest-rate equalization, he too must be prepared to specify some such further sufficiency condition. This he has done in what I shall write down as Theorem 3.

Theorem 3. Suppose that there is but one choice of technology for every industry and that it does not *involve the singular case of 'equal-organic-composition-of-capitals,' i.e. does not involve a common ratio in* all *industries of wage cost to total costs at* any *interest rate, then if all goods are freely tradeable* and are *being produced in common over the different regions (or are capable of being viably so produced under competition), then the interest rates must be equal in all such*

[2]See Samuelson (1975) for careful exposition of the sense in which such a condition is a 'tautology' in some prejorative sense. The present discussion also addresses this matter.

regions – and so must be all real wage rates, w/P_j. *Conversely, the slightest difference in interest rates must induce a pattern of regional specialization.*

The proof follows from the algebraic fact that if two different interest rates produce price vectors that are proportional to each other, those price vectors must be proportional to the direct labor requirements, which is the organic composition condition ruled out in the theorem. (*Remark*: There is no need for the technology to be indecomposable; it need only be 'productive' in the Hawkins–Simon sense.)

Theorem 4. Suppose a one-technique world where only final goods are tradeable and where one or more of the goods involve some transport costs and are observed in equilibrium with some relative price discrepancies between the regions. Then all or some of the rest of the goods (as many as all but one) might have their price ratios equalized by free trade, but that need not equalize interest rates and real wages. Only when some further special sufficiency conditions are given can factor-return equalization be assured by free trade in a subset *of goods.*

One proves this theorem by supplying easy and long well-known examples in which a subset of the price ratios achieve the same values more than once. (Singular cases aside, in which subsets of goods have price ratios invariant to the interest rate, for finite number of goods n, there can only be a finite number of different interest rates prevailing in the various regions that produce the subset of goods in common under free trade in them.)

Theorem 5. There are an infinity of alternative specifiable sufficiency conditions that guarantee equality of interest rates when a certain subset of goods are producible in common under free trade. One such condition, not 'tautologically empty' (nor untrue!) is the 2-good intensity condition given in theorem 6.

Proof of this theorem is provided constructively by the statement and proof of my 1965 condition, formulated so as to apply to an uncountable infinity of Leontief–Sraffa–Mainwaring matrices.

Theorem 6. Supposing that trade is permitted only for the goods intended for final consumption use (raw-material inputs not *being importable) and that under free trade goods 1 and 2 are both viably producible within two regions, and the technology (which could involve more than one choice of techniques) is such that the price ratios of these two goods moves monotonically with the interest rate, then the interest rates and* all *real wages must be equal in the two regions.*

Mr. Mainwaring is in doubt as to the meaning of my 1965 language about 'uniform differences in factor intensity.' His ambiguities will vanish if my whole sentence is read with the realization that the words 'so that' precisely define its intended meaning. Theorem 6 will then be seen to state just what was intended in Samuelson (1965, p. 49):

> Now suppose there are uniform differences in factor intensity, so that for some two goods that are simultaneously produced in both countries, say goods 1 and 2, $p_1(r)/p_2(r) = p_{12}(r)$ is a monotone, strictly increasing (or decreasing) function of r. *Then, the interest rate will be equalized by positive trade in those goods alone.*

Belief that this 'reduced-form' sense of 'intensity differences' cannot be given content disappears when one contemplates corollaries to theorem 6 like the following.

Corollary 6.1. If $n = 2$ and there is but one choice of techniques involving no equal-organic-composition singularity, $p_2(r)/p_1(r)$ is a strongly monotone function of r and viability in both regions of both goods under free trade assures factor-return equality.

Mainwaring's theorem makes this corollary unsurprising. But the contents of theorem 3 and of corollary 6.1 are not identical.

Corollary 6.2. Suppose $n > 2$, and $(a_{2+i,1}, a_{2+i,2})$ are all 'sufficiently small' at the same time that $[a_{01}a_{02}]$ is not an eigenvector of

$$\begin{bmatrix} a_{11} & a_{12} \\ a_{21} & a_{22} \end{bmatrix}.$$

Then, $p_2(r)/p_1(r)$ is a strongly monotone function of r, and common production under free trade of goods 1 and 2 assures factor-return equality.

My 1975 paper gives still other valid corollaries. And I shall leave to the reader to show that, for $[a_{ij}]$ 'sufficiently near' to a matrix in which the first k goods are autonomously decomposable and not of equal-organic composition, then observing those goods produced in common under free trade will assure us – by an obvious extension of Mainwaring's own reasonings – of equalization of interest rates and of *all* factor returns. (This result is understood to hold when $n > 2$ under the stipulation that interregional trade is permitted only in goods destined for final use, a restriction whose rationale will soon be made clear.)

Specialization

I now wish to break some new ground. As soon as any price ratios are *not* equal for whatever reason – because of differences in interest rates or because of some transport costs or tariff impediments – neither I nor Mainwaring can apply the Sraffa cost *equalities*; the non-substitution theorem loses validity now that the labors of 2 regions constitute 2 rather than a single primary factor. It was to sidestep these complications that my theorem 6 contained the restriction against producing with raw materials that can be imported from abroad at prices cheaper than they can be produced at home.

Now let the regions satisfy Mainwaring conditions of theorem 6 and have different interest rates, r' and r'' respectively. Their autarky real costs relative to the paid-in-advance domestic wage rate can be written as $[A_{0j}\{r'\}]$ and $[A_{0j}\{r''\}]$, where

$$[A_{0j}\{r\}] = [a_{01}, \ldots, a_{0n}](1+r)[I - a_{ij}(1+r)]^{-1}. \tag{1}$$

But with $r' \neq r''$, and an induced pattern of regional specialization, the actual prevailing (P_j/w)'s in each region will be *lower* than the autarky real prices.

As soon as free trade leads to specialization *and importing of inputs*, local and international price ratios are no longer given by domestic cost ratios in either country. The 2-good case will illustrate how the pattern of equilibrium prices now depends on the strength of international reciprocal demands.

Under autarky, real costs in the respective countries are given by

$$\begin{aligned} A_{0j}\{r'\} &= [a_{0j} + A_{01}\{r'\}a_{1j} + A_{02}\{r'\}a_{2j}](1+r'), \\ A_{0j}\{r''\} &= [a_{0j} + A_{01}\{r''\}a_{1j} + A_{02}\{r''\}a_{2j}](1+r''), \\ &\qquad (j = 1, 2), \qquad r' < r'', \end{aligned} \tag{2}$$

$$A_{01}\{r'\}/A_{02}\{r'\} < A_{01}\{r''\}/A_{02}\{r''\}. \tag{3}$$

Since autarky costs of good 1 are relatively cheaper in region $'$, this first region will specialize in good 1 where it has comparative advantage, importing its needed inputs of good 2 from the other region. The unknown terms of trade between the goods will be given by the inequalities

$$A_{02}\{r'\}/A_{01}\{r'\} > (P_2/P_1) > A_{02}\{r''\}/A_{01}\{r''\}. \tag{4}$$

Now the relative cost of production in region$'$ of the good in which it has comparative disadvantage, good 2, is irrelevant. And its relevant cost of production and *real* price for good 1, $(P_1/w') = p_1'$, will depend on the supply-

and-demand-determined price ratio at which it can import good 2, (P_2/P_1). The relevant equations in each country become:

$$\begin{aligned} p_1' &= [a_{01}+p_1'a_{11}+p_2'a_{21}](1+r') \qquad (5)\\ &= [a_{01}+p_1'a_{11}+p_1'(P_2/P_1)a_{21}](1+r')\\ &= a_{01}(1+r')/[1-a_{11}(1+r')-(P_2/P_1)a_{21}(1+r')]\\ &< A_{01}\{r'\} \quad \text{because of (4)},\\ p_2'' &= a_{02}(1+r'')/[1-(P_1/P_2)a_{12}(1+r'')-a_{22}(1+r'')]\\ &< A_{02}\{r''\} \quad \text{because of (4).}\\ p_2' &= (P_2/P_1)p_1' < A_{02}\{r'\} \quad \text{because of (4)},\\ p_1'' &= (P_1/P_2)p_2'' < A_{01}\{r''\} \quad \text{because of (4).} \end{aligned}$$

To sum up: The prevailing real prices, (p_j') and (p_j''), become determinate functions of the $(n-1)$ supply-and-demand parameters determined by *reciprocal* demands, (P_j/P_1). Under the usual regularity conditions on tastes, there will always be at least one market-clearing equilibrium $(P_j/P_1)^*$ under free trade. And, if we stipulate proper transport cost functions or tariff duties, there will be a correspondingly altered set of equilibrium real prices $(p_j'^*)$ and $(p_j''^*)$.[3] I leave to the reader the verification that theorem 4's agnosticisms apply in even a more complex way once we permit importing of inputs produced only abroad.

Even if $A_{02}\{r\}/A_{01}\{r\}$ is a monotone increasing function of r, it could be the case for $n > 2$ that some *other* goods are forced into a specialization pattern by transport costs or by $r''-r'$ differences while goods 1 and 2 are observed in free-trade coexistent world-wide production. Once some of the inputs for 1 and 2 are imported from abroad at real prices not reflecting domestic autarky costs, the behavior of $A_{02}\{r\}/A_{01}\{r\}$ is no longer relevant for observable price and production decisions. So there may well be no $r'' = r'$ equalization implied. The limitation of theorem 6 to trade in final goods is seen to be a limiting one and my present wording must be meticulously adhered to.[4] [Warning: Strength-

[3]Suppose $(\alpha_1', \alpha_2', \ldots, \alpha_n')$ and $(\alpha_1'', \alpha_2'', \ldots, \alpha_n'')$ are the melting-of-the-iceberg fractions that characterize how much of the region ′ exports arrive in the other region, and likewise for region ″ exports. Cf. Samuelson (1954) for discussion of the transfer problem under these (α_j) shrinking coefficients. Then p_j'/p_1' and p_j''/p_1'' are no longer equal when $\alpha_j' \neq 1 \neq \alpha_j''$; but each enjoys an equilibrium value.

[4]This is a good place to amplify my answer to Bhagwati's 1960 query referred to in Samuelson (1965). Now there is no need to be in steady states. Let there be 2 inputs: labor, L, and 'leets,' K. Let 3 goods, (q_1, q_2, q_3), be producible from (L_i, K_i) by

$$q_i = F_i(L_i, K_i) = L_i f_i(K_i/L_i), \qquad f_i'(\cdot) > 0 > f_i''(\cdot),$$

$$\sum_1^3 L_i = L, \qquad \sum_1^3 K_i = K, \qquad q_3 = \dot{K}+\delta K, \qquad \delta > 0.$$

ening the meaning of 'capital intensity differences' will not necessarily obviate the need for such a limitation (although, a sufficient strengthening might do so, as in the case of 6 goods *just like* good 1 and 6 goods *just like* good 2, a case that effectively brings us back to the $n = 2$ case where the unqualified 1965 criterion happens to work).]

Needless to say, in the real world nonproducible natural resources make the 1-primary-factor model of Leontief–Sraffa of limited realism, a caution to be kept ever in mind when thinking about the 'Leontief Paradox' and other relationships.

Here q_1 and q_2 are two tradeable consumer's goods, and q_3 is gross output of new (not-necessarily-tradeable) leets, which depreciate at rate δ.

Now suppose that goods 1 and 2 differ uniformly in factor intensities, $[f_1(k)-kf_1'(k)]/f_1'(k) > [f_2(k)-kf_2'(k)]/f_2'(k)$, and suppose we observe goods 1 and 2 being produced in both regions under free trade. Then even in an unsteady state, when $\dot{K}/K > 0 = \dot{L}/L$ in one or both regions, real interest rates, real leets net rentals, and real wages will be equalized between regions. The real interest rates are given by $r' = r'' = f_3'(k_3)-\delta$, $k_3 = k_3' = k_3''$. Note that we could add further consumption goods $(q_4, q_5, \ldots)$, which need not trade freely.

References

Bliss, C.J., 1967, Collected scientific papers of Paul A. Samuelson, Economic Journal 77, 338–345.

Mainwaring, L., 1978, The interest rate equalisation theorem with nontraded goods, Journal of International Economics 8, no. 1, 11–19.

Samuelson, P.A., 1954, The transport problem and transport costs, II: Analysis of effects of trade impediments, Economic Journal 64, 264–289. Reproduced as Chapter 75 in: Collected scientific papers of Paul A. Samuelson, vol. II (MIT Press, Cambridge, MA, 1966).

Samuelson, P.A., 1965, Equalization by trade of the interest rate along with the real wage, in: Trade, growth, and the balance of payments (Essays in honor of Gottfried Haberler) (Rand McNally, Chicago) 35–52. Reproduced as Chapter 71 in CSP, vol. II.

Samuelson, P.A., 1975, Trade pattern reversals in time-phased Ricardian systems and intertemporal efficiency, Journal of International Economics 5, 309–363. Reproduced as Chapter 251 in: Collected scientific papers of Paul A. Samuelson, vol. IV (MIT Press, Cambridge, MA, 1977).

Sraffa, P., 1960, The production of commodities by means of commodities (Cambridge University Press, London).

FREE TRADE'S INTERTEMPORAL PARETO-OPTIMALITY

Paul A. SAMUELSON

M.I.T., Cambridge, MA 02139, U.S.A.

Received October 1977

Emmanuel's thesis of 'unequal exchange' – that free trade at equalized profit rates and unequal wage rates (1) involves deadweight loss to the world, and (2) explains a one-way trend toward deterioration of poor country's well-being and double-factoral terms of trade – is found on analysis to be incorrect. Careful time-period analysis shows that such free trade is actually *intertemporally Pareto optimal*, despite misleading steady-state comparisons.

In *Unequal Exchange* Mr. Emmanuel (1972) considered a model in which:

> ...the capital factor is mobile but the labor factor is immobile on the international plane ... Instead of equal wages and unequal rates of profits, I adopted the assumptions of unequal wages and of profits subject to standardization and tending to equalization. These premises led me to take on all points the opposite line to the official theory of international trade. (p. 267)

What does an audit show for these opposite-line claims? Does it confirm any hope to explain the trend toward deterioration of the double factorial terms of trade of the Third World vis a vis the affluent nations by means of the concept of *unequal exchange* (in which there is embodied in the goods that the poor regions export more labor than is embodied in the goods that the rich regions export in return)? My post-mortem found no merit in this hope – a hope which if not in Emmanuel's mind has certainly been in that of his sympathetic reviewers and readers. (Incidentally, since Mr. Emmanuel (1978) objects[1] to my words 'real wages,' any reader is authorized to strike out the adjective 'real': and even to replace it with the adjective 'money.' My conclusions critical of his analysis are equally good or bad either way.)

More important than semantic contents of the words 'unequal exchange' is the serious question: 'Does free and balanced trade, at positive profit rates equalized by competition, perhaps involve (and even "explain") some important

[1]Cf. A. Emmanuel, 'A note on "Trade pattern reversals",' the preceding paper in this issue of the *JIE*.

quantum of "deadweight loss" that might be recovered to increase the economic well-being of the Third World?' I interpreted sentences like the following to suggest that Mr. Emmanuel believed in such nonoptimallty of competitive free trade in time-phased systems:

> Finally, after we had studied the relative disadvantages that low-wage countries may suffer from free trade, it remained to refute the premise that a general and absolute advantage accrues automatically to the world as a whole from free trade and the international division of labor, by showing that under conditions of regional disparity in rewarding of the factors, and in particular the labor factor, nothing guarantees that specialization in accordance with the rewarding of the factors shall correspond to specialization in accordance with the quantities of the factors and thereby result in the sought-for world optimum. (p. 267)

Since Mr. Emmanuel is not an easy author to decipher, I may have paid him the undeserved compliment of having formulated the notion of deadweight inefficiency. In any case some unwary readers of the papers I have cited by Mainwaring and Metcalfe–Steedman may trap themselves into believing that true deadweight loss is involved in steady-state equal-profit free trade at other than the Golden Rule rate. My 1975 paper on 'trade reversals' has effectively refuted the notion of true deadweight loss by affirming its opposite – namely the *intertemporal* Pareto-optimality of steady competitive states at *equal* profit rates (Emmanuel's chosen case!).

A few words can clear up all confusions. Consider a time-phased *closed* economy with zero population growth, zero technical change, and labor the only primary (nonproducible) factor of production. Observe a steady competitive state with a positive profit rate. Then it is indeed obvious that less will be produced and consumed than would be available in a steady competitive state at a *zero* profit rate. This merely says that only in the Golden Rule state is consumption maximal.

Does it follow that there is available some deadweight loss out of whose removal we might enhance the well-being of everyone or of those with least ownership of labor power and most in need of substance? Not at all. The closed system in steady competitive equilibrium at a positive profit rate is *intertemporally, efficient*: in moving to the Golden Rule with higher consumption forever, one must necessarily sacrifice something of consumer's goods along the transient path. One cannot, so to speak, get something for nothing, since competition has already ensured efficiency: one must 'abstain' and 'wait' even in the most perfect of planned socialist societies in moving to the Golden Rule configuration.

Exactly the same holds for international trade in time-phased systems. The specialization reversals that are observed in comparing Golden Rule steady states and equalized-positive-profit steady states can be removed, as I showed, only by sacrificing some consumption goods at one time in order to get more at another. Q.E.D.

References

Emmanuel, A., 1972, Unequal exchange: A study of the imperialism of trade (Monthly Review Press, New York); originally: 1969, L'exchange inégal (Librarie Francois Masparo, Paris).
Emmanuel, A., 1978, A note on 'Trade pattern reversals', Journal of International Economics 8, no. 1, 143–145.
Samuelson, P.A., 1973, Deadweight loss in international trade from the profit motive?, in: C. Fred Bersten and William G. Tyler, eds., Leading issues in international economic policy: Essays in honor of George N. Halm (D.C. Heath, Lexington, MA).
Samuelson, P.A., 1975, Trade pattern reversals in a time-phased Ricardian system and intertemporal efficiency, Journal of International Economics 5, no. 4, 309–363.
Samuelson, P. A., 1976 Illogic of neo-Marxian doctrine of unequal exchange, in: D. A. Belsley, E. J. Kane, P. A. Samuelson, R. M. Solow, eds., Inflation, trade and taxes: Essays in honor of Alice Bourneuf (Ohio State University Press, Columbus, OH).

ANALYTICS OF FREE-TRADE OR PROTECTIONIST RESPONSE BY AMERICA TO JAPAN'S GROWTH SPURT

by Paul A. Samuelson

Japan has for many years exported a multitude of goods to the United States. In more recent times the same has become true of a number of Pacific Basin countries, notably South Korea, Taiwan, Hong Kong, and Singapore. Although Japan also imports from the United States, so great has been her value of exports to us that there has resulted a chronic deficit in the U.S. current balance of payments with Japan.

Of course there is no reason why trade should be balanced bilaterally between any pair of countries. A long-run equilibrium might well involve Japan's importing most of her energy and raw material requirements both from North America and from other staple producers in the Mid-East and the developing countries; Japan could afford to pay for these imports by means of her copious receipts from her exports to the United States; and America might complete this long-run triangular balance of trade by selling to the staple-producing countries more in value of high technology manufactured items than the value of those countries' exports to the United States.

The existence of capital movements make it both unnecessary and unlikely that current goods-and-services items in the international balance of payments for any country will be even in *multi*lateral balance. After World War I the United States for

Reprinted by permission.

decades on end displayed a positive surplus on current account, matched by our investing abroad and thereby accruing an ever larger net ownership of assets abroad. What was earlier the pattern for the United States could be, and in recent years has been, the pattern for Japan. Japan has run chronic overall surpluses on current account and has used those surpluses to finance an increase in her holdings of foreign assets. When South Korea and other Pacific Basin countries stop growing so fast and therefore no longer have such an insatiable appetite for infusions of foreign capital, they too may move into the stage of capital exporting now characteristic of Japan.

Flexible market systems should be capable of adjusting to long-run trends that have shown themselves in the past and can be expected to continue into the future. Surprise developments and transient adjustment processes aside, economic theory tells us that there should be a pattern of international real wage rates and terms of trade that could keep down mass unemployment both in the trade-deficit and the trade-surplus regions. Furthermore, macroeconomic theory shows that there is a pattern of monetary-cum-fiscal policies, along with stipulated exchange rate regimes (such as floating exchange rates, or an international gold standard with pegged rates), that can achieve tolerably stable price levels and exchange rates.

Problems of Transitional Adjustment

To be sure, actual economic history often falls short of these theoretical patterns of equilibrium. The business cycle we still have with us. The modern mixed economy still is plagued with a host of problems that go under the name of "stagflation." Israel and Latin America remind us of the possibility of three-digit price inflations. Besides, needed transitional adjustments often do not take place smoothly: competitive imports of autos and steel can exacerbate the problems of mass unemployment in the Detroit and Pittsburgh regions; human misery and economic waste may be involved before destitute auto and steel workers are able to find acceptable jobs in new industries; and, in a populist democracy, labor and industrial interests that have been hard hit by foreign competition can lobby successfully for government programs that interfere with and severely delay the market adjustments which the models of economic theorists call for.

Redistributions of income toward those who are the unlucky victims of change may often take place. At the same time that the electorate deems these transfers to be a fair thing, they may serve to slow down the inevitable adjustment. Also, it is generally the case that our welfare states do not have the effective ability to avoid creating significant overall deadweight losses from their well-intentioned interventions.

Why Not Protect?

Economists differ on many matters. But one area where they seem to disagree least is the field of international trade, the one I am now writing about. Generally economists favor free trade. Paradoxically, that which economists are most nearly in agreement on is precisely the set of doctrines which non-economists find hardest to understand and follow. By non-economists I mean ordinary folk on Main Street: editors, lawyers, and general business people; mayors, governors, legislators, and Presidents; and, for that matter, intellectuals and scientists who do not happen to be trained economists.

Ordinary people take it as axiomatic that when U.S. factories lose out in competition with Japanese factories, this must be a bad thing for America. They take for granted that it means more unemployment here; lower real wage rates in the industries afflicted with new competition from imports; and on the average lower real wage rates for the whole of the American economy. What is bad for the average wage of labor, they perceive in this case to be bad as well for American capital return and for the capitalist class here.

Plain folk here do not spend much time contemplating what this same process means for wages abroad. But if the matter engaged their attention, they would no doubt argue by symmetry that America's loss of comparative advantage in many branches of manufacturing, and Japan's gain in advantage, would in all likelihood raise Japanese real wage rates and returns to capital. Free trade, as they reckon it, has lowered our real per capita income and raised Japan's.

Protection to Undo Harm from Imports?

Almost you might say as a matter of sociobiology, ordinary Americans have primary concern for American prosperity, and it is not deemed sufficient consolation by them that the Japanese have gained what they have lost. After you explain to them that the new innovations in productivity underlying all this can be expected to raise the *total* of world product—so that it is likely to be the case that anything which America has lost is going to be more than matched by the gains abroad—it is still only human nature for Americans to resent what they regard as a disturbance to the status quo hurtful to America.

What they perceive as a hurt to the United States is perceived to come from the new element of imports from abroad. Understandably then, their first thought is to remove the offending source—namely, to legislate protective quotas that will prevent the competition from Pacific Basin exports.

Most intelligent business people I talk to see the matter in exactly this way. And so do their workers. If Japan can outcompete us in one branch of manufacturing, soon she'll be able to do so in other lines and, ultimately, in all lines. With manufacturing jobs lost, where will those workers go except to the ranks of the unemployed? Even if some get work in the services industries, surely their enhanced supply will lower the general wage rate there? And isn't there something really basic that is inherent in manufacturing—as in agriculture—so that the services apex of the pyramid will dangle in air unsupported if it lacks a solid manufacturing base? Besides, after a little while won't the Japanese, who have bested us in manufacturing, take over in high technology? With or without guidance from MITI, won't our rivals beat us out in the high-speed computing area? And still later in the jet aircraft sector and in microbiology?

The traditional services sectors: can they in this age of satellite communications and instantaneous computer mail retain their invulnerability from foreign competition? Perhaps our haircuts will some day come most cheaply from robot clippers, built abroad and even controlled by foreign-source programs? An unusually clever non-economist might conceivably formulate the following rebuttal to free trade:

> When you look to the services sector for succor from foreign competition, you are relying for employment opportunity on those sectors that have *natural* built-in quota-protection. If you think such protected non-tradeables are our salvation, why not achieve more of such good salvation by *artificially contrived protection where mother nature has failed to provide protection for us*, as in manufacturing?
>
> If we must in the end rely on naturally protected non-tradeables for our employment of labor and capital, how shall we be able under free trade to pay for manufacturing items needed for our consumption? Surely, better an autarky achieved by protection legislation than an *unbalanced* specialization pattern occasioned by whatever industries happen to involve goods so bulky or perishable, and so costly to ship, as to be kept invulnerable from competing imports?

I have painted a simple picture of a small profession of academic economists, all united around the proposition that free trade is a good thing, confronting a host of non-economists who believe that protection, and only protection, can undo the harm to the American high standard of living that results from the cancerous growth of imports from the Pacific Basin. Are all economists really agreed? Well, almost all.

Lord Kaldor of Cambridge, and a few economists in the British Labour Party, do believe that protection of manufactures will be a net boon to the U.K. citizenry. This school favors import quotas, and does so from the standpoint not of the laborers and capitalists in the industries directly affected but from the standpoint of the whole nation's best interest.[1]

Free Trade Dogmatisms

The naive devotee of free trade denies the major premise of the non-economists—denies flatly that free trade can hurt anybody. Instead, the dogmatist asserts, free trade makes *everybody* best off. Buying from the cheapest source can only maximize the wellbeing of American consumers—which means all of us inasmuch as laborers and capitalists are necessarily consumers.

Such a simplistic statement is an overstatement. It is valid to state that free trade increases worldwide efficiency. In the technical parlance of economists, free trade does tend when competition obtains to achieve "Pareto-optimality" for the world. (This means that it puts the world out on the global production-possibility frontier, so that any gain by one group could only be realized at the expense of another group's loss.) What the doctrine of free trade cannot say is that a competitive innovation in one country (call it Japan) must end up making people better off there. Nor can it say that such an innovation must end up making people outside of Japan better off. What can be validly stated is that one of these groups must be bettered; and, that any group(s) hurt could be more than compensated by those helped—so that, potentially, the *innovation is capable* of blessing everyone with benefit.[2]

Purpose of Present Analysis

Here in this brief investigation I hope to analyze what the effects are on the welfares of the different regions of a great burgeoning of productivity in the Pacific Basin.

Can this hurt the United States? Must it do so? When, if ever, is the benefit likely to exceed the harm?

And how is a Pacific country like Japan affected? Must innovation there raise welfare there? Can it? On what qualitative properties of the domestic and world economies does the result depend?

Finally, how are third regions likely to be affected by an innovation in Japan that improves her bilateral balance with the United States?

Benefit of Cheaper Imports

The free trade doctrine has one essential point that is definitely valid. Innovations in Japan that improve her productivities in industries exporting to America will cheapen the prices of our imports relative to the prices of our export and non-tradeable local goods. This improvement in our terms of trade unequivocally raises our standard of living. There is a presumption that it will raise the real wage which clears the American labor market; raise the real rents of American natural resources; and, raise the real return to American capital goods.

As already asserted, these changes under free trade that help us may well hurt others, namely the Japanese. These innovations in Japan's export industries can be expected to raise Japanese real wage rates reckoned in terms of the outputs of those industries. But now that America's terms of trade have gone up, Japan's will have gone down. This means that more of Japan's goods must be paid for each unit of the goods she imports from the United States. Therefore, Japan's real wage in terms of the goods she must import may well go down. And, depending upon how inelastic our demand is, they may go down by so much as to outweigh any real-wage gains in terms of the innovated goods, thereby resulting in a net loss in Japanese real income from Japan's innovation. This is not to deny that an innovation in Japan's export industries may help us both in those cases where our reciprocal demand functions are very elastic.

Harm from Competition with Our Exports

Suppose the Japanese innovation is in an industry that previously had been one where we were exporting to Japan. The dogmatic free trader is in error when denying that such an innovation can lower the American standard of living. In truth a big enough innovation by Japan, if it takes place in an industry that previously involved American corporative advantage, is sure to hurt our welfare. That is a theorem in the pure theory of international trade.

Begin with a case where the United States exports a high-technology good and balances that trade by an import of a low-technology good from Japan. Let an innovation improve Japan's productivity in our high-technology sector. In a 2-good Ricardo-Mill model of comparative advantage, at first Japan will still not be able to produce as cheaply our good of original comparative advantage. So, at first the invention has no effect on anyone, for the reason that it is not adopted.

But let the innovation become so great as to make the ratio of Japan's productivity to America's productivity be the same in the one industry as in the other.[3] Then all trade ceases. There is no longer any advantage in trade. Each of us is in autarky. Japan does not regret the disappearance of trade. Now she can get her high-tech goods as cheap at home as by trade, which is cheaper for her than used to be the case when she had to import those goods to optimize her standard of life.

The successful innovation by Japan in our industry of erstwhile comparative advantage has indeed helped Japan. What has this done to us? It has hurt us by eliminating *all* of our erstwhile consumers surplus from trade! Our previous favorable terms of trade have deteriorated to the level under autarky. (No quota can help in this case since the harm done is itself the spontaneous drying up of cheap imports.)

Moral: Free trade giveth and free trade taketh away.

Some qualifications are in order. The 2-good Ricardo-Mill model is very special. But its main results remain valid in more complex models.

Thus, consider a many-good Mill model. Japanese innovations in the goods of *their* comparative advantage do improve U.S. welfare. Etc. But consider now an innovation by them in a borderline traded good that both of us produce. That must hurt us. I do not refer to the short-run unemployment created here as some of our factories lose competitive markets. What I refer to is the lowering of the overall real wage rate here that is needed to clear the labor market now that our international terms of trade are deteriorated by the invention abroad. (It is the induced worsening of our real wage in terms of Japan's traditional export goods that lowers the American real wage.)

The same deterioration in our welfare occurs when Japan's innovation gives her a new comparative advantage in a good that previously we had alone produced (and exported). Thus, start with us exporting cars and planes in return for Japan's cloth. Let innovation in the Japanese car industry produce a new equilibrium, one with us now trading planes for her cloth and cars. Even when our labor market works perfectly to find jobs in the aircraft industry for all workers displaced from the auto industry, this will have to be at an American real wage that is absolutely less than before—at least, at first, until still further auto-industry innovation there cheapens cars enough to offset our harm.

The Ricardo model involves a single factor of production in each country: labor. Will an Heckscher-Ohlin model involving more than one factor of production yield essentially our same results—namely, innovations abroad that cheapen our imports are good for us, while innovations abroad that displace goods in which we have had a comparative advantage are bad for us? Yes. The general analysis confirms these presumptions.

Suppose America has so much land relative to labor that competitive equilibrium will make us export food to Japan for her labor-intensive cloth. Suppose such trade, in the Lerner-Samuelson manner, completely equalizes real wages and real rents in both countries. Now let a labor-augmenting invention in the Japanese cloth industry take place. In effect this raises Japan's effective labor supply and the world's labor supply relative to unchanged world land supplies. This tends to lower the real wage of each unchanged American laborer, lowering it most in terms of now-relatively-dearer food as some U.S. labor shifts from cloth to food production. The supply of cloth is raised worldwide relative to the supply of food, thereby raising the food price/cloth price ratio which constitutes the American terms of trade. The induced rise in our rent outweighs the induced drop in our real wage rates (reckoned in either food or cloth): for the nation as a whole, or for the representative American who owns both his mean share of our total land and of our total labor, real per capita income has been raised by the Japanese innovation in their industry exporting to America.

Now for the case hurting us. Let Japan introduce a land-augmenting innovation in her food-producing industry, which competitively coexists with our food exports but which can supply only part of her food needs. This increases the world supply of land, the factor America has in abundance. It reduces our terms of trade, the ratio $P_{\text{food}}/P_{\text{cloth}}$. Although the U.S. real wage goes up now that the relative price of the labor-intensive good is bid up, the drop in our real rents outweighs the rise in our real wage.[4]

Beside the Ricardo and the Heckscher-Ohlin cases, there is the Haberler-Jones-Samuelson model in which goods everywhere are produced by an immobile specific input and a transferable labor input. In such models each nation could be producing something of every good, while importing something of some goods and exporting something of the remaining goods. Again, in such a model, Japanese innovations in industries that export to us improve American welfare. And innovations in her industries that compete with our exports definitely reduce American welfare.

As a final qualification we must recognize that transport costs imply that some goods may not always be competitively traded. If Japan improves her productivity in immobile housebuilding, her resulting increase in real income can tend to raise or lower the price ratio of her import and export goods. $P_{\text{food}}/P_{\text{cloth}}$ in our earlier example. To the degree that the innovation cheapens the relative price of the good(s) we import from Japan, U.S. welfare rises. To the degree that it cheapens the relative price(s) of the goods we export, that hurts our welfare.

A Rival for Irreplaceable Resources

Before World War II, America had a virtual monopoly so far as enjoying a high standard of living was concerned. Since 1950, Europe and Japan have narrowed our superiority gap. These days a high standard of living chews up irreplaceable geologic resources at an awesome rate. Successful innovation and capital formation in countries like Japan brings them near to the high American lifestyle. Along with our quarter of world GNP that is enjoyed being at the high level of living, these other affluent countries have newly come to employ another one-quarter of world GNP also at a high level. And this, in effect, accentuates the Club of Rome problem. To the degree that America is or will be a net importer of unrenewable petroleum products and metals, the dogmatic free trader would be wrong to deny that America could be hurt by this new progress in Japan and elsewhere.

Consider a three-region world. Japan and America both import oil from the Mideast. Japanese innovations, even if they were neutral in effects on the United States—Japan terms of trade, could greatly raise Japan's real income. That could raise her demand for the oil whose marginal real costs to them (and to us!) can be expected to be pushed up. This does tend to hurt American welfare.[5]

The Foolishness of Autarky

More could be given by way of analysis bearing on how progress in Japan affects America's wellbeing. But my several paragraphs above do indicate how a more complete analysis would generally go. I now turn to the important question of how America in her own self-interest should react to the phenomenon of new competition for our manufactures from the Pacific Basin or elsewhere.

Economists, as already noted, will generally reply by favoring free trade. In effect, they will argue—as I myself have largely done in two or more places[6]—that to the degree that Pacific Basin advance alters comparative advantages and hurts the trend of U.S. real income, reacting to this development by legislating American quota and tariff protections will only add to the first harm a second, self-inflicted harm.

When exogenous forces diminish the consumers surplus a country has been deriving from international trade, it is foolish to react so as to wipe out all the consumers surplus that is still left to you from trade. This is a common sense rebuttal to any view that a former high standard of earnings and of life can be reattained by embracing autarky and repelling the imports that have killed off previously prosperous industries. I suppose it is still important to insist upon the truism that, under free trade, a country cannot be beat down to a standard of living below that of autarky itself.[7]

Selective Protection

Shooting down autarky as a sage policy is almost too easy a sport. Protectionists rarely espouse outright autarky. They wish us to have our cake and eat it too. They counsel taking advantage of cheap imports where those imports do not step on the toes of domestic interests, while at the same time we control severely imports of goods that compete with our domestic producers.

Selective protectionism is almost never a scientific program designed to maximize the sum total of U.S. consumers surplus from international trade. It is in real life a mishmash of political compromises, depending more upon who has lobbying clout than on the niceties of demand and supply elasticities. Political laissez faire, in which those groups who can muster legislative votes gain the quotas that politically powerless groups fail to get, is led by no invisible hand to maximize the country's welfare. Thus, owners of special land which is needed to produce a particular good that is subject to import competition will find that the tariff maximizing their rent income is a prohibitive tariff—and this no matter what might be the economic interest of most consumers.

The Small Country Case

This clash between interest groups and the general welfare is seen most clearly in the case of a small, open country. Being small relative to the great international market, prices of goods are what they are and cannot be sensibly affected by anything the small country does. It is essentially a price taker. And this remains so no matter what policy it follows on free trade, autarky, or in between. For such a country, which can buy and sell all tradeables at price ratios set outside itself, a strong theorem applies:

> Free trade is optimal for a small, open economy. Any interference from it reduces the total of national income that can be spent to consume the various goods. Or, what says the same thing, any positive program of selective protectionism reduces the nation's consumer surplus from international trade. Any gain in one group's economic rents derivable from protection will be at the expense of greater losses imposed on other groups—so that, in principle, the losers could bribe the gainers in order to achieve unanimity on optimizing free trade.

These days the small and open economy is very much in fashion, particularly in macroeconomics. There are many reasons why this should be so. A Belgium or Bengal has little unilateral power to affect international price ratios: when the small country expands its currency, it can expect that its exchange rate will eventually float to compensate for any differential rate of growth in its price level and factor prices.

But the United States is not a small country. It receives about 25 percent of world GNP. And Western Europe acting in concert is not a small country, receiving as it does almost an equal fraction of world GNP. Even Japan receives about 10 percent of world GNP, which implies that it does have some discernible ability to affect price ratios. (When we move down to the viewing level of particular industries and firms operating under conditions of imperfect and monopolistic competition, even a region much smaller than Japan may cease to be merely a passive price taker.)

Obviously, any discussion of optimal trade policy must grapple with problems encountered by countries of limited but not miniscule size.

Optimal Protectionism

At the purist level of analytical trade theory, it is not true that each nation does best for itself by adhering to free trade. Indeed, it is a theorem that:

> If all but one nation adheres to free trade, that one nation will do best for itself by judiciously departing from free trade by just enough to turn its terms of trade in its own favor. The degree of protectionism must not be too large, because then the relative-price gain will be so large as to have wiped out much of the volume of quantity trade that benefits from the price-improvement factor.

This stated result is obvious to any economist who thinks on it. Constantly it is being rediscovered: I can testify to that as having in my youth thought to have discovered it for the first time. Although John Stuart Mill had glimpsed aspects of this theorem, original credit for it in the trade literature ought probably go to the names of Edgeworth and Bickerdike. (In terms of modern duopoly and game-theory literature, the one country acting sophisticatedly while the others react passively qualifies under the heading of an Edgeworth-Stackelberg solution.)

Although the general notion of a scientific-optimality program of protection is straightforward, to implement it and calculate its implied vector of tariff rates and quota amounts requires fairly detailed knowledge of the general equilibrium model underlying the trade situation. Broadly speaking, we restrict some of our export supplies to the degree that demands for them are less than infinitely elastic; and we hold in our demand for imports to the degree that this restraint reduces their effective price we must pay. Since long-run demands and supplies tend to be more elastic than short-run, restraint on the degree of departure from free trade is needed.

Intuitively, I feel that some of the political pressures overlap with the needs of an optimal program. Examples: Protectionists don't much mind imports of goods we don't produce. Protectionists are incensed when an industry that is almost competitive nevertheless gets wiped out by free trade; an optimal program might find some merit in emphasizing protection near the borderline where our comparative advantages end and theirs begin.

Undoubtedly, however, the restrained impediments to trade

called for by the optimum program would be overrun by the interests who pursue legislative lobbying.

Free Trade As a Tolerable Compromise?

Game theory says that any one can gain by breaking away from the free trade that the rest are pursuing. But it is naive for me to think that I am the only one in the mob who will deviate from free trade. What is open to one is open to any other. It is likely that many, or all, will depart from free trade.

This shifts us from the asymmetric Edgeworth-Stackelberg mode to some more symmetric mode. A solution that is in the spirit of the Nash-Cournot mode, so beloved by modern game theorists, is where each country patterns its deviations from free trade to optimize its own welfare function, under the constraint that all other countries are doing much the same—but that whatever it is they are going to do they are now already doing, and your new decisions won't cause them to alter their strategies. (Since what you do as a Nash roleplayer does alter what they do as a Nash roleplayer, it seems to me not very logical for anyone to pretend that all Nash opponents' strategies are frozen independently of one's own strategy. But science is often a set of conventions agreed upon, and the younger generation of scholars do concentrate on Nash equilibria.)

One consequence of a Nash solution with every country seeking an optimal protectionist policy is that it involves positive deadweight loss for the world as a whole. Free trade with various side payments or compensations could get rid of all deadweight loss, permitting everyone to be better off than in the Nash solution. However, I see no likelihood that international negotiations and charters could be achieved that would ensure a free trade regime.

Still, the average gain achieved by each departer from free trade might be so low under the Nash-like status quo as to make it desirable to promote the shibboleth of free trade. As people become persuaded they will benefit little from protectionism, acting on that belief will in considerable measure perpetrate a self-fulfilling prophecy.

Therefore, at the same time that I have done my duty in telling the full analytic truth about free trade, I have tried in the present paper to frame the exposition so that readers may persuade themselves that protectionism, like war, is a game in actuality that is not worth the candle. Just as the theoretical gains that a nation might sometimes gain from war are so tenuous and small relative to the losses that war imposes on all or most, so too the theoretical gains from perfectly gauged protection are so uncertain and limited as to persuade many a rational person that in practice free trade is the best policy not just for all but also for each.

Endnotes

1. I shall be analyzing the merits and demerits of protection. Let me say however, in connection with the Kaldor view, that some of its argument for protection is related to the Friedrich List view that infant industries and not-yet-optimally-developed economies can by protective tariffs or quotas be given the time and stimulus to develop a new comparative advantage that will have become so strong and permanent as to permit later repeal of all the protection. Most experience with actual quotas suggests that the opposite of the intended effect in fact takes place: under protection the infants (and, in only lesser degree, the young economies) far from being stimulated to change their infantile ways are rather given the wherewithal to continue in their previous way and put off called for reforms.

   Experts in trade theory will understand the subtle distinctions that need to be made between (1) induced or natural shifts in constant-returns-to-scale productivities, and (2) the Adam Smith and Allyn Young phenomena of increasing returns to scale.
2. In the case where Japan benefits and America loses, there is no remote probability that Japan would actually make unilateral payments by way of partial, full, or over-compensation. Nor would anyone expect her to do so, or to have to do so.
3. Here is a concrete example. Begin with a situation where our productivity is four times Japan's in the high-tech good; and twice hers in the low-tech good; so that our real wage is somewhere between twice and four times hers, depending upon the relative sizes of our labor forces and the intensity of world tastes for the respective goods. Now let Japan innovate in the high-tech field, doubling her labor productivity there. All comparative advantages have been eliminated, now that her productivities relative to ours are the same 50 percent in both lines: at the market-clearing ratio between our real wage rates, which must make ours twice as large, both of us will be effectively in autarky.
4. The above results are exact when both places have the same homothetic tastes. The same results hold even when Japan's innovation in her import industry (or, alternatively, in her export industry) is other than "augmenting in terms of one factor only." But then we aren't able to argue in terms of any simple equality of worldwide factor prices. Leontief's famous trade paradox, which alleged that the United States imported goods more capital-intensive than her exports, invited the explanation that each U.S. worker was the equivalent of x Japanese workers, whereas our capital stock was less than x times hers—making us relatively capital-poor per efficiency-unit of labour. I know of little evidence for such a strong hypothesis. By contrast, researches of Dale Jorgenson in the 1970s alleged that Japan had attained the *same* production functions as America (in terms of labor and "capital"), but that America still had more capital/labor than Japan and that explained our real-wage and real-income superiority. Jorgenson's hypothesis and Leontief's are incompatible in a two-factor world. Since Jorgenson's other

researches purported to show that the rise in OPEC energy prices had lowered the marginal product of our capital more than that of our labor, that ought to have reduced the differential between the two regions' real wage rate. I am in doubt as to whether there has been any speedup since the mid-1970s in the rate at which our wage superiority over Japan is being wiped out. On all this, see W.W. Leontief, (1953), "Domestic production and foreign trade: The American capital position re-examined", *Proceedings of the American Philosophical Society*, 97, 332-349; also Dale Jorgenson and Mieko Nishimizu, "U.S. and Japanese Economic Growth, 1952-1974: An International Comparison" *Economic Journal*, Vol. 88, No. 352 (December 1978), pp. 707-726, and Dale Jorgenson, "Econometric and Process Analysis Models for the Analysis of Energy Policy," in R. Amit and M. Avriel (eds.) *Perspectives on Resource Policy Modelling: Energy and Minerals* (Cambridge, Mass.: Ballinger, 1982), pp. 9-62.

5. As mentioned in endnote 1, it may be necessary to distinguish between reversible and irreversible shifts in costs and returns. Replaceable resources, such as lumber or fish harvests, could involve marginal costs that rise with demand for them. Japan's becoming more affluent, if it competes with our demands for fish and timber and thereby raises rents and wages in third areas, will thus have a tendency to lower our welfare by raising our imports' costs. In the case of oil and ores, the production function relates their current annual output positively to current labor input and negatively to the cumulative integral of all past outputs mined from the earth. It follows that a known rise in the trend of Japan's affluence, with its implied increment in the trend of her demand for the resource we also aspire to, must involve a sharper rise in the cost to us of importing these desired goods. So again, Japan's affluence does tend to hurt America's real income prospects.

   This case of competition with us in third markets differs in essence and results from a two-country Ricardian case where Japanese innovations lower *all* goods' labor costs there pretty much in a balanced way. As far as we are concerned, such a balanced way in which Japan gains affluence is like an increase in her effective labor supply relative to ours. Without going into the question of whether her income elasticities tend to be larger for our goods than for hers, there is a general presumption that an increase in her labor supply relative to ours will amplify the supplies of goods in which she has comparative advantage and will thereby deteriorate her terms of trade to our welfare advantage. When tastes everywhere in the world were homothetic and the same, it is an ironclad theorem of the Ricardo-Mill model that a rise in her labor supply relative to ours must raise our real wage. Whether the rise in Japan's total effective labor supply will lower or raise the real wage per hour of Japanese work depends on the overall elasticity of derived demand for her labor: the result can go either way, with elasticity optimists betting that both countries get some gain in welfare from the innovations.

6. P.A. Samuelson, "To Protect Manufacturing?" *Zeitschrift für die gesamte Staatswissenschaft* (ZgS), 137 (1981), 407-414, Journal of Institutional and Theoretical Economics (A Symposium); also, "International Trade for a Rich Country," my little Nobel lecture before the Swedish-American Chamber of Commerce, New York, May 10, 1972. This item also appears as chapter 250 in *Collected Scientific Papers of Paul A. Samuelson*, Vol. 4 (Cambridge, Mass.: MIT Press, 1977).

7. As a Kaldorian would insist, this dictum of statical comparative advantage has to be qualified for cases where temporary protection does successfully

alter domestic production functions and thereby change dynamic comparative advantages in the future. A whole school of Latin American protectionists, enlisted under the banner of Raoul Prebisch, has put forth similar arguments on behalf of developing countries. Mainline economists, such as Jagdish Bhagwati and Anne O. Krueger, have interpreted the statistics of economic history to cast some doubt on the wisdom of import-substitution protectionism. Export promotion, as pursued by South Korea, Taiwan, Singapore, and Japan itself, they have interpreted as having been the more successful policy alternative. But of course economic history does not perform controlled experiments to teach economic scholars where truth lies. Brazil differs from South Korea in many ways besides their differences in policy on protectionism. So, even when one studies several countries that do or do not stress import impediments, there remains room for judgment and for ambiguity.

323

Japan and the World at the Century's End

It was George Bernard Shaw who joked: "Those who can, do. Those who can't, teach." I say seriously, "Often those who are not very good at understanding the present or past, retreat to the safe waters of *futurology*." If you make your predictions for far enough ahead, it will be a long time before you are found out.

I have another reason for avoiding today the mantle of the futurologist. This involves a role that is as hard to perform well as, paradoxically, to make it pitifully easy to do. All you need do is flatter your host audience. If today is Tuesday and this is Belgium, put forward the daring view that it is Belgium that will lead the pack in the twenty-first century. For, where nothing can be proved, anything can be proved. A founding deity of futurology decided one day that Japan would turn out to win the growth sweepstakes. Immediately, he gained the love and consulting fees of the whole Japanese society. And his arrow did hit near the mark. Pressing his luck, he later decided that France was the wave of the future. Again, he garnered the admiration of the patriotic French. But this time the actual bull's eye failed to present itself in front of his theoretical arrow.

While poetry has its charm, verse that is free of all constraints degenerates by the Second Law of Thermodynamics to boring babble. The probabilities of specific developments in the world economy over the remaining years of the century are diffuse. But they are, I believe, constrained by the realities of the present and the trends of the recent past. Although you and I have to be uncertain whether the American recovery that began in November of 1982 will end in 1986 or in 1985, we can be confident that its spreading abroad will accelerate production around the globe. Paradoxically, we are safer in predicting that the United States real output will grow at about a $2\frac{1}{2}$ precent annual rate between 1985 and 1995 than we are at guessing whether the rate next year will be much below or above that number.

My approach to forecasting will therefore be prosaic rather than poetic. I know the epical forecasts of Karl Marx and Oswald Spengler; I know the lyrical extrapolations of Arnold Toynbee, Henry Adams, and of my teacher Joseph Schumpeter. But their accuracy in comparison with the actual record of history does not tempt me toward emulation.

Prospects for Growth

On August 28, 2000, at 10:20 A.M., Japan will displace the United States as the society with the world's highest real per capita income. Am I sure of this? Of course not. But I judge it to be just short of an even-money bet. Certainly it is a great deal more probable than that the Soviet standard of living will by the year 2000 come close to the American or even attain to three-quarters the American level.

As near as the experts can estimate, the USSR real per capita income now is barely half that of the USA. And in the last decade it has hovered around this same fractional level. To expect any country to triple its real income per head in a mere sixteen years is to expect the incredible: but that is what it would take for the Soviet real income levels to catch up to the American by century's end.

For the Japanese the task is a more manageable one. To grow from being 72 percent as affluent in 1984 as the Americans to being fully as affluent by 2000 requires that Japan's real income per capita grow at an annual rate of 5 percent per annum while ours is growing at half that rate. It is a tall order but not an impossible one. Before 1973 I would have deemed it a cinch. But since the OPEC revolution of the 1970s, the task looks to be a more formidable one.

The numbers I am relying on in making my guesses are fascinating ones hot off the press. They are constructed by Professors Robert Summers and Alan Heston of the prestigious University of Pennsylvania team on real income estimates. Summers and Heston give annual data for more than a hundred nations, including the major socialist contries, year by year from 1950 to 1980. I have made my own back-of-the-envelope updatings to 1984.

America Still Number One

First, these statistics puncture the myth that Switzerland, Sweden, West Germany, and some other Western European countries have passed America in real per capita incomes. The World Bank Atlas continues to publish crude data based on each country's domestic nominal income, measured in its own currency and then deflated by prevailing foreign exchange rates. It knows better. It knows that different currencies' purchasing power over goods, as measured by deflating each by its exchange rate, displays a persistent bias. Kravis, Summers, and Heston, by deflating a region's nominal income *through use of actual prices paid there for goods and services*, tell a different story—and a more convincing one.

Kuwait and some special oil principalities aside, the US still comes first in per capita real income. Then comes Canada some 7 percent behind. Then, 10 to 20 percent behind America, come Norway, West Germany,

Sweden, France, Switzerland, and Denmark. At around two-thirds to three-quarters of the US living level are clustered Belgium, Japan, Austria, the Netherlands, Finland, and Britain.

What is not realized is that, since 1975, the United States has been doing reasonably well relative to those in the tier just behind her. This is a phenomenon one would perhaps not have expected back in 1970. At that time experts thought that France and Italy would outpace the other principal non-Japanese economies in rate of growth. But Italy has lost ground on the US since then; and it was only in the early 1970s that inflation-ridden France showed vigorous growth.

Case Studies

Each decade has its success stories. For a time Israel kept pace with Japan. But in the last two decades the need for Israel to devote more resources to military defense has taken its toll.

Still again, there is the curious case of Sweden and Switzerland. Supposedly so different in ideology, these two economies forged ahead at the same time. And since 1975 they have decelerated more or less in synchrony. Can this be because both lack oil and must pay higher prices for their needed energy? Although the Swedish reversals have been well publicized, for some reason Switzerland is not seen in her true disappointing light—a shortfall of performance that can only partially be explained away by the sending back of many of those who were guest workers in Switzerland.

Indeed, as the cases of Belgium, Denmark, and the Netherlands show, the Common Market economies have been performing in a disappointing way this last decade. Austria and Finland, not economies that used to be much admired, have surprised themselves and us in the post-1973 epoch.

Even more remarkable has been the growth of the Pacific Basin countries we jokingly call "the Gang of Four": South Korea, Hong Kong, Singapore, and Taiwan. These have been doing in the seventies and eighties what Japan did in the fifties and sixties. Led by soaring exports, they have engaged in a takeoff that rapidly raises their productivity and living standards and that serves to reduce the gap between them and both Japan and the United States.

Uncontrollable Experiments

Often economists try to use these Pacific Basin countries, in comparison with a control group of Latin American countries, to test whether it is a better development policy to stress *export stimulation* or to use tariffs and quotas to protect local industry and promote *import substitution.* Since Korea grows faster than Brazil and Singapore grows faster than Argentina, it is an easy conclusion that export stimulation is a better policy than import substitution. The exercise, I agree, is an interesting one. But I must warn against drawing too sweeping conclusions from controlled experiments that are in reality not controlled.

Maybe what the exercise proves is that Mongoloids are a superior race to Caucasoids of the Latin variety. I don't think you can prove any such thing, but I do want to call attention to the number of things that are not held equal in any such comparative case study.

Or, to take another fanciful line, maybe the experiment merely proves that dictatorships are better for economic development than populist democracies. Certainly Taiwan, Korea, and Singapore are not quite your models of Wilsonian democracy; and the social unrest in countries like Argentina, Uruguay, and Chile, I do believe, an economist must take into consideration in interpreting past economic history and in making shrewd guesses about future growth trends.

In making judgments about Japan's future, I certainly take into account that she is a democracy, which like Mexico is de facto a one-party-victorious system. Being an open democracy, Japan in some sense does expose to an observer's eyes the temperature of the opposition forces present in the society; so long as the leading party holds its edge, the prospects for rapid changes in the rules of the game remain limited. By contrast, when I appraise where South Korea will be in 2000, I must apply some discount factor to her recent rates of prodigious growth in order to allow for the risk that her imposed political order may be only quasi-stable.

Having mentioned Latin America, let me call attention to the fact that her post–World War II growth has generally been disappointing. My old teacher Jacob Viner once suggested that the old Schoolmen edicts against interest and usury might be one cause of modern-day stagnation in those Catholic lands. Cultural inheritances can be more important than genetic inheritances.

The story is not a monolithic one. Brazil and Mexico grow better than the US, while Argentina and Chile stagnate over the long pull. In Brazil's case, she is a tropical country with the racial heterogeneity often met in such regions. That she should be able almost to double between 1950 and 1980 her fraction of US real income per head is a notable and all too rare phenomenon in the LDCs. Mexico in the last thirty years has been able to rise from having 24 percent of the US level to almost 32 percent.

The LDC Story

All of my numbers adjust growth numbers for concomitant changes in population numbers. And by referring growth rates to their magnitude vis-à-vis the US, I am roughly making allowances for the fact that in this age of science and communications, par for the course is not holding your own in real consumption terms but rather in achieving some modest degree of advance.

The sad relative performance of African countries must surely be in good part due to the fact that they continue to have high birth rates at the same time that modern science reduces their death rates. By the old Malthusian process, they have dissipated their potential for economic progress by adding more stomachs at as fast a rate as they add to their ability to command the necessities of life. Years ago the English Nobel economist James Meade mentioned that the island in the Indian Ocean called Mauritius had all the problems associated with an LDC. As its population virtually doubled since 1950, can we be surprised that its per capita real income rose only 30 percent, while America's was rising by 75 percent and Japan's was rising by more than 600 percent?

After the old colonial tyrannies were terminated in Africa, the perpetual biological tyrannies were given their full sway to operate. Fortunately, the frustration of material economic advance by population explosion did not mean in this age of scientific medical advance that life expectancies would suffer in the LDCs. In fact, the last half of the twentieth century has seen widespread improvements in the average span of life all over the globe. The quality of health has at the same time also averaged out a widespread improvement almost everywhere—the recent Soviet deterioration in life expectancies being a surprising puzzle.

As we look toward century's end, we can with reasoned confidence predict that peacetime death rates will continue to fall, as the poorer regions slowly converge toward where the affluent regions have recently been.

The Pattern under Socialism

I find it sad to see that India has failed to close the huge gap between her living standards and those of the industrial West. Freed of colonial domination, she has professed to go the way of socialism. At the same time, save for one lapse into authoritarianism by Mrs. Ghandi, India has adhered to democracy. Still the record of the last third of a century shows no pattern of catching up. And the same disappointing record is shown by Sri Lanka, Pakistan, and Bangladesh.

It is hard for me to think of a socialist country that has done exceptionally well in the growth competition. Social democratic governments have sometimes performed well—as in the cases of Sweden and Austria. These economies however are more in the nature of welfare states that redistribute incomes rather than conventional socialisms in which the government owns and operates the means of production.

Certainly none of the Eastern European socialisms can boast of remarkable rates of growth. Professor Irving Kravis of the University of Pennsylvania presents estimates for Mainland China that are perhaps higher than most. These show China starting out in 1950 about even with India. But by 1980, China has twice India's per capita real income, being at 14 percent of the US level as against India's being at 6 percent.

Many of the African countries newly liberated from colonial bondage made a brave new start with constitutions guaranteeing civil liberties and with brand new five-year plans. Too often the constitutions never became reality as dictatorship prevailed. And most of the five-year plans were hardly worth the paper they were written on. As mentioned, the high African birth rates leave many of those economies at the mercy of any spell of drought or other bad weather.

The Kiss of Oil

Having oil is one easy path to growth. Norway comes third in the world, instead of remaining as Sweden's poorer cousin, because of the discoveries of North Sea oil and gas. One observes that both Iraq and Iran more than doubled in real incomes from 1965 to 1975 because of oil.

However, as the case of Iran reminds us, a nation richly endowed with geologic resources can still suffer reverses in productivity after it goes through a political and social revolution. From 1975 to 1980, Iran dropped from 37 percent of the US level in the Shah's time to 24 percent under the Khomeini. During that same interval of time, Iraq rose from 24 percent of our level to 42 percent.

Similarly, oil helped Nigeria break out of the African doldrums. And it was oil that earlier helped Venezuela break away from the Latin American crowd.

Since geologic resources can be used up as well as being newly found, there can arise the problem economists call "the Dutch disease." This refers to the case where discovery of an exhaustible resource (1) first adds to a nation's prosperity, (2) soon distorts its comparative advantage away from traditional manufactures, and (3) ultimately, once the geologic resources are exhausted, leaves the country no longer in a position to resume its original lines of activity. Temporary bursts of prosperity can manifestly do you a lot of harm.

Affluence and Satiation

So long as Japan sees that it still has a gap to overcome before catching up to the American level, motivation to work hard and effectively remains strong. However, in the most advanced societies, such as Scandinavia or

North America, people are able to enjoy a fairly comfortable standard of living without working too hard and are able to turn over much of the dirty and distasteful duties to guest workers who are still motivated by their relative poverty.

Surely it is not irrational for those who have achieved this measure of affluence to want to enjoy more leisure, taking longer vacations, working on the job at a relaxed pace, and losing their old acquiescence in a hierarchical system of industrial command. Therefore, in estimating what the growth potential is in my own country, I do feel it necessary to take into account some depressing effect of affluence on work efforts.

It follows that, in judging Japan's own future growth scenario, I have to try to judge whether the high morale of Japanese workers and managers will be undermined by the achievement of high real incomes. I used to warn facetiously: The day that the Japanese can wake up in the morning and say, "Now we are number one—ahead of the Americans," will be the day when the whole nation suffers a nervous breakdown as it loses the motivating goal of catching up and going to the top.

I have to warn against exaggerating the achievement of affluence. How naive in the 1980s appears J. K. Galbraith's view of the 1950s that Americans had essentially solved the problem of scarcity. Even the upper classes did not then have all they wanted. And, by definition, few Americans were in the upper classes. In the decades since, real incomes have grown. But also people's felt needs have grown.

Before the young Karl Marx had done much study of economics, he fell into the trap that besets socialist thinkers. It is the trap of believing that society's scientific knowledge is so great as to permit everyone to enjoy the highest imaginable (and desirable) standard of living with relatively little effort—if only evil kings and evil capitalistic markets did not prevent consummation of this desirable state of utopia. That was not a rational judgment in the 1840s. Nor was it in 1867. And the end of scarcity for most of the globe is not a feasible condition in 1984 or 2000. Even if socialism could outperform the mixed economy—and the evidence for this is hard to come by—there will still be operating a desperate competition between the law of diminishing returns and the new innovations of scientists and entrepreneurs. To think otherwise is to be uninformed.

One effect of affluence is to reduce the population's rate of saving. In a well-run macrosystem, what reduces saving propensities will in the long run reduce the level of net capital formation. True supply-side economics affirms that one of the few ways that a society can speed up its rate of productivity growth is by the mechanism of accumulation of more and better capital goods. (One does not have to be a naive neoclassical economist to attach importance to this fundamental.)

Japan still has a high saving rate in comparison with the US, where personal net saving is barely 6 percent of disposable income and where the Reaganomic colossal structural-budget deficit has lowered our society's overall thriftiness. America's largely unfunded social security system also tends to reduce private citizens' need to save for their old age, while at the same time *not* building up under government ownership any increment of capital goods out of which retirement needs can be provided. Success breeds success in a chicken-egg-chicken... process: when Japan grows fast, that provides the wherewithal to finance a high level of capital formation. It is quite otherwise in many poor LDCs. And, ominously, if Japan stumbles in her growth pace, lack of success can begin to breed lack of success.

As already asserted, affluence also works to reduce work effort. It is rational to spend some of one's new real income on leisure; rational to refuse to do unsafe, unpleasant work when one can afford to make such refusals. One rather surprising fact, which works against Galbraith's sweeping thesis that Americans are long since satiated with private goods and services, is the slowness with which our average work week has been reduced since 1945 and indeed since 1920. We don't work on weekends any more, but the 5-day 40-hour week is still remarkably common. One expects that the Japanese will increasingly want to enjoy vacations as the century comes to a close, and to reduce their average working week. On the other hand, retirement ages in Japan have always seemed remarkably early to Western observers. Now that life expectancy in Japan is well into the mid-seventies, I suspect your customs will change and it will become more usual for men and women to retire at older and older ages.

The same affluence that reduces personal effort in the workplace also affects the effort that young people exert at school and university. In Scandinavia and in North America the acids of modernity undermine the bourgeois disciplines of eduction. I take it for granted that my children needn't be as good spellers as my generation had to be. Let us hope that word-processor programs will bail them out, just as the hand calculator will compensate for what they don't learn about the process of taking square roots. It would seem naive to expect that marijuana will stay confined to the college dormitory without entering into the factory and office work place.

Japan will probably find itself regressing toward the mean of the human race. Your pressure-cooker competition for place at university has its advantages and disadvantages. I suggest that, rather than replacing your meritocracy by a selection process that reverts to favoritism by class and affluence, that you identify early your elite scholars and free them from the routines of exam competition. As you gain in releasing creativity and spontaneity, I hope you will not have to pay too high a price in deterioration in language and mathematical skills. (Although it is a digression, I cannot refrain from noting the difficulties that all Japanese have with the difference between their language and those of the Western societies. This cleavage can hardly to exaggerated in its importance. If by the year 2000 some technological improvement could bridge the gulf or greatly reduce it, that would be an economic development of the first magnitude. Yet I honestly do not have the imagination to conceive how such an important breakthrough in linguistics and *Weltanschauung* might even begin.)

Deadweight Loss from Intervention

Populist democracy has the temptation and power to interfere with the workings of the market mechanism. This is for good and for evil. It is for good when redistributive taxation and expenditure alters the pre-tax incomes dealt out by market pricing in the direction of greater equity and human equality. It can be for evil when kings and nobles usurp much of the social income; or when evil politicians feather their own nests at the expense of the vast majority; or when plutocrats are able to use their wealth to bribe those who run the state to run it in the interests of the plutocrats.

Those evils of intervention are fairly obvious, but they are not the important evils that concern me most in analyzing what is next ahead for the remaining years of the century. Mancur Olsen's important work, *The Rise and Fall of Nations* (Yale University Press, 1982), makes the fundamental point that the struggle between different interest groups in a democracy is likely to end up in deadweight loss for the whole society. (In economists' parlance, "Pareto inefficiency" is the all-too-likely outcome of the game-theoretic struggles between different classes and interest groups.)

Thus it may be commendable to take from the over-rich and give to the needy poor. But in doing this, the welfare state all too often impairs the incentives for the poor to do the actions that will lessen their poverty. And the process of taking away superfluous income from the affluent classes inevitably in some degree blunts the incentives of those taxpayers to produce useful goods and services. As wool from the affluent sheep is shorn by the state to give to those deemed worthy, the sheep who produce the wool are motivated to produce less of such wool. The production extinguished in the process is unavailable for transfer to the poor. It is deadweight loss.

At the 1980 World Economic Congress in Mexico City, I suggested that maybe one should not look at a Sweden to get a glimpse of the economic future. Instead it may be the Argentinian pattern that presages what is waiting for us ahead. This was a pessimistic viewpoint to enunciate. For Argentina is par excellence an example of an economy whose relative stagnation does not seem to stem from climate, race divisions, Malthusian poverty, or technological backwardness. Its society, not its economy, seem to be sick. Its political system does not function in a way conducive to productivity. And these sicknesses in sociology and government do impair the economic health of the Argentine economy.

Hierarchy and dominance are undermined in modern populist democracy. As the effective rights of individuals increase, an approach toward anarchy results. I do not wish to pronounce on the aesthetic or ethical merits of anarchism and individualism. All that concerns me is the problem for economic efficiency and progress that any requirement of unanimity occasions. It is practically impossible to be on Pareto-efficiency frontiers or near them when logrolling and competitive negotiating enter into every economic decision making.

Take the issue of nuclear energy. Even if there were strong technical advantages in use of fission rather than fossil fuels, outside of the authoritarian USSR and People's Republic of China the prospects for nuclear energy seem poor. Small groups of fearful environmentalists are likely to prevail in their opposition to nuclear power plants. Their very resistances can succeed in making it true that nuclear energy becomes non–cost effective. For a country like Japan that must import its energy, this dilemma is especially painful.

Supporting Obsolete Operations

A few years ago I was even more concerned than I am now over another source of deadweight loss, which can be called the Mussolini syndrome. Modern mixed economies are under great pressure to keep factories operating even when they cannot meet the market test of finding a demand for their products at prices that will cover costs. During the Great Depression, Mussolini found it necessary to support the Italian stock market and to have his government take over ownership in many private corporations. This is an understandable extension of conventional open-market operations by the central bank in government securities.

But once government owns a company, its workers and voters generally will put pressure on it to continue to offer jobs even after markets for its products have disappeared. Pretty soon it can become a meaningless charade to carry on economic activities that accomplish no purpose other than to maintain job opportunity and workers' incomes.

The problem is aggravated if, as in Italy and Sweden, ostensibly private corporations are subject to government pressure or bribes to keep workers hired even when there are not profitable tasks for them to do. If these practices become sizable in the public and private sectors, the very meaning of such measures as *real national product* can begin to come into question.

Within my country we have faced several dramatic cases that cried out for rescue by the government: The Penn Central Railroad network; the Franklin National Bank on Long Island; the Lockheed Aircraft Company; the Chrysler auto company; and the Continental Illinois Bank in Chicago. In no case has the government in the end displayed indifference to the demands put on it.

Where confidence in the whole banking system is in jeopardy, I think the case for intervention is a strong one. Similarly, railroads are public utilities that are part of social overhead costs. But suppose Detroit truly loses long-run comparative advantage in the production of cars. Just because one auto manufacturer is large and hires many thousands of workers, whose unemployment would have a noticeable impact on the whole region, is not a valid reason for keeping it permanently alive by subsidy resuscitation.

What is not yet a significant problem for the United States is for other economies indeed a serious one. Recently I traveled through Egypt where a soft form of socialism prevails. A traveler garners the impression that almost anyone can count on the government for at least a low-paying job. Energy is grossly underpriced and the failure to establish use charges for special water and sewage facilities leads, inevitably to haphazard and inadequate hydraulic installations and operations. In Norway I observed a huge shipbuilding works that was being kept from bankruptcy only by the oxygen of government subsidy. Yet, the reassignment of a score of carpenters precipitated a walkout by thousands of workers. To a stranger there was an air of unreality about the whole event.

I do not draw the conclusion that the government must never interfere with the workings out of the economic marketplace. Rather, I argue that it must keep alert when it is interfering to what inefficiencies it may explicitly or implicitly be augmenting. The outside world regards the Japanese system as one shot through with government paternalism in economic matters. It is not clear how—and whether!—you have been able to avoid inflicting deadweight loss while conducting such operations.

Class Struggle and Over-High Real Wage Rates

The natural working out of dynamic comparative advantage suggests that routine manufacturing in affluent economies will lose out to competition from low-wage regions. The process works itself out most benignly when workers in the industrialized nations are sucked out of manufacturing by job opportunity in the services sectors. More painful is the situation in which workers who lose their good jobs in manufacturing require a long time to find suitable jobs elsewhere.

At all times in the welfare state, but especially in a decade like the 1970s when energy prices quadrupled and raw material prices escalated, there is a temptation for workers to hold out for real wage rates that are too high to clear the market with jobs for all. The result tends to create and involve an overvalued currency: dollar and mark exchange rates so high as to accelerate the exodus of manufactures toward the sprinting Pacific Basin LDCs.

As Michael Bruno of Hebrew University has suggested, real wage rates in Western Europe may have been less flexible in the 1970s than they were in the United States and Japan. Some of the high unemployment since 1973, and much of the long-run unemployment in places like Argentina, may be traceable to labor's pricing itself out of the market. The workers hope to appropriate to themselves the largest feasible fraction of the national income by bargaining militantly for ever-higher wage rates. Whether or not this hope is a correct perception about reality is not clear from either the experience of economic history or the logic of plausible model building.

Nevertheless, the enhanced humanity of the modern welfare state and the responsiveness of activistic populist democracy to pressures from the electorate do tend to help workers hold out stubbornly for real wage rates even when they are too high. Authoritarian systems that are fearful lest they lose their power provide, along with bread and circuses, promises to the workers of higher nominal wage rates—promises that cannot be honored in *real* terms since excessive wage increases are canceled out by induced rises in the price level.

Again, many Latin American case studies could be cited. By contrast, during the mid-1980s American workers have responded to the competition from foreign manufactures, and to the labor surpluses created by our crusades against inflation, by moderating their nominal wage demands. Whether this moderation will persist after the present recovery reduces the excesses of manpower and capital-capacity slack prevailing in the system, that is a question that only the future can tell.

My brilliant MIT colleague Martin Weitzman has been doing pioneering research into the imperfections of the usual form of capitalistic wage contract. Many of the basic Keynesian difficulties and disharmonies he is able to trace to these wage contracts. By contrast, he shows what vast advantages for the macroeconomic system—its degree of unemployment, its instability, and its stagflation dilemmas—that might come from various forms of profit sharing by workers. Japan, he believes, provides a system of bonuses and lifetime ties to employers that more nearly approximate the optimal Weitzman profit-sharing mode. If he is right, this is an aspect of your system that you would lose only to your considerable disadvantage. Don't just count your blessings. Take action to preserve and extend them!

More important than my conclusion about Japan's likely convergence toward the US level of affluence by the year 2000 was my mode of reaching it.

1. Although geography is frowned on as an explanatory factor by modern savants, I give positive weight to Japan's temperate climate. And I do give minor negative weight to Japan's need to import so much of her raw materials. No matter how vibrant remains Japan's entrepreneurship, the capacity of the rest of the world to absorb and tolerate the expansion of Japanese exports needed to pay for the raw materials she would consume after attaining the American level of affluence will be limited. Some slowdown in 1984–2000 non-Japanese growth rates, I fear, will serve as an inhibitor of Japan's achieved growth rate. Put your best minds to work to *reduce your dependence on export-led growth.*

2. Race is a forbidden category in modern explanations. Nevertheless, eschewing fanciful genetic explanations, I think that the whole cultural complex characteristic of the yellow peoples of the far east is a plus for future growth. (Warning: Outside of China the Chinese excelled at entrepreneurship in a way that they seem not to have done inside of China. So it is not genes that I am calling attention to.) The homogeneity of you Japanese, while it may make for monotony, certainly does simplify your problem—as a South African, American, or French Canadian would readily admit. It is your good luck that the market system's equilibrium gives you more equality than elsewhere in the OECD or the developing nations.

3. The fact that ever since 1945 the Japanese people have forsaken glory and military power has been a strong plus for your economic development. I would warn that reverting to earlier patterns would be, from an economic viewpoint, a serious retrogression.

4. Political economy is more than pure economics. If Japan had the internal political instability of an Israel or the lack of social cohesiveness of an Argentina or Chile, I would have to be more guarded in my diagnosis of your potential for progress. Often I have thought that your leading party would be successfully challenged—either because of its own inadequacies or because of the dynamics of the opposition or merely because people get bored with the same old thing. So far that has not happened. So far the antipathy toward the market system even when it seems to be working fairly successfully has remained merely a characteristic of your academic and intellectual classes. Whatever the long-run merits of a rise in radical influence, for the 1984–2000 time frame a New Deal–like regime—or even a Calvin Coolidge regime of crude capitalism—is probably more conducive

to success in the growth derby than would be a ferment of political turmoil along the lines of 1900–1915 Tsarist Russia.

5. Finally, will success itself blunt your hunger for success? As Japan finds it can afford the humanitarian measures that the Scandinavian societies long ago pioneered, will embracing them sap the Schumpeterian vitality of the system? A Milton Friedman insists that it must. I am less dogmatic.

Like the man from Missouri who has to be shown, I want to see how you work out your future destiny. I hope you will surprise me pleasantly and that you will teach the West how to combine the mindless efficiencies of the market with the humanitarian safeguards of the good society—which means the free society.

To Protect Manufacturing?

by

*Paul A. Samuelson**,

Cambridge, Mass.

The third quarter of the Twentieth Century was a golden age of economic progress. It surpassed any reasoned expectations. And we are not likely to see its equivalent soon again.

International trade contributed mightily to the postwar miracle, something that could not be taken for granted in 1945. The depression decade of the 1930s saw the breakdown of the gold standard; it involved competitive tariffs, quotas, and selective exchange controls designed to protect overvalued currencies and domestic employment. The Bretton Woods system was set up in 1944 out of the fear that, after war's end, there would be a continuation by other means of the interferences with free trade and the international division of labor that had become customary during the 1930s.

When we congratulate ourselves on getting rid of the Bretton Woods fixities of parities, it is only fair to remember that the quantum of international trade surpassed the miracle rates of domestic growth in the sensational 1950s and 1960s; and it was under the Bretton Woods regime that this salutary development took place. Japan, the Common Market countries, and all those regions that have increased their share of world GNP at the expense of North America, the leader, should keep the flowers growing on the grave of the Bretton Woods system, in grateful remembrance of its transitional role in rectifying the initial peacetime undervaluation of the American dollar. It was not a good thing for the world that the United States enjoyed in 1945 almost half of real world GNP. And it is not a bad thing for the United States that our share has been reduced to about one-quarter of world GNP: our people have grown in average per capita affluence while Sweden, West Germany, and Switzerland have gained somewhat on us; under healthy world development the U.S. share of the world total will continue to drop, even though our 6 percent of world population continues to be at the top of the scale in *per capita real GNP (correctly* calculated à la Professors Kravis, Summers, Heston, and their Pennsylvania colleagues).

---

* Paul A. Samuelson is professor of economics, Massachusetts Institute of Technology.

Free Trade at Bay

My concern is with the future. Comparative advantage is not static. Economic law suggests to me that much of manufacturing industry will try to leave Western Europe and North America under free trade. This is not a new thing. It is not a peculiar consequence of the presentday regime with its reliance on floating exchange rates. But it is an intensification of older trends that will certainly put a strain on the ideology of free trade.The political pressures for protectionism, I suspect, are about to intensify.

The purpose of economic theory is to alert us to the direction of change, to a reasoned evaluation based on evidence of the probabilities and improbabilities. Along with this positivistic service, economic theory also has the normative purpose of setting out the likely consequences of alternative policy programs. Until electorates and leaders learn what are the menus of choices, they cannot arrive at their optimal selection of acts.

The plain person, unburdened with knowledge of economics, is prone to fear that free trade will wipe out jobs and decimate real incomes. Some sophisticated economists, such as Nicholas Kaldor and other U.K. Labour Party analysts, agree with the notion that loss of manufacturing jobs by free trade will bring loss of national standard of living.

A diametrically opposite conclusion is presumed by the unthinking ideologue of free trade: to him, so to speak by very definition, what free trade brings is the optimum; on this view, a world without tariffs and artificial trade impediments, would have to bring to every region and every person an ever increasing real income. Although Kaldorian mercantilism might be empirically either wrong or right, the deductive syllogism that free trade maximizes each market participant's welfare is logically false. Even under the strict conditions most suitable for perfect competition particular market participants win and lose from ever-occurring shifts in supply and demand.

The correct *theoretical dogma* on free trade is this:

> Under conditions suitable for perfect competition, free trade is efficient in the sense of wiping out *global deadweight loss*. If you deviate from free trade, those who gain from so doing gain less than those who lose lose – in the sense that the losers could afford to bribe the winners to desist from protectionism.

It is naive to think that it is politically feasible (or even desirable) for protectionism in Western Europe and North America to be bought off by such developing industrial states as South Korea, Taiwan, Singapore, or Hong Kong. Aside from political unfeasibility, bribes from the less affluent to the more affluent are not ethically aesthetic.

The free trader, emancipated from false theoretical dogma, will rely rather on an empirical long-run presumption:

> Eschewing trade impediments with their concomitant deadweight losses is likely to bring benefit to a *random* person or regime, in the *long* run, *averaging* out the happenstance of particular gains and losses resulting from supply-and-demand shifts in tastes and technologies. ("What you lose on the swings, you gain on the round-abouts...")

Concretely, as applied to Europeans and Americans apprehensive about their losing comparative advantage in manufacturing, the free trader argues:

> It is not clear that the already industrialized societies lose more than they gain from the development in the new industrial regions of comparative advantage in manufacturing. Cheaper imports have contributed much to the real living standards of the affluent nations. What Nagoya gains is not necessarily what Detroit, Turin, and Düsseldorf lose. What South Korea gains, may be part of what North America and Western Europe stand to gain.
>
> Moreover, suppose it should turn out to be the case that supply-and-demand shifts are tending to hurt the richer nations. Not all hurts can be usefully assuaged by protectionism. Often quota and tariff interferences will add some self-inflicted wounds and leave you twice badly off, at the same time that some deadweight loss is being borne by the developing nation.

How Can Imports Hurt Us?

Noneconomists naively assume a fixed number of jobs. If Japan gets some good jobs that Germans used to have, that is supposed to be a clear cut loss to the German nation.

Economists know better. We know that good German jobs in the textile industries are often lost when better German jobs in the chemistry and machinery industries raise general wage rates above what can keep the German textile industries alive in the face of Taiwanese competition. Japan, having won much of New England's share of the world textile market, in turn loses textile jobs to Korea when Japanese textiles can't hold their workers against the pull of better paying Japanese industries.

Suppose that the Gang of Four – South Korea, Taiwan, Singapore, and Hong Kong – improve their technology dramatically. How does that affect U.S. and German workers and capitalists if we continue with the same slowly improving technology?

I must distinguish[1] whether the Asian improvement came

1. in goods they traditionally export to the West,
2. in goods that have such heavy transport costs that they don't enter into trade on the export or import side,

[1] See DORNBUSCH, FISCHER, and SAMUELSON [1977] for a convenient model to analyze these problems.

3. in goods that can't in any case be produced in the face of Western competition,
4. in goods that we used to export to them but which now they can export competitively to us or at least produce for domestic consumption,
5. in some combination of the above four catagories.

Case 1. The first of these categories is the one dogmatic free traders concentrate on. It is an unmixed blessing to the West to get our imports cheaper. Our terms of trade improve. Our *real* wage rates rise. Our consumers' surplus from international trade rises. Job opportunity rises even in our non-tradeable-goods industries and in the industries where our exports are unchallengable. The resulting increase in our general wage rates, the free trader will admit, does drive out of existence some borderline industries previously just hanging on to their markets in the face of actual and potential Asian competition. But, the free trader can correctly point out, these industries lose workers because workers are bid away by now more-productive job opportunity.

Abroad, one can't be sure. Probably real wage rates rise there as a result of their technological advances. Certainly that must follow if their new supplies are not so flooding world markets as to turn their terms of trade against themselves by so much as to make their technical improvements be immiserating changes.

Case 2. Europeans of goodwill can bless technical changes that make local Korean goods more available to previously poor Koreans. To the extent that this releases resources into Korean export industries and also enhances Koreans' demands for goods imported from the West, this case's technical change will improve the West's terms of trade, its real incomes, its consumers surplus from trade. Though Asians may lose consumers surplus, they probably are net benefitters from the technical change. (Only if demands for their exports are so inelastic as to make the induced deterioration of their terms of trade great enough to offset the boom of domestic productivity, would Asians be hurt in this second case.)

Case 3. I mention this case though it has no effects whatsover. A great change is unlikely to occur, or be recognized, in an industry that Asia can't afford. If now Asia still can't afford the industry, even if it comes closer to being able to do so, there will be no effect on anyone.

Case 4. Here the honest free trader must admit that the West could be hurt by better productivity abroad. The West loses consumers' surplus from trade as the West's terms of trade are hurt by undermining of her export-goods prices relative to her import-goods prices.

The extreme case, would be where South Korea came to have *exactly* Germany's *comparative* productivities, industry by industry. (Warning: even if *every* Korean industry came to have exactly one-half Germany's real productivity, when Korea's real wage rate were one-half Germany's all trade between the two countries would cease.) If Asian technical change occurs thus in all the goods Germany used to export, and all trade ceases, Germany has lost the consumer surplus formerly enjoyed from trade[2]. This is the germ of truth – one of the few germs of genuine truth – in the Marxian notion that the West might lose something if the East became exactly like the West.

Job opportunity in the West might temporarily suffer if money wages lagged in Asia behind the growth in productivity, creating an export surplus there and a trade deficit in the West. Floating exchange rates would take care of this: as the Western currencies depreciated relative to the Eastern, full employment equilibrium would be restored in both places; the final drop in Western *real* wage rates cannot be blamed on the mechanism of floating, since it is an unavoidable implication of Case 4's technical change.

Note this: Even when the West is hurt, there is nothing that can be done about this hurt in the case where the East comes to have the exact same comparative productivities industry by industry as the West. Even acting in concert, the West has no monopoly power to exploit vis-à-vis the East. Admittedly, in less extreme versions of Case 4, if concerted action by the West exploits some of its monopoly power that had previously been unexploited, some (or all) of the induced loss in Western welfare might be mitigated – a problem I return to later.

Before leaving positivistic analysis of how Western welfare is affected by Eastern inventions, I ought to deal with Club of Rome problems. Oil and other geologic deposits are limited. If a Korea joins the ranks of the affluent nations much as Japan had done before, Korea will have real bidding power for OPEC oil and limited food supplies. Western Europeans and North Americans will have lost a little of the privileged access to bidding for those scarce resources which their previous exclusive affluence had given them. Again, the Marxian suspicions of conflict of interest between the rich and less-rich regions is seen to have some basis in fact.

Protectionist resistance to manufacturing imports is not a weapon well gauged to counter the West's potential loss in welfare. The West's knife may cut against itself in scratching at its rival. Let us see why.

Monopoly Power to the Rescue?

I have no wish to rebut dogmatic protectionism by dogmatic libertarianism. A fairminded economist must admit that North America and Western Europe, if they could collude to act concertedly in their own self interest, may be big enough to possess some genuine degree of exploitable market power (monopoly power). It is not a theoretical impossibility that, in departing from free

[2] If Asian technical change proceeds even farther, cheapening relative costs of the goods that have shifted over from being their imports to being their exports, such further changes are covered by my previous Case 2 and don't have to be analyzed here in Case 4.

trade in a way that is optimal from their selfish viewpoint, they might force a loss on the newly industrializing regions that exceeds the global deadweight loss induced by newly contrived imperfection of competition.

Theoretical possibilities have to be judged in terms of practical possibilities and empirical quantitative importance. I know that a tight cartel of the affluent nations is unfeasible: I doubt that a loose confederation, in which the separate European and American countries simultaneously give in to their domestic union and business manufacturing interests, has much monopoly power to exploit.

What Is to Come?

Rational world economic development will probably call for the following end of century trends:

1. Manufacturing, particularly the simpler processes that all can imitate rather easily, will move toward the developing world.

2. North America and Europe will shift resources toward sophisticated technologies, service industries, and headquarter functions – in that way contributing both to their own self-interests and the interests of the less affluent.

3. The successful developing societies will gain on the leaders in real per capita incomes, just as the United States was gained on in the 1945–80 period.

Most of the newcomers' gains will come out of *their own enhanced productivities* and not out of the hides of the peoples less affluent than them or more affluent than them. However, to the degree that global geologic resources are unrenewable and limited, the new bids for such resources by Koreans and Japanese must contribute a little toward more unfavorable terms of trade facing Indians, Chinese, Eastern and Western Europeans, and Americans all over the New World.

4. Only after the LDC's that have not yet experienced a manufacturing take-off succeed in their hoped-for industrial revolutions and only after they have succeeded in controlling their explosive population growths; only then will the affluent nations stand to lose some of the historic consumer surplus that they have enjoyed from international trade – trade that historically involved imports of fiber, food, and ores produced in the tropics by low-wage populations. Hong Kong and Singapore, to say nothing of Taiwan and Korea, have up to this time harmed the West little by reducing their exports of staples. If that happy day comes when South-east Asia, Africa, and Latin America afford a comfortable middle class standard of living to their stabilized populations, we should be content to depend upon mechanized mines and farms for our needed raw materials, uncomplainingly paying the necessary costs for the goods we need.

5. With the demise of colonies, the evidence mounts that India is not poor because Sweden is rich or because Citibank is profit seeking. If all the globe

were as poor as India, the next few generations of Indians (and of Mainland Chinese too) would face less favorable rather than more favorable prospects. Such a conclusion runs squarely contrary to the run-of-the-mill Marxian ideology. Before 1917, when the quantitative importance of colonialism could only be guessed at and prior to availability of experience with actual real growth under Soviet and East European socialism, the evidence bearing upon the putative validity of the Marxian ideology was necessarily scanty. In the Age of Lenin and Castro, the reasoned odds narrow down.

Qualifications

Comparative advantages are to be reckoned in dynamic not static terms. Mexican manufactures not yet viable in 1981 will undoubtedly hold their own in 1991. If empirical evidence and cogent logic supported Kaldor's contention that U. K. manufacturing will experience in the future productivity growth far exceeding that of non-manufacturing activity, a case could be made for temporary quotas to protect British industries. Both logic and experience make me skeptical that such a bootstrap operation would raise U. K. real earnings or minimize their rate of decline. For France, West Germany, Canada, and United States, a similar verdict seems indicated.

Some protectionism must realistically be expected to be in the cards. Particularly as I warned in my 1972 little Nobel Lecture, "International Trade for a Rich Country" (Samuelson [1972]) it will be a bit like Marie Antoinette's admonition on diet to counsel the affluent nations to become headquarters economies, if the mutually-beneficial flow between countries of capital principals and earnings will be rendered impossible by sovereignties that refuse to tolerate or honor a code of foreign investments. If a rational global division of labor is inhibited by nationalistic opposition to foreign investment holdings, some manufacturing industry ought to remain in the affluent West. Under floating exchange rates the industrial nations will achieve the efficient kind of protection that economists approve of – namely, real exchange rate depreciation down to the point where domestic manufactures can still survive against import competition.

At this point *union* protectionism will loom as an important influence. In my own country, trade unions are not in a vibrant epoch of growth. Only in manufacturing and in government can they maintain a tenacious hold. With the electoral shift toward the right and toward contained government expenditures, union progress in the public industries has slowed down. Now the tendency for manufacturing to migrate also hits the unions in their heartland.

The economic effects of trade unions are difficult to agree upon. But this much is clear from the history of the railroad and coal sectors:

> *Unions are important in determining how an industry dies.* It is against their very nature for trade unions to engineer reductions in real wage rate to fend

off declines in employment. A Detroit worker may not be worth \$ 18 an hour, compared to a Nagoyan worker paid \$ 8 or a median American earner paid \$ 10 or less. Even if maintenance of the auto builder's wage at levels of \$ 18 an hour will gradually phase out much of the American industry, captains of the trade union ship will go down with all their flags flying, taking down all hands to sink with them. This is not because union officials are stupid or vicious. It is because they are human, determined to do what they have been created to do – to fight for highest possible wage conditions for their members.

The public at large, including median wage earners, knowing all about inequalities in a market economy and realizing that they each might win the lottery ticket of an \$ 18 an hour job, are unlikely to judge the union officials and members harshly. The small self-interest of many in enjoying cheap imports weighs less as a political influence on legislators contemplating quotas than does the concerted self-interest of the few who work or invest in the auto and steel industries. Particularly is this so when most people fail to perceive that protecting a high paid job may actually be at the expense of *lowering average national real wage rates.*

We economists are needed, to weigh the costs and benefits and appraise the merits and demerits of the contending parties. This is an area where we can be proud of our craft.

References

DORNBUSCH, R., FISCHER, S., and SAMUELSON, P. A. [1977], "Comparative Advantage, Trade, and Payments in a Ricardian Model with a Continuum of Goods", *American Economic Review,* 67, 823-839.

SAMUELSON, P. A. [1972], "International Trade for a Rich Country"; pp. 571-593, in: J. E. Stiglitz (ed.), *Collected Scientific Papers of Paul A. Samuelson,* Vol. IV, Cambridge, Mass. (1977).

325

AMERICA'S INTEREST IN INTERNATIONAL TRADE

Educated at the University of Chicago (B.A. 1935), and Harvard University (M.A. 1936, Ph.D. 1941), Professor Samuelson has long been known in this country and abroad as an influential thinker and educator in the field of economics. His worldwide reputation was confirmed when he was awarded the Nobel Prize in Economic Sciences in 1970. He is an active consultant and lecturer, and his basic textbook, "Economics," appears in over thirty foreign languages, and has sold more than 3,000,000 copies.

The United States is a great continental economy. The American people, being richly endowed with land and natural resources, can produce at home most of what they consume.

Little wonder then that U.S. international trade forms only a small fraction of our total national income. So to speak, we Americans go whole hours never thinking of exports and imports. Our whole lives we hear and speak but one language—English. Not for us the intricacies of foreign exchange, except on the occasional jaunt to the Eiffel Tower and the Grand Canal.

Uneasy U.S. Lead

Well, what's so bad about that? Aren't we Americans still the best off people in the whole world? For all foreigners' command of many languages and their being "export minded," how come they're not as rich as we are?

It is true that the United States per capita real gross national product is still higher than that in Switzerland. Or in Sweden and West Germany. But just barely! By the end of this new decade, the false claims you read in the papers concerning those countries passing us by are likely to be finally true. And before the century ends—just twenty years from now—Japan and most of Western Europe will be edging ahead unless recent economic trends are reversed.

A century ago Britannia ruled the waves, and ruled the markets of international trade. London Bridge has not fallen down. But Britons still alive have had to endure a stagnation in their standards of life and witness an eclipse of their nation's status and power. It is not a pattern to envy or emulate.

Opportunity at Long Last

What I see ahead for America's export position is not doom. Instead, the evidence now suggests a reasoned basis for optimism.

What was threatened in the 1950's, and lost in the 1960's and 1970's, can be regained in the 1980's. At long last United States costs have become competitive. There is opportunity waiting to be grasped.

Two questions must be addressed.

>What is the U.S. interest in international trade?

>What, if anything, should we be doing in this matter—"we" being American consumers, American corporations and banking concerns, American workers, and the United States government?

The Way We've Come

As the Eighties begin, the United States imports more goods than we export. Not only do we have an adverse Balance of Trade: our deficit is so large that we cannot pay for it with our dividends and interest earned from past investments abroad. And so we even run a deficit on a current account basis.

This is something new and unusual. In every year before 1971, America had a strong trade surplus. Indeed, at the end of World War II, the United States was in a position of economic supremacy—a position so extreme that we could not maintain it, nor would we have wanted to if we could.

With Japan, Germany, and Italy defeated and with occupied Europe an industrial shambles, the United States, by my estimate, produced half the world Gross National Product at war's end, even though we represented but 6 per cent of world population.

We produced 60 per cent of world manufactures. Although we imported more consumer goods than we exported in every year before World War II, in the late 1940's America was in the singular position of being a net exporter of consumer goods.

All that is history. It is also history that our Marshall Plan and Aid programs enabled the rest of the world to rebuild. We sent consultants abroad to spread American know-how. Our firms established foreign operations. We invested in foreign corporations.

The 1950's and 1960's were miracle years for Japan and West Germany, and for Europe generally. Result:

America lost export share. Our imports soared. Our rate of productivity growth was eclipsed abroad. As American goods became expensive relative to costs abroad, we ran ever larger deficits in our international accounts.

Under the modified rules of the gold standard, as encoded in the Bretton Woods system of pegged exchange rates, there was nothing we could do to correct the situation. We stood and watched as our gold reserves hemorrhaged away.

Where We Are

What happens when an irresistible force meets an immovable object? There must result an inconceivable disturbance.

And so, in August 1971, the Bretton Woods house of cards came tumbling down. President Nixon was forced to suspend gold convertibility. Exchange rates were freed from their pegs. For business here and abroad, exporting became a new ball game.

As J. Pierpont Morgan said about stock prices, we can say about competitive exchange rates, "They will fluctuate."

Now, when a Detroit or Worcester machine tool manufacturer sells a lathe to France, it must keep in mind possible future moves in the franc and dollar exchange rate. Considerable time must elapse between receipt of order, production of tool, shipping of merchandise, and final receipt of funds transmitted back into the dollars the producer needs to pay its workers and suppliers and to report to its stockholders.

With stability of exchange rates gone to the ashheap of history, has the volume of international trade been able to survive? Yes, and even to grow.

So banking relationships and foreign exchange hedging have taken on a new importance. To ensure funds for next summer's research trip to Geneva, I now go to the International Monetary Market in Chicago and buy my needed Swiss francs. Or, when it proves competitively cheaper, I turn to the foreign exchange department of a knowledgeable bank.

The new system does work. The total volume of fruitful international trade continues to grow. And now that modern methods of communications and transport have shrunk the size of the world, the quantum of trade grows even faster than the total of domestic transactions.

A Competitive Dollar

I have saved the good news for the end. What's favorable about the present situation as the 1980's begin is the following remarkable fact, only now being recognized outside the fold of financial experts:

The dollar has floated down over the years in the foreign exchange markets more than our prices and costs have been rising. Just when we need to be competitive in exporting in order to pay for the OPEC oil that has become so scarce and expensive, American workers and capital goods have their products priced in a favorable way.

Here is a small example, but one that is typical. For years canny self-interest forced me to buy automobiles produced abroad. One year a Toyota, another a Fiat, and twice a Volkswagen.

Now I am driving a Detroit-made car. Is this because I am a patriot? I am a patriot, but I would never conceive it a betrayal of country to buy merchandise where value received is greatest. You and I can today buy an American made car because foreign wage rates, when translated into dollars at ruling exchange rates, are now so high in relation to relative productivities, as to make that the most attractive buy.

American industry is on the threshold of similar opportunity in sector after sector. Juicy markets abroad will not fall into our laps without our doing something about it. But now our promotional people have products that can sell, once the true story about costs has been made clear.

Surmounting Barriers

It is true that we need to become export minded. Official ambassadors and consuls abroad are primed to help our exports win their way abroad. But good intentions are not enough.

More of our business people must learn foreign languages and be willing to spend tours of duty abroad. In Sweden and Italy, even when prices and costs swell at home, corporations go to great ends to keep their prices on exports competitive with those abroad. Exactly the same story is told in Germany and Japan. Indeed it is told everywhere. Everywhere? Almost everywhere. For here in America we are an exception, an unenviable exception.

The Reasons Why

International trade is not an Olympic sporting event, in which the American flag can look down on foreign emblems only if our factories and farms succeed in outselling the wares from those abroad. America's interest in export and trade rests on the rock bottom fact that our standard of living depends upon a healthy and growing network of world trade.

There are metals and materials that are found only abroad. The list of these is becoming longer as our industrial machine depletes the rich deposits existing on this continent at the time of its discovery by Columbus. There are products of tropical and polar climates that we are in no position to produce with advantage.

The above examples are obvious. But they do not exhaust the list, nor are they quantitatively the most important reasons for our vital stake in international trade. Upon examination, we see that they are only the visible tip of a much larger iceberg.

With each decade, the fractional importance of U.S. imports and exports grows. The post-1973 oil crisis, with its attendant huge transfer of dollars to the OPEC countries, is an omen for the future.

Daniel Boone might justly subscribe to self-sufficiency. Pre-1939 America could still nurture the illusion of an economy largely self-contained.

Today, two hundred twenty-five million Americans can look forward to years ahead of greater plenty, when life will not be short, nasty and brutish. But we cannot escape the price of our plenty and progress—an increased interdependence with the trading economies abroad.

The Future of American Industry in a Changing Economy

There is a specter haunting American economic life. It appears our manufacturing industry is trying to leave the North American continent, headed primarily for the Pacific Basin. As one alarmist recently put it, "Are we becoming a nation of hamburger stands?" Is Detroit to become a wasteland while car manufacturing moves to Nagoya, Japan?

As our employment languishes, many have observed, the gang of four— South Korea, Taiwan, Singapore and Hong Kong—record double-digit growth rates.

In the meantime, West Germany, France, Switzerland and the United States show a different, sadder story. One number indicating real GNP is manufacturing employment. Switzerland is still showing negative numbers and, in fact, will never be back to the manufacturing employment of eariler periods.

The United States is not exempt from this trend. Manufacturing has been leaving the North American continent for quite some time. I've been in New England now for 45 years and throughout this period observed the textile industry go south and the shoe industry disappear. This has been a constant part of the picture.

Just a couple of years ago I was in South Carolina where people complained bitterly they were losing the textile industry to Puerto Rico, Juarez Mexico, Taiwan and South Korea. And I had to say, speaking as a New Englander, "Couldn't happen to a nicer bunch of guys because it's your turn now."

It's everybody's turn. Even Japan is not immune because, like the U.S., it can no longer keep its textiles for one basic reason: When you have routine manufacturing that can be done with general knowledge and friendly American consulting firms, that manufacturing will be done somewhere in the world for $4 an hour. Such labor drives out of competitive existence things done in more prosperous countries' markets at $10 and $12 an hour labor. It was always thus.

Economists Agree

This is, of course, a major political issue; it is an area where economists, I think, are in the most agreement. But it's an agreement on which we're least able to convince the public. Generally speaking, if you ask economists how they feel about supply side economics, debt financing, monetarism, or post-eclectic Keynesianism, you will get many-faceted arguments. But when a ballot is taken at an economic association meeting on the desirability of quota protection, the profession closes ranks and shows itself, compared with the general public, to be fairly unregenerate free traders. What's so obvious in the academic classroom is anything but obvious to the public. That's understandable. Because we're now talking about important interests, not something abstract.

I go back a long way in economics to a time when the American Federation of Labor was protectionist. Then, over a long period, even the labor movement became free trader. Of course when the textile industry begins to suffer, the economist for the textile workers' union can no longer be for free trade. It would be as if the president of the American Tobacco Company came into the office one morning and said, "I've studied all the evidence and changed my mind. Cigarette smoking is harmful to your health. We are merchants of death."

When the dynamic laws of comparative advantage gradually change, the interests affected by trade also change.

This is not something to complain about. The special interests may get angry but the real issue is: How should we feel as members of the public? Where is the interest of all as against the interest of the special?

I think opinion polls would show that if you asked the question properly, you would get a large part of the American public to give lip service to free trade but to speak in favor of protecting American jobs.

This is an election year, and I have to be especially nonpartisan. But I have to say objectively that the Democratic Party on this issue will be much worse, much farther from the economists' line, than the Republican Party. The cause of containing protection would be best served by a landslide victory for the incumbent. Walter Mondale, who appealed to and received the help of labor, has supported 95 percent domestic content quotas. That means you must be able to show that 95 percent of the total value at all the stages of fabrication, including all the parts, originated in the U.S. That is a degree of protectionism probably never seen in the history of America, which in the last century was very much the land of the protected tariff.

As far as we economists are concerned, tariffs are an innocuous, mild form of the protectionist virus because they are simply rationed by the purse. But even a voluntary quota by the Japanese automobile industry is not one whit different in its cause and effect than a quota imposed by government. The economic effects are the same.

Comparative Advantage

Comparative advantage is a theory going back to 1871 to the time of David Ricardo. His argument was this: Anybody can see that the tropics are capable of producing bananas while the temperate regions cannot produce bananas but can produce steel. There thus would be a profitable interchange between the cold, northern region and the tropical region.

That's the theory of comparative advantage. Ricardo showed that even if a country like England could produce every good cheaper than a country like Portugal, it would still be to the advantage of both England and Portugal to engage in a fruitful, international division of labor.

There was only one exception to his rule. If the difference in productivity is overwhelming—let's say England is ten times as productive as Portugal in every single category—then there would be no basis for comparative advantage. But never is one country better than another in every single enterprise.

Ranking the Rich

How does this affect the U.S. today? This nation is still the most affluent in the world in real terms. It is not true that Sweden, Switzerland, West Germany, Denmark and France have surpassed us in per capita affluence. I'm leaving out Kuwait and a few countries like that—only oil and no people—because we could hold up Greenwich, Connecticut in favorable comparison.

But if you call the U.S. 100, the country next in affluence is Canada at 93. And believe it or not, Norway (the poor cousin of Sweden) is 90, Sweden is 85, Denmark and Switzerland are 80 and Japan is 72 percent in terms of overall per capita affluence.

These calculations derive from a very elaborate University of Pennsylvania project involving 34 countries. It used actual prices people pay and made the conversions in terms of what can be bought by each of those units. It means India is still poorer than the U.S. but it's not—as GNP per capita would indicate—one-fortieth of the U.S. It's more like one-sixteenth in affluence.

The simple-minded protectionist would despair at this ranking because it only makes the problem worse. How is it possible, he would say, for highly paid American workers to compete if we are the most affluent?

At the same time, the poor countries that pay low wages wonder, how can we compete with the U.S. when it has all that marvelous equipment and has so much capital formation available to every worker? How can we compete against the leviathan of the highly productive, affluent country?

The economist, analyzing these two views by the theory of comparative advantage, says there are many things in which the U.S. cannot compete. Any routine manufacturing which can be done by labor anywhere in the world and by machines anywhere will, under a regime of free trade, go elsewhere.

Losing Jobs

Unfortunately, this has social costs. Fourteen years ago I was on a radio program and was asked, what we were going to do about the shoe industry in Boston which is losing employment?

I went right down the sawdust trail of orthodox economics and said, "Well, those workers should get jobs elsewhere where they have more comparative advantage."

Two things followed: The head of the Shoe Workers' Union called and said, "Professor Samuelson's words will go down in the annals of infamy like those of Marie Antoinette who said, 'Let them eat cake.' Professor Samuelson says, Let Them Get Higher Productivity Jobs Elsewhere."

And I got a letter from a shoe worker in Brockton who wrote, "I've lost my job. I didn't have a high school education when I got that job. It's the only industry I've ever worked. I'm 57. Social security comes in at 62. Come off it, Professor Samuelson. You know I'm not ever going to have another job."

So this comparative advantage doctrine, which dictates how average earners in the U.S. will be affected by trends in international trade, must at a second glance take into acount job reshufflings. It should take into account questions of equity. It then leaves the hard science of economics and enters the value-judgment-laden world of political economy.

The orthodox free trader would say, "Too bad. Everybody is made better off by anything that happens in the market. The technological progress made by less affluent countries is an unqualified boon to consumers in affluent countries."

Prosperity Worldwide

Actually, the whole world has done well economically since the end of World War II. After 1945, the U.S., which was not destroyed, had almost 50 percent of the world's GNP with only 6 percent of the population. As Germany, France, Japan and the others recovered, that 50 percent dropped steadily to 25 percent, where it now stands.

But the Henry Kissingers of the world have to realize that you just can't do with 25 percent of world GNP what you could do with 50 percent. Moreover, 20 years from now, we will probably no longer be at 25 percent. Although we are still on top, trends indicate that one or another of those nations will be a little hungrier than we are. The higher savings, higher investment nations will have somewhat surpassed us.

Nevertheless, 20 years from now, I believe we will be more prosperous per capita than we are now. This takes into account the problem of exhausting limited world resources and the unsolved problems of stagflation.

It is thanks to the great progress of poorer countries that dynamic technological change is happening.

Manufacturing employment in the Pacific Basin is increasing at the rate of three to four percent a year and the overall real GNP is rising 10 percent a year.

Interestingly, the places that are doing best and following the capitalists' recipes the most are not your run-of-the-mill Woodrow Wilson democracies. Like Korea, they fit a new category called *capitalistic fascism* or *fascist capitalism*. The efficiency and energies of the market economy are unleashed in these imposed systems.

I'm not advocating imposed systems because they never know the temperature in the oven underneath them. Humanitarians like me are always telling them to let up, drop censorship, don't do this, be it Moscow or Seoul. But they don't know what will happen when they let up. And, to be honest, neither do I.

These countries are going through a very rapid learning process using American consultants. Knowledge cannot be kept from mingling. Rubber used to be grown in Brazil where it was a crime to remove a sapling from the country. Now almost no rubber is cultivated in Latin America, having gone to Asia along with the general knowledge of how to grow it.

The TV-stereotyped image of industry, with sparks flying and textile looms throbbing, is the first kind of industry to go abroad. At the same time, the growth of the new manufacturing powers represent an increasing penetration of the export market in the world economy.

Now, a free trader of the old-fashioned sort would say: "All this will help America." I'd agree the cheapening of imports does help us in many respects. But when Japan and the Pacific Basin countries bid with us and against us for the limited supply of world resources that are exhaustable, it is a minus from the selfish American viewpoint.

We used to be the ones chewing up nature's resources at a great rate 15 and 20 years ago. Now, these other countries are also chewing them up. When they begin to have technological innovation in goods which we previously exported, it can be shown this has had an element of lowering our standard of living.

Clearly, dynamic comparative advantage changes can harm or help the more affluent country. You must put together a very elaborate calculus involving advantages and disadvantages. After doing this, I suspect the total balance would come out plus.

Policy Choices

But just for argument's sake, let's suppose it's a total minus. What does that imply for policy?

America's monopoly access to equipment and America's managerial and scientific know-how which existed in the past is gone. What can be done about it? Can you unscramble eggs that have been scrambled?

Those who would like to do the unscrambling say, "Let's take a sledge hammer and meet the problem head on. Put in protective quotas."

My analysis of this response, speaking for 95 percent of the economics profession, is that when you get a new, cold wind from abroad, it doesn't pay to shoot yourself in the foot. You just inflict a secondary wound on yourself by having protective quotas. You do not succeed in a bootstrap operation of lifting up and restoring the mean standard of living.

Protection does, of course, serve to keep a lot of the highest paid workers employed. You may want to help the low-paid 57-year-old shoe worker. But if you protect the higher paying, noncompetitive jobs, you cannot continue to have good job opportunities for younger workers, particularly those in unions.

The high-paying jobs are bought very expensively, at a high social cost. I don't know if it's good politics to do that, but it's not good economics in terms of any kind of efficiency. It may also be bad ethics to lower the standard of living of lower-paid workers.

Headquarters Economy

I think the true economic case is quite strong and, by the way, not pessimistic. U.S. employment in manufacturing has been holding up much better than western Europe's. Our comparative advantage in high technology, airlines, computers and in semiconductors is still very strong. We are becoming less a manufacturing, industrial economy and more a headquarters economy.

The occupational census of 1990 or 2000 may well look like the 1980 occupational census of the Denver region. It's already a headquarters area. Now please don't go away and denounce me as another Marie Antoinette who has said, "Let them live in Fairfield, Connecticut and occupy headquarters jobs." But that is the direction in the world division of labor that is taking place. It is consistent with an increase in relative living standards rising much faster in the Pacific Basin.

As a citizen of both the United States and the world, I want India and Pakistan and the really poor countries to join in this movement.

Latin America, incidentally, which has practiced heavy protective quotas, has not done well economically.

Protectionism has been less hot an issue the last year or so because the business cycle has turned upward. When employment, profits, production and consumption go down in the business cycle, agitation for protection goes up—even though we know that the long-run trends in basic steel and automobiles will not be solved just by return to full employment.

Alternatives

But alternatives are there for people who are mobile and flexible. Japan is now losing its textile industry, but the loss has been painless because other jobs were available for the workers. The new job opportunities—to be absolutely honest—are not always at the same high wages because skills may become obsolete. But in economics the correct way to keep score is to look forward. You have to cut losses. Old skills which are no longer valuable should be given up. Overall change can occur with the least transitional harm to people who are victims of dynamic readjustment.

The kind of protection economists favor, the even-handed, efficient kind of protection, is to have the dollar on current account float downward until our goods can pay their way. There's no dispensation in saying America is different from anybody else.

ON DEFICITS

A substantial fraction of our accumulated wealth abroad has been spent by our balance of trade and our current account deficits. We are, at the moment, the most thriftless society in existence. We have a structural deficit that is going to get worse.

Now Japan has had just as big a structural deficit as percentage of GNP as we have, at times. West Germany has. But the Japanese save 23 percent of their incomes. The Germans save 18 percent. Italians and French save 15 percent. We save 4.5 percent.

We have a crowding-out effect. We're using savings from abroad and selling out the nest egg we accumulated since the end of World War I when we became a major capital exporting country. Two or three more years of deficit at this rate, and it will mean that foreigners own as much in America as we own abroad.

ON REPORTING THE ECONOMY

The job of an economist is not to make good copy. In fact, there's a conflict between accurate economic analysis and interesting, good copy. I've been a consumer of economic information from the press and also, in a small way, a producer of it. So I'm very cognizant of this conflict.

It's pointed up by an old but true story about Harry Truman who used to say, "What I want is a one-armed economist." He meant, "I'm fed up with this 'on the one hand this and on the other hand that.' "

My response is clear-cut. You think you want a one-armed economist but you don't. One-armed economists in my profession come in two varieties: those with only a right arm and those with only a left arm. Then you need an eclectic, well-informed economist like me to adjudicate which of them is right.

The same is true about covering the beat of the world or U.S. economy. Predicting and monitoring the business situation, as in the case of the weather, involves a great deal of momentum. Just saying it's going to go along about the same as it has today, or the next quarter as it has today, gives you a remarkably good batting average. Of course, nobody bats a thousand in this league. If you bat 500, you might as well use a coin. And so, the difference between the little girls and the big girls is whether you have a batting average of 700 or 799. You have to take account of the momentum, and you have to disregard the Elliot Janeway kind of reporting which is always calling for the end of the world or the beginning of a new world. An editor who hears this will probably say, "Well, gee, Professor Samuelson, you may be right. It may be good economics, but it's always dull journalism."

For an economist there's no problem. For you reporters there is. I'd rather be right than interesting. But I don't think you have that particular choice.

When people blame the media because it's too hyper, I think they're blaming a beast for doing what it is built by evolution to do. It's what the public wants. The public does not want a boring economics lecture evening after evening.

But if you follow the press very carefully, I have to say that you do get an over-hyped impression of what is happening. Take the business cycle earlier this year. We had a slightly bad Christmas period so there was a terrible amount of flack that the recovery was over. Then it turned out that the January and February numbers were colossal and the economy was overheating. Then there was a bad March. You know, it was as if, since the beginning of time, there haven't always been variations in the weather.

ON INDUSTRIAL POLICY

Industrial policy is an advertising slogan looking for a product. There exists no promising way of planning one. It would become, I predict, a stalking horse for protectionists. FACS

PART IV

Stochastic Theory

327

Stochastic Land Valuation: Total Return as Martingale Implying Price Changes— A Negatively Correlated Walk*

If efficient speculative price were a true random walk, in the long run it could end up anywhere—a virtual denial of economic law. The archetype case of land that earns stochastic rents shows that its ideal efficient-market price is not a random walk but rather a stationary time series with an ergodic probability distribution. Speculative price changes are therefore negatively autocorrelated in the longest run. Economic law is thus confirmed when total return is a martingale. Competitive price is not a tale told by the idiot of chance. Methods useful for economics are applied to a Markov matrix example.

1. Introduction

The first asset analyzed for capitalized value was land. *Twenty-Years Purchase*, corresponding to a 5 percent interest rate per annum, goes back to the Middle Ages. It is appropriate therefore to use land with a stochastic rent as the archetype for analysis of efficient-market speculative price. The deducible Brownian-like movement of ideal price and ergodic probability distribution for the price to be expected in the far future provide the natural generalization of deterministic equilibrium. It will be seen that ideal price is *not* a random walk: When *total return* is a martingale, land-price changes must be biased toward negative autocorrelation in a perfect market.

2. Axiom of Expected Values

Instead of assuming that net cash rents of land are deterministic payments $(x_{t+1}, x_{t+2}, \ldots, x_{t+T}, \ldots)$ made to you at the end of 1, 2, ..., T, ... periods, I now assume that they are random variables $(X_{t+1}, X_{t+2}, \ldots, X_{t+T}, \ldots)$ whose joint probability distribution is known to all even though future draws from that universe are not yet knowable:

* I owe thanks to the National Science Foundation and Sloan Foundation for partial support and to Aase Huggins for editorial aid. This is the third article in the series that contains Samuelson (1965a, 1973).

$$\text{Prob}\{X_{t+1} \le x_1, X_{t+2} \le x_2, \ldots, X_{t+T} \le x_T, \ldots | X_t = x_0, X_{t-1} = x_{-1}, \ldots\}$$
$$= Q(x_1, x_2, \ldots, x_T, \ldots | x_0, x_{-1}, \ldots). \tag{2.1}$$

In the deterministic case, market price at time t is given as the following *present discounted value*:

$$p_t = \sum_{T=1}^{\infty} x_{t+T}(1 + r)^{-T}, \tag{2.2}$$

where r is the appropriate rate of interest, here taken as an exogenous parameter that happens to be a constant over time.

The present analysis proceeds from the axiom that stochastic price at time t is given by the present discounted value, using the r appropriate for this class of risks,[1] of the *conditional expected values* of future rents,

$$(E\{X_{t+1}|X_t = x_t, X_{t-1} = x_{t-1}, \ldots\}, \ldots, E\{X_{t+T}|X_t = x_t,$$
$$X_{t-1} = x_{t-1}, \ldots\}, \ldots),$$

namely,

$$p(t|x_t, x_{t-1}, \ldots) = \sum_{T=1}^{\infty} E\{X_{t+T}|x_t, x_{t-1}, \ldots\}(1 + r)^{-T}. \tag{2.3}$$

At time t, $p(t|x_t, x_{t-1}, \ldots)$ is not a random variable inasmuch as previous data $X_t, X_{t-1}, \ldots$ are known. Before time t, when $(X_t, \ldots)$ are not yet known, $p(t|X_t, X_{t-1}, \ldots)$ is a random variable in that it is a function of random variables. Ordinarily, an observed sequence of land prices $\{p_t\}$ will show some kind of stochastic variation in accordance with being a stationary time series whose properties are deducible from $Q(x_1, x_2, \ldots, x_T, \ldots | x_0, x_{-1}, \ldots)$.

From the latter one can compute T-period-ahead conditional probabilities:

$$\text{Prob}\{X_{t+T} \le x_T | X_t = x_t, X_t = x_{t-1}, \ldots\} = Q_T(x_T | x_t, x_{t-1}, \ldots),$$
$$T = 1, 2, \ldots, \tag{2.4}$$

$$E\{E_{t+T}|x_t, x_{-1}, \ldots\} = \int_0^{\infty} x\, dQ_T(x|x_t, x_{t-1}, \ldots). \tag{2.5}$$

Here I use the notation of Stieltjes integrals to handle discrete probabilities

1. If this land's rents are probabilistically independent of other assets' returns and if each person's optimal share of its ownership is a negligible fraction of his total wealth, the appropriate interest rate to use in discounting might be deduced to be the interest rate on safe cash, or epsilon plus that safe rate. In any case, this paper takes r as the exogenously given discount parameter appropriate to this category of risk, a useful but not deeply based hypothesis.

and probability densities. (It is a simple generalization to augment $(x_t, x_{t-1}, \ldots)$ in (2.4) by information on any and all other vectors of information knowable by now.)

3. Case of Independence

If the probabilities of rents at different times are *independent* and *identically* distributed, Q factors into

$$Q(x_1, x_2, \ldots, x_T | x_0, x_{-1}, \ldots) \equiv Q(x_1)Q(x_2)\ldots Q(x_T), \tag{3.1}$$

independently of $(x_0, x_{-1}, \ldots)$. Therefore, despite the variability of rents ex post, at every t there are ex ante exactly the same future odds for rents, and therefore the same capitalized price is always obtained:

$$\begin{aligned} p(t|x_0, x_{-1}, \ldots) &\equiv \int_0^\infty x\, dQ(x)[1 + (1+r)^{-1} + (1+r)^{-2} + \ldots] \\ &\equiv \int_0^\infty x\, dQ(x)/r = E\{X\}/r. \end{aligned} \tag{3.2}$$

This is the same capitalization formula as (2.2)'s for a deterministic perpetuity, but with each year's *expected* value of rent being what is capitalized and with the r appropriate to the posited risks.

4. Serial Interdependence

There is no reason to rule out the possibility that weather and other determinants of land rent do run in streaks and display probabilistic interdependences of a direct or inverse type. In this general case, ideal price today will depend on recent rents, being high when these shift the odds in favor of high rents in the nearby future—and thus requiring present price to be higher than future price can be expected to be.

Now, varying $x_t, x_{t-1}, \ldots$ will cause p_t to assume higher and lower values. Now (3.2) must be recalculated using expected values that depend on recent rents:

$$p(t|x_t, x_{t-1}, \ldots) = \sum_1^\infty (1+r)^{-T} \int_0^\infty x\, dQ_T(x|x_t, x_{t-1}, \ldots), \tag{4.1}$$

$$\partial p(t|x_t, x_{t-1}, \ldots)/\partial x_{t-i} \not\equiv 0 \quad (i = 0, 1, \ldots). \tag{4.2}$$

If this last year's drought increases the odds for a drought this coming year and low rents, then p_{t+1} will have to be expected to *exceed* present p_t, which itself will have to be low to properly "discount" bad nearby prospects.

Even in such cases of strong positive autocorrelation in $\{X_t\}$, we must still expect a bias toward *negative* autocorrelation in $\{P_t - p_{t-1}\}$. Note that this rules out that $\{p_t\}$ can be a random walk with probabilistically *independent* price changes $[p_{t+T} - p_t, p_t - p_{t-k}]$. If $\{X_t\}$ exhibits negative autocorrelations, all the more reason to expect negative autocorrelation in price changes.

A useful example is the case where rents $\{X_t\}$ are generated by the linear autoregressive process

$$X_{t+1} = aX_t + U_t, \qquad |a| < 1, \tag{4.3}$$

where $\{U_t\}$ is a nonnegative variable distributed independently of $[U_{t\pm k}, X_t, X_{t-1}, \ldots]$ and identically for all t.

For this case

$$\begin{aligned} p(t|x_t, x_{t-1}, \ldots) &= \sum_{T=1}^{\infty} (1 + r)^{-T} E\{X_{t+T}|x_t, x_{t-1}, \ldots\} \\ &= \sum_{1}^{\infty} (1 + r)^{-T} a^T x_t \\ &= x_t(a[1 + r - a]^{-1}). \end{aligned} \tag{4.4}$$

Since the resulting random variable P_t is seen to be exactly proportional to the random variable X_t, its time differences will have to follow the distribution implied by (4.3) for $X_t - X_{t-1}$.

The latter's autocorrelation coefficients are calculated by

$$\begin{aligned} r_T &= r[P_{t+T} - P_{t+T-1}, P_t - P_{t-1}] \\ &= -\tfrac{1}{2}(1 - a)a^{T-1}, \qquad T = 1, 2, 3, \ldots. \end{aligned}$$

For all a, r_1 is negative: It is a good bet that $p_{t+1} - P_t$ will be of opposite sign to $p_t - p_{t-1}$; and the odds for this rise as a falls further below unity. For a negative, as when rain now betokens sunshine soon, the period after next is likely to have the same-signed price change as has just occurred; however, as will be seen, over the longer run, negative autocorrelation of price changes is implied by underlying economic law. Only when $a = 1$ and rents are free economically to wander anywhere by chance—a bizarre model—will $\{P_t\}$ be a true random walk.

5. Ergodic Probability Distributions

In the longest run, $\{p_{t+1} - p_t\}$ changes must show negative autocorrelation in accordance with "regression toward the mean." *Economic law ultimately constrains blind chance.* It does not obliterate chance, but rather averages it out ergodically.

Exactly what does this mean?

I explicitly assume that the stochastic laws of rent variability have the stationary time-series property that makes the distant future virtually "forget" the present chance variations. That is, (2.1) and its (2.4) have the *ergodic* property:

$$\lim_{T\to\infty} Q_T(x|x_0, x_{-1}, \ldots) = Q(x) \tag{5.1}$$

independently of $(x_0, x_{-1}, \ldots)$.

Here $Q(x)$ is the *ergodic probability distribution*, asymptotically approached in the far future by rent, after present-day draws for rent have become irrelevant ancient history. Just as a stable deterministic system is *damped*, so our stationary time series generating all market relations is ergodic.

If rent is ergodically distributed, so will be ideal price. That is, (5.1) implies

$$\lim_{T\to\infty} \text{Prob}\{P_{t+T} \leq p | X_t = x_0, X_{t-1} = x_{-1}, \ldots\}$$

$$= \lim_{T\to\infty} \Pi_T(p|x_0, x_{-1}, \ldots) = \Pi(p) \tag{5.2}$$

independently of $x_0, x_{-1}, \ldots$. Here $\Pi(p)$ is the ergodic probability distribution that the infinite sequence $\{p_t\}$ must satisfy (see Samuelson 1971).

Given any observed p_t, the mathematical expectation of $p_{t+T} - p_t$ will *not* be zero for large T, as with a martingale. Instead it will be opposite in sign to present p_t's divergence from the unconditional mean price

$$E\{p_t\} = \int_0^\infty p\, d\Pi(\bar{p}). \tag{5.3}$$

That is, for T large and $p_t \neq \bar{p}$,

$$[E\{p_{t+T}\} - p_t][p_t - \bar{p}] \to (p_t - \bar{p})^2 < 0 \qquad \text{as } T \to \infty. \tag{5.4}$$

Important note: No one can make profit by speculating against the discernible negative autocorrelation in the sequence of price quotations for land. When p_t is expected to rise, the component of its total yield represented by rent payments ("dividends," so to speak) are expected to be lower than average—so that total return is a martingale process.

The first-order autoregressive process of (4.3)'s example can illustrate the ergodic $\Pi(p)$ distribution. For it, if the white-noise $\{U_t\}$ has a Gaussian distribution, $N(0, \sigma_x^2 a^2[1 + r - a]^{-2})$, then $\Pi(p)$ will have the Gaussian distribution

$$N(0, \sigma_x^2 a^2[1 + r - a]^{-2}[1 + a^2 + a^4 + \ldots])$$
$$= N(0, \sigma_x^2 a^2[1 + r - a]^{-2}[1 - a^2]^{-1}. \tag{5.5}$$

There is, of course, no reason why $\{U_t\}$ need be Gaussian. (Indeed, the possibility then implied of negative land rents and prices could raise economists' eyebrows.) Knowing U_t's characteristic function, we can construct by repeated multiplications and by taking limits the (not necessarily Gaussian) characteristic function of $\Pi(p)$.

6. Functional Equations

It can be a formidable task to perform the relevant multiple integrals to calculate an explicit infinite-series summation of (2.3). Fortunately, this can often be avoided by solving a certain functional equation.

The deterministic case suggests how to make the appropriate stochastic generalization.

In the deterministic case, instead of summing

$$p_t = \frac{X_{t+1}}{1 + r} + \frac{X_{t+2}}{(1 + r)^2} + \ldots, \qquad r > 0, \tag{6.1}$$

we can write the appropriate expression for *total yield* of r in terms of steady state $(X, p; r)$:

$$r = \frac{X_{t+1}}{p_t} + \frac{p_{t+1} - p_t}{p_t}, \tag{6.2}$$

$$p_t(1 + r) = X_{t+1} + p_{t+1}. \tag{6.3}$$

For $X_{t+1} = X_t = X$ and $p_{t+1} = p_t = p$, this gives the correct steady-state answer to the infinite series

$$p = X/r. \tag{6.4}$$

In the stochastic case, (6.3) involves expected values and becomes

$$p(t|x_0, x_{-1}, \ldots)(1 + r) = E\{X_{t+1}|x_0, x_{-1}, \ldots\} + E\{P_{t+1}|x_0, x_{-1}, \ldots\}. \tag{6.5}$$

In the steady or ergodic state, where t and $t + 1$ do not differ and where

$$p(t|X_t = x_0, X_{t-1} = x_{-1}, \ldots) = f(x_0, x_{-1}, \ldots) = p(\cdot|x_0, x_{-1}, \ldots),$$

(6.5) becomes the functional equation

$$f(x_0, x_{-1}, \ldots)(1 + r) = \int_0^\infty x\, dQ_1(x|x_0, x_{-1}, \ldots)$$
$$+ \int_0^\infty f(x, x_0, x_{-1}, \ldots)\, dQ_1(x|x_0, x_{-1}, \ldots). \qquad (6.6)$$

In case $Q_1(x|x_0, x_{-1}, \ldots)$ depends only on x_0, which is the simplest Markov case involving today's rent depending only on yesteryear's, the functional equation becomes

$$f(x_0)(1 + r) = \int_0^\infty x\, dQ_1(x|x_0) + \int_0^\infty f(x)\, dQ_1(x|x_0). \qquad (6.7)$$

In case $Q_1(x|x_0)$ corresponds to a probability density

$$Q_1(x|x_0) = \int_0^x q(u, x_0)\, du, \qquad (6.8)$$

(6.6) becomes the Fredholm integral equation

$$f(y) = g(y) + \int_0^\infty q(u, y) f(u)\, du,$$

$$g(y) = \int_0^\infty u q(u, y)\, du. \qquad (6.9)$$

With $g(y)$ and $q(u, y)$ known functions, $f(y)$ is given as the solution to the integral equation.

Suppose that $f'(x)$ is signed and that the autonomous conditional probability of P_{t+1} given p_t is

$$\text{Prob}\{P_{t+1} \leq p_1 | P_t = p_0\} = \Phi(p_1; p_0), \qquad (6.10)$$

$$\partial\Phi(p; p_0)/\partial p = \phi(p; p_0) \qquad (6.11)$$

if p has a density. Then the ergodic probability density $\Pi'(p)$ must satisfy the basic integral equation

$$0 \leq \Pi'(p) = \int_0^\infty \phi(p; z)\Pi'(z)\, dz, \qquad (6.12)$$

$$\int_0^\infty \Pi'(p)\, dp = 1.$$

7. Markov Example

A Markov-process example is easily solvable and illustrates the logic of the general case. It is worth analyzing for its own sake.

Suppose that rent X_t can take on only two values: high and low, or 2 and 0. Suppose that the probability of a high rent being followed by a high rent is α and that α is also the probability that a low rent will be followed the next year by a low rent. Then, given r, our land pricing is completely determined.

If $\alpha = \frac{1}{2}$, the rents are probabilistically independent. Stochastic price never fluctuates: It is always the mean rent divided by the interest rate, as in (3.2):

$$p_t \equiv p \equiv \frac{\frac{1}{2}(2+0)}{r} = \frac{1}{r}. \tag{7.1}$$

If weather and rents run in spells, $\alpha > \frac{1}{2}$ as when $\alpha = 0.9$, price will fluctuate stochastically: Whenever rent has just been high, p_t must be low in expectation that p_{t+1} may be higher and that rent will average out low in the period ahead. But still, by my symmetry assumptions, X_t averages out to 1 in the long run, 2 and 0 being equally likely.

Because of my symmetry assumptions, whatever α is, r^{-1} will be the ergodic mean of p_t.

With rent taking on but two distinct values, 2 and 0, corresponding to each of them will be the two values that p_t can take on: $p(\cdot|2)$ and $p(\cdot|0)$, where

$$\tfrac{1}{2}p(\cdot|2) + \tfrac{1}{2}p(\cdot|0) = r^{-1},$$

$$p(\cdot|0) = 2r^{-1} - p(\cdot|2). \tag{7.2}$$

Now the functional equation of (6.7) becomes two simple linear equations in two unknowns. However, by use of knowledge of (7.2), we can eliminate $p(\cdot|0)$ as an unknown and ignore one of the two equations as redundant. We are left with the following linear equation to solve for unknown $p(\cdot|2)$:

$$\begin{aligned} p(\cdot|2)(1+r) &= [\alpha 2 + (1-\alpha)0] + [\alpha p(\cdot|2) + (1-\alpha)p(\cdot|0)] \\ &= \alpha 2 + \alpha p(\cdot|2) + (1-\alpha)[2r^{-1} - p(\cdot|2)]. \end{aligned} \tag{7.3}$$

This solves for

$$p(\cdot|2) = r^{-1} + \frac{2\alpha - 1}{2(1-\alpha) + r},$$

$$p(\cdot|0) = r^{-1} - \frac{2\alpha - 1}{2(1-\alpha) + r}. \tag{7.4}$$

For $\alpha = 0.9$ and $r = 0.20$,

$p(\cdot|2) = 5 + 2 = 7,$

$p(\cdot|0) = 5 - 2 = 3.$

Thus, if the historical sample for rents happened to be [..., 2, 2, 0, 2, 0, 0, ...], the respective prices observed would have to be [..., 7, 7, 3, 7, 3, 3, ...]. No rational speculator could be tempted by the low price of 3, thereby hoping to make an excess total return: The "bargain" is there only because the marketplace realizes that next periods' rents are likely to be so low as to require the promise of likely capital gain to deliver the equilibrium total yield.

8. Total Return's Martingale

Note that $\{p_{t+1} - p_t\}$ is not that of a random walk or martingale but rather that of a negatively autocorrelated sequence: Low $p_t - p_{t-T}$ tends to be followed by high $p_{t+T} - p_t$, and vice versa after high $p_t - p_{t-T}$ has been observed. What does have to satisfy a martingale would be a cumulation of total yields through time. Thus, define the random variable Z_t to be dollars of *excess total return* actually experienced between t and $t + 1$:

$$Z_{t+1} = X_{t+1} + p_{t+1} - (1 + r)p_t. \tag{8.1}$$

Looking ahead, the conditional expectation for this must in an ideal market be zero. The same must be true for the conditional expectation of the Cesaro sum of such future yields as

$$C_{\theta,t} = Z_{t+1} + Z_{t+2} + \ldots + Z_{t+\theta}. \tag{8.2}$$

It is not quite true that $C_{\theta,t}$ for fixed t and growing θ undergoes a "random walk" in the sense that $[C_{\theta+1,t} - C_{\theta,t}, C_{\theta+1-k,t-k} - C_{\theta-k,t-k}]$ are strictly independent for all k. But it is true that $C_{\theta,t}$ is a martingale:

$$E\{C_{\theta+1,t}|C_{\theta,t}\} \equiv C_{\theta,t}. \tag{8.3}$$

Also, if all the algebraic total return outcomes were ploughed back, into similar land investments, the resulting multiplicative process would asymptotically approach (when normalized) a log-normal distribution. (Because of the *theorem of almost-certain virtual ruin in the long run* (see Samuelson 1965b, p. 17), the present discounted value of these log-normal deviates will, with probability approaching unity as $T \rightarrow \infty$, be negligibly above zero.)

9. Fundamentalism and Chance

Samuelson (1973) showed that the expected values of each future dividend to be paid out at time θ obeys the martingale property as we move toward that date, moving from $\theta - T$ to $\theta - T + 1$, to $\theta - T + 2 \ldots$, and finally from $\theta - 1$ to θ itself. The present paper confirms the same truth, glimpsed by Cootner (1964):

Fundamentalist evaluation of asset prices is completely compatible with stochastic jitter of such prices in efficient markets that react to jitter in relevant data. What is vulgarly called the "random walk" model, when properly defined by the martingale property of total return, is a confirmation of economic law as against drifting random walk. Reality imposes, so to speak, reflecting barriers that serve to herd maverick chance back toward equilibrium. Efficient markets realize all this and cause prices already to have discounted this, so that there is no excess profit to be made from the intercorrelated price changes.

References

Cootner, P. (ed.). 1964. *The Random Character of Stock Market Prices*. MIT Press, Cambridge, Mass. See especially chapter 11 by Cootner, chapter 2 by L. Bachelier, and chapter 3 by M. G. Kendall.

Samuelson, P. A. 1965a. "Proof that Properly Anticipated Prices Fluctuate Randomly." Industrial Management Review 6: 41–49. Reprinted in *Collected Scientific Papers of Paul A. Samuelson*, vol. III, chap. 198. MIT Press, Cambridge, Mass., 1972.

Samuelson, P. A. 1965b. "A Rational Theory of Warrant Pricing." *Industrial Management Review* 6: 13–39. Reprinted in *Collected Scientific Papers of Paul A. Samuelson*, vol. III, chap. 199. MIT Press, Cambridge, Mass., 1972.

Samuelson, P. A. 1971. "Stochastic Speculative Price." *Proceedings of the National Academy of Sciences* 68: 335–337. Reprinted in *Collected Scientific Papers of Paul A. Samuelson*, vol. III, chap. 206. MIT Press, Cambridge, Mass., 1972.

Samuelson, P. A. 1973. "Proof that Properly Discounted Present Values of Assets Vibrate Randomly." *Bell Journal of Economics and Management Sciences* 6: 369–374. Reprinted in *Collected Scientific Papers of Paul A. Samuelson*, vol. IV, chap. 241. MIT Press, Cambridge, Mass., 1977.

Samuelson P. A. 1976. "Is Real-World Price a Tale Told by the Idiot of Chance?" *Review of Economics and Statistics* 58: 120–123. Reprinted in *Collected Scientific Papers of Paul A. Samuelson*, vol. IV, chap. 242. MIT Press, Cambridge, Mass., 1977.

PAUL COOTNER'S RECONCILIATION OF ECONOMIC LAW WITH CHANCE

PAUL A. SAMUELSON*
Massachusetts Institute of Technology

It would be a negation of economic law if competitive price truly moved in a classical random walk. In enough time it could wander anywhere. Still, an economist would be ill-advised to ignore the probabilistic jitter inherent in speculative prices. Paul Cootner perceived the dilemma that most economists ignored. His proposed solution has been accorded too little notice and approbation.

In this paper, I hope to resurrect briefly one of his important contributions to modern finance theory and to economic theory in general. Besides offering an alternative reconciliation of my own between choice and law, I use this occasion for a fitting remembrance of Paul Cootner, the scientist and the human being.

**I owe thanks to the National Science Foundation and the Sloan Foundation for partial financial aid, and to Aase Huggins for editorial assistance. Fred Westfield, Francis Bator, Charles Kindleberger, and Robert Bishop have shared their memories with me.*

Paul was a young 20 when he came to the M.I.T Graduate School from the University of Florida.[1] Now many of our students come from Yale, Harvard, and other strong centers for economic research. While M.I.T.'s fame was still growing, we used the cash that Rupert Maclaurin raised for our department to bid on talent wherever we could smell it. I was always surprised at how much money could buy for a new department, if only a department were interested in acquiring scientific potential.[2] It helped that Harvard, Yale, and Princeton seemed to shy away from mathematical theorists at that time. (M.I.T. made some mistakes of its own. Our committee didn't offer Kenneth Arrow[3] a fellowship, for instance, even though Harold Freeman and I recognized his potential. Despite Melvin Reder's great recommendations from Oskar Lange and others, our committee made a Type A error in his case too. For Freudian reasons, I fail to recall other similar examples.)

By chance, there were two mathematical economists at the University of Florida: Montgomery Anderson and Cecil Phipps, both somewhat at odds with the American mainstream in that area. I seem to recall Paul's having some differences in viewpoint with one or both of them; but probably it was their presence that brought him to graduate work in theoretical economics and to M.I.T.'s attention.

Although Cootner was admitted to M.I.T. for his mathematical and statistical skills, he rather annoyed Charlie Kindleberger, our new graduate registration officer, by switching his interests to economic history and sociology. I gave him an A on a term paper dealing with Veblen. Only later did I learn from Paul that he had used the same paper to fulfill requirements for two courses. Morris Adelman gave him a C on the same Veblen paper. Perhaps we were both right; in any case I have always been considered an easy marker.

If I ever knew what led Paul into the study of speculative price, I've forgotten. Possibly it was the insistence of his fellow graduate student Fred Westfield that the stock market was more rewarding than baseball scores. Commodity futures, rather than common stock prices, first engaged Paul's interest.[4]

[1]Paul was born in Logansport, Indiana near Lake and Porter counties where I spent my early years. We two country boys pretended to pity our friends from the effete East.

[2]The records show that Cootner cost us only our $800 tuition fee. After his first slump in grades, he lost his scholarship; but after redeeming himself, he had it restored. He did research assistance for Charles Kindleberger and for Albert Kervyn (now Professor at Louvain, then a visitor at M.I.T.'s Center for International Studies). He assisted in the elementary course, under Robert Bishop, who testified that he did well.

[3]The record shows that Cootner's hope in November 1954 to get a job offer from Arrow at Stanford was in vain. The record elsewhere shows, however, that the reason seems to have been Bernard Haley's feeling that the temporary opening should go to an all-but-thesis Stanford student.

[4]Although Paul Cootner was precocious, finishing college before turning 19, because of his oscillations in interests (and possibly his 1953–55 army service), he was not an early publisher. His first items in the *Index of Economic Journals* date from 1960, after his appointment to the Sloan School by Eli Schapiro.

COOTNER AND NORMAL BACKWARDATION

Hendrik Houthakker and I both believed in "normal backwardation" of commodity prices, along the lines Keynes had tersely sketched in the early 1920s and in the *Treatise on Money*.

This is *not* to be confused with the natural tendency of the spot price to rise from the end of one harvest to the beginning of the next. That is a trivial consequence of the positive cost of storing a commodity through time; and such a price rise is the pattern necessary if an arbitrager is to recover his money from such a storing operation.

Keynes' *normal backwardation* is, for example, the alleged tendency of a March 1982 wheat futures contract to rise in price on the average from the end of the previous harvest in June of 1981 to its March 1982 expiration. Someone has to hold the seasonal stock of wheat, Keynes argued. While it is held, its price can rise or fall, an unpleasant risk that millers and bakers will be glad to pay a positive insurance premium against. The long speculators are collecting the (average) positive insurance premium needed to coax out their speculative activity. When those with a comparative advantage in baking bread and milling grain seek this insurance by (short-) selling futures contracts as a hedge against their holding of physical wheat, they must pay the normal backwardation as a positive insurance premium to coax out a supply of long-buying speculators (who being risk-averse will take on the price-fluctuation risk only when provided an average premium to do so).

Lester Telser, then a young scholar at the University of Chicago, expressed Knightian doubts: many speculators act as if they *like* to shoulder risks; their supply price may average out to zero, or even be negative in denial of normal backwardation. To put the matter to a definitive test is not easy when the time series concerned are such "noisy ones" and where the concept of a "stationary time series" can be in serious doubt.

Cootner on the whole sided with Keynes. But he took seriously the work of Holbrook Working which, over the decades at the Stanford Food Research Institute, was only beginning to be given the credit it deserves in the history of "efficient markets." As Michael Brennan noted at Brown University, Working's data suggested that the supply curve of storage called for a *fall* in the spot price of a good when its existing stock is *low* relative to normally needed inventory levels. Millers, bakers, and processors generally act as if they get a positive return from the safety of owning enough inventory to protect themselves against costly interruptions of their milling and baking activities. Instead of being hedgers who short-sell, during seasons of low inventory they will be hedgers who buy long. Cootner reasoned: "When a speculator is induced to do the short-selling needed to provide the industry with a long-hedge, he will be willing to tie up any substantial fraction of his wealth in that risky asset only if he receives a *positive premium* for short-selling." Thus, the Cootner-Keynes Doctrine of *Dual* Normal Backwardation can be described as follows: During the early postharvest months when the total of inventories is necessarily large, the industry (and ultimately the consumers it serves) will want to hedge-short and will be in equilibrium paying a *positive* Keynesian premium to speculators who hold futures long. But in that part of the annual cycle when inventories are characteristically low, the industry will want to hedge-long and will on the average pay a (anti-Keynesian) positive premium to speculators who hold short-sales of futures. In this last phase futures tend to fall on the average: normal "forwardation" or contango.

Again, the empirical evidence for this doctrine is mixed, as we might expect with such "noisy" time series. Nicholas Kaldor and other writers in the tradition of Keynes' liquidity-preference theorizing had argued on a priori reasoning about "convenience yield of holding scarce inventory," in the same direction as the Working-Brennan-Cootner *supply curve of storage;* J. R. Hicks had also done so in *Value and Capital.* But the last word is not yet in. My own 1971 exact model of stochastic speculative price was able to justify much of what Working's data show, but the 1971 model was not able to deduce the "negative storage cost" branch.

THE RANDOM WALK INFILTRATES ECONOMICS

It was probably I who called Cootner's attention to Maurice Kendall's 1953 survey of the statistics of speculative price. For spot and futures prices of commodities, for single stocks and index numbers of stocks, the noneconomist Kendall found *white spectra*—almost zero autocorrelations. As he said, to the initial outrage of the economists in his audience at the Royal Statistical Society, it was as if the devil drew the price changes out of an urn. This accords with the classical Wiener definition of a random walk (a process with independent increments):

$$\text{Prob}\{X(t+T) - X(t) \leq x\} = P_T(x), \quad -\infty < T < \infty \tag{1}$$

independently of $[X(t), X(t \pm K), t, \ldots]$.

Later one noticed that Holbrook Working had been reporting on much the same thing. It was around 1957 that Jimmie Savage wrote to economists asking if any of us knew about the mathematical theory of speculation of the French savant L. Bachelier. I recalled hearing of Bachelier from my mathematical friend at the Harvard Society of Fellows, Stan Ulam, and from a patronizing reference in Feller and Kolmogorov. But I couldn't locate the popular 1914 Bachelier book Savage referred to. By good luck, Savage's query led me to Widener Library's copy of Bachelier's great 1900 Sorbonne thesis. I believe it was Cootner, as editor of his classic M.I.T. Press collection *The Random Character of Stock Market Prices,* who encouraged the English translation of Bachelier.

But before I concentrate on the effort to correct Bachelier's strict model of the arithmetic random walk, I should say a few words about Paul Cootner's general interest in commodity prices.

Most commodity analysts have themselves tried their hand at beating the board of trade. Playing the game on paper is not quite the same as playing it for blood. Paul was no exception. I recall with wry amusement the various syndicates operating in our newly occupied Sloan Building. During one soybean mania, it turned out in retrospect that we could have cut out the middleman and saved ourselves commissions: on the third floor of the economics department were the soybean bulls; the soybean bears were on the fourth floor of the Sloan School; possibly all of us succeeded in making losses. I betray no secrets when I recall the names of heroes from those capers: Paul Cootner, of course; visiting Professor Hendrik Houthakker; Dick Eckaus; Sidney Alexander; Ed Kuh; and your humble servant. Bob Solow was too proud to fight.

I learned something from those experiences. It is a mug's game for a dentist—or an associate professor of econometrics—to think that he and the telephone can have an edge over those who count the cocoa pods in Africa and follow the minute-by-minute arrival of new information. If we made money on balance it must have been because Ed Kuh's father was a lifetime member of the Board of Trade, and blood is thicker than water. (Edwin Kuh, Sr. delighted me with his answer to my basic question, "What makes markets move?" He pondered for only a moment and answered thoughtfully: "New news, not yet digested." As Pareto said to Schmoller when the latter told him that of course there was no place in town where he could get a good meal for a mark, "So there is economic law after all!")

The second reason we may have kept from losing our shirts was that Paul Cootner began to apply his Brennan-Cootner notions seriously, as in the case of formal porkbelly models that involved dynamic regression relations between futures price spreads, stocks, putative supplies, and demand disappearance. These fundamentalist paradigms, in the hands of a sensitive and informed analyst, did seem to work.

Were it not for my contacts with Cootner, I would probably not have been one of the committee members to supervise Helmut Weymar's prize-winning M.I.T. thesis on cocoa. The world would be the poorer (and so would I). Later when Weymar transferred from Nabisco to found the Commodities Corporation in Princeton, Paul Cootner served to help formulate the rational system of controls on profit centers; and Cootner's pork model was put to further practical test.

As Wittgenstein said, on that which we cannot speak, we have to keep silent. I lack knowledge of Cootner's further activity in the fields of practical finance. The sole reason why I touch at all in a scholarly discourse on these personal matters is one of scientific importance: Paul Cootner's theoretical work never suffered from the kind of naivete that so often mars the works of those who analyze scars but never felt a wound; if a Casanova is not the definitive authority on sex, neither is a eunuch.

THE GEOMETRIC BROWNIAN MOTION

From now on I can stick to Cootner's belief that blind chance is held in by walls of economic law. The Brownian dance, of Bachelier, Einstein, and Wiener—as described in (1) above—implies that the price of a Cadillac can become anything relative to that of a pea or a share of IBM.

When I tried to develop a rational theory of option pricing (along with thesis writing Richard Kruizenga) in the middle 1950s, before we knew of Bachelier's Brownian analysis, I soon discovered that the ordinary random walk (in its binomial or Gaussian versions) led to economic monstrosities:

1. It implied that the value of a call would grow as the square root of its duration, leading to the absurdity that a long-lived option will eventually *exceed* in value the common stock it enables you to buy for a price.
2. The absolute Brownian Motion, or classical random walk, implied that after a long time, T, the value of your (limited liability) stock would with a probability of one-half become *negative*. That is, from (1),

$$\lim_{T \leftarrow \infty} \text{Prob}\{X(t + T) < 0 | X(t) = x_0 > 0\} = \tfrac{1}{2}, \tag{2}$$

even though under limited liability the probability of negative price for a common stock is necessarily zero.

My natural repair to the Bachelier longrun anomaly was to stipulate the Geometric Brownian Motion. Invoking the dictum of Gertrude Stein and Josef Schumpeter, that "a dollar is a dollar," I assumed the familiar *law of proportionate or ratio effect:*

$$\text{Prob}\{X(t + T)/X(t) \le x\} = Q_T(x), \tag{3}$$

independently of $[X(t), X(t \pm K), t, \ldots]$. This led, as the physicist M.F.M. Osborne observed empirically at much the same time, to the Log-Normal Wiener process. In other words, under certain assumptions about the probable continuity of the $X(t + T)$ price sample and the finiteness of moments of its changes, this implied the Log-Normal result

$$\text{Prob}\{\log_e[X(t + T)/X(t)] \le y\} = L(y; \mu T, \sigma T^{1/2}) \tag{4}$$

where

$$\begin{aligned} L(y; \mu, \sigma) &= \textstyle\int_{-\infty}^{y} (2\pi\sigma)^{-1/2} \exp[-(u - \mu)^2/\sigma^2] du, \\ \mu &= \text{expected value } \{\ln X(t + 1) - \ln X(t)\}, \text{ and} \\ \sigma^2 &= \text{variance } \{\ln X(t + 1) - \ln X(t)\}. \end{aligned} \tag{5}$$

Thus

$$\text{Prob}\{X(t+T) < 0 | X(t) = x_0 > a\} \equiv 0 \tag{6}$$

Also, the expected present-discounted value of an expiring call option that has T years to run, and which applies to a non-dividend-paying stock, only asymptotically rises to the value of the stock itself as $T \to \infty$. Thus, the Bachelier anomalies were avoided once the Absolute or Arithmetic Brownian Motion of physics is replaced by the Geometric Brownian Motion of economics.

Most of modern option theory, as in the case of the justly famous Black-Scholes arbitrage formula, operates in terms of Log-Normal probability distributions.

Benoit Mandelbrot has usefully pointed out that fat-tailed distributions of the Lévy (or Pareto-Lévy-Mandelbrot) type may occur in speculative stochastic processes. Paul Cootner was an informed student of such processes,[5] with their implication that meandering chance could lead the real world away from economic law even more quickly and extremely than the Wiener process had suggested. The Cootner innovation I deal with here aimed to cut back variances from the Log-Normal model, not amplify them in the Mandelbrot fashion.

MARTINGALE WHITE NOISE

To set the stage for Cootner's proposed innovation, I must provide one last piece of background information. In 1965,[6] I provided a clear-cut deductive theorem for the efficient-market paradigm. In accordance with that paradigm's major tenet—"There are no easy pickings"—I axiomatized the notion that speculative market price already "discounts" available digestible news by the requirement that a futures price equal the mathematical conditional Expected Value of some future variate. The Expected Value is taken according to some exactly specified stochastic process.

From this one deduces that the Expected Value will, according to that stipulated stochastic process, have a change through time with an Expected Value of zero. (The *total return* could be positive if these values are themselves present-discounted values: The "zero" here, then, means zero *excess* return over the yield required for this kind of risky asset.)

In short, the correct model is not a Gaussion process, nor even a Log-Normal random walk. Rather, it is a *martingale:*

$$\begin{aligned}\text{Expected Value}\{X(t+1) - X(t)|X(t) = x_0,\\ X(t-1) = x_{-1}, \ldots; Y(t) = y_0, \ldots\} = 0.\end{aligned} \tag{6'}$$

[5]See Cootner (1964, pp. 333–37), a revision of his remarks at the 1962 Econometric Society meeting. Cootner's innovations that I analyze here are contained in his 1962 *Industrial Management Review* paper, cited here as Cootner (1964, pp. 231–52).

[6]See Samuelson (1965a; 1976; 1980). Samuelson (1965b) provided the arguments for the Geometric Brownian Motion and applied that and other distributions to the problem of rational warrant pricing. Samuelson (1973) provided a survey of speculative prices and gives an extensive bibliography.

Although both Bachelier's random walk and a martingale process imply the white autocorrelation spectrum that Kendall and other writers have found, the martingale is broader and very different from the random walk. In particular it does not imply that $X(t + 1) - X(t)$ is probabilistically independent of $X(t)$. Therefore, a martingale process need not have the rapidly meandering spread, away and beyond the intervals that economic law would seem to dictate for economic variables, that even a Log-Normal process would have to have.

Even though proportionate or logarithmic variables do eliminate the negative prices that the conventional random walk is prone to, we still have conditional geometric means that exhibit trends of exponential decay or growth, ratios of arithmetic means to geometric means that grow ad infinitum with T, logarithmic variances that swell with the square root of elapsed time; and absolute variances that explode even more rapidly.

COOTNER'S REFLECTING BARRIERS

"Although GM stock could, by chance alone, rise or fall very much," Paul Cootner in effect argued:

> surely that company's share of the car market and the automobile's share of the GNP is determined within broad boundaries by consumer tastes, technologies, and resource scarcities. When chance moves GM's prices to the extremes of the channels within which its economic destiny lies, there should be a tendency for further price perturbations in that extreme direction to be resisted. Even though the bulk of the investors who are not especially well informed can reasonably regard GM's stock price as pretty much a random walk, the experts who follow auto stocks and have much money riding on them will know to bet against further deviations outside the "equilibrium" channels. . . . At the extremes of the normal channels, the experts will be able to recognize *correctly* that the price movement is biased to move back toward the mainstream. Instead of white or zero autocorrelation that is consistent with a random walk and which pretty much prevails in the mainstream of the channel, near the channel's walls negative autocorrelation (perhaps weakly so) will prevail much as if we had a stochastic process with "reflecting barriers." The result is that the distant-future probabilities for GM's stock prices do not continue to grow in spread, but rather approach asymptotically a limiting probability distribution—an "ergodic" probability distribution.

MATHEMATICAL DESCRIPTION

The Cootner model can be described as follows. At any time, suppose economic law ordains that the norm toward which aleatory market price tends to be pulled is $\overline{X}$. (This will not remain constant, but itself is subject to certain trends, certain systematic changes as related Y variables change, and even certain probability distributions. For expository purposes, I keep $\overline{X}$ a constant.)

Knowing the present price of a security (whose dividend is zero or has been separately allowed for in its market price), we have thus defined the conditional probability distribution of next period's price:

$$\text{prob}\{X(t+1) \le x_1 | X(t) = x_0\} = P_1(x_1|x_0). \tag{7}$$

Here I have assumed that $[X(t-1), X(t-2), \ldots]$ have no separate influence on $X(t+1)$ which is not already caught in $X(t)$—a Markov assumption.

By reiteration of this conditional probability distribution from today to tomorrow and from tomorrow to the next day, we deduce the Chapman-Kolmogorov implied conditional probabilities for any number of periods ahead:

$$\begin{aligned} \text{prob}\{X(t+T) \le x_T | X(t) = x_0\} &= P_T(x_1|x_0), \\ P_2(x_2|x_0) &= \textstyle\int_0^\infty P_1(x_2|x_1)P_1(dx_1|x_0) \\ P_3(x_3|x_0) &= \textstyle\int_0^\infty P_2(x_3|x_1)P_1(dx_1|x_0) \\ &\cdot \quad \cdot \quad \cdot \quad \cdot \\ P_T(x|x_0) &= \textstyle\int_0^\infty P_{T-1}(x|y)P_1(dy|x_0). \end{aligned} \tag{8}$$

Here, I handle both cases of probability densities and discrete probabilities by the notation of Stieltjes integrals: namely, $\int_0^\infty df(x) = \int_0^\infty f(dx)$. Thus, if $f'(x)$ exists everywhere, $\int_0^\infty f(dx) \equiv \int_0^\infty f'(x)dx$. If probabilities are positive at the points $x = a$ and $x = b$, $p_a = 1 - p_b$, then $f(x)$ will have jumps there: $f(x) = \int_0^x f(dx)$ will be zero for $0 < x < a$; p_a for $a \le x < b$; and 1 for $b \le x \le \infty$.

Cootner, in effect, assumes that $P_1(x_1|x_0)$ is a martingale, or nearly so, when x_0 is near to its economic norm of $\overline{X}$.

It pays no one to risk his money betting that the stock is over- or underpriced. Random chance rules in this no-man's land of neutrality:

$$\text{Exp}\{X(t+1)|x_0\} = E_1(x_0) \approx x_0, \ |x_0 - \overline{X}| \text{ not too large.} \tag{9}$$

But when $X(t) = x_0$ pulls too far away from the $\overline{X}$ that professionals take the trouble to calculate, what then? Cootner assumes there is enough capital-gain bait there to induce them to buy or sell. In doing this informed buying or selling, the cool professionals tend to move $X_1(t+1)$ back toward $\overline{X}$, thereby on the average garnering an ex post profit. So

$$\begin{aligned} \text{Exp}\{X(t+1)|x_0\} &= E_1(x_0) < x_0 \text{ if } x_0 >> \overline{X} \\ \text{Exp}\{X(t+1)|x_0\} &= E_1(x_0) > x_0 \text{ if } x_0 << \overline{X}. \end{aligned} \tag{10}$$

If (10) supplants (9) when chance takes the economic variable far astray from the equilibrium called for by economic law, as we look far ahead at distant T, the Central Limit Law with its Gaussian spread proportional to $\sqrt{T}$ is negated.

Instead Cootner faces an *ergodic probability distribution:*

$$\begin{aligned} \lim_{T\to\infty} P_T(x|x_0) &= P_\infty(x) \\ \partial P_\infty(x)/\partial x_0 \equiv 0 &= \lim_{T\to\infty}\{\partial P_T(x|x_0)/\partial x_0\}. \end{aligned} \tag{11}$$

This need not be approximately rectangular; but Cootner's hunch would be right if (10) holds to a violent degree very near to specified extreme walls and not at all elsewhere.

I believe Cootner had unpublished tests of his hypothesis beyond those he reported in 1962. Those 1962 testings were not very powerful ones. The issue of kurtosis is only loosely relevant. The weak signs of negative autocorrelations, reported by Larson (1960) and others, are more germane.

As applied to stocks of small companies in inactive markets characterized by relatively high transaction costs, Cootner's hypothesis—that price can systematically deviate so far from its norm as to enable profitable bets to be made with confidence—might be plausible. But, as applied to actively traded stocks like IBM, GM, or Vanguard Index Trust (the S & P 500), I must confess to doubt. Member firms and specialists encounter very low transaction costs; they can sell short without penalty of upticks or penalty capital requirements. Even small profit opportunities, if they are almost sure things in the steady state of repeated quasi-independent transactions, could make one rich beyond the dreams of avarice. At best, it seems to me, Cootner's violations of the martingale property would have to be only weak even in the extreme zones.

In the next section I shall vindicate most of Cootner's hunches about the systematic deviations from a true random walk that are involved in the real world of economics made up of both economic law and aleatory chance.

MARTINGALE BETWEEN WALLS

Now I shall deny Cootner's (10). I shall affirm, everywhere between the walls of a channel defined around the economic par of $\overline{X}$, the martingale property of (9):

$$E_1(x_0) = \int_0^\infty x P_1(dx|x_0) \equiv x_0. \tag{12}$$

From (8) and (12), we can deduce that, for *any* number of periods ahead, knowing only $X(t) = x_0$, the expected value of $X(t + T)$ must also be x_0 if $E_1(x_0)$ must equal x_0.

The proof is by induction:

$$\begin{aligned} E\{X(t + T)|X(t)\} &= E_T(x_0) = \int_0^\infty x P_T(dx|x_0) \\ &= \int_0^\infty x \int_0^\infty P_{T-1}(dx|y)P_1(dy|x_0) \\ &= \int_0^\infty E_{T-1}(y)P_1(dy|x_0) \end{aligned} \tag{13}$$

If in (13) we can assume that $E_{T-1}(x_0) \equiv x_0 \equiv E_1(x_0)$, we deduce that $E_T(x_0) = x_0$, namely that

$$E_T(x_0) = \int_0^\infty E_{T-1}(y)P_1(dy|x_0) = \int_0^\infty y P_1(dy|x_0) = E_1(x_0) = x_0. \tag{14}$$

Now let us look at two overly simple examples of martingale processes, representing markets so efficient that no one can make a (disequilibrium) profit, but in which, nevertheless, the prices are contained within Cootner walls

EXAMPLE 1: Around $\overline{X} = 1$ are two walls, one at $X^M > \overline{X} = 1$ and the other at $\overline{X} = 1 > X^L \geq 0$. $[X(t), X(t+1), \ldots, X(t+T), \ldots]$ will probabilistically fluctuate over the channel around $\overline{X}$ defined by these Cootner Walls or Barriers.

Wherever $X(t) = x_0$ is in the admissible channel, let $X(t+1)$ be able to go to two positions only: half way to the upper wall and half way to the lower wall. But I adjust the probabilities of these two exclusive places so as to make the bet a fair game: If x_0 is nearer to X^M than to X^L, I adjust the probability so that the move will be a small positive one, greater enough than $\frac{1}{2}$ so that the mathematical expectation of the smaller gain just balances the mathematical expectation of a larger loss. In short, $P_1(x|x_0)$ must in this example be such that

$$\begin{aligned} \text{prob}\{X(t+1) &= \tfrac{1}{2}x_0 + \tfrac{1}{2}X^M | X(t) = x_0\} \\ &= 1 - \text{prob}\{X(t+1) = \tfrac{1}{2}x_0 + \tfrac{1}{2}X^L | X(t) = x_0\} \\ &= p(x_0) = \frac{x_0 - X^L}{X^M - X^L}. \end{aligned} \tag{15}$$

The stochastic process has now been well defined. Although it is a zero-profit process—a martingale—it is certainly not a random walk. In particular, the variance of $P_T(x|x_0)$ does not grow indefinitely like $\sqrt{T}$. Indeed, the variance never can get as big as $(X^M - X^L)^2$.

Note that there cannot be an ergodic distribution in the sense of (11). The initial x_0 never does wash out of the mean of $P_T(x|x_0)$, even when T is large. $E_T(x_0) \equiv x_0$ contradicts $\lim_{T\to\infty} P_T(x|x_0) = P_\infty(x)$, independently of x_0.

It does not contradict

$$\begin{aligned} &\lim_{T\to\infty}[P_{T+1}(x|x_0) - P_T(x|x_0)] \equiv 0 \\ &\lim_{T\to\infty} P_T(x|x_0) = P_\infty(x|x_0) \\ &\textstyle\int_0^\infty x P_\infty(dx|x_0) \equiv x_0. \end{aligned} \tag{16}$$

The next example throws further light on the phenomena.

EXAMPLE 2: Again we have two walls. For definiteness we can set $\overline{X} = 1$, $X^M = 2$, $X^L = .0$. Now suppose that $X(t)$ can take on only a countable infinity of values, namely 1,

$$\begin{aligned} 1 + 2^{-1} &= 2 - 2^{-1}, 1 + 2^{-1} + 2^{-2} = 2 - 2^{-2}, \ldots, 1 + 2^{-1} + \ldots + 2^{-k} \\ &= 2 - 2^{-k}, \ldots; 1 - 2^{-1} = 2^{-1}, 1 - 2^{-1} - 2^{-2} \\ &= 2^{-2}, \ldots, 1 - 2^{-1} - 2^{-2} - \ldots - 2^{-k} = 2^{-k}, \ldots. \end{aligned}$$

I may number these alternative positions such that any $X(t)$ can take as, respectively, positions

$$[0, 1, 2, \ldots, +k, \ldots] \quad [-1, -2, \ldots, -k, \ldots]. \tag{17}$$

Now, suppose that $X(t) = i$ can become $X(t+1)$ equal to either $i+1$ or $i-1$. To keep the process a martingale, the probability that it will go to $i+1$, $p(i)$ must be just right, compared to the probability it will go to $i-1$, $1 - p(i)$:

$$\begin{aligned} p(i)[2 - 2^{-i-1}] + [1 - p(i)][2 - 2^{-i+1}] &= 2 - 2^{-i}, i > 0 \\ p(i) &= \frac{2}{3}, i > 0 \\ p(0) &= \tfrac{1}{2}, \text{by symmetry} \\ p(i)[2^{-i+}] + [1 - p(i)][2^{-i-1}] &\equiv 2^{-i}, i < 0 \\ p(i) &= \frac{1}{3}, i < 0. \end{aligned} \tag{18}$$

We can write this in the form of an infinite-dimensional Markov matrix:[7]

$$\text{prob}\{X(t+1) = j | X(t) = i\} = a_{ij}, \sum_j a_{ij} \equiv 1 \tag{19}$$

The $[a_{ij}] = \underline{a}$ matrix becomes

$$\begin{matrix} \ldots 0 & \frac{2}{3} & 0 & \frac{1}{3} & 0 & 0 & 0 & 0 & 0 \ldots \\ \ldots 0 & 0 & \frac{2}{3} & 0 & \frac{1}{3} & 0 & 0 & 0 & 0 \ldots \\ \ldots 0 & 0 & 0 & \frac{1}{2} & 0 & \frac{1}{2} & 0 & 0 & 0 \ldots \\ \ldots 0 & 0 & 0 & 0 & \frac{1}{3} & 0 & \frac{2}{3} & 0 & 0 \ldots \\ \ldots 0 & 0 & 0 & 0 & 0 & \frac{1}{3} & 0 & \frac{2}{3} & 0 \ldots \end{matrix} \tag{20}$$

We would have an ergodic probability if we could find a column vector of one sign that is a right-hand characteristic vector of a, namely a vector with the properties

$$\Pi = [\ldots \Pi_{-2} \Pi_{-1} \Pi_0 \Pi_1 \Pi_2 \ldots]^T > 0, \sum_{-\infty}^{\infty} \Pi_i = 1. \tag{21}$$

Selecting Π_0 to be a finite number, I reach a contradiction to the existence of such a Π vector. So, we are confirmed that there could not be an ergodic probability distribution like that in (11): the matrix a^t cannot in the limit become a matrix, a^∞, all of whose rows are alike.

[7]See Champernowne (1953) for somewhat similar use of such matrixes with an infinity of rows and columns.

One asks this question: As $t \to \infty$, does a^t approach a limit, a^∞, albeit with rows that depend upon i?—that is, are the first two relations in (16) confirmed? If the answer is in the affirmative, one sees roughly what these distant probabilities must be like.

First, all probabilities display for any T symmetry around the middle of the channel. Ignoring the x points (a set of measure zero) at which $\text{prob}\{X(t + T) \le x|x_0\} \ne \text{prob}\{X(t + T) < x|x_0\}$, we must have

$$P_T(1 + u|1 + v) = 1 - P_T(1 - u|1 - v). \tag{22}$$

In particular, for $x_0 = 1$, the probability densities or histograms must be symmetric about 1.

Second, near one of the walls and away from the middle, one expects the distant probability distribution to be skewed off in the direction of the remote wall.

Third, the rate at which a perpetual warrant converges to the value of the stock itself is slower than in the Log-Normal case.

Fourth, and this is Cootner's essential point, we can reject the preposterous element in a random walk: we are spared the need to expect that as, in the far future, actual price will be dispersed ever further around the definable par set by technology and tastes.[8]

I fear that my attempt to vindicate Cootner's notion of reflecting barriers within the framework of fair-game returns fails. My conjecture is that as T approaches ∞, $P_T(x|x_0)$ approaches the following bimodal distribution with probabilities concentrated on the walls themselves:[9]

$$\begin{aligned} \text{prob}\{X(\infty) = X^M|X(t) = x_0\} = \frac{x_0 - X^L}{X^M - X^L} = \\ 1 - \text{prob}\{X(\infty) = X^L|X(t) = x_0\}. \end{aligned} \tag{23}$$

[8]I am tempted to add a third example. In it, we would have a Log-Normal distribution at all times. But the (μ,σ) of the distribution are each functions of x_0 rather than being constant. To preserve the martingale property, $\mu(x_0) + \frac{1}{2}\sigma(x_0)^2 \equiv 0$; for $x_0 >> \overline{X}$, $\mu(x_0)$ can be made so negative as to reflect the system back toward the par of $\overline{X}$; for $x^0 << \overline{X}$, alas, the most we can algebraically increase $\mu(x_0)$ is to just below zero, where $\sigma(x_0)^2 \approx 0$; however, I doubt whether this is enough to keep $P_T(x|x_0)$ in (15) from going to 1 for small positive x. Making $E\{X(t + 1) - X(t)\}$ equal a positive constant rather than zero will not, I fear, evade the essential difficulty.

I ought to add a remark for the reader who is troubled that the total yields indicated by my martingales are zero rather than positive. Actually, the reader should feel free to regard my $X(t)$ as present-discounted values calculated using some positive-nominal or real rate of interest. (This could be little above the safe rate of interest or as much above it as this class of riskiness requires. To be more rigorous than this in my specification would require following Arrow's approach to all possible states of nature that can obtain.)

[9]In both of my examples, the probability that your next move will decrease the distance to the nearest wall exceeds $\frac{1}{2}$. So you might think that this outward bias explains the drift to the walls. But that seems to be an invalid argument. Consider the following example: From $X(t) = x_0$, you move, with probability $\frac{1}{3}$, halfway to the nearest wall; or with probability $\frac{2}{3}$, you move half as far in the opposite direction. Then, despite this "inward bias," (23)'s ultimate piling up of probabilities at the walls will still obtain. One proves this mathematically along the following lines: Let any point, x_0,

The reader will note the superficial resemblance of this formula to that applying to the gambler-ruin problem: If you begin to make fair gambles at x_0 and vow to quit when you win $X^M - x_0$ or lose $x_0 - X^L$, the probability that you will quit a winner is $(x_0 - X^L)/(X^M - X^L)$ as above.

If a martingale must pile up its probabilities at the boundaries, I cannot achieve Cootner's intuitive goal by means of a martingale. At the least, if we are to derive an ergodic probability, $P_\infty(x)$, we must let Cootner have near the walls some (possibly weak) systematic violations of the martingale property.

Actually, an almost-efficient market is what a realist ought to expect. To get the risk-averse investor to commit a finite fraction of his funds to take on a new gratuitous (independent) risk, you must first offer a little bait. And a little bait is all that Cootner needs to make his case.

Fortunately, as the next section will show, once we introduce the dividends or cash outpayments that must eventually be forthcoming (or at least available), then we shall find that white noise for total yield implies *negative autocorrelation* for asset price changes—a clear negation of the so-called random walk.

ALTERNATIVE REJECTION OF THE RANDOM WALK

I believe Paul Cootner was right to doubt that the speculative price of a stock, bond, grain futures, grain physical, machine tool, or acre of perpetual land would wander endlessly (like $\sqrt{T}$) away from its rendezvous with its equilibrium dictated by economic law. His reflecting barriers were a valiant attempt to evade the unacceptable.

Recently I have shown how the paradoxes and dilemmas evaporate. In as yet unpublished research, I consider the archetypical case of land with a perpetual stochastic yield. The present-discounted value of such a stream of rents does "vibrate stochastically." But it is not Brownian motion—neither Wiener-Bachelier Absolute Brownian Motion, nor Osborne-Samuelson Geometric Brownian Motion. Instead the random variable of capitalized land price, previously referred to as $X(t)$, approaches an ergodic probability distribution as in (14):

$$\lim_{T\to\infty} P_T(x|x_0) = P_\infty(x), \int_0^\infty x P_\infty(dx) = \overline{X} \qquad \textbf{(24)}$$

$x_1, \ldots, x_T, \ldots$ have defined for it a Liapunov function—$f(x) = \text{Max}[X^M - x, x - X^L]$. We see that the expected value of this, conditional on x_0, rises in each passing period. Therefore, $P_\infty(x|x_0)$ cannot be other than given in (23) which defines the only class of distributions that achieve $\text{Max}_x \text{Exp}[f(x)]$ at $X^M - X^L$. As an alternative proof, note that, $P_T(x|x_0)$ must by Jensen's inequality have a greater variance than $P_{T-1}(x|x_0)$ has when both must have the same mean of x_0. Therefore, if a $P_\infty(x|x_0)$ existed with a finite probability of interior points, we would have a contradiction in the "next period." $P_\infty(x|x_0)$ with all its probabilities piled on the walls would alone be immune to this self-contradiction.

The stochastic jitter around $\overline{X}$ is not white noise. Its autocorrelellogram shows negative serial autocorrelations in the long run: When x_0 begins away from the mean of $\overline{X}$, we can expect regression toward that mean in the far future (even if the land's net rents are probabilistically independent over long intervals of time and are identically distributed over every time period.)

What can follow a random walk is the cumulation of *total yield* (random dividend plus implied stochastic changes in capitalized value). Twin brothers who own independent plots of land, and who compute the cumulative historical products of their respective total yields, will find that the differences between their two computed portfolios diverge endlessly and in exact correspondence with the Geometric Random Walk. It is quite proper that this should be the case—at the same time that every plot of land is constrained to bubble stochastically around its par set by Economic Law. The point is that no one can make any money by betting on a repulsion of land price from its "reflecting barriers." What makes it likely that land's low present price will rise by next year (or fall by then) is that its net rent is likely to be low this coming year (otherwise its present price could not have fallen so low in our efficient market).

As a scholar, Paul Cootner combined the unusual qualities of depth and versatility. His early death cheats economic science of our rational expectations, a fact that compounds our personal loss.

References

Arrow, K. J., *Essays on the Theory of Risk-Bearing.* Amsterdam: North Holland Publishing Company, 1971.

Bachelier, L., *The Theory of Speculation.* Paris thesis translated into English in Cootner's 1964 anthology referred to below.

Black, F., and **M. S. Scholes,** "The Pricing of Options and Corporate Liabilities," *Journal of Political Economics* 81, no. 3 (1973), 637–54.

Brennan, M. J., "The Supply of Storage," *American Economic Journal* 48 (1958), 50–72.

Champernowne, D. G., "A Model of Income Distribution," *Economic Journal* 63 (1953), 318–51.

Cootner, P., "Returns to Speculators: Telser vs. Keynes," *Journal of Political Economy* 68 (1960), 396-404; and "Rejoinder," ibid., 415–18.

———, "Stock Prices: Random vs. Systematic Changes," *Industrial Management Review* 3 (1962), 24-45, reproduced in *The Random Character of Stock Market Prices,* P. Cootner, ed. Cambridge, Mass.: M.I.T. Press, 1964.

Cootner, P., ed., *The Random Character of Stock Market Prices.* Cambridge, Mass.: M.I.T. Press, 1964 and 1967, hereafter referred to as *Cootner Anthology.* For Cootner's own contributions, see pp. 1–6, 79–83, 189–97, 231–52, 333–37, 373–75.

Hicks, J. R., *Value and Capital.* Oxford: Claremont Press, 1939, 1946.

Houthakker, H. S., "Can Speculators Forecast Prices?" *Review of Economics and Statistics* 39 (1957), 143–51.

———, "Systematic and Random Elements in Short-Term Price Movements," *American Economic Review* 51 (1961), 164–72.

Kaldor, N., "Speculation and Economic Stability," *Review of Economic Studies* 7 (1939), 1–27.

Kendall, M. G., "The Analysis of Economic Time Series, Part I: Prices," *Journal of the Royal Statistical Society* 116 (1953), 11–25; reproduced in *Cootner Anthology,* pp. 85–99.

Keynes, J. M., Quoted in *Manchester Guardian* (March 29, 1923).

———, *Theory of Money,* London:Macmillan, 1930.

Kruizenga, R. J., "Put and Call Options: A Theoretical and Market Analysis," Ph.D. dissertation, M.I.T., 1956; reproduced in *Cootner Anthology,* pp. 392–411.

Larson, A., "Measurement of a Random Process in Futures Prices," *Food Research Institute Studies* 1 (1960), 313–24; reproduced in *Cootner Anthology,* pp. 219–30.

Mandelbrot, B., "Variation of Speculative Prices," *Journal of Business* 36 (1963), 394–419; reproduced in *Cootner Anthology,* pp. 307–32.

Osborne, M. F. M., "Brownian Motion in the Stock Market," *Operations Research* 7 (1959), 145–73 (reproduced in *Cootner Anthology,* pp. 100–128).

Samuelson, P. A., "Intertemporal Price Equilibrium: A Prologue to the Theory of Speculation," *Weltwirtschaftliches Archiv,* (1957); reprinted in *CSP* 2, 1965.

______, "Proof that Properly Anticipated Prices Fluctuate Randomly," *Industrial Management Review* 6 (1965a), 41–49; reprinted in *CSP* 3, 1972.

______, "Rational Theory of Warrant Pricing" and "Appendix: A Free Boundary Problem for the Heat Equation Arising from a Problem in Mathematical Economics," by H. P. McKean, Jr., *Industrial Management Review* 6 (1965b), 13–39; reprinted in *CSP* 3, 1972 and in *Cootner Anthology,* pp. 506–22.

______, "Stochastic Speculative Price," *Proceedings of the National Academy of Sciences* 68 (1971), 335–37; reprinted in *CSP* 3, 1972.

______, "Proof that Properly Discounted Present Values of Assets Vibrate Randomly," *The Bell Journal of Economics* 4 (1973), 369–74; reprinted in *CSP* 4, 1977.

______, "Is Real-World Price a Tale Told by the Idiot of Chance?" *The Review of Economics and Statistics* 58 (1976), 120–23; reprinted in *CSP* 4, 1977.

______, "Stochastic Land Valuation: Total Return as Martingale Implying Price Changes—A Negatively Correlated Walk," unpublished manuscript, 1980.

Telser, L. G., "Reply" (to Cootner's "Returns to Speculators: Telser Versus Keynes"), *The Journal of Political Economy* 68 (1960), 404–15; also in *Selected Writings on Futures Markets,* vol. II, A. E. Peck, ed., Chicago Board of Trade, 1977.

Weymar, F. H., *Dynamics of the World Cocoa Market.* Cambridge, Mass.: M.I.T. Press, 1968.

Working, H., "Theory of the Inverse Carrying Charge in Futures Markets," *Journal of Farm Economics* 30 (1948), 1–28; reprinted in *Selected Writings of Holbrook Working,* Chicago Board of Trade, 1977.

______, "The Theory of Price of Storage," *American Economic Review* (December 1949), 1254–62.

WHY WE SHOULD NOT MAKE MEAN LOG OF WEALTH BIG THOUGH YEARS TO ACT ARE LONG

Paul A. SAMUELSON*

Massachusetts Institute of Technology, Cambridge, MA 02139, USA

> He who acts in N plays to make his mean log of wealth as big
> as it can be made will, with odds that go to one as N soars,
> beat me who acts to meet my own tastes for risk.

Who doubts *that*? What we do doubt[1] is that *it* should make us change our views on gains and losses - should taint our tastes for risk.

To be clear is to be found out. Know that life is not a game with net stake of one when you beat your twin, and with net stake of nought when you do not. A win of ten is not the same as a win of two. Nor is a loss of two the same as a loss of three. *How much* you win by counts. *How much* you lose by counts.

As soon as we see *this* clear truth, we are back to our own tastes for risk. Mean log of wealth then bores those of us with tastes for risk not real near to one odd (thin!) point on the line of *all* the tastes for risk – and this holds for each N, *with* N *as big as you like.*

Why then do some still think they should want to make mean log of wealth big? They nod. They feel 'That way I *must* end up with more. More sure beats less'. But they err. What they do not see is this:

> When you lose – and you *sure can* lose – with N large, you can
> lose real big. Q.E.D.

Long since, in Samuelson (1963, p. 4), I had to prove what is not hard to grasp:

> If it does not pay to do an act once, it will not pay to do it
> twice, thrice,..., or at all.

*I owe thanks for aid to NSF Grant 750-4053-A01-SOC.

[1]Cf. the views of Ophir (1978, 1979) and Latané (1978).

Can we bring the dead rule back to life by what it tells us about the mean growth rate? No. Here's why not.

> For large N, when you act at each turn to make the mean of log of wealth big, you will make your *mean growth rate* big in this sense:
>
> As N grows large, the odds go to one that my mean growth rate (per turn) will end up real close to a rate less than that which you (with big odds) *end up* close to.

Who doubts *that* truth? But *it* does not rule out this clear truth.

> For N as large as one likes, your growth rate can well (and at times must) turn out to be less than mine – and turn out so much less that my tastes for risk will force me to shun your mode of play. To make N large will *not* (say it again, *not*) make me change my mind so as to tempt me to your mode of play. Q.E.D.

No doubt some will say: 'I'm not sure of my taste for risk. I lack a rule to act on. So I grasp at one that at least ends doubt: better to act to make the odds big that I win than to be left in doubt?' Not so. There is more than one rule to end doubt. Why pick on one odd one? Why not try to come a bit more close to that which is not clear but which you ought to try to make more clear?

No need to say more.[2] I've made my point.[3] And, save for the last word, have done so in prose of but one syllable.

[2]We should spare the dead. When a chap has said he now doubts that '...this same rule [of max of mean of log of wealth] is approximately valid for all utility functions [...insofar as certain approximations are permissible...]...', we should take him at his word and free his shade of all guilt. For a live friend to still say: 'given the qualifications it seems to me that this [above quoted] statement of Savage is very difficult to refute', as the French say, gives one to cry. Those key words are false when we make them clear. When we don't make them clear, there is nought to talk about (to say Yes or No to). As the French say too, it is a case of put up or... For more on this, see Latané (1959, p. 151; 1978, p. 397) and Samuelson (1959, p. 245).

[3]Let me tie down one loose end. Look at this Odd Rule:

> From Acts $A(N)$ and $B(N)$ pick Act $A(N)$ if, for their two end wealths, $W_A(N)$ and $W_B(N)$, with odds of more than one half (or more than $1-\varepsilon_N$, $0<\varepsilon_N \ll 1$), $W_A(N) > W_B(N)$.

This Odd Rule is odd since it can put you in this Fix:

> You may well pick $A(N)$ from $A(N)$ and $B(N)$, and pick $B(N)$ from $B(N)$ and $C(N)$, and yet still pick $C(N)$ from $A(N)$ and $C(N)$.

References

Latané, H.A., 1959, Criteria for choice among risky ventures, Journal of Political Economy 67, 144–155.

Latané, H.A., 1978, The geometric-mean principle revisited: A reply, Journal of Banking and Finance 2, 395–398.

Ophir, T., 1978, The geometric-mean principle revisited, Journal of Banking and Finance 2, 103–107.

Ophir, T., 1979, The geometric-mean principle revisited: A reply to a reply, Journal of Banking and Finance, this issue.

Samuelson, P.A., 1963. Risk and uncertainty: A fallacy of large numbers, Scientia 1–6. Reproduced in: 1966, Collected scientific papers of Paul A. Samuelson – I (MIT Press, Cambridge, MA) 153–158.

Samuelson, P.A., 1969, Lifetime portfolio selection, Review of Economics and Statistics 51, 239–246. Reproduced in: 1972, Collected scientific papers of Paul A. Samuelson – II (MIT Press, Cambridge, MA) 883–890 (cf. p. 889).

Thorp, E., 1971, Portfolio choice and the Kelley criterion. Reproduced in: W.T. Ziemba and R.G. Vickson, eds., 1975, Stochastic optimization models in finance (Academic Press, New York) 599–619.

This Fix *can* come for *all* N, as large as we choose to make N. It can do so though the truth of Thorp (1971, p. 603) holds,

$$\operatorname*{plim}_{N\to\infty} W_A(N) = \bar{W}_A > \bar{W}_D = \operatorname*{plim}_{N\to\infty} W_B(N), \qquad \bar{W}_B > \bar{W}_C = \operatorname*{plim}_{N\to\infty} W_C(W),$$

rules out

$$\operatorname*{plim}_{N\to\infty} W_C(N) > \operatorname*{plim}_{N\to\infty} W_A(N).$$

That is so since $\bar{W}_A > \bar{W}_B$ and $\bar{W}_B > \bar{W}_C$ means $\bar{W}_A > \bar{W}_C$.

But I'd not said: 'When you act to make mean of log of wealth large, you could get in the Fix'. To see why you can't, we need only note that

$$\text{mean of log of } W_A(N) = L_A(N) > L_B(N) = \text{mean of log of } W_B(N),$$

and

$$\text{mean of log of } W_B(N) = L_B(N) > L_C(N) = \text{mean of log of } W_C(N),$$

rules out

$$L_C(N) > L_A(N),$$

and it does so for *all* N, as when N is as small as one.

Some goals are strange, but need not be as bad as the odd rules some seek to base them on.

Economics of Futures Contracts on Basic Macroeconomic Indexes: An Economist's Appraisal

By Nobel Prize Economist Paul A. Samuelson

When futures contracts on farm products were new, many people rejected them as mere devices for gambling. This is a natural reaction. And it would be a healthy reaction if all that an organized exchange provides is a casino where players can satisfy their lust for risk legally and cheaply.

Gradually, there evolved understanding that futures contracts do perform an important economic function. Farmers and millers have an interest in their availability. So do consumers and workers. Society is the beneficiary. All this is true even though a considerable number of the people who buy and sell futures are out and out speculators, desirous of taking chances, and not infrequently poorly informed optimists destined to lose their investments.

Now there are proposals to offer futures contracts on the consumer price index, the rate of housing starts, the rate of auto sales and the total of corporate profits. If approved, these contracts could offer advantages to many commercial and manufacturing businesses similar to those enjoyed by farmers and millers from more traditional futures contracts.

No one can be surprised that some hostility and considerable skepticism greeted the proposal new futures contracts be set up. "Why legalize a casino for people to make bets on the economy's future? Next thing you know, they'll be proposing a casino for futures on the weather." Such reactions had to be expected. But they do not come from economists or from persons engaged in the serious activities of manufacturing and commerce. Indeed, as far as economists are concerned, it follows from the deep analysis of optimal risk allocation and risk bearing of Nobel Laureate Kenneth J. Arrow[1] of Stanford University, that some day the insurance against weather contingencies that Lloyds of London and other agencies now sell to producers may be supplemented to society's advantage by the setting up of new futures contracts that do involve weather and climate outcomes.

A corn future, or a soybean future, came to be acceptable once it was understood that each of these enable a farmer or miller to buy for a price some protection against the contingency that bountiful harvests will knock down the price that can be received for the farmer's grain or the miller's flour and meal. Few understand the details of "hedging." It is enough to realize that consumers (who benefit from bountiful crops) can afford to deal in competitive futures markets with producers (who are hurt by bumper crops): together they make a hedge possible; also, third parties who are speculators (knowledgeable about market information and/or tolerant of risk) help to make it possible for producers and consumers to achieve the hedged protection they desire and need.

No pricing mechanism is perfect. It is known to err. But studies over the last fifty years by Dr. Holbrook Working and a great number of statistical economists have verified that futures markets do on balance render a useful social service in reducing unnecessary price variability, promoting price movements that serve as signals for storage and production decisions. That in a nutshell is why futures markets are as socially valuable

1. The definitive scientific references are Kenneth J. Arrow, "The Role of Securities in the Optimal Allocation of Risk-Bearing," *Review of Economic Studies*, 31 (1963-4), pp. 91-6; Gerard Debreu, *Theory of Value* (New York: John Wiley & Sons, 1959, Chapter 7 on Uncertainty.

as stock markets, bond markets and even labor markets. That is why the device has spread from grains to meats to metals, and more recently to currency futures, interest-rate and bond contracts, stock and bond options, and indexes of common stock prices.

Some may agree that the switch to cash settlement of new futures contracts snapped the link between futures and underlying economic fundamentals. Agricultural futures contracts are "settled" by the delivery of physical commodities. On maturity of a wheat futures contract, the seller delivers to the buyer the contracted quantity of wheat. Many new futures contracts are settled in cash equivalents but physical delivery is not essential either to futures or to their economic value. Actually, most futures are settled by cancelling sales and purchases. Indeed, a contract like the Kansas City Value Line stock index could not from its geometric-mean nature be "settled" by delivery of a portfolio of common stocks. There is no such animal on land or sea. Although the S&P 500 contract in Chicago could in principle be settled by delivery of a definable portfolio of 500 different equities, that is not what can be legally done. Proper understanding of a futures is quite independent of the possibility of settling it by delivery of one or another physical entity, and consists rather of the risk-reduction and optimal risk-sharing that the contract makes possible.[1]

It is therefore no valid criticism of the new contracts that they are not designed to be settled by delivery of some physical item. Even if the contract involving the Consumers Price Index could be terminated by the delivery of a weighted basket of the commodities that make it up, that would be an absurd, inefficient, and costly way of settling final claims. There is nothing in the economic principles of risk allocation that rests on and requires settlement in a physical object. Gambling fever in the wheat pit is not cleansed by terminal settling in spot grain.

Dr. Holbrook Working's scholarly findings have established that no bourse remains viable and manages to pay its overhead expenses unless it provides a legitimate insurance function. The gambling function pays its way perhaps in Las Vegas and Atlantic City, but not in Wall Street and Lasalle Street!

I write as an economist, not as a floor trader. I am not able to predict with precision whether corporations, which are much affected by unforseeable inflation, will learn quickly how to acquire hedging insurance by means of the new price-level contract. Maybe the learning process will take so much time that such a contract would prove not viable. But as an economist I do know from Arrow's basic theory, and from ancient principles, that the availability of macroeconomic futures contracts lowers the deadweight loss in the economic system attributable to risk and uncertainty. Economists' theories will be better when they can perceive what the *expected rate of inflation* really is.

What is infinitely more important, the players in the economic game—two hundred and fifty million Americans—will be better off when the exchange institutions evolve that help to signal risks, reduce them, and allocate the residual irreducible risks optimally.

1. When I buy, and you sell, a March '84 wheat future on the Board of Trade, it will vary each day and hour until then. A rise in tomorrow's price for physical wheat delivered tomorrow may cause the market's estimate of what wheat's price will be in March of 1984 to vary. Agreed. It is wrong to criticize on this account a housing-starts contract, arguing that only once a month does the government publish a new housing-start number. Every day, hour, and minute—as news comes in about Federal Reserve actions, bond-price variations, dollar exchange-rate weakness and strength—a rational jury has reason to alter what it thinks will be the number of housing starts announced by the government *next year*. Nothing in practical experience of economic theory requires that a useful and viable contract have connected with it a thing just like itself (but other than itself) that is hourly quoted in the marketplace. Criticism of the macroeconomic futures on this account seems ill-informed.

Hanging In There

Most of us are going to be poorer later on. It is part of the biological facts of life that we can expect to live on past our period of prime earning power. The rainy day for which people proverbially save is that final retirement stage of life.

The Gettys and Rockefellers, and all those who amass huge fortunes to pass on to their children and grandchildren and to the charitable foundations of their choice, are dramatic exceptions to the general rules of economic life. As MIT's Franco Modigliani has spent his own lifetime in studying, it is *life-cycle saving* that best explains the dynamics of capital formation in the U.S. and in other countries at various stages of economic development.

Although 1977 was a year of fairly vigorous growth for the American economy, the common stocks people held generally declined in value. Pension assets, held by corporations for employees' eventual retirement, suffered from the same general malaise. Those people who earned 6 per cent on their savings accounts were about the only ones who kept up with the increase in the cost of living, but after they paid a quarter of their return in income tax, the real value of their principal actually declined.

CLUTCHING AT STRAWS

Only two kinds of assets held their value. The social-security payments that most of us have coming when we reach our 60s and 70s have been escalated in accordance with the consumer price index. Despite the periodic rumors of insolvency that get spread, families' first line of defense in the form of social security rests securely on the growing earning capacity of the nation, and this provides assurance of a basic minimum for the future.

Also, the values of people's homes continued to grow in most parts of the country. Building costs continue to advance remorselessly, and older homes are buoyed up by the rising prices that have to be charged for new dwellings. Indeed, many a young family has found it necessary to buy a more expensive home than it can afford and only the rise in housing prices has bailed it out from its frenzied overcommitments.

Given the disappointing performance turned in by traditional modes of investment in recent years, people are naturally tempted by some less conventional alternatives. I am frequently asked:

"Can one prudently do better buying diamonds? Oriental rugs? Paintings, sculptures, prints or antiques? Stamps? Farm land, citrus groves, tax-sheltered oil deals? Sun-country condominiums, mountain or shore properties? Gold bars, coins (for example, U.S. eagles, French napoleons, South African krugerrands), gold-mining shares?

"Can one recoup, or at least preserve real value of principal, by buying call options on IBM or GM? Or by buying put options? Or by selling either of such options? Are the odds favorable in soybean futures, pork bellies, silver or copper? Can one provide for old-age needs by taking judicious flyers in foreign-exchange futures (the mark, yen, pound, Swiss franc)?"

NO PHILOSOPHER'S STONE

Careful investigation shows that none of these gambits pays off for the average intelligent amateur. Each new line begins favorably for those who happen to be early birds. And special knowledge and diligence tend to be rewarded as in any form of activity.

Actually, in well-organized competitive markets there is no place to hide when the winds of liquidation are blowing. You are naïve to be taken in by rumors of neighbors who are making killings in London commodity options or in private-mint commemorative issues of coins.

Don't misunderstand: a judicious small position in a closed-end gold fund, or in gold coins bought at low premium, sometimes makes sense; I know a chemist who will die rich because he spends hours studying catalogs and auctions of prints, a field in which he has become expert. But these are not examples easy to imitate. In times adverse to conserving net worth, it is all the more important to hew to investment's golden rules:

Diversify broadly, hold down turnover, keep all fees minimal.

When asked what he had done during the Terror of the French Revolution, the Abbé Sieyès replied, "I survived." Conditions for surviving were never easier than now for those who trouble to become well-informed.

Coping Sensibly

The small investor can now, for the first time, invest in common stocks and bonds in an efficient and convenient way. I am talking about people who don't have $10 million; who don't want to take *unnecessary* gambles; who operate under no Napoleonic delusions of being able to pick winners that will quadruple their money; who begrudge every minute devoted to keeping tax and personal records, and wish to think about their investments only at New Year's and when preparing their tax returns.

Disinterested experts in finance prescribe for such people as follows:

1. Depending on your tolerance for the irreducible risks involved in owning common stocks, decide what portion of your nest egg you wish to keep in common stocks: 0, 100, 30 or 70 per cent. No one can decide this for you. You must decide at what point you'll sleep best at night, and whether eventually stocks will provide a better inflation hedge than they have done these last dozen years. (Many will settle for 50-50.)

2. For what common stocks you do decide to own, follow the golden rules of prudence:

Diversify broadly, hold down costly turnover, keep all fees (and bookkeeping!) minimal.

3. The same rules (diversification, etc.) apply to your holdings of tax-free and ordinary bonds. If you have taxable income of $20,000 or more, probably the bulk of your bonds should be "municipals"—i.e., state and local issues that escape all Federal tax because Congress refuses to close this loophole. Less affluent people will probably do as well in local savings accounts as in anything else.

Now you know *what* to do. *How* do you do it?

MUTUAL-FUND POOLING

For most people the best and simplest device is a no-load mutual fund, either of the common-stock, bond-income, money-market variety, or a combination of all three.

There are hundreds of such funds. A couple of dozen of them have the lowest fees and superior diversification practices. I personally resist the temptation to switch to that small fund which happens to have scored the best "performance" record recently.

When at long last I became a grandfather, my gift to young James went into the First Index Investment Trust, which at low expense tries to match the 500 diversified stocks of the Standard & Poor index. True, many funds beat the S&P in 1977; but James has a long life ahead of him and I want to go with the long-run odds. (Needless to say, I could do about as well with the Dreyfus, Fidelity, Scudder, and T. Rowe Price organizations, or a half-dozen other full-line services.)

A CASE IN POINT

For definiteness, here is a sample setup for a 53-year-old engineer earning $30,000 a year. Similar percentages might apply to a widow who just inherited $200,000.

1. Put *half* your net worth into a no-load, low-turnover stock fund like the First Index Investment Trust. Let all dividends and capital gains be automatically reinvested. Draw at your convenience what you want to live on or for vacations. (You will get only a half-dozen simple reports each year; from the year-end slip, you can file your tax return in ten minutes.)

2. Put one-third of your assets in a no-load municipal bond fund (like the Federated Tax-Free Income Fund or Warwick Municipal Bond Fund). You can write checks against this account, using it as a reserve of liquidity. As above, the bookkeeping is minimal. Municipal funds now yield about 5 per cent free of Federal tax, and run some risks of capital gains or losses.

3. Keep one-sixth of your portfolio in a local insured bank, to pay small bills and for convenient instant access.

This is a stripped-down version. Your self-employed person's Keogh pension plan, being subject to zero immediate tax, might go to a high-yielding income fund (like the Fidelity Aggressive Income Fund). The risks of holding "junk" bonds can be made tolerable by broad diversification.

Also, those who think they are good at "timing" market swings can switch costlessly from one fund in an organization to another—e.g., reducing First Index holdings in favor of Warwick Municipal, both run by the Vanguard Group. Other variations are possible for opinionated sophisticates.

Most of you, though, will want to stick to basics. Then the finance prof will award you an A for probity, and you can forget about economics.

Gold and Common Stocks

A lot of people claim to be able to forecast turns in the stock market, and a few occasionally have done so; but no persons or groups have provided evidence of any consistent success. What most of us are best at is explanations after the fact.

Anyone reasonably facile with his pen can provide Monday-morning rationalizations for what happened in Wall Street last week. I know. Once, to accommodate a sick friend, I ghost-wrote his brokerage letter for a spell; no one noticed the difference even though I purposely engaged in double-talk, cliché, and empty tautology. Indeed, to tell the immodest truth, his fan mail swelled a bit.

In April, common stocks suddenly spurted upward, and on high volume. This time, even after-the-fact explanations were hard to fabricate and carried less than the usual impression of saying something.

This summer, Wall Street has experienced another sudden rise. The volume of daily transactions set a new record. Large and small companies shared in the advance. Once again, convincing reasons for the move are scarce.

GOBBLEDYGOOK

Here are specific examples.

Traders think they know that rising interest rates are bad for stock prices, for the reason that when bonds fall in price they pull down the prices of such competing assets as stocks. Yet the post-April rise in common stocks was directly in the face of weakening bond prices and rising interest rates. (No wonder that the beleaguered market-letter writers had to appeal to oil strikes in the Baltimore Canyon, savvy European investment money, covering by short sellers, fear by institutional investors lest they miss the boat and, finally, panic by writers of naked or uncovered call options caught short.)

Whatever the merits of the rationalizations of the April rise, they aren't needed to explain the recent boomlet. This time, bonds have shared the bull market, as one minority of experts opines that the peak of interest rates is now here.

Sufficient to the time is the nonsense thereof. A new theme claims that President Carter and the Fed have turned soft on inflation. So interest rates are to fall at the same time that living costs accelerate? Also, are we now to go back to the belief that common stocks are a *good hedge* against inflation, rather than the rotten hedge of the last dozen years?

It used to be said that the stock market is a leading indicator, moving in anticipation of business. Yet, it is only recently that the consensus forecasters have veered to the view that the U.S. is about to go into a mini- or growth-recession. So are we supposed to infer that stock prices now point ahead to day-after-tomorrow sunshine rather than tomorrow's rain?

STRANGE BEDFELLOWS

My purpose in poking fun at pseudo explanations of the summer market rally is not to cast doubt on the validity of the rise in equity prices. I do have some suspicions concerning the permanence of the rises in bond prices; but stocks are another matter, and I could provide ammunition for the Wall Street bulls as well as bears.

What I think needs pointing out is that there are some anomalous features in recent events. Gold and the Dow are rising at the same time.

The unpegging of the price of gold permitted its price to rise during the 1970s from the old official par of $35 to quadruple that level. That created a handsome profit to those who hoarded it for whatever reason. Once official pegging was well in the background, the most rational reason for maintaining a modest fraction of one's assets in gold shares (or even coins and bullion) has been the well-founded belief that gold tends to move in the *opposite* direction to most American securities. A coal dealer can prudently buy ice shares even if their mean return is skimpy, provided that they will come through for him just when his coal assets are proving disappointing.

That is why, once certain gold-share funds dropped to a discount below net-asset value, I added a few to my portfolio. The recent market run-up that appreciated run-of-the-mill shares also chanced to send up those token gold holdings. Pure luck, undeserved and unlikely to reoccur.

Good questions outrank easy answers. Ponder this one: "After a dozen years of irreversible inflation, should share prices still be at their average 1966 levels?"

Time to Sell?

An hour before President Carter announced his new program to save the dollar, I was enjoying my periodic dental checkup. "Now let's turn to serious matters," said my friend in white. "Should I sell out all my common stocks?"

That is not a question to ask a professor of economics. I hope to live with my dentist for a good long time. It is a no-win situation ever to give advice: if it turns out well, people naturally preen themselves on their acumen in accepting the hypothesis you've nominated; if it turns out otherwise, they remember just where they learned it first.

Nonetheless, I overheard myself emitting some cautionary bromides. One does not really sleep better when 100 per cent out of stocks. Those locked-in 9 per cent yields on long-term bonds can look very sour should inflation accelerate. Even though common stocks have turned out to be a rotten hedge against inflation these last dozen years, experience shows that over the long pull . . .

You know how such soothing syrup runs and can yourself fill in the hollows.

THE IN-AND-OUT PLOY

The rest of the morning, as I licked my gums, I pondered over what I had done. True, the Dow Jones averages leaped 30 points that very day in the wake of the President's unanticipated decisiveness. True, I was addressing someone over 21.

But I also harbor a Hippocratic oath: an economist, other things equal, should do no harm; in formulating the odds and stating the main reasons behind them, he should come clean on the uncertainties. Once, when asked for an off-the-record comment on one of the brilliant economists of our time, I said about my friend: "The gods gave him every talent—except the gift of 'maybe'."

Still, I found myself stubbornly unrepentant. Let me sketch the reasons.

First, I can make a case for selling out now. Stock prices in the past have tended to turn down *before* the economy went into recession. ("The market has forecast nine of the last five recessions," some sage once observed.) A respectable plurality of the good economic forecasters has recently come down on the side of a 1979 recession. Next spring one may well be able to buy those same stocks back at lower prices. In the meantime, a nice quick profit on the reviving bond market may be obtainable.

I can also punch holes in this gambit. It would require nimble timing. Chances are you'd not get back in equities until *after* the balloon had gone up, and then perhaps only at prices even higher than now. Experience reveals few who succeed in playing the in-and-out game. Everyone knows what you know. Why will *you* be lucky Alphonse? Perhaps Wall Street is already discounting the worst that will happen.

MONEY-MARKET ASTIGMATISM?

So I'm left with the hard question. *How are American stocks priced relative to their intrinsic values?* Although economists have learned to respect the wisdom and efficiency of the marketplace's checks and balances, on this question they do have an interesting point of view.

A persuasive case can be made that *equities are now cheap from a long-run point of view.* Why? Because the public incorrectly evaluates the effects of inflation on equity values.

The conventional wisdom overdiscounts for the false element in inflationary profits. It underestimates the *implicit* gains in money capital values that accrue when anticipatable inflation is raising the reproduction cost of America's earning assets. It fails to notice the gain that the common stockholder filches from the lending bondholders when they are paid off in melting dollars.

To be sure, there are genuine ways in which fake inflation profits do get overtaxed—as when historic-cost depreciation allowable against tax liability fails to cover replacement-cost depreciation. But my point remains after we have made all such needed corrections.

When we can expect prices to rise 5 per cent a year instead of being stable, it is rational for bond yields to go from 5 per cent to 10—or, to put it another way, for bonds' price-earnings ratios to fall from 20 to 1 to 10 to 1. But it is not rational for inflation to halve the P-E ratio of common stocks. Yet this is what has happened in Wall Street.

In summary, common stocks might be a good hold. Maybe.

No-Fuss Canny Investing

My wife used to listen to Julia Child with high hopes, then put down her pencil saying, "An omelet is just not worth all that trouble."

This is the way many sensible people feel about the chore of managing their life savings. If the price of prudence is reading Barron's, Forbes and the Institutional Investor, keeping track of the Commerce Department's leading indicators and figuring out how the raindrops are falling in the soybean counties, then that is just too high a price for a busy biochemist, lawyer or housespouse to pay.

Good Habits: For such people I have good news. There is a way of managing your savings that requires a minimum of work on your part. But you will ask, "Isn't there an easy way and a *right* way? What am I sacrificing by way of safety and mean return when I succumb to the easy way?"

Again, good news. Essentially, nothing imprudent is involved in doing things the simple way—provided you get started with good habits. When I was training my wife to be a widow, I researched the subject at some length. What I learned about the science and art of asset selection confirmed what the late Al Capp once told me about cartooning: "I found that if I spent more than a couple of days a week on my 'Li'l Abner' comic strip, I tended to louse it up."

So it is with your suburban neighbor who calls his broker every day and subscribes to The London Financial Times. His portfolio churns and churns, making more money for the broker than for himself. (I don't have to be reminded that there are exceptions to my generalization: what I am reporting is the *average* success achieved by the active money managers working for the most respected financial organizations.)

Here then is the main recipe for no-fuss canny investing: make great use of no-load mutual funds, preferably those with low expense ratios. Here are some examples:

- Your child is born, and will need to go to college in 1998. Give her now a tax-free gift of $6,000 per year for one or two years. Put the proceeds in a money-market fund—any of the big ones will do—and let the assets accumulate at her low-income-bracket rate. In most states there are minor-custodian acts and you won't need a lawyer; just spend half an hour each year preparing her tax return from the slip of paper the fund sends you. (Query: is there no better procedure? Answer: who can tell what will happen in the next two decades? But research by Prof. Zvi Bodie of Boston University, among others, suggests that shortest-term fixed-principal assets do have the *least variance* in *real* purchasing power.)
- You and your spouse together earn $50,000 per year and are taxed accordingly. Instead of keeping your ready cash in a sizable checking or savings account, use one of the tax-exempt money-market funds that let you write checks of more than $500 on your funds. Then pay small bills by bank check, replenishing your funds by writing a large check on the tax-exempt fund. Use such a check to pay your property taxes or finance a trip to Europe.
- You are a widow of 60 left $300,000 in insurance. This must last the twenty-odd years of your life expectancy. I wish there were some annuity you could buy that would guarantee your real purchasing power. But there isn't. All you can do is minimize risk, not escape it.

The Easy Way: The trust department of a local bank can serve you. Or you can match its performance by dividing your principal among three mutual funds. (If they are with the same organization, you can conveniently make switches with a single phone call.) One-third might go into a broadly diversified common-stock fund. Just which fund is not important; what's important is that you not be entirely out of equities in these uncertain times. One-third might go into a bond fund and the final third into a money-market fund, taxable or tax exempt depending on your tax bracket. (Warning: once you've chosen the path of broad diversification, don't then expect to make a killing with choices that double and triple in value.)

If you do it right, your record-keeping will be minimal since the funds' custodian banks will do it all for you. If you study prospectuses, you'll be able to find good funds whose annual expense ratios are well below 1 per cent of asset value.

Do a little research at the beginning. Then relax, knowing you've minimized the irreducible risks and bookkeeping. Besides, you can always change your mind at minimal cost, and start churning your portfolio whenever you feel lucky.

Crackpot Investing

People ask me what they should read to protect their savings. It's a hard question. Most of the best sellers on how to invest are likely to do you more harm than good.

That's my view. I base it on decades of personal experience, both as a private investor and as an economist called on to advise nonprofit organizations and forced on occasion to discuss financial methods with friends.

What's one man's opinion against another's? Howard Ruff is glad to pit his hunches against mine. Millions buy his books warning against collapse of the banks, destruction of the dollar by hyperinflation and the breakdown of law and civilization.

Dupes: There are authors aplenty who do well purveying advice like this:

- Sell your stocks and bonds.
- Liquidate bank accounts.
- Buy land, stock a cabin in the woods with food sufficient to outlast a holocaust and keep rifles handy to fend off the shiftless dupes who will try to move in on your prudential turf when the chips are down.

My point is not to exchange fishmonger vituperation with those who differ from the conventional wisdom. Franz Pick, Harry Schultz, Harry Browne, Eliot Janeway, Joe Granville and other well-heeled pundits laugh all the way to the bank thinking it is I who doze in a fool's paradise.

Since economics is not an exact science, they could turn out to be right. But such evidence as there is suggests that you ought not to bet on it.

The essence of science is not personal anecdotes. Science, even inexact science, is *public knowledge,* reproducible for analysis by everyone. For 50 years now, professors at the nation's business schools have been studying the batting averages of chartists and technicians. The goals of security analysts have been compared with subsequent statistical performance by the totality of mutual funds, pension and insurance services and investment counselors.

The findings are uniformly the same. Some do well, some do badly. A few do very well, a few do very badly. Monkeys put to typewriters in the British Museum will, if you wait long enough, reproduce without error the Encyclopaedia Britannica. So scientists must apply statistical tests of significance to find whether there's much impressive in the batting average of those few best performers in each epoch.

What is the upshot? The vast preponderance of the evidence suggests that stocks are bought and sold in "efficient markets"—that is, in markets where the checks and balances of many would-be investors result in prices that reflect discountable news and which probabilistically divide the bulls and the bears evenly.

To sum up: there are no easy pickings. Unless you have special sources of information and speedy ways of analyzing the incoming flow of news, you are not able from past patterns of stock prices to achieve excess risk-corrected returns. Those few with exceptional information and ways of successfully interpreting the uncertain imponderables of chance are very few indeed. It's about as hard to spot them as to spot stock bargains. And you'll find that you probably have to pay them full economic rent for their unusual abilities.

Pudding's Proof: So much for stock selection. Even if a Granville's record is mediocre at picking specific stocks, what's the evidence on the ability of the various services to succeed at the game of "timing"? As against merely buying and holding stocks, can you hope to gain from advisory services that tell you for a few hundred dollars annually to get out of the market before a bad year like 1974, and get back in before a good year like 1975?

Here, too, most of the evidence is discouraging. This does not deny that a particular adviser can have a hot run of favorable calls. But south Florida is full of would-be Joe Granvilles, and one of them—like a monkey in the museum—can several times succeed in buying stocks when the Dow Jones index is at 800 and selling them when it is at 1,000 without astonishing the statisticians.

Merlin the Magician never reveals his proprietary methods. Still, Barnum warns us to weigh what is revealed for plausibility and relevance. On that basis I'd counsel caution and skepticism.

A final warning. You can lose money in anything: gold, real estate, collectibles or a general index of stocks. Diversification is what holds down risk.

CANNY INVESTING

FOREWORD

A good economic textbook should have something to say about the important problems of life. In this newsletter, I address myself to the personal finance problem common to all professors, drawing on the economic principles that the beginning student will learn from Samuelson's ECONOMICS, 11th edition.

To show that it can be done, all the words I use are of one syllable, except for bold face technical terms—such as Money Market Funds, Diversification, and so forth. After the piece on how to invest, I add some words to economists to explain how a skeptic can test what is said. So short a piece can't be the whole truth. But it is an important part of that truth.

Paul A. Samuelson

This is not for all folks. It aims at those who aren't rich or poor. At those who want to spend most of their time on work and play, not on fun and games with wheels of chance or pages of stock and bond data. I speak to those who shun risk save in a good cause.

I could call this *NO-Fuss Investing.* It uses no tricks. It scores no coups. What it does do is keep down all costs. It cuts risk but there is no way to bank on a sure thing.

Could you lose your wealth? Yes, you can lose your wealth.

Will you beat the chap down the street? You might not. But chances are you will.

What you won't beat is the *champ* down the street. He draws luck. Or he may know how to do what few can do, what I and you can't do: see *first* what is to come.

You and I must play safe: We opt for **Diversification.**

That means we dare not put all our eggs in one urn. That way they all go bad at once; or else all score well at the same time. With more than one urn, when some go bad, we stand to have some turn out well.

Thank the moon, which gives us light at night *when we need it most!* **Diversification** is the life raft in need when fate turns her face from us.

Some No Nos

To start, get clear on a few points.

1. *Should you own your own home?* That's up to you. It's not true that to rent is a fool's game. It might be. It might not be. I take it you've made up your own mind on this.

2. *Is your* **INSURANCE** *right?* Most times **TERM INSURANCE** is best, the **GROUP** kind you get through your job. There is no set rule on how much to buy. I take it you will pick as much **TERM** as is right for you. Then to get a good yield on what you want to save, you'll go down the street and not fool with **WHOLE LIFE INSURANCE.** Though it could save tax, its fees are high and its yield low.

3. *Should you hold gems?* Stamps? Gold coins or bars? Rugs from the East? Old chairs and chests? Land or shore homes?

If you are first to buy. . . . If you can buy and sell at low fees, which won't be at a store in town . . . . If you know more than the mob does about fine prints . . . .

If, if and if. Then you might do well.

But for most it's a mug's game. Here's why.

You say to me: "Buy land. They don't make more of it." I must say to you: "We all know that fact. It's *now* in land's high price. To beat the game, you and I must know now what the rest have yet to learn."

4. **COMMODITY FUTURES** are not for you. Few know the ins and outs of these. Most lose their shirts. When prices of what we buy might soar, a fund that holds **COMMODITY FUTURES** might give us a hedge. (Dr. Zvi Bodie of Boston University has shown this.) But I say all that's for pros with big, big bucks and stout hearts.

At last: What To Do

Put your wealth in three forms

1. CASH at the bank to write small checks on
2. STOCKS of lots and lots of firms
3. MONEY MARKET FUNDS whose yields are set day by day, and which you can write big checks on.

That's all you need to do. (Yes, bonds are meant to be left out of this list. Here, for the sole time, I give you *my own* view. And I could be wrong.)

1. Bank Cash

One rule holds: KEEP THIS LEAN

Your yield will be low on this loose cash. Pay a fee for each check if you must. You might want a **NOW ACCOUNT,** one that lets you write checks but still pays you a yield of 5¼% per year.

But why give up the 17% you now can get on the funds that you don't tie up in the bank? (If your tax rate is high, that might make it pay to hold more bank cash to keep check fees down. But it is not for the rich that I write.)

2. Stocks

Hold **NO-LOAD DIVERSIFIED MUTUAL FUNDS,** those with low fees. ("No load" means there is *no* fee to buy or sell!)

The Fund's bank will keep the books for you and hold your shares. At year's end, they'll send a slip to let you know what **DIVIDENDS** you got and must put on your tax form. That's all there is to it.

If your **MUTUAL FUND** holds stocks of all kinds, you have no need to sell an old fund and buy a new one. Not so when you hold a few stocks on your own. Once they go up too far, you must sell them and buy those stocks that are still cheap. That means fees to sell and buy. It means a tax on your gains—a low tax but still a tax.

With a broad Fund you can hold until you get old and are in need. Or until you take that trip to Rome. Or want to pay down on a new home. Or send your child to Yale.

The point is that you won't have to trade stocks to take good care of your wealth. And you can sleep well, since you know you have done all that it is wise to do.

3. **MONEY MARKET FUNDS**

These take your cash and pay a yield set each day by the bids of all the big and small banks.

You can get your dough back by a phone call. Or by a wire. Or they will let you write big checks—checks just like those on your own bank!

Can you lose your mite? Yes. The FDIC does not make good your loss if yields rise and your Fund takes a loss on some notes it holds. I face up to this risk. I weigh it. In the end I deem it small for funds that stick to notes that all come due in weeks and not months or years. I get so much on day to day funds as to make me think it worth the risk of a small loss once or twice in ten years. (I stay with Funds that keep their price at $1.00 on the head. Some Funds let their price go up and down. And some reach out for notes from off shore and that take months to come due. They could be good buys but they do bring some risks.)

To me MM Funds are like banks by mail, brought to us by the age of IBM. These funds keep the books for me. They put my yields back in the Fund if I tell them to. They send me a slip so I can fill out my tax form. None of this is at all hard.

What counts is that **MONEY MARKET FUNDS** give me the high yields that rich men can get. (Of course the Funds do charge me a fee: and I would balk when this is put at more than 1/2% per year. If we ran our banks right, some home bank could give me the same good deal. But that time has not yet come.)

How Much In Each?

I can't tell you if you should put half your spare wealth in **Stocks** and half in **MM Funds.** That's up to you.

You may want to play safe in terms of cash. So you could opt to put 80% in **MM Funds** and put 20% in **Stocks.** (I will say that 0% in stocks seems rash. It flies in the face of **DIVERSIFICATION.**)

Down at the job, they may now put much of what you'll get in old age in cash. So you at home might opt for 85% in stocks, and 15% in MM Funds. (I will say that *all* in stocks scares me. It thumbs its nose at **DIVERSIFICATION.**)

I ought to point out that we all have a great need for a hedge against price hikes. Since 1965, there has been no good hedge. But so far **MONEY MARKET FUNDS** have been at least as good a hedge as stocks. But the past is no sure guide on what's to come.)

One last word on why there are no long bonds in my list. Bonds have been a bad hedge when price hikes fool us. The age may come when their prices fall so low as to make me want to take the risk that they run. But that age seems not yet here. (At best, if my tax rate were low, I might buy a "Junk Bond Fund" that holds scores of low grade bonds. Their yield is high, since some few may go bust. But here I speak to the plain chap, who lacks spare time for frills like this.)

What Names, Please?

I don't pick stocks. You have to pick your own **NO-Load Diversified Mutual Stock Fund** or Funds. You must pick your own **Money Market Fund.**

It helps me to go to a big group, one that holds both kinds of funds in the same house. One phone call does all the work. And were I so rash as to try to time the ups and downs of stocks and yields, by phone I can switch 20% of my **Stocks** into **MM Funds** or 20% of my **MM Funds** into **Stocks.** I doubt that you or I can catch such swings. But if you think you can, here is how to try at no cost for the move.

Just to show what kinds of groups there are, I take from the ad pages the names of four big fund groups. By free 800 phone, you can learn more on each one or on still new groups.

Dreyfus Funds (New York)
Fidelity Funds (Boston)
T. Rowe Price Funds (Baltimore)
Vanguard Funds (Valley Forge, Penn.)

Good Luck

I've laid out the bare bones. Much more could be said on the fine points. But this should do for a start.

You are on your own. And you know you can lose.

Postscript to Scholars

Professors of economics will know that my argument here rests upon modern findings with respect to "efficient markets." Samuelson's ECONOMICS, 11th edition, deals with this topic early in the course. Cf. pp. 69-71.

Many researchers have contributed to our knowledge on this subject: Holbrook Working of Stanford, who studied grain prices; Sir Maurice Kendall, then of the LSE, who found speculative prices moved almost as if in a random walk; the late Paul Cootner, who edited an MIT Press collection of papers on the randomnesses of price changes; numerous researchers who have shown that the best money managers, at funds and banks and insurance companies, at your college and mine, do not on the average do better on a risk-corrected basis than would a fund that invested broadly in all the stocks that could be put into the overall index of stock prices. (The Standard & Poors 500 Stock index is better than the Dow-Jones Industrials, but even it is only a tolerable sample of the whole market.)

Some important names in the field of modern finance whose work I've drawn upon, include: Irwin Friend (Pennsylvania), Eugene Fama and Myron Scholes (Chicago), Fischer Black and Robert C. Merton (MIT), John Lintner (Harvard), Zvi Bodie (Boston University), William Sharpe (Stanford), Richard Roll (UCLA), Stephen Ross, James Tobin, and Harry Markowitz (Yale).

The subject of "efficient markets" of course borders on the important new subject treated in ECONOMICS 11th ed. (Chs. 17, 18, 41 and elsewhere), namely the school of "rational expectationists." The random component in stocks' price changes provides a good example for the rational expectationist school, but as is warned on p. 310:

> *[Less] well verified by the evidence is the view that ordinary consumers and businesspeople correctly sort out the odds concerning the economy's future cycle movements. Speculative manias and panics do surprise people; and experience shows that these are self-fulfilling processes while they are happening. (p. 310, 11th ed.)*

I don't have to tell economists that no investment advices can be foolproof. The first lesson given here could be followed by others. (As an example, if you must hold diamonds, don't hold them in your Keogh pension account where taxes don't matter. Hold high-yielding funds in that account, and in your more heavily taxed personal account hold gems if you must. Also, if you have a loss on a no-load stock fund that you've held less than a year, you're in good shape to register that as a Short Term Capital Loss. You do so easily by planning to switch into another stock fund inside the same house of the group you deal with. I could go on and on, but that would be down a curve of diminishing returns.)

I still have a few copies of my Newsweek columns covering related ground, entitled: No-Fuss Investing, and Crackpot Investing. I'll send copies while they last to instructors who write for them.

Paul A. Samuelson
MIT, March 1981

FOREWORD

To tackle how a common resultant effect is traceable to a number of separate factors that all contribute to it, R.A. Fisher and a host of statisticians have developed the useful "factorial" approach. Here is a simple example of it.

You want to diversify your stock portfolio. How much Ford stock should you buy compared to General Motors or Toyota stock? You already have GM shares in quantity and many U.S. corporations stocks. It is useful for you to try a factorial approach: How important is the auto-industry component in Ford's future price changes? How important is the geographical component of Ford's being in the U.S.? These factors it shares with GM, which you already own. Finally, there is a residual factor having to do with the particular management staff and corporate style peculiar to Ford itself. Professor Banerjee shows how to use the tools of least-square regression and Fisher's analysis of variance in order to estimate the separate factorial components.

What has this to do with index numbers? Next year the dollar volume of U.S. GNP will change. Some of that change will be due to outputs' growth; some due to price changes of the goods and services. Economists and statisticians try to separate an observed change in GNP, say a 3% increase, into its two parts: say a 1% increase in the index number of prices plus a 2% increase in the index numbers of quantities. For many years, in many learned journals both accessible and inaccessible, Professor Banarjee has been pursuing the factorial approach to constructing such price and quantity indexes. He has innovated many formulas and discoveries. He has rediscovered by his approach some of the formulas old and new in the economic and statistical literature. Readers will be grateful to find, in one book (this book), a comprehensive exposition of the Banerjee factorial approach.

My own work in index numbers follows another line: the "economic theory of index numbers." When prices move next year so that I will need twice as many dollars as this year to be able to live as well as I did this year, I want the Price Index (calculated for me) to read 200. Also, if next year I buy a batch of goods that I could have bought this year only with three times the income I actually had now, I want the Quantity Index (calculated for me) to read 300.

The economic theory of index numbers faces many difficulties. If your tastés differ from mine, or your income differs enough to make the pattern of your consumption differ from mine, then a purist must calculate different P and Q indexes for you and for me. So it is obvious that no one of the common index formulas can be the right formula; the arithmetic mean of price changes (using early-period weights or late-period weights) cannot be the right one; nor can a weighted geometric mean or any other kind of mean be the Holy Grail we are looking for. There is no one Holy Grail within the economic theory of index numbers.

The practical statistician replies with a question: Aren't some formulas better approximations to what you economists want than other formulas? Dr. Banerjee nominates various of his factorial formulas as tolerable approximations. Indeed, some of his formulas duplicate well-known approximations proposed by such economists as Stuvel and Marshall-Edgeworth.

Fair enough. But some factorial formulas raise purists' doubts. Take the very first index formulas in the book, those of Stuvel-Banerjee. When every price exactly doubles between two periods, their Price Index generally does not read 200. The economic theory of index numbers cannot tolerate this. To be sure, Banerjee's formulas that immediately follow do escape this objection. And taking symmetric means of polar pairs of them might meet some of us purists' hopes. How does a mechanical least-squares procedure cater to the economists' hopes? It cannot, unless a wise Dr. Banerjee guides its path.

Is it proper for me to write a Foreword to an approach that differs from mine? Yes, in a true democracy a Democrat may welcome a good hearing for a Republican. Science is, or should be, a true democracy. In the adversary procedure that is scholarship, let every view be worked out so as to set its best foot forward. Then the jury of competent peers can best decide. In this spirit, I hail K.S. Banerjee's valuable contribution.

Paul A. Samuelson

MIT, Cambridge, MA

January, 1985

PART V

Classical Economics

Thünen at Two Hundred

By PAUL A. SAMUELSON
Massachusetts Institute of Technology

I have benefited from suggestions by Ronald Jones and Edwin Burmeister, and from editorial assistance by Aase Huggins. Partial support from the Sloan Foundation is gratefully acknowledged.

1983 IS A YEAR of centennials: the death of Karl Marx, the births of Maynard Keynes and Josef Schumpeter. But also, running exactly a century before Schumpeter's life clock (1883–1950) was that of Johann Heinrich von Thünen (1783–1850), the economist who met a payroll and, in recording and analyzing his Junker estate accounts, not only created *marginalism* and *managerial economics*, but also elaborated one of the first models of *general equilibrium* and did so in terms of realistic *econometric* parameters.

Thünen was a loner with a one-track mind. By 1803—still a minor!—he had already glimpsed the equilibrium of his *Isolated State:* a town surrounded by a homogeneous plain, trading city goods for the rural fruits of labor and land; and with the inner rings nearest the town specializing on the goods dearer to transport, while the farther out low-rent-generating acres are growing the goods cheaper to transport.

Knowing Adam Smith, Thünen arrived at his own model determining wages and rents before David Ricardo (or Edward West or Robert Malthus). But publishing only in German, and in several installments of a lengthy and intricate book, Thünen's work of genius is primarily admired by the public at a distance while serving as an occult mine for hundreds of German dissertation writers to sift over and sniff at.

Among geographers and location theorists, Thünen is a founding God. What John Bates Clark did at the end of the nineteenth century in formulating a theory of distributive shares, in terms of the marginal productivities of factors of production, Thünen had already done in the 1842 and 1850 installments to his original 1826 *The Isolated State.* Since J. B. Clark (like his son John Maurice Clark) was notorious for never reading anybody and having to work out his ideas for himself, and since to this day a full translation of Thünen into English is lacking, we undoubtedly face here another example of Robert K. Merton's doubletons of independent scientific discovery.[1] Only Alfred Marshall among the modern greats "professed" to be much influenced by Thünen: and Schumpeter is probably right to insin-

[1] Again in the Merton manner, Clark's 1889 breakthrough had simultaneous quasi-independent marginal-productivity discoveries on the part of such diverse scholars as Stuart Wood, Philip Wicksteed, Vilfredo Pareto, Enrico Barone, Léon Walras, Knut Wicksell, and Alfred Marshall. On the sociology and history of science, see Robert K. Merton (1973).

uate the quoted verb, since Marshall's sanctimonious acknowledgement provides a self-serving downplaying of Marshall's more important borrowing from Augustin A. Cournot.[2]

Whatever his neglect, Thünen would merit first-rank fame in the annals of economic theory if he had written no more than the following brief lines:

> The significance of capital we have measured by the increase in the product of the labor of a man which results from an increase in the capital with which he works. Here labor is a constant, capital a varying magnitude.
>
> When, on the other hand, we consider capital as remaining constant and the number of workers as varying, we realize in a large business that the significance of labor and the share of labor in the product is determined by the increase in the product which results from the addition of another laborer [Thünen, *Der Isolierte Staat,* 1930 ed., p. 584; trans. in Douglas, 1934, pp. 36–37].

With these lines, the primitive implicit marginalism involved in classical Ricardian rent theory graduates into neoclassical marginal productivity.

Before proceeding to substantive analysis of Thünen's system, let me mention that two clouds have always hung over his name. The first, and less important one, was connected with Eugen von Böhm-Bawerk's need to clear the way for his own positive theory of capital and interest by annihilating all earlier theories (and theorists) of the subject. Thünen is indicted and convicted by Böhm as holding a "productivity theory of interest": in allegedly *merely assuming* that capital projects exist that do yield a saving of labor greater than the labor needed to produce the capital goods themselves, Thünen is accused by Böhm of the logical fallacy of *petitio principii*—he is begging the question that needs to be faced and resolved. However, as Böhm's admirer Knut Wicksell had to point out, the scientist has no choice but to beg every such question in the sense that ultimately a Newton must accept how it is that apples do fall; and that it is not in the power of an Einstein to deduce why Mercury must lag in the way that telescopes confirm it does and that the truth of general relativity theory would entail. (Böhm's own "third cause of interest," the alleged and merely assumed superior technical productivity of time-involving processes, is ultimately just as question begging and inescapably so.)[3]

The other reason for Thünen's disrepute in certain quarters is Thünen's own fault. He spent years and gallons of ink on his weird doctrine of the natural wage, and I use the adjective "weird" advisedly. One of my purposes in an appendix is to show that critics have been both too harsh and too kind to Thünen on the topic of his natural wage. When historians of thought parrot the phrase that Thünen was the first to apply the differential calculus to political economy, they could add that Thünen was also one of the first to misapply it to our subject. In this paper's text I confine myself mostly to Thünen's timeless land-and-labor model, a magnificent edifice and one that still can benefit from modern treatment.

Here are a few suggestions to a reader in a filial mood wishing to salute Thünen's bicentennial. Arthur H. Leigh (1946) provides the best modern survey of Thünen's capital theory and natural wage labyrinth. Horst C. Rechtenwald (1973) gives a photograph and abridgments from Leigh, along with an evaluation by Edgar Salin (1958). Erich Schneider (1934) provides a good biographical account. Mark Blaug

[2] For Clark on Thünen, see J. B. Clark (1914, pp. 321–24). For Marshall's testimony, see Arthur C. Pigou (1925, pp. 359–60) and J. A. Schumpeter (1954, pp. 465–68).

[3] Cf. E. von Böhm-Bawerk (1884, 1889). None of this is to deny that there are arbitrarinesses in Thünen's program to measure capital in terms of stored-up labor. One purpose of my Appendix is to clean up Thünen's capital model so that it is logically consistent and complete.

(1962, 1968) overlaps with Schumpeter (1954, pp. 465–68). An abridged translation of *The Isolated State,* with some biography and emphasis on geographers' location theory, is provided by Peter Hall, ed. (1966). For the economics treasures in Part Two, Section 1 of *The Isolated State,* see the translation provided in Bernard W. Dempsey (1960, pp. 187–367). But read with caution the extensive defenses of Thünen's natural wage. Hall (1966, p. xii) recommends as a definitive commentary on Thünen's theory of agricultural location that in German by Asmus Petersen (1944). Martin Beckmann and Thomas Marschak (1955) give a brief look at Thünen's system from a modern viewpoint.

Thünen's Rings

Someone, somewhere, must surely have provided an exact and complete version of Thünen's space model. Here is my stripped-down version.

All labor is alike, free to move either to country or town. All land is alike except for distance from town. All people (laborers or landowners), wherever they permanently reside, have identical (homothetic) tastes at all income levels, involving a city-produced good (cloth) and two country-produced goods (vegetables dear to transport, and grain cheap to transport).

I ignore the fact that the city good might require for its production raw materials from the countryside. To keep all capital out of this Act 1, I assume cloth is produced instantaneously by labor alone at constant returns to scale.[4] Each farm good has its smooth first-degree-homogeneous production function that is concave in its labor and land inputs. (In short, neoclassical conditions obtain: the law of diminishing returns; constant returns to scale; well-defined limit ratios for [Δoutput/Δland, Δoutput/Δlabor], and so forth.) The case of fixed coefficients, where marginal products are not defined, will also be discussed in an example. Three possibilities are of interest: both farm goods have the same labor/land intensities; grain is the more land/labor intensive of the two goods at all wage/rent ratios; grain is the less land/labor intensive in the above sense.

The simplest version of Thünen's rings of specialization is then supposed to follow:

1. Immediately around the town comes a circle where only hard-to-transport vegetables can bid successfully for the limited nearby acres of land.
2. Outside of this first ring comes an annulus in which easier-to-ship grain is grown. (With more farm goods, Thünen envisages more distinct zones of specialization. Also, for him, the same product may have to be produced farther out by a different and more "land intensive" method.)
3. At the farthest extremity of cultivation comes the endogenously determined *external margin,* where land rent has fallen to zero because the cost of transporting town cloth outward and farm products inward has lowered farm-goods' prices relative to prices for city-goods and has reduced the economical density of labor to land. Beyond this frontier land is a free good.

Some questions remain open to this day:

(a) Are vegetables shipped outward as well as inward, in exchange for the grain needed by residents of the first circle? Could the grain received from this outward trade ever be for barter with city workers for first-circle residents' cloth needs?

(b) Can people in a zone of specialization produce also some of the other goods they

[4] It is agreed that a town is a town because certain activities involve, at least for a range, *increasing* returns to scale, specialization, and the division of labor. I assume the town is large enough so that all internal and external economies of scale in cloth production have been exhausted, after which all variations in cloth output involve proportional variations in town labor input, and market competition can be treated as if it were perfect.

desire for their own consumption? Must they?

(c) So long as the rural good that is cheapest to transport is also most labor-intensive, and therefore most sparing in its requirement for limited nearby land, the pattern of specialization zones is quite intuitive. But suppose the good dear to transport is also the good that is most land/labor-intensive, can it still usurp the inner position where land is so scarce?

(d) Can it really be universally true that the labor/land intensity drops with distance from the city? As in the case just mentioned, when the farm good cheapest to transport happens to be most labor intensive, couldn't we encounter higher labor/land intensity in the farther-out ring than prevails in the circle nearest to town?

Rigorous proofs are seen not to be superfluous luxuries. They are indispensable for true understanding and for answering long-open questions.

The One-Farm-Good Case

To tune up our analytical engines, start with the simplest case of essentially cloth and grain only. (If vegetables had the same transport cost and production function as grain, the two-farm-good model would degenerate essentially into the present one-farm-good case.)

Intuition tells us:

1. A preassigned labor supply will divide itself, at the direction of competition's Invisible Hand, between town labor, L_0, and labor smeared out over the plain in a density relative to land that diminishes along radial spokes emanating from the city.

2. Town labor receives in wages all of the town cloth product, its real wage in cloth being set by the technical productivity constant in the cloth-labor production function.

3. Town labor spends part of its real income on cloth. Part it barters for grain, paying the delivered-price of grain (the price in terms of cloth at the town center of the Thünen circles), as set by the auction market to balance supply and demand involving town and rural exports.

4. Remember all rural labor, in close to town or far out, must get the same real wage in utility terms—which must also equal town labor's utility wage. People migrate from low to high utility-wage places, thereby bidding down wages at the latter places, bidding up wages at the former, and achieving stationary equilibrium only when real-utility wage equalization has been attained.

5. Of course, equality of real wage, near and far from town, does not mean that workers at the two places enjoy equal real wage rates in both grain and in cloth. Actually, neither of these can be equal along different circumferences. At far circumferences, real wage rates in cloth are low because of transport-cost-losses in moving cloth and grain; but out there real wage rates in grain must be compensatingly high as a condition of equilibrium under labor mobility. Labor thins out there until, by the law of diminishing-returns acting in reverse, its grain wage-product has risen enough to keep labor contented in utility terms. (As Thünen knew, if some people liked country life or country goods more than others did, people would sort themselves out to where they most want to be and it would not be meaningful to say wage rates are equal everywhere; what is meaningful is that auction markets bid up and down the delivered price ratios between grain and cloth, until labor's location is endogenously determined and all markets clear. I ignore all differences in tastes.)

6. Land is not mobile. Its rent far from town, measured in either grain or cloth, can and will stay permanently lower than the real rents of similar acres that are located nearer town. The rent rate (in grain) of land r radial miles from town, $y(r)$ is

determinate as soon as the labor/land intensity at that place r, $L(r)$, is known. Both $y(r)$ and $L(r)$ fall off with distance r and do so in accordance with simultaneous equations. Today, thanks essentially to Thünen, J. B. Clark, and Philip H. Wicksteed (1894), we know that the real rent rate at any place is the same whether determined as a Ricardian residual or as a neoclassical marginal productivity. At the outer perimeter of cultivation, land rent has dropped to zero (the condition that defines endogenously the external margin of cultivation).

Where do landowners live and consume in this scenario? One possibility, perhaps in Thünen's mind and convenient for me to stick with here, is that rent collectors are permanently rooted on the acres they own. (A second possibility would be that of absentee ownership, where all rents earned on land are paid in kind there but are exchanged for consumption goods in town. A third possibility, which also calls out for future examination, is to make landowner's location an endogenous variable to be determined by their own utility maximization as footloose rentiers.)

7. Now that I've supplied technology and tastes, my model will be complete when I've specified the exact nature of transport costs to move grain and cloth (and vegetables when we return to multiple farm products). Thünen devotes much thought to realistic transport technology for his time and region. Often this involves an element of cost that is constant for each mile a particular good travels. Thus, from an F.O.B. price intercept, the delivered C.I.F. price would rise linearly.

My transport-cost functions are made even simpler in this first stripped-down version. Samuelson (1954) introduced the "iceberg" model to obviate in trade models the need to handle new industries whenever positive transport costs are met. By serendipity, Thünen himself had already noted the case where grain is moved by oxen, who must eat some of that grain while moving it a mile—so that some fraction of the grain moved can be conceived of as melting away in the iceberg fashion as the necessary cost of moving it a unit distance.

My iceberg assumption entails that

a) Price of town cloth delivered r miles from town, $P_0(r)$, must rise like $P_0^0 e^{a_0 r}$, where P_0^0 is the F.O.B. price of cloth in town and a_0 is the percent of melting of cloth per mile of transport. (On convenient semi-log diagrams, $P_0(r)$ rises linearly from its in-town intercept; and, it will be seen, $P_1(r)$ falls linearly.)

b) If price of grain delivered in the city is P_1^0, then it becomes cheaper as we move out r distance into the plain. Its price at $r, P_1(r)$, decays away like $P_1^0 e^{-a_1 r}$, where a_1 is the melting coefficient for grain. All this presupposes that cloth is in fact moving outward in positive amounts between 0 and r; and that grain is moving inward in positive amounts between r and 0.[5]

Figure 1 plots the town-good and country-good case, giving only a quarter arc of the perfect circles. Town is at the circles' center in 1(a). The outer circumference is at the boundary of purposeful cultivation, R miles from town. To depict the declining labor density of cultivation along each radius, the circles are drawn more closely bunched together near town. By radial symmetry, along any one intermediate circumference, r and $[W(r)/P_0(r), W(r)/P_1(r), y_1(r)]$ are everywhere the same, as will be total production and aggregate consumptions of resident laborers and landowners, $[q_1(r), c_0(r), c_1(r)]$.

Figures 1(b)–1(f) show the equilibrium variation with distance from town of the different variables. The intercept depicting in 1(b) the grain-cloth price ratio in

[5] Actually, my version has need only for *relative* prices, not absolute prices: for $[P_i(r)/P_j(r), W(r)/P_i(r), y_1(r)]$. If you could imagine a transport-free gold numeraire you might use it to express fictional absolute prices—a harmless and redundant convention.

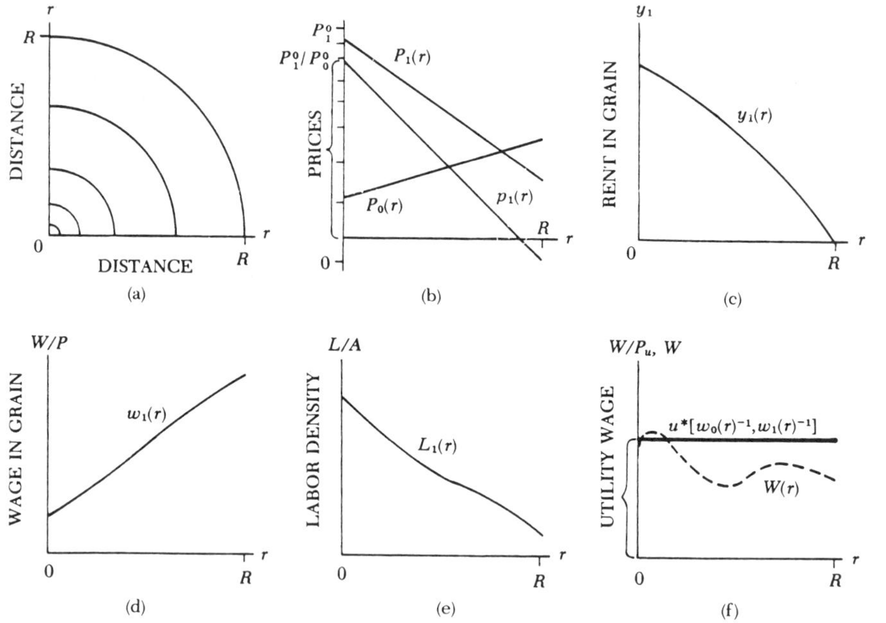

Figure 1.

town, $(P_1/P_0)^0$ as shown by the bracket, plays a key role in generating *all* the other relations once technology and transport-cost parameters are known.

In 1(b), the exponential decay of the grain-to-cloth price ratio follows from my "iceberg" assumption, as an outward flow of "melting" cloth and an inward flow of "melting" grain have their terms of trade set to agree with no-arbitrage-profit conditions. (The diagram is semi-log to make the exponential curves graph as straight lines.)

In 1(c) the grain rent rate drops with r as fewer and fewer laborers are able to earn the common utility wage on each acre of land.

In 1(d) is shown the rise in grain wage needed to compensate the workers for the higher relative cost of town goods when the latter must be carted far from town (and exchanged for the grain that is destined to be expensively carted into town).

In 1(e) is shown how sharply labor/land density must drop off as the grain wage rises and the grain rent falls.

Finally, 1(f)'s solid line shows the horizontal pattern of wage utility, $u^*(r)$. The broken curve shows the nominal wage at each point r: whether it rises or falls as we leave town depends on whether the fraction of income that people spend on cloth relative to what they spend on grain is at each r greater than a_1/a_0; when cloth is preponderantly important, the nominal wage, $W(r)$, must rise to compensate for the rise in $P_1(r)/P_0(r)$; etc. The bracketed intercept for u^* is one of our two basic endogenous unknowns, along with the bracketed $(P_1/P_0)^0$ in 1(b).

Important remark: We have here a set of simultaneous equations, whose solution yields our determinate equilibrium. If $(P_1/P_0)^0$ is initially set too high in 1(b), then the town level of wage-earners' utility would be too low. That means too many workers would be able to live in the country earning the initial level of town utility. The external boundary would be too far away for true equilibrium: so much grain would be grown over the swollen acreage as to inundate town with grain, leading to erosion of the too-high initial $(P_1/P_0)^0$ ratio.

The reader can show how too low an initial $(P_1/P_0)^0$ would lead to too-high common utility, to too-few rural workers and too-small acreage and grain production, and thus to a subsequent bidding up of $(P_1/P_0)^0$. All the related diagrams will be permanently compatible only after the system finds, by trial and error of competition, the correct equilibrium level for $(P_1/P_0)^0$.

Mathematical Derivation

An *indirect utility* function conveniently handles the demand functions for the town and farm goods, defined for people in terms of the prices they face at their given location, (P_0, P_1), and their total income, Y:

$$u^*[P_0/Y, P_1/Y] = Yu^*[P_0, P_1], \tag{1}$$

where we embody the assumption that all consumers have identical, homothetic tastes. The amounts they demand of the respective goods, $[C_0, C_1]$ are known from modern duality theory to be given by

$$C_i = V_i[P_0/Y, P_1/Y] = Y\,V_i[P_0, P_1],\ (i = 0,\ 1) \tag{2}$$

where

$$V_i[P_0/Y, P_1/Y] = -\partial \log_e u^*[P_0/Y, P_1/Y]/\partial(P_i/Y). \tag{3}$$

The production functions for cloth and grain are given respectively by

$$Q_0 = f_0 L_0 \tag{4}$$

$$Q_1 = A_1 f_1[L_1/A_1],\ f_1'[\ ] > 0 > f_1''[\ ] \tag{5}$$

where L_0 is town labor and (L_1, A_1) are labor and acres of land used for grain production. If we write the density of labor to land at any radial distance r from town as $L_1(r)$ and the density of grain grown there as $q_1(r)$, (5) takes on the normalized form

$$q_1(r) = f_1[L_1(r)]. \tag{6}$$

The area of a circle with radius R is given by

$$\int_0^R dr[\int_0^{2\pi} r d\theta] = \int_0^R 2\pi r dr = \pi R^2. \tag{7}$$

Therefore, the total of labor applied to the farm good, spread around the countryside out to the frontier R and with the labor/land density of $L_1(r)$, is given by

$$2\pi \int_0^R L_1(r) r dr = L_1 = L - L_0. \tag{8}$$

Here L is the total of labor supply preassigned by Thünen, and which is to be endogenously divided between town and the various acres of the countryside.

The real wages are given respectively by the marginal products

$$W/P_0 = w_0(0) = f_0; \tag{9}$$

$$W/P_1 = w_1(r) = f_1'[L_1(r)],\quad L_1(r) > 0,\ 0 < r \leqq R < \infty. \tag{10}$$

In town there is no rent. (With Thünen we neglect site-value scarcity within a city. Our town is an idealized point.) The rural rent, expressed in grain, is given by

$$y_1(r) = f_1[L_1(r)] - L_1(r) w_1(r),\quad 0 < r \leqq R. \tag{11}$$

With Thünen we make the realistic assumption that at some low-enough positive labor density, λ_1, further abundance of land would add nothing to total product.

By definition of R as the external margin, it is the root that makes the following expression zero

$$y_1(R) = 0 = f_1[L_1(R)] - L_1(R) f_1'[L_1(R)] \equiv f_1[\lambda_1] - \lambda_1 f_1'[\lambda_1]. \tag{12}$$

For all values of $L_1(r)$ satisfying the following

$$0 < L_1(\mathrm{r}) < \lambda_1 < \infty, \qquad (13)$$

land rent will be positive.

It remains only to write down how the price ratio of grain to cloth must fall as we make the r distance to town greater. Spatial arbitrage ensures that for every r, where that grain destined for town is auctioned off for what it will bring locally in terms of cloth of town origin, we must have

$$P_1/P_0 = p_1(r) = p_1(0)e^{-a_0 r}e^{-a_1 r}, \quad 0 \leq r \leq R. \qquad (14)$$

From (9), (10), and (14), we deduce the real-wage relation

$$\begin{aligned} w_0(r) &= p_1(r)w_1(r) \\ &= p_1(0)e^{-a_0 r}e^{-a_1 r}f'[L_1(r)]. \end{aligned} \qquad (15)$$

Knowing both real wage rates in terms of $p_1(0)$, we can write down the real wage rate in utility at each point in space and equate them all to town workers' utility wage:

$$\begin{aligned} u^*[w_0(0)^{-1}, w_1(0)^{-1}] &= f_0 u^*[1, p_1(0)] \\ &= u^*[w_0(r)^{-1}, w_1(r)^{-1}] \\ &= w_1(r)u^*[p_1(r)^{-1}, 1] \\ &= w_1(r)u^*[p_1(0)^{-1}e^{a_0 r}e^{a_1 r}, 1]. \end{aligned} \qquad (16)$$

This tells us how fast the grain real wage must rise with distance from town

$$w_1(r) = f_0 u^*[1, p_1(0)] / u^*[p_1(0)^{-1}e^{a_0 r}e^{a_1 r}, 1]. \qquad (17)$$

From (17) and (10) we deduce how fast labor density must fall as we move away from town. For each value of $p_1(0)$, we put $f_1'[L_1(r)]$ on (17)'s left-hand side and solve the resulting implicit relation for its $L_1(r)$ root. When r is large enough to make the calculated $L_1(r)$ root small enough to equal (13)'s λ_1, we have found the limiting R of profitable land cultivation.

We still lack the final basic relation needed to solve for the $p_1(0)$ parameter. We can provide this for Thünen if, borrowing a leaf from the modern book of international trade theory, we require balance-of-trade equilibrium between (i) what town workers will want to buy of delivered grain (spending their $f_0 L_0$ wage income and facing the delivered price ratio, $p_1(0)$ in town) and (ii) the grain that will get to town after rural laborers and landowners have decided how much of the grain that they produce they will want to devote to exports (a decision made in terms of total grain income at each place and in view of the price ratio for the two goods that prevails at that place).

The demand functions of (2), combined with our transport-cost designations, enable us to write down the final balance-of-trade relation as follows:

$$\begin{aligned} &[L - \int_0^R 2\pi r L_1(r)dr]\, V_1[1, p_1(0)] f_0 \\ &= \int_0^R 2\pi r f_1[L_1(r)]\{1 - V_1[1/p_1(r), 1]\} e^{-a_1 r}dr. \end{aligned} \qquad (18)$$

Our previous discussion has established that every function that appears in (18) is determined once $p_1(0)$ is known. So (18) is itself essentially one implicit equation in the one unknown variable $p_1(0)$. That it will have a unique positive root under our postulated conditions can be demonstrated by modern analytical tools. Thünen's intuition is confirmed—a nice 200th birthday offering!

Remark: With each additional farm good, we have the additional requirement that its physical supply voluntarily brought to town must match the amount of it that will be voluntarily bought in town. The way that lands at each r distance from town are allocated to the productions of different farm goods are new unknowns, solvable so as to maximize land rent at each place. The spatial price and real-wage patterns are, as before, determined by spatial arbitrage conditions and by the labor mobility that equalizes utility wages. When Thünen perceived what spatial pricing and specialization patterns are admissible under competition, he was anticipating the methods and results of Kuhn-Tucker nonlinear programming (P. A. Samuelson, 1959, Appendix).

Examples

Suppose all people spend half their incomes on town-produced cloth and half on rural-produced grain. Negating neoclassical smoothness of the production function for grain, let 1 of grain require f_1^{-1} units of labor input and 1 of land input.

The indirect utility function and demand functions are given by

$$u^* = \tfrac{1}{2} I/(P_0 P_1)^{1/2} = \tfrac{1}{2}(w_0 w_1)^{1/2} \quad (19)$$

$$c_0 = \tfrac{1}{2} I/P_0,\ c_1 = \tfrac{1}{2} I/P_1. \quad (20)$$

The production functions are given by

$$\begin{aligned} Q_0 = f_0 L_0 &= f_0(L - L_1) \\ &= f_0[L - \int_0^R 2\pi r L_1(r) dr] \end{aligned} \quad (21)$$

$$q_1(r) = \mathrm{Min}[f_1 L_1(r), 1]. \quad (22)$$

Between town and the frontier where $r = R$, we have

$$\begin{aligned} &q_1(r) \equiv 1,\ L_1(r) \equiv f_1^{-1} \\ &q_1(r)/L_1(r) \equiv f_1. \end{aligned} \quad (23)$$

Now that our $f_1[L_1(r)]$ lacks a defined derivative at $L_1(r)$ of f_1^{-1}, we have lost our marginal productivity definition of the real wage in grain. We know that $w_1(r)$ cannot exceed f_1; how much it falls short of f_1 determines the magnitude of land rent, $y_1(r)$.

Fortunately, for each value of the $p_1(0)$ parameter, there can be only one spatial pattern of the real grain wage that will give workers everywhere the same utility wage as in town. Our determining relations are, from (16),

$$\begin{aligned} (u^*)^2 &= w_0(0) w_1(0) = f_0^2 p_1(0)^{-1} \\ &= w_0(r) w_1(r) = w_1(r)^2 p_1(r) \\ &= w_1(r)^2 p_1(0) e^{-a_0 r} e^{-a_1 r} \end{aligned} \quad (24)$$

$$\begin{aligned} w_1(r) &= f_0 e^{(1/2) a_0 r} e^{(1/2) a_1 r} / p_1(0) \\ f_1 &= w_1(R) \\ &= f_0 e^{(1/2) a_0 R} e^{(1/2) a_1 R} p_1(0)^{-1} \end{aligned} \quad (25)$$

$$R^* = 2(a_0 + a_1)^{-1} \log_e [p_1(0) f_1 / f_0]. \quad (26)$$

The basic balance of payments relation of (18) then becomes

$$\begin{aligned} &\tfrac{1}{2} f_0[1 - \int_0^{R^*} 2\pi r f_1 dr] / p_1(0) \\ &= \tfrac{1}{2} \int_0^{R^*} 2\pi r [1 - \tfrac{1}{2}] e^{-a_1 r} dr. \end{aligned} \quad (27)$$

We solve this for

$$\begin{aligned} p_1(0) &= \frac{f_0[L - \pi(R^*)^2]}{\int_0^{R^*} \pi r e^{-a_1 r} dr} \\ &= a_1^2 \frac{f_0[L - \pi(R^*)^2]}{\pi[1 - e^{-a_1 R^*} - a_1 R^* e^{-a_1 R^*}]}. \end{aligned} \quad (28)$$

With $p_1(0)$ known, $[p_1(r), w_0(r), w_1(r), y_1(r), c_0(r), c_1(r), L_1(r), L_0, C_0(0), C_1(0)]$ and all relevant unknowns can be solved for.

The reader can replace $\mathrm{Min}[f_1 L_1(r), 1]$ by the CES function $[f_1^{-1} L_1(r)^{-1} + 1^{-1}]^{-1}$ and solve the resulting example, making use of the marginal productivity relation (10) now that $q_1(r)/f_1[L_1(r)]$ is open to an infinity of choices. (Remark: If labor's marginal product goes to infinity as its density to land goes to zero, show that "iceberg" transport costs entail that $R = \infty$ and land's rent never quite disappears; the Cobb-Douglas choice for $f_1[L_1(r)]$ of $L_1(r)^{1/2}$, or the CES choice of $[L_1(r)^{1/4} + 1]^4$, will illustrate.)

Two or More Farm Goods

One sees how any number of farm goods are to be handled in the Thünen model. The present impressionistic sketch can stay with the case of two farm goods. In addition to L_0 devoted to production in town of cloth, Q_0, we have a pair of farm goods: $L_1(r)$ is the density of labor applied to production of vegetables, a commodity expensive to transport because its $e^{a_1 r}$ is high; $L_2(r)$ is the density of labor applied to production of grain, an easily transported good with $e^{a_2} < e^{a_1}$.

When we go beyond Thünen's simplest picture of separate zones, each of which specializes on a single good—and we cannot avoid doing so—we shall need to determine the fractions of the land at each place in the given zone that are devoted to the respective farm goods.[6] I write these fractions as:

$$[g_1(r), g_2(r)] \geqq 0,\ g_1(r) + g_2(r) = 1. \quad (29)$$

We have as many production functions and marginal productivity relations as there are farm goods:

$$q_i(r) = f_i[L_i(r)],\ (i = 1,2) \quad (6')$$

$$w_i(r) = f_i'[L_i(r)], f_i'[\ ] > 0 > f_i''[\ ]. \quad (10')$$

In the demand relations of (1)–(3), we flesh out $u^*[P_0, P_1]$ and $V_i[P_0, P_1]$ to become $u^*[P_0, P_1, P_2]$ and $V_i[P_0, P_1, P_2]$—and so forth for goods $(0, 1, \ldots, n)$.

Our total labor supply in (8) now becomes

$$L = L_0 + \sum_1^2 \int_0^R 2\pi g_j(r) L_j(r) r dr. \quad (8')$$

Now our spatial-arbitrage price gradients become more complicated. It being assumed that town laborers require something of every farm good and all country folk require some positive amount of cloth, there must be an innermost circle within which every farm good is travelling toward town and is exchangeable at each radius point for outmoving cloth. Call the radius of this innermost circle $\underline{R}$, with $\underline{R}$ not greater than the R of the external margin. Inside this inner circle, (14) generalizes easily to

$$P_j/P_0 = p_j(r) = p_j(0)e^{-a_0 r}e^{-a_j r}, \quad 0 \leqq r \leqq \underline{R} < R\ (j = 1,2). \quad (14')$$

Similar relations would hold for all of n goods, whatever n might be.

Suppose that Thünen was right in believing, outside an inner circle that exports vegetables to town, there is an outer annulus that exports to town only grain. Then throughout this outer zone, (14′) does assuredly apply for $j = 2$, corresponding to grain. It, however, need not apply for perishable vegetables. What does obtain? Only the spatial arbitrage inequality applies:

$$P_1/P_0 = p_1(r) \geqq p_1(0)e^{-a_0 r}e^{-a_1 r}, \quad \underline{R} \leq r \leq R. \quad (14'')$$

If the strong inequality obtains in (14″), it cannot be the case that vegetables are being shipped from $\underline{R} + h$ inward to $\underline{R}$ where they would be exchangeable for cloth. Although $p_1(\underline{R} + h)$ can exceed

$$p_1(\underline{R})e^{-a_0 h}e^{-a_1 h},$$

it cannot exceed this by more than a limit set by its transport cost relative to cloth's transport cost. Spatial arbitrage requires that

$$e^{-a_0 h}e^{-a_1 h} \leqq \frac{p_1(\underline{R} + h)}{p_1(\underline{R})} \leqq e^{-a_0 h}e^{a_1 h}. \quad (30)$$

Were the left-hand strong inequality to hold, vegetables would be just capable of being shipped inward from $\underline{R} + h$ to $\underline{R}$; were the right-hand strong inequality to hold, both vegetables and cloth could be shipped outward for exchange with grain there.

In the important singular case where grains and vegetables have technologies that involve the same labor/land intensities—so that the $f_i[L]$ are the same $f[L]$ function in (6′)—it can be deduced that

[6] A small conceptual problem arises when more than one good is produced at points that are all the same r distance from town. How is the land corresponding to an element of circular area to be allocated to the different productions? To ensure that no unnecessary rural cross-shipments be introduced, I imagine space covered by a fine network of hexagonal fields. In every local region, however small, the relative number of hexagons devoted to each good is made to agree with the desired production ratios. Thünen, as a realistic observer, never pushed the assumption of constant returns to scale to its logical limit as I am doing; he thought of actual Prussian farms.

This is a place to mention the element of jointness of production that is entailed by cultivation systems that follow rotation of different crops so as to enhance land's steady-state productivity. I duck all joint products here and do so with a better conscience because of the tactic of leaving to the Appendix discussions of time phasing (of which crop rotation would be one special case).

outward export of vegetables is quite forbidden. (If this outrages readers' intuition, which suggests to them that each zone might profitably specialize completely and exchange products to mutual advantage, remember that constant returns to scale does not afford the Smith-Young advantages to specialization that we intuitively expect in many real-life situations.)

At $r = \underline{R}$, by definition of $\underline{R}$ as the watershed between the zones from which town consumers get their vegetables and their grain, the ratio $p_2(\underline{R})/p_1(\underline{R})$ is precisely unity—the critical and invariant cost ratio of the two farm goods. Nearer in than $\underline{R}$, the vegetables have risen more in price than the grain because of the postulated difference in accruing transport costs. So, inside the inner ring, vegetables displace grain in profitability.

Unwary readers think to reverse this argument as one moves outward from $\underline{R}$. But this begs the question of the proper flow of goods and does so by proffering a false answer. Beyond $\underline{R}$, communities have the option of growing their own vegetables, and were they to exercise this option no transport costs would accrue on them.

Competition's Invisible Hand will contrive that people out there import cloth in barter for grain exports, while being self-sufficient in vegetables. This is a provable theorem, not a probability.[7]

Thus, $p_2(r)$ falls exponentially all the way to the external margin. However, with similar labor/land intensities for the two goods, $p_1(r)$ falls at its exponential rate only to the $\underline{R}$ watershed. Beyond that, $p_1(\underline{R} + h)/p_2(\underline{R} + h)$ stabilizes at the cost ratio of unity, with $p_1(\underline{R} + h)$ falling between $\underline{R}$ and R only at grain's slower exponential rate.

In this singular case of equal factor intensities, it is indeed the case that the overall rural labor/land ratio, no matter how demand-tastes parcel out the $[g_1(\underline{R} + h), g_2(\underline{R} + h)]$ fractions, will fall uniformly as the distance from town grows. (With fixed coefficients, that of course couldn't be true—even though land rent would still fall steadily. With a few different techniques to choose from out of a book of Robinsonian blue prints, as one moves out of town the labor/land ratio will discontinuously travel down steps, alternating between steps and their riders. A nice example of such a finite-number of activities model is provided by Thünen's assertion of the three-field system as paying only on land far enough from town to bear low rent-wage ratios.)

Geographical Summary of Two-Farm-Good Case

Figure 2 provides almost full verification of Thünen's specialization rings in the case where the farm goods have the same factor intensities.

The inner zone of 2(a) grows only vegetables, some of which are exported to town in exchange for cloth. The outer zone exports grain to town, but also grows vegetables for worker and landowner consumption.

In the semi-log diagram of 2(b), the price of vegetables (in cloth) at first falls faster as we move outward from town than does the price of grain. This reflects the latter's relative cheapness to transport. Beyond A, where r is at $\underline{R}$, the watershed between the zones, only grain moves to town. Everywhere in the outer-zone the price ratio between vegetables

[7] If I knew Thünen's text better, I could judge whether this is an old finding. As a realist, Thünen knew about farmers growing their own vegetables: but that could merely reflect his correct apprehension that kitchen gardens are a natural *joint* product, a phenomenon ruled out here. In the same way, I would have to refuse full marks to a student who thought he was proving the present theorem by pointing to the realistic fact that vegetables would spoil completely before they could be shipped very far out beyond $\underline{R}$: in the present iceberg model, some would get through and thus we are back to having to distinguish between a *quantitative* and a *qualitative* necessity.

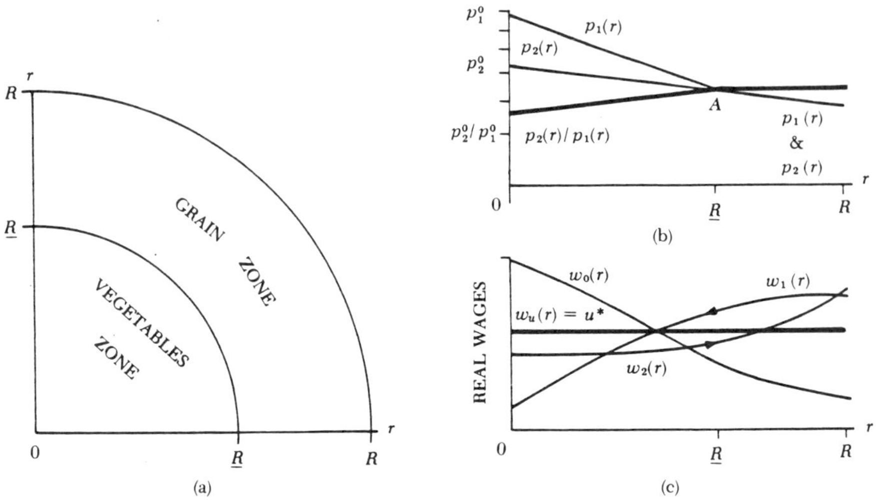

Figure 2.

and grain stays at its unit relative costs of production. Hence, despite vegetables' dearness for transport, its price now drops relative to cloth's at the same gentle rate that grain's transport costs entail. (The prices follow straight lines on semi-log charts.) In 2(c), the real wage rate in cloth falls steadily. To compensate, the real wage rates in the farm goods have to rise. The real wage in utility is thus able to be the same everywhere. With the real wage rates of farm-goods rising, real land rents must correspondingly fall. Reading Thünen's text closely, we can only with charity attribute to him comprehension of the post-1953 factor-price-frontier concept. Like David Ricardo, he glimpsed this tradeoff frontier from a considerable distance and through some haze.

Factor Intensity Complications

I have left to the end the intricate question of whether a good that is most expensive to transport, if it were sufficiently land-intensive, could find itself priced out of the town's innermost neighborhood by virtue of the natural scarcity of such near-to-town land. Peter Hall writes: "It is necessary to stress this [intensity] point because . . . in the German literature . . . there has been the most fundamental confusion about it" (1966, pp. xxx–xxxii). He goes on to quote reprovingly H. Weighman's assertion that "the central feature of the Thünen system is that intensity of cultivation rises towards the market"; and Theodor Brinkmann's similar contention: "Zones near to the market are locations of specifically intensive types of land use."

By contrast, Hall insists that ". . . the pattern of location which Thünen describes . . . in no way follows any simple rule of intensity . . . Thus in the second ring . . . there is forestry, a very extensive [low labor/land] activity . . . And in the sixth or outermost ring we find a whole series of intensive cash crops such as oilseeds, hops, tobacco and flax" (p. xxx). Hall, warning against over-simple definitions of "intensity," concludes with the flat claim: ". . . the general rule will be that the site nearest the [town] market will be appropriated by that product which experiences the greatest cost reduction nearer the market, or in other words, the greatest cost increase away from the market" (p. xxxii).

In my iceberg model, where all costs are unambiguously defined, such a general rule, if it is to have any content, must presumably be interpreted to assert: vegetables, whose cost gradient is steepest as one moves away from town, must outbid grain for acres nearest to town *even if vegetables are much more land/labor intensive.* Hall (1966, p. xxxii, n. 2) associates A. Petersen with this viewpoint of his.

My investigation of the point bears out that Hall is right in asserting that nearest to town, no matter how land-sparing the good cheap to transport is, it will be outbid by the good dearer to transport (and no matter how land intensive that good is.) But it would be wrong to assert the truly general rule that *the exports cheap to transport always arise farther out than the exports dear to transport.*

To provide a counter example to the most general rule, while at the same time putting to a severe and successful test Hall's assertion about the acres nearest to town being usurped by the good dearest to transport, I employ the following strong model.

Vegetables, dear to transport, are producible by land alone. Grain, cheap to transport, requires both labor and land and is unequivocally less land/labor intensive than vegetables. (Thus, let 1 of grain output require as inputs 1 of labor and 1 of land.)

We shall discover that equilibrium for this model involves four zones:

Paradoxically, the far hinterlands grow vegetables only, even though that is the good dearest to transport.

As Hall claims, the innermost zone also grows vegetables only, even though this is a good that is anything but sparing in its use of scarce nearby acres.

All town imports of grain come from the next nearest second zone. That zone also grows the vegetables that its laborers and landowners consume.

Then comes a third zone that grows grain destined for home use and to be shipped outward in exchange for vegetables and inward in exchange for cloth. (Some regions in the third zone might also grow their own vegetables, one supposes.)

As already mentioned, stretching forever without limit, comes the model's final zone of vegetable production.[8]

Why are all acres very far out used for vegetables? If no labor will go there—and footnote 8 shows that a high enough price of cloth will make workers refuse to go far out—those acres might as well produce what it is that they can produce. The total vegetables, produced over the infinite plain, would be infinite; but after transport cost, only a finite amount will get through to any inner radius.

Why can't innermost acres be used exclusively for grain? Suppose that were so, from $r = 0$ out to $r = \hat{R}$, a watershed where both goods can first be produced. At $\hat{R}$, vegetables are just beginning to pay. If, for the first time, they are beginning to pay it must be (for constant utility wages) because $p_1(\hat{R})/p_2(\hat{R})$ has risen relative to where it had been inside the first zone. But, being dearer to transport, its relative price has to have fallen. And so we have our needed logical contradiction

[8] Any violence done to the reader's intuition by this final result can be attributed to my polar model's strict assumptions: iceberg transport costs; literally zero labor required for good 1; fixed coefficients for good 2. In actual life, delivered cloth could become so expensive for workers far enough out that, realistically, no cheapness of the farm goods could induce them to live out there. That would define a *finite* external margin (which is ruled out by my extreme assumption that vegetables require land only). Far out landowners have rent per acre that yields ever-lower utility. Therefore, we might suppose that each ekes out a living by owning ever more acres. Since the model requires zero work of the landowners, this is no problem. But the mind does rather boggle at the prospect of an indivisible human being straddling over ever more expansive acres and doing all consuming on them.

from our false supposition, and we can rule out the supposition.

Why can't both goods be produced in the innermost zone? This also would lead to a contradiction: it would not permit real utility wages to stay the same and arbitrage-proof price gradients to prevail.

In the third and fourth zones, grain and cloth are moving outward and meeting vegetables moving inward. So $p_1(r)$ must resume falling with the same exponential gradient as in the first zone. Likewise $p_1(r)/p_2(r)$ must now fall with a gradient set by $e^{-a_1}e^{+a_2}$. How $p_2(r)$ behaves depends upon $e^{a_2}e^{-a_0}$; if cloth is cheaper to transport than grain, $e^{a_0} < e^{a_2}$, then $p_2(r)$ will rise; if $a_2 < a_0$, then $p_2(r)$ is ultimately falling.

Concluding Reflections and Solutions

Thünen's system is seen to be a grand one, and one grandly worked out by him. Hall's claim for it as "the world's first economic model" is a pardonable exaggeration (1966, p. xxi).

Thünen's model has in it elements of all of the following systems:

1. The Ricardo-Torrens theory of comparative advantage.
2. The Malthus-West-Ricardo theory of rent.
3. The Heckscher-Ohlin and Stolper-Samuelson theory of factors-and-goods pricing.
4. The Marx-Dimitriev-Leontief-Sraffa system of input-output.[9]

Moreover, Thünen has correctly perceived how his versions of those models operate under competition. Not only has he understood their positivistic features but, in addition, he has anticipated the Allyn Young, Frank Knight, and Dennis Robertson demonstration that charging competitive land rents is what leads to normative social efficiency (albeit possibly great inequalities and inequities).

Thus, Thünen would understand at once a demonstration by a modern economist that it would be wrong to allocate workers homesteads on which they alone are to work—wrong, even if the size of their acres was made lower near to town in order to achieve ethical equity. As each homesteader sought to acquire more land, or to hire more workers, preventing them from doing so would lead to deadweight loss. I think Thünen would also soon understand the point that an egalitarian society would want to distribute its land rents in *lump sum* transfer payments, the size of which payments would have to be geared to the worker's location, with transfer of goods being in the Pareto-efficient patterns that competitive spatial arbitrage would dictate.

It would be a mistake to think of Thünen's theory as applying to the frontier's wage. His is a complete theory of distribution. Moreover, he avoids the curse of general equilibrium models, in which all that can be said is that everything depends on everything else. His comparative statics is beautifully simple.

An increase in labor supply will raise land rent, extending the circle of cultivation. It will lower real wage rates.[10] (A

[9] To eliminate any vestige of time-phasing, I have ignored Thünen's insistence that town products use farm goods as raw materials and farm products use town products as inputs.

A part of Thünen's capital theory is his own assumption that rural production does require town products as inputs, and vice-versa for town production. This accelerates the drop in rent with distance from town and accentuates the thinning out of factor intensities on far-out acres. If Thünen's capital good, K, is producible by labor and itself without need for land inputs, I'd expect K to be produced in town and everywhere that it is used, thereby eliminating deadweight cross-haulage.

[10] As Thünen realized, when there is enough total labor, a second, third, . . . , and nth town will become viable. So, if the plain were really infinite in acreage, the longest-run returns to labor would be constant rather than diminishing. In each short run, when the number of towns is temporarily fixed, more L means more rent; but when a new town is formed and attracts labor away from settled to virgin lands, rents decline to a base level that corresponds to a

higher supply of capital—as in my Appendix rehabilitation of Thünen's capital theory—will tend to raise both wages and rents unless some particular pattern of substitutability between separate pairs of the three factors happens to obtain. Thus, if capital goods are robots, produced in town and serving as close substitutes for labor, an increase in their supply will be much like a higher-supply of L and will raise rents while lowering wages.)

A decrease in transport costs will also widen the circle of cultivation. But it will lower land rents and raise real wage rates.

By coincidence, Thünen anticipated contemporaneous as well as later theoretical discoveries. It is not surprising that his independent researches went beyond the findings of the mainstream of economics. Here is but one example.

Ricardian trade theory traditionally assumes zero factor mobility between countries or regions and 100 percent commodity mobility between countries or regions. Thünen's model works out the opposite case. Within a region, labor moves freely (on immobile land); goods move only at a cost. Where labor will locate was not a question that traditional trade theory considered, but Thünen did.

* * *

Modern geographers claim Thünen. That is their right. But economists like me, who are not all that taken with location theory, hail Thünen as more than a location theorist. His theory is a theory of general equilibrium.

Thünen belongs in the Pantheon with Léon Walras, John Stuart Mill, and Adam Smith. As Schumpeter would say, it is the inner ring of Valhalla they occupy.

hexagonal network of towns. With the earth a finite globe, all of whose good acres ultimately get settled, still further L must imply lower real wage ceteris paribus as land scarcity invokes the law of diminishing returns.

Appendix: Thünen's Natural Wage and His Capital Theory

Thünen who spent much of the last twenty years of life perfecting his "Natural wage," found his handiwork so good that he had its formula put on his gravestone.

His natural wage is the geometric mean of the Subsistence wage rate and the worker's Average Product: in his notation,

$$w^* = \sqrt{ap}.$$

In his 1934 Chicago lectures Paul Douglas, himself a do-gooder but already hooked on a marginal-product theory of wages, explained this natural wage as more the product of Thünen's warm heart than his cool intellect—a partial atonement on his part for the sad, hard fact that an extra worker brings down the earnings of charter-member workers even though these work as hard as before and are as deserving (P. H. Douglas, 1934, pp. 34–37). As a beginning student, I regarded this natural wage as a naive Aristotelean golden mean between the least that labor could be paid in the steady state and the most. Half a century later I can discern only a superficial resemblance between Thünen's formula and John Nash's threat-bargaining theory.

Actually, as the reader of Schumpeter (1954, pp. 465–67) or of Arthur H. Leigh (1946, 1968) will know, Thünen deduced his natural wage from a (rather odd) maximum problem, finding that wage as the root of a first-derivative equation. Almost universally Thünen has been hooted at for his natural wage.[11] One cannot say that posterity has been biased against him: in

[11] Bernard W. Dempsey (1960) is an exception. At the same time that we owe him gratitude for providing an English translation of Thünen's Volume II, Father Dempsey's defenses of the natural wage is subject to the same objections as are directed here against Thünen's own derivations.

my reading of the evidence, commentators have been both too hard and too soft on him; but the fact remains that a scrupulously just autopsy will find that Thünen's natural wage lacks both positivistic verisimilitude and normative optimality.

For the present purpose I reviewed a dozen commentaries on the derivation of the natural wage, but singly or all together they do not quite provide the needed fair and complete post-mortem.

Schumpeter's Version

Thünen, like Ricardo, is under the illusion that he can get rid of the complication of land and its rent by focussing on the external margin with zero rent. Grain is produced there by labor, and also by "capital" in Thünen's special sense of past labor stored up.

Schumpeter's scenario for Thünen is perhaps the simplest one. In effect, Schumpeter (1954, pp. 465–68) poses a Jevons-Wicksell point-input and point-output model. Labor at time t produces grain at time $t+\theta$ in the future. Call grain output p and labor-inputs' wages w. (These can be measured in numeraire of grain or anything else.) Profit or total interest is $p - w$. The rate of interest, earned on each unit of wage outlay and expressed as a percentage return for a time period equal to the lag θ, is $(p - w)/w$ and is called z.

Thünen envisages workers who can own capital; or, what is the same thing, capitalists who may also work for wages. It is rather odd, for the last century or this one, to regard workers' wages as the prime source of saving. If the interest rate z is positive, there must be positive profits earned on past accumulations and it would be strange for Thünen not to regard such incomes as also a source of saving. Thünen in effect turns Marx and Kalecki upside down and makes wages rather than profits the source of saving. Accordingly, I shall keep the story uncluttered by assuming that all non-wage income gets consumed: current saving, y, comes for each of society's identical workers from the surplus of their w wages over a postulated subsistence level of consumption, a: $y = w - a$. (Remark: Malthus, Ricardo, and Marx meant by "subsistence wage" the rate workers had to get to maintain and reproduce their supply of labor. Thünen's "subsistence wage" is to be understood mostly as equalling what consumers spend on consumption out of their wage income—beyond their property income that, in my model, they also spend on consumption. Leigh and others have denied that a is a recognizable constant; I see no reason not to give Thünen all the rope he needs, so that we can assay the logic of his conceptions.)

During and since World War II, economists have learned that experts in operations analysis often devote much hard and clever effort in maximizing some maximands that are not sensible goals for policy. Thünen offers a similar case. Posterity has scoffed at his assumption that society will, or ought to, want to maximize the current return earned on current saving.

Thünen says:

$$\text{Maximize } z \times y = [(p - w)/w]\,[w - a]. \tag{A1}$$

That is Thünen's major felony. It is a crime against normative economics, and against the positivistic economics of competitive behavior under laissez faire.

He compounds this felony by a major misdemeanor, which is a crime against logic. In Thünen's maximization, and with Schumpeter blowing no public whistle, a and p are both held constant at prescribed levels; only w is to be varied, and it is allegedly at our disposal to vary w arbitrarily.

There is no logical objection to regarding consumption out of wages as being frozen at a. (Only the facts are against the relevance of this.) But, as we shall see, it runs counter to the logic of Thünen's own model, to believe that what changes w won't also change p.

Mathematically, Thünen carries out an absurd purpose:

Subject to $p = \bar{p}$ and $a = \bar{a}$, $w \geqq 0$,

$$\max_w \Phi(w) = \max_w \left[\frac{p-w}{w}(w-a)\right], \tag{A2}$$
$$= \Phi(w^*)$$
$$w^* = +\sqrt{ap}. \tag{A3}$$

Here w^* is the root of

$$0 = \Phi'(w) = (d/dw)[(p-w)w^{-1}(w-a)]$$
$$= -1 + (ap)w^{-2} \tag{A4}$$
$$\Phi''(w) < 0 \text{ for } w > 0.$$

Thünen, who knew that a tree growing on rent-free land ought to be cut at an age when its percentage instantaneous biological growth rate of saleable lumber is just as big as the interest rate at which money grows, ought to understand the following proper analysis of the Wicksell-Jevons model that Schumpeter should have squared his exposition with.

Grain output at $t + \theta$, $Q(t + \theta)$, is produced by labor input at $t, L(t)$:

$$Q(t+\theta) = f(\theta)L(t) > 0, f' > 0 > f''. \tag{A5}$$

If W/P_Q is the grain real wage rate and r is the instantaneous rate of interest, then competition implies for (A5) in the steady state:

$$f'(\theta)/f(\theta) = r,\ dr/d\theta < 0$$
$$f(\theta)e^{-r\theta} = W/P_Q,\ d(W/P_Q)/d\theta > 0 \tag{A6}$$
$$r = \rho(W/P_Q),\ dr/d(W/P_Q) < 0.$$

The last of these relations, the modern factor-price-frontier, Thünen and Ricardo only occasionally perceived.

What is the earnings flow from current saving of (W/P_Q) minus a? On an instantaneous rate basis, Thünen's zy becomes

$$r \times [(W/P_Q) - a]$$
$$= \frac{f'(\theta)}{f(\theta)}[f(\theta)\exp\{-f'(\theta)f(\theta)^{-1}\} - a]. \tag{A7}$$

This is a monstrous maximand. But if it is to be maximized, Thünen should differentiate every one of its terms with respect to θ. (Or, expressing θ as a function of either one of r or W/P_Q, he will get the same result by differentiating *all* expressions by the chosen independent variable.)

In no case will the correct solution involve a geometric mean of Thünen's tombstone type. Specifically, it will *not* be anywhere near the case that

$$W/P_Q = +\sqrt{af(\theta)}.$$

There is no reason why (A7)'s maximand should even have a maximum. As we'll see, Thünen's criterion can call for an indefinitely large θ.

It is a case of what might be called the Sentimental Fallacy to think that a society, not now in the golden-rule state of maximal per-capita consumption, can by an act of will (or of capital expropriation by edict), attain that zero-interest nirvana. It is a mathematical theorem that neither Peking nor Manchester can go from a non-golden-rule technological steady state to a golden-rule steady state without experiencing sacrifice of current consumption in favor of (higher) future consumption. Starting from present θ, not equal to a larger θ^* that corresponds to maximum Thünen ry, our feasible current ry is less than that maximum, which itself may not be reachable for less than a century of $w - a$ thrift.

In short, there is no reason to want to go to Thünen's goal, and every reason to realize that you can't now be there anyway.

Vindicating Thünen's Logic on Capital

Schumpeter's scenario is only one such. I want to move to Thünen's own model, which involves a permanent-lived durable good (a "leet" or machine) that is produced instantaneously out of labor alone. (If a short lag occurred between input of labor and output of the machine, footnote 13 will show that this involves no essential complications.) Despite Leigh's reproving comments, I find Thünen's sure-footed treatment in 1850 of this case as highly commendable. He has anticipated correctly one instance of the modern Solow-Uzawa two-sector flow model of capital.

Let K be the stock of capital (of "leets"), measured in physical terms. The total labor supply of L is held constant. L is divided between the new machine industry, L_K, where it works alone; and the grain industry, L_Q where it works with K to produce grain. The production functions are:

$$dK/dt \text{ or } \dot{K} = bL_K = b(L - L_Q) \qquad \text{(A8)}$$

$$Q = F[K, L_Q] = L_Q f[K/L_Q], \quad f' > 0 > f''. \qquad \text{(A9)}$$

Combining (A8) and (A9), we have society's production-possibility frontier that is valid both in steady states and in general:

$$Q = F[K, L - b^{-1}\dot{K}]. \qquad \text{(A10)}$$

The interest rate, r, and the real wage in grain, W/P_Q, are given respectively by

$$r = \partial\dot{K}/\partial K = \frac{\text{rent in grain of capital goods}}{\text{cost in grain of capital goods}} = \frac{F_1[K, L - b^{-1}\dot{K}]}{F_2[K, L - b^{-1}\dot{K}]b^{-1}}. \qquad \text{(A11)}$$

The wage rate is given by marginal productivity:

$$W/P_Q = F_2[K, L - b^{-1}\dot{K}]. \qquad \text{(A12)}$$

Here, $F_i[K, L_Q]$ stands for $\partial F/\partial K$ and $\partial F/\partial L_Q$ respectively. Thünen deserves highest marks for getting all this right.[12]

Since the right-hand sides of (A11) and (A12) depend only on the single parameter $K/(L - b^{-1}\dot{K})$, r and W/P_Q are connected by the factor-price-frontier tradeoff:

$$r = \rho(W/P_Q), \; dr/d(W/P_Q) < 0. \qquad \text{(A13)}$$

Having vindicated Thünen's capital model,[13] we must indict him for mistreating it. If Thünen insists on maximizing $r[(W/P_Q) - a]$—which happens to maximize the *grain* value of earnings on current saving and not their value in wage

[12] See Arthur H. Leigh (1968, Vol. 16, p. 19, first complete paragraph): what I call $(K/L, F_1, F_2)$ Leigh writes as $(q, \alpha, w = p - \alpha q)$. My maximand in (A14) Leigh writes as $[\alpha(p - \alpha q)^{-1}(p - \alpha q - a)]$. What Thünen should not be permitted to do is to differentiate this expression with respect to α without making p and q change as my (A14) and earlier relations show they must. Doing it right completely negates Thünen's derivation that $p - \alpha q$ or w will equal $+\sqrt{ap}$.

[13] Leigh, along with earlier critics of Thünen, is concerned whether circularity vitiates Thünen's capital-theory formulation. Here is how one vindicates Thünen in a discrete-period model. We write for him

$$K(t+1) - K(t) + \delta K(t) = bL_K(t)$$

where δ is the rate of (exponential) depreciation. Combine this with

$$\begin{aligned} Q(t+1) &= F[K(t), L_Q(t)] \\ &= F[K(t), L - L_K(t)] \\ &= F[K(t), L - b^{-1}K(t+1) + b^{-1}(1-\delta)K(t)]. \end{aligned}$$

Then the interest rate z and real grain wage become

$$z = \frac{F_1[K(t)/L_Q(t), 1]}{F_2[K(t)/L_Q(t), 1]b^{-1}} - \delta$$

$$W/P_Q = F_2[K(t)/L_Q(t), 1]/(1+z).$$

Any circular interdependence constitutes virtuous and not vicious circularity. QED.

Incidentally, the charge by Erich Carrell, discussed in Hall (1966, p. xxii, n.l), that there is some inconsistency or circularity in Thünen's space model is completely rebutted in my present version of Thünen's model.

units or leets units!—he should do so recognizing all the interdependences between r and W/P_Q that his own model calls for:

$$\underset{K/L_Q}{\text{Max}}\left[\frac{F_1[K/L_Q,1]}{F_2[K/L_Q,1]b^{-1}}(F_2[K/L_Q,1]-a)\right]. \tag{A14}$$

The resulting maximizing $(W/P_Q)^*$—if it exists, and it need not—has absolutely no relation to Thünen's geometric mean:

$$(W/P_Q)^* \neq \sqrt{aF[K/L,1]}. \tag{A15}$$

The Ramsey-Solow Santa Claus Case

Enough can be too much. However, the one-sector model of Frank P. Ramsey (1928) and Robert M. Solow (1956) is so simple as to permit a wrapup of the issues.

Here, with proper choice of units,

$$\begin{aligned} Q+\dot{K} &= F[K,L] = Lf[K/L], f'>0>f'' \\ r &= F_1[K/L,1] \\ W/P_Q &= F_2[K/L,1] = W/P_{\dot{K}}, \\ p &= F[K/L,1] \\ r &= \rho(W/P_Q),\ \rho'<0. \end{aligned} \tag{A16}$$

If people are all alike, we can set L equal to unity. If what they save, y, is always $(W/P_Q)-a$, then the system's evolution over all time must from (A16) satisfy

$$\dot{K} = F[K,1]-KF_1[K,1]-a. \tag{A17}$$

Thünen's maximand, ry, is precisely the system's instantaneous growth rate

$$\begin{aligned} \dot{F} &= \dot{K}\,\partial F[K,1]/\partial K = r\dot{K} \\ &= F_1[K,1](F[K,1]-KF_1[K,1]-a) \\ &= r(F[K,1]-Kr-a). \end{aligned} \tag{A18}$$

His bizarre saving stipulation, when taken literally as I have done, makes the system overshoot the golden-rule state once it gets there. His is a cancerous mode of behavior. It is an instance of the Sentimental Fallacy to believe that we can alter any system's growth rate *after* we have committed it to having its consumption frozen at a constant profit income, and with existing $K(t)$ given to us as a heritage of the long past. Still we can humor Thünen and ask on his behalf the meaningful question: For what K—what K/L—does his system achieve *its* fastest growth rate? To answer this, we seek the maximum of Thünen's ry:

$$\begin{aligned} \underset{K}{\text{Max}}[r(w-a)] &= \underset{K}{\text{Max}}\ \dot{F} \\ &= \underset{K}{\text{Max}}\ (F_1[K,1]F[K,1] \\ &\qquad - KF_1[K,1]^2 - aF_1[K,1]). \end{aligned} \tag{A19}$$

The answer is a surprising one. Possibly no such maximum exists. Thus, if $F[K,1]$ were Cobb-Douglas, of the Wicksell type $K^{1/2}$, $\dot{F}$ like F will grow forever, obeying

$$\dot{F} = \tfrac{1}{2}[1-aK^{-1/2}]>0,\ K>a^2. \tag{A20}$$

The system has no inflection point, no Thünen maximum point, since

$$\ddot{F}>0,\ \tfrac{1}{4}a<K<\infty. \tag{A21}$$

If $f[K,1]$ were quadratic, the system would also grow cancerously. Once it reaches Thünen's inflection point, it will not tarry there. Nor should it. But, alas, once it reaches the golden-rule bliss point, it will overshoot disastrously—as all its capital formation is wasted or even worse can become harmful.

The Ramsey-Solow model shows us that a wage equal to Thünen's geometric mean between a and labor's average product could well be a rotten wage, worse than the competitive marginal-product wage. Thus, for $F[K,L]$ a Cobb-Douglas function, the marginal-product wage $F[K,L]$ becomes as $(K/L)\to\infty$ an *infinite multiple* of Thünen's $\sqrt{ap}$. If the elasticity of substitution is less than unity, as $K/L\to\infty$ the competitive wage becomes all of the average product, p, and this approaches an infinite markup on $\sqrt{ap}$. If the elasticity of substitution is always above unity—a dubious possibility—Thünen's $\sqrt{ap}$ would eventually grant the workers an infinite multiple of their rising competitive wage.[14]

Final Reflections

1. Conceptual difficulties in Thünen's theory of distribution between labor, land, and capital have been shown to be capable of being cleared up while still his essential vision is preserved.

At 200 we hail Thünen more admiringly than was possible at 100 or at the time of his death.

2. Posterity has been right to criticize Thünen's arbitrary maximand of current earnings on current saving out of wages. Where posterity has nodded is in failing to realize that Thünen fell victim to the Sentimental Fallacy in specifying the wrong technological constraints within which his maximizing was to take place.

3. Curiously, just as technical change was ushering in a century of rising agricultural real wage rates in Europe—a trend that would have been even more favorable were it not for New World competition (an element that does not really belong to Thünen's most abstract isolated state)—Thünen succumbed to pessimism over laissez-faire wage trends and labored away on his utopian alternative.

How did so deep and subtle a mind get mired in the doctrine of the natural wage? Who can say? I venture the hypothesis that it was because Thünen was an autodidact—a lone scholar without colleagues, students, readers, or critics within his own lifetime—that his generous impulse to reform the world drove him to a grandiloquent recipe for the world.

Having taken measure of the chaff and the kernel of his analysis, posterity can cherish his heritage.

[14] I have had to free myself of the 1934 impression that the natural wage is something necessarily in excess of the marginal-productivity wage. I believe Thünen regarded it as exceeding the marginal-productivity wage that laissez faire would bring about spontaneously, probably regarding it rather to be equal to the marginal-productivity wage that property-owning workers can and should contrive for themselves. Such an interpretation is a disquieting one, for it implies that Thünen did not understand that his own system, given its short-run labor supply and stock of capital (even if a growing one), will determine only one present-day marginal-productivity real wage.

When contemplating capital and labor, Thünen treats the two factors symmetrically. The return on each is interchangeably treated as a residual or as a marginal product; thus, Thünen presents a heuristic proof of Euler's Theorem along the lines of Joan Robinson (1934) or Paul Samuelson (1972). I don't recall that he treated land in a labor-land context other than as a residual. He sensed that even with zero transport costs, if land were limited relative to labor, it would bear rent even if all acres were alike. We see that it was no exaggeration, in Samuelson (1983), to hail Johann Heinrich von Thünen as one of the great microeconomists of all time, a peer of Augustin Cournot and the often over-rated David Ricardo.

REFERENCES

BECKMANN, MARTIN J. AND MARSCHAK, THOMAS. "An Activity Analysis Approach to Location Theory," *Kyklos*, 1955, *8* (fasc. 2), pp. 125–41.

BLAUG, MARK. *Economic theory in retrospect.* Homewood, IL: Richard D. Irwin, [1962] 1968, Ch. 8.

BÖHM-BAWERK, EUGEN VON. *Capital and interest.* Vols. I–III, South Holland, IL: Libertarian Press, [1884, 1889], 1959.

CLARK, JOHN B. *Distribution of wealth.* NY: Macmillan, [1899] 1944.

DEMPSEY, BERNARD W. *The frontier wage: With the text of the second part of the Isolated State.* Chicago: Loyola U. Press, 1960.

DOUGLAS, PAUL H. *Theory of wages.* NY: Macmillan, 1934.

HALL, PETER, ed. *Von Thünen's isolated state.* London: Pergamon Press, 1966.

LEIGH, ARTHUR H. "Von Thünen's Theory of Distribution and the Advent of Marginal Analysis," *J. Polit. Econ.*, Dec. 1946, *54*, pp. 481–502.

———. "J. H. VON THÜNEN," in *International encyclopedia of the social sciences.* NY: Macmillan and Free Press, 1968, pp. 16–20.

MERTON, ROBERT K. *The sociology of science.* Chicago: U. of Chicago Press, 1973.

PETERSEN, ASMUS. *Thünen's Isolierte Statt: Die Landwirtschaft als Glied der Volkswirtschaft.* Berlin: Parez, 1944.

PIGOU, ARTHUR C., ed. *Memorials of Alfred Marshall.* London: Macmillan, 1925.

RAMSEY, FRANK P. "A Mathematical Theory of Saving," *Econ. J.*, Dec. 1928, *38*, pp. 543–59.

RECKTENWALD, HORST C., ed. *Political economy: A historical perspective.* London: Collier-Macmillan, 1973, pp. 135–56.

ROBINSON, JOAN. "Euler's Theorem and the Problem of Distribution," *Econ. J.*, Sept. 1934, *44*, pp. 398–414.

SALIN, EDGAR. "Johann Heinrich von Thünen in seiner Zeit," *Zeitschrift für Agrargeschichte und Agrarsoziologie: Sonderheft: Johann Heinrich von Thünen, 6,* 1958, abridged.

SAMUELSON, PAUL A. "The Transfer Problem and Transport Cost, II: Analysis of Effects of Trade Impediments," *Econ. J.*, June 1954, *64*, pp. 264–89.

———. "A Modern Treatment of the Ricardian Economy: I. The Pricing of Goods and of Labor and Land Services," *Quart. J. Econ.*, Feb. 1959, *73*(1), pp. 1–35.

———. "A Quantum-Theory Model of Economics: Is the Coordinating Entrepreneur Just Worth His Profit?" *Essays in honour of Paul Rosenstein-Rodan.* Eds.: JAGDISH BHAGWATI AND RICHARD S. ECKAUS. London: Allen and Unwin, 1972, Ch. 18. See corrected version in *Collected scientific papers of Paul A. Samuelson.* Vol. 4. Eds.: HIROAKI NAGATANI AND KATHLEEN CROWLEY. Cambridge, MA: MIT Press, 1977, Ch. 214.

———. "1983: Marx, Keynes and Schumpeter," speech given at Eastern Economic Association, March 10, 1983; *Eastern Econ. Assoc. J.*, forthcoming.

SCHNEIDER, ERICH. "Johann Heinrich von Thünen," *Econometrica*, Jan. 1934, *2*, pp. 1–12.

SCHUMPETER, JOSEF A. *History of economic analysis.* NY: Oxford U. Press, 1954.

SOLOW, ROBERT M. "A Contribution to the Theory of Economic Growth," *Quart. J. Econ.*, Feb. 1956, *70*, pp. 65–94.

THÜNEN, JOHANN H. VON. *Der Isolierte Staat in Beziehung auf Landwirtschaft und Nationalökonomie.* Third ed. Ed.: HEINRICH WAENTIG, Jena: Gustav Fischer, 1930. See Peter Hall and Bernard W. Dempsey for English translations.

WICKSTEED, PHILIP H. *Coordination of the laws of distribution.* London: 1894. Reissued in *London School of Economics Scarce Tracts,* No. 12. London: 1932.

1986 Correction and Addendum

Professor Robert Dorfman of Harvard, in Dorfman (1986), has pointed out that I erred in putting an inequality in (A15). I agree with him and with a related criticism of me in Jürg Niehans paper (1986). Dorfman demonstrates:

von Thünen laid the groundwork for ... misunderstandings by deriving his formula at least four times in *Der Isolierte Statt* (1950), in Chapters 11, 15, 16, and 18, all in somewhat different ways. Furthermore, the derivations in Chapters 15, 16, and 18 all suffer from the mistake in differential calculus of which Samuelson complains, while the argument in Chapter 11, where his reasoning is set forth least obscurely, is not carried through to completion.

Using present notation, Dorfman is seen to derive the geometric-mean equality of (A15) from (A14) in the following way:

$$\begin{aligned} &\operatorname*{Max}_q \frac{F_1[q,1](F_2[q,1]-a)}{F_2[q,1]} \\ &= \operatorname*{Max}_q \frac{f'(q)[f(q)-qf'(q)-a]}{f(q)-qf'(q)} \\ &= G(q^*), \qquad F[q,1] \equiv f(q), \quad f''(q) < 0, \end{aligned} \tag{A14}$$

where q^* is a root of

$$\begin{aligned} 0 = G'(q) &= f''(q)\{[f(q)-qf'(q)]^2 - af(q)\} \\ &= f''(q)\{w^2 - ap\} \rightarrow w^* = \sqrt{ap} \qquad \text{QED.} \end{aligned}$$

Samuelson's (1986) affirmative reply provides a similar valid arithmetic-mean formula to replace Thünen's when his technology of (A8)–(A9) is replaced by next section's Ramsey-Solow one-sector technology. Now (A19) can be written

$$\begin{aligned} &\operatorname*{Max}_q \{F_1[q,1]F[q,1] - qF_1[q,1]^2 - aF_1[K,1]\} \\ &\equiv \operatorname*{Max}_q \{f'(q)[f(q)-qf'(q)-a]\} = \operatorname*{Max}_q H(q) = H(q^\dagger), \end{aligned} \tag{A19}$$

where $q^\dagger$ is a root of

$$\begin{aligned} 0 = H'(q^\dagger) &= f''(q)[f(q) - 2qf'(q) - a] \\ &= f''(q)[2w - p - a] \rightarrow w^\dagger = \tfrac{1}{2}a + \tfrac{1}{2}p. \end{aligned}$$

This derivation corrects faulty arithmetic-mean derivations that appear in the Thünen literature under the names of A. Marshall and G. F. Knapp.

Thünen's valid chapter 11, linking up the wage and the interest rate to the capital/labor ratio, as Dorfman shows, does lead to the $\sqrt{ap}$ formula; although Thünen did not show this explicitly in chapter 11, he must have calculated its truth and (mistakenly) thought his needed proof was provided by uncogent calculus exercises such as the following:

$$(\partial/\partial w)[(\bar{p} - w)(w - a)/w] = 0.$$

In my interpretation of Dorfman, labor's marginal product will equal (subsistence $\times$ labor's average product)$^{1/2}$ in the following state: the state where, when a *single* small worker saves the surplus of his wage over the specified subsistence level a, it brings him the maximum possible perpetual increment of rye. If all workers did it, society's increment of perpetual rye could *not* be at a maximum in such a Thünen $\sqrt{ap}$ state.

Incidentally, Professor Dorfman has shown that exponential depreciation is compatible with the $\sqrt{ap}$ formula, provided only that p is interpreted as average product net of depreciation. I have proved the same generalization for the $\frac{1}{2}(a + p)$ formula of the one-sector case.

References

Dorfman, Robert. 1986. "Comment: Thünen at Two Hundred." *Journal of Economic Literature* (to be published).

Niehans, Jürg. 1986. "Johann Heinrich von Thünen." *The New Palgrave Dictionary of Political Economy* (to be published).

Samuelson, Paul A. 1986. "Yes to Robert Dorfman's Vindication of Thünen's Natural-Wage Derivation." *Journal of Economic Literature* (to be published).

The Canonical Classical Model of Political Economy

By PAUL A. SAMUELSON
Massachusetts Institute of Technology

I owe thanks to the National Science Foundation for partial financial aid, and thanks also to helpful criticisms from George Stigler, William Baumol, and Mark Blaug, most of which I took to heart.

1. Adam Smith, David Ricardo, Thomas Robert Malthus, and John Stuart Mill shared in common essentially one dynamic model of equilibrium, growth, and distribution. When the limitation of land and natural resources is added to the model of Karl Marx, he also ends up with this same canonical classical model.

In its present version the model is stripped down to its minimal essentials. For brevity I employ modern mathematical tools, but only to characterize in modern terms the relations that were actually common to all these writers.

The reader should of course be warned that any simple codification of the classical economists' discursive writings must be an oversimplification: in some of their passages they qualify what they have written elsewhere; in some they provide negations and contradictions. Not a few of the stereotypes about the classical writers are, to paraphrase Voltaire, myths agreed-upon by later commentators—distortions that both improve and libel the originals. The relevant object of study for a modern scholar is the corpus of original texts and the commentaries on them, the latter not being genuinely of less interest than the former once we have succeeded in telling them apart.

To the fascinating question of whether classical political economy does, or can be made to, offer an *"alternative paradigm"*—in the sense of Thomas Kuhn [11, 1962]—to modern mainstream economics, the present investigation provides an instructive answer. So to speak, within every classical economist there is to be discerned a modern economist trying to be born. A Ricardo or Mill did not so much replace supply and demand by quite different mechanisms but rather sought to be able to say something significant and limiting about their properties, quite in the same way that we moderns endeavor to do. I describe and analyze here the basic classical model in its essential form.

2. Real output is divided interchangeably between *consumption* and *capital formation* (on a net or gross saving-investment basis). Ignoring details concerning the input-intensity differences between goods of different industries (much as can be done in a modern one-sector one–capital-good model), the classicists in effect assume that output is produced by a pro-

duction function involving land input and a *dose* of labor-*cum*-capital input. Competition among (1) landowners, (2) entrepreneurs who hire labor and needed raw materials to work with hired land, and (3) owners of labor and capital goods out to make the most favorable terms for themselves—all this leads to a determinate breakdown of competitive earnings and cost between (a) land rent and (b) the *combined return to the composite dose of labor-capital.* The breakdown of the combined return to the dose between its two components would be indeterminate as far as the demand side of the problem is concerned (at least this would be so if we stick literally to the fixed-proportions assumption usually alleged to be adhered to by the classical writers). The needed conditions come from the supply side.

3. The classical long-run theory postulates that the workers' wage rate is ultimately determined by (α) the real *subsistence* level needed to ensure reproduction and maintenance of the working population. Just as the classicists had a long-run horizontal supply curve for the subsistence wage, so they had a long-run horizontal supply curve for capital at (β) the *minimum-effective rate of accumulation,* that profit rate just low enough and just high enough to cause capital to be *maintained* with zero net algebraic saving. The long-run equilibrium number of total doses, with the implied long-run plateau of population and of capital stock, is just big enough so that the law of diminishing returns brings down the combined return of the dose to the *sum* of the needed wage-subsistence and needed minimum-profit rates. When accumulation has gone that far and population has grown in balanced proper degree, then in the absence of further technical change total land rent is *maximal.* Equilibrium prevails forever. (Mill went on to emphasize that technological innovation, continued in the long-run steady state, would imply *rising output forever;* we can show on Mill's behalf that, if the technical change is *land-augmenting* at a steady exponential rate, then labor and capital will grow forever at the same balanced exponential rate, just enough to match the growth of land measured in "efficiency units" and with the long-run wage rate and profit rate each just high enough above their respective bare minima to elicit the implied growth rates of the factors.)

4. The long-run equilibrium is stable in the sense that the system, if disturbed from it, will spontaneously return toward it. To grasp the short-run transient development of the system, suppose labor and capital goods begin in the balanced proportions needed for the technological dose, but with each at a level short of the long-run equilibrium level. Land rent then will begin below its long-run equilibrium; by the same token, the aggregate return to the composite dose will begin in excess of the long-run subsistence levels. The short-run breakdown of the dose's aggregate return among capital and labor will be determined by competitive auctioneering at that fractional breakdown just *needed to keep the two components of the dose growing at the same balanced rate* (which will be a uniquely determinate growth rate).

Thus, if population adjusts so rapidly to any surplus of real wage above subsistence that we can practically assume the truth of (what can be termed) Ricardo's "short-circuited" approximation, then the transient wage rate will be insignificantly different from the long-run subsistence level. The rate of profit is then determinate as a *residual* in the short run. And being thus determined *above* the long-run minimal profit rate, the system's saving propensities will determine the rate at which capital accumulates and population grows apace. Asymptotically, the growth of doses of capital as applied to a limited supply of land leads down the trail of diminishing returns to the rendezvous of long-run equilibrium.

Suppose we go beyond the short-circuited version and recognize that just as it takes an increment of profit rate to elicit positive saving and growth of capital, so too there must be an increment of real wage rate over the subsistence level to elicit the needed transient growth in population. Still, we shall find that there is a determinate short-term breakdown between the components of the dose's aggregate return that will be just enough to keep both labor and capital growing in the needed fixed-proportions way. The only difference in this more realistic scenario is what Smith envisioned so much more clearly than Ricardo—namely, that the real wage is higher in the transient state of progressive growth. Only in the final equilibrium when growth ceases is society in Smith's *dull* state of minimal real wages. Ricardo's predecessor and successor, Smith and Mill, are both more realistic than is Ricardo himself on wages adjustments. (By contrast, Ricardo is more realistic in 1817 [21] than Smith in 1776 [29] when it comes to recognizing that continuing new inventions will greatly delay the fall of the profit rate to its minimum and perhaps continue to do so permanently.)

Even Mill is not realistic enough in his modelling of innovation and the lagging supply of population in advanced economies. What observers like Kuznets have observed this past century is that the growth of technology has been enough *to keep the real wage growing at something like an exponential rate,* with the growth in population and saving not being fast enough to wipe out the rising trend in real wages. By contrast, the rate of profit has meandered more or less trendlessly depending on the qualitative structure of technical change, much as if population growth were more a bottleneck than were saving. It is curious that the Marxian variant of classicism, with its soft-pedalling of the limitations of land and natural resources, ought logically to have led to an even more optimistic scenario for the laws of motion of capitalistic profits than the Ricardo-Smith version.

Long-Run Equilibrium Diagrammed

5. *Figure* 1 shows the canonical classical equilibrium in the long run or steady state. The DD' relation, which looks like a modern demand relation, gives the competitive return to the composite dose of capital-*cum*-labor: the greater the number of doses competing for the same fixed supply of various qualities of land, the higher will be bid up land rents and the lower will be the dose price available to be divided between labor's wage rate and capital's profit-or-interest rate.

The DD' relation looks like a Clarkian neoclassical marginal-product curve for the variable composite doses applied to fixed land(s). But we shall be more in tune with the classicists' own mode of thinking if we delay giving DD' that admissible interpretation.[1] Perusal of the accompa-

[1] The numerical tables in the last part of Chapter II on rent of Ricardo [21, 1817] leave sketchy his notion that "successive portions of capital [doses 1, 2, 3, and 4] yielded 100, 90, 80, 70 [with total rent therefore being (100–70) + (90–70) + (80–70) + 0 = 60 and the total return to the 4 units of doses being {(100+90+80+70) − 60}/4 = 280/4 = 70]." It is clear that Ricardo believed that extra available doses would both work with lands of lower quality not previously worth cultivating and work old lands more intensively, thus altering both the *extensive* and *intensive* margins of cultivation.

Until the last half century, no one seems to have worked out rigorously the processes going on implicitly in the background, although Mountifort Longfield [12, 1834] came close to doing so as far as "reduced-form" descriptions are concerned. We shall outdo the classicists and underplay neoclassical versions of marginalism by first utilizing the following model, which is analyzed in Samuelson [24, 1959; 28, 1977].

(a) A strip of land declines continuously "eastward" in "fertility." (b) Every grade of land is cultivated

LONG-RUN EQUILIBRIUM

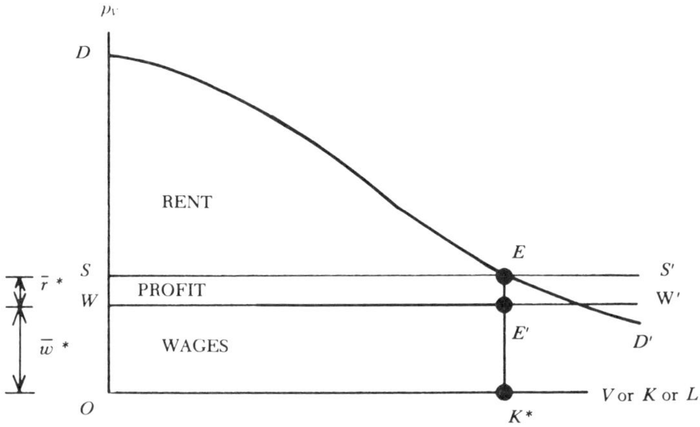

Figure 1. Long-run equilibrium is at *E*, where the *DD'* curve of return to the doses of *V*, made up of balanced proportions of *L* and *K* applied to a fixed profile of lands, just intersects the *SS'* supply curve that measures the wage subsistence and the minimum profit rate needed for steady reproduction of labor and capital. The equilibrium long-run wage rate is $\bar{w}^*$ and the long-run profit rate is $\bar{r}^*$, both exogenous parameters. Distribution of total product, *OK*ED*, is between the residual rent triangle *SED* and the dose's rectangle *OK*ES*. The breakdown between wages and profit is given by the rectangle's breakdown into *OK*E'W* and *WE'ES*. (Possibly $\bar{r}^*$ could be zero. *DD'* can be given the ultra-classical interpretation as the *average product* of the dose on the *external* margin of a continuum of lands of different grades; but, also, it could be the dose's common *marginal product* at the varying *intensive* margins of all lands used.)

by composite doses of exactly the same internal *relative* labor-capital proportions. (c) Fixed proportions of dose to land prevail at each grade's longitude, with (d) return of product per doses applied declining continuously as we move eastward. Then, when total available doses are few, all land to the east is not worth cultivating; as doses increase in availability, they all are applied ever further eastward (with no change in density of doses on prime westward land, but of course with increased *differential rent* earned on those prime acres). For each total of doses available, there is an external frontier of zero-rent land: the height of *DD'* at any given *V* is the *average product* (not the yet-to-be invented "marginal product") of output per unit of *V*, namely *Q/V* there. Footnote 7 below will show when *DD'* also can be interpreted as a true marginal product of the variable composite dose, *V*.

nying footnote shows how we might also interpret *DD'* as the curve of *average product of the varied dose* out at the moving external frontier of zero-rent grade of land.

6. The supply of labor is given by the horizontal line *WW'*, representing the subsistence cost of reproduction of labor in steady-state numbers. Followers of Smith, Ricardo, and Mill were prepared to recognize non-physiological components in the subsistence level of wages required by workers before their patterns

of marriage, procreation, migration, and labor-force participation were just adequate to keep total labor employed constant. Marx shifted the determinants of WW' away from Malthus's emphasis on biological elements of marriage, procreation, and mortality toward his own emphasis on the reserve army of the unemployed, labor-saving inventions, and in-migration to the industrial regions from the over-populated rural areas.

So long as we choose conventional units for labor, capital goods (or "leets"), and composite doses that agree in numerical magnitude, the height of WW' represents the *real wage rate* per unit of labor, $\bar{w}^*$, that must prevail when labor power's cost of reproduction is just achieved and its long-run total is in stationary equilibrium.

7. Superimposed on WW', to achieve the long-run supply response SS' for the composite dose, is the long-run profit per unit of capital goods needed if the profit rate per annum is to be at the effective rate of accumulation, $\bar{r}^*$, just enough to choke off further net saving but not so low as to cause dissaving and eating up of the previously existing stock of capital goods.

8. The distance WS, or $E'E$, represents both the rental rate of capital goods *and* the ("own") profit rate per unit time (such as .10 when 10 percent is the rate of profit to be earned on assets) when our numeraire for output is capital-goods per unit time. When differences in factor intensities between the consumption- and the capital-goods industries are ignorable, as in *Figure* 1, there is no difference between using consumption goods or capital goods as numeraire provided both kinds of goods are actually being produced—as will be the case for any stationary or growing system.

This long-run profit rate might, in some theories, be zero (after, of course, all allowances for depreciation and replacement of principal have separately been allowed for; after any needed actuarial premia for probable accidents and losses had been properly allowed for; and after any wages of managing capital assets had been provided for). If $\bar{r}^*$ is zero, SS' would coincide with WW' and E with the intersection of DD' and WW': the vertical distance between them measures the long-run *perpetual net rental* (if any) to be earned by owners of maintained capital-goods (leets) in the steady state when they are just motivated to cease net saving or dissaving.

9. The *residual of land rent* is measured on the diagram by the curvilinear triangle SED. It is what is left of total product, OK^*ED, after the composite doses are paid their needed long-run aggregate of OK^*ES. Whereas J. B. Clark and such neoclassicals as Philip H. Wicksteed, Knut Wicksell, Léon Walras, and Paul Douglas would split up the non-rent aggregate between labor and capital by a marginal-product calculation in which variability of the labor-to-leets components is brought to the optimal degree of substitution, the present classical paradigm denies such smooth substitutability *within* the composite dose and at best tolerates it between land and the composite of the fixed-components dose.

From the horizontal long-run supply curves of the components, WW' and SS', and from them alone comes the classical system's determinate *long-run* distribution theory of the non-land factor shares.[2]

[2] If $V = \text{Min}[L, K]$ were replaced by a neoclassical-first-degree-homogeneous smooth function, $v[L, K]$ with well-defined partial derivative, $\partial v[L, K]/\partial L$, the same $\bar{w}^*$ and $\bar{r}^*$ levels would prevail in the long run: but now the 2-dimensional *Figure* 1 would be inadequate to depict the determination of the resulting L^* and K^* levels: marginal productivity conditions, involving DD' and $\partial v[L, K]/\partial L$ would be the necessary and sufficient conditions to determine the extra unknowns of the rephrased problem, as in §19 below.

10. As noted in the Physiocratic version of the classical system of Samuelson [23, 1959], under long-run equilibrium all goods can be decomposed into their (marked-up) socially-necessary *land* contents: a shift in tastes and final demand from one good to another, toward more cloth and less corn, would have no effect on long-run prices. But such a shift toward less–land-intensive and more–labor-intensive goods would lower rent's share in ultimate national income; it would also raise the plateaux of population and of capital in any model where they combine in doses of the same proportions in all industries (an implausible special case). The point is obvious that any classicist who thinks he can separate "value" from "distribution" commits a logical blunder. He also blunders if he thinks that he can "get rid of land and rent as a complication for pricing" by concentrating on the external margin of no-rent land: where that external margin falls is an *endogenous* variable that shifts with tastes and demand changes so as to vitiate a hoped-for labor theory of value or a wage-*cum*-profit-rate theory of value.

11. For given technological knowledge, there is defined a unique steady-state ("factor-price") frontier relating (α) the *profit or interest rate* to (β) the *real wage rate* (expressed in terms of market basket of subsistence goods or in terms of any specified good) and (γ) the *rate of land rent* earnable by a composite unit of *all* grades of land weighted by their actual importance in the system. With the profit rate and the real wage given at their long-run supply levels, the rent rate is maximal at the long-run rendezvous of the system. (For fixed profit rate, the trade-off between real wage and rent rates can be shown to be convex, no matter how many the sectors or capital goods.)

Any reader uninterested in the rigorous analysis of this classical model may skip the next section's mathematical exposition and concentrate on the subsequent section's graphical analysis of classical growth and development.

Mathematical Version of the Canonical System

12. To define the system's behavior both in long-run equilibrium and also in transient movements toward equilibrium, here are the equations implied by this version of the classical system.

Real output, Q, is divided into real consumption, C, and net capital formation, dK/dt. It is produced at time t out of land and a composite dose of labor and capital goods ("leets"), $V_t = \mathrm{Min}[L_t, K_t]$, where the units in the dose and in L_t and K_t are related so that one dose involves one unit of labor and one unit of capital goods. With land (possibly of various grades) fixed, we can omit the symbol for it (T, standing for a scalar, a vector, or even possibly a function of a parameter denoting a continuum of grades) in the economy's production function.

The basic production function becomes

$$Q = 1(C) + 1(dK/dt) = f(V). \quad (1)$$
$$V = \mathrm{Min}[L, K], \quad (2)$$

where $f(V)$ is a *concave* function with $f'(V) \geq 0$, $f''(V) \leq 0$. [Warning: only the expositional need to compress the model into a single sector and the desire to exaggerate the differences between classical and neoclassical writers can justify so simple and strong an axiom of fixed proportions. When we relax this by quoting passages in classical writings, we need to augment the system with extra equations that help determine the extra unknowns.]

Total land rent, R, is given residually by

$$R = f(V) - Vf'(V). \quad (3)$$

The non-rent real return to the total dose, p_V, expressed in output units as numeraire, is equal to the sum of the wage component and the profit component: it is given by

$$f'(V) = p_V = 1w + 1r, \qquad (4)$$

where w is the real wage in output units, r is both the own rate of interest and the real rental rate of capital goods expressed in output units (*i.e.*, interchangeably in capital-good or consumption units), $f'(V)$ is the increment in product resulting from an extra dose of V, applied to fixed land(s); its reciprocal is the competitive marginal cost of output in terms of extra needed V requirements.[3]

13. As *Figure* 1's WW' and SS' horizontal lines indicated, w and r have to be at the well-defined $\bar{w}^*$ and $\bar{r}^*$ levels in long-run equilibrium. Thus, *Figure* 1's E is defined by the long-run equilibrium equations:

$$f'(V^*) = \bar{w}^* + \bar{r}^* = p_V^* \qquad (4^*)$$
$$R^* = f(V^*) - V^*f'(V^*) \qquad (3^*)$$
$$L^* = K^* = V^* \qquad (2^*)$$
$$Q^* = C^* + 0 = f(V^*). \qquad (1^*)$$

Any increase in the subsistence wage, $\bar{w}^*$, or in $\bar{r}^*$, must lower V^*, R^*, K^*, and L^*, Q^*, and C^*. The absolute shares ($\bar{r}^*K^*$, $\bar{w}^*L^*$) can move in either direction relative to R^*: if $\bar{r}^*/\bar{w}^*$ rises, the profit/wage share rises, but how a change in $\bar{w}^*+\bar{r}^*$ affects the $(\bar{w}^* + \bar{r}^*)V^*/R^*$ ratio must depend on how changes in V affect the elasticity of the $f(V)$ curve (more precisely, on what we today call the elasticity of substitution of the $f(V)$ production function).

[3] As will be seen later, when one of the L or K inputs exceeds its needed proportions—*i.e.*, when $L/K > 1$ or $K/L > 1$—the price of the redundant's input in (4) is zero, corresponding to a free good. So (4) must be augmented under ruthless perfect competition by

$$w = 0, \quad L > K \qquad (4a)$$
$$r = 0, \quad K > L \qquad (4b)$$
$$w + r = f'(\mathrm{Min}[L, K]), \quad L \gtreqless K. \qquad (4c)$$

For all their talk about the importance of the problem of distribution between land rent, labor wages, and profits, the classicists succeeded in saying little definite (and correct!) on levels of and changes in relative factor shares.

14. The dynamic laws of growth of population, $(dL/dt)/L$, and of the accumulating stock of capital, $(dK/dt)/K$, must be specified for the canonical model. When the real wage rate, w, is above the subsistence real wage rate, $\bar{w}^*$, the population grows—and grows at a greater rate the greater is the excess in wage rates:

$$\epsilon(dL/dt)/L = \lambda[w - \bar{w}^*]; \qquad (5)$$
$$\lambda[0] = 0, \quad \lambda'[\ ] > 0.$$

Here ϵ is a non-negative parameter determining the slowness of the growth response of labor supply to surpluses over subsistence wages: if $\epsilon = 0$, the adjustment is instantaneous of short-run w to long-run $\bar{w}^*$ level of subsistence as L grows at whatever pace is needed to achieve $\bar{w}^*$; this is what I call the Ricardian "short-circuited" version of dynamics. If ϵ is a large positive parameter, evidently the more realistic case historically, the population grows only slowly during a high-wage era. By definition, in the long run, $(dL/dt)/L = 0$ when $w = \bar{w}^*$.

15. For Smith, Ricardo, and Mill, saving and investing never fail to be equated at full-employment conditions; only Malthus expressed doubts, envisaging in 1820 [15] the possibility of oversaving and violation of what we know loosely as "Say's Law." The rate of saving-investment is positive when r exceeds $\bar{r}^*$, the effective rate at which net accumulation ceases. Crudely, we write:

$$(dK/dt)/K = \sigma[r - \bar{r}^*]; \qquad (6)$$
$$\sigma[0] = 0, \ \sigma'[\ ] > 0,$$

where $\sigma[r - \bar{r}^*]/r$ is the fraction that saving will bear to total profit incomes.

16. Our dynamic canonical classical system is almost complete.[4] If it *always* started with initial L_0/K_0 in the balanced configuration of unity and remained always in a balanced configuration, it would in fact generate determinate motions of all our variables: $L(t)$, $K(t)$, $V(t)$, $w(t)$, $r(t)$, $p_V(t)$, $C(t)$, $Q(t)$.

One such complete version is the "short-circuited" case already referred to. In it, we make the unrealistic polar Ricardian assumption that population adjusts virtually instantly, so that w falls or rises immediately to the $\bar{w}^*$ subsistence wage rate. Now (5) is replaced by:

$$w = \bar{w}^*, \quad L(t) \equiv K(t) \equiv V(t) \qquad (5')$$

Our new system [(1)–(4), (5′), (6)] can now be reduced to

$$(dK/dt)/K = \sigma[f'(K) - \bar{w}^* - \bar{r}^*], \quad K(t_0) = K_0 \qquad (7.1)$$
$$Q = f(K) \qquad (7.2)$$
$$C = f(K) - dK/dt \qquad (7.3)$$
$$L = V = K \qquad (7.4)$$
$$w = \bar{w}^* \qquad (7.5)$$
$$R = f(K) - Kf'(K). \qquad (7.6)$$

The equilibrium at the K^* root of $f'(K) = \bar{w}^* + \bar{r}^*$ is globally stable: for any initial positive K_0,

$$\lim_{t\to\infty} [K(t), L(t), r(t), R(t), \ldots] = [K^*, L^*, \bar{r}^*, R^*, \ldots], \qquad (7.7)$$

where the starred long-run equilibria are precisely those of (1*)–(4*). The global stability follows from the fact that $\sigma[x]$ always has the sign of x and $-dK/dt$ therefore always the sign of $K - K^*$.

17. Not even Ricardo adhered to the short-circuited version in which the population is instantly variable so that the wage rate could be regarded as adjusting to the long-run $\bar{w}^*$ rate instantaneously. Ricardo realized that labor as well as capital would have to share in the transient surplus of the dose's return: how much of the maximum "wage fund" that could go to wages rather than to profits was never worked out in proper supply-and-demand detail by the classical writers but was left implicit by Ricardo and his contemporaries. Our supply relations (5) and (6) explicitly bridge the logical gap. (See *Figures* 3(a) and 3(b) for the diagrammatic details.) The full classical system of (1)–(6), if started out with initially balanced (K_0, L_0) sufficiently near to (K^*, L^*), will forever after grow with K/L in the needed balance and with neither factor redundantly free. Subject to such balanced conditions, the canonical system of (1)–(6) can be reduced to the determinate dynamical system:

$$(dK/dt)/K = \sigma[f'(K) - w - \bar{r}^*], \quad K_0 = L_0 = V_0 \qquad (8.1)$$

$$(dK/dt)/K = (dL/dt)/L = \sigma[f'(K) - w - \bar{r}^*] = \epsilon^{-1}\lambda[w - \bar{w}^*]. \qquad (8.2)$$

Between (8.1) and (8.2) we can eliminate w as an unknown, solving for it uniquely in terms of K:

$$w = \omega(K; \epsilon) \qquad (8.2')$$
$$\partial w(K;\epsilon)/\partial K < 0,$$
$$\omega(K^*;\epsilon) \equiv \bar{w}^*.$$

The less is ϵ, the faster w approaches final equilibrium, the sign of $\partial\omega/\partial\epsilon$ being that of $-(K - K^*)$.

Our determinate system becomes:

$$(dK/dt)/K = \sigma[f'(K) - \omega(K;\epsilon) - \bar{r}^*] \qquad (9.1)$$
$$0 \equiv \sigma[f'(K^*) - \omega(K^*;\epsilon) - \bar{r}^*]$$
$$\lim_{t\to\infty} K(t) = K^*$$

for all K_0 near enough to K^* for (8.2) to have the solution of (8.2′). The smaller is ϵ, the closer the solution of the full-fledged canonical system (1)–(6) to the short-circuited version.

[4] With the (4a) and (4b) relations of footnote 3, the dynamic system would be complete (as will be discussed later in footnote 6).

18. There remains only the task of showing that the canonical system is determinate and globally stable from any *initial conditions* of positive K and L, balanced or unbalanced.[5]

Suppose we start the system off with excess supply of one of the factors— say with more of capital goods (leets) than can be manned by labor. With $K_0 > L_0$, the short-term rentals of redundant capital goods would fall to zero under ruthless competition. At a current profit rate of zero (really negative if we recognized depreciation), there would be no profit income to save, and presumably there would be every incentive for all holders of capital assets to want to dissave at as rapid a rate as possible. Meantime labor's wage is getting all of the gross return to the composite dose, and population growth will be rapid. Therefore, very quickly, K/L will diminish toward balanced proportions without redundancy— the case already analyzed in (8) or (9).

Similarly, if we begin with redundant L/K, labor will be a free good with a zero competitive price or wage. Under laissez faire, people will die like flies; even if poor-law relief slows down the process of genocide, after an interval L/K will have dropped to balanced proportions suitable for the earlier analysis. (If one more realistically replaces perfectly fixed proportions by some variability of techniques, the r/w factor-price ratio will not gyrate so violently to zero or infinity and the more neoclassical model of §19 will better approximate reality.)

In every case, ours is a deterministic system for $(L, K, dL/dt, dK/dt)$ and the other variables.[6]

Digression on
Neoclassical Elaboration
of the Classical Model

19. Ricardo and Marx were not so naive observers as to believe literally in fixed proportions between capital goods and labor. Their knowledgeable commentaries on current events presuppose recognition that, at certain price and profit rates, substitutions will be made that would not be competitively viable at other price and profit rates. So it is a caricature to insist on fixed-proportion doses, $V = \text{Min}[L,K]$.

On the other hand it would be ahistorical to read into the classicists a full-fledged post-Clarkian model of neoclassical type. Nonetheless, if we wish to flesh out the torsos of their logically incomplete models, we must supply the equations missing for their additional unknowns. And, once we commit ourselves to (α) free-entry and widely-shared knowledge, (β) constant-returns-to-scale technology, and (γ) smooth variability of the (L_t,K_t) components of the V_t dose, ruthless competition will enforce the neoclassical marginal productivity relations in the canonical model whether or not the classicist is yet aware of those relations and is able to apprehend them. (Before Isaac N.'s birth, apples and the moon fell toward the earth in accordance with inverse-square-of-distance gravitational laws!)

To evaluate the question of how different the classical paradigm was from to-

[5] Strictly speaking, if initial L_0 is astronomically large, starvation and insurrection might kill off the system in one fell swoop. To do justice to this realism, we would have to make $\lambda[w - \bar{w}^*]$ minus infinity at $w = 0$ and perhaps make $f(V)$ turn down for overly large V. Along with the classical writers, I forbear from modelling scenarios of *extinction* from overpopulation. Darwin would no doubt deem this a fault.

[6] The dynamic system is most generally defined by

$$dL/dt = \epsilon^{-1}\lambda[g_1(L, K) - \bar{w}^*]$$
$$dK/dt = \sigma[g_2(L, K) - \bar{r}^*]$$

$$g_1(L, K) + g_2(L, K) = f'\ (\text{Min}[L, K]),\ K \gtreqless L$$

$$g_1(L, K) \equiv 0,\ L > K;\ g_2(L, K) \equiv 0,\ K > L.$$

For any initial (L_0, K_0), this system will approach §13's (L^*, K^*) asymptotically.

day's mainstream economics, it is worth sketching briefly the consequences of replacing $f(\text{Min}[L,K])$ by smooth constant-returns-to-scale technology. To relate the discussion more easily to classical "wage-fund" notions, I work with discrete-time variables, $K_{t+1} - K_t$ instead of dK/dt, and so forth. Writing $(T_1, T_2, \ldots) = \mathbf{T}$ for prescribed amounts of different grades of land, we have:

$$Q_{t+1} = C_{t+1} + K_{t+1} - K_t = F(L_t, K_t; T_1, T_2, \ldots), \quad (10.1)$$

where $F(\ )$ is a first-degree-homogeneous, concave function.[7] For this section, F's partial derivatives are assumed to be well-defined everywhere, in contrast to $\text{Min}[L_t, K_t]$'s assumed non-substitutability. The present section does not rule out that $F(\ )$ might have the separability property of $F(v[L,K]; T_1, T_2, \ldots) \equiv f(v[L,K])$, where $v[L,K]$ is now a smoothly substitutable first-degree-homogeneous and concave function. In this last case, $\partial F/\partial L$ and $\partial F/\partial K$ would be equivalent to $f'(v[L,K])\partial v[L,K]/\partial L$ and $f'(v[L,K])\partial v[L,K]/\partial K$, with $wL + rK = f'(v[L,K])V$ still.

We complete our system with the relations:

$$r_t = \partial F(L_t, K_t, T_1, \ldots)/\partial K_t \quad (10.2)$$

$$w_t = \frac{\partial F(L_t, K_t, T_1 \ldots)/\partial K_t}{1 + r_t} \quad (10.3)$$

$$R_{t+1} = F(L_t, K_t, T_1, \ldots) - r_t K_t - w_t L_t(1 + r_t). \quad (10.4)$$

Note that the workers who are paid *at the beginning* of the period receive only their *discounted* marginal productivity. Note that the total of profit includes (α) interest on wages advanced to the workers (in consumable output) plus (β) the interest earned on the capital-goods used in production K_t. Land gets as residual rent under competitive bidding that part of end-of-period product not preempted by competitive bidding for laborers and capital goods; if rent is payable in advance, competitive arbitrage will ensure that it too will be discounted by the $1/(1 + r_t)$ factor.

Long-run equilibrium comes when all dated variables are starred constants determined by (10.1)–(10.4), when (10.2)–(10.4) have had inserted inside them $\bar{w}^*$ and $\bar{r}^*$ exactly as in §13.

To generate the dynamic growth path of the classical system, we complete it by the supply conditions of saving and of population growth:

$$\frac{K_{t+1} - K_t}{K_t} = \sigma[r_t - \bar{r}^*], \quad (10.5)$$

$$\sigma[0] = 0 < \sigma'[\ ]$$

[7] As Ricardo and J. H. von Thünen understood, larger totals of L and K involve more intense cultivation of previously cultivated grades of good land—say of T_1, at the same time that T_2 newly comes into cultivation. In the background, the function $F(\ )$ has been defined implicitly *as if* by a maximization process. Thus

$$F(L, K; T_1, T_2, \ldots) = \underset{L_i, K}{\text{Max}} \{F_1(L_1, K_1, T_1) + F_2(L_2, K_2, T_2) + \ldots\}$$

subject to

$$L_1 + L_2 + \ldots = L,$$
$$K_1 + K_2 + \ldots = K.$$

If $F_i(\ )$ are concave in (L_i, K_i) and $\partial F_i(\ )/\partial L_i$ and $\partial F_i(\ )/\partial K_i$ are well-defined, or if, for the composite dose $V_i = \text{Min}[L_i, K_i]$, $\partial F_i(V_i, T_i)/\partial V_i$ is well-defined for $F_i(\ )$ concave in V_i, then for all lands actually in use, there will be common marginal productivities of the transferable factors, equal as the case may be to $\partial F(L,K; T_1, T_2, \ldots)/\partial L$ or $\partial F(L,K; T_1, T_2, \ldots)/\partial K$ or to $\partial F(V; T_1, T_2, \ldots)/\partial V$. Therefore, in *Figure* 1 and later figures, the DD' curve of $f'(V)$ represents not merely the *average* product at the *external margin* of continuous-grade lands (as in my footnote 1's' ultra-classical interpretation); DD' alternatively represents the true *marginal* product (at the *internal* margin on every land used of whatever grade) of the variable dose there applied. Note that residual rent, $R = F(V; T_1, T_2, \ldots) - V\partial F(V; T_1, T_2, \ldots)/\partial V$, can *also* be given the post-classical interpretation as being a *marginal-product imputation to lands:* it is logically $R = [T_1 \partial F(V; T_1, T_2, \ldots)/\partial T_1] + [T_2 \partial F(V; T_1, T_2, \ldots)/\partial T_2] + \ldots$ when $F(V; T_1, T_2, \ldots)$ is smooth and obeys constant-returns-to-scale—whether or not Adam Smith had ever known anything of the work of his contemporary, Leonhard Euler!

$$\frac{L_{t+1} - L_t}{L_t} = \lambda[w - \bar{w}^*], \qquad (10.6)$$

$$\lambda[0] = 0 < \lambda'[\ ]$$

$$\lim_{t\to\infty} [L_t, K_t, r_t, w_t, \ldots] = [L^*, K^*, \bar{r}^*, \bar{w}^*, \ldots]. \qquad (10.7)$$

The stability property of (10.7) holds under wide conditions.[8]

It would not be hard to include in (10.5) explicit handling of the wage-fund component in the total asset base upon which capitalists earn profits. For that matter, the capitalized value of land could, in the fashion of A. R. J. Turgot [34, 1770] and Franco Modigliani [18, 1966], be included in the asset base of life-cycle saving. But to handle these items and the public debt rigorously would be to mete out more than justice to the classical writers.

Actually, the classical economists did less than justice to their own model. To suppose that the real wage of any period must merely be the ratio of however many workers present themselves for jobs, divided into that part of C_t which capitalists have decided not to consume but instead have dedicated to the wage fund is not so much a falsehood as a triviality. There could be a period so short in which that version of the wage fund might even be formally correct. (But even this is dubious: the potatoes coming into Manchester need not go by that night into some worker's belly; they might be stored for another day or be destined for the stomach of one of Jane Austen's genteel rentiers.) For a more sympathetic appraisal of wage-fund, see George Stigler [32, 1976].

In the long-run steady state, the fraction of C^* that is adapted to wage-earner's consumption will have been *endogenously* determined. In the transient growth phase of the classical system where each month or year is not very different from its predecessor or successor, the competitive system will anticipate and forestall unpleasant surprises: so the "wage fund" will have been adapted to the viable real wage and total of employed population rather than itself constituting a *deus ex machina* to predetermine wages. John Stuart Mill had reason to dither when various of his wage-fund expositions came under attack—which is not to disagree with the attack in Frank W. Taussig [33, 1896] on the vulgar view of Henry George that

[8] For $\sigma'[\ ]$ and $\lambda'[\ ]$ sufficiently small, the difference equations of the above neoclassical model will be at least locally stable. For any number of factors, $(T, L, K, \ldots) = (x_0, x_1, x_2, \ldots)$, the following version will be stable:

$$(dx_i/dt)/x_i = s_i[p_i - \bar{p}_i^*], \quad (i = 1, \ldots, n)$$

$$p_i = \partial F(1, x_1, \ldots, x_n)/\partial x_i = \partial f(x_1, \ldots, x_n)/\partial x_i$$

$$s_i[0] = 0 \leq z s_i[z] x_i, \qquad x_i > 0$$

$$F(x_0, x_1, \ldots, x_n) = x_0 f(x_1/x_0, \ldots, x_n/x_0)$$

$f(x_1, \ldots, x_n)$ a strictly-concave function.

We may set $x_0 = 1$; and denote by $(x_1^*, \ldots, x_n^*)$ the unique roots of

$$\bar{p}_i^* = \partial f(x_1, \ldots, x_n)/\partial x_i, \quad (i = 1, \ldots, n).$$

Then, for all positive (x_i^0),

$$\lim_{t\to\infty} x_i(t) = x_i^*, \qquad (i = 1, \ldots, n).$$

To prove this theorem on global stability, consider the following maximization process of *total rent*,

$$R(x_1, \ldots, x_n) = F(\bar{x}_0, x_1, \ldots, x_n) - \sum_1^n \bar{p}_j^* x_j$$

$$\dot{R} - \sum_1^n [F_j(\bar{x}_0, x_1, \ldots, x_n) - \bar{p}_j^*] \dot{x}_j = \sum_1^n [F_j(\ ) - \bar{p}_j^*] x_j$$

$$s_j[F_j(\ ) - \bar{p}_j^*] > 0 \text{ when } x_j \neq x_j^*$$

$$\therefore \lim_{t\to\infty} R(t) \equiv \text{Max } R = R^*$$

$$\lim_{t\to\infty} x_j(t) = x_j^*, \ (j = 1, \ldots, n).$$

Note that $\dot{R} = dR/dt$, etc., and that the sign-preserving property of $z_j s_j[z_i] x_j$ has been exploited in the above proof of global stability. I owe thanks to Hiroaki Nagatani of the MIT graduate school for suggesting that $d\{R^* - R(t)\}/dt$ be used as a Lyapunov function for this stability proof. When dx_i/dt is replaced in this footnote's first equation by $x_i(t+1) - x_i(t)$, it can be shown that the resulting difference equations will assuredly be locally stable provided all $s_i'[0]$ are small enough positive numbers.

SHORT-CIRCUITED CASE

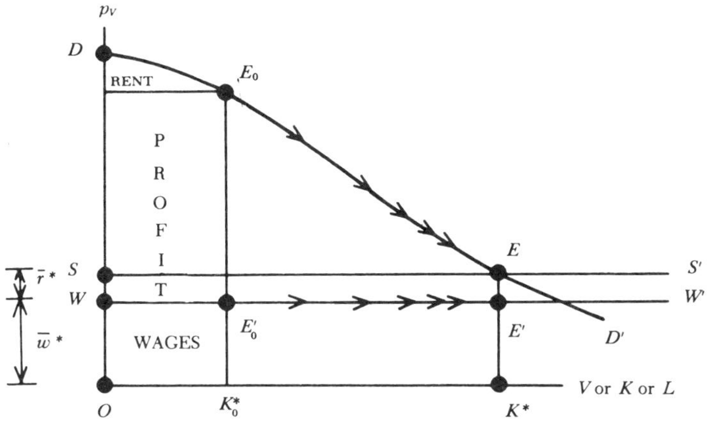

Figure 2. When population supply adjusts virtually instantly, $w(t)$ is always at $\bar{w}^*$ along WW'. With capital (and labor) initially scarce at K_0, rent begins low as shown by the small triangle at E_0: *all* the gain to the composite dose goes to profit as a short-term residual, as shown by E_0' being down on WW'. But the excess of $r(t)$ over $\bar{r}^*$ generates accumulation, as shown by the growth arrows at E_0 and E_0'. Gradually, as $E_0 \rightarrow E^*$ and $r(t) \rightarrow \bar{r}^*$, growth shuts itself off as shown by the shortening of the arrows near the long-run equilibrium E.

production of outputs by inputs is instantaneous and automatically synchronized, a view that seemed to have been surprisingly condoned by J. B. Clark [7, 1899] and Frank Knight in his many writings of the 1930's, and a view properly questioned in Eugen von Böhm-Bawerk [2, 1906; 3, 1907] and echoed a generation later by Fritz Machlup [13, 1935] and Friedrich von Hayek [9, 1936].

* * *

After this neoclassical digression, the reader may return to the canonical classical system. Whether or not he has sampled the mathematical expositions of §12–19, he should be able to follow the next section's graphical depiction of the canonical classical model's path of dynamic development.

Diagrammatics of Classical Growth Theory

20. *Figures* 2, 3(a) and 3(b) provide a self-contained derivation of how the classical system is self-propelled into development by capital accumulation and parallel population growth whenever it initially starts from scarcity of capital and labor relative to their long-run equilibrium rates when they barely earn their costs of reproduction.

For pedagodical simplicity, it is well to begin with the "short-circuited" version of virtually instantaneous population adjustment and the real wage practically always at the subsistence level $\bar{w}^*$. *Figure* 2 portrays this archetypical case, essentially embodying the equations of (7) from §16. The legend should be self-explana-

CANONICAL GROWTH

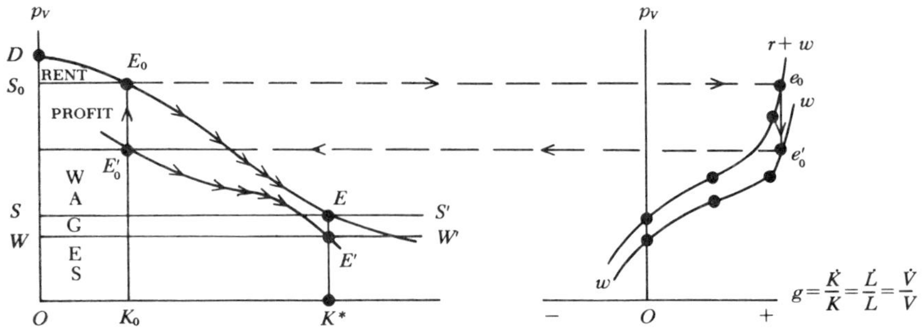

3(a) 3(b)

Figure 3. Labor and capital grow in concert from initial E_0. But now competition determines a fractional breakdown of the dose's surplus return between *both* components of the dose, $w(t) - \bar{w}^*$ as well as $r(t) - \bar{r}^*$, at those fractions that just succeed in evoking the same balanced growth in the supplies of the respective factors $L(t)$ and $K(t)$. The $E_0'E'$ locus in 3(a) gives the breakdown of the fruits of transient progress between capitalists and laborers: the faster the relative supply responsiveness of population, the nearer will $E_0'E'$ be to WW' and the greater profit's transient share; the steeper is $E_0'E'$ northwest of E', the greater the transient share of labor in the above-subsistence surplus. (Short-run distribution of total product, of OK_0E_0D, is shown by the rent triangle S_0E_0D; the dose's remaining rectangle $OK_0E_0S_0$ is divided between profit share and wages share by E_0' on the $E_0'E'$ locus.)

3(b) shows exactly how the $E_0'E'$ locus is determined. The locus ww shows the real wage needed to elicit each algebraic growth rate of labor in balance with the composite dose, $g = \dot{K}/K = \dot{L}/L = \dot{V}/V$ (where $\dot{L} = dL/dt$, etc.). The $r + w$ locus shows the p_V composite returns needed for the combined dose to grow, its needed wage rate plus needed profit rate, to induce balanced growth g—with $w(t)$ read from the lower curve and $r(t)$ from the interval between the curves. One begins at the computational cobweb E_0 in 3(a) then moves horizontally to e_0 in 3(b) and down to e_0'. Going back to 3(a) gives appropriate height of E_0' in 3(a) and appropriate short-run distribution of non-rent income between profit and wages, thus filling in at each new time any logical gaps in the "wage-fund" palaver of the classicists.

tory, as the system moves the short-run equilibrium point E_0 down the path of diminishing returns on fixed land: as E_0 approaches E^*, with $w(t)$ always on the WW' level of $\bar{w}^*$ and $r(t)$ therefore falling toward $\bar{r}^*$, the motive for saving shuts itself off and the system eases itself asymptotically into long-run equilibrium with minimal profit and wage rate and maximal land rent.[9]

[9] If scarcity of land is ignored, the law of diminishing returns is negated and DD' becomes a horizontal line above WW'. This yields the perpetual exponential growth of Marx's *Tableau of Extended Reproduction*, with the growth arrows never shortening and with finite E undefinable.

21. *Figures* 3(a) and 3(b) are interrelated diagrams that handle the more general case. Eschewing the naiveties of the short-circuited pole, they portray the short-term equilibrium in which the transient shortfall of capital and labor leads to both wage and profit being above their ultimate subsistence levels in relative degrees determined by the short-run elasticities of these factors' growth responses: the auction markets for goods, lands, labor, and capital determine short-term equilibrium factor and goods prices that provide allocation between profits and wages of the composite dose's transient surplus return.

To supplement the legends of *Figures* 3(a) and 3(b), the reader will want to understand what determines the dynamic path $E_0''E'$ in 3(a), the path that summarizes how much goes to above-subsistence wages and how much to what Schumpeter would have called *transient* profits (which, he thought, would soon cease to exist in the absence of technical change and entrepreneurial innovation because $\bar{r}^* = 0$ for Schumpeter).

To test his understanding, the reader should be able to realize that Smith's cheerful rise in real wages would be enhanced if the ww curve were made more vertical in 3(b) and the $r + w$ curve were made virtually parallel to it.[10] By contrast, the short-circuited case will be understood as that in which ww is virtually horizontal while $r + w$ is not. In every case, the dashed-line cobweb $E_0e_0e_0'E_0''$ determines the position of the points on the $E_0''E'$ path of wage-profit allocation and the decelerating growth rate of the classical system as land scarcity invokes the law of diminishing returns and the relapse into long-run equilibrium.

Ricardo's readers should not have been shocked by his third edition discovery that invention of machinery could depress the real wage and lower the population and the total of product in the short and long run. Already in his earlier editions, and quite independently of the *durability* of capital goods, there was present to a truly sophisticated eye the possibility that DD' could twist *upward and inward*, the *only* limitation on the *long*-run viability of an invention being that it *raise* the *SED* rent triangle!

Final Qualifications and Extensions

22. The classicists earned for our subject Carlyle's title of the dismal science precisely because their expositions erred in overplaying the law of diminishing returns and underplaying the counterforces of technical change. They lived during the industrial revolution, but scarcely looked out from their libraries to notice the remaking of the world.

Thus, as innovation plucks the DD' string outward, it would in all likelihood lift real wages and profit rates above their minima. Before they and the string can dampen down, a new invention plucks again the string. Therefore, a Brownian dance or Schumpeterian fluctuation of real wages and profits at average levels *above* the minima would be the proper and realistic generalization of the notion of gloomy equilibrium. Indeed, if one steps up the rate of innovation enough, an upward trend in the level of E_0'' and real wage may be called for as the putative laws of motion of developing capitalism, which could have made economists in

[10] *Figures* 3(a) and 3(b) in effect solve the simultaneous equations (8.1) and (8.2) for each inherited level of K and its accompanying balanced L. In the pre-balanced stage where one of L or K might be redundant, the diagrams must be reinterpreted. Thus, suppose K/L initially unbalanced above unity. Then only the ww curve in 3(b) is relevant: we run from E_0 over to it and short-run E_0'' coincides with E_0; V_t grows with L_t and, being redundant, K_t's level is irrelevant. Once L_t rises to K_t, 3(a) and 3(b) apply as shown. To handle the case of initially redundant L_0, the reader should vertically subtract ww from $w + r$, labelling the result as rr; then, erasing ww, he should proceed as in the previous several sentences but with the factors being interchanged in the logically obvious way.

Carlyle's eyes the complacent scientists and the apologists for the system.

Just as one example, suppose land-augmenting technical change takes place according to Malthus's *arithmetic* progression. Then if he could analyze correctly his version of the canonical system, he would find that population comes to grow in an *arithmetic* and not in a *geometric* progression [14, 1798]. An amusing irony? Perhaps, but not a joke on Malthus: for, asymptotically, the real wage would then indeed approach his subsistence wage, $w(t) \rightarrow \bar{w}^*$. But, whatever the warrant for geometric progressions in biological reproduction, Malthus never had any plausible reasons behind his gratuitous effusions about arithmetic progressions. If the wrangler had remembered from his Cambridge education three rather than two kinds of progressions, Malthus's impact would have been weakened, but his analysis would have been less special.

23. The present model narrows the classical focus to a single sector. Thereby, one succeeds in freeing their distribution theory from the dreaded complications of value theory. Thereby, one fabricates the Ur-Ricardo model, which determines the system's profit rate from the corn sector alone: having only one sector, it is the corn sector that Ladislaus von Bortkiewicz [5, 1907], Piero Sraffa [30, 1951], Nicholas Kaldor [10, 1956], and others liked to think about; and, contrary to enemies of neoclassicism, there is nothing in the model of a corn-sector-that-determines-its-own-profit-rate which is alien to neoclassicism.

But of course many of the classical problems—as for example the actual share of wages to profits or rent—were recognized by them to depend on many-sector demands. Reducing the Corn-Law tariff on imported food shifted the mix of English production to less land-intensive goods and lowered rent's share. Ricardo knew that in 1815 and 1821: no external margin can logically save his pseudo-labor-theory-of-value from "the complications of value theory and resource scarcities." In my bicentennial appreciation of Smith [28, Samuelson, 1977], I sketched a many-commodity version of the present system, and in my classroom lectures on Ricardo, I show how a 2-primary-factor time-phased system *must* depart from the simplicities of a labor-only technology. It would be easy here to deal with many capital goods of differing durabilities.[11] But it is ludicrous to think that problems that haunt a post-neoclassical writer today—the 1966 Hahn problem of foresight to determine the warrantable allocation among microsectors and durable goods, reswitching, *etc.* [8, 1966]—were themselves absent from the century of 1750–1850 or were better handled by some lost paradigm of the capitalist writers. Under a powdered wig you find the usual head, like yours and mine, sometimes inflated and sometimes sage, but quite innocent of magic charms and skeleton keys to banish complexity.

24. Much of what has been called history of economic thought deals with questions like, "What did Ricardo mean when he said . . . ?" And "Was Smith right and Malthus wrong in alleging . . . ?" On this occasion it has not been my purpose to find and quote the pages in which Smith or Marx or Mill did or did not define an exogenous reproduction wage or profit rate, $\bar{w}^*$ and $\bar{r}^*$. Like the Bible, the canon of classical political economy contains passages that seem to assert and to deny the same thing. If, in some mood or for some problem, an ancient writer denies some axiom of what has here been called the canonical classical system, that does not

[11] Thus, we might replace K in (2) by the vector $\mathbf{K} = (K_1, K_2, \ldots)$ and dK/dt in (1) by $\Sigma c_j(dK_j/dt)$, recognizing that depreciation of each K_i occurs at the rate $\delta_i K_i$.

dispose of the problem. It raises the question of what he then intended to provide for the now-missing equation of the new system.

The canonical model is not so realistic in its features or pretty in its logic that any classicist, if he really understood it in all its interrelations and implications, would want to go into a very hot oven to defend it. As you read the letters of debate and agreement between Malthus and Ricardo, the treatises of Smith and Mill, you realize that theirs was not an age where one set out in Whitehead-Russell or even Spinoza purity the structures of their models. Their quarrels lasted because often they were quarrels over misunderstandings and definitions. (I was intrigued a few years ago when Professor Dorfman came from Harvard to my MIT seminar to report on Malthus's theoretical system: it turned out—Say's Law aside—to be isomorphic with my earlier report to the seminar on Ricardo's system, even though Dorfman and I had never compared notes! Yet Ricardo and Malthus thought they had different and irreconcilable views on microeconomics, and most commentators have judged Ricardo the victor in the debate.)

On reflection, I think that the present version of the classical system agrees in behavioral essentials with that understood by John Ramsey M'Culloch, William Nassau Senior, Samuel Bailey, Karl August Dietzel, Francis Y. Edgeworth, Edwin Cannan, Frank W. Taussig, Jacob Viner, and Piero Sraffa. I have checked my relations and behavior equations against those of Nicholas Kaldor [10, 1956], Luigi L. Pasinetti [20, 1960], Mark Blaug [1, 1978], Hans Brems [6, 1960], and Samuelson [22, 1957; 23, 1959; 24, 1959; 25, 1971; 26, 1974; 27, 1977] and believe they all tell essentially the same classical story. Left to the Appendix is a cursory sampling of the semantic quarrels of the classical writers.

Literary Appendix on Doctrinal Disputes Among Classicists

I ought to address myself, even if briefly, to the following queries. "Have you not minimized the basic differences between the classical writers in formulating for them a common canonical model? After all, didn't Ricardo set out to write his *Principles* in considerable degree because he thought Smith in error on important matters?"

The considered answer I would give is this: "Yes, Ricardo differed with Smith; and thought those differences important. But upon detailed examination, we find that their differences do not mainly involve differences in their behavior equations, short-run or long-run, but rather involve their semantic preferences about what names could be given to the same agreed-upon effects. To moderns, it is for the most part a quarrel about nothing substantive, being essentially an irrelevant argument carried out by Ricardo, often with somewhat unaesthetic logic."

I shall illustrate with no less than Ricardo's Chapter 1, Section 1 [21, 1817]: Here Ricardo wishes to relate changes in any good's "value" to changes in its embodied labor content alone; and here he chides Smith for replacing embodied labor content by how many hours of labor a good can command (or, in some Smithian moods, by what need not be quite the same thing, by the amount of corn or means-of-subsistence goods basket that the good in question may trade for or command).

A 3-good version of the canonical model will show Smith and Ricardo in absolute agreement on *all* substantive facts. Corn, ballet, and gold are each producible by land, labor, and possibly out of themselves as needed raw materials or durable goods in a time-phased way. Here are test cases.

Case 1. Land is redundant and rent

zero. The profit rate is zero ($\tilde{r}^* = 0$). In this initial rude state, each good has a market price in proportion to its labor contents; each good commands precisely those same labor contents. A drop in labor requirements for a good like gold cheapens gold relative to corn and ballet and relative to a day's labor. Gold has dropped in "value," both writers agree. (Note: "money prices" expressed in gold rise for corn, ballet, and a day's labor.)

Case 2. Replace the invention in gold production by a similar one in corn production only. Now only corn has dropped in "value" for Ricardo. Gold and ballet have remained unchanged. The same holds for Smith's labor-command version of value. But now of course Smith's corn-command measure of value must diverge from Smith's labor-command measure: in terms of the former, Smith would say that gold, ballet, and a day's labor have risen in "value" and corn by definition has not changed.

If this were the end of the matter, despite Einstein's shrugging of shoulders, Ricardo's terminology and Smith's here-identical first-version terminology would seem slightly preferable to Smith's second-version terminology. I suspect Smith would agree for this case.

Case 3. But Smith—and Ricardo in Chapter 1, Section 1—would not expect the matter to end with this new short-run equilibrium. With the real wage now above the (previous) subsistence level, population would grow and in *Figures* 2–3 we would move along E_0E'. With land superabundant and the population adjustment parameter ϵ in (5) very fast (as suggested by Ricardo's words "in no long time" or "probably at the end of a very few years"), the corn invention would raise the profit rate above zero (actually to 100 percent per period if the labor requirements for corn halved) keeping the corn wage down near $\bar{w}^*$ and making Smith's two versions now agree with each other. But now they differ from Ricardo's version.

And which is semantically more appealing? I believe the jury will say, if *case* 3 is at all the common one in history, then Smith's terminology is more appealing: For Smith, the rise in the prices of gold and ballet in terms of both corn and a day's work (these last are in the same exchange rate as before) represents an increase in their "value." Moreover, Smith's quantitative degree of rise in their "value" does *exactly* match their rise in relative price. By contrast, Ricardo says that gold and ballet are completely unchanged in "value," while corn has halved in "value"; relative to corn's "value," they have exactly doubled in "value"—whereas actually, both men agree that their prices could have increased respectively by 10 percent and 999 percent or by 99 percent and 1 percent or by *any* quantitative degrees, depending on what a 100 percent profit rate does in marking up their competitive prices!

Ricardo's debating gaffe is to chide Smith for departing from concepts appropriate only for a $r = 0 = R$ world, and then in Section 1 himself adopting such departures as the ammunition for his criticisms of Smith.

Case 4. To amplify the point, let's suppose land is scarce and rent no longer zero. For simplicity, posit $\tilde{r}^* = 0$ and concentrate on comparing long-run equilibria. Suppose all wages are spent on subsistence corn, which is produced by land and labor. Suppose all rent is spent on a luxury good (say gold), which is produced by labor alone. *Figure* 1, with *WW'* and *SS'* coinciding, determines the corn employment level at E (and coinciding E'). Knowing the ratio of the *SED* rent triangle to the wage rectangle formed by E, we know the ratio of labor employed in gold to that employed in corn. So our 2-good canonical long-run equilibrium is determinate in all details.

Now let a labor-augmenting invention in the corn industry make one laborer be the equivalent to two laborers. After a transient rise in profit and wage rates, $r(t)$ and $w(t)$ settle back to 0 and $\bar{w}^*$ by that determinate change in corn labor that reflects the shifted E intersection. In the end, the prices of corn, a day's labor, and gold are in *exactly the same ratios* as they started out. Both of Smith's verbiages well describe the facts: neither corn nor gold have changed in command over a unit of labor; gold is unchanged in its command over corn; only rent has risen in its command over everything else, corn, gold, and a unit of labor.

Ricardo, by contrast, is in a pickle. Gold's embodied labor is unchanged; but corn's embodied labor, measured by *total corn labor/total corn*, rises if rent's share of corn cost rises and falls if that rent share falls: either case is possible depending on a 1932 elasticity-of-substitution undreamed of by Ricardo or Mill. Who would find it useful to follow Ricardo in saying that corn's "value" has changed when *all* (P_c, P_g, W) ratios are unchanged?

There is one way out for Ricardo—a disastrous one. Suppose Ricardo measures corn's embodied labor content, not by *average* labor content, L_c/Q_c, but by *"marginal* labor content"—measured by labor per corn output on *external* margin land, or on the *internal* land margin's $1/(\partial Q_c/\partial L_c)$. To coin a phrase, this neoclassical version of Ricardo (call it Clark-Ricardo) is a disaster for his debate with Smith *because, using it, Ricardo finds himself here in exact agreement with* the labor-command *doctrine of Smith* that *Section* 1 is attacking![12]

[12] As Viner [35, 1930, pp. 79–80] pointed out in his famous review of Cannan, a marginal-labor theory of value is isomorphic with a marginal-land theory of value or with a marginal-fertilizer theory of value: when n goods are each producible out of transferable-indifferent labor and transferable-indifferent fertilizer, it is as trivial to say that any competitive price ratio, P_i/P_j, is equal to relative marginal-fertilizer–requirement ratios as to marginal-labor–requirements. It would be anticlimactic if the labor theory of value, from John Locke through Marx, reduced down to this (envelope) triviality.

* * *

Other beefs with Smith by Ricardo reduce to similar semantic snarls.[13] We are left with the essential unity of the classical model, the progressions and retrogressions being primarily in the modes of explanation.

[13] One such is Ricardo's accusation that Smith makes land rent price determining. After a careful audit, we should agree with the dissenting verdict of Stigler [31, 1952, p. 205]: ". . . the tenor of Smith's theory of rent, which was not given a coherent statement, was that aggregate rents are a residual, but that the rent of any one use of land is a cost determined by alternative uses of land. Ricardo ignored the multiplicity of uses of land." Another Ricardian *non sequitur*, Sraffa [30, 1951, p. xxxvii], is his invalid inference that Smith's equating of price to the *sum* of wages + rent + profit implies that Smith believed that such a price was necessarily higher than in the rude state (when productivity was so low as to make rent zero and the earnable-profit zero). Again, it is the critic, Ricardo, who seems to have nodded.

Professor Stigler points out to me that I have been rather charitable to Smith in attributing to him knowledge of diminishing returns; and less than just to Ricardo in not crediting his Chapter 1 with having succeeded in showing that changes only in wage rates will not affect relative values. I ought to mention that the similarity of Ricardo and Malthus ends when we deal with the macroeconomics of Say's Law. Professor Blaug also doubts that the differences between Ricardo and Smith are usefully dismissed as being merely semantic; in any case, upon review, I find no thought experiments proposed by Ricardo to which he has given a different substantive answer than would Smith's system; outright slips by Smith seem if anything less than those in Ricardo and are of secondary importance in both cases.

References

1. Blaug, Mark. *Economic theory in retrospect.* Third edition. London; New York and Melbourne: Cambridge University Press, [1962, 1968] 1978.
2. von Böhm-Bawerk, Eugen. "Capital and Interest Once More: I. Capital vs. Capital Goods," *Quart. J. Econ.*, Nov. 1906, *21*, pp. 1–21.
3. ______. "Capital and Interest Once

More: II. A Relapse to the Productivity Theory," *Quart. J. Econ.*, Feb. 1907, *21*, pp. 247–82.
4. ______. "The Nature of Capital: A Rejoinder," *Quart. J. Econ.*, Nov. 1907, pp. 28–47.
5. VON BORTKIEWICZ, LADISLAUS. "On the Correction of Marx's Fundamental Theoretical Construction in the Third Volume of 'Capital,'" *Jahr. Nationalökon. Statist.*, 1907, *89*, pp. 319–35; reprinted in English in *Karl Marx and the close of his system, by Eugen von Böhm-Bawerk and Böhm-Bawerk's criticism of Marx, by Rudolf Hilferding; with an appendix by L. von Bortkiewicz.* Edited by PAUL M. SWEEZY. New York: Kelley, 1949.
6. BREMS, HANS. "An attempt at a Rigorous Restatement of Ricardo's Long-Run Equilibrium," *Canadian J. Econ.*, Feb. 1960, *26*, pp. 74–86.
7. CLARK, JOHN BATES. *The distribution of wealth: A theory of wages, interest and profits.* New York: Macmillan, 1899.
8. HAHN, FRANK H. "Equilibrium Dynamics with Heterogeneous Capital Goods," *Quart. J. Econ.*, Nov. 1966, *80*, pp. 633–46.
9. VON HAYEK, FRIEDRICH A. "The Mythology of Capital," *Quart. J. Econ.*, Feb. 1936, *50*, pp. 199–228.
10. KALDOR, NICHOLAS. "Alternative Theories of Distribution," *Rev. Econ. Stud.*, 1956, *23*, pp. 83–100.
11. KUHN, THOMAS S. *The structure of scientific revolutions.* Chicago: University of Chicago Press, 1962.
12. LONGFIELD, MOUNTIFORT. *Lectures on political economy.* Dublin: R. Milliken and Son, 1834.
13. MACHLUP, FRITZ. "Professor Knight and the 'Period of Production,'" *J. Polit. Econ.*, Oct. 1935, *43*(5), pp. 577–624.
14. MALTHUS, THOMAS R. *An essay on the principle of population* [First Essay on Population]. London: J. Johnson, 1798.
15. ______. *Principles of political economy.* London: J. Murray, 1820.
16. MARX, KARL. *Capital: A critique of political economy.* Vol. 1, 1867; Vol. 2, 1885; Vol. 3, 1894.
17. MILL, JOHN STUART. *Principles of political economy.* Boston: Little & Brown, 1848.
18. MODIGLIANI, FRANCO. "The Life Cycle Hypothesis of Saving, the Demand for Wealth and the Supply of Capital," *Social Res.*, June 1966, *33*, pp. 160–217.
19. MORISHIMA, MICHIO. *Marx's economics: A dual theory of value and growth.* New York and London: Cambridge University Press, 1973.
20. PASINETTI, LUIGI L. "A Mathematical Formulation of the Ricardian System," *Rev. Econ. Stud.*, Feb. 1960, *27*, pp. 78–98.
21. RICARDO, DAVID. *On the principles of political economy and taxation.* London: J. Murray, 1817.
22. SAMUELSON, PAUL A. "Wages and Interest: A Modern Dissection of Marxian Economic Models," *Amer. Econ. Rev.*, Dec. 1957, *47*, pp. 884–912; reprinted in *The collected scientific papers of Paul A. Samuelson.* Vol. 1. Edited by JOSEPH E. STIGLITZ. Cambridge, Mass.: MIT Press, 1965, pp. 341–69.
23. ______. "A Modern Treatment of the Ricardian Economy: I. The Pricing of Goods and of Labor and Land Services," *Quart. J. Econ.*, Feb. 1959, *73*, pp. 1–35; reprinted in *The collected scientific papers of Paul A. Samuelson.* Vol. 1. Edited by JOSEPH E. STIGLITZ. Cambridge, Mass.: MIT Press, 1965, pp. 373–407.
24. ______. "A Modern Treatment of the Ricardian Economy: II. Capital and Interest Aspects of the Pricing Process," *Quart. J. Econ.*, May 1959, *73*,

pp. 217–31; reprinted in *The collected scientific papers of Paul A. Samuelson.* Vol. 1. Edited by JOSEPH E. STIGLITZ. Cambridge, Mass.: MIT Press, 1965, pp. 408–22.

25. ———. "Understanding the Marxian Notion of Exploitation: A Summary of the So-Called Transformation Problem between Marxian Values and Competitive Prices," *J. Econ. Lit.*, June 1971, *9*(2), pp. 399–431; reprinted in *The collected scientific papers of Paul A. Samuelson.* Vol. 3. Edited by ROBERT C. MERTON. Cambridge, Mass.: MIT Press, 1972, pp. 276–308.
26. ———. "Marx as Mathematical Economist: Steady-State and Exponential Growth Equilibrium," in *Trade, stability, and macroeconomics: Essays in honor of Lloyd A. Metzler.* Edited by GEORGE HORWICH AND PAUL SAMUELSON. New York: Academic Press, 1974, pp. 269–307; reprinted in *The collected scientific papers of Paul A. Samuelson.* Vol. 4. Edited by HIROAKI NAGATANI AND KATE CROWLEY. Cambridge, Mass.: MIT Press, 1977, pp. 231–69.
27. ———. "A Modern Theorist's Vindication of Adam Smith," *Amer. Econ. Rev.*, Feb. 1977, *67*(1), pp. 42–49.
28. ———. "Correcting the Ricardo Error Spotted in Harry Johnson's Maiden Paper," *Quart. J. Econ.*, Nov. 1977, *91*(4), pp. 519–30.
29. SMITH, ADAM. *An inquiry into the nature and causes of the wealth of nations.* London: W. Strahan and T. Cadell, 1776.
30. SRAFFA, PIERO. "Introduction," in *Works and correspondence of David Ricardo.* Vol. 1. Cambridge: Cambridge University Press, 1951, pp. xiii–lxii.
31. STIGLER, GEORGE J. "The Ricardian Theory of Value and Distribution," *J. Polit. Econ.*, June 1952, *60*, pp. 187–207.
32. ———. *The scientific uses of scientific biography,* with special reference to J. S. Mill. Toronto: University of Toronto Press, 1976, pp. 55–66.
33. TAUSSIG, FRANK W. *Wages and capital: An examination of the wage fund doctrine.* London and New York: Macmillan, 1896.
34. TURGOT, ANNE ROBERT JACQUES. *Réflexions sur la formation et la distribution des richesses* (1770). Translated as *Reflections on the formation and the distribution of riches.* New York: Macmillan, 1898.
35. VINER, JACOB. "Book Review of Edwin Cannan's *A Review of Economic Theory,*" *Economica,* 1930, *10*(28), pp. 74–84.

Noise and Signal in Debates Among Classical Economists: A Reply

By PAUL A. SAMUELSON
Massachusetts Institute of Technology

1. It is high praise when so expert a scholar as Samuel Hollander (1980) hails my canonical classical model (1978) as likely to become "the *locus classicus* for the next generation of textbook writers." Like Fletcher I care not who makes a nation's laws if I can shape its textbook writers' songs.

But with power comes responsibility. I must weigh and respond to the doubts Dr. Hollander raises about some positions I took in the three-seventeenths of my positivistic text that digresses to interpret particular historical controversies.

I shall be brief and deal only with most essential points.

2. I am glad that Dr. Hollander does find in the *Wealth of Nations* the canonical model that I attributed to the classical writers and to it. My readers will be grateful to him for documenting the case that it is there.

3. Ricardo and his contemporaries may, however, be in no need of enemies if their defenders must write on their behalf that they missed what was in the *Wealth of Nations* because the relevant material was "scattered" and appears in out of the way chapters where such esoteric subjects as colonies are discussed. To say that something in an earlier well-known author is "irrelevant" because it was "overlooked" seems just another way of saying it has been overlooked—a *description* of a misdemeanor and not an *extenuation*. A stronger defense of Smith against such misunderstandings can be provided by modern economics, I believe, and now wish to explain.

4. Experienced readers know that Ricardo all too often (1) does not succeed in expressing what he means to say. And (2) that which he does mean to say is often *not* correct until properly qualified. What complicates the matter is that (3) Ricardo often reveals somewhere in his work that he has glimpsed the needed qualification.

Thus, the following Factor-Price–Frontier Theorem was certainly glimpsed by Ricardo.

THEOREM. (α) In a given competitive technology, there is a trade-off relation between the equilibrium (1) *profit* rate, (2) *real wage* rate (in terms of any good or subsistence basket of goods), and (3) *real rent* rate (or set of real rent rates if, instead of a single homogeneous land, we assume a vector of heterogeneous lands). Mathematically,

$$\begin{aligned} 0 &= \text{profit rate} + f(\text{real wage, real rent}) \\ &= p + f(w,r) \end{aligned}$$

where $f(w,r)$ is a quasi-concave monotone-increasing function—i.e., one with convex contours. (See *Figure* 1 for plots of this trade-off.)

(β) It follows that, if the real wage stays *in the long run* at a prescribable subsistence level as the result of population adjustment, there can be no decline in the profit rate unless land's scarcity rent rises.

FACTOR-PRICE–FRONTIER TRADE-OFF

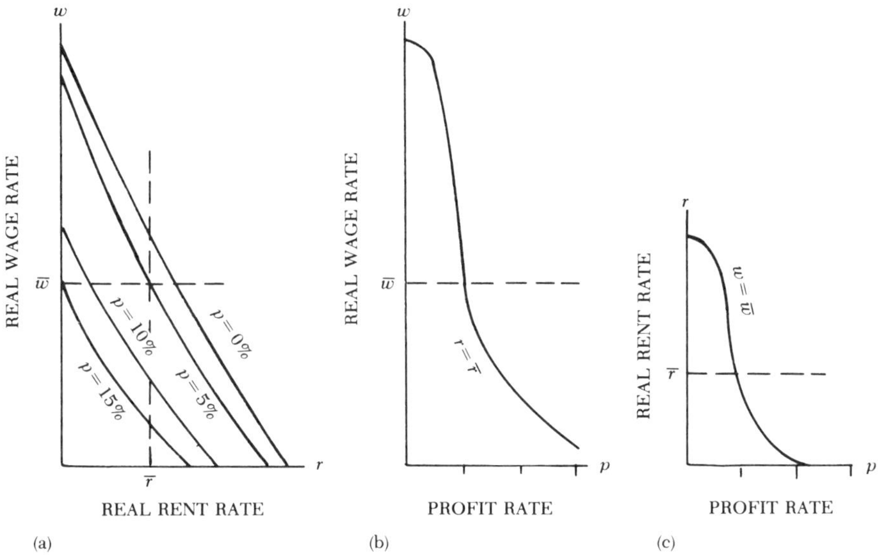

Figure 1. Competitive equilibrium requires that, when any two of (w,r,p) are higher, the remaining one must be lower. With technology unchanged, the iso-profit contours in (a) must be convex, but no such curvature restrictions need occur in (b) and (c). In Ricardo's longest run in which the subsistence wage is kept by population adjustment to $\bar{w}$, (c) depicts the trade-off that Ricardo perceived. Smith also perceived this. So long as we avoid the unrealistic "short-circuited version of the Ricardian system," in which population adjusts infinitely quickly, capital accumulation that outpaces population can move the system upward on (b)'s contour (or even *north*westward of it); so Smith is free of logical error in having accumulation bid down the profit rate without regard to land and diminishing returns. He would, however, be wrong if he thought that labor could command the same amount of subsistence corn while the profit rate was falling, technical change was possibly going on, and the scarcity rent of land was not rising; but can such a belief be fairly pinned on Smith?

Ricardo never stated the above post-1953 truth in my clear language. But, to repeat, he obviously did grasp it.[1] What

[1] To illustrate my remark that what Ricardo wants to say is often not true without qualification, let me mention the case well known to the classical writers of *joint production*. The above Factor-Price–Frontier Theorem is *not* true for it. Thus, when capitalists and rich landowners shift their tastes for shoes made of hides that are jointly produced with workers' meat, Ricardo must concede that the profit rate, real subsistence wage rate, and real rent rate could *all simultaneously fall*. In what follows I explicitly rule out joint production as the disputants would obviously want me to.

we grant to him, Ricardo was unwilling to grant to Adam Smith. However, when I read what the *Wealth of Nations* has to say about the rude state, about China, Bengal, and other regions whose fertile lands get "filled up" with their complements of people, I find Smith's understanding to be commendable. (Book I seems by itself adequate. But so are later Books.)

5. I must now investigate the possibility that what Smith does at times grasp, he at other times denies or at least overlooks.

In particular, was Adam Smith at fault in speaking so often of a process whereby extensive accumulation of capital will bid down the profit rate without Smith's making explicit or implicit reference to diminishing returns on fixed land?

My verdict is in Smith's favor. The following valid third paragraph of the Factor-Price-Frontier Theorem demonstrates why.

> (γ) It also follows that, whenever the accumulation of capital (or the vigorous attempt to accumulate it) sufficiently exceeds the pace of population growth, there can be a decline in the rate of profit and a rise in the real wage during whatever run of time the process is continuing—and this even in a colony without land scarcity or even where the existent land scarcity is not becoming more pressing, and indeed even where land rent were to be forced *down* by the creation of new capital items that happen to be competitive in production with land. [Thus, envisage a movement northwest along or near a contour in *Figure* 1b.]

If Ricardo denies this truth, he errs. If he and other contemporaneous readers affirm it, they must withdraw their charge and absolve Smith of *logical error* in numerous passages where he writes that an increase in capital can bid down the profit rate (and can cogently claim this even in the absence of mention of the fact of diminishing returns and of such diminishing returns being present).[2]

Once Dr. Hollander acquits Dr. Smith of logical error, Smith's "celebrated notion of 'competition among capitals'" is seen to have little cogent bearing on Ricardo's quashed indictment. It is like the red herring of whether Smith momentarily deviated into the heresy of questioning what is today called Say's Law (or James Mill's Law, or Francis Hutcheson's, or Smith's, or Ricardo's). You can affirm Say's Law and still agree with Adam Smith's contention that fast capital accumulation can depress the profit rate without necessarily raising remuneration of land.

6. Patently, Smith's terminology is not that of modern purists. I would not call land's return a "monopoly" return—even

[2] Only in what I called the "short-circuited version" of the Ricardian system will we be moving *in every run* on a contour of *Figure* 1c and would Ricardo's indictment of Smith be strictly sustained. I must mildly protest that Dr. Hollander does me an injustice in saying that my article fabricated a myth in discussing this short-circuited version. I presented that version as a pedagogic device; the fact that this polar case contained the prefix "Ricardian" was not meant to indicate that Ricardo himself believed in it but rather that it applied to Ricardo-like systems. However, I do not mind doing here what I refrained from doing in the article on the canonical model, namely joining with the host of commentators on Ricardo who complain over his exaggerating the speed with which long-run relations are realized. Schumpeter, not unfairly, called this "the Ricardian vice"—one of several such. Citing some sentences where Ricardo lapses into good sense will not wash away the stain. I should add that other classicals, Smith not excepted, sometimes perpetrate similar misjudgments about the long and short run—as some writers now living have been observed to do. It is an interesting curiosity that Ricardo himself criticized Adam Smith's facile assumption that population adjusted quickly enough to make it approximately true that labor always commands about the same ration of subsistence corn. (In the 1980 Eleventh edition of my textbook, *Economics* [1980, p. 257], I reproduced the behavior of the subsistence wage rate calculated by E. H. Phelps Brown and S. V. Hopkins [1956], and I was surprised to see how well Adam Smith's doctrine of "labor command" stood up empirically in the period 1550–1800.)

if its return covers no cost—so long as no landowner is big enough to affect market rents. But substantively Smith's rent theory and mine are one.

Similarly, when a plentiful rye harvest bids down the price of rye, I would not speak of "an increase in competition" for fear that a modern reader of Chamberlin might infer that I was asserting that the degree of *market imperfection* had changed. But, still, Smith's theory of what is going on in the rye market and mine are the same one.

Therefore, I am not tempted to throw a very large stone when Smith indulges in expressions like "increased competitions of capitals." He and I are agreed that the equilibrium interest or profit rate is likely to be lowered when the investment-saving rate soars and biological reproductive propensities remain the same. And so should Ricardo when we call to his attention the facts that it takes nine months to make a baby and more than a decade for that baby to ripen into a worker.

I put to the counsel for Ricardo the following questions: "Will you please shift downward in *Figure* 3(b) of Samuelson's canonical classical model the $r + w$ locus to reflect a sudden increase in thriftiness. Now I ask you to state the answers to these three questions: (i) What happens to the rent rate? (ii) What happens to the profit rate? (iii) What happens to the real wage rate? Must you not agree with the answers: (i) Rent changes not at all in the first instance. (ii) The profit rate is bid down. (iii) The real wage is bid up." I rest Adam Smith's case.

7. In conclusion, I want to make clear that I believe West, Malthus, and Ricardo did in 1815 add much value to the classical doctrines. Every historian of science appreciates how vague are the brilliant perceptions of the earliest writers and how constructive is the achievement of later writers in synthesizing and clarifying ideas. I do not wish to say, "It was all in Adam Smith from the beginning," but to rescue him as I would John Stuart Mill from the discount that they suffer as theorists on the bourse of posterity opinion. Puffing Ricardo simply sets him up as a great short sale.

Still, I must say, *"Touché,"* when Dr. Hollander gently reproves me for my incautious boyish words alleging that all classical writers believed in the same behavior equations. Like us, they were too human to be above error and self-contradiction.

REFERENCES

HOLLANDER, SAMUEL. "On Professor Samuelson's Canonical Model of Political Economy," *J. Econ. Lit.*, 1980, *18*(2), pp. 559–74.

PHELPS BROWN, E. H. AND HOPKINS, S. V. "Seven Centuries of the Prices of Consumables Compared with Builders' Wage-Rates," *Economica N.S.*, Nov. 1956, *23*, pp. 296–314.

SAMUELSON, PAUL A. "The Canonical Classical Model of Political Economy," *J. Econ. Lit.*, Dec. 1978, *16*(4), pp. 1415–34.

———. *Economics.* Eleventh edition. New York: McGraw-Hill, 1980.

A Modern Theorist's Vindication of Adam Smith

By PAUL A. SAMUELSON*

Inside every classical economist is a modern economist trying to get out. In rereading the *Wealth of Nations,* it seems to me that with a little midwifery sleight of hand, one can extract from Adam Smith a valuable model that vindicates him from criticisms of Ricardo and Marx and from the general supercilious discounting of Smith as an unoriginal theorist who is logically fuzzy and eclectically empty. My general finding, as reported in these brief literary words here today and in a companion mathematical appendix, provides a vindication of Adam Smith and serves, in my mind at least, to raise his stature as an economic theorist, both absolutely and in comparison with his predecessors and successors.

I. Views on Smith

Smith is admired for his eclectic wisdom about developing capitalism, and for his ideological defense of competitive *laissez faire* as against blundering Mercantilist interferences with the market. His analysis of the division of labor, like Allyn Young's analysis of increasing returns in the 1920's, is thought to be seminal for the understanding of change, for the Chamberlinian deviations from perfect competition, and for the young Marx's concept of *alienation* of the overspecialized worker.

But there you have it. As a pure theorist, Adam Smith is written down precisely because of his fuzzy eclecticism. His natural prices and wages are thought to be merely the resultants of long-run supply and demand. His pluralistic decomposition of price and of Net National Product *(NNP)* into components of wages, land rent, and of profit is criticized as emptily tautological. After his good start with the labor theory of value, Smith is thought to have blotted his copybook by introducing *ad hoc* and not-fully-explained deductions from labor's full share by landowners and capitalist owners of stock. Even Smith's accounting decomposition of national income into value added elements of wages, rents and profits has been attacked in *Capital,* Volume 2, as involving vicious-circle reasoning. Too often theorists contrast Adam Smith to his disfavor with his brilliant predecessor, David Hume, and brilliant successor, David Ricardo.

II. The Case for Smith

My reading is otherwise.

1) Smith's value-added accounting is shown to be correct by Leontief-Sraffa modeling.

2) His pluralistic supply-and-demand analysis in terms of all three components of wages, rents, and profits is a valid and valuable anticipation of general equilibrium modeling.

3) His vision of transient growth from invention and capital accumulation, which is brought to an equilibrium end with a low rate of profit and a high total of land rent, is *isomorphic* with the model of Ricardo, Malthus, and Marx. But Smith is less guilty than these three of believing in a rigid subsistence-wage supply of labor in the short and intermediate run; so Smith's transient rise in wage rates is a credit to his model's realism, wherever it deviates in emphasis from its successors.

As a theorist, I do find things to criticize in Smith. Thus, he seems never to have known how to put net capital formation into his Net National Product concept. His exposition is 1776, not 1876 or 1976, in its vagueness. However, with careful reading, we do infer in the *Wealth of Nations* a complete and valuable theoretical model.

Finally, I omit in this brief paper discussion of

*Massachusetts Institute of Technology.

pseudo-problems that have monopolized the Smith-Ricardo literature.

Although my axioms are those of the 1776 Adam Smith, my analysis from them utilizes 1976 mathematical methods, including convenient duality theory. Today, heavy mathematics will be eschewed and reference merely made to the accompanying mathematical appendix.

III. Smith's Assumptions

i) Goods, e.g., food and clothing, are produced in a time-phased way out of land and "doses" of labor-cum-raw-materials.

ii) To arrive at net consumable outputs of goods, e.g., food and clothing, one must subtract from the gross production of each the amounts of that respective good used as input components of the various industry doses.

iii) A ration of subsistence goods per laborer, e.g., m_1 of food and m_2 of clothing, is required to produce and reproduce the population. When the worker's money wage can buy more than the subsistence vector, population grows at a positive percentage rate; when the money wage buys less than subsistence, population declines exponentially; at the subsistence wage, population is constant.

iv) Workers never save and invest. Owners of land and of raw material inputs spend their wealth on food and clothing as they will. So long as the profit rate is above some minimal subsistence rate for saving, which might be zero after allowing for stochastic losses and management expenses, nonworkers do positive saving, which is never aborted. Below that minimal profit rate, nonlaborers decumulate or dissave; at the minimal profit rate, net saving and net accumulation is zero.

v) Perfect competition prevails. Land use is auctioned off for rentals. Free entry and constant returns to scale prevail. Knowledge is, or soon becomes, general.

IV. Smith's Implications

A logician, turning his deductive crank, would deduce the following properties of Smith's system.

1) Suppose it begins in long-run equilibrium. Wages are at the subsistence level. The profit rate is minimal. Depending on the pattern of nonlaborer tastes for food and clothing, land rent will be high or low; land-intensive food price will be high or low relative to clothing price; the size of the population and of the various components of raw material inventories will be high or low depending on nonlaborer tastes; and so will depend the relative distribution of *NNP* between land owners' rent and workers' wages, to say nothing of capitalists' profits if the minimal interest rate is not zero.

Most of this Ricardo missed. Some Malthus caught. Smith denies none of this, but offers little in detail.

2) Now let there be an invention. It will be viable only if, in some industry, it raises one or more of the following: the real wage there, the real rent there, or the profit rate. Except for the singular case where its incidence happens to be solely to raise land rent everywhere, the invention must transiently raise one, or more probably both, of the profit rate and the real wage rate. This initiates population growth and capital accumulation. We are in Smith's "cheerful" transient state of growth—like England rather than China or India. But ultimately, as in China and Holland, the land fills up; the law of diminishing returns on fixed land operates.

3) The system relapses into Smith's "dull state" of equilibrium with subsistence profit rate, subsistence real wage rate, and *enhanced* land rent. In effect, Smith's system maximizes rent!

4) If inventions keep recurring, the system goes through a Brownian motion in which profit rates and real wage rates average out *above* their subsistence levels, perhaps being trendless.

5) The model captures the general behavior of economic history these last two centuries if only Smith modifies his demographic hypothesis that population explodes whenever the real wage is above an unchanged subsistence level. If the needed ration of subsistence itself grows exponentially in time, then the presumption is that (a) the real wage will oscillate around an upward-rising exponential

trend, with the labor force possibly growing slowly; (b) the profit rate will meander, averaging out positive and inducing growing capital inventories; (c) land rent will tend to rise, subject to any land-saving biases in invention and to the subtraction from its rise due to the rise in real wages; (d) once we allow for alternative ways of producing the same things and for any biases in inventions, relative wage and nonwage shares of *NNP* cannot be predicted to show any definite trends; but that does not mean that minor changes contrived in labor supply can necessarily much alter the relative wage share.

These last few propositions sound much like what Simon Kuznets reports for the laws of motion of western economies, even if Ricardo and Marx failed to come as close to them as did the *Wealth of Nations*. Hats off, I say, to Adam Smith.

6) If we add to the above model a declining supply of primary "land"—that is, declining stocks of nonreproducible natural resources, such as rich seams of metal ores and coal and exhausted geologic deposits of oil and gas—we are prepared for the Club of Rome's future.

It becomes a race between invention (spontaneous and induced) and dwindling natural resources per head: the profit rate can be expected to meander in no predictable way, the real wage to grow at a slower rate (or even to suffer a declining trend). Nonwage and nonprofit share, always so important in explaining the great historic fortunes, may possibly rise. Analysis can carry prophecy no further.

V. Verdict

It is serendipitous to be able to announce, not the Scottish verdict *unproven,* but the happy finding that Adam Smith comes through with flying colors from a modern postmortem, provided we conduct it with the modicum of charity due an early pioneer.

Mathematical Appendix

The following equations vindicate Adam Smith from the principal indictments against him, and also reveal the half-untruth present in his INVISIBLE HAND doctrine.

Productivity Assumptions

Smith assumes that any of commodities, $(q_1, \ldots, q_n)$, is produced by its industry out of its labor inputs, $(L_1, \ldots, L_n)$, its land inputs $(T_1, \ldots, T_n)$, and out of produced inputs such as raw materials (or durable equipments) purchased by the various industries: so q_j will require for its production, along with T_j and L_j, also $(q_{1j}, \ldots, q_{nj})$. Smith's production functions embodying known technology can be written as

$$(1)\quad q_j(t+1) = F_j[T_j(t), L_j(t), q_{1j}(t), \ldots, q_{nj}(t)] \qquad (j = 1, \ldots, n)$$

Note the time-phasing of production in (1): inputs are needed prior to the appearance of output. In (1), T_j could be a vector of elements representing heterogeneous lands of different grades.

To arrive at net available *consumption* amounts of the ith goods, $[C_i(t)]$, one writes:

$$(2)\quad C_i(t) = q_i(t) - \sum_{j=1}^{n} q_{ij}(t) \geq 0, \qquad q_{ij}(t) \geq 0$$

Whereas a modern neoclassical economist might wish to assume that inputs can be substituted for each other in a smooth way so that $F_j[\;]$ all have well-defined partial derivatives, a classical economist like Smith usually thought that a variable "dose" of labor-cum-raw-materials could be applied to fixed land more intensively or less intensively. So one rewrites (1) as

$$(3)\quad q_j(t+1) = F_j[T_j(t), V_j(t)]$$

$$(4)\quad V_j(t) = \text{Min}\,[L_j(t)/a_{0j}, q_{1j}(t)/a_{1j}, \ldots q_{nj}(t)/a_{nj}]$$

The a_{ij}'s are non-negative. When some a is zero, it is as if its argument is absent from the expression Min[ ].

The production functions in equation (3) are postulated to have simple properties once the scale of production goes beyond the initial levels at which the division of labor does not pay. Each $F_j[\ ]$ is concave, homogeneous-first-degree, and differentiable:

$$(5)\quad F_j[\lambda T, \lambda V] \equiv \lambda F_j[T,V]$$

$$F_j[T+\Delta T, V+\Delta V] - F_j[T,V] \geq F_j[T+2\Delta T, V+2\Delta V] - F_j[T+\Delta T, V+\Delta V]$$

$$\partial F_j[T,V]/\partial V > 0, \quad F_j[T,V] - V\partial F_j[T,V]/\partial V \geq 0$$

Finally, Smith even before Malthus and Marx believed that human labor itself had a reproduction cost at that level of *subsistence* (food, clothing, etc.) at which a family could manage to reproduce itself by mortality survival and procreation. The long-run reproduction cost of total labor, $\Sigma_1^n L_j = L$, is defined per unit of L by the nonzero column vector of needed subsistence: m_1 of q_1, m_2 of q_2, ..., m_n of q_n:

$$(6)\quad \mathbf{m} = [m_i] = \begin{bmatrix} m_1 \\ \vdots \\ m_n \end{bmatrix} \geq 0$$

If the real wage exceeded the subsistence vector **m**, L_t would grow; if it fell below **m**, L_t would decline; at exactly **m**, Smith's stationary state would prevail. Evaluating the iron ration of subsistence at its market prices, $\Sigma_1^n P_j m_j$, we compare it with the market wage, W, thereby to determine the rate of population growth. Smith's simplest Malthusian relation, I write as

$$(7)\quad (L_{t+1} - L_t)/L_t = f[1 - \sum_1^n (P_j/W)m_j]$$

$$f[0] = 0, f'[\ ] > 0, f[\ ] \geq -1$$

Clearly, when the real wage is at the subsistence level **m**, population growth ceases.

Smith's Early "Rude State"

For one page, Smith does have a "labor theory of value," writing (*Wealth of Nations*, Book I, ch. 6):

> In that early and rude state of society which precedes both the accumulation of stock ["capital"] and the appropriation of [scarce] land, the proportion between the quantities of labour necessary for acquiring different objects seems to be the only circumstance which can afford any rule for exchanging them for one another... what is usually the produce of two days' or hours' labour, should be worth double of what is usually the produce of one day's or one hour's labour. . . .
>
> In this state of things, the whole produce of labour belongs to the labourer. . . .

We can make logical, even if not historical and anthropological sense of this, by postulating that land is so abundant as to be redundant and *free*, with the ratio $\Sigma_1^n T_j/\Sigma_1^n L_j$ so great as to make land ignorable. To make inventories of raw materials and crude tools ignorable takes a greater stretch of the imagination. I cut the knot by postulating that outputs and inputs are *simultaneous* rather than lagged as in equations (1) and (3).

With land redundant, so that no increase in T_j has any incremental effect on q_j output, one rewrites equations (2) and (3) in the rude state as

$$(8)\quad q_j(t) = \alpha_j V_j(t) = V_j(t),\ (j=1, \ldots, n)$$

$$= \mathrm{Min}\,[L_j(t)/a_{0j}, q_{1j}(t)/a_{1j}, \ldots, q_{nj}(t)/a_{nj}]$$

Here, by proper choice of dimensional units of goods or of doses, we can suppress the $[\alpha_j]$ coefficients.

Indeed, if the rude state is in exact stationary equilibrium, we can ignore all timing designations and define that exact state by the following specializations of (1)–(8):

$$(9)\quad L - \sum_1^n L_j = 0$$

$$q_i - \sum_{j=1}^n q_{ij} - m_i L = 0, \qquad (i=1, \ldots, n)$$

By virtue of equation (3)'s definition of the

fixed components of the doses, these relations become

$$(10)\quad L - \sum_{1}^{n} a_{0j}q_j = 0$$

$$-m_iL + q_i - \sum_{1}^{n} a_{ij}q_j = 0, \quad (i = 1, \ldots n)$$

These linear equations can have a positive solution $(L, q_1, \ldots, q_n)$ only if the following technological conditions for the rude state are exactly met:

$$(11)\quad 0 = \begin{vmatrix} 1 & -a_{01} \ldots & -a_{0n} \\ -m_1 & 1-a_{11} \ldots & -a_{1n} \\ \cdot & \cdot & \cdot \\ \cdot & \cdot & \cdot \\ \cdot & \cdot & \cdot \\ -m_n & 1-a_{n1} \ldots & \end{vmatrix}$$

$$= \det[\mathbf{I} - a_{ij} - m_ia_{0j}]$$

$$= \det[\mathbf{I} - \mathbf{a} - \mathbf{ma_0}]$$

where $\mathbf{a_0}$ is the row vector of *direct labor* requirements, $[a_{0j}]$, $\mathbf{m}$ is the column vector of subsistence requirements per worker, $[m_i]$, and $\mathbf{a}$ is the n-by-n square Leontief matrix of input-output coefficients, $[a_{ij}]$.

We now vindicate Smith's equating the competitive pricing relations of his rude state with their embodied total labor requirements (direct plus indirect). There are of course no further components of the prices of the goods, $[P_1, \ldots, P_n] = [P_j] = \mathbf{P}$, than the wage component involving the money wage, W: land rent is zero, and interest (or profit) is impossible in a world of instantaneous production.

Competition assures

$$(12)\quad \mathbf{P} = [P_j]$$

$$= [Wa_{0j} + \sum_{i=1}^{n} P_ia_{ij} + 0 + 0] > 0$$

$$= W[A_{0j}] = \mathbf{WA_0}$$

where

$$(13)\quad \mathbf{A_0} = [A_{0j}] = \mathbf{a_0}[\mathbf{I} - \mathbf{a}]^{-1} > 0$$

$$= \mathbf{a_0} + \mathbf{a_0a} + \mathbf{a_0a}^2 + \ldots,$$

a convergent series.

Positivity and convergence in equation (13) is guaranteed by equation (11) plus the postulate that every good must indirectly, if not directly, require some labor if it is to be a good worth talking about in the rude state.

That the real wage can just buy the iron ration of subsistence was assured by Equations (11)–(13), which imply

$$(14)\quad \mathbf{Pm} = W = (\mathbf{A_0m})W, \qquad \mathbf{A_0m} = 1$$

Incidentally, (14) tends to vindicate the empirical usefulness of Smith's notion of "labour command theory of value," as against Ricardo's semantic objections.

Stationarity of the rude states' population now follows from equation (7), which takes the form in the rude state of

$$(15)\quad (L_{t+1} - L_t)/L_t = f[1 - \mathbf{A_0m}]$$

$$= f[0] = 0$$

Smith's identification of *net national product* in the rude state with wages only, or with the susbsistence consumptions of the workers, is verified:

$$(16)\quad NNP - WL + 0 + 0$$

$$- \sum_{1}^{n} P_jC_j = (\mathbf{A_0C})W$$

$$= (\mathbf{A_0m})WL$$

Investment and Malthusian Growth

Smith quickly turns the page on his rude state in which the labor theory of value holds. By the division of labor or otherwise, let some set of the elements of $(\mathbf{a_0, a, m})$ decrease. That raises equation (11)'s determinant from zero to positive. That raises the real wage above the subsistence level. That causes population initially to grow at an endogenous positive rate, like $(1 + g)^t$. If we still keep production instantaneous, capital and positive profits cannot yet occur. The workers get all the fruits of the invention, and devote part of that fruit to procreation and longevity. Now

$$(17)\qquad \mathbf{Pm} < W,\ \mathbf{A_0m} < 1,\ \mathbf{C} \geq \mathbf{mL}$$

$$(L_{t+1} - L_t)/L_t = g = f[1 - \mathbf{A_0m}] > 0$$

$$L(t) = L(0)(1+g)^t,\ q(t) = q(0)(1+g)^t, \ldots,\quad t \geq 1$$

This initial state of exponential growth, à la Malthus (1798) and von Neumann (1932), must begin to decelerate once land becomes scarce. Eventually, workers elbow each other, trample down fields, and so forth. Land must be rationed by positive rentals, which for Smith were to go to the private appropriaters of land, selling their scarce inputs in a competitive market.

As L grows more and more relative to the fixed total of land, $\Sigma_1^n T_j = T$, positive rent income arises. Depending upon how landowners spend their rent incomes on consumption goods, and workers their surplus wages on goods, an equilibrium will emerge at each level of (T, L, $C_1, \ldots, C_n$) for all prices ($P_1, \ldots, P_n$, W, R). Smith's resolution of each P_j into W and R components was essentially correct, despite doubts in Marx (1885). And, even in the absence of profit and differences in time-phasing of production, Smith's solution does contradict the attempt in Ricardo (1817) to measure price ratios in terms of goods' labor contents alone.

Equilibrium Restored

At any stage of growth, for the given available technology and land, T, and for any prescribed pattern of feasible total consumption, ($C_1, \ldots, C_n$), one can solve the planner's efficiency problem of minimizing needed total labor, L:

$$(18)\qquad L = M(T; C_1, \ldots, C_n), \qquad C_i \geq 0$$

$$= \underset{T_i, V_i}{\mathrm{Min}} \sum_1^n a_{0j} V_j, \quad \text{subject to}$$

$$\sum_1^n a_{ij} V_j - F_i[T_i, V_i] + C_i \leq 0, \quad (i = 1, \ldots, n)$$

$$\sum_1^n T_j - T \leq 0,\ V_i \geq 0,\ T_i \geq 0$$

This is a standard problem in nonlinear programming, as in Kuhn and Tucker (1951). On the assumption that every good needs something of both land and variable factors, the necessary and sufficient conditions for the solution can be written down in terms of equalities involving "dual variables," or Lagrangean multipliers, or "shadow prices," which are interpretable as the non-negative price ratios $[P_1/W, \ldots, P_n/W, R/W]$, where R stands for the rental of land. (If T is a column vector of lands, R will be a row vector of rentals.) The unique conditions of equilibrium involve for scalar T,

$$(19)\qquad (P_j/W)\,\partial F_j[T_j/V_j, 1]/\partial V_j = a_{0j} + \sum_1^n (P_i/W) a_{ij}$$

$$(P_j/W)\,\partial F_j[T_j/V_j, 1]/\partial T_j = R/W, \quad (j = 1, \ldots, n)$$

$$\sum_1^n a_{ij} V_j - F_i[T_i, V_i] = C_i, \qquad (i = 1, \ldots, n)$$

$$\sum_1^n T_j \leq T,\ R\left(T - \sum_1^n T_j\right) = 0,\ T_j > 0$$

These are $3n + 1$ independent equations that are just sufficient to determine the $3n + 1$ unknowns of the problem: ($V_1, \ldots, V_n$; $T_1, \ldots, T_n$; $P_1/W, \ldots, P_n/W$, R/W). But equation (19), aside from having the planner's optimality interpretation, are precisely the *competitive* equilibrium conditions under Smith's postulated production conditions.

This identifies a valid element in Smith's INVISIBLE HAND doctrine: *self-interest, under perfect conditions of competition, can organize a society's production efficiently*. (But, there need be nothing ethically optimal about the $[C_i]$ specifications and their allocations among the rich and poor, the healthy and the halt!)

We indicate Smith's resolution of the price of every good into its total wage and rent components by deriving from (18) each good's total-land-and-labor requirements. We solve for the respective pairs:

$$
\begin{aligned}
(20)\ L_1^* &= M(T_1^*; C_1, 0, \ldots, 0) \leftrightarrow C_1 = \phi_1[T_1^*, L_1^*] \\
L_2^* &= M(T_2^*; 0, C_2, \ldots, 0) \leftrightarrow C_2 = \phi_2[T_2^*, L_2^*] \\
L_n^* &= M(T_n^*; 0, 0, \ldots, C_n) \leftrightarrow C_n = \phi_n[T_n^*, L_n^*]
\end{aligned}
$$

These $\phi_j[\ ]$ functions give the totals of land and labor required, directly *and* indirectly, to produce a net amount of each consumption good. These Smithian functions, never before written down explicitly in quite this way, are concave and first-degree-homogeneous; if the $F_j[\ ]$ functions are smoothly differentiable, as even Ricardo assumes in his arithmetic examples, so too will be the $\phi_j[\ ]$ functions. Hence, as in Shephard (1953), they will have dual unit-cost functions

$$(21)\ \phi_j^*[R, W] = \underset{T_j, V_j}{\text{Min}} \{(RT_j + WV_j)/\phi_j[T_j, V_j]\}$$

The ϕ_j^* functions have all the concavity, homogeneity, and differentiability properties of the $\phi_j[\ ]$ functions.

So, we sustain Smith against the objection that his eclectic breakdown of prices into wage and rent components is a trivial, surface relation. We write down for Smith:

$$
\begin{aligned}
(22)\quad P &= \phi_j^*[R, W] + 0 \\
&= R\partial\phi_j^*[R, W]/\partial R + W\partial\phi_j^*[R, W]/\partial W
\end{aligned}
$$

These partial equilibrium relations are well-determined by Smith's relations of general equilibrium in equation (19).

Finally, we solve for the new Smithian steady state of zero population growth after diminishing returns has brought the post-invention wage rate down to the subsistence level: we seek the L^* root of

$$(23)\quad L = M(T; m_1L + \gamma_1, \ldots, m_nL + \gamma_n)$$

where $(\gamma_1, \ldots, \gamma_n)$ represents landowners choice of composition of their consumption goods. As Malthus realized, the equilibrium population will be larger or smaller depending upon whether rent collectors tend to spend their incomes on goods of high or low "labor intensity." Thus, their demand for "retainers" will mean greater L^* than will their demand for food or for hunting grounds.

In long-run equilibrium states where (13) holds and the real wage is at the subsistence level, the Physiocratic Land Theory of Value holds, as described in "A Modern Treatment of the Ricardian Economy" (Samuelson 1959). Landlords are faced by a linear budget constraint in choosing their γ's, namely:

$$(24)\qquad \tau_1\gamma_1 + \ldots + \tau_n\gamma_n = T$$

where the $[\tau_j]$ coefficients involve the total "socially necessary land" involved in each C_j's production, directly and indirectly and after including the land needed to produce the needed labor's subsistence.

Realistic Time-Phasing of Production

Since output is not instantaneously producible from inputs, inventories of raw materials and of subsistence wage goods are needed for steady-state production and for growth. Smith correctly recognized that the rate at which capitalist owners of such capital goods would be willing to save in order to "accumulate" them would set a limit on the system's growth and thereby generate a positive profit rate. With land fixed, new inventions ceasing, and population growing whenever the real wage exceeds subsistence, Smith correctly saw that continued saving and accumulation—contrived by capitalists' consuming less of their current profits than is available to them—must eventually induce a falling trend in the rate of profit. Finally, at a zero profit rate (over and above stochastic average losses) or at some low positive rate below which decumulation will occur, Smith's system reaches its longest-run equilibrium.

Let r^* be Smith's long-run, low positive rate of profit at which capitalists and landowners will spend all their incomes on current consumptions. With land fixed at T, no new inventions and no change in workers' subsistence (m_i), Smith correctly wrote his equilibrium in a tripartite breakdown of national income and each competitive price into wages, rents, and profits. His complete system becomes:

$$\text{(25a)}\quad F_i[T_i, V_i] - \sum_1^n a_{ij}V_j = m_iL + \gamma_i, \qquad (i = 1, \ldots, n)$$

$$\text{(25b)}\quad P_j\partial F_j[T_j/V_j, 1]/\partial V_j = (Wa_{0j} + \sum_1^n P_ia_{ij})(1 + r^*)$$

$$\text{(25c)}\quad P_j\partial F_j[T_j/V_j, 1]/\partial T_j = R(1 + r^*), \ (j = 1, \ldots, n)$$

$$\text{(25d)}\quad \sum_1^n a_{ij}V_j = L, \ \sum_1^n T_j \leq T$$

$$\text{(25e)}\quad \sum_1^n P_jm_j = W > 0, \ V_j \geq 0, \qquad T_j \geq 0, \ P_j \geq 0, \ R \geq 0$$

For r^* and **m** sufficiently small, and for T and the ratios of nonworkers' taste parameters given $[\gamma_i/\gamma_1]$, these are $3n + 3$ equations for the equal number of unknowns: n V's, n T's, n (P/W)'s, γ_1, R/W, L. A meaningful solution is guaranteed to exist by virtue of the postulated properties for $F_j[\ ]$.

Independently of the (γ_i) and (m_i) parameters, there is always a factor-price-frontier tradeoff between the real wage in terms of any good, W/P_j, the real rent, R/P_j, and the profit rate, r^*:

$$\text{(26)}\quad W/P_j = -\psi_j[R/P_j; r^*], \ \partial\psi_j/\partial r^* > 0$$

$$\partial\psi_j/\partial(R/P_j) > 0, \ \partial^2\psi_j/\partial(R/P_j)^2 \leq 0$$

For $r^* = 0$, $\psi_j[\ ;0]$ is derivable from equating to unity $\phi_j^*[R/P_j, W/P_j)$. For $r^* > 0$ and all inputs used up in each single use, replacing the true $F_j[\ ]$ functions by $(1 + r^*)^{-1}F_j[\ ]$ will give rise to new $\phi_j[\ ]$ and $\phi_j^*[\ ]$ functions exactly as in equations (18) to (22). Then the fundamental factor-price frontiers defined by Smith's system can be defined by

$$\text{(27)}\quad \phi_j^*[R/P_j, W/P_j; 1 + r^*] = 1$$

For fixed $1 + r^*$, (27) defines convex contours.

With $r^* > 0$, equation (24)'s τ's have to be marked up, but are still constants so long as the m's are constants.

Prior to the system's having settled down into its long-run, time-phased steady state, one can provide for Smith's model an *endogenous* process of growth. Recognize the nonsimultaneous character of (1), and the need for capital inventories implied by such time phasing. So long as the initial rupture from the rude state is so recent that land is still redundant and rent zero, the system can grow in an initial golden age. Its rate of balanced exponential growth and the accompanying intermediate-run rate of interest or profit will provide the endogenous roots at which the supply of saving out of capitalists' profits are just large enough to provide the inventories for widening of capital goods and the advancing of wage goods for the multiplying population. If (7)'s population-growth function f[ ], is given; if (6)'s $[m_i]$ and (23)'s (γ_i) for nonlaborers are known; and finally if the fraction of profit that will be saved is a known function of the interest rate $s[r]$—then there will be an intermediate growth and profit rate, $(g^\dagger, r^\dagger)$, at which golden-age saving will equal golden-age warranted investment. Had Smith been able to write down the full conditions of this transient golden-age equilibrium, he would have anticipated Marx's expanded-reproduction tableaux of *Capital, Vol. II* and would have provided Harrod and Domar with an endogenous natural rate of growth.

Needless to say, once exponential growth runs into the constraint of scarce good land, positive rent will have to be reckoned with and recourse to ever-worse land, or ever-more-crowded best land, will imply a steadily dropping growth rate and a steady fall in the profit or the wage rate (or, most probably in both), as the post-rude *cheerful* state sinks into Smith's long-run *dull* state.

Quesnay's 'Tableau Economique' as a Theorist would Formulate it Today

Paul A. Samuelson[1]

1 INTRODUCTION

Schumpeter used to shock his Harvard classes by declaring that of the four greatest economists three were French.

In view of Schumpeter's boundless admiration for the Newtonian general equilibrium of Walras, and his delight in the elegance of Cournot's partial-equilibrium analysis, two-thirds of his contention we could understand. But to admit François Quesnay into the Pantheon – presumably because his *Tableau Economique* was a precursor of general equilibrium and of Schumpeter's own beloved *circular flow* – that seemed a bit much.

The *Tableau* began in comedy. Mirabeau (1760), who is known not to have understood it, is quoted maliciously by Adam Smith for his extravagant puffery:

> There has been since the world began, three great inventions . . . The first is the invention of writing . . . The second is the invention of money . . . The third is the Oeconomical Table . . . the great discovery of our age.

Fire, the wheel and the invention of brandy must apparently come further down the list.

Overvaluation invites short selling. Contemporaries of the Physiocrats, such as Linguet, cast scorn upon the *Tableau* as the mystic mumbo-jumbo of a mad sect, dismissing it as charlatanical nonsense. Alexander Gray's (1931) useful compact history refers to the *Tableau* as 'an embarrassing footnote' in the history of economics. Gide and Rist (1926) consider the degree of enthusiasm expressed by Mirabeau and other idolisers as 'almost incredible'. Schumpeter, when he came to write down his magisterial *History of Economic Analysis* (1954), treats Quesnay as a bit of a bore and a crank: there Schumpeter writes with patronising coolness about the *Tableau*.

It was Karl Marx who resurrected the *Tableau Economique*, devoting a whole chapter in his *Theories of Surplus Value* to the *Tableau* and writing: 'Never before had thinking in political economy reached such heights of genius.' Marx's own analytical work on models of *steady reproduction*, and of *expanded* (exponential) *reproduction*, seems to have been stimulated by his puzzling over Quesnay's arithmetic. To be able to say this heaps much praise on the Physiocrats since, I would argue, Marx's own finest *analytical* work came in this area of circular interdependence.

My old teacher Wassily Leontief (1941) had Quesnay very much in mind when he referred to his own endeavour to construct a statistical '*Tableau Economique* of the United States'. It is thus not surprising that members of Leontief's workshop – the late George Malanos (1946), Almarin Phillips (1955), Shlomo Maital (1972), and others – should have offered interpretations of the *Tableau* in terms of modern Leontief–Sraffa input–output systems. (Dialectically, Harry Johnson (1974) reacted against such a *technological* interpretation, preferring a Keynesian *multiplier–expenditure* interpretation to an input–output one.) Tibor Barna (1975) gives a version of the *Tableau* in modern guise, disaggregating the sectoral flows and providing an expanded matrix of transactions.

W. A. Eltis (1975, p. 168), who has analysed the various tableaux against the background of all the writings of Quesnay and Mirabeau, states:

Almost all the problems (assertions that have no clear

> logical basis . . . apparent gaps in the arguments, inconsistencies, and puzzling calculations . . .) are solved, however, and the inconsistencies removed when Quesnay's published works are read as a whole.

Eltis is one of the few modern authors bold enough to tackle Quesnay's zig-zags or diminishing geometric progressions.

Although I recognise the role obscurity can play in commanding respect and evoking attention to a scientific work, my own bent is against mystification and abracadabra. Hume and Cantillon, Quesnay's predecessors, and Turgot, Quesnay's successor, are more to my personal taste than Mirabeau and Quesnay. But in recalling the praises and abuses the *Tableau* has evoked, I shall give Ronald Meek (1962, pp. 259–60) the last word:

> The *Tableau* is far from being the ideal and airy thing which it is sometimes made out to be: on the contrary, it is one of the most striking examples in the whole history of economic thought of the achievement of a harmonious unity between abstract theory and concrete investigation.

2 PRESENT PURPOSE

I shall not add one more explication of the many versions of the *Tableau* and its appended materials. Instead, my intent here is to try to put the fundamental Physiocratic insights into modern goatskins.

How would a student of Robert Solow or Piero Sraffa, starting from scratch, draw up a table that illuminates the envisaged equilibrium? My interest is theoretical and methodological. The point is not to capture the quantitative and sociological features of the *ancien régime*, and it is not to illuminate Quesnay's own modes of thought and exposition. Although my debts to Phillips (1955), and particularly to Maital (1972), will be obvious, the programme set out here hitherto seems never to have been carried though to completion.

Two features are central to Quesnay:

(1) Land enjoys a special asymmetric position in the Physiocratic system, and our model must reflect that.

(2) By the same token, if labour's 'sterility' is to stand in stark contrast to land's, logic requires us to push to the limit the Classical hypothesis that an unlimited supply of labour can be endogenously created at a specifiable subsistence wage (which could involve only agricultural food – 'corn' – but which could also involve manufactures).

When I first began to lecture on *Dogmengeschichte* several decades ago, I hoped to be able to understand Quesnay's zig-zag notions. It would be nice in this modern formulation to be able to clear up definitively these mysterious geometric progressions; for, I am sure, it is these puzzling patterns of spending flows that captivated the *Tableau's* admirers and critics. Alas, even the recent explorations of Izumi Hishiyama (1960) and Eltis (1975) do not satisfy my analytical conscience. So the best I can do is to use the complete model introduced here to indicate why Quesnay's zig-zags never did fulfil a useful purpose in the analysis of his own system and the crystallisation of his own insights.

3 ASSUMPTIONS

Assume two industries or departments: *agriculture*, which produces food and raw materials; *manufacturing*, which produces clothing, shelter, other finished goods, and (in later elaborated versions of the model) various capital goods.

(1) Farm products – (Ricardian) 'corn' for short – are produced by the given supply of (scarce) land and by labour. (Later, you can allow for durable capital goods' inputs, for seed and other raw materials produced in agriculture.)

Quesnay deals with three classes of people: landowners or *proprietors* (possibly including the Crown and the clergy); the *productive class* of 'farmers' and farm labourers; and *artisans*, the 'sterile' class of people who labour on manufactures (and which includes what we would call 'bourgeois' employers of their own and other people's labour).

As Barna observes, one can easily disaggregate or consolidate the particular classifications of Quesnay. In a first pass at the subject, I find it useful to divide factors of production into fixed *land* (used exclusively, or primarily, in agriculture) owned by landowners or proprietors, and into *labour*, whether employed in manufacturing (as artisans) or in agriculture (as farmers or hired workers). Prior to complicating the model by explicitly introducing time-phasing and pure interest into it, the difference between a rural farmer and a rural labourer is only one of degree of skill and status. Like the Physiocrats, I envisage one farmer as a congealed unit of more than one unskilled labourer; so long as the gear ratio in this equivalence is not allowed to be an endogenous economic variable, we can avail ourselves of the simplification used later by Marx and speak simply of so many units of socially necessary ('least-common-denominator') labour without regard to the breakdown by industry and occupation.

(2) Manufactures are produced by labour (with land of negligible use in the simplest model) and by raw materials produced on the farm. For simplicity, I begin with the assumption of *fixed proportions* among labour, co-operating raw materials, and output of manufactures.

A caveat is in order concerning the preliminary neglect of time-phasing. For land to be truly the only ultimate source of net product, *à la* Quesnay and Henry George, we are best advised to contemplate a model that is essentially *timeless*. (Or, if the steady states do involve synchronised time leads and lags, either these intervals are so short that the interest component of total costs and incomes is negligible; or else the rate of interest and profit – these are the same thing in the absence of uncertainty and market imperfections – have been established at so low a rate per period as to be effectively ignorable. In any case, as Barna observes, the *Tableau Economique* must be supplemented by a separate statement on capital account, since its own explicit current flows do not register the needed capital information.)

I do justice to the Physiocrats' vision that land's return is the only *produit net*, the only true surplus by virtue of the fact that its supply is given by nature without a needed cost. By contrast, labour's productivity merely repays labour's needed cost of subsistence; and raw materials' contribution to competitive revenue merely repays its competitive purchase price (which is, in turn, the sum of the land inputs in it and the subsistence cost of the labour needed for it as inputs). To do full justice to this essentially correct Physiocratic vision, I best sacrifice Quesnay's own ambiguous terminologies: the contribution of farm *labourers* is just as 'sterile' as the contribution of manufacturing *labourers*; the former are not 'the productive class' in the true sense of the word 'productive' – for the reason that it is the land they work with *that is alone productive* in producing the Physiocrats' *produit net*. Personally, like Adam Smith, I would avoid the adjective 'sterile' and merely insist that those costs that are paid to labour merely recoup in long-run equilibrium the subsistence cost whereby labour is maintained. Later, when one admits that manufactures also require some land, one realises that it is not the industry that is 'sterile' in the sense of lacking *net* product but rather only the labour and raw materials used there and anywhere which are 'sterile'. In departing from Quesnay's precise categories and terminologies, I actually better bring out his essential vision.

My technological stage directions will be complete after I have given the quantitative *technical coefficients* of labour and raw materials in manufacturing, and have given for agriculture what we would today call the 'production function' relating corn output to the land supply and the varying quantities of farm labour. But before doing this, I need to specify the composition and scale of the *subsistence real wage*. And I need to specify, as Quesnay's models do, how landowners spend their *produit net* or land rents on the consumption of farm products or of manufactures.

Quesnay's zig-zags must have seemed simpler to him if he always assumed 50–50 allocation of spendings. So I partially indulge that penchant and assume that landlords spend half their rents on manufactures and half on farm products.

But, with a bow towards greater realism, I postulate that the subsistence wage consists only of agricultural products (of 'corn'). It is immaterial how high or low I assume the subsistence wage to be, provided only that the quality of the land and the laws of technology enable a finite population of landless labour to be supported by the given land under a regime of competition for their services.

Quesnay and earlier writers definitely glimpsed at least vaguely the notion of what would today be called a 'production function'. They realised that under better technology France would be able to enjoy a higher level of total land rent while still paying the same competitive subsistence wage. Since mine is to be a modern treatment, I go beyond their vague perceptions and assume in Ricardo's fashion that the greater the rural labour supply employed, the lower must be its corn wage and the higher must be the total of landowners' *produit net*. The equilibrium that we will observe in the *Tableau Economique* for this society will involve a quantity of agricultural labour that is endogenously determinate. Here are the modern equations:

$$\text{Agriculture } Q = F(\text{land, farm labour}) = F(T, L_F)$$
$$= Tf(L_F/T), f'(\ ) > 0 > f''(\ ) \qquad (1.1)$$

For fixed land (or lands), we can set T equal to unity and ignore it in all our equations.

West (1815), Malthus (1798), Ricardo (1817), and J. B. Clark (1899) realised that under a regime of competition by landowners for labourers, there would be a determinate level of farm L_F^* that would just earn the stipulated corn wage, $\bar{w}$. This L_F^* is the root of the equation (that the neoclassicals would call marginal productivity):

$$f'(L_F^*) = \bar{w} \qquad (1.2)$$

Rent (in corn) can then be computed as the residual:

$$R^* = f(L_F^*) - \bar{w}L_F^* \qquad (1.3)$$

To keep the arithmetic simple, I will let rent be half of total farm product, the rest being farm workers' wages.

Half of this rent goes for corn consumption. The other half goes to buy manufacturing product, the only source of demand for such product. Under competition these manufactures sell only at their cost of production – the sum of the subsistence corn needed to feed the manufacturing artisans and the corn raw material needed for production of manufactures. Thus the residual rent, left over after farm labour gets its subsistence and the only *produit net* in the system, is divided three ways: into landowners' own corn consumption, into the corn needed for *manufacturing* labour's subsistence, and into the corn needed by industry as raw materials. (What the ratio of these last two components is depends upon the technology in manufactures: to keep the arithmetic simple, I pick one-to-one as that ratio in my examples.)

4 BIRD'S-EYE VIEW

The stage has now been completely set. The play must now go on for ever more according to its coded laws of motion:

(1) Landowners buy from agricultural and manufacturing producers, paying from their stream of competitive money rents and receiving in return the physical goods that constitute their standard of life.

(2) The farm sector, besides selling to landowners, sells its product to labourers who need subsistence – i.e. they sell both to farm labour and to manufacturing labour. The farm sector also sells its product as raw materials for industry.

(3) Out of the total revenues it receives, the farm sector pays competitive rents for the land it needs. It also pays out wages to farm labour, paying the competitive wage that the existing supply of such labour can command (at auction, so to speak).

(4) The size of the farm population supplied is determined in final equilibrium at that level which will fetch the needed subsistence wage. (Were L_F too large, the corn wage would sink below the subsistence $\bar{w}$ and the population would decline; were L_F below L_F^*, the corn wage would exceed $\bar{w}$, thereby evoking a growing supply of farm labour. QED.)

(5) The sole receipts of the industrial sector, under my first simplifying assumptions, come from consumption purchases by landowners spending their rent incomes. In the competitive equilibrium these receipts are just enough to offset the subsistence wages that are forced by competition out of the indus-

trial employers (who may be self-employed) plus the cost of the raw materials that have to be bought from the farm sector. There are no land factors in the industrial sector that can earn a *produit net*; the labour and raw-material inputs merely recover their costs of production and reproduction.

A picture or numerical table to sum this all up might well have pedagogical convenience. But it is an illusion to think that such a picture or *gestalt* provides a magic engine of analysis for the discovery of new truth and the marshalling of rigorous proof. Consider, for example, a typical problem propounded by Quesnay: What if landowners alter their 50–50 spending of rents, and increase the fraction spent on manufacturing products? A one-point-in-time *tableau*, geared to the previous spending proportions, cannot answer the question of what the new equilibrium will be. Barna (1975, p. 493) cogently criticises Quesnay's procedures:

> Quesnay, as usual, begins the computation with the landlords spending their income. At the end of the first round landlords find that they did not collect in rent as much as they had originally spent, and hence the second round starts with a smaller outlay. There is thus a cumulative decline in the 'base' of the *Tableau* and everybody will be worse off then before.
>
> This conclusion clearly does not follow from the *Tableau's* assumptions. Within the framework of a static Leontief model, a shift in demand from agricultural produce to manufactures should bring about a reduction in agricultural activity and an increase in manufacturing. There will be a redistribution of incomes away from landlords. But there is no reason why total national income should change.

In the rockbottom Physiocratic model adumbrated here, the effect of the specified change in tastes is clear. And its correct description seems not to have been achieved by Quesnay and Mirabeau or, according to my best recollection, by any of the commentators on them. Here is that correct description:

A shift in landowners' tastes towards manufacturers must

lead to a new long-run equilibrium with *increased* labour population, all of which goes into manufacturing. Total rent (*produit net*) is *just as before* (whether measured in terms of corn or in terms of manufactures)! What Ricardo calls 'gross revenue' – which, in the Kuznets manner, adds the total of wages to the total of Ricardian 'net revenue' (equals rent or *produit net* in this interestless world) – will be *higher* in the new equilibrium, precisely as Ricardo came to argue in the notorious chapter on machinery that he added to his third edition. (See p. 393 in the 1951 Sraffa edition of Ricardo's *Principles.*)

Barna's point is well taken that you could never conclude all this from the *Tableau Economique* itself. You would have to go to the table's underlying logic to arrive at this result.[2]

5 AT LAST A TABLE

Three sectors are in our model: agricultural production, manufacturing production, and the production of labour (out of subsistence wages). Table 1.1, with three columns, shows

TABLE 1.1

Tableau Economique

	Purchasing sector				
Output	Agriculture	Manufacturing	Labour	Landowners	Totals
Agriculture (product)	0	25	*125*	**50**	200
Manufacturing (product)	0	0	0	**50**	50
Labour (supply)	*100*	*25*	0	0	*125*
Land	**100**	0	0	0	**100**
Value totals	200	50	*125*	**100**	(475)

the costs of these respective industries broken down by the inputs those costs are spent on. Each input appears in its respective row – including the input of land (which is not itself producible in the system and so appears as a row appended *outside* the 3 x 3 input–output elements of the system). Finally, I append a final column to show how landowners spend their incomes.

I end up with a familiar *open-end* Leontief *tableau*, consisting of 3 x 3 internal elements plus appended exogenous row and column for Physiocrats' land and landowners. The *tableau* is expressed in money terms: dollars, livres, pounds, corn-*numéraire* units, etc. It can also be given a physical-units interpretation.[3]

The bold-face numerals denote *produit net* items, the only true surplus in the Physiocratic system and attributable to land alone, with its *zero cost* and *positive productivity. Produit net* (or Ricardian '*net* revenue') is **100**, and reckonable in two equivalent ways: as a flow of rent *income* (or cost), it is the **100** in the first column and land row (carried over in the totals column on the right as the last row's item); as a flow of (final) product, it is shown as **50** and **50** in the landowners' column of consumption expenditure.

To get modern national income of *225 à la* Kuznets (or (Ricardo's '*gross* revenue'), we must add wage incomes to rent income. I have italicised these wage value-added items: in the third row for labour, note the wage items *100* and *25*, and their sum on the far right. As a matching Kuznets flow of (non-intermediate) product, we must add to landowners' consumptions of corn and manufactures the corn that goes for workers' subsistence. This is shown in the first agricultural row in labour's third column – by the italicised numeral there, *125*. (This last of course appears as a repetition in column 3's bottom total, where *125* is seen.) To relate modern national income to the smaller Physiocrats' *produit net*, I have introduced brackets to enclose the two magnitudes.

Finally, as is well known to users of input–output tables, the grossness of our data depends upon the arbitrary fineness of our disaggregation. The over-all total of 475, shown at lower right in the circle as a grand total of the whole table, has no intrinsic significance: it involves not only the double-counting of the agricultural output that is used as raw-material input for industry; but, more singularly in modern eyes, it includes labour power as a produced item in the system; and, of course, it includes both landowners' earnings *and* their equivalent spendings, a palpable case of double-counting.

To help relate my presentation to that of Quesnay, Meek, Phillips, and Maital, I consolidate my 4 x 4 (open-end) table into the more conventional 3 x 3 (*open*-end!) format. Now labour will no longer be given its own row and column. Instead, I now put the farm labour back in the 'productive' sector of agriculture, treating the subsistence wage that workers receive there as 'corn raw-material input necessary to produce corn output'. Likewise the manufacturing labour and their corn wages are treated merely as the costs of the sterile classes ('artisans'), who produce manufactures out of an equivalent market value of farm product as input – out of actual raw farm materials themselves used in manufactures *plus* the subsistence corn in the artisans' stomachs while they produce manufactures.

Arithmetically, this consolidation involves eliminating column 3 and row 3 but adding row 3's items into the respective first-row items. This gives Table 1.2, a formal variant of Table 1.1. The *produit net* items are again put in bold face, both on the side of income earned and the side of equivalent flow of final product (net, after allowances to keep labour

TABLE 1.2

Tableau Economique

Sectoral outputs	Agriculture (productive classes)	Manufacturing (sterile artisans)	Land-owners	Totals
Agriculture	100	50	**50**	200
Manufacturing	0	0	**50**	50
Land	**100**	0	0	**100**
Value totals	200	50	**100**	350

alive and recouping their human reproduction costs). Table 1.2 does not conveniently tabulate Kuznets's national income of 225, since intermediate product of corn used to produce manufactures is mixed up with the requisite numbers.

Both my tables side with Maital against Phillips on the issue of whether Quesnay's *Tableau Economique* is best rendered by a *closed*-end Leontief table or by an *open*-end one. In Phillips's closed-end case, land and landowners are treated symmetrically with any other input or class. To make wine you really do need grapes; but it is stretching convention to say that to produce proprietors you need so many luxuries of this kind and so many of that. It is better to open end the array, pulling land out as a *primary* input and pulling landowners' final consumptions out as items dictated by exogenous tastes.

The Physiocratic asymmetry of land comes of course from their theory of reality. The table is made to reflect it, and it would not be useful to say that the *Tableau Economique* somehow 'proves' the correctness of this insight. Nor would it be useful to blame it for failing to provide such 'proof'.

I shall leave to the interested reader the task of making a pretty picture of my table, with pedagogically useful arrows indicative of spending channels. Perhaps there is a best, canonical pattern that such a diagram should take, but I do not dare to pronounce on the matter.

* * *

There remain two quite different tasks. There is the task of discussing zig-zags, the geometric progressions somchow supposed to be indicative of 'dynamic' spending processes. And also there is the task of facing up to time-phasing and to some of the durable capital-goods processes that Quesnay had explicitly in mind. (This will involve not only Quesnay's 'depreciation of capital' but also Turgot's true interest rate.) On both these issues I shall be very brief.

6 THE CHIMERA OF ZIG-ZAGS

So far there has been no need to even mention the mysterious zig-zags of the Quesnay literature. A typical one, I suppose, is very roughly of the form shown in Figure 1.1. Or, since my model has neither workers spending their subsistence wages on manufactures nor corn producers needing manufactures as raw material or durable capital, after the second round no new flows come to the sterile sector of manufacturing. So the slightly less transparent pattern shown in Figure 1.2 might perhaps be the indicated zig-zag.

In the preceding paragraph I have used the tentative words 'I suppose' and 'might perhaps' because no definite prescip-tions are possible until one has already settled what the intrinsic logic of the zig-zag is – which is the objective of the immediate investigation and ought not to be presumed settled in advance.

First, let me dispose of an empty point. Formally, unity can be written as

$$1 = \tfrac{1}{2} + \tfrac{1}{4} + \tfrac{1}{8} + \ldots + (\tfrac{1}{2})^n + \ldots$$

And, for any positive x, we can write the convergent series

$$1 + x = 1 + [x/(1 + x)] + [x/(1 + x)]^2 + \ldots$$

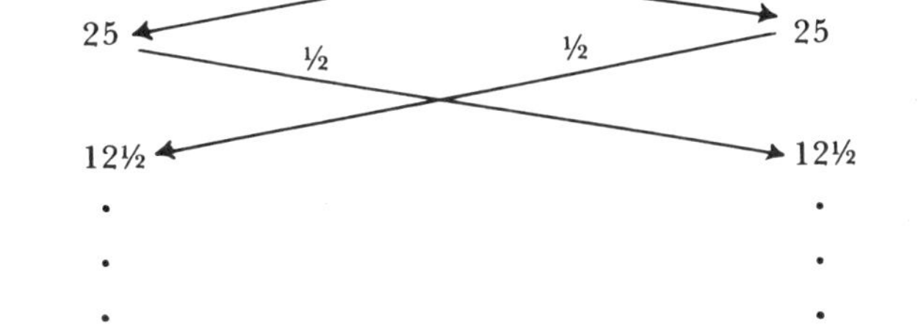

FIGURE 1.1

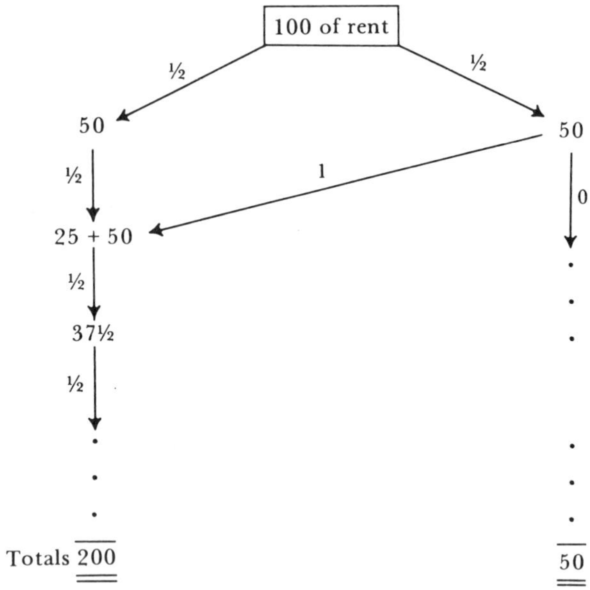

FIGURE 1.2

But *cui bono*? In the first flush of the Keynesian dawn many of us could write one-plus-one only as $1/(1-\frac{1}{2})$. At least we then had the excuse that the Kahn–Keynes–Metzler dynamic multiplier could usefully take the difference-equation form:[4]

$$y(t+1) = \tfrac{1}{2}y(t) + b$$

$$y(t) = \frac{1}{1-\frac{1}{2}} + [y(0) - 2]\,(\tfrac{1}{2})^t$$

$$\lim_{t\to\infty} y(t) = 2b = [1 + \tfrac{1}{2} + (\tfrac{1}{2})^2 + \ldots]\,b \qquad (1.4)$$

No doubt Harry Johnson (1974) had something like this in mind when he hankered for a multiplier–expenditure interpretation of the Quesnay zig-zag *Tableau* in preference to a technical input–output approach of the Phillips (1955) type. But I am not aware that Johnson ever made good his claim that the Quesnay zig-zag could usefully model *the* actual dynamic steps forward either (i) when the system is in its postulated steady state, or (ii) when it is dynamically being perturbed from an old steady state to a new one.

The essence of circular flow – the essence of what Schumpeter admired in Quesnay – is the repetition *without leakage* of the equilibrium. From this viewpoint we do not want to break 100 down into dwindling fractions, but instead want it and all the other elements to *repeat* in conserved magnitude:

$$100 = \ldots = R(t-1) = R(t) = R(t+1) = \ldots \qquad (1.5)$$

No doubt the keen reader will cogently reply to my argument of the previous paragraph:

> True, equilibrium involves stationariness. But every student of J. M. Keynes (1936) and Fritz Machlup (1939) knows that a plateau can be made up of the convergent sum of (an infinity of) overlapping elements – just as a stationary population can be the sum of all the age classes, with each cohort of new births forming a dwindling sequence as each passing year adds a year of age.

This logic is impeccable. But it leaves moot whether there is a *useful* dynamic paradigm that moves forward in time according to the Keynesian manner and which is in some measure illuminated by Quesnay's traditional zig-zags.

My own desultory researches make me agnostic. Code the elements in Table 1.2 as follows:

$$\begin{bmatrix} 100 & 50 & 50 \\ 0 & 0 & 50 \\ 100 & 0 & 0 \end{bmatrix} = \begin{bmatrix} z_1 & z_2 & z_3 \\ & & z_4 \\ z_5 & & \end{bmatrix} \qquad (1.6)$$

My stage directions, and Quesnay's when he accepts my assumptions about tastes and technology, lead to the homogeneous difference equations:

$$\begin{aligned} z_3(t+1) &= \tfrac{1}{2} z_5(t) = z_4(t+1) \\ z_1(t-1) &= \tfrac{1}{2}[z_1(t) + z_2(t) + z_3(t)] = z_5(t-1) \\ z_2(t-1) &= z_4(t) \end{aligned} \qquad (1.7)$$

These are incapable of being put in 'causal form' either forward or backward in time. Thus, for arbitrary $[z_j(0)]$ it is not the case that a unique sequence is generated for $[z_j(+\mid t\mid)]$ or for $[z_j(-\mid t\mid)]$. However, for $[z_j(0)]$ proportional to Table 1.2's equilibrium values, that same set of values gives a solution that satisfies the equations forever more. This suggests that Quesnay's attempted use of the tableau was flawed at the core: once he altered his parameters and ruptured the old equilibrium, its initial conditions could not begin a path to the new equilibrium. What he inferred to be a property of the real world was only a property of his misconceived programme – something his readers might have come to realise.

Is it quite hopeless, then, to seek some kind of geometric progression that correctly relates to our equilibrium system? Not quite. There is the teleological backward-in-time process known in the input–output literature as a Cornfield–Leontief (matrix) multiplier (and which is not to be confused with the dual pricing multiplier of Gaitskell–Dosso).[5]

Here is how to describe the process. Begin with 100 units of landowner expenditure that generates 50 each of the two sectors' consumptions. To produce these at initial $t = 0$, we needed to produce at $t = -1$ the raw materials and worker fodder called for by the paradigm's technology of input–output coefficients. But to produce these inputs at $t = -1$, we needed *their* inputs to be produced at $t = -2$. These in turn needed their inputs to be produced three periods back.

We are in an infinite regress, going not forward into the far future, but hypothetically backward to the beginning of time. Although the span of time is infinite, the series is a dwindling one with a convergent sum. It is actually the matrix power series of note 4 (see p. 75).

It would be somewhat farfetched to claim that Quesnay's zig-zags were a vague anticipation of the planner's teleological matrix multiplier. There is, however, one instance of the matrix multiplier in which its elements are *exactly* in geometric progression from the very beginning (and not just asymptotically *à la* note 4). Consider a two-sector example in which land and raw materials produce those sectoral outputs without explicit mention of labour. Let half of the cost of manufactures be agricultural raw materials and half of corn's cost be manufacturing raw materials, the other half being land rent in each sector. This singular case involves neither sector requiring its own self as input.

Figure 1.3 shows the Cornfield–Leontief teleology in quasi zig-zag form. This is not much of a harvest for several decades of mulling over Quesnay's zig-zags, you will agree. But it is the best I can do, and that best does not seem good enough.[6] It seems gratuitous to read this interpretation into Quesnay himself.

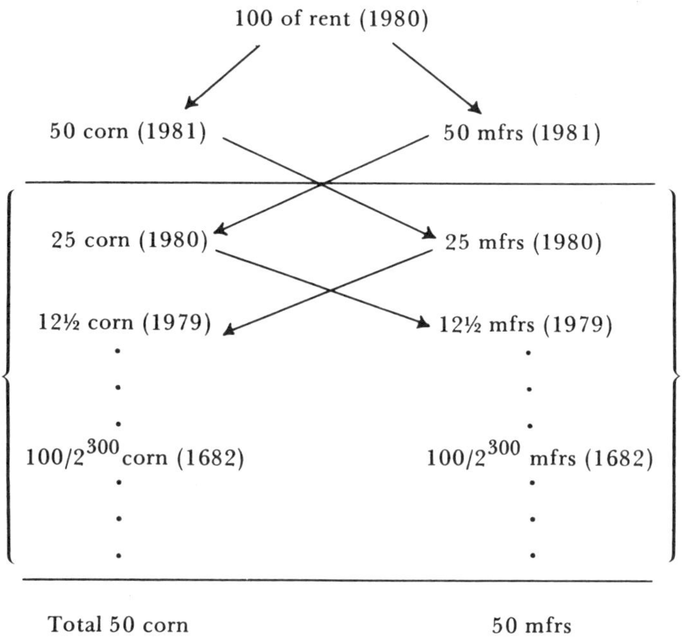

FIGURE 1.3

7 CAPITAL GOODS

Quesnay was one of the first Classical economists to concentrate on 'advances' – as when the farmer begins with a barn and with seed, and a worker is provided with the subsistence he needs to last out the growing season. Turgot, not quite a

Physiocrat but at heart a 'fellow traveller', gave what Böhm-Bawerk called the first scientific theory of the interest rate: if land with a permanent annual *produit net* sells for a finite price, as in the medieval 'twenty years' purchase', then that interest rate calculated as annual-yield-to-principal sets the level that capitalists must competitively earn on their outlays for wages, for raw materials, and for barns or durable tools.

Neither Quesnay nor the *Tableau Economique* adequately handles the fundamentals of the profit rate and the time-phasing problem. That would be too much to ask of the eighteenth century. What I shall do is provide the simplest *Tableau* that consistently recognises interest.

My model preserves the subsistence-wage theory. It sticks to the stationary state. Just as rent income is spent half-and-half on agriculture and manufactures, so will be the profit-interest income of capitalists. Indeed, we could for the present purpose alternatively lump together *proprietors* and *rentiers* into the *capitalists*.

Since it already had the circulating-capital item of raw materials needed for manufacturing and had subsistence workers who were 'advanced' their subsistence pay, my previous model can be made to serve the present purpose – once we alter its 'timeless' properties and time phase it so that all outputs come one period *after* the application of all inputs. For brevity, I stick with the earlier model and forbear to introduce durable-capital items.

Where shall I get a determinate positive rate of profit from? Turgot's vision of the process is good enough for us, and recently in the Abba Lerner *festschrift*, Samuelson (1979) sketched a Turgot–Modigliani life-cycle model of interest. Here is its thumbnail outline.

At a zero interest rate, land would be of infinite value. Capitalists looking forward to a finite life (for themselves and the next few generations they care about) would overspend their incomes. So equilibrium can take place only at some positive rate of interest. If that rate per period, call it r, is too high, the capitalised value of land will be less than people need for their old-age livelihoods, and would-be savers will bid up assets' values until *the interest rate is at that equilibrium level where generation after generation there will be zero net* *saving*. So r^* will be the determinate long-run rate of interest.[7]

At a positive profit rate the same land cannot support so many workers if their competitive wage rate is to equal the needed subsistence level in corn. So L_F^* will be lower than in the zero-r^* case. That means that landowners' corn rent, R^*, payable at the end of the harvest, will be lower than before. The determinate levels for these will be given as (L_F^*, R^*) roots of

$$\bar{w} = f'(L_F^*)/(1 + r^*) \tag{1.8}$$

$$R^* = f(L_F^*) - \bar{w}f'(L_F^*) \tag{1.9}$$

$$\text{Agricultural profit}^* = \bar{w}L_F^* r^* \tag{1.10}$$

The rentier group of capitalists, who advance farm workers their wages, are seen to earn the profit rate on these advances (just as the landowners' rent earns them the same percentage on the capitalised value of their acres).

Now that the population working the land has been lowered by the presence of interest, it takes relatively more land to produce each unit of corn. This tends to raise the price of corn relative to the rent per acre, an effect that is reinforced by the profit mark-up on the wage component of corn's cost. The price of manufactures includes *two* profit mark-ups in my model's technology: the one mark-up already in the price of the corn raw material, and the profit mark-up on the wage and raw-material components of manufactures' cost.

*　　　　*　　　　*

To dramatise the effect upon the *tableau* of profit, I shall assume a 50 per cent interest rate. The task of writing down a new *Tableau Economique* consistent with the technology and tastes of our previous zero-profit *Tableau Economique* provides a testing for a modern theorist. So it is no wonder that the eighteenth-century writers fall short of accomplishing this goal.

Table 1.3 bases itself on a quasi-realistic agricultural production function in expression (1.1) above (p. 51). Raising r^* from zero to 50 per cent per period reduces total population

TABLE 1.3

Tableau Economique (cum profit)[a]

Purchases by ⟶ *Sales of* ↓	*Agriculture*	*Manufacturing*	*Labour*	*Capitalists*	*Landowners*	*Totals*
Agriculture	0	20	*60*	*20*	**40**	40
Manufacturing	0	0	0	*20*	**40**	60
Labour	*40*	*20*	0	0	0	*60*
Profit (or interest)	*20*	*20*	0	0	0	*40*
Land rent	**80**	0	0	0	0	**80**
Totals	140	60	*60*	*40*	**80**	380

$r^* = 0.5$.

[a] All these values are in terms of corn as *numéraire*. If desired in manufactures as *numéraire*, multiply every item by two-thirds. Values in monetary units (dollars, livres, . . .) depend upon monetary assumptions – such as the money supply and its transactions velocity.

by more than half – from 125 to 60; lowers land rent by 20 per cent, from 100 of corn to 80; raises P_M/P_F from 1 to 1.5. With landowners and rentiers each spending half their incomes on farm goods and manufactures, the composition of the new *tableau* becomes determinate and takes the magnitudes shown in Table 1.3.[8]

With positive profit, my open-end *tableau* enlarges from a 4 x 4 to a 5 x 5 array: a new (fourth) row has been added for the profit component of sectors' costs; and a new (fourth) column has been added for capitalists' consumption expenditure of their profit on agricultural and manufacturing products.

The brackets show modern national income, equal in corn *numéraire* units to 180. Land's share of the reduced total product has dropped from one-half to four-ninths, now that profit usurps a share; labour's share has dropped from one-half to three-ninths. The real value of land's rent has dropped by one-fifth in terms of corn, and by even more in terms of manufactures. Each worker gets the same subsistence wage in corn as before, but now the real wage in terms of manufactures is down by one-third.

To pierce the veil of market values, Table 1.4 presents the exact physical magnitudes underlying Table 1.3.

8 CLOUDING UP *PRODUIT NET*

Once Turgot and Quesnay admit profit into their system, there arises some embarrassment in treating land rent as the sole component of *produit net*. Or, to sidestep circularity in the defining of *produit net*, I can put it this way:

(1) Manufacturing revenues no longer *merely* cover the 'cost elements' in manufactures. Subsistence fodder to reproduce workers seems to be a more legitimate 'cost' than capitalists' interest and profit is.[9] Unless one elevates 'waiting and abstinence' to the level of genuine real costs, they could seem to involve elements of 'surplus' or even of 'exploitation'. Land rent is indeed a surplus, but with the saving grace that the land is at least 'productive' whatever be the demerits of the land's owners.

TABLE 1.4

Tableau's physical magnitudes[a]

Sectors	*Agriculture*	*Manufacturing*	*Labour*	*Capitalists' consumption*	*Landowners' consumption*	*Totals*
Agriculture	0	20 corn	60 corn	20 corn	40 corn	140 corn
Manufacturing[b]	0	0	0	13 mfrs	26 mfrs	40 mfrs
Labour	40 labourers	20 labourers	0	0	0	60 labourers
Land	1 land unit (of 100 acres)					1 land unit

[a] The sole capital in this model is 80 of corn, 20 advanced as raw materials for manufacturing and 60 advanced as subsistence wages.
[b] Second-row items are those of Table 1.3 multiplied by two-thirds.

(2) There are models in which interest can be given a semblance of true productivity but my Table 1.3's example differs from Table 1.1's not a bit in technology. Involving less of population and of farm raw material needed for manufactures, Table 1.3 possesses even less of useful capital goods than Table 1.2 did. So one can understand why Marx would not have been tempted to regard its profits as either legitimate costs or as the return to a 'productive' input.[10]

Twentieth-century theorists try harder than eighteenth-century theorists did to keep normative attitudes from contaminating correct analysis of positivistic fact. So it is as well if the honorific category of *produit net* begins to get complicated in realistic models.

9 CONCLUSION

Embarrassing or not, the *Tableau Economique* has been an interesting footnote in the history of economic thought. Dr Quesnay was not a young man when he first fabricated it. After studying Quesnay's many jousts with the problems it raises, one is not surprised to learn that Madame Pompadour's physician believed he had matched his contribution to economics by his contribution to mathematics in the form of a successful squaring of the circle.

Where early pioneers are concerned, posterity must be grateful for what they accomplished and must not scold over mere imperfections.

MATHEMATICAL APPENDIX

1. Here is how the *Tableau Economique* of my Tables 1.1 and 1.2 are rigorously determined when $r^* = 0$. The steady-state production functions for the agriculture and manufacturing sectors are given by

$$\begin{aligned} Q_1 &= F[T, L_1] \\ &= f(L_1) \text{ if } T = 1, f'(\ ) > 0 > f''(\ ) \qquad \text{(A.1)} \\ Q_2 &= \text{Min}[Q_{12}/a_{12}, L_2/a_{L2}] \qquad \text{(A.2)} \\ &= \text{Min}[Q_{12}/\tfrac{1}{2}, L_2/\tfrac{1}{2}] \text{ in my example} \end{aligned}$$

The corn subsistence wage of $\bar{w}$, which can be unity by proper choice of corn and labour units, determines L_1^* by

$$f'(L_1^*) = \bar{w} \tag{A.3}$$
$$= f'(100) = 1 \text{ in my example}$$

Corn output and corn rent are given by

$$Q_1^* = f_1(L_1^*) \tag{A.4}$$
$$= f_1(100) = 200 \text{ in my example}$$
$$R^* = Q_1^* - \bar{w}L_1^* \tag{A.5}$$
$$= 200 - 1(100) = \tfrac{1}{2}Q_1^* = 100 \text{ in my example}$$

In the equilibrium of (A.1) every competitive farm firm has production coefficients given by

$$\begin{bmatrix} a_{L1}^* \\ a_{T1}^* \end{bmatrix} = \begin{bmatrix} L_1^*/Q_1^* \\ T/Q_1^* \end{bmatrix} = \begin{bmatrix} L_1^*/f_1(Q_1^*) \\ 1/f_1(Q_1^*) \end{bmatrix} \tag{A.6}$$
$$= \begin{bmatrix} 1/2 \\ 1/200 \end{bmatrix} \text{ in my example}$$

The following prices can be set at unity by virtue of my choice of units and coefficients $[P_1^*, P_2^*, W^*, W/P_1 = \bar{w}]$. With $T = 1$ earning 100 units of rent, the rent rate per unit is 100:

$$P_1^* = W^*a_{L1}^* + (\text{rent rate})a_{T1}^* \tag{A.7}$$
$$= 1(\tfrac{1}{2}) + 100(1/200) = 1 \text{ in my example}$$

$$P_2^* = W^*a_{L2} + P_1^*a_{12} \tag{A.8}$$
$$= 1(\tfrac{1}{2}) + 1(\tfrac{1}{2}) = 1 \text{ in my example}$$

Since $R^* = 100$ and I have made Quesnay's assumption that half of the income is spent on agriculture and on manufacturing:

$$P_1 C_1^* = R^* = P_2 C_2^* \tag{A.9}$$

$$C_1^* = 1(50) = \tfrac{1}{2}(100) = 50 = C_2^* \text{ in my example} \tag{A.10}$$

$$L_2^* = a_{L2} Q_2^* = a_{L2}(C_2^* + 0) \tag{A.11}$$

$$= \tfrac{1}{2}(100) = 50 \text{ in my example}$$

Total corn must equal subsistence for all $(L_1^* + L_2^*)$ workers plus raw materials for manufacturing plus landowners' corn consumption:

$$Q_1^* = \bar{w}(L_1 + L_2) + Q_{12} + C_1 \tag{A.12}$$

$$= 1(150) + 25 + 50 = 225 \text{ in my example}$$

Also

$$Q_2^* = C_2^* + (Q_{21}^* + Q_{22}^*) \tag{A.13}$$

$$= C_2^* + 0 = 50 \text{ in my example}$$

This completes my Table 1.1 as:

$P_1^* Q_{11}^*$	$P_1^* Q_{12}^*$	$P_1 \bar{w}(L_1^* + L_2^*)$	$P_1^* C_1^*$	$P_1^* C_1^*$
$P_2^* Q_{21}^*$	$P_2^* Q_{22}^*$	0	$P_2^* C_2^*$	$P_2^* Q_2^*$
$W^* L_1^*$	$W^* L_2^*$	0	0	$W(L_1^* + L_2^*)$
R^*	0	0	0	R^*
Σ	Σ	Σ	Σ	$\Sigma\Sigma$

which is equal to

0	25	125	50	200
0	0	0	50	50
100	25	0	0	125
100	0	0	0	100
200	50	125	100	375

2. An equivalent treatment of the subsistence wage requirements involves eliminating the row and column for labour. Instead, add the subsistence corn requirements of industries to the first row's a^*_{1j} coefficients. These now become $a^*_{1j} + \bar{w}a_{Lj}$. My Table 1.2 is then given by:

$P^*_1 Q^*_{11} + P^*_1 \bar{w} L_1$	$P^*_1 Q^*_{12} + P^*_1 \bar{w} L^*_2$	$P^*_1 C^*_1$	$P^*_1 Q^*_1$
$P^*_2 Q^*_{21} + 0$	$P^*_2 Q^*_{22} + 0$	$P^*_2 C^*_2$	$P^*_2 Q^*_2$
R^*	0	0	R^*
Σ	Σ	Σ	$\Sigma\Sigma$

which is equal to

100	50	50	200
0	0	50	50
100	0	0	100
200	50	100	(350)

3. There is no reason why, in models more general than my version of Quesnay, land might not be required in more than the first sector. Then $(a_{Tj}) = (a_{T1}, a_{T2}, \ldots)$ might have a_{T2} and other a_{Tj} non-zero.

Also, there is no reason why subsistence should be solely in corn. Instead, the ration needed per worker for subsistence could be the column vector $[m_i]$, with

$$\begin{bmatrix} m_1 \\ m_2 \end{bmatrix} = \begin{bmatrix} \bar{w} \\ 0 \end{bmatrix} \text{ in my example} \qquad \text{(A.14)}$$

But in general m_2, and m_j other than m_1, could *also* be positive.

It would still be true, in the case of $r^* = 0$, that *produit net* equals land rent. Our equilibrium would be given by

$$1 = \sum_1^n (P_j/W) m_j \qquad \text{(A.15)}$$

If land is a homogeneous scalar – or even if it were a vector of different-quality lands but with each quality of land having the *same* relative efficiency in every use (as when grade B has half grade A's effectiveness in every sector)[11] – the relation (A.15) together with the minimum-cost conditions would determine real wage rates, real rent rates, relative prices, and L_j^*/Q_j^* ratios that are independent of the pattern of landlord tastes for consumption. And the real *produit net* would be a total independent of such tastes. See Samuelson (1977b, equations 25) for an 'Adam Smith' model of this type.

4. Recognising time-phasing, the production functions for the two sectors become

$$Q_1(t+1) = F_1[T(t), L_1(t)]$$
$$= f_1[L_1(t)] \text{ for } T(t) \equiv 1 \quad \text{(A.16)}$$
$$f_1'[\ ] > 0 > f_1''[\ ]$$
$$Q_2(t+1) = \text{Min}[L_2(t)/a_{L2}], Q_{12}(t)/a_{12}] \quad \text{(A.17)}$$
$$[L_2(t), Q_{12}(t)] = [a_{L2}, a_{12}]Q_2(t+1) \quad \text{(A.17')}$$

$Q_{12}(t)$ is the corn raw material used up in producing manufactures.

Writing $[c_j(t), C_j(t)]$ for consumptions of good j by capitalists and landowners respectively, total outputs are allocated according to

$$Q_2(t) = c_2(t) + C_2(t) + 0 \quad \text{(A.18)}$$
$$Q_1(t) = c_1(t) + C_1(t) + \bar{w}[L_1(t) + L_2(t)] + Q_{12}(t) \quad \text{(A.19)}$$

In the steady state

$$[Q_j(t), Q_{ij}(t), c_j(t), C_j(t), L_j(t)] \equiv [Q_j, Q_{ij}, c_i, C_j, L_j] \quad \text{(A.20)}$$
$$W/P_1 = \bar{w} = f_1'(L_1)/(1+r^*) \quad \text{(A.21)}$$
$$= f_1'(40)/(1+0.5) = 1 \text{ in Table 1.3}$$
$$Q_1 = f_1(L_1) \quad \text{(A.22)}$$
$$= f_1(40) = 140 \text{ in Table 1.3}$$

$$R = Q_1 - L_1 f_1'(L_1) \tag{A.23}$$
$$= 140 - (40)(1.5) = 80 \text{ in Table 1.3}$$

$$P_2 = (Wa_{L2} + P_1 a_{12})(1 + r^*) \tag{A.24}$$
$$= P_1(\bar{w}a_{L2} + a_{12})(1 + r^*)$$
$$= P_1(\tfrac{1}{2} + \tfrac{1}{2})(1 + 0.5) = P_1(1.5) \text{ in Table 1.3}$$

$$c_1 + C_1 = \tfrac{1}{2}[\text{Total profit + Rent}] \tag{A.25}$$
$$= \tfrac{1}{2}[r^*(L_1 + L_2) + r^*Q_{12} + R]$$

$$c_2 + C_2 = (P_2/P_1)^{-1}[r^*(L_1 + L_2) + r^*Q_{12} + R] \tag{A.26}$$

$$L_2 = a_{12}Q_2 = \tfrac{1}{2}(c_2 + C_2) = Q_{12} \tag{A.27}$$

Solving (A.25) – (A.27) simultaneously determines for Table 1.3

$$[L_2^*, Q_2^*, Q_{12}^*, c_1^*, C_1^*, c_2^*, C_2^*] = [20, 40, 20, 20, 40, \tfrac{2}{3}\,20, \tfrac{2}{3}\,40]$$

5. Quesnay's durable capital goods can be handled expeditiously if any such good is assumed to depreciate exponentially. Thus, replace the Q_{ij} symbol in (A.17) appropriate for the case where the input is all used up in one use by K_{ij}, with $d_{ij}K_{ij}$ being used up in one-period's use. For $d_{ij} = 1$, we have our previous case.

Now, in (A.19), replace the symbol $Q_{ij}(t)$ by $[K_{ij}(t) - K_{ij}(t-1)] + d_{ij}K_{ij}(t-1)$. This takes account of the fact that net investment equals gross investment minus depreciation. Then (A.24) becomes

$$P_2/P_1 = \bar{w}a_{L2}(1 + r^*) + a_{12}(d_{12} + r^*) \tag{A.28}$$

Generally, if we are given for all input–output coefficients the depreciation fractions $[d_{ij}]$, what Leontief and Sraffa write for circulating-capital systems as

$$[I - a_{ij}(1 + r^*)]^{-1} \tag{A.29}$$

we now merely write as

$$[I - a_{ij}(d_{ij} + r^*)]^{-1} \qquad \text{(A.30)}$$

My text skips such inessential complications.

NOTES TO CHAPTER 1

1. The author owes thanks to the American National Science Foundation for financial aid, and to Kate Crowley and Aase Huggins for editorial assistance.
2. In Barna's short run, when the total of farm and manufacturing labour has not yet grown, some L_F will shift to manufacturing. Corn rent will fall. The real wage will rise, both in terms of manufactures and subsistence corn, but more in terms of the latter. Kuznets's national income (Ricardo's gross revenue) will necessarily *rise* reckoned in corn and fall reckoned in manufactures. The terms of trade will temporarily shift against agriculture. All this, however, was not worked out in its entirety until the time of Stolper and Samuelson (1940). What needs mentioning in connection with the short-run case is that *it* does *not* constitute a Leontief–Sraffa one-primary-factor model. With homogeneous land and labour *both* primary factors, Leontief's assumption of fixity of production coefficients would lead to indeterminacies of equilibrium; under the Ricardian assumption of *land–labour substitution*, as in equation (1.1) above, the classical model apes neoclassical properties.

   Quesnay's arithmetic never seems to have led him to the *fundamental theorem of Physiocracy*: that is, no change in tastes can alter the total of long-run *produit net* in a homogeneous-land model where *all other* outputs and inputs are producible at constant returns out of themselves.
3. The base of 100 for land rent is arbitrary: we can define our units of homogeneous land so that there are initially 100 of them. Then, if their number should double or halve, the equilibrium level of *all* other *extensive* variables will double or halve, while all *intensive* price and quantity ratios will be invariants. We can select as our physical units of agricultural product exactly what half a land unit produces (when it has the matching labour to work with). For our units of labour, we define as one labour unit the amount needed (along with land) to produce two units of corn. In terms of these

units the subsistence wage is one corn per period. It follows that the price of corn in *numéraire* units of land rent will be exactly one. Similarly, we are free to select as our physical unit for manufactures the amount of it that requires as raw materials exactly one-half of our farm-product units. Then our example's technology tells us that $P_M/P_F \equiv 1 \equiv P_M/\text{rent rate}$.

Adopting the above conventional definitional units, every item in the table becomes a physical magnitude as well as a dollar or livre magnitude. Thus, in column 1, 100 units of land along with 100 workers produce 200 of corn; in column 2, 50 of manufactures is produced by 25 workers and 25 units of farm-product raw materials. The rows can still be added to get totals of physical items. Interpreted as a *physical tableau*, the table's columns cannot be added since cheese-plus-chalk or corn-plus-manufactures-plus-labour-plus-land makes no sense.

4. If $y(t)$ is a column vector of n elements, B a vector of constants, 1 is replaced by the n-by-n identity matrix I, and $\frac{1}{2}$ is replaced by $a = [a_{ij}]$, a matrix of positive elements with column sums positive proper fractions, then expression (1.4) generalises to the 'matrix geometric progression'

$$y(t+1) = ay(t) + B$$

$$y(t) = [I-a]^{-1}B + y(0)a^t$$

$$y(t) = [I-a]^{-1}B + [y(0) - (I-a)^{-1}B]a^t$$

$$\lim_{t\to\infty} y(t) = [I-a]^{-1}B = [I + a + a^2 + \ldots]B > 0 \qquad (1.4a)$$

The respective elements in a^t or a^tB do not themselves decay in simple geometric progressions (being the *sum* of exponentials), but for a a *primitive* matrix such elements *asymptotically* decay at a common exponential rate. However, as seen in my text, the matrix generalisation cannot vindicate the Johnson spending-chain interpretation but if anything its reverse in time.

5. See Dorfman, Samuelson and Solow (1958) for details.

6. For steady-state purposes, there is no harm in netting out each sector's *own* raw-material requirements. But when the pre-1980 pattern is a genuine planner's programme, phased in real time, technology usually will not allow us to have an $[a_{ij}]$ matrix with zeros in the diagonal. And then the matrix series of note 4, $B + aB + a^2B \ldots$, will *not* be the simple geometric progressions of Hishiyama (1960) and Eltis (1975), except penultimately.

Remark: the 1980 and earlier *land* inputs needed to produce the 1980 consumptions are not shown in my zig-zag table. The reader may use the blank middle column to write in the requisite entries 25 (1980), 12½ (1979), ... The sum there will be 50 of land units, representing the *direct* land requirements of the (50 corn and 50 mfrs); the missing 50 of land units is the *indirect* land embodied in the outer columns' totals.

7. Admittedly, r^* will be determined *simultaneously* along with the other equilibrium values (L_F^*, L_M^*, P_M^*/P_F^*, . . .). For brevity I shall take r^* as already given: at 50 per cent, $r^* = 0.5$, in Table 1.3's dramatic example (p. 65). I mention, but ignore, the possibility of multiple equilibria.
8. See the mathematical appendix (pp. 72–3) for precise equilibrium conditions behind Tables 1.3 and 1.4.
9. See Samuelson (1959a, 1959b) for the Physiocratic version of Ricardo, a version I have essentially plagiarised for Table 1.3. In that version the supply price needed to keep saving neither negative nor positive was the Pickwickian 'cost of reproduction of capital' and all market value was expressible in terms of 'embodied-dated-land-content-marked-up-by-that-profit-rate'.
10. Quesnay used the term 'interest' to name what we call 'capital depreciation'. Suppose we stay with $r^* = 0$ and postulate *exponential* depreciation, with d_{ij} being the fraction of each intermediate input that is used up in any single period's use. Then we can still accomplish what Karl Marx struggled over and doubted could be done: we can express final goods' values in terms of the sum of the values added by land rent and profit or interest on capital items. See the mathematical appendix for some of the details.
11. If, however, T is a vector of heterogeneous lands (T_1, T_2, . . .) that do not enter into *all* production functions in the same linear aggregate, $\alpha_1 T_{1j} + \alpha_2 T_{2j} + \ldots$, then a change in landowners' tastes might well affect $(P_j/P_1)^*$ and (L_j^*/Q_j^*) ratios. Also, real *produit net*, reckoned as $\Sigma_k (R_k T_k/P_j)$, will then generally be altered by changes in tastes.

REFERENCES TO CHAPTER 1

BARNA, T. (1975) 'Quesnay's "Tableau" in Modern Guise', *Economic Journal*, vol. 85, pp. 485–96.

CLARK, J. B. (1899) *The Distribution of Wealth: A Theory of Wages, Interest and Profits* (New York, Macmillan).

DORFMAN, R., SAMUELSON, P. A. and SOLOW, R. (1958) *Linear Programming and Economic Analysis* (New York, McGraw-Hill).

ELTIS, W. A. (1975) 'Francois Quesnay: a reinterpretation I: the Tableau Economique', *Oxford Economic Papers*, vol. 27, pp. 167–200.

GIDE, C. and RIST, C., (1926). *A History of Economic Doctrines*, 2nd English edn (Paris: Société anonyme du Recueil Sirey).

GRAY, A. (1931) *The Development of Economic Doctrine* (London, Longman, Green).

HISHIYAMA, I. (1960) 'The Tableau économique of Quesnay: its analysis, reconstruction and application', *Kyoto University Economic Review*, vol. 30, no. 1, pp. 1–46.

JOHNSON, H. (1974) 'Some reflections on Quesnay's *Tableau Economique*', (in Spanish), *Economia*, vol. 2, pp. 76–85; also in French, *Revue d'Economie Politique*, vol. 2, 1975, pp. 397–407.

KEYNES, J. M. (1936) *The General Theory of Employment, Interest and Money* (London, Macmillan).

KUCZYNSKI, M. and MEEK, R. L. (1972) *Quesnay's Tableau Economique* (London: Macmillan).

LEONTIEF, W. (1941) *The Structure of the American Economy, 1919–39* (New York, Oxford University Press).

MACHLUP, F. (1939) 'Period analysis and multiplier theory', *Quarterly Journal of Economics*, vol. 54, pp. 1–27.

MAITAL, S. (1972) 'The Tableau Economique as a Leontief model', *Quarterly Journal of Economics*, vol. 84, pp. 504–7.

MALANOS, G. J. (1946) 'The evolution of the General Theory', Ph.D. thesis, Harvard University.

MALTHUS, T. R. (1798) *An Essay on the Principle of Population* (First Essay on Population) (London, J. Johnson).

MEEK, R. L. (1962) 'Problems of the 'Tableau Economique', in *The Economics of Physiocracy* (London, Allen & Unwin).

MIRABEAU, MARQUIS DE (1756–60) *L'ami des hommes (Friend of Mankind)*, (Avignon). (Reprinted by Scientia, Verlag Aalen, 1970.)

PHILLIPS, A. (1955) 'The Tableau Economique as a simple Leontief model', *Quarterly Journal of Economics*, vol. 69, pp. 137–44.

QUESNAY, F. (1758) *Tableau Oeconomique* (so-called 'first edition' as reproduced and translated in appendix A of Kuczynski and Meek, 1972).

RICARDO, D. (1817) *On the Principles of Political Economy and Taxation* (London, J. Murray).

SAMUELSON, P. A. (1959a) 'A modern treatment of the Ricardian economy: I. the pricing of goods and of labor and land services', *Quarterly Journal of Economics*, vol. 73, pp. 1–35. Reprinted in *The Collected Scientific Papers of Paul A. Samuelson*, vol. 1, ch. 31, ed. J. E. Stiglitz (Cambridge, Mass., MIT Press, 1966).

SAMUELSON, P. A. (1959b) 'A modern treatment of the Ricardian economy: II. capital and interest aspects of the pricing process',

Quarterly Journal of Economics, vol. 73, pp. 217–31. Reprinted in *Collected Scientific Papers of Paul A. Samuelson*, vol. 1, ch. 32.

SAMUELSON, P. A. (1977a) 'Correcting the Ricardo error spotted in Harry Johnson's maiden paper', *Quarterly Journal of Economics*, vol. 91, pp. 519–30.

SAMUELSON, P. A. (1977b) 'A modern theorist's vindication of Adam Smith', *American Economic Review*, vol. 67, pp. 42–9.

SAMUELSON, P. A. (1979) 'Land and the rate of interest', in *Theory for Economic Efficiency: Essays in Honor of Abba P. Lerner*, ed. H. I. Greenfield (Cambridge, Mass., MIT Press).

SCHUMPETER, J. A. (1954) *History of Economic Analysis* (Oxford University Press).

SRAFFA, P. (1951) *The Works and Correspondence of David Ricardo*, vol. 1 (Cambridge University Press) Editor's Introduction, pp. xiii–lxii.

STOLPER, W. F. and SAMUELSON, P. A. (1940) 'Protection and real wages', *Review of Economic Studies*, vol. 9, pp. 58–73. Reprinted in *The Collected Scientific Papers of Paul A. Samuelson*, vol. 2, ch. 66, ed. J. E. Stiglitz (Cambridge, Mass., MIT Press, 1966).

TURGOT, A. R. J. (1769) *Reflections on the Formation and the Distribution of Riches* (New York, A. M. Kelley, 1963).

WEST, SIR E. (1815) *Essay on the Application of Capital to Land* (Baltimore, Johns Hopkins Press, 1903).

Chapter 12 Land and the Rate of Interest

Paul A. Samuelson

Can society be worse off from possessing something useful? Keynes believed a laissez-faire system might be permanently harmed from having land:

That the world after several millenia of steady individual saving, is so poor as it is in accumulated capital-assets, is to be explained, in my opinion, neither by the improvident propensities of mankind, nor even by the destruction of war, but by the high liquidity premiums formerly attaching to the ownership of land and now attaching to money. (*General Theory*, p. 242)[1]

The effect of land as displacing capital formation has a truth, I believe, beyond that glimpsed here by Keynes. One must bring to bear upon the problem the Modigliani life-cycle saving model, an hypothesis that seems to throw more light on the cross-sectional and historical facts of capital formation than any other single explanation.

For, as can be seen in the quotations and verified from the full passages out of which they are taken, Keynes based his case primarily or even exclusively, on the role of land in satisfying liquidity preference and thereby exacerbating the problem of ineffectual demand and job opportunity: when the marginal efficiency of capital is already so low that what is needed is interest rate reduction to coax out enough investment to sustain full employment, Keynes feared that the existence of storable money, of other liquid assets such as jewelry or old masters, *and of land* would inhibit the needed capital formation by keeping the market's money rate of interest

I owe thanks to the National Science Foundation for financial aid. As will be obvious, the ideas expressed here go back to work done long ago; but the few-period life-cycle model, so useful in writings of Diamond (1965) or Samuelson (1958, 1967, 1968, 1975a, 1975b), provides a simple way to explain a basic property of land. My debt to Franco Modigliani's seminal writing on the life-cycle model is obvious: cf. Modigliani (1954, 1963, 1970, 1974) and still unpublished writings.

too high (above zero, for example, rather than at zero or below zero by the differential needed to coax from risk-averse investors the requisite volume of capital formation).

As thus stated, Keynes's argument proves too much, and, more importantly, too little. The argument claims too much because it can be argued—Lerner and Kaldor[2] have so argued—that Keynes erred in likening land to money: he can be charged with forgetting that the price of land is a variable that can be bid up to whatever level is needed to bring the interest rate down indefinitely close to zero. But, as stated, Keynes's argument claims too much, quite aside from the Lerner and Kaldor attacks on the cogency of his syllogisms. If land starves productive investment of its needed finance *only when capital is already so abundant that liquidity traps threaten and Keynes's euthanasia of the rentier class is imminent*, then land has presumably *not* really made the world "so poor . . . in accumulated capital-assets," as Keynes has claimed.

Quite aside from depression periods of gross inadequacy of effective demand, it can be shown that land does have the effect, other things being equal, of keeping steady-state capital levels lower per head than would otherwise be the case.[3] By not noting this, Keynes's own argument claimed much too little. Even if profit rates and interest rates are high—say 15 and 8 percent—and employment is full, the existence of land has effects on the long-run interest rate. Moreover, land is not unique in this respect: slavery in the ante-bellum South, to the degree that it *merely*[4] gave white capitalists a new asset to hold in the form of capitalized human labor-earnings power, the present analysis can show, likewise reduces the level to which plant and equipment expenditures will be pushed! Land is in many ways not at all like money in creating these long-run effects. What land is like is a long-lived machine, indeed an infinitely-lived asset if it is "Ricardian land" that we envisage, the "inexhaustible (unaugmentable) gift of nature."

As will be seen, the effect of land in keeping the long-run interest rate higher in the steady-state than it would otherwise be is no different in kind from the effect of *any change in technology that could be recognized as involving "greater durability" of capital assets*—greater "wealth-to-income" ratio.

Planning versus Laissez-Faire

No one, and certainly not Keynes, believed that having more of something productive, whether it be land or anything itself, would be anything other than a *potential blessing* to a well-run society. Only under private property in land and laissez-faire market conditions might the blessing become a curse. It is well, at the beginning, to go through some welfare-economics analysis to see how truly optimal development will be aided rather than hurt by more plentiful productive land.

If private ownership in land induced private saving behavior that would result in less reproducible capital in the long-run than is needed in a golden-rule state, a planned society could (a) nationalize land ownership, or (b) tax it in Henry George fashion, or (c) offset its effects by socially determined thrift. Familiar Ramsey analysis of optimal control, applied to a stationary economy (at first assumed free of technical change), shows what is needed to bring the system ever nearer to the golden-rule state of maximum per capital steady-state consumption. A Ramsey labor-land-(heterogeneous) capital model can approach that state at an optimal rate—optimal in the sense of maximizing, from the initial stock of capital goods, the expected lifetime utility level of a representative person who might be born in *any* future generation. One can verify by straightforward analysis what is my essential common-sense point, that having a higher land supply, B, does raise and not lower this attainable expected lifetime well-being of the representative person.

Even under laissez-faire, could it be the case that salting *all* land would make people better off in the steady state? Certainly if zero land implies zero output and zero consumption, this could hardly be the case.[5] At most, Keynes and other writers who worried about the investment-reducing influence of land ownership intended to say only that people will not be as well off under private property in land as they *might be*.

On reflection, though, one must wonder whether that is saying anything interesting. Even in the absence of land—that is, if it were so plentiful as to be "free"—is there really any Schumpeterian presumption that laissez-faire will lead to long-run golden-rule equilibrium? Of course not. Nor was this claim made by Senior, Böhm-Bawerk, or Fisher. Quite the contrary. Their arguments were to show why the interest rate in a stationary society would be *positive* rather than at the golden-rule level of zero; and, often, why this was only proper.[6] Paradoxically, it was Marx, and also Kalecki, who envisaged a process in which the golden rule state might conceivably be attained—namely, the process in which all profits are saved and only the non-capitalists consume.

Keynes's point about land as an inhibitor of real capital formation can, however, be shown to be stating something meaningful. To see this, agree that rigorous life-cycle models—such as those in Modigliani (1954,

1963, 1970, 1974), Diamond (1965), Cass and Yaari (1967), or Samuelson (1958, 1967, 1968, 1975a, 1975b)—prove that laissez-faire leads to divergence from the golden-rule state of maximum expected lifetime well-being. We can then introduce land into such a model and deduce that private ownership of land well may[7] keep up the long-run interest and profit rate and lower permanently the level of permanent per capita consumption.

The following sections will give the needed analysis.

Life Cycle Analysis

Begin with the simplest model. All people are alike. Each lives two periods, consuming c_1 in his working period and c_2 in his retirement period. Inheriting nothing and bequeathing nothing, his budget equation under laissez-faire is

$$c_1+[c_2/(1 + r)] = w \tag{12.1}$$

where w is the real wage and r is the interest rate.

Subject to (12.1) he acts to maximize his lifetime well-being $u(c_1, c_2)$. What he doesn't consume while working, $w - c_1$, he lives off when retired, then having c_2 consumption equal to $(w - c_1)(1 + r)$. The counterpart of his principal is society's stock of capital goods (inclusive of land, B, if land is not so plentiful as to be free).

The schedule of each generation's asset holding depends on w and $1 + r$, being derived as follows:

$$\begin{aligned} &\operatorname*{Max}_{c_i} u(c_1, c_2), \text{ subject to } c_1 + [c_2/(1 + r)] = w \\ &\qquad = u(c_1\{w, 1 + r\}, c_2\{w, 1 + r\}) \end{aligned} \tag{12.2}$$

$$\begin{aligned} w - c_1 &= w - c_1\{w, 1 + r\} \\ &= a\{w, 1 + r\}, \text{ per capita life-cycle asset holding.} \end{aligned} \tag{12.3}$$

Note that a curly-brackets expression, such as $f\{x, y\}$ denotes a function of the variables (x, y).

Long-run equilibrium comes when the total of assets that life-cycle savers want to hold, $L(t)a\{w, 1 + r\}$, is equated to the total of productive assets of society that enterprises find profitable to (bring and) keep in existence at the long-run interest rate $1 + r^*$. (There may be more than one such equilibrium rate that clears the market, some perhaps locally unstable.)

The simplest technology to try in our model is the Ramsey-Solow-Meade one-sector case with one capital good ("leets"). This postulates

$$\begin{aligned} Q(t+1) &= C(t+1) + K(t+1) - K(t) \\ &= F[L(t), B(t), K(t)] \\ &= L(t)f[b(t), k(t)] \end{aligned} \tag{12.4}$$

where $f[b, k]$ is a concave function, smoothly differentiable in the standard neoclassical case and strictly concave,[8] and where $[b, k] = [B/L, K/L]$.

We must stipulate something about the supply of labor. Thus, we might posit a given stationary supply, $L(t) \equiv L_0$. Or, provided land were permanently excessive in supply (if that were imaginable), we could have labor grow exponentially, like $L_0(1 + g)^t$, or with the proper choice of dimension to make $L_0 = 1$, like $(1 + g)^t = R^t$.[9] Or, instead of assuming a fixed labor supply, we might postulate a subsistence living wage[10] at which $dL(t)/dt = 0$, and above or below which labor grows or decays at prescribed rates.

Begin with a given labor supply, L_0, and arbitrary capital stock, $K_0 = k_0 L_0$. What must k be so that it represents k^*, an equilibrium ratio of capital, associated with a long-run equilibrium profit or interest rate r^*? The conditions for long-run equilibrium for k^*, r^*, w^*, and for β^*, the rent of land per unit, can be written down, when the price of capital and consumption goods is taken to be unity by our choice of such numeraire units.

$$\bar{b} = \bar{B}/L_0, \text{ a prescribed constant} \tag{12.5a}$$

$$r = \partial f[\bar{b}, k]/\partial k \tag{12.5b}$$

$$\beta = \partial f[\bar{b}, k]/\partial b \tag{12.5c}$$

$$w = f[\bar{b}, \bar{k}] - rk - \beta\bar{b} \tag{12.5d}$$

$$La\{w, 1 + r\} = K + (\beta\bar{B})/r \text{ or}$$

$$a\{w, 1 + r\} = k + (\beta\bar{b})/r \tag{12.5e}$$

Marginal productivity relations are given by (12.5b) and (12.5c), and for that matter, in view of Euler's theorem on adding up, by (12.5d). Our life-cycle saving condition is embodied in (12.5e), which says that at the long-term r^*, the cross-sectional total of what people of all ages have saved must equal the earnings assets of the firms in the economy, land plus capital goods. Land's value comes from capitalizing its perpetual income stream at the long-run interest rate; the equilibrium capital stock, $K^* =$

k^*L_0, is adjusted to the long-run interest rate; a simultaneous equation solution is, of course, needed to define this statical equilibrium, since in this paper I do not present in detail the dynamic transient paths by which, starting out from $K_0 < K^*$, the system evolved into K^* and r^*.

Equations (12.5a–12.5e) suffice to determine our 5 unknowns, β^*, r^*, w^*, k^*, b^*. Indeed, substituting (12.5a)–(12.5d) into (12.5e) gives us a single implicit equation in k, namely

$$a\{f[\bar{B}/L_0, k]-(k\partial f[\bar{B}/L_0, k]/\partial k) - (\bar{B}/L_0)(\partial f[\bar{B}/L_0, k]/\partial b), \quad 1 + (\partial f[\bar{B}/L_0, k]/\partial k)\} = k+(\partial f[\bar{B}/L_0, k]/\partial b)(\bar{B}/L_0)/(\partial f[\bar{B}/L_0, k]/\partial k). \tag{12.6}$$

So our system is "determinate"[11]: after solving (12.6) for a k^* root, we calculate r^*, β^*, and w^* from (12.5b)–(12.5d).

Turgot Vindicated

Before vindicating Keynes's dictum that land ownership tends to keep up the interest rate, we can set to rest the problem that Böhm-Bawerk wrestled with—namely, *Why* is there a positive interest rate?

It will be recalled that, prior to Marshall's 1890 *Principles*, Böhm-Bawerk was probably the world's best-known economist. From the mid-1880s until his 1914 death, he wrestled in three fat volumes with the puzzle of interest. In the volumes that preceded and followed his own *Positive Theory of Capital* (1888), Böhm engaged in tireless polemics, reviewing all old and new theories of interest and finding them all inferior to his own preferred version.

Thus, Böhm divided earlier theories into such categories as *productivity* theories (naive and otherwise), *exploitation* theories (Marx and all that), *abstinence* theories, and so forth. And, of course, he found each lacking: the productivity theories were naive, the exploitation theories begged the issue, etc., etc. Although he is painstaking and tireless, his logic chopping tends to be tedious and boring, besides being so often casuistical and sterile. I do not propose to review his merits and demerits here: it is enough to say that I agree with the general evaluation of Wicksell and Fisher that, for all Böhm-Bawerk's hooplah and merits, in the end he must do what he castigates others for doing—namely, he must "explain" interest in no other way than to point to the supply-and-demand forces that operate in consumption and production loan-assets markets of the world, involving (1) the desires of people to demand both future and present goods, and (2) the ability of businesses to find time-phased production operations that pay competitively at different market profit rates. In short, at his best, Böhm glimpses a Fisher model of intertemporal general equilibrium; and if he had extended to many an earlier writer the charity we extend to him, he could have spared us hundreds of pages.

What is relevant for my present analysis of land and the interest rate is Böhm's initial analysis of Turgot's so-called *fructification* theory of interest. Right at the beginning, after Böhm has warmed up by demolishing the amateurish strictures on usury and interest of the Bible, Aristotle, and the Church's Schoolmen, he turns to Turgot, "the greatest of the physiocrats," and "the first to attempt a scientific explanation of all interest on the fact that the owner of any capital employed in a fruitful field always has the option of a different field. That is to say, he can use it for the purchase of land which is then capable of yielding land rent."[12]

I shall not go into the question of whether the theory attributed to Turgot does that author full justice.[13] It is enough for us that Böhm attributes to Turgot the view that the permanent fertility of land is the source of a positive interest rate: for if one can buy land at 20 (or 30 or . . .) years purchase, then by competitive arbitrage all alternative opportunities to invest that are equally safe must also yield 0.05 or 5 per cent per annum (or $30^{-1} = 0.333$ or . . .).

Böhm seems to think that 20 year's purchase, or any finite n year's purchase begs the question by assuming what needs to be "proved" and "explained." Salty Edwin Cannan (1929, p. 280) did not at all agree, writing "If the question, Why is there a rate of interest? is put in the form 'Why is there a ratio between capital-value and income-value?' it looks rather silly, . . ." The only legitimate scruple that Böhm should have investigated (but hardly began), and that Cannan might have more humbly explored, is whether an acre of good land could in equilibrium have an *infinite* value relative to any finite bushel of grain or quantum of money purchasing power.

My old teacher, Joseph Schumpeter, with his quaint theory of zero interest rate in the stationary circular-flow general equilibrium, may have had some such infinity notion in mind.[14] Within the context of a reasonable life-cycle model, we can put the whole matter to definitive rest. We can provide for the "first scientific" writer on interest, Turgot, a perfectly plausible and consistent model for a positive rate of interest; so, even prior to Böhm-Bawerk's own 1888 "positive" solution, Böhm might better have conceded that truth had already been glimpsed.

Turgot's Purest Case

Forget for the present purpose about the existence of any produced inputs, K or $K_1, K_2, \ldots$. Let there be the labor of people, who like all men are mortal, and let there be permanent land in limited amount: as with Sir William Petty, labor sires out of land the progeny of annual product, $Q = Lf[B/L], f''[b] < 0$. Grant Turgot the reasonable supposition, which need not even have been explicit, that whatever are people's preferences about future and present, they will want to consume in their lifetimes *some finite* portion of the total principal that is theirs to consume or to bequeath. Then Böhm should have admitted the truth of the following Turgot-like Theorem.

If land has a perpetual net yield and at least one mortal wishes to enjoy a finite portion of the assets at his disposal rather than bequeath it, we have sufficient conditions for a necessarily positive steady-state interest rate.

To prove the obvious, rewrite (12.6) so that $a\{w, 1 + r\}$ has included in it the effects of whatever (finite!) bequests or inheritances people decide on; and suppose that K is absent from $F[L, B]$. We then have

$$L_0 a\{\partial F[L_0, \bar{B}]/\partial L, 1 + r; \text{inheritance}\} = \frac{\bar{B}}{r} \partial F[L_0, \bar{B}]/\partial B \qquad (12.6')$$

Equation (12.6′) is the Turgot-Modigliani equation for the land-begotten positive interest rate, positive because at $r = 0$ the infinite right-hand side would have to exceed the left-hand side.[15] To be conciliatory, we can willingly admit that two of Böhm's three blades are here operative: along with his third "productivity" cause of interest (involving land's permanent observed yield, not "proved" or "explained" but accepted), Böhm can save face by claiming that his second cause of interest, "time preference" of some kind, is invoked by our assumption that men someday die and do not entail their land against any sale. Turgot could gladly agree to the emendation; and could point out that, putting some capital goods back into (12.6′) would still leave its smallest r^* root positive, with nothing fundamental having been begged in the discussion.

Figure 12.1 illustrates the Turgot equilibrium of (12.6′) in the simplest case of zero inheritance and bequeathal. The unknown interest rate, r, is on the vertical axis; on the horizontal axis is the total of per capita assets to be held, $a\{w, 1 + r\}$, which in this simplified Turgot case consists only of the land that workers buy when young and live off when old. Since the rent income of land per capita is determined by $\bar{b} = \bar{B}/L_0$ times land's marginal product, $\partial F[L_0, \bar{B}]/\partial B$, dd is a rectangular hyperbola. The "sup-

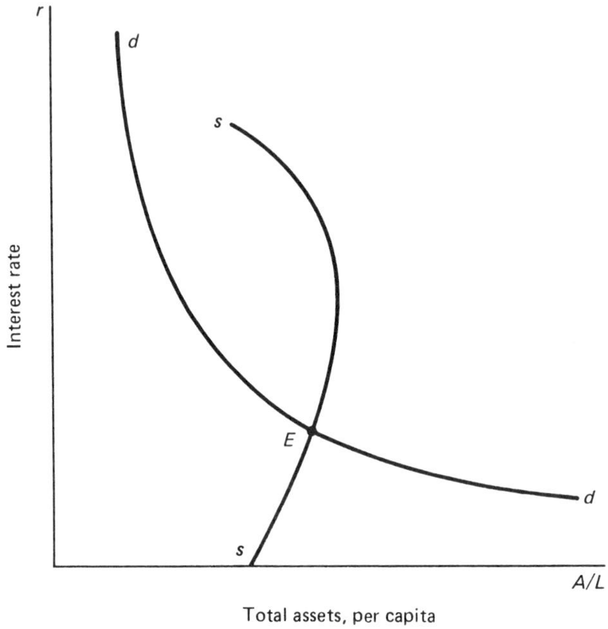

Figure 12.1 In the pure Turgot model, the constant amount of land rent is capitalized by $1/r$, giving *dd* as a unitary-elasticity demand by firms for assets that owners are to hold. From life-cycle saving considerations, the supply of asset holding by families is given by *ss* (being simply $\bar{w} - c_1\{\bar{w}, 1 + r\}$ in the two-period life-cycle model). The equilibrium interest rate is shown at r^*, what Böhm calls the first "scientific" demonstration of a positive interest rate. If the supply of land increases and if that raises total rent along an elastic marginal-product curve, *dd* shifts out to $d'd'$, raising r^* in the fashion alleged by Keynes.

ply schedule" of what people will want to hold for Modigliani life-cycle reasons is given by *ss*: at $r = 0$, it begins at a finite intersection on the horizontal axis to the west of *dd*; therefore, Turgot's model does provide a rigorous demonstration that the interest rate cannot fail to be positive.

An increase in the supply of land, in $\bar{B}$ and $\bar{b}$, could raise or lower the *dd* hyperbola; but, on the customary presumption that the marginal-product demand for land is *elastic*, it will shift *dd* upward and most likely raise r^* much as Keynes alleged would be the case.

Keynes Vindicated

Now we can demonstrate the germ of putative truth in Keynes's contention that the existence of private ownership in land serves to inhibit capital formation. It is his conclusion I support, though I jettison his liquidity-mechanism reason in favor of life-cycle reasons. The procedure to be followed is that involved in analyzing the incidence of a tax, or of the change in comparative-statical equilibrium values produced by a specified change in some parameter.

Subtracting the right-hand "demand side" of (12.6) from the left-hand "supply side," we rewrite it and its implied equilibrium changes in the short form:

$$H[k; b] = 0 \tag{12.7a}$$

$$\frac{dk^*}{db} = -\frac{\partial H[k^*; b]/\partial b}{\partial H[k^*; b]/\partial k} \tag{12.7b}$$

To evaluate (12.7b)'s algebraic sign, one usually applies dynamic stability analysis to a spelled-out short-run scenario of the system being described. Then, if this dynamic analysis establishes that the sign of (12.7b)'s denominator is positive, one can infer that Keynes alleged inhibition by land of the level of capital will follow from (12.7b)'s numerator being shown to be positive. This is not the place to pursue in depth such needed dynamic stability analysis.

It is enough to indicate an important warning or qualification. Even in a simple *leets* model, the land-incidence problem is a bit more delicate than was the public-debt-incidence problem for Diamond (1965). That is (1) because an increase in land, ΔB or Δb, must *directly* raise society's total output per capita, $f[b, k]$, and will thus generally have a *direct* effect on both the w and the r in $a\{\omega, 1 + r\}$, but in unknown directions or degrees. And (2) because the effect of Δb on total land rent per capita, βb in $\beta b/r$, has already been seen to be not necessarily positive in sign. Hence, the final sign pattern in (12.7b) need not be unambiguously definite, and Keynes's sweeping conclusion does have to be qualified.

Figures 12.2 and 12.3 indicate how the actual picture might look. These two-dimensional diagrams bear a vague resemblance to those of Tobin (1967, p. 234, Figure 1). However, two dimensions cannot capture all of the present story, since the W in $a\{w, 1 + r\}$ need not bear a systematic technical relationship to r once land complicates the simplest leets model. As footnote 16 discusses,[16] there is one singular case in which B/L or the land-rent rate does not affect the (r, w) factor-price frontier; my Figures 12.2 and 12.3 may be assumed to apply to that singular (and unrealistic!) case.

In Figure 12.2, the total demand relation of dd gives $k + (\beta b/r)$ as a function of r; note that $(\beta b/r)$ is added horizontally to the (sans-land) neo-

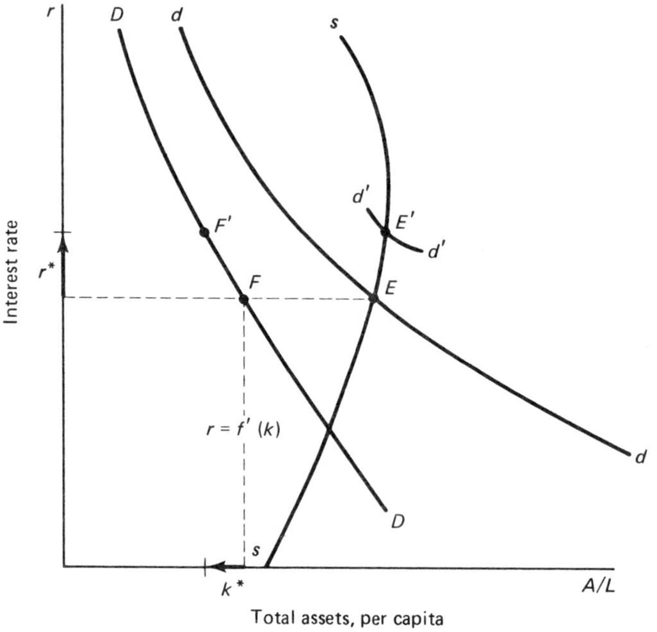

Figure 12.2 Supply, *ss*, is as in Figure 12.1. But now *dd* is the lateral sum of *DD*, the reproducible *k* assets, and land's capitalized asset value—giving *dd* as shown. The intersection of *ss* with *dd* is shown yielding a higher r^* than would the sans-land intersection with *DD*—thus providing a confirmation of Keynes's conjecture.

classical *dd* demand relation that comes from inverting $r = f'(k)$. The *ss* supply relation plots $a\{\ ,\ \}$ against r alone, it being understood that each r gives rise to a unique w along the factor-price frontier $w = \omega(r)$.

The intersection at F defines the equilibrium point of (k^*, r^*) that is due west of E. Now note how an increase in land, B, and in its total rent βB, shifts equilibrium from F to F', and shifts E to E', confirming Keynes's hypothesis that land inhibits k^* and raises r^*.

Figure 12.3 shows some of the multiple equilibria that can occur when we go beyond the neoclassical 1-sector leets model (or, for that matter, recognize that the Modigliani *ss* locus can be twisty). Allowing for Wicksell effects, heterogeneous capital goods like $(k_1, k_2, \ldots)$ rather than scalar k alone, or more simply following Liviatan and Samuelson (1969, p. 456, Figure 1) and postulating the kind of "complementarity" that joint-production leets models may display, we can replace the monotone $f'(k)$ *DD* schedule of Figure 12.2 by the twisty *DD* shown in Figure 12.3. Adding land's rectangular hyperbola to *DD* gives the twisty *dd* locus. Note the

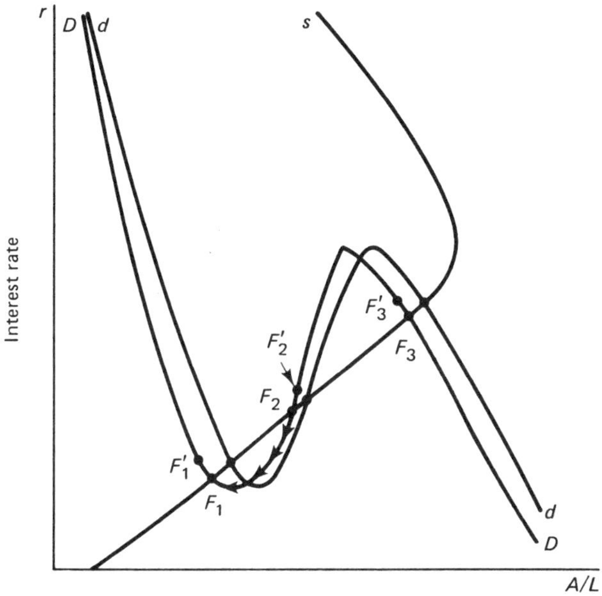

Figure 12.3 Sans land, *DD* here reverses its direction because of Liviatan-Samuelson "complementarity" of joint production. Multiple equilibria occur at F_1, F_2, and F_3, with F_2 being "locally unstable." Adding land shifts *DD* out to *dd*. As Keynes claimed, k^* falls from F_1 to F_1'; and r^* falls from F_3 to F_3'. However, k^* does not rise from F_2 to F_2', but instead it falls "catastrophically" from unstable F_2 to stable F_1'—as shown by the dynamic arrows.

sans-land equilibria at F_1, F_2, and F_3; and how the addition of land leads to new equilibria points for (k^*, r^*) at F_1' and F_3'; but, perhaps surprisingly, the initial unstable F_2 point is shifted, not to F_2' in its neighborhood, but rather is shifted "catastrophically" all the way to F_1' in an extreme vindication of Keynes's conjecture. How dynamic stability affects the comparative-statics shifts in an r^* as a result of shifts in *dd* is briefly discussed in a footnote.[17]

Conclusion

What Keynes never successfully demonstrated by liquidity trap analysis —that the existence of private ownership in land serves to keep up the long-run interest rate—has been shown to be plausible in a model of life-cycle saving. However, certain exceptions were shown to require qualification in various complicated, but not impossible, cases. On the other hand, by introducing Hicks-neutral or Harrod-land-augmenting technical change, the analysis provided here for stationary population and zero-golden-rule states could be generalized to Harrodian exponential-growth systems: Keynes's presumption still holds, that existence of capitalizable land rent will help surfeit the life-cycle need for assets to support one's old age, and will thereby tend to keep the profit rate higher than it would otherwise be.[18]

How important is Keynes's point about land? From his portentous rhetoric, one must weigh this question seriously. Smith, Malthus, Ricardo, Wicksell, the Maynard Keynes of the *Economic Consequences of the Peace* (1919), and last week's Club of Rome, have all expected scarcity of land and natural resources to become increasingly important, with a presumed (but not logically inevitable) rising share in national income of pure rent. The historical facts seem, so far, to have been otherwise. The measurements in Denison (1974, pp. 57–59) of the separate sources of growth, the most careful estimates we have, seem to show pure land rent has a trend of declining relative share of NNP, now being less than 5 per cent of the total. Agricultural economists, such as Theodore Schultz and Gale Johnson of the University of Chicago, have stressed the cardinal importance of land-saving technical change, both in history and at the present time. If they are right, Keynes's point will continue to be of only moderate import, representing more a rhetorical flourish on his part than a pithy insight.

Notes

1. See also p. 241 and p. 358 in J. M. Keynes, *The General Theory of Employment, Interest and Money* (London: Macmillan, 1936) where he writes ". . . there have been occasions in history in which the desire to hold land has played the same role in holding up the interest rate at too high a rate which money has played in recent times. . . . As I have mentioned above, there have been times when it was probably the craving for the ownership of land, independently of its yield, which served to keep up the rate of interest."

2. See A. P. Lerner, "The Essential Properties of Interest and Money," *Quarterly Journal of Economics* 66 (1952): 172–193, particularly its penultimate section. Lerner observes, ". . . what is perhaps the most challenging and memorable part of the chapter [the famous Chapter 17 of the *General Theory* on own rates of interest] . . . is the assertion that '. . . land has played the same role in keeping up the interest rate. . . .' " Lerner goes on to argue: "This intriguing speculation seems, however, to fall to the ground . . . [since] there is nothing to stop the value of land from rising . . . as there is in the case of money . . . [and hence no reason] for keeping up the marginal efficiency of land (and, therefore, in equilibrium, the rate of interest)." N. Kaldor, "Keynes' Theory of the Own-Rates of Interest," an essay not published until it appeared as Chapter 2 in his *Essays on Economic Stability and Growth* (London: Gerald Duckworth & Co., Ltd., 1960),

pp. 58–74, arrives at a critique of Keynes similar to that of Lerner. J. Robinson, "Own Rates of Interest," *Economic Journal* 71 (1961): 596–600, accepts Kaldor's criticism of Keynes, on the proviso that landowners display all the properties of the capitalist class. But, she goes on to argue, often landowning gentry have sold out to thrifty capitalists only in order to maintain consumption, acting in this respect like the rentier heirs to businesses who sell those businesses to conglomerates and other promoters of takeovers: thus, the thrift that might have gone to provide the finance for "productive investment" is diverted into offsetting consumption. Her 1961 lines were prophetic of what the pseudonymous Adam Smith wrote about in *Supermoney* (New York: Random House, 1972). The Robinson argument, as stated, is not incompatible with the Marshall classical view that Keynes was attacking: in the sentence on p. 242 that follows my original quotation from Keynes, Keynes wrote: "I differ in this from the older view as expressed by Marshall . . . : '. . . the accumulation of wealth is held in check, and the rate of interest so far sustained, by the preference which the great mass of humanity have for present over deferred gratifications, or, in other words, by their unwillingness to "wait." ' " But, if we suppose that widows and orphans and selling-out gentry have exceptional risk-aversion, they may favor gilt-edge and even "hoarding" and contribute some exacerbation of an effective demand problem in depressed periods of low interest rates, an effect not in Marshall's mind.

3. This is quite apart from any alleged "high liquidity-premiums formerly attaching to the ownership of land and now attaching to money." (Actually, land is not a liquid asset in the sense of offering a narrow spread between bid and asked and a stable, predictable mean of those limits; there is no reason to think it ever was liquid in this sense, except in made-up history. But, in any case, the issue is irrelevant for what follows.) Also, a possible willingness to hold land at lower yields than other assets—for social climbers or arrivers—has no particular relevance to the analysis that follows.

4. As stated, this argument has to be qualified if it is the case that investment in human capital—education and training of slaves, even number of Negro births—is itself pushed further under slavery's profit motive than under emancipation.

5. A less obvious case is one in which we destroy a little land, reducing B to $B - \Delta B$. Is the long-run steady-state interest rate that results a little higher or a little lower? The later analysis will show that the answer is ambiguous, depending inter alia on whether less land raises or lowers land's relative share in current product and what its effects are on labor's relative share and on capital's yield.

6. If the representative man lives forever (or is part of a self-reproducing clan, or plans vividly for his posterity), and if he applies systematic time preference to consumptions of a future date, the optimal solution to his Ramsey saving-consuming problem is to stay forever away from the golden-rule state of maximum per capital consumption. An ethical observer who regards such subjective time discounting as "myopic" will, of course, regard a closer approach to the golden-rule as more optimal: but, no matter what "reswitching" can occur, a move to the highest plateau of permanent consumption from a lower one cannot be feasible without incurring the need to "wait," "abstain," and "do without" something at one time in order to get something later. Much of Nassau Senior will have to go under socialism, but not that part based on irreducible technology.

7. The words "may well" are used here rather than "must" for at least two reasons: (1) It can be shown that laissez-faire can sometimes lead to interest rates

below the golden-rule rate; and then, like increments of public debt in Diamond (1965), more land may then improve the level of capital formation. (2) Multiple equilibria are always possible, and, as soon as one leaves simplest neoclassical capital models (one-sector "leets," etc.), we know that multiple equilibria are particularly likely: so, depending upon the branch that a laissez-faire system happens to end on, a new increment of land may have complex effects upon the displacement of equilibrium. This ambiguity is reduced if the change in land impinges on an equilibrium that is sufficiently near to the golden-rule state.

8. Ramsey (1928), Solow (1956), Meade (1961) are standard references. Ricardo (1817) is often presumed to be assuming that labor and capital must be applied to corn land in a fixed-proportions dose. In that case, which also has some attraction for modern economists like Robinson (1956), Kaldor (1955), and Pasinetti (1962), $F[L, B, K]=\phi[B, \min(L, K/k\dagger)] = L\phi[b, \min(1, k/k\dagger)$, where $k\dagger$ is a particular technical constant denoting the ratio of capital to labor in the fixed dose. If land is superabundant and free, $k\dagger$ is the "capital-output ratio" times "the product produced by one labor working with its requisite amount of capital." See Samuelson [1977] for an interpretation of Adam Smith along these lines. Even in this non-neoclassical case, long-run r^* may still be determined—as a unique or a multiple root. (Warning: with land limited and no technical change, and the wage needed for life being finite, we'll deduce that a positive r^* will emerge even if net investment and saving is ultimately zero: the $r^* = g/s$ tautologies do not apply in this model, becoming at best the indeterminate form 0/0.

9. Alternatively, suppose that land is limited in supply and useful: but suppose that when B/L is indefinitely small, a real wage can be earned that will support life. Then, we can have $L(t)=R^t$, $K(t) = k^*R^t$, and $B/L(t) = b(t) \to 0$ in a golden-age exponential-growth state; however, with rent becoming negligible, Keynes's point evaporates in importance. As still another alternative, we can suppose that exponential technical change takes place to offset land's scarcity; then, provided that $u(c_1, c_2)$ is homothetic, we can still define exponential-growth states.

10. If workers must be paid their wage at the beginning of each period, we have to count advanced wages as capital assets along with B and K. To sidestep this complication I assume the wage is paid post-factum and the same for land rent.

11. Uniqueness of a solution for k^* is not assured. To see this, denote by $a_i\{\ \}$, $f_i[\ ]$, $f_{ij}[\ ]$, the partial derivatives of the relevant function with respect to the indicated argument. Then the Jacobian of the difference between the two sides of (12.6) is given by

$$J = a_1\{\ \}(-kf_{22}-bf_{12}) + a_2\{\ \}(f_{22})-1-(bf_{12}/f_2)+(f_{22}f_1b)/(f_2)^2$$

Even though a one-sector leets model cannot involve reswitiching or perverse "Wicksell-Swan" effects, J need not be one signed. However, it is easy to show that the smallest r^* root must be positive; and it will be unique if various strong restrictions are placed on $u[c_1, c_2]$ and on $f(b, k)$.

In the Ricardo case of fixed-dose of L and K, we replace (12.5c) by $\beta = \partial f[b, \min(1, k/k\dagger)]/\partial b$, and replace (12.5b)'s marginal-productivity condition by $k = k\dagger$. Then (12.6) becomes a single equation for r^*:

$$a\{f(b, 1] - rk\dagger - b\partial f[b, 1]/\partial b, 1 + r\} = k\dagger + (b\partial f[b, 1]/\partial b)/r.$$

The sign of its relevant Jacobian depends on $-a_1\{\ \}k\dagger + a_2\{\ \} + b\beta/r^2$, which can be ambiguous and yield multiple r^*: if, however, $a_2\{\ \}/a_1\{\ \}$ is sufficiently large, r^* will be a unique positive number.

12. Turgot is discussed in Chapter 4 of Böhm-Bawerk (1884 and 1959). These quotations are taken from pp. 39–40. Turgot's chief relevant work is given as his 1769 *Réflextions sur la formation et la distribution des richesses*, particularly Sec. 57, 58, 59, 61, 63, 68, and 71.

13. Marshall, in a letter to Wicksell—for which see Gardlund (1958, pp. 339–345) —seems to deny that it did; and Marshall may be right even though Wicksell ended not thinking so; in any case, since Marshall is often not at his best when reading sense into safely-dead economists, we can here leave the matter moot. I might add that Turgot's instincts seem to lead him beyond the pieties of the Physiocratic system; periodically he guiltily pays lip service to the overimportance of land.

14. I must write "may" since Schumpeter would neither abandon his theory nor cogently defend it; indeed it was hard to get him to talk on the subject, and perhaps more than mere modesty was involved. In various *Festschrift* and obituary writings on Schumpeter, I have adverted to the problem of infinite land value at a zero interest rate, as in Samuelson (1943, 1951, 1972).

15. All this is not so obvious as to make proof unnecessary. For reversing the argument to remove land from the production function and to put K back into it, we can specify a case in which $r^* = 0$ *is* the long-run root. Thus, let people (or the planning unit for the state) live forever and have zero subjective time preference. Then, as with Ramsey (1928),

$$\text{Max}\sum_0^\infty U[C(t)] \text{ s.t. } C(t) = F[K(t), L_0] + K(t) - K(t+1)$$

leads, from any $K(0)$, provided $\partial F[K^*, L_0]/\partial K = 0$ has a finite K^* root, to $K(t) \to K^*$, $r = F[K, L_0]/\partial K \to r^* = 0$ as $t \to \infty$. So it is permanent land that is needed to assure that a zero or negative root is *never* possible for the laissez-faire market's supply-demand equation.

16. For a three-factor Solow-Meade function, $Lf[K/L, B/L]$, we have a three-dimensional factor-price frontier, $w = \omega[r, \beta]$. However, $\partial\omega[r, \beta]/\partial\beta \equiv 0$ when $f[k, b] = f(k) + \bar{\beta}b$, the singular case where there is a unique (w, r) tradeoff.

17. The Liviatan-Samuelson joint-production technology is defined by $C_{t+1} = F[L_t, K_t; K_{t+1} - K_t]$, with the steady-state relation between the profit rate and the per capita K/L, given by the rate of partial derivatives, $r = -F_2[1, K; 0]/F_3[1, k; 0] = \delta(r)$. With the proper "complementarity," away from $r = 0$, $\delta'(r)$ can change sign shown by *dd* in Figure 12.3. To avoid ambiguity, let me spell out the (somewhat arbitrary) "dynamics" assumed here. Let $r_t = \partial f(b, k_t)/\partial k$, $\beta_t = \partial f(b, k_t)/\partial b$, $w_t = f(b, k_t) - r_t k_t - \beta_t b$; and denote $a\{w_t, 1 + r_t\} - k_t - (\beta_t b/r_t)$ as $H[k_t]$. Then our posited dynamics adjustment is guided by $k_{t+1} - k_t$, a function of $H(k_t)$, with the property $0 < [k_{t+1} - k_t]/H[k_t] \ll 1$.

Near stable equilibria, F_1 and F_3, a shift in *dd* can be expected to raise r^* in the Keynes's manner. How does unstable F_2 get shifted? Toward lower rather than higher r^*? However, as indicated in Samuelson (1971, p. 343, Figure 153) one must avoid such a fallacious interpretation of the *correspondence principle* linking perverse comparative-statical shifts with dynamically unstable fixed points a system that begins precariously at unstable F_2 will be shifted by the slightest jarring of *dd* to the vicinity of F_1 and not to the new intersection near F_2; thus, even in this "unstable" case, a "global correspondence principle" yields concordance between dynamics and comparative statics.

18. Since life-cycle saving can lead to r^* *below* the golden-rule level of the system's natural growth rate, readers of Keynes should realize that what he called a curse could in such cases as these be a blessing!

References

BÖHM-BAWERK, E. VON, *Capital and Interest*, vol. I. (South Holland, Illinois: Libertarian Press, 1959).

CANNAN, E., *A Review of Economic Theory*. (London: P. S. King and Son, Ltd., 1929).

CASS, D., and M. YAARI, "Individual Savings, Aggregate Capital Accumulation and Efficient Growth," In K. Shell, ed., *Essays on the Theory of Optimal Economic Growth*, (Cambridge, Mass.: The MIT Press, 1967), pp. 233–268.

DENISON, E. F., *Accounting for United States Economic Growth, 1929–1969*. (Washington, D.C.: The Brookings Institution, 1974).

DIAMOND, P. A., "National Debt in a Neoclassical Growth Model," *American Economic Review* LV (December 1965): 1126–1150.

FISHER, I., *The Rate of Interest: Its Nature, Determination and Relation to Economic Phenomena*. (New York: Macmillan, 1907).

GARDLUND, T., *The Life of Knut Wicksell*, trans. Nancy Adler. (Stockholm: Almquist and Wicksell, 1958).

KALDOR, N., "Alternative Theories of Distribution," *Review of Economic Studies* 23 (1955): 83–100; reprinted in *Essays on Value and Distribution*, pp. 228–236. (London: Gerald Duckworth and Company, 1960).

KALDOR, N., "Keynes' Theory of the Own-Rates of Interest," 1955; reprinted in *Essays on Value and Distribution*, chapter 2.

KEYNES, J. M., *The Economic Consequences of the Peace*. (London: Macmillan and Company, 1919).

KEYNES, J. M., *The General Theory of Employment, Interest and Money*. (London: Macmillan and Company, 1936).

LERNER, A. P., "The Essential Properties of Interest and Money," *Quarterly Journal of Economics* 66 (1952): 172–193; reprinted in *Essays in Economic Analysis*. (London: Macmillan and Company, 1953).

LIVIATAN, N., and P. A. SAMUELSON, "Notes on Turnpikes: Stable and Unstable." *Journal of Economic Theory* 1, No. 4, (December 1969): 454–475; reprinted in R. C. Merton, ed., *The Collected Scientific Papers of Paul A. Samuelson*, vol. III. (Cambridge, Mass.: MIT Press, 1972), chapter 141.

MEADE, J. E., *A Neoclassical Theory of Economic Growth*. (New York: Oxford University Press, 1961).

MODIGLIANI, F., and R. BRUMBERG, "Utility Analysis and the Consumption

Function: An Interpretation of Cross Section Data." In *Post Keynesian Economics.* (New Brunswick, New Jersey: Rutgers University Press, 1954).

MODIGLIANI, F., and A. ANDO, "The 'Life Cycle' Hypothesis of Saving: Aggregate Implications and Tests," *American Economic Review* 53 (March 1963): 55–84.

MODIGLIANI, F., "The Life Cycle Hypothesis of Saving and Intercountry Differences in the Saving Ratio." In *Induction, Growth and Trade: Essays in Honor of Sir Roy Harrod,* W. A. Eltis, M. F. Scott, and J. N. Wolfe, eds. (Oxford: Clarendon Press, 1970).

MODIGLIANI, F., "The Life Cycle Hypothesis Twenty Years Later." In M. Parkin, ed., *Contemporary Issues in Economics.* (Manchester: University of Manchester Press, 1974).

PASINETTI, L., "Rate of Profit and Income Distribution in Relation to the Rate of Economic Growth," *Review of Economic Studies* 29 (1962): 267–279.

RAMSEY, F. P., "A Mathematical Model of Saving," *Economic Journal* 38 (December 1928): 543–549.

RICARDO, D., *On the Principles of Political Economy and Taxation.* (London: John Murray, 1817, 1819, 1821; Dent and Sons, Ltd, 1912, 1957).

ROBINSON, J., *The Accumulation of Capital.* (Homewood, Illinois: Richard C. Unwin, Inc., 1956).

ROBINSON, J., "Own Rates of Interest," *Economic Journal* 71 (1961): 596–600.

SAMUELSON, P. A., "Dynamics, Statics, and the Stationary States," *Review of Economics and Statistics* XXV, No. 1 (February 1943): 58–68; Essays in Honor of Joseph Schumpeter, reprinted in J. E. Stiglitz, ed., *The Collected Scientific Papers of Paul A. Samuelson,* vol. I, (Cambridge, Mass.: The MIT Press, 1966), chapter 19.

SAMUELSON, P. A., "Schumpeter As A Teacher and Economic Theorist," *Review of Economics and Statistics* XXXIII, No. 2 (May 1951): 98–103; reprinted in J. E. Stiglitz, ed., *The Collected Scientific Papers of Paul A. Samuelson,* vol. II (Cambridge, Mass.: The MIT Press, 1966), chapter 116.

SAMUELSON, P. A., "An Exact Consumption-Loan Model of Interest With or Without the Social Contrivance of Money," *Journal of Political Economy* 66 (1958): 467–482; reprinted in J. E. Stiglitz, ed., *CSP,* vol. I, chapter 21.

SAMUELSON, P. A., "A Turnpike Refutation of the Golden Rule in a Welfare-Maximizing Many-Year Plan." In K. Shell, ed., *Essays on the Theory of Optimal Economic Growth.* (Cambridge, Mass.: The MIT Press, 1967), chapter XIV, pp. 269–280; reprinted in R. C. Merton, ed., *The Collected Scientific Papers of Paul A. Samuelson,* vol. II (Cambridge, Mass.: The MIT Press, 1972), chapter 137.

SAMUELSON, P. A., "The Two-Part Golden Rule Deduced As the Asymptotic Turnpike of Catenary Motions," *Western Economic Journal* VI, No. 2, (March 1968): 85–89; reprinted in R. C. Merton, ed., CSP, vol. III, chapter 138.

SAMUELSON, P. A. "On the Trail of Conventional Beliefs About the Transfer Problem." In J. Bhagwati et al., eds., *Trade, Balance of Payments, and Growth: Papers in International Economics in Honor of Charles P. Kindleberger.* (Amsterdam: North-Holland Publishing Company, 1971), chapter 15, pp. 327–351; reprinted in R. C. Merton, ed., CSP, vol. III, chapter 163.

SAMUELSON, P. A., "Paradoxes of Schumpeter's Zero Interest Rate," *Review of Economics and Statistics* LIII, No, 4, (November, 1972): 391–392; reprinted in H. Nagatani and K. Crowley, eds., *The Collected Scientific Papers of Paul A. Samuelson*, volume IV (Cambridge, Mass.: The MIT Press, 1978), chapter 217.

SAMUELSON, P. A., "The Optimum Growth Rate for Population," *International Economic Review* 16, No. 3, (October 1975a): 531–538; reprinted in H. Nagatani and K. Crowley, eds., *CSP* IV, chapter 221.

SAMUELSON, P. A., "Optimum Social Security in a Life Cycle Growth Model," *International Economic Review* 16, No. 3, (October 1975b): 539–544; reprinted in H. Nagatani and K. Crowley, eds., *CSP* IV, chapter 220.

SAMUELSON, P. A., "A Modern Theorist's Vindication of Adam Smith," *The American Economic Review* 67, No. 1, (February 1977): 42–49.

SCHUMPETER, J. A. *Theorie der wirschaftlichen Entwicklung*. Munich: Duncker and Humblot; English trans. R. Opie. *The Theory of Economic Development*. (Cambridge, Mass.: Harvard University Press, 1961).

SMITH, A. (G. J. W. Goodman), *Supermoney*. (New York: Random House, 1972).

SOLOW, R. M., "A Contribution to the Theory of Economic Growth," *Quarterly Journal* LXX, (February 1936): 65–94.

TOBIN, J. "Life Cycle Saving and Balanced Growth." In W. Fellner et al., eds., *Ten Economic Studies in the Tradition of Irving Fisher*, (New York: John Wiley and Sons, Inc., 1967), chapter 9, pp. 231–256.

TURGOT, A. R. J., *Reflections on the Formation and the Distribution of Riches*. (New York: A. M. Kelley, 1963).

Any man's death diminishes me . . .
—John Donne

Economists everywhere were especially diminished on May 8, 1977, when Dr. Harry G. Johnson died in mid-career. Professor Samuelson's memorial to Harry Johnson expresses and helps relieve our keen sense of loss.

CORRECTING THE RICARDO ERROR SPOTTED IN HARRY JOHNSON'S MAIDEN PAPER*

PAUL A. SAMUELSON

INTRODUCTION

Leontief used to say, just as there may be special significance in a person's first kiss, a scholar's first paper perhaps tells us something special. An interest in the history of doctrine generally breaks out late in life; surprisingly, Harry Johnson's first three papers were on Ricardo, Malthus, and J. S. Mill. He has put in the record how he first found an error in Ricardo, and the story tells us something about

* Written in memory of Harry Johnson's days in Cambridge, Massachusetts, exactly thirty years ago. I owe thanks to the National Science Foundation for partial aid.

Schumpeter's notorious encouragement to young scholars and about the Ricardo worship of those days.[1]

Actually, Ricardo's quill often slipped. It was acute of him to sense in 1817 that an invention could raise or lower land rent, relatively or absolutely and both at unchanged output or at unchanged doses of input of labor-cum-capital. But his attempt to distinguish between two kinds of inventions according to whether the invention saves on land or saves on the variable input of labor-cum-capital is strictly speaking untenable. (A parameter that raises the dependent variable in a monotone-increasing, two-variable function lowers the isoquant locus of requirement in *both* directions.)

Ricardo's luck was better when it came to mentioning some strong cases. Thus, toward the end of his Chapter 2 on rent, he correctly noted that an invention, if it merely produced an increment of output proportional to the variable doses of input, would leave rent unchanged at the old input levels and would give all its fruits to labor and capital. But then he proceeded to stub his toe in the attempt to specify an invention that would leave corn rent unchanged at the old output.

TRUTH LOST, AND FOUND

In the rent chapter's third-from-last paragraph (*any* edition of Ricardo's *Principles*), Ricardo writes:

> If four portions of capital [i.e., 4 successive unequal-size increments of the dose of labor-cum-capital, *V*], 50, 60, 70, 80, be employed on the [always fixed available

1. "Just before I arrived in Cambridge [England], I had published a short note in *The Quarterly Journal of Economics* on 'An Error in Ricardo's Exposition of His Theory of Rent' [for which see Johnson, 1948]. . . . On arrival in Cambridge I found Dobb and Sraffa much excited by my note, which they were sure was wrong; Sraffa even proposed to publish a criticism of my note, thereby breaking nineteen (I think) years of silence. . . . I was shown a stack of notes that had passed between them, notes replete with such phrases as 'Johnson's fallacy is . . . .' I would have been overjoyed to have smoked Sraffa out of his long silence, especially as I knew for sure that my mathematics were correct. But unfortunately or fortunately Sraffa eventually looked up Edwin Cannan's history of thought and found the error already noted there, whereupon he dropped the subject. (That taught me two lessons: one about the scholarship of Cambridge, and the other about the scholarship of Joseph Schumpeter, who had got me to write up and publish the note. On balance I far prefer Schumpeter's style: if one does not know the literature, and a young man can prove an error one had not noticed, it is better to encourage him than to assume that he must be wrong; better still, of course, to check the literature to guard against unnecessary originality in the establishment of errors.)" This is from Johnson (1976, pp. 186–87). Cf. Cannan (1893, pp. 328–30) for his early exact anticipation of the Johnson critique. In it Cannan correctly recognizes the arbitrariness of Ricardo's logical and empirical shifting of productivity functions; but neither he, nor Ricardo, nor, as far as I can tell, any of Ricardo's many editors and commentators, ever correctly defines the criterion a technical change must satisfy if it is in fact to be capable of being a *viable improvement*.

supply of] land, giving each the same results [i.e., each such increment of input giving the *same* increment of corn output, which we can set at unity for q], and any improvement [i.e., invention] . . . should enable me to withdraw 5 from each so that they should [now] be 45, 55, 65, and 75, [then] no alteration would take place in the corn rent [allegedly earned by landlords when q is still 4].

As Johnson (1948, pp. 792–93) says:

> But his example is erroneous, and fails to illustrate his proposition [of constant corn rent at $q=4$]. . . . contrary to Ricardo's conclusion, corn rent has been increased by the introduction of the improvement. . . . Both before and after the improvement, aggregate rent is equivalent [in exchange] to [the same] 60 units of capital [-cum-labor, of course; and, as Johnson notes, the price of the dose V, P_V, necessarily rises relative to corn, making rent in corn *necessarily* rise].

Not only has Johnson correctly diagnosed that Ricardo made an error, but more than that he has recognized that it happens to be an interesting error. Ricardo's new postulated technical change, we moderns would say, is *dual* to the case he had previously analyzed correctly—that case where the product curve of the variable dose had been shifted *uniformly* upward and rent in q was unchanged at the same input levels: if we regard q output as dual to V input, and the marginal-product curve against V, $f'(V)$, as dual to the marginal-cost curve of incremental V needed to elicit more of q, $C'(q)$, then Ricardo's present case involves a uniform vertical shift downward in the $C'(q)$ locus.

By duality, that does leave rent unchanged at q (measured not in corn but rather by the *producers' surplus* area of V, the dual-variable input *numéraire*). Johnson's recognition that rent is thus always the same in terms of input numéraire units, in effect, represents a discovery of this duality theorem (an independent rediscovery after Cannan's 1893 discovery).

One ought to add that Ricardo would have achieved his desired constancy of corn rent at the old output level if he had cut (50, 60, 70, 80) *by the same percentage amount* rather than *by the same absolute* amount of 5: thus, he would have avoided error by lowering all numbers by, say, one-fifth, to (40, 48, 56, 64). To achieve his result, he should have postulated *a purely-V-augmenting technical change*—where the production function $q = F(T,V)$ is changed to $q = F(T, [1+k]V)$ by invention.[2]

2. Following the suggestions of Professor Robert Dorfman, I have devoted the final sections of my Mathematical Appendix to what is called there an "*ultra*-classical" model, in which there are lands of every grade of fertility, each producing corn with a fixed complement of the variable dose V. The *reduced form* relation between q and V that results is indistinguishable from a (neoclassical) relationship involving variable proportions of V and a homogeneous scalar of land. All of the Johnson and other points are completely confirmed in the ultra-classical model. On my reading of Ricardo, he perceived both the *intensive* and *extensive* margin: Johnson aptly cites Longfield (1834, pp. 132–35), for a subtle understanding of these relationships.

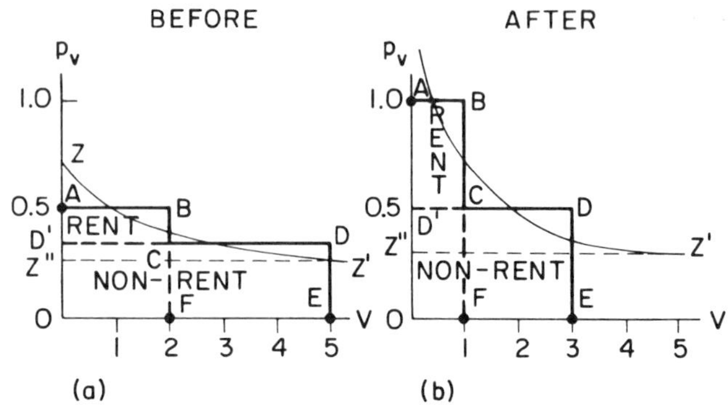

FIGURE I

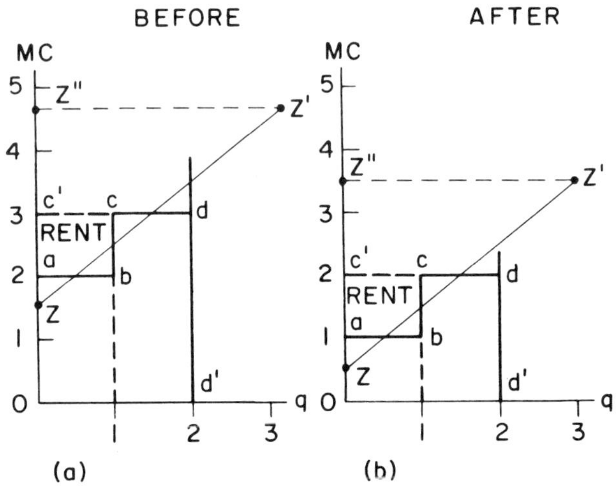

FIGURE II

GRAPHICAL DEPICTION

Johnson's prose is terse. The reader must work his own way through the arithmetical examples and must prove for himself that the coarseness of the units does not affect the universality of the duality theorem or jeopardize its proof. Figures I and II will tell the conclusive story, and will do so most simply if we alter the four-step example to an equivalent two-step example: we replace (50, 60, 70, 80) and (50–5, 60–5, 70–5, 80–5) by (2,3) and (2-1, 3-1) = (1,2).

In Figure Ia the area $ABCDE0$ gives the total product of $q = 2$ prior to the invention: the 2 of corn is divided between the rent area

$ABCD'$, measuring $(\frac{1}{2}-\frac{1}{3})\ 2 = \frac{1}{3}$ of corn; and the nonrent rectangle $D'DE0$, measuring $\frac{5}{3}$ of corn, equal to the base of $5V$ times the corn-price of V of $\frac{1}{3}$ per unit.

After the invention, Figure Ib's new $ABCDE0$ again gives corn a total product of 2: now it is divided between the enlarged rent area $ABCD'$ of $(\frac{1}{1} - \frac{1}{2}) = \frac{1}{2}$ corn; and now the new nonrent rectangle of $D'DE0$ involves the residuum of $\frac{3}{2}$ corn, equal to the base of $3V$ times the enlarged return to the dose of $\frac{1}{2}$ corn per V. The 50 percent rise in corn rent just matches the 50 percent rise in the return to each unit of labor-cum-capital, as Johnson recognized.

Figures IIa and IIb tell the same before-and-after story in terms of cost $C(q)$, where cost is measured not necessarily in terms of money but rather in terms of the numéraire of variable doses of labor-cum-capital. Now the rising locus *abcd* depicts pre-invention marginal or incremental cost. The producers' surplus area $c'cba$ gives residual rent measured in terms of V-input numéraire, representing $(3\text{-}2) \times 1 = 1$,—out of the total $c'dd'0$ cost area of $6V$, which is the base of $2q$ times the altitude's price of corn of $3V$ per unit. The residual nonrent five-sixths of the total cost represents the actual 5 of V inputs.

Figure IIb shows the after-invention marginal-cost locus, now shifted downward from Figure Ia's by 1 unit. Consequently, the producers' surplus area is the same as before (expressed in input units). Q.E.D.

Also shown in Figures IIb and IIa are the smooth-curve versions of Ricardo's linear progressions. The light zz' locus in IIb is that of IIa's zz' shifted downward by 1 unit: hence, Johnson's conclusion of unchanged rent in input units, the triangular area $z''z'z$, is seen to be generally true. The ZZ' curves in Ia and Ib come from their dual zz' curves in IIa and IIb. Since the yield in corn of a dose is the *reciprocal* of the marginal cost of a unit of corn measured in V, the ordinates of ZZ' are the reciprocals of those of zz but plotted against V rather than q. The rent triangle of ZZ' in Ib, $ZZ'Z''$, is seen to be larger than that in Ia, confirming Johnson's diagnosis of universal error in Ricardo.

Remark. Ricardo and the other writers introduce the extraneous complication of what is happening to *money* rent as against corn rent. I have avoided this consideration, sticking rigorously to rent measured in corn or in V-input units. Since England had no gold mines to connect up money and V-input units and since Ricardo's international trade theory breaks the nexus between domestic labor units and foreign-goods' exchange values, we avoid the confusions of Ricardo's commentators by my practice, and we lose nothing of Johnson's analysis.

The Error Corrected

If the invention made every new unit of labor-cum-capital the equivalent of each two old units, the invention would be purely-V-augmenting and would give Ricardo unchanged corn rent. We can use the same Ia diagram to represent the new picture *provided we double all its vertical distances and halve all its horizontal dimensions,* preserving *all* corn areas!

Instead of drawing a new Ic picture, the reader can redefine the unity point on the horizontal axis of Ia at F, where 2 used to be; and he can redefine the new unity point on its vertical axis at A, where ½ used to be; then rescaling the two axes, he will still read off the unchanged corn rent area as Ricardo desired (and the unchanged non-rent area will now, when divided by half the doses, give twice the return per dose).

Now that we have correctly arrived 160 years later at Ricardo's intended case of unchanged corn rent at unchanged corn output, what does he really achieve? The *actual* incidence of such an invention will neither in the long nor in the short run leave the old q unchanged: Ricardo was strangely rash in his casual remarks about real-world incidence of exogenous events. (*Example.* James Mill admired as much as anything in Ricardo his following "truth": ". . . the proposition . . . 'That improvements in agriculture raise the profits of stock, and produce immediately no other effects'" (Sraffa, 1951, p. xiv). But this proposition can be easily shown to be quite untrue! (And not even plausible as an approximation within Ricardo's own system.) What is useful in Ricardo's analysis is his appreciation of some of the complexities of what *might* happen from inventions.

The correct analysis throws light on Ricardo's third edition bombshell, in which he pointed out that a viable invention of machinery could *decimate* the demand for labor (or for capital, or for labor-cum-capital). This has been a much misunderstood point. First, Ricardo misunderstood it; then McCullough; later Wicksell thought Ricardo in error on the point, as did Stigler still later. Most recently Hicks, in acknowledging the validity of the point, unnecessarily ties it up with the durability of machinery and the transient adjustment process.

Actually, the correct V-augmenting invention that Ricardo sought can, quite aside from introduction of durable machinery, induce short-run or long-run genocide of population and euthanasia of the capitalists. All we need is a ZZ' returns locus in Ia that is quite inelastic: as a result when each worker becomes like ten workers, most of them must die before the rest can earn a subsistence wage. At the beginning of his first edition, David Ricardo had this result staring him in the face!

Conclusion

Whether Leontief has or has not overstated the importance of *first* beginnings, Harry Johnson's critique of Ricardo was indicative of much to come. It shows power and economy.

Mathematical Appendix

A brief but rigorous summary is worth giving. Ricardo in effect assumes a "classical" production function relating output q to inputs land T and doses of labor-cum-capital V, namely

$$q = F(T,V) = Tf(V/T) \tag{1}$$

$$= f(V) \quad \text{if } T = 1 \text{ by dimensional convention}$$

$$f'(V) > 0 > f''(V).$$

The variable dose V is min[labor/λ, capital/γ].

To allow for invention, put in the production function a technical-change parameter τ, writing the relation as

$$q = F(T,V;\tau) = Tf(V/T;\tau) \tag{2}$$

$$0 < \partial F(T,V;\tau)/\partial\tau \equiv T\partial f(V/T;\tau)/\partial\tau.$$

For q constant, and either one input held constant, a rise in τ will reduce the need for the other input whether it be land or the variable dose. So Ricardo's attempted dichotomization of inventions fails.

Equation (1) can always be solved for its inverse, to give the total cost of q, $C(q)$, expressed not in dollars but in requirements of V:

$$V = C(q) = f^{-1}(q) \tag{3}$$

$$C'(q) > 0,\ C''(q) > 0.$$

When the technical change parameter τ is present and we denote partial derivatives by letter subscripts, $\partial C/\partial q = C_q$ and so forth:

$$V = C(q;\tau) \tag{4}$$

$$C_q(q;\tau) > 0,\ C_{qq}(q;\tau) > 0,\ C_\tau(q;\tau) < 0.$$

Rent in terms of corn can be expressed as a function of V, or as a function of q. These are, respectively,

$$R = f(V;\tau) - V\partial f(V;\tau)/\partial V \tag{5}$$

$$R = q - \frac{C(q;\tau)}{C_q(q;\tau)}. \tag{6}$$

For Ricardo's erroneous specification, we have (4) in the special form:

$$V = C(q) - \tau q \tag{7}$$

$$\begin{aligned} R &= q - \frac{C(q) - \tau q}{C'(q) - \tau} \\ &= \frac{qC'(q) - C(q)}{C'(q) - \tau} \\ &> \frac{qC'(q) - C(q)}{C'(q)}, \quad \tau > 0. \end{aligned} \tag{8}$$

$$\begin{aligned} R \text{ in terms of } V &= \text{previous } R \times [C'(q) - \tau] \\ &= qC'(q) - q\tau + q\tau - C(q) \\ &\equiv qC'(q) - C(q). \end{aligned} \tag{9}$$

This last is independent of τ, as noted in the Cannan-Johnson instance of the duality theorem.

Suppose, however, that we correct Ricardo's specification and consider a purely-V-augmenting relation:

$$q = f([1+k]V), \quad V = C(q)[1+k]^{-1}. \tag{10}$$

Then

$$\begin{aligned} R &= q - \frac{[1+k]^{-1}C(q)}{[1+k]^{-1}C'(q)} \\ &= q - \frac{C(q)}{C'(q)}, \end{aligned} \tag{11}$$

independently of $[1 + k]$.

Rent in terms of V numéraire units is then

$$\begin{aligned} R[1+k]^{-1}C'(q) &= [1+k]^{-1}C'(q)q - [1+k]^{-1}C(q) \\ &= [1+k]^{-1}\{C'(q)q - C(q)\}, \end{aligned} \tag{12}$$

a declining function of the $[1 + k]$ improvement factor.

Also, (12)'s expression for rent in corn can be related to V:

$$R = f([1+k]V) - V[1+k]f'([1+k]V), \tag{13}$$

a rising function of $[1 + k]$. The return available for *each* V can decline as a result of the invention's $1 + k$, if only $f'(\ )$ is an inelastic schedule such that $[1 + k]f'([1 + k]V)$ falls with $[1 + k]$—proving that inventions can lower the demand for labor-cum-capital in any degree.

Such an immiserating effect the reader will recognize to be impossible in that first kind of invention, which Ricardo got right in its giving all its fruits to labor and capital and none in the first instance to corn rent. For it Ricardo specified

$$q = f(V) + \tau V \tag{14}$$

$$(15) \qquad R = f(V) + \tau V - Vf'(V) - V\tau$$
$$= f(V) - Vf'(V), \text{ independently of } \tau.$$

Q.E.D.

I have refrained from discussing how Ricardo thought the return to the dose V was to be divided between wages and profits in the long and the short run, and how his views ought to be judged today on these matters.

Finally, here is an *ultra*-classical model based on a continuum of grades of land, each indexed by a continuous parameter of location x with $T(x)$ being the quantity of land of the quality appropriate to each such point. In modern notation, like that of Samuelson (1959, pp. 21–28), we have between x and $x + dx$ the production relations,

$$(16) \qquad q(x)dx = F[T(x), v(x); x]dx$$
$$= v(x)F[T(x)/v(x), 1; x]dx, \qquad \text{"homogeneity"}$$
$$= \min\left[\frac{T(x)}{\theta(x)}, \frac{v(x)}{\omega(x)}\right] dx, \qquad \text{"fixed coefficients,"}$$

where $v(x)$ is the amount of the dose of labor-cum-capital applied at x, and where $\theta(x)$ and $\omega(x)$ are input-output coefficients of the respective factors.

For simplicity suppose that land's fertility declines as x rises from 0 to positive numbers:

$$(17) \qquad \omega'(x) > 0, \quad 0 \leq x.$$

It follows that low-x acres will be used before high-x acres: as the total of the dose V increases in availability, the range of cultivated land $0 \leq x \leq X$ will show a monotone-increasing relationship between the X index of the extensive margin and V.

Our reduced-form relationships between output totals of corn q and input total of V are defined by

$$(18a) \qquad V = V[X] = \int_0^X v(x)dx = \int_0^X \omega(x)T(x)\theta(x)^{-1}dx$$

$$(18b) \qquad q = Q[X] = \int_0^X q(x)dx = \int_0^X T(x)\theta(x)^{-1}dx.$$

These relations are based on the fact that, for $x > X$, $v(x)$ and $q(x)$ are zero; but for intramarginal good land, for $0 < x < X$, we have full utilization with

$$(18c) \quad q(x) = v(x)/\omega(x) = T(x)/\theta(x), \quad v(x) = \omega(x)T(x)/\theta(x).$$

(If there were smooth, indefinite substitutability instead of fixed coefficients, (18) would be replaced by

$$(18') \qquad \partial F[T(x), v(x); x]/\partial v(x) \equiv \partial F[T(0), v(0); 0]/\partial v(0)$$

(18″)
$$q = \int_0^\infty F[T(x), v(x); x]dx$$
$$V = \int_0^\infty v(x)dx,$$
with $q = f(V)$, $f'(V) \equiv \partial F[T(x), v(x); x]/\partial v(x)$.)

Relations (18) are parametric equations in X defining the production-function relations:

(19)
$$q = f(V)$$
$$dq/dV = f'(V) = \frac{Q'[X]}{V'[X]} = \omega(X)^{-1}$$
$$d^2q/dV^2 = f''(V) = V'[X]^{-1}d\{\omega(X)^{-1}\}/dX$$
$$= -\omega'(X)\omega(X)^{-2}V'[X]^{-1} < 0.$$

Thus, the observable input-output relationship from the ultra-classical model is seen in (19) to have exactly the properties of the simplest neoclassical model.

So all the previous proofs of this Appendix apply to the ultra-classical case. Still it will be of interest to verify the Johnson and other theorems utilizing only ultra-classical modes of exposition.

Let the total rent at x and everywhere be, respectively,

(20a) $$R(x) = r(x)T(x)$$

(20b) $$R[X] = \int_0^X R(x)dx.$$

The common prices of V and of corn are P_V and P_q, independently of x. At every point x, competition enforces

(21) $$P_q q(x) = P_V v(x) + R(x), \quad 0 \leq x \leq X$$
$$q(x) \equiv 0, v(x) \equiv 0, R(x) \equiv 0, \quad X < x < \infty.$$

Combining (16) and (21), we express rent as

(22a) $$R(x) = P_q T(x)\theta(x)^{-1} - P_V\omega(x)T(x)\theta(x)^{-1}, \quad 0 < x \leq X$$
$$R(X) = 0 = P_q T(X)\theta(X)^{-1} - P_V\omega(X)T(X)\theta(X).$$

Since X is the zero-rent external margin, by definition

(22b) $$R(X) = 0, \quad P_q/P_V = \omega(X).$$

Total rent $R[X]$ is calculated by integration to be

(22c) $$R[X] = P_q Q[X] - P_V V[X].$$

In terms of V as numéraire, total rent becomes

(22d) $$R[X]/P_V = \omega(X)Q[X] - V[X].$$

In terms of q as numéraire, total rent becomes

$$(22e) \qquad R[X]/P_q = \{R[X]/P_V\}\omega(X)^{-1} = Q[X] - \omega(X)^{-1}V[X].$$

Now recognize that Ricardo wants to assume that $\omega(x)$ is reduced at every x by an absolute constant τ to become $\omega(x) - \tau$. Immediately we see from (18) that, at the same q and X, total V is lowered by $-\tau q$, to $V[X] - \tau q[X]$ from $V[X]$. From (22d) we see that rent in V units is unaffected by τ, being

$$(23d) \qquad R[X]/P_V = [\omega(X) - \tau]Q[X] - \{V[X] - \tau Q[X]\} = \omega(X)Q[X] - V[X], \text{ independently of } \tau.$$

From (22e) and (23e) we see that rent in corn must therefore be higher at the same X or q:

$$(23e) \qquad \frac{R[X]}{P_q} = \frac{\omega(X)Q[X] - V[X]}{\omega(X) - \tau} > \frac{\omega(X)Q[X] - V[X]}{\omega(X)} \quad \text{for } \tau > 0$$

Q.E.D.

By contrast, if Ricardo had reduced $\omega(x)$ to $k\omega(x)$ at every x, where $0 < k < 1$, he would have achieved unchanged rent in corn or q units, achieving

$$(24) \qquad \frac{R[X]}{P_q} = \frac{k\omega(X)Q[X] - k\int_0^X \omega(x)T(x)\theta(x)^{-1}dx}{k\omega(X)} \equiv \frac{\omega(X)Q[X] - \int_0^X \omega(x)T(x)\theta(x)^{-1}dx}{\omega(X)}.$$

Finally, to contrive Ricardo's first kind of invention, that of (15) and for which he achieved a correct analysis, we must have at each x Hicks-neutral technical change at the rate $[1 + \tau\omega(x)]$. Now our production function becomes

$$(25) \qquad f[T(x), V(x); x] = [1 + \tau\omega(x)] \min\left[\frac{T(x)}{\theta(x)}, \frac{V(x)}{\omega(x)}\right].$$

It can be verified that at any X (18a) is unaltered by neutral technical change and $V[X]$ is unchanged by τ. However, τ enters into (18b) to give

$$(26) \qquad q[X] = \int_0^X T(x)\theta(x)^{-1}dx + \tau V[X].$$

To demonstrate that rent in corn does remain unaltered at specified V or X, we recalculate (24) based on new (25) rather than old (16). This gives

$$(27)\quad \frac{R[X]}{P_q} = \int_0^X T(x)\theta(x)^{-1}dx + \tau V[X] - \frac{1+\tau\omega(X)}{\omega(X)} V[X]$$
$$= \int_0^X T(x)\theta(x)^{-1}dx - \omega(X)^{-1}V[X],$$

independently of X.

Q.E.D.

Thus, the ultra-classical model is seen to obey all the valid laws of the homogeneous-land model, an important finding.

MASSACHUSETTS INSTITUTE OF TECHNOLOGY

REFERENCES

Cannan, E., *A History of the Theories of Production and Distribution, 1776–1848* (London: Staples, 1893).
Johnson, H. G., "An Error in Ricardo's Exposition of His Theory of Rent," this *Journal,* LXII (1948), 792–93.
——, "Cambridge as an Academic Environment," in D. Patinkin and J. C. Leith, eds., *Keynes, Cambridge, and the General Theory* (1976), pp. 173–200.
Longfield, M., 1834, *Lectures on Political Economy.*
Ricardo, D., *On the Principles of Political Economy and Taxation* (1817, 1819, 1821).
Samuelson, P. A., "A Modern Treatment of the Ricardian Economy," this *Journal,* LXXII (1959), 1–35, 217–31.
Sraffa, P., ed., *The Works and Correspondence of David Ricardo,* Vol. I, Editor's Introduction (Cambridge: Cambridge University Press, 1951), pp. xiii–xxii.

PART VI

Mathematical Biology

MAXIMIZING AND BIOLOGY

PAUL A. SAMUELSON*

Armen Alchian has made important contributions to many different fields of economics. Here are only a few that come to my imperfect memory.

Cost progress functions in the airframe industry — one of the earliest and still best examples of "learning by doing."

Optimal replacement timing for an auto or other durable good — a pre-Bellman exercise in what we have come to recognize as dynamic programming over a finite- or infinite-time horizon.

The economic history of price-level movements. Can the ancient Hume notion be valid?—that, while prices are rising, there is a shift to profits at the expense of real wages and contractual rents. I.e., can this Hume notion be valid over a period of centuries? or even decades? Kessel and Alchian were among the first to realize the *a priori* implausibility that a recurring inflation will continue to be unanticipated virtually forever. They had the established data and myths of the Hamiltonian School of Economic History against them. But never underestimate the survival power of a good and plausible idea: in the end it can kill off many an alleged fact. The real neutrality of anticipatable inflation is now, thanks in part to Alchian, part of the tool-kit of modern economics.

The workings of markets where, because of imperfect knowledge and other realistic factors, *prices do not operate to ensure a clearing of supply and demand.* Alchian's ideas and writings in this area have not only influenced countless elementary textbook readers, but they have also influenced such fertile writers in the theory of search and the natural rate of unemployment as Donald Gordon, Leijonhufvud, Phelps, Friedman, Robert Hall, and others too numerous to try to list.

I could go on and on, cribbing from the recent and early issues of the *Journal of Law and Economics* or from the *American Economic Review.* But one of Alchian's seminal contributions appealed most naturally to me as a general topic of interest that overlaps with my own longtime researches.

I refer to his 1950 paper on "Uncertainty, Evolution and Economic Theory." This put forward the valuable notion that profit-maximizing has even greater validity in economics than you would realize from observing that subset of entrepreneurs, consumers, and producers who

*Massachusetts Institute of Technology. I owe thanks for financial aid to the National Science Foundation. This is an abridged version of my remarks made at UCLA at the April 1977 symposium in honor of Armen Alchian, himself a pioneer in the area between economics and biology. Reserved for a future occasion is a more thorough analysis of neo-Darwinian concepts of inclusive fitness, as developed by Hamilton, R. Trivers, E. O. Wilson, and many others. Rather than modify the exposition in terms of more recent analysis by Joel Yellin and me, I have left it in its original form.

consciously calculate the profits that would result from different decisions and who consciously and coolly select out of all possible decisions those optimal ones which do maximize profits. Alchian emphasizes that any large number of guinea pigs who fail to approximate some maximization of profits (or utility or present-discounted value) will find themselves shoved aside in the struggle for competitive coexistence by those who do, unknowingly or knowingly — it does not matter much, act as if to maximize a profitability criterion.

Alchian used the language of Darwinian selection theory to dramatize the points he was making about the non-biological field of economics. But, he has told us in 1953 debate with Edith Penrose that in point of historical fact his argument was originally perceived and formulated without any reference at all to biology or the metaphors of Darwinian evolution. Only in the final drafts did Alchian introduce the vocabulary and examples of biology to reinforce and explicate his new way of looking at economics.

Economics can benefit from biology, but, also, it can return the compliment two-or-many fold. The methods of economics can hope to fructify the analysis of biology.

In recent years Becker, Demsetz, Hirshleifer, and other economists who have been influenced by Alchian have invaded the field of biology. And, independently, certain biologists such as E. O. Wilson, William Hamilton, and Trivers have developed certain analytical notions not unworthy of a Chicago School economist.

Let me illustrate. Back in 1964 Hamilton sought to explain something called "reciprocal altruism." A mother will go into a fire to save her baby; it would seem that she is built that way, in the sense that those mothers who in the past have lacked the genetic propensity or inherited propensity to make such sacrifices have tended not to have surviving offspring to be observed in present-day populations. Morgan, Trivers, and others have assayed to set testable quantitative models of altruism. A Sicilian says: "Me for me. After me, my mother. After me and my mother, my brothers. After us, the members of my village." Perhaps Sicilians go no farther. Hamilton and Trivers recognize that there is a geometric progression in the correlations of shared genes between mother and child, between mother and nephew or niece, ..., between mother and cousins of different degrees: call the relevant progression 1, 1/2, 1/4, 1/8, ..., $1/2^n$, ... The hypothesis is set up that the degree to which the mother will give up caviar or berries or the degree to which she will plunge deeper into a burning building can be related to the degree of percentage sharing of genes.

As a result the observed mother is defended from the grave charge of neglecting her own self-interest. She need not be drummed out of the club of selfish egotists. It is just that she responds to a different drumbeat. Here genes, Alchian-like, are successfully acting to perpetuate themselves, to maximize the probability of survival. Those mothers who don't behave in this way are shouldered aside by those who do.

You will agree that this is an interesting area of speculation. It has even given rise to bitter polemics among the geneticists. Not surprisingly it has led some writers, Wilson is one, to occasionally put forward some rather tall claims for the future importance of what they call Sociobiology for the sociology and ethics of the future. Like any crude Quantity Theorist, Wilson alternates between careful and cautious qualifyings and breathtaking claims and proclamations. Like any Quantity Theorist, Wilson succeeds in raising against himself a host of critics who alternate between overreaction and needed cautionary warning.

My time here is very limited. Since a fraction of my efforts as a modern-day economic theorist has been concerned with the analysis of maximizing formulations in economics, physics, and mathematical systems, the bouquet that I am bringing to Armen Alchian's birthday party or potlatch is a fresh analysis of some of the misleading and romantic notions about maximizing that are loosely used in all-too-much of biological writings on evolution. Most of the lines that follow were written in the last fortnight, partly for a different purpose, mainly to substitute some light for heat in the polemics that have emerged over the proponents and critics of something called Sociobiology. I venture to hope that coals designed for export from Newcastle may merit a measure of honor in their home county.

MAXIMIZING AND BIOLOGY

Metaphors of maximization are used repeatedly in biological discussions of evolution. To test whether the usefulness of a maximizing formulation, such as has been developed in economics and physics, is really borne out of sociobiology, some concrete demographic models have been taken from standard Lotka theory. They have been combined with scarcity of resources and the law of diminishing returns. It then turns out that the resulting coupled non-linear system of difference equations can only sometimes be given a maximizing interpretation. When this can be done, it is shown that no knowledge on the part of the participants or the observers of any preexisting problem to be solved is required. But, even when a maximizing interpretation is possible, it is shown that teleological concepts such as "egotism," "reciprocal altruism," "adaptation," or "fitness" are redundant ways of describing the positivistic fact that Nature's cookie sometimes crumbles in such a way as to make certain patterns recurrent and viable, while certain other patterns are only transiently persistent. Most important of all, for almost every choice of the parameters of a model no maximand can be found to be definable and whose solution constitutes the observable and testable behavior equations. Not only are the imperialist-economists pretensions debunked by this audit, but in addition various of the concepts of biologists such as R. A. Fisher are seen to be severely limited in scope and application.

1. *Introduction.* In economics and physics there are certain patent advantages to formulating analysis in terms of an *extremum* problem (a maximum or a minimum). Are there similar advantages to be had in the domain of biology and evolution? Can one usefully define a concept like "fitness" and gain insight thereby into the mathematical description of biological behavior? This is a topic worthy of exploration, even by an outside amateur.

2. *Linear demography.* Begin with the standard post-1911 Lotka-Leslie model of demography.[1] Write total births of a variety at time $t = 0, 1, 2, \ldots$ as b_t. Write age-specific *survival* parameters as $[a_j] = [1, a_1, a_2, a_3, 0]$, and age-specific *fertility* parameters as $[m_j] = [m_1, m_2, 0]$, where $m_1, m_2 > 0$ and $1 \geqslant a_1 \geqslant a_2 \geqslant a_3 \geqslant 0$. Then the population's births grow according to

1. In the Addendum I give an alternative formulation in terms of simple differential equations. Ignoring age effects, these equations may be deemed more easily understandable by some readers.

$$(1) \qquad b_t = (m_1 a_1) b_{t-1} + (m_2 a_2) b_{t-2} + (0 a_3) b_{t-3}$$

$$= c_1 b_{t-1} + c_2 b_{t-2}, \qquad c_1, c_2 > 0.$$

$$(2) \qquad \lim_{t \to \infty} (b_t / g^t) = \text{constant for all positive initial } (b_0, b_1)$$

where g is the positive root of

$$(3) \qquad 1 = c_1 x^{-1} + c_2 x^{-2} = f(x)$$

and where $g - 1$ has the sign of $1 - c_1 - c_2$.

3. *Expanding, dilute universe.* So far the model encounters no scarcity of overall resources. Provided $1 - c_1 - c_2 > 0$, the system grows forever, approaching balanced exponential growth at rate $g - 1$. Darwin would hardly recognize such a world (although von Neumann would). In it we could have, side by side with this variety, a second variety or species that might also enjoy growth relations like (1) - (3). Both independent systems grow in their own way, never interacting or interfering prior to our assuming some conditions of scarcity or limited overall resources.

The second system could be written in capital letters that match in meaning those already encountered, namely: B_t, A_j, M_j, C_j, G, $F(X)$, etc.

4. *Recognizing diminishing returns.* More realistically, limitation of space and resources in the environment must ultimately be encountered by an exponential growth (at least when technical change is ignored). This is the lasting message of Malthus. We can most simply model this effect of the "law of diminishing returns" by assuming that the fertility parameters,[2] m_j, are lowered by an increase of total numbers of adults in the limited environment, $n_t = a_1 b_{t-1} + a_2 b_{t-2} + a_3 b_{t-3}$.

Therefore, the net fertility coefficients, c_j, are no longer parameters but instead become (weakly) *decreasing* functions of overall size, $c_j[n_t]$, with $c_j'[n_t]$ and $\Sigma_1^2 c_j'[n_t]$ negative numbers (sufficiently small in magnitude).

The linear dynamics of Lotka-Leslie in (3) is now replaced by the nonlinear system

$$(4) \qquad b_t = c_1[a_1 b_{t-1} + a_2 b_{t-2} + a_3 b_{t-3} b_{t-1}] b_{t-1}$$

$$+ c_2[a_1 b_{t-1} + a_2 b_{t-2} + a_3 b_{t-3}] b_{t-2}.$$

Now that resource limitations are recognized, it can be shown that (4)

2. It would be more realistic to have the survival fractions, a_j, also lowered by an increase in n_t; however, we avoid some extraneous complications by sacrificing this element of realism, and lose nothing essential in so doing.

defines a stable stationary equilibrium for population, b^* and $n^* = b^*\Sigma_0^3 a_i$, where b^* is the positive root of

$$(5) \qquad 1 = c_1[b\Sigma_1^3 a_i] + c_2[b\Sigma_1^3 a_i]$$

and

$$(6) \qquad \lim_{t \to \infty} b_t = b^* > 0, \qquad n^* = b^*\Sigma_0^3 a_i$$

for all positive initial (b_0, b_1, b_2) not too much in excess of b^*.

Similar to (4) - (6) are the equations for the second variety when it alone occupies an environment:

$$(4') \qquad B_t = C_1[\sum_1^3 A_i B_{t-i}]B_{t-1} + C_2[\sum_1^3 A_i B_{t-i}]B_{t-2}$$

$$(6') \qquad \lim_{t \to \infty} B_t = B^*, \qquad N^* = B^*\Sigma_0^3 A_i$$

where B^* is the root of

$$(5') \qquad 1 = C_1[B\sum_1^3 A_i] + C_2[B\sum_1^3 A_i].$$

5. *Interacting varieties.* Now we can couple the two systems by having both varieties (try to) occupy the same limited environment. The simplest assumption (admittedly over-simple!) is to have fertility parameters m_j and M_j, and hence c_j and C_j, all *depend inversely on total numbers of both varieties*, $n_t + N_t$, as an increase in that total lowers the sustenance available to each and every adult of any age:

$$(7) \qquad c_j[n_t + N_t], \quad c_j'[\ ] < 0; \quad C_j[n_t + N_t], \quad C_j'[\ ] < 0.$$

Now our trajectories are generated by the *simultaneous non-linear difference* relations

$$(8) \qquad b_t = \sum_{j=1}^2 b_{t-j}c_j[\Sigma_1^3 a_i b_{t-i} + \Sigma_1^3 A_i b_{t-i}]$$

$$B_t = \sum_{j=1}^2 B_{t-j}C_j[\Sigma_1^3 a_i b_{t-i} + \Sigma_1^3 A_i B_{t-i}].$$

A stationary equilibrium in which both varieties coexist in positive numbers would require *simultaneous* satisfaction of the two relations

$$(9) \qquad 1 = \sum_{j=1}^{2} c_j[n^* + N^*],$$

$$(10) \qquad 1 = \sum_{j=1}^{2} C_j[n^* + N^*].$$

It is infinitely unlikely that the same value of $n^* + N^*$ can satisfy two independent relations like (9) *and* (10).

Almost certainly, as the system is now modelled, one variety will drive out the other. Thus, suppose

$$(11) \qquad 1 = \sum_{1}^{2} c_j[\nu^*] > \sum_{1}^{2} C_j[\nu^*];$$

then the first variety will oust the second asymptotically. Thus, (8) must have solutions with the asymptotic property

$$(12) \qquad \lim_{t \to \infty} b_t = b^* \text{ of } (5), \quad n^* = \nu^* = b^*\Sigma_1^3 a_i;$$

$$\lim_{t \to \infty} B_t = 0 = \lim_{t \to \infty} N_t.$$

These relations will be certainly valid for all initial positive b's and B's near $(b^*, b^*, b^*; 0, 0, 0)$. I believe they will be more globally valid, holding for example also for initial (n_t, N_t) near $(n_t, \nu^* - n_t)$ provided the absolute values of $c_j'[\ ]$ and $C_j'[\ ]$ are sufficiently small.

Actually, we can sharpen the second relation of (12) to read

$$(13) \qquad \lim_{t \to \infty} \frac{B_t}{(1 - |D|)^t} = \text{constant}$$

where $1 - |D|$ is the fractional root of X in

$$(14) \qquad 1 = C_1[\nu^*]X^{-1} + C_2[\nu^*]X^{-2}.$$

One can also sharpen the first relation in (12) to read

$$(15) \qquad \lim_{t \to \infty} \frac{b_t - b^*}{(1 - |d|)^t} = \text{constant}$$

where $1 - |d|$ is the fractional root of x in

$$(16) \qquad 1 = \sum_1^2 c_j[n^*]x^{-j} + \sum_{i=1}^3 \left(\sum_1^2 c_j'[n^*] \right) a_i x^{-i}.$$

The constants in (13) and (15) will depend on the initial conditions $(b_0, b_1, b_2; B_0, B_1, B_2)$.

I omit details of the proof of these various assertions and forbear from investigating how far one can go in weakening the various restrictions sufficient for global stability.

6. *Maximizing interpretation.* So to speak, variety 2 is driven out of existence by variety 1 because variety 1 "uses the limited environment more 'efficiently.'"

What warrant do we have for such a *teleological* formulation with its appeal to fuzzily defined "efficiency"? At bottom, we have the brute fact described in (11) — that variety 2 loses numbers at density of occupation of the environment where variety 1 can hold its own.

We may even put the matter more provocatively. In this model, variety 1 has according to (11) a viable steady state scale, n^*, which exceeds the viable steady state scale for variety 2 of N^*. Nature is a *cancer*, worshipping so to speak mere size and arranging "survival of the growingest."

We can even make predictions about reversals in survival dominance when, for any reason (such as mutation, environmental change, Congressional fiat, or custom change), changes occur in the $(a_j, c_j[\ ]; A_j, C_j[\ ])$ propensities. Thus, if (11) is reversed to become

$$(17) \qquad 1 = \sum_1^2 C_j[\nu^*] > \sum_1^2 c_j[\nu^*]$$

the variety dying out will spring back into life and decimate endlessly the previously dominant variety.

7. *Triage for the aged?* Why does any species tolerate infertile oldsters (post-menopausal females, for example)? Wouldn't setting a_3 at zero create a super subspecies that will oust the others in time?

The answer is No in this literal model. Thus, if we make the varieties differ only in having $A_3 = 0 < a_3$, but with all other $a_j = A_j$, $c_j[\nu] \equiv C_j[\nu]$, the two varieties will be in razor's-edge labile equilibrium. Now (11) turns out to involve no inequality, becoming

$$(18) \qquad 1 = \sum_1^2 c_j[\nu^*] = \sum_1^2 C_j[\nu^*].$$

Now (n^*, N^*) are indeterminate so long as their sum equals ν^*.

Is this result counterintuitive? No. The oldsters carry their weight in the sense that more of $a_3 b_{t-3}$ does not lower the per capita sustenance of the fertile first-variety groups any more than they lower the sustenance of the rival second-variety group. So to speak, Nature doesn't seem to care whether She gets her same maximal number by fewer B^* births than b^* births!

One's intuitive feeling that oldsters are an evolutionary burden, so that arteriosclerosis and old-age cancer have adaptive value in Nature's scheme, comes from the suspicion that the older groups may draw more sustenance than their presence contributes to the group in question. To realize this suspicion, *let the sustenance available to the fertile groups be lowered by the presence of more oldsters.* Thus, let the "wage" available per capita to the fertile be w and W respectively, each equal to the same declining function of the total number of *fertile and working* adults, $\omega(a_1 b_{t-1} + a_2 b_{t-2} + A_1 B_{t-1} + A_2 B_{t-2})$, but allocated equally among *all* adults of the variety in question so that oldsters are a burden on *their* colleagues, not on those of the *other* variety. Then $c_j[\;]$ and $C_j[\;]$ now become

$$(19)\qquad c_j\left\{\frac{a_1 b_{t-1} + a_2 b_{t-2}}{a_1 b_{t-1} + a_2 b_{t-2} + a_3 b_{t-3}}\;\omega(\Sigma_1^2 a_i b_{t-i} + \Sigma_1^2 A_i B_{t-i})\right\}$$

$$C_j\left\{\frac{A_1 B_{t-1} + A_2 B_{t-2}}{A_1 B_{t-1} + A_2 B_{t-2} + A_3 B_{t-3}}\;\omega(\Sigma_1^2 a_i b_{t-i} + \Sigma_1^2 A_i B_{t-i})\right\}$$

$$(20)\qquad c_j'\{\;\} > 0,\quad C_j'\{\;\} > 0;\quad \omega'(\;) < 0.$$

It can now be verified that, if the second variety somehow practices triage and sets $A_3 = 0$ while matching all the other parameters and functions of the first variety, then the second variety will wipe out the first variety and rule alone in the environment, with B^* the root of

$$(21)\quad 1 = C_1\{\omega(B\Sigma_1^2 A_i)\} + C_2\{\omega(B\Sigma_1^2 A_i)\} > \sum_{j=1}^{2} c_j\left\{\frac{\Sigma_1^2 a_i}{\Sigma_1^3 a_i}\;\omega(B\Sigma_1^2 A_i)\right\}$$

8. *Egotistic "individualism" versus "adaptive group altruism."* What wins out always in these models is the greatest "growingness" or "viability" of the variety, regardless of how any typical individual fares in one "lifetime." Normally, an oldster does not feel thrilled at the prospect of his own demise. If egocentrism means anything beyond an empty tautology or convention, it means that individuals have an ordering with respect to survival and other propensities $(a_1, a_2, a_3; A_1, A_2, A_3)$ and so forth. To say that an "individual" *wants to commit* suicide and

set $A_3 = 0$ is to turn egotism upside down (as in converting "Mother love" into "Mother's peculiar self interest," or fabricating "masochism" as a dummy variable to save the face of a nomenclature involving egotistic or egoistic pleasure seeking). To say "An individual really selfishly wants to die early because (he realizes?) that is the only way his species did not long ago cease to exist" is, I think, a comical defense of selfish, canny egotism.

The theorist of individualism himself commits suicide, or perhaps self-abortion, if he must emasculate the only content of his formulation by such headstands.

Whatever the merits of the imperialist-economists in their bid to take over sociobiology (today, but tomorrow biology and next Friday quantum mechanics), the present explorations have not given much comfort to their aspirations and claims. To describe some altruism as "egotism simulating altruism" reveals something about the describer that lacks substantive interest.

9. *More general sustenance imputations.* The reader will have noticed my arbitrary assumption that the sustenance available per capita to fertile individuals of both species depends on the *same* linear magnitude, $n_t + N_t$. This is excessively special.

It would be more realistic to recognize that different varieties desire and need different end products of the environment; and that adults of different varieties need not be similar producing agents. Thus, we might replace (7) or (19) by more general formulations involving wage functions, $w(\ )$ and $W(\ )$, such as

$$c_j\{w(n_t, N_t)\}, \quad C_j\{W(n_t, N_t)\} \tag{22}$$

$$c_j'\{\ \} > 0, \quad C_j'\{\ \} > 0. \tag{23}$$

The *per capita* "wage functions" can themselves be given a variety of alternative forms. One simple possibility is to have each variety good at producing what it needs:

$$c_j\{w(n_t, N_t)\} \equiv c_j\{\omega(n_t + \alpha N_t)\}, \quad 0 < \alpha < 1 \tag{24}$$

$$C_j\{W(n_t, N_t)\} \equiv C_j\{\omega(N_t + \alpha n_t)\}.$$

$$\omega'(\ ) < 0; \quad c_j'\{\ \} > 0, \quad C_j'\{\ \} > 0. \tag{25}$$

Now the razor's-edge of competitive coexistence has been widened by α's being made fractional. For $[c_j\{\ \}]$ functions not too different from $[C_j\{\ \}]$ functions there will assuredly exist positive roots, n^* and N^*, of

(26) $$1 = \sum_{1}^{2} c_j\{\omega(n + \alpha N)\}$$

$$1 = \sum_{1}^{2} C_j\{\omega(N + \alpha n)\}\ .$$

Now, *what can the system be described as maximizing?*

This is a fair question to put to economists such as A. Alchian, G. Becker, or P. Samuelson. It is a fair question to put to admirers of R. A. Fisher's contributions to natural selection. What "fitness" concept is definable for systems like these? It is not enough to regard Fisher as a genius; it would be even better to explicate his important contributions in this regard.

Still more general imputation schemes will occur to the theoretical economist. I mention only one such.

10. *Animal economics.* Here both sets of adults are differentially productive in creating a common harvest. Total sustenance, θ, is given by a concave "production function"

(27) $$\theta = \Theta(n_t, N_t)$$

(28) $$\partial\Theta(U_1, U_2)/\partial U_i > 0 \qquad (i = 1, 2)$$

(29) $$[\partial^2\Theta(U_1, U_2)/\partial U_i \partial U_j] \qquad \text{neg. definite.}$$

The sharing of the harvest, θ, among the two varieties, is given by

(30) $$k(n_t, N_t) + K(n_t, N_t) \equiv \theta(n_t, N_t).$$

Now

(31) $$c_j\{k(n_t, N_t)/n_t\}, \qquad C_j\{K(n_t, N_t)/N_t\}$$

(32) $$\partial c_j\{\ \}/\partial n_t < 0, \qquad \text{etc.}$$

The equilibrium is defined by (n^*, N^*) roots of

(33) $$1 = \sum_{1}^{2} c_j\{k(n^*, N^*)/n^*\}$$

$$1 = \sum_{1}^{2} C_j\{K(n^*, N^*)/N^*\}.$$

What is being maximized? Is there any Lyapunov magnitude, such as $(n_t - n^*)^2 + (N_t - N^*)^2$, that declines as the system approaches its asymptotic equilibrium?

Is the equilibrium necessarily stable? Why should it be, even locally?

Serious mathematical biology seems still in its infancy with its work cut out for it.

11. *Finale*. The present analysis seems to emerge with a debunking indictment of the claims for maximizing and teleological constructs in biology, evolution, sociobiology, and imperialist-economics (which threatens to absorb sociology, law, and biology by its pretentious applying to them the jargon of economists).

Nevertheless, the notion of useful maximizing approaches can be defended against some of the criticisms levied against it. If biological behavior equations happen to provide the maximizing solution to some definable problem, that does not mean that any mind must know in advance anything about that problem (including anything about its very existence or nonexistence).[3] Apples fall in Lincolnshire to minimize Hamilton's Action integral, and to minimize the Maupertuis-Euler-Lagrange-Jacobi Least-Action expression. They did so before Newton was born. Apples don't know they are doing so. The fact that Maupertius chanced on his enunciation of this extremum principle because of Cartesian moonshine and deistic prejudices has nothing to do with its validity or its limitations.

Although I am sympathetic with R. Lewontin's testings of the concept of "adaptation," the above remarks qualify the force of his criticism that "The concept of adaptation implies that there is a preexistent form, problem or ideal to which things are fitted by a dynamical process" (Lewontin, 1977, p. 3). The word "preexistent" can be made to lack force in this argument.

Similarly, Lewontin (pp. 4-6) seems to make the usefulness of the concept of *ecological niche* hinge on whether there is a *unique* ultimate equilibrium configuration in nature that is the sole solution of the relevant maximand (and which constitutes the rendezvous of the process from the beginning). However, it is well known that there are many calculus of variations problems with multiple branches, some of which provide *local* maxima. It would be useful in biology and economics if certain configurations could be ruled out as being peculiarly non-maximizing, being dominated by other configurations with a greater probability of being observed in a longer-lasting state. *Partial orderings* that do not attain a *complete ordering* could also be valuable.

3. Repeatedly in my own work in economics I have had occasion to define useful maximands that no actor in the scenario knows about. Thus, in my 1978 Machlup *Festschrift* analysis of industry derived demand for factors, I build up from consciously-profit-maximizing firms an *industry maximand* that gets itself maximized by the resultant actions of the mob. The point is that this leads to observable and testable Maxwell-reciprocity relations on price elasticities.

The present viewpoint places emphasis on whether the observed biological variables behave *as if* generated by an extremum formulation, not on whether there "really" is a problem to be solved and which gets solved. In a sense, therefore, my critique cuts deeper than Lewontin's if, in the end, I am able to set forth quasi-realistic systems that could *not* have been generated by a meaningful maximization process.

The system of (8), which does admit of an *ex post* maximizing interpretation, is a nice example in which there is no need for a "preexistent" problem that "requires" solving. Two brute systems, when coupled, interact to "fill the space with the greatest number of individuals." Nature didn't will it. Understand it. That is merely the way the cookie crumbles.

Samuel Butler described a chicken as an egg's way of making another egg. (From Leontief's input-output viewpoint, man may be merely pig-iron's way of making more pig-iron!) But one can as well regard genes as somatic cells' instruments for reproducing if not themselves then their form. In an indecomposable n-variable dynamic system, no subset of variables could in general be singled out for a critical reproductive role.

In every case we are dealing merely with positivistic interactions that happen to conduce to persistence and with less long-lived interactions that happen not to.

Teleological language is, at best, a mnemonic shorthand to save time for fuller and more prosaic analytical description.

REFERENCES

Samuelson, P. A., "Maximum Principles in Analytical Economics," Nobel Memorial Lecture, *Les Prix Nobel en 1970*, Stockholm, Nobel Foundation, 273-288, 1970.

Lanczos, C., *Variational Principles of Mechanics*, University of Toronto, 1949.

Becker, G., "Altruism, Egoism, and Genetic Fitness: Economics and Sociobiology," *Journal of Economic Literature*, *14*, 817-825, 1976.

Alchian, A. A., "Uncertainty, Evolution, and Economic Theory," *Journal of Political Economy*, *58*, 211-221, 1950.

Fisher, R. A., *The Genetical Theory of Natural Selection*, Oxford University Press, 1930.

Wilson, E. O., *Sociobiology*, Harvard University Press, 1975.

Keyfitz, N., *Introduction to the Mathematics of Population*, Addison-Wesley, 1968.

Lewontin, R., "Adaptation," Harvard University Working Paper, 1977.

Complete genetic models for altruism, kin selection and like-gene selection

Paul A. Samuelson

Economics Department, Massachusetts Institute of Technology, Cambridge, Massachusetts 02139, USA

Tractable difference-equation models, involving as many dynamic relations as there are unknown variables, are formulated to investigate like-gene selection. Unambiguous verdicts can then be rendered on intuitive conjectures and counter-conjectures that appear in the literature on altruism and kin selection. Thus, the 1978 Tullock view, that helping others with genes not exactly like your own lacks fitness, is verified to be incorrect. On the other hand, the 1978 correction of Tullock by Frech, with its dependence on environmental limitations and its omission of necessary and sufficient conditions for steady states with coexisting altruists and non-altruists, is provided with needed corrections, qualifications and amplifications. The scenarios considered, which include the fitness of incest and inbreeding and their unfitness, shed light on the 1976 Dawkins criticism of E. O. Wilson's 1975 association of kin selection as falling between individual and group selection. Ground is prepared for evaluation of the usefulness of a maximizing criterion in formulating neo-Darwinian systems of evolution.

1. Introduction

The concepts of 'kin selection' and 'inclusive fitness' have been fruitfully applied to the problem of altruism's survival and evolution by W. D. Hamilton (1964, 1971), Trivers (1971), E. O. Wilson (1975) and many others. The purpose here is to define and analyze some complete models, involving as many independent dynamic equations as there are unknowns in systems that exhibit and exemplify relationships akin to kin selection. Although these equations could have arisen in economics or abstract game theory, they are patterned and interpreted along the lines of standard mendelian mating models, as for example those in textbooks like that of Crow & Kimura (1970).

Such a model can resolve precise debates like the following. Along Hamiltonian lines, one may expect that a gene which causes one brother to undergo some sacrifice to save his brother or close kin will be a gene that will survive and flourish under natural selection. Tullock (1978) has objected, using the language of the economist's 'free-rider' problem in the provision of common public goods to argue: since your brother has some genes unlike your own, the act of altruism is indiscriminately favoring them at the same time as favoring your type of genes. Frech (1978), properly, refutes this version of Tullock's argument, showing it to be both bad biology and economics: corrected of error, the Tullock attention to the shared and unshared genes actually vindicates the basic insight of kin selection, namely the enhanced fitness of altruism the greater the proportion of shared genes, its fitness *not* disappearing when the shared component fails to be 100 per cent. (Example: Tullock would be right that I may be programmed to be more altruistic to my identical twin than to my fraternal twin, wrong to argue that this must make me indifferent to the latter.)

The present models can test the validity of Frech's point that altruism toward a less-than-fully-close relative is in general strengthened by environmental pressures limiting the total number of competing genotypes. This is shown not to be true in general. Also, using the methods of classical economists like Ricardo, which were rediscovered by Verhulst (1838) and are used by such modern biologists as May (1973), my models fail to corroborate Frech's contention that environment limitations lead generally to mixed equilibria with coexisting altruists or non-altruists.

2. 'Like-gene' selection

Two siblings, because they share the same parents, are likely to share many genes; but, by remote chance, two brothers could have no genes in common. Remote chance is of course rare, and when there is a large number of loci–e.g. with alleles A_1 or a_1, A_2 or $a_2, \ldots, A_n$ or a_n, $n \gg 1$–the law of large numbers assures that brothers tend to share more genes in common than do cousins or strangers.

The present models work with a small number of loci–'A or a' only, or 'A_1 or a_1 and A_2 or a_2' only. Again, offspring of the same couple are more likely to be of similar genetic composition than are strangers. But now, it will not be rare to find 'unrelated' individuals who are close in genetic composition, sometimes even closer than are pairs of brothers. Instead of 'kin-selection', one finds it convenient to begin with something even stronger, with what might be called 'like-gene' selection. By Hamiltonian-like reasoning, we can expect that the inherited propensity to perform acts of altruism toward those with genes like your own will, under individual selection, be found to possess fitness and that individuals with such genetic propensities will tend to proliferate and gain at the expense of those lacking such altruistic propensities. The analysis tests whether like-gene altruists oust the rest; or whether their proportions merely grow up to a critical preponderance.

3. Single-factor model

Begin with the simplest case (that which a biologist might call 'haploid, monoecious, biparental'). Each individual is genetically either an A or an a. The total number, N, is the sum of the respective numbers, N_A amd N_a:

$$N(t) = N_A(t) + N_a(t) = N(t)[n_A(t) + n_a(t)]$$
$$N_A(t) \geqslant 0, N_a(t) \geqslant 0, n_A(t) + n_a(t) = 1. \tag{1}$$

Here the n's are the *intensive* proportions.

At random these A's and a's mate: when A mates A, only A's result; from a and a, only a's; from A and a (or what we can regard as indistinguishably the same thing, from a and A), half the time A's result and half the time a's. The fertilities that determine the numerical magnitude of births, $B_A(t)$ and $B_a(t)$, may depend upon the density of total $N(t)$ relative to the limited environment's carrying capacity; but, in the simplest models, the fertilities of different matings can be assumed to be the same independently of parents' genotypes. Let $\beta[N], \beta'[N] \leqslant 0$, be the function relating the common fertility to the state of the environment; it is a special symmetric quasi-linear version of the general $\beta[N_A, N_a]$ case.

Assume that going from t to $t+1$ goes from one adult generation to the next and that there are no overlapping generations. (Explorations have assured that the results are similar in age-structured or differential-equation models with overlapping generations.) Births are assumed to occur a small fraction of a generation, θ, after matings: $0<\theta<1$. Only the respective fraction $[l_A, l_a]$ of $[B_A(t+\theta), B_a(t+\theta)]$ will survive to become adults at $t+1$, $[N_A(t+1), N_a(t+1)]$. The mortality parameters, l_A and l_a, may be affected by genetic propensities toward altruism; although they might well be density-dependent, it is an inessential simplification to assume that l_A/l_a is independent of N.

In writing our dynamic equations, we save space by using the following notation: $N(t+1)$ is denoted by $EN(t)$ or $EN, N(t)$ by N; and likewise for other variables, $N_A(t), \ldots, n_a(t), \ldots$ Now our mendelian assumption of random mating defines the complete system:

$$B_A(t+\theta) = \beta[N]N^{-1}[N_A^2 + N_AN_a] = N_A\beta[N]$$
$$B_a(t+\theta) = \beta[N]N^{-1}[N_a^2 + N_AN_a] = N_a\beta[N]$$
$$N_A(t+1) = l_AB_A(t+\theta), N_a(t+1) = l_aB_a(t+\theta); 0 \leqslant l_A \leqslant 1, 0 \leqslant l_a \leqslant 1. \quad (2)$$

Eliminating the explicit B's, we have our basic second-order non-linear difference equations

$$EN_A = N_Al_A\beta[N]$$
$$EN_a = N_al_a\beta[N]. \quad (3)$$

The problem can now be posed:

How will a genetic propensity for any one A to help another A, even at a cost to his own survival, affect the relative survival rates (the l's) of the two genotypes and thereby (3)'s asymptotic equilibrium proportions of the two categories?

Any of the examples standard for kin selection will suffice. Suppose that an individual of genotype A is heritably disposed to be altruistic toward any other individual identifiable as having the phenotype of A: like helps like, by definition of the 'like-gene altruism'. Suppose those with a lack such altruism.

If the altruism is of the rash type, where the mean incremental sacrifice of the helper exceeds the mean incremental survivorship induced in the helped, we can expect l_A to have been lowered below l_a and can expect N_A/N_a to decrease. The cases of surviving interest–history must come to be concerned with survivors!–is where the like-gene altruism is such as to push l_A/l_a above unity. Then like-gene selection will take place: the ratio for the relevant growth rates is given merely by l_A/l_a. To see this another way, decompose (3) into dynamic relations that determine the development of the *intensive* variable, $n_A(t) = N_A(t)/N(t)$, and the *extensive* variable of total number, $N(t)$. Adding (3)'s two equations, and dividing their sum into the (3)'s first equation, can be verified to give

$$EN = N\beta[N][l_An_A + l_an_a]$$
$$= N\beta[N][l_a + (l_A - l_a)n_A] \quad (4.1)$$

$$En_A = n_A \frac{l_A}{l_a + (l_A - l_a)n_A} = f[n_A; l_A, l_a]$$
$$= f[n_A] \text{ for short.} \quad (4.2)$$

Note that the environment's limitation on overall growth has disappeared from (4.2)'s relationship for the intensive proportions. Thus, it is not the case in general that kin selection for altruism is strengthened by environmental limitations and density dependencies. As is so properly emphasized in the neo-Darwinian literature, *individual* selection operates in ignorance of and indifference to *group* selection. One would see this most strongly when realizing that 'altruism' is an algebraic magnitude: in its negative guise as malevolence or (rational?) spite, A's may be predisposed to lower l_a rather than raise l_A, with the inevitable consequence that the carrying capacity of the environment is *lowered* as long as any a's still persist; some quite different species might gain a permanent foothold at the expense of the one, during the transient phase when a's are not yet extinct.

A plot of $f[n_A]$ shows it intersects the 45° line at $n_A = 0$ and $n_A = 1$, confirming that a steady state is possible with only A's present or only a's present. So long as $l_A = l_a$, *any* initial proportions will indifferently perpetuate themselves: this labile or neutral equilibrium has the same degeneracy properties as the Hardy–Weinberg equilibrium; however, in this simpler haploid model, it does not even take one transient generation for the system to come into its equilibrium as is required in the Hardy–Weinberg diploid model.

When $l_A > l_a$, $f[n_A]$ arches above the 45° line between the origin and the (1, 1) point of only A's: with positive slope less than unity at the latter point, $0 < f'[1] < 1$, it is assured that any occurrence of a's will be followed by their elimination by selection; with positive slope greater than unity at the origin, it is assured that introducing ever so few A's into a population of a's will result in dominating proliferation of the like-gene altruists–in confirmation of the usual heuristic reasonings on kin selection. Fig. 1 tells the story.

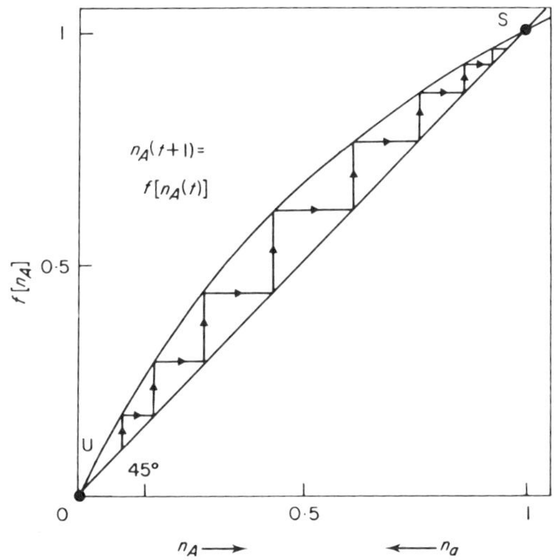

Fig. 1. Like-gene selective fitness. The arrows of iteration, $n_A(t+1) = f[n_A(t)]$, show that S is a stable equilibrium with like-gene altruism fitness and U is an unstable equilibrium of non-altruists only. Note: $l_A/l_a = 2$ here

The equilibrium states for (3) or (4), with $l_A > l_a$, are derived as

$$\lim_{t\to\infty} n_A(t) = n_A^* = 1, \lim_{t\to\infty} n_a(t) = n_a^* = 0 \tag{4.3}$$

$$N(t) = \beta^{-1}[\text{Max}(l_A, l_a)^{-1}] = \beta^{-1}[l_A^{-1}]. \tag{4.4}$$

where $\beta^{-1}[\ ]$ is the inverse function to $\beta[N]$, and where the stationary solution $n_A^* = 0$, $N_a^* = \beta^{-1}[l_a^{-1}]$, is locally and globally unstable at U.

If samples are not infinitely large, when $l_A = l_a$ the n_A intensity will undergo a Brownian wobble around its initial $n_A(0)$ value (ultimately reaching 0 or 1 in long enough time, with a probability of a's ultimately becoming extinct, that probability being $n_A(0)$ itself). With $l_A > l_a$, this random walk is biased to drift toward an *increasing* fraction of altruists; now the probability that the altruists will eventually become alone existent, although it is not 1, will definitely be above 1/2–and that probability of eventual sole domination by altruists will increase, along with the speed with which its ultimate victory is obtained, the greater is l_A/l_a and/or $n(0)$ itself.

4. Anthropomorphic fallacies

So far no light at all has been cast on Tullock's puzzle. When an A helps another A in this one-factor model, it is so to speak helping its identical twin, all but 'helping itself' genetically speaking. If I make the model diploid, as in section 6 below, we face the possibility that an individual of genetic composition AA at one locus may be programmed to help an individual with genotype and phenotype of Aa at that same locus, a case in which the selfish gene is partially missing its egotistic target–which is Tullock's concern.

However, before going on to a diploid model, let us give Tullock's argument rope by considering a two-locus haploid model. Now, at two loci, individuals occur of genotypes A_1A_2, A_1a_2, a_1A_2, and a_1a_2, in numbers $N_{ij}(t)$ where $(i, j = 1, 2)$. Again, I posit birth fertilities independent of genotype: $\beta_{ij}[N] \equiv \beta[N]$, $\beta'[N] < 0$. But now we must prepare to let differences occur in l_{ij}'s as a result of like-gene selection being built into possession of A_1 rather than of a_1.

First, suppose that individuals of both A_1A_2 and A_1a_2 types will sacrifice some of their own survival in order altruistically to improve the survival of any encountered individual who is perceived to be either of A_1A_2 or A_1a_2 types. Ruling out (as evolution will ultimately do!) rash altruism, we may stipulate:

$$l_A = l_{11} = l_{12} > l_{21} = l_{22} = l_a. \tag{5}$$

Now, when an A_1A_2 helps an A_1a_2, he might seem to be wasting his generosity on the latter free rider; likewise, when an A_1a_2 helps the unmatching genes of an A_1A_2, at the same time he is helping the matching genes. (Tullock could properly object to this *symmetric* example of quixoticism: each such generous group happens to be compensated by like gallantry on the part of the class it helps. So demonstration that selection wipes out the a_1's does not provide a cogent example for Frech to refute Tullock.)

On reflection, one realizes that as far as A_1 and a_1 frequencies are concerned, the presence of the second factor A_2 or a_2, so long as it is made to be independent of the first factor in every respect, will have no effect whatsoever. Mathematically, we can reduce the following four relations to two aggregative ones:

$$EN_{ij} = N_{ij}l_{ij}\beta[N], (i, j = 1, 2). \tag{6}$$

Summing over j and recognizing that

$$N_A(t) = \sum_{j=1}^{2} N_{1j}(t), N_a(t) = \sum_{j=1}^{2} N_{2j}(t), \tag{7}$$

we find by virtue of (5)'s two equalities

$$EN_A = N_A l_A \beta[N], EN_a = N_a l_a \beta[N].$$

But these are precisely our original one-factor relations of (3). So we are assured that, as long as $N_{11}(0) + N_{12}(0) > 0$ and $l_A > l_a$,

$$\lim_{t\to\infty} [N_{21}(t), N_{22}(t)] = [0, 0].$$

If both A_2's and a_2's are initially present, they will be asymptotically present in positve ratios. The limiting frequency of A_2 compared to a_2, of $(N_{11} + N_{21})/(N_{12} + N_{22})$, will be increased if initial N_{11} is increased at the expense of N_{21} and initial N_{22} at the expense of N_{12}.

In this trumped-up example of a second *independent* factor, it is a red herring to speak of wasted selfish altruism. A more interesting case is the following one, in which only members of $N_{11}(t)$ are altruists, but are myopic ones who indiscriminately favor members of $N_{11}(t)$ or $N_{12}(t)$. Necessarily l_{12} will be pushed above $l_{21} = l_{22} = l_a$ because members of N_{12} are recipients of N_{11}'s altruism. That altruism will cost something, enough to put l_{11} below l_{12}. If, still, it leaves l_{11} above l_a, we are much as in the previous independent case: the frequency of $N_a/N_A \to 0$ as $t \to \infty$, taking $N_{21}(t)$ and $N_{22}(t)$ to zero; this follows because any mean survival rate of A between l_{11} and l_{12}, $\tilde{l}_A$, must exceed l_a. Therefore, A_1's must grow faster than a_1's:

$$\frac{EN_A/N_A}{EN_a/N_a} \geqslant \frac{\text{Min}\,(l_{11}, l_{12})}{\text{Max}\,(l_{21}, l_{22})} > 1 + \delta > 1. \tag{8}$$

The interesting case, in which Frech can validly claim that indiscriminate similar-gene altruism will lead to *coexisting* survival of both altruists and non-altruists, comes when N_{11}'s altruism lowers l_{11} *below* $l_{21} = l_{22} = l_a$. Now

$$\lim_{t\to\infty} \frac{N_{11}(t)}{N_{11}(t) + N_{12}(t)} = \frac{l_{12} - l_a}{l_{12} - l_{11}} > 0 \text{ for } N_{11}(0) + N_{12}(0) > 0. \tag{9}$$

The ultimate proportions of A_2's and a_2's are not predictable, since this depends on the happenstance of initial $[N_{ij}(0)/N(0)]$ ratios. In summary

$$\lim_{t\to\infty} N(t) = \beta^{-1}[l_a^{-1}] = N^* > 0$$

$$\lim_{t\to\infty} [N_{ij}(t)] = [a_i b_j] N^*$$

$$\sum_1^2 a_k = 1 = \sum_1^2 b_k$$

$$0 < a_1 = \frac{l_{12} - l_a}{l_{12} - l_{11}} < 1$$

and where b_1 is a homogeneous function of degree 0 in $[N_{11}(0), N_{12}(0), N_{21}(0), N_{22}(0)]$, which is monotone-increasing in the arguments $[N_{11}, N_{21}, -N_{12}, -N_{22}]$. No explicit formula for b_1^1 is expressible, but it can be calculated to any degree of accuracy by calculating limiting ratios $(N_{11} + N_{21})/N$ for various initial conditions $[N_{ij}(0)]$.

In concluding this section, one should note that genes are not supposed to be consciously selfish or consciously any other thing. It is merely that selection favours survival of certain genotypes with certain accompanying phenotypes, a statement that is shown to be more than an ex-post repeating of the facts of biological competition by our being able to predict all of the above stated directions of dynamic change.

5. Selection for incest or close-breeding

If like-gene and kin-selection favor traits of altruism, what could be a stronger instance of this than the heritable propensity to benefit the genes of those like yourself by the act of mating solely with them? To illustrate the possible fitness of such inbreeding, I drop for the first and only time the postulate of *random* or non-assortative mating.

To keep the model haploid and monoecious, suppose that each individual has both eggs and sperms. Let only the former be effectively limited in numbers and be determinative of the total number of births. Because the total of sperms is so great as to give them a redundant role, the number of them that contribute to the next generation of births is set by the number of eggs alone and the choice among successful sperms by genotype is governed by the eggs.

By mutation or otherwise, let all eggs of composition A choose to mate only with A sperms: all their offspring are A's. The a eggs mate at random, with N_A/N proportion of A sperms and N_a/N proportion of a sperms: the resulting offspring of such matings involve births of A's to a's in ratio $\frac{1}{2}N_A/(N_a + \frac{1}{2}N_A)$, since half the mixed matings yield offspring of each genotype, and since all of the aa matings yield a's. To isolate how selection affects incest, I posit equal death rates for both genotypes, $l_A = l_a = l$.

Now our dynamic relations become

$$EN_A = l\beta[N][N_A + \tfrac{1}{2}N_A N_a N^{-1}] = N_A l\beta[N][1 + \tfrac{1}{2} - \tfrac{1}{2}n_A] \tag{11}$$

$$EN_a = l\beta[N][N_a^2 N^{-1} + \tfrac{1}{2}N_A N^{-1}] = N_a l\beta[N][1 - \tfrac{1}{2}n_A].$$

From (11) we deduce

$$EN = Nl\beta[N] \tag{12.1}$$

$$En_A = n_a[\tfrac{3}{2} - \tfrac{1}{2}n_A] = \phi[n_A], \tag{12.2}$$

$$1 = \phi[1], \phi'[1] = \tfrac{1}{2} < 1 \tag{12.3}$$

$$0 = \phi[0], \phi'[0] = \tfrac{3}{2} > 1. \tag{12.4}$$

From (12.2) – (12.4), we deduce the global stability of the incestuous equilibria

$$\lim_{t\to\infty} n_A(t) = 1 \text{ for } N_A(0) > 0 \tag{12.5}$$

$$\lim_{t\to\infty} N(t) = \beta^{-1}[l^{-1}] \tag{12.6}$$

6. Diploid models and harmful recessives

Of course, in realistic biological life the fitness of incestuous or like-gene mating propensities is held down by the likelihood that harmful recessives will be brought out by the inbreeding. To do justice to this possibility we must introduce, for the first time, a diploid model. Now

$$\begin{aligned} N &= N_{AA} + N_{aa} + (N_{Aa}) \\ &= N[n_{AA} + n_{aa} + (1 - n_{AA} - n_{aa})] \\ &= (N_{AA} + \tfrac{1}{2}N_{Aa}) + (N_{aa} + \tfrac{1}{2}N_{Aa}) \\ &= N_A + N_a = N[n_A + n_a]. \end{aligned} \tag{13}$$

Now suppose that heterozygous Aa eggs mate ('incestuously') only with Aa heterozygous sperms while all other eggs mate strictly at random with all categories. However, suppose that homozygous aa's represent a lethal recessive:

$$l_{aa} = 0 < l_{Aa} = l_{AA} = l. \tag{14}$$

After the first period $t = 0 + 1$, for $t \geqslant 1$, $N_{aa}(t) \equiv 0$ and our dynamic relations become:

$$EN_{AA} = l\beta[N]\left[\tfrac{1}{4}N_{Aa} + \frac{1}{2}\frac{N_{Aa}}{N}N_{AA} + \frac{N_{AA}}{N}N_{AA}\right], t \geqslant 1$$
$$= l\beta[N]N\tfrac{1}{4}[1 + n_{aa} + 2n_{AA}^2] \tag{15.1}$$
$$EN_{Aa} = l\beta[N]\left[\tfrac{1}{2}N_{Aa} + \frac{1}{2}\frac{N_{Aa}}{N}N_{AA}\right]$$
$$= N_{Aa}l\beta[N]\tfrac{1}{2}[1 + n_{AA}]. \tag{15.2}$$

From (15.1) and (15.2), we can deduce

$$En_{AA} = \frac{1 + n_{AA} + 2n_{AA}^2}{3 + n_{AA}} = \psi[n_{AA}], 1 = \psi[1], 0 < \tfrac{1}{4} = \psi'[1] < 1 \tag{15.3}$$
$$EN = Nl\beta[N]\tfrac{1}{4}[3 + n_{AA}]. \tag{15.4}$$

From (15.3), $n_{AA}^* = 1$ is a stable equilibrium, so that here incest will indeed bring out the postulated lethal recessives and the gene for incest will be selected out of the population

$$\lim_{t\to\infty} [N_{AA}(t), N_{Aa}(t), N_{aa}(t)] = [N^*, 0, 0] \tag{15.5}$$
$$\lim_{t\to\infty} N(t) = N^* = \beta^{-1}[l^{-1}]. \tag{15.6}$$

Thus, the like-gene selection, despite its favoring births with a rather than A, in the diploid case with adverse recessives is overcome by the selection against those recessives. It is reassuring that the present simple models do not contradict but rather confirm the conventional wisdom in these matters–reassuring not for that wisdom but for these models!

7. Free riding in the diploid case

A final verdict can be determined on how kin and like-gene selection is affected by (1) environmental limits and (2) elements of free riding due to coincidental favoring of unlike or 'unrelated' genes along with like ones. A single locus will bring in complications aplenty!

Assume three genotypes, in respective numbers

$$[N_{AA}(t), N_{aa}(t), N_{Aa}(t)] \equiv [N_{11}(t), N_{22}(t), N_{12}(t) + N_{21}(t)]$$
$$N_{ij}(t) \equiv N_{ji}(t), (i, j = 1, 2). \tag{16}$$

Warning: although the same N_{ij} notation is used here as in the two-locus haploid model, they are not at all the same models; thus, for the latter, $N_{12} \neq N_{21}$, since the number of individuals with A_1 at one locus and a_2 at the other bears no necessary relation to the number with A_2 at one locus and a_1 at the other; however, simply by convention (and in agreement with what Mendel already observed to be true about the indifference of whether an *Aa* received an *A* from a sperm and an *a* from an egg or received an *a* from a sperm and an *A* from an egg), we can here work with $N_{12}(t) \equiv N_{21}(t)$.

At least 64 patterns of altruism can be distinguished: *AA*'s might favor *AA*'s or, alternatively might favor *Aa*'s, or . . . ; or *Aa*'s might favor *Aa*'s only, or *AA*'s and *aa*'s; or . . . The number of sets of favorers is $2^3 = 8$, the number of favoreds is also 8, giving $8^2 = 64$ distinct patterns to analyze. Indeed, if we allow malice or negative altruism–and why shouldn't we?–the number of patterns is enormous, being in the trillions of trillions since $2^{64} > 10^{18}$.

Some patterns are so obvious as to lack interest. If *AA*'s are altruistic toward *aa*'s, *A* clearly eliminates itself from survival in favor of a: $n_{aa}(t) \to 1$ as $t \to \infty$. Some patterns we have already provided complete analysis for: if AA's help each other much at little risk to themselves, $l_{AA} > \text{Max}\,[l_{aa}, l_{Aa}]$ and $n_{AA}(t) \to 1$.

Analysis can now clinch the point that when AA helps Aa only, a Tullock disciple would be correct to declare: helping unrelated genes–i.e. helping alien a at the same time as helping like A, will do more for the opposition than it does for the home team–with $l_{Aa} > l_{aa} > l_{AA}$, $n_{aa}(t) \to 1$. Here, the free riders gain so much more than the dues payers, that the somewhat-like-gene altruism proves suicidal.

However, to believe that all free-riding involves quixotic altruism is to fall into logical fallacy. Let Aa's be predisposed to help AA's at small self-sacrifice. Then Aa's are, so to speak, helping half-brothers. However, now

$$[n_{aa}(t), n_a(t)] \to [0, 0] \text{ for } l_{AA} \gg l_{aa} > l_{Aa}. \tag{17}$$

Clearly, all that matters for the outcome of altruism propensities is encapsulated in our knowledge of the relative strengths of the three mortality parameters, $[l_{AA}, l_{aa}, l_{Aa}]$. Normalizing their scale, which will not affect *intensive* outcomes, we can set their sum equal to unity. Fig. 2's barycentric diagram shows the region in the equilateral triangle that corresponds to survival of A's only, of a's only, or of both in coexistence equilibrium (stable or unstable).

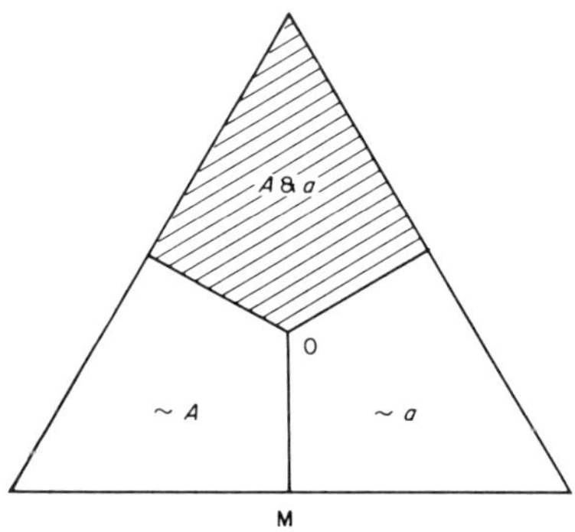

Fig. 2. Stability diagram. The three parameters, $[l_{AA}, l_{aa}, l_{Aa}](l_{AA} + l_{aa} + l_{Aa})^{-1}$, *are represented respectively by the distances from any specified point in the equilateral triangle to, respectively, the triangle's left-hand, right-hand, and bottom sides. Then, any system corresponding to a point in the dark region marked A&a will give rise to a mixed equilibrium with* n_A^*/n_a^* *the greater the farther to the right of the altitude that point is. Any point inside ~ A will give rise to steady state with* $n_A^* = 0 = 1 - n_a^*$*; one inside ~ a implies A's triumphant. The OM watershed is vulnerable to the slightest mutation or perturbation*

For any dark point in the space of l parameters, *both* A's and a's ultimately coexist–as indicated by the label 'A & a'. Thus, any altruism pattern that is *symmetric* between A and a and which favors the survival of N_{Aa} heterozygotes, will represent a point on the triangle's altitude above the ortho-center, O. For any such point, $l_{Aa} > l_{aa} = l_{AA}$, $[n_{AA}(t), n_{aa}(t), n_{Aa}(t)] \to [k, k, 1 - 2k] > 0$. A small mutation that finally moves us off the razor's edge of the altitude, say one that makes A a bit more altruistic than is a, will not lead to extinction of the altruistic gene but only to its representation below fifty-fifty.

A point on the lowest third of the altitude, on OM, will represent a fifty-fifty equilibrium, maintained because each of A and a happen to be equally foolish. But such a singular equilibrium will be unstable: the slightest mutation of A to become more sacrificial will move the point leftward from the altitude into the region marked 'no A' or '$\sim A$', where $n_A(t) \to 0$.

By what exact formulas are Fig. 2's regions demarcated? As in Samuelson (1978) one analyzes the stability of the following complete model.

$$EN_{ij} = l_{ij}\beta[N]N_iN_jN^{-1}, (i,j = 1, 2) \tag{18.1}$$

$$l_{11} = l_{AA}, l_{22} = l_{aa}, l_{12} = l_{21} = l_{Aa}.$$

Summing over j, we deduce

$$EN_i = N_i\beta[N]N^{-1} \sum_{j=1}^{2} l_{ij}N_j, (i = 1, 2) \tag{18.2}$$

$$= N_i\beta[N] \sum_{j=1}^{2} l_{ij}n_j.$$

Summing over i, one deduces one extensive relation for EN, and autonomous relations for the intensive magnitudes, $n_i(t) = N_i(t)/N(t)$, or if desired for $n_{ij}(t) = N_{ij}(t)/N(t)$. A convenient set is the following

$$EN = N\beta[N] \sum_{i=1}^{2}\sum_{j=1}^{2} n_il_{ij}n_j \tag{18.3}$$

$$= N\beta[N]Q[n_1, n_2; l_{11}, l_{12}, l_{22}]$$

$$= N\beta[N]Q[n_1, n_2] \text{ for short.}$$

$$En_i = n_i \sum_{j=1}^{2} l_{ij}n_j/Q[n_1, n_2], (i = 1, 2)$$

$$= \tfrac{1}{2}n_i \frac{\partial Q[n_1, n_2]/\partial n_i}{Q[n_1, n_2]}. \tag{18.4}$$

Only one of the last pair of relations is independent, each implying the other. So we may replace (18.4) by the equivalent:

$$En_A = n_A \frac{l_{AA}n_A + l_{Aa}(1 - n_A)}{l_{AA}n_A^2 + 2l_{Aa}n_A(1 - n_A) + l_{aa}(1 - n_A)^2} \tag{18.5}$$

$$= h[n_A; l_{AA}, l_{Aa}, l_{aa}]$$

$$= h[n_A] \text{ for short}; h[1] = 1 = h[0].$$

Equating En_A to n_A in [18.5], we can solve the resulting cubic equation for its three real roots. True stationary value for the dynamic difference equation of [18.5] are given by $n_A^* = 1$ and $n_A^* = 0$, representing respectively the cases when only A or only a are present. Only when the third root is a positive fraction can it represent a feasible biological equilibrium. Since the cubic implied by (18.5) can be factored into

$$(l_{AA} - 2l_{Aa} + l_{aa})n_A(n_A - 1)\left(n_A + \frac{l_{Aa} - l_{aa}}{l_{AA} - 2l_{Aa} + l_{aa}}\right),$$

an intermediate stationary solution with coexisting A's and a's will occur if, and only if,

$$l_{Aa} > \text{Max}\,[l_{AA}, l_{aa}]. \tag{18.6}$$

The dark region in Fig. 2's triangle satisfies this requirement. It can be shown that such a mixed equilibrium is globally stable in the sense that

$$\lim_{t\to\infty} n_A(t) = \frac{l_{aa} - l_{Aa}}{l_{AA} - 2l_{Aa} + l_{aa}} \text{ for } 0 < n_A(0) < 1. \tag{18.7}$$

This follows from the fact that, if we superimpose $h[n_A]$ onto Fig. 1, then (8.6)'s condition requires it to form a figure-eight appearance with the 45° line, arching above that line between the origin and their intersection, and arching below that line between the intersection and the point $(n_A, h[n_A]) = (1, 1)$.

Notice that the relation (18.4) encapsulates everything that can be readily stated about individual selection, in terms of the intensive magnitude, $n_A(t)$, alone. The phenomenon of 'crowding' or of 'scarcity limiting the population growth of the group'–words quoted from Frech (1978, p. 181)–is embodied in the monotone-decreasing $\beta[N_1 + N_2]$ function. But this $\beta[N]$ function cancels out of the like-gene or kin-selection relation for $n_A(t)$. Frech nods when asserting (p. 181): 'When crowding is admitted, Tullock's results are simply wrong'. Those results, when they are wrong, are wrong in my models even when there is no possible crowding because $\beta[N]$ is a constant and what biologists call 'r-selection' prevails rather than their 'K-selection'. Cf. Wilson (1975, p. 99) for these definitions. And where Tullock's argument happens to be right–as when AA's help Aa's–it is right *even with* crowding and $\beta'[N] \ll 0$. In none of my models is the p. 185 statement true that 'Crowding actually *reverses* the free rider effect, so that it works to the detriment of the non-altruists'. Neither can the occurrence or non-occurrence of crowding limitations affect the permissibility of mixed equilibrium with positive n_A^* and n_a^*, or the intensity of that mixture.

Again, p. 185 is false in asserting that 'the crowding pressure must be considered in determining the crucial inclusive fitness gain/loss ratio (of Hamilton)'. Of course, the parameters $[l_{AA}, l_{aa}, l_{Aa}]$, and their ratios, might be different at high N densities. But reflection suggests that there are no obvious sign patterns to the partial derivatives of the function of N that would realistically describe $l_{ij}[N]/l_{pq}[N]$ ratios.

What does seem plausible is to make the mortality parameters, l_{ij}, depend on the *ratios* of the genotypes present, writing for example l_{AA} as a function of $[n_{AA}(t), n_{aa}(t)]$. Thus, when AA is predisposed to help AA, if n_{AA} is very small it may be hard to find a like-gene object for your altruism. This opens the gate for threshold-level instabilities: ultimately, if the mutant gene A could get established in some numbers, $n_A(t) \gg 0$, $l_{AA}[n_A]$ might become so large as to make $n_A(t) \to n_A^* \gg 0$; but, for $n_A(0)$ small, $n_A(t) \to 0$ might be inevitable.

I have not in this paper considered such dependencies of l_{ij} on relative proportions. The complexities introduced are sufficiently great to warrant reserving this problem for a more appropriate occasion. This can be done, I believe, with a better conscience because it is realistic to involve *neighborhood* effects in our models in random mating. A rare AA might never meet another AA if *all* individuals in a vast region are imagined to be pooled together. But if we mean by random mating that in each local region individuals mate at random with their near neighbors, then an advantageous mutant A will grow faster in its region of origin: spreading outward from that region, just as a developing crystal spreads out homogeneously, will be regions or demes of increasing A density. Our earlier formulas, when averaged or blended with the pre-mutation version of those formulas, will accurately describe observable developments, thereby permitting us to retain the analytical simplicities of random-mating models.

8. Conclusion

The formulation of *complete* dynamic models enables us to adjudicate between opposing contentions concerning kin selection, and to demonstrate precisely and unambiguously the intuitive conjectures that sprinkle the literature.

A final example may be mentioned. Dawkins (1976, pp. 101–2) objects somewhat opaquely to an attempt, like that in Wilson (1975, Ch. 5), to consider *kin* selection as somehow intermediate between *individual* and *group* selection. Fig. 2's triangle can show that there is a connection between viable like-gene selection and teleological maximum of group fitness.† Wilson might take some comfort from the fact that, when you examine the one of the three roots of (18)'s cubic equation that represents (globally) *stable* asymptotic equilibrium, you find that the individual selection always moves to that equilibrium n_A^* which does yield *maximum* N^* for the group as a whole—as compared to any other n_A^* equilibrium compatible with the specified l's. Thus,

$$\lim_{t\to\infty} N(t) = \beta^{-1}\left[\frac{1}{\text{Max}\,[l_{AA}, l_{aa}, n_A^{*2} l_{AA} + 2n_A^*(1-n_A^*)l_{Aa} + (1-n_A^*)^2 l_{aA}]}\right], \quad (19.1)$$

where

$$n_A^* = \frac{l_{Aa} - l_{aa}}{2l_{Aa} - l_{AA} - l_{aa}} > 0. \quad (19.2)$$

However, this same complete model shows that Wilson would be wrong, and Dawkins right, in the sense that a mutation toward 'altruism' which managed to establish itself could be one which leaves the new N^* worse than before any mutation occurred. Individual selection really doesn't care what it is doing to group fitness, even if sometimes it does add to that. I ought to add that cases like the latter in which individual and group fitness happen to agree are more common than chance alone would account for—precisely because such cases survive to be observed. The same logic that makes individual selection interesting can make group selection interesting. Neo-neo-Darwinists know that.

Acknowledgements

I owe thanks for partial financial aid to an NIH Grant, 2-R01-HD09001-03, the National Science Foundation, 75-04053A01-SOC, and the Sloan Foundation. Intellectual stimulus from Joel Yellin is gratefully acknowledged.

References

Crow, J. F. & Kimura, M. (1970). *An Introduction to Population Genetics*. New York: Harper and Row.
Dawkins, R. (1976). *The Selfish Gene*. Oxford: Oxford University Press.
Frech, H. E., III. (1978). *J. Social Biol. Struct.* **1**, 181.
Hamilton, W. D. (1964). *J.* Theor. Biol. **7**, 1.

† The sorties into non-assortative matings along kin or like-gene lines, analyzed in sections 5 and 6, provide a different defense for the Wilson association. Any method of inbreeding or ingroup altruism that diminishes the net fertility of pairings involving couples not both of the same homozygous genotypes will lead to patterns of individual selection that tend to agree with those of group selection. Thus, let there be relatively few matings of N_{AA} with N_{Aa} or N_{aa} compared to matings with N_{AA}, and likewise for N_{aa}, or let the coefficients $\beta_{Aa}(N)l_{Aa}$ be low compared to $\beta_{AA}(N)l_{AA}$ with the surviving gene being the one that maximizes the *group* fitness parameter $N^* = \text{Max}\,(\beta_{AA}^{-1}[l_{AA}^{-1}], \beta_{aa}^{-1}[l_{aa}^{-1}])$, just as group selection would call for—even though only *individual* selection is involved. The 'purpose' of species differentiation is thus suggested.

Hamilton, W. D. (1971). In *Man and Beast: Comparative Social Behavior*, J. F. Eisenberg and W. S. Dillon, eds., Washington, D.C.: The Smithsonian Institution, 57–91.
May, R. (1973). *Model Ecosystems*. Princeton, N.J.: Princeton University Press.
Samuelson, P. A. (1978). *Proc. Natn. Acad. Sci. U.S.A.* **75,** 4062.
Trivers, R. L. (1971). *Q. Rev. Biol.* **46**, 35.
Tullock, G. (1978). *J. Social. Biol. Struct.* **1**, 3.
Verhulst, P. F. (1844). *Mem. Acad. R. Bruxelles* **18,** 1.
Wilson, E. O. (1975). *Sociobiology: The New Synthesis.* Cambridge, Mass.: Harvard University Press.

FRONTIERS IN DEMOGRAPHIC ECONOMICS†

Modes of Thought in Economics and Biology

By PAUL A. SAMUELSON*

Sociobiology, particularly in connection with its obsessive interest in Hamiltonian altruism, has veered closer towards economics. Reactions within economics against highfalutin borrowings of the methodology of mathematical physics led Alfred Marshall and a host of later writers to hanker for a "biological" approach to political economy. A dispassionate audit of what resulted from this urge would have to report a disappointing paucity up to now of fruitful finds or insights.

But independently of this anti-physicism strain in economics there developed within economics an "evolutionary approach." It is not social Darwinism that I am referring to (although an insidious temptation in that direction is sometimes involved). Rather, several writers explored the notion that—what survives under competition, whether in the jungle or the marketplace, may resemble what is achieved in a maximum problem's solution—even though no participants in the struggle may have any perception and awareness that they as individuals are maximizing anything or awareness that the group ends up doing so. Some names associated with this notion are Armen Alchian (1950), Milton Friedman (1953), and Sidney Winter and Richard Nelson (1982). My *Foundations* (1947) discussions of the stability of surviving forms, borrowed explicitly from the physiologist philosopher L. J. Henderson (1917), is somewhat in this same vein.

There is really no trace of anti-physicism in such an approach. Indeed, the case where soap bubbles unconsciously form the shapes that maximize elaborate integrals in the calculus of variations is very much like the case where leaves and branches of a tree, competing for access to the sunlight, achieve maximal shapes.

When Edward Wilson's manifesto for sociology first came out (1975), I predicted that it would meet a resonant response in Chicago-school economics. Everything has proceeded on schedule to validate my forecast. A hard-boiled economist who shares his income with his child can now cease to feel guilty about this superficial violation of the doctrine of "no free lunch." Hamiltonian inclusive fitness shows that this is just a selfish gene's way of making more of itself—no less respectable a process than that in which I cannily outsell or outproduce my neighbor.

I. Population as Part of Economics

Population analysis is at the intersection of social science and biology. Once upon a time, throughout the heyday of classical economics, demography belonged to political economy. The supply of labor was one of the important endogenous variables in the systems of Smith, Malthus, Mill, and Marx. I have expressed in many places how superficial and empty the concept of a subsistence wage has always been. Although economies in the pre-industrial revolution era differed widely in their per capita levels of real income, writers blithely embraced the paradigm of a horizontal SS supply curve for labor, as if the cost of production and reproduction of labor was an identifiable exogenous parameter. There must be something very tempting about this vacuous notion, since so many different scholars did succumb

†*Discussant:* Gordon Tullock, Public Choice Center, Virginia Polytechnic Institute and State University.

*Department of Economics, Massachusetts Institute of Technology, Cambridge, MA 02139. I owe thanks to the Sloan Foundation for partial support.

to it. And, by the age of Mill and Marx—indeed, even in Ricardo's time and Malthus's later editions—the level of the subsistence wage rate was freed from physiological dimensions and became a dummy variable shot through with conventional standards of life hankered after by (some) workers. At this stage a meaningful false theory had been replaced by a meaningless nontheory that could never be vindicated or rejected by any pattern of historical facts.

II. Paradigm Lost and Regained

One feature of neoclassical economics that distinguishes it from the classical version is the removal of population as a variable subject to economists' equilibrium analysis. Knut Wicksell, an autodidact in a backwater of northern Europe, was the last neoclassicist to preoccupy himself with demography. Marshall, Edwin Cannan, Frank Knight, and A. C. Pigou all were content to have the trend of population growth imported from the fields of sociology and technical demography. The pioneers of modern demography—Alfred J. Lotka, Robert R. Kuczynski, David Glass, Kingsley Davis, Ansley J. Coale, Nathan Keyfitz, and others—were not primarily economists and made little pretence to be. The classical subsistence wage theory is dead forever—dead as a theory of constancy of wage even as applied to the poor regions of Africa and Asia where gross reproduction rates are still enormously high and where population density perceptibly reduces per capita productivity. So the real wage rate is definitely not an exogenous variable for today's economics. Nevertheless, in recent years economists have begun to infiltrate the field of demography. This is part of the imperialist movement in which we economists try to apply our methodologies to everything—to the law, to the sociology of the family (courtship, marriage, divorce, cohabitation). I have in mind writings by such economists as Richard Easterlin, Paul Schultz, Gary Becker and a whole Chicago school, Ronald Lee, Harvey Leibenstein, and many others.

As might be expected, noneconomists have sometimes resented invasion of their turf. Demographers are not as titillated as we are by letting the decision to have or not have a child be likened to the decision to buy or not buy a new car. Easterlin aside, the economists' models did not predict in advance the magnitude of the post-1939 baby boom; nor the post-1957 resumption of the trend toward small family sizes. Slutsky-like analysis of the income-and-family size relationship labors like a lion with concepts of *quality* and alternative earning power of spouses, only to produce the mouse that sometimes these days it is fashionable to have 1 or 2 children and sometimes to have 2 or 3. Weak and hard-to-reproduce evidences for extrasensory perception, people find boring. Similarly, a weak tendency for people to have more or to have less of their children during cyclical recessions does not excite noneconomists.

Economists are smart and hard-working people, now being produced in copious supply relative to the traditional problems feasible to make progress on. Like lemmings oppressed by the workings out of the law of diminishing returns, economists will continue to swarm into the area of demography. Hard work and intelligence will get themselves heard, even when somewhat hamstrung by unpromising initial hypotheses and methods. So, in the end, economists' demography will carve out an ecological niche for itself.

III. Anecdotes and Anecdotes

A Kuhnian expert in the dynamics of scientific schools will observe how sociobiology extrudes into the traditional grounds of the social sciences. Francis Galton, Karl Pearson, and Ronald Fisher sought genetic explanations for differences in performance and class position. Although R. A. Fisher was a genius in genetics and mathematical statistics, his 1930 classic, *The Genetic Theory of Natural Selection*, seems naive in the degree to which he hypothecates a genetic basis for observed differences in behavior. No cogent evidence is given for his views and indeed it is not clear what evidence would be cogent.

We are beginning to identify today, by means of biochemistry and molecular biology, particular diseases with particular singularities in DNA data. But just how the courage observed in offspring is related to the genes for courage inherited from their ancestors is as yet a completely nonoperational question. The same has to be said of "altruism," "intelligence," "sexuality," and most of the attributes discussed in the final chapters of Wilson. These final chapters, I noticed at first reading, depend largely upon hypothetical anecdotes and case studies. Initially, I thought this a weakness of the material dealing with man and with higher primates, an understandable let down from the higher level of scientific rigor characterizing the earlier chapters dealing with the solid facts of animal and plant biology. But on further examination and reflection, I discovered that much of what goes under the name of natural history involves a similar marshaling of selective anecdotes. Chemistry and meteorology are not like that. And neither is economics. In economics we have data aplenty. Our subject is inexact but we do apply quantitative analysis (statistical and otherwise) to formulate and test our hypotheses. When you read about Volterra's struggle for existence between predators and prey, or Wilson's programs for a genetic-based ethics, you are not in the constrained world of fact and interpretative hypothesis but rather in the imaginative realm of speculative possibility.

To be sure, more and better observations will be made available by future scholars working in this vineyard. But the point to be made is how far away we now are from a satisfactory state of knowledge in these between-disciplines domains.

Rather than belabor these points about realism and relevance, I wish for the rest of the present endeavor to deal with purely deductive matters, to illustrate by some examples involving sex ratios how unalike (and alike) are the deductive paradigms common to economics (and perhaps sociology) and those of sociobiology and genetic demography.

IV. Different Moods

There are important differences between a typical genetic process and an economic or sociological process. Genetic evolutionary selection, as when there is survivability advantage in a malarial environment for the genotype that is heterozygous for the sickle cell trait, involves no consciousness or overt purpose: any teleological aspect is an "as if" phenomenon. Ofttimes genetic change is glacially slow, involving hundreds of generations. So to speak, there is no "action at a distance" in demographic genetics: funeral by funeral, mating by mating, each allele must make its way. By contrast, in economics what one firm innovates to do now can in principle sweep the whole industry by quick imitation.

As a typical process in biology, consider a society that relies solely on the rhythm method for its birth control (a specification already shot through with sociology and convention). Given enough time the strategy will partially or wholly self-destruct—as those genetically disposed to have irregular menstrual cycles leave more of their offspring to be represented in subsequent populations. But the biological time scales involved run into hundreds of years, by which time there will have occurred scores of alternations of sociological ideologies.

The sex ratio is a useful topic for our comparison.

V. Balanced Sex Ratio

Human babies are almost as likely to be girls as boys: typically males are in small excess, 106 to 100; but females have lower mortality so that by adulthood the sex ratio is in virtual balance. Animal populations, whether monogamous or not, are observed often to have nearly balanced sex ratios at birth, with whatever unbalance that implies in maturity.

R. A. Fisher gives an ingenious argument why individual natural selection might be expected to evolve toward a balanced sex ratio at birth or conception. Here is my attempt to paraphrase his logic:

> Suppose all genetic strains but yours tend to produce an excess of male over female births. If your strain tends to produce a more balanced sex ratio of

births, other things equal, each of you will be better represented with grandchildren than each of the other crowd —this for the reason that, for producing the grandchildren generation, the totality of *all* sons have exactly equal representation with the totality of *all daughters* (even when the respective totals are unequal!), with the implication that each daughter brings you more in relative grandchildren representation than each son does. So, in each generation, the unbalance of the sex ratio at birth tends to be reduced. Only a sex ratio at birth in balance is immune to evolutionary drift.

To see how mathematical geneticists put this heuristic argument on a rigorous analytical basis, refer to I. Eshel (1975), Joel Yellin and myself (1977), and the Gibbs Lecture of Samuel Karlin (1984). To illustrate the logic it suffices for me here to sketch the rock-bottom simplest case.

VI. Darwin's Mindless Invisible Hand

Adult male and females, $[M, F]$ mate to produce this period's births, B. The fractions $[g, 1-g]$ determine the breakdown of newborns between males and females. The mortality fractions $[p_m, p_f]$ specify how many of the newborn males and females survive to be adults in the next period. With mortality specified, our model is complete once we specify the mating-fertility function determining the output of births out of the inputs of adult males and females. I write this as

$$(1)\quad B(t) = M(t)F(t)b[M(t), F(t)],$$

where $MFb[M, F]$ is much like the economists' production function, being monotone increasing (and perhaps concave). Examples would be $cMF/(M+F)$, $cMF/(\frac{1}{3}M+\frac{2}{3}F)$, $cMF/M^{1/3}F^{1/2}$.

Combine (1) with our mortality and sex-ratio assumptions

$$(2)\quad M(t) = p_m[gB(t-1)],$$
$$F(t) = p_f[(1-g)B(t-1)]$$

to derive an autonomous first-order difference equation determining births and all demographic variables:

$$(3)\quad B(t) = g(1-g)p_m p_f B(t-1)^2 \times b[p_m gB(t-1),\ p_f(1-g)B(t-1)] = \phi[B(t-1)], \qquad t \geq 1.$$

Thus, if $MFb[M, F]$ is first-degree homogeneous, we find Malthus-Lotka exponential growth:

$$(4)\quad B(t) = B(0)R^t,$$
$$B(0) = M(0)F(0)b[M(0), F(0)]$$
$$1 \gtreqless R = g(1-g)p_m p_f b[gp_m(1-g)p_f].$$

If both sexes played a symmetric role in the MFb function, maximal group fitness would require that any superiority of females in mortality ought to be compensated by having an excess of males at birth $g > \frac{1}{2}$. The above Fisherine argument denies that the Invisible Hand of individual selection will lead to this group fitness state, leading instead to balanced sex ratio at birth $(g = \frac{1}{2})$ whatever that implies for unbalance in the adult sex ratio!

Now introduce genetic selection. The old genetic strain that (M, F, B, g) above belonged to, I now write as (M_A, F_A, B_A, g_A). A mutation creates also a new genetic strain, with (M_a, F_a, B_a, g_a). (To keep the discussion simplest, I don't deal with diploid inheritance, which would require us to introduce $[M_{AA}, M_{aa}, M_{Aa}, F_{AA}, \ldots]$, etc.) The axioms of the Fisherine syllogism are very strict:

1. The genotypes differ *only* in sex ratio: $g_A \neq g_a$.
2. The same survival fractions $[p_m, p_f]$ apply to both genotypes.
3. Where fertility-mating is concerned, an individual of genotype A has *exactly* the same properties as any like-sexed, like-aged individual of genotype a. This implies random or nonassortative mating and that total

births, $B = B_A + B_a$, are determined as before by *total* (M, F) numbers:

$$(5)\quad B_A + B_a = (M_A + M_a)(F_A + F_a) \times b[M_A + M_a, F_A + F_a].$$

For short, the last factor on the right will be written as b.

4. The last axiom specifies that offspring of parents both of the same genotype are of that genotype; half the offspring of parents of different genotype average out to be of the father's genotype, half of the mother's, and sampling irregularities are assumed ignorable in a large enough population.

The axioms translate in a straightforward way to give the following first-order difference equation system determining how the vector $[B_A(t), B_a(t)] = [B_A, B_a]$ transforms itself into $[B_A(t+1), B_a(t+1)] = [B_A', B_a']$:

$$(6A)\quad B_a' = \{g_a(1-g_a)B_a^2 + \tfrac{1}{2}[g_A(1-g_a) + g_a(1-g_A)]B_AB_a\}\{p_m p_f b\}.$$

$$(6a)\quad B_A' = \{g_A(1-g_A)B_A^2 + \tfrac{1}{2}[g_A(1-g_a) + g_a(1-g_A)]B_AB_a\}\{p_m p_f b\};$$

Suppose we are interested only in ratios of genotypes, $B_a/B_A = x(t)$, and in the ratio of the sexes at birth, as measured by $g(t)$ the properly weighted average of $[g_A, g_a]$. We can divide (6a) by (6A) and cancel out completely both any differences in the sexes' mortality fractions and any special features of the $b[M, F]$ function that happen to obtain!

We then get the autonomous first-order difference equation in $[x(t), x(t+1)]$:

$$(7)\quad x(t+1) = x(t)\times \frac{g_a(1-g_a)x(t)+\tfrac{1}{2}[g_A(1-g_a)+g_a(1-g_A)]}{g_A(1-g_A)+x(t)\tfrac{1}{2}[g_A(1-g_a)+g_a(1-g_A)]}$$

It can then be shown graphically or analytically that, for $0 < x(0) < \infty$, as $t \to \infty$ the overall sex ratio $g(t) \to \tfrac{1}{2}$ if (g_A, g_a) straddle $\tfrac{1}{2}$; if they are both on one side of $\tfrac{1}{2}$, $g(t) \to$ the (g_A, g_a) nearest to $\tfrac{1}{2}$.

Warning: Balance of the sexes at birth would obtain in this model even if males lived longer than females, $p_m > p_f$, and even if females were more important for nurturing and if a small fraction of the available males would suffice for purposes of procreation. Fitness of the *group*, when it calls for balanced sex ratio of adults or such adult unbalance as implies a strong unbalance at birth, will be sacrificed to that maximizing *individual fitness*. Economists understand well that what's good for each may be bad for all sellers—as in Prisoner's Dilemma, or in perfect competition.[1]

VII. Economic and Sociological Processes

New techniques are making it possible to know in advance what will be the sex of a baby. With knowledge may come power to control. Thus, if one learns by amniocentesis that an embryo is female, and if one prefers a male, an abortion might be decided on. If such customs become common, some far-reaching sociological changes could occur. And these would have economic ramifications.

Nor is all this new. Animal breeders and folklore have held that the probabilities of the different sexes can be affected by timing patterns within the menstrual cycle. Indeed, it is reported in *Too Many Women?* by M. Guttenberg and P. F. Secord (1983) that the

[1]See Fisher (pp. 142–43), W. D. Hamilton (1967), Wilson (pp. 316–17), R. L. Trivers and D. E. Willard (1973), for alternative models that alter conclusions about balanced sex ratios by bringing in considerations of "parental investment" and other interactions between genotype and fertility or mortality functions and parameters. Where an economist would say: "Parents will invest in one sex or the other up to the point of equality of *marginal* advantage," biologists more often speak of equality of investments in the two sexes. Equality of derivatives and equality of ordinates are not always the same thing! Actually, selection would lead to two-thirds of newborns being male if the (M, F) symbols in (1)–(7), instead of meaning (males, females), had to be interpreted to be (pairs of males, single females)—as when each female uses up twice the "energy" or "mass" of one male.

Talmudic practices followed by nineteenth-century orthodox Jews of Eastern Europe resulted in a sex ratio as distorted as 146/100. Also, the mystery of the alleged excess of male births occurring in the World War I epoch may even be resolvable by prosaic factors having to do with scheduling of army leaves and discharges during that period.

Whatever the mixture of science fiction and fact characterizing present knowledge, it is not unlikely that better control over gender is just around the corner for reasons that have nothing to do with genetic change. How do economists model such a process? I shall deal only with an archetypal example.

Scarcity tends toward value. The more women there are, other things equal, the lower might be expected to be their relative wages and lifetime earnings. Feminists might therefore look with some approval upon a future trend toward more sons rather than daughters.

Working against this in the political sphere is that scarcity leads to weakness of voting position and respect. "Expand thy numbers," is the injunction each identity group responds to. Here I shall stay with the economist's case where per capita real incomes are hurt by abundance of numbers.

The simplest case is where the real national product, Q, is produced by the male and female adult labor forces, (M, F), with the imputed real wage to each being determined by respective marginal products:

$$(8) \quad Q = Q[M, F] = Mq[F/M], \quad q' > 0 > q'';$$

$$W_m = \partial Q[M, F]/\partial M = q'[M/F];$$

$$W_f = \partial Q[M, F]/\partial F = \phi(W_m), \quad \phi' < 0.$$

Warning: a polar feminist model that supposed male and female inputs to be identical factors of production would make Q be $c(M + F)$ and necessitate qualifying much of the following analysis.

If some people indulge a strong enough preference for sons, that will skew the adult sex ratio upward, tending to raise female wage rates and lower male rates. If women are no less productive than men, in the sense that $Q[M, F]$ is a symmetric function equalling $Q[F, M]$, then the female wage will exceed the male. Such an elevation in relative remuneration may serve *partially* to reverse the sex ratio imbalance.

One past reason for preferring sons may have been their superior earning power. Although daughters may perhaps be counted on to be more nurturing to you in your old age, sons may have the greater wherewithal to support you. Or the vanity of having the family name carried on may, under our patriarchal culture, be better served by sons. But now that the contrived scarcity of females raises their earnings, you have a new economic motive to indulge your preference for males less.

The new equilibrium, under the postulated symmetry of $Q(M, F)$ and specified preference bias toward males, will be toward an excess of males but an excess limited by their induced impoverishment. The approach to the new equilibrium could involve successive over- and undershoots (as in the economist's "cobweb" model, where each person doesn't realize how many others are also doing the same thing). Or the approach may be gradual in the fashion of adaptive expectations. To keep up with the latest fad, we could even fabricate a rational expectations model: in it, people make a best guess about what the future development of the sex ratio will be; they take account of what is implied by this for relative earnings of their sons, daughters, grandsons and granddaughters, and in terms of this make their decisions; and, miracle of miracles, when all do this they together contrive what it is that they each expect.

Again we discover the possibility of a conflict between *group* (economic) selection and *individual* (economic) selection. If two unfriendly societies compete, the more prosperous one (Sparta) may eliminate the other. However, the $M/(F+M)$ ratio that maximizes total Q (of Athens) may not be the sex ratio that best pleases its representative citizen. So each following self-interest may achieve the destruction of all.

Observation: genetic evolution can work to offset economic unbalancing of the sex ratio. To see this best, suppose $p_f = p_m$ and that only a subset of the population exercise gender control by abortion or otherwise. The groups who do and do not control gender need not be genetically defined. None the less, the dynamic Equation (7) could still apply, provided only we can suppose that when both parents belong to one group, so will the offspring. And that when the parents belong to different groups, half the offspring will be like one parent and half like the other.

What will follow? The Fisher logic will then apply to this non-particulate-inheritance setup. With what result? Our defined process of sociological selection will lead to a rebalancing of the sexes! Indeed, the process can lead to a serendipitous balancing if there are two groups, one favoring sons and one daughters: each can then get their heart's desire, with their numerical weightings evolving to keep the overall birth ratio in balance though no one is aware of the equilibrating process.

Mere deduction cannot prove anything definite about real world sex ratios. If we alter the razor's-edge symmetries of the Fisherine premises—admit nonrandom matings, etc., etc.—we of course can no longer deduce balanced sex ratios. Realistic economic models are not too likely to honor the precise "other things equal" premises implicit in the Fisherine deduction.

VIII. Finale

There is much territory between economics and biology that is still virgin ground. It will be tilled increasingly in the future. We should not be surprised if the first explorations are both crude and pretentious. Wisdom and maturity are the last settlers to arrive in pioneering communities.

REFERENCES

Alchian, Armen A., "Uncertainty, Evolution and Economic Theory," *Journal of Political Economy*, June 1950, *58*, 211–21.

Eshel, I., "Selection on Sex-Ratio and the Evolution of Sex-Determination," *Heredity*, 1975, *34*, 351–61.

Fisher, R. A., *The Genetical Theory of Natural Selection*, Oxford: Clarendon Press, 1930.

Friedman, Milton, *Essays in Positive Economics*, Chicago: Chicago University Press, 1953.

Guttenberg, M. and Secord, P. F., *Too Many Women?—The Sex Ratio Question*, Beverly Hills: Sage Publications, 1983.

Hamilton, W. D., "Extraordinary Sex Ratios," *Science*, 1967, *156*, 477–88.

Henderson, L. J., *The Order of Nature: An Essay*, Cambridge: Harvard University Press, 1917.

Karlin, S., "Mathematical Models, Problems, and Controversies of Evolutionary Theory," *Bulletin (New Series) of The American Mathematical Society*, April 1984, *10*, 221–73.

Samuelson, Paul A., *Foundations of Economic Analysis*, Cambridge: Harvard University Press, 1947.

Trivers, R. L. and Willard, D. E., "Natural Selection of Parental Ability to Vary the Sex Ratio of Offspring," *Science*, 1973, *179*, 90–92.

Wilson, Edward, O., *Sociobiology*, Cambridge: Belknap Press, 1975.

Winter, Sidney G. and Nelson, Richard R., *An Evolutionary Theory of Economic Change*, Cambridge: Belknap Press, 1982.

Yellin, J. and Samuelson, P. A., "Genetic Fitness and the Sex Ratio: Natural Selection in Nonlinear Models of Population Growth," unpublished NIH paper 1977.

Comparison of Linear and Nonlinear Models for Human Population Dynamics*

JOEL YELLIN

School of Humanities and Social Science, Massachusetts Institute of Technology, Cambridge, Massachusetts 02139

AND

PAUL A. SAMUELSON

Department of Economics, Massachusetts Institute of Technology, Cambridge, Massachusetts 02139

Received June 8, 1976

In standard demographic practice, population projections are commonly based on one-sex linear models of the Lotka–Leslie type. We demonstrate here that such projections based solely on time-invariant, age-specific male fertilities and mortalities are incompatible with those based solely on female fertilities and mortalities. This incompatibility obtains even in the singular case where effective male and female fertility functions are equal, and generate equal ultimate rates of growth. In standard demographic practice, the incompatibility is initially masked, since one-sex fertility functions are generally calculated from the same initial-time data and thereby tautologically forced to concur initially; however, with the passage of any finite time, the incompatibility reasserts itself—the only exception being the uninteresting case where the system is already in the stationary age and sex distribution of balanced exponential growth.

An example is adduced of a nonlinear (age-free) system whose true rate of ultimate growth is correctly bracketed by the male and female one-sex rates of ultimate growth. Analysis of more general two-sex models shows that the two one-sex growth rates, calculated for *arbitrary* male and female initial age distributions, need not bracket the true rate. We show, however, that models exist such that with appropriate choices of initial conditions, this bracketing will occur.

1. INTRODUCTION

The standard, linear demographic model (Sharpe and Lotka, 1911; Leslie, 1945) is based on one sex only. In general, such a model provides at best a linear approximation to real, two-sex dynamics. As a linear system, the Lotka–Leslie

* Research supported in part by a grant from the National Institutes of Health (NIH No. 5 R01-HD 09081-02).

model obeys the principle of superposition: when one adds equal increments of fertile-aged individuals of one sex, one observes equal increments of subsequent population. This suggests a manifest absurdity, since adding any increment of individuals of one sex to a world with zero of the other sex can never generate any population whatever.

So long as the sex ratio happens to be nearly normal, the linear approximation may seem to serve well. This explains why Sharpe and Lotka, in their original specification, could work with a male version of the model in computing the intrinsic rate of autonomous increase. Since, however, it is easier to identify an infant's mother than father, and since it is plausible that age-specific female fertility may be more time-invariant than age-specific male fertility, subsequent writers (Lotka, 1913; Dublin and Lotka, 1925; and Kuczynski, 1928)have tended to work with the female version of the model.

Just as demographers were beginning to master the mathematics of the Lotka model, World War I mortality for males resulted in a measurable discrepancy between the calculated male and female *net reproductive rates*, as noted in Lotka (1929). Thus, Kuczynski (1932) calculated that during 1920–1923 France had a female NRR of 0.98, suggesting an ultimate exponential decay of total population; at the same time his male NRR of 1.19, calculated from data of the same period, implied an ultimate positive exponential growth of total population.[1] This dramatic discrepancy was difficult to shrug off. Ultimately, Hajnal (1947), Karmel (1947), Pollard (1948), Kendall (1949), Goodman (1953, 1967), Keyfitz (1968, 1971), Pollard (1973), Das Gupta (1972, 1973, 1976), and many other writers grappled with two-sex models, either with or without explicit marriage functions, and explicit nonlinear functional relationships.

In this paper we continue research on nonlinear two-sex models begun in Yellin and Samuelson (1974). We demonstrate here that, in general, the female-dominant and male-dominant versions of the one-sex model are mutually contradictory. This incompatibility tends to be masked by the fact that, in using the data of the same base year to estimate separate female and male age-specific fertilities, one forces the two models to be compatible for the base year—a spurious agreement lost with the passage of any finite time. A more subtle camouflaging of this basic incompatibility occurs also for any situation in which the true system is fortuitously at or near a stable age distribution: Each one-sex model must then parasitically mirror the true two-sex exponential rate of increase.

Despite the literal inconsistency of the male and female one-sex models—with each other and with the true nonlinear dynamics—one might hope that the two asymptotic rates of growth derived from the male and female models would

[1] A similar but smaller discrepancy between male and female NRR's occurred for the United States: in 1972 and 1973, the male NRR exceeded unity while the female NRR was below unity; after 1973 both dipped below unity.

always bracket the true rate of growth, or at least do so in a wide set of circumstances. As shown below, such bracketing need not obtain. Indeed, we adduce a nonlinear case for which the male and female one-sex rates of increase must be exactly equal (by virtue of symmetry in the postulated male and female mortalities and fertility propensities), with a common value that systematically differs from the true two-sex rate of ultimate increase.

2. Inconsistencies of One-Sex Models

Let $B(t)$ be the total of births at time t, characterized by a fixed male/female sex ratio $(1-\gamma)/\gamma$. Let $B(A, A'; t)$ be the (age-specific) number of births to fathers of age A and mothers of age A', at time t. Then

$$B(t) = \int_\alpha^\beta \int_\alpha^\beta B(A, A'; t)\, dA\, dA', \qquad 0 < \alpha < \beta < \infty, \tag{2.1}$$

where α and β are the earliest and latest ages at which a person of either sex is fertile.

Given time-independent male and female age-specific survival fractions $(p_M(A), p_F(A'))$, then at time t the numbers of males and females of ages A and A', respectively, are related to previous births, B, by

$$N_M(A; t) = (1-\gamma)\, p_M(A)\, B(t-A); \tag{2.2a}$$

$$N_F(A'; t) = \gamma p_F(A')\, B(t-A'). \tag{2.2b}$$

In the standard one-sex models, one fixes age-specific fertility functions, postulating the time-invariant relations:

$$m_M(A) = (1-\gamma) \int_\alpha^\beta B(A, A'; t)\, dA' / N_M(A; t); \tag{2.3a}$$

$$m_F(A') = \gamma \int_\alpha^\beta B(A, A'; t)\, dA / N_F(A'; t). \tag{2.3b}$$

In (2.3), one divides the total male births to males of age A by the number of males of age A; and likewise for the females. This calculation is typically performed for any one time t_0. The resulting fertility functions, $m_M(A)$ and $m_F(A')$, are then assumed to be time-independent for subsequent $t \geqslant t_0$, permitting calculation of the respective, implied ultimate rates of increase. Such an assumption of constant subsequent one-sex fertilities will be shown below to be, in general, at best an approximation to the true population dynamics, even in the absence of genuine historical shifts in mortality and fertility.

Combining (2.2) and (2.3), and using (2.1), one obtains two, rather than one, standard Lotka integral equations:

$$B(t) = \int_{\alpha}^{\beta} m_M(A)\, p_M(A)\, B(t - A)\, dA; \tag{2.4a}$$

$$B(t) = \int_{\alpha}^{\beta} m_F(A)\, p_F(A)\, B(t - A)\, dA. \tag{2.4b}$$

The pair of equations (2.4) *overdetermines* the system, inasmuch as both relations are nontrivially satisfiable only if

$$m_F(A)\, p_F(A) \equiv m_M(A)\, p_M(A). \tag{2.5}$$

In other words, unless the net one-sex effective fertilities are fortuitously such that (2.5) holds, the two one-sex models will be patently incompatible.

The identity (2.5) is a necessary[2] but not a sufficient condition for compatibility of the trajectories actually generated by the alternative one-sex models. In order for two linear integral equations to produce the same solution, it is not enough that they have the same weighting kernels in their integrands: They must also have exactly the same boundary conditions. Therefore, even if (2.5) holds for all $t > t_0$, if the $N_M(A; t_0)$ and $N_F(A'; t_0)$ functions are arbitrarily and independently prescribed, $B(t)$ will be overdetermined for $t > t_0$, being constrained to follow two incompatible paths.

One most easily sees this incompatibility in the following way. By definition, we have for all t, most particularly for t_0 itself, the relations of Coale (1972, p. 55):

$$B(t_0) = \int_{\alpha}^{\beta} \int_{\alpha}^{\beta} B(A, A'; t_0)\, dA\, dA' \tag{2.6}$$

$$= (1 - \gamma)^{-1} \int_{\alpha}^{\beta} m_M(A)\, N_M(A; t_0)\, dA \tag{2.6a}$$

$$= \gamma^{-1} \int_{\alpha}^{\beta} m_F(A')\, N_F(A'; t_0)\, dA'. \tag{2.6b}$$

However, if the equality of (2.6a) and (2.6b) must hold for *arbitrary* initial $N_M(A; t_0)$ and $N_F(A'; t_0)$ functions, we clearly have a contradiction, whether or not (2.5) is valid.

[2] Euler (1761), in a private communication to Süssmilch, assumed that all males and females marry exactly at age 20, all dying at age 40. At ages 22, 24, and 26, they produce one boy and one girl baby. He showed that an ultimate geometric progression of even-year births is implied. Euler's symmetry postulate for the two sexes thus does satisfy the identity (2.5), in the form: $p_M(22) = p_M(22) = p_M(24) = p_F(24) = p_M(26) = p_F(26) = 1$; $p_M(22)\, m_M(22) = p_F(22)\, m_M(22) = 1$; $p_M(24)\, m_M(24) = p_F(24)\, m_F(24) = 1$; $p_M(26)\, m_M(26) = p_F(26)\, m_F(26) = 1$.

The incompatibility of the alternative one-sex equalities of (2.6a) and (2.6b) would be glaring were it not for the custom—a reasonable one—of estimating the $m_M(A)$ and $m_F(A')$ functions a posteriori from the same data at $t = t_0$. Tautologically, this does avoid the (2.6) contradiction, as will be presently demonstrated. But, for any time subsequent to t_0, the contradiction between the mutually incompatible one-sex models reasserts itself.

To demonstrate that in such a case (2.6) is tautologically satisfied, assume the usual procedure of estimating or "identifying" empirical fertilities $\hat{m}_M(A)$ and $\hat{m}_F(A')$ from data for $B(A, A'; t)$, $N_F(A; t)$, $N_M(A; t)$, and γ at $t = t_0$. We then have the defining relations

$$\hat{m}_M(A) = (1 - \gamma) \int_\alpha^\beta B(A, A'; t_0)\, dA'/N_M(A; t_0), \tag{2.7a}$$

$$\hat{m}_F(A') = \gamma \int_\alpha^\beta B(A, A'; t_0)\, dA/N_F(A'; t_0). \tag{2.7b}$$

From (2.7), we then easily see that the identity

$$(1 - \gamma)^{-1} \int_\alpha^\beta \hat{m}_M(A)\, N_M(A; t_0)\, dA = \gamma^{-1} \int_\alpha^\beta \hat{m}_F(A')\, N_F(A'; t_0)\, dA'$$

$$= \int_\alpha^\beta \int_\alpha^\beta B(A, A'; t_0)\, dA\, dA' = B(t_0)$$

is satisfied. Q.E.D.

But now let the system autonomously develop its own post-t_0 development in the usual Lotka manner (2.4b), according to the $\hat{m}_F(A)\, p_F(A)$ schedule. The data so generated cannot agree with those following from (2.4a), using the male $\hat{m}_M(A)\, p_M(A)$ schedule.

Of course, the tautological constraint (2.6) must hold for all t, not just for initial t_0, if *both* one-sex models are to be valid. Specifically, (2.1) and (2.7a) plus (2.7b) imply

$$B(t) \equiv (1 - \gamma)^{-1} \int_\alpha^\beta \hat{m}_M(A)\, N(A; t)\, dA = \gamma^{-1} \int_\alpha^\beta \hat{m}_F(A')\, N_F(A'; t)\, dA', \quad t \geqslant t_0. \tag{2.6c}$$

This requirement in general will be violated by *each* of the one-sex dominant models. In particular, (2.6c) is in disagreement with the determinate motions generated by the male-dominant relations (2.1), (2.2), (2.3a), and arbitrary initial choices $N_M(A; t_0)$ and $N_F(A'; t_0)$. Equation (2.6c) is also inconsistent with the determinate motions generated by the female-dominant relations

(2.1), (2.2), (2.3b), and those same initial age distributions. Any true two-sex model will, in general, also violate (2.6c).

To see explicitly that these statements are correct, we may differentiate the identity (2.6c) with respect to time, obtaining

$$\begin{aligned} dB(t)/dt &= (1-\gamma)^{-1} \int_\alpha^\beta \hat{m}_M(A)\, [\partial N_M(A;t)/\partial t]\, dA \\ &= \frac{1}{1-\gamma} \int_\alpha^\beta \hat{m}_M(A) \left[p_M(A)^{-1} \frac{dp_M(A)}{dA} N_M(A;t) - \frac{\partial N_M(A;t)}{\partial A} \right] dA \\ &= \frac{1}{\gamma} \int_\alpha^\beta \hat{m}_F(A) \left[p_F(A)^{-1} \frac{dp_F(A)}{dA} N_F(A;t) - \frac{\partial N_F(A;t)}{\partial A} \right] dA. \end{aligned} \tag{2.8}$$

The transition from the first to the second line in (2.8) makes use of differentiation of (2.2a); similarly, use of (2.2b) has been made in the last line of (2.8).

If (2.8) is an identity in t, it must certainly be valid at $t = t_0$. At $t = t_0$, this leads to the asserted contradiction: *arbitrarily* assignable $\partial N_M(A; t_0)/\partial A$ and $\partial N_F(A'; t_0)/\partial A'$ functions will violate (2.8), even if (2.5) should be valid. We have used up all the tautological rope available in having already estimated $\hat{m}_M(A)$ and $\hat{m}_F(A')$, and can no longer avoid the asserted contradiction to the simultaneous validity of the parallel one-sex models.

There is, however, a fortuitous singular case where the contradiction has no leverage to reveal itself. Suppose we begin at t_0 with a stable age distribution for both sexes, appropriate to some exponential rate of growth, e^{ut}. The rate u might come from some model remote from the Lotka system. Or it might actually come from a Lotka female-dominant model, with a "true" $m_F(A')$ function. In that case, we know there cannot be a true $m_M(A)$ that obtains under perturbations of the stable age distribution; however, no matter how births are allocated to fathers by age, observations for $t \geqslant t_0$ will yield a "pseudo" $m_M(A)$ function that echoes the $\exp(ut)$ we started with. This echoing will be shown to be purely formal.

Assume that the initial stable age distribution is generated by a nonlinear two-sex model that differs in its qualitative essentials from *either* Lotka model. Despite any such differences, the initial $B(A, A'; t_0)$—assumed to be already in the equilibrium e^{ut} configuration—yields to a naive statistician hell-bent to estimate linear-Lotka parameters, pseudo $\hat{m}_M(A)$ and/or $\hat{m}_F(A')$ functions that each give for the intrinsic or asymptotic rate of increase, the same root, $r = r_M = u$ and $r = r_F = u$, in the standard equations

$$1 = \int_\alpha^\beta p_M(A)\, \hat{m}_M(A) e^{-rA}\, dA = \psi_M(r); \tag{2.9a}$$

$$1 = \int_\alpha^\beta p_F(A')\, \hat{m}_F(A') e^{-rA'}\, dA' = \psi_F(r). \tag{2.9b}$$

To show this, we observe from (2.2) and (2.7) that

$$p_M(A)\,\hat{m}_M(A) = B(t-A)^{-1}\int_\alpha^\beta B(A, A'; t)\,dA'; \tag{2.10a}$$

$$p_F(A)\,\hat{m}_F(A) = B(t-A)^{-1}\int_\alpha^\beta B(A', A; t)\,dA'. \tag{2.10b}$$

Also, for an initial stable age distribution with growth rate u.

$$B(A, A'; t) = B(A, A'; t_0)\exp[u(t-t_0)]; \tag{2.11a}$$

$$B(t) = B(t_0)\exp[u(t-t_0)]. \tag{2.11b}$$

Inserting (2.11) into (2.10), we have

$$p_M(A)\,\hat{m}_M(A) = e^{uA}B(t_0)^{-1}\int_\alpha^\beta B(A, A'; t)\,dA'; \tag{2.12a}$$

$$p_F(A)\,\hat{m}_F(A) = e^{uA}B(t_0)^{-1}\int_\alpha^\beta B(A', A; t)\,dA'. \tag{2.12b}$$

Substituting (2.12) into (2.9) we then have

$$1 = \psi_M(r) = B(t_0)^{-1}\int_\alpha^\beta e^{-rA+uA}\,dA\int_\alpha^\beta B(A, A'; t)\,dA'; \tag{2.13a}$$

$$1 = \psi_F(r) = B(t_0)^{-1}\int_\alpha^\beta e^{-rA+uA}\,dA\int_\alpha^\beta B(A', A; t)\,dA'. \tag{2.13b}$$

Clearly, $r = u$ is a root of both (2.13a) and (2.13b). Explicitly, at $r = u$, (2.13) becomes

$$1 = \psi_M(u) = B(t_0)^{-1}\int_\alpha^\beta\int_\alpha^\beta B(A, A'; t_0)\,dA'\,dA; \tag{2.14a}$$

$$1 = \psi_F(u) = B(t_0)^{-1}\int_\alpha^\beta\int_\alpha^\beta B(A, A'; t_0)\,dA\,dA'. \tag{2.14b}$$

Q.E.D.

When the identity (2.5) holds, we have the stronger identity $\psi_M(r) \equiv \psi_F(r)$ in (2.9), and $r_M = r_F$ regardless of initial conditions. Therefore, even though the initial perturbation in the sex ratio occasioned by a war will lead to alternative and incompatible subsequent dynamic extrapolations from the male and female one-sex models, so long as (2.5) holds, the incompatible models must nonetheless generate the *same ultimate* growth rates, r_M and r_F.

As is well known, the superior mortality experience of females is partially compensated in real life by the excess fraction of boy babies born,

$(1-\gamma)/\gamma \approx 1.05$. Does natural selection perhaps work in the very long run to preserve some tolerable approximation to (2.5), as systems that depart from that identity generate sex-ratio distortions harmful to survivability[3]?

3. Approximation Procedures

Despite their incompatibility with each other and with nonlinear two-sex models, the alternative one-sex models have appeal as possibly giving useful approximations to the unknown true rate of increase [see Lotka (1922), Das Gupta (1976)]. Some limited support for this hope is provided in this section by a blending theorem which follows below, and by an example of a nonlinear system in which the bounding procedure happens to be always valid.

One procedure followed by demographers uneasy with exclusive reliance on one sex alone is to regard reality as some kind of a weighted average of each linear one-sex model. It can be shown that the intrinsic growth rate from such a blend is indeed an internal mean of the one-sex growth rates.

Blending Theorem. *Let $W_0(A)$ and $W_1(A)$ be positive net fertility weighting functions such that*

$$B_i(t) = \int_\alpha^\beta W_i(A)\, B_i(t-A)\, dA, \qquad (i = 0, 1), \tag{3.1}$$

where

$$W_i(A) > 0 \qquad \text{for} \quad 0 < \alpha < \beta < \infty.$$

Consider the blended system

$$B_\omega(t) = \int_\alpha^\beta [\omega W_0(A) + (1-\omega)\, W_1(A)]\, B_\omega(t-A)\, dA,$$

$$\equiv \int_\alpha^\beta W_\omega(A)\, B_\omega(t-A)\, dA, \qquad 0 \leqslant \omega \leqslant 1, \tag{3.2}$$

which has an asymptotic rate of exponential growth r_ω, defined as the sole real root of

$$1 = \int_\alpha^\beta W_\omega(A) e^{-rA}\, dA = \psi(r; \omega). \tag{3.3}$$

[3] There is a considerable literature on the adaptation by natural selection to approximate equality between the numbers of males and females in the fertile years; see, for example, Fisher (1930).

Then the blended system's rate of growth is indeed bounded by the respective one-sex growth rates, r_0 *and* r_1:

$$\mathrm{Min}[r_0, r_1] \leqslant r_\omega \leqslant \mathrm{Max}[r_0, r_1]. \tag{3.4}$$

Proof. By the implicit function theorem

$$\begin{aligned} \frac{dr_\omega}{d\omega} &= -\frac{\partial\psi(r_\omega\,;\,\omega)/\partial\omega}{\partial\psi(r_\omega\,;\,\omega)/\partial r} \\ &= \frac{\psi(r_\omega\,;0) - \psi(r_\omega\,;1)}{-\partial\psi(r_\omega\,;\,\omega)/\partial r}. \end{aligned} \tag{3.5}$$

From the definition of (3.3), the last denominator is clearly positive. Since $\psi_0(r)$ and $\psi_1(r)$ each cross the horizontal axis only once, between r_0 and r_1 they are necessarily of opposite sign, verifying that the numerator is also one-signed for ω on the interval [0, 1]. Therefore, r_ω moves monotonically between the maximum and minimum of (r_0, r_1) as ω moves from 0 to 1 or 1 to 0. Q.E.D.

The following example of a nonlinear two-sex model shows that it is sometimes possible to satisfy the hope of deriving legitimate bounds on the true rate of increase from calculating one-sex rates of increase. Consider the following age-free model of Kendall (1949), involving totals of male and female populations, $N_1(t)$ and $N_2(t)$:

$$dN_1/dt = (1-\gamma)\,B[N_1, N_2] - \delta_1 N_1\,; \tag{3.6a}$$

$$dN_2/dt = \gamma B[N_1, N_2] - \delta_2 N_2, \tag{3.6b}$$

where $(\gamma, 1-\gamma, \delta_1, \delta_2)$ are positive constants. The model also assumes the homogeneity property:

$$B[\lambda N_1, \lambda N_2] = \lambda B[N_1, N_2] \geqslant 0, \tag{3.6c}$$

with

$$B[0, N_2] = 0 = B[N_1, 0];$$

$$\partial B/\partial N_i \geqslant 0 \qquad \text{for} \quad (N_1, N_2) \geqslant 0.$$

By inserting a trial solution, $N_i(t) = c_i e^{ut}$ in (3.6), one observes that this model will have a stable exponential mode proportional to $\exp(u^*t)$ provided roots (u^*, k^*) can be found for

$$\begin{aligned} u &= \frac{(1-\gamma)\,B(1,k)}{1} - \delta_1 = \frac{\gamma B(1,k)}{k} - \delta_2 \\ &= r_1(k) \qquad\qquad\qquad\quad = r_2(k). \end{aligned} \tag{3.7}$$

Since the *calculated* male ultimate growth rate, $r_1(k)$, is an increasing function of k and since the *calculated* female growth rate, $r_2(k)$, is a decreasing function of k, at any initial k different from k^* one of these respective one-sex estimates, $r_i(k)$, will be above u^* and one will be below u^*. The bracketing property is thus seen to hold.

The nonlinear model (3.6) is instructive also as a warning *against* one-sex approximations. Suppose, as in Samuelson [1976, (11.17)] or Keyfitz (1971), we select for $B(N_1, N_2)$ the reasonable form of the harmonic mean, $2[N_1^{-1} + N_2^{-1}]^{-1}$. Then, by making one of the death rates very large, say $\delta_2 \gg \delta_1 > 0$, the system (3.7) will have no root for positive k^* and hence no exponential growth mode. The sex ratio, we know, then goes asymptotically to infinity or to zero: $\lim_{t\to\infty} N_1/N_2 = \infty$ or 0. What then happens if we blindly calculate one-sex intrinsic growth rates at any time t? The calculated $r_i(k)$ will bracket a range of numbers, but since there is no true u^*, positive, negative, or zero, this estimated range is illusory. Furthermore, as the next sections will show, calculating one-sex growth rates cannot in general provide reliable bounds on the true rate.

4. Discrete Time and Age Model

To bring out essentials and avoid the needless complexities of analyzing functionals, we may suppose that time takes on discrete values, $t = \ldots -1, 0, +1, +2, \ldots$. These times are defined so that females and males are fertile only in age periods 1 and 2, which may be thought of as roughly corresponding to age groups 15–30 and 30–45. Thus, as in (2.2),

$$\begin{aligned} N_M(A; t) &= p_M(A)(1-\gamma)\, B(t-A), \qquad (A = 1, 2), \\ N_F(A'; t) &= p_F(A')\, \gamma B(t-A'), \qquad (A' = 1, 2), \end{aligned} \tag{4.1}$$

where A and A' are now discrete age variables, measured in the same periods as t.

In this notation, (2.1) becomes

$$\begin{aligned} B(t) &= \sum_{A=1}^{2} \sum_{A'=1}^{2} B(A, A'; t) \\ &= B(1, 1; t) + B(1, 2; t) + B(2, 1; t) + B(2, 2; t). \end{aligned} \tag{4.2}$$

We now make the usual assumption that the system is scale-free, or homogeneous-first-degree. Thus, for any A and A',

$$B(A, A'; t) = f^{AA'}[N_M(1; t), N_M(2; t), N_F(1; t), N_F(2; t)], \tag{4.3}$$

where

$$f^{AA'}[\lambda x_1, \lambda x_2, \lambda x_3, \lambda x_4] \equiv \lambda f^{AA'}[x_1, x_2, x_3, x_4], \qquad (A, A' = 1, 2)$$

and

$$\begin{aligned} B(t) &= \sum_{A=1}^{2} \sum_{A'=1}^{2} f^{AA'}[N_M(1; t), N_M(2; t), N_F(1; t), N_F(2; t)] \\ &\equiv f[N_M(1; t), N_M(2; t), N_F(1; t), N_F(2; t)], \end{aligned} \tag{4.4}$$

which defines the function f. By homogeneity,

$$f[\lambda x_1, \lambda x_2, \lambda x_3, \lambda x_4] = \lambda f[x_1, x_2, x_3, x_4] \geqslant 0. \tag{4.5}$$

Substituting (4.1) into (4.4), we derive

$$\begin{aligned} B(t) &= f[(1-\gamma)\, p_M(1)\, B(t-1), (1-\gamma)\, p_M(2)\, B(t-2), \\ &\qquad\qquad \gamma p_F(1)\, B(t-1), \gamma p_F(2)\, B(t-2)] \\ &= \beta[B(t-1), B(t-2)], \qquad t \geqslant t_0 + 2, \end{aligned} \tag{4.6}$$

where

$$[B(t-1), B(t-2)] \geqslant 0.$$

Note that (4.6) holds 2 periods or more after the initial $N_M(A; t_0)$ and $N_F(A'; t_0)$ have been arbitrarily prescribed, but does not necessarily apply for $t = t_0$ or $t = t_0 + 1$, when sex ratios can still reflect the initial mortality perturbations.

Defining the growth ratio of births as

$$R(t) = B(t)/B(t-1),$$

we can reduce (4.6) and (4.7) to the first-order relation

$$\begin{aligned} R(t) &= \beta[1, R(t-1)^{-1}], \qquad t \geqslant t_0 + 2 \\ &= \Gamma[R(t-1)], \end{aligned} \tag{4.7}$$

where the function $\Gamma[\ ]$ is defined by (4.7).

If there exists a positive root, $R^* = 1 + r^*$, of

$$R = \Gamma[R], \qquad |\Gamma'[R]| < 1, \tag{4.8}$$

then either r^* [or $\ln(1 + r^*)$] represents the ultimate true intrinsic growth rate of the nonlinear two-sex model. The asymptotic stable age and sex distributions can then be calculated by setting $B(t) = c(1 + r^*)^{t-t_0}$, and applying the relations (4.1).

We reserve detailed treatment of the general case (4.6) for a subsequent paper. Here we wish to analyze some interesting special cases, where the functions $f^{AA'}[\ ]$ depend only on $N_M(A)$ and $N_F(A')$, as certain weighted geometric means or otherwise[4]. In particular, two special patterns are worth examining in detail: the *diagonal* case where fathers and mothers are always of the same age; and the *symmetric* case where male and female mortality and fertility propensities are the same.

5. The Linearizable Diagonal Case

Here, by definition, pairings of male and female of *different* ages are irrelevant for fertility, so that

$$B(t) = f^{11}[N_M(1;\,t),\, N_F(1;\,t)] + f^{22}[N_M(2;\,t),\, N_F(2;\,t)]. \tag{5.1}$$

Using the relations (4.1) and the homogeneity property (4.3) of $f^{AA}[\ ]$ we see that (5.1) becomes the linear relation

$$B(t) = G_1B(t-1) + G_2B(t-2), \qquad t \geqslant t_0 + 2, \tag{5.2}$$

where the time-independent constants G_A are defined by

$$\begin{aligned} G_A &= f^{AA}[(1-\gamma)\, p_M(A)\, B(t-A),\, \gamma p_F(A)\, B(t-A)]/B(t-A) \\ &= f^{AA}[(1-\gamma)\, p_M(A),\, \gamma p_F(A)] \geqslant 0 \qquad (A = 1, 2). \end{aligned} \tag{5.3}$$

Since (5.2) has the standard linear form, we know that the general solution is

$$B(t) = b_1R_1{}^t + b_2R_2{}^t, \tag{5.4}$$

where b_1 and b_2 depend on the initial conditions for B. Inserting (5.4) into (5.2), we observe that the parameters $(R_1\,,\, R_2)$ are roots of the quadratic equation

$$R^2 - G_1R - G_2 = 0. \tag{5.4$'$}$$

It follows easily from (5.4′) that one root, call it R_1, is positive and the other negative, with $-R_1 < R_2 < 0 < R_1$. This further implies the asymptotic behavior

$$\lim_{t\to\infty} B(t)R_1^{-t} = b_1\,.$$

[4] The fact that $f^{AA'}[\ ]$ does not depend on $N_M(A \pm 1;\, t)$ or $N_F(A' \pm 1;\, t)$ is a serious restriction that will have to be dropped in the most general analysis of (4.6).

From (5.4′), we observe that if $G_1 + G_2 = 1$, then $R_1 = 1$, and the growth rate $r^* = 0$.

By making the initial sex ratios sufficiently distorted we can certainly contrive that the male and female one-sex NRR's (and hence, the one-sex ultimate growth rates) calculated for $t_0 \leqslant t < t_0 + 2$ be one above and the other below unity, even when $G_1 + G_2 = 1$ and the true ultimate growth rate of the population is zero.

However, provided there initially exist some males and females of the same age, after 2 periods at most, when $t \geqslant t_0 + 2$, the sex ratios will have normalized. We will then have, for all subsequent t,

$$\begin{aligned} \hat{m}_M(A) &= \frac{(1-\gamma) f^{AA}[(1-\gamma)\, p_M(A), \gamma p_F(A)]}{(1-\gamma)\, p_M(A)}, \qquad t \geqslant t_0 + 2 \\ &= G_A/p_M(A), \qquad (A = 1, 2) \end{aligned} \tag{5.5a}$$

and similarly,

$$\hat{m}_F(A) = G_A/p_F(A). \tag{5.5b}$$

Clearly, from (5.5) the one-sex models do satisfy—for the diagonal case (5.1)—the crucial identity (2.5). Therefore, feeding into them the same initial $B(t_0 - 1)$ and $B(t_0 - 2)$ values will generate for the male and female models identical $B(t)$ values ever afterward, and the *same* values for all demographic variables. Moreover, both one-sex models now satisfy precisely the same linear relation as the correct diagonal two-sex models

$$\begin{aligned} B(t) &= \hat{m}_M(1)\, p_M(1)\, B(t-1) + \hat{m}_M(2)\, p_M(2)\, B(t-2) \\ &\equiv \hat{m}_F(1)\, p_F(1)\, B(t-1) + \hat{m}_F(2)\, p_F(2)\, B(t-2) \\ &\equiv G_1 B(t-1) + G_2 B(t-2), \qquad t \geqslant t_0 + 2 \end{aligned} \tag{5.6}$$

for common initial values $[B(t_0), B(t_0 + 1)]$. The model of Euler (1761) (mentioned in footnote 2), has the form of the diagonal case.

This diagonal case is the most favorable one for one-sex approximations. For it, once the initial perturbations have had time to disappear, the one-sex models do more than predict the correct *ultimate* two-sex growth rate: they actually give correct *transient* growth patterns. Of course, the diagonal model is not realistic, since parents in real life often do have different ages.

6. The Symmetric Two-Sex Case

Just as the diagonal model is most favorable for one-sex approximations, our present case is in a sense the most disastrous one for would-be bracketeers.

The basic postulate here is the relation

$$B(1, 2; t) \equiv B(2, 1; t), \tag{6.1}$$

which implies that marriages between older women and younger men produce equal numbers of offspring as do marriages between older men and younger women. From (2.3) or (2.10), we observe that—provided we begin at a time t which has been preceded by at least 2 periods in which the normal mortality coefficients $[p_M(A), p_F(A)]$ are applicable—the one-sex effective fertility coefficients are equal for the male and female case, and the identity (2.5) is satisfied. Under those circumstances the one-sex ultimate growth rates have a common value

$$R_0{}^* = 1 + r_M{}^* = 1 + r_F{}^*. \tag{6.2}$$

Now the question of bracketing becomes equivalent to whether the $R_0{}^*$, calculated, as in (5.5), for *arbitrary* $[B(t_0), B(t_0 + 1)]$ in

$$\begin{aligned}&[N_M(A; t_0 + 2), N_F(A'; t_0 + 2)]\\ &\quad = [(1 - \gamma)\, p_M(A)\, B(t_0 + 2 - A), \gamma p_F(A')\, B(t_0 + 2 - A')],\end{aligned}$$

is equal to the true value R^* asymptotically characterizing the nonlinear system.

We shall show that no matter how many periods we project the true symmetric model forward, if we do not begin in stable growth, the one-sex models will always produce a systematically biased estimate of that growth. Fortunately, the degree of bias attenuates as the chosen initial conditions approach the stable configuration.

To specify an easy example of such nonbracketing, we can work through the symmetric case for the "geometric-mean" family (whose general analysis is provided in Section 8 below). With the choice of geometric-mean form for $f^{AA'}[\ ]$, we have

$$\begin{aligned}&f^{AA'}[(1 - \gamma)\, p_M(A)\, B(t - A), \gamma p_F(A')\, B(t - A')]\\ &\quad = [f_A B(t - A)]^{1/2}[f_{A'} B(t - A')]^{1/2}, \qquad (A, A' = 1, 2),\end{aligned} \tag{6.3}$$

where we have introduced the pair of positive coefficients (f_1, f_2).

Note that (6.3) implies, in addition to the sex-symmetry constraint (6.1), the additional age-symmetry relation

$$B(1, 1; t)/B(1, 2; t) \equiv B(2, 1; t)/B(2, 2; t). \tag{6.4}$$

Following (2.1) and (4.2), we can now use (6.3) to derive the basic dynamical equation

$$\begin{aligned} B(t) &= \sum_{A=1}^{2} \sum_{A'=1}^{2} B(A, A'; t) \\ &= f_1 B(t-1) + 2 f_1^{1/2} f_2^{1/2} B(t-1)^{1/2} B(t-2)^{1/2} + f_2 B(t-2). \end{aligned} \tag{6.5}$$

The nonlinear system (6.5) can be converted into an *exact linear system* by the transformation of variables:

$$z(t) = B(t)^{1/2}. \tag{6.6}$$

Then (6.5) becomes the *linear difference equation*

$$z(t) = f_1^{1/2} z(t-1) + f_2^{1/2} z(t-2), \qquad t \geqslant t_0 + 2. \tag{6.7}$$

The solution of (6.7) is again of standard form

$$z(t) = c_1 \rho_1{}^t + c_2 \rho_2{}^t, \tag{6.8}$$

where the ρ_i are the roots of

$$\psi(\rho) = \rho^2 - f_1^{1/2}\rho - f_2^{1/2} = 0, \tag{6.9}$$

with

$$-\rho_1 < \rho_2 < 0 < \rho_1,$$

as in (5.4′) above. Therefore, the general solution for $B(t)$ is

$$B(t) = z(t)^2 = c_1^2 \rho_1^{2t} + c_2^2 \rho_2^{2t} + 2 c_1 c_2 \rho_1^t \rho_2^t, \tag{6.10}$$

with the asymptotic behavior

$$\lim_{t\to\infty} B(t)(\rho_1{}^2)^{-t} = \lim_{t\to\infty} B(t)(R^*)^{-t} = \text{constant}. \tag{6.11}$$

It is convenient to prepare the system so that, without loss of generality $\rho_1 \equiv R^* = 1$ (and $r^* = 0$). To do so, we work with a new dynamic variable $B(t)(R^*)^{-t}$; in terms of this variable, the new (6.5) has coefficients (f_1, f_2) satisfying

$$f_1^{1/2} + f_2^{1/2} = 1. \tag{6.12}$$

For comparative purposes, we must now compute the ultimate growth rate of the one-sex models whose common dynamic equation (2.4) has the form

$$B(t) = g_1 B(t-1) + g_2 B(t-2). \tag{6.13}$$

Here the coefficients g_i are defined from the chosen initial conditions, in accordance with (2.10) and (6.4), as

$$g_A = p_F(A)\, m_F(A) = p_M(A)\, m_M(A) = \frac{B(A, 1; t_0) + B(A, 2; t_0)}{B(t_0 - A)}. \tag{6.14}$$

The dominant one-sex growth rate implied by (6.13) is then

$$R_0^* = \tfrac{1}{2}[g_1 + (g_1^2 + 4g_2)^{1/2}], \tag{6.15}$$

which gives $R_0^* \gtreqless 1$ depending on whether $g_1 + g_2 \gtreqless 1$.

For the geometric-mean case (6.3), the calculated g's are related to the f's, and to the initial conditions on $B(t)$, by

$$g_1 = f_1 + [f_1 f_2 B(t_0 - 2)/B(t_0 - 1)]^{1/2}; \tag{6.16a}$$

$$g_2 = f_2 + [f_1 f_2 B(t_0 - 1)/B(t_0 - 2)]^{1/2}. \tag{6.16b}$$

If we use the constraint $f_1^{1/2} + f_2^{1/2} = 1$, then from (6.15) and (6.16) R_0^* can be written in the form

$$R_0^* = H[f_1, B(t_0 - 2)/B(t_0 - 1)]. \tag{6.17}$$

It is straightforward to show by explicit calculation that

$$\left.\frac{\partial H[x, y]}{\partial y}\right|_{y=1} = 0; \qquad \frac{\partial^2 H[x, y]}{\partial y^2} > 0, \tag{6.18}$$

so that $\hat{R}_0^* \geqslant R^* = 1$, independently of the value of f_1 and of the initial conditions. The one-sex estimated growth rates are therefore systematically positively biased, except in the trivial initial stable configuration in which $B(t_0 - 2)/B(t_0 - 1) = 1$, where $\partial H[f_1, 1]/\partial y = 0$ and $R_0^* = 1$.

It is important to note that the positive growth bias evidenced in the example above is not an inevitable property of the general symmetric case.

For example, consider the somewhat more general situation in which

$$\begin{aligned} B(t) &= G_1 B(t - 1) + G_2 B(t - 2) + 2\phi[B(t - 1), B(t - 2)] \\ &= G_1 B(t - 1) + G_2 B(t - 2) + 2\phi[B(t - 2), B(t - 1)], \end{aligned} \tag{6.19}$$

where (G_1, G_2) are defined as in (5.2), and ϕ is a homogeneous, symmetric function

$$\begin{aligned} \phi[B(t - 1), B(t - 2)] &= f^{12}[(1 - \gamma)\, p_M(1)\, B(t - 1), \gamma p_F(2)\, B(t - 2)] \\ &= f^{21}[(1 - \gamma)\, p_M(2)\, B(t - 2), \gamma p_F(1)\, B(t - 1)] \\ &\equiv \phi[B(t - 2), B(t - 1)]. \end{aligned} \tag{6.20}$$

It is straightforward to show that—though there is systematic bias of the common one-sex growth rate—the algebraic sign of that bias is dependent on the detailed properties of ϕ.

To verify that this is the case, we may once again prepare the nonlinear system (6.19) so that it neither grows nor decays, with $R^* = 1$ and $r^* = 0$. Following (6.13) and (6.14), it is then convenient to define the quantity

$$p_M(1)\, m_M(1) + p_M(2)\, m_M(2)$$

$$= \frac{B(1, 1; t_0) + B(1, 2; t_0)}{B(t_0 - 1)} + \frac{B(2, 1; t_0) + B(2, 2; t_0)}{B(t_0 - 2)} \tag{6.21}$$

$$= G_1 + \phi[1, R_0^{-1}] + \phi[R_0, 1] + G_2 = \mu(R_0),$$

which represents the common, one-sex NRR. For $R_0 = R^* = 1$, as in the stable age distribution,

$$\mu(R^*) = 1. \tag{6.22}$$

However, in the neighborhood of $R_0 = 1$, $\mu(R_0)$ must deviate from 1. Writing $\partial\phi[x_1, x_2]/\partial x_i$ as $\phi_i[x_1, x_2]$, we find

$$\mu'(R_0) = \phi_1[R_0, 1] - \phi_2[1, R_0^{-1}]R_0^{-2}, \tag{6.23}$$

so that

$$\mu'(1) = \phi_1[1, 1] - \phi_2[1, 1] = 0, \tag{6.24}$$

by the symmetry of ϕ.

Furthermore,

$$\mu''(R_0) = \phi_{11}[R_0, 1] + \phi_{22}[1, R_0^{-1}]R_0^{-4} + 2\phi_2[1, R_0^{-1}]R_0^{-3};$$

so that

$$\mu''(1) = 2\phi_{11}[1, 1] + \phi[1, 1]. \tag{6.25}$$

In (6.25) the symmetry and homogeneity of ϕ have again been used. There is no reason for $\mu''(1)$ to vanish, even though its first term may well be negative. Consequently, in the neighborhood of the stable age distribution, the one-sex models will almost always give rate of growth estimates that are *both in excess* or are *both* in *deficiency*, even though they must agree with each other in the symmetric case.

7. The General Theorem

We now return to the general case, which is neither *diagonal* nor *symmetric*. We state for it the following:

Theorem 1. (i) *Starting from arbitrary initial conditions,* $[N_M(A;t_0),$ $N_F(A';t_0)]$, *the one-sex growth rates calculated for* t_0 *will* not *necessarily bracket the true rate.*

(ii) *However, except for the singular symmetric case* (6.1), *there will always be a choice of initial conditions on* $R(t_0-1)=B(t_0-1)/B(t_0-2)$ *sufficiently close to the stable* $R^*=1+r^*$ *so that the two calculated one-sex rates of growth,* $1+r_M{}^*$ *and* $1+r_F{}^*$, *do bracket the true rate of ultimate growth,* $1+r^*$.

An example of extreme asymmetry will illustrate the meaning and scope of this theorem. Suppose older women display zero fertility; and further suppose that some young mothers have children with young fathers, and some with older fathers. The system is then neither diagonal nor symmetric.

Equation (4.2) then takes the form

$$\begin{aligned} B(t) &= B(1,1;t)+B(2,1;t) \\ &= F_1N_M(1;t)^{1/2}N_F(1;t)^{1/2}+F_2N_M(2;t)^{1/2}N_F(1;t)^{1/2}, \qquad t\geqslant t_0. \end{aligned} \tag{7.1a}$$

Here, (F_1, F_2) are constants, and we again use the geometric-mean form for our fertility relations. For $t\geqslant t_0+2$, (7.1a) becomes

$$B(t)=GB(t-1)+HB(t-1)^{1/2}\,B(t-2)^{1/2}, \qquad t\geqslant t_0+2, \tag{7.1b}$$

where G and H are constants defined by relations like (5.3).

We may prepare the system, as before, so that

$$r^*=0, \qquad 1+r^*=R^*=1=G+H. \tag{7.2}$$

To illustrate part (i) of the theorem above, we take a numerical example, with $G=H=\frac{1}{2}$.

Using our license to select $[N_M(1;t_0), N_M(2;t_0), N_F(1;t_0)]$ arbitrarily, we may set them at, say, [1, .25, 9]; for numerical convenience we also set $[p_M(1),$ $p_M(2), p_F(1), p_F(2)]=[1,1,1,1]$, and $\gamma=1-\gamma=\frac{1}{2}$. Now we can verify that the one-sex NRR's do fail to bracket unity, instead both exceeding unity. Explicitly, the male one-sex model gives

$$\begin{aligned} B(t) &= \hat{m}_M(1)\,p_M(1)\,B(t-1)+\hat{m}_M(2)\,p_M(2)\,B(t-2) \\ &= 2B(t-1)+\tfrac{1}{6}B(t-2); \end{aligned} \tag{7.3a}$$

while the female model gives

$$\begin{aligned} B(t) &= \hat{m}_F(1)\, p_F(1)\, B(t-1) + \hat{m}_F(2)\, p_F(2)\, B(t-2) \\ &= 1.75\, B(t-1), \end{aligned} \tag{7.3b}$$

where we have used (2.10) and (7.1). The growth rates are

$$1 + r_M = 1 + (7/6)^{1/2}; \tag{7.4a}$$

$$1 + r_F = 1.75, \tag{7.4b}$$

which explicitly verifies the assertion that the one-sex NRR's can deviate from 1 in the same direction.

To illustrate part (ii) of the theorem, we will show that, for any $t \geqslant t_0 + 2$, the one-sex growth rates for this completely asymmetric case *always* bracket the true rate $R^* = 1$.

From (7.1) and (2.10), the one-sex dynamical equations become, for $R_0 = B(t_0 - 1)/B(t_0 - 2)$

$$B(t) = GB(t-1) + (1-G)/(R_0)^{1/2} \cdot B(t-2); \tag{7.5a}$$

$$B(t) = [G + (1-G)(R_0)^{1/2}]\, B(t-1). \tag{7.5b}$$

The relations (7.5) yield the ultimate growth rates

$$R_M^* = G + (1-G)(R_0)^{1/2}; \tag{7.6a}$$

$$R_F^* = \frac{G + [G^2 + 4(1-G)R_0^{-1/2}]^{1/2}}{2}. \tag{7.6b}$$

From (7.6), it is easy to verify that, for every R_0 differing from $1 = R^* = 1 + r^*$, the NRR's for males and females will be on opposite sides of unity. Hence, one-sex bracketing is assured as soon as the initial mortality perturbations disappear.

As we move toward symmetry from this case of extreme asymmetry, the region for R_0 around R^* for which bracketing is assured naturally shrinks (shrinking away to nothing at perfect symmetry).

8. The General Geometric-Mean Case

It is worthwhile to summarize the properties of the general "geometric-mean" case:

$$B(t) = \sum_{A=1}^{2} \sum_{A'=1}^{2} F(A, A')\, B(t-A)^{1/2}\, B(t-A')^{1/2}, \qquad t \geqslant t_0. \tag{8.1}$$

An exponential solution of (8.1) exists, of the form $B(t) = b_1(R^*)^t = b_1\rho_1^{2t}$ where ρ_1 is the real positive root of the fourth-degree polynomial

$$1 = F(1, 1)\,\rho^{-2} + [F(1, 2) + F(2, 1)]\,\rho^{-3} + F(2, 2)\,\rho^{-4} = \psi(\rho). \qquad (8.2)$$

For $B(t_0 - 1)/B(t_0 - 2) = R_0$ sufficiently near the true R^*, the calculated one-sex growth rates will, singular symmetric cases aside, bracket R^*. Also, given an initial stable distribution with $R_0 = R^* = 1 + r^*$, one may verify that the growth rates $1 + r_M$, $1 + r_F$, and $1 + r^*$, will all coalesce.

Remark. A fourth-degree polynomial has 4 roots, $(\rho_1, \rho_2, \rho_3, \rho_4)$, some of them possibly complex. It is tempting, extrapolating uncritically from linear analysis, to assert that any dynamic path for $B(t)$ can be written in the series form

$$B(t) = b_1\rho_1^{2t} + b_2\rho_2^{2t} + b_3\rho_3^{2t} + b_4\rho_4^{2t}. \qquad (8.3)$$

This is nonsense for a true nonlinear system. Only ρ_1^2 has genuine significance for an exact real-time solution or for an asymptotic solution. Any other solution of the form ρ_{1+i}^{2t} does *not* correspond to an admissible, nonnegative $B(t)$. Also, since the principle of superposition does *not* hold for a nonlinear system, weighted sums of two or more such distinct exponentials will not be solutions of the nonlinear recurrence relation (8.1), even if it is possible for each of them to be.

Actually, along with $\rho_1^2 = R^*$, there is another relevant "root"—call it R_2—but it is not one of the ρ_{1+i}^2 when the dynamic system is nonlinear. This secondary growth rate is the nonpositive root of the *characteristic quadratic equation* of the *associated linear system*—the linear difference-equation system whose solutions approximate closely to the true time development of the divergences from $B(t) = b(1 + r^*)^t$, when those divergences are small. That associated linear system is defined, for the general nonlinear case (4.6), as

$$x(t) = \beta_1 x(t - 1) + \beta_2 x(t - 2), \qquad (8.4)$$

where

$$\beta_i = \partial\left[\sum_{A=1}^{2}\sum_{A'=1}^{2} F(A, A')\,B(t - A)^{1/2}\,B(t - A')^{1/2}\right]\Big/\partial B(t - i), \qquad (i = 1, 2),$$

evaluated at $B(t - 1)/B(t - 2) = R^*$.

The characteristic quadratic equation associated with (8.4) is

$$\begin{aligned} 0 &= 1 - \beta_1 R^{-1} + \beta_2 R^{-2} \\ &= (1 - R^* R^{-1})(1 - R_2 R^{-1}), \qquad -R^* < R_2 < 0 < R^*. \end{aligned} \qquad (8.5)$$

The significance of R_2 results from the following property of the real-time solutions of the true nonlinear system (8.1). When (8.1) holds, the ratio $B(t)/B(t-1) = R(t)$ must satisfy a nonlinear relation of the form (4.7). Any such relation can be shown to lead to the asymptotic property

$$\lim_{t\to\infty} \frac{R(t) - R^*}{R(t-1) - R^*} \cdot R^* = R^* \Gamma'[R^*] = R_2 < 0. \tag{8.6}$$

There is no relation between R_2 and any of the nondominant roots, $(\rho_2^2, \rho_3^2, \rho_4^2)$, of (8.3).

An important caveat is in order in connection with the geometric-mean model (8.1). As already remarked, *it is not realistic for* $B(A, A'; t)$ *to depend only on* $N_M(A; t)$ *and* $N_F(A'; t)$. Whenever monogamy is important, the more there are of either sex of ages *other than* A and A', the greater the chance that they will attract some of the existing individuals of ages A and A', and thereby bar people of those ages from having a child together.

The harmonic mean function

$$B(t) = \sum_{A=1}^{2} \sum_{A'=1}^{2} F(A, A') \, [.5N_M(A; t)^{-1} + .5N_F(A'; t)^{-1}]^{-1} \tag{8.7}$$

has certain advantages of realism over models based on the geometric mean, $N_M(A; t)^{1/2} N_F(A'; t)^{1/2}$. In the latter, if $N_M(1; t)$ is great enough, indefinitely more births $B(1, A'; t)$ occur than there are potential mothers $N_F(A'; t)$. The harmonic mean lets any one sex serve ultimately as a bottleneck, which seems only realistic.

It can be verified that the harmonic and geometric means will have virtually identical properties near the stable age distribution. In a forthcoming paper we show that when $B(A, A'; t)$ are realistically made to depend on the numbers of males and females of ages *other than* A and A', then even the *existence* of an exponential growth rate and of a stable distribution may be denied, a nonlinear effect already noted in Yellin and Samuelson (1974), Samuelson (1976a), and discussed in connection with Eq. (3.7) above.

References

Coale, A. J. 1972. "The Growth and Structure of Human Populations: A Mathematical Investigation," Princeton Univ. Press, Princeton, N.J.

Das Gupta, P. 1972. On two-sex models leading to stable populations, *Theor. Popul. Biol.* **3**, 358–357.

Das Gupta, P. 1973. Growth of U.S. Population, 1940–1971, in the light of an interactive two-sex mode, *Demography* **10**, 543–565.

Das Gupta, P. 1976. An interactive nonrandom-mating two-sex model whose intrinsic growth rate lies between one-sex rates, *Theor. Popul. Biol.* **9**, 46–57.

Dublin, L. I. and Lotka, A. J. 1925. On the true rate of natural increase of a population, *J. Amer. Statist. Assoc.* **20**, 305–339.
Euler, L. 1761. Private communication to Süssmilch, described, *in* "Contributions to Mathematical Demography" (Smith, David and Keyfitz, Nathan, Eds.), Springer-Verlag, Berlin/Heidelberg/New York.
Fisher, R. A. 1930. "The Genetical Theory of Natural Selection," Oxford Univ. Press (Clarendon), London.
Goodman, L. A. 1953. Population growth of the sexes, *Biometrics* **9**, 212–225.
Goodman, L. A. 1967. On the age-sex composition of the population that would result from given fertility and mortality conditions, *Demography* **4**, 423–441.
Hajnal, J. 1947. Aspects of recent trends in marriage in England and Wales, *Popul. Stud.* **1**, 72–92.
Karmel, P. H. 1947. The relation between male and female reproduction rates, *Popul. Stud.* **1**, 249–274.
Kendall, D. G. 1949. Stochastic processes and population growth, *J. Roy. Statist. Soc. Ser. B* **11**, 230–264.
Keyfitz, N. 1968. "Introduction to the Mathematics of Population," Addison-Wesley, Reading, Mass.
Keyfitz, N. 1971. "The Mathematics of Sex and Marriage," Proceedings of the Sixth Berkeley Symposium on Mathematical Statistics and Probability, Vol. 4, pp. 89–108.
Kuczynski, R. R. 1928. "The Balance of Births and Deaths, Vol. I: Western and Northern Europe," Macmillan, New York.
Kuczynski, R. R. 1931–1932. "Fertility and Reproduction," Falcon Press, New York.
Lotka, A. J. 1913. A natural population norm, *J. Wash. Acad. Sci.* **3**, 241–248; 289–292.
Lotka, A. J. 1929. Review of "The Balance of Births and Deaths, Vol. I" (R. Kuczynski), *J. Amer. Statist. Assoc.* **24**, 332–333.
Pollard, J. H. 1973. "Mathematical Models for the Growth of Human Populations," Cambridge Univ. Press, Cambridge, Mass.
Samuelson, P. A. 1976. Time symmetry and asymmetry in population and general dynamic systems, *Theor. Popul. Biol.* **9**, 82–122.
Sharpe, F. R. and Lotka, A. J. 1911. A problem in age-distribution, *Phil. Mag.* **21**, 435–438.
Yellin, J. and Samuelson, P. A. 1974. A dynamical model for human population, *Proc. Nat. Acad. Sci. USA* **71**, 2813–2817.

FISHER'S "REPRODUCTIVE VALUE" AS AN ECONOMIC SPECIMEN IN MERTON'S ZOO*

Paul A. Samuelson

Department of Economics
Massachusetts Institute of Technology
Cambridge, Massachusetts 02139

Robert K. Merton released from the closet the truth that scientists are human and work for the coin of applause from other scientists for their own innovations. Just as men will steal for bread and the ducats to buy bread, scholars will sometimes break the rules of the club in their pursuit of fame; or bend the rules; or put away temptation to do so, reluctantly if not firmly.

Nor is this surprising. Any stakes worth fighting for are worth being tempted about. I like to repeat my conversation with a dear colleague, H. A. Freeman. "Harold," I asked, "if the Devil came to you and in return for your immortal soul offered you a theorem, would you accept the Faustian bargain?" He replied without hesitation, "No." Then he went on to add, "But I would for an *inequality*."

Crimes are only in the eyes of the jury. I spoke of the rules of the club. The canons of scientists' etiquette were not ready-made on the seventh day of Genesis. If I knew in the sixteenth century the formula to solve a cubic equation, I wouldn't reveal it to you. I'd conquer examples with it for kudos and lucre. To protect my priority, I'd enunciate an anagram that conveyed nothing to the ignorant but proved to a Leibnitz or Wallace come-lately that my flag was already at the North Pole awaiting his arrival.

Clifford Truesdell claims that his hero Euler was the first scholar who tried in his writings to provide accurate accounts of just what his predecessors had done, citing earlier authors not merely for their errors, omissions and imperfections, but to inform the reader of the correct state of development of the subject under consideration. This suggests that present standards are but two centuries old, which is not long enough apparently for them to have penetrated all branches of discourse or reached all practitioners in any.

Crime for the most part really doesn't pay. The bank teller's lavish weekend has a price tag of hardtack for a decade. A fudged experiment or plagiarized lemma has a half-life of one academic semester. The talent needed to make crime pay can earn higher economic rent plowing the straight and narrow furrow.

To the sociologist and historian of science what is of interest is not the gross felony or even the indictable misdemeanor. Rather it is the study of the different styles of conduct open to the scientist who knows how to operate within the laws of the game. One is reminded of the fine art of tax *avoidance*, which is never to be mistaken for the crime of tax *evasion*.

People differ. A few are completely generous. They share their caviar with casual strangers, present their graduate students with crucial experiments and seminal hypotheses, and in the guise of anonymous referees reformulate whole articles. Again, Euler comes to mind. From the babbling of Maupertuis about teleology, Euler distilled the Principle of Least Action and presented it as Maupertuis' brain child. When he

*This work was supported in part by grants from the National Science Foundation 75-040530A01-SOC, National Institutes of Health 2-RO1-HD09081-03, and the Sloan Foundation.

learned that the brilliant young Lagrange was about to publish researches on the calculus of variations, Euler held up his own deep memoir on the subject so as not to dim the light of the rising sun.

Euler could afford to be generous, you will say. He had an infinite treasure-house of good things. True. But John Bernoulli, perhaps Euler's most profound contemporary (although the claims of his brother James and son Daniel are comparably great), also had a treasure-house. Yet John proposed the famous brachistochrone problem in the calculus of variations primarily to try to show up his older brother James (he failed in this fratricidal ploy†); and John even pre-dated his unpublished writings in order to rob his own son of merited scientific priorities. If we dismiss John as pathological, we are given pause by the case of Gauss. No one was more generously endowed with genius and scholarly contributions than Gauss. Still the record is skimpy when it comes to generous acts on his part: when Wolfgang Bolyai, one of his few friends, reported that his son Johann had discovered and axiomatized non-Euclidian geometry, instead of congratulating the young genius for his genius, Gauss merely wrote back that his own unpublished works on the subject had followed the same track years before. Even if Johann Bolyai had not been depressed by this beyond the point of consummated suicide, Gauss's admirers will admit that truth is no defence for such a crime.

My interest on this occasion is neither with saints nor rascals. The former are all too few. The latter are born all too plentiful. Thus, Laplace was unscrupulous to a fault in appropriating the work of others and sufficiently absent-minded to plagiarize his own earlier works. (Yet before we throw stones, we are given pause by the fact that Laplace was uniquely able to add value to his purloined rubies and to recognize their intrinsic worth.) In my field of economics, the great Swedish scholar of the World War I epoch, Gustav Cassel, was notorious for never acknowledging the sources of his contributions. "Ten per cent Leon Walras and 90 per cent water," is how my old teacher Schumpeter used to dismiss Cassel. Cassel's secretary, in her biography of him, attributed his bad scholarly manners to Cassel's hatred of his father, which is supposed to have blocked from his memory all he learned in his earlier decades (and, apparently, to have fastened that habit on him for life!).

Foibles of Genius

Here I want to concentrate on the pattern of men who are so highly original that they find it more economical to work out a thing themselves, even if in doing so they are repeating without acknowledgment what is already in the literature—easier to forge a ballbearing than find one in inventory. Albert Einstein was such a scholar. So, I believe, was Enrico Fermi. R. A. Fisher, who revolutionized both mathematical statistics and neo-Darwinian genetics, provides me with a fine example for Mertonian dissection.

In my own field of economics, Columbia's John Bates Clark never read anything.

†The Mertonian jury of historians of science can never be permanently discharged; its verdicts are always tentative and subject to change. The conventional view, by G.A. Bliss and others, is that James Bernoulli is really the victor in the brachistochrone duel with John: although John has the more brilliant and glib solution through his analogy with the way geodesics of light bend in a medium of variable refraction index, James' more clumsy variational technique in fact established the firm foundations upon which later writers built the calculus of variations. Imagine then my surprise to learn from the speech of the great Carathéodory at Harvard's 1936 Tercentenary that John's local analysis may be deemed the first instance of the modern deeper approach.

Not only was he the first to discover the marginal productivity model of income distribution (an accomplishment that makes me proud to wear his medal). Clark also rediscovered, a decade late and in defective form, the theory of marginal utility. His son, John Maurice Clark, also a famous scholar, also read nothing. "We used to have to put a book in front of Maurice," Frank Knight once told me, "and open the book to the proper page, to get him acquainted." Perhaps this was just as well. J. M. Clark's most famous finding, his 1917 enunciation of the Acceleration Principle—relating the *level* of investment spending to the *rate of change* of consumption (or total final) spending—might never have occurred if he had known of Bickerdike's 1914 anticipation, or Hawtrey's 1913 approach, or Aftalion's . . .

Einstein himself didn't know whether or not he had heard of the Michelson-Morley experiment on the equal velocity of light in all directions when he axiomatized his special theory of relativity. Whittaker, who had a grudge against Einstein, reproached him for his cavalier ignoring of Poincaré's contemporaneous work: what Whittaker failed to mention was that there was nothing personal about this, Einstein rarely pauses to recognize property rights of any earlier scholars. When Fermi wrote up his lecture notes on thermodynamics, he assigned an assistant the task of spiking them with footnote references. When someone would come to Richard Feynman with an approximation result in physics, Feynman would often take down a notebook from his shelf and verify from his unpublished version of the exact solution that his visitor had indeed correctly identified the first term in the complete expansion. Men have been shot for less.

My own titanic colleague, Sir John Hicks of Oxford, always tells us how he came to his ideas. "I could have kicked myself," his prefaces relate about a delayed perception. "Already, I had perceived the broad outlines of my theory . . ." What his footnotes rarely contain is informed and precise appraisal of past and present parallel researches. Sometimes this results in what Gunnar Myrdal years ago called "attractive but unnecessary Anglo-Saxon originality." Sometimes, as in the rediscovery of Markowitz's well-publicized portfolio model of efficient mean-variance tradeoff, it results in anti-climax. Redundancy, I am prepared to argue, is only a minor blemish: it causes a few trees to be unnecessarily axed, the spilling of some rather cheap ink, a waste of readers' limited time and attention. But, before you go hacking with Ockham's razor, be sure you don't cut muscle along with fat. Because the sun does not rise until a scholar of Hicks' originality opens his eyes in the morning, we get a fresh view of any subject he addresses. Often I find novel Hicksian insights in the treatment of old topics. (I once explained to Joan Robinson, after she remarked that English economists wouldn't mind reading American economics if only they knew where to begin on that vast continent, "We New World economists take unfair advantage: we can read both English and American.")

R. A. Fisher, A Case in Point

It is Sir Ronald Fisher—R. A. Fisher to my generation of statisticians—that I am concerned with here. Fisher was a genius—if that term has a meaning. He founded, and revolutionized, the subject of statistics. For the quarter century after 1912, statistics *was* R. A. Fisher. Great as Fisher was in the domain of mathematical statistics, one is told he was equally great in the domain of genetics. It is regarded as a reproach that the Nobel Prize in biology was never awarded to R. A. Fisher, J. B. S. Haldane, and Sewall Wright. Fisher's *The Genetical Theory of Natural Selection*[1] is a classic, regarded with the awe to be accorded a bible and containing some of the mysteries and obscurities of that sacred work.

Here I shall deal with one small gem from this book, Fisher's novel and ingenious concept of "reproductive value." He bequeathed us scores of such jewels, many of which might serve my purpose as well were it not for the accident that, in training for understanding Fisher's nearby Fundamental Theorem of Natural Selection, my attention was fastened upon the ambiguities implicit in Fisher's reproductive-value concept and his exposition of it, creating in me an itch that could not be scratched out until I found myself writing four (brief, unrefereed) articles on the subject.

Since some of my words might seem less than fulsome, I ought to begin with a deposition of R.A. Fisher's greatness. Like the great John Maynard Keynes, Fisher probably increased the impact of his lasting discoveries and novelties by the polemical mode of his scientific writing. Had Fisher been able to narrate the steps in reasoning by which he came to his theorems, they might have lost a sense of magic that invests them. Each reader might then be able to say, "Shucks, there with the grace of God might go I, and what's so remarkable about anything as freely got as that?" Obscurity is neither a necessary nor a sufficient condition for magnifying one's impact; but, conjoined with a message worth sending, it can bull up market price. The labor theory of value applies in the history of ideas. After you have hunted through 2 million words in *Das Kapital,* you esteem the catch. The wood I chop warms me twice. Newton in geometric Latin is more profound than in the freshman textbook. Unheard melodies are sweeter yet.

I wrote had Fisher "been able to," rather than "willing to," because there is a question as to whether his was not the intuitive mind that arrives at a gestalt without being able to rationalize its historical steps. My old Harvard teacher, Edwin Bidwell Wilson ("E.B."), who was a good acquaintance of Ronald Fisher and a genial admirer and observer, used to comment on Fisher's poor eyesight. "Perhaps that is why Fisher was so good at the n-dimensional geometry by which he derived his 'F' and other notable distributions," E.B. used to say. "Certainly it explains the extraordinary number of printing errors that permeate his fundamental memoirs." Or, to take another example of Fisher's remarkable flights of intuition, Sir Maurice Kendall has commented somewhere on the mystery of Fisher's mode of discovering the intricate k-statistics so useful when sampling moments, semi-invariants, and cumulants of theoretical probability universes. Not only could Kendall not reconstruct the paths of reasoning, but Fisher could also not do so on interrogation.

Was it Virginia Woolf (or Stephen) who said, "How do I know what I think until I hear myself saying it?" The quip that Hegel didn't really understand his own philosophy until he read the French translation is a minor truth next to that which claims that an idea does not really exist until it can be plagiarized. We have all had a brilliant Coleridgian colleague whose head is full of deep perceptions that can't quite be grasped. How do chimeras parse *cogito ergo sum?* My point is that, after perusal of Fisher's texts and reflection on them, I am left with the hypothesis that not infrequently his unclarities are not perverse thumbnosings at the reader, not fudgings over the fine details of the syllogism or its limitations, but rather they faithfully mirror unclarities in his own thought. Why, in connection with matters that he wrote on over a period of more than a quarter of a century, he did not choose to devote the time to think them through, one can only speculate about.

Cassel, his secretary exonerated on the grounds of friction with his father. Fisher's rudeness has been excused on the grounds that he was as much sinned against as sinning. My generation of students were like children observing their elders at a drunken party, so titillated were we at the display of fireworks by Karl Pearson and Ronald Fisher. Was there ever another generation of savants with similar scholarly manners? It used to be said that Planck and Einstein were such nice people that they elevated a whole generation of German physicists (no mean act of levitation).

Example works both ways. When I expressed to E.B. my shock at the motion of thanks emitted by Fisher after an invited 1935 speech by Jerzy Neyman before the *Royal Statistical Society*,[2] it was explained to me that Karl Pearson had treated Fisher so badly as to make this understandable. And Alfred North Whitehead once boasted at Harvard's Society of Fellows that he had been the only person in Britain who managed to stay on good terms with both the Mendelian advocate, William Bateson, and the Galtonian advocate, Karl Pearson. Each, he said, was impossible to use as a referee: the slightest commendation in a manuscript of work from the enemy camp was enough to outweigh any excellence it possessed.

Science, some sage said, advances funeral by funeral. Fisher was out of tune with his times after 1940. Statistical decision making he denounced as a fascistic tool. Confidence intervals did not gain his confidence. Bayesian tools he eschewed; but after decades of declaiming against equi-probability of the unknown, Fisher explained that his fiducial probability involved a proper assumption of balanced ignorance. Neyman-Pearson rejection regions based on minimizing Type B errors were rejected by Fisher as the figment of those who did not understand practical matters—and this from the man who chided Gregor Mendel for reporting ratios *too near* to 3-to-1, and who casually releases in *Statistical Methods for Research Workers* the bombshell that *too-small* values of chi-square are as bad as the *large* ones upon which his tables are built!

Genius can get away with methods unforgivable in talent? That is the reverse of truth, precisely because of Merton's syndrome of the Matthew Effect.[3] To him who hath shall be given—and given also the power to take away. Because Fisher's work in design of agricultural experiments was so good, his unfortunate work on smoking and longevity proved so very unfortunate in misleading statisticians of his claque. Because his analysis of genetic models was so pathbreaking, Fisher's final chapter, in which he seriously purports to deduce the decay of civilization from the propensity of heritably unfecund heiresses to capture as mates and render insterile the most successful (and genetically able) elements of the population, was taken with comical seriousness. My point is that it takes the wisdom of Maxwell's Demon to separate out the good from the bad in the *oeuvres* of an acknowledged genius—the more reason for refusing him license.‡

Fisher's Version of the Lotka Model

My purpose is to describe, and comment on, two distinct components of Fisher's 1930 exposition: his rendering without citations of A.J. Lotka's model of population that is self-propelled by invariant age-specific mortality and fertility schedules; Fisher's own discovery and cryptic explication of the novel concept of "reproductive value" of each age-group.

Here, in selected words of Fisher, is the first of these.[4]

> . . . a life table . . . shows for each year of age, of the population considered, the proportion of persons born alive who live to that age . . . ℓ_x [being] the relative number living to age x, the death rate at age x is given by: $\mu_x = -d \log_e(\ell_x)/dx$.
>
> The life table concerns itself only with death and not at all with reproduction. To repair this deficiency it is necessary to introduce a second table giving rates of reproduction in a manner analogous to the rates of death at each age. Just as a person alive at the beginning of

‡A. E. Housman was asked about an item that he refused to reprint in a collection of his classic writings, whether he did not think it good. He replied: "It is good, but not good enough for me."

any infinitesimal age interval dx has a chance of dying within that interval measured by $\mu_x dx$, so the chance of reproducing within this interval will be represented by $b_x dx$, in which b_x may be called the rate of reproduction at age x. Again, just as the chance of a person chosen at birth dying within a specified interval of age dx is $\ell_x \mu_x dx$, so the chance of such a person living to reproduce in that interval will be $\ell_x b_x dx$. . . . If we combine the two tables . . . of death and reproduction, we may . . . calculate the expectation of offspring of the newly born child . . . $\int_0^\infty \ell_x b_x dx$ [which] determines whether . . . reproductive rates are more or less than sufficient to balance the existing death rates. If its value is less than unity . . . [the] population . . . would . . . certainly ultimately decline in numbers at a calculable rate. Equally, if it is greater than unity, the population biologically speaking is more than holding its own, although the actual number of heads to be counted may be temporarily increasing . . . . corresponding to any system of rates of death and reproduction, there is only one possible [stable age distribution] . . . proportional to $e^{-mx}\ell_x dx$ . . . [where m is the one and only existent real solution to] $\int_0^\infty e^{-mx}\ell_x b_x dx$ . . . equated to unity. . . . The number m, is thus implicit in any given system of rates of death and reproduction, and measures the relative rate of increase or decrease of a population when in the steady state [and] . . . m may appropriately be termed the Malthusian parameter . . .

Those familiar with A. J. Lotka's post-1911 researches on a population that is self-propelled toward stable exponential growth by invariant age-specific mortality and fertility parameters will recognize in Fisher's above account a useful description of the Lotka model. There is, however, no mention of Lotka's name and no reference to work of other earlier writers such as R. R. Kuczynski, who had independently and as a disciple of Böckh published on the related concept of *net reproduction rate*.[5]

Inasmuch as Fisher was an undergraduate in 1911 when Sharpe and Lotka[6] appeared, and since he was then presumably more interested in mathematics and astronomy than in the life sciences, one can doubt that Fisher knew this earliest work—or that of Lotka[7,8] (1913, 1922). Indeed a person of Fisher's originality may well have worked out the whole theory by himself in ignorance of its prior existence—a doubleton that Robert Merton would not be surprised at. On the other hand, Lotka's 1925 classic, *The Elements of Physical Biology*,[9] achieved wide circulation and might have been expected to pique Fisher's curiosity. Its Equation (33), p. 118, clearly presents the relation that Fisher invoked to determine the Malthusian parameter m; several of Lotka's remarks on selective slaughtering of the old rather than young do smack of the "reproductive value" concept; and Fisher's p. 29 remark that the human death rate is at its minimum at age 12 could well have come from Lotka's p. 151 observation rather than from the more obscure original Raymond Pearl source.

All this presents the Mertonian detective with a nice problem in maximum likelihood or Bayesian estimation. What are the subjective odds that, if a definitive document is later found that *settles* whether Fisher did or did not know about the Lotka system, we as informed scholars will bet that it will reveal Fisher's discovery not to have been independent? To formulate these odds, one naturally turns to other discoveries of Fisher. Fisher[10] presents without citation of von Neumann's work on game theory what is clearly a formulation of the mixed-strategy saddlepoint solution to a 2-person zero-sum game (that of "her" discussed in Todhunter's standard history of probability). My considered guess is that Fisher did not then know of von Neumann's 1928 German mathematical article on game theory[11] (but he might have vaguely heard of Borel's less complete speculations?). When as an undergraduate Fisher proposed his 1912 maximum-likelihood criterion for estimation, one can doubt that he knew of similar work a century earlier by Gauss (or, for that matter, but here we are on trickier ground, of the more recent work in Edgeworth (1908) that contained at least implicitly the notion of "efficiency" of the maximum-likelihod estimator). The written remark of H. L. Seal[12] (1967) is relevant to our forming subjective probability judgements: ". . . we have heard it stated that Fisher in private conversation showed himself familiar with the work of the earlier mathematicians in Europe."

Seal adds what I can only agree with: "It is no discredit to the genius whose published output is large and continuous that he failed to take the time to review all previous literature." I should also add that, personally, it provides an even greater challenge to me to try to add to what my predecessors have done, *within the constraint* of formally pointing out their accomplishments: just how high is the altitude reached by the shoulders of the giants that bear me is the necessary base from which I can estimate my pygmy reach. And one should note that, when Fisher wished to mete out faint praise to Karl Pearson, he was capable of quoting the little known 1872 work of Helmert on the derivation of what came to be called Pearson's chi-square distribution.

We do not have to go to the works of an Einstein or Fisher to discern a not uncommon gambit, part of Stephen Potter's one-upmanship as played by scholars, in which a safely-dead scholar is used to eclipse a live rival. If I am to be anticipated, pray that it be by someone centuries back! To call m the Malthusian parameter, rather than say "the Lotka intrinsic rate of natural increase" may not have been such an unconscious ploy, but we cannot rule out that it was.

UNDOUBTED ORIGINALITY

I move on now to the part of Fisher's discussion that is unquestionably novel—his defining of "reproductive value of each age group" in terms of an almost mystical analogy to the economics of compound interest. Again his own words can be adequately sampled.[13]

> In view of the close analogy between the growth of a population supposed to follow the law of geometric increase, and the growth of capital invested at compound interest, it is worth noting that if we regard the birth of a child as the loaning to him of a life, and the birth of his offspring as a subsequent repayment of the debt, the method by which m is calculated shows that it is equivalent to answering the question—At what rate of interest are the repayments the just equivalent of the loan? . . . the Malthusian parameter of population increase is the rate of interest at which the present value of the births of offspring to be expected is equal to unity at the date of birth of their parent [$1 = \int_0^\infty e^{-mx}\ell_x b_x dx$].
>
> . . . The analogy with money does, however, make clear the argument for another simple application of the combined death and reproduction rates. We may ask, not only about the newly born, but about persons of any chosen age, what is the present value of their future offspring; and if the present value is calculated at the rate determined as before, the question has the definite meaning—To what extent will persons of this age, on the average, contribute to the ancestry of future generations? The question is one of some interest, since the direct action of Natural Selection must be proportional to this contribution. . . . by the analogy of compound interest the present value of the future offspring of persons aged x is easily seen to be given by the equation
>
> $$v_x/v_0 = \frac{e^{mx}}{\ell_x}\int_x^\infty e^{-mt}\ell_t b_t\, dt.$$
>
> Each age group may in this way be assigned its appropriate reproductive value . . .
>
> A property that well illustrates the significance of the method of valuation, by which, instead of counting all individuals as of equal value in respect of future population, persons of each age are assigned an appropriate values v_x, is that, whatever may be the age constitution of a population, its total reproductive value will increase or decrease according to the correct Malthusian rate m, where as counting all heads as equal this is only true in the theoretical case in which the population is in its steady state.

Mere commonsense says: Choosing to save the child does more for the future population than to save the grandparent; if the child may die before puberty, saving the adolescent is more economical still. Fisher advances from this commonplace to an exact quantitative evaluation of the proper tradeoff between persons of different ages when it comes to determining the level at which the population will eventually double and redouble.

Moreover, as always, when we explain commonsense we go beyond it to the rare atmosphere of new truth. In a declining population—like ours in which few children die but many lack brothers and sisters—the new babe has more reproductive value than the nubile maid. Why? That is what Fisher's formula spits out when you insert a negative interest rate into its slot. "But *why*?" you insist on asking. Perhaps for the reason the talmudists agreed the moon is more important than the sun: true the moon gives less light than the sun, but it does so during night's darkness when we need it most. The babe's gift will come later and will have melted away less by the time it arrives.

What is most awesome about Fisher's exposition is its oddness. A mysterious if not mystical analogy is made to economics. Just as a bond's yield is that rate of interest which will discount its future cash payments to its present market price, Fisher says a population's growth rate is that interest rate which will discount all a new babe's future births to the unit life bestowed on her. Who enters into this contract? Enforces it? Perceives it? Why, at each age of life, should the present discounted-value of her future expected offspring, calculated with the growth rate that the population does not *yet* experience (but will ultimately experience) be a proper measure of what each initial member of that age group will contribute to the ultimate level of a population's growing?

As Professor Keyfitz has mentioned in our private conversation, once the problem is well-posed of determining how the initial age distribution determines the coefficient of the dominating exponential in the model's exact solution, the solution in terms of a certain characteristic row vector or eigenfunction is complicated but not mysterious. What is amazing is how Fisher apparently bypassed the straightforward and leaped to the solution immediately by means of the compound-interest analogy. As a demographer and sociologist, Professor Keyfitz may be excused for not perceiving intuitively the economic interest approach. But I am an experienced economist, one who has made his profits so to speak from the study of compound interest and capital theory, and yet I must confess—nay insist—that the argument is a mysterious one and even (looked at from the standpoint of a general, not necessarily linear, model) an inconclusive one. If someone told me that Fisher had actually found his solution in the straightforward way and then—after the fact!—puzzled out how to express it in compound interest terms, I would not find that hard to believe. And yet there is no evidence for such a scenario and no warrant for asserting its validity.

It occurred to me to investigate what Fisher's biologist readers have made of his compound interest analogy. As might have been expected, they seem simply to take it on faith, reiterating its assertions. As a representative specimen, E. O. Wilson's magisterial *Sociobiology*[14] may be cited. In the course of its excellent, brief description of reproductive value, the relevance of the Malthusian parameter as a discount factor is not only not really explained, but is in fact omitted from some of the key literary explanations.

Mathematical Proof

Before turning to my positive analysis of the economic valuations definable by demographic or biological models, let me give a brief account of the straightforward approach to reproductive value that a mathematician would take. Write $B(t)$ for (female) births at time t; $N(x, t)$ for the number (of females) of age x at time t (i.e., the "density" of females between x and $x + dx$), where $N(0, t) \equiv B(t)$; ℓ_x for the fraction of new-born (female) babies who survive to age x; and b_x for the rate at which women of age x bear female babies. Then Lotka's model—and Fisher's!—is definable by

$$B(t) = \int_0^\beta \ell_x b_x B(t-x)\,dx + \int_0^\beta (\ell_{x+t}/\ell_x)\, b_{x+t} N(x,0)\,dx$$

$$= \int_0^\beta \ell_x b_x B(t-x)\,dx + G(t), \qquad 0 < \alpha < \beta < \infty \tag{1}$$

$$0 \leqq G(t);\ G(t) \equiv 0,\ t > \beta;\ \ell_x b_x > 0 \quad \text{for} \quad \alpha < x < \beta$$

The Volterra integral equation of the second kind in (**1**) is known to have an explicit solution of the form

$$B(t) = G(t) + \int_0^t \phi^*(t-y) G(y)\,dy$$

$$= 0 + \int_0^\beta \phi^*(t-y)\left[\int_0^\beta \ell_{x+y}/\ell_x) b_{x+y} N(x,0)\,dx\right] dy,\ t > \beta \tag{2}$$

$$= \int_0^\beta N(x,0)\left[\int_0^\beta \phi^*(t-y)\, \ell_{x+y/\ell_x}) b_{x+y}\,dy\right] dx, \quad t > \beta$$

$$= \int_0^\beta N(x,0) v(x,t)\,dx,\ t > \beta \tag{3}$$

$$= 0 + \int_0^\beta v(x,t)\, N(x,0)\,dx,\ \text{t} > \beta$$

where $\phi^*(t-y)$ is the resolvent kernel to the kernel $\ell_{t-y} b_{t-y}$ (as discussed in Samuelson[15]) and where $v(x, t)$ is the generalization *to any* t for Fisher's reproductive value of an initial age element. By convention, $\phi^*(t)$ vanishes for negative t.

By definition, $v(x,t)$ represents the contribution to births t periods later of an initial female of age x:

$$v(x,t) = \int_0^\beta (\ell_z/\ell_x) b_z \phi^*(t - z + x)\,dz \tag{4}$$

In the limit as $t \to \infty$, $\phi^*(t)$ becomes essentially exponential, ce^{mt}, and so

$$v(x)/v(0) = \lim_{t\to\infty}[v(x,t)/v(0,t)] = \int_x^\beta (\ell_z/\ell_x) b_z \exp[m(x-z)]\,dz \tag{5}$$

in agreement with Fisher's formula.

The resolvent kernel $\phi^*(t)$ has the clear interpretation as the stream of subsequent female births occasioned t periods from now by a unit pulse of female babies now. Just as the inverse of a Leslie matrix can achieve the solution of a problem with any initial conditions, so the resolvent (or "inverse") kernel can do the same in the continuous case. The sole integral equation for $\phi^*(t)$ is

$$\phi^*(t) = \ell_t b_t + \int_0^t \ell_{t-z} b_{t-z} \phi^*(z)\,dz \tag{6}$$

$$= \ell_t b_t + \int_0^t \ell_{t-z} b_{t-z} \ell_z b_z\,dz \tag{7}$$

$$+ \int_0^\beta \ell_{t-x} b_{t-x}\left[\int_0^\beta \ell_{x-z} b_{x-z} \ell_z b_z\,dz\right] dx + \cdots$$

where (**7**) is a uniformly converging iteration series.

An interesting approach to $\phi^*(t)$ comes from pretending that $\ell_x b_x e^{-mx}$ is the death-rate function for some associated process. Such a death-rate function defines a renewal (or, better, "replacement") function, $R(t)$, by the standard renewal integral equation

$$R(t) = \ell_t b_t e^{-mt} + \int_0^t \ell_{t-z} b_{t-z} e^{-mt+mz} R(z)\,dz \tag{8}$$

$$\lim_{t\to\infty} R(t) = \left[\int_0^\infty \ell_x b_x e^{-mx}\,dx\right]^{-1} \tag{9}$$

$$\phi^*(t) = R(t)e^{mt} \tag{10}$$

$$\approx \left[\int_\infty^0 x\ell_x b_x e^{-mx}\,dx\right]^{-1} e^{mt},\ t \gg 1$$

The equivalence of (**8**) and (**6**) is seen after (**9**) is substituted into (**6**) and (**8**) results.

Note that this straightforward proof does not utilize either Laplace transforms or the Hertz-Herglotz infinite exponential expansions of Sharpe and Lotka. So long as b_x vanishes after some finite age, there is no lack of rigor in the second of these approaches, as has been shown by Lopez.[16] Using it, we find that (**1**)'s solution can be written as

$$B(t) = Q_0 e^{mt} + \sum_{j=\pm 1}^{\pm\infty} Q_i e^{m_j t} \tag{11}$$

$$= Q_0 e^{mt}[1 + \epsilon(t)],\ \lim_{t\to\infty} \epsilon(t) = 0$$

where

$$Q_0 = \frac{\int_0^\beta N(x,0)\int_x^\beta (\ell_z/\ell_x)\, b_z \exp[(x-z)m]\,dz}{\int_0^\beta z\ell_z b_z e^{-mz}\,dz} \tag{12}$$

and the (m_j, m_{-j}) are conjugate complex roots with coefficient of their real part less than m.

The reader may be referred to Keyfitz[17] for the best treatment known to me of Fisher's reproductive value as applied to the Lotka-Leslie one-sex linear model, the one case for which it is exact.

Fisher writes as though his reproductive value formula would apply—no doubt with various straightforward but minor qualifications—to realistic biparental (i.e. bisexual) models involving both fathers and mothers. He seems to believe that the sexes are tautologically equal in total reproductive value (in that every baby has exactly 1 mother and 1 father), and hence either can stand for half the whole. Fisher also recognizes that a mere increase in numbers will cause the effective environment to deteriorate and make his ℓ_x and b_x functions be also functions of total numbers, such as $\int_0^\infty N(x, t)dx$. This destroys the strict linearity of his model and vitiates the principle of superposition on which his intuitive syllogisms depend. Also, but this is presumably not substantively a strong effect, Fisher recognizes that females beyond the menopausal climacteric of age β may add to the future population by the care they provide for their kin; again, such plausible effects cannot be correctly handled by making $b_{\beta+x}$ positive instead of zero. Since, however, Samuelson[18–21] has gone into these aspects at sufficient length, my concluding section on the economics of reproductive valuations will touch upon them only in connection with the demonstration of lack of *logical* connection between various of Fisher's propositions.

Economics of Biological State

I conclude by investigating more deeply the analogy between economists' price and Mother Nature's scarcities.

1. It is standard to calculate the present-discounted-value of persons of different ages. This is done for juries in damage awards, for clients of life insurance to help determine their coverage needs, for scholars studying "human capital" and the economics of education. [See Dublin and Lotka[22], Walsh[23].] However, it is usually *not* to the b_z fertility function that the (ℓ_z/ℓ_x) conditional survival fractions and $\exp[r(x-z)]$ discount factor are applied, but rather to some measure of wage earnings by age.§ And the interest rate used, r, is as Fisher noted generally not of the same magnitude as the Malthus-Lotka m. [See, however, Samuelson[25] for a "biological" interest rate; and Phelps[26] for the concept of the golden-rule interest rate, equal to the economy's natural growth rate of labor (in biological or efficiency-unit terms) and which leads to production methods that maximize consumption per head.]

2. Purely by the definition of present-discounted-values and without reference to any biological relations as such, any repeated investment project whose initial cost is precisely equal to what is needed to make it just pay will at every instant of time earn on the portfolio of accumulated and reinvested returns the postulated market interest rate. Fisher's demonstration that the calculated total reproductive value, $\int v(x)N(x,t)dt$, grows *from the beginning* at his postulated rate m is a brilliant instance of this general truth. (Example: You buy a bond or truck that gives you at stated intervals cash payments and then a final payment. Its initial cost to you is set at the present-discounted-value of such an income stream; and each cash payment you plow back into similar new purchases, never withdrawing any net cash from your total portfolio of such investments. Then, as shown in Samuelson,[27] your principal grows at each instant at the constant interest rate postulated. What Fisher does not touch upon is the still more general tautology: even if the interest rates are *not* constant over time, being $r(t)$ rather than r, it will still be true that your portfolio grows at each t at the exact percentage rate $r(t)$ provided that all costs of investment projects are at their true present-discounted-values.

3. Now I examine processes that generate their own growth: 2 rabbits give you 4 every period; or a Lotka-Leslie model postulates that female babies produce so many female adults who produce so many female babies at different ages. If we reckon the interest rate in terms of money, and if the r is not equal to the Malthus-Neumann rabbit "own rate of interest," it would violate the rules of competitive arbitrage for the money price of a rabbit to be constant over time. If the rabbit interest rate is 20 percent per annum and the money interest rate is 5 percent, then the money price of rabbits must fall in proportion to $(1.05/1.20)^t$.

In the rabbit case, so long as there are no overlapping generations, the population and births will grow exponentially from the beginning at the $(1.20)^t$ rate. No reproductive value weighting is needed, and 1 rabbit does equal the present-discounted-value of its 1.2 offspring at the rabbit-own-rate-of-interest of $m = .2$.

§A partial exception occurs when Fogel and Engerman[24] seek to explore the economics of ante bellum slavery in those regions and sectors where slaves are bred to breed slaves. Then, ignoring byproducts such as slaves' useful non-breeding services, they tend to find that nubile females are worth more than post-menopausal elders or newborn female babies. However, the proper present discounted value computations are done with the interest rate earnable on comparable investments and not on some biological Malthusian rate. Furthermore, the imputed value of land and other services needed to cooperate with people in keeping them fit and able to reproduce babies must be reckoned in, by methods obvious to economists but much more complex than Fisher needed for the idealized Leslie model.

For the Lotka-Leslie case in which females are mothers at various ages of life, there is defined by the process what Boulding[28] would call "the internal [own] rate of return of interest," which is precisely the Lotka-Fisher rate m that discounts the sum of all future female daughters into equality with unity.

Thus, the only female-baby own-rate-of-interest that could be constant over time in a perfect competitive market is the Malthus-Fisher m of the Lotka-Leslie process.

4. The Lotka process, particularly in its Leslie[29] version involving discrete time units and age intervals, is a special and simple instance of the von Neumann[30] self-generating general-equilibrium model, in which any good can be producible as output out of inputs that are the system's output one period earlier. Specifically here,

$$\begin{gathered} b_x \text{ female babies and } p_x \text{ females of age } x+1 \\ \text{are produced by} \\ 1 \text{ female of age } x \end{gathered} \tag{13}$$

Here $[b_x] = [b_1, b_2, \ldots, b_\beta, b_{\beta+1} = 0]$ with $b_\beta > 0$, $b_{\beta-1} > 0, \ldots$. Also $[p_x] = [p_1, p_2, \ldots, p_{\beta-1}, 0, 0]$, with $0 < p_j = \ell_{j+1}/\ell_j \leq 1$.

Then competitive steady-state price equilibrium requires of the interest rate r and the respective prices of a female of age x, $[\pi_x] = [\pi_1, \pi_2, \ldots, \pi_\beta, \pi_{\beta+1}]$, that the following cost-of-production relations obtain

$$\pi_1 b_x + \pi_{x+1} p_x = \pi_x(1+r), \; (x = 1, 2, \ldots, \beta) \tag{14}$$

This says that I must earn the common interest rate on my outlay in buying 1 female of age x as input when she produces for me b_x daughters and turns into p_x females of age $x + 1$ and I can sell these joint products at their respective prices.

In matrix terms we have, where bold face type denotes a matrix or vector;

$$\mathbf{N(x, t+1)} = \begin{bmatrix} N(1, t+1) \\ \cdot \\ \cdot \\ \cdot \\ N(\beta+1, t+1) \end{bmatrix} = \begin{bmatrix} b_1 & b_2 & \cdots & b_\beta & 0 \\ p_1 & 0 & \cdots & 0 & 0 \\ 0 & p_2 & \cdots & 0 & 0 \\ \cdot & \cdot & \cdots & \cdot & \cdot \\ \cdot & \cdot & \cdots & \cdot & \cdot \\ 0 & 0 & \cdots & p_{\beta-1} & 0 \\ 0 & 0 & \cdots & 0 & 0 \end{bmatrix} \begin{bmatrix} N(1, t) \\ \cdot \\ \cdot \\ \cdot \\ \cdot \\ N(\beta+1, t) \end{bmatrix} \tag{15}$$

$$= \mathbf{LN(x, t)}$$

$$\begin{aligned} \boldsymbol{\pi}\mathbf{L} &= [\pi_1, \ldots, \pi_\beta, \pi_{\beta+1}]\mathbf{L} = [\pi_1, \ldots, \pi_\beta, \pi_{\beta+1}](1+r) \\ &= \boldsymbol{\pi}(1+r) \end{aligned} \tag{14'}$$

Equation 15 is the familiar Leslie-Bernardelli discrete-time version of the Lotka system. [See Keyfitz[31] for a useful account.] Equation 14′ is the matrix version of (**14**). Clearly its solution requires prices to be row-vector eigenfunctions of L and 1 + r to be the Malthus-Lotka-Fisher eigenvalue of asymptotic growth. Except for inessential scale coefficient (**14′**) has the following unique solution, which is Fisher's solution adapted to discrete time periods

$$[v_1\ v_2 \cdots v_\beta 0]\mathbf{L} = [v_1\ v_2 \cdots v_\beta 0](1 + m)$$

$$v_1 = 1 = \sum_1^{\beta+1} (p_1 \cdots p_{j-1})b_j(1 + m)^{-j} = \sum_1^{\beta+1} \ell_j b_j(1 + m)^{-j}$$

. . . .

$$v_x = \sum_x^{\beta+1} (\ell_j/\ell_x)b_j(1 + m)^{-j+x-1}, \quad 1 \le x \le \beta + 1 \tag{16}$$

. . . .

$$v_\beta = b_\beta(1 + m)^{-1}$$

$$v_{\beta+1} = 0$$

The subtle reader will protest: In (**15**) you made your quantity iterations for **N(x, t)** dynamic. Why did you not do the same in (**14′**) for the *dual* price vector $\bar{\pi}_\mathbf{x}(\mathbf{t})$, replacing (**14′**) by

$$[\bar{\pi}_1(t + 1) \cdots \bar{\pi}_\beta(t + 1)] \begin{bmatrix} b_1 & \cdots & b_{\beta-1} & b_\beta \\ p_1 & \cdots & 0 & 0 \\ \vdots & & \vdots & \vdots \\ 0 & \cdots & p_{\beta-1} & 0 \end{bmatrix} \tag{15′}$$

$$= \bar{\pi}_x(t + 1)\bar{L} = \bar{\pi}_x(t)$$

That reader has a point: since the population is for a long time in transient nonsteady states, why should the steady-state price be appropriate during those states?

The best answer I can give, and it seems a somewhat feeble one, is this. There is only one normalized initial $\bar{\pi}_\mathbf{x}(\mathbf{0})$, namely that chosen to be proportional to $[1, v_2, \ldots, v_\beta]$, such that the iteration

$$\bar{\pi}_\mathbf{x}(t + 1)\bar{\mathbf{L}} = \bar{\pi}_\mathbf{x}(t) \tag{16}$$

$$\bar{\pi}_\mathbf{x}(t + 1) = \bar{\mathbf{L}}^{-1}\bar{\pi}_\mathbf{x}(t) \tag{17}$$

does not for some finite t give solutions with some negative components. [See Wan[32] for discussion of these so-called Furuya-Inada and F. Hahn properties of permanently extendable equilibrium systems.]

If anything, our admiration grows for Fisher's blindfolded gallop over eggshells. His sureness of foot in reaching useful results is astounding. Those of us not geniuses had better not shut our eyes in exploring such treacherous new ground. The following section shows the need to discipline intuition by logical proof.

To apprehend the subtle general (lack of!) logical connection between correct steady-state economic prices and true reproductive value of initial population elements, consider a rockbottom simple case of a biparental population model. Babies of both sexes are created in equal numbers; their mothers are all young women; their fathers are young or less-young men, but of course the latter display less fertility than the former. With the age-specific-mortality of men specified, and also the fertility function specified in terms of the 3 arguments—young women, $F(t)$, young men $M(1,t)$, and less-young men, $M(2,t)$,—we have a determinate nonlinear dynamic system that will approach an asymptotic mode of balanced exponential growth. Here, as in Yellin and Samuelson[33] are its dynamic relations

$$\tfrac{1}{2}B(t+1) = F(t+1) = M(1, t+1) = b[F(t), M(1,t)\ M(2,t)] \quad \textbf{(18.1)}$$

$$M(2, t+1) = \ell M(1,t), 0 < \ell \leq 1$$

$$b[\lambda x, \lambda x_2, \lambda x_3] \equiv \lambda b[x_1, x_2, x_3], \partial b/\partial x_i = b_i[x_1, x_2, x_3] > 0 \quad \textbf{(18.2)}$$

$$\sum_1^3 x_j b_j[x_1, x_2, x_3] \equiv b[x_1, x_2, x_3]$$

$$\lim_{t\to\infty} \frac{B(t)}{(1+m)^t} = v[F(0), M(1,0), M(2,0)]/[1 + \tfrac{1}{2}\ell] \quad \textbf{(18.3)}$$

where $1 + m = M^*$ is the unique positive root for M in the steady-state relation

$$b[1, 1, \ell M^{-1}] - M = 0, \quad 0 < 1 + m \gtrless 1 \quad \textbf{(18.4)}$$

The question is now well-posable. How is the true reproductive-value function, $v[F(0), M(1,0), M(2,0)]$, related—if at all—to the correct steady-state prices applied to the initial elements of the population?

In Fisher's exposition, this question is answered in an affirmative and quantitative manner. But, as we shall now see, in general biparental models it is *not* the case that calculating present discounted values of the charter members of the population, at the true asymptotic Malthusian growth rate or at *any* other interest rate, will give the true reproductive value.

I now calculate these present discounted values in what modern advanced economics has shown to be the only way that they can be defined. First, we must calculate the rents (in terms of babies of course) that each person of each sex will earn during each period of life. Modern advanced economics tells us that when 2 or more inputs cooperate in producing an output [strictly speaking, by a homogeneous-first-degree, differentiable function like $b[x_1, x_2, x_3]$ in (**18**)], the separate contribution that can be imputed to each is identifiable by the respective partial derivative of the production function (its so-called "marginal productivity"). Hence, at *any* time, which may be the *original* time and need not be a time in which the system has settled into its long-term stable-age distribution steady state, these rents are given by

$$q_F(t) = \frac{\partial b[F(t), M(1,t), M(2,t)]}{\partial F(t)} \quad \textbf{(19)}$$

$$q_{M_i}(t) = \frac{\partial b[F(t), M(1,t), M(2,t)]}{\partial M(i,t)}, \ (i = 1, 2)$$

The steady-state rents are therefore

$$q_F^* = b_1[1, 1, \ell(1+m)^{-1}]$$
$$q_{M_1}^* = b_2[1, 1, \ell(1+m)^{-1}] \quad \textbf{(20)}$$
$$q_{M_2}^* = b_3[1, 1, \ell(1+m)^{-1}]$$

The steady-state present-discounted-values of each age-and-sex group would then be

$$\begin{aligned} v_F^* &= b_1[1, 1, \ell(1+m)^{-1}](1+m)^{-1} \\ v_{M_2}^* &= b_3[1, 1, \ell(1+m)^{-1}](1+m)^{-1} \\ v_{M_1}^* &= b_2[1, 1, \ell(1+m)^{-1}](1+m)^{-1} + b_3[1, 1, \ell(1+m)^{-1}](1+m)^{-2} \end{aligned} \quad \textbf{(21)}$$

In the last row above, we have to take proper notice that a young man will father babies in 2 stages of life, and we must discount more heavily the fruit that will come only later.

Any numerical example will verify that true total reproductive value, such as is well defined in **(18.3)**, is *not* given by a Fisher-like calculation of

$$v_F^* F(0) + v_{M_1}^* M(1, 0) + v_{M_2}^* M(2, 0) \quad \textbf{(22)}$$

Why not? Because the charter member's own fruit is *not* that which they'd earn working with numbers in the other groups that are in the ultimate balanced ratios, but rather what they contribute when working with the *actual initial* unbalanced ratio.

What would be the present discounted values of the original groups calculated at their *actual* future economic rents? Evidently, the following obtains at *any* t:

$$\begin{aligned} v_F(t) &= b_1[F(t), M(1, t), M(2, t)]\,(1+m)^{-1} \\ v_{M_2}(t) &= b_2[F(t), M(1, t), M(2, t)]\,(1+m)^{-1} \\ v_{M_1}(t) &= b_3(F(t), M(1, t), M(2, t)]\,(1+m)^{-1} + \ell v_{M_2}(t+1)(1+m)^{-1} \end{aligned} \quad \textbf{(23)}$$

Again, it is *not* the case that the following equality holds:

$$V(t+1) = (1+m)V(t) \quad \textbf{(24.1)}$$

$$V(t) = v_F(t)F(t) + \sum_1^2 V_{M_j}(t)M(j, t) \quad \textbf{(24.2)}$$

However, and here my quill takes on Fisherine style, it can be seen (or shown) that

$$\lim_{t\to\infty} [B(t)(1+m)^{-t}/V(t)] = 1 \quad \textbf{(25)}$$

So to speak, penultimately, use of current present discounted values (or even discounted values that employ steady-state prices) will give a "good approximation" to true reproductive value. But I fear this is the case of a candle that gives a light near the bright noon of day when we need it least. If the system is already in its penultimate state *near* the stable-age-distribution configuration, it suffers little from transient oscillations in its relative age distribution and we have no great need to damp them down.

The reader may examine a nonlinear case already known to be soluble and satisfy himself that applying Fisherine present-discount-value formulas in cookbook fashion will not procure the desired soufflé of true reproductive value.

I may sum up these deeper economic investigations of biology thus. Fisher did not prove, nor even conjecture clearly, that present discounted value calculated with steady-state or other prices does (1) provide a scalar that grows from the beginning at the ultimate Malthusian rate, (2) provide a proper measure of an initial age element to the system's ultimate growth level. In general, such a conjecture would be false. Like Tartaglia (who had a formula for the roots of one kind of polynomial, the cubic), and unlike Sturm or Gauss (who knew how to calculate all the roots of any polynomial, and knew when there existed no closed-form formula for doing so), R. A. Fisher glimpsed the rule valid [only!] for the Lotka one-sex linear model and stated that rule in anagramic mystery. Fisher's command over his readers is revealed by their docile acceptance for half a century of his abracadabra. (Perhaps he was his own first conquest.)

Conclusion

It will not escape Robert K. Merton's attention—I insist on the "K." since he and I have a "C." in common—that the present exercise also belongs in his zoo. Pioneering work, Littlewood and Hardy agreed, is usually clumsy. It is hard to be elegant while conquering Everest for the first time. Later, Lilliputian tailors provide a more elegant dress or axiomatization. Often that dress is a shroud, of more interest to the embalmer and taxidermist of science—its philosopher, historian, and sociologist—than to its card-carrying tillers. Still, as they say down at the census, even undertakers' services are part of the Gross National Product, along with those of the midwife.

Acknowledgments

I have benefitted from joint researches with Joel Yellin of Massachusetts Institute of Technology, and from writings and conversation of Nathan Keyfitz of Harvard. Kate Crowley gave much appreciated editorial assistance. Robert K. Merton alerted me to what might otherwise have been taken for granted. After this paper was set up in type, I was able to read the fine biography of R. A. Fisher by his daughter, Joan Fisher Box.[34] It corrects my surmise that Fisher's interest in biology post-dated his undergraduate days. But, with qualifications, I find it confirming of my general conclusions.

References

1. Fisher, R. A. 1958. *Genetical Theory of Natural Selection.* Dover Publications, Inc. New York. Second revised edition of 1930 Oxford University Press first edition.
2. Neyman, J. 1935. Statistical Problems in Agricultural Experimentation. *J. R. Stat. Soc.* **2:** 107–154.
3. Merton, R. K. 1973. *The Sociology of Science.* The University of Chicago Press, Chicago.
4. Fisher, R. A. Ref. 1. In all cases I quote from the 1958 revision; but, actually, as is readily apparent from study of the smaller type in which changed lines were set, no substantial changes from the 1930 text occur in any of the quoted passages.
5. Kuczynski, R. R. 1928. *The Balance of Births and Deaths,* Vol. I. Macmillan. New York.
6. Sharpe, F. R. & A. J. Lotka. 1911. A Problem in Age Distribution. *Philosophical Magazine* **21:** 435–438.
7. Lotka, A. J. 1913. A Natural Population Norm. *J. Wash. Acad. Sci.* **3:** 241–248; 289–292.
8. Lotka. A. J. 1956. *Elements of Mathematical Biology.* Dover Press. New York. See this publication for a list of relevant pre-1930 Lotka writings.
9. Lotka, A. J. 1925. *Elements of Physical Biology.* Wilkins and Wilkins. Baltimore. This is the original edition from which the amplified 1956 posthumous Dover edition of reference 8 was derived.

10. FISHER, R. A. 1934. Randomisation, and An Old Enigma of Card Play. *Mathematical Gazette* **18**:92–297.
11. VON NEUMANN, J. 1928. Zur Theorie der Gessellschaftsspiele. *Mathematische Annalen* **100:** 295–302.
12. SEAL, H. L. 1967. The Historical Development of the Gauss Linear Model. *Biometrika* **54:** 1–24. The quotations are taken from p. 2.
13. FISHER, R. A. Ref. 1: 23–26.
14. WILSON, E. O. 1975. *Sociobiology*. Harvard University Press. Cambridge, Mass.
15. SAMUELSON, P. A. 1976. Resolving a Historical Confusion in Population Analysis. *Hum. Biol.* **48:** 559–580. Equation 19. Reproduced as Chapter 236 in *The Collected Scientific Papers of Paul A. Samuelson,* Vol. 4. H. Nagatani & K. Crowley, Eds. 1978. The MIT Press. Cambridge, Mass.
16. LOPEZ, A. 1961. *Problems in Stable Population Theory*. Office of Population Research. Princeton, N.J.
17. KEYFITZ, N. 1977. *Applied Mathematical Demography*. John Wiley & Sons. New York.
18. SAMUELSON, P. A. 1977. Generalizing Fisher's "Reproductive Value": Linear Differential and Difference Equations of "Dilute" Biological Systems. *Proc. Nat. Acad. Sci. U.S.A.* **74:**5189–5192.
19. SAMUELSON, P. A. 1977. Generalizing Fisher's "Reproductive Value": Nonlinear, Homogeneous, Biparental Systems. *Proc. Nat. Acad. Sci.* U.S.A. **74:** 5772-5775.
20. SAMUELSON, P. A. 1978. Generalizing Fisher's "Reproductive Value": Overlapping and Nonoverlapping Generations. *Proc. Nat. Acad. Sci.* U.S.A. **75:** 4062–4066.
21. SAMUELSON, P. A. 1978. Generalizing Fisher's "Reproductive Value": "Incipient" and "Penultimate" Reproductive-Value Functions When Environment Limits Growth; Linear Approximants for Nonlinear Mendelian Mating Models. *Proc. Nat. Acad. Sci. U.S.A.*
22. DUBLIN, L. I. & A. J. LOTKA. 1930. *Money Value of a Man*. The Ronald Press Company. New York.
23. WALSH, J. R. 1936. The Capital Concept Applied to Man. *Q. J. of Econ.* 255–285.
24. FOGEL, R. W. & S. L. ENGERMAN. 1974. *Time on the Cross*. Little Brown. New York.
25. SAMUELSON, P. A. 1958. An Exact Consumption-Loan Model of Interest with or without the Social Contrivance of Money. *J. Polit. Econ.* **66:** 467–482. Reproduced as Chapter 21 of *The Collected Scientific Papers of Paul A. Samuelson,* Volume 1. J. E. Stigilitz, Ed. 1966. The MIT Press. Cambridge, Mass.
26. PHELPS, E. S. 1966. *Golden Rules of Economic Growth*. W. W. Norton. New York.
27. SAMUELSON, P. A. 1937. Some Aspects of the Pure Theory of Capital. *Q. J. Econ.* **51:** 469–496. Reproduced as Chapter 17 of *The Collected Scientific Papers of Paul A. Samuelson,* Vol. I. J. E. Stiglitz, Ed. 1966. The MIT Press. Cambridge, Mass.
28. BOULDING, K. 1934. Applications of the Pure Theory of Population Change to the Theory of Capital. *Q. J. of Econ.* **45:** 645–666.
29. LESLIE, P. H. 1945. On the Use of Matrices in Certain Population Mathematics. *Biometrika* **33:** 183–212.
30. VON NEUMANN, J. 1945. A Model of General Economic Equilibrium. *Review of Economic Studies* **13:** 1–9. Translation of 1931 and 1936 German version.
31. KEYFITZ, N. 1968. *Introduction to the Mathematics of Population*. Addison-Wesley Publishing Co. Reading, Mass.
32. WAN, H. 1971. *Economic Growth* (Chapter 11). Harcourt Brace Jovanovich. New York.
33. YELLIN, J. & P. A. SAMUELSON. 1977. Comparison of Linear and Nonlinear Models for Human Population Dynamics. *Theor. Popul. Bio.* **11:** 105–126.
34. BOX, J. F. 1978. *R. A. Fisher: The Life of a Scientist*. John Wiley & Sons. New York.

Generalizing Fisher's "reproductive value": Linear differential and difference equations of "dilute" biological systems†

(one-sex demography/eigenvectors/density dependence/asymptotic importance)

PAUL A. SAMUELSON

Department of Economics, Massachusetts Institute of Technology, Cambridge, Massachusetts 02139

Contributed by Paul A. Samuelson, August 22, 1977

ABSTRACT R. A. Fisher's 1930 "reproductive value" is defined as the contribution made by a population's *initial* age elements to its asymptotically dominating exponential growth mode. For the Leslie discrete-time model, it is the characteristic row vector of the Leslie matrix, and for the integral-equation model of Lotka the similar *eigenfunction.* It generalizes neatly to a 2-sex model of *linear* differential equations, and to general *n*-variable linear systems. However, when resource limitations end the "dilute" stage of linearity, reproductive value loses positive definability. The present linear analysis prepares the way for generalizing reproductive value to nonlinear systems involving first-degree-homogeneous relationships.

For a linear female-dominant demographic system like that of Sharpe and Lotka (1), or its discrete-time version of Leslie (2), R. A. Fisher (3) defined the "reproductive value" of an initial population element of a given age. Eschewing his analogies to the compound-interest concepts of economics, we may tersely define Fisher's concept as *the contribution made by the system's initial conditions to its asymptotically dominating exponential-growth mode.*

Review of discrete-time demography

Utilizing convenient matrix notation, we write our system as

$$x(t+1) = Lx(t) \qquad [1]$$

in which $x = [x_i]$ is the column vector of a number of females of age j; in which $[L_{1j}] = [m_j]$ is the row vector of nonnegative age-specific fertilities, with $m_n > 0$ if we ignore all post-fertile ages older than n, and with $m_k m_{k+1} > 0$ for some choice of k between 1 and $n-1$; and in which the only nonzeros in *L's last* $n-1$ rows are the positive age-specific survival fractions in the sub-diagonal, $0 < L_{i+1,i} = p_i \leq 1 = l_0, p_1p_2 \ldots p_k = l_k \leq l_{k-1}$ for $1 \leq k < n$.

Now with L assured to be a *primitive* (nonnegative, acyclic, irreducible) Perron–Frobenius matrix, it is well known that the system approaches an exponential rate of growth

$$\lim_{t\to\infty} \frac{x_i(t+1)}{x_i(t)} = 1 + r, \; (i = 1, \ldots, n), \; x(0) > 0 \qquad [2.1]$$

$$-1 < r \lesseqgtr 0,$$

in which $1 + r$ is the positive root of

$$\psi[\lambda] = \sum_1^n m_j l_{j-1} \lambda^{-j} = 1 \qquad [2.2]$$

$$\lim_{t\to\infty} \frac{\sum_1^n x_j(t)}{(1+r)^t} = v[x_1^0, \ldots, x_n^0]. \qquad [2.3]$$

This is a uniquely defined function, fulfilling Fisher's purpose and obeying

$$v[x_1^0, \ldots, x_n^0] = \sum_1^n v_j x_j(0) = vx(0) \qquad [2.4]$$

$$\lim_{t\to\infty} \frac{x_i(t)}{\sum_1^n x_j(t)} = \bar{x}_i, \; \sum_1^n \bar{x}_i = 1 \qquad [2.5]$$

v and $\bar{x}$ being row and column eigenvectors of L corresponding to its characteristic root of largest absolute value, $1 + r$:

$$L\bar{x} = (1+r)\bar{x}, \; 1\bar{x} = 1, \; 1 = (1, 1, \ldots, 1) \qquad [3.1]$$

$$vL = v(1+r), \; v\bar{x} = 1. \qquad [3.2]$$

[Remark: $\sum_1^n x_j(t)/\sum_1^n c_j x_j(t)$, where $c_j > 0$, approaches a constant as $t \to \infty$; so there is no intrinsic bias from adding units of different age on a one-for-one basis.]

Fisher's vector of *reproductive value* is, by definition, proportional to v. (He seems to suggest a normalization for v that makes the reproductive value at birth unity, *my* v/v_1; then his v_j/v_1 gives each age's reproductive value compared to that at birth.) It may be noted that, if we include in L some rows and columns for post-fertile ages, we shall have L reducible and shall have *zeros* for $[v_{n+1}, v_{n+2}, \ldots]$.

Explicit formulas for $\bar{x}$ and v are given, as by Samuelson (ref. 4, p. 396; ref. 5, pp. 400–401), by

$$\bar{x}^T = [\bar{x}_j] = b[1, l_1(1+r)^{-1}, \ldots, l_{n-1}(1+r)^{-n+1}] \qquad [4.1]$$

$$b^{-1} = 1 + l_1(1+r)^{-1} + \ldots + l_{n-1}(1+r)^{-n+1} \qquad [4.2]$$

$$\begin{aligned} v = [v_j] &= a\left[\sum_{k=j}^n m_k l_{k-1}(1+r)^{-k}/l_{j-1}(1+r)^{j-1}\right] \\ &= a[1, m_2(1+r)^{-1} + m_3(l_2/l_1)^{-2} + \ldots \\ &\quad + m_n(l_{n-1}/l_1)(1+r)^{-n+1}, \ldots, m_{n-1}(1+r)^{-1} \\ &\quad + m_n(l_{n-1}/l_{n-2})(1+r)^{-2}, m_n(1+r)^{-1}] \end{aligned} \qquad [4.3]$$

in which

$$a = 1/b\bar{g} \qquad [4.4]$$

$$\begin{aligned} \bar{g} &= -(1+r)\psi'[1+r] \\ &= [1, \ldots, m_n(1+r)^{-1}] \begin{pmatrix} 1 \\ \vdots \\ l_{n-1}(1+r)^{-n+1} \end{pmatrix} \end{aligned} \qquad [4.5]$$

Here b is the stable-age birth rate, $x_1(t)/\sum_1^n x_j(t)$, and $\bar{g}$ is the stable-age "average length of a generation" (i.e., the weighted average age of mothers when giving birth, the weights being the stable-age $[\bar{x}_i] = \bar{x}$).

† This is the first of two related papers. Part 2, "Nonlinear, homogeneous, biparental systems," will appear in the December 1977 PROCEEDINGS.

Keyfitz (ref. 6, pp. 56–58) has provided a useful interpretation of this $v[x_1{}^0, \ldots, x_n{}^0]$ function. It is the size that a stable-age population would have to be *today* to lead to the same *ultimate* population level as our system will generate out of its actual initial conditions $\mathbf{x(0)}$. This defined "equivalent" stable-age system grows from the beginning at rate $1 + r$, and it continues to be "equivalent" to our actual system at ts after $t = 0$; therefore, $v[x_1(t), \ldots, x_n(t)]$ must be a scalar with the remarkable property of growing immediately (and not just asymptotically) at rate $1 + r$. Mathematical proof of this Fisherine property follows.

From the orthogonality properties of the full set of column and row eigenvectors of $\boldsymbol{L}$, we have

$$\begin{aligned} V(t+1) &= \mathbf{v}\mathbf{x}(t+1) = \mathbf{v}\mathbf{L}\mathbf{x}(t) = (1+r)\mathbf{v}\mathbf{x}(t) \\ &= (1+r)V(t) = (1+r)^t V(0) = (1+r)^t[\mathbf{v}\mathbf{x}(\mathbf{0})]. \end{aligned} \quad [5]$$

This verifies that Fisher's total reproductive value does grow from *the beginning* like $(1 + r)^t$, whereas any different linear combination of the $x_i(t)$s will only *asymptotically* grow like $(1 + r)^t$. Reference may be made to Vincent (7), Goodman (8), and Keyfitz (6) for computations and interpretations of reproductive values.

Review of continuous-time case

The integral-equation counterpart of Eqs. [**1–5**] can be written in terms of total female births, $B(t)$, and of number of females of age y at time t, $N(y,t)$, once we are given invariant age-specific survival and fertility functions, $m(y)$ and $l(y)$, as follows:

$$B(t) = \int_\alpha^\beta m(y)N(y,t)dx,\ 0 < \alpha < \beta < \infty. \quad [\mathbf{6.1}]$$

$$N(y,0) = N^0(y) \geq 0, \text{ a given nonnegative function}$$

$$N(y,t) \equiv \frac{l(y)}{l(y-\theta)} N(y-\theta, t-\theta),\ y \geq \theta,\ t \geq \theta \quad [\mathbf{6.2}]$$

$$l(0) = 1;\ l'(y) \leq 0 < l(y),\ 0 \leq y < \gamma;\ l(y) \equiv 0,\ \gamma \leq y$$

$$m(y) > 0,\ 0 < \alpha \leq y \leq \beta < \gamma;\ m(y) \equiv 0,\ \beta < y$$

Provided $\int_0^\beta N^0(y)dy > 0$, it is known that

$$\lim_{t\to\infty} \frac{\partial N(y,t)/\partial t}{N(y,t)} \equiv \rho \lesseqgtr 0. \quad [\mathbf{7.1}]$$

Fisher's *reproductive value* at age y is then definable as

$$\lim_{t\to\infty} \frac{\int_0^\beta N(y,t)dy}{\exp[\rho t]} = \int_0^\beta v(y)N^0(y)dy \quad [\mathbf{7.2}]$$

$$\lim_{t\to\infty} \frac{N(y,t)dy}{\int_0^\gamma N(u,t)du} = \overline{N}(y),\ \int_0^\gamma \overline{N}(y)dy = 1 \quad [\mathbf{7.3}]$$

in which ρ is the real root of

$$\psi(R) = \int_\alpha^\beta m(y)l(y)e^{-Ry}dy = 1 \quad [\mathbf{7.4}]$$

and

$$\overline{N}(y) = bl(y)e^{-\rho y} \quad [\mathbf{7.5}]$$

$$b^{-1} = \int_0^\beta l(u)e^{-\rho u}du \quad [\mathbf{7.6}]$$

and

$$v(y) = a\int_y^\beta m(u)[l(u)/l(y)]e^{-\rho(u-y)}dy \quad [\mathbf{7.7}]$$

$$\int_0^\beta v(y)\overline{N}(y)dy = 1 \quad [\mathbf{7.8}]$$

$$a = 1/b\overline{g}$$

$$\overline{g} = -\psi'(\rho) = +\int_0^\beta ym(y)l(y)e^{-\rho y}dy. \quad [\mathbf{7.9}]$$

As in the discrete-time case of Eq. **4.4**, $\overline{g}$ and b are stable-age average generation length and birth rate (on a pre-menopausal population base).

Specifically, Eq. **7** shows that $N(y,t)$ can be written asymptotically as follows

$$N(y,t) \approx \overline{N}(y)e^{\rho t}\left[\int_0^\beta v(u)N^0(u)du\right]. \quad [\mathbf{8}]$$

It is worth mentioning that, when fertility and mortality depend on total population, T, with

$$T(t) = \int_0^\gamma N(y,t)dy, \quad [\mathbf{9}]$$

$$\partial m(y,T)/\partial T < 0, \qquad \partial l(y,t)/\partial T < 0$$

the *nonlinear* integral equation for $B(t)$ becomes

$$B(t) = \int_\alpha^\beta m(y,T)l(y,T)B(t-y)dy,\quad t \geq \beta < 0 \quad [\mathbf{10.1}]$$

and

$$\lim_{t\to\infty} B(t) = B^*,\quad \lim_{t\to\infty} T(t) = T^* \quad [\mathbf{10.2}]$$

in which T^* is the positive root for T in

$$1 = \int_\alpha^\beta m(y,T)l(y,T)dt \quad [\mathbf{10.3}]$$

and

$$B^* = T^* \Big/ \int_0^\gamma l(y,T^*)dy. \quad [\mathbf{10.4}]$$

Leslie (ref. 9, section 5) and the vast Verhulst (10) and Pearl and Reed (11) literature recognize the realism of Eq. **10**'s nonlinearity.

For the nonlinear model of Eqs. **9–10**, there is *no* existent useful $v(y)$ function that Fisher can find to employ to form

$$V(t) = \int_0^\beta v(y)N(y,t)dy$$

for which

$$V'(t)/V(t) \equiv \text{a constant}.$$

Similarly, for the *logistic* model of Verhulst and Pearl and Reed, which prevails in the post-dilute stage,

$$\dot{x} = x(a - ax\hat{x}^{-1}) \quad [\mathbf{10.5}]$$

$$\lim_{t\to\infty} x(t) = \hat{x} \text{ for all } x(0) > 0 \quad [\mathbf{10.6}]$$

and reproductive value of $x(0)$ is inevitably zero.

In other words, the concept of "reproductive value" loses existence for general nonlinear demographic systems. Unfortunately, the reality any theory of natural selection must face, as Fisher (ref. 3, pp. 41–46) clearly understands, is of the nature of Eq. **10** above rather than Eq. **6** above. Only in early *dilute* stages of Malthus–von Neumann growth (ref. 12) will Eqs. **1** and **6** have relevance; but it is precisely then that selection loses its sting!

In Price and Smith (13) some difficulties with Fisher's $v(y)$ concept are noted when $m(y)l(y)$ in Eq. **7.4** is a varying function of calendar time. The present critique cuts deeper: even if the *structure* of the nonlinear system shows *no* change with calendar t, Fisher's concept of "reproductive value" encounters grave definitional problems.

Linear differential and difference equations

Not all nonlinear systems render reproductive value nugatory. To pave the way for an important class of manageable nonlinear systems, those involving biparental nonlinearities of the type introduced by Kendall (14), we need first to generalize the concept of reproductive value for the linear differential equations of biparental reproduction like those of Goodman (15).

Thus, consider the *linear* version of Eq. **1** that ignores age differences but recognizes two sexes, x_1 for males and x_2 for females. So long as the $[x_i]$ are still so small that the resource limitations of the finite environment are not yet binding, we may model the system's "dilute" stage by the following linear version:

$$\dot{x}_1 = \gamma_1(\beta_1 x_1 + \beta_2 x_2) - \delta_1 x_1 \qquad [11]$$

$$\dot{x}_2 = \gamma_2(\beta_1 x_1 + \beta_2 x_2) - \delta_2 x_2$$

$$\gamma_1 + \gamma_2 = 1;\ \gamma_i, \delta_i, \beta_i > 0,\ \dot{x}_i = dx_i/dt.$$

This can be written in matrix notation as

$$\dot{x} = \boldsymbol{A}\boldsymbol{x}. \qquad [12]$$

As is well known,

$$\lim_{t\to\infty} \frac{\dot{x}_i(t)}{x_i(t)} = \rho \lesseqgtr 0, \quad (i = 1,2) \qquad [13.1]$$

$$\lim_{t\to\infty} \frac{\sum_1^2 x_i(t)}{e^{\rho t}} = v[x_1^0, x_2^0] = [\boldsymbol{v}\boldsymbol{x}(\boldsymbol{0})] \qquad [13.2]$$

$$\lim_{t\to\infty} \frac{x_i(t)}{\sum_1 x_j(t)} = \bar{x}_i, \quad \sum_1^2 \bar{x}_i = 1, \qquad [13.3]$$

in which ρ is the largest real characteristic root of

$$\det[\boldsymbol{A} - \lambda \boldsymbol{I}] = (\rho - \lambda)(\lambda_2 - \lambda),\ \rho > \lambda_2 \qquad [13.4]$$

and $\bar{x}$ and v are ρ's normalized eigenvectors.

$$\boldsymbol{A}\bar{x} = \rho\bar{x}, \quad \sum_1^2 \bar{x}_j = 1 \qquad [13.5]$$

$$\boldsymbol{v}\boldsymbol{A} = \boldsymbol{v}\rho, \quad \boldsymbol{v}\bar{x} = \sum_1^2 v_j\bar{x}_j = 1 \qquad [13.6]$$

$$V(t) = \boldsymbol{v}\boldsymbol{x}(t) \text{ obeys } V'(t) = \rho V(t). \qquad [13.7]$$

Clearly $[v_1, v_2] = \boldsymbol{v}$ is the exact rendition of Fisher's reproductive value for a *linear* 2-sex model. To verify this, consider the female-dominant version discussed by Goodman (ref. 15, p. 213) in which $\beta_1 = 0$.

In this case, males have no role in determining the ultimate growth rate of the system. Does $\boldsymbol{v}$ show this? Indeed it does, because now $[v_1, v_2] = [0, v_2]$. Thus, other things equal, it would be well to harvest only males for game, their reproductive value and role in system growth being zero.

Qualifications and generalizations

As observed by Kendall (14), Goodman (8, 15), and Yellin and Samuelson (16), and as Fisher does not fail to notice, the additive form for the biparental birth function of Eq. **11** has the unrealistic property that increasing the numbers **of one sex alone** adds unflaggingly to the birth rate. How the concept of reproductive value is to be generalized for a more realistic nonadditive birth function must remain as a separate task for analysis.

The linear relations of Eq. **12** can easily be generalized to $n \geq 0$. If either A is a *primitive* Perron–Frobenius matrix, or if A has off-diagonal elements all positive, we are guaranteed that it has a real root ρ that is dominant, and whose characteristic *row* vector provides an appropriate measure of "reproductive value."

Similarly, if we replace $\boldsymbol{L}$ in Eq. **1** by any *primitive* matrix, $\boldsymbol{B}$, so that our biological system takes the form

$$[x_i(t + 1)] = [b_{ij}][x_i(t)], \qquad [\mathbf{14.1}]$$

then for a dominating $1 + r$, we have the characteristic row vector

$$\boldsymbol{v}[b_{ij}] = \boldsymbol{v}(1 + r),\ v > 0. \qquad [\mathbf{14.2}]$$

Thus, reproductive value is proportional to $\boldsymbol{v}$. Even if some b_{ii} are negative, provided $\alpha\boldsymbol{I} + \boldsymbol{B}$ is for some real α a primitive matrix, all our results will apply. Of course, $(1 + r)^t$ for a difference equation system corresponds to $(e^\rho)^t$ for a differential equation system: indeed, $1 + r = e^\rho$ and the systems **12** and **14** are identical for equally spaced values of t if $\boldsymbol{B} = e^{\boldsymbol{A}}$.

What if the system is not irreducible, so that $\boldsymbol{A}$ or $\boldsymbol{B}$ are reducible matrices such that (*i*) either part of the system comes to grow at a slower exponential rate than the rest, or (*ii*) the whole system's ultimate level is independent of some of the variables' initial conditions? Then, as we've already seen in the female-dominant model below Eq. **13**, some of the biological variables have a *zero* reproductive value in the Fisher sense.

What if the system is *cyclic*, so that B generates *asymptotically* a dominating $(1 + r)^t$ component, but one with coefficients for each exponential component that are each functions of the initial $[x_i(0)]$ that are periodic functions of integral period m? Then, strictly speaking, we have m different $v[x_1^0, \ldots, x_n^0]$ functions, $v[k; x_1^0, \ldots, x_n^0]$, in which $v[k + m; x_1^0, \ldots, x_n^0] \equiv [k; x_1^0, \ldots, x_n^0]$ If we take a Cesaro mean of the biological solution,

$$\{\boldsymbol{x}(0) + \boldsymbol{x}(1) + \ldots + \boldsymbol{x}(t)\}/t = \boldsymbol{Y}(t)$$

then a specifiable $\bar{v}[x_1^0, \ldots, x_n^0]$ will give its reproductive value.

Finally, differential and difference equations like **12** and **14**, but with no simple sign restrictions on the a_{ij} and b_{ij} coefficients, could chance to have dominant exponential-growth modes $v[x_1^0, \ldots, x_n^0]\bar{x}\exp[\rho t]$ or $v[x_1^0, \ldots, x_n^0]\bar{x}(1 + r)^t$. But now the $\sum_1^n v_j x_j(0)$ expression might involve some *negative* reproductive-value v_i coefficients. Before spending much time in giving such phenomena a biological interpretation, we have to remind ourselves that the linear modelling of a real-world system is at best useful for the restricted domain of the variables in which the system can be regarded as "dilute." *Logistic* and other saturation relationships, like that in Eq. **10**, will soon enough apply in situations where natural selection has genuine relevance.

My greatest debt is to my collaborator Joel Yellin of the Massachusetts Institute of Technology. I owe thanks to the National Science Foundation Grant 7708959 and National Institutes of Health Grant 1 R01 HD 09081 for partial financial aid.

1. Sharpe, F. R. & Lotka, A. J. (1911) "A problem in age distribution," *Philos. Mag.* **21**, 435–438.
2. Leslie, P. H. (1945) "On the use of matrices in certain population

mathematics," *Biometrika* **33,** 183–212.
3. Fisher, R. A. (1930) *The Genetical Theory of Natural Selection* (Clarendon Press, Oxford).
4. Samuelson, P. A. (1943) "A simple method of interpolation," *Proc. Nat. Acad. Sci. USA* **29,** 397–401. Reproduced as chapter 49 in *Collected Scientific Papers of Paul A. Samuelson,* Vol. I, ed. Stiglitz, J. E., (MIT Press, Cambridge, MA, 1966).
5. Samuelson, P. A. (1943) "Efficient computation of the latent vectors of a matrix," *Proc. Nat. Acad. Sci. USA* **29,** 393–397. Reproduced as chapter 50 in *Collected Scientific Papers of Paul A. Samuelson,* Vol. I, ed. Stiglitz, J. E. (MIT Press, Cambridge, MA, 1966).
6. Keyfitz, N. (1968) *Introduction to the Mathematics of Population* (Addison-Wesley, Reading, MA).
7. Vincent, P. (1945) "Potentiel de'accroisement d'une population stable," *J. Soc. Stat. Paris* **86,** 16–29.
8. Goodman, L. A. (1967) "On the reconciliation of mathematical theories of population growth," *J. R. Stat. Soc. Ser. A,* **130,** 541–553.
9. Leslie, P. H. (1948) "Some further notes on the use of matrices in population mathematics," *Biometrika* **35,** 213–245.
10. Verhulst, P. F. (1838) "Notice sur la loi que la population suit dans son accroissement," *Correspondance mathématique et Physique Publiée par A. Quetêlet (Brussels)* **10,** 113–121.
11. Pearl, R. & Reed, L. J. (1920) "On the rate of growth of population of the United States since 1790 and its mathematical representation," *Proc. Nat. Acad. Sci. USA* **6,** 275–288.
12. von Neumann, J. (1945) "A model of general equilibrium," *Rev. Econ. Stud.* **13,** 1–9.
13. Price, G. R. & Smith, C. A. B. (1972) "Fisher's Malthusian parameter and reproductive value," *Ann. Hum. Genet.* **36,** 1–7.
14. Kendall, D. G. (1949) "Stochastic processes and population growth," *J. R. Stat. Soc. Ser. B,* **11,** 230–264.
15. Goodman, L. A. (1953) "Population growth of the sexes," *Biometrics* **9,** 212–225.
16. Yellin, J. & Samuelson, P. A. (1974) "A dynamical model for human population," *Proc. Nat. Acad. Sci. USA* **71,** 2813–2817.

Generalizing Fisher's "reproductive value": Nonlinear, homogeneous, biparental systems*

(biparental models/dilute homogeneous systems/asymptotic growth states)

PAUL A. SAMUELSON

Department of Economics, Massachusetts Institute of Technology, Cambridge, Massachusetts 02139

Contributed by Paul A. Samuelson, August 22, 1977

ABSTRACT **Biparental demographic models violate linearity. However, in their early "dilute" stages before limited environment resources bring need for competitive selection, first-degree-homogeneous relations obtain. For them, a reproductive-value function of the *initial coordinates* is defined to recapitulate their contribution to the asymptotically dominating mode of exponential growth: now the generalized Fisher reproductive value of one sex is altered by relative numbers of the other sex. The new reproductive-value function is also derived for general systems of homogeneous-first-degree differential and difference equations, and is shown to grow *from the start* at the asymptotic growth rate.**

Review of general linear case

Samuelson (1) provided a comprehensive review of the concept of reproductive value defined by Fisher (2). For the discrete-time Leslie (3) matrix version and for the Sharpe–Lotka (4) integral-equation version of linear demographic systems, reproductive value summarizes the relative quantitative contribution to the system's long-run growth of each initial-condition element: thus, it is the normalizable dominant characteristic (row) eigenvector of the Leslie demographic matrix and the integral-equation equivalent in the continuous-time case.

Generalizing from the one-sex-dominant models of conventional Lotka demography, Samuelson showed how to define and calculate the reproductive-value vector, $[v_1,v_2] = \mathbf{v}$, for a *linear* biparental system like that discussed by Kendall (5) or Goodman (6):

$$\dot{\mathbf{x}} = \mathbf{A}\mathbf{x} \qquad [1]$$

$$= \begin{bmatrix} dx_1/dt \\ dx_2/dt \end{bmatrix} = \begin{bmatrix} \gamma_1\beta_1 - \delta_1 & \gamma_1\beta_2 \\ \gamma_2\beta_1 & \gamma_2\beta_2 - \delta_2 \end{bmatrix} \begin{bmatrix} x_1 \\ x_2 \end{bmatrix}$$

$$\gamma_1 + \gamma_2 = 1; \quad \gamma_i,\beta_i > 0$$

$$\mathbf{x}(t) \approx \{\mathbf{v}\mathbf{x}(\mathbf{0})\}\, \mathbf{x} e^{\rho t}$$

$$\det[\mathbf{A} - \lambda \mathbf{I}] = (\rho - \lambda)(\lambda_2 - \lambda), \quad 0 \gtreqless \rho > \lambda_2$$

$$\mathbf{A}\mathbf{x} = \rho \mathbf{x}, \quad [1 \quad 1]\mathbf{x} = 1$$

$$\mathbf{v}\mathbf{A} = \mathbf{v}\rho, \quad \mathbf{v}\mathbf{x} = 1$$

$$\mathbf{v}\mathbf{x}(t) = e^{\rho t}\, \mathbf{v}\mathbf{x}(\mathbf{0}).$$

Bold-face type in the equations above denotes matrices and vectors. The above relations recapitulate Samuelson (ref. 1, equations **12–13**).

First-degree-homogeneous biparental case

It is proposed here to show how Fisher's concept of reproductive value can be properly generalized for the manageable biparental nonlinear models of the type discussed by Kendall (5), Goodman (6), Pollard (7), Yellin and Samuelson (8), and others. Instead of the linear system in **1**, we encounter

$$\dot{x}_1 = \gamma_1 B[x_1,x_2] - \delta_1 x_1 \qquad [2]$$

$$\dot{x}_2 = \gamma_2 B[x_1,x_2] - \delta_2 x_2$$

$$\gamma_1 + \gamma_2 = 1; \quad \gamma_i,\delta_i > 0.$$

Here, as before, δ_i is the force of mortality for the ith category. The sex ratio at birth is a constant, $\gamma_1/\gamma_2 \gtreqless 1$. What is new is the jointly interacting *biparental* birth function, $B[x_1,x_2]$, which is biologically nonlinear: with zero males, births are zero; with zero females, births are zero; as one increases the number of one sex alone, the number of the other sex held constant, one encounters the law of diminishing returns in births; however, if one doubles *both* sexes together, births double so long as the environment's limitation of resources is not yet binding on the *dilute* system.

This means that $B[x_1,x_2]$ is a homogeneous-first-degree, concave, monotone-increasing function:

$$B[x_1,x_2] \equiv \lambda^{-1}B[\lambda x_1,\lambda x_2] \equiv x_1 f[x_2/x_1] \geq 0 \qquad [3]$$

$$0 \equiv B[x_1,0] \equiv B[0,x_2]; \quad f'[v] > 0 > f''[v], \quad v > 0.$$

What is not clear is whether, for x_i frozen, a large enough increase in x_j can raise the rate of birth above any preassigned level, as with the "geometric-mean" example

$$B[x_1,x_2] = a x_1^{\alpha} x_2^{1-\alpha}, \quad 0 < \alpha < 1 \qquad [4.1]$$

$$\lim_{x_2\to\infty} B[1,x_2] = \infty = \lim_{x_1\to\infty} B[x_1,1]$$

or whether, as would actually seem more realistic, limiting the number of one sex must limit the level of possible rate of births no matter how numerous is the other sex—as with the "harmonic-mean" example:

$$B[x_1,x_2] = a\frac{x_1x_2}{\alpha x_1 + (1-\alpha)x_2}, \quad 0 < \alpha < 1 \qquad [4.2]$$

$$\lim_{x_2\to\infty} B[1,x_2] = a(1-\alpha)^{-1} < \infty > a\alpha^{-1} = \lim_{x_1\to\infty} B[x_1,1]$$

Still other examples are

$$B[x_1,x_2] = a\, \mathrm{Min}[x_1/c_1, x_2/c_2] \qquad [4.3]$$

$$B[x_1,x_2] = a[\alpha x_1^{\theta} + (1-\alpha)x_2^{\theta}]^{1/\theta}, \quad 0 \neq \theta < 1. \qquad [4.4]$$

The asymptotic solution of **2**'s nonlinear biparental model has the essential exponential-mode properties of the Lotka–Fisher model, or of **1**'s 2-parent linear model.

More precisely, for $|\delta_1 - \delta_2|$ and $|\gamma_1 - \gamma_2|$ not too large (or,

* This is the second paper of a pair; the first paper is ref. 1.

in **4.1**'s case where $B[1,x_2]$ and $B[x_1,1]$ are unbounded, for *any* positive δs and γs), and for initial $[x_i^0]$ positive:

$$\lim_{t\to\infty}\frac{\dot{x}_i}{x_i} = \rho \gtreqless 0, \quad (i = 1,2), \quad x(0) > 0 \qquad [5.1]$$

$$\lim_{t\to\infty}\frac{x_i(t)}{\Sigma_1^2 x_j(t)} = \bar{x}_i > 0, \quad \sum_1^2 \bar{x}_j = 1 \qquad [5.2]$$

$$\lim_{t\to\infty}\frac{\Sigma_1^2 x_j(t)}{e^{\rho t}} = v[x_1^0,x_2^0] \equiv \lambda^{-1}v[\lambda x_1^0,\lambda x_2^0] \qquad [5.3]$$

in which (ρ; $\bar{x}_1,\bar{x}_2$) are the unique positive real roots of

$$\rho = \gamma_1 f[x_2/x_1] - \delta_1 \qquad [6.1]$$

$$= \gamma_2 f[x_2/x_1](x_2/x_1)^{-1} - \delta_2 \qquad [6.2]$$

$$x_1 + x_2 = 1, \quad x_i > 0 \qquad [6.3]$$

and in which $v[x_1^0,x_2^0]$ is a determinate *generalized reproductive-value function* calculable from the existent solutions to **2,** $[X_i[t;\ x(0)]$, and **5.3**'s limit.

[Remark: As shown by Yellin and Samuelson (ref. 8, table 1, sections 9–11) and by Samuelson (ref. 9, p. 110), there need *not* always be an exponential solution to a homogeneous demographic system: instead, the sex ratio may diverge to infinity—as for example when $f[\quad]$ is derived from **4.2** and the death rate of one of the sexes is *very* much larger than the other, so that the sex ratio goes to zero or infinity as both groups hasten to extinction.]

The reader will note the complete parallelism of the nonlinear relations of **5–6** to the already established linear reproductive-value relations given in **1**.

The reproductive-value function

It remains to investigate the properties of **5.3**'s reproductive-value function, $v[x_1^0,x_2^0]$, which is the desired nonlinear *generalization* of Fisher's linear reproductive-value concept, $v_1x_1^0 + v_2x_2 + \ldots$.

Actually, it can be shown from the homogeneity property of $B[x_1,x_2]$ that $v[x_1^0,x_2^0]$ must have a similar first-degree-homogeneous property

$$v[\lambda x_1^0,\lambda x_2^0] \equiv \lambda v[x_1^0,x_2^0] \geq 0, \quad \lambda > 0 \qquad [7.1]$$

$$v_i[\quad] = \partial v[x_1^0,x_2^0]/\partial x_i^0 > 0, \quad (i = 1,2), \quad [x_j^0] > 0 \qquad [7.2]$$

$$1 = \frac{x_1^0 v_1[x_1^0,x_2^0]}{v[x_1^0,x_2^0]} + \frac{x_2^0 v_2[x_1^0,x_2^0]}{v[x_1^0,x_2^0]}. \qquad [7.3]$$

Now that we have our generalized reproductive-value *function*, we shall find that it lacks some of the properties that Fisher was able to find in the linear case of $v[x_1^0,x_2^0] = v_1x_1^0 + v_2x_2^0$. No longer can Fisher speak of the reproductive value of one segment of the population *without regard to its plenitude relative to other segments*. How much an extra female is "worth" to Australia in 1911 cannot be put in a table like that of Fisher (ref. 2, figure 2, p. 28) without regard to how many males there are in Australia—as Fisher implicitly realizes elsewhere in his discussion. On the other hand, he seems to nod in inferring (ref. 2, p. 159):

> If we consider the aggregate of an entire generation of such offspring [ready to reproduce, which would seem to be (x_1^0,x_2^0) in our modelling] it is clear that the total reproductive value of the males in this group is exactly equal to the total value of all females, because each sex must supply half the ancestry of all future generations of the species.

What can this mean? That half of $v[x_1^0,x_2^0]$ in some sense belongs to each sex? The least ambiguous measure of each sex's *separate total* reproductive value would seem to be given by $x_i^0\partial v(x_1^0,x_2^0)/\partial x_i^0$ from **7.3**. For each of these to be *always* one-half because every diploid birth has both a mother and father, this last prosaic biological fact would have to imply that $v[x_1^0,x_2^0]$ is of the equally weighted geometric-mean type

$$v[x_1^0,x_2^0] \overset{?}{=} c[x_1^0x_2^0]^{1/2} \qquad [8]$$

This, however, is quite invalid—as any experimentation with actual admissible instances of $B[x_1,x_2]$ in **2** will confirm. Indeed I have not yet been able to find even one admissible $B[x_1,x_2]$ function for which **8** obtains!

What is a different and more trivial matter is that, under the singular assumption of *complete symmetry,*

$$B[x_1,x_2] \equiv B[x_2,x_1], \quad \gamma_1 = \gamma_2 = \tfrac{1}{2}, \quad \delta_1 = \delta_2 = \delta \qquad [9]$$

it is obvious that $v[x_1^0,x_n^0]$ is then a symmetric function, with each sex of "equal reproductive value" *when the sex ratio is balanced* (and *only* then):

$$v[x_1^0,x_2^0] \equiv v[x_2^0,x_1^0] \qquad [10.1]$$

$$x_1^0v_1[x_1^0,x_2^0] = x_2^0v_2[x_1^0,x_2^0] = \tfrac{1}{2}v[x_1^0,x_2^0] \qquad [10.2]$$

when

$$x_1^0 = x_2^0. \qquad [10.3]$$

The *reproductive value* of *each* member of a sex, as measured by $\partial v[x_1^0,x_2^0]/\partial x_i^0$, will rise as it becomes scarce and x_i^0/x_j^0 falls; but one cannot predict in advance how the *total* reproductive value of *all* members of that sex moves when x_i^0/x_j^0 falls, because $x_i^0(\partial v[x_1^0,x_2^0]/\partial x_i^0)$ may rise or fall in the general case.

A counterexample

To grasp the meaning of these corrections to the conventional view, begin with the case that would seem most favorable to the Fisher quotation—the case of complete symmetry and **4.1**'s geometric mean:

$$\dot{x}_1 = \beta(x_1x_2)^{1/2} - \delta x_1,$$
$$\dot{x}_2 = \beta(x_1x_2)^{1/2} - \delta x_2; \quad \beta,\delta > 0. \qquad [11]$$

For $x_1^0 = 0$, obviously the solution is given by $[x_j(t)] = [0,x_2^0e^{-\delta t}]$. However, as soon as we move ever so little from either axis, making *both* $[x_j^0]$ positive, the system's asymptotic growth rate becomes the *faster* growth rate $\exp[(\beta - \delta)t]$. As will be seen below, the exact solution can be written as

$$x_i(t) = v[x_1^0,x_2^0]e^{(\beta-\delta)t}\{1 + \epsilon(t)\} \qquad [12.1]$$
$$= [\tfrac{1}{4}x_1^0 + \tfrac{1}{4}x_2^0 + \tfrac{1}{2}(x_1^0x_2^0)^{1/2}]e^{(\beta-\delta)t}\{1 + \epsilon(t)\}$$

$$\lim_{t\to\infty}\epsilon(t) = 0 \text{ for all positive } (x_1^0,x_2^0). \qquad [12.2]$$

From **12.1** we see that even in this case most favorable to Fisher's purported equal sharing of reproductive value among the two (needed!) sexes, it is actually the case that the *scarcest* sex has the *least* total reproductive value.

To verify **12** and handle more realistic cases of nonvanishing $|\gamma_1 - \gamma_2|$ and $|\delta_1 - \delta_2|$, we may analyze the one nonlinear case shown by Kendall (ref. 5, equation **72**) to be exactly solvable. Put **4.1**'s symmetric geometric mean into **2** to get

$$\dot{x}_i = \gamma_i 2\beta(x_1x_2)^{1/2} - \delta_i x_i, \quad (i = 1,2) \qquad [13]$$
$$\gamma_1 + \gamma_2 = 1; \quad \gamma_i,\delta_i,\beta > 0; \quad [x_j^0] > 0.$$

Transform the $[x_j]$ to new variables $[y_j]$:

$$x_1^{1/2} = y_1,\ x_2^{1/2} = y_2;\ x_1 = y_1^2,\ x_2 = y_2^2;\ x_i > 0 \quad [14.1]$$

$$\dot{x}_i = 2y_i\dot{y}_i, \quad (i = 1,2). \quad [14.2]$$

Then **13** is transformed into the exactly linear system, with the following properties

$$\dot{y} = \begin{bmatrix} \dot{y}_1 \\ \dot{y}_2 \end{bmatrix} = Ay = \begin{bmatrix} -\frac{1}{2}\delta_1 & \gamma_1\beta \\ \gamma_2\beta & -\frac{1}{2}\delta_2 \end{bmatrix} \begin{bmatrix} y_1 \\ y_2 \end{bmatrix} \quad [15.1]$$

$$\det[A - \lambda I] = \lambda^2 + \tfrac{1}{2}(\delta_1 + \delta_2)\lambda + \tfrac{1}{4}(\delta_1\delta_2 - 4\gamma_1\gamma_2\beta^2) \quad [15.2]$$

$$= (\rho - \lambda)(\lambda_2 - \lambda), \quad 0 \gtreqless \rho > \lambda_2$$

$$A\begin{bmatrix} \bar{y}_1 \\ \bar{y}_2 \end{bmatrix} = \rho\begin{bmatrix} \bar{y}_1 \\ \bar{y}_2 \end{bmatrix}; \quad \bar{y}_i \geq 0, \quad \bar{y}_1 + \bar{y}_2 = 1 \quad [15.3]$$

$$[v_1\ v_2]A = [v_1\ v_2]\rho, \quad v_j \geq 0 \quad [15.4]$$

$$v_1\bar{y}_1 + v_2\bar{y}_2 = v\bar{y} = 1 \quad [15.5]$$

$$y_i(t) = [v_1y_1^0 + v_2y^0]\bar{y}_ie^{\rho t} \times \{1 + c_i\exp[(\lambda_2 - \rho)t]\} \quad [15.6]$$

$$x_i(t) = y_i(t)^2 = [v_1^2x_1^0 + v_2^2x_2^0 + 2v_1v_2(x_1^0x_2^0)^{1/2}]\bar{y}_i^2e^{2\rho t} \times \{1 + 2c_i\exp[(\lambda_2 - \rho)t] + c_i^2\exp[2(\lambda_2 - \delta)t]\}, \quad (i = 1,2). \quad [15.7]$$

Hence, for our nonlinear system **13**, the correct reproductive value is calculated to be

$$v[x_1^0,x_2^0] = (v_1)^2x_1^0 + (v_2^2)x_2^0 + 2v_1v_2(x_1^0x_2^0)^{1/2} \quad [16.1]$$

$$\partial v[x_1^0x_2^0]/\partial x_i^0 = (v_i)^2 + v_1v_2(x_j^0/x_i^0], \quad j \neq i \quad [16.2]$$

$$x_i\{\partial v[x_1^0,x_2^0]/\partial x_i\} = (v_i)^2x_i^0 + v_1v_2(x_1^0x_2^0)^{1/2}, \quad \text{a rising function of } x_i^0. \quad [16.3]$$

Warning: For an $x_i^0 = 0$, the $e^{2\rho t}$ growth mode becomes irrelevant: so it is dangerous to go all the way to the limit $x_i^0 \to 0$, for the reason that the Kendall transformation of variables in **14** fails on either x_i axis. Always in **5** and **6** it is important to avoid cases where either x_i vanishes and where $\exp(-\delta_it)$ solutions supercede the exponential growth modes of **6**.

Invariant growth rate of reproductive value

Because we know from the established linear analysis that $vy(0)$ in **15.6** grows *from the beginning* like $e^{\rho t}$, we know that $\Sigma_1^2 v_jx_j(t)^{1/2}$ has the invariant growth rate of ρ. Its square has the invariant growth of 2ρ. So **16**'s reproductive-value function $v[x_1^0,x_2^0]$ does grow *from the beginning* at the nonlinear system's asymptotic growth rate of 2ρ. But, is this important Fisher property valid only for nonlinear systems that are merely a disguised transformation of a linear system in other variables—as in **13–14**, which is admittedly a special, Santa Claus, case?

Fortunately, we can give the following proof that the nonlinear system's reproductive-value function, $v[x_1(t),x_2(t)]$, defined by **5**, has Fisher's invariant growth rate property.

We have

$$\lim_{\tau\to\infty} \frac{\sum_1^2 x_j(t + \tau)}{e^{\rho\tau}} = v[x_1(t),x_2(t)], \quad \text{by 5.3's definition} \quad [17.1]$$

$$\equiv e^{\rho t} \lim_{t+\tau\to\infty} \frac{\sum_1^2 x_j(t + \tau)}{\exp[\rho(t + \tau)]}, \quad \text{by substitution}$$

$$\equiv e^{\rho t}v[x_1(0),x_2(0)] \quad \text{Q.E.D.} \quad [17.2]$$

Thus, for the most general nonlinear system that approaches asymptotically to a balanced state of exponential growth, we can define a reproductive-value function with the usual Fisher properties. Indeed, there is nothing of black magic involved in this invariant growth rate of the reproductive-value function from the beginning: that property is implicit in its original definition.

Generalizations

We have completed the task of properly defining a nonlinear function of so-called reproductive value. There remains the task of showing how this applies to any number of coordinates, $(x_1, \ldots ,x_n)$, $n \geq 2$; and the task of showing how the concept is defined for *difference* rather than *differential* equations.

Consider the alternative first-degree-homogeneous systems:

$$dx_i/dt = f^i[x_1, \ldots ,x_n], \quad (i = 1, \ldots ,n)$$
$$= \lambda^{-1}f^i[\lambda x_1, \ldots ,\lambda x_n], \quad \lambda > 0 \quad [18.1]$$

and

$$x_i(t + 1) = F^i[x_1(t), \ldots ,x_n(t)], \quad (i = 1, \ldots ,n) \quad [18.2]$$
$$= \lambda^{-1}F^i[\lambda x_1(t), \ldots ,\lambda x_n(t)], \quad \lambda > 0.$$

These can represent essentially the same system in the following sense. Write down the solution of **18.1** at $t + \tau$ in terms of its non-negative initial conditions at t, $[x_j(t)]$:

$$x_i(t + \tau) = X^i[\tau;\ x_1(t), \ldots ,x_n(t)], \quad (i = 1, \ldots ,n) \quad [18.3]$$
$$= \lambda^{-1}X^i[\tau;\ \lambda x_1(t), \ldots, \lambda x_n(t)].$$

The indicated first-degree-homogeneity of **18.3**'s solution follows from that of **18.1**. Now set $\tau = 1$ in **18.3** to derive

$$x_i(t + 1) = X^i[1;\ x_1(t), \ldots ,x_n(t)], \quad (i = 1, \ldots ,n). \quad [18.4]$$

It will now be obvious that **18.4** is identical in form and substance to **18.2**: hence, it is seen that the differential-equation system **18.1** generates at equally spaced intervals of *t exactly* the same solution as **18.2** does.

The same exponential-growth mode will exist for **18.1** as for **18.2**, $[\bar{x}_i](e^\rho)^t$ or $[\bar{x}_i](1 + r)^t$;

$$1 + r = e^\rho, \quad \rho = \log_e(1 + r) \quad [19.1]$$

and where the $\bar{x}$s are the positive solutions of the equivalent alternative sets

$$\rho\bar{x}_i = F^i[\bar{x}_1, \ldots ,\bar{x}_n], \quad \sum_1^n \bar{x}_i = 1, \quad [19.2]$$

$$(1 + r)\bar{x}_i = F^i[\bar{x}_i, \ldots ,\bar{x}_n], \quad (i = 1, \ldots ,n). \quad [19.3]$$

It is of course not necessary that there exists a solution in **19**, or that it be unique, or even that an existent unique solution be "locally stable." Thus, Yellin and Samuelson (ref. 8, table 1) give examples of null solutions and of locally unstable solutions that can obtain in feasible demographic models. In reducible examples—one such is the trivial case where $\dot{x}_1/x_1 = \dot{x}_2/x_2 = \rho$—**19** has an infinity of solutions; hence, there is a different reproductive-value function for each x_i or for any of an infinite number of homogeneous-first-degree functions of x_1 and x_2! Unfortunately, the standard Hardy–Weinberg case in genetics possesses just such degeneracy.

It is shown by Solow and Samuelson (10), that, provided the partial derivatives $(F_j^i[x_1, \ldots ,x_n])$ are all positive numbers in the non-negative orthant $[x_i] \geq 0$, such unique solutions will exist. Indeed, if the off-diagonal elements of $(F^i_j[\quad])$ or of $(f^i_j[\quad])$ are positive for $[x_i] \geq 0$ and the diagonal elements are bounded, that will suffice to guarantee a unique and stable exponential growth mode, $\bar{x}_i(1 + r)^t$.

The generalized *reproductive-value function* is now easily defined as $v[x_1^0, \ldots, x_n^0]$ in **20.2**

$$\lim_{t \to \infty} \frac{x_i(t+1)}{x_i(t)} = 1 + r > 0, \quad (i = 1, \ldots, n) \qquad [20.1]$$

$$\lim_{t \to \infty} \frac{\sum_1^n x_j(t)}{(1+r)^t} = v[x_1^0, \ldots, x_n^0] = \lambda^{-1} v[\lambda x_1^0, \ldots, \lambda x_n^0]. \qquad [20.2]$$

This completes the generalization. One should conclude with a warning: Every environment has ultimately limited resources that serve in the end to terminate the dilute first-degree-homogeneous stage of Malthus and von Neumann (11). In that case, reproductive value is by definition zero because the initial conditions $[x_1^0, \ldots, x_n^0]$ wash out in the limit:

$$\lim_{t \to \infty} X^i[t; \; x_1^0, \ldots, x_n^0] \equiv x_i^*, \quad (i = 1, \ldots, n). \qquad [21]$$

In concluding, one must warn that the concept of reproductive value has often been used in a loose way. There remains the analytic task of auditing its claims, as for example in connection with optimal harvesting and other problems. Unfortunately, the homogeneity assumptions underlying dilute systems then become peculiarly vulnerable and the whole concept of reproductive value must be handled with care.

My greatest debt is to my collaborator Joel Yellin of Massachusetts Institute of Technology. I have benefitted from helpful conversations with Nathan Keyfitz. Gratitude goes to Vicki Elms for editorial assistance. I owe thanks to National Science Foundation Grant 7708959 and National Institutes of Health Grant 1 RO1 HD 09081 for partial financial aid.

1. Samuelson, P. A. (1977) "Generalizing Fisher's 'reproductive value': Linear differential and difference equations of 'dilute' biological systems," *Proc. Natl. Acad. Sci. USA* **74**, 5189–5192.
2. Fisher, R. A. (1930) *The Genetical Theory of Natural Selection* (Clarendon Press, Oxford).
3. Leslie, P. H. (1945) "On the use of matrices in certain population mathematics," *Biometrika* **33**, 183–212.
4. Sharpe, F. R. & Lotka, A. J. (1911) "A problem in age distribution," *Philos. Mag.* **21**, 435–438.
5. Kendall, D. G. (1949) "Stochastic processes and population growth," *J. R. Stat. Soc. Ser B* **11**, 230–264.
6. Goodman, L. A. (1953) "Population growth of the sexes," *Biometrics* **9**, 212–225.
7. Pollard, J. H. (1973) *Mathematical Models for the Growth of Human Populations* (Cambridge University Press, New York).
8. Yellin, J. & Samuelson, P. A. (1974) "A dynamical model for human population," *Proc. Natl. Acad. Sci. USA* **71**, 2813–2817.
9. Samuelson, P. A. (1976) "Time symmetry and asymmetry in population and deterministic dynamic systems," *Theor. Pop. Biol.* **9**, 82–122.
10. Solow, R. M. & Samuelson, P. A. (1953) "Balanced growth under constant returns to scale," *Econometrica* **21**, 412–424.
11. von Neumann, J. (1945) "A model of general economic equilibrium," *Rev. Econ. Stud.* **13**, 1–9.

Generalizing Fisher's "reproductive value": Overlapping and nonoverlapping generations with competing genotypes†

(dilute systems/homogeneous functions/Hardy–Weinberg model/biparental genetics)

PAUL A. SAMUELSON

Department of Economics, Massachusetts Institute of Technology, Cambridge, Massachusetts 02139

Contributed by Paul A. Samuelson, June 6, 1978

ABSTRACT How to go beyond Fisher's 1930 linear eigenvector definition of reproductive value has been established for dilute systems whose dynamic relations are first-degree-homogeneous functions so that intensive ratios are scale-free. Here such an extension is applied to standard mendelian models. It is shown that, aside from singular cases like that of the Hardy–Weinberg razor's-edge labile equilibrium, such general systems are irreducibly nonlinear and admit of reproductive-value functions that are calculable only in an *infinite* number of steps.

Before an age-structured dynamic system in population genetics settles down into its state of balanced exponential growth or stationarity, it may first display quasi-oscillatory transients that depend on its initial conditions. The concept of *reproductive value* was introduced by Fisher (1, Chap. 2) to summarize how the ultimate level of the system's growth mode depends upon the initial values of the separate phase variables. Keyfitz (2) represents one valuable use of essentially this concept in his measurement of the "momentum" of a population that suddenly shifts from high-growth fertility to stationary-growth fertility. How high the population will continue to grow, in the ensuing several decades required to iron out the distortions in the system's initial age distribution inherited from past high fertility, can be estimated by Keyfitz's ingenious variant of the Fisher concept.

A possible purpose of reproductive value is to provide an appropriate surrogate model that is *immediately* in equilibrium and replaces the more complicated true system's initial gyrations and transients. Thus, consider a simple diploid model with AA, aa, and Aa (or aA) numbers, involving *overlapping generations and age-phased differences in mortality and fertility.* Then the simple Hardy–Weinberg property is lost in which the proportions of AA, aa, and Aa genotypes settle down *immediately* to their equilibrium values. Can we perhaps hope to approximate from the beginning such a system's ultimate equilibrium proportions and scale by means of some clever (*finitely*-calculable!) weightings of the initial age-and-genotype classes along the lines of Fisher's reproductive-value concept or from its patent generalizations in Samuelson (3, 4)? Some such hope seems to have been nurtured, but detailed investigation of its practicality has been neglected in the two generations since Fisher's classic 1930 treatise. The present paper explores the application of reproductive value to some standard nonlinear models of simplest mendelian genetics. The limitations of the concept, as well as its successes, are revealed.

The Hardy–Weinberg case

First, consider the simplest monoecious model of nonoverlapping generations, involving genotypes AA, aa, and Aa or aA. If all genotypes have the same fertilities and mortalities and mating is independently random rather than assortative, the Hardy–Weinberg law will obtain and the system will settle down in one generation to its ultimate genotype proportions. The common mortalities and fertilities could depend on the size of the total adult population, $N(t)$, relative to the carrying capacity of the environment without necessarily affecting this truth about *intensive* proportions or ratios; moreover, the *extensive* dynamic relation relating total $N(t+1)$ to $N(t)$ could be such that ultimately the system's malthusian parameter of growth dampens down to zero. Until a sequel, such density-dependent effects will be ignored in order to parallel Fisher's original derivation of reproductive value.

Denote the respective numbers at time t of adults of types AA, aa, and Aa (aA is included with Aa) by $[N_{AA}(t), N_{aa}(t), N_{Aa}(t)]$. The total population, $N(t)$, is defined at each time by the relations

$$\begin{aligned} N &= N_{AA} + N_{aa} + N_{Aa} \\ &= (N_{AA} + \tfrac{1}{2}N_{Aa}) + (N_{aa} + \tfrac{1}{2}N_{Aa}) \\ &= N_A + N_a = (p+q)N. \end{aligned} \quad [1]$$

The totals of A and a alleles, N_A and N_a, are implicitly defined in Eqs. 1, as are the intensive proportions.

Under completely nonassortative mating, with no differential selective effects on fertilities or mortalities, the number of births of type AA and of adults of that type will each be proportional to the product N_A^2; those of type aa will be proportional to N_a^2; those of type Aa will be proportional to $2N_AN_a$. The factor of proportionality appropriate for adults of the next generation, which will itself be the product of fertility and mortality-survivorship factors, can be written as λ/N. (If increases in N lower λ because of saturation effects of higher densities in a limited environment, λ is short for $\lambda[N]$, where $\lambda'[N] \le 0$. In a sequel, the effects on the concept of reproductive value of having $\lambda[N]$ drop below $\lambda[0] = \lambda$ will be analyzed in detail.)

Our assumptions lead to the following dynamic recursion relations for successive generations of $[N_{AA}(t), N_{aa}(t), N_{Aa}(t)]$, where the operator symbol E is used to shorten the written difference equations by being given the meaning $EN_{AA} = N_{AA}(t+1)$,

$$EN_{AA} = N^{-1}[N_{AA} + \tfrac{1}{2}N_{Aa}]^2\lambda \quad [2.1]$$

$$EN_{aa} = N^{-1}[N_{aa} + \tfrac{1}{2}N_{Aa}]^2\lambda \quad [2.2]$$

$$EN_{Aa} = 2N^{-1}[N_{AA} + \tfrac{1}{2}N_{Aa}][N_{aa} + \tfrac{1}{2}N_{Aa}]\lambda. \quad [2.3]$$

Under our assumptions of common fertilities and mortalities, the total population satisfies a simple relation that is indepen-

† This is paper no. 3 in a series. Paper no. 2 is ref. 3.

dent of its relative genotype composition: adding the above three relations yields

$$EN(t) = N(t)\lambda. \qquad [2.4]$$

The behavior of the subaggregates is determinable from adjoining to Eq. **2.4** the following relation deducible from Eqs. **2.1–2.3:**

$$Ep(t) = p(t), \quad t \geq 0$$

$$EN_{AA}(t) = N(t)p(t)^2, EN_{aa}(t) = N(t)[1 - p(t)]^2. \qquad [2.5]$$

Eqs. **2.5** are the embodiment of what is called the Hardy–Weinberg law, in which the system settles down in one generation to its stable $(p^2, q^2, 2pq)$ proportions (see for example ref. 5). From them and Eq. **2.4** we can write down at once the system's explicit solution, which grows from the beginning proportionally to the geometric progression $(1 + r^*)^t$:

$$N(t) = (1 + r^*)^t N^0, \quad t \geq 0; \quad 1 + r^* = \lambda \qquad [3.1]$$

$$N_{AA}(t) = p(0)^2(1 + r^*)^t N^0$$

$$N_{aa}(t) = q(0)^2(1 + r^*)^t N^0$$

$$N_{Aa}(t) = 2p(0)q(0)(1 + r^*)^t N^0 \qquad [3.2]$$

$$N_A(t) = p(0)(1 + r^*)^t N^0, p(0) + q(0) = 1$$

$$N_a(t) = q(0)(1 + r^*)^t N^0. \qquad [3.3]$$

This simple Hardy–Weinberg case has no need for a surrogate system based upon some prior calculated reproductive value. It is its own surrogate. The question is whether systems that are not so degenerately simple as the Hardy–Weinberg case can be artifically given its simplicity by means of artful calculation of fisherine reproductive values.

Nonuniform fertilities and mortalities

The general case will involve different fertilities and mortalities for the different genotypes, $(\lambda_{AA}, \lambda_{aa}, \lambda_{Aa})$ rather than the common λ of the Hardy–Weinberg example. For almost all values of these three λs, the system's asymptotic growth mode will have its $[\dot{n}_{AA}, \dot{n}_{aa}, \dot{n}_{Aa}; p^*, 1 - p^*]$ proportions generally independent of the positive initial conditions $[N^0_{AA}, N^0_{aa}, N^0_{Aa}]$. Hence, essentially one reproductive-value function $v[N^0_{AA}, N^0_{aa}, N^0_{Aa}]$, will be definable. Now the general dynamic relations become

$$EN_{AA} = N^{-1}N_A^2\lambda_{AA} = N^{-1}[N_{AA} + \tfrac{1}{2}N_{Aa}]^2\lambda_{AA}$$

$$EN_{aa} = N^{-1}N_a^2\lambda_{aa} = N^{-1}[N_{aa} + \tfrac{1}{2}N_{Aa}]^2\lambda_{aa}$$

$$EN_{Aa} = 2N^{-1}N_A N_a \lambda_{Aa}$$

$$= 2N^{-1}[N_{AA} + \tfrac{1}{2}N_{Aa}][N_{aa} + \tfrac{1}{2}N_{Aa}]\lambda_{Aa}. \qquad [4]$$

Relations **4** are like those met in standard mendelian genetics, as in ref. 5, but with this generalization: the total number, N, is not assumed to necessarily stay the same from generation to generation; how the total $N(t)$ changes will ultimately depend upon how large $N(t)$ is in comparison with the environment's carrying capacity; but so long as $N(t)$ is small enough so that the system can be regarded as dilute, how fast $N(t)$ grows depends only upon the proportions of the different genotypes (or, under random mating, on the proportions of the gene totals).

In terms of total genes as phase variables, $[N_A(t), N_a(t)]$, the dynamic laws of motion of the system **4** can be written under random mating as

$$EN_A = [N_A + N_a]^{-1}N_A[N_A\lambda_{AA} + N_a\lambda_{Aa}]$$

$$EN_a = [N_A + N_a]^{-1}N_a[N_a\lambda_{aa} + N_A\lambda_{Aa}]. \qquad [5]$$

Replacing $[N_A, N_a]$ by phase variables

$$N = N_A + N_a, Z = N_A - N_a; z = Z/N$$

$$N_A = \tfrac{1}{2}[N + Z], N_a = \tfrac{1}{2}[N - Z] \qquad [6]$$

we have as an equivalent to Eqs. **5**

$$Ez = \frac{[1 + z]^2\lambda_{AA} - [1 - z]^2\lambda_{aa}}{[1 + z]^2\lambda_{AA} + [1 - z]^2\lambda_{aa} + 2[1 + z][1 - z]\lambda_{Aa}} = \psi(z) \qquad [6.1]$$

$$EN = \tfrac{1}{4}N\{[1 + z]^2\lambda_{AA} + [1 - z]^2\lambda_{aa} + 2[1 - z^2]\lambda_{Aa}\}. \qquad [6.2]$$

Eq. **6.1** is an autonomous difference equation for $z(t)$ alone. To solve for a stationary solution, $z(\infty)$, we equate Ez and z in Eq. **6.1**. The resulting cubic equation in z has three real roots: $(1, -1, z^*)$. The first two correspond to axis solutions where but one of the homozygous genotypes obtains:

$$N_{aa}(t) \equiv 0 \equiv N_{Aa}(t), [z(t),p(t),q(t)] \equiv [1,1,0] \qquad [7.1]$$

$$N_{AA}(t) \equiv 0 \equiv N_{Aa(t)}, [z(t),p(t),q(t)] \equiv [-1,0,1]. \qquad [7.2]$$

Provided the third root, call it z^*, falls on the interval $-1 < z < +1$, we have genotypes coexisting in equilibrium. The equilibrium will be stable:

$$\lim_{t \to \infty} z(t) = z^* = \psi(z^*) \text{ if } -1 < \psi'(z^*) < 1. \qquad [8.1]$$

The ultimate geometric rate of growth of $N(t)$, proportional to $(1 + r^*)^t$, is at a rate given by

$$1 + r^* = \tfrac{1}{4}\{[1 + z^*]^2\lambda_{AA} + [1 - z^*]^2\lambda_{aa} + 2[1 + z^*][1 - z^*]\lambda_{Aa}\} \qquad [8.2]$$

$$\lim_{t \to \infty} \frac{N(t)}{(1 + r^*)^t} = v[N^0_{AA},N^0_{aa},N^0_{Aa}], \text{ by definition} \qquad [8.3]$$

$$\lim_{t \to \infty} [N_A(t),N_a(t)](1 + r^*)^{-t} = [p^*,q^*]v[N^0_{AA},N^0_{aa},N^0_{Aa}]$$

$$= [\tfrac{1}{2} + z^*,\tfrac{1}{2} - z^*]v[N^0_{AA},N^0_{aa},N^0_{Aa}] \qquad [8.4]$$

$$\lim_{t \to \infty} [N_{AA}(t),N_{aa}(t),N_{Aa}(t)](1 + r^*)^{-t}$$

$$= [\dot{n}_{AA},\dot{n}_{aa},\dot{n}_{Aa}]v[N^0_{AA},N^0_{aa},N^0_{Aa}]$$

$$= [(1 + z^*)^2\lambda_{AA},(1 - z^*)^2\lambda_{aa},2(1 + z^*)(1 - z^*)\lambda_{Aa}] \times \frac{v[N^0_{AA},N^0_{aa},N^0_{Aa}]}{4(1 + r^*)} \qquad [8.5]$$

Case of heterozygous fitness

An interesting example of the previous section's analysis is the case where the heterozygous state, *Aa*, is superior in fitness to either of the homozygous states, *AA* or *aa*. We then expect that there will be a stable ultimate equilibrium with both A and *a* coexisting. It will simplify the arithmetic to set λ_{AA} and λ_{aa} equal, a transparent symmetric case. Thus, suppose

$$\lambda_{AA} = \lambda_{aa} = \lambda < \lambda_{Aa} = \lambda\gamma, \quad \gamma > 1. \qquad [9]$$

From the symmetry of *AA* and *aa*,

$$[z^*,p^*,q^*] = [0,\tfrac{1}{2},\tfrac{1}{2}]$$

$$[\dot{n}_{AA},\dot{n}_{aa},\dot{n}_{Aa}] = [\tfrac{1}{2},\tfrac{1}{2},\gamma](1 + \gamma)^{-1} \qquad [10.1]$$

$$1 + r^* = \tfrac{1}{2}(1 + \gamma)\lambda > \lambda \qquad [10.2]$$

$$v[N^0_{AA},N^0_{aa},N^0_{Aa}] \equiv v[N^0_{aa},N^0_{AA},N^0_{Aa}]. \qquad [10.3]$$

If the heterozygous state had lacked fitness, $\gamma < 1$ and $p^* = q^* > \tfrac{1}{2}$, the interior equilibrium would have represented an *unstable* equilibrium: any slightest perturbation of N_{AA}/N_{aa} away from unity would have been followed by further movement in the same direction—until only one homozygous genotype remained.

From its intrinsic definition in Eq. 8.3, $v[N_{AA}(t),N_{aa}(t),N_{Aa}(t)] = V(t)$ is a scalar that grows from the beginning at the percentage rate $(1 + r^*)$:

$$V(t + 1) = (1 + r^*)V(t). \quad [11.1]$$

Similarly, the following surrogate vector grows like $(1 + r^*)^t$:

$$[n^{*}_{AA},n^{*}_{aa},n^{*}_{Aa}]V(t) = \mathbf{V}(t)$$
$$\mathbf{V}(t + 1) = (1 + r^*)\mathbf{V}(t). \quad [11.2]$$

One interprets this as a surrogate system, which replaces the true $[N^0_{AA},N^0_{aa},N^0_{Aa}] = \mathbf{N}^0$ and implied true $N(t)$by new Fisherine initial conditions that are in equilibrium proportions, $\mathbf{V}(0)$: after the period of transient delay, this surrogate system ultimately closely approximates the original system—in the vectoral sense that

$$\lim_{t\to\infty} \frac{\mathbf{N}(t) - \mathbf{V}(t)}{(1 + r^*)^t} = 0 \quad [12]$$

However, we were not able to use this concept of reproductive value $\mathbf{V}(0)(1 + r^*)^t$ to *learn* what the equilibrium will be: rather, it was the case that *after* we had *already* learned what the equilibrium was we were then able to arrive at Eq. 8.3's definition of reproductive value. It remains true that the recipe for cooking the pie of reproductive value must begin with the instruction: First, you must catch your bird.

Biparental genetic models

Now we can come to grips with reproductive value in a two-sex model where males, $M(t)$, are of respective genotypes AA, aa, or Aa; and where females, $F(t)$, are likewise. Using letters with obvious mnemonic properties to denote sex, we write down the many convenient notational identities:

$$\begin{aligned}
N &= M + F = (m + f)N, f = 1 - m \\
&= [M_{AA} + M_{aa} + M_{Aa}] + [F_{AA} + F_{aa} + F_{Aa}] \\
&= [m_{AA} + m_{aa} + m_{Aa}]N + [f_{AA} + f_{aa} + f_{Aa}]N \\
&= [F_{AA} + \tfrac{1}{2}F_{Aa}] + [F_{aa} + \tfrac{1}{2}F_{Aa}] \\
&\qquad + [M_{AA} + \tfrac{1}{2}M_{Aa}] + [M_{aa} + \tfrac{1}{2}M_{Aa}] \\
&= [M_A + M_a] + [F_A + f_a] = [m_A + m_a + f_A + f_a]N \\
&= N_A + N_a = [n_A + n_a]N \\
&= N_{AA} + N_{aa} + N_{Aa} = [n_{AA} + n_{aa} + n_{Aa}]N. \quad [13]
\end{aligned}$$

To avoid the complexities involved with natural selection for the male-female sex ratio at birth, $g/(1 - g)$, I shall usually assume that g is the same parameter for all genotypes of the parental matings and offsprings. I begin by assuming no overlapping of generations and that all mating is strictly independent-random.

The dynamic relations for the six phase variables $[M_{AA}(t), \ldots, F_{Aa}(t)]$ now are assumed to be

$$\begin{aligned}
EN_{AA} &= g^{-1}EM_{AA} = (1 - g)^{-1}EF_{AA} = N^{-1}M_AF_A\lambda_{AA} \\
EN_{aa} &= g^{-1}EM_{aa} = (1 - g)^{-1}EF_{aa} = N^{-1}M_aF_a\lambda_{aa} \\
EN_{Aa} &= g^{-1}EM_{Aa} = (1 - g)^{-1}EF_{Aa} \\
&= N^{-1}[M_AF_a + M_aF_A]\lambda_{Aa}. \quad [14]
\end{aligned}$$

Deducible from Eqs. 14 are

$$\begin{aligned}
EN &= N[m_Af_A\lambda_{AA} + m_af_a\lambda_{aa} + (m_Af_a + m_af_A)\lambda_{Aa}] \\
&= N\theta(m_A,m_a,f_A;\ \lambda_{AA},\lambda_{aa},\lambda_{Aa}) \text{ for short, } t \geq 0 \\
&= Ng(1 - g)[n_A^2\lambda_{AA} + (1 - n_A)^2\lambda_{aa} \\
&\qquad + 2n_A(1 - n_A)\lambda_{Aa}],\ t \geq 1 \quad [15.1]
\end{aligned}$$

$$\begin{aligned}
En_A &= \frac{m_Af_A\lambda_{AA} + \tfrac{1}{2}(m_Af_a + m_af_A)\lambda_{Aa}}{\theta(m_A,m_a,f_A;\ \lambda_{AA},\lambda_{aa},\lambda_{Aa})},\ t \geq 0 \\
&= \frac{n_A^2\lambda_{AA} + n_A(1 - n_A)\lambda_{Aa}}{n_A^2\lambda_{AA} + (1 - n_A)^2\lambda_{aa} + 2n_A(1 - n_A)\lambda_{Aa}},\ t \geq 1 \\
&= \phi[n_A] \text{ for short; } |\phi'[n_A]| < 1. \quad [15.2]
\end{aligned}$$

Relation 15.2 is an autonomous first-order difference equation for $n_A(t)$ alone, just as Eq. 6.1 was for $z(t)$; indeed, relations exactly like 15.1 and 15.2 could have been written in place of 6.2 and 6.1 for the monoecious case. For, as is noted by Crow and Kimura (5, P. 45), so long as the relevant sex ratios are uniform, the dioecious case can be reduced *after one extra generation* to the monoecious case. Therefore, we need not duplicate the details of our earlier analysis. Thus, greater fitness of the heterozygous state will lead to a unique equilibrium of coexisting genotypes, approached asymptotically over infinite time from any initial conditions that involve positive (M_A, F_a) or (M_a, F_A). The results of Eqs. 8 apply once we follow obvious steps in calculating $[N_{AA}(1),N_{aa}(1),N_{Aa}(1)]$ from $[M_{AA}(0), M_{aa}(0),M_{Aa}(0),F_{AA}(0),F_{aa}(0),F_{Aa}(0)]$.

Also, in the Hardy-Weinberg case when all λs are equal, results just like Eqs. 2 and 3 apply—but now only after two generations rather than one. This means that the ultimate (p^*, q^*) mendelian probabilities are equal to the $[p(1), 1 - p(1)]$ numbers; and although these are not the same as the crude $[p(0), 1 - p(0)]$ numbers derived from pooling the originally present genotypes without respect to their partition between initial males and females, they are easily calculated in a small finite number of steps from the initial $[m^0_A,m^0_a,f^0_A,f^0_a]$ data by use of Eqs. 15 as applied to $t = 0$. Hence, there could in this case be analytical profit from the concept of reproductive value.

Linearlizable cases of overlapping generations

There are some special cases where a diploid genetic model could yield to Fisher-Lotka linear eigenvector algorithms. One such is where (*i*) male and female mortalities are identical, (*ii*) the male/female sex ratio at birth is always the same $g/(1 - g)$, or (*iii*) only parents of the same age mate together and at rates independent of the numbers of persons of other ages (see ref. 6). Another is that where all who mate do so at random without regard to their respective ages and where their fertilities and sex ratio of offspring are the same at all ages of the parents. When B_t is thus linearly determined by $(B_{t-1}, \ldots, B_{t-K})$, the 1930 Fisher concept applies. When its true nonlinear relation is perturbed only slightly away from such a singular linear case, the latter's eigenvector gives *approximate* reproductive-value weights that *approximately* wipe out initial age oscillations.

Age-phased reproductive value

Now I face up to the fact that adults reproduce at more than one age, so that generations cannot be nonoverlapping. If there is only one parent and the system is dilute, the standard linear demographic models of Sharpe and Lotka (7) and Leslie (8) could give Fisher his simple 1930 reproductive value formulas. But when biparental reproduction is involved, none of this remains generally valid.

I now apply the methods and definitions of refs. 3 and 4 to show how reproductive value is to be properly computed for such nonlinear systems in their dilute, homogeneous stages. Begin with a dioecious, diploid model where at first only one genotype is involved. Denote the number of males at time t by $M(x,t)$ and the number of females of age x' at t by $F(x',t)$. Suppose time and age are observed at discrete equally spaced intervals, $(t = \ldots, -1, 0, 1, 2, \ldots)$ and $(x,x' = 0, 1, 2, \ldots, K)$, where K is the oldest relevant age and age 0 represents new births.

As in standard demography, begin by assuming invariant age-specific mortalities for each sex (initially independent of genotype). The fraction of males newborn at age 0 who survive to age x is written as $[l_M(x)]$; the similar fraction of surviving females is written as $[l_F(x')]$:

$$1 = l_M(0) \geqq l_M(1) \geqq \ldots \geqq l_M(K) > 0$$
$$1 = l_F(0) \geqq l_F(1) \geqq \ldots \geqq l_F(K) > 0. \qquad [16]$$

Then, much as in refs. 9 and 10,

$$M(x,t) = \frac{l_M(x)}{l_M(x-\theta)} M(x-\theta, t-\theta), \quad x \geqq \theta, \quad t \geqq \theta$$
$$= l_M(x)M(0,t-x) = l_M(x)B_M(t-x), \quad t \geqq x \qquad [17.1]$$
$$F(x',t) = \frac{l_F(x')}{l_F(x'-\theta)} F(x'-\theta, t-\theta), \quad x' \geq \theta, \quad t \geq \theta$$
$$= l_F(x')F(0, t-x') = l_F(x')B_F(t-x'), \quad t \geqq x'.$$

Our assumptions about fertilities cannot be so conventional, having to go beyond those of the standard one-sex demographic model. Total births of each sex at t equals the sum of the births of that sex born at t to parents of all ages x and x':

$$B(t) = M(0,t) + F(0,t) = B_M(t) + B_F(t) \qquad [17.2]$$
$$= \sum_{x=0}^{K} \sum_{x'=0}^{K} [g(x,x') + \{1 - g(x,x')\}]B(x,x',t) \qquad [17.3]$$

Here $g(x,x')$ is the fraction of births that are male born to a father of age x and mother of age x'. (Initially, genotype is considered irrelevant.) For x or x' outside the fertile ages, $B(x,x',t) = 0$ and we have no need to define $g(x,x')$.

Although ages of human fathers and mothers often tend to bunch close together, it is only realistic to recognize that births to parents of ages x and x' might depend on more than their own respective numbers, $M(x,t)$ and $F(x',t)$. Thus, the number of females 1 year younger than a given female will reduce her chance to mate with a male of any age. The number of infants, although each is in an infertile age, may well influence the probability of their relatives bearing offspring. Even if no one mated with a person more than one period different in age, it could still be the case that the fertility of 20 year olds could be influenced by the relative numbers of middle-aged persons. Therefore, our general fertility function must become

$$B(x,x',t+1)$$
$$= f[x,x';M(0,t),\ldots,M(K,t)F(0,t),\ldots,F(K,t)]$$
$$= f[x,x';\mathbf{M(t)},\mathbf{F(t)}] \text{ for short.} \qquad [17.4]$$

So long as the system remains sparse or "dilute" relative to the environment's limited resources, $f[\ ]$ can be expected to be a first-degree-homogeneous function of all of its arguments, albeit not linear in them, i.e.,

$$f[x,x';qM(0,t),\ldots,qF(K,t)]$$
$$\equiv qf[x,x';M(0,t),\ldots,F(K,t)], \quad q > 0. \qquad [17.5]$$

The generality of $f[\ ]$ in Eqs. **17**, like that of $f^{ij}[\ ]$ in Eqs. **20** is more than enough to permit the usual geneticist's quasi-random-mating specialization (as in Eqs. **18**). However, the generality of Eqs. **17** is not excessive: to handle the fact that humans mate with people near their own age but are affected in doing so by the number of people present of varying ages, one must go beyond the conventional mendelian formulas.

Combining Eqs. **16–17.5**, we derive valid recursive relations for $[B_M(t),B_F(t)]$, holding after K periods have passed and all the initial living individuals have been replaced by individuals whose numbers have been obeying our postulated mortality and fertility laws:

$$B_M(t) = \Phi_M[B_M(t-1), B_M(t-2),$$
$$\ldots, B_M(t-K), B_F(t-1), \ldots, B_F(t-K)]$$
$$= \Phi[\mathbf{B_M(t)}, \mathbf{B_F(t)}] \text{ for short}$$
$$B_F(t) = \Phi_F[\mathbf{B_M(t)}, \mathbf{B_F(t)}]$$
$$\Phi_M[q\mathbf{B_M(t)}, q\mathbf{B_F(t)}] \equiv q\Phi_M[\mathbf{B_M(t)}, \mathbf{B_F(t)}]$$
$$\Phi_F[q\mathbf{B_M(t)},q\mathbf{B_F(t)}] \equiv q\Phi F[\mathbf{B_M(t)},\mathbf{B_F(t)}]. \qquad [17.6]$$

Although an exponential-growth solution to Eqs. **17.6** is no longer guaranteed now that Φ_M and Φ_F are nonlinear functions and possibly no longer monotone-increasing in all of their arguments, under specifiable conditions of some plausibility there will be a stable exponential solution of the form:

$$[B_M(t),B_F(t)] = c[1,\beta^*](1 + r^*)^t. \qquad [17.7]$$

Here $[1 + r^*,\beta^*]$ are the positive roots for $[R, \beta = B_F/B_M]$ in

$$1 = \Phi_M[R^{-1},\ldots,R^{-K},\beta R^{-1},\ldots,\beta R^{-K}]$$
$$\beta = \Phi_F[R^{-1},\ldots,R^{-K},\beta R^{-1},\ldots,\beta R^{-K}] \qquad [17.8]$$

and c is a scalar proportional to generalized fisherine reproductive value and dependent on the system's initial conditions.

From any initial state of positive $[M(0,0),M(1,0),\ldots,F(0,0),\ldots,F(K,0)]$,

$$\lim_{t\to\infty} \frac{B_M(t+1)}{B_M(t)} = \lim_{t\to\infty} \frac{B_F(t+1)}{B_F(t)} = 1 + r^* \qquad [17.9]$$
$$\lim_{t\to\infty} \frac{N(t)}{(1+r^*)^t}$$
$$= v[M(0,0),M(1,0),\ldots,M(K,0),F(0,0),\ldots,F(K,0)]$$
$$= v[\mathbf{M(0)},\mathbf{F(0)}] \text{ for short} \qquad [17.10]$$
$$\lim_{t\to\infty} \frac{M(x,t)}{M(0,t)} = l_M(x)(1 + r^*)^{-x}$$
$$\lim_{t\to\infty} \frac{F(x',t)}{F(0,t)} = l_F(x')(1 + r^*)^{-x'}. \qquad [17.11]$$

In Eq. **17.10**, $N(t)$ is the sum of all individuals of all ages and sex, $\Sigma_x[M(x,t) + F(x,t)]$, and $v[\mathbf{M(0)},\mathbf{F(0)}]$ is the well-defined reproduction-value function of the system, generalized to nonlinear homogeneous systems, with $v[\ ]$ itself being first-degree-homogeneous in its arguments. Any other extensive variable of the system beside N, as for example $M(3,t)$, has defined for it a reproductive value function that is its appropriate equilibrium proportion times $v[\ ]$ of Eq. **17.10**.

The relations **17** provide a complete and general solution for the nonlinear, biparental case of overlapping generations. It shows that the infinite number of computations implied by Eq. **17.10** is the irreducible number. Only in special, singular razor's-edge cases that lack structural stability (and hence almost never occur in nature however frequently they appear in textbooks and treatises), like the cases given in the previous section, can the 1930 interest-rate-discount eigenvector formulas of Fisher be applicable.

An interesting nonlinear case is that special one in which (*a*) effective relative fertilities of each sex show a systematic invariant relationship with adult age, but where (*b*) the adult mating patterns are random with respect to age. Let $[\omega_M(x), \omega_F(x)]$ be the weights of relative fertilities by age: thus $\omega_F(40)/\omega_F(20) = 1/3$ means that one 20-year-old female is like three 40-year-old females in effective fertilities.

From these relative-fertility weightings, we derive the effective number of procreating males and females at time t, $W_M(t)$ and $W_F(t)$:

$$W_M(t) = \sum_{x=0}^{K} \omega_M(x)M(x,t)$$

$$W_F(t) = \sum_{x'=0}^{K} \omega_F(x')F(x',t). \quad [18.1]$$

Each member of the $W_M(t)$ category is as likely to mate with any given member of the $W_F(t)$ category as with any other, the number of births at $t + 1$ being proportional to the product $W_M(t)W_F(t)$. Now we can replace Eqs. **17.3–17.4** by the special relationship

$$B(t+1) = g^{-1}M(0,t+1) = (1-g)^{-1}F(0,t+1)$$
$$= \beta \frac{W_M(t)W_f(t)}{W_M(t) + W_F(t)}. \quad [18.2]$$

Adjoining to Eqs. **18.1–18.2** the unchanged mortality relations **17.2**, our general recursion relations of **17.6** reduce down to

$$B(t) = \Phi[B(t-1), \ldots, B(t-K)], \quad t \geq K$$
$$= q^{-1}\Phi[qB(t-1), \ldots, qB(t-K)] \quad [18.3]$$

$$= \frac{\left[\sum_0^K W_M(x)\phi_M(x)gB(t-x)\right] \times \left[\sum_0^K W_F(x')\phi_F(x')(1-g)B(t-x')\right]}{\beta^{-1}\sum_0^K [W_M(x)\phi_M(x)g + W_F(x)\phi_F(x)(1-g)]B(t-x)} \quad [18.4]$$

Then

$$\lim_{t\to\infty} \frac{B(t+1)}{B(t)} = 1 + r^*, \quad [18.5]$$

where $1 + r^*$ is the positive R root in

$$1 = \Phi[R^{-1}, \ldots, R^{-K}] = \psi(R), \ \psi'(R) < 0 \quad [18.6]$$

$$\lim_{t\to\infty} \frac{N(t)}{(1+r^*)^t} = v[M(0,0), M(1,0), \ldots, F(0,0), \ldots, F(K,0)] \quad [18.7]$$

$$\lim_{t\to\infty} \left[\frac{M(x,t)}{M(0,t)}, \frac{F(x,t)}{F(0,t)}\right] = [l_M(x), l_F(x)](1+r^*)^{-x}. \quad [18.8]$$

Independently, Crow‡ has proposed certain genetic variants of the scenario of Eqs. **18.**

Age-structured genotype demographics

Now we may assume males and females of age x at time t are also characterized by their genotype: AA, aa, Aa, . . .; or, to simplify notation, by A^1A^1, A^2A^2, A^1A^2, A^2A^1, A^3A^3, . . . , A^sA^s where A^iA^j represents the presence of alleles A^i and A^j. Now we have

$$N = \sum_{x=0}^{K}\left\{\sum_{i=1}^{s}\sum_{j=1}^{s} M^{ij}(x,t)\right\} + \sum_{x'=0}^{K}\left\{\sum_{i=1}^{s}\sum_{j=1}^{s} F^{ij}(x',t)\right\}$$
$$= \sum_{x=0}^{K}\left\{\sum_{i=1}^{s} M^{i}(x,t)\right\} + \sum_{x'=0}^{K}\left\{\sum_{i=1}^{s} F^{i}(x',t)\right\}. \quad [19]$$

Always, by our convention, $M^{ij}(x,t) = M^{ji}(x,t)$ and $F^{ij}(x',t) = F^{ji}(x',t)$. Now we have mortality functions by genotype: $[l_M^{ij}(x), l_F^{ij}(x')]$, with

$$M^{ij}(x,t) = l_M^{ij}(x)M^{ij}(0,t-x) = l_M^{ij}(x)B_M^{ij}(t-x)$$
$$F^{ij}(x',t) = l_F^{ij}(x')F^{ij}(0,t-x') = l_F^{ij}(x')B_F^{ij}(t-x'). \quad [20.1]$$

Now our **17.6** fertility relations give $B_M^{ij}(x,x',t)$ and $B_F^{ij}(x,x',t)$ in terms of the vector $[M^{11}(0,t), \ldots, M^{11}(K,t), M^{12}(0,t), \ldots, M^{12}(K,t), M^{22}(0,t), \ldots, M^{ss}(L,t), F^{11}(0,t), \ldots, F^{ss}(K,t)] = [\mathbf{M(t)},\mathbf{F(t)}]$ for short. With prescribed mortality relations of Eqs. **20.1**, we can express this last pair of vectors in terms of the past values $[B_M^{ij}(t-1), \ldots, B_M^{ij}(t-K), B_F^{ij}(t-1), \ldots, B_F^{ij}(t-K)] = [\mathbf{B_M(t-x)}, \mathbf{B_F(t-x)}]$ for short. Thus, for $(i,j = 1, 2, \ldots, s)$,

$$B_M^{ij}(t) = \Phi_M^{ij}[\mathbf{B_M(t-x)},\mathbf{B_F(t-x)}]$$
$$= q^{-1}\Phi_M^{ij}[q\mathbf{B_M(t-x)},q\mathbf{B_F(t-x)}]$$
$$B_F^{ij}(t) = \Phi_F^{ij}[B_M(t-x),B_F(t-x)]$$
$$= q^{-1}\Phi_F^{ij}[q\mathbf{B_M(t-x)}, q\mathbf{B_F(t-x)}]. \quad [20.3]$$

Under plausible regularity conditions on the $\Phi^{ij}[\ ]$ functions, we define a stable exponential mode of asymptotic growth

$$\lim_{t\to\infty} \frac{N(t+1)}{N(t)} = 1 + r^*, \text{ the positive } R \text{ root of} \quad [20.4]$$

$$B_M^{ij} = \Phi_M^{ij}[R^{-1}B_M^{11}, R^{-2}B_M^{11}, \ldots, R^{-1}B_M^{22}, \ldots, R^{-K}B_F^{ss}],$$
$$B_F^{ij} = \Phi_F^{ij}[R^{-1}B_M^{11}, R^{-2}B_M^{11}, \ldots, R^{-1}B_M^{22}, \ldots, R^{-K}B_F^{ss}],$$
$$(i,j = 1, \ldots, s) \quad [20.5]$$

$$\lim_{t\to\infty} [B_M^{ij}(t), B_F^{ij}(t)]N(t)^{-1} = [B_M^{ij}, B_F^{ij}], \quad [20.6]$$

$$\lim_{t\to\infty} \frac{\mathrm{N(t)}}{(1+\mathrm{r}^*)^{\mathrm{t}}} = v[\mathbf{M(0)},\mathbf{F(0)}], \quad [20.7]$$

etc.

The present analysis will disappoint readers of Fisher who hoped that the simplicity of his asserted "fundamental theorem of natural selection" could be restored to validity by appeal to reproductive-value weightings (as where in the 1958 edition of ref. 1, p. 38, Fisher says ". . . the ease of its [the 'fundamental theorem's'] interpretation may be increased by appropriate conventions of measurement. For example, the frequencies should strictly be evaluated at any instant by the enumeration, not necessarily of the census population, but of all individuals having reproductive value, weighted according to the reproductive value of each."

The reader of the present series of papers on reproductive value will realize that, trivially special cases aside, there exist no such individual's weighting to save the theorem. Left for another occasion is exploration of various generalizations of the reproductive-value concept in the direction of defining the *approximate* effect of initial conditions on *penultimate* behavior of the system or on its early behavior under dilute conditions, and use of approximate 1930 eigenvector reproductive value to smooth out oscillations in age deviations of systems perturbed only slightly from singular linear cases.

I have benefited from discussion with Joel Yellin of the Massachusetts Institute of Technology, James F. Crow of the University of Wisconsin, and Nathan Keyfitz of Harvard, but not necessarily earned their approval in all respects. I owe thanks to Kate Crowley for editorial assistance, and to National Science Foundation 75-04053-A01-SOC and NIH R01-HD09081-02 for partial financial support.

1. Fisher, R. A. (1930 and 1958) *Genetical Theory of Natural Selection* (Clarendon Press, Oxford), 1st Ed. and 2nd Ed.
2. Keyfitz, N. (1971) *Demography* **8,** 71–80.
3. Samuelson, P. A. (1977) *Proc. Natl. Acad. of Sci. USA* **74,** 5772–5775.
4. Samuelson, P. A. (1977) *Proc. Natl. Acad. Sci. USA* **74,** 5189–5192.
5. Crow, J. F. & Kimura, M. (1970) *An Introduction to Population Genetics Theory* (Harper and Row, New York).
6. Euler, L. (1761) in *Die göttliche Ordnung*, ed. Süssmilch, J. P. Vol. 1, pp. 291–299.
7. Sharpe, F. R. & Lotka, A. J. (1911) *Philos. Mag.* **21,** 435–438.
8. Leslie, P. H. (1945) *Biometrika* **33,** 183–212.
9. Samuelson, P. A. (1976) *Theor. Popul. Biol.* **9,** 82–122.
10. Yellin, J. & Samuelson, P. A. (1976) *Theor. Popul. Biol.* **11,** 105–126.

‡ Crow, J. F. (1977) *Gene frequency and fitness change in an age-structure population*, Working paper from Department of Genetics, University of Wisconsin, Madison, draft of May 1, 1978.

Generalizing Fisher's "reproductive value": "Incipient" and "penultimate" reproductive-value functions when environment limits growth; linear approximants for nonlinear Mendelian mating models†

(dilute growth stage/diminishing returns/genetic selection)

PAUL A. SAMUELSON

Department of Economics, Massachusetts Institute of Technology, Cambridge, Massachusetts 02139

Contributed by Paul A. Samuelson, September 1, 1978

ABSTRACT In the usual Darwinian case in which struggle for existence leads to density limitations on the environment's carrying capacity, R. A. Fisher's reproductive-value concept reduces to zero for every initial age group. To salvage some meaning for Fisher's notion, two variant reproductive-value concepts are defined here: an "*incipient* reproductive-value function," applicable to a system's early dilute stage when density effects are still ignorable; and a "second-order *penultimate* reproductive-value function," linking to a system's initial conditions near equilibrium its much later small deviations from carrying-capacity equilibrium. Also, slowly changing age-structured mortality and fertility parameters of Lotka and Mendelian mating systems are shown to suggest linear reproductive-value surrogates that provide approximations for truly nonlinear diploid and haploid models.

The classic 1930 definition of reproductive value, in Fisher's book (ref. 1, chapter 2), was formulated in terms of a population that can grow forever at an exponential rate determined by *linear* mortality and fertility relations of the Sharpe and Lotka (2) or Leslie (3) type. However, as Fisher noted, a finite environment cannot support indefinite growth; every Malthusian parameter of logarithmic increase must drop from being a positive constant to a level "always near zero" (ref. 1, p. 47), as, for example, where Fisher replaced d log N/dt = constant by d log $N/dt = Ae^{-t/c} \to 0$ as t $\to \infty$ (ref. 1, p. 45).

Fisher did not explicitly mention that when total number approaches a determinate equilibrium level, $N(t) \to N^*$, representing the environment's *carrying capacity*, the reproductive-value function becomes independent of initial age groups of the population and loses its *raison d'etre*. See Samuelson (4) for elucidation of this fact of nondefinability of relative reproductive-value importance of the different initial elements in precisely those cases in which the struggle for existence and the scope for selection becomes most acute.

Here I show how something can be saved from the ruins by means of a definable "incipient reproductive-value function" and of a "second-order reproductive value" gauging penultimate effects of initial elements. Also, it is shown that nonlinear systems that are perturbed not very far away from a linear system can, to a good approximation, utilize the 1930 Fisherine reproductive-value eigenvector of that linear system to dampen down transients and afford a rough measure of reproductive value.

1. Coupled logistic systems

Consider a simple two-sex model in which the neonatal sex ratio of births is given at unity, in which females alone are determinative of births, but are subject to density effects of the limited environment that depend on total number, $N(t)$. The death rates of each sex are constants and all age-specific effects are ignorable. Denote the number at time t of [females, males, both sexes] by $[x_1(t), x_2(t), N(t) = x_1(t) + x_2(t)]$.

The dynamics of the system in its simplest case is given by

$$dx_1/dt = x_1[b - cN] - \delta x_1 \qquad [\mathbf{1.1}]$$

$$dx_2/dt = x_1[b - cN] - \delta x_2$$

$$b > \delta > 0, c > 0.$$

With male and female death rates equal to δ and with births equal by sex to $x_1[b - cN]$, from equal initial conditions, $x_1^0 = x_2^0$, the system obeys the familiar logistic relation:

$$dN/dt = N[b - cN] - \delta N \qquad [\mathbf{1.2}]$$

$$d[x_1 - x_2]/dt = -\delta[x_1 - x_2] \qquad [\mathbf{1.3}]$$

$$x_1(t) = x_2(t) = \tfrac{1}{2}N(t) \qquad [\mathbf{1.4}]$$

$$N(t) = \frac{N^*}{1 + Ke^{-\alpha t}} \qquad [\mathbf{1.5}]$$

$$N^* = (b - \delta)/c, \alpha = b - \delta, K = N^*N(0)^{-1} - 1 \qquad [\mathbf{1.6}]$$

$$\lim_{t \to \infty} [N(t), x_1(t), x_2(t)] = [N^*, \tfrac{1}{2}N^*, \tfrac{1}{2}N^*]. \qquad [\mathbf{1.7}]$$

From any positive initial conditions, not necessarily symmetric, the above relations **1.3, 1.7**, and **1.6** remain valid: thus, the system always converges to its carrying capacity independent of positive initial conditions $[x_1^0, x_2^0]$. Indeed, even if we let death ratios differ somewhat by sex, $\delta_1 \neq \delta_2$, and let the sex ratio of births differ somewhat from unity, we can see from continuity considerations that a stationary equilibrium, $[x_1^*, x_2^*, N^*]$, is globally stable.

Let me now apply the natural generalizations of refs. 4 and 5 to the definition of reproductive value:

$$v[x_1^0, x_2^0] = \lim_{t \to \infty} \frac{N(t)}{\left[\lim_{T \to \infty} \frac{N(T + 1)}{N(T)}\right]^t} \qquad [\mathbf{1.8}]$$

$$= N^* = (b - \delta)/c, \text{ from } [\mathbf{1.7}]$$

$$\partial v[x_1^0, x_2^0]/\partial x_i^0 \equiv 0, (i = 1, 2). \qquad [\mathbf{1.9}]$$

† This is paper no. 4 in a series. Paper no. 3 is ref. 8.

It is quite impossible to measure which initial element has the most importance for ultimate reproduction because no initial element has any lasting importance in a globally stable system, by the very definition of global stability.

Remark: Keyfitz (6) measures the "momentum" of a population when its *linear* parameters of age-specific net fertility drop proportionally from a positive intrinsic growth rate to a zero intrinsic growth rate. But such a zero rate for a tuned linear model is not at all the same thing as the zero-rate rendezvous of a nonlinear model subject to explicit density effects on birth and death rates. The "momentum" concept, like the reproductive-value concept, undergoes a sea change when linearity and first-degree homogeneity are emasculated by the law of diminishing returns. Demography lost its original roots in economics because the miracle of the industrial revolution offset in the last century the threat of diminishing returns and resource scarcity. Darwin's thicket was vouchsafed no similar dispensation, and in this age of the Club of Rome our own respite may be running out.

2. Incipient reproductive value

For (x_1^0, x_2^0) sufficiently small, the logistic system shows almost exponential growth. Let us denote by capital letters, $[X_i(t)]$ rather than $[x_i(t)]$, an early dilute system associated with our actual nonlinear system **1.1**. This associated system is written by suppressing as zero the terms in **1.1** involving the products $x_1(x_1 + x_2) = x_1 N$, terms that are minute when all x_i are small:

$$dX_1/dt = (b - \delta)X_1,\ dX_2/dt = bX_1 - \delta X_2. \qquad [2.1]$$

Writing the associated solutions as $[X_i(t; X_1^0, X_2^0)]$, we find

$$X_1(t; X_1^0, X_2^0) = X_1^0 \exp[(b - \delta)t] \qquad [2.2]$$

$$X_2(t; X_1^0, X_2^0) = X_1^0 \exp[(b - \delta)t] + [X_2^0 - X_1^0]\exp[-\delta t]$$

$$\lim_{t\to\infty} \frac{X_1(t) + X_2(t)}{\exp[t(b - \delta)]} = v^0[X_1^0, X_2^0], \text{ by definition} \qquad [2.3]$$

$$= 2X_1^0 + 0X_2^0.$$

Relation **2.3** defines our proposed "incipient reproductive-value function." It is the ordinary reproductive-value function, established in refs. 4 and 5, but now applied to the density-dependent system's *associated* early-stage, dilute or homogeneous, system. Its meaning can be described as follows.

Consider the actual, true, exact system with its correct solution $[x_i(t; x_1^0, x_2^0)]$. If initial (x_1^0, x_2^0) are "small enough," so that "for a long time" the limiting effects of the environment can be "largely ignored," the relative effect of initial x_1^0 rather than of initial x_2^0 on where the system will be "after a very long (but not too long) time" is gauged by the partial derivatives of [**2.3**]'s proposed incipient reproductive-value function $v^0[x_1^0, x_2^0]$, namely by $[\partial v^0/\partial x_1^0]/[\partial v^0/\partial x_2^0]$.

I have put quotation marks around the phrases in the above paragraph that heuristically describe an *exact* limit process. Here is that exact limit process:

$$\lim_{\epsilon\to 0} \frac{X_i(t; \epsilon x_1^0, \epsilon x_2^0)}{x_i(t; \epsilon x_1^0, \epsilon x_2^0)} = 1, (i = 1, 2) \qquad [2.4]$$

$$\lim_{\epsilon\to 0} \epsilon^{-1} \frac{\sum_1^2 x_j(\log \epsilon^{-1}; \epsilon x_1^0, \epsilon x_2^0),}{\exp[(b - \delta)\log \epsilon^{-1}]} = v^0[x_1^0, x_2^0]. \qquad [2.5]$$

Now we can go from the logistic example to the general case of a density-dependent demographic or genetic system. Consider, as in ref. 5's equation 18, the general difference-equation system:

$$x_i(t + 1) = f_i[x_1(t), \ldots, x_n(t)], (i = 1, \ldots, n) \qquad [2.6]$$

such that it admits of a stable stationary equilibrium,

$$x_i^* = f_i[x_1^*, \ldots, x_n^*] > 0, (i = 1, \ldots, n) \qquad [2.7]$$

$$\lim_{t\to\infty} x_i(t; x_1^0, \ldots, x_n^0) = x_i^*, [x_j^0] > 0 \qquad [2.8]$$

and also admits of an incipient dilute stage of first-degree-homogeneous growth potentialities

$$\lim_{\epsilon\to 0} \frac{f_i[\epsilon X_1, \ldots, \epsilon X_n]}{\epsilon} = F_i[X_1, \ldots, X_n] \qquad [2.9]$$

$$\equiv q^{-1} F_i[qX_1, \ldots, qX_n].$$

Then the *incipient reproductive-value function* for the true system **2.6** is defined as the ordinary reproductive-value function, call it $v^0[x_1^0, \ldots, x_n^0]$, of the *early-stage homogeneous system associated with* [**2.6**], namely

$$X_i(t + 1) = F_i[X_1(t), \ldots, X_n(t)]\ (i = 1, \ldots, n) \qquad [2.10]$$

$$\equiv q^{-1} F_i[qX_1(t), \ldots, qX_n(t)]$$

$$v^0[x_1^0, \ldots, x_n^0] = \lim_{t\to\infty} \frac{\sum_1^n X_j(t; x_1^0, \ldots, x_n^0)}{(1 + r^*)^t}, \text{ by definition} \qquad [2.11]$$

in which

$$\lim_{T\to\infty} \frac{\sum_1^n X_j(T + 1; x_1^0, \ldots, x_n^0)}{\sum_1^n X_j(T; x_1^0, \ldots, x_n^0)} = 1 + r^*. \qquad [2.12]$$

Then if the initial conditions in [**2.6**] are all small enough, after a long time its total number will have increased at an annual rate of $1 + r^*$, with a factor of proportionality given by $v^0[x_1^0, \ldots, x_n^0]$. More precisely, we have defined our *incipient reproductive-value function* by

$$\lim_{\epsilon\to 0} \frac{\sum_1^n X_j(\log \epsilon^{-1}; \epsilon x_1^0, \ldots, \epsilon x_n^0)}{\epsilon(1 + r^*)^{\log \epsilon^{-1}}} = v^0[x_1^0, \ldots, x_n^0]. \qquad [2.13]$$

3. Second-order reproductive value

Having taken care of [**2.6**]'s earliest stage, we now can take care of its penultimate stage, that stage "just before" it attains stationary equilibrium.

By virtue of [**2.8**]'s equilibrium being independent of initial $[x_1^0, \ldots, x_n^0]$, we have

$$\partial v[x_1^0, \ldots, x_n^0]/\partial x_i^0 = \partial N^*/\partial x_i^0 = 0. \qquad [3.1]$$

This means that, if we define the finite-time approximation to ordinary reproductive value,

$$v[T; x_1^0, \ldots, x_n^0] = \sum_1^n x_j(T; x_1^0, \ldots, x_n^0), \qquad [3.2]$$

then

$$\lim_{T\to\infty} \partial v[T; x_1^0, \ldots, x_n^0]/\partial x_i^0 = 0. \qquad [3.3]$$

But it may well still be the case that, for $i = 2, \ldots, n$,

$$\lim_{T\to\infty} \frac{\partial v[T; x_1^0, \ldots, x_n^0]/\partial x_i^0}{\partial v[T; x_1^0, \ldots, x_n^0]/\partial x_1^0} = \text{a definite limit} \qquad [3.4]$$

$$= \lim_{T \to \infty} \theta^i[T; x_1^0, \ldots, x_n^0] = \theta^i[x_1^0, \ldots, x_n^0].$$

Necessarily, as one can verify, $\theta^i[T; x_1^0, \ldots, x_n^0]$ must satisfy for *all* finite T the $(n-1)(n-2)/2$ independent integrability conditions

$$\frac{\partial \theta^i[T; \mathbf{x}^0]}{\partial x_j^0} - \frac{\partial \theta^i[T; \mathbf{x}^0]}{\partial x_1^0}\theta^j[T; \mathbf{x}^0] = \frac{\partial \theta^j[T; \mathbf{x}^0]}{\partial x_i^0} - \frac{\partial \theta^j[T; \mathbf{x}^0]}{\partial x_1^0}\theta^i[T; \mathbf{x}^0], \quad (i \neq j; i, j = 2, \ldots, n) \quad [\mathbf{3.5}]$$

Therefore, in that wide class of cases in which [**3.4**]'s limit exists, it can be written in the form

$$\theta^i[x_1^0, \ldots, x_n^0] = \frac{\partial v^2[x_1^0, \ldots, x_n^0]/\partial x_i^0}{\partial v^2[x_1^0, \ldots, x_n^0]/\partial x_1^0} \quad [\mathbf{3.6}]$$

for an infinite number of different $v^2[\mathbf{x}^0]$ functions, all of the form $f\{v^2[\mathbf{x}^0]\}$, in which $f\{\}$ is an arbitrary function and $v^2[\mathbf{x}^0]$ is any one admissible function in [**3.7**]. I shall now show how, constructively, one excellent choice for $v^2[x_i^0, \ldots, x_n^0]$ can be defined and computed.

If [**2.6**] is globally stable, almost always its equilibrium point, $[x_j^*]$, will have associated with it distinct characteristic values $(\lambda_1, \lambda_2, \ldots, \lambda_n)$:

$$0 = \Delta(\lambda) = (\lambda_1 - \lambda)(\lambda_2 - \lambda) \ldots (\lambda_n - \lambda)$$
$$= \det[\partial f_i[x_1^*, \ldots, x_n^*]/\partial x_j - \lambda\delta_{ij}], \quad [\mathbf{3.7}]$$

in which $\delta_{ii} = 1$, $\delta_{ij} = 0$, and $[x_j^*]$ are the stationary values defined in [**2.7**]. Because the stationary point is postulated to be globally stable, it must be locally stable: therefore, almost always, the (possibly complex) characteristic values, $[\lambda_j]$, associated with the $[x_j^*]$ point, will all be less than unity in absolute value:

$$|\lambda_j| < 1, (j = 1, \ldots, n). \quad [\mathbf{3.8}]$$

We can renumber and order them so that

$$1 > |\lambda_1| \geq |\lambda_2| > |\lambda_{3+j}| \quad (3 + j = 3, 4, \ldots, n). \quad [\mathbf{3.9}]$$

Actually, the equality will almost never occur in [**3.9**] except when λ_1 and λ_2 are complex-conjugate roots. Begin with λ_1 real.

Then, if $D(t)$ is written for $\sum_1^n x_j(t; x_1^0, \ldots . x_n^0) - \sum_1^n x_{n,j}^*$

$$\lim_{t \to \infty} \frac{D(t)}{\left[\lim_{T \to \infty} \frac{D(T+1)}{D(T)}\right]^t} = v^2[x_1^0, \ldots, x_n^0]. \quad [\mathbf{3.10}]$$

This defines for us our *second order*, or *penultimate*, reproductive-value function, which measures the relative importance of the initial-state variables in determining the *final deviations* from equilibrium.

If λ_1 and λ_2 are conjugate-complex numbers and such a limit does not exist, then, for very large t, the triplet of numbers $[x_j(t+1) - x_j^*, x_j(t) - x_j^*, x_j(t-1) - x_j^*]$ will very nearly satisfy a second-order difference equation

$$[x_j(t+1) - x_j^*] = 2u[x_j(t) - x_j^*] - (u^2 + \omega^2)[x_j(t-1) - x_j^*]. \quad [\mathbf{3.11}]$$

Thus, one could identify (u, w) in $\lambda_{1,2} = u \pm iw$.

The singular case of repeated λ roots will lack structural stability and, in a sense, will "almost never" occur. However, if roots are close together in absolute value, the number of decimal places that will have to be retained to permit accurate determination of λ_1 and of $v^2[x_1^0, \ldots, x_n^0]$ could be inordinately large.

Still higher-order v functions than $v^2[\,]$ could be calculated from limits such as the following

$$\lim_{t \to \infty} \frac{N(t) - N^* - \lambda_1^t v^2[x_1^0, \ldots, x_n^0]}{\lambda_2^t} = v^3[x_1^0, \ldots, x_n^0]. \quad [\mathbf{3.12}]$$

4. Linear approximations to "slow" nonlinearities

A standard linear Lotka–Leslie system is of the form

$$x_1(t+1) = \sum_1^n m_j x_j(t) \quad [\mathbf{4.1}]$$
$$x_{i+1}(t+1) = p_i x_i(t), \; (i + 1 = 2, \ldots, n), \; 0 < p_i < 1$$
$$0 = m_1 = \ldots = m_r < m_{r+k}, \; (r + k = r + 1, \ldots, n)$$

Here the ms and ps are constants and the 1930 Fisherine dominant eigenvector procedure works to define reproductive-value weights. See ref. 4.

To make the system nonlinear (and realistic), suppose that instead of being constants the age-specific fertilities and mortalities are functions of total population number, $N(t) = \sum_1^n x_j(t)$, but are weakly changing functions of N. Thus,

$$m_j = m_j[N(t)], \quad [\mathbf{4.2}]$$
$$l_j = p_1 p_2 \ldots p_{j-1} = l_j[N(t)] \quad [\mathbf{4.3}]$$
$$1 = l_1 > l_2 > \ldots > l_n > 0$$
$$0 < m_j'[\,] \ll 1$$
$$0 < l_j'[\,] \ll 1.$$

The system will be globally stable from any initial point such that $x_1(0) + x_2(0) + \ldots + x_n(0) > 0$,

$$\lim_{t \to \infty} N(t) = N^*, \text{ the root of} \quad [\mathbf{4.4}]$$
$$1 = \sum_1^n l_j[N^*]m_j[N^*] \quad [\mathbf{4.5}]$$
$$\lim_{t \to \infty} x_i(t) = l_i[N^*]N^*/\sum_1^n l_j[N^*]. \quad [\mathbf{4.6}]$$

In view of [**4.3**]'s smallness of $m_j'[\,]$ and $l_j'[\,]$, from any initial $[x_j(t^0), N(t^0)]$, we would expect that, for $t - t^0$ not too large, the true nonlinear system's solution, $[x_j\{t - t^0; \mathbf{x}(\mathbf{t}^0)\}]$, will not differ much from the solution to an associated standard Lotka–Leslie linear system, namely from $[X_j\{t - t^0; \mathbf{x}(\mathbf{t}^0)\}]$, the solution to

$$X_1(t+1) = \sum_1^n m_j[N(t^0)]X_j(t) \quad [\mathbf{4.7}]$$
$$X_{i+1}(t+1) = \frac{l_{i+1}[N(t^0)]}{l_i[N(t^0)]}X_i(t), \; (i + 1 = 2, \ldots n)$$
$$[X_j(t^0)] = \mathbf{x}(\mathbf{t}^0), \; N(t^0) = \sum_1^n x_j(t^0) = N^0.$$

Therefore, for $t - t^0$ not too large an integer, the 1930 Fisherine eigenvector weights calculated from the $m_j(t^0)$s and $l_j(t^0)$s —call them $[v_j\{N^0\}]$—ought to iron out quite quickly the transient age distribution disturbances entailed by an unbalanced choice of initial $[x_j(t^0)]$.

Thus, for initial $N(t^0)$ very small, this section's approximation, $\sum_1^n v_j\{N[t^0]\}x_j(t^0)$, ought to be near to our *incipient reproductive-value function*, $v^0[x_1^0, \ldots, x_n^0]$, as defined most generally in [**2.13**]. Likewise, for initial $N(t^0)$ already very near to ultimate N^*, this section's 1930 approximation ought to be near to our exact *second-order reproductive-value function*, $v^2[x_1^0, \ldots, x_n^0]$, as defined in [**3.10**] or [**3.6**].

To generalize the approximation results of this section, consider the nonlinear system

$$\mathbf{x}(\mathbf{t} + \mathbf{1}) = [x_i(t+1)]$$

$$= [a_{ij}\{x_1(t), \ldots, x_n(t)\}][x_i(t)]$$
$$= \mathbf{a}\{\mathbf{x}\}\mathbf{x}(\mathbf{t}), \qquad [\mathbf{4.8}]$$

in which the elements of the $\mathbf{a}\{\mathbf{x}(\mathbf{t})\}$ matrix are not constants but rather are functions of the coordinates of the system.

Let $\mathbf{v}\{\mathbf{x}(\mathbf{t})\} = [\mathbf{v}_j\{\mathbf{x}(\mathbf{t})\}]$ be the dominant row eigenvector of $\mathbf{a}\{\mathbf{x}(\mathbf{t})\}$ so that

$$\mathbf{v}\{\mathbf{x}(\mathbf{t})\}\mathbf{a}\{\mathbf{x}(\mathbf{t})\} \equiv \mathbf{v}\{\mathbf{x}(\mathbf{t})\}\lambda_1\{\mathbf{x}(\mathbf{t})\}, \qquad [\mathbf{4.9}]$$

in which $\lambda_1\{\mathbf{x}(\mathbf{t})\}$ is a scalar function. Then, trivially, the scalar

$$v[t, t^\circ] = \mathbf{v}\{\mathbf{x}(\mathbf{t}^\circ)\}\mathbf{x}(\mathbf{t}) \qquad [\mathbf{4.10}]$$

satisfies

$$V[t^\circ + 1, t^\circ] = \lambda_1\{\mathbf{x}(\mathbf{t}^\circ)\}V[t^\circ, t^\circ] \neq V[t^\circ + 1, t^\circ + 1]. \qquad [\mathbf{4.11}]$$

Because $V[t, t]$ represents a changing definition as t changes, there is little value in [**4.11**]'s formal relation. See Price and Smith (ref. 7, equation 16) for a derivation similar to [**4.11**].

However, if the elements of $\mathbf{a}\{\mathbf{x}\}$ are only slowly changing functions of $\mathbf{x}$, then the error in

$$\frac{V[t + 1, t + 1]}{V[t, t]} - \frac{V[t, t]}{V[t - 1, t - 1]} \qquad [\mathbf{4.12}]$$

will be very small *even from the beginning.*

Relations **4.8**–**4.12** suggest a good approximation to [**2.11**]'s $v^\circ[X_1^\circ, \ldots, X_n^\circ]$ for arguments that are "near" [**2.10**]'s stable balanced-growth mode, $[X_j^*]$, the root of

$$\sum_1^n X_j^* = 1$$
$$(1 + r^*)X_i^* = F_i[X_1^*, \ldots, X_n^*] \qquad [\mathbf{4.13}]$$
$$= \sum_{j=1}^n (\partial F_i[X_1^*, \ldots, X_n^*]/\partial X_j)X_j^*. \qquad [\mathbf{4.14}]$$

Corresponding to the $1 + r^*$ characteristic root of the matrix $(\partial F_i[X_1^*, \ldots, X_n^*]/\partial X_j)$, let there be the normalized left-hand eigenvector, $(v_j\{\mathbf{X}^*\})$, such that

$$(v_j\{\mathbf{X}^*\})(\partial F_i[X_1^*, \ldots, X_n^*]/\partial X_j) = (v_j\{\mathbf{X}^*\})(1 + r^*) \qquad [\mathbf{4.15}]$$
$$(v_j\{\mathbf{X}^*\})(X_i^*) = 1.$$

Then for $\mathbf{X}^\circ$ "near" $\mathbf{X}^*$, $v^\circ(X_1^\circ, \ldots, X_n^\circ)$ should be well approximated by the Fisherine surrogate $\sum_1^n v_j\{X^*\}X_j^\circ$.

5. Discussion

These approximations seem to vindicate the view that James F. Crow‡ has communicated to me: if the random matings of different genotypes all have fertilities and mortalities that are very nearly alike (the case of slow selection), then, even if the nonlinear genetic model involves overlapping generations, the initial transient age distortions ought to iron themselves out long before genotype equilibrium is approached; very soon then, the model behaves much like a simple one-generation model whose proportions can be approximately estimated by means of Fisherine "reproductive value weights."

The following model, suggested both by Crow (‡, equations 46–48) and Samuelson (ref. 8, equation 18), is illustrative. Let $n_{ij}(x, t)$, the number of A_iA_j genotypes of age x at time t, be self-propelled according to the usual age-specific mortality assumptions and the random-mating patterns of simplest Medelian systems:

$$n_{ij}(x + 1, t + 1) = \frac{l_{ij}(x + 1)}{l_{ij}(x)} n_{ij}(x, t) \qquad [\mathbf{5.1}]$$
$$= l_{ij}(x + 1)n_{ij}(0, t - x), \; t \geq x \qquad [\mathbf{5.2}]$$
$$(x = 0, 1, \ldots, A; i, j = 1, 2, \ldots, m)$$
$$1 = l_{ij}(0) > l_{ij}(1) > \ldots > l_{ij}(A) \qquad [\mathbf{5.3}]$$
$$n_{ij}(0, t + 1) = \frac{W_i(t)W_j(t)}{\sum_1^m W_k(t)} \qquad [\mathbf{5.4}]$$
$$W_i(t) = \sum_{j=1}^m \sum_{x=0}^A n_{ij}(x, t)\omega_{ij}(x) \qquad [\mathbf{5.5}]$$
$$= \sum_{j=1}^m \sum_{x=0}^A n_{ij}(0, t - x)l_{ij}(x)\omega_{ij}(x) \qquad [\mathbf{5.6}]$$
$$0 \leq \omega_{ij}(x) = \omega_{ji}(x)$$
$$n_{ij}(x, t) \equiv n_{ji}(x, t) \text{ if } n_{ij}(x, 0) \equiv n_{ji}(x, 0). \qquad [\mathbf{5.7}]$$

Under specifiable conditions on the positivity of the various $[\omega_{ij}(x)]$ parameters, one can prove that the system moves from almost all positive initial conditions to an exponential steady state:

$$\lim_{t \to \infty} \frac{n_{ij}(x, t)}{\sum_x \sum_r \sum_s n_{rs}(x, t)} = \nu_{ij}(x) \geq 0 \qquad [\mathbf{5.8}]$$

$$0 < \lim_{t \to \infty} \frac{\sum_x \sum_i \sum_j n_{ij}(x, t + 1)}{\sum_x \sum_i \sum_j n_{ij}(x, t)} = \bar{\lambda} \gtreqless 1 \qquad [\mathbf{5.9}]$$

$$\lim_{t \to \infty} \frac{n_{ij}(x, t)}{\bar{\lambda}^t}$$
$$= \nu_{ij}(x)v[n_{11}(0, 0), \ldots, n_{rs}(x, 0), \ldots, n_{mm}(A, 0)]. \qquad [\mathbf{5.10}]$$

Here $v[\mathbf{n}(\mathbf{x}, 0)]$ is the generalization of Fisher's 1930 reproductive-value function provided by Samuelson (4, 5, 8).

Crow‡ has conjectured that bounds on $\bar{\lambda}$ are provided by what I shall call crypto-growth rates, λ_{ij}, definable as the largest positive root of the Lotka–Leslie equation

$$1 = \psi_{ij}(\lambda) = \sum_{x=0}^A l_{ij}(x)\omega_{ij}(x)\lambda^{-1-x}. \qquad [\mathbf{5.11}]$$

Crow's plausible conjecture is that

$$\text{Min}\,[\lambda_{11}, \ldots, \lambda_{ij}, \ldots, \lambda_{mm}]$$
$$\leq \bar{\lambda} \leq \text{Max}\,[\lambda_{11}, \ldots, \lambda_{ij}, \ldots, \lambda_{mm}]. \qquad [\mathbf{5.12}]$$

Furthermore, one can calculate the obvious crypto-reproductive-value weightings that correspond to $[\omega_{ij}(x); \lambda_{ij}]$; call them $[v_{ij}(x)]$. Crow‡ suggests that they be used to smooth out early transients in ratios such as $\sum_j\sum_x n_{ij}(x, t)/\sum_j\sum_x n_{kj}(x, t)$. Thus, ratios of $\sum_j\sum_x n_{ij}(x, t)v_{ij}(x, t) = V_i(t)$, such as $V_i(t)/V_k(t)$, are shown in Crow's numerical experiments to be quite steady.

I find this plausible, at least when

$$\omega_{ij}(x) = \omega(x) + \epsilon_{ij}(x) \qquad [\mathbf{5.13}]$$
$$|\epsilon_{ij}(x)| \ll 1, \qquad [\mathbf{5.14}]$$

because neglecting $\epsilon_{ij}(x)$ completely gives for $\sum_i\sum_j n_{ij}(x, t) = n(x, t)$ the strictly linear dynamic relation

$$n(0, t + 1) = W(t) = \sum_{x=0}^A n(0, t - x)\omega(x)l(x) \qquad [\mathbf{5.15}]$$

‡ Crow, J. F. (1978) "Gene frequency and fitness change in an age-structured population" (Department of Genetics, University of Wisconsin, Madison, WI).

$$\sum_{0}^{A} v(x)n(x, t+1) = \gamma \sum_{0}^{A} v(x)n(x, t), \qquad [5.16]$$

in which γ is the largest positive root of

$$1 = \psi(\lambda) = \sum_{0}^{A} \omega(x)l(x)\lambda^{-1-x}, \qquad [5.17]$$

and in which $[v(x)]$ represents the corresponding Fisher reproductive-value vector. See Charlesworth (9) for a similar model with much the same results. Also, *Section 3*'s discussion of how a nonlinear system's penultimate deviation from stationary-equilibrium approximate to a balanced vector of exponential decay seems to me to be in agreement with the finding of Kimura (10) concerning the early near constancy of the Wrightian *mean selective value* of two haploid alleles competing for a limited environment.

I am grateful to Kate Crowley for editorial assistance. My greatest debt is to patient instruction and argumentation from Prof. James F. Crow of the University of Wisconsin. I owe thanks for partial support to National Science Foundation Grant 750-4053-A01-SOC and to National Institutes of Health Grant R01-HD 9081-02.

1. Fisher, R. A. (1930) *The Genetical Theory of Natural Selection* (Oxford University Press/Clarendon, London).
2. Sharpe, F. R. & Lotka, A. J. (1911) *Philos. Mag.* **21**, 435–438.
3. Leslie, P. H. (1945) *Biometrika* **33**, 183–212.
4. Samuelson, P. A. (1977) *Proc. Natl. Acad. Sci. USA* **74**, 5189–5192.
5. Samuelson, P. A. (1977) *Proc. Natl. Acad. Sci. USA* **74**, 5772–5775.
6. Keyfitz, N. (1968) *Introduction to the Mathematics of Population* (Addison-Wesley, Reading, MA).
7. Price, G. R. & Smith, C. A. B. (1972) *Ann. Hum. Genet.* **36**, 1–7.
8. Samuelson, P. A. (1978) *Proc. Natl. Acad. Sci. USA* **75**, 4062–4066.
9. Charlesworth, B. (1974) *Theor. Popul. Biol.* **6**, 108–133.
10. Kimura, M. (1978) *Proc. Natl. Acad. Sci. USA* **75**, 1934–1937.

PART VII

Biographical and Autobiographical Writings

MY LIFE PHILOSOPHY*

by Paul A. Samuelson**

Ethics

Many economists—Alfred Marshall, Knut Wicksell, Léon Walras, . . .—became economists, they tell us, to do good for the world. I became an economist quite by chance, primarily because the analysis was so interesting and easy—indeed so easy that at first I thought that there must be more to it than I was recognizing, else why were my older classmates making such heavy weather over supply and demand? (How could an increased demand for wool help but lower the price of pork and beef?)

Although positivistic analysis of what the actual world is like commands and constrains my every move as an economist, there is never far from my consciousness a concern for the ethics of the outcome. Mine is a simple ideology that favors the underdog and (other things equal) abhors inequality.

I take no credit for this moral stance. My parents were "liberals" (in the American sense of the word, not in the European "Manchester School" sense), and I was conditioned in that general *Weltanschauung*. It is an easy faith to adhere to. When my income came to rise above the median, no guilt attached to that. Nor was there a compulsion to give away all my extra coats to shirtsleeved strangers: my parents would have thought me daft to do so, and neurotic to toss at night for not having done so. Some personal obligation for distributive justice liberals do expect of themselves; but what is far more important than acts of private charity is to weight the counterclaims of efficiency and equity, whenever public policy is concerned, in the direction of equity. As my University of Chicago teacher and friend Henry Simons used to say, "Any *good* cause is worth incurring some *costs* for. Everything should be pushed beyond the point of diminishing returns (else, why desist from pushing it still further?)."

Persons who will not volunteer to serve in the army can with good logic vote to pass a fair conscription law that will entail their being drafted with the same positive probability as any other persons. I have generally voted against my own economic interests when questions of redistributive taxation have come up. The fact that I have favored closing tax loopholes has not precluded seeking some advantage from those left in the tax code. But too avid an effort in that direction would seem not only unaesthetic but also a source of some discomfort and self reproach.

Without exception all the economists I know regard themselves as humanitarians. This includes communists who toe the Stalinist line and Chicago-school zealots for laissez-faire. Yet we all pretty much know what to expect of each other when it comes to policy recommendations and judgments. It is not unanimity. If political economy were an exact, hard science, then more agreement on probable outcomes would occur. If economics were no science at all, only a tissue of value judgments and prejudices, then soliciting an opinion from an economist would tell the Prince or Parliament nothing about the merits or demerits of the proposal under deliberation but only give a reconfirmation that Economist Jones is a bleeding-heart liberal and Economist Smith a selfish elitist.

Political economy as we know it falls in-between. Economists do agree on much in any situation. Where Milton Friedman and I disagree, we are quick to be able to identify the source and texture of our disagreements in a way that non-economists cannot perceive. The disparity of our recommendations is not an unbiased estimator of the dispersion of our inductive and deductive beliefs. With my *social welfare function* (or, in Waldian statisticians' terminology, my "loss function") concerning the relative importance of unemployment and business freedoms, I

* I owe thanks to the Sloan Foundation for partial financial support, and to Aase Huggins for editorial assistance.
** Institute Professor, MIT.

could disagree 180° with his policy conclusion and yet concur in diagnosis of the empirical observations and inferred probabilities. Yet, such is the imperfection of the human scientist, an anthropologist studying us academic guinea pigs will record the sad fact that our hearts do often contaminate our minds and eyes. The conservative will forecast high inflation danger on the basis of the same data that lead the dogooder to warn against recession. (Conscious of this unconscious source of bias, as the subsequent discussion will elaborate on, I make a special effort toward self-criticism and eclecticism—with what success, the record must testify to.)

An economist who has been preoccupied over the years solely with *Pareto optimality* wrote me long ago that I would be surprised to know how liberal he is. Indeed I would be. Reflecting on his writings, I wondered how he knew he had a heart: it had been so long since he had used it. Organs atrophy without exercise. "Use it or lose it," is nature's law.

It is not only the arteries that harden with age. Economists are said to appear to grow more conservative as they rise in seniority. This they often deny.

In my own case, I do not perceive that my value-judgment ideology has changed systematically since the age of 25. For a decade now mainstream economics has been moving a bit rightward. But I have not been tempted to chase it. What does tend to change with the accumulation of years and experience is one's degree of optimism about what is feasible and one's faith in good intentions alone. My enhanced skepticism about government ownership of the means of production or the efficacy of planning is not a reflection of ossifying sympathies and benevolence, but rather is a response to the testimony of proliferating real-world experiences.

I am conscious of one occasion in which my respect for the market mechanism took a quantum leap upward. This change had nothing to do with improved performing of the market system. Nor was it related to any new arguments brought forward by Hayek about generating and utilizing information, or to any old arguments about market efficiencies and freedoms by Adam Smith, Frederic Bastiat, or Frank Knight. Rather my changed viewpoint came from observing the communist witchhunting episode of the 1950s.

The McCarthy era, in my judgment, posed a serious threat of American fascism. I knew plenty of people in government and the universities whose civil liberties and careers came into jeopardy. I observed at close hand the fears and tremblings that the Harvard and MIT authorities experienced, and these were the boldest of the American academic institutions. As Wellington said of Waterloo, it was a close-run thing that Senator McCarthy was discredited: the Richard Nixon "enemy list" was a joke in comparison, and my being named on it only added to my fading credentials as a New Dealer. What I learned from the McCarthy incident was the perils of a one-employer society. When you are blackballed from government employment, there is great safety from the existence of thousands of anonymous employers out there in the market. I knew of people who got some kind of work in private industry, usually smaller industry since large firms tend to try to keep on the safe side of government. To me this became a newly perceived argument, not so much for laissez faire capitalism as, for the *mixed* economy.

How did free-market advocates among the economists score as defenders of personal freedoms and civil liberties? This was a subject of great interest to me and over several years I kept a quiet tally of the behavior and private utterances of scores of the leading American and continental libertarians, almost all of whom I knew intimately. Like a visiting anthropologist I would ask innocent questions designed to elicit relaxed and spontaneous views. If it was churlish to keep a record of private conversations, then I was a churl. The results surprised and distressed me. Worshippers of laissez faire à la Bastiat and Spencer were insensitive and on the whole unsympathetic toward the rights and personal freedoms of scholars. Alone among the members of the Mt. Pelerin Society the name of Fritz Machlup stood out as one willing to incur personal costs to speak up for John Stuart Mill values. It is not the failure of people to be heroes that I am speaking about. There is little of the heroic in my own makeup and I have learned not to expect much of human nature. What my research found was a sad lack of genuine concern for human values.

I was taught at the University of Chicago that business freedoms and personal freedoms have to be strongly linked, both as a matter of brute empirical fact and of cogent deductive syllogism. For a long time I believed what I was taught. Gradually I had to acknowledge that the paradigm could not fit the facts. By most Millian criteria, regimented Scandinavia was freer than my America—or certainly at least as free. When I used to bring up these inconvenient facts to my conservative friend David McCord Wright, he would warn: "Just you wait. British and Swedish citizens, it is true, have not yet lost their freedoms. But it cannot last that the market is interfered with and people remain politically free." We have all waited for more than thirty years now.

Friedrick Hayek wrote his bestseller, *The Road to Serfdom*, at the end of World War II, warning that partial reform was the sure path to total tyranny. Cross-sectional and time-series analysis of the relationship between politics and economics suggest to me important truths.

1. Controlled socialist societies are rarely efficient and virtually never freely democratic. (There is considerable validity then for the nonnovel part of Hayek's warning.)

2. Societies which resisted partial reforms have often been those overtaken by revolutionary change. If it is the free market or nothing, often it has then had to be nothing. Indeed, after midcentury the finest archetypes of efficient free markets have often been quasi-fascist or outright fascist societies in which a dictatorial leader or single party *imposes* a political order—without which imposition the market could not politically survive. Chile with its military dictatorship cum-the-Chicago boys is only one dramatic case. Taiwan, South Korea, and Singapore are less dramatic but more representative cases.

3. I can nurture a dream. Like Martin Luther King, I have a dream of a humane economy that is at the same time efficient and respecting of personal (if not business freedoms). Much of producing and consuming decisions involve use of the market mechanism. But the worst inequalities of condition that result from reliance on market forces—even in the presence of equality of ex ante opportunity—can be mitigated by the transfer powers of the democratic state. Does the enhancement of equity by the welfare state take no toll in terms of efficiency? Yes, there will be some tradeoff of enhanced total output against enhanced equality, some tradeoff between security and progress. I call the resultant optimizing compromise *economics with a heart*, and it is my dream to keep it also economics with a head.

My Methodology

It is some relief to move from the exalted realm of philosophical ethics to the mundane realm of scientific methodology. However, I rather shy away from discussions of Methodology with a capital M. To paraphrase Shaw: Those who can, do science; those who can't prattle about its methodology.

Of course I can't deny that I have a methodology. Its just that there seems little appeal in making it explicit to an outsider. Or for that matter, in spelling it out to my own consciousness.

I am primarily a theorist. But my first and last allegiance is to the facts. When I began study at the University of Chicago, Frank Knight and Aaron Director planted in me the false notion that somehow deduction was more important than induction. This was a confused tenet of Austrian methodology at the time, and I certainly do not mean by the word "Austrian" the logical positivism of the Vienna Circle. Rather, such direct and indirect disciples of Carl Menger as Ludwig von Mises, Friedrich Hayek, and Lionel Robbins seemed to put on their own heads the dunce caps of the classical Ricardians who believed that by thinking in one's study one could arrive at the basic immutable laws of political economy. I remember believing Director when he pooh-poohed Wesley Mitchell's empirical work on business cycles, claiming instead that the greatest breakthroughs in the subject were coming from Hayek's a priorisms on the subject.

I grew out of this phase fast. Once Lionel Robbins explained lucidly in the first edition of his *An Essay on the Nature and Significance of Economic Science* his claims for Kantian a priorism in economics, his case was lost. Logical positivism is now judged to be an oversimplified doctrine, but it was enormously useful in deflating the pretensions of deductionists. If one had to choose between the methodologies of the warring brothers—Ludwig the economist and Richard von Mises the mathematical physicist—Richard would win hands down.

Let me not be misunderstood. I abhor the sins of scientism. I recognize that, as social scientists, we can have relationships with the data we study that the astronomers cannot have with the data they study. I am aware that my old friend Willard van Orman Quine, one of this age's greatest logicians, has cast doubt that anyone can in every case distinguish between "analytic" a priorisms and the "synthetic" propositions that positivists take to be empirical facts. Furthermore, Wesley Mitchell's empiricisms on the business cycle do seem to me to have been overrated—not because they are empirical, but rather because his was an eclecticism that never had much luck in discovering anything very interesting, as the lifecycle profile of his post-1913 career sadly reveals. Some of the skepticisms of Knight and Jacob Viner concerning the empirical statistical studies that their colleagues Paul Douglas and Henry Schultz were attempting, I readily admit, were well taken—just as some of Keynes's corrosive 1939 criticisms of Jan Tinbergen's econometric macromodels were. But it is on *empirical* grounds that these empirical attempts have to be rejected or accepted, and not because deductive syllogisms can claim a primacy to vulgar fact grabbing. What was wrong with the German Historical School was not that it was historical, but rather that its sampling of the facts was incomplete and incoherent. The facts don't tell their own story. You can't enunciate all the facts. And if you could, the job of the scientists would just begin—to organize those facts into useful and meaningful *gestalts*, into patterns that are less multifarious than the data themselves and which provide economical *descriptions* of the data that afford tolerably accurate extrapolations and interpolations.

Whatever logical positivisms' faults and superficialities are in science at large, it gets an undeservedly bad name in economics from being confused with Milton Friedman's peculiar version of positive economics. Much of what is in Friedman's 1953 essay on this topic is unexceptional and a story so old as to seem almost platitudinous. But what is novel in his formulation and commands most attention is that which I have called "the F twist"—the dictum that a scientific theory is none the worse if its premises are unrealistic [in the usual meaning of "unrealistic" as stating hypotheses that are false and/or far-from-true assertions about what obtains in the actual world], so long as the theory's "predictions" are usefully true. Thought suggests, and experience confirms, that such a dogma will be self-indulging, permitting its practitioners to ignore or play down inconvenient departures of their theories from the observable real world. A hypothesis's full set of predictions includes its own descriptive contents; so, literally understood, an unrealistic hypothesis entails some unrealistic predictions and is all the worse for those false predictions—albeit it is all the better for its (other) empirically-correct predictions. We are left then validly with only the prosaic reminder that few theories have all their consequences exactly correct; and it can be the case that a scientific theory is deemed valuable because we have reason to give great weight to those of its predictions that happen to be true and to give little weight to those that are found to be false. In no case is unrealistic falsity a virtue; and there is danger of self-serving Humpty-Dumptyism in letting the theorist judge for himself which of his errors he is going to extenuate or ignore.

Unpopular these days are the views of Ernst Mach and crude logical positivists, who deem good theories to be merely economical descriptions of the complex facts that tolerably well replicate those already-observed or still-to-be-observed facts. Not for philosophical reasons but purely out of long experience in doing economics that other people will like and that I myself will like, I find myself in the minority who take the Machian view. "Understanding" of classical thermodynamics (the archetype of a successful scientific theory), I find to be the capacity to "describe" how fluids and solids will actually behave under various specifiable conditions. When we are able to give a pleasingly-satisfactory "HOW" for the way of the world, that gives the only approach to "WHY" that we shall ever attain.

Always when I read new literary and mathematical paradigms, I seek to learn what descriptions they imply for the observable data. The paradigms full set of entailed descriptions is what is of interest and forms the basis for a complete judgment on it. My work in revealed preference, in *Foundations of Economic Analysis*, and in the several volumes of *Collected Scientific Papers*, consistently bears out this general methodological procedure.

I dislike being wrong. Long before knowing of Karl Popper's writings, I sought to be my own strictest critic. Why give that fun to the other chap? All this explains why I am an eclectic economist. It is not because of inability of making up my mind. I am eclectic only because experience has shown that Mother Nature is eclectic. If all the evidence points to a single-factor causation, I have no internal resistance to accepting that. But there is a big "if" involved in the previous sentence.

Being prepared to be eclectic does not have to inhibit bold theory building. One creates boldly knowing that this does not commit one to exaggerated belief in the sole potency of one's brain child.

We all have secret vanities. He prides himself on his good looks. She takes satisfaction in her sense of humor. I do delight in producing still another beautiful model that illuminates important terrains of economics. But in my heart of hearts I nurture the claim that I have good judgment. Be wise, sweet maid, and let them who will be clever. My theories must run the gauntlet of my judgment, an ordeal more fearsome than mere peer review. (Of course one can have one's cake and eat it too by presenting a theoretical gem as an unpretentious mirror of some aspects of some corner of the economic terrain under observation.) Why let sagacity degenerate into well-informed nihilism? The mindless naysayer is no better than the mindless yeasayer. Neither adds anything to the silent scientist's cipher.

Joseph Schumpeter, who all his life whored after beautiful theories, just before he died testified at the 1949 National Bureau conference on business cycles: If he had to choose between mastery of mathematics and statistics, or of economic history, he would have to choose mastery of economic history. I won't disagree. But I deny the need for dichotomous choice. Give apes in the Widener library a data bank of all that's there and you don't get a master economic historian. What you get back is the data bank and a curator.

Let me make a confession. Back when I was 20 I could perceive the great progress that was being made in econometric *methods.* Even without foreseeing the onset of the computer age, with its cheapening of calculations, I expected that the new econometrics would enable us to narrow down the uncertainties of our economic theories. We would be able to test and reject false theories. We would be able to infer new good theories.

My confession is that this expectation has not worked out. From several thousands of monthly and quarterly time series, which cover the last few decades or even centuries, it has turned out not to be possible to arrive at a close approximation to indisputable truth. I never ignore econometric studies, but I have learned from sad experience to take them with large grains of salt. It takes one econometric study to calibrate another: a priori thought can't do the job. But it seems objectively to be the case that there does not accumulate a convergent body of econometric findings, convergent on a testable truth.

Does this mean that I belong to the camp who regard truth as in the eye of the beholder? Who deny the existence of an objective truth out there, in political economy as well as in astronomy and biochemistry? Who recognize in the truth of mainstream economics only the class interests of the bourgeoisie, and in the truth of Marxian economics either the class interests of the nascent proletariat or the objective truth of the final classless and universal society?

No. Observing myself over fifty years and a vast number of scientists in various disciplines, I do recognize that truth has many facets. Precision in deterministic facts or in their probability laws can at best be only partial and approximate. Which of the objective facts out there are worthy of study and description or explanation depends admittedly on subjective properties of the scientists. Admittedly, a given field of data can be described in terms of alternative patterns of description, particularly by disputing authorities who differ in the error tolerances they display toward different aspects of the data. Admittedly, observations are not merely seen or sensed but rather often are perceived in gestalt patterns that impose themselves on the data and even distort those data.

But still, having admitted all of the above, as you observe scientists and study the developments of disciplines when schools evolve and paradigms are born and die, it is forced upon you that *what ultimately shapes the verdicts of the scientist juries is an empirical reality out there.* When a Marxist scores a triumph it is not by employing a useful alternative to 2+2=4 logic, or cultivating a different Hegelian dialectic. We esteem a Pavlov, Lysenko, Haldane or Bernal, Landau or Baran for what they can or cannot accomplish with respect to animal experiments, plant breeding, hydrogen-bomb explodings or phase transitions, or insights into the observable paths of economic development.

When Thomas Kuhn's book on the *Structure of Scientific Revolution* came out in 1962, I made two lucky predictions: one, that in the physical and life sciences its thesis would have to be modified to recognize that there is a cumulative property of knowledge there that makes later paradigms ultimately dominate earlier ones, however differently the struggle may transiently look; two, that Kuhn's doctrine of incommensurability of alternative paradigms would cater to a strong need in the social sciences and would develop a brisk market with us, as polemicists become able to say, "That's all very well in your paradigm, but your white is black in my paradigm—and who's to say that we'uns have to agree with you'uns." Kuhn has correctly discerned the warts on the countenance of evolving science. His readers must not lose the face for the warts.

How I Work

As a theorist I have great advantages. All I need is a pencil (now a ball pen) and an empty pad of paper. There are analysts who sit and look vacantly out the window, but after the age of 20 I was not one of them. I ought to envy the new generation who have grown up with the computer, but I don't. None of them known to me sit idly at the console, improvising and experimenting in the way that a composer does at the piano. That ought to become increasingly possible. But up to now, in my observation, the computer is largely a black box into which researchers feed raw input and out from which they draw various summarizing measures and simulations. Not having access to look around in the box, the investigator has less intuitive familiarity with the data than used to be the case in the bad old days.

I have been blessed with an abundance of interesting problems to puzzle out. Many artists and writers run into long fallow periods when new creative ideas just will not come. Luckily, that has not been my experience. Perhaps I am insufficiently self-critical to recognize when problems of lower quality are involved. In any case mine has never been the Carlylean view of Schumpeter that only the greatest ideas count, and only a few great men are important in history and in the development of science. One tackles the most important unsolved problem at hand. Then the next one. If that leads down the path of diminishing returns in the absence of dramatic new challenges and breakthroughs, so be it.

"What are you working on now?" This is a question I have been asked all my life. And never in my life have I known how to answer it. At any one time I have several balls in the air. And always there is an inventory of questions just below the threshold of my explicit attention. Some of these slumber in that limbo for two decades. There is no hurry; they will keep. Some morning (or at night in a dream) the evolving wheel of chance will turn their number up.

Poets testify that often their lines gush up from within. They merely write down what their muse is dictating. That sounds rather highfalutin, but there is something in it. When I was young I used to explore a topic; write down equations and syllogisms dealing with different aspects of it; then outline the final work. After that the final draft could be written out. Perhaps what I am describing is the optimal way to write a paper.

Increasingly after the age of thirty five that is not how I have in fact operated. Instead I have often let the paper write itself. A problem is posed. One begins to solve it, writing out the steps in the solution. One development leads naturally to another, as one exposits in writing. Finally, what can be solved of the problem has been solved. The paper is finished. What has been finished is not something that has ever been envisaged, waiting only to be written down. All this is reminiscent of Franklin Roosevelt's dictum, "How do I know what I think until I hear myself saying it?"

This means that some articles might be composed in half a day. Of course the first draft need not be the final draft. There may follow many hours of revisings, involving additions, deletions, rearrangements, and corrections. Perhaps it would be better to follow the first draft with a completely new rewrite. But that is not my usual practice, as I trade some perfection against more time for new topics. This means I am a prisoner of my first drafts, and it is a source of exquisite pain if a manuscript is lost: my mind rebels at having to reconstruct a lost argument, and impatience is likely to make a recollected version abridge some essential matter.

Prolific scholars are addicted to writing. A day spent in committee meetings is for me a day lost. After an interval of fasting, you are hungry. After an interval of doing no analytical research, there is so to speak a fluid inside you that wants to get free. I used to think that the unconscious mind, which Henri Poincaré described so beautifully as working away at specific puzzles the mathematician is interested in, was accumulating findings on the particular problems that routine duties prevented me from dealing with. But I have come to think that not to be quite correct. For, *any* new topic can capture one's enthusiastic and fruitful attention after a period of deprivation. One snowy day in New England I was told at the airport gate that Washington was snowed in. A friend hearing me inquire, "Can you go to New York?" asked, "Are you just bound to go somewhere this day?" That's exactly what it's like with the creative urge: It doesn't have to spend itself on the theory of capital that has been engaging the scholar's recent attention; it just wants to go about doing something creative, and its motors seem revved up to be effective in whatever direction it is pointed.

Reporters used to speak of a nose for news. What is important in scholarship is an aesthetic sense for what is an important problem. Otherwise the facile mind can spend itself on patterns that are merely pretty. For recreation I would rather play tennis than play chess, or read pedestrian detective stories than solve the mathematical conundrums that appear in the back pages of learned journals. My unconscious motivation, I suspect, is that chess and problem-solving involve the same energies as innovative scholarship does. They will usurp some of the limited supply of precious brainpower that might better go toward learning something new; and, involving use of the same workday muscles so to speak, those recreations do not provide as refreshing rest periods. I daresay that the powerful pure mathematician faces a different problem from the applied scientist. A great mathematician is only as great as his greatest deeds. The revolutionary idea that might lead to great deeds comes very rarely. One marks time in between and one might as well mark time while keeping the brain tuned up in chess or bridge as in any other way. However, I do not have too much confidence in the distinction that I have just made. For it certainly does not cover the case of prolific mathematicians such as Poincaré or Euler. A mathematical snob like G. H. Hardy might judge that much of Euler and Poincaré could just as well have never been written. But even from the snobbish viewpoint, we must reckon with the fact that some of their best work would not have gotten done if it had not been an outgrowth of some of their less transcendental achievements.

I said that my working tools are only pen and paper, and that an airplane cabin provides as good an environment for research as a library study. That is true as far as analytical creativity is concerned. On the other hand to stay well informed on what it is that is important to be done, a scholar must have access to books and to learned journals. In this regard I have always been very lucky. Whatever works the MIT libraries have not had, the neighboring Harvard libraries can be counted on to provide. There are very few great scholars, working off by themselves with paper and pen far from the centers of creative economic thought. Those who pride themselves on being most autonomous usually end up most idiosyncratic.

Long ago I set myself the grandiose challenge of not being merely subjectively original. More useful to science—and more truly fulfilling if you can bring it off—is to try to stay informed on what other scientists have done and to advance the frontier by your own quantum jumps. In terms of the old song: "Good work if you can get it. And you can get it if you try."

356

Economics in My Time

The last five or six decades have seen American economics come of age and then become the dominant center of world political economy. When I began the study of economics back in 1932 on the University of Chicago Midway, economics was literary economics: A few original spirits—such as Harold Hotelling, Ragnar Frisch, and R. G. D. Allen—used mathematical symbols; but, if their experience was like my early ones, learned journals rationed pretty severely acceptances of anything involving the calculus. Such esoteric animals as matrices were never seen in the social science zoos. At most, a few chaste determinants were admitted to our Augean stables.

Do I seem to be describing Eden, a paradise to which many would like to return in revulsion against the symbolic puss-pimples that disfigure not only the pages of *Econometrica* but also *The Economic Journal* and *The American Economic Review*?

Don't believe it. Like *Tobacco Road*, the old economics was strewn with rusty monstrosities of logic inherited from the past. Its soil generated few stalks of vigorous new science, and the correspondence between the terrain of the real world and the maps of the economics textbooks and treatises was neither smooth nor even one-to-one.

The Great Takeoff

Yes, 1932 was a great time to be born as an economist. The sleeping beauty of political economy was waiting for the enlivening kiss of new methods, new paradigms, new hired hands, and new problems. Science is a parasite: The greater the patient population, the better the advance in physiology and pathology; and out of pathology arises therapy. Nineteen thirty-two was the trough of the Great Depression, and from its rotten soil was belatedly begot the new subject that today we call macroeconomics.

Do I refer to the Keynesian revolution? Of course I do. But people are wrong to associate with that name the particular policies and ideologies found fifty years ago in the writings of John Maynard Keynes, Alvin Hansen, Joan Robinson, Abba Lerner, and Michael Kalecki. The New Classical School, through the quills of Robert Lucas, Tom Sargent, and Robert Barro, reverse those Keynesian doctrines 180°. Nevertheless, the present-day equations found in monetarism, eclectic mainstream Keynesianism, or rational expectationism are a galaxy removed from what were in Walras and Marshall—or in Frank Knight and Jacob Viner, my great neoclassical teachers in Chicago. The macromethodology innovated by Keynes's 1936 *General Theory* constitute both the 1985 swords that slash at Keynesianism and the shields that defend mainstream macroeconomics.

So far in this introduction I have been talking about the internal logic and development of economics as a science. It has been an inside-the-seminar-room survey of the subject, where of course the observations of the economic world have been brought into that seminar room. As a result of outside influences the period 1932–1975 was a favorable one for economists like me in that it was an epoch of tremendous university expansion and job opportunity. If one can borrow from the vulgar terminology of economic science fiction, my generation of economist activity was buoyed along by the great wave of a Kondratieff expansion.

The New Deal and welfare state created a vast new market for economists in government. Then came the war, which was carried on by armaments, cannon fodder, and economists: When the business cycle was put into hibernation by the wartime command economy, whenever problems of quantitative resource allocation ran out, economists could chance their arm on the new science of operations research, a game at which only the rare brilliant physicist could best the run-of-the-mill economists.

Then came the postwar boom in education. Where there had been in 1935 only a few strong centers for economic research—Harvard, Chicago, Columbia, and a few others—now everywhere in the land there grew up excellent graduate departments. No longer did one wait to be made a full professor at 45; the typical new Shangri-la in the firmament of postwar economics was created by an activist department chairman, given the go-ahead signal by his administration, to go out and hire hotshot stars at twice his own salary. Like beardless colonels in the wartime air corps, 30-year-old full professors deigned to grace prestigious academic chairs.

Pax Americanus

The shear numbers of American economists gave them unfair advantage over economists abroad. In addition, Hitler gave us even before the War the cream of the continental crop. Just as Chicago is the biggest Polish city after Warsaw and New York the greatest Swedish city after Stockholm, America obtained practically the whole of the Austrian school in economics. Along with such names as Einstein, von Neumann, and Fermi, go such American economist names as Koopmans, Leontief, Schumpeter, Marschak, Haberler, Kuznets, and many others. Later, as strength draws to itself strength, there began to appear in the American lineup the names of Hurwicz, Debreu, Theil, Bhagwati, Coase, Fischer, and many others.

Again and again I have seen in recent decades the tremendous stimulus that top postdoctoral scholars from abroad have received from a year's sojourn in the States, hopping on the grand tour from Cambridge to Stanford. They go back home fired up to change the old world. For half a decade their reprints keep coming. Then, almost in accordance with some second law of thermodynamics, the Schumpeterian burst subsides.

Evidently science itself is not subject to the law of constant returns to scale. The book of Matthew applies: "To him who hath shall be given." Unfair, you say? Well, as Jack Kennedy observed, "Who said life is fair?"

Life at the Top

I have seen economists grow in public esteem and in pecuniary demand. Surveys have shown that the highest paid scientists, physical and biological scientists as well as economists, are not to be found in private industry but rather in the universities—perhaps in and out of the universities would put it more accurately. I don't know scholars who have agents. But some do have lecture bureaus. And being a public member on corporate boards has become a new way of life.

It is a heady experience to advise the Prince on a sabbatical tour of duty in Washington. Newspaper columnists from academia serendipitously acquire the omniscience they need for the job.

"And gladly teach" used to refer to the lecture hall and seminar table but now includes telling congressional committees there is no free lunch and telling TV audiences to buy cheap and sell dear.

Trees do not grow to the sky. Every Kondratieff wave has its inflection point. The 1932–65 expansion in economists' prestige and self-esteem has been followed by some leaner years. We have become more humble and, as Churchill said, we have much to be humble about. Economists have not been able to agree on a good cure for stagflation. That disillusions non-economists. And, to tell the truth, it punctures our own self-complacency. We shop around for new paradigms the way alchemists prospect for new philosophers' stones. Just because a National Bureau paper is silly does not mean it is uninteresting. Just because it is profound does not mean that it is admired.

Mea Culpa

So far, I have been talking about economics. The title of this series, "My Evolution As An Economist," suggests that I should be talking about *me.* Mr. Dooley said that Theodore Roosevelt was going to write a book about the Spanish American War called *Me and Cuba.* It would begin with

Teddy's tribute, "My black sergent was the bravest man I ever knew. He followed me up San Juan Hill."

I can claim that in talking about modern economics I am talking about me. My finger has been in every pie. I once claimed to be the last generalist in economics, writing and teaching such diverse subjects as international trade and econometrics, economic theory and business cycles, demography and labor economics, finance and monopolistic competition, history of doctrines and locational economics. Kilroy, having been there, must share the guilt. (Goethe wrote that there was no crime he ever heard of that he didn't feel capable of committing. Bob Solow's reaction was that Goethe flattered himself. And perhaps what I called "crime" is a mistranslation of what Goethe meant only as "error.")

Here is my worst error. Do you remember the infamous wrong prediction by economists that after World War II there would be mass unemployment? I was not part of the multi-agency team that produced the official 1945 forecast of doomsday. But, if you look at the yellowing files of the New Republic, you will find a well-written article by this humble servant that involves a large squared forecasting error on the downward side. My friend and mentor, Alvin Hansen, who believed in a postwar restocking boom, could have taught me better. And so could Sumner Slichter and a host of Keynesians and non-Keynesians.

I reproach myself for a gross error. But I would reproach myself more if I persisted in an error after observations revealed it clearly to be that. I made a deal of money in the late 1940s on the bull side, ignoring Satchel Paige's advice to Lot's wife, "Never look back." Rather I would advocate Samuelson's law: "Always look back. You may learn something from your residuals. Usually one's forecasts are not so good as one remembers them; the difference may be instructive." The dictum "If you must forecast, forecast often," is neither a joke nor a confession of impotence. It is a recognition of the primacy of brute fact over pretty theory. That part of the future which cannot be related to the present's past is precisely what science cannot hope to capture. Fortunately, there is plenty of work for science to do, plenty of scientific tasks not yet done.

Other Testimonies

I shall not shirk talking more specifically about my own development as a scholar and scientist. But, since I do not believe in that kind of elegant variation which follows "he said" by "he averred" and then by "vouchsafed the speaker," I shall not try to duplicate some earlier autobiographical writings. Peppered through many of the technical articles in the four volumes of my *Collected Scientific Papers* are various personal reminiscenccs. But the richest vein of this kind of ore will be found in, first, my 1968 Presidential Address before the World Congress of the International Economic Association. It is cunningly entitled "The Way of an Economist," ambivalent words denoting both the economic road traveled and the personal style of the Sigfried traversing that road. Similarly, today in speaking of "Economics in My Time," I also mean economics in my own peculiar rhythms and style.

A second source is my 1972 "Economics in a Golden Age: A Personal Memoir," which appeared in the *Daedalus* book Gerald Holton edited called *The Twentieth Century Sciences: Studies in the Biography of Ideas* (W. W. Norton, New York).

A third source, one whose title was imposed on me, is *My Lifetime Philosophy*. This appeared in the 1983 series for students of *The American Economist*, XXVII, No. 2, pp. 5–12, and will be in the forthcoming fifth volume of *Collected Scientific Papers of Paul A. Samuelson.*

The Scientist Delineated

Here briefly, in the third person for objectivity, is the superficial outline of my scientific career.

PAS has always been incredibly lucky, throughout his lifetime overpaid and underworked. A bright youngster, favored by admiring parents, he shone at school until the high school years when he became an underachiever. The calendar lies in naming May 15, 1915, as his time of birth. Truly he was born on the morning of January 2, 1932, at the University of Chicago.

He was made for academic life. An A student at Chicago and an A + one at Harvard, PAS wandered by chance into economics. Economics turned out to be made for him as the Darwinian genes from generations of commercial ancestors encountered their teleological destiny.

Every honor he aspired to came his way, and came early. He got the undergraduate social science medal his undergraduate year. Just when commencement loomed near, the Social Science Research Council created a new experimental fellowship program in economics, whose first award supported him handsomely at Harvard. Having drawn from Chicago giants like Knight, Viner, Henry Schultz, Henry Simons, Paul Douglas, John U. Nef, and Lloyd Mints, he levitated to the Harvard Yard to learn from Joseph Schumpeter, Wassily Leontief, Edwin Bidwell Wilson, Gottfried Haberler, Edward Chamberlin, and Alvin Hansen. Before his SSRC fellowship gave out, he overcame the opposition of the Society of Fellows to economics and rode on the shoulders of Vilfredo Pareto into the sacred circle of Junior Fellows. The philosopher Willard van Orman Quine, the mathematician Garrett Birkhoff, the double-Nobel physicist John Bardeen, the chemists Bright Wilson and Robert Woodward, and the polymath Harry T. Levine were his companions in arms in the Society of Fellows. There he hit his stride, and began to turn out articles faster than the journals could absorb such quasi-mathematical stuff.

It is not true that PAS began life as a physicist or mathematician. Well into his undergraduate course he discerned that mathematics was to revolutionize modern economics. Proceeding to learn mathematics, PAS still remembers how a Lagrange multiplier first swam into his ken and how, with a wild surmise, it gave him independent discovery of the Edgeworth-Stackelberg asymmetric solution for duopoly—an insight that has kept him immune to the false charms of Nash-Cournot purported solutions.

His *Foundations of Economic Analysis*, written mostly as a Junior Fellow but usable later for the Ph.D. union card, won the David A. Wells Prize at Harvard. Later it helped him receive in 1947 the first John Bates Clark Medal of the American Economic Association, awarded for scholarly promise before the age of forty. Its quality was thrice blessed: Later still it contributed to his 1970 Nobel Prize in economics, the second time that fabricated (or "forged") honor was awarded, and the first time to an American.

Hegira Down the River

If PAS was born as a child his freshman year at Chicago, he was born a second time as a man that 1940 October day he succumbed to a call from MIT. MIT's force met no detectable Harvard resistance, so the movable object moved. It was the best thing that could have happened to PAS. A boy must always remain a boy in his father's house. On his own acres a man can build his own mansion, and after 1941, PAS, along with magnificent colleagues, was able to help build up what became recognized as a leading world center for economics. Living well is the best revenge, Hemingway's crowd used to say; but, in sober truth, the example of MIT's Norbert Wiener, who in his days of fame still brooded over his ejection from the Harvard Yard, led PAS ever to cherish his Harvard connections and labor for the greater glory of Cambridge and Middlesex County.

Peer recognition came early and often: from the American Academy of Arts and Sciences, the National Academy, American Philosophical Society, and British Academy. Just as it is the first million that is the hardest, one honor leads to another. After the first dozen of honorary degrees, all it takes is longevity to double the number. The first such degree—from Chicago, alma mater and basilica of a church he no longer believed in—PAS found most touching. When Harvard honored a prophet in his own country, he also liked that.

Vice presidencies and presidencies in professional societies came his way: the Econometric Society, the American Economic Association, the International Economic Association. As yet there is no Galaxy Political Economy Club.

A scholar at a new place for economic study like MIT receives plenty of offers from all over the world. PAS revealed a preference to be an immovable object, and when made an Institute Professor in 1966, with magnificant research opportunities and optional teaching duties, he in effect returned to the womb of a perpetual Junior Fellowship. Having arrived in Paradise, he stayed there.

But not without excursions to the outside. Many a tutorial he gave to congressional committees. Often when he became a consultant to a federal agency, that precipitated its demise. The US Treasury and the Federal Reserve Board did, however, survive his academic counsels. Murmuring that the United States is too precious to be turned over exclusively to big picture thinkers like John Kenneth Galbraith and Walt Whitman Rostow, PAS gave economic tutorial to Adlai Stevenson and Averell Harriman and worked his way as adviser to Senator J. F. Kennedy, Candidate Kennedy, and President-Elect Kennedy. Moses-like, PAS did not pass into the promised land beyond the Potomac, but as an *éminence grise* he had the fun of backing the poker hands of such magnificent Joshuas as Walter Heller, James Tobin, and Kermit Gordon at the Kennedy Council of Economic Advisers.

What can the good fairies give the man who has everything? George Stigler, referring to Samuelson's 1947 *Foundations* and his newly published 1948 bestselling textbook *Economics*, introduced him with the words, "Samuelson, having achieved fame, now seeks fortune." Soon the smoke of burning mortgage could be sniffed in Belmont, Massachusetts. More than this, J. K. Galbraith's prophesy in a *Fortune* review, that a new generation would receive its eçonomics from Economics, turned out to be right on the mark. PAS was heard to mutter complacently, "Let those who will, write the nation's laws if I can write its textbooks." Being denounced by William Buckley for blaspheming God and man at Yale, the textbook took on a new aura of respectability and sales soared all over the world.

A quarter of a century ago, the author of *Economics* commented on the new layer of fame that accrues to a scholar who writes a bestseller, stating modestly:

> Writing a beginning textbook is hard work. But its rewards have been tremendous —and I do not mean simply pecuniary rewards. Contact with hundreds of thousands of minds of a whole generation is an experience like no other that a scholar will

ever meet. And writing down what we economists know about economics has been truly an exciting experience. I can only hope that some of this excitement will rub off on the reader.

By Joy Possessed

Stop! Enough is enough. Of such *Who's Who* boilerplate, enough is too much. What has been described above could be said of many a successful go-getter. A West Pointer who hated soldiering might settle for a Faustian bargain in which promotions and blue ribbons compensate for a wasted life.

The rewards that have counted for me in scholarship and science is the marvelous hunt through enchanted forests. I began to write articles for publication before I was twenty-one. I have never stopped. I hope never to stop. When Harry Johnson died, he had eighteen papers in proof. That is dying with your boots on! (Even for Harry, who never did things by halves or held down to the golden mean, eighteen was overdoing it.)

My mind is ever toying with economic ideas and relationships. Great novelists and poets have reported occasional abandonment by their muse. The well runs dry, permanently or on occasion. Mine has been a better luck. As I have written elsewhere, there is a vast inventory of topics and problems floating in the back of my mind. More perhaps than I shall ever have occasion to write up for publication. A result that I notice in statistical mechanics may someday help resolve a problem in finance.

Like a gravid spouse I achieve the release of publication. Have I published too much? Others must form their judgment on this. Speaking for myself, in my heart of hearts I have regretted almost no chapter, article, note, or footnote my quill has penned. And I have rued many an excision, forced on me by editors of only finite patience or self-imposed for reasons of space and aesthetic measure.

Perhaps this betrays the lack of taste that marks the gourmand and not the gourmet? I hope not. I certainly sympathize with the view expressed in the following conversation of the classicist-poet A. E. Housman. A friend asked him why he was not including in a collection of his writings on Latin a certain item: "Don't you think it good?" "I think it good," Housman replied, "but not good enough for me." And not infrequently when I read some scholars latest work, I have asked of Robert Solow what G. H. Hardy asked of J. E. Littlewood: "Why would a man who could write such an article do so?"

The able scholar with writer's block elevates by the mere passage of time the standards each future work must hurdle. It is easy to write a letter every day but, when you have not done so for five years, there is really nothing to report.

Repeatedly I have denied the great-man or great-work notion of science.

Every drop helps, the old farmer said as he spat into the pond. One does the best one can on the most pressing problem that presents. And, if after you have done so, your next moves are down a trajectory of diminishing returns, then still it is optimal to follow the rule of doing the best that is there to do. Besides, at any time a Schumpeterian innovation or Darwinian mutation may occur to you, plucking the violin string of increasing returns.

Between Mozart and Brahms, I'm for Mozart. I am thankful for the precious gold pieces Pierro Sraffa left us. But economics would be the better if he had also blessed us all with some dozens of rubies and pearls. And, as I remember his eloquent but sad eyes, one wonders whether he would not have been the happier man if—as William James puts it—he had been born with a bottle of champagne to his credit. Maynard Keynes, who suffered from no writer's cramp, when asked at the end of his life what he'd have done different if he had it all over again to do, replied: "I'd have drunk more champagne."

Earlier I confessed to having always been overpaid and underworked. Even good friends might agree with the first of these adjectives, but several will protest at the second, perhaps protesting, "Come off it, you work all the time, weekends and during vacations and, if legend holds, often during the reveries of the midnight hours." True enough. It is precisely my point though that working out economic analysis is play, not work. I am notorious for shirking tasks I hate to do. I minimize administrative duties, displaying an incompetence in their performance that chokes off additional assignments. Like Dennis Robertson, I always wash the forks last in the realization that should an atomic holocaust be imminent there may never be a need to do them.

If I am required to fill out an elaborate questionnaire, that liability is likely to stimulate me to write a new model in the theory of trade or in population genetics. Anything to put off the evil day of duty.

Remembered Kisses

Novels about painters, musicians, poets, or scientists notoriously fail to convey what they do in the working hours of the week. Come to think of it, novels about allegedly great business tycoons similarly fail to capture what it is precisely that they do.

Therefore, speaking to an audience of economists, I should be more specific and describe some particular acts of scientific gestation. How did I first notice the problem? When did a breakthrough occur? What were the steps of development? And how, in retrospect, was the pattern of knowledge affected by the research?

But where to begin? I toyed with the experiment of describing the big ledger that, for a year like 1983, served as a partial diary of research doodlings. Thus, the January 1 entry might be jottings on how to devise a numerical example of a linear programming system that violates globally a crude version of the Le Châtelier principle in economics. This never got published. Yet. It refers back to work done in 1949, and indeed in 1937 when I was a student at E. B. Wilson's knee—or perhaps shoulder. One might then trace in the daybook a return on January 2 and 3 to the problem, and perhaps discern how it modulates into a related problem.

Suffice it to say that, in the course of a year, there will be half a hundred such finger exercises. But it would be misleading to believe that my 1983 research is well described, or even sampled, by the chance items that happen to get jotted down in one bedside journal. Therefore I had better reserve for another and longer day detailed discussion of how some familiar result was conceived and came into being. (The impatient reader can be referred for a sample to my 1982 contribution to the Jørgen Gelting Festschrift, which I entitled "A Chapter in the History of Ramsey's Optimal Feasible Taxation and Optimal Public Utility Prices.")

Chasing the Bitch Goddess of Success

Let me close with a few remarks on the motivations and rewards of scientists. Scientists are as avaricious and competitive as Smithian businessmen. The coin they seek is not apples, nuts, and yachts; nor is it coin itself, or power as that term is ordinarily used. Scholars seek fame. The fame they seek, as I noted in my 1961 American Economic Association Presidential Address, is fame with their peers—the other scientists whom they respect and whose respect they strive for. The sociologist Robert K. Merton has documented what I call this dirty little secret in his book, *The Sociology of Science.*

I am no exception. Abraham Lincoln's law partner and biographer, Herndon, observed that there was always a little clock of ambition ticking in the bosom of honest and whimsical Abe. No celebrity as a *Newsweek* columnist, no millions of clever-begotten speculative gains, no power as the Svengali or Rasputin to the Prince and President could count as a pennyweight in my balance of worth, as against the prospect of recognition for having contributed to the empire of science.

Once I asked my friend the statistician Harold Freeman: "Harold, if the Devil came to you with the bargain that, in exchange for your immortal soul, he'd give you a brilliant theorem, would you do it?" "No", he replied, "but I would for an inequality." I like that answer. The day I proved that no one could be more than 60,000 standard deviations dumber than the mean, that Samuelson inequality made my day. The fact that subsequent writers have both generalized beyond it and discovered antecedents of it in earlier writings has not altered my pleasure in it. For that is the way of science, and sufficient to the day is the increment to the house of science that day brings.

Being precocious, I got an early start. Unconsciously and consciously, I was a young man in a hurry because I felt that the limited life span of my male ancestors tolled the bell for me. My father died young, when I was 23. I was supposed to resemble him, and the effect on me was especially traumatic. What I was to do I would have to do early, is what I thought. Actually, modern science granted me respite. Heredity, always, is modifiable by environment. Whatever the reason, I have been granted bouncing good health, a factor given too little weight in allocating merit to scientists and in explaining their achievements. A respected friend of mine, sometimes unfairly marked down as an underachiever, has been subject all his life to debilitating migraines. I say he is the meritorious one for having, as the Bible says, used his pound so judiciously.

There is another aspect to early, full (even over-full) recognition. It relaxes you. Why fret about priorities when, in the time you might spend in recriminations and turf-claiming, you can dip your hook into the waters and be pulling out other pretty fish?

I long ago enunciated the doctrine that scholars work for their self-esteem, in the sense of what they all agree to judge meritorious. However, once your need for glory in the eyes of others has been somewhat appeased, you become free to work for your own approval. The job you will think well done is the one that brings true bliss. Perhaps part of this involves the faith that what one craftsman will like, so eventually will the rest.

There was never a time when I didn't strive to please myself. There have been those who thought that my fooling around with thermodynamics was an attempt to inflate the scientific validity of economics; even perhaps to snow the hoi polloi of economists who naturally can't judge intricacies of physics. Actually, such methodological excursions, if anything, put a tax on reputation, rather than enhancing it. So what? Taxes are the price we pay for civilization. Such work is fun. And I perceive it adds to the depth and breadth of human knowledge.

Someone asked me whether I enjoyed getting the Nobel Prize. I thought before answering. "Yes," I replied, "few things in life bring undiluted pleasure, but this one did." The honor was a pleasant surprise and came early, but not so early as to worry even me. Friends whose opinions I valued were pleased. If there were contrary opinions. I was too obtuse to be aware of them. My family enjoyed the Stockholm hoopla. Some colleagues in science have looked back with pain at the public interviews and turmoil that took them out of their laboratories. I bore up well, and discovered that it takes only a few days of dependence upon one's own chauffer to develop an addiction.

Indian Summer

Sociologists of science study how the Nobel award affects a scholar. Do the laureates go into an era of depressed fertility? Do they write fewer or more joint papers and more often list their names first or list them last? Does citing of them accelerate? What is the propensity to change fields—for a physicist to tackle the problem of the brain, for a chemist to become an expert on peace or the minimum wage?

To me it was a case where my cup runneth over—almost. The last vestiges of guilt disappeared when I chose to go off the main turnpike of my discipline of economics—to explore R. A. Fisher's notion of survival value, or James Clerk Maxwell's image of a Demon who cheats the second law of thermodynamics of its certainty. I still monitor business trends and the latest fads like a hawk. I still write articles in the many different provinces of political economy. But the last generalist no longer feels it necessary to keep on top of—I mean to try to keep on top of—all the literatures of economics.

As I veer toward the traditional three-score-and-ten, how do I feel about it? Goethe, who like Wagner and Verdi had a great long run, wrote that the difference between age and youth was that, in youth when you called on it, it was always there in response. By contrast, only on the best good days could the octogenarian attain the peak performance. To myself, I am 69 going on 25. All the days seem as good as ever. But, as the lyricist says and reason insists, the stock of what's left of the good times must shrink as you reach September.

BERTIL OHLIN (1899–1979)*

Paul A. Samuelson

Massachusetts Institute of Technology, Cambridge, Mass., USA

Ohlin will live forever as one of the great innovators in the theory of international trade. He was also a pioneer in the development of modern macroeconomics. For fifty years he advanced the banner of the vintage second generation of notable Scandinavian economists—a worthy follower of the Swedish giants, Knut Wicksell, David Davidson, Gustav Cassel, Eli Heckscher; a companion in arms of Gunnar Myrdal, Erik Lindahl, Tord Palander, Gustav and Johan Åkerman; the teacher and mentor of Erik Lundberg, Ingvar Svennilson, and so many names that I dare not enumerate.

We must be grateful that Bertil was so precocious: for in midlife he slighted our science of political economy for the arena of practical politics; but, at the same time, he was able to complete his scientific mission. Since creative economic theory is a mushroom that lives on the wood of experience, Ohlin's political preoccupations were not without benefit to his scientific work. Ohlin's insufficiently appreciated originality in perceiving already in the 1940s the stagflation of over-full-employment grew out of his Parliamentary preoccupation with economic policy. Precisely because Sweden is so advanced as a mixed economy, it served as an analogue computer to simulate the shape of things to come for us in the United States, and Britain, and Japan. Ohlin as leader of the political party that represented more than a class interest had a grandstand seat from which to relay to his economist colleagues abroad the omens for our future.

I set myself the task of evaluating Ohlin's scientific legacy. Someone from his own country and circle can best testify to his personal style and professional biography. What I may do is report on how Bertil Ohlin appeared to foreign economists, particularly to my generation.

The Scientist as Colleague

Bertil Ohlin was notoriously handsome, in a profession not notorious for appearances and even in a country that sets a high standard. We expect bankers and undertakers to be tall and courtly as befits their ritualistic duties. But just

* I owe thanks for partial financial aid to the National Science Foundation, grant no. 75-04053AOI-SOC and to Kate Crowley for editorial assistance.

as blondes are discounted as frivolous and empty-headed, we prefer that the surgeons who operate on us have attained their positions primarily by merit. By sheer brilliance, the young Bertil lived down his good looks. One other thing: Swedish academics were in my time supposed to be stiff and formal. When Gunnar Myrdal gave the 1938 Godkin Lectures at Harvard I learned not to believe this canard of punctiliousness. Bertil Ohlin confirmed my skepticism. And no one of the thousands who have been lovingly insulted in the witty introductions of Erik Lundberg will doubt that the bourgeois Scandinavia of Strindberg and Ibsen has evolved away from its pure Victorian archetype.

I must dwell on one more personal matter. It has been often said that Albert Einstein and Max Planck were such nice men that they elevated a whole generation of German physicists. I was told 40 years ago that when Gunnar Myrdal and Bertil Ohlin chose different political parties, they resolved not to let this lead to personal bitterness of scientific dispute in the manner of their elders, Cassel, Bagge, Heckscher, and Wicksell. As far as the testimony of my own experience is concerned, such a pact was never broken. In any case, the force of this example has been important in my own life. Over what will soon be five decades, Milton Friedman and I have had some occasions to disagree on policy choices and doctrines, without that affecting our friendly relations. Not only is this better for manners and for the liver. It also makes for better science. To coin a phrase, the scientists whom the Gods would destroy, they first make angry. The decline of England's primacy in economics I must in part attribute to the personal acrimony that long ago infected the senior common rooms of that other Eden.

Years of Apprenticeship

By his own confession, Bertil Ohlin was born into a large "upper-middleclass family" in the South of Sweden. Educated in private schools, the precocious boy entered the University of Lund at a young age, but alas did not have the advantage of personal instruction from Knut Wicksell. Attracted by Heckscher's wartime writing, Ohlin went on to the Stockholm School of Economics for advanced study, completing his graduate work at the University of Stockholm under Gustav Cassel and Gösta Bagge.

His initial 1922 thesis, and subsequent 1924 doctoral dissertation, constituted early Swedish versions of his classic 1933 *Interregional and International Trade*. Ohlin has testified to the importance in his training of the Harvard teachers he met during his 1923 year in Cambridge, Massachusetts: the grand old man of classical theory, Frank Taussig, the brilliant Allyn Young, who was to die too young, Thomas Nixon Carver in rural economics, and especially John H. Williams. I have heard both John and Bertil speak with evident nostalgia of the year they spent together arguing; and although the skeptic who was my old teacher seemed to me hardly Ohlin's cup of tea, we must take at face value their mutual admiration and affection and recall that both shared skepticism of the pure classical model of international trade.

Bertil told me that only once in his life had *mathematics written a paper for him.* The incident is an interesting one. Most economists follow Thünen and Irving Fisher in thinking that a tree should be cut down when the percentage rate of growth of wood in it just equals the instantaneous market rate of interest. In 1849 a German forester named Martin Faustmann showed this to be wrong: since cutting a tree releases its ground for a new tree, so long as land is scarce enough to earn positive rent, you should cut the tree earlier, when its growth rate of wood is so very big as to cover *both* the opportunity cost of money (Thünen's interest rate) *and also* the opportunity cost of the land it keeps from other uses. Faustmann corrected Thünen's conventional wisdom by maximizing the present discounted value, not of one tree's lumber receipts in *its* lifetime but of, the *infinite stream of trees* that includes the original tree and all of its successors on the site.

The Faustmann dynamic-programming solution has been rediscovered a dozen times since 1849, once by me, as I describe in my 1976 survey of forestry economics. When that lecture was privately circulated, Professor Karl Jungenfelt, Ohlin's colleague, called to my attention the 1921 maiden paper that Ohlin contributed to the Wicksell *Festschrift*: this independently derives the correct Faustmann condition and stoutly refutes the contention of Ohlin's mentor Heckscher. Except for the celebrated Appendix to his 1933 book, this seems to be the only time when Ohlin used the talent for mathematics that he displayed in early years. It is a matter of regret to me that along with Ohlin's prodigious and original literary economics, we did not also get from him more by way of technically analytical contributions.

One who pages through the *Index of Economic Articles* will form a false notion of how prolific Bertil Ohlin was. His papers in English and in standard learned journals are only the tip of the tip of the iceberg.* Aside from his numerous scientific works in Swedish and German, Ohlin seems to have written a daily newspaper commentary for years. This must bring him into the league of Einaudi, Heckscher, and Pareto for sheer number of economic publications. The reader will, I believe, nevertheless be able to form a just impression of Ohlin's scientific importance by consulting the following main items: his 1933 *Interregional and International Trade*; his late-1920s debates with Keynes on the transfer problem; his 1937 *Economic Journal* articles on the Stockholm School's independent anticipation of Keynesian income analysis; and his various biographical and bibliographical commentaries on Scandinavian and world economic developments. Richard Caves (1978) gave a useful analytical

* Bertil Ohlin compiled a bibliography of his work for publication in *The Scandinavian Journal of Economics 80*, 93–99, 1978.

appraisal of Bertil Ohlin's contribution to economics on the occasion of the 1977 Nobel Award to him (and to James Meade); and Erik Lundberg, in *Challenge* (September/October, 1980), has written Ohlin's obituary.

I must be selective here in my appreciation. After discussing Ohlin's seminal contribution to international trade theory, I examine in some detail his 1929 views on the transfer problem against the background of modern formulations. And I conclude with an evaluation of the sense in which Ohlin and his Swedish contemporaries did or did not independently arrive at Keynes's *General Theory*.

Ohlin's International Trade Model

To say that Bertil Ohlin lives on in the Valhalla of great contributors to the theory of international trade is to say much, for trade theory has always been the queen realm of economic theory. Mill's chapters on international values provide the first complete model of general equilibrium—one essentially isomorphic with Jevons' chapters a generation later on competitive exchange and with Walras's equilibrium. Marshall's youthful 1879 *Pure Theory of International Trade* outshone analytically anything he ever succeeded in doing in his later *Principles*. Nowadays trade theory benefits from general theory, but in the latter's history the direction of interdependence went largely the other way—as the survey in Chipman (1965–6) documents.

It also says much to claim that Ohlin's name belongs on the same shelf with such names in the field of international trade as Hume, Torrens-Ricardo, J. S. Mill, Mangoldt, Marshall, Taussig, and Edgeworth. If Alfred Nobel's will had provided for prizes in economics beginning in 1901 along with the prizes in physics, chemistry, medicine, literature, and peace, I think that by 1940 Bertil Ohlin would have received one—either by himself, or sharing one with either or both of Jacob Viner and Gottfried Haberler or with Eli Heckscher.[1]

Bertil Ohlin is to be grouped as one of the great triumvirate: Jacob Viner, Bertil Ohlin, and Gottfried Haberler, whom I list in chronological order of birth. Viner, Taussig's star pupil and a nova in his own right, was the learned and skillful rear-guard defender of the classical one-factor model of interna-

[1] One cannot forbear playing the game of might-have-been. Here is the most likely scenario of awards from 1901 on: Böhm-Bawerk, Marshall, J. B. Clark, Walras, and Wicksell; Carl Menger, Pareto, Wicksteed, Irving Fisher, and Edgeworth; Sombart, Mitchell, Pigou, Adolph Wagner, Allyn Young, and Cannan; Davenport, Taussig, Schumpeter, Veblen, and Bortkiewicz; Cassel, J. M. Keynes, Heckscher, J. R. Commons, and J. M. Clark; Hawtrey, von Mises, Robertson, H. L. Moore, and F. H. Knight. My list breaks off at 1930 and the dawn of the modern age. Of course there would have to be the usual grumblings and criticism. Why were Eugen Slutsky and Frank Ramsey missed? If Davenport, why not Carver and Fetter? Why Böhm before Menger? If Mises, why not Foxwell, Nicholson, Aftalion, Seligman, Spiethoff, von Wieser, Bowley, Pierson, Birke, Einaudi, Pantaleoni, or Barone? If Veblen, what about Hobson, Luxemburg, the Webbs, Hilferding, or Lenin himself? The listing I have given compliments the taste of the Swedish Royal Academy of Sciences, being a compromise between (1) what I with hindsight judge to be true scientific merit, and (2) what would likely have been recognized as merit by conscientious but fallible committees.

tional trade. Ohlin was the Jacobin Pretender, who chose to regard the extreme differences in degree between a multi-factor model and a one-factor model as a difference in kind. Gottfried Haberler, who generalized to the case of factors of production additional to labor but made their multiplicity manageable by means of the brilliant device of the Fisherine *production-possibility frontier* (or technological *transformation* locus), preferred eclectically to call his innovations *evolutionary* developments in the spirit of Ricardian comparative-cost analysis. This triumvirate paved the road for the outburst of post-1932 work by Abba Lerner, Leontief, Meade, Samuelson, Ronald Jones, McKenzie, Metzler, Pearce, Chipman, and present-day authors too numerous to mention.

Throughout the twenties, Ohlin championed the cause of what he regarded as a new paradigm: the *mutual interdependence* theory of international and interregional trade. Ohlin's thought shows the clear influence of two great teachers: Cassel, with his purloining of Walras's system of general equilibrium; and Heckscher, with his 1919 *tour de force* that developed from Wicksell's system the tendency for factor returns to be equalized by means of free trade in goods alone. Ohlin added much value to their microeconomics. In addition he stressed two important elements of his own.

Much as Böhm-Bawerk had endeavored to establish with his interest theory a general model of *intertemporal* prices, Ohlin endeavored to make his trade theory part of a general *locational analysis* of *spatial* pricing and goods and factor movements. He hoped to go beyond the locational analysis of Cournot, Thünen, Launhardt, Alfred Weber, Lösch, Palander (his kinsman), and to integrate this with the theory of interregional and international trade. I do not regard as optimal Viner's tart observation that locational theory owes more to international trade theory than vice versa, but I share the widespread feeling that location theory has never fulfilled its exciting promise (and its promises).

The second additional microeconomic point that Ohlin always stressed was the role of *increasing returns* in international specialization and exchange. Here he was following in the tradition of Adam Smith, Allyn Young, and the late Frank Graham. Even with regional symmetry in tastes, technology, and factor proportions, the occurrence of increasing returns can give rise to viable and mutually beneficial exchange. There are grave problems in formulating an elegant and informative theory of such processes. For one thing, if overall demand is still so small as to leave unexhausted the economies of large scale production, the viability of perfect competition is brought into question. Although Ohlin and a host of writers before and after him have called for a useful theory of *imperfect competition and international trade*, that call has thus far not evoked a very exciting response. A further difficulty intrinsic to the increasing returns case is the likelihood of some indeterminacies in the pattern that emerges. So to speak, often two advanced regions could toss a coin to decide which of two increasing-returns industries should be placed in each of the respective countries: whichever gets a head-start first may, by hysteresis, rule the roost forever. The phenomenon of increasing returns negates the nice convexity properties that are so beloved by us lazy mathematical economists hell-bent for elegance of formulation. Instead, we are in a world of multiple local maxima, one in which things often get worse before they get better. A horrible combinatorial problem of description and computation faces us, with all the unmanageable complexities of digital programming and much worse.

I agree with Ohlin that it is an injustice to his 1933 classic to think of it as simply a stepping stone[1] between the original article of Heckscher and the 2-by-2 (or n-by-n) models of Stolper–Samuelson or Lerner–Samuelson. In Ohlin's text implicitly, and explicitly in his original mathematical appendix, Ohlin does deal with an n-good r-factor technology, identical and neoclassical in two regions, with every person's factor supplies given constants, and with each person having his individual demand preferences to determine how he spends his laissez-faire imputed income. (Actually, Ohlin's literary text is more general than his appendix, following Heckscher in supposing that people's factor supplies expand when their respective factor returns endogenously rise, and coming to grips with transport costs.) Ohlin's equations system, which is a bit more general than the fixed-coefficient version usually associated with Cassel, essentially rediscovers some of the general equilibrium trade models that Pareto had developed in the Italian literature of the 1890s. Ohlin's 1933 appendix made little dent on later writers, perhaps because everything is left at the formalistic level of counting equations and unknowns without regard to specifying characteristic curvature properties and specializing to strategic models. Thus, had Ohlin considered the two-good two-factor case, with uniform homothetic demands, there would have been much less left for youngsters like me to do later.

Here is the core content to be found in the Heckscher–Ohlin model. Two regions, with the same smooth neoclassical production functions, the same tastes for *two* goods (at *all* income levels!), and the same endowments of the *two* factors, will have *no* reason to trade—inasmuch as their autarky price ratios will all be exactly equal. If their factor endowments are kept equal but their tastes are allowed to differ, each in autarky will have a relatively dear

[1] Rereading Heckscher (1919) for this eulogy, I find that Ohlin definitely did go beyond Heckscher. Heckscher gives shrewd conjectures, but he never presented a *complete* model and necessarily lacked cogent proofs of the key theorems latent in his model. Example: Heckscher has three factors, not two; yet he never explicitly specifies as many as three goods; he gives but a necessary condition for the n-by-r $[a_{ij}]$ matrix to be of rank r—namely that two goods have columns not linearly dependent—which is far from sufficient. He never works out how his $[a_{ij}]$ reaches leastcost configurations in terms of ruling factor prices $(w_1, ..., w_r)$. His exposition is meandering, derivations shaky, and he fails to describe exactly the alternative possible cases where (ii) specialization precludes factor-price equalization and (i) simultaneous production of r ("linearly-independent") goods in *both* regions does succeed in equalizing factor prices. Still, Heckscher's 1919 paper is a work of genius. Ohlin's appendix, save for his one basic slip and his neglect of rank problems, does bring to completion, not the Heckscher system, but rather the Heckscher–Ohlin system!

price for the good it demands in unusual degree. *So taste differences can (and in this case will) generate partial specialization, each country importing the good it has relatively greater desire for.* What might have seemed novel in 1919 is the interesting fact that, after trade, equilibrium can make factor returns equalized in both countries; since, prior to trade, in each country that factor was relatively dear which is required in relatively great intensity by the good unusually desired there, Heckscher–Ohlin can say, "Free trade in goods 'relieves' the autarky scarcity of the factor that is in relative great need because of taste differences."

Now keep tastes the same in the two countries, but let factor endowments differ *a little* between the regions. We see that factor disparities will generate production differentiations and trade. The relative endowment scarcity of a region's factor will cause the good that requires relatively much of it to be dear under autarky. So, opening up trade will cause a region to import the good it found to be relative scarce under autarky; the pattern of importing and of exporting thus relieves the scarcity of the factor that the region is skimpily endowed with. Again, *free trade in goods is (singular cases aside) as effective as free migration of factors would be in wiping out modest differences in regions' factor returns due to geographical scarcities.*

Now consider induced changes in factor supply. If trade eliminates (or even simply reduces) factor-price discrepancies, the induced lowering of the return of that factor initially scarce in a region will cause its endowment to shrink and become scarcer still. Trade, like migration, equalizes factor returns; but, in opposition to migration, trade *widens* endowment differences.

What happens when the difference in factor endowments between the regions becomes larger and larger? Think of labor and land, and of labor-intensive clothing and land-intensive food. What is essentially the same analytical question is this: Compare your region with its labor/land endowments with a succession of regions whose factor proportions depart ever further from yours. All those regions that are so near in factor endowments to yours that both of you produce positive amounts of the same two goods in common, they will end with the same *real* factor returns as yours. But consider a region whose autarky real wage is much higher than yours. Its labor/land endowment is much skimpier than yours and it will find that it has too little of labor to be able to produce competitively under free trade the clothing that requires relatively much of its scarcest factor. Producing only one of your two goods, food, and finding that it must produce it with relatively less of its scarce labor than you use to produce food, that exotic region must clearly end up in free-trade equilibrium with a real return to its ultra-scarce factor that is still relatively high, even if not so high as it was in autarky.

In sum, free trade in goods goes all the way in equalizing factor returns between regions that produce two goods in common; but free trade in (technically-different) goods goes only part of the way toward equalizing the factor returns that in autarky were made grossly divergent by *large* differences in factor endowments. So long as two indispensable goods each systematically require relatively more of one of the two factors of production, completely free trade results in but three distinct geographical areas:

(i) A "central area of non-specialization" in which all subregions produce both goods and enjoy equalized real factor returns and good's terms of trade.

(ii) An area made up of regions that have so relatively little of labor as to be able to compete in the world market solely with production of that good which needs relatively much of land. The real wage of that scarce factor is everywhere in this region higher than in the non-specializing region of (i), being kept highest in (ii)'s subregions where endowments are skimpiest in that factor. Producing (and exporting) only that good which uses relatively much of the abundant land labor raises the rent return of that factor above its low autarky prices, but cannot raise it to the level in (i).

(iii) Finally, on the other side of region (i) is that in which the land is so relatively scarce as to raise *its* rent return above the equalized level in (i). Here all subregions produce (and export) only the second clothing good which requires much of the labor in abundant supply here; the more abundant that labor factor is in subregions, the farther below the region (i) level will the real wage be (albeit not so far below as prevailed before free trade in goods).

Within region (i) relative prices of the goods are the same, but subregions with relatively much of any factor will export relatively more of *its* good. Within region (i), and similarly for region (ii), subregions with least of a factor suffer the worst terms of trade to import the good that needs that scarce factor, and they presumably consume relatively less of that dear good.

Now recognize that exchanging goods always involves some positive transport costs, even if only infinitesimally so. This alters the above world patterns in an obvious way.

1. The outer regions that specialize solely on one good are each slightly shrunk by positive transport cost.

2. The central region in which both goods are produced is slightly *widened* by transport costs. Each point in it trades a bit less. The *strict equality* within it of factor returns and goods' terms of trade is lost, as now its subregions of greater relative labor density have somewhat lower real wage (and higher rent return to the other factor). Such regions also have slightly lower cost ratios and terms of trade for clothing versus food.

In sum, the positivity of transport costs (or of tariffs) will make equalization of factor prices by trade necessarily only *partial* rather than *complete*.

All these simple verities,[1] which were latent in the Heckscher and Ohlin

---

[1] My above description deals with the case of a *continuum* of regions or countries, possessing a *continuum* of labor/land endowments. If there are only two regions, the modification is straightforward. When their endowments are sufficiently near together, both produce both goods; except for a (small) wedge between real factor returns caused by

models, still needed to be logically derived and clarified in 1948–9 when I re-examined the question of factor-price equalization by trade. In particular, as I now reread carefully Ohlin's treatment of his own mathematical appendix (and also his text) I find that Heckscher's obscure exposition seems to have led Ohlin into a logical error—into Ohlin's denying, even under the zero transport cost assumption (a denial spelled out in his mathematical appendix), that factor price equalization could be *necessarily complete* in the central region. For Ohlin, that central region falsely shrinks to a frontier or watershed point between two regions of sole specialization.

What threw Ohlin's logic momentarily off on so basic a point? I now believe he did fall prey to what Samuelson (1948) called the "Ellsworth fallacy". Ohlin realized that equality of factor returns under autarky would kill off *all* trade. He forgot what Heckscher had glimpsed, that positive trade could persist under factor-price equalization that had been made possible only by that trade itself. (In Ohlin's appendix notation, with $n=2$, $r=2$, and factor-endowment ratios near enough alike in the two regions, his post-trade equations mandate a solution with equalized factor returns—a necessity he overlooked.)

Around 1949 there still remained some questions needing clarification. Here are a few of them.

1. What if food and clothing don't stay respectively more land and labor intensive at *all* wage/rent or land/labor ratios?

Answer: Then the above simple three-region world pattern could easily become a four-region (or multi-region) pattern. Now two distinct central regions could produce *both* goods at the common world price ratio: but having distinct factor endowments, they would do so with factor returns equalized in each region but at respective levels that gave lower real wage to the region of greater labor/land density. Between two such non-specializing regions we can expect there to be a region that specializes in but one of the goods. Somewhere in this separating region will be the "cross-over" point, where there occurs the critical land/labor endowment at which the two goods *exchange* relative factor intensities.

2. What if there are two factors and only one good?

Answer: No trade is possible. The autarky wage/rent discrepancies produced by labor/land endowment discrepancies persist.

3. What if there are two factors and more than two goods?

---

assuming (small) positive transport costs, factor returns are completely equalized by trade. With three or m regions, the same conclusions follow. When two regions become sufficiently disparate in factor endowments, each specializes in goods intensive in the factor it is generously endowed with; trade wipes out only part of the autarky differentials in factor returns and it does so more effectively when transport costs are zero or very small. With three or more regions, we may obviously have those that are close together in endowments forming a common non-specialization region of equalized factor returns—surrounded on two sides by outer regions that specialize in the single good that most uses their abundant factors. For them, trade moderates a fraction of their autarky factor-return discrepancies.

Answer: Having many goods that differ widely and systematically in their land/labor intensities widens the central area(s) within which complete factor-price equalization occurs.

These areas are bordered (and possibly separated) by areas in which essentially only a subset of goods is produced, those in demand which best utilize their abundant factor.

4. What if there are two goods and three (or more) factors? With more factors than goods, $r>n$, few simple generalizations will be uniformly valid.[1]

5. What if there are three goods and three factors. (Or n goods and r factors, with $r=n>2$?)

Answer: If the n goods are "technologically distinct" at the autarky price ratio(s), then two regions with geographical endowments close enough together will produce all n goods in common and have equalized factor prices. But any other region, with one or more factors sufficiently far away in factor endowments may cease to produce one or more of the goods and will thereby generate for itself post-trade factor returns different from the central core.[2]

---

[1] In my 1971 paper, "Ohlin Was Right", I considered a special model in which one versatile factor, labor, works in each of two industries with a respective specific (land) factor. In this useful case, one which Jones (1971) has also analyzed, I was able to show that there could exist a tendency for goods trade to *partially* equalize factor prices—in conformity with some of Ohlin's contentions.

Thus, consider four regions: a "central region" with moderate labor and moderate food-land and clothing-land; another region with much super-abundant labor relative to those lands; a third region with super-abundant food-land; a fourth region with super-abundant clothing-land.

The autarky pricing pattern is clear. Compared to the central region, the labor-abundant region would have low real wage (in terms of both food and clothing); *both* its lands would tend to have high-real rent (in terms of both goods). The food-land-abundant region would have high real wage in food, but low real wage in clothing; low food-land rent in terms of food and presumably in terms of clothing; and fairly high clothing-land rent in terms of both goods.

Trade in goods cannot do much to raise the real wage in the labor-abundant region; but, by causing the least-labor-requiring good to be imported, something may be done to relieve the labor superfluity. Each region, tending to concentrate on producing the good that most utilizes its superabundant non-transferable land, will thereby tend to raise the low real rent of that land. But, even without transport costs, free trade equilibrium is compatible with all four regions producing something of both goods in common and with factor returns differing in the direction of the autarky pattern even if in less degree of differentiation.

[2] McKenzie (1955, 1967) has shown that, even if n goods are "linearly independent globally", with n factors of production there may be *more* than one "central" region producing *all n* goods, each region with factor returns equalized *internally* but at rates different from those in other central regions. "Diagonal dominance" simplifies the possible patterns. Thus, suppose food, clothing, and shelter are respectively very land-intensive, female-labor intensive, and male-labor intensive, but all goods require something of all factors. Then the following regional pattern is a reasonable one to expect: three extreme regions, each of which are respectively heavily endowed with but one of the three factors and which produce and export only that good which needs much of the scarce factor in question; a central region whose subregions are all moderately well endowed with all 3 factors, and within which complete factor price equalization takes place; between the central region and each of the 3 extreme 1-good regions are 3 respective regions in which 2 goods only are produced, those 2 that do not need much of the factor most skimpily present. Outside the central region, as the endowment of any one factor becomes ever more swollen its real return falls ever farther, as the other factors' real returns rise and the terms of trade of the good that requires it rises vis a vis the other 2 goods.

The Debate on Reparations

To go beyond the question of what Ohlin contributed to the microeconomics of foreign trade, I can indicate the flavor of his contribution to its macroeconomics by devoting a few words to Ohlin's debate with Keynes on the transfer problem. This debate, which pitted the unknown David from Sweden against the world famous Goliath, brought Ohlin his first international reputation. And ever since, Ohlin's name has been associated with the vital notion that *income flows have an equilibrating effect on balance-of-payments discrepancies that obviates some of the needed equilibrating effects from changes in (absolute and relative) prices.*

After Versailles Keynes exaggerated the difficulties for Germany of having to pay reparations. Keynes uncharacteristically sided with what was then considered orthodox opinion: Pigou and Taussig believed that, in addition to the *primary burden* on the paying country of paying the real transfer, there was a strong presumption that the transfer would *induce* a secondary burden in the form of a *deterioration of the payer's (net) terms of trade* (the ratio of her export prices to her import prices). Indeed, if Germany had to contract to pay enough in terms of her input goods, facing inelastic Marshallian reciprocal demand, Germany would be unable by *any* expansion of her exports to raise the requisite real transfer. All this is quite aside from any *budgetary* difficulties Germany might face in raising enough domestic-currency taxes from her citizens to effectuate the contracted transfer. Note that Keynes' argument could be given a purely barter formulation—quite aside from any possible difficulty or impossibility for Germany to *convert* its taxes collected in Germany currency into a suitable international form acceptable by the recipients abroad of the transfer payment.

Keynes evidently *shifts* Germany's Marshallian reciprocal-demand curve as a result of the transfer effort but illogically leaves the receivers' Marshallian reciprocal-demand curve *unshifted* by the income transfer. (At least Keynes does this part of the time. He is confused; for, at times, as in Ohlin's first quotation from Keynes, Keynes does presume income shiftings for *both* curves.) Few discussants of fifty years ago kept analytically distinct questions of barter, from questions that hinged on whether the transfer did cause, and did need to cause, at least an initial *flow of gold* from the paying country to the receiving country.

Let me sample Ohlin's 1929 mode of thinking. Ohlin (1929, p. 170) quotes Keynes as follows:

> If £1 is taken from you (Germany, B) and given to me (Britain, A) and I choose to increase my consumption of precisely the same goods as those of which you are compelled to diminish yours, there is no Transfer Problem.

I note that this holds even if Britain's reciprocal-demand curve vis-à-vis Germany is "inelastic". So Keynes *is* shifting *both* curves as a result of (opposing) income flows. Ohlin then quotes Keynes further:

> But clearly only a proportion of their (i.e., German's) abstention from consumption will be in respect to foreign goods (that Britons will want to spend their transfer-increased incomes on. So, Germany will have to increase its exports to make up the implied discrepancy. So, to get this done ...) ... the solution of the Transfer Problem requires a reduction of the Germany gold-costs of production relative to such costs elsewhere. (Samuelson's parentheses.)

Ohlin agrees with Keynes that much of income gets spent on home-produced goods that are non-tradeable: he agrees that if Germany pays 100 to Britain, only 20 may be directly spent on freely-traded goods. Ohlin presumably could also agree, that of the 100 of income lost to Germans, 80 would be withdrawn from spending on non-tradeable goods produced and consumed in Germany. Says Ohlin (1929, p. 173):

> Mr Keynes and the economists who share his views think this is the end of these 80 ... I venture to suggest that, on the contrary, ... (this) sets in motion a mechanism which indirectly creates an export surplus in (Germany, the payer) of about the same magnitude (of 80, presumably in addition to the easy and automatic 20).

Ohlin is a bit mysterious and cryptic on exactly how these powerful *indirect* effects come about. He hints (1929, p. 173) that, on the gold standard, "... there is an increase in monetary buying power in A (Britain, the receiver) and a decrease in B (Germany, the payer) which may be much larger than the 80 or 100 ... A secondary 'inflation' (in A) and 'deflation' (in B) of may be necessary to bring about the adaptation of production and trade quickly enough".

Ohlin, like most of the great economists I have known, had a flair for judging the facts of experience. Thus, in his reply to Keynes, Ohlin pointed out that Germany was then *borrowing more* than she was paying in reparation: so, on Keynes theory, we should expect the facts to show a *favorable* shift in Germany's terms of trade and not the reverse. Knowing the investigations of Taussig and his Harvard students, Ohlin (p. 176) could write: "... experience speaks very strongly in favor of the conclusion that adjustments of the trade balances go much easier and even quicker than the orthodox theory would have it." This is a good riposte to Keynes's warning against those optimists who apply to the transfer problem "the theory of liquids to what is, if not a solid, at least a sticky mass with strong internal resistances".

At this date there is no point in quoting Ohlin's elasticity optimism against Keynes's elasticity pessimism. Ohlin's theoretical point is deeper: he points out that it is not *ceteris paribus* price elasticity that is the key ingredient. Why did Ohlin assert: "It is not necessary that A's export prices should rise and B's fall." In Samuelson (1971, p. 351) I drafted an argument that Ohlin could have had subconsciously in mind from the pristine Heckscher–Ohlin model. It shows that Keynes was *not* right in concluding from the smallness of 20/100 that the payer's terms of trade *had* to fall.

Let A and B produce two different tradeable goods, on each of which everyone spends 10 percent of income. Let each spend 80 percent on their respective nontradeable good, produced in similar ways out of labor and land. Before and after reparations, Heckscher–Ohlin factor-price equalization takes place.

Then, even though only 20 percent is spent on goods exportable and importable, with similar taste patterns it follows that reparations cause *zero change* in the payer's terms of trade:

1. Germans' loss in income makes them cut down on home goods (80 %), on the good exported (10 %), and on the good imported (10 %).
2. Britons' gain in income is divided the same way.
3. The shift in German resources away from home-good production and into production of more tradeables, and the opposite shift in British resources, can be proved to take place at *unchanged* factor-price and goods-price ratios—in complete refutation of Keynes's orthodox expectations and arithmetic!

As a realist, Ohlin realizes that the above perfect balance need not obtain. But the example shows the error in Keynes's logical analysis. If income shifts can do *all* the work in the above case despite the monumental importance of non-tradeable goods, then even in more realistic cases income shifts can do most of the work, obviating the need for Keynes's draconian price concessions.

As shown in the continuum Ricardian model of Dornbusch, Fischer, and Samuelson (1977) and its Heckscher–Ohlin counterpart model of *ibid.* (1980), Ohlin's 1929 analysis is right on the mark in its analysis of how the absorption of British resources into home-goods production may well raise British factor costs and export-goods costs, at the same time that the opposite process is taking place in the paying country to lower home-goods production, factor costs and German export-good costs.

In such cases, Ohlin does admit that the presence of non-tradeables may result in *some* orthodox price effects. But Ohlin is surely right in stressing that the concomitant income shifting in reciprocal-demand curves is not what was envisaged and understood in the orthodox writings of Mill, Taussig, and Keynes. Goliath's rhetorical bluster and political resentment against the Treaty of Versailles were not able to upset the neutral rationality of the youthful David!

Stockholm Foreshadowings of Keyne's *General Theory*

When we young economists read the *General Theory* in 1936 and Ohlin's 1937 articles on the Stockholm school, we formed the opinion that around 1933–4 the Swedes had more or less independently arrived at the same theory of effective demand as Keynes had. The fact that Ragnar Frisch, an Oslo admirer of Wicksell, had written in 1934 on "circulation planning" reinforced this impression: there, Frisch (1934) set up a model in which a sector's expenditure in one period was to be a fraction of its expenditure in an earlier period, giving rise to a convergent exponential decay to equilibrium reminiscent of a simple Kahn–Keynes multiplier model. Michael Kalecki's claim, and Joan

Robinson's on his behalf, to have been led before 1936 to essentially Keynes' *General Theory* by his studies of Marx, seemed to be a third or fourth simultaneous discovery—a case of multiple discovery that, like Darwin and Wallace or Newton and Leibnitz or Leverrier and Adams or Schrodinger and Heisenberg, Robert K. Merton (1973) has taught historians of science to expect to be the rule rather than exception.

In 1980 further reading has made me shade this conventional view as over simple. The Frisch fragment seems only tangentially related to the determinate Keynesian system. Kalecki's determinate equations for the determination of profit by the level of investment comes closest to duplicating the Keynesian system: if Kalecki had made explicit his latent notion that the total of non-profit incomes are in a determinate relation to the total of profit, we could claim on his behalf discovery of a model isomorphic to the Keynesian relation: $Y \equiv C+I=f(Y)+\bar{I},\ f(0)>0<\delta<f'(Y)<1-\delta.$

I have to agree with Don Patinkin that, in a *formal* way, Swedish post-Wicksellians like Myrdal made the *price level* rather than the *output level* the equilibrium variable in their syllogisms. But I have to agree with Ohlin's rejoinder to Patinkin that, after 1932, Ohlin and his Stockholm colleagues took for granted that changes in $Y=PQ$ would involve changes for real output, Q, in the same direction as for prices, P. We should accept at face value statements of Ohlin like the following one, Ohlin (1978, p. 144):

> If investment falls to a size smaller than savings, which is compatible with full employment, then a situation of full employment will degenerate into a contraction (of *real* output and *not* just prices).

Such an Ohlin view, if held in 1933, would have been as untenable to a J. B. Say or to a Robert Lucas as was Keynes' 1936 model. The present survey of Bertil Ohlin's style as an economist has confirmed that he was not a virtuoso of equations and graphs or even a meticulous specifier of complete sets of independent non-redundant logical relations. So why expect from him in 1933 policy contexts a full-blown abstract model?

Note that my partial defense of Ohlin does not throw him the usual sop, in the form of some admiring words about the Swedish School's innovations concerning the terminology of *ex ante* and *ex post* magnitudes. Keynes' expositions were far from optimal and did need modification; but I have to confess that the *ex ante–ex post* novelties have had only a limited role to play in the 1940–1980 progress of modern macroeconomics and its necessary preoccupation with expectations.

A Man and His Time

My task is done. The lasting achievements of Ohlin surveyed here are only a sample of an extended universe. Bertil Ohlin has left his permanent mark on the science of political economy.

Scand. J. of Economics 1981

Success must surely bring fulfillment. Bertil Ohlin, it seems to me as a professional friend, had a happy life. He was lucky in his birth and opportunities and, what is more important, he capitalized on his luck. Except that he never became Prime Minister—often a bridesmaid, never a bride—every honor came to him and did so early. Wife, children, kin, teachers and pupils, friends, good enemies—was there any perfection he lacked?

Bertil Ohlin was also part of his times and his place. For an economist, century's end was a good time to be born—the best since the century's middle. To have been born in 1875 would have been to be born too late; and to have been born too early. Bertil told me he began his serious economic study in 1915, the year of my birth. By the time he was 20, he was rubbing elbows with the members of Stockholm's Political Economy Club, where gathered around a single table were *all* the great minds of Swedish economics. Ohlin saw Knut Wicksell plain—*very heaven* in my envious view.

Had Scandinavia not existed, we should have had to invent it—to run our international agencies and provide the cosmopolitan binding between the disparate language empires. Bertil Ohlin early earned the right to serve such organizations as the League of Nations. I would suppose he knew personally *all* the great economists of his day.

Numbers were small then, in a way that young scholars today can barely perceive and *envy*. A few score people attended professional conventions. Just by surviving, you were virtually sure to be president of the economics association. The *Economic Journal* offered a forum for a dozen regulars: the world read their agreements and their disagreements. (The other side of the coin of cozy smallness was the fact that, if you were *outside* the charmed circle, that was that. Disciples succeeded to chairs of their masters; and if the young Pigou was made professor at 30, that meant two generations had to give up all hopes of elevation.)

Sweden, the tortoise of steady growth, went in Bertil Ohlin's lifetime from being a poor country in frigid Europe to near equivalence with the richest country in the world, the United States. Sweden's bourgeois culture was bound to create a cadre of good economics scholars. Freed from the tyranny of law school domination, and with a homogeneous society to serve as its laboratory for policy experiments, Swedish economics outperformed its natural potential. Knut Wicksell, Eli Hechscher and, for all his personal traits, Gustav Cassel deserve much credit. And part of what they deserve credit for is producing the Ohlins and Myrdals of our times.

Swedish economists are forever saying, "We're not what we used to be." Every great tradition must expect to encounter regression toward the mean. Probably in the dawn of 1927 Swedish economists were repeating that same lament. Perhaps there is even some truth in the self-diagnosis that Swedish economists have been too much seduced out of their libraries and away from their computers by the heavy opportunities for public service. If there is,

Bertil Ohlin would want to shoulder some of the reproach for his own lifecycle example. But where people in a living science are concerned, we are not quite dealing with a stationary time series. No one can predict when a young Wicksell or Ohlin will walk into the seminar room. Let us hope we shall recognize her or him when that time comes.

References

Caves, Richard: Bertil Ohlin's contribution to economics. *The Scandinavian Journal of Economics 80*, 86–99, 1978.

Chipman, John: A survey of the theory of international trade. Parts 1–3. *Econometrica 33*, 477–519, 685–760, *34*, 18–76, 1965–66.

Ellsworth, P. T.: *International economics*. The Macmillan Company, New York, 1938.

Gale, D. & Nikaidô, H.: The Jacobian matrix and global univalence of mappings. *Mathematische Annalen 159*, (2), 81–93, 1965.

Heckscher, Eli F.: The effect of foreign trade on the distribution of income. *Ekonomisk Tidskrift 21*, 497–512, 1919. Reprinted as Chapter 13 in *Readings in the theory of international trade*. Homewood, Illinois: Richard Irwin, 1949. (English translation.)

Keynes, J. M.: *The general theory of employment, interest, and money*. Macmillan, London, 1929.

Lundberg, Erik: Bertil Ohlin. *Challenge*, September/October 1980, 54–57.

Marshall, A.: *Pure theory of international trade*. 1879. (1879 edition for private circulation only; facsimile reprint, London School of Economics and Political Science, London, 1930.)

Marshall, A.: *Principles of economics*. Macmillan, London, 1890.

McKenzie, L. W.: Equality of factor prices in world trade. *Econometrica 23*, 239–257, 1955.

Ohlin, Bertil: Till frågan om skogarnas omloppstid (On the question of forest rotation). *Ekonomisk Tidskrift*, "Festschrift to Knut Wicksell".

Ohlin, Bertil: *Interregional and international trade*. Harvard University Press, Cambridge, 1933.

Ohlin, Bertil: Some notes on the Stockholm theory of savings and investment. Parts I and II. *Economic Journal 47*, 53–69, 222–240, 1937.

Ohlin, Bertil: Keynesian economics and the Stockholm School: A comment on Don Patinkin's paper. *The Scandinavian Journal of Economics 80*, 144–147, 1978.

Patinkin, Don: On the relation between Keynesian economics and the 'Stockholm School'. *The Scandinavian Journal of Economics 80*, 135–143, 1978.

Samuelson, P. A.: International trade and the equalisation of factor prices. *Economic Journal 58*, 163–184, 1948. Reproduced as Chapter 67 in *The collected scientific papers of Paul A. Samuelson*, vol. 2 (ed. Joseph E. Stiglitz), The MIT Press, Cambridge, 1966.

Samuelson, P. A.: International factor-price equalisation once again. *Economic Journal 59*, 181–197, 1949. Reproduced as Chapter 68 in *CSP*, vol. 2.

Samuelson, P. A.: Prices of Factors and Goods in General Equilibrium, *Review of Economic Studies 20* (1), 1–20, 1953–54. Reproduced as Chapter 70 in *CSP*, vol. 2.

Samuelson, P. A.: Summary on factor-price equalization. *International Economic Review 8*, 286–295, 1967. Reproduced as Ch. 161 in vol. 3, *The collected scientific papers of Paul A. Samuelson* (ed. Robert C. Merton), The MIT Press, Cambridge, 1972.

Samuelson, P. A.: Ohlin was right. *Swedish Journal of Economics 4*, 365–384, 1971. Reproduced as Chapter 254 in *The collected scientific papers of Paul A. Samuelson*, vol. 4 (ed. Hiroaki Nagatani and Kate Crowley), The MIT Press, Cambridge, 1977.

Samuelson, P. A.: Economics of forestry in an evolving society. *Economic Inquiry 14*, 466–492, 1976. Reproduced as Chapter 218 in *CSP*, vol. 4, Chapter 218, 146–172.

Stolper, W. F. & Samuelson, P. A.: Protection and real wages. *Review of Economic Studies 9*, 58–73, 1941. Reproduced as Chapter 66 in *CSP*, vol. 2.

Arthur Okun, 1928-1980

At all times it is a personal tragedy when a top scientist or artist is cut off in the prime of life. In difficult times like these it is a national loss when an experienced and wise policy economist dies.

Arthur Okun was a young and rising star in the Camelot days when President John F. Kennedy was turning a stagnant economy around and initiating a decade of sustained economic growth. Douglas Dillon, Walter Heller, James Tobin and Kermit Gordon deserved the public notice that their successful efforts brought them. But they and the President knew how much our success depended on a younger cadre of able economists—on scholars like Arthur Okun and Robert Solow.

The Public Interest: Academia's loss was the public's gain when Okun decided not to go back to Yale. For Arthur Okun was the consummate macroeconomist. He even has a law named after him: *Okun's Law,* a rule of thumb relating the unemployment rate and the change in real gross national product, which has stood up remarkably well considering the inexactness of economics. His was the definitive postmortem on how the Kennedy-Johnson tax cut had worked out (not miraculously, but on the whole, well).

Trained at Columbia by Arthur Burns, he had the eclectic judgment to combine Keynesian insights with the emerging realities. Okun could estimate econometric regressions with the best of the mathematical virtuosi. But many have that skill.

Economic value comes from scarcity. The rare and precious quality that Okun possessed was *good judgment combined with resourcefulness.* I sit on the board of a nonprofit organization whose bonds are invested by a bank that relied on Okun for macroeconomic advice. His *practical* forecasts were a fountain of good sense. Brokerage houses sought his views because they were worth having.

If you know economists, you will realize how lavish my praise is when I report that I never heard Arthur Okun say a foolish thing. He was often wrong, as all economists turn out to be. But his long-run batting average was good, and even his wrong judgments were cogently based on such evidence as could be known in advance.

Having mastered the lesson of how to move the United States economy to high employment, Okun devoted the last dozen years of his life to seeking ways to make price stability compatible with full use of society's resources. He sought a better *incomes policy*—not a perfect one but a better one than what we've been stuck with.

His reason and knowledge made him dubious of mandatory wage-price controls as a permanent solution. But his econometric research correctly predicted that contriving a recession to fight inflation would produce disappointing benefits and staggering human costs.

Okun believed that there must be some compromise program, partly voluntary and partly compulsory, that would bring Presidential leadership to bear on the more flagrant sectors of stagflation—perhaps a "social contract" that persuaded workers to forgo real wage increases made untenable by OPEC, but which ensured those who complied against being victimized. Like the physicist Max Planck, who devised the radical quantum theory as "an act of desperation," Okun was willing to try tax penalties against excessive wage and price increases. He died still grappling with our No. 1 problem of stagflation.

Double Vision: It is well that we have organizations like the Brookings Institution that can provide a research base for policy-oriented economists between tours of government duty. And I welcome the rise in size and stature of the American Enterprise Institute. It is natural that the latter should attract economists who average out to a more conservative viewpoint. But it is healthy that both these Washington think tanks should attract economists spread across the political spectrum.

Harry Truman is sometimes quoted as saying, "What I want is a one-armed economist, who won't pussyfoot with 'on the one hand this, on the other hand that'." With respect, this is foolish. What he'd have is a cripple. For one-armed economists come in two dogmatic varieties, those with a right arm only and those with only a left. And *then* you need a two-armed eclectic to adjudicate between them.

Arthur Okun looked at both sides of an issue, and then, in striking his judicious compromises, he employed a cool hand in the service of a warm heart.

359

Lloyd Metzler
(April 3, 1913–October 26, 1980)

At mid-century, Lloyd Metzler was one of the half dozen leading economists in the world. Though only thirty-seven, his creative works in the field of international trade, the macroeconomics of dynamic business cyles, and the fundamentals of capital theory made it inevitable that he would win for himself the highest prizes in our subject. After his years at Harvard and in Washington, he was called to Yale and then went on to the University of Chicago. There his classes were attracting students from all over the world.

Lloyd was not only in the pantheon of top economists, he was undoubtedly the single best-liked economist. Often brilliant youngsters are brash and abrasive. They are admired and feared, but not always loved. Lloyd was the exception. He was relaxed. Affable, gentle, unassuming, and kind. You wanted to take care of Lloyd. So, naturally, his good friends were amused and pleased when in Washington he met and married Edith.

It is my pleasant task to say a few words about Lloyd Metzler, the peerless scientist. Here in my hand I have his imperishable intellectual remains. These varied chapters give him a lasting place in the history of political economy. When you consider that they are the fruits of a dozen golden years, your appreciation is deepened of what the word "genius" means.

That we should hold this memorial service in the Harvard Yard is fitting. Widener Library was Lloyd's first stamping grounds after he came to Harvard in 1937 from Kansas. Later, when the Littauer building was new, he switched his battleground to the other side of where we now meet. In my mind's eye, I can still see Lloyd Metzler walking across the Harvard Yard, with his little dachshund in tow, engaged in animated badinage with Bob Bishop or Dan Vandermeulen. A young resident of Winthrop House, destined to be president of the United States, used to be disturbed in his studies by our revels in Lloyd's Winthrop House tutorial suite.

What I have just called Lloyd Metzler's golden years coincided with what in a memoir I called "the Golden Days of the Harvard Yard." Let me quote a few lines to describe the brilliant company in which Lloyd Metzler was first among equals.

> [I] sing of the Age of Hansen—and of Schumpeter, and of Leontief, and (for me) of E. B. Wilson. And I can sing for all my comrades at arms—Alan and Paul Sweezy,

Kenneth Galbraith, Aaron [R. A.] Gordon, Abram Bergson, Shigeto Tsuru, Alice Bourneuf, Richard Musgrave, Wolfgang Stolper, and others who were already established when I arrived in the graduate school, September 1935; and for many years yet to come—Lloyd Metzler, Robert Triffin, Joe Bain, James Tobin, Robert Bishop, John Lintner, Richard Goodwin, Henry Wallace, Cary [E. C.] Brown, Emile Depres, Walter and William Salant, Sidney Alexander, Benjamin Higgins, to say nothing of postwar diamonds such as James Duesenberry, Robert Solow, Carl Kaysen . . . .

First, a few facts about Lloyd's life before he was reborn in 1937 at Harvard. He was born in Lost Spring, Kansas. What could be more American than that? He was the middle son of middle class parents: His older brother became a civil engineer; his younger brother a hydraulical engineer. Lloyd was the black sheep who became an economist. His father apparently did not do well in the arts of retail commerce, and Lloyd lived in a number of Kansas towns. To be near K. U., the family finally moved to Lawrence, Kansas. There the spellbinder populist, John Ise, rescued Lloyd from the swamp of the business school. Just as Ise had done with Ed Mason and as he was to do with John Lintner, Challis Hall, and a host of other sons of the middle border, Ise sent Metzler on to his old graduate student at Harvard.

Harold Hitchings Burbank, noting the Germanic "z" in Lloyd's name and recognizing his egregious talent, probably mistook him for a Jew. Actually, Lloyd and my wife, Marion Crawford, when in their cups used to sing the Protestant Sunday School songs of their midwestern childhoods. The one I remember best went like this:

Jesus wants me for a sunbeam
To shine for Him below.
A sunbeam, a sunbeam,
Jesus wants me for a sunbeam
To shine for him below.

Like other able people Burbank didn't favor, Lloyd was put in the galleys of Frickey and Crum, to serve as assistant in the undergraduate courses in statistics and accounting. Since I never had that honor, I can with good grace report that the cream of the graduate school, those who have won the Wells Prizes and top honors of our profession, all came from this Burbank ghetto. It became a mark of distinction and one that Lloyd richly deserved.

There is no need for me to say anything about Schumpeter, Williams, Mason, and Hansen. Their fame is understood. What is in order is to speak of Wassily Leontief and E. B. Wilson. We few mathematical economists at Harvard were blessed by these great teachers. We had monopoly access to them in small seminar encounters. At that time, Wassily still had no tenure at Harvard. E. B. Wilson, the last student of Willard Gibbs, was a polymath who turned from mathematical physics to become Dean of the School of Vital Statistics. He was one of America's few experts on R. A. Fisher's new statistics. And he understood Pareto's mathematical economics. Wilson spotted Metzler's genius. One of President Conant's few stupid decisions was to retire Wilson at the earliest possible age, and this in a period of teacher shortages, thereby depriving the post-Metzler generations of the consumers' surplus that Metzler, I, Bergson, Tsuru, Alexander, and some other happy few enjoyed.

That, however, was par for the critics of mathematical economics. In the year that Metzler came to Harvard, Sidney Alexander was Keynes's last tutee at Cambridge University. Keynes seriously advised Alexander not to waste his time with mathematical economics—the same Keynes who was supposed to be a shrewd judge of future markets and trends!

At Harvard, Lloyd Metzler was right in the midst of the new developments in monopolistic competition, welfare economics, and the Keynesian revolution. With Wordsworth he could chant:

Bliss was it in that dawn to be alive,
But to be young was very heaven.

Already in his Wells Prize thesis, Metzler set straight the multicountry multiplier controversies. Mathematically, he anticipated the Frobenius matrix theorems that go today under the name of Metzler-Mosak-Markov. Leontief-Sraffa input-output, Hicksian gross substitutes, and transition probabilities also satisfy these same elegant identities.

Inventory fluctuations were known to play a key role in the business cycle. Metzler's masterly model of dynamic difference equations converted an empirical jigsaw into a meaningful paradigm of explanation. Scholars will get Nobel prizes for lesser achievements and have done so.

World War II, most men found, served as an interruption of scholarly research. Not so with Lloyd Metzler. While doing his bit for the war effort at OSS, Metzler simultaneously continued his research at the Washington Federal Reserve Board. Though most scientists returned with pleasure to university life after the war. Lloyd regarded government as a favorable research environment. He went to Yale with mixed feelings. Then on to Chicago where he carried on the magnificent Viner tradition in international trade and served as the token New Dealer Keynesian. His fertile Chicago period earned for him the title formulated later by Uzawa: the great Chicago economist.

In the forenoon of Metzler's brilliant promise, tragedy struck. It was as if the gods were envious. A brain tumor robbed the economics profession of part—too large a part—of Lloyd Metzler's genius. When Mendelssohn died young, in a sense his mission had been completed. Not so with Mozart. His last works show no signs of diminishing returns. And so it was with those magnificent *JPE* papers of Lloyd Metzler's around 1950. With Edith Metzler's help, Lloyd continued to teach and he continued to write. But one cannot help but want to complain that the gods cheated us out of Metzler's full contribution.

Yet we must not complain. All in all, Lloyd Metzler added enormously to economic science. And that sense of humor and sweet nature lives on in our happy memories.

2 Nobel Laureates' Theories on Trade

By PAUL A. SAMUELSON

An Appraisal

Economists will be pleased that this year's Nobel Memorial Prize in Economic Science has gone to James Meade of Britain and Bertil Ohlin of Sweden. Both have done outstanding scholarly work in the field of international trade and finance. Each man has demonstrated that those who are best in pure science are often outstanding policy advisers and public servants. And both have been prolific discoverers of new theories and empirical patterns in divers topics of modern political economy that transcend international exchange.

When the central bank of Sweden endowed a Nobel award in economics to parallel those in physics, chemistry, medicine, literature and peace, it was considered only a matter of time before Gunnar Myrdal and Bertil Ohlin would be recipients. The Swedish Royal Academy of Science, anxious to maintain a scientific objectivity, was too diffident to name one of its own in the early years.

More than 50 years ago, Professor Ohlin's classic work, "Interregional and International Trade," appeared in its Swedish version. It is still not outdated, and it explains why he received a professional chair at the very early age of 25.

Professor Ohlin, a disciple of two great Swedish masters, Eli Heckscher and Gustav Cassel, showed how to explain and understand the geographical patterns of trade: The New World, endowed with much land relative to labor, naturally specializes in producing food, the land intensive commodities. It trades food for labor-intensive Old-World goods. And, as Professor Heckscher and Professor Ohlin showed, such trade raises the demand for land here and for labor there, serving thereby to reduce the initial geographical disparities between wages and rents.

Professor Ohlin's first international reputation among men of affairs came when he challenged, successfully. John Maynard Keynes's assumption that Germany could not pay the reparations imposed on it after World War I. Keynes said that Germany's attempt to generate a surplus of exportable goods would force down the prices for its exports in comparison with the prices to be paid for its imports.

What Professor Ohlin pointed out was Keynes's failure to realize that, to the degree that the Allies spent their receipts on the "same" goods that Germany would have bought, there need be no extra burden on Germany's export-import prices.

Independently of Keynes' development of his theory of fiscal stimulus to fight unemployment, the Stockholm School of Ohlin, Myrdal, Hammarskjold and others pioneered modern macroeconomics.

Alas for economics as a science, at this point in his career Bertil Ohlin was elected to Parliament and became the head of the Liberal Party, one of the leading parties in opposition to the ruling Labor Party. Over three decades, Professor Ohlin helped to shape the Swedish middle way, even though it was never to be given to him to serve as prime minister.

A strikingly handsome man, Bertil Ohlin was able to maintain friendly and civil relationships with his old classmate Gunnar Myrdal, despite their basic political differences. Just as the fine characters of Einstein and Planck served to elevate a generation of German physicists, so the Ohlin-Myrdal debates set a pattern for economists to emulate all over the world.

Versatility is one hallmark of a great mind. Bertil Ohlin was one of the first economists to recognize the post-World War II patterns of overfull employment. Like Lord Beveridge in Britain and Alvin Hansen in the United States, he warned more than 30 years ago that the modern mixed economy would encounter the gravest difficulties with the problem that we now call stagflation—the tendency in the humane welfare state to have wages and prices rise even before full employment is in sight.

Don With a Heart

Born in 1907, James Meade rceived his Oxford training in economics before the Great Depression. In the early 1930's he put in a tour of duty at Cambridge University just at the time that Keynes was developing his revolutionary general theory of economics. Professor Meade, along with other young economists destined for future fame—John Robinson, Sir Roy Harrad, Lord Kahn—served in the "Circuits," the workshop on which Keynes tried out and tested his novel ideas.

His first international fame came from his brilliant editing in the late 1930's of the League of Nations World Economic Surveys. During World War II he served with Keynes in running the British economy; with R. Stone, Professor Meade helped set up the first British national income accounts.

As professor at the London School of Economics, he devoted seven years to his great four-volume treatise, "The Theory of International Policy." It combines his analytical finesse with a burning interest in promoting welfare. The last of the utilitarians who trace from Jeremy Bentham, James Meade would give his cloak to a shivering beggar, not only because he feels it is right and fair to do so, but also for the reason that the beggar will receive more pleasure from it than a well-off professor of political economy.

Called to a chair at Cambridge 20 years ago, Professor Meade voluntarily retired early from it to avoid doctrinal wranglings with colleagues and to devote himself to another four-volume restatement of all of economics. My students will be rediscovering many of the important Meade theorems for decades to come.

Paul A. Samuelson, professor of economics at the Massachusetts Institute of Technology, won the Nobel Memorial Prize in Economic Science in 1970.

A Nobel for Forecasting

The recession ended in late summer, making it the shortest one on record. If it had been any shorter, the game warden would have made us throw it back.

Autumn had scarcely begun when we knew the upturn had commenced. We have the giant computer to thank for this promptness in knowledge.

In 1798, when Malthus was warning that England faced overpopulation and mass starvation, no one had a clue to what was really happening to the total size of the population. Dr. Richard Price, an eminent authority, was convinced that the British population had shrunk by a third since the Glorious Revolution of 1688. We now know that Price was wrong, but no one then had any way of resolving the issue.

As recently as 1937 the United States was surprised to find itself in a steep recession. Gen. Robert Wood, then the head of Sears, Roebuck and Co., testified that when he went into the Canadian bush on a hunting trip everything looked all right. When he emerged, the economic heavens had fallen in. Accurate data, promptly available on a broad sector of the economy, are indeed a post-World War II development.

Age of Klein: Of software and the man I sing. On Dec. 10 in Stockholm, Prof. Lawrence R. Klein of the University of Pennsylvania will justly receive the Nobel Prize in Economics for his scientific innovation of macroeconomic forecasting.

We are all in Klein's debt: not just the hundreds of econometricians who ply their craft at banks, consulting firms, universities, corporations and government agencies but also judgmental forecasters like me who eschew formal mathematical models.

A malicious colleague once asked, "Paul, how soon will the computer make you obsolete?" Since he was malicious, I let him have the truth: "Not in a million years." Even if I am wrong by a factor of 10, the point is made. Inside every computer is a fallible human being, the person who wrote its program, who specified its important variables and designed their general structure.

I retell the story so that it can be provided with its needed correction. It is idle to pose the debate in the form of judgment versus quantitative science. For in plain truth every judgment of the modern age rides piggyback on the output of hundreds of operating computers. When, abacus in hand, I confront the blank back of an envelope, my views are already contaminated by knowledge of what is being said by Klein's Wharton model, Otto Eckstein's model at Data Resources, Inc., the UCLA and Ann Arbor models and a dozen other econometric systems.

As Larry Klein's graduate-school teacher at MIT, I must recognize that water can rise above its source. It does so every academic generation. Klein was MIT's first Ph.D. in economics. It's been down the hill of diminishing returns ever since.

America is a great country. Klein got to MIT on the basis of his straight-A record. (*All* A's? Well, he did get one B in practical typing at Central High, Omaha. And one B in economic history at the University of California at Berkeley.)

Work to Do: Science is a process of creative self-destruction. Nobel prizes mark not completions but milestones on a continuing journey.

Economists forecast better than they did. They forecast better than chance, better than do naïve rules like "Same tomorrow as today," better than noneconomists can do, whether they be astrologer, banker or candidate for public office.

Nevertheless, economics remains an inexact science. Most of the consensus forecasters, those few dozen analysts with a batting average worth following, expected that 1979 would be the year of recession, not 1980. They were not completely wrong. The history books do show 1979 to be a year of *growth recession*—a growth rate well below the trend. But it may turn out to be that the difference between a growth recession and a full-fledged one is just enough to make President Carter lose the election. Whether the new recovery will be the weak one most forecasters expect is still a matter of betting odds.

Although forecasting has improved, we may be reaching a plateau. An *indeterminacy principle* seems to dog us, beyond which we cannot penetrate.

Somewhere in Consolidated High or Los Angeles State there is a future laureate who will make Lawrence Klein obsolete. More power to her!

1981 Nobel Prize in Economics

When Albert Einstein's first marriage broke up, he promised his wife as alimony the proceeds he would be getting from the Nobel Prize. So certain was he to get it that this was like money in the bank. The only wonder was that it was so late in coming, and that the Royal Swedish Academy of Sciences went out of its way to make clear that the award had not been given for Einstein's work in relativity. (In rebuke, Einstein devoted his Nobel Lecture to the subject of relativity.)

It was just as certain that James Tobin would receive the Nobel Prize in Economics. It was never a question of whether, only of when. The breadth of Tobin's work in empirical macroeconomics and the depth of his many analytical innovations make this a popular award in a field of not-so-hard science, where not all awards are greeted with unmixed enthusiasm.

I shall try to give a sample of Tobin's researches. But first it is worth examining the scholar as a person. For James Tobin is the archetype of a late 20th-century American scholar.

Son of the Middle Border

Tobin had to win the Nobel Prize because he can't help winning any prize that's out there. This began at nursery school in Champaign, Illinois, that oasis of culture and incubator for Nobel Laureates in diverse fields. Michael Tobin, his father, was publicity director for athletics at the University of Illinois, and his eruptions at the conservatism of Colonel McCormick's *Chicago Tribune* recruited Jim early into the camp of liberalism.

Prior to 1935 Harvard College was still a finishing school for Grottlesex graduates and commuting Bostonians. President Eliot's creation of a university had been followed by President Lowell's nurturing of a college. The new President Conant was engaged in the alchemy of converting Harvard into a meritocracy. James Tobin, fresh from University High and quite ignorant of the Porcellian and other final clubs, was one of the first of the meritocrats, entering with the class of '39 as one of the new National Scholars. Sandwiched between John F. Kennedy's class of '40 and Joseph Kennedy, Jr.'s class of '38, the end of the decade's class is worth contrasting with the beginning of the decade's. The class of '31, which contained both Douglas Dillon, the future financier, and Paul Sweezy, the future interpreter of Marx, included more millionaires than socialists. The class of '39, with Alan Lerner, Leonard Bernstein, and James Tobin, foreshadowed the new Harvard that was being formed.

One must be born at the right time. For a future quantum physicist, 1897 was a good birth year. Lucky Jim was a freshman when John Maynard Keynes's revolutionary *General Theory of Employment, Interest and Money* burst upon the economic world (*1*). Never having acquired immunity from orthodox antibodies, Tobin was a pushover for the new heresies. His teachers were nine to two against Keynes; but one of the two was Alvin Hansen (*2*), and the issue was never in doubt.

After a tour of duty in the prewar Washington agencies preparing for military mobilization, Tobin joined the Navy, picking up the customary gold watch for best officer in his training class. His sea duty is recorded in *The Caine Mutiny*, written by his classmate Herman Wouk (*3*). Tobin is the high-foreheaded, silent mandarin portrayed there. In a profession not noted for its taciturnity, Tobin is indeed a silent person, who passes on to those he has newly met not every clever thing he knows.

Returning to Harvard at war's end, Tobin was elected into the Valhalla of the Society of Fellows. Promising Junior Fellows often become tenured Harvard professors. But when Yale called, James Tobin acted in the way economics pretends everyone acts: he took the best offer held out to him.

The old Yale economics department was notoriously conservative. It tells us something about William Buckley's sophistication as a youngster that in his *God and Man at Yale*, he regarded that assembly of scholars as a hotbed of subversion (*4*). So rapid is the metabolism of a university, that in half a decade Lloyd Reynolds and James Tobin built up a team that put the Yale economics department in the first few of American departments. I once quipped to Alvin Hansen, "Yale is the best Harvard department outside of Cambridge." His sober reply was, "Harvard should be so good."

Important for Yale and the development of econometrics was the decision of the Cowles Foundation to transfer its research unit from the University of Chicago. Everyone was happy: Chicago could document undisturbed the efficiencies of the marketplace; Yale could recruit Jacob Marschak, Gerard Debreu, and Tjalling Koopmans (Nobel Laureate, 1975) while hanging on to James Tobin; the science of econometrics could enter a golden age.

All biography loses interest after success comes. Suffice it to say that James Tobin lived happily ever after in New Haven, and during The Game can be heard to boo Harvard like any apoplectic old blue from Bones.

Portfolio Theory

I must be selective in sampling Tobin's scientific contributions. Here is one, important for itself, and vital as a precursor to the exciting development of modern portfolio theory.

Keynes, faced with the Great Depression, had to explain why people held so much idle cash relative to their annual dollar incomes. Irving Fisher, Yale's reformer zealot and America's greatest economist of the pre-1930 era, believed that the velocity of circulation of money, V, was a fundamental constant (rather like the speed of light). To understand the depression drop in V, Keynes devised a theory of "liquidity preference" along the following lines:

> Although you can buy long-term bonds that pay an annual coupon yield, you will still keep some of your wealth in the form of zero-interest cash because you fear that interest rates will soon rise back to their prosperous-times level, thereby causing bond prices to fall by even more than the bonds' interest returns.

This is perhaps not a bad theory for the years in the 1930's when memories of pre-1929 were very fresh. But young Tobin came up with a better theory to fit the 1950 facts, which were that investors could rationally expect that bond prices might go up *or go down* depending on the uncertainties of future interest rates.

Tobin knew the mathematical probability theory of Pascal, Fermat, Laplace, and Kolmogorov (*5*). He recognized that the expected ("mean") value of a risky security's total return—its interest coupon or cash dividend, corrected by its percentage change in market price—can typically be taken to exceed the zero-return of cash (or the minuscule yield on absolutely safe cash equivalents).

But Tobin also knew the St. Petersburg paradox and the work of Daniel Bernoulli, Laplace, and Bentham which suggested that people are typically risk-averse (*6*). The thousand dollars we stand to gain in a fair-coin toss does not mean so much to us in utility terms as the thousand dollars we stand to lose. So Tobin, like economists and philosophers before him, assumed that what counts to us in making our portfolio decisions is maximizing the expected value of the utility of money outcomes, not the mere expected value of money itself (*7*).

The moral: Risk-averse people who are subject to the law of diminishing utility will want to put part of their wealth in a risky security that promises a higher mean return than safe cash does. But they will not want to put all their wealth into the asset that could leave them very badly off. "Don't put all your eggs in one basket" is the philosophy they follow. Other things equal, a drop in the expected return on stocks and bonds, and their increased variabilities associated with depression, should make us expect that people will hold more cash in depression relative to total wealth and total income. The drop in money's velocity is explained once its V is made to be a rising function of the prevailing interest rate, $r : V = f(r), f'(r) > 0$.

James Tobin also measured econometrically the dependence of V on r (*8*), a result congenial to neoclassical pre-Keynesian orthodoxy and verified by all statistical investigators with the exception of some monistic Monetarists.

I have skipped in this account Tobin's ingenious approximation, by means of which a security's mean, μ, and its variance (or mean squared deviation), σ^2, are used as proxies for its whole probability distribution. This convenient approximation, which, independently of Tobin, Harry Markowitz was also exploring at the Cowles Commission (*9*), applies well under various conditions

(10): (i) if my marginal utility schedule is nearly linear; (ii) if the probabilities I face are bunched (as they will be if I can instantly rebalance portfolios subject to a Wiener-Itô-Merton process of the type Einstein analyzed for Brownian motion) (11); or (iii) if the security is almost subject to a Gaussian probability distribution (for which μ and σ are sufficient parameters).

The mean-variance analysis was applied to portfolio choices among cash and many securities: Confronted with the mean returns per dollar of cash on each of n risky securities, and given the n^2 variances and covariances of the n securities' joint probability distribution, Markowitz and Tobin solve by a quadratic-programming algorithm for the set of "efficient" portfolio weightings that provide minimum total portfolio variance for each tolerated total portfolio mean. Investors with little risk tolerance will select an efficient (mean, variance) portfolio heavily weighted by cash, which sacrifices mean returns for safety; investors with more nearly constant marginal utility will hold less cash in their efficient portfolio and achieve higher mean returns at the cost of variability.

The theory accords with common sense. Despite the difficulty in getting estimates from past data of means and variances that are relevant for the future, the theory is useful in practice. In the hands of W. F. Sharpe and John Lintner, it has developed into the important capital-asset-pricing model, according to which markets will be efficiently priced already so that prudent investing calls for the broadest possible diversification into everything out there in the marketplace, and with very low turnover (12).

Post-Keynesian

When I described Tobin as an archetypical present-day scholar, I had in mind his concern for policy as well as for theory and empirical inference. He served, along with Walter Heller and Kermit Gordon, on the famous Camelot Council of Economic Advisers to President John F. Kennedy. A supply-side economist before Arthur Laffer had matriculated or David Stockman had been weaned, Tobin was one of the architects of the investment tax credit designed to promote capital formation and productivity. To his disappointment, politics thwarted Tobin's proposed consideration of austere overbalanced budgets and low-real-interest credit policies to shift our full-employment mix toward less consumption and more investment. (This is the opposite of what Wall Street believes the Reagan program will be.)

The Nobel Committee was less enchanted with Milton Friedman's monetarist theories than the lay press is, and was more admiring of his contributions to our understanding of a market system's workings and merits. They went out of their way to stress the latter contributions. (Friedman, like Einstein, gave the Stockholm lecture he chose to give.) Similarly, in 1981 the Swedish commentators have expressly ignored Tobin's role as one of the few prepared to debate the ideologies and findings of Monetarists—who go beyond the view that "Money does matter" to the view that, when it comes to macroeconomic inflation control, "Only money matters." Whatever the Royal Swedish Academy wishes to stress, James Tobin is known as a macroeconomist whose value judgments weight heavily the real costs in the short run of combating inflation. His optimal rules for conducting monetary and fiscal policies are not content with mere attempts to stabilize the growth rate of Money 1B, or Money 2, or of any one of the two dozen alternative definitions of the total money supply.

The Reagan team is unlikely to heed Tobin's counsel. But democracy can never afford to disregard the findings of scholars just because their value judgments are momentarily out of fashion.

What Price Prizes?

Alfred Nobel did not include economics in his will. From 1901 to 1969, there was no Nobel Prize in Economics, just as there still is no such prize in mathematics. When the Bank of Sweden decided to fund an economics prize to celebrate its own 300th anniversary, the committee set up by the Swedish Royal Academy of Sciences endeavored to lean over backward in eschewing layman's popularity and emphasizing the elements of science within political economy.

Making James Tobin the 19th laureate—the 10th American laureate—I feel adds to the luster of my own medal. It gives hope to each creative scholar anywhere in the world that she, or he, may also earn the esteem of scientific peers, which is indeed the coin that all researchers work for.

—PAUL A. SAMUELSON

References and Notes

1. J. M. Keynes, *General Theory of Employment, Interest and Money* (Macmillan, London, 1936).
2. Most influential of the early books by Hansen, the leading American Keynesian, were: A. H. Hansen, *Fiscal Policy and Business Cycles* (Norton, New York, 1941); *A Guide to Keynes* (McGraw-Hill, New York, 1953).
3. H. Wouk, *The Caine Mutiny* (Doubleday, New York, 1954).
4. W. F. Buckley, Jr., *God and Man at Yale* (Regnery, Chicago, 1951).
5. I. Todhunter, *A History of the Mathematical Theory of Probability* (Cambridge Univ. Press, Cambridge, 1865).
6. The nature of that paradox and the literature it spawned are surveyed in P. A. Samuelson, *J. Econ. Lit.* **15**, 24 (1977). Important writers in the revival of expected-utility notions were F. P. Ramsey, J. Von Neumann, O. Morgenstern, J. Marschak, B. de Finetti, and L. J. Savage.
7. J. Tobin, *Rev. Econ. Stud.* **25**, 65 (1958).
8. ——, *Rev. Econ. Stat.* **29**, 124 (1947).
9. H. Markowitz, *J. Finance* **7**, 77 (1952); *Portfolio Selection: Efficient Diversification of Investments* (Wiley, New York, 1959).
10. Sufficient conditions are discussed in P. Samuelson, *Rev. Econ. Stud.* **37**, 537 (1970). Tobin [J. Tobin, *ibid.* **36**, 13 (1969)] withdrew one other alleged defense of mean-variance analysis.
11. R. C. Merton, *Rev. Econ. Stat.* **51**, 247 (1969).
12. W. F. Sharpe, *Portfolio Theory and Capital Markets* (McGraw-Hill, New York, 1970) provides a useful survey of the capital-asset-pricing model pioneered by J. V. Lintner, J. Mossin, and himself.

The author is Institute Professor in the Department of Economics at Massachusetts Institute of Technology, Cambridge 02139. He received the Nobel Prize in Economics in 1970.

The 1983 Nobel Prize in Economics

Gerard Debreu, the 21st scholar to receive the Nobel Prize in Economics since the award was established in 1969, is a mathematical economist's mathematical economist. Formed in the crack *École supérieur normale* of France, Debreu came to this country as a postdoctoral scholar, enriching the environment at the Cowles Foundation for Economic Research in its University of Chicago and Yale incarnations. For almost two decades he has graced the economics and mathematics departments at the University of California, Berkeley, serving as a magnet there for scholars from all over the country and indeed the world.

I emphasize Debreu's French origins because of the deplorable headlines that stress the clean American sweep of the 1983 prizes. Credit always adds up to more than 100 percent: if you moved to Harvard 1 day before you got the prize, Harvard would bask in your reflected glory; and so would the kindergarten back in good old Champaign. Back in Paris, when Debreu was coming of age, Professor Maurice Allais, an engineer turned economist, had largely worked out on his own during the Occupation of Paris the fundamentals of advanced economics. Himself of Nobel caliber, Allais gathered around himself after World War II a brilliant cadre of graduates from the engineering faculties which trace back to Napoleon. Marcel Boiteux, then a brilliant young mathematical economist and now the head of the state-owned electricity system in France, was one of them. And so was Debreu.

America did give Debreu's native genius and fine mathematical training the scope for its full development. Jacob Marschak and Tjalling Koopmans, themselves new Americans who gave and received here, recognized Debreu's talents. The names of the scholars Debreu worked with, or whose work he paralleled and built upon, tells much of his quality and opportunities: John von Neumann, Abraham Wald, Kenneth Arrow, Leo Hurwicz, John Nash, Samuel Karlin, Herbert Scarf, Robert Aumann, Roy Radner, Karl Vind, Werner Hildenbrand, Robert Dorfman; the triumvirate A. W. Tucker, H. W. Kuhn, and D. Gale; Brouwer and Kakutani, W. Fenchel, S. Eilenberg, K. Menger, W. Blaschke, S. Smale, . . . Throughout there hovers over his shoulder the pervasive shade of N. Bourbaki (*1*).

First Fame

Debreu's classic, *The Theory of Value: An Axiomatic Analysis of Economic Equilibrium*, was published when he was still in his 30's. Although barely 100 pages, it is a gem of terseness, elegance, and universality. A paragraph from the preface imparts its flavor.

> The theory of value is treated here with the standards of rigor of the contemporary formalist school of mathematics. The effort toward rigor substitutes correct reasonings and results for incorrect ones, but it offers other rewards too. It usually leads to a deeper understanding of the problems to which it is applied, and this has not failed to happen in the present case. It may also lead to a radical change of mathematical tools. In the area under discussion it has been essentially a change from the calculus to convexity and topological properties, a transformation that has resulted in notable gains in the generality and the simplicity of the theory.

The words "contemporary formalist school of mathematics" are well chosen, for it is the mathematics à la Bourbaki that has overtaken economic theory. Herbert Simon once observed that the level of mathematical rigor met in *Econometrica* exceeds that in *Physical Review*—a finding that Simon did not intend as a compliment to economics. I believe it was Debreu himself who speculated that the applied science which most nearly taxes the resources of sophisticated modern mathematics is, paradoxically, the soft discipline of economics. In a field not completely free of baroque preciousness, Debreu is known for his unpretentious no-nonsense approach to the subject.

Existence of Equilibrium

In order to illustrate the new techniques let me discuss the problem of whether there is an equilibrium solution for goods' prices under competitive supply and demand.

Suppose we are many economic individuals, each endowed with one apple and three oranges. We all have the same tastes, which can be summarized by the following: Each of us persons always spends half of our income on apples and half on oranges.

Does there exist an equilibrium price ratio, $P_{\text{apples}}/P_{\text{oranges}}$, that clears competitive markets? Is the equilibrium unique?

For this trivial case the answers are trivially clear: Yes, and Yes; at the equilibrium price ratio of 3.0, and only there, will the totals of supply and demand clear the market (and, actually, with each of us consuming what we initially own and being content to exchange nothing).

No Debreu or Bourbaki is needed for this conclusion. But, as the Swedish Royal Academy of Sciences hinted at in its citation of the award, it is by means of Brouwer and Kakutani fixed-point theorems in topology that Debreu, and independently Lionel McKenzie, proved that more complicated systems do have at least one nonnegative equilibrium solution.

Beautiful? Yes. Comprehensive? Yes. It was Sophie Tucker who said, "I've been rich. I've been poor. Believe me rich is better." Having lived as a scholar in both the pre- and post-Debreu era, I can testify that the modern proofs are better than what used to pass muster for demonstration of determinate economic equilibrium. Here's how our wave-of-the-hand expositions used to go. We used to count our number of unknowns—in this case one unknown price ratio. And then we counted our number of independent equations—in this case that the function of P_a/P_o representing aggregate supply of apples be equated to the function representing aggregate demand for apples. If we could show equality between number of equations and unknowns, we took that to be an adequate indication of a determinate economic equilibrium.

What's wrong with that? Plenty. Our functions, even the ones in this trivial problem, are not linear. There are no theorems on rank of matrixes that guarantee the existence of a solution of nonlinear relations. (Even for linear systems that are neither under- nor overdetermined, economists learned the hard way that meaningless negative solutions might be implied by the mathematical formalisms.)

For readers who were away from school the morning they dealt with fixed-point theorems, let us draw a square and pencil in the 45-degree diagonal connecting its southwest and northeast corners. Is there any way to draw a curve that goes from the square's east side to its west side without taking pencil off the paper, such that the curve and the diagonal have no single point in common? Brouwer's fixed-point theorem in one dimension proves that there is indeed no possible way. Similarly, under specified conditions about people's tastes and goods endowments, there is no way for curves of supply and demand to be drawn without having at least one intersection point in common.

Warning: we must not purport to prove too much. Suppose people behave as Thorstein Veblen said they do, and value goods highly just because they are expensive in price. Then, the old-fashioned economist would argue, the higher its price goes the higher it will be further pushed, with no determinate equilibrium possible.

Let's test the new techniques on this case. Suppose in our earlier examples of apples and oranges that the fractions of income spent on each are not constants but instead are proportional to their respective absolute prices. McKenzie's existence theorem asserts that economic equilibrium is still determinate. "How can this be?" the literary economist asks. A postmortem reveals that P_a/P_o of infinity and zero are counted in by the mathematician as an existent solution, and it is precisely such odd results that the literary economists had in mind when speaking of indeterminateness of equilibrium price (*2*).

Topology to the Rescue

It is not easy to convey to nonspecialists the intricacies of economic theory. Our oranges and apples case is one whose demand behavior can be generated by assuming that each of us acts to maximize a Weber-Fechner utility function of the form: log apples plus log oranges.

Even more generally, for you (two apples, three oranges) is better than (one apple, four oranges); and, more generally, it can be shown that you will prefer (x apples, y oranges) to (X apples, Y oranges) whenever the product xy exceeds XY. What Debreu, and independently Hirofumi Uzawa, were able to show is this: if equality of xy and XY always implied indifference on your part between the two batches of goods, then there must exist a utility function, $u(x,y)$, whose maximization generates your demand functions. However, the same spending of half your income on each good could be the result of a preference structure on your part in which, when xy equals XY, you break the tie by preferring the goods batch having the most of apples. That would mean you have a *lexicographic* ordering that cannot be described by a scalar utility function. Using topological methods of Eilenberg and others, Debreu proves that a utility function must exist if both the following sets are *closed*: the sets of all points you deem at least as good as *any* prescribed (apples, oranges) batch; the sets of all points you deem no better than such a prescribed batch.

Here is still another topological success. In your Weber-Fechner utility function, the extra utility you get from adding simultaneously an apple and an orange is exactly equal to the sum of the extra utilities you get from an extra apple by itself and from an extra orange by itself. (This is in contrast, presumably, to the case where tea and lemon added together give you more than the sum of what each does separately, or the case of tea and coffee where the two together give less than the sum of each separately.) Nicholas Georgescu-Roegen, and Debreu independently, use topological methods to derive conditions for such additive independence which are in the form of testable functional equations and are of a structure different from the differential equations used by Abel and 19th-century mathematicians.

Style of the Scholar

Debreu writes sparingly. He never corrects errors of others, publishing only to establish novel results. In his adopted land where the art of lecturing is these days little cultivated and prized, Debreu is one of those who fills the blackboard with a neat sequence of axioms, lemmas, theorems, and corollaries. Eschewing faculty club and airline chefs, he prefers to dine Chez Debreu.

Gerard Debreu is not as American as apple pie. But he is as American as Enrico Fermi or Christopher Columbus.

—PAUL A. SAMUELSON

The author is Institute Professor in the Department of Economics at Massachusetts Institute of Technology, Cambridge 02139. He received the Nobel Prize in Economics in 1970.

Notes

1. General N. Bourbaki is the mythical character under whose name the top French mathematicians have published a comprehensive series of studies designed to put all of mathematics on a rigorous and sophisticated foundation.
2. The problem is more than a semantic one. Years ago Milton Friedman advocated that the pound sterling be allowed to depreciate to restore equilibrium in Britain's balance of payments. Critics objected saying that, when demand elasticities are perverse, a depreciation might worsen the unbalance. To support Friedman's position, the late Egon Sohmen argued that a large enough depreciation would as a matter of logic alone *have* to produce an equilibrium. Jagdish Bhagwati and the late Harry Johnson produced counterexamples in which the so-called existent equilibrium involved a zero dollar price for the pound.

The 1984 Nobel Prize in Economics

The Alfred Nobel Prize for Economics, on this 16th occasion of its award, goes to Sir Richard Stone of Cambridge University. Rather than divide the honor among scholars, as has often been done in the past, the Royal Swedish Academy of Sciences chose to stress the importance of Stone's work in formulating the system of integrated national-income accounts that have proved so useful in the post World War II era (*1*).

Economist peers will second this emphasis, while at the same time insisting that Stone has two other important achievements to his credit: innovations in econometric measurement of demands for groups of goods and services (*2*); and in linear matrix models permitting extrapolation and testing of growth relations (*3*). In framing his will, Alfred Nobel set a bad precedent for the physical sciences. A Lord Rayleigh could not win a Nobel Prize for a lifetime of deep and versatile work in all branches of theoretical physics, but fortunately could be fitted in under the rubric of being a discoverer of a new and rare component of the atmosphere. Arnold Sommerfeld, for all his innovations over an extended period of time, was not so lucky. Fortunately, committees know how to fudge on their own procedures, so that a Percy Bridgman as well as a lucky bystander could win the laurel leaves and lucre.

Social scientists, eager as always to ape the more exact sciences, can be counted on to take over the vices as well as virtues of their pace setters. Fortunately, though, the 1984 prize goes to a scholar prolific both in the empirical and theoretical sides of political economy and one recognized for having rung the bell of novel accomplishment several times.

The Anatomy of Social Accounts

First researches, like first loves, are important. J. R. N. Stone first gained world renown almost a half century ago for measurement of families' budget patterns with respect to spending and saving (*4*). Anyone who doubts that there is such a thing as economic law need only look at these well-documented ancient regularities. Stone's statistical investigations of the propensities to consume and save assumed an especial importance in the brave new dawn of John Maynard Keynes's revolutionary 1936 *General Theory of Employment, Interest and Money* (*5*).

During World War II itself, in the Offices of the War Cabinet's think tank attached to Keynes, Stone worked closely on setting up national-income accounts with James Meade (himself to share the 1977 Nobel Prize for innovation in international trade analysis). Those ideologically distanced from Lord Keynes—the late Lord Robbins and Sir Dennis Robertson for example—have testified to the exhilarating quality of that charmed circle. It was there that Stone and Meade made their first U.K. estimates, and forged the tools of interlocking accounts appropriate to a nation and, by extension, to a region or the whole world.

Cambridge University was not a friendly environment in the postwar years for a Department of Applied Economics in which people actually dirtied their hands manipulating empirical data. Stone fortunately wore the right tweeds, and as a Fellow of King's College and a protégé of Maynard Keynes was able to protect a revolving corps of able researchers. Not all of them spoke with top drawer accents and it must be admitted that many were colonials and Americans. But science, as we are told, recognizes no distinctions of class or race. Still it was considered rather much when a chair designated for finance and accounting went to a don (Stone himself) who had never met a payroll and whose double-entry items referred to societies and sectors and not to corporations and wholly owned subsidiaries.

Good wine travels far. What was good for the United Kingdom was found to be good for the United States and became the pattern for the United Nations community generally as the Stone square matrices of interlocking fund flows became the *lingua franca* of world statisticians: involved was a *production* account, and one each for *consumption, accumulation*, and *foreign finance*.

Physiology of the Circular Flow

Parallel with these accounts at the national level, there was being developed by Wassily Leontief at Harvard a similar system of input-output relations, in which a vector of industries is seen to be connected by a vast matrix of transaction flows—the dollars received by industry i from the total expenditure flow of industry j (*6*). The general notion of such a *Tableau Économique* goes back a long way, to Francois Quesnay, Madame Pompadour's physician at the court of Louis XV and founder of the Physiocratic school of economics. Despite exaggerated claims by Quesnay's disciples—as that the *Tableau* was the greatest invention since fire and writing—both Karl Marx and Joseph Schumpeter could admire this first attempt to grapple with an economy's general equilibrium.

A scholar has predecessors, co-workers, and successors. Simon Kuznets in America had pioneered in defining and measuring national income and deservedly received the 1971 Nobel Prize for this work. Stone followed in his tradition, and in the tradition of such other laureates as Jan Tinbergen, Leontief, and Lawrence Klein. Going beyond the formal anatomy and taxonomy of social accounts, Stone set up behavior-equation hypotheses to rationalize and project future saving and income growths. A large team at Cambridge has produced volumes dealing with linear growth models (*7*).

The jury still seems to be out on how useful these exercises have been. Criticism is easy, and for every scholar who complains that these systems are oversimplified there is also a pedant who is bored by their multivarious detail. Supply-side economics is not an easy subject and it is even more difficult at the level of microeconomics than at the macroeconomic level.

Measurement in Terms of Theory

In the announcement of this year's Nobel award, the Royal Swedish Academy of Sciences stated: "*Economic theory* is at the back of Stone's system for national accounts, and these therefore provide a systematic base for economic analysis, forecasts and economic policy." Thus, behind the dollar or pound numbers of the gross national product (GNP), an economic theorist tries to discern some real scale of output of goods and services.

What is needed is some proper index number of prices that can be used to deflate the dollar totals. Thus, suppose we all spend two-thirds of our incomes on food and one-third on clothing. And suppose our total of dollar incomes doubles between 1980 and 1985 while food prices have all doubled and clothing prices have all stayed the same. How much, if at all, has our real income gone up?

In this Santa Claus example an exact answer is possible: real income has gone up almost exactly 26 percent (more precisely, it is $\sqrt[3]{2}$ times what it had been). To arrive at the correct answer, we calculate the correct weighted average of price changes: with expenditure fractions so constant and simple, our index number of prices must be

$$100(P^{85}_{\text{food}}/P^{80}_{\text{food}})^{2/3}(P^{85}_{\text{clothing}}/P^{80}_{\text{clothing}})^{1/3}$$
$$= 100(2)^{2/3}(1)^{1/3} \simeq 158.74$$

Deflating the index number of GNP, 200, by 158.74 gives, after multiplication by the conventional 100, the desired answer of 125.992—a 26 percent rise.

When making calculations for all the countries in the Organization for Economic Cooperation and Development, Professor Stone proposed reasonable use of conventional price index numbers as deflators (*8*). The same general philosophy has been common among experts. Do correct theoretical methods matter? Indeed they do. Thus, it was recently thought that half-a-dozen countries had surpassed the U.S. real per capita level of income: West Germany, Sweden, Switzerland, and so forth. And that is what the World Bank Atlas recently used to show even though the experts there knew better.

When the United Nations and World Bank commissioned a team at the University of Pennsylvania—A. Heston, I. Kravis, and R. Summers—to do the research correctly, these used the same general methodology that Stone follows. They eschewed using merely exchange rates as deflators, knowing that short-term depreciations of the dollar would excessively lower the U.S. estimates. Instead they gathered prices actually paid in each country and constructed from them the proper index numbers needed as deflators (*9*). Result: America is still more than 10 percent above the European nations named.

There is one further theoretical innovation of Stone's that is closely related: the Stone-Geary or Klein-Rubin system of demand functions. Rich people are known to spend a smaller fraction of their income on food than poor people do. So instead of assuming fixed fractions—the so-called Cobb-Douglas model—Stone gets a better fit by assuming people spend on each good a fixed fraction of the income they have left after they have bought a fixed market basket of the goods (*2*). This too is an oversimplification, but it is one in the good cause of arriving at tolerable econometric fits to whole systems of observations. Fairly recently, the Kravis-Summers-Heston team has verified that such a model does approximately fit their data on more than a score of countries, ranging from poor Kenya and India to Hungary, Britain, Japan, and the United States.

Style That Makes the Man

Though Sir Richard has led teams and done joint work with many, including Lady (Giovanna) Stone, he is rather a loner and has a reserved personality. Meticulous in citing earlier work by others, probably he has arrived by his own route at much of his final work. With jaunty cap, he strides across the heath, shooting stick in hand. Poker-faced, he savors a good cigar and sips fine wine. Probably, in all his life he has never spilled gravy on his velvet waistcoats.

Competent scientists, it is reported, usually have narrow interests. Brilliant scientists reputedly have broad interests. Certainly that is the case with Richard Stone.

As you read one of his well-drafted essays or memoirs, suddenly you spy an unexpected nugget. Here is one example, culled from chapter 1 of his 1966 collection of essays (*10*).

Jean D'Alembert, the brilliant 18th-century mathematician and physicist, made rather a jackass of himself when dealing with probability. Confronted with the divergent series arising in the St. Petersburg Paradox, he alleged that all probabilities below a certain critical fraction could be treated as zero. With such humpty-dumptyism, what series could fail to converge!

More notorious was D'Alembert's insistence that, in two tosses of a fair coin, the probabilities of two heads, two tails, and of a mixed outcome of heads and tails are each one-third. By contrast, conventional minds reckon as having equal probabilities, of one-fourth each, the different cases: HH, TT, HT, TH. Stone offers D'Alembert the following ingenious defense. Not being able to be certain that the coin is indeed fair, perhaps I must consider the probability of a heads to be p, which can be more or less than one-half and might be deemed by me to be equally likely to be anywhere on the interval (0,1). In that case, the probability of HH is p^2, with expected value for it and for TT and for (HT or TH) all equal to one-third! (*11*).

To perceive how great have been both the quality and quantity of Stone's researches, the reader is referred to the *Festschrift* in his honor, which contains a bibliography of 169 Stone publications in the years 1936 to 1979 (*12*). And finally I should mention that, in an economics profession known for its standoffishness, Richard Stone has done fruitful interdisciplinary work in the realms where demographic and economic analysis overlap.—PAUL A. SAMUELSON

The author is Institute Professor in the Department of Economics of Massachusetts Institute of Technology, Cambridge 02139. He received the Nobel Prize in Economics in 1970.

References and Notes

1. R. Stone, "Definition and measurement of the national income and related totals," Appendix to *Measurement of National Income and Construction of Social Accounts* (United Nations, Geneva, 1947).
2. ———, *Econ. J.* **64**, No. 255 (1954).
3. ———, *Discovery* **22**, No. 5 (1961).
4. J. R. N. Stone and W. M. Stone, *Rev. Econ. Stud.* **6**, No. 1 (1938).
5. J. M. Keynes, *The General Theory of Employment, Interest and Money* (Macmillan, London, 1936).
6. W. W. Leontief, *The Structure of American Economy, 1919–1929* (Harvard Univ. Press, Cambridge, Mass., 1941).
7. R. Stone, Ed., *A Programme for Growth* (Chapman & Hall, London, 1962–1971), vols. 1–11.
8. R. Stone, *Quantity and Price Indexes in National Accounts* (Organization for Economic Cooperation and Development, Paris, 1956).
9. I. Kravis, A. Heston, R. Summers, *World Product and Income: International Comparisons of Real Gross Product, Phase III* (Johns Hopkins Univ. Press, Baltimore, 1982).
10. R. Stone, *Mathematics in the Social Sciences and Other Essays* (Chapman & Hall, London, 1966), pp. 20–21.
11. Stone's defense works for three or more tosses as well: that is, the integral between 0 and 1 of p^n is indeed $1/(n + 1)$, and so on. However, in the case where we have two coins with respective probabilities (p_1, p_2), which are deemed independent and each equally likely to be anywhere between 0 and 1, the jury must still vote to hang D'Alembert since the probability of HH is one-fourth, the product of two factors, each the integral between 0 and 1 of p_i (dp_i).
12. A. Deaton, Ed., *Essays in The Theory and Measurement of Consumer Behaviour in Honour of Sir Richard Stone* (Cambridge Univ. Press, Cambridge, 1981), pp. 325–337.

365

Seventieth Birthday Remarks

Like Proust's madeleines, my childhood picture that fond Risha dug up from the files brought a rush of forgotten memories. And it will stay in my mind as the motif of this particular occasion. In the last few years I have participated in a number of scholarly affairs arranged by kind friends to honor my academic achievements. This one is different. It is purely personal.

When you saw that picture, it made you think of a serious little boy: as one colleague said—the thinker, 3 going on 19. To me it brought back the years I spent on the farm with Aunt Frieda and Uncle Sam. They were not my real relatives but the foster parents I spent much of the years between two and five with. Isaac Newton and Bertrand Russell both had the experience of having no parents in their early and formative years. This may well have scarred them both personally—even though it may also have unleashed their creative abilities. Maybe I, too, was permanently scarred by being sent away from home in tender years; I have never been on the psychologist's couch to find out. One dollar a day for room and board was the market rate in those days, but what came as a free joint product was Aunt Frieda's love. My brother Bob a few years later could testify also to the warmth of that love. I didn't like the transitions from the home and foster environments, but once in either regimen I seemed to thrive. In retrospect I have thought it liberating to have been in two cultures: the urban one of my immigrant parents and the rural old-American one of Aunt Frieda. If there were any unhappy years in my life, they were those of adolescence: twelve to fourteen.

As that picture reveals, I had golden locks and was treated as something of a *wunderkind* from the beginning. Much was expected of me, and hamlike I responded. In retrospect I think my older brother got shortchanged. I say older brother because Harold was two and a half years my senior. But it tells us something about my earliest gravity that a family maid once said to my mother: "I always send the younger one to do the errands because that's only right." "But," my mother expostulated, "you always send Harold." Isn't Paul the oldest?" the maid replied. Both brothers, including Robert Summers here on my left, achieved career fulfillments with help from no one, entirely on their own.

At a Chicago Commencement ceremony a few years ago, I truthfully said, "I was not born in 1915 but rather at 8 A.M. on January 2nd, 1932, the morning I began college in Louis Wirth's lecture on Malthus's population theory." My IQ probably peaked at the age of ten, when I knew everything except, as I reproached my father, it had never been vouchsafed to me that Samuel Gompers was a labor leader. In high school I marked time as an underachiever: What is more American than that? In the university I finally came into my own. And ever since I have been overpaid and underworked. MIT has been my indulgent alma mater, and the world, my oyster. Luck of course comes to the prepared mind, but as Napoleon said, it is better in picking a general to look for luck rather than merely for above-the-ordinary military stupidity.

Now I am seventy. I cannot believe this. To myself I seem about thirty-nine. As Paul Rodan used to say: "I grow fat; my friends grow old." Thomas Mann expected to die young, just when his father did, and he planned his life accordingly. As the great day of his critical birthday approached he waited for something to happen. The day came and passed with no events. So he just carried on until the end came in his late seventies.

All of the males on both sides of my family succumbed early to cardiac conditions. To my surprise, the University of Chicago medical department limited my freshman athletic participation because of hypertension. So, being a rational expectationer, I presumed that anything I was to accomplish would have to be done early. Perhaps this is the genesis of the canard that the brash Paul Samuelson subsequently mellowed. Actually, I never was brash, being only generous in correcting the obvious mistakes of my teachers and superiors. As Warren Hastings said in his trial for Indian frauds, "When I consider my opportunities, I marvel at my moderation."

Having been regarded as being just like my father, I found his early death had a profound effect on me. For years I had a recurrent dream that really he was still alive. Gary Becker would say it was a selfish concern based upon self-identification with him. In historical fact, before I reached the age of 50, trivially simple therapies came along that left me with the vigorous good health that I had always enjoyed. So, like Thomas Mann, I just carried on.

And that is what I propose to do for another twenty years. Doing my research, correcting my betters, and perfecting my tennis game. I appreciate my luck in having Risha as companion. Present here are the six children who know they have the love that I have never been good at expressing. And, at latest count, there are eight grandchildren—all present here. Not least of my blessings are these many dear friends I see before me.

As some sage has said, behind every successful and fulfilled person, you'll find a surprised deity. I am the nonexception that does indeed prove the rule.

INTRODUCTION TO THE ENLARGED EDITION

TIME LENDS DISTANCE. When I read words written four decades ago, I see them with an objectivity as if they were composed by another scientist. And yet, blessed with a good memory, I have access now in 1983 to the process of creative genesis for this book's theories that no one else can ever enjoy.

John Livingston Lowes won scholarly esteem for himself, and added to Coleridge's immortal fame, when he explored in *The Road to Xanadu* the books and poems Coleridge was known to have read before *The Rime of the Ancient Mariner* was written, tracing in one or another of these works the inputs of images, metaphors, and conceits out of which the great poem's contents were forged. Posterity is grateful to Lowes. But how much more valuable it would be if we had from Coleridge himself an accurate sampling of the creative travail that went into his masterpiece.

Science is not art. Yet, despite the lack of complete identity between art and science, there is much in common among different creative processes. How Mozart produced his music, Shakespeare his plays, Frost his short poems and Milton his great epics, Tolstoy and even Trollope their novels—what would we not give to learn? No less interesting to those of us who consider science the most exciting game in the universe would be autobiographical accounts of the young and old Newton, of Euler at work and Clerk Maxwell at play.

We are eternally grateful to Henri Poincaré for his detailed exposition of the role that the subconscious plays in the discovery of mathematical theories: how one wrestles consciously and unsuccessfully with a theorem, then puts it aside, as if out of mind, but apparently not really out of mind; for suddenly, in a Coleridgean dream—or, in the case of Poincaré when he was stepping on a bus while doing his military service—the successful solution arrives as if the unconscious had all along been grinding away on the puzzle. I once advised the head of the Harvard University Press to publish James Watson's double-helix manuscript—exactly in its first naked form, with its original title, *Honest*

Jim—for the insight it gave into one aspect of science: the struggle for priority and fame. If a man would write such an account, let him be read, even if it is an exaggeration of what is a normal element in the scientific way of life.

We have all been bored by pedants' postmortems on the essence and nature of humor. And working scientists, to tell the simple truth, have neither the time nor the patience to bother with the history of their subject: they want to get on with making that history. Philosophers of science, historians of science, sociologists of science, may not be without honor in their own houses; but the customers who take in their washings, and swap garments with them, are unlikely to be working scientists still in the prime of life. Still, the attention that an assistant professor's dissertation cannot command to a discussion of how Helmholtz achieved his scientific contributions may just possibly be attracted by Helmholtz's own account. Again, this suggests a role for autobiography in science. The laboratory notebooks of Michael Faraday are more precious to me than the Domesday Book or the Rosetta Stone.

Autobiography has its pitfalls. No better example of that could be found than in the case of Coleridge. Research shows that his statements to have written this or that poem at the age of seven, or eleven, or forty-three can never be taken at face value—and there is the further danger that the "original" poem in question is in fact a translation from Schiller's German. Coleridge has high claims to the title of greatest plagiarist of all time. Genius is above scandal. But just what there is to be forgiven or praised posterity does want to know.

Watson's account of DNA is Watson's account. It is part of a truth and belongs in the record, even though it does less and more than justice to its narrator. Isaac Newton did not falsify the story of his transcendental achievements. He did not do so either consciously or unconsciously. But he was not generous to rivals and you would not be able to discern from Newton's *Principia* how he arrived at his major discoveries and insights. Even Albert Einstein, the sweetest of human beings and one with so many early achievements to his credit that he had no need for puffery or priority claims, does not seem in late-life accounts to have managed to give plausible accounts of the origins of all his notions. Not to have known of the Michelson-Morley experiment by name is not the same thing as not to have known of equivalent empirical findings. Innumerable writers Einstein studied did know of Brownian motion; in what sense, then, can one interpret Einstein's claim not to have known of it when writing his 1905 paper on stochastic processes?

Content analysis will confirm that autobiographers cannot help but give themselves the benefit of the doubt. Accounts by scientists of their earlier works are invaluable, but such accounts are only one subset of the data and hypotheses that nominate themselves for inclusion in the adversary procedure that constitutes the corpus of science.

Let the reader beware. I have made a conscious attempt to render correctly my role in the creation of modern theoretical economics. But I urge that the grain of salt I have to apply to the present dish be kept at hand by those who have the objectivity of distance as well as of time.

Apotheosis of the Calculus

The first edition of *Foundations of Economic Analysis* was a culmination and also a beginning. It finally achieved for economics a synthesis of Cournot's Newtonian calculus method of maximizing with Walras's equations of general equilibrium. Certain problems were settled for all time: consider, for example, observable demand functions that achieved for a consumer the maximum of an ordinal utility function subject to given income and prices—call them $q = f(P/\text{income})$ in matrix notation. If they satisfied the Slutsky conditions of having a symmetric, negative semi-definite matrix, $S = [\partial q_i/\partial p_j + q_j \partial q_i/\partial(\text{income})]$, $S = S^T$, $PS \equiv 0$, $X^T SX \leqq 0$ for arbitrary column vector X, then it was shown that nothing more could be asked of them by the theory. No young Hotelling, Hicks, Allen, Pareto, or Slutsky could later come along and add a new requirement once closure had been attained by rigorous proof.

But beyond the counting of equations and testing of Newton-Weierstrass quadratic forms and bordered determinants, *Foundations* began the systematic use of *finite inequalities* in modern economics. To say that raising price from p_1 to p_2 will lower quantity bought from q_1 to q_2 along a demand curve, $q = f(p)$, one need not be able to say that $f'(p)$ is almost everywhere negative on the interval (p_1, p_2). It will do to know that $(p_2 - p_1)(q_2 - q_1) = \Delta p \Delta q < 0$ for every two distinct points on the demand curve. Where Newtonian calculus helps, economists are grateful. But where it doesn't apply, as when price can take on only integral (or rational) values, we are even more grateful for more general methods. When I stumbled on the notion of revealed preference in 1937, I was shoved into the task of trying to free classical mathematical analysis from its calculus corsets.

The original version of this book abounded with questions for further research and development. Future Arrows, Houthakkers, Debreus, Shephards, Samuelsons, and McKenzies were to apply to economics the unifying tools of convex set theory, partial orderings and lattices, fixed-point theorems, nonstandard analysis, and all of the paraphernalia of Bourbaki mathematics. Gerald Debreu once commented to me—soberly—that the discipline which most fully uses in its daily work the frontier refinements of mathematical analysis is modern economic theory. That is a sobering thought indeed.

Newtonian Paradise Regained

So fertile were the analytical methods of A. Wald, J. von Neumann, K. J. Arrow, H. Wold, T. Koopmans, D. Gale, H. Kuhn and A. W. Tucker, G. Debreu, L. S. Pontryagin, R. J. Aumann, and Abraham Robinson that by the time *Foundations* celebrated its official twentieth birthday, its pages of Newtonian calculus were old hat. But then the mathematician Steven Smale wandered into economics, pointing out in effect that if only one added the magic incantation of "almost always," the classic assertions of the calculus were reinstated into respectability. Thus, if a demand function is smooth everywhere on an interval except at a set of points of measure zero, it is necessary and sufficient for it to be strictly monotone-decreasing that "almost everywhere" its derivative, $f'(p)$, be negative. Willard Gibbs's phase rule in thermodynamics—which his disciple and my master, E. B. Wilson, pointed out is no more than the economist's counting of equations and unknowns—after all does have a substantive *generic* content even in the land of Bourbaki.

More can be less. Much of mathematical economics in the 1950s gained in elegance over poor old Pareto and Edward Chamberlin. But the fine garments sometimes achieved fit only by chopping off some real arms and legs. The theory of cones, polyhedra, and convex sets made possible "elementary" theorems and lemmas. But they seduced economists away from the phenomena of increasing returns to scale and nonconvex technology that lie at the heart of oligopoly problems and many real-world maximizing assignments. Easy victories over a science's wrong opponents are hollow victories—at least almost always.

Fortunately, some of the inequalities of revealed preference have a validity even when utility functions are not quasi-concave and do possess indifference contours that reverse their curvatures. Thus, suppose Q^1 is the cheapest way for me to buy at P^1 at least a specified level of well-being, $\bar{U} \leqq U(Q)$, and suppose Q^2 is the cheapest way to achieve at least that well-being when prices have changed to P^2. Then, even if $U(Q)$ is not a well-behaved quasi-concave function, and even if it is not defined for all real numbers in the non-negative orthant $(q_1, \ldots, q_n) = Q \geqq 0$, the inequality of the Weak Axiom of Revealed Preference is still valid: $\Delta P \cdot \Delta Q = \Sigma_1^n(p_j^2 - p_j^1)(q_j^2 - q_j^1) \leqq 0$. This follows from the basic logic of maximizing. One of the most joyful moments of my life was when I was led by listening to E. B. Wilson's exposition of Gibbsian thermodynamics to infer an eternal truth that was independent of its physics or economics exemplification. (A student who studied only one science would be less likely to recognize what belonged to *logic* rather than to the nature of *things.*)

BLESSED LACK OF UNITY

Foundations is three books. I am glad that I did not stick to my original thesis intention of concentrating solely on the implications for observable economic data of the hypothesis that individuals or firms act to maximize specifiable functions. Most of Part I did focus on that problem. But every time an interesting topic beckoned, I departed from the narrow path in hot pursuit.

Four instances will suffice. Chapter III begins with "A Calculus of Qualitative Relations." That is admitted not to fall under the rubric of maximizing behavior. But it is a novel topic, valuable for its own sake, and years later it led such economic theorists as K. Lancaster, W. M. Gorman, and T. Quirk to develop and codify what can be said on the basis solely of qualitative relationships (such as algebraic sign of influence of one variable on another). This calculus has had applications even in ecology.

A second valuable digression (or partial digression) was Chapter VI's section "The Economic Theory of Index Numbers." Index number theory is shown to be merely an aspect of the theory of revealed preference. Thirty-five years after that analysis appeared there has been but one major advance in index number theory—namely W. E. Diewert's formalizing concept of a "superlative index number," which is a formula based upon two periods (p_j, q_j) data that will be exactly correct as an ordinal indicator of utility for some specified family of indifference contours. (Only a few different "superlative" formulas are known; perhaps the set of simple superlative formulas is a limited set.) What my book's discussion around equations (76) and (77) settled, and what needed still to be settled back in the mid-1930s when the *Review of Economic Studies* rejected the pearl I cast before them, was the fact that no index number would ever be found that would do the exact job that early economists wanted of an index number. Thus, let half the goods double in price and half of them triple. Trivially, the cost of living has increased somewhere between 100 and 200 percent. But, even if we know exactly what you and I spend on each good before and after the price changes, it is impossible in principle for the same scalar formula—$f(P^a, Q^a; P^b, Q^b)$—to represent correctly for the two of us with different (not yet known!) tastes the exact amount by which our respective costs of living have risen. Knowable in principle from knowledge of our respective complete indifference contours are the ratios of new-to-old dollars each of us needs in the new P^b price situation to be as well off as we were in the initial P^a price situation; but—and this is the point of revealed preference—knowledge of but two (P, Q) situations (or of a limited number of such situations) can at best put bounds on each one of our sought-for ratios.

Before leaving this second digression I ought to mention that my notorious opposition to the usual consumers-surplus palaver was similarly based on objection to nonoptimal revealed-preference inferences. If you know my q_1 responses to changes in

p_1, while p_2 and my income are held constant—and that is what you know when you observe my "demand curve"—you are not able to infer my many indifference contours in the region surrounding the observed (Q) points. Therefore, you cannot calculate the deadweight-loss magnitudes needed for various welfare purposes. If you have more knowledge about me—for example, how income changes my Q purchases—a more accurate mapping of my contours is made possible. Revealed preference is the theory that analyzes just what can be inferred from available (P,Q) observations. When consumers surplus is done right, it becomes revealed preference theory and reveals its own redundancy.

A third digression had to do with Chapter V's "A Note on the Demand for Money." Young scholars tend to want to tell you all they know. And I was young. Now that I am not young, I am glad that this section got included. For the need existed to bring money into conventional demand theory, and to do so in a way that would deduce as a theorem the essential difference between coffee that you want for its own sake and money that you want only for its ability to enable you to buy and sell goods like coffee. Because the stock of money, M, enters the ordinal utility function along with the price vector, P, in the homogeneity form of P/M, a rational basis for the Quantity Theory is provided free of the gratuitous $MV = PQ$ formulation. Neoclassical economics is better than Monetarism!

Finally, it is pleasant to note Chapter V's final paragraphs in which the invention of money-market funds is indicated and the prospect is envisaged in which transaction money comes near to earning the full interest yield of an economy, with all the puzzles for a determinate theory of velocity of circulation that this would imply.

Welfare Economics

The second of the three books contained in *Foundations* is Chapter VIII's summary of Abram Bergson's new welfare economics. Until that chapter was available, only those who knew Bergson's seminal 1938 *Quarterly Journal* article or Oskar Lange's 1942 *Econometrica* article could find their way through the swamp of assertion, truth, ambiguity, denial, and misunderstanding that went under the name of the "new welfare economics." In a 1981 *Festschrift* to Bergson, I have written that his breakthrough of a *weakly separable* individualistic social welfare function "came like a flash of lightning, describable only in the words of the pontifical poet: 'Nature and Nature's laws lay hid in night: / God said, Let Newton be! and all was light.' "

Suddenly one recognized Lerner's marginal proportionality RULE and Pareto-optimality conditions for what they really are—members of the subset of conditions *necessary* for welfare optimization that are statable independently of the form of the interpersonal ethical norms specified for the (separable, ordinal) social welfare function. Just as Hegel is said to have understood his philosophy for the first time when he read its French translation, Vilfredo Pareto could have learned what it was he meant exactly to say when he read Bergson's 1938 classic. That Bergson's approach could stimulate new breakthroughs as well as unify past paradigms is shown by the fact that my 1954 application of it to the theory of public goods both gave new life to the old Wicksell-Lindahl theories and led to new cheat-proof algorithms by W. Vickrey, T. Groves and J. Ledyard, E. Clarke, G. Tullock, and J. Buchanan. Judged by frequency of citation, the 1954 effort succeeded in making its original point that mathematics does have a creative role to play in modern economics.

After four decades there is still misunderstanding concerning an individualistic social welfare function (of what is called Bergson-Samuelson type). Because Kenneth Arrow, in his 1951 classic *Social Choice and Individual Values*, gave the same name ("social welfare function") to the Constitutional Voting Function that he proved could not possibly exist with the properties one wishes for it, economist tyros think the Bergson-Samuelson Social Welfare Function has been proved not to exist. Experts know better. But some of the avant-garde make the curious mistake of thinking that the requirement that a Bergson-Samuelson Individualistic Social Welfare Function be "ordinal" implies that some one person is a dictator whose preferences are to prevail on all interpersonal judgments. This is a misunderstanding, as I have argued in *Economica* (1977) and in the Bergson *Festschrift*. Here is one more try.

Suppose society has one hundred chocolates to allocate between Jane and Dick: q_1 for Jane, q_2 for Dick, $q_1 + q_2 = 100$, $q_i \geq 0$. An Individualistic Social Welfare Function, ISWF, that is ordinal might have ethical indifference contours in the (q_1,q_2) plane defined completely as rectangular hyperbolae: If $q_1^a q_2^a > q_1^b q_2^b$, the allocation (q_1^a,q_2^a) is ethically better than (q_1^b,q_2^b); if $q_1^a q_2^a = q_1^b q_2^b$, the two allocations are ethically indifferent. Then subject to the constraint of one hundred chocolates to divide among sweet-toothed Jane and Dick, neither of whom is envious or altruistic, suppose the ethical judgment is made that the best state of the world is an even division of fifty each.

Everything is ordinal. Agreed? Nothing up anyone's sleeve. Agreed? Then what is the shouting about?

Somehow readers of the social choice literature have associated the good old word "ordinal" with a compulsion to use *rank-order* ratings of *changes*. They've stumbled into an axiom that is unhappily named a "neutrality axiom." It goes something like the following: "If it is ethically better in *some* situation to prefer a move that raises Jane and lowers Dick in individual welfares, then *every* choice that raises Jane and lowers Dick must be ethically preferred." You will say, how stupid an axiom is that entails one person's being an absolute dictator. I am not one to disagree. But wise or stupid, such an axiom has nothing to do with the usage of the word "ordinal" in the Edgeworth-Pareto-Hicks-Samuelson literature. The Bergson ordinal Individualistic Social Welfare Function is alive and well.

John Harsanyi (1955) has made one valuable addition to the Bergson ISWF. He has shown that, after all, there is something to be said for the Bentham form that merely adds different persons' *cardinal* utilities with appropriate ethical weights. Harsanyi deduces this simplification by extending the individualistic ethic—which agrees that ethically one state of the world is better than another if all persons unanimously deem it to be—to the stochastic realm.

Mathematical Appendix C, section 5, will give some details of the argument, but here is a sketch of how it goes. Suppose each of N persons wants to act in choosing among probability situations in accordance with a few Ramsey-von Neumann axioms of consistency and "rationality." It follows that each will act to maximize the Expected ("mean") Value of his existent *cardinal* utility function. Suppose Bergson's Ethical Observer, choosing ethically among probability situations, wishes to do so in accord with those few Ramsey-von Neumann axioms; then She, or He, will act to maximize the Expected Value of an existent cardinal Social Welfare Function. Further, suppose that this SWF is an Individualistic Social Welfare Function in the sense that, when all persons agree that State A is better than State B, the ISWF agrees that A is ethically better than B. Harsanyi's point is that it is plausible to let A and B be probabilistic states as well as certainty states. If you grant him this point, then by logic it follows that the ISWF can be written in Bentham's additive form: $\lambda^1 u^1(q) + \lambda^2 u^2(q) +$, where only the non-negative ethical weights $(\lambda^1, \lambda^2, \ldots)$ are at the choice of the ethical system.

Before leaving the topic of welfare economics, I might mention that Chapter VIII throws light on how primitive the pre-1940 understanding was on some basic issues. My teachers, giants of the subject such as Jacob Viner, Frank Knight, and Joseph Schumpeter, could not explain to me or to themselves what was the germ of truth in Adam Smith's doctrine of the Invisible Hand, which was supposed to lead to something or other in a competitive market. Or consider the fashionable belief, then prevailing, that constant returns to scale is incompatible with stability of perfect competition. Even Pierro Sraffa's classic 1926 article, which launched the modern Chamberlin-Robinson theory of imperfect competition, was flawed in its contention that the boxes of increasing cost and of constant cost represented one box too many. Accepted literally, Sraffa's argument would deny validity to the following simplest case of general equilibrium: corn is produced by labor and land by a first-degree homogeneous production function; cloth is produced solely by labor at constant returns to scale. Then a shift of tastes toward food and away from clothing will raise P_{corn}/P_{cloth}, lowering the wage/rent ratio and labor's share in national income. Sraffa's logic can be caricatured to allege that such a model is logically self-contradictory and so (*sic*) we need a new theory of imperfect competition. I remember how delighted—and doubtful!—Schumpeter was with the Chapter IV section "Indeterminacy in Purest Competition?" which set this matter straight.

A VIRGIN CONTINENT

This leads to a needed observation. Newton said: Aw shucks, because I stood on the shoulders of giants I saw so far. True. We all benefit from our scientific predecessors. I in particular pored over the works of Ragnar Frisch, Jan Tinbergen, Harold Hotelling, Griffith C. Evans, E. B. Wilson, Wassily Leontief, Nicholas Georgescu-Roegen—to mention only my then living elders.

Newton might also have added, less modestly, that he raised the platform from which his posterity could climb. And if Newton had not been so solitary a thinker and so transcendent a genius, he could have benefited from the work of contemporaries. Every racing cyclist knows how fast the ride is for the contender who travels just behind the pacesetter, enjoying the vacuum his efforts create as an externality. I pored over the works of J. R. Hicks, R. G. D. Allen, Abram Bergson, A. P. Lerner, Nicholas Kaldor, and all the great theorists of the day. Admittedly, it is easier on the ego to develop what is already in the air while nurturing the self-deception of subjective originality. But early on I decided that the higher prize was to get on with the subject's advancement by utilizing and acknowledging whatever was already to be found in the literature, eschewing what Gunnar Myrdal acidly called "unnecessary Anglo Saxon 'originality'." Then, if one could leap a cubit from those ethereal heights, the fulfillment was the greater.

There is something still more important. I was lucky to enter economics in 1932. Analytical economics was poised for its take-off. I faced a lovely vacuum that young economists today can hardly imagine. So much remained to be done. Everything was still in an imperfect state. It was like fishing in a virgin lake: a whopper at every cast, but so many lovely new specimens that the palate never cloyed.

Learned journals were then allergic to mathematics: having the leisure as a Junior Fellow at Harvard to pour out papers, my problem was to avoid saturating any one journal. I doled out the articles to as many different publications as would tolerate them. Again and again editors wrote: "Please shorten and make less mathematical." I swallowed the temptation to protest: "Which do you want? Both are impossible. And neither is optimal." The last laugh is to the scientist: the quality of the papers that editors rejected was, if anything, a bit better than the rest.

Being a Junior Fellow was the life for me. The pay was good. I owned a pen and the library was near. I used to think that I would gladly settle for the three-year term's becoming a life sentence. Later when I had the chance to teach scores of the world's most promising scholars, I ceased to regret the ending of paradise. But later still, when MIT made me an Institute Professor, I again reveled in the Indian Summer of a junior fellowship renewed for life. Paradise enow!

Foundations of Economic Analysis had successes in generating a wide variety of substantive theories. But what interested its young author most—and what I have tried to keep in mind in preparing this enlarged edition—was the success it could achieve in formulating a general theory of economic theories.

367

Forewords to the Japanese Edition of *The Collected Scientific Papers of Paul A. Samuelson*

Foreword to Volume 1

These papers deal with what today we call *macroeconomics*—a surprisingly recent term. A dozen years ago, Dr. Edwin Nourse, President Truman's venerable first Chairman of the US Council of Economic Advisers, wrote to Professor Alvin Hansen of Harvard, asking: "Who invented the word 'macroeconomics'?" Hansen wrote back: "I don't know. Probably Samuelson. I'll ask him."

I must answer for much. But I don't believe it was I who coined this now-standard word. It was not in the index of the 1948 first edition of my *Economics*! My hunch was that Ragnar Frisch of Oslo deserved the credit, in connection with his famous 1933 Cassel *Festschrift* piece in which, like Wicksell's rocking horse's motions, the business cycle was envisaged as resulting from random or quasi-regular exogenous shocks applied to the endogenous economic system with its propensity to cumulate and resonate with those shocks. Library research proved this Frisch hunch wrong: He, Tinbergen, and Kalecki used the expression "macrodynamic" and had not yet contrasted *micro*economics and *macro*economics. Actually, my researches revealed that the first use of "macroeconomics" was in the second of its two primary present-day meanings and came around 1946—as in Lawrence Klein's *Econometrica* article on "aggregation," in which Clark-Douglas total output is to be expressible as a function of the total of a few inputs like labor and "capital." The primary use of "macroeconomics," to describe Keynes-like models of how output and unemployment are determined by "effective demand" considerations—the subject matter of these present papers—came soon after. Now we take the word for granted.

What I must plead guilty to when I approach St. Peter's Gate to Heaven—if it is a crime—is first devising the 45°-line diagrams in which $C + I$ Keynesian schedules of consumption-plus-investment intersect with the 45°-line to determine Keynes's simplest "multiplier" model of (underemployment) equilibrium determination. Professor Axel Leijonhufvud, in his 1966 "On Keynesian Economics and the Economics of Keynes," has tried to argue that this basic model (and its patent Hicks-Hansen generalization to the $L - M$ and $I - S$ diagrams) is a perversion of the Master's subtle thinking, perpetrated by such Keynesian disciples and epigoni as me, Kahn, Joan Robinson, Harrod, Hansen, Hicks, Meade, Reddaway, Lerner, Kalecki, Lange, Modigliani, Smithies, Kaldor, Tobin, Colin Clark, and other names so illustrious that they turn Leijonhufvud's own sword against himself.

With respect, Dr. Leijonhufvud has things wrong. His history is distorted; more important, he fails to grasp the essence of scientific methodology. On the first point, Keynes himself read *prior* to publication most of the expositions that Leijonhufvud says pervert Keynes's own theory; many of these papers he published in the *Economic Journal*, of which he was the dictatorial editor. He had plenty of opportunity, at the time of their publication in the latter 1930s of protesting; yet he did not. And Keynes showed himself eminently capable of complaining about his disciples: His last days, many can testify, seem to have been occupied in writing self-contradictory letters concerning how his revolutionary contributions are to be properly interpreted, applied, and modified. Yet, examining the texts of his oral and written second thoughts does *not* lead to the view that Keynes himself was not one of the "Keynesians" Leijonhufvud tries to denigrate.

More important than errors of historical fact is failure to realize that Kuhnian truth that it is "tractable" paradigms with unambiguous content, imperfect though they inevitably must be, which constitute creative science at work. Even if Keynes's 1930 *Treatise* or 1936 *General Theory* or innumerable post-1936 writings had contained more numerous, and more successful, "intuitions" concerning the complexities of uncertainty and money markets of the type that Leijonhufvud glorifies, their importance would have come when a Tobin or a Modigliani or a Leijonhufvud succeeded in extracting from their moonglow a prosaic, tractable, describable, testable, and understandable model or paradigm. Nobel laureate Sir Peter Medawar put the matter well when he insisted that science has to grapple with the tractable.

Keynes, the Merlinian magician, artist, and sage dies when his own heart stops beating; what cannot be passed on to his public and co-workers dies with him. Isaac Newton and Albert Einstein have returned to grass, their bones returned to dust. But their behavior equations live on for scholars, scholars not necessarily possessed of genius, to use and to improve upon. Historians, I came to realize as a young man, never get things quite right; and each generation has a need to fabricate and forge its own myths; just as the Athenians tired of hearing the name of Aristides the Just, there is a modern thirst to put down Keynes. When *Time Magazine* asked me a decade ago, "Is Keynes dead?" I gave the only proper reply: "Yes, Keynes is dead. And so are Newton and Einstein." I suppose I could have added the name of Darwin.

Foreword to Volume 2

A scientist's papers are like his children. To a parent, all children must be equal. But as George Orwell would agree, some are even more equal than others. The theoretical articles in this volume were fun to write, and I must confess I still find them fun to reread.

Somewhere I've quoted my teacher Leontief's remark that you can tell much about a scholar from his first article. This is in the spirit of the myth that no girl ever gets over her first love. Actually, the first papers of Maynard Keynes are nothing remarkable—good, but not transcendentally excellent. Mozart was incapable of bad music but his juvenalia are great primarily as indicators of even greater things to come. My own first paper dealt with measuring utility cardinally from observations of saving by age. It received favorable notice, but it took another decade before my friend and colleague Professor Franco Modigliani made his fundamental breakthrough with his theory of life-cycle savings.

What one admires in a great mind like Euler is the deepening through time of his analytical formulations. A score of years later he will be spiraling upward in his handling of the fundamentals of analytical physics and pure mathematics. I took pride in the fact that my 1958 "Exact-Consumption Long Model" had immeasurably more depth and sophistication than did my first article, which had dealt with that same subject twenty-one years earlier.

My first paper that was perceived to have important originality was the 1938 note launching the theory of revealed preference. I've testified how it grew out of my saucy retort to my teacher Gottfried Habeler. When he said, "But how do you know indifference curves are convex?" I retorted with twenty-two-year-old cheek: "Well, if they're not, the index number theory of your Ph.D. thesis won't be valid." I listened to what my tongue was saying and realized that I could with advantage turn the conventional theory of ordinal utility on its head. Using observed $\sum p^i q^j$ demand-and-budget observational data, I could provide testable axioms that had the same intrinsic content for competitive demand theory that indifference and utility models have.

One should dilute boasts about triumphs with confessions of interesting failure. My 1938 "Weak Axiom of Revealed Preference" was necessary and sufficient for the *two-good* case. I realized that the "integrability problem" of the *three-or-n-good* case required more. I even formulated what the young Hendrik Houtthaker gained proper immortal fame for in his maiden 1950 paper, "Strong Axiom of Revealed Preference." But I was unable to see how to prove this, and none of the great world mathematicians who were my friends at the time were able to respond to my plea for either a proof or a refutation.

Although my *Foundations of Economic Analysis* soft-pedaled the topic of revealed preference, it carried on with emphasis on finite inequalities. This was to be the wave of the future. In the age of Gerard Debreu, the Newton-Weierstrass vanishing of first derivatives and denial of indefiniteness of quadratic forms was often to be replaced by convex-set theory and general topological methods. (In the last decade, under the inspiration of the mathematician S. Smale, the Newtonian slant was to be given a new birth—as conditions that apply "almost everywhere.") The honest scientist realizes he does not start from scratch. He adds value to what his predecessor created. I acknowledge that my inspiration to seek the generality of finite inequalities came from a great teacher and polymath now too little remembered. Edwin Bidwell Wilson was the last disciple of Yale's great Willard Gibbs. A talented mathematician, "E. B." contributed to mathematical physics, statistics, psychometrics, biomedicine, mathematical economics, and was a pioneer in writing down the stability conditions for the newfangled aeroplane. Wilson instilled in me at Harvard Gibbs' search for finite generality. Before convex set theory became fashionable and when I had never heard of a Legendre transformation, I perceived the Gibbsian insight that the nonconvex segments of indifference contours would be avoided by price-taking consumers and would be observationally missing. From these hints and those of Harold Hotelling in 1932, other Harvard theorists and I were well launched into what was to become known as duality theory. Since thermodynamics had enriched my understanding, I made a small repayment in the little-noticed appendix to my 1960 Hotelling *Festschrift* paper, where I suggest a new axiomatic foundation to classical thermodynamics (in the Carathéodory vein). And elsewhere, independently of many another writer, I was able to make sense out of the Le Châtelier principle.

In writing a foreword, I must not abuse the patience of the reader. But permit me some more reminiscences.

You might think that a scientist's best papers receive instant recognition and approbation. Actually, some of mine that have come to gain most reknown were first refused by editors and referees. (The Stolper-Samuelson article on protection and real wages was turned down by the *AER*. The 1958 paper mentioned above encountered rough weather from the *JPE*.) Vexing as this may be in the short run to a proud parent, hostility from the neighbors never succeeds in undermining one's brainchild in one's own eyes. Indeed, my paper on "The St. Petersburg Paradox as a Divergent Double Limit" has remained all the more dear to me despite its failure to engender enthusiasm and notice in most quarters.

My final remarks have to do with how a privileged cardinal utility may be defined from ordinal choices in probability sitautions. The von Neumann and Morgenstern axioms on this I found untempting. Similarly, the Savage-Friedman verbiage was not up to those authors' capabilities. It was Jacob Marschak's 1950 formulation, stimulated I seem to remember by his conversations with the young and brilliant Herman Rubin, that gave one the needed hint. But it was private correspondence with the mathematician [L.] Jimmie Savage that finally converted me to what has subsequently become the standard theory of Ramsey-de Finetti-Savage, that elegant axiomatization of both subjective probability and utility.

Without regard to my own toils in the vineyard, I am struck by the degree to which the work of economists has been fruitful for anyone interested in the philosophical and mathematical terrains of uncertainty and decision making. I laughed when the youthful Robert Solow said to me, "Either you're the sort of person who thinks that probability is the most interesting thing in the world. Or you're not. And if you're not, I feel sorry for you." Thirty-one years later, I do not laugh.

Autobiographers impute too much credit to themselves. I must right the balance by asserting my debts: to my teachers, Jacob Viner, Josef Schumpter, Wassily Leontief, E. B. Wilson, Gottfried Haberler; to fellow students Abram Bergson, Lloyd Metzler, and many others; to fellow scholars Harold Hotelling, Henry Schultz, R. G. D. Allen, John Hicks, Nicholas Georgescu-Roegen—and later, Lionel McKenzie, Herman Wold, Leo Hurwicz, Ronald Shepard, John Chipman, Hendrik Houthakker, Sydney Afriat, Marcel Richter, and many others.

Foreword to Volume 4

This volume on *Economic Dynamics* falls into two main parts. The first part is deterministic rather than stochastic or probabilistic. Its early chapters represent work done in my early twenties, when I led the good life as a Junior Fellow in the Society of Fellows of Harvard University. Along with Garrett Birkhoff and Stan Ulam, world famous mathematicians, with Quine, the mathematical logician, with Bob Woodward and John Bardeen in chemistry and physics, we thought of ourselves as an intellectual aristocracy. Our only duty was to do important research. Most of my *Foundations of Economic Analysis* was written then. But what Pareto started and John Hicks developed, it was my good luck to bring to a final synthesis: how maximization provides a general basis for qualitative comparative statics and how, through the heuristic but seminal "correspondence principle," dynamic stability conditions relate to comparative statics.

My own debts were not primarily to Pareto or Slutsky. Rather they were to the great thermodynamicist, Willard Gibbs of Yale, who served as my symbolic grandfather through the channel of my Harvard master, Edwin Bidwell Wilson, a polymath in physics and statistics, who had been Gibb's last disciple and assistant. Since I owed a debt to thermodynamics for inspiration on how to *deduce* the negativity of firm's demand slope, it pleased me to be able to balance the accounts by providing for thermodynamics a rigorous explanation and derivation of what the Le Châtelier principle was all about. That a specified increase in pressure on a gas would reduce its volume more when its temperature is kept at original room temperature than when the gas is insulated from all heat exchange was seen not to be an ad hoc empiricism but rather a determinantal theorem on definite quadratic forms—a truth only obscurely glimpsed in the great textbooks on classical thermodynamics.

Much of the above work was done in a brief period of youthful inspiration. Not less satisfying was the work on efficient markets and stochastic optimization that makes up this volume's final sections. It is inspiring to see a genius like Euler returning again and again to the same scientific problems, but spiraling upward in elegance and exactitude of understanding. In a more mundane way, I derive pleasure in tracing the evolution of my contributions to ideal speculative price: First, spatial equilibrium; then intertemporal equilibrium in a nonstochastic setting; then the probabilistic generalization of deterministic *equilibrium* in the form of an asymptotic *ergodic* (or "equilibrium") *probability distribution.* The tyranny of mean-variance approximations is repelled; and, by the notion of "compact probabilities," the nature of the approximation is laid bare. My only regret is that many of the related papers must appear in still other volumes.

I would be ungrateful if I did not voice my thanks to Professors Shinohara and Sato for marshaling so distinguished a team of translators. The magnificent King James version of the Bible was the work of a committee, and hereto we have in the vineyard of science another example of a collective creation. I realize how I am blessed and record my thanks.

Foreword to Volume 5

International trade is the flagship of the economic theory fleet. Historically, the theory of general equilibrium owes more to trade theory than trade theory owes to pure theory. I might say with only a little exaggeration: J. S. Mill's 1829–1848 theory of international values is the first complete model of competitive equilibrium, preceding Jevons's 1862–1870 effort and Walras's 1874–1878 breakthrough.

The great names in trade theory can be listed briefly: Hume, Torrens-

Ricardo, J. S. Mill, Mangoldt, Marshall, Edgeworth, Pareto, Taussig, Viner, Haberler, Ohlin, A. P. Lerner, Meade, McKenzie, Metzler, Chipman, Mundell, and a few others. But it was still the case just fifty years ago that the highest authorities were not clear in their minds on the normative and positivistic findings of the subject.

In my own work I learned most from the collaboration with Wolfgang Stolper on *Protection and the Real Wage*. After that the analysis of equalization of factor prices could follow rather naturally.

From my first effort in trade theory I came to appreciate the not-yet-named concept of Pareto optimality. Early on I realized that more could be said on the optimality of free trade than the great masters had managed. But I also realized that you could not treat a country as if it were one person and simply say: "If Robinson Crusoe chooses to trade, he must be better off than under autarchy. Ergo, the same applies to a nation." The convexity notion that underlies the theory of revealed preference, which I was developing in the last half of the 1930s, was seen to give a useful handle to the investigation.

People used to ask, "What use is mathematics in economics?" We need only look at the famous Keynes-Ohlin debates on postwar reparations to see how needed was the kind of discussion provided in my 1952 and 1954 *Economic Journal* papers. (Jacob Viner as editor of the *Journal of Political Economy* had rejected my submission on the subject made around 1937. Scientists are not perfect!)

Science itself is not perfect. And yet generation after generation of scholars can be satisfied with incomplete and erroneous paradigms. An example is Hume's brilliant, but faulty, proof that gold drains will heal themselves via the quantity theory of money. (The last couple of papers of this volume touch on Hume's work while avoiding the familiar errors.) Only a few years ago, in my Sohmen *Festschrift* piece that appeared too late for inclusion in this volume, I elaborated on the correctness of Arnold Collery's view that Hume should never have let readers think that the surfeit of gold in the surplus country could come to raise its price for any freely tradable good above the price for that good in the deficient country (all prices being expressed in a common currency, such as gold, and due allowance for transport costs and tariff impediments being made). The proper theory would work even when all goods are perfectly tradable and have one price everywhere; the proper theory covers nontradables as well as tradables. Also, whether goods are easily or poorly tradable, the correct grain of truth in the *purchasing-power-parity* dogma hinges on the hypothesis that in the longest run the money supply is neutral as far as *real magnitudes* and *nominal ratios* are concerned. These good-sense relations were poorly perceived in the standard literature.

So impregnable is the theory of comparative advantage that it is as valid for socialist as for capitalist societies. Only occasionally have Marxist economists tried to improve upon it, and with disastrous results. Take for example a doctrine like that of "unequal exchange." For a time A. Emmanuel's book of that name had some vogue among French intellectuals. What valid points are scored in it?

Consider the simplest case: A million workers in poor Asia are in trade equilibrium with a million Europeans, importing from the latter their manufactures and exporting to them food and raw materials. The European real wage rate is, say, ten times that of Asia; and the European labor productivity per hour is say twenty times greater in manufactures and five times greater in food. To say that ten hours of Asian labor sells for one hour of European labor says no more and no less than that the European wage is tenfold higher and that the balance of trade is in equilibrium.

What follows for policy? That Asian workers should be welcomed to Europe? That spread of technical knowledge should gradually bring the geographical labor productivities into closer alignment? That the affluent have an ethical imperative to aid the poor? The labor theory of value is of no real help in assessing these issues. Even where the labor theory of value would apply in each continent under autarchy, when trade is possible and labor supplies are geographically immobile, we are then in a two-primary-factor theory of value—as Ricardo sensed and Mill knew. The labor theory of value is destroyed.

When we bring in profit rates, geographically unequal or equalized by capital flows, the labor theory of value is even less applicable. Harmful rather than helpful to understanding is the 1867 Marxian paradigm of *Das Kapital*, which hypothesizes an equal "rate of surplus value" (or percentage markup on direct labor costs alone) in the different industries of a country. What captured the interest of Emmanuel's readers was the false impression they received that somehow a large amount of deadweight loss is entailed by competitive market equilibrium in international trade. Actually, this is incorrect. Intertemporal Pareto optimality can be proved to be a property of perfectly competitive markets. A similar misleading impression tempts the reader when time-phased heterogeneous capital goods are involved in international trade. In the fourth volume of my English *Collected Scientific Papers*, I have discussed reversals of geographical specialization patterns of the following type (and so have other writers, such as J. E. Metcalfe and I. Steedman): At a zero-interest-rate, golden-rule state, Asia has comparative advantage in producing and exporting raw materials while Europe specializes in manufactures. All this is straight Ricardo. But at a common positive interest rate it could be the case that Asia's manufactures are relatively cheaper and that trade patterns reverse. Any readers of Emmanuel who think that this confirms his notion of unequal exchange make a gross error.

True, at the positive-profit-equilibrium, less may be produced and consumed of *every* good, perhaps by everybody. *But that is no valid sign of exploitation or of deadweight loss. It is consistent with intertemporal Pareto optimality.* It is merely an open-economy instance of what can happen under autarchy in a Crusoe economy or under utopian communism. The missing output is not waste, for there is a mathematical theorem affirming that the only way to get from a *non*–golden-rule technology to a golden-rule technology is by going through some sacrifice of current consumptions in favor of more future consumptions. The need for "waiting" or "abstinence" is as unavoidable under socialism as under capitalism—and this truth holds in the most general models of Sraffa and Joan Robinson, where reswitching and Wicksell effects may be present!

Because the principles of interregional trade are so important for human welfare, the political trend toward protection properly worries present-day economists. Our professional counsel was never more needed.

Foreword to Volume 6

Linear programming erupted as a useful theory soon after World War II. Within barely half a dozen years it reached most of the perfection it could ever attain. Economists played an important role in its development, particularly since linear programming had close and reciprocal relationships to game theory and to modern statistical decision theory. Aside from the name of George Dantzig, the discoverer of the practical simplex algorithm, I single out such names as Tjalling Koopmans, L. Kantorovitch, John von Neumann, Jerzy Neyman, Pierre Massé, Abraham Wald, the triplets A. W. Tucker, David Gale, and Harold Kuhn, and F. L. Hitchcock. I realize that some of these names—Neyman and Massé for example—will come as a surprise to informed readers. But as one who lived both before and after the age of inequalities in economic theory, I recall being struck by both of these authors' concern with maximization of one linear expression subject to a constraint on another linear expression.

During the war itself, operations research was born as a discipline of systematic optimization. Physicists, statisticians, economists, and mathematicians pooled their talents. Economics, which had always been valuable for describing how a society works, became practical in its own right: Businessmen and engineers had to set up and solve analytical problems; business schools had to teach future businessmen the rudiments of doing so.

Along with this volume's sampling of my articles related to linear programming, the R. Dorfman, P. Samuelson, and R. Solow book *Linear Programming and Economic Analysis* (McGraw-Hill, New York, 1958) will be of interest. Intuitive literary economists had anticipated the duality theorems of linear and general Kuhn-Tucker programming. At the beginning of the 1930s, Gustav Cassel's limited version of the Walrasian system, with its constant coefficients of production, brought home to economists that a mere counting of equations and unknowns was not enough to ensure the existence of a unique (or of at least one) meaningful equilibrium solution. Negative outputs obviously lacked economic meaning. The Viennese banker Rudolph Schlesinger, was one who worried about the problem. Von Neumann's 1931 *A Model of General Equilibrium* did provide a proof of existence of an equilibrium, but not for a full general equilibrium system. In Germany Hans Neisser, in Denmark Frederik Zeuthen, in England J. R. Hicks, and in America Henry Schultz all developed similar worries. (I recall being told by Neisser that it was an anodyne back in 1932 when Hitler was knocking on the door demanding power to think and correspond about this intellectual problem.) Pursuing economic intuition, Zeuthen and others perceived that, when supply exceeded demand at a zero price, rather than have price go negative, the system would be satisfied to have a free good be in excess supply, as a strong inequality replaced the equilibrium equality condition. Abraham Wald, as a penniless mathematician, was hired by Schlesinger to clear up the matter, and the result was Wald's powerful (if overstrong) proof of uniqueness of equilibrium. Subsequently, convex set methods and fixed point theorems became the preferred method of proving existence of competitive equilibria, as the writings of G. Debreu, K. Arrow, H. Uzawa, L. McKenzie, J. von Neumann, H. Kuhn, H. Scarf, and other moderns have shown.

Both the nonsubstitution theorem and the turnpike theorem go back to my 1948–1949 Guggenheim Fellowship sabbatical. When people extol individualism and deplore subsidized group research, I always point out that the magnificent King James version of the Bible was composed by a committee; that Kenneth Arrow's two Nobel-stature contributions to economics were financed by the Office of Naval Research and the Rand Corporation. I may add that it was at Rand in 1949 that the above two theorems were first enunciated.

I look back with satisfaction on the fourteen items in this volume. One of them, although I did not realize it at the time, had already been discovered in the mathematical literature. Another one I consider a finger exercise for youthful hands. But the other dozen needed doing and were fun to do.

Foreword to Volume 8

Theory and Policy

In my textbook *Economics* I wrote that all the great economists were interested in doing good—with the possible exception of two. Adam

Smith's *Wealth of Nations* was a handbook of economic development. David Ricardo was led to study economics in order to appraise the Corn Law duties on imports and to prescribe for the inflationary overissue of the currency during the Napoleonic Wars. Knut Wicksell, Alfred Marshall, and Leon Walras all began as passionate reformers. John Maynard Keynes ended as one. Although Karl Marx in some moods professed to set down the *scientific* laws of socialist and capitalist development, you will read on his tomb in Highgate Cemetery the thesis on Feuerbach: "Hitherto, the philosophers have only sought to *explain* the world. But the point is to *change* it." Even Vilfredo Pareto and Joseph Schumpeter, my two possible exceptions, pretended to be satisfied with the half loaf of positivistic scientific explanation only after the world refused to go their preferred aristocratic way.

Personally, I have always been concerned with economic policy to improve human welfare. That is the ultimate goal. And making some progress toward that hard goal adds zest to the self-contained pleasures of elegant analysis and magisterial description.

Economists are supposed to become more conservative as they grow older. If so, I am a partial exception to the rule. By my mid-twenties I had outgrown the philosophy of the Manchester School that my teachers at the University of Chicago (Frank Knight, Henry Simons, Jacob Viner, Aaron Director) had preached. With each new decade of life I do not so much become more conservative as become more aware of the stubborn *feasibility constraints* within which successful reform must operate.

I would be sad to notice in myself any atrophying of social sympathies. But I would despise myself for sentimental wishful thinking. To let the warmth of my heart addle my brain and distort my perception of the reality around me would be the ultimate scientific and aesthetic sin—a sure sign of senility.

Although one remains the same, the center of current thought keeps shifting around one. When I was an early Keynesian, my textbook was bitterly attacked by know-nothing reactionaries as dangerously radical. (William F. Buckley, Jr.'s 1951 *God and Man at Yale* was a typical criticism of *Economics*.) Having educated a generation, that same textbook became something of a bible and was often considered a fossil of orthodoxy. (In Australian backwaters there are still activist students who regard Samuelson economics as the doctrine of the establishment devils.)

Actually, as I write in the early 1980s, the economics profession is becoming perceptibly more conservative. The Chicago School, with its simple dogmatisms and attractive program of researchable projects, gains adherents all the time. Many scholars stop short at mere Pareto optimality—as if "efficiency" has an intrinsic meaning and content distinct from "efficiency for what?" All the more important, therefore, are scholars who make it a point of honor never to consider questions of efficiency without at the same time consciously bringing into consideration their bearing on "equity." The fact that *equity* is a hard concept to define so as to command unambiguous agreement is not a reason to ignore it: This is a reason to devote more time to it.

People who read my popular books or columns sometimes ask me the question: "Is there any important relation between your esoteric mathematical researches at the frontier of political economy and your simple commonsense writings on economic policy?" My honest answer is yes.

Good sense is hard to come by. You recognize it only after you have it. Much fancy theorizing has to be its own reward, radiating beautiful light yet not emanating heat to power the engines of policy. But occasionally, often when you least expect it, a beautiful model illuminates a complicated problem of practical policy. Of many possible examples, I shall mention only one.

In 1958 I wrote one of my favorite theoretical papers, "An Exact Consumption-Loan Model of Interest with or without the Social Contrivance of Money." Even in my own eyes it broke new theoretical ground and, autobiographically, I was pleased to realize that in the brilliance of my early twenties I could not have contrived this product of my forties. My present point is that this analytical breakthrough—which gave economists a handle on intergenerational transfers between those who are now young and old and who will in the next period be old and dead—proves to be the indispensable tool for understanding the problems of *social security* under different population trends.

Policy owes much to economic theory. But it is a two-sided exchange. The history of economics shows that the quandaries of policy have splashed the theorist with the challenges needed to fructify his efforts. That is why, as Keynes knew, political economy is such a satisfying science to pursue as a life career. It holds its own proudly in the good company of mathematics, physics, and biology.

Foreword to Volume 9

This volume translates papers in which I discuss the great: Ricardo, Marx, Keynes, Schumpeter, ...—the living as well as the dead. It is fun. But what makes it greater fun is that it is serious, too.

Thus I take Marx seriously. I don't revere him (or anyone else); chew over his quotations; insult him by fulsome praise that never comes to grips with the logic and the empirical relevance of his economics for this century or the last. Like Joan Robinson, I pay Marx the compliment of treating him like any contemporary scholar.

Like Macaulay I award grades to earlier writers: an *A*+ for Smith and Walras and Keynes; strong *A*'s for Hume, Ricardo, J. S. Hill, Jevons, Pareto, Wicksell, and Marshall. Like Whig historians, the standards I try to use in judging a writer's innovations for their own times are those of the best in economics of the present day. This, I know, is not the only way to study history of science. And, since I am a mainstream modern economist, I realize this gives rise to the special weightings that people who know my work will expect and allow for. Fifty years hence, new graders will give new grades. My job is to anticipate as best I can what the later jury will conclude. As I turn these pages, what interests me may interest you. Here are a few sample reactions.

1. Robert K. Merton, the sociologist who innovated the sociology of science, has taught us not to be surprised that a Leibnitz is anticipated by a Newton or a Wallace by a Darwin. Doubletons and multiple quasi-independent discoveries are to be expected rather than singletons in science. So it is little wonder that my 1946 obituary essay on Keynes and the *General Theory* should have foreshadowed some of the 1962 Kuhnian notions of how one ruling paradigm is finally displaced by another: "It takes another theory to kill a theory—not merely a bold fact." "Funeral by funeral science advances," is my Planckian aphorism. Merton will not marvel that my 1961 AEA Presidential Address should record anticipations of his finding: so to speak," ... scholars work for the only coin worth having—our own applause."

2. These after-dinner ventures into history of economists and autobiography are like a fruitcake: packed with inside stories and nutmeats, laced with high spirits. When the IEA came to publish my 1968 Montreal Presidential ruminations on the economist's way, the Secretary-General came to me in perplexity: "The editor of the French version of the World Congress proceedings claims your address is untranslatable. What shall we do?" Reminding him of Robert Frost's definition of poetry as what evaporates in translation, I suggested, "Do the best you can with the prose." I wonder whether the Japanese version will live up to what I wrote in the first sentence of my 1967 foreword to the Japanese version of my *Foundations*: "The only thing better than a classic is its Japanese translation." If Hegel in French is clearer than in the original, perhaps new poetry will creep into Samuelson prose à la Japanese.

3. David Ricardo, like Alfred Marshall, goes down in my book as a bit overpraised. But rereading my physiocratic version of the Ricardian system, I still find it good and not yet overpriced in the bourse of economic opinions. Where land is the only primary bottleneck; where labor is producible at

constant cost out of classicists' subsistence "corn"; and where Ricardo, Mill, and Smith hypothesized that capital goods will only cease accumulating net at some specifiable long-run level of the profit or interest rate—there the land theory of value will usurp the sovereignty of the popular labor theory of value. Every good will then sell at its total socially necessary *land content* (direct plus indirect and with inputs marked up à la compound interest at the long-term subsistence-profit rate). That is not inconsistent with this: All goods that don't require land (directly or indirectly in any way other than through labor) will *also* sell at their socially necessary embodied labor requirements; but this last is a more superficial and subordinate truism. For the physiocratic Ricardian model, the famous nonsubstitution theorem holds: Changes in composition of final demands have no long-term effects on relative (land-quanta) prices!

Even when we relax this strict Ricardian version, we realize how naive Ricardo would have to be to think that he could save a meaningful labor theory of value by "getting rid of the complication of land" through the device of concentrating on the *external* margin of no-rent land. I could hardly believe my eyes when I read the editors' introduction to Sraffa's edition of Ricardo's *Principles*: Could the sophisticated Pierro Sraffa be taken in by such a palpable boner concerning the use of the external margin? My perplexity abated when recently reading some autobiographical lines by the late Maurice Dobb in the *Cambridge Journal of Economics*. There I learned that Dobb rather than Sraffa has written this introduction!

Doctrinal history aside, as soon as goods require primary land as well as primary labor, the crude nonsubstitution theory fails, and the embodied labor and land requirements of each unit of each good become *endogenous* equilibrium unknowns rather than *exogenous* explanatory parameters. The labor theory of value simply fails. (And when we abandon a subsistence theory of wages as wildly unrealistic, so does Ricardo's physiocratic land theory of value fail.) "Good riddance," says the serious student of income distribution.

4. It was not land that economists usually argued about in criticizing the labor theory of value. What they worried about was interest or profit, and how that modified mere wage costs in a realistic world of *time-phased* applications of labor and produced-goods' inputs. The point is obvious. Smith saw it; Ricardo couldn't avoid it, even in the last months of his life when he tried unsuccessfully to find a defense for his labor theory of value. Shrimp picked up on the shore by direct labor alone and the wood for tall shipmasts from ancient trees—their relative prices had to be shifted by changes in the profit or interest rate even when labor inputs stayed the same. Malthus saw that. Torrens saw that. It didn't take a Böhm-Bawerk to see that. Macaulay's schoolboy saw it, and so did Hans Christian

Andersen's truthful child. Sraffa's 1960 discovery of a "standard commodity (basket)" alters this fact not a whit.

So, what Ricardo hoped to avoid he couldn't avoid: To explain the distribution of national income between wages and profits, he had to grapple with the complications of commodity-demand theory. For, if tastes shifted from shrimp to masts, or from shrimp-*cum*-masts today to those goods in the future, relative prices and factor shares would *endogenously* change. When Stigler seconded the defense of Ricardo's labor theory of value as a "93% (correct) theory of value," he betrayed his affection for the man and conceded the untenability of Ricardo's labor-theory-of-value hankerings.

The test of the decadence of a subject is this: After the last word has been said, does the literature cycle back on itself and repeat ... repeat ...?

I pass on to Marx.

5. Twenty some years ago I wrote articles for the *Nihon Keizai Shimbun* on a puzzle: Why, from the 1920s on, did Japanese intellectuals become captivated by Marx? After two articles, which Paul Sweezy pointed out to me still didn't solve the puzzle, I gave up on the third. I still don't know the answer. But the fact remains: Whereas not 10 percent of economists in the United States, Britain, and Western Europe know or care much about Marxian economics, some half of Japanese academic economists eschew mainstream economics in favor of Marxian economics.

From 1900, when Keynes began to study economics, to 1946, when he died, no specter of Marxian economics haunted the reveries of Anglo-Saxon economists. Perhaps J. B. Clark, Böhm-Bawerk, and neoclassicals of a century ago were haunted by the specter of Karl Marx. I would like to see the case for this documented one way or the other. But when Joan Robinson turned to study *Das Kapital* in the World War II era, that was a tribute to her curiosity and catholicity, not a reflection of the *Zeitgeist*. To most of my teachers—Schumpeter and Leontief were exceptions, but they were foreigners!—Marx was a bore, not a bogeyman. Paul Sweezy's interest in Marx, even if it had arisen in 1929 when the threat of communism was dormant, would I dare say not have won him tenure at Harvard any more than would have an esoteric interest in St. Thomas Aquinas.

Abba Lerner considered himself a socialist, even at one time an admirer of Trotsky. But the study of economics at the LSE cured him of any real interest in Marx. Kei Shibata and Oskar Lange alone in the 1930s put up a case for Marx that mainstream economists found worth debating. Mainstream economics, they in effect said, is good at microeconomic realism; under stationary capitalistic business-cycle ebbs and flows, it is even good at macroeconomic prediction and control. It wins hands down under such *statical* conditions. But, argued Shibata and Lange, Marxian economics is superior in explaining the "laws of motion" and long-term development of the capitalistic system (economy and governmental structure). At dynamics, Marxian economics, they thought, wins the palm. So, the reader is to infer, some convex combination of mainstream and Marxian economics would eventually win out as the best academic political economy.

That hypothesis I have always found interesting. What were the 1850–1939 trends of history? What are the likely 1940–1990 patterns? How can we best explain past, present, and likely future structures of economic inequality?

A student once said: "Professor Samuelson, you would be afraid to become a Marxian even if your observations and reason told you it is a superior mode of analysis." I replied (in what I think was an honest and candid way): "I would take aid from the Devil if that would help crack the puzzle of economic reality. I have professional tenure. My books have given me financial independence. Having made one reputation in mainstream economics, I could only benefit from being first to make a second one working the other side of the street. Besides, if the political climate got rough, I am Machiavellian enough to work out of the closet: Gaining insights by Marxian magic, I could forge language and symbolism to disguise their origin, passing them off as a new variant of mainstream economics."

So, I continue to read and reread Marx. And Engels, Luxemburg, Lenin, Hilferding, Bortkiewicz, Bauer, Kalecki, Sweezy, Dobb, Tsuru, Robinson, Baran, Meek, Morishima, Johansen, Okishio, Mandcl, Stcadman, Pasinetti, von Weizsäcker, Emmanuel, and many more. Were it not a harmless hobby, I must confess that I would have to apologize for the time spent. I do not get my principal back in terms of real-world insights, much less earn an opportunity-cost surplus yield on my invested time.

To my non-Japanese readers I have never elaborated this finding:

> When one has corrected false syllogisms about the "transformation problem," or even assumed the validity of key approximations (such as equality of all industries' organic compositions of capital), I am *not* advanced in the understanding of the trends of the mixed economy (or of capitalism in the advanced or underdeveloped worlds) by the s_j/v_j ratios of Marxian surplus value. Neither dynamic competitive capitalism nor monopoly capitalism yield their secrets to the skeleton key of Marxian modeling. To understand the Lorenz curves and Pareto parameters of unequal distributions of wealth and income, I am only thrown off by the matrix bickering of modern Marxian discourse (to which bickering I might be said to have contributed my own mit).

Let me give three examples. (1) Getty and Sheik X of the Persian Gulf are billionaries. Natural resource fortunes built the dormitories and chapels of the great American universities. Where in volumes 1, 2 or 3, in the *Grundrisse* or in the *Manifesto*, do I glimpse modes of understanding for these basic phenomena?

(2) Edwin Land of Polaroid camera fame or David Packard of the Hewlett-Packard electronics company typify America's post–World War II elite, with their hundreds of millions of dollars of new wealth. Joseph Schumpeter might help me understand them. So might Graham and Dodd's textbook of security analysis. Lenin's imperialism? Luxemburg's accumulation of capital? Garenagni's reswitching? Of what help are these?

(3) The Mitsuis, Mitsubishis, or land-appreciation fortunes of Japan call out for explication. The "reserve army of the unemployed," "the law of the falling rate of profit," "the law of immiserization of the working classes," "the law of Moses to accumulate and accumulate"—what light do these euphonious phrases cast on that which is to be seen and which needs to be understood?

No real light of understanding has *ever* come from the Marxian novelties of analysis. Here are a few examples. Let us waive the question of whether there is a meaningful tendency for the rate of profit to fall under capitalism. Even if there were, it is sterile to try to "explain this" by appealing to an alleged tendency for some organic-composition-of-capital ratio, $\sum c_j/\sum v_j$, to rise.

Indeed, as late as 1959, I had to rescue the Marxian literature from the delusion that *both* the rate of profit and the real wage could by law have a tendency to fall in a competitive market model involving labor as the only primary factor of production. To provide the needed rescue, neoclassical or Sraffian methods turned out to be superior to Marxian methods.

My original purpose in writing up my lecture on the transformation problem was not to show up Marx's own error. Or even to correct it. Rather I gave for the first time a set of conditions under which Marx's faulty algorithm would in fact be nontrivially correct. And *even then*, it was my intention to show, there turn out to be *no* insights into the nature of wage exploitation and its laws of motion of development under capitalism to be derived from Marx's model of equalized s_i/v_i ratios—Marx's one point of purported innovation aimed to improve on bourgeois economics. Thus, even if one agrees with Meek and Baumol that Marx's purpose was to "explain" the total of capitalist profits, $\sum S_j$, and the profit rate, $\sum S_j/\sum(C_j + V_j)$, by means of Marx's new concept of equalized rates of surplus values, s_i/v_i, he actually failed in that purpose and by logic was necessarily bound to fail. Professor Morishima—who is a national treasure: nay, an international treasure—has given in his classic book much of interest to a modern Marxian. But, so far I have been able to find no reason to change my mind on this all-vital point.

Too often Marxian vectoral calculus is the opiate of the Marxians (and the anti-Marxians who labor in the *hope* of producing value). Mao was a great leader. Yet his words of wisdom on economics might shame a sophomore (something that, I fear, might be said also of the great genius Albert Einstein!). But I must not complain about vectoral mathematics. The *Journal of Economic Literature* asked me whether they should publish a detailed account of the literary thoughts of a certain great Japanese Marxian scholar. I counseled yes. But, when I came to study those pages, I was forced to wonder whether the results justified the space used up. Not Russia, China, Yugoslavia, America, Japan or 1844 Manchester seemed illuminated by the discourse. Even the mindless statistics of Wesley Clair Mitchell and the German Historical School seem easier to defend against the complaints of overworked students than the sterilities of semantic word chopping. Few read that *JEL* article. And in most of them it led to supercilious depreciation.

If the nineteenth-century model of Marx fails to explain statical and dynamical facts, is it perhaps still worthwhile as a tool for *normative control* in the good society of the future? No, alas. As Lerner and Lange, Ramsey and Koopmans, Kantorovitch and Danzig have elaborated, the efficiency shadow prices of utopia must systematically deviate from the labor values of *Capital's* volume I, and must do so in the direction of Böhm-Bawerk's critique of the labor theory of value. (That is, the optimal approach to the golden-rule state and the pricing appropriate to resource allocation in it, must, whether or not reswitching and other phenomena obtain, mimic the general equilibrium solution of a specifiable competitive market system. Since perfectionism is not feasible, pragmatic planning will compromise with certain approximations and rules of thumb in which intertemporal price-and-profit ratios play a role.)

I must not abuse the hospitality of the editors with too long an overture. So I invite the reader on.

368

FOREWORD

Mathematics is the handmaiden of the sciences. But mathematics also has a life of her own, gaining as much in her own development and fulfillment from the sciences as she gives to them. To help describe how apples and planets fall, and how ropes hang, Newton and Leibniz developed the calculus. By serendipity, that mode of analysis permitted economists to perfect the theory of general equilibrium two centuries later.

Sometimes the logical tools are forged long before their practical use becomes apparent. The calculus of variations was formulated in the eighteenth century and, in its classical form, perfected a century ago. Lying dormant for decades, it was brought back to life by the kiss of the dynamic programmer in pursuit of optimal control. Quaternions were something of an anticlimax until the spin matrices of quantum mechanics brought them back into vogue. Albert Einstein's quest for a general theory of relativity was helped by the fortuitous earlier development of the Ricci tensor calculus. Applied researchers even reinvent the wheel, as when Werner Heisenberg's rules for combining the elements in the array of quantum observables turned out to mimic the rules for matrix multiplication. Probability theory would remain a rather dry branch of measure theory were it not for its usefulness in describing how dice fall, multitudes die, and atoms collide.

Barely a century ago, the Norwegian Sophus Lie developed the theory of what have come to be called *Lie transformation groups*. Their original primary application was to the classical mechanics of Lagrange and Hamilton. Now Ryuzo Sato of Brown University is making a pioneering attempt to apply the Lie theory to modern economics. Here are only a few of his explorations.

1. It is popular to speak of "labor-saving inventions," which enable nine men to do the work of ten. This is the special case of a "factor-augmenting invention," in which land or labor or any input becomes equivalent in efficiency to a multiple of itself. Dr. Sato treats such technical processes, and more general ones, as examples of Lie groups.

2. I once posed the open question: What demand functions are *self-dual*, in the sense that their natural duals have *exactly the same mathematical form as themselves?* (The unit-elastic Cobb–Douglas case, in which any good's relative expenditure $p_i q_i / I = k_i$, is an obvious case; but what other cases are there in which

$$\mathbf{q} = \mathbf{f}(\mathbf{y}), \qquad \mathbf{y} = \mathbf{f}(\mathbf{q}),$$

$$\mathbf{q} = [q_1, \ldots, q_n], \qquad \mathbf{y} = [p_1/\sum_1^n p_j q_j, \ldots, p_n/\sum_1^n p_j q_j],$$

and $\mathbf{f}(\mathbf{y}) = [f_1(\mathbf{y}), \ldots, f_n(\mathbf{y})]$?) Dr. Sato, using the methods of Lie groups, has extended the answers given by Professor Wahidul Haque and others.

3. Here is the final example from a long list of possible examples. Along an intertemporally efficient path of a *closed* von Neumann system, in which every good of a set of goods and its rate of growth are producible out of those *same goods as inputs* by a *constant-returns-to-scale* technology, the ratio of the total value of the capital goods to total income is a fundamental constant. Dr. Sato now shows that this 1970 finding of mine is essentially the only "energy integral" that such a dynamic system can in general possess.

I believe that Ryuzo Sato is the only scholar who has studied the application of Lie groups to economics. Not until economists have given his impressive treatise a thorough reading shall we be in a position to put useful bounds on the value added to economics by this powerful and elegant technique. The ball is now in our court.

Massachusetts Institute of Technology PAUL A. SAMUELSON

PART VIII

Current Economics and Policy

3 The World Economy at Century's End

Paul A. Samuelson

USA

I FUTUROLOGY

George Bernard Shaw declared, 'Those who can, do. Those who can't, teach'. Today's cynic says, 'Those who are able to predict, make their econometric forecasts. Those who can't, become futurologists'. So, at the beginning, let us make a deposition that no scientist can pinpoint the distant future with any accuracy. What separates the sage from the dilettante is the plausibility of the odds quoted, the degree of interest and relevance in the tale told. History has shown us that the luck of clowns has often beaten that of sages. But for every number on the wheel there is some clown to give it backing; and so, once again, we must judge the worth of a prophet by the *ex ante* plausibility of his model.

1980 is twenty years from the twenty-first century. To discern the road ahead whom should I learn from? Nostradamus is not my cup of tea. There is really nothing in Adam Smith, David Ricardo, or even Robert Malthus that will serve my purpose. The world does not have a rendezvous with a classical steady state characterised by population just big enough to yield minimum subsistence wages.

Can the vision of Karl Marx be my guide? Since Marx was writing more than a century ago, it would be no fair criticism of him if we found his paradigms obsolete. But, actually, the laws of motion of the capitalistic system as recorded in the economic historians' annals for the century after the 1867 publication of *Das Kapital* are not those sung by Karl Marx; nor are the recorded patterns of real output and wage/property income shares deducible from the Marxian paradigms of surplus value and organic composition of capital. Marx, the political scientist, merits a better report-card grade than Marx the political economist. At least one-third of humanity lives under socialism; and nowhere, not even in Switzerland or Chicago, does anyone live under laissez faire nineteenth-century style.

Many are called as prophets. Henry Adams, Oswald Spengler, Leon Trotsky and Pitrim Sorokin, Arnold Toynbee, John Maynard Keynes, Friedrich Hayek, Joseph Schumpeter, Herman Kahn, the Club of Rome. Though many are called, few are chosen as seers by the score-keeping historian.

II KEYNES AND THE CONQUEST OF POVERTY

Not all prophets are equally bad. As Justice Oliver Wendell Holmes would put it, the cynicism of Joseph Schumpeter gives us a better run for our money than the mysticisms of Arnold Toynbee. Forty years after Friedrich Hayek wrote down his nightmare of the welfare state leading remorselessly to the totalitarian murder of freedom, Scandinavians enjoy freedom second to none that the world has ever seen; and, contrary to the logic of *The Road to Serfdom*; societies such as Chile and Singapore with maximal market freedoms live under dictatorships that suppress civil liberties.

For the purpose of today's discussion, I want to concentrate on the visions for the future of two great economists: John Maynard Keynes and Joseph Schumpeter. Each was born in 1883, the year that Karl Marx died. Each died not long after the Second World War.

Of the two, Keynes was the more optimistic. In 1930, before the Great Depression, Keynes wrote a remarkable essay called, 'Economic Possibilities for our Grandchildren'. He looked ahead for onc hundred years – to the period I am focusing on today. He prophesised that by the early twenty-first century the stock of capital would have doubled, and doubled again, and redoubled still once more. As Keynes points out, there is nothing remarkable in this, only the grinding away over a long time of compound-interest growth at 2 per cent per annum. Reinforcing the accumulation of capital, Keynes predicted, would be technological innovation, the fruits of science, engineering and managerial rationalisation. With population under volitional control, this had to mean a four-to-eight fold increase in per capita living standards in progressive countries.

So, three decades before Galbraith, Keynes foretold the withering away of the problem of economic scarcity. Four decades before the sociobiology of Edward O. Wilson, Keynes warned that the human race had evolved in the grim Darwinian struggle for existence. He worried whether, once the machine freed us from the necessity to fight for our daily bread, our muscles would go flaccid and our boredom would drive us into a collective nervous breakdown. Anomie, neurosis, soft and hard drugs in the affluent suburbs – all these fit in nicely with the Keynesian horoscope.

In fact, Keynes correctly foretold the miracle progress that the modern mixed economy actually enjoyed in the third quarter of the twentieth century. I have checked his back-of-the-envelope econometrics against the recorded findings of Simon Kuznets and Colin Clark, and it is remarkable how lucky Keynes turned out to be in his extrapolations.

But it is only in fairy tales that one can write down the ending: 'And so they lived happily ever afterwards'. Just as Karl Marx ended up historic history with a classless society in which the state had withered away and resources somehow got themselves economically organised, so the paradigm of Keynes ends in a kind of Swedish utopia. In this utopia the successful interactions of the accelerator and the multiplier are brought about by the not-for-profit Bank of England and they serve to free the Bloomsbury élite to spend their days in artistic creation and their nights in the pleasures of friendship.

III SCHUMPETER'S SCHIZOPHRENIC SCHEMATA

Perhaps in 1965, under the spell of John F. Kennedy's Camelot, one could have confidence in the verisimilitude of the Keynesian trajectory of economic development. In 1980, with the disappointing memories of the 1970s fresh in mind, the darker horoscope of Joseph Schumpeter gains in relevance. Schumpeter wrote *Capitalism, Socialism and Democracy* a decade after Keynes presented his vision of the future. The Great Depression showed Schumpeter how prone the political systems of Europe and North America were to depart from the conventional patterns and practices of constitutional democracy. Since Joseph Schumpeter had earlier lived through the decay of the feudal society in Austria-Hungary, and had observed with some distaste its replacement by fragile bourgeois establishments, he was better prepared than most of us for the happenings of the Hitlerian age.

You must also remember that Schumpeter was isolated in Cambridge, Massachusetts during the Second World War. Students were few. Most of his colleagues had been called into the war effort. Living in

Cambridge and commuting to Cornwall, Connecticut, Schumpeter was not in very close touch with how the war was actually proceeding. Thus, I can testify from personal memory, that as late as 1943 or 1944 Schumpeter still expected that Hitler would end up victorious. When the actual reality came to be realised, he was saddened by the expectation that the Soviet Union would be the true victor of the war. In Schumpeter's view, we had been engaged with the wrong ally in fighting the wrong enemy. Since Joseph Schumpeter was not a very diplomatic person and since he took pleasure in shocking people, you can be sure that his views were not very popular in those wartime days.

I think it would be wrong, however, to believe that Schumpeter's view of the future was formulated after 1940. If we read him with care, we can see that already in the 1920s Schumpeter had arrived at the following schemata of history.

SCHUMPETER'S AXIOM 1: THE ECONOMIC SYSTEM ITSELF IS ESSENTIALLY STABLE

Walrasian general equilibrium always has a solution and such a solution would be capable of realising itself if the political and sociological system would permit economic laws to operate.

To be sure, Schumpeter had a dynamic theory of innovation and development. Entrepreneurial innovation, which Schumpeter associated with a particular sociological type, would be enabled by the money-creating banking system to upset and disturb the Walrasian equilibrium. Booms and high temporary profits would result from bursts of innovation. But then the mills of imitative competition would grind fine and erode away the transient profits. In all likelihood the return to Walrasian equilibrium would be accompanied by an overshot. But, in time, a laissez-faire capitalistic system would find its way back to a new Walrasian equilibrium with a higher standard of living, shared by workers and owners of natural resources.

I gloss over as not important for the present purpose the hoopla that Schumpeter liked to make about the different cyclical rhythms of capitalism. He took more seriously than a grown man should, the taxonomy of Kondratieff long waves, Juglar major business cycles averaging about eight years in duration, and the forty-month Kitchin–Crum shorter business cycles. His two-volume 1938 *Business Cycles* book goes into all this, but it never really commanded much attention in those first heady days of the Keynesian Revolution. And as Schumpeter himself fully recognised, it would not materially affect the validity of his underlying vision if the reader rejected Schumpeter's belief in superimposed business cycles. I may add that a disbelief in Schumpeter's zero-interest steady state need also have no material effect upon our acceptance or rejection of Schumpeter's vision of the innovational development process of creative destruction.

Before proceeding to Schumpeter's Axiom 2 from his Axiom 1 about the stability of the economic system in purely economic terms, I ought to point out that this part of Schumpeter pretty much agrees with Keynes's 1930 horoscope. In writing up his 1942 book, Schumpeter may have forgotten Keynes's 1930 arithmetic. But on his own he constructs a similar compound-interest accumulation of capital that is helped in stimulating productivity by an ongoing process of technological change. With a wave of his hand Schumpeter dismisses as preposterous the post-1936 Keynesians' worry over the possibility of saving being in excess of investment. Keynes in 1930 can be forgiven for not being concerned with the dilemma of an economy that stagnates below its full-employment potential because of a mismatch between saving propensities and motivated investment opportunities. Schumpeter can claim no similar defence when he airily dismisses the stagnationist apprehensions of post-Keynesian writers. Here Homer nods badly. Instead of invoking theoretical arguments of the Pigou-effect type, or marshalling anti-Hansen empirical trends in George Terborgh's manner, Schumpeter merely asserts that most saving activity is itself motivated by investment opportunity. So, depression psychology aside, Schumpeter claims that consumption will spontaneously rise to fill the gap whenever investment fails to be buoyant. For once, the ebullient Schumpeter shows his age.

There is one minor difference between the optimisms of Keynes and Schumpeter. Keynes in 1930 is really talking about the future successes not of capitalism but of what we have since come to call *the Mixed Economy*. Schumpeter, by contrast, is dealing with the polar case of *unfettered capitalism*. This archetypical mode is set up by Schumpeter not as a projection of what is likely to prevail in the future, but precisely as a contrafactual stalking horse to help make his point concerning the political demise of capitalism. This leads me to Schumpeter's Axiom 2, with its Hegelian negation of his Axiom 1.

SCHUMPETER'S AXIOM 2

Although the capitalistic system is *economically* stable, capitalism is essentially *politically unstable.*

The very successes of market capitalism in delivering the goods of material progress, Schumpeter proclaimed, would lead to capitalism's undoing. That rationality of capitalism which makes for productivity will serve to corrode the irrational sentiments of social cohesiveness. The spoiled children of affluence will reject their parents and heritage. Their self-hate will lead to boredom and anomie. As I mentioned in my 1970 Nobel Lecture, Schumpeter, like Keynes, was an early sociobiologist. He believed that the economic problem of scarcity had selectively evolved the fitter modes of rational thinking. The need to be *homo economicus* was the Darwinian struggle that created *homo sapiens.*

As *Capitalism, Socialism and Democracy* approaches its fortieth birthday, what stands up best in its analysis is this striking thesis of Schumpeter that capitalism's very success will be its undoing. Joseph Schumpeter, looking down from Valhalla on the Iranian revolution against the Shah, must be crowing, 'I told you so!' In his view the same fate would have been meted out to Peter the Great were it not that the feudal elements of superstition and religion conspired to protect Peter from the Shah's destiny.

Schumpeter, like Thorstein Veblen, does not really document conclusively the interesting dogmas that he promulgates. Like Oliver Twist, we readers ask for 'More'.

Back in 1969, that Vietnam War era of New Left student revolts on American campuses, I wrote a column for *Newsweek* entitled 'Memories'. It dealt with the great evening in my life back at Harvard forty years ago when giants walked the earth in the Harvard Yard. Because of its relevance to the outlook for 1999, permit me to quote my *Newsweek* words.

> Joseph Schumpeter, Harvard's brilliant economist and social prophet, was to debate Paul Sweezy on 'The Future of Capitalism'. Wassily Leontief was in the chair as moderator, and the Littauer Auditorium could not accommodate the packed house.
>
> Let me set the stage. Schumpeter was a scion of the aristocracy of Franz Josef's Austria. It was Schumpeter who had confessed to three wishes in life: to be the greatest lover in Vienna, the best horseman in Europe, and the greatest economist in the world. 'But, unfortunately,' as he used to say modestly, 'the seat I inherited was never of the topmost caliber.'
>
> Half mountebank, half sage, Schumpeter had been the *enfant terrible* of the Austrian school of economists. Steward to an Egyptian princess, owner of a stable of race horses, onetime Finance Minister of Austria, Schumpeter could look at the prospects for bourgeois society

with the objectivity of one whose feudal world had come to an end in 1914. His message and vision can be read in his classical work of a quarter century ago, *Capitalism, Socialism, and Democracy.*

WHOM THE GODS ENVY

Opposed to the foxy Merlin was young Sir Galahad. Son of an executive of J. P. Morgan's bank, Paul Sweezy was the best that Exeter and Harvard can produce. Tiring of the 'gentlemen's C' and of the good life at Locke-Ober's with Lucius Beebe, Sweezy had early established himself as among the most promising of the economists of his generation. But tiring of the conventional wisdom of his age, and spurred on by the events of the Great Depression, Sweezy became one of America's few Marxists. (As he used to say, you could count the noses of American academic economists who were Marxists on the thumbs of your two hands: the late Paul Baran of Stanford; and, in an occasional summer school of unwonted tolerance, Paul Sweezy.)

Unfairly, the gods had given Paul Sweezy, along with a brilliant mind, a beautiful face and wit. With what William Buckley would desperately wish to see in his mirror, Sweezy faced the world. If lightning had struck him that night, people would truly have said that he had incurred the envy of the gods.

So much for the cast. I would have to be William Hazlitt to recall for you the interchange of wit, the neat parrying and thrust, and all made the more pleasurable by the obvious affection that the two men had for each other despite the polar opposition of their views.

MEETING OF OPPOSITES

Great debaters deserve great moderators, and that night Leontief was in fine form. At the end he fairly summarized the viewpoints expressed.

'The patient is capitalism. What is to be his fate? Our speakers are in fact agreed that the patient is inevitably dying. But the bases of their diagnoses could not be more different.

'On the one hand there is Sweezy, who utilizes the analysis of Marx and of Lenin to deduce that the patient is dying of a malignant cancer. Absolutely no operation can help. The end is foreordained.

'On the other hand, there is Schumpeter. He, too, and rather cheerfully, admits that the patient is dying. (His sweetheart already died in 1914 and his bank of tears had long since run dry.) But to

Schumpeter, the patient is dying of a psychosomatic ailment. Not cancer but neurosis is the patient's complaint. Filled with self-hate, he has lost the will to live.

'In this view capitalism is an unlovable system, and what is unlovable will not be loved. Paul Sweezy himself is a talisman and omen of that alienation which will seal the system's doom.'

All this I had long forgotten. And a few years ago when I reread Schumpeter's book, I graded him down for his gloomy views on the progress that would be made by the mixed economy – capitalism in an oxygen tent, as Schumpeter put it. His failure to predict the miraculous progress of the postwar years earned Schumpeter a C in my eyes. However, 1969 university happenings reveal an alienation of privileged youth entitling Schumpeter to a report-card recount.

IV THE MIRACULOUS MID-CENTURY SPRINT

How are we to judge the respective merits of the views about the future in Keynes and Schumpeter? What would be most useful about my evaluation of these great economists resides in the fact that describing their hits and misses is an instructive way of formulating my own hunches about the years still ahead.

First, Keynes and Schumpeter did a pretty good job in estimating what modern economists call 'the trend of potential GNP' for the advanced nations of the world. This is not a task of superhuman complexity. Lay persons, and some crochety professionals, do manage to make gross errors in this regard. Mad dreamers see the end of the world at hand each weekend. Science fiction writers foretell incredible improvements in the standard of living just around the corner, and they find a ready audience among those disaffected with the here-and-now. But the sober analysis of statistical trends by a Simon Kuznets or Arthur Okun tells a less exciting but more credible tale. The greatest economists of my lifetime have been extraordinarily wise in guessing by rule of thumb what the more elaborate models of the cliometricians will derive after tedious calculation.

On the whole I judge that Schumpeter substantially underestimated the actual performance of the world economy in the third quarter of the twentieth century. His point was that 'fettered capitalism – capitalism in an oxygen tent' – could viably survive. But I do not see that he had the imagination or luck to perceive in advance the actual economic miracle enjoyed by Germany and Japan, Sweden and Switzerland, Western Europe generally and in particular the original Common Market countries.

This magnificent performance, if Schumpeter had been apprised of it, by the logic of his thought he would have had to regard as taking place *despite* the encroachment of the mixed economy on the prerogatives of market capitalism. I, by the advantage of hindsight, am forced to the quite opposing conclusion that the miracle decades of the 1950s and 1960s were actually *enhanced* by those encroachments of the mixed economy on laissez faire capitalism. Japan Inc. has neither the Walrasian structure of perfect competition nor the oligopolistic structure of Schumpeter's dynamic monopoly capitalism. The bureaucracy of the Bank of Japan and MITI played a vital role in the miracle.

All around the world, the post-Keynesian environment provided macroeconomic stimulus to employment and gave effective protection against deflation and persisting slump. After the successful Marshall Plan and MacArthur occupation of Japan, the ultimate fragilities of the Bretton Woods mechanism for a long time escaped recognition. In a fool's paradise, dollar undervaluation turned into dollar overvaluation, a disequilibrium that was papered over for the decade of the 1960s by uneasy acceptance of a flood of dollar IOUs.

I have often pondered over this basic question: Why did not Western Europe catch up with the United States after the First World War in the way that came to pass after the Second World War? I cannot fault Schumpeter for failing to prophesy this remarkable overtaking of America. But that failure does reveal him to be only human.

Sweden is an example I often use to calibrate Schumpeter's insights and outsights. Sweden may yet confirm Schumpeter's cynical pessimism, but if so Schumpeter's pessimism was certainly enunciated twenty-five years too early. From 1945 to 1970 neutral Sweden pulled off a veritable hat trick. Eschewing Schumpeter's old-fashioned socialism in the form of a governmental ownership of the means of production, Sweden achieved much egalitarianism by means of expanded tax-financed welfare payments. What is remarkable is the fact that she was able *to redivide the social pie without reducing its size or slowing down its rate of growth.* Fair shares coexisted with 8 per cent annual improvements in manufacturing productivity – something that Australians and New Zealanders only dream about but which rarely gets confirmed in the history books of any nation.

Alas, poor Hayek! His 1945 readers were quite unprepared for the statistical triumphs recorded a score of years later in the annals of the

OECD. Latter-day Marxists had to counter the demonstrated augmentations of proletarian real wage increases by the complaint 'What is material prosperity to an *alienated* worker?' Similarly, Doctors Hayek and Friedman on the right have had to take a leaf from the book of Ludwig von Mises and pooh-pooh as meaningless the index numbers of soaring real output calculated for economies like those in Western Europe which substantially second-guess the market place. And when that fails to serve as a sufficient discount, it is still open to them to complain, 'What is material prosperity to individuals who have lost their libertarian freedoms?'

V INEVITABILITY OF SOCIALISM?

To live is to change one's mind. Not uncommonly a sage will come to repudiate his own earlier classic. I could document from my own personal contacts with Joseph Schumpeter that he no longer believed in the 1940s what he taught me on my first 1935 afternoon in the Harvard Graduate School – namely that no large company like Du Pont or General Motors could continue to stay on top under the onslaught of new innovators. In his later writings Schumpeter was converted to the view that the modern large corporation has in a sense acquired the secret of perpetual youth and innovational rejuvenation.

But we happen to know that, up to the evening before he died, Schumpeter continued to believe that capitalism was on course to its rendezvous with socialism. Schumpeter's death was that which is a gift of the Gods. He died at his battle station, scholar's quill in hand, at the peak of his powers. He had all but finished the penultimate paragraph of his American Economic Association speech entitled 'The March to Socialism'. For once Schumpeter was trapped into the conventional wisdom. And it will help us peer with the rest of this decade's future if we engage in unsparing analysis of where Schumpeter may have gone wrong in his extrapolations.

Socialism may once have had a simple definition where the state owned the means of production – the land and mines, the factories and tools, inventories of raw materials and finished goods – that was socialism. By contrast under capitalism land, labour and capital goods were all privately owned and got allocated through the push-shove equilibrium of market competitions.

All this would have been understood by early socialist writers, by such Fabians as the Webbs and Shaw, and by the followers of Marx. They, and their capitalist critics, would have agreed that the October Revolution of Lenin converted Tsarist capitalism into socialism. And they would have agreed that an evolutionary acquisition by the British Government of ownership of the coal mines, railroads, banks and steel mills would have represented a march along the road from capitalism to socialism.

If you interpret Schumpeter's confident prediction that capitalism was on its way to socialism to mean that he expected the third quarter of the twentieth century to witness a burgeoning of governmental takeovers of the means of production, then we would have to award Schumpeter a failing grade on his forecast.

I believe Schumpeter realised this point. But he never really seemed to have clarified his thinking on the matter. When you broaden your definition of socialism so that you cannot be caught out in technical error, you may make the concept so fuzzy as to rob it of much of its usefulness.

Here is a personal anecdote to illuminate Schumpeter's ambiguities. Once at a cocktail party he said to me: 'I'd expect a socialist like you to believe that'. I was quite taken aback, being genuinely surprised, and asked, 'Do you really take me to be a socialist, Joe?' I pressed the point beyond that of perfunctory politeness to clear up my understanding of what Schumpeter's general views were. 'After all', I pointed out, 'I was brought up by the Chicago School under Frank Knight and Henry Simons. I first resisted the Keynesian revolution in macroeconomics. Do you regard anyone who believes in fiscal policy stabilisation and in New Deal welfare programmes as a socialist? By what single criterion would you, after knowing me these many years, define me to be a socialist?'

Schumpeter squirmed a bit. After all he was a polite man, and diplomatic behaviour does not compel unsparing truth. Finally, Schumpeter explained, 'My dear Paul, I was merely making reference to what you will not deny, that you lack respect for the pietistic verities of capitalism'.

There I must admit he had me. I fear I lack respect for most things; it is an imperfection in my nature. But leaving personalities, notice how broadening the definition of socialist to cover those who are cynical or even objective about capitalism – notice how this trivialises the proposition that, in the last half of the twentieth century, socialism will come to prevail.

For one thing it reduces to a redundant tautology Schumpeter's proposition that ideological disaffection with capitalism will create socialism. Disaffection cannot be said to create disaffection: disaffection *is* disaffection just as a rose is a rose and two and two are four, propositions not capable of being empirically refuted or meaningfully corroborated.

Somewhere Schumpeter proposes a more useful broadening of the word 'socialism' beyond its original connotation of state ownership of the means of production. He speaks of 'an extension of the public sector at the expense of the private sector' as constituting an extension of socialism. But in using this terminology Schumpeter comes back to being very close to Keynes and the New Deal liberals in the American sense of the word liberal. In the Schumpeter–Sweezy debate I referred to, it sounded ominous when Schumpeter predicted that the patient was dying even if only of a psychosomatic ailment. Death is, after all, no joke. But his listeners would have been less enthralled by his diagnosis if he had patiently explained to them that all he meant to say was that the patient was turning over a new leaf, entering upon a new life of jogging and vitamins and noble thinking along mixed economy lines.

I must repeat that Schumpeter's thought was confused. He really did not expect the mixed economy, whose evolution he correctly perceived, to be a well-functioning and stable way of running the railroad of modern social living. The fact that Schumpeter was, on the whole, wrong in this regard for the third quarter of the century should not blind us to the possibility that some of the malfunctionings he feared may be looming up more closely ahead in the last quarter of this century.

VI LATIN AMERICA AS PARADIGM

The human mind thinks in terms of overdramatic case-studies. I suggest that to understand the future there may be a more useful paradigm than that suggested by Scandinavia, the Netherlands, or a typical mixed economy of Western Europe or North America. I am not proposing that we concentrate on the Yugoslavian experiment or on the pattern of an Eastern European economy such as Hungary or Poland. Instead I have in mind the Latin American example.

Suppose someone in 1945 had asked: 'What part of the world do you expect to experience the most dramatic take-off in the next three decades?' Probably I would have given an answer something like the following: 'Argentina is the wave of the future. It has a temperate climate. Its density of population provides a favourable natural resource endowment per employee. By historical accident its present population is the fairly homogeneous progeny of Western European nations. And

Argentina is in 1945 at that intermediate stage of development from which rapid growth is most easily expected.'

How wrong I would have been. Nor would my prophecy have been much better if I had substituted Chile for Argentina. In point of fact the southernmost countries of Latin America have fallen most markedly below their post-war potentials for development. The reasons do not seem to be narrowly economic. We cannot explain what has happened by appeal to Malthus's law of diminishing returns. There has been no exogenous shift in world demands peculiarly unfavourable to that region of the world. Their sickness, Schumpeter would claim, is political and sociological rather than economic. It has to do with the breakdown of social consensus. It has to do with the workings out of the logic of populist democracy. A conservative like Schumpeter or Pareto or Sorel would agree in their diagnoses with the class-struggle analyses of Marxian writers. But with this difference. The Marxians would welcome battling between classes that gums up the working of capitalism. This is part of the temporary labour pains necessary if the benevolent permanent condition of communism is to get born. For Pareto and Schumpeter, by contrast, the death throes of the achieving market economy have the inevitability of a Greek tragedy, but are nevertheless in themselves pointless and regrettable.

Not being an expert on Latin America, I cannot pretend to give a definitive interpretation of its political malaise. It is superficial to blame the lack of progress on the dictator Juan Péron. Years after Péron had left Argentina, and before his return, chronic inflation and stagnating growth characterised that part of the world. It is ironical that Uruguay was once called the Switzerland of Latin America. (It is ironical in a different sort of way that Lebanon was once called the Switzerland of the Near East.)

VII THE WAY WE LIVE NOW

Oslo, Washington and New Delhi are a long way from Buenos Aires and Santiago. But is it far-fetched, as we try to peer into the decades just ahead and do so against the backdrop of the 1970's era of worldwide stagflation, to fear that many of our mixed economies will begin to suffer from their own version of the Argentinian sickness?

My implicit prediction is not that the recent inflation rates of 5 to 20 per cent will be revving up in the decade ahead to the South American rates of 30 to 200 per cent per annum. I do not regard that as particularly likely and it is not an essential part of my thesis that it should occur.

My point is a deeper one. We have eaten of the fruit of the Tree of Knowledge. Whether for Schumpeter's reason that capitalist success must breed alienation from it or for other reasons that I will advance, democratic societies do not adhere to self-denying practices and let the Walrasian game of pure economics play itself out. *The same self-interest that provided the gasoline to make the classical game of markets operate must be expected in today's political sphere to motivate interferences with the laissez faire scenario.*

This could be dignified as a theorem of von Neumann's theory of games.

> Social equilibrium à la Queen Victoria or Calvin Coolidge is unstable. If all groups but one adhere to its modes of behaviour, then it definitely pays the remaining persons to form a collusion and use the state to depart from the laissez faire beloved by Ludwig von Mises or Fredric Bastiat.

It will not do to object to my implication with the riposte: 'But if all collusions and cliques try to second-guess the market, they may well *all* end up worse off than where Smith's Invisible (and unthinking) Hand would have taken them'. For it is also a theorem in the theory of non-zero-sum games that the Golden Rule state, which would make everybody happiest if all uniformly adhered to it, may itself be unstable. If some adhere to the behaviour it calls for, it pays others to depart from it in their own interest. Religion and superstition are invoked to propagandise for the Golden Rule precisely to alleviate this incipient instability.

Do not interpret me as saying that the mixed economy is intrinsically bad. It is not my belief that *any* interferences with laissez faire are on balance harmful. The neo-classical economists of goodwill had a noble and feasible vision. They advocated redistributive taxation and transfers to reduce the stark inequalities of laissez faire. Marshall, Wicksell and Pigou are instances in point. Economists also advocated macroeconomic stabilisation, whether of the Irving Fisher 1920 variety, the Keynes–Ohlin 1937 variety, or the Tobin–Friedman 1980 variety. And do-gooders like me envisage a role in the mixed economy for democratic policies designed to influence the fraction of high-employment GNP going to capital formation, and envision a measure of democratic planning to deal with externalities and probabalistic problems of the future.

All this is a noble vision, most of you will allow. But what guarantee is there that the forces of democracy will converge to those interferences with the market economy that are nicely optimal, forsaking all other temptations that involve deadweight loss and distortion?

Our reason does raise doubts. Experience, alas, does not quell these doubts. Examine the history of half a hundred former colonies that have achieved national independence in our time. For how many of them has the date of emancipation coincided with a Rostovian takeoff in the economic sphere? You know how sad the brute facts are in this domain. Even after we allow for a shake-down period of decline, the mismatch between performance and aspiration embalmed in formal five-year plans is painfully evident.

VIII STAGFLATION AS AN INHERENT FEATURE OF THE MIXED ECONOMY

My concern is not that of an élitist looking down with pity on the immaturities of developing countries. The bell I fear to be hearing tolls for the most affluent countries of North America and Western Europe – and also for Japan and Australia.

At this very moment the United States is in a genuine recession, and much of the world is in a growth recession. Well, what is so unusual about that? The history of capitalism was a history of boom and bust. There is the difference that *this recession is one deliberately contrived by governments*. If you had attended in this last year conferences of international economic authorities, you would have found that most of the central bankers and treasury officials present, to say nothing of a thinner majority of the academics in attendance, hoped for a recessionary slowdown. The reason is plain. They viewed the 'flation' part of the modern disease of stagflation as a greater evil than the 'stag' part. Neither their experience nor their reason tempted them to advocate mandatory price and wage controls as a better antidote than a contrived slowdown. A secondary factor reinforcing their advocacy was their hope that OPEC prices might be better contained if a deceleration of world activity lowered the demand for energy.

It is my thesis that stagflation is an intrinsic characteristic of the mixed economy. Back in 1973, I prepared a memorandum on *Worldwide Stagflation* for the West German Council of Economic Advisors. In it I gave a pessimistic diagnosis of the modern disease of stagflation. I hope my thesis is wrong, because it is so fundamental and traces the roots of stagflation into the basic nature of the modern welfare state. In summary, I attribute the mixed economy's stagflation to the fact that ours is now a humane society in which the presence of unemployment and industrial slack is not permitted to have the downward repercussion on prices and wages that was characteristic of the cruel and ruthless capitalism of the history books.

I would think it a mistake to regard West Germany, Switzerland and Japan as immune to the scourge of stagflation. It is true that elderly bankers all over the world envy these three countries for their relative degree of success in avoiding accelerating two-digit price inflation. Switzerland has even for brief periods enjoyed stable prices. West Germany averaged an inflation rate in the late 1970s of below 4 per cent. Japan's price index could not match these stellar performances but until recently was able to do better than most OECD countries.

But do not forget that this success on the price level front was purchased by all three countries at a fairly heavy cost in terms of vigour of output growth. The production index in Switzerland has barely recovered to the pre-1973 level. For the decade of the 1970s real GNP growth in West Germany was slightly worse than that of the United States, and in the last half of the decade was definitely worse. If Switzerland and West Germany had not been able to sweep some of their unemployment under the rug by putting its burden on guest-workers, the crusade against inflation would have lost some of its adherents. Although it is true that Japan continues to display more rapid real growth than the other principal OECD countries, when I calculate how much Japan has fallen below its extrapolated trend profile, I estimate that the cost has been fairly steep for her to fight stagflation.

In concluding I must record the guess that world growth in the last quarter of the century must be estimated to be lower than that in the third quarter. My colleague Charles P. Kindleberger is a coiner of expressive titles. Kindleberger speaks of the 'menopausal economy'. This is not Wagnerian *Götterdämmerung*. Progress ebbs not with a bang but with a whimper.

Such biological analogues may offer an expressive tag, but they provide no true explanation. Opium puts you to sleep because of its dormative property. We age because of our aging. Modern economics can hope to do better than that by way of analysis.

Undoubtedly one reason for slower growth ahead is the fivefold increase in the real OPEC price of energy. This is usually called a cartel price, but to me what requires explanation is not so much why the price is now high as why the oil price was so very low in the years preceeding

1973.[1] Today's OPEC price may be more what economists ought to call competitive price than monopoly price. The major competitive cost is not the few dollars needed to suck oil out of the ground. The basic marginal cost is that of future alternative use. If all oil were auctioned off the way all wheat is, I would guess its price would vary from $20 to $80 a barrel from month to month. A Three Mile Island incident that clouds the future of nuclear energy everywhere except in the Soviet Union and China, would rationally raise the equilibrium price of oil by several tens of dollars. The ability and willingness of Saudi Arabia to provide the umbrella of price stability is the one feature of OPEC that does smack of monopolistic cartel rather than competition. To sum up, beside oil, other natural resources will presumably set limits on average global growth now that so many countries have achieved the stage of industrialisation that exhausts irreplaceable resources at a rapid rate.

As a second factor making for deceleration in future growth rates, there is the let-up in effort and discipline that comes from affluence itself. It is rational, not irrational, for Swedes and Americans to take longer vacations, slow down the work pace on the job, talk back to the foreman, and neglect the fine arts of spelling and algebra. South Korean workers are hungrier than Belgian workers and some of their technological disadvantage can be offset by this factor of personal eagerness. As Germans and Japanese prosper, they too will in all likelihood acquire the stigmata of affluence.

There is a third, less certain, reason for slower productivity change ahead. Schumpeter's process of innovation and technical change reached its zenith during the Second World War and the catch-up period thereafter. History is always a race between the law of diminishing returns and the discovery of scientists. The rate of advance in pure science and applied engineering is far from a stationary time-series. It is quite unpredictable in its oscillations, and these oscillations are not at all like a white-noise process. The temporary period of Schumpeterian monopoly power to extort the rents of innovation becomes a shorter period in this age of rapid communication and public regulation. All in all, we cannot count with any confidence on a renewed burst of productivity emanating from scientists, engineers and managers.

[1] I think those prices were below true competitive price. My hypothesis to explain this hinges on the fact that the dozen giant oil companies could not count on their property rights to drill for oil at the optimal rate. So, ignoring true (future) opportunity cost, they rushed to produce oil at more than warrantable competitive rate in the pre-OPEC days.

IX THE DEVIL'S FIX THAT DOES NOT FIX

Clever members of my audience will have discerned one possible solution to the dilemmas of the mixed economy that I have dwelled upon. Vilfredo Pareto was a clever man. And so was Georges Sorel. Reading between Schumpeter's lines, I believe we can see that the same solution as theirs was tacitly in his mind even though it was only on a few private occasions that Joseph Schumpeter drew as advocate the obvious moral from his own insight.

What I am alluding to is of course the fascist solution. If the efficient market is politically unstable, then fascist sympathisers conclude: '*Get rid of democracy and impose upon society the market regime*. Never mind that trade unions must be emasculated and pesky intellectuals put into jail or exile.'

The 1980 Eleventh Edition of my *Economics* has a new section devoted to the distasteful subject of capitalist fascism. So to speak, if Chile and the Chicago boys had not existed, we should have had to invent them as a paradigm. It is relevant to quote some of my words – the more so because conservatives who dislike how democracy works out are unwilling to follow their logic to the fascist conclusion these days and use constitutional limits on taxation as their form of imposed capitalism. Here are the words to describe fascistic capitalism:

> Generals and admirals take power. They wipe out their leftist predecessors, exile opponents, jail dissident intellectuals, curb the trade-unions, and control the press and all political activity.
>
> But, in this variant of market fascism, the military leaders stay out of the economy. *They* don't plan and don't take bribes. They turn over all economics to religious zealots – zealots whose religion is the laissez faire market, zealots who also take no bribes. (Opponents of the Chilean regime somewhat unfairly called this group 'the Chicago Boys,' in recognition that many of them had been trained or influenced by University of Chicago economists who favored free markets.)
>
> Then the clock of history is turned back. The market is set free, and the money supply is strictly controlled. Without welfare transfer payments, workers must work or starve. Those unemployed now hold down the growth of the competitive wage rate. Inflation may well be reduced if not wiped out.
>
> If the production index rises and foreign investments pour in, what is

there to complain about? Political freedom aside, *there does tend to be a significant increase in the degree of inequality of incomes, consumption, and wealth* under the archetypical pattern here envisaged.
EXAMPLE: The World Bank almanac shows superlative real growth for Brazil in the 1970s: but it also shows that the lowest 20 per cent of the population there receive only 2 per cent of total household incomes, while the highest 20 per cent are getting 67 per cent – an unusual disparity.

What do Brazil, South Korea, Singapore, Mexico and Taiwan have in common? They are regarded as examples of *successfully developing countries*. Their manufacturing grows and captures markets in the affluent nations and the LDCs. But they are also *one-party political systems, some of them outright dictatorships*.

I do not wish to leave you with the impression that fascistic capitalism is a good thing, or even that it will work. What do Mussolini, Nkruma, Sukarno, Amin, Khan and the Shah have in common? All of them were dictators who professed to make the trains run on time and to promote the growth of the GNP. For a time some of them even seemed to succeed in their purpose, but I need to quote my textbook final words on imposed Capitalism:

> History records no known case where fascism succeeds, even on its own economic terms, for any sustained period. Alas, such systems cannot evolve into normal democracies. Their business freedoms are maintainable only by being *imposed* on the populistic voters. The dictators dare not ease up on repression. They never know how much dissent is being bottled up. As in Iran, it is only later that one learns how class divisions have been festering and widening.

X DREAMING

Personally, I must agree with Winston Churchill when he said that although democracy is not a very good system, it is nevertheless better than any other system. My dream is to make the mixed economy work better.

We must try not to shrink the social pie and kill off its growth by our struggles over the dividing of the pie. The goal is the old Marshallian one of using a cool head to realise the aspirations of a warm heart.

Is it utopian to retain and promote the *humane* qualities of the *mixed economy* while conserving the *efficiencies* of the market mechanism? Yes, it is utopian. But the rational pursuit of this goal provides our generation of economists with a worthy challenge.

REFERENCES

Keynes, J. M. (1930). 'Economic Possibilities for our Grandchildren', in *Essays in Persuasion* (London: Macmillan, 1933).
Schumpeter, J. A. (1942, 1947). *Capitalism, Socialism and Democracy* (New York: Harper & Row).
Samuelson, P. A. (1973). 'Worldwide Stagflation', reproduced in *Collected Scientific Papers* of Paul A. Samuelson, Vol. IV, H. Nagatani and K. Crowley (eds) (Cambridge, Mass.: MIT Press, 1977), Chapter 268, 801–7.
—— 1980. *Economics*, 11th edn (New York: McGraw-Hill), pp. 815–16.

ACKNOWLEDGEMENT

The editor and publishers are grateful to *Newsweek* for permission to quote the extract from 'Memories' by Paul Samuelson. Copyright 1969 by Newsweek, Inc.

PAUL A. SAMUELSON

Evaluating Reaganomics

It is possible that Ronald Reagan's landslide victory in 1980 will be reckoned by historians to be the second most important American electoral triumph in the twentieth century—second only to Franklin Roosevelt's 1932 victory over Herbert Hoover that culminated in the New Deal and the welfare state. Whether or not the conservative attempt succeeds in moving the United States back toward the pre-1929 pattern of market capitalism, with limited government regulatory and transfer operations, thc Rcagan program did begin with a challenge to conventional mainstream economics.

The story is not over. But what does the evidence on Reaganomics suggest so far? Are economists like me obsolete, fossils who perhaps do not even know that they are fossils? Was the Keynesian revolution all a big mistake—at best a temporary concession to transient populist distress, at worst a half-century detour from the main road of correct economic science?

It is hard to bc nonpartisan about contemporary policy issues; value judgments so easily contaminate one's positivistic descriptions, interpretations, and forecasts. Nonetheless, I shall do my best. You are forewarned because you know me as a post-Keynesian, a one-time adviser to Adlai Stevenson and John F. Kennedy, an unrepentant idolator of Franklin Delano Roosevelt.

I caution at the beginning that my present task is not to evaluate the merits of eclectic post-Keynesianism against the merits of such contesting paradigms as monetarism, rational expectationism, Marxism, Kenneth Galbraithism, and much else. That is a hard task but one worth doing. It is a job, however, for the seminar room and the computer console. Treatises and monographs, rather than the spoken word in a public

PAUL A. SAMUELSON is Institute Professor of Economics at M.I.T. This article was presented as the Horowitz Lecture in Tel Aviv, March 8, 1984.

lecture, are requisites for so mighty a task. Reaganomics is the object my microscope is focused on here.

A melange of views

Reaganomics is not a coherent program. Certainly you could not put Ronald Reagan on a psychoanalyst's couch and, by interrogating him on what he believes, identify just what the content of Reaganomics really is.

Nor is there one economic adviser of the President whose views approximate closely to the core of Reaganomics. His last chief economic adviser, Professor Martin Feldstein of Harvard, does not agree with much of Reaganomics. But Feldstein's academic predecessor, whose name you will have forgotten, also found himself uncomfortable with much that went under the name of Reaganomics.

We are confronted with a doctrine that is less than the sum of its partly-cancelling parts. All one can do is enumerate some of the factions that have sought to formulate the Administration's policies. This is a task that a gossip columnist can do as well as or better than I. But only someone like me can relate these competing blocs to the doctrinal schools of thought that characterize modern economic science.

• *Business interests*. Reagan, an ideologue at the right wing of the Republican party, has from the beginning received support from business interests in California and Texas. They play hard political ball. Their ideology is minimal; self-interest sums it up. Laissez-faire and Chicago-style market economics are what they champion for the most part. But they have not had to read Hayek, Friedman, or Knight—or had to ponder over Harberger's consumer-surplus triangles of deadweight loss—to arrive at their positions. And they will as naturally seek a quota or tariff as buy cheap and sell dear, and will do so without the slightest feeling of ideological inconsistency.

I do not imply that there is something special about a conservative government's being responsive to the desires and interests of people of property. That's the nature of the beast of government. When a Democratic administration is in office, the special desires of trade unions and of various lower-income groups receive more favorable attention. On the whole, the record of the Reagan Administration in resisting protectionist pressures has been no worse than that of Democrats and may well have been somewhat better.

When a Reagan appointee—be it James Watt or Ann Burford—gets in terrible disrepute with the general public for some flagrant kowtowing to private interests, don't think for a moment that the President has been unlucky in his appointments. These officials, like much of the cabinet, subcabinet, and independent agency bureaucracy, were selected for their positions precisely because they could be counted on to favor a drastic reversal of previous practices. Only when carrying out these duties results in actions that are more than the political market will bear does the press become aware of what is going on all the time.

• *The Chicago-school wing*. American academic economics is becoming increasingly conservative. Anyone who believes that the economics profession is shot through with leftists has not recently attended a meeting of the Western Economic Association or done content analysis of our leading learned journals. Pareto optimality preoccupies much of microeconomics. What the schoolmen called distributive justice is not where the action is today.

That someone like Milton Friedman, confronted with the alternatives to Ronald Reagan, should think well of Reagan comes as no surprise. This admiration, as is so often the case in life, is reciprocated. Both adhere to the philosophical tenet that a strictly limited government role in the GNP is a good thing—a good thing in itself and quite beside the improvement in economic efficiency that it will entail. Personal freedom, and in significant degree that means freedom from government, is an ultimate good, perhaps even the ultimate good.

Professor Friedman, of course, represents many things. Aside from having within him elements of Knightian doctrines, he is an exponent of that special paradigm of macroeconomics called monetarism. Although Ronald Reagan goes whole hours not thinking about the Granger-causality of M_1 and M_2, his Treasury does contain a Beryl Sprinkel and his Council of Economic Advisers does have a William Poole. On the whole, the Reagan team has given its vague blessings to the Federal Reserve when it has seemed to be approximating to some version of the monetarist rule about steady-growing money supply—except when Reagan supply-siders and election-worriers have disliked the recessionary stagnation entailed by the corset of monetarism.

The wing of elderly conservatives who are obsessed with restoring the gold standard has been repulsed by the Reagan economists, who by and large favor floating exchange rates. I am about to describe the Reagan supply-siders, who do incline toward Robert Mundell's regime of stable exchange rates; but, as the conservative counterrevolution devours its young, these supply-siders were the first to go.

• *Radical-right supply-siders*. What received the most publicity as most novel in Reaganomics was what was called supply-side economics. The prominent names here include Arthur Laffer, Congressman Jack Kemp, the old David Stockman, Paul Craig Roberts, Norman Ture, and still others.

These supply-siders did not have very distinguished academic credentials. Laffer himself first rose to public prominence when, for Nixon's secretary of the Treasury, George Shultz, he prepared (with David Ransom) a famous $1,084-billion prediction for GNP that seemed enormously high to Nixon's chief economic adviser, the mainstream conservative scholar Paul McCracken. This forecast, which was perhaps the first to employ some of the techniques of the school we now call rational expectations, was proved in the event to be as excessive as the consensus forecasters of the time had judged it to be. (Later revisions made its numbers less ridiculous, but its implied *gains* were not borne out by the revised numbers, and that is what counts in judging a forecast.) This first venture in forecasting by rational expectations foreshadowed the irrational bloopers that this school's crystal ball has so characteristically generated on those relatively few occasions when its practitioners have chanced their arm in the hazardous game of predictions.

(Otto Eckstein's Data Resources, Inc. has for many months presented alternative economic forecasts based on Robert Barro's model involving economic surprises in the growth of the money supply. The squared errors of predictions have been Gargantuan in size and irrational in composition. Related methods of forecasting by Claremont Associates of John Rutledge and others were sought by the new Reagan Administration, but the results occasioned no loss of sleep or failure of nerve on the part of the consensus forecasters and their old-fangled Keynesian macromodels. Less unlucky has been the H.C. Wainright group in Boston, which attempts to derive benefit from rational expectations. I shall come later to the qualitative batting averages of the leading rational expectationists.)

Supply-side economics is not a new story; such Keynesian stalwarts as Robert Solow (estimator of econometric production functions) and Arthur Okun (of Okun's Law fame) long worked this furrow. And a long list of scholars—including Simon Kuznets, Colin Clark, John Kendrick, Moses Abramovitz, Edward Denison, and Angus Maddison—have investigated what contribution capital formation (human and tangible) and technical innovation and development can make to a society's productivity. This standard supply-side economics deals with long and slow processes that shape a society's progress.

Kemp-Laffer-Stockman supply-side economics is a different thing. Its authors prepared for the new President an initial document, declaring that he had inherited a crisis situation (a "Dunkirk") due to governmental overregulation and disastrous overtaxation. A dramatic program of deregulation and tax reduction would be the kiss to bring back to vigorous life the sleeping beauty of American capitalism.

The famous Laffer Curve, revealed not on stone tablets but on the back of a Chinese restaurant's menu, argued the impeccable logical syllogism: if the tax rates are zero, total tax receipts are zero; if tax rates are excessively high, bordering on taking all, tax receipts are again zero. Somewhere in between, at the zenith of the arch formed by two branches of the taxation curve, revenues are at their maximum.

To this banality was added the gratuitous premise that America in 1980 was in fact already deep into the falling branch of the curve. So, less is more; cutting tax rates for three years running would raise, rather than lower, tax collections. It would reduce inherited Keynesian deficits rather than add to them.

Whatever the merits and the rationalizations, Reaganomics started out by forcing through Congress massive tax cuts: three-year Kemp-Roth income tax cuts; fast depreciation; and other corporate tax-incentive benefits.

Can the supply-side logic have prevailed? Keynesian liberals like me testified before congressional committees that there was no cogent evidence in economic history, nor plausible presumption in sensible analytics, for the contentions of the radical-right supply-siders. Conventional conservative economists like Alan Greenspan, Herbert Stein, and Arthur Burns for once made common cause with the Solows, Modiglianis, and Tobins in warning against the rashness of massive tax cuts before one knew what the economic conditions would be like in 1981–84. Even Professor Feldstein, enamored as he was of the favorable *substitution* effects on incentives that would follow from tax cuts on corporations and the high-bracket taxpayers, testified in favor of delaying final decisions on the later-year cuts.

All to no avail. Why? Because the Laffer logic was convincing? I doubt that its economic logic explains the story.

Wall Street, in early 1981, panted for the tax cuts simply for their favorable *income* effects.

White House tacticians knew that the President's landslide victory was not yet a mandate. Strike while the iron's hot, was their watchword.

Wall Street misgivings and a Reagan recession

Economists like Friedman were long on record as believing tax cuts always to be in season. They discerned a law of politics: whatever the rascals in Washington are given in tax revenues, they will spend. Cut down on what they are given, then, as a lever to force down what they spend. You will note that Friedman could believe the Laffer argument to be 180 degrees wrong and still join with the supply-siders in favoring the three-year Kemp-Roth tax cuts.

The Achilles heel of this ploy to cut tax rates to force down spending lay in the fact that a sovereign nation can finance expenditures out of deficits. To borrow back the phrase that Paul Volcker took from me, Reaganomics involved a game of Russian roulette. If the revenue slashes induced commensurate slashes in nondefense welfare spending, a conservative could argue that the game had a favorable outcome. But if, as actually happened, revenues were decimated in defiance of Laffer's Law and that shortfall did not force from a Democratic Congress the desired Reagan-Friedman expenditure cuts, then the harmful bullet came up.

Once Wall Street got its heart's desire, it quickly worked out the consequences. The tax cuts meant huge structural deficits ahead. They meant high nominal and real interest rates. They meant the crowding out of some would-be domestic investors by the need to finance Treasury bonds. They meant interest rates high enough here to attract foreign savings, a process likely to bid up an American dollar already overvalued on current account. With the dollar dear relative to the mark and yen, jobs in our export and manufacturing industries would become even harder to get than in typical periods of recession and crusading against inflation.

So, immediately in mid-1981, Wall Street did what came naturally. It dumped its bonds, bidding up interest rates in the process and knocking down the housing industry (which had in any case hardly recovered from the 1980 Carter recession).

Reaganomics thus gave America the Reagan Recession of 1981–82. The new President had inherited an economy recovering from the short 1980 recession. Within only a year, an exceptionally short lifespan for a postwar expansion, Reaganomics was able to abort the recovery. To be sure, Volcker's Federal Reserve aided and abetted the operation. But it did so with the blessing of the Reagan team, the only protesters being the supply-siders who out-Keynesed the Keyserlings in their obsession with expansion.

Rationalizations of early failure

By autumn of 1981 it became evident that the claims of Lafferism were not going to materialize, and that a large structural deficit would be the harvest of the Reagan tax cuts. The three major paradigms of macroeconomics reacted in different ways to provide interpretations of what the effects of the deficit would be.

The simple Keynesian view is that a larger deficit will mean, other things equal, lower unemployment and higher real product. Since the economy was recognized to be in recession, post-Keynesians like me testified before congressional committees in early 1982 along the following lines:

1. We told you so, that Reaganomics wouldn't work out as promised. Events are right on target.

2. Since the economy has already suffered the effects of the Reagan deficits on interest rates, let us at least get the program's benefits in employment. So enact the 1982 tax cuts, but reserve judgment about whether the 1983 cuts should go into effect.

Monetarists (Beryl Sprinkel being a typical spokesman) defended the Reagan deficits along the following lines. All that matters for aggregate demand is the size and growth rate of the money supply. So the deficit and the debt as such do not matter, provided that the Federal Reserve does the right thing. The right thing, of course, involves adhering to a strict money-growth *rule*, with no bending in the direction of financing the deficit out of contrived increments in the money supply.

This quoted argument adheres closely to the views on money and aggregate demand of Milton Friedman, as expressed for example in the *International Encyclo-*

pedia of the Social Sciences. But what is good monetarism is bad neoclassical economics.

Secretary of the Treasury Donald Regan—surprisingly, for a recruit from Merrill Lynch—hewed to the line put out by the Treasury staff that there would be no "crowding-out effect" from enlarged deficits. If fiscal policy has no interest-rate effects and the money supply is controlled by the Fed, then there would indeed be no reason for deficits to impinge on aggregate demand.

But what is there in monetarism to make a monetarist deny that systematic budget deficits affect the market-clearing interest rates at which investment balances out with reduced total saving propensities? Nothing. Even Milton Friedman expects large deficits to affect the mixture of aggregate investment and aggregate consumption at the natural rate of unemployment.

A monetarist who admits that there is a crowding-out effect and an enhanced interest rate ought to recognize, on neoclassical grounds, that the velocity of circulation of money will speed up when the opportunity cost of one's cash balance is high in terms of sacrificed yield on alternative earning assets. So such a monetarist ought to recognize, after all, that a large deficit does tend to raise nominal GNP.

But how could such a sensible monetarist be differentiated from an eclectic post-Keynesian? The late Harry Johnson, who had a stochastic position on monetarism—some months he castigated it, some months he defended it—argued at the 1970 World Econometric Congress in Cambridge, England that monetarism had at least generated subtle, sophisticated analyses and measurements of the demand for money. James Tobin, rising to the opportunity, replied with the citation of a dozen studies of the demand for money, all but one of which identified a systematic positive correlation between velocity and the interest rate. The one exceptional scholar, who claimed not to be able to find any such appreciable positive correlation, was Milton Friedman.

A third strand of defensive argument appealed to the rational expectations paradigm of Robert Barro, Thomas Sargent, and Robert Lucas. Using an argument associated with Barro, which had earlier been deduced in Robert Hall's doctoral dissertation at MIT, some defenders of Reaganomics denied any interest-rate or crowding-out effects of structural deficits. Rational people, they contended, who could foresee the higher future taxes that would be put on them and their heirs to service and pay off the accumulating deficits, would reduce their private thriftiness by exactly as much as public thriftlessness was augmented by the deficit. David Ricardo had used similar reasoning to argue that people who live forever will realize that they are not a penny richer because they own the public debt. Although Ricardo was notoriously foolish in confounding short-run practicalities with long-run theoretical possibilities, he was much more cautious than modern supporters of Barro and warned against accepting his argument as being fully applicable.

Since the many taxpayers I knew were not cutting down on their consumption by as much as their share of the deficit in order to leave their heirs as well off as if there were to be no future public debt, I could not believe that respected economists took this argument seriously. I burst out laughing when one of the ablest young macroeconomists put it to me.

"You don't believe that," I asserted.

"Indeed I do, and so do all the good economists under forty," I was told.

We used to expect graduate students to lose all good sense for a spell, and were not alarmed by this since we had the comfortable reassurance that later it would come back. For once, however, I felt old; the doubt kept asserting itself that maybe in this generation the loss of practical knowledge might be permanent and irreversible.

In any case, this bizarre notion of infinite time horizon has fallen into disrepute and oblivion. Instead of the Reagan deficits being accompanied by rises in the personal saving rate, they have coexisted in 1982–84 with historically low personal saving rates. Controlled experiments are never possible in economics, but the bulk of experience seems strongly at variance with the far-fetched Barro-Hall-Ricardo hypothesis.

Disillusionment with rational expectations

The Washington supply-siders, I have already mentioned, appealed to rational expectations in their tirades against Keynesianism. Scholars more respectable than the supply-siders argued that if Washington followed creditable policies to bring down the inflation rate, the cost of doing so would be surprisingly low.

Thus, in 1980 when I attended a Minneapolis conference in honor of Walter Heller's sixty-fifth birthday, a disciple of Sargent pressed on me at the Federal Reserve Bank of Minneapolis a review by Sargent of how easy it had been in 1923 to bring the German, Austrian, and Polish hyperinflations to an end. The moral of this retold ancient story, it was suggested to me, is that in the 1980s it would be easier to descend from double-digit inflation rates to reasonably stable price levels.

My reply at the time was that the student of mine explosions cannot expect to learn much from analyses of atomic bomb detonations. The retold Sargent story, I said, made me perhaps a shade more sanguine on the possibility of doing something about an inflation like Israel's. But the historic fact that short-term changes in nominal GNP, in P × Q, have tended generally to be divided about two-thirds in Q and one-third in P, suggested that extrapolating Sargent's tale would lead to serious error.

Now, four years later, we can examine the testimony of experience. It tells, I think, against the views of Sargent, Lucas, and William Fellner. It tells in favor of the predictions by Robert J. Gordon and George Perry.

The achieved reduction in U.S. inflation rates did not come easy or cheap: the costs in lost output and jobs was just about what an Okun, Gordon, or Perry would have predicted in 1980. (I suspect that Fellner and Lucas had a salutary effect earlier, in getting Gordon and Perry to lower their cost estimates a bit below previous, more pessimistic guesses.)

Rational expectationists, such as Lucas, were too canny to risk the credibility of their theory on the rosy predictions of the supply-siders. When economic history seemed to move in the direction of their Keynesian opponents, they and Fellner could always say that the Administration's policies had not been "credible."

This is precisely the position I had predicted *ex ante*. No conclusive, or even useful, test of the credibility hypothesis would ever be possible. Even though the recession contrived by the policies of the Reagan years had exceeded in amplitude and duration anything forecast by the best consensus forecasters, there is no meaningfully formulatable definition of credibility that can be put to empirical testing. It is incredible to any rational observer of the democratic process that any central bank could announce in advance a decelerating money-supply path—and be believed that it would stick to that policy through thick or thin! Hence, much of the rational expectationist palaver was irrelevant speculation concerning how many angels can stand on the point of an ill-defined pin. When the novelty of the credibility nomenclature wore off, boredom swiftly took over.

Elsewhere in my Jerusalem lecture, I have recounted how and why events in the early and late 1930s made me recognize the need for a Keynes-like theory of effective demand, which is precisely the kind of theory not dreamed of in the philosophy of neutral-money neoclassical paradigms. Such paradigms are consistent with Say's Law and classical macro-orthodoxies. The Lucas-Sargent school of rational expectationists has recently revived precisely this view. In light of America's 1979–1984 experience, have Keynesian I-S and L-M paradigms in fact retained any usefulness in the present day and age?

The events and interpretations that I have been giving for the Reaganomics era suggest to me that we need a nonclassical theory of effective demand in order to understand the contemporaneous developments in nominal and real GNPs and the fluctuations in the velocity of circulation of money.

How could it be otherwise, when the Gordon finding remains true up to the present minute—that intermediate fluctuations in normal P × Q are still divided up in the respective proportions of about one-third and two-thirds? Lucas's market-clearing formalisms can no more account for these modern phenomena than they can account for the Great Depression itself. Since Sargent's tales of 1923 currency stabilizations turned out to have so little relationship to the cost-benefit history of our most recent crusade against inflation, it appears that there is still need for a theoretical apparatus that can try to come to grips with systematic fluctuations in aggregate output.

I don't want to be misunderstood. I am not putting in a plug for 1936-style Keynesianism, or for 1959 Keynesianism of the type represented by the bulk of the 1959 Radcliffe Committee in the United Kingdom. Nor am I intending to cast doubt on the many important findings about the considerable efficiency of speculative markets. Yes, arbitrage does work well to keep option prices near to Black-Scholes and similar theoretical formulas, yes, the spectra are quite white for price differences of stocks, staple goods, and their futures contracts. Yes, workers and entrepreneurs do catch on more quickly to what is happening than they used to do in the 1930s and 1940s.

Therefore, Robert Lucas and Thomas Sargent have done well to stress the difference between surprising policy moves and anticipated policy moves. But it is a far cry from these admitted facts to a belief in neutral money in the short run, or to an expectation that it is a useful model which assumes that major markets are always cleared and that there is little deadweight loss involved in the business cycle.

The school of rational expectations has been accorded spurious honor because of the genuine honor earned by efficient-market theory. Saying this is not to say that rational expectationism is without honor; it is to say that we must fairly identify what are its earned honors.

Here is an important example. I can fairly safely assume that a seasonal wheat price will develop in accordance with rationally expected price. For if it does not, some well-informed people can sell short or buy long and make a mint of money wiping out the divergencies from Muthean wheat price. Does that justify my assuming that the Fortune 500 entrepreneurs act like a best-informed econometrician who can work out where the GNP and price level can be expected to be? No. There need be no single well-informed analyst in the whole crowd of American executives. Admittedly, in forecasting, the consensus of the crowd can be pretty good even when no one forecaster can be counted on as reliable. (Remember the quite respectable history of odds at the race tracks!) But what I am now asserting is that the whole consensus crowd can be expected to be wrong, and to stay wrong for long periods of time, on what is going to happen to the macro data of the economy. Even if God told me in advance that the crowd was wrong, there is no way I could make money in the short run by betting against the crowd and setting it aright. The case of spot wheat prices or of General Motors calls is another matter. It is not even necessarily the case that, over several cycles or several Ponzi-processes and tulip manias, the consensus can be counted on to learn not to be too volatile and not to be too sluggish. In the long run the consensus group is dead, in the sense of being made up of new generations with imperfect memories.

Fine-tuning by the Fed

All this is not academic. In mid-1982 the first Reagan recession refused to come to an end. Unemployment exceeded 10 percent. The stock market sagged. The President's popularity plummeted. The demand regressions for M_1 were displaying large squared deviations. The Federal Reserve was being blamed for its corset of monetarism by many in the public and by a few in the Reagan Administration (e.g., by Treasury high brass, Reagan the practical man, and by all the supply-side zealots). Three bills to curb the independence of the Fed as a central bank were introduced in Congress, two by Republicans (including one by Jack Kemp).

No wonder the Federal Reserve was tempted to throw off the corset of monetarism it had been imposing on itself since 1979. Both political expediency and its perception that bank deregulation had altered the significance of M_1-to-GNP relationships conspired to motivate a fundamental change toward credit easing.

What could be expected to be the rational reaction? Monetarists would counsel: stay the course. I myself believed then that, despite rational expectationism, the Fed had a window of opportunity to turn the economy around. I recognized that there was a risk of such actions igniting fears of inflation, because of the possibility that Wall Street would react perversely to signs of central bank expansionism. If that happened, the Fed's departure from monetarism would in fact raise nominal and real interest rates.

In historical fact, it was all a tremendously successful maneuver. Wall Streeters rejoiced at the Fed's move. They bid up bond prices. Immediately, common stocks took their cue from bonds. The Dow-Jones index soared in August 1982. Again, in October 1982, real and nominal interest rates fell. For the year following August 1982, stock prices generally rose by 60 percent.

This massive reduction in nominal and real interest rates brought the residential construction business back to life. Durable goods like autos began to sell well again. In the standard textbook pattern, the Fed's easier-money program brought the 1981 Reagan recession to its end in November 1982.

It was a consumer-led recovery. As usual, plant and equipment investment were lagging time series. As usual, the deceleration of inventory decumulation helped to end the recession.

Looked at another way, the colossal budget deficit finally had its Keynesian stimulating effects once the high real interest rates occasioned by fears of future deficits were offset by easier Federal Reserve credit policy.

The surprisingly strong recovery

Except for orthodox monetarists, everyone was happy: speculators, investors, job seekers, profit-seeking entrepreneurs, politicians in the White House. The expert consensus forecasters, weighing the evidence from early 1983, predicted only a modest first-year recovery. Martin Feldstein, chairman of the Council of Economic Advisers, began with a pessimistic forecast that was below what the evidence suggested to the consensus crowd. Events soon forced him to rejoin the crowd.

By the middle third of 1983, the real economy was growing at the exuberant annual rate of 8 to 9 percent. In the autumn the Fed, as if determined to infuriate hard-line monetarists, turned down the rate of M_1 growth below its boisterous spring pace. (There is no particular warrant, in modern economic theory or in historical experience, for the view promulgated by monetarists that a high standard deviation of M growth is as such depressing to an economy. So their explanation for why the Fed's post-1979 attempt at monetarism had produced the 1981 recession is, to say the least, problematic. Also problematic is a naive identification of the cause of high M variance as being stupidity or duplicity by the Federal Reserve authorities. When the demand functions for the various definitions of money—M_1, M_2, M_3, M_0, . . . ,M_{99}—are shiftable, it is not surprising that policy should result in high standard deviations in their growth rates. As Arthur Burns observed, studies of experience do not bear out the view that the money market is unable to adjust to temporary aberrations in M growth rates.)

Just when sophisticated monetarist models were incurring large errors of estimation, Milton Friedman's speeches and *Newsweek* columns were warning against an inflationary recession by mid-1984. Karl Brunner, more cautiously, expressed similar misgivings. I find it hard to fabricate a plausible macromodel in which separate channels of causation operate in parallel, according to which the lag between dP/dt and dM/dt is longer than an independent lag between dQ/dt and dM/dt. So on *a priori* grounds the probability of both inflation and recession in early 1984 seemed low to me. Under sensible filtering, the actual pattern of dM/dt did not seem to me very frightening. But—and this is my major point—when one took into proper account the vast bulk of the relevant non-M data, a nonmonetarist would bet with strong odds against a recession before the November election.

Summing up the Keynesian tide

Readers will by now have recognized that my title was cunningly chosen. I have used "Evaluating Reaganomics" as a device for testing different macroparadigms against the evidence of recent experience. Here is the verdict:

A Hamlet-like student, poised in neutral equilibrium between eclectic post-Keynesianism, monetarism, and rational expectationism, would have to be pushed in the direction of post-Keynesianism by the brute factual experiences of America in the 1980s.

That is my message. That is my finding. Economics is not an exact science, so I cannot prove the correctness of this result in the way that one proves the Pythagorean Theorem or confirms the constancy of the speed of light.

Let me also point out that there are U.S. patterns of behavior in the 1980s that still require new explanatory theories and that mandate some eclectic blending of the competing schools of thought. We don't really understand why the short-term real rate of interest stays so high these days, or for that matter why long-term real interest rates stay higher than they seemed to be in most of the last many decades. (Why, by the way, don't such high real rates choke off homebuilding? One minor reason seems to be people's myopia: if mortgage lenders offer buyers floating-rate loans, and structure them to involve low initial monthly cash payments, apparently buyers will purchase new and old homes.) Why the dollar does not float downward is still a puzzle. Its strength on capital account could use a plausible theory, and one that permits prediction of the future.

When I say that post-Keynesianism has received some vindications from experience, I am also saying that some of the standard hypotheses of neoclassical microeconomics have been borne out by experience. Thus, good-sense supply-side economics would expect that tax reductions which reduce the wedge between pre-tax and post-tax returns might well strengthen investment demand, *ceteris paribus*. The record, I think, bears this out. Adjusting for cyclical factors and for the height of real interest rates, we do seem to observe stronger demands for equipment than past regressions would call for. The Reagan tax cuts, I would suppose, do explain part of this story.

Should we economists be pleased that for once, at least, our mainstream theories have seemed to be about right? Yes, perhaps. But I remind myself that science is most exciting when new findings are being made. There is still plenty of excitement—too much excitement, some citizens would say—in the world of political economy.

CHAPTER FOUR

THE U.S. FISCAL CRISIS OF THE 1980s

Paul A. Samuelson

The U.S. electorate cannot resolve its internal debate on how large the public sector's share of the GNP shall be. The impasse has led to sizable deficits, not only in recession times, and also to questions about the prospect for high employment in the mid-1980s. To try to resolve the ethical debate by finding the right one of the dozen definitions of the budget to balance, and declaring that it must be balanced by constitutional or self-imposed decree, is both naive and an evasion of the democratic decision that needs to be made.

Each fiscal policy leads to a different total of current thriftiness and capital formation, having different effects on consumption of future and present generations. It is an illusion to think that there is one "neutral" solution that lets private family and corporate decisions optimally adjudicate between present and future generations. Even rabid individualists cannot defend letting those now alive and commanding a bare majority of voters do whatever they wish when their actions must have profound effects upon those still to come. Most of what is perceived as a present fiscal crisis dissolves on analysis into understandable frustration on the part of those more critical of government's role in the economy than the effective majority of the voters and their representatives has been since 1980.

In time of trouble, people look for a religion. Often it is for a new religion, since one would not be in trouble had the current religion not proved wanting. But a reversion to an older religion may be grabbed at for a solution.

CRISIS IN FISCAL POLICY

The U.S. economy is now in trouble. After a decade of floundering, we found ourselves in the early 1980s mired in a recession. Whatever the index numbers say, the person in the street does not perceive that inflation is on its way to being cured. The steady rise in living standards that U.S. citizens could always take for granted has been thwarted by OPEC oil scarcity and by Club of Rome's problems with irreplaceable natural resources and the law of diminishing returns. Affluence has brought anomie: The decay of the work ethic has undermined the affluence—leaving the anomie. While Athens degenerates in spirit and substance, the feared Sparta grows in military power—to parity at best, and at worst to superiority.

The choice of the topic of these essays is testimony that the general unease about economic policy narrows down in focus to a perceived crisis in fiscal policy. By conventional definition, the U.S. federal deficit is seen to be at a record high. Looking ahead to the middle of the decade, the informed eye sees continued record deficits. If all of this were the work of the left-of-center Democratic administration, there would be less mystery in the process. But, ironically, the agitation about departure from fiscal grace occurs during the term of office of a conservative Republican and following an apparent election landslide against New Deal programs.

What worries those who seek a balanced budget is not that Ronald Reagan is a big spender. Only in the area of national defense has the Administration promoted new expansionary expenditure programs.

Sophisticated advocates of budget balance can shrug off that part of the current deficit attributable to the loss in tax receipts engendered by the 1981 recession. What they cannot shrug off is the deficit envisaged still to be with us long after recovery has brought the United States back to the low levels of unemployment characteristic of good phases of the business cycle.

TAX REDUCTION TO FORCE EXPENDITURE REDUCTION

In 1980, the Laffer-Kemp wing of the Republicans professed to believe that the massive reductions in tax rates would actually lead to a great upsurge in tax revenues, implying no deficit at all, but rather a surplus available to permit interest rates to fall and to permit further tax-rate reductions. That did not happen, but it was the intention.

The monetarists, regarding the level of the budget and of its algebraic surplus or deficit as pretty much irrelevant to the strength of total GNP spending, had reason to be concerned by deficits (as against high-expenditure levels), only to the degree that a deficit in being would generate effective political pressures on the Federal Reserve to depart from steady constraints on the rate of money-supply growth. A large deficit, being equivalent to a large element of public dissaving, might be expected to put some upward pressure on nominal and real interest rates; and to the degree that the Fed was still subject to nonmonetarist hankerings to resist a rise in interest rates, any such crowding-out effect of deficits would put in jeopardy the Fed's successful achievement of its monetarist targets.

Many rational expectationists could agree with the above considerations. But the purists in this camp were inclined to doubt that a so-called deficit would itself have any substantial effects upon anything. So long as people foresee that they and their heirs must incur the tax obligation to pay for current expenditures not covered by current taxes, they will behave in much the same way as they would if there were no tax reductions and, hence, no deficit. (The too-large spending of 1981 to 1982 would, of course, have some substantive effects in comparison with a lower level of federal expenditures; but so long as people plan, in effect, as if they and their heirs will live forever and have to pay their taxes in the future, if not in the present, they will act in the end in the same way—whatever the level of current taxes and the implied so-called deficit. So the argument goes.) The record of rational expectationists in illuminating the probabilities of short-term economic developments has been almost as bad as that of the most imaginative supply-side theorists. But the logic of the paradigm plays down even the crowding-out effects upon investment of deficits.

All the separate wings of the Reagan teams could agree on the desirability of reducing the *total* of government expenditures. The weight of the private market in the GNP was to be increased, so to speak; the weight of the public sector to be decreased. An increase in efficiency would result from deregulation and from reducing the wedge between pretax and posttax returns. Quite aside from efficiency gains, the philosophical virtue of *freedom* would be promoted by such a successful reduction in the total of federal spending (or at least a lowering of the trend of such spending in comparison with previous implied paths). Presidential leadership and threats were deemed desirable to ensure that Congress cut entitlement and other federal programs in order to realize the desired goal.

Many, but not all, Republican economists favored tax reductions as a way of putting pressure on Congress to cut expenditures. What the rascals do not have they cannot spend, was the argument. Inasmuch as a sovereign government has the power to run deficits, those who favored the tax reduction as a ploy to bring down spending must have been implicitly relying on a propensity of Congress to be unwilling to countenance an unlimitedly high deficit. Some conservatives, and also some nonconservatives, warned Congress in early 1981 that this tax-reduction ploy could degenerate into a form of Russian roulette. If it worked, well and good from the standpoint of those conservative in ideology. But what if it failed to bring down spending commensurate with the reduction in tax revenues? Then it would create the kinds of deficits that the United States actually faces.

Anyone who monitors Wall Street and investor brokerage opinions will learn that some of the highness of the real rate of interest during the first year of the Reagan recession must be attributed to the boomeranging of the Reagan tax-reduction program (a program that was gleefully supported by many Democrats who had tax-reduction items of their own to add onto those advocated by the Administration). The depressing effects of high real rates of interest on housing and other durable-goods spending meant that the U.S. economy got little or none of the antirecession benefit of the deficit; and, indeed, every dollar of tax reduction might well have led to a reduction in total spending, employment, and production. Such an induced reduction in the velocity of circulation of money was not desired by anybody; of course, any attempt by the Federal Reserve to try to offset by upward revisions of M targets would have had to be rejected by monetarists as "no-no" fine tuning.

DISTRUST OF DEMOCRACY

If the ordinary workings of representative legislatures lead to such continued levels of public expenditure and deficits, it is natural that there be resort to referenda and constitutional amendments to achieve once and for all what is not achieved by congressional procedures. Economists are asked to specify which of the many competing definitions of the balanced budget is the best one. Once economists identify it for the people, the people are asked to freeze into successful practice the appropriate level of tax-rate structure and to constrain total spending by the total of such available tax receipts.

This is not the place to examine the problems and advantages that might inhere in a system of constitutionally imposed fiscal totals. My primary task is to point out why it is arbitrary to select *any* one definition of budget as the right and neutral one to be balanced.

There is a value-free part of economics that constitutes its scientific core. And, not less important when it comes to any policy applications, there are the values and ethical goals that democracies wish to realize, to argue about, and to compromise over. Positive economic science cannot pronounce that it is desirable for any of the budget concepts to be balanced. What inescapably belongs in the nonscientific realm of value-welfare judgments is the decision on how positive or how negative the deficits ought to be (as defined in each of the dozens of relevant ways). For, according to the positivistic macroeconomics characterizing the real world, each different size and sign of deficit has different substantive effects on the present and future generations of the citizenry. (This is an understatement. There are even discernible trade-offs between present consumption by people who are now alive and their consumption when they are older. The citizenry, recognizing vaguely its own myopias and private-saving idiosyncracies, may rationally choose one size of surplus or deficit over another in order to achieve the optimum feasible compromise.)

There are some present-day models in which the size of the deficit is so subject to being offset by private reactions as to make that size of no substantive importance. As already indicated, such models are not realistic.

HOW FISCAL POLICY MATTERS

In 1933, one of every four workers was unemployed. The system was producing less than two-thirds of what it would have been capable of producing if the years 1929 to 1932 had been years of average productivity growth and employment.

Few economists would expect that the U.S. system could be brought back to a normal employment and production level by a 1933 program that would have tried to balance the budget by a normal 1929 tax structure, and that called for a 1933 to 1940 monetary commitment to a steady 4 percent growth in some measure(s) of the total money supply.

What could be expected to be the outcome of such a program by well-informed macroeconomists? First, they would expect that the normal tax structure would fail to balance the budget. Second, the main reason for this actual deficit would be their confident expectation that the system would remain stuck for years at abnormally high levels of excess capacity and unemployed labor. Third, for how long output might continue *not* to grow would be a question hard to forecast. How fast it might grow once the corner was turned would also be a question that no jury of eclectic economists could be expected to agree on.

This bit of history is not resurrected as an experiment because we are in times as parlous as those of 1933. Nor because I believe we are about to go into an economic tailspin. The reason is to remind us that the economic system cannot always be usefully understood by the tools of market-clearing microparadigms.

WHERE FISCAL POLICY DOES NOT MATTER

A mathematical theoretical Walras-Debreu system would find a full-employment equilibrium path even if it started out from initial conditions like those of 1933.[1] It would not need a crash program of bank expansion to bring it back toward full employment. Indeed, such a program would merely raise its various price levels pretty much in balance. A Walras-Debreu system would not benefit in its real magnitudes of output, consumption, and employment from a program of massive deficit spending, involving tax reductions, expanded transfer payments, and enlarged public purchases of real goods and services. Preparation for war by a 1936 Adolf Hitler might raise prices in a Walras-Debreu system, but it could not achieve most of its effects in the form of higher levels of job activity and consumption satisfactions.

Thus, there are the tremendous differences between actual economic history and the refined theoretical micromodels of economists. Those same differences occur between actual business-cycle developments and the pure models of rational expectationists.

To see this, consider the 1923 stabilizations of hyperinflation in Germany, Hungary, Austria, and Poland. As Thomas Sargent has recently pointed out, quick termination of these hyperinflations—with rather little unemployment and stagnation—would be how a rational-expectationist model might be expected to operate.[2] But Robert Gordon's examination of 14 attempts to fight inflation in the United States and abroad—and report that all but a very few of them seemed to involve considerable sacrifices in real output, employment, consumption, and capital formation—indicate how a rational expectationist's model is supposed not to work.[3]

A REALISTIC FISCAL PARADIGM

The art of political economy is to know when and how to modify abstract models to take account of the discrepancies between them and the real world. My reading of how the real world works suggests the following:

• Usually higher public expenditure, lower tax rates and collections, and greater (algebraic) deficits in short and intermediate runs add to output and employment. They also add something to the algebraic rate of price-level growth. A breakdown of nominal GNP change into about two-thirds output and one-third price change applies until the system reaches abnormally low levels of unemployment and excess plant capacity; then most of the GNP change is dissipated in mere price-tag changes.

• Speeding up the growth of the M (money) aggregates has similar effects, quantitatively and qualitatively. When the growth in M is itself occasioned by a so-called "need to finance the deficit," any partially offsetting reduction in V (velocity) induced by the increases in M, will be weaker. So, normally, simultaneous increases in M and fiscal variables are especially potent.

• Overbalancing the budget (as conventionally defined) by increasing tax revenues relative to public outlays is compatible with high-level employment and vigorous output growth if (and only if) suitably compensating easiness of credit and of real interest rates is achieved. The short- and intermediate-run M target that is required for just-adequate total spending is not the same when a deficit is crowding out capital formation and thereby speeding up V in $MV = PQ$ (money times velocity equals price times quantity). A higher dM/dt growth is tolerable, and may sometimes be mandatory, when public thriftiness via the budget is reinforcing private propensities to save on the part of families and corporations.

These propositions are based on the assumption that some tolerable or desirable behavior of the price level is specified as a constraint for the short or intermediate run under contemplation. Thus, with a whopping deficit, an M growth rate of 3 percent might be much more inflationary than one of 5 percent would be with an overbalanced budget.

• It would be misleading to believe that people in 1982 react as slowly as they used to in 1933. Therein lies the saving germ of truth in the rational expectationists' emphasis. Their explicit and implicit forecasts have so often gone astray since the late 1970s because rational expectationists extrapolated into the short run of a year or two many of the effects that will be correct in the long run of several years or more. But their larger squared errors of estimation should not blind us to the truth that the participants in the economic scenario today are quicker to act than they used to be.

What used to take one or two decades might be compressed into little more than half a decade.

RECENT AMBIGUITIES

Concretely, there are possibly special times when an increment of M contrived by the Federal Reserve could so trigger off inflationary expectations as to lead to higher, rather than lower, nominal and real rates of interest. The weight of the evidence still suggests that in most times a short-run rise in dM/dt will increase capital formation and real GNP, and do this via the mechanism of lower costs of credit and its greater availability, and also via the mechanism of higher wealth capitalizations in corporate- and family-spending functions. However, since expectations are so volatile, and indeed irrational, I am prepared to believe that there have been recent times in which M effects have been opposite in sign to their normal reactions.

Similar "perversities" in fiscal-policy reactions can occur. To explain the puzzle of over-high real interest rates in the year before July 1982, it was useful to put the dummy variable of the size of the deficit into the function of income and the money stock that determines the level of the structure of interest rates. This is an ad hoc procedure, whose main defense was that it worked to predict what was happening and was consistent with what was heard on Wall Street.

But notice what this tinkering with standard macroanalysis does to the system's comparative statics. If a rise in public spending and reduction in tax rates swell the deficit and thereby raise real interest rates, the induced reduction in housing and other durable-goods spending could more than offset the expansionary effects of the fiscal deficit on real GNP. (In technical terms, the positive signs that normally hold for ∂ output/∂ deficit and ∂ output/∂ ($-$Taxes) could well be reversed!)

Does all this sound academic? It is anything but. The debate between Chairperson Martin Feldstein and Secretary of Treasury Regan on whether the 1983 cut in personal taxes should be advanced from July to January hinges on precisely this question.

How to resolve the puzzle? If the economy stays very weak and the fiscal stimulus contemplated is a large enough one, one would have to bet that the normal positive sign would hold for the partial derivatives. But given the small magnitude of the tax cut and the uncertainty about the sign of the partial derivative, I cannot generate much enthusiasm for either side of the quarrel.

WHICH BUDGET BALANCE?

Once you understand the paradigm that I consider to be realistically applicable in the modern age, my denial that there can be found a unique definition of the budget that we ought to aim to balance as a condition of optimality or of neutrality is understandable. Overbalancing the budget, while at the same time ensuring by Federal Reserve policy that the enhanced overall social thriftiness will not be aborted by induced unemployment, implies a higher capital stock in the future achieved by lower current consumption now. Is that mix a good thing? A bad thing?

There is no way to give a definite answer to these questions within the realm of positivistic economics. If you think future generations ought to enjoy more and the present generation less, you will answer the question affirmatively. If you think the present generation deserves more consumption, you will answer negatively.

Why should the citizenry not decide the matter? A naive approach is to say: "People in their private capacities as family spenders or voters of corporation proxies favoring high or low dividend payments should solely decide. If the right one of the dozen or so alternative definitions of the budget is balanced, public thriftiness will be kept "neutral and optimal capital formation will result."

Such a contention is gratuitous, and has no basis in any system of philosophy or welfare economics. Certainly, in a democracy, the citizenry must decide on everything: on what weight must be given to the needs, merits, and desires of present and later generations; on what social compacts are to prevail, involving what compromises between the "rights" of individual persons and lawful limitations of their behavior. But to conclude without argument that the citizenry must decide to endure that amount of thriftiness implied by the balanced budget is to beg the question at issue.

For more than a quarter of a century, I have been urging the merits of budget surpluses offset by enough credit easiness to keep employment as full as it ought to be. This is for the purpose of encouraging a higher investment-consumption mix at high employment. Such a long-run goal ought to be rejected (or accepted) on its merits and not by the happenstance of constitutional amendments and referenda.

I must guard against being misinterpreted. A rise in taxes and an expenditure cut in early 1983 may well undermine—not enhance—actual investment. The Fed could react to fiscal austerity—or, what is the same thing, less fiscal looseness—by letting it depress the economy further, thereby stepping up the fight against inflation.

Until a recovery is ensured, until the tax-incentive reforms of the 1981 act have some scope for coaxing out capital formation, the economy will operate within the paradox of thrift—with increased thriftiness probably reducing actual achieved investment. It is here that I want not to be misinterpreted in the espousal of a long-range program of fiscal austerity. True, we are not all dead in the long run; but that long run is distinguishable from the present short run that is relevant for immediate U.S. policy. So long as the economy is still in our present short run, I warn against an austere fiscal program appropriate for the long-term future.

CONCLUSION

Public spending out of control is a calamity. Public spending that is inefficient and not responsive to democracy's desires and needs is a pity. Discipline is needed at all times. But to try to fabricate a religion that will impose discipline by creating new shibboleths or trying to resurrect the old makes little sense and, in any case, will not work. When people no longer believe in hell fire, threatening them with the heat of perdition serves little purpose. Pretending to believe, in order to frighten ourselves into doing that that we cannot make ourselves do on its merits, is a charade. For better or worse, a democracy has to face up to the substantive issues.

NOTES

1. Leon Walras, *Elements of Pure Economics*. Homewood: Richard D. Irwin, 1954, translations of 1874–1926 editions by W. Jaffe; Gerard Debreu, *Theory of Value*. New York: John Wiley and Sons, 1959.

2. Thomas J. Sargent, "The Ends of Four Big Inflations." Paper presented at the October 1980 Conference on Inflation, Washington, D.C.

3. Robert J. Gordon, "Why Stopping Inflation May Be Costly: Evidence from Fourteen Historical Episodes." National Bureau of Economic Research, Working Paper 682, March 1, 1981.

What happened and why?

Myths and realities about the Crash and depression*

The realities are harder to find than the myths, but the search adds to understanding.

Paul A. Samuelson

Nations, like families, live on myths. Who can forget the time Mother dropped Junior into the buttermilk? Who would want to forget Black Thursday on Wall Street when the Dow Jones Averages collapsed in announcement that the 1920's boom had come to an end and the Great Depression of the 1930's begun?

Myths serve a Jungian purpose whether they be true or only well told. In my boyhood memories are Jack Dempsey and Gene Tunney; Bill Tilden and Bobby Jones; Leopold and Loeb; Capone (Al) and Diamond (Legs); Scott and Zelda. So how can I forget helping my high school algebra teacher make her selection between Hupp Motors and RCA? My Aunt Sophie's loss in Ford Limited of Canada is part of the economic history of our times.

HISTORY AS ANTIQUARIAN CHRONOLOGY

There are at least two kinds of history. One kind is a rattling good tale — told by an antiquarian, signifying nothing (but its own content). Samuel Eliot Morison's classic account of the rise and fall of the clipper ship can illustrate this kind of history at its best. It teaches us nothing about the economics of wind and steam, the dynamics of Schumpeterian creative obsolescence. But then it was not intended to convey any lesson. Such history is a one-time thing. Don't ask, don't even speculate over, what would have happened if Napoleon had defeated Wellington at the Battle of Waterloo. Such contra-factual scenarios have no operational meaning for this kind of history.

You can't do better than to read Frederick Lewis Allen's, *Only Yesterday*, to learn about the 1929 stock market crash from the antiquarian point of view. If your curiosity is whetted, you can spin out the tale by reading John Kenneth Galbraith's *The Great Crash* or Charles Kindleberger's romp through the *Manias, Panics and Crashes*. Although the number of sold-out bulls who defenestrated from Manhattan high-rise edifices has been somewhat exaggerated, and although by sober audit it appears that my Aunt Sophie lost only $600 (1929 dollars), the sheer magnitude and duration of the drop in common stocks after October 1929 nominates the Crash for a lasting place in the repertory of our national legends. Like the magnificent German hyperinflation of 1920-1923, the pathology merits many a wake and jubilee. So no apology or rationalization is needed for the present 50th birthday *potlatch* in honor of the Great Crash.

HISTORY AS INCIPIENT SCIENCE

But there is a second kind of history. It constitutes the journal book of science, preserving the records of observations, the case studies and anecdotes of experience, and the findings of experiments. Inside every broad-bottomed historian of this category there is a wee skinny scientist trying to break out. People read this kind of history to learn a moral, to gain a useful understanding. Those who write this kind of history try — and at their lucky best succeed in the attempt — to present a selection of past happenings that will provide *an evidential basis for causal understanding and (perhaps even) prediction.*

When financial journalism and current commentary are done well, they are to me indistinguishable from economic history, being so to speak merely contemporaneous economic history hot off the griddle. Similarly, a bang-up job of economic history for some past century and distant place, when done at its best, must display and marshal evidence according to the same canons of cogency and relevance we require of scientific memoirs and treatises.

I address myself on this occasion to the second kind of history. I ask, and you will want me to do so:

Aside from its intrinsic interest as a scary melodrama, what in retrospect can we deem to be the deeper economic significance of the Great Crash?

After all, Frederick Lewis Allen deviated from the path of pure chronologist. Kenneth Galbraith cannot resist the temptation to infer — and gladly preach. If you told my colleague, Charlie Kindleberger, that Mother displayed a *chronic* propensity to lose hold of offspring, his own scientific propensity to generalize, to forge patterns of regularity, to invent dummy variables of "accident-proneness" and "death-wishes", would inevitably burst loose. No wonder then that Kindleberger professes to find something in common between the South Sea Bubble, The John Law Swindles, and the 1929-1933 Boom-and-Bust — the alleged failure for a Gallahad lender of last resort to emerge.

TRIAL BALANCE

In order to come into court with clean hands, I must at the beginning make a deposition of ignorance. Although authorities assert with confidence distinguishable (and sometimes conflicting) causal interpretations of the Great Crash, we simply do not have the controlled experimental data and the critical observations that would permit a dedicated jury of experts to agree on a verdict. Still, I find the evidence persuasive against two extreme views.

First, there is the vulgar belief that Wall Street epitomized and encapsulated the excesses of the 1920's boom era. The October 1929 crash, in this view, did not merely reflect the end of the boom and the beginning of the depression. It was in its own right a fall in capital values *and the causal progenitor* of the depressed decade to come. Reason and experience, I think, must reject this naive view that the economy at large is merely the tail wagged by the dog of the stock market.

The second polar view, fortunately no longer so prevalent among academic economists, is the view of *the equity market as little more than a sideshow* to the Wagnerian main act of the gross national product. Monomaniacs who concentrate only on the rate of growth of the money supply write history as if the stock market crash is no worse than a bad cold and the failure of several thousand banks just part of the growing pains of capitalism. Fortunately, when you cut through their rhetoric you find there is nothing in monetarists' presentation of statistical evidence, or indeed in the wider historical record, that should tempt us to follow them down their Niagara of monomania.

The speculative casino may well be the tail of the macroeconomic dog. But in Einstein's system where the sparrow that falls to earth wrinkles the four-dimensional space for all things in the universe, there is *feedback* from tail to body! (The quantitative strength of that feedback, and its exact time-phasing, alas, cannot be determined by the cross-spectral analysis of the naive econometricians. When the latter observe the spot price of wheat, Y, rises *after* the futures price, X, has risen, he errs if he infers that "X causes Y." Actually, the correct *anticipation* of Y's rise is the cause of X's rise — something crude observations on leads and lags will never reveal to you.)

FOSSILS FROM OLD DEBATES

On occasions like this it is meet to remember ancient arguments. We can count on their being reinvented by each new generation. Here are some random samplings of memory.

1. Farm prices collapsed long before 1929. This reinforced the desire to believe: *Agriculture holds the key to industrial prosperity.* Remember the World War I slogan: "Food will win the war and write the peace"? It didn't; and didn't. Funeral by funeral, this old paradigm faded out of economics.
2. Ernest Henderson, the co-founder of the Sheraton Hotel chain, was the last to hold the view that the tail of stock prices controls inexorably the dog of GNP. (In 1962 he implored me to tell President Kennedy that the Blough confrontation over steel would cause grass to grow on Main Street. Henderson's self-confidence proved misplaced.)
3. Harold Moulton of Brookings was convinced that stock market gains hyped up consumption spending in the 1920's. The data do not unequivocably support his quantitative estimates. We must be content with good stories. (Tex Guinan, the henna'd mistress of ceremonies of the speakeasy age, claimed she could tell how each day's market had gone by the tempo of that night's spending. Well — maybe.)
4. Keynes, Hawtrey, and other great macroeconomists believed the monetary authorities were unduly alarmed by the 1928-1929 Wall Street speculation. Lesser lights — Carl Snyder and W. Randolph Burgess of the New York Federal Reserve Bank and

C. J. Bullock of Harvard — identified inflation of share values and collateral loans as the seeds of disaster. Keynes and Hawtrey feared that the attempt to subdue Wall Street might asphyxiate Main Street. Synder and Bullock feared that failure to take action soon enough against stock speculation would lead later to Main Street stagnation.

In retrospect we must award the palm to the lesser lights — even if they were not right for the right reasons. If only 1928 Keynes had 1936 Keynes' understanding of how variable the velocity of circulation of money, animal spirits, and the marginal efficiency of investment can be as a result of collapses in asset prices and the resulting burdensomeness of contractual debts!

5. Just before my time students had to wrestle with the Talmudic quandry. "Does the stock market absorb credit, robbing legitimate 'agriculture, trade, and industry' of their needed fix of M?" (There is nothing old under the sun. Earlier this year I read a pointless Argus market letter arguing that money-market funds don't use up or constitute M. Ignored was whether or not the same V_i would pertain to various M_i whether or not money-market funds exploded in size. Pointless analyses of the Eurodollar market similarly choke our in-baskets.)
6. On the supposition of the 1913 founders of the Fed that one wants to protect the legitimate monetary needs of agriculture, trade, and industry from the parasitic predations of speculation, how does the Central Bank go about doing so in a universe where "money mingles"? The old Banking School versus Currency School debates of the nineteenth century had a revival 50 years ago when the Qualitative School (centered around Columbia's H. Parker Willis) jousted with the orthodox Quantitative School (of Fisher, Warburton, Mintz, Currie, *et al.*). Neither paradigm scored a knockout blow. The Columbia Business School camp faded away. The Quantity Theory contingent jumped aboard the Keynesian bandwagon or went into Cook County hibernation awaiting a new spring and a new Pied Piper.
7. Meanwhile, as equity prices of the Cowles Composite Index dropped by three-quarters from 1929 to 1932, and their reported P/E ratios rose tenfold, "efficient markets" and "rational expectations" uniformly prevailed. How do we know this (aside from being told so by the Federal Reserve Bank of Minneapolis)? Because, it stands to reason that they must have — just as it stands to reason that there are no free lunches. (As Hume "proved": You can prove nothing about the real world by 'it stands to reason' assertions.)

SUMMING UP

Tersely, here is what a postmortem will show.

1. The 1920's was a period of genuine U.S. advance. The housing boom peaked years before the 1929 Crash. The Florida real estate boom confirmed what Ponzi had shown earlier in Boston.

   Speculative price moves in phases that can for a considerable time (of indeterminable length!) be self-fulfilling.[1] When they level off and cease to be self-fulfilling the nominal and real carnage can be considerable.
2. Overall the P/E and yield characteristics of the 1920's bull market showed no great pathology. (Playing as I often do the experiment of studying price profiles with their dates concealed, I discovered that I would have been caught by the 1929 debacle. This led me to say to Lionel (now Lord) Robbins: "I don't understand something. How did a person of Keynes' temperament avoid going broke a second time, in 1929 as well as earlier?" Robbins replied: "Actually, Maynard did go broke in 1929. But he just managed to survive — and of course subsequently came back strong.") When my textbook mentioned Keynes' genius at finance, I received a letter from Professor P. Sargent Florence of the University of Birmingham: "Keynes may have made his own fortune and that of King's College, but the investment trust of Keynes and Dennis Robertson managed to lose me my fortune in 1929."
3. The coincidental indicators turned down in mid-1929, for once leading rather than lagging behind the stock market, which peaked only in the autumn. From mid-1929 to the end of 1930, a somewhat "normal" recession ensued. There followed, domestically and internationally, a non-inevitable avalanche of bank failures, debt suspensions, and bankruptcies. A self-fulfilling vicious circle of deflation and depression followed. Existing orthodoxies of law and ideology intensified the debacle.
4. Modern analysis, and the corpus of accumulated factual experience, suggest:
   a) Stock values are an appreciable part of wealth or net worth.
   b) An increase in stock prices raises wealth and, other things equal, the rate of consumption and investment spending. (What is the same thing, it raises animal spirits and M's velocity.)
   c) Rising stock prices, for the same level of expected earnings, lowers the effective cost of capital investment.

d) The rise and fall of stock prices is *only one of numerous factors* acting to raise and lower the overall pace of total spending.

We are entitled to infer the eclectic and prosaic conclusion:

The Great Crash of 1929 was one of several important, and somewhat fortuitous, factors that reflected and intensified the Great Depression. Events since then are consonant with those of the post-1933 recovery, the 1937-1939 business cycle, the 1962 Kennedy-Blough confrontation, and the 1966-1979 macroeconomic world experience.

No more can as yet be validly said. And, Wittgenstein reminds us, on that which we cannot say it is as well to be silent.

[1] A mathematical footnote is mandatory. Long before the multiplier and accelerator were dreamed of, society suffered from self-fulfilling exponential price explosions of the form $P_t = (1+k)P_{t-1} = P_0(1+k)^t \rightarrow \infty$ as $t \rightarrow \infty$. There is no reason why such a self-warranting tulip mania should end when it does end. My *Collected Scientific Papers,* Chs. 73 and 150, discuss the basic lack of determinateness of Ponzi self-warranting processes. The basic arbitrage relation, $P_{t+1} - P_t = rP_t - N_t$, has for its solution not only $\Sigma^\infty N(1+r)^{-t}$ but also that normal solution plus the arbitrary Ponzi term $A^1(1+r)^t$!

The Crash of '29: Lessons for '79

By Paul A. Samuelson

Nature has style. Fifty years ago, just as the long boom decade of the 1920s was coming to its end, the great stock market crash trumpeted that end. Appropriately, it all happened in the fall of the year.

What lessons can we learn from the experience? Do not expect too much. Karl Marx once said, "History repeats itself, the first time as tragedy, the second time as farce." He was wrong.

History never quite repeats itself. If you legislate rules against speculation in tulips just after the Dutch Tulip Mania of the 17th Century, that cannot serve to prevent the next century's South Sea Bubble. Some of the worst excesses of Wall Street have been cleaned up by the post-New Deal Securities and Exchange Commission. But right now there is a scandal brewing in the speculative market for silver, as foreign interests engineer a partial "corner" so that there is not enough deliverable silver to fulfill all the contracts that avaricious sellers have made.

Let me, however, throw caution to the winds and try to summarize the relevance for our own times of the fireworks on Wall Street just 50 years ago:

Lesson Number 1. *Everything can be overdone.*

John J. Raskob, vice president of General Motors and treasurer of the Democratic Party in the late 1920s, was confident that anyone could get rich in the stock market. It was your *duty* to get rich, he wrote, and claimed it could all be done by saving $15 a week! Was he laughed out of court? Not at all. He was saying what people wanted to hear. And for half a dozen years, his predictions seemed always to turn out right.

So, when people ask me whether the present boom in housing could burst, my answer is the obvious one.

Higher building costs and burgeoning new families provide good fundamentals for the real estate market. But when families with $35,000 a year incomes are buying houses that cost $200,000 and paying 12 per cent on their mortgages, they obviously are depending upon a continuing rise in housing prices at exponential rates that have never been permanently maintainable in the past.

Lesson Number 2. *Nothing is forever.*

If you bought the 30 stocks of the Dow-Jones Industrial averages at the September, 1929, peak of 381, by the end of the year you had lost almost half your nest egg. (If, as was likely at the time, you bought your shares putting up only 10 or 20 per cent as margin, you were cleaned out by October.) If you held on to your shares—and passed up the fortune from selling short that President Kennedy's father then made—by 1933 you would have lost 90 per cent of your wealth.

The trauma of such losses soured a whole generation on common stocks. Their long memories helped youngsters like me pick up stocks dirt cheap in the first years after World War II. As the Bible says, there is a time to remember and a time to forget. Many learned only half this lesson.

The first big Florida land boom fizzled out in 1927. But values later came back and surpassed their peak—a phenomenon that has happened several times in Florida since.

Lesson Number 3. *Markets will not regulate themselves; governmental rules of the road are necessary.*

Although common stocks would have fallen in value even if there had been no fraud, back in the 1920s there was a good deal of hanky-panky. You could run a bucket shop, taking people's bets as to whether equity prices would go up or down; and, if someone made a big hit against you, you could quietly disappear with their funds.

You could spread rumors to bull a stock up. Having taken money from the optimists, you could then spread opposite rumors to send that stock down—down far enough to catch the short sellers. You could entice ribbon clerks into risking their eating money by tempting them with liberal credit.

It is hard to prove scientifically that the SEC has materially improved the workings of the market. Fools and wise people can still lose their shirts in Wall Street. But when you observe the boiler-room operations in the commodity option market, an area that used to fall between stools of the regulators, a reasonable inference is that regulation is definitely in the public interest.

Lesson Number 4. *The 1929 crash did not cause the Great Depression of the 1930s.*

Nor was it primarily the *effect* of that depression. The crash came long before the 1929-30 recession had degenerated into the malignant depression.

To be sure, the decline in stock values did help to depress consumer spending. And it did make funds for investment purposes harder to get. But what needs emphasizing is the *multiplicity of interacting causes* that must be pointed to if we are to understand the collapse of the capitalistic system. What happened in Wall Street was only *one* of these numerous factors, and in my judgment not even in the class with the leading ones.

As an example, the failure of 8,000 banks was much more important in explaining what happened on Main Street than was the bankruptcy and moral turpitude of some prosperous Long Island residents.

Lesson Number 5. *Yes, "it" can happen again.*

That is, in the second half-century since 1929 we can expect to have cataclysmic declines in common stock prices. Stock prices fell sharply in 1937. They even fell during the first years of World War II, despite all the inflation implied by that conflict. Their behavior since 1965, I would argue, has been just as deflationary as anything seen in 1929.

We now know you can lose money in bonds. (For that matter, with a little ingenuity, you can lose in gold, diamonds, Swiss francs, antiques, oriental rugs, stamps, Picassos, or cash itself.) But let no one be kidded into the belief that there is no risk of ups and downs in common stocks.

Let no one jump from the statement that Wall Street can crash again in the future to the conclusion that the United States has any appreciable likelihood of undergoing in the future a great depression like that of the 1930s. Nothing is impossible in economics. So you cannot categorically rule out of our horoscope the possibility of another 10-year worldwide depression, in which most residential mortgages become frozen and half our banks go down the tubes.

Although that rerun of the 1930s is not impossible, I believe its probability to be so low that no prudent person would be well advised to pay to Lloyds of London any appreciable premium to insure against its happening. Why this change of odds? Because humans are getting smarter? Because economics has become more of an exact science?

No, the vice presidents at General Motors today average out to about the same IQs and savvy as John J. Raskob. A President Carter, or a President Reagan, can count on getting somewhat better economic advice than Herbert Hoover was able to command in 1929, but one ought not make too much of that. *The big difference is that the electorate has lost its faith in shirt-sleeve fundamentalism in economics.*

We have all eaten of the fruit of the Tree of Knowledge and there is no going back to the orthodoxies of the 1930s.

If all it takes to keep thousands of banks from going under, taking with them the lifetime savings of the citizenry, is the printing of bits of green paper, you may be sure that those bits of paper will be forthcoming in the last decades of the 20th Century. And that is the reverse of what was true even in the black day of 1931! Then mankind did crucify itself on the cross of belief in orthodoxies: Thou shalt not unbalance the budget. Thou shalt keep a gold reserve.

Them days is gone forever. And this makes all the difference.

* * *

You would like me to end up with the most important lesson of all. You would like to know whether stocks are now, at their deflated value, a good buy.

It was announced recently in the newspapers that Harvard University thinks this is a good time to pick up some bargains in common stocks. Harvard can afford the best economic advice that money and loyalty to Alma Mater can buy. But before you act on someone else's optimism, let me remind you that John D. Rockefeller and Andrew Mellon gave out the free advice that stocks were a bargain after Black October, 1929. They were wrong. Dead wrong. Harvard acted boldly, and successfully, in acquiring bargains in 1974, during the last recession. That perhaps explains their confidence now, but by itself it is not enough to convince a skeptic.

Lesson Number 6. *Never ask a professor of economics for stock market advice.*

He might give it to you. He might tell you that the stocks of American corporations are now selling for considerably below their reproduction costs. He might tell you that Wall Street denizens are triple-discounting for the affect of inflation. He might tell you that some day common stocks will turn out at last to be a pretty good hedge against obvious inflations. You might believe him and make—or lose—a fortune.

2 The Role of Profits in a Mixed Economy: Changes in the Perceived Reality

Paul A. Samuelson

Profit is today a fighting word. The capitalistic way of life, free private enterprise, its admirers tell us is a system of profit and loss. Profits are the lifeblood of the economic system, the magic elixir upon which progress and all good things ultimately depend.

One man's lifeblood is another man's cancer. In other quarters, profit is simply an exploitative surplus which fat men with an unfair penchant for arithmetic skim off from the gross national product, leaving the worthy true producers of that gross national product with a mere subsistence.

The fireworks of semantics set off by the word *profit* are merely a reflection of the tension and debate going on in every modern mixed economy concerning the proper role of the market-oriented private sector and the state-financed public sector. And it is part of the related perpetual floating debate going on between those who strive for greater egalitarianism both of opportunity and of condition and those who favor the status quo ante bellum, and by *ante bellum* I mean prior to the war over the proper way of taxing pretax income and wealth.

The swing group in these perpetual struggles is composed of those who hanker for less inequality, other things being equal, but who are concerned with the tactical and strategic considerations involved with the deadweight loss that may be incurred in the further pushing of equalizing measures and with what the political traffic will bear in a milieu where the electorate will not always put their money where their rhetoric points.

You will have to forgive me, therefore, if the logical thread of the discussion leads me to stray from the narrow province of profit theory. These will not be digressions or detours but rather necessary explorations of connected territories.

You will also have to forgive me if, as first speaker, I poach on some of the topics in which Professors Arrow and Lundberg have prime property rights. I have an exaggerated respect for the rights of private property, but what would be the advantage of going first if one could not skim off the cream of the discussion in an imperialist fashion?

My self-judged task is to analyze profit from the standpoint of the professional economist. It is proper that I give warning of what is most definitely not going to be my focus on this occasion. This is worth doing because the approach that I am *not* taking is very much the approach that many business people take toward the problem. Let me paint with an impressionistic brush the picture as they see it. Here goes the story.

Once upon a time business enterprise was respected. Calvin Coolidge was accurate when he said that, "the business of America is business," and it was a sad day for all the American people–workers as well as farmers–when Coolidge's statement came to be regarded as a sign of his crudity and of his having sold out to plutocracy.

Today it is another story. Profit *is a dirty word.* Business *is a dirty word.* Businessman *is a dirty word. The public is woefully uninformed on what fraction of the dollar spent goes to profit. What has happened to our educational system that students do not learn in high school and in college economics courses that only a few pennies of each sale dollar go to profits? And why don't our college professors get across the message that even those few pennies left over after heavy taxation do not go simply to finance the riotous and unnecessary consumption expenditures of a few wealthy families, but rather that it is out of those pennies of profits that plowed-back earnings will finance the capital formation we so desperately now need? The high real wages of tomorrow will materialize only if the needed increments to capital take place–just as the present-day highest standard of living in the world is enjoyed by the American working person only because the fruits of past thrift have filtered down to him in higher productivity and real wages.*

This being the truth about profits and business–the economic facts of life–what business needs is to get its story across. Although businessmen, as doers, are often at a disadvantage with the glib intellectuals, they must learn to go out on the public platform. They must testify before congressional committees. They must take out full-page ads that educate readers on the function of profits. They must encourage proper economics courses and teaching at the school, college, and inplant-course level. And, within the limits of their powers and influence, businessmen should seek to discourage the dissemination of falsely critical alternative doctrines.

The picture I have painted is a bit of caricature, as brevity makes more or less inevitable. But a no less devastating caricature could be made of the typical position of the antagonists toward business. If I were to read to you short selective passages from *Monopoly Capitalism*, the view of profits given by two eminent American Marxian scholars, Paul Baran and Paul Sweezy, the impression could be given that the cancerous surplus now swallows up much of the United States GNP, and that final disaster is kept at bay only by virtue of cold-war expenditures and imperialism, and by ever more frantic advertising expenditures and other conspicuous wastes.

Mine is not the task of analyzing ideologies, or of sifting out the correct and incorrect hypotheses concerning the real economic world that implicitly lie behind the various articulations of ideology that focus around the topic of profit. Mine is the more prosaic task of looking at what is happening in the last half of the twentieth century to profit and to the general share of the national income that goes to property—looking at all this, I remind you, from the standpoint of the professional economist—to try to understand the process and, perhaps from this understanding, to achieve some feel for the probabilities about future economic developments.

Here is a preview of some hard problems that analysis hopes, in the end, to grapple with:

Has the trend for the rate of profit been downward in the last decade or so in the United States? Has there not been a similar trend discernible for Western Germany and Sweden, for France and Japan, for Italy and Britain, and for the nonsocialist world generally?

If this downward trend can be verified, what are its principal causes? Is it, as many businessmen believe, due primarily to the rapacious demands of the trade unions? Some left wing writers—I think of two from Oxford—essentially agree that profits are down because militant wage bargaining has transferred them to the workers. Unlike the complaining businessmen, however, they look upon this process with favor rather than disfavor. Are either of these groups right in their diagnoses?

Aside from the exactions from profit by plundering labor, it has been argued that governmental regulations serve as a burden on capital's earning power. Control of pollution and agitation by environmentalists undercut the margin of profitability. The extra costs of achieving the last degree of atmospheric and water purity come right off the top of profits. An Alaskan pipeline budgeted to cost $700 million ends up in such a political regime costing $5 billion to $10 billion. A substantial fraction of all the funds available for new gross capital formation is preempted from going into capacity expansion and commercial productivity improvement because it must be siphoned into meeting safety and environmental standards imposed by government and public opinion. No wonder, according to this view, that the profit rate is down.

Or is an alternative explanation valid, one which posits that since World War II there has been a great accumulation of new capital all over the Western world? Capital competes with capital, and in this view it is the competitive "deepening" of capital that explains the putative decline in profit rates.

Keynes, in his now classic 1936 *General Theory*, spoke speculatively about the "euthanasia of the rentier." For this lecture's purposes, this can be translated to mean that capital accumulates enough to bring its return essentially down to zero or close to that level. Can the mixed economy survive, can the capitalist sheep perform their vital function when so little of the wool they grow is left to them?

Obviously, a model that alleges a worldwide decline in the profitability of capital incident to a vast deepening of accumulated capital is a bit at variance with the loud talk we have been hearing of "capital shortage." The president of the stock exchange has calculated with his Hewlett-Packard computer that our capital needs over the next several years are prodigious. Secretary of the Treasury William Simon, a seasoned veteran of Wall Street, points to the new capital needs created by the fivefold increase in OPEC energy prices. George Terborgh and other shrewd observers of current economic history voice concern that fictitious paper profits generated by inflation conceal the true drop in real profit returns and in real corporate savings in the 1970s. The United States has for decades been devoting a smaller fraction of GNP to gross capital formation than have West Germany and Japan; U.S. investment ratio has been smaller even than that of France, Italy, the Netherlands, or Scandinavia. More than a dozen years ago, Simon Kuznets, in one of his classic National Bureau of Economic Research quantitative monographs, put forth the hypothesis that this under-saving by America might well be the result of overspending by the American government. Treating public expenditure as the collective counterpart of private-consumption expenditure, one might argue that it was because the affluent United States was already consuming so much in the pre-Kennedy-Johnson-Nixon years that it was able to invest so little. This raises the question of how to reconcile an implied dearth of capital with low rather than high pretax real returns, and how to explain the puzzle of stagnating real values of equities in a decade of inflation when their reproduction costs have been soaring.

Textbook Treatment of Profit

If you are assigned a topic and have no good ideas on it, your first refuge as an intellectual scoundrel is to go to the dictionary and pluck out a definition of the subject. A second way of marking time before buckling down to hard thought is to turn to an elementary economics textbook for its definitions and classifications. With your indulgence, let me summarize what Chapter 31 of my *Economics* says about profits. Its first sentence says: "In addition to wages, interest, and rent, economics often talks about a fourth category of income: profit." I believe this follows in the tradition of Adam Smith, and on this 200th anniversary of Smith's *The Wealth of Nations*, it is mandatory for a lecturer to bring in the doctrines of that exalted founder of economics.

Smith, like Ricardo and other classical economists, thought it one function of economics to describe and explain the *distribution* of the national income. Smith, however, unlike David Ricardo, did not regard the question of how the social pie is to be divided as the prime and fundamental question of political economy. He was interested as well in the conditions conducive to *growth of the size of the total pie.* We already have here an explicit formulation of a dialectical debate that rages unresolved 200 years later. Conservative writers–Vilfredo Pareto will serve as a good example–urge the public to concentrate on *increasing the total* of national product, resting assured that the different classes of society are likely to share in any increment of the total. Radical critics of the bourgeois order take the opposite tack and insist upon the opposition of interests of the different classes, so that what one class can hope to gain in fractional share of total income must come out of the fractional share of another class.

Just as Adam Smith would break down national income into the wages of labor, the rent of land, the interest on reproducible capital, and a fourth category of entrepreneurial profit, so too did Adam Smith regard the price of any competitive product as being the sum of four necessary components.

First is wage cost to compensate for the *sweat and disutility of human labor.*

Second is interest cost to compensate for what Nassau Senior would 50 years later declare to be *the psychic sweat of the human abstinence and waiting involved in the act of saving for the future rather than consuming now.* Ferdinand LaSalle, the great rival of Karl Marx in the German socialist movement, had a good deal of fun in rhapsodizing about the Herculean sweat of Baron Rothschild in saving his millions of pounds. Still, in terms of apologetics for the different elements of cost and class sharing of income, Smith's first two components are understandable.

When it came to the third component, land rent, David Hume, Adam Smith, David Ricardo, and the American Henry George parted company with the pre-Revolution French Physiocrats who had glorified argiculture as the only productive industry and land as the only producer of true net product. People like to quote Adam Smith to show that he was not a stuffy reactionary. With respect to land owners, Smith pointed out that they love to reap where other men have sown. Land is productive, but not its owners, who are providing no true or honorary sweat deserving of a return. From this follows the notion that true rent–the return to the inexhaustible, nonaugmentable Ricardian land that is the gift of nature–is a most suitable object of taxation, both from an ethical viewpoint and from the viewpoint of involving the least efficiency distortion.

This concept of land rent as an unnecessary surplus is worth keeping in mind. Bernard Shaw and other Fabians later generalized this Ricardo-George doctrine to *all property*, alleging that their return is an unnecessary surplus that can largely be taxed away without production or other nondistributive consequences.

In our own day, an independent mind like Joan Robinson becomes a bit impatient with the idea that the interest and profit return to capital is something "deserved": whatever it took to bring the vector of heterogeneous capital goods into existence, now that they are in existence there is no real reason why the fruits of their combined collaboration with labor should not go almost wholly to labor. Indeed, one can specify technological models in which, if the laboring class as a collusive group militantly insist upon a high real wage that takes most of the total social pie, the resulting low level of profit involves no great penalties in terms of maintenance of production. Mrs. Robinson, and other members of the Cambridge-Italian neo-Keynesian school, may agree that the rate of saving and long-term growth of the system may be less if the more thrifty capitalists have their incomes decimated; but even this could be overcome by having the state do the saving conducive to more rapid growth.

Austrian economists less radical than Robinson—I have Böhm-Bawerk, Gottfried Haberler, and Lionel Robbins in mind—like to dispense with psychic disutility in favor of "opportunity-cost" theories of price determination. For such Austrians, the inelasticity of supply of all the factors, nonland as well as land, means that their rents can be taxed without distorting substitution effects and deadweight loss. They differ from Robinson in that they regard the returns to property as being well determined by economic laws independently of power bargaining—as if, so to speak, by a vast Cobb-Douglas, J.B. Clark Austrian production function for aggregate output. But in terms of policy, their model lends itself to agreement with her conclusion, in that redistributive taxation by the state could, in effect, make workers the owners of the nonhuman factors of production, or at least of their fruits.

Those who call themselves socialists fall into at least two groups: Marxists and the others. Modern economists like Abba Lerner, James Meade, and Oskar Lange (before he went back to Poland after World War II) have tended to become impatient with the vulgar Marxian notion that the labor theory of value has some factual or scientific validity. To insist that labor is the sole source of value in a system where labor, land, natural resources, and various productive inputs that have been manufactured in the past are allocated in a time-phased way to produce streams of different kinds of outputs, consumer goods, and intermediate outputs—this they regard as *unuseful.* All that is required according to egalitarians of this non-Marxian viewpoint is to say:

Nonhuman inputs are productive in creating outputs along with human inputs. But the technical indispensability *of those nonhuman factors has nothing to do with the* indispensability of their owners. *Their owners are quite dispensable. They can be dispossessed of their ownership by capital levies, by expropriation without compensation, by expropriation with full or partial compensation, or by redistributive taxation of the incomes they derive from property.*

It is true that people like Abba Lerner have been saying this for more than 40 years without being particularly listened to by the Marxists or, for that matter, by the propertied interests and electoral majorities. But not being listened to is a fate they share with Marxians and with numerous other critics of the existing mixed-economy order.

I began to list Adam Smith's four components of price and of national income. Before getting to the fourth I digressed into the views of later writers. Most of my discussion about the fractional returns to property and labor, as those shares work themselves out in the marketplace or as they are altered by governmental policies, could be carried on without ever even mentioning the word *profit.* Indeed, the words *interest* or *capital yield* could for the most part do the work of the word *profit.* And on the whole, Smith does work with a three-sector model of wages, rent, and interest.

But if memory serves, Adam Smith did sometimes make the further distinction between profit and interest. Thus, in the informed-man-of-the-world fashion that characterizes Smith's writings, he somewhere speaks of the rate of interest as being 6 percent at the same time the rate of profit is 12 percent. How neat that one is just double the other, but no neater than the convenient fiction of pre-Smith and post-Smith writers that national revenue, like an estate revenue, is split up into even thirds: one-third for the worker, one-third for the operator or employer, and one-third for the land owner.

When an eighteenth century writer put the rate of profit above the rate of interest, what did he have in mind? First, he usually had in mind *the differential return to some kind of management:* extra effort by the entrepreneur in handling funds and making productive decisions—and perhaps extra cleverness on his part in so doing. Today we would tend to call this the wages—high wages to be sure—of responsible managers. Because they make decisions so important for huge sums of money, the wages they command are high. Because they handle such large sums, Smith thought it made good sense to pay them well lest they abuse their trust or handle it carelessly. Because great talent in doing these important things is rare, the wage rents that are earned by those with such scarce genetic and educational advantages are handsome. A modern intermediate writer would treat these differentials completely as wages rather than profits, except for the realistic possibility that it may be optimal to give such high-talented workers a profit-sharing interest in the fortunes of the concern. This makes it something of a hybrid, poised between wages and interest or profit.

There is a second notion that early writers had in mind when speaking of a profit premium over and above the safe rate of interest. The capitalist owner of an enterprise was regarded as the risk taker of last resort. He paid out wages and rent; he paid out interest on capital borrowed from a passive rentier group; he produced with these acquired inputs; and he bought merchandise for sale. However, the ability to sell goods at satisfactory price is never assured in advance. One ship venture may be very profitable; but positive profit premium over and above the interest rate might well be cancelled off in the next venture which would be unsuccessful.

From the point of view of *profit as the chance algebraic premium above and below the interest rate*, one might on the average find no positive profit share and no positive average differential of profit over and above the interest rate. However, for that to be the case, risks in the long run would have to be fairly predictable even though chancy in the short run. And furthermore, capitalists would have to be fairly neutral with respect to risk taking, ready to accept a ducat if the fair coin turns up heads and lose a ducat if the coin turns up tails. However, suppose it is more realistic to assume that just as it is a human propensity to wish to shun the disutility of work and to shun giving up consumption today in favor of consumption tomorrow, so it is a human propensity to wish to shun the disutility and sweat of risk taking. In that case, those industries which are subject to heavy irreducible risks would in the long run find that their goods would be priced so as to cover not only the wage of labor, the rent of land, and the interest rate of needed capital, but also the positive risk or insurance premium needed to cover the disutility of risk taking. By means of reinsurance and hedging in speculative markets, the irreducible risks might be cut down and shifted more evenly over the community; but to the extent that an irreducible residuum of riskiness remains, a Smithian would expect price to include some compensation for it. Similarly, some component of the GNP, hard as it might be to identify and measure, would be the *profit return to risk taking.*

Chapter 31 of the elementary textbook had to point out that the current statistics on profits put out by the Department of Commerce by no means measure this fourth concept of profit. Corporation profits plus earnings of nonincorporated enterprise are a catchall of *implicit interest return* on capital provided by the owners of the businesses—in the case of smaller business, of *implicit wage earnings* of the proprietors, farmers, and professional people. There may be *some component of risk premium,* but how large it is or even what its algebraic sign is, there is no way of inferring from the figures themselves.

That chapter also had to point out several difficulties with the Smith and post-Smith concepts of profits:

1. Frank Knight has questioned whether people are risk averse, arguing that often they embrace risk without compensation or even pay for the privilege. Although he could be right, the bulk of the stock market evidence on the tradeoff between risk and return suggests that people as a whole do act as if they are risk averse. But Knight's skepticism goes on to argue that most uncertainties in real life are not at all amenable to the mathematical probabilities of risk. Thus, when the National Bureau reports that a person would have done better buying second-class bonds from 1920 to 1950 than buying gilt-edge highest-quality bonds, a Knightian would reply: "History is a one-time story. If the United States had not come out of the Great Depression as it did—and that was a perfectly possible outcome on which mathematical odds cannot be defined—gilt-edge bonds would have done better." So most of pure profit might be regarded as simply the discrepancy in an uncertain world between what people thought might happen and what actually happens.

2. Schumpeter put great stress in his theory of profit on the unforeseeable gains the innovator can temporarily get before imitators come in to compete away his necessarily temporary surplus returns.

3. Adam Smith was for the most part thinking of the interest and profit earnings of reasonably competitive enterprises. In a Galbraithian view of the world, most of the large corporations do not live in the dream world of effective competition. I do not know what Galbraith's theory of the share of profits is: his last books have not told us why they are as large as they are, and why they are not larger. The late Michael Kalecki of Poland attempted to create a theory of the profit share based on an alleged constancy of "the degree of market imperfection." But even when one reformulates his model to make it applicable to the real world, it is dangerously like one of those theories which the logicians can reduce to the tautology "Things are what they are because that is what they are." One does not get excited by the remark that morphine puts us to sleep by virtue of its soporific quality, but that bored reaction should not blind us to the fact that morphine does put one to sleep. As I have tried to understand the trends in the distribution of income, remarks about the degree of deviation of actual market conditions from the competitive model have not seemed to have predictive or explanatory content.

4. Time limitations require me to be dogmatically brief concerning proposed macroeconomic theories of income distribution. Nicholas Kaldor in 1955 floated the theory that spontaneous changes in investment spending, instead of producing changes in money and real GNP, in fact have no effects in moving a system from its full-employment position: the only effect of the changes in the investment multiplicand is to change the share of profits enough to bring full-employment saving into equality with the new level of investment. Kaldor has been called "Jean Baptiste Kaldor" for this full-employment model. However, events of the 20 years since its creation have not given us full employment or evidence confirming the model. The more cautious long-run theories of Robinson and Pasinetti have been of little explanatory value in interpreting what seem to have been the facts about profits in the last two decades.

Marxian Paradigms for Profit

Having quoted mainstream economists from Adam Smith to post-Keynesian writers, I must be ecumenical and take note of Marxian formulations. The law of the declining rate of profit is one tenet of such analysis. Karl Marx hoped to lay bare the laws of motion of developing capitalism by means of his novel analysis of surplus value.

The broad historical facts of the last century have involved a rising trend in real wages, a fractional share of wages in national income that is either constant or gently rising, and long-term meandering of the real rate of profit or interest.

A basic Marxian model that postulates a definable reproduction cost for wage labor is capable of defining a determinable rate of steady-state profit provided all goods are producible by time-phased labor and themselves as inputs.

The resulting steady-rate rate of profit will be constant in the absence of technical change. The level of this equilibrium interest or profit rate is definable without any recourse to Marx's novel algorithm in which the rate of surplus-value markup is reckoned on direct labor costs alone and is uniform between industries. The methods of Sraffa, Leontief, and other modern analysts benefit in no degree from Marx's novelties of analysis. But even if one waives this controversial point, the predictive implications of postulating a reproduction cost for labor at a meaningful, conventional subsistence level would be incompatible with the actual historical facts of a meandering profit rate and rising real wage rates. Logically, the paradigm should have implied a rising rate of profit from 1867 to 1976, a stagnant pattern for real wages, and a falling fractional labor share in the national income. (To grapple with the damnable difficulties of understanding and predicting real-world complexities, one will accept help from any source, however unpopular it might be with the conservative interests of plutocracy. Alas, perusal of the analyses proferred by Marxists abroad or at home has not deemed to reward analysts of the past, present, and future.)

Falling Profit, a Normal Thing?

If the expert jury does conclude that the profit rate has been falling worldwide this decade, that would not be a finding abhorrent or even surprising to Adam Smith and David Ricardo. Like Karl Marx, Smith and Ricardo each predicted the profit rate would fall. While the system was growing through accumulation, the fall in profit rate, Smith thought, would temporarily raise the real wage rate above the reproduction cost of labor. The fact of population growth itself, Smith thought, was a sign of wage prosperity. Ricardo saw perhaps more clearly than Smith that growth could not continue in a balanced exponential mode forever. The scarcity of land would invoke the law of diminishing returns. Since labor would always emerge from the fertile womb in the abundance needed to bring the real wage down to labor's cost of reproduction, Ricardo deduced that capital accumulation would reduce the interest rate to a minimum, and that a lower profit rate and an unchanged real wage rate had to imply that land rent collectors were the ultimate beneficiaries of progress.

By 1912 Schumpeter's classic *Economic Development* argued in a similar fashion for a decline in the rate of interest and profit to zero. By 1912 the human womb was no longer so fertile. Hence Schumpeter expected that both labor owners and land owners would reap the benefit of the capital deepening. At least this was Schumpeter's schemata in the absence of innovation and technical change. Why were Smith, Ricardo, and Schumpeter so comfortable with the prospect of virtual euthanasia of the interest-receiving classes? Remember that all three were essentially believers in Say's law, according to which there could never be underspending and involuntary unemployment.

Malthus, Sismondi, Hobson, Keynes, and most nonacademic economists were not so confident that there is a law of conservation of purchasing power which rules out unemployment and excessive hoarded savings. Marx believed that capitalists would be stimulated by any incipient drop in the profit rate to initiate labor-saving inventions to hold down real wages. He perhaps did not sufficiently realize that this would be likely to negate his law of the declining rate of profit. Rosa Luxemburg, Lenin, and other post-Marxian analysts of imperialism held that advanced capitalistic countries would need desperately to rely on colonies and exploitive foreign investment to put off the evil day of euthanasia and mass unemployment.

Innovation versus Diminishing Returns

It is almost exactly 40 years ago that Keynes's *General Theory* set off the Keynesian revolution. The universe of economics has not been the same since. Let me sum up the outlook for the rate of profit just prior to that bombshell. Schumpeter, Irving Fisher, Cannan, Pigou, and Hicks all agreed with the Smith-Ricardo march toward low profit rates to the drumbeat of capital accumulation and deepening. But as an offset to movements down static curves of diminishing returns, they all envisaged a quasi-random chain of invention and technical change. They expected the result to be a more or less endless Brownian vibration of the profit rate at average levels determined by the pace and character of invention relative to the rapidity of capital accumulation. Their model seemed to provide an appropriate fit to the stylized facts of capitalistic development: rising real wage rates, relatively constant factor shares, and meandering rates of profit.

Joan Robinson has taught us to recognize that this simplified parable of neoclassical economics is overly simple. My colleague, Robert Merton, working in a tradition first explored by Oxford's James Mirrlees, has shown how a one-sector, one-capital-good model subject to white-noise, Harrod-neutral technical change can be given an exact formulation. For it, the real wage does rise on the average; the real rate of profit does display a Brownian wobble according to an ergodic probability distribution; and depending on how closely the oscillating production function approximates the elasticity substitution of unity, the resulting factor shares tend to change little over time.

Mrs. Robinson regards such a flexible "leets" model as hopelessly unrealistic (*leets* is *steel* spelled backward, an inside joke). Such a model evades the problem of limitations on technical substitutability. It evades the problem of how to reduce a changing vector of heterogeneous capital goods to some scalar quantum measure of platonic capital. It evades what is called the "Hahn problem," which more than a decade ago Frank Hahn posed in the following form.

Given multivarious demands and capital goods, how does an unplanned market system know what path of productions and prices to aim for and follow?

There are an infinite number of alternative paths it could follow this next year with apparent equality of yield in every industry. Yet, as Hahn and other writers have suggested, only one of the infinity of paths can be a *permanent* equilibrium path, self-warranted by its own fulfillment. In the absence of omniscient planning or of a utopian system of perfect futures markets quoting prices on everything from now 'til Kingdom Come, how does a mixed economy organize itself with even a tolerable approximation to effective performance?

Writeoffs on REIT loans and urban condominiums provide examples that the Hahn problem is a genuine one. The wonder is that the examples are not more numerous. Most of the time, it is the macroeconomic malfunctioning of the system—inflations, slumps, and stagnations—that occasions greatest concern. Only intermittently do microeconomic malfunctionings force their way to the top of the agenda for economists' concern.

One understands the real world the best one can. Often that "best" is unsatisfactorily good. One may pragmatically evade the Hahn perplexity by conceiving of the real world as a generalized Merton-Solow model of many industries and alternative processes involving congeries of heterogeneous inputs. As tastes and technology change in ways only partially predictable, the system, so to speak, keeps re-aiming its motions toward configurations that are more or less self-warranting and maintainable, avoiding Ponzi-like tulip manias and necessarily transient changes in the terms of trade between various goods.

This admittedly fuzzy and less-than-satisfactory model, looked at from the perpsective of the longer-run economic historian, may be hypothesized to have some of the general properties of the oversimple Solow-Merton "leets" model:

It displays rising real wage rates from technical change. It displays meandering average profit rates over a decade depending on whether the life-cycle accumulation of capital is checked fully or partly by labor-saving or capital-saving technical change. The relative share of labor (inclusive of the return to "human capital" in the form of past investments into education and training) need not change systematically much in one direction or the other relative to the share of property (inclusive of rents from land, interest, dividends, and imputed accounts to equity ownership).

There is no logical necessity that the real world actually behaves much like this fuzzy paradigm. But as the Nobel biologist Peter Medawar reminds us, serious scientists struggle with the *tractable*: and until a better wheel comes to town, serious players at the game of understanding developments in the modern mixed economy will have to use the best wheel available. Some young economist in the room may win a Nobel Prize for devising such a better wheel—and I wish her Godspeed on the task!

Rectifying Investment Distortion

Taking a Toynbean world view—and no lesser viewpoint is relevant—I do *not* on balance discern a dearth of capital, except in the trivial sense that having more of all producible inputs would bring per capita consumption potential nearer to the maximal golden-rule state. If fewer of us wasted time, if the first seven laws of thermodynamics could be repealed, if, other things being equal, one had more capital goods—it is an uninteresting truism that productivity would be enhanced. And if my Aunt Sally had wheels, she'd be a stage coach.

There is a less trivial sense in which "capital shortage" is worth investigating. Any income tax system like the American one puts a wedge between the pretax return to society of having more capital and the posttax return to the investor deciding whether to trade off some current consumption goods against some future consumption goods. In addition, as Martin Feldstein has been analyzing, modern systems of state-financed old-age pensions may inhibit the level of capital formation in comparison with what the people would choose to save and invest in a private system that is kept running at full employment by central-bank policies that ensure no aborting of thrift in stagnation.

A case can therefore be made along lines argued decades ago by Myrdal, Tobin, me, and others of "socialization of thrift" in the following sense:

The central bank keeps real interest rates low enough to induce real capital formation at a pace sufficient to offset the extra savings generated by tight fiscal policies dictated by an enlightened electorate.

Attractive as this possibility might seem to be, in actual life, Burns, Wallich, and their fellow governors of the Federal Reserve System find themselves acting out the role of inflation fighters of last resort: fiscal ease voted by the people is used to offset monetary tightness contrived by the Central Bank. I blame no one for this Greek comedy—or perhaps tragedy—but must point out that the scenario is a reversal of the Myrdal-Tobin-Samuelson script.

Capital "Glut"?

Having made the preceding concessions to the notion of a possible capital shortage, I must state that the bulk of the evidence points in the opposite direction. As I survey the many studies made on real profit yields, the story seems to be thus: in Western Europe or North America, in Japan or Australasia, real earning rates of capital show a declining trend during the last decade or two. The decline is more acute in Italy and Britain than in the United States and Germany. But qualitatively the pattern is similar everywhere.

The study by William Nordhaus of Yale, in the 1974 *Brookings Papers on Economic Activity*, provides an excellent example. After correction for aberrations of inflation accounting, both before and after taxes there is a steady downdrift of the real profit rate. A dozen similar studies for Sweden, West Germany, Britain, and elsewhere tell the same story.

My MIT colleague Fischer Black reminds me how difficult it is to detect a genuine trend in the real return on capital. To know it, you must have a firm measure of capital's value at the beginning and end of the period. Since stock market valuations are so much like a random walk—a tale about white noise told by 30 million idiots and prudent men—the proper corrections to historic book values are hard to come by. Still there must be some pattern of evidence suggestive of stationary or declining real yields even for a Wiener-Itô-Merton stochastic diffusion process. And my Bayesian probabilities make me inclined to bet that the 1960-1974 trend, if not the 1950-1976 trend, has been somewhat downward.

Nordhaus provides an explanatory hypothesis for the fall of the profit rate. Perhaps, he speculates, it has fallen because risk-averse investors regard profits as less chancy than they used to be. On reflection, I am inclined to doubt this explanation. Investors have never seemed so jumpy and unsure of themselves as in the 1965-1975 decade. The failure of the stock market to serve as a hedge against inflation in this last decade has induced in the bourgeoisie a failure of nerve hardly consonant with the Nordhaus explanation.

From Glut to Dearth?

Capital glut rather than capital shortage provides a better scientific fit to the actual facts. But of course capital glut at one time can induce capital shortage at another. Perhaps the surprising strengths in real profit rates in 1975-1976 are the first signs that an element of capital shortage is beginning to be generated by the very stagnation of the Nixon-Ford 1970s epoch.

Those would be the signs a scientist would look for. Rather than agreeing with the fashionable postulate that an increased degree of oligopoly power explains the surprising improvement in profitability, one might keep a watchful eye out for the possibility that the OPEC energy crisis and the recession shortfalls in fixed investment are beginning to induce a rise in competitive capital yields.

However, given the facts on excess capacities in many different lines, it would be premature to declare the demise of capital glut and the arrival of capital shortage.

Puzzle of Falling Equity Values

A 10-hour speech could not do justice to the basic problems posed in these Diebold lectures. Only a few words can be spared to discuss the paradox of a stagnant stock market over a decade of inflation.

Perhaps the 1975-1976 rise will blow away the paradox. But even with the Dow Jones Industrial Index back once again to 1000, the following oddity requires explanation:

A decade ago the equity averages were about the same as today. Thus you can buy the earning assets of the U.S. economy for not very much more money than it would have cost 10 years ago. (I exaggerate a bit, since one must correct for new debt and make other adjustments.) Yet in the last 10 years, the cost of living, labor, and raw materials have all risen steadily and irreversibly. If you were to buy those same earning assets (plant, equipment, inventories, intangibles) in the commodity markets–at their production costs (or reproduction costs after depreciation adjustments)–you would find the total price has soared in comparison with 10 years ago.

All this has been nicely documented by estimates of Tobin and Bischoff at Yale. How do we explain this paradoxical discrepancy?

1. An important possibility is that equities were grossly overvalued in 1965. Newton's law of action and reaction then accounts for part of the discrepancy.

2. A second argument is fashionable but partially misleading. When a system goes from a low 1965 inflation rate to a higher equilibrium rate of 1975 inflation, nominal interest rates gradually adjust upward. So to speak, the price/earnings (p/e) multiple of bonds is lower at higher anticipated inflation rates. The argument goes on to assert: "Since common stocks must compete with bonds for the investors' favor, a drop in the equilibrium price/earnings price multiple of bonds must dictate a corresponding drop in price/earnings multiple of common stocks. So the post-1965 drop in real value of common stocks, far from being paradoxical, actually represents the needed once-and-for-all adjustment to a new equilibrium rate of inflation."

There is some grain of truth in this argument. But inflation-induced distortions in real tax rates aside, careful analysis can show cogent models in which the price/earnings multiple of common stocks should be the same at a high rate of anticipated inflation as at a low rate once all transient adjustments have taken place. (I do not wish to pronounce here on the merits or demerits of the view of John Lintner and others that, when inflation first accelerates and *while* the system is adjusting to a new higher permanent rate of inflation, the p/e ratios of stocks will systematically (and even rationally) fall. My colleague at MIT, Fischer Black, doubts this. Only an extended analysis could narrow down and appraise the disagreements.)

3. A third explanation offered for stagnation of stock prices has nothing essentially to do with inflation. Stipulating a deepening of capital which lowers the interest or profit yield on capital, shouldn't we expect this to show itself in a decline of rentier earnings and common stock prices? The economic theorists can by no means agree in giving necessarily affirmative answers to these separable questions.

First, the increase in the total of capital might be greater in percentage terms than the drop in the yield in each unit of capital. Thus *total* capitalists' yield might rise rather than fall. To be sure, this would be little comfort to your great aunt living off an unenlarged quantum of capital. To the person looking at his shares of a corporation that has been paying out its earnings in dividends and preserving the same size of operations, the size of those dividends per share would admittedly go down. But that is to say no more than that the yield on capital, expressed as an interest rate or profit rate, has gone down in accordance with the stipulated hypothesis.

Although a deepening of capital might result in no fall in its absolute total yield, even an unchanged absolute total could become a declining fractional share of the growing total of real national income. So the propertied classes might lose relative position.

Worse than that, it may be realistic to expect that the overall elasticity of substitution between capital goods and human labor is low enough so that property's absolute share is made to decline by the deepening of capital. Part of the malaise of the upper-middle-income and upper classes might result from this possibility.

Suppose for the sake of the argument that it is. Does that explain the fall in the real value of a typical common stock? The theorist must point out that a drop in interest rates is definitely not the same thing as a drop in the capitalized value of the earnings of a property. A postulated halving of the rate of interest, say from 10 down to 5 percent, would double the price/earnings multiple of a dollar of perpetual earning stream. It is a merit of the oversimplified Solow one-sector "leets" model that in it, a deepening of capital which lowers the profit rate unmistakeably has absolutely no effect on the value of a unit of old capital expressed in terms of a market basket of consumption goods.

We are still left, then, with a puzzle over explanation of the stagnating real values of all equities. It is not beyond the ingenuity of the economic theorist to dream up some pattern of capital-saving innovation which would destroy forever much of the value of existent capital goods. These dreary days it is hard for a physician to distinguish between paranoia and rational concern. Still, I would have to regard it as premature to put much credence in a scenario alleging dire outlook for incomes from property.

Conclusion and Outlook

An old hand at college lecturing learns to pace himself so that the end of the classroom hour arrives just as he has brought the discussion to the springboard between the past and the future. The present is that part of the past which has the greatest relevance for the future.

Moses-like, I have been leading you chosen people through the wilderness of the economic present. Like Moses, it is not given to me to enter omnisciently into the promised future. I must leave to Joshua—I mean to Professors Arrow and Lundberg—the triumph of resolving the uncertainties of the future, responding successfully to the title of these third John Diebold lectures, "New Challenges to the Role of Profit." As an economic theorist, I will venture only the following speculation about the promised land of the last quarter of the twentieth century.

I suspect that economic historians will judge the third quarter of the twentieth century to have been a vintage epoch for the mixed economy. Every year in Bordeaux is not a vintage year. Regression toward the mean is as real in economics as it is in biology. Though one expects the economic order to end neither in a bang nor a whimper, it would be rash of me to project for the quarter century ahead the sprint of economic growth of the quarter century behind us. Therein I suspect lies the true challenge to the role of profit, rather than from trade union headquarters, national capitals, or campfires of the Sierra Club.

3. Paul A. Samuelson

The Public Role in the Modern American Economy

This is not the first time that groups like the NBER have taken a broad look at the cosmic future. Let us hope we are a bit luckier in the present exercise.

One almost hesitates to mention the 1929 *Recent Economic Trends*, commissioned by the confident President Herbert Hoover and blessed by Wesley Clair Mitchell, our founder and patron saint, then at the apex of his scholarly career. That group of economists took a careful look at the United States economy and reported it to be in great shape with a sunny future ahead. That was in 1929!

Then again I recall that, before World War II was over, a National Bureau group consisting of a Harvard statistician and a Wall Street financier published a volume on the subject I am asked particularly to comment on today: the future state of the government finance. It was a sorry performance. It is easy to see in retrospect how woefully it underestimated the scale of post-1945 fiscal activity. But even at the time, this objective study reeked of wishful thinking and of editorializing in favor of the conservative views of its authors. I remember my old master Alvin Hansen commenting to me that no one alive would ever see a federal budget less than twice this volume's predicted numbers. And, as Hansen later explained to me when I asked him how he thought his prewar doctrine of secular stagnation had actually worked out in the postwar epoch: "Paul, my numbers for federal expenditure, fiscal deficits, and tax revenues—which were considered so outlandish in 1939 and 1944—turned out to be far short of the actual mark. Nature never got the chance to perform the needed experiment for us to know what would have happened if the postwar budget had been always in balance at a low level" (and, I may add in 1980, if the low birthrate had continued after 1939—the only trend anyone had a right to extrapolate in 1939).

So, it is well that I as a commentator am chastened by the demonstrated complexity in forecasting the future and in understanding the present before it has become history. But it is also well that at least some of the scholars who have prepared the surveys that we are all to discuss should have been bold in their speculations and should have nominated theses for us to agree with or try to shoot down. It is part of the eclectic diversity of the National Bureau, preserved in each of its reincarnations, that its authors should differ in substance and style. Thus, Professor Mansfield has cautiously reported some of the available facts about productivity and research, mentioned a few of the current hypotheses some have put forward to explain them, but has eschewed advancing a grand thesis of his own. Professor Easterlin, from the same university, has perceived the postwar movements in birthrates through the spectacles of his own self-generating every-other-generation cycle, giving his brainchild all the rope it can use. Professor Break, whose paper surveys my topic of government finance, has chosen to present the domestic facts in an analytical mode, so that at least our theories can know what it is they are purporting to explain.

What I want to do today is to examine critically some broad views about government that people outside of economics have been hotly debating. Here is (what, prior to hearing some of the speakers at this conference, I thought to be) a caricature, almost a parody, of what most businessmen believe. In a lower keyed version, but still in essentially the same thesis, I suspect it is a view that the majority of college graduates would essentially subscribe to. The thesis follows:

> The Roosevelt New Deal brought in some needed reforms. But this last half century has witnessed an overshoot of government regulations, taxation, and deficit spending. The vigor of the market economy has thereby been sapped—just as it has been in so many of the mixed economies abroad. United States inflation, stagnation in productivity, class struggle, and popular unrest is the inevitable consequence of the cancerous growth of the public sector engineered by powerseeking bureaucrats and politicians.
>
> Britain provides an archetypical case to prove that the hand of government withers progress and efficiency, and fails to make good on the "equity" it promises. As well, a comparative survey of all the mixed economies will bear out the same perverse correlation between the usurpations of the public sector and shortfalls of economic performance—Switzerland versus Sweden, Japan and West Germany versus Italy and the United States, and so forth.

Notice that I have included nothing in the above statement about the importance of limiting government for the sake of liberty itself. A Hayek, even if you could demonstrate to him a mixed economy where government planning, stabilization, and redistribution really worked well, would reject it in the same way he would reject a well-run jail. Such a view is still a minority view with the electorate, but where it does gain support from fellow travelers is to the degree that the actual "jails"—by which I mean the mixed economies as we know them—are not well run.

Tasting Puddings

What I wish to do here is to display that "respect for the facts" which Arthur Burns once proclaimed must be the National Bureau's watchword.

Is all of the above thesis borne out by the available facts?

Is any of it?

What is the cautious reading of experience on these controversial matters?

These are not easy questions. Since time is scarce, let me reveal at the beginning that I do not think the caricature as stated is unequivocally supported by the historical record. That doesn't mean it's wrong. It might be correct. But a fair-minded jury is under no compulsion to swallow its contentions on the basis of the empirical observations available.

Wishes of Bureaucrats

Here is one part of it that I find farfetched. Bureaucrats would of course like to have their empires grow; and politicians do prefer, other things equal, to be elected rather than defeated. It does not follow from this that I am able to make sense about trends, and to make good predictions, by assuming that it is the desires and psyches of Washington inhabitants that I must look to in explaining actual political happenings.

Social security is a good instance. As George Break observes, it has been one of the fastest growing elements of public expenditure and taxation. Those numerous clerks in Baltimore have been of least importance in the process. I have known most of the head actuaries in that program from the beginning. Their causal role has been, if not negligible, certainly minor. Indeed it was over their objections that so many of the evolving features have become dominant. Why then the growth? It was immanent from the beginning—once the national decision was made to introduce a general insurance scheme. Few of us had the imagination and courage to extrapolate what was immanent. But that is the usual story in these matters. My point is not that this has all been a beneficent thing. Franco Modigliani and Martin Feldstein may turn out to be right that the social security system is the cause of a reduced effective rate of saving and investing in the American economy. My point is that how Main Street and Congress feel about this matter, and not how civil servants do, is what has given us whatever it is we now have.

My old teacher, Josef Schumpeter, tried to set forth a theory of public finance based on the realpolitik of getting elected. I welcome modern revivals of this seminal idea. But all theories of revealed preference must be subject to the check of comparison with empirical data. And the innuendo that it is the power wishes of government officials that explains the police state is not a hypothesis that stands up well to explain the complexity of facts that need explaining.

Post Hoc, but . . .

The middle third of the twentieth century goes into the record book as the era in which the tax share of the public sector soared. The final third, we can confidently predict, is not going to be able to show a similar acceleration. This is so, if only because of the nature of a fraction, which has to be bounded by one. But it is also so because, as the market sector shrinks, one can expect there will be a resistance and backlash rather like that we have begun to see in recent years.

How has real GNP fared in this middle third of the century in which governments grew like a cancer? Would a Hayek have predicted in 1933 that the patient would show the debilitation of cancer? Would a Schumpeter in 1942 have written about "capitalism in an oxygen tent" on its march to socialism? Of course. And that is what I was taught at the University of Chicago was the likely future to look forward to after 1935.

But when we turn to the real world, we see it has been a different story. Of course, the recoveries from the world depression consequent upon deficit financing in North America, Germany, and elsewhere in Europe are easy to understand in terms of short-term fluctuations. But what Schumpeter was writing about in *Capitalism, Socialism and Democracy* was the long pull. If he came back to Vienna, Bonn, and Cambridge today, he would be as surprised as that urbane mind could admit to, by what the Kuznetses and Denisons have measured to be the postwar miracles of growth by the mixed economy.

Am I arguing that, *because* the public sector was burgeoning from 1932 to 1970, that is *why* world GNP outperformed the growth rates previously witnessed under the gales of creative capitalistic destruction? No. What I am precisely warning against in this commentary is such a facile attempt to read into the chaos of facts the theses you want to believe about them (theses which may even have important germs of truth in them).

Thus, Switzerland and Sweden show almost identical paths of Kuznetsian progress. If I gave you their two time series blind, you couldn't tell them apart. More than that. It is a great mistake to think that Switzerland is a Walrasian economy and Sweden a totalitarian state. If you examine the long vector of attributes of these two, you will find them surprisingly alike; and also you will find some surprising reversals of the usual stereotypes.

Debaters and lawyers are always trying to overstate their cases. I recall how, just after the mid-1940s, conservative friends used to point to Belgium and Holland. Belgium, they claimed was a market economy and it was prospering. Holland was allegedly a controlled economy and it was stagnating. If you inquired about the different degrees of bombing of the ports of Antwerp and Rotterdam, they lost patience with your pedantry. But of course in a few years, both economies showed marked departures from laissez-faire; and their relative growth rates showed no simple patterns of dominance.

What is relevant to the present session is to look at the numbers Dr. Break has given for the United States and compare them with similar numbers abroad. Everyone knows that Germany and France, to say nothing of the Low Countries and Scandinavia, have grown more in the postwar than has the United States. Is it then the case, as the above thesis would require, that these fast growing countries show a larger fraction for the market economy than we do? I have just had the occasion to prepare the eleventh edition of my elementary textbook *Economics*. Every four years I get reeducated on the world economy, and an economic historian could do worse—as Bob Gordon has indicated in footnoting his paper for this conference—than to use these successive revisions as a documentary source to chronicle both the change in events and in beliefs about them.

What I found, when preparing a table of comparative shares of GNP that taxes take, was that Switzerland and the United States each tax about the same fraction of national income. That paragon of growth and the free market, West Germany, has a larger total tax fraction than the United States or the United Kingdom do. And Germany, unlike America or Israel, has little call to spend on national defense. The Netherlands and Sweden are two nations whose public sectors have leaped above half their GNPs. Has Providence punished them for this profligacy?

Not yet. Their growth rates have for decades been exceeding our best performances. I happen to think that their future productivity trends will be adversely affected by this heavy load. But that thought of mine is not a National Budget thought: It is not a finding of statistical analysis or even a deducible lemma from a compelling model; but like so many of my best insights it is a Bayesian hunch that could never deserve the Mitchell-Burns imprimatur. If you match your hunches against mine, who is to be the referee to adjudicate between them?

Even Britain cannot serve as the whipping youth for the determined empiricist. For all the talk about the "British sickness," the United Kingdom's government's fraction of GNP expended on goods and services has averaged out to less than those reported for the United States in Dr. Break's tables. And, just to confuse the parable, Britain's productivity trend in the third quarter of the century turns out to have surpassed that of the United States—just as growth rate in the United States production index has outperformed production growth in Switzerland and Germany in the 1970s.

I've made my point: Only ideologues can see simple morals writ large in historical record. The facts tell their own story, but it is not the *simple* story that so many want to hear.

Welfare and Mutual Reinsurance

Thanks to earlier National Bureau authors, we have been reminded that conventional measures of product and productivity do not capture all the elements of welfare that the citizenry are concerned with. William

Nordhaus and James Tobin constructed their rough Measure of Economic Welfare (MEW) to make clear that there are offsets to the reduction in productivity which may result from environmental pollution standards and from occupational safety regulations. My neighbors and I go to the polls and by majority vote make sure that if *we* should happen to be unemployed, or blind, or penuriously old, we shall still receive some minimum of income payments. In agreement with Alan Blinder's paper, even though the ordinary measures of income inequality—e.g., Gini coefficients of Lorenz curves, Pareto-curve parameters—show no strong trends for the last three decades, it is my observation that there has been a perceptible reduction in lifetime inequality. Fewer people do go to bed hungry in present-day America; and life is not so short, nasty, and brutish for the poor as I can remember it being in my youth.

None of this is accomplished in a Pareto Optimal way. From the beginning of time such a state of thermodynamic efficiency has never been remotely approached. If economists were to wait for that day in which income redistributions are done in the Pareto Efficient way, they would wait forever. And society's members would wait with them.

Economists are a minority, no more numerous than chiropractors. Noneconomists go whole hours without thinking about Pareto Optimality. It is noneconomists who constitute our clients. We are their not-so-efficient servants. They are our not-so-clear-thinking masters.

Once democracies decide to second-guess the outcome of the market, the programs take on a momentum of their own. When I was a young student of what was to come to be known as macroeconomics, we all took for granted that F.D.R.'s new expenditures on welfare and unemployment compensation would have to last only so long as the economy remained significantly below its full employment potential. *After* recovery was achieved, those expenditures would recede in the simple anticyclical manner. That was the naïve expectation I shared.

Of course it didn't happen. You might think that this was the result of "politics"—a reflection of the weakness in the voting system that tends to make it easier to expand the economy than to restrain and contract it. Well, you would be wrong in thinking so. There may well be such a political bias in the workings of the mixed economy. But what I came to realize belatedly in the late 1930s—and it came from the writings of Bill Haber of the University of Michigan, writings that did not appear in refereed proper economic journals—that once society decided that people should not fall below certain minimum levels of well-being and income, the total of the welfare load would grow and grow. And so it has, no longer to my surprise, these last forty years.

My Worries

I have reached the age to scold and nag. So I must not fail you. Although for the most part my own value judgments applaud the economic trends that have been the trends of my times, my reason and experience with economic models leave me with a concern. Markets are more effective for many facets of economic activity than people have been able to make fiats and commands be. Any new nation freed from colonial bindings can give itself a socialist constitution and type out a crisp Five-Year Plan. But so often, we know from experience, these good intentions are not worth the paper they are written on.

The mixed economy is *mixed*. That is its strength: to mobilize for human ends the mechanisms of the market and to police those mechanisms to see that they do not wander too far away from the desired common goals.

The market can be a strong horse under us. But every horse has its limits. Those limits may not show up at once. A Sweden or Holland can for a time pile onto the horse ever greater relative loads. No one is wise enough to state exact limits beyond which the mechanism must begin to falter. But that doesn't mean limits are not there.

The problem for the United States, I have come to think, is to move beyond our good intentions. Our challenge is to preserve the useful features of the market—as when we want whatever slack there is in the economy to put effective downward pressure on prices and wage costs. But that should not mean that we have to submit to all the thoughtless consequences of the market's solution. To paraphrase Alfred Marshall of ninety-five years ago, economists need to put their cool heads to the service of their warm hearts. And that's what the American economy itself needs urgently to do in the years ahead.

Thoughts on Profit-Sharing

by

PAUL A. SAMUELSON

Cambridge (Mass./USA)

The modern mixed economy, however far it may have moved from historic capitalism, is still characterized by a considerable degree of inequality of annual incomes, lifetime incomes and consumption expenditures, and ownership of wealth. Humanitarians would like to see the degree of equality increase, both equality of opportunity and of actual realized living standards. Many of the policies and institutions of the mixed economy have for their purpose greater equalization of real incomes: graduated taxation of incomes (and of wealth), social security pensions and health insurance, unemployment compensation, and minimum welfare assistance from the State for families with low earning power or with various handicaps.

The trade union movement has had for one of its general goals the hope of raising the share of workers in total national income and lessening the interest and profit share of capital and the rent share of owners of land and natural resources. Militant collective bargaining has not, however, seemed to be very successful in promoting greater real wage share. One need not be a believer in the relevance of simple neoclassical models of distribution to be impressed by the tendency of a push for higher money wage rates to lead to inflationary rises in the prices of the goods workers buy – so that a problem for macrostabilization is created without any great success in reducing the income share of property or of the more affluent professional classes. Whatever be the realistic forces that determine the division of the GNP between property return and human-earnings return, they do seem to be stubborn forces that resist alteration merely because a militant rank and file or trade-union leadership desire such an alteration. (To be fair, one must admit that, in the absence of militant collective bargaining, the achieved share of GNP going to wage-and-salary earners *might* have been lower than it is. But even those economists sympathetic with the aspirations of workers cannot produce much hard evidence that militance and power pay off in terms of relative income distribution.)

Given the stubborn persistence of unequal incomes, persons of goodwill periodically turn to profit sharing as a hopeful way of promoting equality. If rich men generally enjoy the fruits of property, let every worker become an owner of property. "Wouldn't *two* incomes be even better than *one*? Of course it would," so goes the oft-heard simple refrain.

Outright and Gradual Appropriation of Capital

Early in the century, revolutionary socialists followed this logic boldly. Let the workers unite, successfully execute a revolution, seize political power, and then expropriate all property. The citizenry incorporated would then own the fruits of its own labor and also own and enjoy the fruits of the nationalized plant, equipment, land, and mines of the nation. One hundred percent of the national income or Net National Product would then go to the universal class of citizen-workers – to be allocated by a rational planning process between current consumption and capital formation to increase future consumptions.

To many this logic seemed too drastic. Expropriation without remuneration to them seemed extreme. Peaceable evolution rather than violent revolution became the slogan of Fabian socialists and non-Marxian social democrats. I have long thought that sentimental illusion permeated some of the thinking of this well-meaning group. Let me illustrate.

Consider land reform. *Ricardo, Henry George,* to say nothing of the eighteenth-century Physiocrats, regarded the surplus rent produced by land as something that might be taxed away from the undeserving so-called owners of land. Expropriation of land without compensation or permanent taxation (by the *single* tax) of its net rent, was one possible solution. But, again, to many that seemed drastic: Why strip the Duke of Liverpool of his heritage acres when you are leaving his brothers with their ownership of extensive factories and machines?

So, by way of compromise, evolutionists suggested: "Let all *future* increments of land value be subjected to heavy Henry George taxation." What was not realized is that a substantial part of *present* land value is merely the capitalized value of its future incremental rents – as far as those can be foreseen by anyone. Legislate this away, and *you are partially expropriating existing property values.*

Or, consider polite socialists who say: "Let us legislate, in one fell swoop or in installments, a capital levy whose proceeds are to be used to buy out – at fair market prices – existing acres of land, mines, plants and tools, or existing titles to such productivity in the form of shares of common stock or certificates of bonded indebtedness."

Obviously, this would involve a slow process of liquidation of the propertied classes in favor of ownership by the general working classes. Except that the proposed tax is democratically arrived at, it differs in no essential way from an even-handed law that *directly expropriates* some fraction of private ownership of productive assets.

Abraham Lincoln's Emancipation Proclamation (1863) abolished black slavery – an act of outright expropriation, followed by a gift to the former slaves of ownership in their own future fruits of labor. Could the same have been achieved by arm's-length free purchase by the government of slaves? Would we not still today have some human chattels in the South if that route had been pursued – as some share holders hold out?[1]

I may sum up. For capitalists to lose what they have and for workers to acquire it, an act of expropriation must be involved however one may shudder at the prospect or wish to sugarcoat the process.

Workers' Thrift to Become Capitalists

This sweeping dictum is of course subject to the following exception. Workers may transmute themselves into capitalists by the capitalist act of saving. If those classes which are now rich will in the future dissave, selling out their assets to the more thrifty working classes, we could end up with the workers owning all or most of society's productive assets. But of course it is easier for high income families to accumulate assets than for low income. This does not deny that, in modern Western societies, most personal saving arises from lifecycle needs and opportunities: *Franco Modigliani*'s researches have shown that the best single explanation of saving patterns within and across nations is in terms of accumulation during productive adult years in order to make some provision for consumption in years of retirement from the working force. Moreover, the "permanent income hypothesis" of *Milton Friedman* has stood up well under adversary investigation in its contention that, over broad ranges of income, the fraction of nontransitory income saved is very nearly a constant. Even the neo-Keynesian growth model of *Kaldor* and *Pasinetti* has the property that, if the fraction saved out of income earned by the class who work and own property is large enough relative to the fraction saved out of the incomes of those who never earn wage incomes, eventually virtually all of society's assets will be owned by the non-rentier classes.

Still, accumulating large ownership of property through abstaining from consuming one's current income is a difficult and slow process. There is a Marie Antoinette element in the advice of those conservatives who, wishing to increase the number of voters who will favor the interests of property, sermonize to the working population that they should save their pfennigs to acquire stocks, bonds, and real estate. They optimistically hope to be able to perpetrate something of a swindle, whereby if the housewife is persuaded to acquire a few derisory shares of mutual

---

[1] Under the Czars, Russia abolished serfdom, with *forced* compensation in the form of newly created state bonds. Subsequently the whole nation, including the freed serfs, were taxed to pay interest service on the bonds and principal repayment. A modern cliometrician could calculate estimates of what fractional share of private property in serfs was "expropriated" by this legislation. These days, in Cuba and elsewhere, *de facto* expropriation is thinly disguised by issue of bonds whose coupons and principal will be made derisory by arbitrary terms and by subsequent inflation.

funds, she and her husband will be persuaded to forget that 99% of their spendable income arises from wages rather than from profit and will vote with the conservative rich.

Socialization of Thrift

There is still another way that the fraction of national property owned by relatively few rich groups can be reduced in relative importance. A century ago *W. Stanley Jevons,* sensing that the coal mines of England were gradually being depleted, suggested that general tax rates be increased with their proceeds being used to reduce the internal public debt (and/or, by logical implication, be used to finance net capital formation to be owned by the government or, what is much the same thing, to buy up on behalf of the citizenry at large an enhanced share of existing British earning assets). Decades ago *Gunnar Myrdal* advocated in Sweden the socialization of thrift, whereby the government would run a budgetary surplus, offsetting this by a low interest central bank policy; the full employment composition of output would by these combined measures be shifted toward a higher fractional share for net capital formation and a lower fractional share for current consumption. Similar proposals were independently advocated in the United States by me, *James Tobin,* and others. Had the electorate accepted these proposals, gradually over time the citizenry at large would gain ownership of larger and larger absolute amounts of capital; if such a program could be pushed sufficiently hard, it could even result in a slow asymptotic approach toward 100% ownership of property on behalf of the state. Just as share owners indirectly control corporation policies by their proxy votes, governments could exercise ownership by vote of share proxies, gradually acquiring primary control prior to attaining ownership of more than 50% of each company's stock.[2]

Proposals of the kind just mentioned have not met a resonant response with the voters and their legislative representatives. However, the growth of social security public pension schemes might well have provided an opportunity for the realization of this logic. Under old-fashioned capitalism with its masses of the poor, most people died broke. They were supported in their old age on a niggardly scale by their children. Just as the nuclear family is breaking up in the modern age, a large part of old-

[2] Taxes inevitably involve an element of coercion, not qualitatively different from the coercion involved in capital levy. Also, a contrived increment of taxation would presumably involve graduated progressive rates that impinge more heavily on the rich than poor. So, in a sense, a successful program of socialization of thrift could in part be construed to involve a forced transfer to the less affluent of what would otherwise accrue to the affluent. This is something different from a bloody revolution, in that democratic due process would be involved at every stage of the game. And yet, economically speaking, the evolutionary solution would have something in common with the revolutionary.

age support comes from public systems or from corporation pension plans arrived at by trade union collective bargaining. If governments had decided to fund public pensions on what private actuaries deem to be sound principles, workers would be subjected to extra taxes during their productive years. These taxes would be set at a level high enough to provide a capital fund whose interest and principal would, for workers of each age cohort (born in the same year), just suffice to pay their retirement annuities. The real-capital counterpart of each cohort's actuarial fund would be invested in plant, equipment, and other productive assets. Now the proletariat is not without property: it would truly own the present discounted value of its retirement benefits; and also it would truly own a pro-rated share of society's plant and equipment. The Chairman of the Board of General Motors or Unilever might continue to reign as an elected constitutional monarch or premier. But it would be the government's pension fund that controlled a significant fraction of the share-owner proxy votes.

That the mechanism here outlined is not completely fanciful is shown by what is beginning to happen in Sweden. There, so large a part of the national income is going into pensions as to make it likely that in the decades to come the government will acquire an important ownership stake in Swedish industry. This is quite apart from traditional socialist ownership by the government of particular steel mills, railroads and industries.

As a matter of historical fact the United States and most countries have not been financing their social security systems along so-called sound actuarial lines. It is more nearly the case that each generation of living workers are taxed in order to provide funds to transfer to the existing generation of retired workers. This reality will become increasingly recognizable as time goes by when the various so-called trust funds of the public pension system are seen to be only a fraction of what an actuary would require of a fully funded noncompulsory private system.

Modigliani's lifecycle model of savings gives some support to those critics of social security who claim that under its present mode of financing it serves to lower effective social thrift and capital formation. Professor *Martin Feldstein* of Harvard University has in recent years been one of the most profilic propounders of this criticism. Although my own view is that the matter is a complicated one, in the October 1975 *International Economic Review* I did formulate a model in which governments' establishing of social security displaces private thrift by exactly the amount of publicly contrived thrift. My own preferred reading of reality holds that the general populace is not free of myopia: paternalistic legislation of compulsory public pensions may therefore increase effective lifetime wellbeing, rather than simply provide in a public way that profile of lifetime consumption which would otherwise be provided by spontaneous private decision. (This view of possible merit in paternalism does not necessarily involve disagreement with the *Feldstein* view that present modes of U.S. finance of social security may serve to lower the fraction of GNP devoted to capital formation in comparison with what would prevail in the absence of social security or in the presence of alternative ways of financing social security.)

Realities of the Modern Mixed Economy

Let me sum up this part of the analysis. The simple nineteenth century view that the few rich own essentially most of the wealth and that the many poor own essentially only their wage earning power is no longer tenable under twentieth century affluence. Not only is there mobility among and between the income classes, but in addition ever-larger fractions of the total population take on some of the essential patterns of the so-called middle classes. *Pareto*'s end-of-the-century view that immutable iron laws govern income distribution is simply not borne out by the facts: in *Pareto*'s time, the average man richer than I had mean income three times mine; working through any economic almanac, one finds that these days the average person richer than I has an income twice mine. This is a drastic change, but even within unchanged values for Pareto's coefficient characterizing the branch of highest incomes, there can be significant movement of the population toward greater equality of distribution of income. The Gini-Lorentz coefficient of effective lifetime real incomes, corrected for state transfers and taxations, would show a significantly different picture from that of undiluted capitalism.

Still, I applaud the fact that humanitarians show impatience that mixed economies should make even greater progress toward equality of both opportunity and *a posteriori* realizations in the years to come. So I should now like to turn to some sympathetic but objective analysis of proposed profit-sharing schemes.

Risk-Free Wages as Overhead Risks for Businesses

I have available to me only brief English abstracts from the 1972 and 1975 Annual Reports of the [German] Council of Experts on Economic Development bearing on the issue of Profit-Sharing with Limited Liability. Hence, any views I express are far from authoritative and must be considered as preliminary and tentative. In particular, my criticism and doubts are only for the purpose of furthering the discussion, not for the purpose of dismissing new proposals for reform or of throwing cold water on bold innovations.

A century ago, workers rented their labor for short periods of time in return for wages. At the docks or slaughterhouses workers appeared each morning not knowing whether they would be hired that day, or be sent home in the afternoon. With professors it was otherwise: we had annual contracts, and eventually we had effective lifetime tenure. The employees of large corporations are today treated more like professors. Not only in Japan (but especially there!), wages and salaries tend to become *overhead* rather than *variable* costs for the corporation. Wage earnings are then much like bond interest, and are very unlike discretionary corporate dividends or residual profits. Only with respect to cyclical layoffs do white-collar (and, increasingly, blue-collar) workers of large corporations shoulder the risks of varying supply and demand.

What is safety from risk for the employee is risk to the employing shareowners. Net profits are volatile when revenues vary and costs are fixed. Since workers are generally poorer than capitalists, and since risk-taking is relatively easier for the affluent than for the needy, the described uneven division of risk is perhaps optimal. And to the degree that workers become more affluent in modern times, they can begin to save and accumulate assets, putting some of them into common stocks and other risk-taking instruments. There is no reason why the worker should invest his funds for future life contingencies (education of children, vacation trips, medical catastrophes, old-age comforts) in the shares of the corporation he works for or in related industries. (Indeed, there is a case against investing in an activity upon whose prosperity the worker's job and earnings are already contingent.)

All this argues *against* profit-sharing programs. Here, however, are some arguments in their favor. People spend one-fifth of their lives at work. Their office and factory jobs are as important to them as their school, church, or home neighborhood. They make friends at work. They learn from their supervisors. To cement good relations and express team loyalties, employees may *want* to put part of their nest-eggs into shares of the corporation that employs them.

More important, the output produced by a person's labor input is *not* an immutable engineering constant. The economists' tool of a "production function" cannot be defined independently of workers' morale, attitudes, and wage rates. This truth seriously modifies the validity of conventional microeconomics. Workers may produce more effectively and may promote the profitability of the firm if they have a sense of financial incentive and profit reward when the corporation flourishes. That is why, in the 1920's, private profit-sharing plans were introduced by employers anxious to woo workers away from militant unionism and to coax out high productivity from the workers. During the great Stock Market Boom, many profit-sharing plans guaranteed workers a minimum annual wage with extraordinary bonuses in periods of high corporation profitability; and promotional campaigns were put in to sell company stock to its own workers.

Many, perhaps most, of such plans foundered on the rocks of the Great Depression. However, there still are some companies (Eastman Kodak is one example, many Japanese corporations are other examples), in which a significant fraction of their workers' annual incomes are received in the form of periodic *bonuses* contingent on the profit performance of the employing corporation. Such workers are less like professors, and more like top corporate executives.

In a sense, all this involves some residual-profit income for the working classes. There is no special reason why a socialist should care one way or the other that such schemes be advanced. For the risk-taking owners of the corporation's capital, such schemes represent some dilution of their equity receipts in prosperous years; but, in return, such schemes do lower somewhat the riskiness in bad years of inflexible wage contracts. The comparison is quite like that of a firm's decision to use more or less leverage of equity capital with debt capital: by the Modigliani-Miller theorem, shareholders can offset any enhanced or reduced variance of firm profitability by the way shareholders rearrange their total asset portfolios between safe liquid holdings and volatile capital assets.

It is *not* clear that higher total worker income will result from such profit-sharing schemes. What the worker gives up in assured wage may be just matched by what he receives on the average over the years in variable bonuses. *Only if the overall productivity of the firm is enhanced by the feeling of participation will there be any net gain of society's income* (and any such gain will be divided up among both workers *and* property owners). One must emphasize these trite banalities because enthusiasts for profit-sharing are always making unsubstantiated claims that somehow something-for-nothing is achieved by such schemes.[3]

Let us suppose, however, purely for the sake of the argument, that it makes good sense in terms of productivity for there to be in some large-scale sectors of industry a number of (1) profit-sharing bonus plans, (2) employee-ownership of shares in the employing company, (3) partial investment of employee-employer pension funds in the shares of the firm itself. Still it does not follow that much will be accomplished by such programs in enhancing the fractional ownership share of workers in society's plant and equipment. Rational workers, realizing that an enhanced share of their future consumption standards will now be contingent on the profitability experience of these firms, will other things equal, take on less common-stock ownership of other corporations. They will prudently put more of their savings into their own homes and into fixed-principal assets.

How then do the proponents of new profit-sharing programs envisage that such programs will elevate the relative position of the working class?

i) Do they think that the amounts employers must now contribute by law to profit-sharing funds represent a *net increment* to wage share in national product and a *new decrement* of capitalists' share? I see little warrant for such a supposition: if militant collective bargaining, aided by legislation sympathetic to the worker's position, cannot do much to elevate the wage share of GNP, why should the gimmick of profit-sharing change matters?

[3] The U.S. today has so-called ESOP plans that give some tax loophole advantage to certain kinds of profit-sharing trusts. *Louis Kelso,* a San Francisco lawyer, has made extensive claims for such innovations. Often John-Law schemes, in which somehow, out of bank loans, equity is created from thin air, get involved in the profit-sharing Gospel. Those few economists who have audited the economic theories underlying the proposals and the claims made for them have generally not rendered favorable verdicts on them. I must concur in these negative appraisals.

ii) Is the new profit-sharing legislation essentially a way of cutting down on workers' current-consumption enjoyment of wage incomes and of enhancing workers' effective saving? One can entertain some doubts that it will effectively succeed in any such purpose, rather than being offset by less saving by workers out of their remaining discretionary incomes. But suppose it does achieve a net increment of workers' saving, and thereby ultimately increases the fraction of productive wealth owned by workers. What has that to do with profit-sharing? Why could not the same good (or bad) purpose be achieved by mandatory forced-saving schemes that involve no profit-sharing features *per se?*

Final Caveats

I raise these questions for discussion. If space permitted, I could raise questions favorable to profit-sharing programs. Thus, the problem of "incomes policy", of macroeconomic stabilization, might be alleviated if workers will accept less rigid wage rates in bad times. As workers achieve a middle-class standard of life, they may have the leeway to forego rigid wages in slumps in the good cause of helping to make the economic system resistant to a) creeping inflation and b) stop-go recession-recovery operations. Put this way, such programs might seem more attractive to the propertied classes than to the working classes. Assured steadiness of wage contracts is not a benefit we would want workers to give up lightly (or even want professors to give up lightly). Fiscal stabilizers – varying tax revenues and tax rates, unemployment compensation or income-maintenance supplements – are perhaps to be preferred to workers' altruism. Certainly it serves little useful purpose for people to pull in their belts when the social problem is merely one of inadequate monetary demand.

I must conclude with the candid impression that more in the way of long-run reform may be expected of the new profit-sharing schemes than they can perhaps deliver. And with the reminder that there are various schemes for greater worker participation in firms' decision making that are analytically distinguishable from mere increased equity ownership by the working classes.

Summary

Most of the national income is wages. Most workers receive little property income: education as "human capital", home ownership, and savings for old-age retirement are the major exceptions. Too much writing on profit-sharing is romantically unrealistic. There are no easy ways to expropriate capitalists' property to the workers' benefit. Only if profit-sharing happens to motivate workers to greater productivity is there a costless source for workers' new property. Unfortunately, prudent risk aversion argues against workers' concentrating their life-cycle savings in their own industry or firm. By and large the welfare state, through its budget, redistributive taxation, and social security schemes, has been the major source of workers' receiving some of the fruits of capital in addition to their own work earnings.

THE ROOTS OF INFLATION

Inflation continued to rage in 1978 throughout every region of the world. Indeed, inflation worsened in the United States to the point that Pres. Jimmy Carter late in the year reactivated guidelines for wage-price controls and gave priority to hard-money and tight-budget programs designed to cool off the economy.

The cost of living, as measured by the consumers' price index, had risen by 11% from 1973 to 1974. The reality of two-digit annual price inflation, interacting with the fivefold increase in the price of oil by the OPEC (Organization of Petroleum Exporting Countries) cartel, brought on the worldwide 1974 recession. At a heavy cost in terms of unemployment, lost output, and depressed profits, U.S. price inflation was brought down in 1975–77 to a base level of about 6%.

But in 1978, the fourth year of vigorous economic expansion, food prices began to accelerate at an ominous rate. And the prices Americans pay for services—the cost of medical care, the premium for car insurance—continued their irreversible rise.

It is no wonder then that polls of public opinion report that people of all classes regard inflation as the number one economic problem. To be sure, the overall rate of U.S. unemployment continued to hover around 6%, a rate that would have been considered fairly high back in the decades of the 1950s and 1960s. Among nonwhite minorities, particularly young urban workers without skills, unemployment rates persist at very much higher levels, 25 and even 50%. Nonetheless, the U.S. had done better than the other leading nations in bringing down overall unemployment; from a peak rate of 9% in 1975 to the autumn 1978 rate of around 6% represented a rapid decline. Moreover, the expansion in total jobs was remarkably great, as more and more women chose to work for pay and as those born in the baby boom of the 1950s became of an age to seek jobs.

A tight labour market began to put upward pressure on wage rates. Help-wanted advertising rose as a barometer of skilled worker shortages. Corporations yielded to trade union negotiation for collective bargaining contracts, often granting increases in wage rates and pension benefits of 10% per annum over three-year contracts. Nonunion workers, facing increases in the cost of living of 8 to 10%, suffered a drop in their real wage earnings unless they could achieve commensurate hikes in pay. Unit labour costs inevitably rose, rising particularly in that the late 1970s have been years of disappointing productivity improvements. People these days want to enjoy some of the fruits of affluence in a more relaxed pace of labour. As in prosperous Sweden, absenteeism becomes common. Scientists, engineers, and experts in business management continue to improve technology know-how, but not at the extraordinary pace of the epoch just after World War II.

Fortunately, harvests of food and fibre have not been as disastrously bad in the late 1970s as in the earlier years of the decade. Still, Soviet and Chinese shortfalls in crop production continue to put pressure on staple prices. Successful lobbying by U.S. farmers has led to governmental programs that tend to reduce production whenever abundant supplies threaten to keep farm prices down.

Dollar Depreciation. Along with rising wages and raw material prices, recent U.S. inflation has been aggravated by the depreciation of the dollar. Since the autumn of 1977 the exchange rate for the dollar has fallen most relative to the Swiss franc, the Japanese yen, and the West German mark. The dollar has fallen less compared with currencies of other industrial countries, such as the French franc and the British pound sterling. The U.S. dollar has even risen relative to the Italian lira and the Canadian dollar.

When we measure the average drop in the dollar exchange rate, giving weight to each of the countries according to how much we trade with them, the dollar has lost about an eighth of its value in the last five years. During that same period the Swiss franc has almost doubled on a trade-weighted basis, the mark has risen by about 40%, and the yen by about a third. Since there cannot be two different geographic prices for any staple good that can be cheaply shipped from one region to another, the rise in the dollar price of the mark and the yen must mean a greater rate of American inflation for staple goods than for similar staple goods in West Germany and Japan. No wonder then that the inflation rate has not been so high in those countries as in the U.S. And no wonder that the inflation rate has been higher in Italy and Canada than in the United States.

Fortunately, the extra U.S. inflation induced by depreciation of the dollar has been only a small fraction of the dollar's actual percentage depreciation. This shortfall is fortunate because it means that, to potential foreign importers, the costs of American goods have become much more competitive. As the U.S. is able to export more, the deficit in its balance of trade may at long last stop growing and begin to disappear. Reinforcing this favourable tendency for the dollar *eventually* to float upward rather than downward is the fact that West German and Japanese exports to the U.S. are beginning to run into strong competition from now-competitive American products. Detroit car manufacturers face smaller cost increases than do distributors who must import Toyotas and Volkswagens at prices sharply inflated by the appreciation of the yen and mark.

By late autumn of 1978, President Carter finally took action to help support the floating dollar. He arranged for a U.S. fund of some $30 billion to be used for dollar stabilization; countenanced higher interest rates in the U.S. and slower economic growth; even showed a willingness to run extra risks of an end-of-the-decade recession, if that was the price of fighting inflation and preventing further dollar depreciation.

Diagnostic Facts. Before choosing a prescription to cure a disease, the expert physician must first attempt to diagnose the nature of the disease. And to formulate a reasoned diagnosis, he must achieve an accurate description of all the symptoms displayed. One can summarize the factual symptoms of modern inflation preparatory to diagnosis and therapy as follows:

1. The worldwide recession of 1973–75 did achieve a general reduction of the two-digit price inflation of the frenzied boom years of the early 1970s. By the late 1970s the U.S. inflation rate compared favourably with most other countries, Japan and West Germany being notable exceptions.

2. As the final years of the decade came into view and as memory of the mid-decade recession began to fade, some new worsening of inflation has become apparent.

3. Virtually every industrialized country is now clearly showing symptoms of the new disease called "stagflation" (*i.e.*, the persistence of uncomfortably rising prices and wages *at the same time* that there seem to exist in the contemporary mixed economy uncomfortably high levels of unemployment and of unused plant capacity).

Popular Fallacies and Half-Truths. People know they hate inflation. Each age needs a scapegoat for real and fancied ills. Inflation is the scapegoat for the modern age.

Suppose your wage goes up by 7%. Suppose at the same time that the OPEC cartel is raising the price of oil, that crops are failing in Eastern Europe, Asia, and the Mississippi Valley, that Iowa farmers are gaining at the expense of urban earners, and finally that productivity growth is languishing in your affluent society. Then most or all of your gain in money earnings will be found to be illusory, as the prices you must pay also rise by around 7%. You blame inflation. But really you should blame the oil and food scarcity and the disappointing productivity trends. For, even if there had been no inflation, you would still have to experience the same disappointing growth in your real income. No wonder, then, that careful, objective economists, like G. L. Bach of the Stanford Graduate School of Business, are hard put to find any broad income class that is the particular victim of inflation.

What then are the primary genuine evils involved in present-day inflation? Here is a brief list.

1. Unexpected and unanticipatable changes in the rate of inflation redistribute incomes in a chaotic and destabilizing fashion. There is rarely anything fair about the process. When the inflation rate is high it is also likely to involve great variability and unpredictability, exacerbating class tensions and decreasing the efficiency of resource use.

2. Modern mixed economies are prone to rates of inflation that accelerate rather than stay constant. Democratic governments feel an imperative need to do something about accelerating inflation before it turns into chronic inflation, like the doubling of prices every decade in so many Latin-American countries, to say nothing of galloping inflations like those of the Confederacy in the American Civil War, the German hyperflation after World War I, and the Hungarian and Chinese destruction of their currencies after World War II. There is little exaggeration in saying that the principal cause of recessions in the Age After Keynes is this felt need of governments to fight inflation by deliberate policies that cool off the economy and slow down its rate of real growth.

3. The brute fact of stagflation creates grave dilemmas of policy. Authorities know how to undertake fiscal and monetary policies that will work against inflation. They know how to undertake those same policies in reverse so as to work against unemployment and stagnating real incomes. But in the presence of modern chronic stagflation, that which helps against inflation hurts unemployment; that which helps against unemployment worsens inflation. Disillusionment over the ability of Washington, Bonn, Stockholm, or Tokyo to "fine tune" the economy comes, not from the inability of analysts to forecast future economic conditions, not from inability to appraise the length and variety of time lags before programs have their intended effect on the future economy. The inability of a jury of the best economic experts to agree upon macroeconomic policies that will ensure reasonable price stability and satisfactory full employment comes from the basic tendency in every modern mixed economy for prices and wages to rise in an inflationary degree *even prior* to conditions of overall demand that will provide what democratic electorates deem to be adequate job opportunity and adequate attainment of the economy's potential for real growth.

Older Theories to Explain Inflation. Beginners in economics are often told: "Inflation results when too much money spending bids against too few economic goods." This touches on both demand and supply. If productivity improvements increase the supply of goods, other things being equal, the rate of inflation can be reduced. If people spend their money more rapidly or if the central bank prints billions of new dollar bills for release from helicopters, enhanced demand will bid up the prices of goods once all labour and capital resources have become fully employed and further increases in output are severely limited.

Under the relatively pure form of capitalism that obtained a century ago, before the welfare and stabilizing activities of government made ours a "mixed economy," the elementary propositions of the previous paragraph contained much useful truth. As John Maynard Keynes put it in his revolutionary scholarly work of 1936, *The General Theory of Employment, Interest and Money*, the primary task of government used to be to expand total dollar demand by just enough to create enough jobs for all qualified workers seeking employment.

Thus, in 1932, at the bottom of the Great Depression, there was poverty in the midst of potential plenty. Grass grew in the streets. People wanted work. Capitalists wanted to put their idle machines to work. Defying old-fashioned orthodoxy, government could usefully increase its spending and cut down on its taxing. It could aim deliberately for a budgetary deficit and a growing public debt. This way existing dollars would turn over more rapidly, and new dollars could be created to help finance the budget deficit at unchanged low interest rates. Total spending would come into being to produce a new supply of goods commensurate with the additional spending, and no significant price or wage inflation would have to take place.

What would happen, though, once full employment was reached and excess plant capacity was exhausted? Then further new spending, whether brought about by still larger budget deficits or by concomitant Federal Reserve expansion of the money supply, would bid up prices and wages. This economists would call "demand-pull inflation"—as enhanced spending demand pulls or bids up prices and wages of limited goods, labour supplies, and capital capacities. Old-fashioned inflation was simple for political economy to understand.

Stagflation in the Humane Welfare State. Simple demand-pull inflation, prior to the epoch of stagflation and of "cost-push inflation," was easy for governments to control. They needed only to curb the central bank printing of money and the government's overspending by balancing the budget and running a budgetary surplus. And by curbing the total stock of money and its rate of growth, government policy would confront people and business with interest rates that were high enough and with cash balances tight enough to bring the total of demand spending into balance with the full employment supply of goods.

But 1978 was not 1878, nor even 1928. Today everywhere there is the welfare state. Whereas it used to be a case of either work at whatever wage is offered or starve, now there is the humane state. Unemployment insurance and public welfare payments help to provide a minimum of living standards even if you cannot find employment or will not accept a painfully low wage. Here then is the root cause why unemployed resources no longer put downward pressure on wages and prices: man's humanity to man.

Few would wish to turn the clock back to the inhumane society. In any case, it could not be done politically in any of the modern democracies—the United States, Canada, Japan, Scandinavia, Britain, West Germany, or elsewhere in the developed world. There is thus built into the very nature of the modern mixed economy a problem of *cost-push* inflation intertwined with that of old-fashioned *demand-pull* inflation.

What to do about this modern pathology? John Kenneth Galbraith, the exponent of the new industrial state, believes the only cure is to have an "incomes policy"—permanent governmental controls of prices and wage rates. Milton Friedman, high priest of laissez-faire capitalism, declares that there are no new problems of cost-push inflation. "Adhere strictly to a rule of a constant growth rate in the money supply at an annual rate equal to the slow growth rate of potential high-employment output," Friedman argues in effect, "and in the long run your society will succeed in avoiding price inflation."

Unfortunately a jury of economic experts cannot agree that Galbraith's permanent price-wage controls can be made to work effectively and efficiently in a democratic mixed society. Nor can the jury agree with Friedman's diagnosis that the mixed economies of the last part of the 20th century can be made to behave like the laissez-faire economies of Victorian capitalism.

A core of agreement is discernible among present-day economists. Most of them agree that money matters. Changes in the money supply tend in the longest run to produce changes in the general level of prices in the same direction and (other things being equal) in approximately the same degree. In the shorter run—a year or two ahead—increased money spending can mostly result in expanded production and employment so long as labour markets are slack and industrial equipment is not fully employed.

Those who have studied the several episodes of mandatory wage and price controls, experimented with in the post-World War II period by each of the mixed economies, have usually agreed on the following interpretation: controls work rather effectively in the very short run, for three or six or nine months. But increasingly they become ineffective, inefficient, and inequitable. Bureaucracies to enforce them must proliferate. Courts and tribunals become jammed with litigation. Supplies of staple goods whose prices have been too rigidly frozen simply dry up. In desperation and impatience, voters, legislators, and Cabinets terminate the controls; and, once the lid on prices and wages is removed, much of what you thought you had gained from putting in such an incomes policy is lost as corporations hasten to raise their prices and workers insist upon achieving higher wage rates.

The Political Business Cycle. U.S. experience in the 1970s, and experience elsewhere, confirms the stagflation dilemma faced by the mixed economy. Nations perforce contrive stop-go policies. When the inflation part of stagflation is hurting the electorate most, governments step on the fiscal and monetary brakes to cool off the rate of price rise. The result is an outright recession or a growth recession (in which, although output does not actually fall, it grows more slowly than the increase in labour supply and productivity tend to make possible). When the costly stagnation cure for inflation is vexing the electorate, the government finds itself releasing the throttle of fiscal and monetary expansion. Thus the old-fashioned business cycle of anarchistic market capitalism has been succeeded by the new-fashioned "political business cycle."

Contemporary history confirms that economies suffer from chronic creeping inflation. Political economy waits upon new innovative research to provide better therapies for the scourge of stagflation, much as medical research seeks for breakthroughs in knowledge to cope better with the scourges of cancer and cardiovascular diseases.

Pessimists believe that a U.S. recession by the end of the decade is inevitable. The new Carter program to defend the dollar may itself contrive such tight-money conditions as to bring on an early 1979 recession. If the president and the Federal Reserve back down from their tough crusade against inflation, the pessimists believe that the recession will merely be delayed. And the longer the delay, the more virulent they expect it to have to be.

Optimists take comfort from the apparent success of the Labour government's "social contract" with the British workers, which seems to have helped reduce the U.K. inflation rate from 25% per year to less than half that rate. This gives hope that the Carter quasi-voluntary price-wage guidelines, reinforced by some monetary and budgetary austerity, can make a contribution to inflation control. Inasmuch as Europe and Japan have scarcely recovered from the 1973–75 worldwide recession, there is less reason to fear that slower U.S. growth will plunge the whole globe into a new recession.

Realists understand that inflation is not a problem that will soon go away.

378

RECESSION — Causes and Consequences

By Paul A. Samuelson
and
William F. Samuelson

Business conditions never stand still. One year, sales are booming and jobs plentiful. Another year, the stock market collapses and the bankruptcy courts have standing room only. Economic history books chronicle the sequence of recession, expansion, recession. And in the bad old days of ruthless capitalism, there even occurred major depressions when banks failed by the thousands and grass grew in Main Street.

An Extinct Species? In the United States, pure capitalism has gradually given way to a *mixed economy,* in which the government shapes its tax and expenditure policies to stabilize the ups and downs of business. The Federal Reserve Board acts to control the money supply and counteract the business cycle. Is it therefore the case that recessions are a thing of the past—like smallpox, only a bad memory?

No. It is premature to announce the death of the business cycle. From 1973 to 1975 the whole world experienced a recession—the worst and longest in the post-World War II Age of John Maynard Keynes. As the decade of the 1980's begins, the United States shows all the traditional symptoms of a recession, major or mini. Production drops. People get the bad news of job layoffs. Construction of homes, industrial plants, and manufacturing equipment slows down. Red ink begins to show up on corporate annual reports, and families find it harder to make ends meet.

Although a final cure for tuberculosis is yet to be found, its occurrence these days is rarer than it used to be and its form less virulent. Similarly, we can take real comfort in the fact that recessions are milder in the mixed economy than they were under pre-New Deal capitalism. They are also shorter and occur less often. Our parents and grandparents grew gray and wrinkled with worries our children will scarcely know.

Stagflation. Alas, when you cure one old disease, you may be brought face-to-face with a new one. At the same time that the mixed economy has alleviated the curse of old-fashioned depression and recession, there has arisen the dread new specter of "stagflation"—the odd fact of stagnation in production and employment *coinciding* with inflation in the cost of living.

The economic challenge that confronts the United States also haunts other nations. In Germany and Japan, Sweden and Switzerland, France and Italy, Britain, Canada, and Australia, voters and government officials are ringing out the 1970's and ringing in the 1980's with anxious concern: Is a worldwide recession brewing? Could it turn into a great depression like that of the 1930's? Can the system enjoy reasonably full employment and essential price stability for the things we buy? Can *humane* distribution of the aggregate economic pie be compatible with *efficiency* and *progress* in the production and growth of the total size of that pie?

These are hard questions. To answer them and throw light on probable economic developments just ahead, we must apply the tools of economic science to current business conditions in the United States and abroad.

Defining the Scourge. Begin with the OPEC energy cartel. In 1973, the mideast oil sheikhdoms succeeded in raising five-fold the real price of energy. The increases came just when food and fiber harvests were at a low point all around the world: in Russia and China, Brazil and Ghana, Burma and Iowa. The inflated price of oil was the one straw too many. The U. S. recession of 1973–75 was declared to have officially begun in the last quarter of 1973.

What is a recession? Who decides? The press and Las Vegas oddsmakers have a simple pragmatic definition:

> When the real Gross National Product (total value of all goods and services, corrected for inflationary price rises) declines for *two quarters* in a row—that is a recession.

This rough definition is adequate for most purposes. The National Bureau of Economic Research, a prestigious nonprofit organization that has kept the official score on business cycles, naturally insists on more refined tests and measurements. Yet, for the most part, it arrives at the same conclusions when it applies its own definition:

> "A recession is a recurring period of decline in total output, income, employment, and trade, usually lasting six months to a year and marked by widespread fluctuations in the economy."

By both these tests, the United States had the following postwar recessions: 1948–49, 1953–54, 1957–58, 1960–61, 1969–70, 1973–75. Japan, however, did not have a postwar recession until 1973. Is Japan, therefore, immune to the pulses of optimism and pessimism in world markets, suffering no fluctuation in its own business economy? Hardly. Because the Japanese economy is growing so rapidly, overheating shows up merely as an extraordinary acceleration of its growth rate. A slowdown merely brings the growth rate below its normal level—and does not necessarily cause an actual drop in absolute levels of income and employment.

Therefore, economists these days want to define a new species of recession—a "mini-" or "growth-recession." In 1966–67 the American people had to live with such a recession when a credit crunch curtailed housing starts and shaved 20% off stock prices. The mini- or growth-recession is defined as follows:

> When output and employment grow for half a year or more at significantly less than their average trend rate of growth, an economy is in a growth recession—even if actual growth rates never turn negative.

Are We? Aren't We? In 1979 no one in the United States could decide whether April Fool's Day marked the beginning of a recession. A drop in real GNP was recorded in the second quarter of the year, but many experts were surprised when the third quarter did not also show a decline. By the crude test of journalists and oddsmakers, a true recession did not occur. But by almost everyone's agreement, 1979 would go down in the history books as a year of growth-recession, at least.

An Old Expansion. Why the slowdown? Again, oil scarcity and OPEC price-hikes provided an immediate threat to U. S. economic stability. Empty gasoline pumps and long service station lines at midyear paralyzed consumer buying of the larger cars produced by the American auto industry. The result was a decline in total retail sales. Rising oil prices and soaring food prices contributed to two-digit inflation—i.e., a rise in consumer prices of more than 10% for the year.

The U. S. economy began to slow in 1979 *because* of its successful expansion after the 1975 upturn, the period when U. S. production grew more vigorously than that of West Germany and Western Europe in general. Millions of new jobs had been provided for women, now dedicated to working outside the home, and the great baby boom of the 1940's and 1950's required millions of jobs for young adults.

Thus, the first reason for the 1979–80 slowdown was the fact that the post-1975 expansion was getting old, as business cycles go. The United States began running short of industrial capacity and spare labor power. Signs of "demand-pull" inflation appeared in late 1978: too much spending on and bidding for a limited supply of produceable goods.

Government Policy. The second reason for the recessionary tone of business has been tight money and credit policies. This is not because a president is cruel. Or because Congressmen don't want to get reelected. Or because members of the Federal Reserve Board are less smart and informed than economists in New York or Cambridge.

The dilemma of stagflation requires that steps be taken by the federal government to cool off the economy. High interest rates on loans—15%

for large companies, 20% for less credit-worthy borrowers—are intended to combat inflation. But, one might argue, a high interest rate adds to company costs and thereby leads to inflated prices. Yes, it does so in the shortest run. But if tight money and credit cut down on housing starts, inventory speculation, investment spending, and the purchase of durable goods, this will also chill aggregate spending and cause an easing of the rate of inflation.

That is the theory on which President Jimmy Carter, Secretary of the Treasury G. William Miller, and Federal Reserve Board Chairman Paul Volcker have been operating. Historical experience suggests that this hard-money medicine does eventually help bring down soaring prices. But history also shows that government can overdo the cure, sometimes almost killing the patient in the process. Each advance against inflation comes dear. The poor and unskilled—be they white, black, or brown, on marginal farms or in city slums—take it on the chin when a mixed economy goes on a crusade against stagflation. In the case of stagflation, cures for the "flation" often exacerbate the "stag."

Two Soft Cheers. It is evident that political economy is not yet a perfected science. Fame still awaits the scholar who can find the way to give modern mixed economies real mastery over deep depressions by acquiring a better control over chronic inflation.

Fortunately, the early outlook for the 1980's is not so bleak that only an immediate breakthrough in the cure for stagflation can save us from disorder. Our far-from-perfect economic system has been functioning to make lives longer, healthier, and more secure in a way that the 19th century apologists of capitalism would never have expected.

Living With Stagflation

Today's inflation is chronic. Its roots are deep in the very nature of the welfare state. The best single name for it is "stagflation"—which means that we have rising prices and wages at the same time that we have unemployment and excess industrial capacity.

This is a new disease, one to which no modern mixed economy is immune. It hits the United States and Canada; West Germany and Japan; Britain, France, and Italy; Sweden and Switzerland. To say that our inflation comes from governments' printing too much money—so that too much spendable money chases after too few goods—is to state a truth. But, alas, this is a half truth only. For, were the government to stop printing new money, that would not simply end the inflation. It would also slow down production and, for an uncomfortable spell of years, lower real living standards. Such a cure for the "flation" part of stagflation would worsen the pathology of the "stag" part of stagflation. The cure, in short, seems worse than the disease itself.

Government ceilings on prices and wages would work well only in the short run, only during the first year of such a peacetime program. Experience in a dozen countries, on scores of post–World War II occasions, testifies to that. Price and wage controls should therefore be saved for acute emergencies.

Abolishing the humane society, reverting to the 19th-century jungle of ruthless capitalism and to the dogmas of frozen money supplies and ever-balanced budgets, yes this could ultimately bring an end to chronic inflation. But that would reimpose inequality and suffering not tolerated under democracy. A fascist political state would be needed to impose such a regime and preserve it. Short of a military junta that imprisons trade union activists and terrorizes intellectuals, this solution to inflation is unrealistic—and, to most of us, undesirable.

The best that we can hope for, I believe, is to work the inflation rate down over a long period of time. We must keep the economy from overheating, even though that means more unemployment than we really want. The challenge is to secure the efficiencies of a market economy, while tempering the cruelties and inequities of the market system. Perfection is not attainable. But we can hope to make the humane society work better than in the 1970's.

GOVERNMENT AND BUSINESS

*Paul A. Samuelson**

I was asked recently whether the Nobel Prize had improved my tennis, and I replied only very briefly and only by intimidation. It does have one effect which you will notice. Alcohol may not make one a better driver, but it makes one feel that he is a better driver. Similarly, after receiving a Nobel Prize, one suddenly has an opinion on all matters.

One valuable function that I might be able to perform here is to play the part of the old Irving Kristol before he became the new Irving Kristol. Businessmen generally think of Washington as a mysterious place. They wonder what kind of new horror out of Washington is going to hit them. That is not my view at all. My view is like that of the old farmer who lost his jackass. The farmer sat down and asked himself, "If I were a jackass, where would I go?" Then he went to the place he imagined and found the animal. I always can predict whether some step is going to be taken in Washington by thinking, "If I were Allen Greenspan, what would I do?" It is not difficult for me to make that experiment. What would I do if I were Walter Heller? What would my attitude be if I were Paul Samuelson in that job?

Art Buchwald says that there is a little fellow named Plotkin who really runs the government. If there is some emerging problem that is worrying you, why not try to predict how Plotkin may react to it?

J. P. Morgan and the Changing Scene

Just to prime the pump of discussion, I will recall a little history. During the depression of 1892–1893, the U.S. government under Cleveland was in serious economic trouble, and it turned to J. Pierpont Morgan for help. The President put his problem before J. Pierpont Morgan, and Morgan, like any good investment banker, thought about the matter and decided that this was a worthy cause and that he should do something about it. Morgan mobilized his domestic resources, floated a big gold loan, and rescued the U.S. government. That is an example of the way the system used to run.

Imagine J. Pierpont Morgan's surprise when scarcely a decade later Teddy Roosevelt discovered that there was a dead-letter law, the Sherman Antitrust Act, that had been passed in 1890 while nobody was paying much attention to it. Lawyers in the Department of Justice initiated the first U.S. episode in antitrust by initiating proceedings against one of J. Pierpont Morgan's transcontinental railroads. It is a matter of historical record that when Morgan was notified of this, he sent a note to the President of the United States, Theodore Roosevelt, and said, "You send your man and I'll send my man. They can meet

*Mr. Samuelson is Professor of Economics, Massachusetts Institute of Technology, Nobel Prize Winner in Economics, and Contributing Editor, *Newsweek*.

and dispose of this matter." It was a very rude awakening for J. Pierpont Morgan when he found that business could no longer conduct its business with the U.S. government in that manner. Life has been very different from that time, and it was only another decade until the 1913 Pujo Investigation, when J. Pierpont Morgan discovered how unpleasant the beginnings of populist democracy can be.

The fact that the function and profession of government relations specialists exist is an indication of the importance of the relationships between government and business. Perhaps it ought not to be that way.

I hate to disagree with any part of the Washington Post family, but it is not Plotkin who runs the government. The root of the trouble from the standpoint of somebody who thinks of the simple business of business as business comes from the electorate itself. It is the electorate that selects the kind of civil servant that we have and the kind of advice that is followed. For example, when I was an advisor to President Kennedy, I asked members of the Boston medical community whether the President was receiving the proper treatment for his back and other ailments. In the judgment of most of the Boston medical community he was not. I was told that the Kennedys shop around until they find a doctor who tells them pretty much what they want to hear, and they can always find one. Suddenly my own role as an advisor appeared to me in a new light, which was reinforced by analogous experiences with a large family and a very intelligent wife. My wife, who has no license to practice medicine, was at the time practicing medicine in Massachusetts. When we had a child who was ill, I would ask Marion if she thought the child were really ill, and when she said it was not very ill, we called our high-class pediatrician from Children's Hospital who prescribed aspirin. If Marion said the child was seriously ill, we called our local village general practitioner, and he would prescribe penicillin or the latest antibiotic. We in fact were predetermining the treatment.

National Economic Planning

There obviously has been a trend in government toward centralization of power. The turning point was the 1932 election in which FDR walloped Herbert Hoover at the polls. Something was started then which has been a one-way movement by and large, but since 1952 there has been a tension between centralization and decentralization. Successful candidates try to appeal to some divergent, emerging consensus and then push one way or the other.

What about national planning? Is this one of those important developments that every chief executive officer should have somebody monitoring and watching? In my judgment, it definitely is not. National planning is a paper tiger, unlike environmentalist sentiment that can be stopped, modified, or persuaded, but which must be considered. It is very important for advising economists to try to forecast whether this recovery is going to encounter a shortage of capacity in the paper industry, the aluminum industry, the steel industry, the basic materials industry. And environmental issues are significant factors in making such a forecast.

The national planning campaign is, on the other hand, a media event. Robert Nathan, and, not surprisingly, John Kenneth Galbraith, and a little surprisingly, Robert V. Roosa got together and hired a mimeograph machine, made a statement and signed it. (This is the sort of thing that I do six times a week and rest on Sunday. I sign petitions for good causes directed at getting somebody out of Russia or out of a Chilean jail.) Nathan and others are in favor of planning and are causing a few people to worry. But I would say that this is not a proposal of great importance. In the Eisenhower era, some executives of General Motors were very excited about input-output in the federal government. They were afraid that the input-output model of spending flows analysis was going to control the American economy, but input-output was merely a pedestrian, valuable tool that worked better than aggregate GNP accounts.

National planning is a long way from running eastern European socialist republics, even relatively small ones. It will not be a feature in my forecasting scenarios, even if it plays a much bigger role than it is likely to play in the U.S. government.

Le Plan

There is no ground-swell for national planning among Carter's advisors. At best the talk about planning is similar to the French *Le Plan*, which was not very different from the Committee for Economic Development postwar planning. When a lot of economists thought there was going to be a big postwar depression like that of the 1930's, CED economists tried to estimate what full employment would mean for the American economy in terms of total investments, savings, and so forth. They tried to see how the Fortune 500 corporations would fit in with plans for full employment and what their share of the market would be if there were reasonably full employment. Not all 500 corporations did fit in with the plans, though many of the largest corporations did. When these largest corporations planned in terms of the overall guidelines, the sum of all that the corporations were going to do, combined with the consumer's hunger for durable goods and his involuntary savings brought on by the war, seemed to indicate that full employment was going to be attainable.

Le Plan was primarily indicative planning and not dictatorial planning. The CED, of course, had no sovereignty, no regiments, no sanctions, while deGaulle's civil servants did. A company that was too flagrantly against the plan could be refused access to the capital market. That kind of authority in addition to planning can accomplish quite a lot. However, when economists study the French experience, they find that although the private sector under indicative planning approximated what had been planned in many of the first and successful years, what actually saved the plan from even grosser irrelevance was the fact that so much of the French economy is under direct government ownership. If stimulus was needed in the railroad industry (and the French have probably overspent on high-speed trains in response to the desires of the community), the public sector could overfulfill its part of the plan and be stabilizing. The U.S. government lacks that kind of power.

Speaking now as a dangerous intellectual, I wish the government had more weapons of control. I have adverted to the fact that in 1972–1973 the basic materials industries—paper, aluminum, a number of basic chemicals, steel—were short of capacity, and these are around-the-clock operations. The recession ended that shortage, but most of the computations that I have seen suggest that if this recovery is made to be a drawn-out, healthy one, and the unemployment rate drops down below six percent in 1977 and 1978, there will again be multiple ordering, excess capacity, and bottlenecks in plant capacity. There is almost nothing that the U.S. government can do in advance about this. Although theoretically the investment tax credit might be mobilized to prevent this, it seems very doubtful that it would be effective. My point is that we are very far from the kind of comprehensive planning that Friedrich A. von Hayek worries about when he talks about the road to serfdom. We have the Federal Reserve and fiscal policy, but these are aggregate controls that every democracy has had for more than a quarter of a century.

Discussion

Question: The views of the presidential candidates regarding economics are very confusing to the American public and obviously a most important political matter. How would you characterize them?

Samuelson: I think that President Ford has been extremely unlucky. There appeared to be a strong recovery, even a V-bottom recovery, about April, 1975. That was almost the ideal time for a recession to bottom-out—a year and a half before the election—from the standpoint of the incumbent President. According to most polymetricians, the most important variable favoring an incumbent winning the presidential election is what happens to real income and real output for the year before the election. For a time Ford was in a good position. Unemployment went from a peak of 9.2 percent in May of 1975 to 7.4 percent a couple of months ago, and I think that Allen Greenspan was absolutely candid with the press and the American people when he said he thought that by the end of the year the unemployment number would be down to just below seven percent. Unfortunately, as some statisticians have suspected, there are grave problems in the seasonal adjustment to these numbers, and the number recently went from 7.4 percent to 7.8 percent and 7.9 percent. There is only one report scheduled to come out before the election, and my suspicion is that the unemployment figure will go down but not to a level at which politically it will be a great help to Ford.

Coinciding with this unemployment figure, there has been a second-quarter slow-down in GNP. The GNP figure that is going to come out before the election will appear October 20. For the most part, however, people do not vote by the numbers: most of my neighbors go whole hours without thinking about the GNP and the unemployment rate. What they do worry about is whether a brother-in-law is out of work or whether someone on Route 128 has lost his job, placing their jobs in jeopardy. So it is important to keep in mind that numbers do not mean as much to the voter as does the human suffering involved.

The United States is a welfare state, for better or worse, and there are many supplements that divorce income from current work: welfare assistance, unemployment compensation, supplementary funds from the unions. Therefore, the 7.9 percent unemployment figure exaggerates the problem from the standpoint of human suffering. I ought to add that the figure also understates the problem in certain dimensions. Part-time unemployment is not included in that number, and unemployment among the high-risk groups, such as the unskilled, blacks, and youth, may be as high as 30 percent in the inner city. Part of that 7.9 percent is attributable to the fact that many families twenty years ago had six children. Large families have gone out of fashion, but those children have now come into the labor force. Another factor is the trend toward female participation in the labor force, and this trend is related to the change in family pattern. It is not very diplomatic of the President to say that these are only women who have no jobs, but there is a certain truth in that. Women do go in and out of the labor force and have a high propensity in the best of times to show higher unemployment rates than men do. In part this happens because women have rotten jobs. (I have decided that women are just men without money.) If an

MIT male graduate loses his job on Route 128 as assistant vice president or vice president making $35 thousand, it is a tragedy because there is no similar job for him. His female counterpart may be earning $15 to $17 thousand and probably less than that. School teaching, for example, is a relatively high-paid job among females. In short, the woman's job is seldom a very good one, and if she loses it, she can get another not-very-good job quite easily. Consequently, certain parts of the labor force show higher rates of unemployment than do others.

When one standardizes to allow for a change in the composition, one still finds that the unemployment rate after the worst recession in the whole post-war period is higher than that of the 1950's and 1960's, and is working its way down very slowly. The President's gamble of steady-as-you-go concern about inflation has had mixed results. It is inevitable that the Democratic candidate appeals to people in the middle income classes and lower income classes, and that he is more of an activist. I may say, because I know his advisors very well, that Carter takes seriously the problem of handling unemployment by methods other than just spending. He has sensed the mood of the American people, whether one calls this lack of principle or responsiveness to a higher voice, and he knows that the people do not want spending that just causes inflation. Carter's statement that the budget must be balanced by 1980 is a serious constraint on his advisors, and they are trying now to work out some kind of training subsidy program. Jobs which provide better than a minimum wage, but only about $6,000 a year would receive government subsidy if they involve training. It is hoped that such a program could improve the trade-off between unemployment and inflation by including a million or more people. Of course, Carter has to be elected first.

Question: I wonder if you would comment on Herman Kahn's predictions that, first, in the course of the next decade gross world economic product, if there is such a concept, will go up at about five to six percent a year; and second, the world will move into a kind of Golden Age, in contrast to the doomsday others foresee.

Samuelson: I have *opinions* about Kahn's predictions. (*Newsweek* separates fact from opinions.) Kahn is a showman and a futurologist; he nominates ideas. But he can overlook significant factors. For example, he overlooked environmental factors in his first futurology, and told Japan that every Japanese worker was seven feet tall at the time the workers were proving to be ordinary members of the human race. One must examine Kahn's ideas against a background of fact. The State Department publishes every year a report on planetary real product, and that report contradicts what J. Forrester and others have been saying about the 1970's and the 1960's being the twilight of world growth. According to my rough calculation, the U.S. had about half of real world GNP at the end of World War II. The rest of the world was on its back. The United States now is down to just a little over a quarter, and the world as a whole has been growing at a more rapid rate than was true in the heyday of capitalism— I think at a rate of three or four percent a year. At the turn of the century, the best calculations showed that world product was growing at about two to three and a half percent a year, and world population growth was almost comparable to that. There still is a mismatch between population growth in different parts of the world and the real product growth.

I do not view lightly, however, the five-fold increase in the price of energy, and I do not agree with that facile view of my academic colleagues that like every cartel, OPEC will break down. Perhaps this one will break down at some time, but what will break it down will not be tough talk by Henry Kissinger, but alternative sources of supply. At the moment, worldwide economic recovery is still vigorous. It looks as if the next move is higher prices, because the real price of oil has not kept up with worldwide inflation in the last couple of years. We are going to be working with an increased real-cost of resources, because the best resources, like the Mesabi Range, have been exploited first.

On a more optimistic note, that village GP whom I mentioned earlier used to prescribe antibiotics for my children, and I once said to him, "You are kind of free with antibiotics, are you not?" He said, "Yes, that is true. I can be criticized for that. But I have two points to consider: the point of view of my selfish patient, and my conviction that scientists are smarter than bacteria." This is an act of faith, and I do not think that the futurologists can accurately project present technology with respect to resources into the next century. Survival may be a nip-and-tuck thing, but I am personally betting on the home team at MIT.

Question: If government regulation continues to increase, and if national economic planning is instituted, will it bring our creative, free-enterprise system to a screeching halt and result in a static economy?

Samuelson: The intellectual climate among academics has turned against regulation. Academics used to think, perhaps naively, that the ICC and other regulatory agencies were protectors of the consumer against the oligopolist and monopoly. The sunshine of fact has persuaded economists more and more that the regulators have become prisoners of the regulated. In September of 1974. President Ford called a summit meeting of 28 economists representing a broad spectrum of opinion. It was of interest to me that when it was proposed that some 40 sacred cows of regulation ought to be slaughtered in the interests of a more efficient society, about 25 out of those 28 participants agreed. However, I want to point out that that heavy consensus resulted in no action. Every regulatory situation exists because of a constellation of interests. Usually the interests that are promoting an idea or agency, even if they are very narrow, are very sharp, whereas the opposition, in the name of public interest, is very diffused. Just after the oil crisis, the speeds on the German autobahns were controlled for the first time. They were reduced not to 55 miles per hour, but to perhaps 70 mph. This restriction saved a lot of lives, and both political parties were in favor of making it permanent. But both political parties completely caved in to opposing views. I asked people how that was possible, and I learned that a minority was against it. The majority who were for this continued regulation did not care much, but the minority who were against it cared intensely. The handgun situation is a similar thing. In general, interests that are served by inefficient regulation are very concentrated and very strong, and interests served by the public interest are very diffused.

Question: Who are Governor Carter's primary economic advisors and which school of thought do they represent?

Samuelson: He has gotten away from the Harvard-MIT axis. I think John Bowles, the investment banker, recruited Lawrence Klein who is the distinguished Benjamin Franklin Professor of Economics at the University of Pennsylvania and has been the foremost pioneer in computer forecasting. Carter has access to a broad spectrum of opinion under the general direction of Lawrence Klein, who had a more radical past in the 1940's when he was about 20 years old. He now is quite a conservative economist in terms of what is feasible, and this has shown itself in the kind of economic advice which is given. Most political figures do not spend much time on economics. They may have taken ECOA a long time ago, and they are rather stunned when they learn where the feasibility mix is. Although there are conservative economists in the Carter bandwagon, the center of gravity of the economists in a Democratic campaign is perceptibly on the left side of center in comparison with Secretary of the Treasury William Simon, Allen Greenspan, and other advisors of Presidents Nixon and Ford.

Policy Advising in Economics

PAUL A. SAMUELSON

I am sometimes asked, "What is the relationship between the highfalutin' research you do in modern economic theory and the policy advice that you give?"

That is not an easy question to answer candidly and correctly within a limited space. The honest answer I have to give is this: "The connection I believe is very close—but that does not mean that only sophisticated modern analysts can provide good counseling or that there is a strong positive correlation between the scientific fruitfulness of a scholar and his usefulness as a forecaster and policy consultant."

Space does not permit me to do justice to this topic. Here then are only some unsystematic samplings of what needs to be discussed.

Dollar valuation

Let me begin with the illustration of the problem of the depreciating dollar early in 1978. If a person is not well-informed on the recent facts with respect to world trade and finance, the fact that she (or he) is well-versed in Marshall-Lerner stability conditions or in the pretensions of the so-called monetary approach to the balance of payments will not suffice to enable her to provide worthwhile policy prescriptions. On the other hand, command of this body of theoretical knowledge can be an important aid to the economist trying to arrive at a best judgment.

Two examples will be illustrative. A government official recently told me that the downward floating of the dollar was a bad thing inasmuch as our costs have not deteriorated relative to those in Germany, Japan, and elsewhere abroad. He cited the purchasing-power-parity doctrine as a basis for his conclusion and for what he drew as its implication, that the United States should dirty up the float by now supporting the dollar. A second and related view was given Congress by a leading economist who is now an investment banker. He attributed the dollar's weakness not to any "overvaluation" but to the insistence of Americans on importing so much OPEC oil.

I had to remind both of them of some essentials of trade theory. On the supposition that a free citizenry insists on keeping homes hot and cars big, and on the premise that the OPEC recipients of U.S. receipts will not voluntarily invest those receipts in our bonds, stocks, real estate, and other assets, then even if no costs change here and abroad, a currency that was previously in equilibrium (neither overvalued nor undervalued) must now be considered an overvalued currency.

An obvious point, you say? I assure you it is anything but, as a review of current policy discussions will verify.

More important still. What if it be the case, as the investment-bank economist obviously believes whether he realizes it or not, that elasticities of import and export demand are so low or "pessimistic" that degeneration of the dollar serves only to make the balance of payments worse or, at best, improve it by only a derisory amount? Then, how should we run the railroad of international finance? To provide intelligent counsel on this matter, so that the statesmen, bureaucrats, and legislators of the world can make informed and rational decisions, is anything but child's play. Practical men—bankers, editors, lawyers, the sort of people whom we recruit to handle the nation's business—cannot begin to grasp the issues and subtleties involved. High-falutin' scholars

March-April 1978/Challenge

are needed.

Economists as predictors

So far my examples have dealt with analysis. Let me turn to the problem of forecasting for the Prince. He will need to know the consequences of his various alternative actions.

For many decades I have observed how this is done, and have myself participated. It is a sad finding that, for the most part, I can predict on what side of an issue every economist present in the room will be. What is so bad about that? Economists differ in value judgments. Naturally the chap who abhors inequality will be on the side of tax reform; and the *savante* who favors the verdict of the marketplace can be expected to cast her vote against controls and fiats.

It is not these revealed ethical leanings that I am referring to. Rather it is the odd fact that the Professor from Yale who is known to have great concern for the plight of the unemployed will be an odds-on Las Vegas favorite to come to a Washington meeting with the lowest prediction for next year's growth rate; and the elderly New York banker who was trained on the continent, and is famous for his concern over inflation, can be counted on to present the highest estimate for next year's growth rate.

You may find no mystery in this. "Each one is lying in what he regards as a good cause," may be your hypothesis to fit the facts that need to be explained. "Actually, they may well have the same objective beliefs, but their difference in goals causes each to bias his objective belief in his preferred subjective direction."

I doubt that the economists I know have been so rationally Machiavellian as to keep two sets of books knowingly and consciously. Rather one is impressed with how much wishful thinking there is; and, among sophisticated scholars, how much of the other side of the coin of wishful thinking there is, namely "apprehensive thinking." The Chicago economist who detests wage-price controls tosses at night in the conviction they are just around the corner, whereas the Galbraithian cannot fall asleep in his frustration over the fact that controls are just not politically feasible.

No conscious or unconscious deception need be involved, as may be seen in the following incident. Twenty-five years ago, Arthur Burns, as Eisenhower's CEA chairman, used to invite non-Republican economists to academic sessions at Brookings. I shocked the venerable J. M. Clark in mid-1953 by saying: "Although the probability of a 1954 recession is only one-half, we should treat it as if it were two-thirds." Clark asked whether I was not engaging in self-contradiction. I had to explain that Clark's Columbia colleague, Abraham Wald, would understand in terms of his "loss function" my crude way of stating that there is more social evil in a shortfall of 1954 real GNP than in a longfall.

This explains why mere differences in value judgment seem to be reflected so often in apparent differences in objective probability evaluation: Each person shades his objective mean (or modal or median) estimate in the direction most likely to call forth policy decisions that will maximize the expected value of the utility of outcomes *as he ethically evaluates the utility of those outcomes.*

The case for candor

I must warn of the evident danger in following this practice. What you gain in the short run for your notion of equity, you tend to lose in the long run as your credibility evaporates and the Prince comes to regard you as Mr. Johnny-one-note. The boy who in season and out of season cries the wolf of inflation or of unemployment, becomes the boy no one wants to listen to.

My code therefore in journalistic writings and in congressional testimony—a code that I may not always succeed in living up to—is to call the objective probabilities as I scientifically see them. The difficulty in doing so is not primarily that one's chosen prescriptions get in the way. The actual difficulty is that it makes for dull journalism to eschew the clever view, the sensational estimate, and cleave to that predicted gain in next year's GNP or price level such that, if you had to risk most of your eating money on one side or the other, you honestly wouldn't know on which side of your estimate to bet.

The same principles should, I believe, apply in all scholarship. Eschewing being interesting and novel, one tries not to be wrong! It is amazing how eclectic that makes the profoundest scholars. Perhaps Gottfried Haberler, my old teacher, was right when he defended being eclectic against the critics of eclecticism with their more exciting views: "How do we know that Mother Nature is not herself eclectic?"

Foreword

If health care is not already our biggest industry, it soon will be. Our institutions have not caught up with reality. To illustrate, Big Ten universities still have departments of agricultural economics with as many professors as in the department of economics itself. That represents cultural lag: the defense industry, the construction industry, and the health care industry increasingly put food production in the shade; and yet, in Congress and the public press, the romantic image of the family farm still exercises undue political weight.

Massachusetts provides David Kinzer, president of the Massachusetts Hospital Association, with a rich sample of experience. The bell that tolls in Boston tolls for the whole nation. It was the mayor of Newark who said, "Wherever it is that American cities are going, they'll find Newark waiting for them when they get there." Whatever public health crises this country is rushing to meet, Kinzer can already discern in Massachusetts, a pace-setter state in the march toward a welfare state. Once President Carter finally achieves comprehensive medical insurance for all, Americans as a people will be working one to two months every year to pay for the doctors, nurses, hospitals, prescriptions, x-ray scanners, and bookkeepers in the health care industry. And why not? we may argue. How can a nation better spend its affluence than in preventing pain and prolonging years of healthful productivity?

Green dollars, Kinzer shows, cannot themselves lead to humane and efficient deployment of our medical resources. A recipe for comedy is Boy meets Girl, Boy loses Girl, Boy gets Girl. A recipe for political tragedy, and one being performed in all the 50 states, follows the grim sequence: Conservative interests fight off aspirations for universal medical care; progress wins out; tax bill grows at 20 per cent in an economy with four per cent real growth; electorate recoils in panic, and the political process cuts back blindly and stupidly. Read David Kinzer to learn the gory details.

An economist must ask, "Why the special problems in social medicine?" Mousetraps and bubble gum get rationed by market price. Buying too much gum or caviar means I have to do without a second car. Both rich and poor can avoid dead-weight losses from irrationally spending their allotted funds on ordinary goods and services.

And that's the way medical care used to be run. The well-to-do lived long; life for the poor was miserable and short. Before World War II a debutante with a cold could sojourn for a week in a modern hospital for less expense than a good hotel! Her sister could have a baby in Massachusetts General Hospital and order catered food from the Ritz Hotel! Meanwhile, in South Boston, people in their forties died from preventable and curable disease.

That "efficient" system is gone. But the new, more humane system generates its own pathologies. Physicians can order ever more expensive treatments *without regard to cost.* Sometimes venality is involved: To balance the monthly budget, an unnecessary hysterectomy is performed, and performed by one so incompetent as to triple the irreducible risks involved; or, if Purple Shield pays more for a radical than a partial mastectomy, the invisible hand of greed leads to nonoptimal care. More often good intentions rather than selfish avarice lead to explosive costs of medical care: Human life is infinitely precious; still one more expensive test can do no harm—to the patient's pocketbook, the doctor's tax return, or the teaching hospital's research budget. Professor Jeffrey Harris, my colleague at MIT who is both an M.D. and a Ph.D. in economics, points out that 10 per cent of the GNP probably could be lavished on car repairs rather than medical care if garage mechanics were freed of all budget constraints in an environment that extolled the sanctity of extending at any costs the auto's life expectancy.

I write as a liberal. As one who advocates comprehensive health insurance, I recommend that Kinzer's revelations and recommendations be read and discussed. Whether he is right in every diagnosis, and whether one joins in his recommendation of federalizing the financing of Medicaid, we are on a collision course with chaos under the present system.

Cassandra saw the future. And it didn't work! High time we face up to trends and problems already documented in David Kinzer's provocative study.

Paul A. Samuelson
Institute Professor
Department of Economics
Massachusetts Institute of Technology

An Economist's View

An Interview With Dr. Paul Samuelson

Do you think that environmental regulations are adding significantly to current U.S. inflation, unemployment, etc.?

The current combination of inflation and unemployment in this country is what we economists call stagflation. It's related on one hand to fiscal policy and Federal Reserve money supply creation and on the other hand to the way wages and other costs respond in the system to different degrees of unemployed labor supplies and plant capacity. Environmental regulations are really one small and minor factor in that general picture. So the answer is environmental regulations contribute at most insignificantly to current U. S. inflation and unemployment problems.

What do you see as major steps we could take to make environmental regulation more efficient?

It is easy for legislators to put in fiats, to introduce regulations, to set quantitative restrictions on effluents and emissions. Then it's a matter for the police and courts to enforce them.

Economists believe that a better approach often is to make the process of environmental control self-regulating by means of some system of automatic money penalties and rewards. This means that a major needed step is to use more measures that motivate industry to clean up the environment, such as tax penalties, subsidies, and pecuniary enticements.

The steel industry among others has argued that environmental regulations put U.S. industry at a disadvantage with respect to foreign competitors. Do you think there is any truth to this charge? If so should the U.S. attempt to protect its business and how?

At every international conference on environmental improvement, we observe that representatives from the developing countries where life is nasty, short, and brutish, and where the GNP per capita is very low and living standards are minimal, those regions are anxious to acquire some pollution and some deterioration of the environment if that is the price for getting jobs.

In the more affluent countries, such as Sweden, Switzerland, Western Europe generally, the U.S., and Japan, it's realized that the whole purpose of production, the whole purpose of jobs and real income, is the good life, in all of its dimensions.

One very important aspect of the good life is that it last, that we do not die prematurely from environmental blight, that while we're living we're living under skies that are reasonably clear and with water that's reasonably pure. So the affluent countries like the U.S. naturally want to put stiffer regulations on industry than do the developing countries.

Now there are certain industries, which by their nature are more frequently polluting than others. It follows from economic analysis that just where things should be done in the world, what the geographical division of labor should be, ought to be affected by this difference in tastes between the advanced and the undeveloped world. And so an extremely filthy industry, which cannot by any incentive scheme, or any zoning and fiat regulation be made clean, simply ought not be in the middle of a prosperous suburb or in the middle of a prosperous country.

If the steel industry turns out to be one which is irretrievably polluting, and I don't believe that to be the case, then it ought to follow that the jobs which have taken place in this self-confessed dirty industry should take place in some other site where they will do less harm. So if it were the case that the steel industry simply could not compete in the United States on a decent, non-polluting basis, that would be a very powerful argument for letting that industry move abroad.

Now this has nothing to do with national defense. Obviously some crucial amount of steel capacity for national defense purposes, which is much much less than the U.S. ordinarily produces, you would want to keep here. That can be done on an electric furnace basis without the old Pittsburgh and Gary, Ind., approach. (I was born in Gary and I know the nature of the old-fashioned, polluting steel plant. Those plants should go abroad.)

A century from now, even in the poorer parts of the world they will not be allowed to continue the old 1919 methods of polluting the environment.

On the other hand, having said all that, let's just really look at the competitive situation in steel. The U.S. industry has not been losing out to imports primarily because of environmental concerns. The Japanese, who have been some of the most successful in capturing American business on a cost basis, are themselves beginning ing to put in environmental constraints. Some are not much different than now apply in East Chicago, Gary, Pittsburgh, and elsewhere.

So the steel industry, which will be made to pay its way on a non-polluting basis to the degree that it's able to stay here, will continue to be able to compete here, that is if its other problems, which are its rate of technological advance in comparison with what's been happening abroad, are put in order.

The only case for the U.S. Government to come in to protect an industry like this, which is losing ground because it will not or cannot shape up to environmental needs, is that workers in that industry who have staked their occupations and fortunes on it should, as with other industries hurt by competition, receive a transitional subsidy to help them locate in another industry. Beyond that I don't think a strong case can be made for the steel industry to have walls built around it so that on a clean basis it can compete with industry abroad.

Aren't our economic analyses inherently short range and how can they adequately include the value of a lower cancer rate or a cleaner river when data on damages to society are often inconclusive?

It isn't the case that modern economic analysis is or must be only short-range. We realize that costs accrue even if they do not show in the form of a monthly bill to some corporations or to some households. So the correct formulation would be that our economic analysis must be short-run, must be intermediate-run, must be long-run, and we must attempt to quantify as best we can the costs in terms of environmentally-increased cancer rates and costs in terms of democratically-legislated standards for clean air and clean water.

Do you think economists have developed adequate ways of measuring the benefits of pollution control regulations? Or are many of these benefits inherently unmeasurable?

I think we are only at the beginning of making such measurements. But we are at the beginning, and there are many improvements which will come in the future in our ability to meaningfully calculate costs and benefits.

The fact that a thing is hard to measure does not mean that it is zero. And in the past we have been treating costs that were difficult to quantify as if they were zero costs. That is a logical error and we simply have to do the best we can in terms of new yardsticks.

How many hospital beds, how many doctor days, how many nurse years are going to be involved in running our cities the way the Victorian 19th Century city was run? When you apply these new yardsticks, it will be found, and economic historians will corroborate the statement I am making, that far from our now spending too much on the environment, in the remaining decades of the century we will be spending an increasing fraction of our total resources upon this important area.

It's often said that investment in pollution control equipment is "nonproductive." Is this true from an economist's viewpoint? Is such investment less productive than, say, investment in air-conditioning equipment?

If you use the old-fashioned methods of measuring outputs then you may find that in a year when more of our society's resources go into keeping mercury out of our lakes, keeping sludge out of the ocean, the Federal Reserve index of production has not grown as rapidly in terms of mousetraps and conventional goods and services as would otherwise have been the case.

However, economists have always known that what's measured by the Federal Reserve Board index of production or what's measured by the real Gross National Product is only an approximation of something more fundamental. And we are gradually changing our notions of what ought to be the measured Gross National Product.

I introduced into my elementary textbook in economics some few years ago along with the GNP, which is a conventional measure of ordinary goods and services, an auxiliary measure of Net Economic Welfare (NEW) which tries to take into account the improved amenities that are just as important to each living generation as the mousetraps and the other ordinary items.

When you have calculated these auxiliary measures of physical production and of corrected Gross National Product then it's not the case that investment in pollution control equipment is non-productive and is a subtraction from what could otherwise have been produced.

On the contrary, it may be that in any one year's spending on these items in a society not at the bare margin of existence, these may be among the most important welfare-creating expenditures.

Do you then advocate a different kind of yardstick?

Yes. I would, for example, not dispense with our old GNP, but I would always supplement it with these auxiliary measures.

Has environmental spending become a target for some because the GNP doesn't present a true picture of cleanup costs and benefits?

If I were a political scientist and I tried to analyze the mobilized forces of opposition to environmental spending and regulations, then I would not list as important the fact that the conventional GNP is measured wrong. Most voters, most lobbyists, most people in the street go whole hours without thinking of the conventional real GNP.

What a lobbyist does do regarding a particular regulation that he thinks is hard on his industry is when he comes into Congressional committee meetings or into court, he quotes from the GNP to buttress his case. It's important that the measures of environmental benefits be available in order to answer such debating tactics.

But I think that some of the opposition to environmental improvement is rationally based.

A lot of people feel pinched in buying their ordinary mousetraps, in paying for their ordinary schooling, and they're looking for something to economize on and they may have blithely voted too high a standard for environmental purification.

Looking at this problem, the economist doesn't say, "The more the merrier." If pure air is good, why isn't the purest air possible also good? Why shouldn't you be able to swim in the Hudson River off midtown Manhattan, someone may ask. An economist says you should really sacrifice that last little purity of the Hudson because that is the part which is the most expensive to achieve.

To get all the air out of the jar by vacuum pump is literally impossible. To get the first half of the air out, creating half the pressure of the ordinary atmosphere, is pretty cheap, and if it's worth doing most people would say it's a bargain. But they wouldn't say it would be worthwhile to get 99.9 percent out.

So an economist's viewpoint is always cost-benefit analysis. Cleanliness is good, but what do you want to pay for that last little bit? I think the auxiliary measures of economic progress will not only serve as refutation in debates but will also enable us to sharpen up our rational opposition to too much environmental spending. Everything up to a margin is justified and anything carried to excess economists would have to say, as any wise person would, is an aberration of judgment.

Considering some of the intangibles in pollution cleanup, what is the best way to decide environmental policy? By economic analysis or Congressional vote?

There is no substitute for democratic control of the policies of the society. So in the last analysis it is the electorate deciding.

Now under representative government that means that most of the decisions will have to be deliberated on by leigslative representatives. Any legislature must acquire informed, expert knowledge and use it in making judgments.

But as every representative legislature in the world knows and has always known, the Congress, the State House of Representatives, and the committee of aldermen cannot make the day-to-day decisions. What you have to do is set down good guidelines in the form of tax rates on effluents, in the form of zoning regulations. But these must be in forms that are enforceable, understandable, and are optimally designed in terms of the degree of environmental control the democracy ultimately desires.

So voting is important, but we economists believe it's very crucial for the voters and their representatives to set things up in such a way that many policies are self-enforcing. This way, the private pocketbook interests of the steel company are made to coincide with the interests of the community.

Make no mistake about it, under a competitive process no one firm out of the goodness of its heart, out of altruism, can take on the job of a higher level of environmental protection than its competitors. And no industry can ever spontaneously and through its trade associations be counted upon to do the job.

This doesn't mean that the people in an industry are any worse than the people in any other industry, including my own, college teaching. It just means that it's against their money interests to impose a higher standard than we the community insist upon there being imposed.

Therefore, there is no escape, in the last analysis, for democratic control involving the fair-handed coercion through the due process of law.

Polls show that the public is willing to pay for environmental cleanup. What kind of factor is that in economic policy toward the environment? Is it being taken into account adequately?

Yes, although if you're a perfectionist you might despair at the slowness of the process. I've just come back from southern California and I was a little bit appalled by the smog. On the other hand, I recall earlier times when it was worse. It would have been much worse if we had not already imposed what many people in that part of the world regarded as a painful constraint—the need for a higher and more expensive level of pollution control on automobiles.

The job is never finished, but I think the American people are getting on with the job. These problems are not going to go away. On the contrary, they are going to get bigger even as we are more effectively solving them. There is only so much land, and only so much atmosphere and rivers and lakes and underground water. Because of past demography we're putting a very, very heavy load in our modern industrial society on these limited resources of nature.

We've talked about internalizing costs, making environmental protection part of our daily affairs. Are we beginning to do this in our economy? In wastes and pollution?

We have made a beginning. I know plants here in New England which have been in business for 250 years, and the owners tell me they just didn't know until ten years ago what it was their own plants were doing. They were simply doing what their uncles and grandfathers had done before them. It was unthinking.

It reminds me that not until we had a corporate income tax and personal income tax did accounting get developed in this country. Businessmen so often didn't know their own ordinary money costs and revenue.

Similarly, the force of law is bringing home the need to internalize more of these environmental costs. The costs were there. They just weren't perceived until it was too late and they weren't brought home to those people who were causing damages.

Now I'm not pointing my finger at businesses and corporations only. In the last analysis the consumers who want steel, who want products which require certain chemicals for production, must be prepared to pay the bill for making these acceptably safe. And certain products, certain asbestos products for example, will not be able to meet those stringent requirements in the future and they will have to be replaced by substitutes that can.

So it is not just a matter of internalizing costs into some industry or business. It means internalizing them to us, the public, the ultimate consumer, the ultimate electorate whose dollar votes are swinging the patterns within which our economic resources are devoted.

Basically, looking at it over the long run, can we have a clean environment and a strong economy at the same time?

Yes. The productivity of the American system—the technological and managerial know-how, the skill of our labor force, the education and human capital—is such that although we are not growing as fast as in earlier post-WWII decades, we still have a considerable margin of growth. Part of that margin can prudently go into an expansion of the ordinary conventional private goods and services. But part of it can and, if the electorate wanted, should go into the improved good life with respect to a more healthful and more pleasant environment. When we look at the sources of American growth and consider our best future projections, it becomes apparent that there is room for both environmental cleanup and ordinary goods and services.

Is there any special message you would like to give?

Sometimes the enthusiasms of certain proponents of environmental control may appear to ordinary, more conventional citizens as hysteria. But one man's complacency is another man's hysteria, and in order to sell, sometimes you have to oversell.

So on the whole, it seems to me that we have been well served by the more altruistic among us, often the more youthful members of the population, who have raised the consciousness of the rest of us. I think most of us, as we look to what would otherwise be the case, the hell that you could have here in North America in the wake of the post WWII baby boom and industrial affluence boom, realize that things are much better than they otherwise would be, and I for one am grateful. □

This interview was conducted by John Heritage, Assistant Editor of EPA Journal.

Lofty aims alone cannot create efficiency, growth and equity

One of the sad paradoxes of our age is the fact that noble intentions are not enough to create economic efficiency, growth, and equity. Utopian socialists and Marxian Communists rebelled against the nineteenth century regime of capitalism because of their discontent with the fact that laissez-faire market mechanisms still left the masses in relative and absolute poverty.

It was not until 1917, after the Russian Revolution, that the aspirations of socialism could be put to the test. Some sixty years later, as we study the 150 nations of the world, we find that those which have forsaken market pricing are still characterized by lower than average real incomes. More surprising, experience since the end of World War II shows that the economies relying on centralized planning have on the average shown *slower growth* than have the economies that are primarily organized by means of supply and demand mechanisms.

Modified capitalism

It would be archaic to call these latter twentieth-century economies capitalistic. Pure capitalism died in Europe with Queen Victoria at the beginning of this century. It died in the United States after 1929 when Franklin Roosevelt's New Deal replaced Herbert Hoover's rugged individualism.

The best name I know to replace the anachronistic title of capitalism is to speak of the "mixed economy." There is now a mixture of (1) macroeconomic control by the government and a measure of welfare redistribution of income toward the least-advantage classes with (2) most of the production and distribution of Gross National product taking place through the pricing mechanism of the market.

Personal freedoms and business freedoms

I propose here to analyze what can plausibly be said about the relationship between the mixed or modified-capitalistic mode of economics and political democracy.

First, I must stress that they are not the same thing. In Sweden and Britain, *political freedom* obtains. You can criticize the government and sleep well, knowing you won't be sent to jail. Nonetheless, your *business* freedoms — what you can do with your private property and what coercive rules and taxes impinge on you — these are severely limited in comparison with Victorian laissez faire.

Another example to stress the difference between political and business freedoms is the case I call Capitalistic Fascism. If modern Chile had not existed, we would have had to invent it for the purpose of this taxonomy. Perhaps you will recognize some realism in the following parable.

A fairy tale

A military junta seizes power. But unlike most dictators, they are not venal. And, uncharacteristically, they stay completely out of everything economic.

The running of the economy they leave in the hands of a priestly caste. The religion of these high priests is that of market capitalism. They worship free competition. They do not receive high pay and they abjure all pecuniary bribes. It is payment enough for them to see the power of their theological ideology translated into action.

How does the parable work out? After initial painful shocks, economic efficiency does improve. Production grows and grows. Profits grow even more for those who are most active, efficient, avaricious, and lucky. Some of the poor get even poorer as their jobs are eliminated. With welfare redistributions of the state cut to the bone, these unlucky poor suffer, sicken, and some die.

Later, as more and more adjustments are made to accommodate to the new regime, the initial upsurge in economic inequality somewhat abates as the material prosperity begins to filter down to every corner of the land and to every income class. But the steady-state inequality remains higher than before the coup; and the bottom third of the population in income enjoy a rise in living standards only after the total size of the social pie has grown by more than their fractional share has fallen.

Intellectuals fare badly in the new order. Those not jailed or intimidated must lose their jobs, their rostrums and publishing outlets, and the freedom to explore and promulgate new and subversive ideas. Trade union officials are stripped of their autonomy. Legislatures are either closed down or suffered to go through the motions of harmless debate.

Obviously, democracy in the tradition sense has been compromised — at least temporarily. Nevertheless, so long as capitalism is imposed by the force of the dictators, the economic system can continue to operate.

Evolution out of fascism?

Apologists for such an order hope that the suspension of democracy can be only temporary. Once the fruits of economic efficiency begin to filter down throughout the system, it is their hope that the allegiance of the masses will be won over. And then, these ideologues hope, free voting can be restored and the laissez-faire mode of organizing the society can ultimately be given legitimate sanctions. (During the 1920s, the American people really did approve of the Coolidge-Hoover capitalism and there was no need for military or other force to impose it on the society.)

The hope that capitalistic fascism will evolve gradually into democratic capitalism is not logically absurd. Perhaps Japanese society since the United States' Occupation under General Dougals MacArthur provided an actual historical instance. The pre-1945 Japanese masses still believed in the medieval Shinto system built around the Emperor.

Japanese intellectuals, in and outside the universities, came increasingly to believe in one or another version of Marxism. However, so rapid was the rate of growth of Japanese production, exports, and real wage levels that the ruling conservative party has been able to win elections and defeat all oppositions.

As I survey wider experience, I must report that it is anything but certain that capitalistic fascism will be able to evolve into democracy even if on the economic side it does live up to the efficiency claims made for it. Iran is a case in point, only one of many.

Primarily because of his luck in having oil at a time when the OPEC cartel was succeeding in quadrupling the real price of oil, the Shah of Iran was able to deliver to the Iranian people a rapid improvement in standard of life. To be sure the fruits of progress were not shared equally with the poorest classes; and there was much corruption on the part of the elite, and much torturing and killing of dissident elements. Nevertheless, when I would ask the students in my seminar to distinguish between the great leap forward of Japan and Iran, often they could not guess which numbers in the tables and which figures in the charts belonged to Japan and which belonged to Iran.

Events of the last year, in which the whole country turned against the Shah, confirm my point that material progress is not always a condition sufficient to buy off opposition and dissent. I don't suppose this lesson is lost on the military officials in Chile.

Inequality of incomes & wealth can lessen amid competition

How to measure alienation?

Democracy has many disadvantages. And none are brought out more clearly than in the workings of populistic democracy in Argentina since the time Peron first took power.

But for all its disorder, democracy does have one great advantage. A free press and periodic elections provide approximate measures of the degree of discontent and opposition prevailing in the society.

Not so in a repressive dictatorship. The Leader can never know how unhappy or happy his subjects really are. They don't even have a way of knowing themselves since, if it is forbidden to express discontent, you yourself have no way of gauging its intensity and form.

Indonesia provides a good example. The dictator Sukarno seemed to have power well in hand. The Indonesian people are noted for their amiability and serenity. Yet that is the part of the world where the expression "running amuck" originated. And when opposition to the Sukarno regime went past its flashpoint, the resulting deaths had to be numbered in the hundreds of thousands.

Liberals like myself are always urging a Krushchev to relax repressive fiats. Sometimes our pious advice is disregarded because of mere paranoia. But often the dictatorial establishment has reason to fear that what begins as a slight loosening up may unleash an avalanche of dissent.

Some tentative hypotheses

I do not think any confident and definitive conclusions are possible. Ambiguities in political science are even greater than in the imperfect science of economies. But let me hazard a few guesses.

1. Use of the competitive market system is important for efficiency. Professors Jagdish Bhagwati of MIT and Anne Krueger of the University of Minnesota have shown in a recent study for the National Bureau of Economic Research that developing countries which have relied primarily on trade protection in order to foster "import substitution" have not done as well in the recent decades as those which have given freer reign to the market mechanism and who have embraced "export promotion."

We speak somewhat admiringly of the Gang of Four, meaning by this the rapidly prospering LDCs: South Korea, Taiwan, Hong Kong and Singapore. Turning their backs on the Latin American strategy espoused by Dr. Raul Prebisch, these societies show since 1960 growth rates in real income per capita double that of the United States and many times that of all Latin American countries other than Brazil and Mexico.

2. Note that all these successful economies other than Hong Kong involve oligarchic dictatorships rather than traditional democracies. Assassination of the political leader must put into jeopardy the continuation of the successful economic pattern.

3. But turn now to the advanced industrial countries. A Switzerland interferes less with the market place than does a Sweden. Does it follow that the Switzerlands clearly show more rapid economic progress than the Swedens?

The historical record is more complicated. During the last third of a century both countries show very similar rates of economic growth and of real wage improvement.

Conservative economists like Friedrich Hayek or Milton Friedman argue that the more undilutedly capitalistic an economy is the more efficient and progressive will be its performance. But if I use as an important measure of interference with capitalism the fraction of the Gross National Product that goes into government taxation and expenditure, I find that fast growing countries like West Germany, France, Belgium and Holland, and Scandinavia all leave a smaller fraction of the total social pie to the private sector than does the slower growing United States.

The so-called "English disease" does seem to be a real thing. The United Kingdom has been falling behind most countries in Western Europe and North America. Moreover, the British Commonwealth countries of Australia and New Zealand show some of the same symptoms as in the English case. Early in the twentieth century Australia and New Zealand had already attained living standards among the highest in the world. But they too have been experiencing rather languid and disappointing economic growth.

Admittedly, material economic growth is not everything. It is a good life in Australia under the easy-going "fair shares" philosophy that prevails there. Many democracies will be willing to embrace a tradeoff in which greater equality in the sharing of the total social pie is achieved at the cost of some reduction in the potential size and growth rate of that total social pie. But still there are signs in the election turnovers in all three of these English-speaking countries that there are internal doubts concerning whether the optimal tradeoff between equity and efficiency has been realized in recent years.

4. I should warn that my own value judgment puts great weight on lessening the inequality of incomes and wealth that is inherent in the workings of the pure capitalistic market economy. But I believe we can hope to harness the market mechanism to preserve and promote dynamic efficiency without abandoning the humanitarian impulse to provide democratically some minimum welfare standards for those most disadvantaged in the competitive struggle.

I end where I began. Good intentions are not enough. We should cast scorn at mere sentimentality. I would have found it laughable, were it not so pathetic, to hear the rich students at American elite universities declaim, back in the late 1960s, on the virtues of organizing economic life by the high-minded principles of production for social utility rather than for mere private profit. The New Left has much to learn from those imaginative and humane economists in Eastern Europe who urge on the ruling bureaucrats — without much success — that greater use be made there of market-pricing mechanisms, profitability calculations and other incentive devices.

I suspect that some of these same wisdoms will have relevance for the developing countries of Africa, Asia, and Latin America — and for the advanced industrial countries as well.

Afternoon of the Mixed Economy?

Before 1929, capitalism generally prevailed. The Great Depression of the thirties ushered in the mixed economy—the welfare state characterized not so much by traditional ownership of the means of production by the socialist state as by *mutual reinsurance* arrangements to *transfer* incomes from us when we fare well in the marketplace to ourselves when our human needs exceed what we can earn.

Miracle Epoch

Utilizing Keynesian finance, the mixed economies grew during the third quarter of the twentieth century in a truly miraculous way. Western Europe essentially closed the gap between itself and the United States. Japan, a poor and defeated oriental country in 1945, by the 1970s was the third largest economy in the world, surpassing Britain in real per capita income. Even the underdeveloped regions improved their life expectancies and mean standard of life at a rate never equaled under capitalism in its palmiest days. The communist countries of the Soviet sphere and China made some economic progress but performed mediocrely compared to the mixed economies.

No one predicted the 1945–1970 miracles. Not Marx, Trotsky, Mao, or Khrushchev. Not Hayek or Friedman. Josef Schumpeter came the closest. But Schumpeter feared that "capitalism in an oxygen tent" would lose its efficiency and innovational growth. Capitalism's very successes, Schumpeter predicted, would breed alienated intellectuals and neurotic self-doubts—leading inevitably to socialism.

So much for prophesy. And so much for history.

What about the future of the mixed economy?

The Disappointing Seventies

I very much fear that the last quarter of the twentieth century will fail to match the miraculous third quarter. The easy Keynesian victories are well behind us. Club of Rome problems are likely to intensify—even though limits-to-growth hysteria is not justified by OPEC's sevenfold increase in the *real* cost of energy.

Since 1970, the trend of productivity growth has decelerated almost everywhere. If you did not know better, you would be tempted to trace so universal a phenomenon to sunspots or a global cycle in climate.

Without exception, every mixed economy is afflicted with *stagflation*—soaring nominal wages and prices at the same time that the system is threatened with unemployed labor and excess factory capacity. We do know how to expand fiscal programs and credit supplies to ameliorate stagnation in production and real incomes. But, when we help the "stag" part of the stagflation, we hurt the in*flation* part. We do know how to contract fiscal and credit programs to counter inflation. But when we help the "flation" part of stagflation, we make the *stag*nation worse.

This is *not* an academic dilemma. It is a glaring blemish in the workings of the welfare state. You cannot understand the dismal performance of the 1970s—the several recessions around the globe and the anemic recoveries—without realizing that it is the specter of accelerating inflation that compels governments to countenance ever higher average levels of unemployment.

The Humane Society

I am not a conservative economist. I applaud the modern humane society. In my view it would be a tragedy to go back to 1929, with its laissez-faire inequalities. Milton Friedman's vision of the good society, in which all are free to wrest from the marketplace what their endowments and efforts can contrive, is not my ethical vision.

But I am a realist. In the humane society, losing a job or losing market demand for your industry's products fails to put downward pressure on your wage and on the prices of what your industry sells. So, right there lies the key to stagflation. Stagflation is not an accidental disease that happens to afflict the mixed economy. Stagflation is rooted deep in the humane nature of the welfare state.

I abhor Chile with its fascistic capitalism—Chicago economics imposed by political force. But my heart cannot keep my reason from understanding that the behavior laws are different when the only alternative that a worker has to starving is to accept a job at a lower wage. North America and Western Europe are not at all like that, and we should not be surprised to observe an upward bias in the price level of these regions and a need for governments to be contriving ever higher degrees of economic slack to slow down inflation.

Freezing in the Status Quo

Italy nicely points up what you can also begin to see in Sweden, Norway, Britain, France, and the United States. My country subsidizes Chrysler to produce cars that can't be sold to cover their costs of production. We do it to preserve jobs. Or, at least, to preserve them for a while. Later, we may succumb to import quotas and tariffs for the same purpose.

The Italians could teach us a lesson. Mussolini bought common stocks during the 1930s depression to shore up their prices. The government became an important holding company. More than that. The government can tell any large Italian company to continue to employ workers even if there is nothing they can produce for profitable sale.

A humane thing you say? Yes. But down that road lies the swamp of inefficiency. As the Soviet planners know to their despair, meeting the test of market price is one of the few ways a society can be responsive in its production, resource allocations, and technological methods to human wants and needs.

The beauty of a mixed economy is that it is supposed to channel the efficiencies of the market into humane goals. In what my MIT colleague Charles Kindleberger calls the "menopausal economy," ends are lost in the means as pressure groups succeed in preserving attained economic roles even after they no longer are responsive to society's wants and needs.

Argentina as Paradigm

My nightmare is that Schumpeter's scenario of the good-intentioned blundering political system is coming closer. The shadow in our future may not be Sweden à la 1965—combining the miracle of egalitarian policies with annual productivity improvements in manufacturing of 7 percent per annum—but rather Argentina. Blessed after 1945 with temperate climate, promising labor force, and favorable natural resources, *economically* Argentina was poised for miraculous growth. But a sick political and social system—one more concerned over the division of the social pie than its total size and growth—thwarted that economic potential.

The bell that tolls for Argentina may be the bell that tolls for the mixed economy in the age after Keynes.

I hope that my diagnosis is wrong; that political self-restraint can preserve the disciplines of the marketplace and chain them to humane ends.

Postscript on Norway

I am not an expert on the Norwegian economy. By temperament I avoid interfering in the election competitions of any country. Last summer when I visited Paru, at a time when a new civilian government at long last took over from the military, the press at my lectures tried to build me up as an anti-Friedman. That is not my preferred role.

Norway is to be envied. Located in northwest Europe, even without oil, it enjoys one of the highest per capita incomes in the world. And, in addition, Norway does have North Sea oil.

Partly because of these oil reserves in her balance of international payments, Norway was able in the 1970s to withstand the worldwide recessions better than many of her neighbors. If this gift of nature, North Sea oil and gas, is husbanded well, Norwegians can hope to prosper in the future, favorably compared to other advanced nations.

But blessings also present challenges. I have had to ponder over the special oil problems of such diverse places as Alaska, Saudi Arabia, and Peru. When the Oslo Group brought to my attention the fascinating case of Norway, I came to realize the temptations and opportunities oil will involve.

Will Norwegian manufacturing be elbowed out? Should it? To what degree?

Will the bonanza of oil be spent on a consumption binge of the present generation and generation just ahead? Will it be *private* or *public* consumption? How can the depleting oil taken from the ground be transmuted into enhanced capital stock for future Norwegians—so that when the oil is gone, there will exist in perpetuity the fruits of the new trees that oil made possible?

I have spoken of the temptations of the welfare state. An automatic source of oil reserves for the state will not be gauged to lessen those temptations.

I have asked enough questions to keep a team of economists busy for a quarter of a century. I have aired my aspirations and concerns. What I have not done is weigh the merits of different political parties or platforms.

387

World Economy of the Eighties

The 1970s began with high hopes. And why not? The decades of the fifties and sixties had been wonderful ones for world growth. Now that the 1980s are ahead, we realize how disappointing the 1970s turned out to be for most economies of the world. This chastens the experts as they try to peer into the murky future of the decade ahead.

The Dismal Outlook

Prophets of despair are all too plentiful. They speak dolefully of a day of judgment just ahead when energy and other choice natural resource deposits run out. They warn darkly of a breakdown in the structure of international finance. Great banks are to fail as their loans to governments in the developing world go into default.

The dollar's days as a great key currency are numbered, according to the scenario envisaged by the pessimists. Chaos in exchange rates will lead to a Wagnerian breakdown of the system of free trade. Once again the world is to return to autarchy, as quotas and exchange controls multiply.

For two centuries since the beginnings of the industrial revolution, economic growth has been the rule—not only in the industrialized West, but also in the Third World. But what has been almost a tenfold increase in the real price of oil since 1970, coupled with a rash of harvest failures in Russia and Asia, has already brought a decline in real wages to urban workers.

This is only a foretaste of what is to become an avalanche in the 1980s. At least that is what you are led to think when you read the Sunday newspaper scare stories.

Libertarians' Euphoria

Physicists and chemists generally speak with one voice where hard science is concerned. Not so with political economy. For every school of pessimists about the future, there is an opposing camp of optimists. They want us to believe the following rosy story.

Electorates are revolting against the heresies of Keynesian fiscal and monetary policy. Led by Germany, Switzerland, and Japan, governments all over the world are giving first priority to the fight against inflation. Full employment is no longer an unconditional target. Given the political will, austerity in controlling the money supply will succeed in bringing the rates of price increase down from two-digit annual rates to one-digit rates. Then, if governments will only hold on a little longer, in the same way that small pox can be permanently eradicated from the world once we have traced down every last case—so, if we persist, we can win permanent victory over stagflation.

Hence, runs the dream of the optimists, after 1982, most of the world will return to healthy real growth with steady price levels and shrinking role of government. Given free scope, markets and the pricing mechanism will deliver the goods of progress at a breath taking rate. The eighties will be the decade of return to the sanity of markets: That sums up the expectations of this romantic school.

Reasoned Compromises

I must firmly reject both of these extreme poles. The evidence does not justify your expecting a worldwide economic breakdown in the years ahead.

Agreeing that there is a swing toward conservatism in many of the mixed economies of the world, I still have to be skeptical that we have entered on a one-way trend toward government retrenchment. And my studies of how market pricing mechanisms work—their many advantages and disadvantages—raise doubts that the performance records of the 1950s and 1960s can be maintained in the 1980s.

Let me justify my expectation that the 1980s will for most of the world just about match the middling performance of the 1970s. And for the very most affluent nations—the United States, West Germany, Sweden, Switzerland, Japan—the betting odds favor some further deceleration of rates of economic growth. Their lead should, if anything, shrink a little between now and 1990.

US in the 1970s

Few realize that the United States has ranked well in the 1970s in comparison with Europe, Japan, and Australia. The world recession of 1973–1975 did not hit us as hard as it hit Germany, Switzerland, and Japan.

More important, the US economic recovery from 1975 to 1979 was a more vigorous one than in those countries. As the fruits of our baby boom of the 1940s and 1950s came on the labor market, we put millions of young people to work. More than that, we have had a sociological revolution in the economic status of women. As a majority of our females have opted to stay continuously in the labor force, despite marriage and mothering a small family, our economy has put millions of new female workers into productive jobs.

Despite the political stalemate in America over a rational energy policy, our economic system has adjusted to the OPEC shock remarkably well. Slowdown in the growth of real wage rates, and even a drop in them, is an implication of the rise in oil and food prices. Our workers, both in unions and outside them, have more or less gracefully accepted this fate. The same cannot yet be said of workers on the European continent, who still have some painful adjustments to look forward to.

In what respects, then, has the American economic performance in the 1970s been disappointing? In two main respects. First, our productivity growth has been extremely poor, poorer even than can be explained by higher energy prices and demographic shifts toward lower-paid female and younger workers. Second, America has done a poorer job of moderating stagflation than has Japan or Germany. This is admittedly a disappointment. However, I must point to the little realized fact that our system has managed to adjust itself rather well to the inflation understood to be taking place. Thus the depreciation of the dollar, which has been so much deplored by noneconomists, has in fact been a rational adaptation to our higher rate of inflation.

The Years Ahead

Although I expect Japan to grow faster in the 1980s than America does, I expect the rate of growth of her real gross national product to be barely 5 percent per year, just half of what used to be her pace. At that rate, Japan will still not reach the US standard of living by 1990. Germany, France, and Britain have all done worse in the 1970s than they ought to be capable of in the 1980s. Russia and the East European socialist countries are not now in an enviable stage of growth. If peace prevails, South Korea, Taiwan, Hong Kong, Singapore, Malaya, and the Philippines should outperform the USSR in the decade ahead. Concerning China, we must remain agnostic. Her upside potential is promising, but there is no guarantee she will realize it. The OPEC countries have for the most part not been utilizing their great gains well, even though few have been faring as badly as Iran.

I take satisfaction that the developing countries did, on the average, match the 1970s' performance of the industrialized countries. It is an even bet that they may do so again in the 1980s.

My final word of comfort is this. The economic sprint of the 1950s and 1960s was not a natural par. It was nice while it lasted. But regression toward a more average performance does not represent the end of the world. It still ranks well with the performance of historic capitalism.

That Constitutional budget amendment—'tremendous potential for harm'

In our February issue we published "The TRA—Taxpayer's Rights Amendment," a piece, by James Dale Davidson, Chairman of the National Taxpayers Union, suggesting a Constitutional amendment requiring a balanced Federal budget. Here is a view, by an eminent economist, that differs sharply from Davidson's and from similar proposals. It is reprinted from *The AEI Economist*, April 1979. Copyright © 1979 American Enterprise Institute for Public Policy Research; originally, it was presented as testimony before the Subcommittee on Monopolies and Commercial Law of the Committee on the Judiciary of the U.S. House of Representatives.

I have been asked to give my analysis and evaluation of the many proposals to amend the Constitution of the United States to require a balanced Federal budget or to specify some other unambiguous constraint on governmental fiscal policy. Each and all of the proposals that have been made appear, on analysis, to entail grave dangers to the prudent operation of the modern economy. More important than my adverse opinion on this matter are the reasons for this critical evaluation, which I am prepared to discuss in detail. In summary, here are the conclusions to which analysis leads.

A Constitutional Amendment cannot by its nature provide the *flexibility* for future governmental policy that is necessary in so imperfect a science as economics. There is much *historical experience*, with laudable attempts to specify for all time the permitted parameters of economic policy, both here in the United States and in many foreign countries. Without exception—whether it be the case of the automatic gold standard, the many central bank gold-reserve clauses underlying the creation of money, the pegged exchange rates of the Bretton Woods system, the frequent legal requirements at the municipal and state levels to require an annual budget balancing, the Congressional debt-limit resolutions—*each such attempt at permanent fine-tuning has resulted in specific economic crises and inefficiencies.*

Not only has the universal testimony of experience shown that every such attempt to freeze policy in advance has failed in its objective and led, after unnecessary travail, to its abandonment, but in every case *the analysis of economic principle prior to enactment of the once-and-for-ever rules would have been able to predict that those tragic breakdowns would subsequently take place.*

Whenever it is the case that a bare or preponderant majority of the American people *permanently* conclude that the role of the public sector ought to be constrained in its fractional share of the total national income or in its trend rate of increase, our representative democracy is capable of translating that will of the people into effective action. The American republic is not defective in its present organizational structure to secure what are stated to be the goals of the amendment to balance the budget or the amendment to limit the share and growth trend of the public sector. *There is no inherent flaw in our checks and balances and division of responsibility among the Legislative, Executive and Judicial branches of government that makes inevitable a process of "logrolling" designed to swell the level of expenditures and taxes beyond that truly desired by the effective majority of the electorate.* Instead, the elaborated pure theory of public expenditure and of game theory more evenhandedly show that there are countertendencies favoring realization of *both less and more* government expenditures than the pluralistic electorate really desire.

If a temporary upsurge in resentment against taxes, expenditures, and deficits that are conceived to be excessive were to culminate in a Constitutional convention, and if one of the many alternative amendments were to be adopted, an economist can predict, with all-too-weighty odds, that several times in the decades to come the adopted amendment will bring on or exacerbate an economic crisis. If the adopted amendment provides escape valves so easy to invoke that the harm of the amendment can be avoided, the amendment degenerates into little more than a pious resolution, a rhetorical appendage to clutter up our magnificent historical Constitution. If no escape valves are allowed for, a breakdown in the whole economic system is threatened whenever unpredictable future events prove incompatible with the particular nostrum of 1979 that is frozen into the American charter. Analysis shows how illusory it is to dream that there is some wide middle ground of Constitutional formulation that will enable our people to have their cake and eat it, too.

There is no substitute for disciplined and informed choice by a democratic people of their basic economic policies. No wave of the future washes us down the road to serfdom or back to laissez-faire. A government of law (and not of capricious men) involves national decision-making by due process: it does not call for, and indeed is incompatible with, written-out hundred-year economic plans or cookbook recipes for infinity.

I am prepared to discuss the above conclusions, and the empirical data and analytical reasoning on which they are based. But before doing so, I need to make a much misunderstood point.

We live in an age of stagflation. In seeking to end this deplorable condition, one must not make the mistake of believing that its basic root is to be found in overspending by government, or in over- or undertaxing by government, with the chronic budget deficits thereby implied. If only the problem were as simple as that of old-fashioned demand-pull inflation! You would not then need so sage an economist as **Dr. Burns** to head up the

Federal Reserve Board in the 1970s to have given us, long before now, a return to price stability if only demand-pull forces had been involved. A Milton Friedman—quite without referring to fiscal policy, much less Constitutional amendments—could prescribe for old-fashioned demand-pull inflation in a few, crisp *Newsweek* columns. Indeed, I myself believe that the total of aggregate demand spending could be brought up to the requisite full-employment amount by a politically acceptable combination of monetary and fiscal policy *if only there were such a clearly designatable requisite amount of spending for full employment without inflation.*

Our modern chronic dilemmas of policy have been much more complicated, and they will not be resolved or significantly ameliorated by Constitutional amendments. Whatever government policy does to help handle the "flation" part of our stagflation inevitably worsens in the short run the stagnation part of the problem. That stubborn reality will not go away even if 50 out of 50 states agree on some rhetorical formulation. Likewise, whatever government policy does to help handle the "stag" part of stagflation will ineluctably worsen the inflation part of stagflation. We can do better with respect to stagflation than we have been doing in the 1970s. But the task of reducing the element of stagflation in our modern mixed economy cannot be accomplished by once-and-for-all tax and spending formulas.

A few concrete examples will illustrate the tremendous potential for harm implicit in use of the Constitution for freezing policy rules. Our economic system almost came to ruin in the Great Depression: suppose that the Constitution had been amended prior to 1931, requiring that Federal Reserve liabilities and printed currency notes be covered by some magic fraction of gold reserves. I believe present-day experts of all schools of thought, monetarist or otherwise, would agree that the tragic reluctance of the Federal Reserve to then help preserve the banking system that was being rent asunder by bank failures would have been grossly amplified by such a rule, *however wise it would have seemed to economists in 1928 and to the public at large that the amendment was a good thing.*

Again, during the Great Depression, Herbert Hoover's budget fell out of balance against his wishes. His rash raising of tax rates was self-defeating in its attempt to balance the budget. But that rash attempt did most definitely worsen the state of bankruptcy of the economic system. How much worse would have been the pressure on Congress and the Executive to perpetrate these follies if the Constitution itself called for such suicidal policies.

The final example concerns proposals to "index" wages that were being made in the early 1970s by prominent American economists. Of course, these proponents could not predict in advance that OPEC would increase the price of oil fivefold and that a rash of harvest failures all over the world would call for a lower real wage on the part of urban workers. If anyone doubts the endless harm that would have resulted from a Constitutional amendment trying to keep wages at a real level not actually attainable in the market, I have to call attention to the disastrous effect in Italy that has resulted from the legal escalating of all wage rates to match the absolute gains of the highest paid workers—a formula that informed observers blame for much of Italy's sickness in recent years.

Economics is so inexact a science and the future so unpredictable that it is an act of arrogant folly to try to specify Constitutional formulas applicable for the infinite future.

CONTENTS

Volume I

Book One

Problems in Pure Theory: The Theory of Consumer's Behavior and Capital Theory

CONTENTS

Volume II

Book Three

Trade, Welfare, and Fiscal Policy

Book Five

Economics — Past and Present

CONTENTS

Volume III

Book One

Problems in Pure Theory: The Theory of Consumer's Behavior and Capital Theory

Book Two

Topics in Mathematical Economics

Part VIII. Mathematical Investigations

Book Three

Trade, Welfare and Fiscal Policy

Part IX. Trade

Part X. Welfare Economics

Part XI. Dynamics and Statics of Income Determination

Book Four

Economics and Public Policy

Part XII. Pure Theory of Public Expenditure

Part XIII. Principles of Fiscal and Monetary Policy

Part XIV. The Individual and the State

Book Five

Economics—Past and Present

Part XVI. Essays in the History of Economics

Part XVII. Lectures and Essays on Modern Economics

Part XVIII. Comments on Methodology

CONTENTS

Volume IV

Part I. Theory of Consumption and Production

Part II. Theory of Capital and Growth

Part III. On Marxian Economics

Part IV. Mathematical Biology and Economics of Population

Part V. Stochastic Theory of Economics

Part VI. International Economics

Part VII. Welfare Economics

Part VIII. Theory of Money and Inflation

Part IX. Lectures and Essays on Current Economic Problems

Part X. Essays on the Evolution of Economics

ACKNOWLEDGMENTS

The author, editor, and The MIT Press wish to thank the publishers of the following essays for permission to reprint them here. The selections are arranged chronologically, with cross references in brackets to the chapter numbers used in this collection.

Foreword to *Marx's Economics: Origin and Development*, by Alexander Balinky. Lexington, Mass.: D. C. Heath, 1970, xi–xii. [311]

"Government and Business," in *Emerging Issues Affecting U.S. Corporations*. Washington, D.C.: The Public Affairs Council, 1977, 99–106. Copyright by the Public Affairs Council, 1220 Sixteenth Street NW, Washington, D.C. 20036. [380]

"A Modern Theorist's Vindication of Adam Smith," *The American Economic Review*, vol. 67, no. 1, February 1977, 42–49. [342]

"Reaffirming the Existence of 'Reasonable' Bergson-Samuelson Social Welfare Functions," *Economica*, vol. 44, February 1977, 81–88. [294]

"Comparison of Linear and Nonlinear Models for Human Population Dynamics," with Joel Yellin, *Theoretical Population Biology*, vol. 11, no. 1, February 1977, 105–126. [349]

Foreword to *Health Controls Out of Control*, by David M. Kinzer. Chicago, Ill.: teach'em, 1977, ix–xi. [382]

"St. Petersburg Paradoxes: Defanged, Dissected and Historically Described," *Journal of Economic Literature*, vol. 15, no. 1, March 1977, 24–55. [298]

"Two Nobel Laureates' Theories on Trade," *The New York Times*, 15 October 1977. Copyright © by The New York Times Company. Reprinted by permission. [360]

"Generalizing Fischer's 'Reproductive Value': Linear Differential and Difference Equations of 'Dilute' Biological Systems," *Proceedings of the National Academy of Sciences USA*, vol. 74, no. 11, November 1977, 5189–5192. [351]

"Correcting the Ricardo Error Spotted in Harry Johnson's Maiden Paper," *The Quarterly Journal of Economics*, vol. 91, no. 4, November 1977, 519–530. Copyright 1977 by John Wiley and Sons, Inc. [345]

"Thoughts on Profit-Sharing," *Zeitschrift für die gesamte Staatswissenschaft*, Special Issue on Profit-Sharing, A Symposium, Heinz Sauermann and Rudolf Richter (eds.). Tübingen: J. C. B. Mohr, 1977, 9–18. Copyright J. C. B. Mohr (Paul Siebeck). [376]

"Balanced Growth Equilibrium in the General Multi-Class Saving Model," *Quantitative Wirtschaftsforschung: Wilhelm Krelle zum 60. Geburstag*, Horst Albach, Ernst Helmstädter, and Rudolf Henn (eds.). Tübingen: J. C. B. Mohr, 1977, 569–577. Copyright J. C. B. Mohr (Paul Siebeck). [301]

"Comparative Advantage, Trade, and Payments in a Ricardian Model with a Continuum of Goods," with Rudiger Dornbusch and Stanley Fischer, *American Economic Review*, vol. 67, no. 5, December 1977, 823–839. [316]

"When It Is Ethically Optimal to Allocate Money Income in Stipulated Fractional Shares," in *Natural Resources, Uncertainty, and General Equilibrium Systems: Essays in Memory of Rafael Lusky*, Alan S. Blinder and Philip Friedman (eds.). New York: Academic Press, 1977, 175–195. [295]

"Generalizing Fischer's 'Reproductive Value': Nonlinear, Homogeneous, Biparental Systems," *Proceedings of the National Academy of Sciences USA*, vol. 74, no. 12, December 1977, 5772–5775. [352]

"Hanging in There," *Newsweek*, 13 February 1978, 80. Copyright 1978 by Newsweek, Inc. All rights reserved. Reprinted by permission. [331]

"Free Trade's Intertemporal Pareto-Optimality," *Journal of International Economics*, vol. 8, 1978, 147–149. [321]

"Policy Advising in Economics," *Challenge*, March-April 1978, 37–38. [381]

"Coping Sensibly," *Newsweek*, 6 March 1978, 88. Copyright 1978 by Newsweek, Inc. All rights reserved. Reprinted by permission. [332]

"Maximizing and Biology," *Economic Inquiry*, vol. 16, April 1978, 171–183. [346]

"Interest Rate Equalization and Nonequalization by Trade in Leontief-Sraffa Models," *Journal of International Economics*, vol. 8, 1978, 21–27. [320]

"Generalizing Fischer's 'Reproductive Value': Overlapping and Nonoverlapping Generations with Competing Genotypes," *Proceedings of the National Academy of Sciences USA*, vol. 75, no. 8, August 1978, 4062–4066. [353]

"Gold and Common Stocks," *Newsweek*, 21 August 1978, 65. Copyright 1978 by Newsweek, Inc. All rights reserved. Reprinted by permission. [333]

"Pseudo-Maximization to the Rescue of Derived Factor Demand of a Competitive Industry," in *Breadth and Depth in Economics: Fritz Machlup—The Man and His Ideas*, Jacob S. Dreyer (ed.). Lexington, Mass.: D. C. Heath, A Lexington Book, 1978, 87–118. Copyright 1978, D. C. Heath and Company. [297]

"Time to Sell," *Newsweek*, 11 December 1978, 90. Copyright 1978 by Newsweek, Inc. All rights reserved. Reprinted by permission. [334]

"The Canonical Classical Model of Political Economy," *Journal of Economic Literature*, vol. 16, December 1978, 1415–1434. [340]

"Generalizing Fischer's 'Reproductive Value': 'Incipient' and 'Penultimate' Reproductive-Value Functions When Environment Limits Growth; Linear Approximants for Nonlinear Mendelian Mating Models," *Proceedings of the National Academy of Sciences USA*, vol. 75, no. 12, December 1978, 6327–6331. [354]

"An Economist's View," *Environmental Protection Agency Journal*, vol. 5, no. 1, January 1979, 4–5, 36. [383]

"The Roots of Inflation," in *Encyclopaedia Britannica, 1979 Book of the Year.* Chicago, Ill.: Encyclopaedia Britannica, 1979, 60–64. Reprinted with permission from the *1979 Encyclopaedia Britannica Book of the Year.* Copyright 1979, Encyclopaedia Brittanica, Inc., Chicago, Illinois. [377]

"World Economy of the Eighties," speech broadcast over *Westdeutscher Rundfunk*, December 1979. [387]

"The Role of Profits in a Mixed Economy: Changes in the Perceived Reality" (John Diebold Lecture), in *New Challenges to the Role of Profit*, Benjamin M. Friedman (ed.). Lexington, Mass.: D. C. Heath, 1978, 13–29. Copyright 1978, D. C. Heath and Company. [374]

"That Constitutional Budget Amendment—'Tremendous Potential for Harm,'" *AEI Economist*, April 1979, 4–6. [388]

"Myths and Realities about the Crash and Depression," *The Journal of Portfolio Management*, vol. 6, no. 1, Fall 1979, 7–10. [372]

"The Crash of '29: Lessons for '79," *Newsday*, 28 October 1979. [373]

"Paul Douglas's Measurement of Production Functions and Marginal Productivities," *The Journal of Political Economy*, vol. 87, no. 5, part 1, October 1979, 923–939. © 1979 by The University of Chicago. All rights reserved. [302]

"Why We Should Not Make Mean Log of Wealth Big though Years to Act Are Long," *Journal of Banking and Finance*, vol. 3, 1979, 305–307. Copyright North-Holland Publishing Company, Amsterdam. [329]

"America's Interest in International Trade," in *New England Merchants Company, Inc., 1979 Annual*, 4–5. [325]

"Land and the Rate of Interest," in *Theory for Economic Efficiency: Essays in Honor of Abba P. Lerner*, Harry I. Greenfield, Albert M. Levenson, William Hamovitch, and Eugene Rotwein (eds.). Cambridge, Mass.: The MIT Press, 1979, 167–185. [344]

"The Public Role in the Modern American Economy," in *The American Economy in Transition*, Martin Feldstein (ed.). Cambridge, Mass.: National Bureau of Economic Research, 1980, 665–671. [375]

"No-Fuss Canny Investing," *Newsweek*, 4 February 1980, 68. Copyright 1980 by Newsweek, Inc. All rights reserved. Reprinted by permission. [335]

"Arthur Okun, 1928–1980," *Newsweek*, 7 April 1980, 67. Copyright 1980 by Newsweek, Inc. All rights reserved. Reprinted by permission. [358]

"Recession: Causes and Consequences," with William F. Samuelson, in *The Americana Annual 1980, Yearbook of the Encyclopedia Americana*. Danbury, Conn.: Grolier, 1980, 25–28. Reprinted with permission of *The Americana Annual*, copyright 1980, Grolier, Inc. [378]

"Living with Stagflation," in *Collier's Year Book 1980*. London: Macmillan, 1980, 89. Reprinted by permission from the 1980 Year Book, covering the year 1979, annual supplement to Collier's Encyclopedia and Merit Students Encyclopedia. Copyright © 1979 by Macmillan Educational Corporation. All rights reserved. [379]

"Lofty Aims Alone Cannot Create Efficiency, Growth and Equity," *The Japan Economic Journal*, 17 June 1980, 20. Nihon Keizei Shimbun. [384]

"Inequality of Incomes and Wealth Can Lessen amid Competition," *The Japan Economic Journal*, 24 June 1980, 24. Nihon Keizei Shimbun. [385]

"Noise and Signal in Debates Among Classical Economists: A Reply," *Journal of Economic Literature*, vol. 18, June 1980, 575–578. [341]

"Heckscher-Ohlin Trade Theory with a Continuum of Goods," with Rudiger Dornbusch and Stanley Fischer, *The Quarterly Journal of Economics*, vol. 95, no. 2, September 1980, 203–224. Copyright John Wiley and Sons, Inc. [317]

"Fischer's 'Reproductive Value' as an Economic Specimen in Merton's Zoo," *Transaction of the New York Academy of Sciences*, series 2, vol. 39, April 1980, 126–142. [350]

"A Corrected Version of Hume's Equilibrating Mechanism for International Trade," in *Flexible Exchange Rates and the Balance of Payments: Essays in Memory of Egon Sohmen*, John S. Chipman and Charles P. Kindleberger (eds.). Amsterdam: North-Holland, 1980, 141–158. [315]

"A Nobel for Forecasting," *Newsweek*, 3 November 1980, 72. Copyright 1980 by Newsweek, Inc. All rights reserved. Reprinted by permission. [361]

"Lloyd Metzler (April 3, 1913–October 26, 1980)," Memorial Service, 12 December 1980. [359]

"Crackpot Investing," *Newsweek*, 26 January 1981, 67. Copyright 1981 by Newsweek, Inc. All rights reserved. Reprinted by permission. [336]

"Summing Up on the Australian Case for Protection," *The Quarterly Journal of Economics*, vol. 96, no. 1, February 1981, 147–160. Copyright John Wiley and Sons, Inc. [318]

"Justice to the Australians," *The Quarterly Journal of Economics*, vol. 96, no. 1, February 1981, 169–170. Copyright John Wiley & Sons, Inc. [319]

"Afternoon of the Mixed Economy?" *Økonomisk Rapport*, March 1981. [386]

"Canny Investing," *McGraw-Hill Economics Newsletter*, Spring 1981. [337]

"Bertil Ohlin, 1899–1979," *Journal of International Economics*, vol. 11, 1981, 147–163. Copyright North-Holland Publishing Company, Amsterdam. [357]

"Schumpeter's Capitalism, Socialism and Democracy," in *Schumpeter's Vision: Capitalism, Socialism and Democracy After 40 Years*, Arnold Heertje (ed.). London: Praeger, 1981. 1–21. [310]

Foreword to *Theory of Technical Change and Economic Invariance: Application to Lie Groups*, by Ryuzo Sato. New York: Academic Press, 1981, xi–xii. [368]

"Bergsonian Welfare Economics," in *Economic Welfare and the Economics of Soviet Socialism: Essays in Honor of Abram Bergson*, Steven Rosefielde (ed.). Cambridge: Cambridge University Press, 1981, 223–266. [293]

"To Protect Manufacturing?" *Zeitschrift für die gesamte Staatswissenschaft (Journal of Institutional and Theoretical Economics)*, Band 137, Heft 3, September 1981, 407–414. Copyright J. C. B. Mohr (Paul Siebeck). [324]

"1981 Nobel Prize in Economics," *Science*, vol. 214, 30 October 1981, 520–522. Copyright 1981 by the American Association for the Advancement of Science. [362]

"Quesnay's 'Tableau Economique' as a Theorist would Formulate it Today," in *Classical and Marxian Political Economy: Essays in Honor of Ronald L. Meek*. Ian Bradley and Michael Howard (eds.). New York: St. Martin's Press, 1982, 45–78. [343]

"Paul Cootner's Reconciliation of Economic Law with Chance," in *Financial Economics: Essays in Honor of Paul Cootner*, William F. Sharpe and Cathryn M. Cootner (eds.). Englewood Cliffs, N.J.: Prentice-Hall, 1982, 101–117. Reprinted by permission of Prentice-Hall, Inc., Englewood Cliffs, New Jersey. [328]

"The Normative and Positivistic Inferiority of Marx's *Values* Paradigm," *Southern Economic Journal*, vol. 49, no. 1, July 1982, 11–18. [312]

"A Chapter in the History of Ramsey's Optimal Feasible Taxation and Optimal Public Utility Prices," in *Economic Essays in Honour of Jørgen H. Gelting*, Svend Andersen, Karsten Larsen, P. Norregaard Rusmussen, and J. Vibe-Pedersen (eds.). Copenhagen: Danish Economic Association, 1982, 157–181. [296]

"Schumpeter as an Economic Theorist," in *Schumpeterian Economics*, Helmut Frisch (ed.). London: Praeger, 1982, 1–27. [309]

Forewords to the Japanese edition of *The Collected Scientific Papers of Paul A. Samuelson*, vols. 1, 2, 4, 5, 6, 8, 9, M. Shinohara and R. Sato (eds.). Tokyo: Keiso Shobo, 1982. [367]

"Rigorous Observational Positivism: Klein's Envelope Aggregation; Thermodynamics and Economic Isomorphisms," in *Global Econometrics: Essays in Honor of Lawrence R. Klein*, F. Gerard Adams and Bert G. Hickman (eds.). Cambridge, Mass.: The MIT Press, 1983, 1–38. [303]

"Complete Genetic Models for Altruism, Kin Selection and Like-Gene Selection," *Journal of Social and Biological Structures*, vol. 6, 1983, 3–15. Copyright Academic Press, Inc., London. [347]

"The House That Keynes Built," *The New York Times*, 29 May 1983. Copyright 1983 by The New York Times Company. Reprinted by permission. [306]

"Durable Capital Inputs: Conditions for Price Ratios to be Invariant to Profit-Rate Changes," *Zeitschrift für Nationalökonomie*, vol. 43, no. 1, 1983, 1–20. Springer-Verlag. [314]

"The World Economy at Century's End," in *Human Resources, Employment and Development. Volume 1. The Issues*, Shigeto Tsuru (ed.). London: Macmillan, 1983, 58–77. [369]

"Comment [on Axel Leijonhufvud's 'What Would Keynes Have Thought of Rational Expectations?'],” in *Keynes and the Modern World*, David Worswick and James Trevithick (eds.). Cambridge: Cambridge University Press, 1983, 212–221. [308]

"The Keynes Centenary," *The Economist*, 25 June 1983, 19–21. [305]

"Marx Without Matrices: Understanding the Rate of Profit," in *Marxism, Central Planning, and the Soviet Economy: Economic Essays in Honor of Alexander Erlich*, Padma Desai (ed.). Cambridge, Mass.: The MIT Press, 1983, 3–18. © 1983 by The Massachusetts Institute of Technology. [313]

"1983: Marx, Keynes and Schumpeter," *Eastern Economic Journal*, vol. 9, no. 3, July–September 1983, 166–180. [304]

"My Life Philosophy," *The American Economist*, vol. 27, no. 2, Fall 1983, 5–12. [355]

"The 1983 Nobel Prize in Economics," *Science*, vol. 222, 2 December 1983. 987–989. Copyright 1984 by the American Association for the Advancement of Science. [363]

"Economics of Futures Contracts in Basic Macroeconomic Indexes: An Economist's Appraisal," *Futures: Policy and Prospects for a Dynamic Market*. Washington D.C.: National Journal, 1983, 43–44. [330]

"Thünen at Two Hundred," *Journal of Economic Literature*, vol. 21, December 1983, 1468–1488. Copyright American Economic Association. [339]

Introduction to the Enlarged Edition of *Foundations of Economic Analysis*. Cambridge, Mass.: Harvard University Press, 1983, xv–xxvi. Reprinted by permission of the publishers. © 1947 Harvard University Press. © 1983 by the President and Fellows of Harvard College. © by Paul A. Samuelson. [366]

"Second Thoughts on Analytical Income Comparisons," *Economic Journal*, vol. 94, June 1984, 267–278. Cambridge: Cambridge University Press. [299]

"Stochastic Land Valuation: Total Return as Martingale Implying Price Changes—A Negatively Correlated Walk," speech given 19 January 1984, University of California, San Diego. [327]

"The U.S. Fiscal Crisis of the 1980s," in *Reconstructing the Federal Budget: A Trillion Dollar Quandary*, Albert T. Sommers (ed.). New York: Praeger, 1984, 75–86. Copyright 1984. The Conference Board. Reprinted by permission of Praeger Publishers. [371]

"Japan and the World at the Century's End," *NEXT Magazine*, August 1984, 4–15. Tokyo: Kodansha, Ltd. (Original English version provided for translation into Japanese.) [323]

"The Future of American Industry in a Changing Economy," *The Journalist*, Fall 1984, 3–5, 19. [326]

"Unattainability of Integrability and Definiteness Conditions in the General Case of Demand for Money and Goods," with Ryuzo Sato, *American Economic Review*, vol. 74, no. 4, September 1984, 588–604. [300]

"Evaluating Reaganomics" (Horowitz Lecture), *Challenge*, November-December 1984, 4–12. [370]

"Modes of Thought in Economics and Biology," *The American Economic Review*, vol. 75, no. 2, May 1985, 166–172. [348]

"Succumbing to Keynesianism," *Challenge*, January-February 1985, 4–11. [307]

"The 1984 Nobel Prize in Economics," *Science*, vol. 227. January 1985, 20–22. Copyright 1985 by the American Association for the Advancement of Science. [364]

Seventieth Birthday Remarks, 18 May 1985. [365]

Foreword to *On the Factorial Approach to Index Number Problems, Consumption Analysis and Orthogonal Decomposition of National Income: A Summary*, by K. S. Banerjee. College Park, Md.: World Academy of Development and Cooperation, Special Studies Publication, no. 2, 1985, ii–iv. [338]

"Analytics of Free-Trade or Protectionist Response by America to Japan's Growth Spurt," in *Economic Policy and Development: New Perspectives*, Toshio Shishido and Ryuzo Sato (eds.). Dover, Mass.: Auburn House, 1985, 3–18. [322]

"Economics in My Time," in *Lives of the Laureates*, William Breit and Roger W. Spencer (eds.). Cambridge, Mass.: The MIT Press, 1986, 59–76. [356]

INDEX